Lecture Notes in Computer Science   7674

Commenced Publication in 1973
Founding and Former Series Editors:
Gerhard Goos, Juris Hartmanis, and Jan van Leeuwen

Weisi Lin   Dong Xu   Anthony Ho
Jianxin Wu Ying He   Jianfei Cai
Mohan Kankanhalli   Ming-Ting Sun (Eds.)

Advances in Multimedia Information Processing – PCM 2012

13th Pacific-Rim Conference on Multimedia
Singapore, December 4-6, 2012
Proceedings

 Springer

Volume Editors

Weisi Lin
Dong Xu
Jianxin Wu
Ying He
Jianfei Cai
Nanyang Technological University, 639798 Singapore
E-mail: {wslin, dongxu, jxwu, yhe, asjfcai}@ntu.edu.sg

Anthony Ho
University of Surrey, Guildford, GU2 7XH, UK
E-mail: a.ho@surrey.ac.uk

Mohan Kankanhalli
National University of Singapore, 117417 Singapore
E-mail: mohan@comp.nus.edu.sg

Ming-Ting Sun
University of Washington, Seattle, WA 98195, USA
E-mail: sun@ee.washington.edu

ISSN 0302-9743   e-ISSN 1611-3349
ISBN 978-3-642-34777-1   e-ISBN 978-3-642-34778-8
DOI 10.1007/978-3-642-34778-8
Springer Heidelberg Dordrecht London New York

Library of Congress Control Number: 2012951402

CR Subject Classification (1998): H.5.1, C.2, H.3-4, I.5, D.2

LNCS Sublibrary: SL 3 – Information Systems and Application, incl. Internet/Web
and HCI

Typesetting: Camera-ready by author, data conversion by Scientific Publishing Services, Chennai, India

Printed on acid-free paper

Springer is part of Springer Science+Business Media (www.springer.com)

Message from the General Chairs

On behalf of the Organizing Committee, it is our great pleasure to welcome you to the proceedings of the Pacific-Rim Conference on Multimedia (PCM), held in Singapore during December 4–6, 2012. PCM is a leading international conference for researchers and industry practitioners to share and showcase their new ideas, original research results, and engineering development experiences from all multimedia-related areas.

PCM 2012 was the 13th in the series of PCM conferences which has been held annually since 2000 in various cities across the Pacific regions. This year, the technical program consisted of opening keynote addresses, tutorials, a panel, special sessions, and technical presentations of refereed papers. Particularly, we were honored to have two eminent professors, Henry Fuchs from the University of North Carolina and Tat-Seng Chua from the National University of Singapore, give the keynote lectures. PCM 2012 also offered one best paper prize and one best student paper prize.

We would like to express our sincere gratitude to Weisi Lin for his great service in leading the Technical Program Committee. We would also like to thank the other Program Chairs, Dong Xu and Anthony Ho. We thank the Track Chairs, the reviewers, and the special session organizers whose invaluable efforts and dedication led to the high-quality technical program as well as the tremendous success of PCM 2012.

Special thanks also go to the Special Session Chairs, Shuicheng Yan and Jun-song Yuan, for their untiring efforts in recruiting and selecting the special sessions; the Local Arrangements and Finance Chairs, Chan Hua Vun (Nicholas), and Jun Luo as well as Co-chairs Jialie Shen and Kap-Luk Chan, for their tremendous support; Publication Chairs, Jianxin Wu and Ying He for their painstaking efforts in helping produce the LNCS proceedings; Publicity Co-chair, Yonggang Wen, for managing the conference website; Tutorial Chairs, Liang-Tien Chia and Qing-Ming Huang, for recruiting tutorial speakers; as well as all the other chairs for their help in promoting this conference. We are also grateful to the School of Computer Engineering, Nanyang Technological University, for their great support in administration, registration, and finance matters.

We would like to thank the PCM Steering Committee, especially the former and current PCM Steering Committee Chairs and Vice Chairs, Sun-Yuan Kung, Yong Rui, Ling Guan, and Changsheng Xu, for their encouragement, support, and guidance.

Finally, we would like to express our sincere appreciation to all of the authors and attendees for their contributions to PCM 2012.

Jianfei Cai
Mohan Kankanhalli
Ming-Ting Sun

Message from the Technical Program Chairs

The Pacific-Rim Conference on Multimedia (PCM) entered its 13th event this year! On behalf of the PCM 2012 Technical Program Committee, we welcome you to the proceedings of the conference.

During the two days of the conference (December 5–6, 2012), the PCM 2012 technical program included two keynote talks. Two parallel oral sessions were presented daily, and a poster session was be held in conjunction with lunch each day to maximize the technical exchange and interaction in an informal atmosphere. We designed the conference technical program in such a way that the audience would not miss the keynotes and the panel discussion. PCM 2012 also included two high-quality tutorials on December 4, 2012. Under the leadership of Special Session Co-chairs, Shuicheng Yan (National University of Singpore) and Junsong Yuan (Nanyang Technological University, Singapore), we also had four interesting special sessions with 23 presentations.

PCM 2012 gave two best paper awards including the best paper award and the best student paper award. The awards were determined based on the technical merits of the papers. We congratulate the winners.

This year, we received 106 submissions. Led by three Technical Program Chairs and eight Track Chairs, we conducted a careful paper review. The majority of the papers received three or more independent reviews, with 52% of the papers receiving four or more reviews. These reviews served as basis to select the 59 papers accepted for the main conference. Out of the 59 accepted papers, 30 better quality papers were selected for oral presentation (28% of the total submissions). A selected set of PCM 2012 oral papers will be invited to submit the extended versions of the papers to be reviewed for acceptance into a special issue of *Journal of Signal Processing Systems*. We thank Sun-Yuan Kung for his great support in forming the special issue.

The technical program of PCM 2012 would not have been possible without the dedicated effort of volunteers of the entire PCM 2012 Technical Program Committee and the Organizing Committee. We are most grateful to the authors who have submitted their latest research work to PCM 2012, and the Technical Program Committee members who have contributed significantly to the peer-review process (we have acknowledged the Technical Committee members on the PCM 2012 website). In particular, the PCM 2012 Program Chairs are most grateful to the eight Track Chairs: Tao Mei (Microsoft Research Asia, China), Gang Hua (Stevens Institute of Technology, USA), Toshihiko Yamasaki (Cornell University, USA), Chong-Wah Ngo (City University of Hong Kong, Hong Kong), Stefan Winkler (Advanced Digital Sciences Center, Singapore), Chia-Hung Yeh (National Sun Yat-sen University, Taiwan), Guangming Shi (Xidian University, China), and Jie Liang (Simon Fraser University, Canada), for their hard work, cooperation, and professionalism in organizing individual track reviews.

We would like to express our thanks to the PCM Steering Committee, especially to the Committee Chair, Ling Guan (Ryerson University, Canada), and Vice Chair Changsheng Xu (Chinese Academy of Sciences, China) for their support, guidance, and advice. Last but not least, we would like to express our greatest appreciation for the initiative, support, and supervision of the PCM 2012 General Chairs, Jianfei Cai (Nanyang Technological University), Mohan Kankanhalli (National University of Singapore), and Ming-Ting Sun (University of Washington).

Weisi Lin
Dong Xu
Anthony T.S. Ho

Organizing Committee

Honorary Co-chairs

Tat-Seng Chua	National University of Singapore
Srikanthan Thambipillai	Nanyang Technological University

General Co-chairs

Jianfei Cai	Nanyang Technological University, Singapore
Mohan Kankanhalli	National University of Singapore
Ming-Ting Sun	University of Washington, USA

Program Co-chairs

Weisi Lin	Nanyang Technological University, Singapore
Dong Xu	Nanyang Technological University, Singapore
Anthony T.S. Ho	University of Surrey, UK

Special Session Co-chairs

Shuicheng Yan	National University of Singapore
Junsong Yuan	Nanyang Technological University, Singapore

Tutorial Co-chairs

Liang-Tien Chia	Nanyang Technological University, Singapore
Qingming Huang	Chinese Academy of Sciences, China

Publicities Co-chairs

Chang-Sheng Xu	Chinese Academy of Sciences, China
Jian Zhang	University of Technology, Sydney, Australia
Chia-Wen Lin	National Tsing Hua University, Taiwan
Yo-Sung Ho	Gwangju Institute of Science and Technology (GIST), Korea
Tat Jet Cham	Nanyang Technological University, Singapore
Yonggang Wen	Nanyang Technological University, Singapore

Industrial/Sponsorship Co-chairs

Feng Wu   Microsoft Research Asia, China
Zhengguo Li   Institute for Infocomm Research, Singapore

Finance/Registration Co-chairs

Jun Luo   Nanyang Technological University, Singapore
Kap-Luk Chan   Nanyang Technological University, Singapore

Local Arrangement Co-chair

Chan Hua Vun, Nicholas   Nanyang Technological University, Singapore
Jialie Shen   Singapore Management University

Publication Co-chair

Jianxin Wu   Nanyang Technological University, Singapore
Ying He   Nanyang Technological University, Singapore

Steering Committee

Changwen Chen   University at Buffalo
Sadoaki Furui   Tokyo Institute of Technology
Ling Guan (Chair)   Ryerson University
Sun-Yuan Kung   Princeton University
Yong Rui   Microsoft Research Asia
Changsheng Xu (Vice Chair)   Chinese Academy of Sciences

Track Chairs

Tao Mei   Microsoft Research Asia, China
Gang Hua   Stevens Institute of Technology, USA
Toshihiko Yamasaki   Cornell University, USA
Chong-Wah Ngo   City University of Hong Kong, Hong Kong
Stefan Winkler   Advanced Digital Sciences Center, Singapore
Chia-Hung Yeh   National Sun Yat-sen University, Taiwan
Guangming Shi   Xidian University, China
Jie Liang   Simon Fraser University, Canada

Reviewers

Hezerul Abdul Karim
Bedrich Benes
Marco Bertini
Miguel Carrasco
Xiujuan Chai
Yoong Choon Chang
Chin-Chen Chang
Hwann-Tzong Chen
Jia Chen
Chongyu Chen
Chu-Song Chen
Kuan-Ta Chen
Gene Cheung
Chen-Kuo Chiang
Sunghyun Cho
Michael Cree
Ismael Daribo
Xiaoyu Deng
Liya Ding
Lei Ding
Zhao Dong
Gianfranco Doretto
Ling-Yu Duan
How-Lung Eng
Giovani Gomez Estrada
Chiou-Shann Fuh
Xinbo Gao
Margrit Gelautz
Bo Geng
Yo-Sung Ho
Richang Hong
Seiji Hotta
Changbo Hu
Gang Hua
Fay Huang
Zi Huang
Qingming Huang
Rui Huang
Chun-Rong Huang
Naoyuki Ichimura

Daisuke Iwai
Yoshio Iwai
Gangyi Jiang
Shuqiang Jiang
Yugang Jiang
Xin Jin
Li-Wei Kang
Chang-Su Kim
Mario Koeppen
Takio Kurita
Shang-Hong Lai
Tung-Ying Lee
Jaejoon Lee
Wen-Nung Lie
Jenn-Jier Lien
Huei-Yung Lin
Guo-Shiang Lin
Damon Shing-Min Liu
Dong Liu
Xiao Liu
Jing Liu
Qingshan Liu
Huiying Liu
Jonathan Loo
Hong Lu
Haifeng Lu
Yasushi Makihara
Fabrice Meriadeau
Rodrigo Moreno
Hajime Nagahara
Atsushi Nakazawa
Bingbing Ni
Shohei Nobuhara
Ho-Yuen Pang
Christian Pieringer
Lei Qin
Guoping Qiu
Mahdi Rezaei
Laurent Risser
Isaac Rudomin

Hitoshi Sakano
Shin'ichi Satoh
Nicu Sebe
Jie Shao
Jialie Shen
Dong Gyu Sim
Mingli Song
Yu-Wing Tai
Ping Tan
Masayuki Tanaka
Jinhui Tang
Qi Tian
Chien-Cheng Tseng
Carlos Vazquez
Meng Wang
Lei Wang
Yu-Chiang Wang
Yan Wang
Min-Liang Wang
Fei Wu
Hsien-Huang Wu
Xiao Wu
Zhong Wu
Changsheng Xu
Jizheng Xu
Xiangyang Xue
Ming Yang
Xiaokang Yang
Kaori Yoshida
Gang Yu
Zheng-Jun Zha
Guangtao Zhai
Qi Zhao
Yao Zhao
Yantao Zheng
Bo Zheng
Huiyu Zhou
Xiangdong Zhou
Shuyuan Zhu
Roger Zimmermann

Table of Contents

Video Coding and Multimedia Information Processing I

Multimedia Content Analysis II

Video Coding and Multimedia Information Processing II

Image and Video Processing II

Image/Video Processing and Analysis

Video Coding and Multimedia System

Advanced Image and Video Coding

Location-Based Social Media Analysis

Cross-Media Learning with Structural Priors

Efficient Multimedia Analysis and Utilization

Incremental Learning of Patch-Based Bag of Facial Words Representation for Online Face Recognition in Videos

Chao Wang, Yunhong Wang, and Zhaoxiang Zhang

School of Computer Science and Engineering, Beihang University, China
chaowang@cse.buaa.edu.cn, {yhwang,zxzhang}@buaa.edu.cn

Abstract. Video-based face recognition is a fundamental topic in image and video analysis, and presents various challenges and opportunities. In this paper, we introduce an incremental learning approach to video-based face recognition, which efficiently exploits the spatiotemporal information in videos. Face image sequences are incrementally clustered based on their descriptors. With the quantization of the facial words, representation of the face image is generated by concatenating the histograms from regions. In the online recognition, a temporal matrix and a voting algorithm are employed to judge a face video's identity. The proposed method achieves a 100% recognition rate performed on the Honda/UCSD database, and gives near realtime feedback. Experimental results demonstrate the effectiveness and flexibility of our proposed method.

1 Introduction

In recent years, face recognition is always an active topic in the field of biometrics. Compared to traditional face recognition in still images, face videos contain more abundant information, and temporal information becomes available to be exploited in videos to improve the accuracy of face recognition. However, video-based face recognition is impaired by poor video quality, low quality facial images, illumination changes, pose variations and so on. Hence, a robust face recognition method is required in a practical environment.

Wang et al. [1] proposed an online learning model for face recognition in videos. They introduced a novel online learning method which can learn appearance models incrementally from a given video stream. Ajmal Mian [2] presented an online learning approach, in which face images were automatically clustered based on the similarity of their local features.

Others have addressed the recognition problem into exploit the temporal information. Liu and Cheng [3] successfully employed HMMs for video-based face recognition by improving the basic implementation of HMMs. Lee et al. [4] successfully developed a probabilistic appearance manifold approach for tracking and recognition using video sequences. Bayesian inference was employed to include the temporal coherence of human motion in the distance calculation. Gou et al. [5] present an video-based face recognition algorithm which Multi-atlas

W. Lin et al. (Eds.): PCM 2012, LNCS 7674, pp. 1–9, 2012.

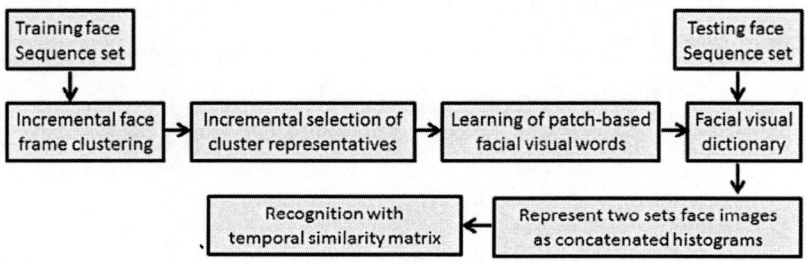

Fig. 1. The block diagram of the proposed method

is employed to represent faces of individual persons under different poses and expressions. But such an approach will be highly dependent upon the accuracy of face tracking in scale space and will also be sensitive to illumination.

In order to exploit facial temporal information, incremental learning system can learn continuously to adapt to incoming training samples. Bag of features (BoF), which represents an image as an orderless collection of local features, can fully exploit the spatial information in face image, and it tends to be robust to pose, illumination and expression changes of a face.

The remainder of paper is organized as follows. Firstly, Sec. 2 depicts the workflow of our face recognition method. Then, the incremental learning of face representatives algorithm are demonstrated in Sec. 3. We do the recognition using our proposed temporal similarity matrix voting algorithm, which described in Sec. 4, and the experimental results is analyzed in detail in Sec. 5. The paper finishes with conclusions and future work.

2   Framework

Fig. 1 depicts the workflow of our face recognition method. In the training stage, firstly, faces are detected from the input video using the Adaboost algorithm [6]. In order to link the detections into face tracks, Camshift [7] algorithm is employed for face tracking. At the same time, the face region is clipped from each frame, and the features of these faces are extracted. During the increase process of face frames, we employ an incremental clustering algorithm to assort the face frames into different class. And by applying the incremental selection of cluster representatives algorithm, representative faces are chosen in each cluster to build the dictionary of facial visual words . After the dictionary is built up, the histograms of face images are generated to representant faces in training set. In the testing stage, the face region is cropped as in the training stage, and all the face frames are represented by histogram using the dictionary obtained in training stage. In the online recognition, each testing frame is matched with the gallery which consists of the cluster representatives and result in a temporal similarity matrix. And the recognition result of the query face video sequence is voted according to the matrixes of all the frames in the video.

3   Incremental Learning of Patch-Based Facial Visual Words

3.1   Incremental Face Frame Clustering

Incremental clustering with matrix cosine similarity [8] distance and K-means are employed in our algorithm. Due to facial expression and movent, the number of clusters is empirically set to 10, and the maximum number per cluster is 20. The first 50 face frames' global features of one subject are used to build a initialized classifier. Successively, if the minimal distance between the new incoming face frame and one cluster centroid less than a threshold, the new incoming face frame will be assigned to the cluster. Else, this face with its features became a new cluster, and the cluster which has least faces is discarded. But if the number of face images in any cluster reach a threshold, the face image with the maximum distance from the cluster centroid is discarded, and replaced with the freshly acquired face. This algorithm restarts when a new subject incoming, and continues until the all videos are exhausted.

In our algorithm, it is possible to make the number of clusters variable by setting a fixed between cluster distance rather than keeping it as a constant. The cluster criteria in this paper is meant to avoid uneven distribution of faces in the clusters e.g. if a person remains still throughout the clustering process, most of the faces will go into one or a few clusters. This means that most of the face information will be redundant. But our desire is to capture different poses and different expressions of a face during the clustering process. Generally, the easiest way to achieve our purpose is to ensure that the faces are evenly distributed among the clusters as far as possible.

3.2   Incremental Selection of Representatives

One of the motivations of clustering is data compression whereby each cluster is represented by its subset. In our proposed method, a selecting scheme is used to chose the representative faces. Within each cluster, the face image which has the minimal distance to the cluster center is chosen as its cluster representative. During the incremental face frame clustering in Sec. 3.1, the classifier is updating, and if a face image has been chosen as a cluster representative, it will not be chosen twice. The selecting scheme ensures that the face features sufficient cover the face and represent the whole cluster. Using the cluster representatives, a facial words codebook is generated by vector quantization (VQ).

3.3   Patch-Based Visual Words Representation

The goal of patch-based facial visual words algorithm is to obtain a feature of face which robust to facial variations in pose, lighting and expression. As shown in Fig. 2 , firstly, face image is divided into $n \times n$ patches, and descriptors are extracted from each patch. Continually, the facial words codebook obtained in Sec. 3.2 is applied to quantize every descriptor, and each descriptor is converted

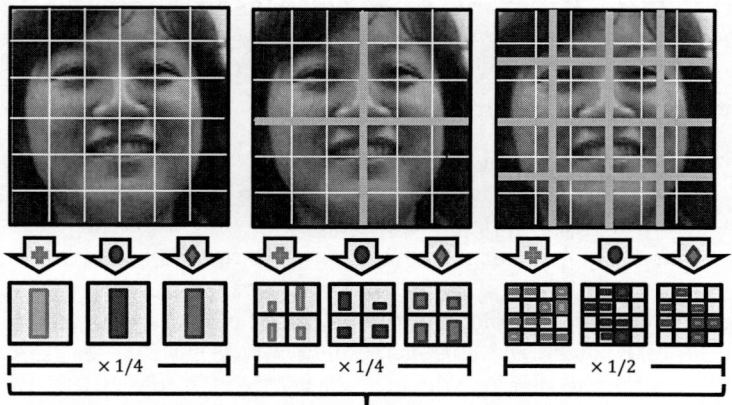

Feature vector representation of face image

Fig. 2. Three-level pyramid instance

into code. Finally, with employing of spatial pyramid matching (SPM) [9] the histograms from all sub-regions are concatenated together to generate the final representation of the face image.

4   Online Recognition with Temporal Similarity Matrix

During online recognition, each query face frame feature f_t (represented by patch-based facial visual words) match with the gallery using matrix cosine similarity [8] distance: $d_{kj} = \rho(f_t, f_{kj}), k = 1, ...C_j$, resulted in $G \times C_j$ similarity matrix. Where G is the number of categories (identities) in the database, C_j is the faces (selected in Sec. 3.2) number of jth category. Fig. 3 displays a part of values in temporal similarity matrix. Notice that the similarity distances are always high in the first line, which suggest that query face frame has more possibility identified as 'Behazd'.

The similarity score between the query face frame and jth category is calculated as follows:

$$s_j = \frac{1}{C_j - 2}(\sum_{k=1}^{C_j} d_{kj} - \max_k(d_{kj}) - \min_k(d_{kj})). \tag{1}$$

We give a weight to each category's similarity score to get the identity likelihood score:

$$score_j = \alpha(W_j s_j - \beta),$$

$$\alpha = \frac{1}{\max_j(s_j) - \min_j(s_j)}, \tag{2}$$

$$\beta = \min_j(s_j).$$

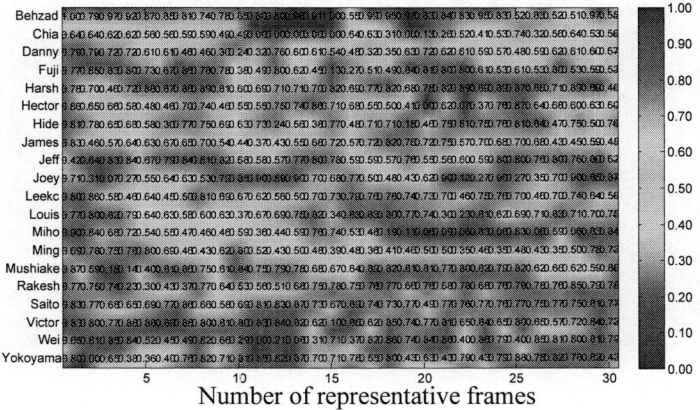

Fig. 3. Temporal similarity matrix

The similarity score is weighted as define:

$$W_j = \frac{NbC_j - \min_{k}(NbC_k)}{\max_{k}(NbC_k) - \min_{k}(NbC_k)}. \tag{3}$$

The valid number of similarity distance of each category $(NbC_1, \ldots, NbC_G)$ is calculated as follows:

$$NbC_j = \sum_{k=1}^{C_j} w_{kj},$$

$$w_{kj} = \begin{cases} 1, d_{kj} > Confidence \\ 0, d_{kj} \leq Confidence \end{cases}. \tag{4}$$

As the each identity likelihood score for query face frame is known, the identification result of the query frame is calculated as:

$$c = \arg\max_{j} score_j. \tag{5}$$

Once we obtain a query face frame's category (identity) c, we cast a vote for c, after we achieve all of votes from the face frames in the query video, the final identity of the face video is the category with the maximum votes.

5 Experiments

The proposed algorithm is implemented in MATLAB R2010a and runs on a Dual Core 2.5 GHz PC with 4GB memory. In experiments, we use the first dataset of Honda/UCSD [4] video database to test our purposed approach. The database includes 20 individuals moving their heads in 2-D and 3-D rotation with different

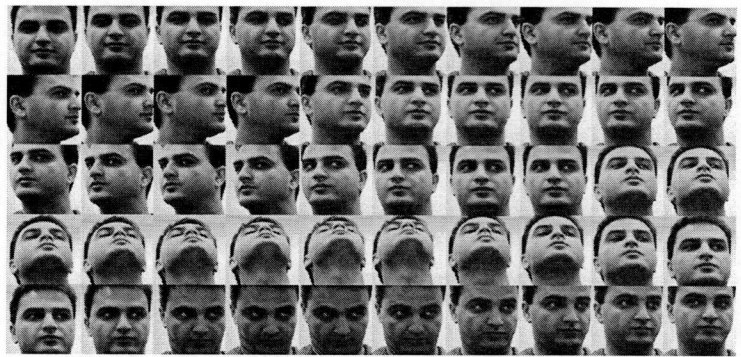

Fig. 4. Sample faces

expression and speed. The face in the video is automatically detected [6] and tracked [7], and the face region is clipped from each frame without registration. Fig. 4 shows sample faces of a person in the database. We can see the face region changes when the pose changes and does not perfectly enclose the face.

Comparisons with Different Type of Descriptors and Different Codebook Dimensions. Dense SIFT [10], dense MB-LBP [11] and dense COLOR histogram are employed to compare their performance, the face images are represented by quantization of the facial visual words with the size of 64. As shown in Tab. 1, recognition results are obtained using each frame's correct and failing categorization, and AUC is the area under the ROC curve. The confidence ($Confidence = 0.7$ in Equ. 4) is used to reject similarity distances which are below a threshold. Notice that the AUC of dense SIFT is higher than the others. It indicates that, when choosing a single descriptor and no prior knowledge about the data set, the dense SIFT with SPM is recommended.

We then test different sizes of facial visual words codebook. In Tab. 2, We can see that when the number of size reaches to 64 the AUC are the highest. And Tab. 3 shows AUCs of different numbers of patches using SIFT. We can see that the patch number of 20×20 works the best in Honda/UCSD database.

Recognition of Identity Changes. In real world scenarios, identities always change in video. In this experiment, in order to study the phenomenon of identity change in face video, the two subjects' test videos in the Honda/UCSD dataset were concatenated together. Faces are represented by quantization of the facial

Table 1. Different types of descriptors

Descriptor	SIFT	MB-LBP	COLOR
Recognition Rate	**91%**	86%	80%
AUC	**97.72**	95.84	96.21

Table 2. Different sizes of the codebook

Size	16	32	64	128	256
AUC	95.28	97.25	**97.72**	96.43	97.13

Table 3. Different numbers of patches

Number	10×10	20×20	30×30	40×40
AUC	94.78	**97.72**	96.06	97.43

visual words with the size of 64 using SIFT. Fig. 5(a) shows the plots of identity likelihood (calculate using Equ. (2)) between the concatenated video and two identities. Recall that a larger value means more possibility belonging to a identity. The slump in the plot of *subject*1 indicate the changing of identity.

Fig. 5(b) shows the vote results of two identities corresponding in Fig. 5(a). The vote results are obtained using continuous ten frames' similarity score as describe in Sec. 4. The value of the vote rate denotes the possibility of a face sequence belong to a identity. During the changing of the identity, the vote rate for *subject*1 begin to decline, while the vote rate for *subject*2 start to rise up. We can clear see that the identity changes are identified using the vote rates.

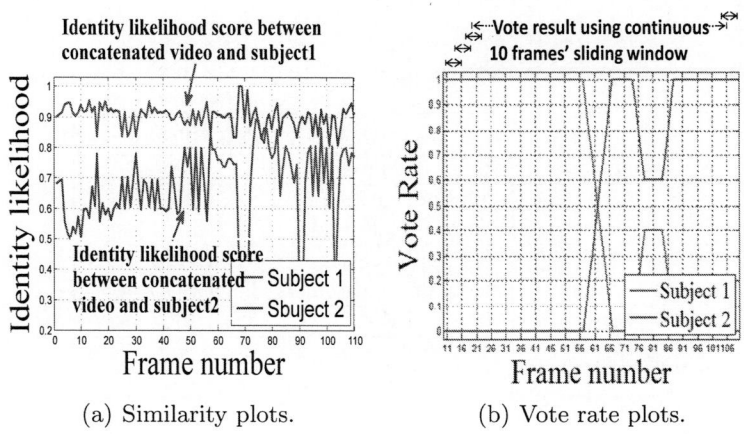

(a) Similarity plots.   (b) Vote rate plots.

Fig. 5. Curves of changing identities

Online Face Recognition in Video. In this experiment, all test videos match with all identities in the training set. Fig. 6(a) shows the vote rate result of subject 'Harsh''s test video. From the vote rate curves, we can see that at time (frame number) 8 to 13 the query video is recognized as 'Behzad'. But the vote rate for 'Harsh' increase from 9 to the end of the video sequence, and the test video is recognized as 'Harsh' at last.

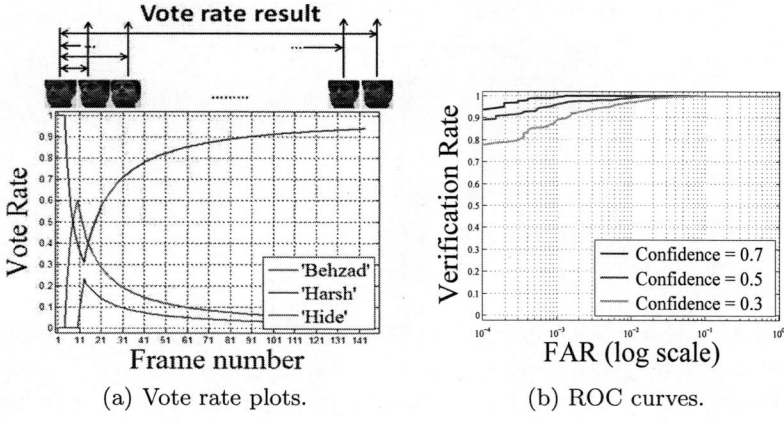

(a) Vote rate plots.   (b) ROC curves.

Fig. 6. Curves of changing identities

In Fig. 6(b), we calculate the Verification Rate and False Accept Rate (FAR) of each test video, using the vote results from the beginning to every time in successive video sequence. The confidence (*Confidence* in Equ. 4) is used to reject similarity distances which are below a threshold. At a FAR of 0.0012 and using confidence of 0.7, the verification rate is 100%. And we can see that the increasing confidence can reduce the FAR.

Table 4. Recognition Rates of different approaches in the literatures

Literature	Approach	Recognition Rate
Lee et al. [4]	Appearance manifolds	92.1%
Wang et al. [1]	Online learning of appearance model	96.5%
Gou et al. [5]	Multi-atlas	94.3%
Ajmal Mian [2]	Feature clutering	99.5%
Kim et al. [12]	HMM	100%
Proposed method	Online learning of face representation	100%

At last, we compared the face videos' Recognition Rate of our proposed method against five approaches including Lee et al. [4], Wang et al. [1], Gou et al. [5], Ajmal Mian [2] and Kim et al. [12] on the Honda/UCSD database. The summary of verification results in Tab. 4 clearly indicates that the performance our purposed method can be compared to the previous works.

6   Conclusions

In this paper, we propose an incremental learning of patch-based facial visual words method for face recognition in videos. Our work extends the BoF and

SPM methods to patch-based bag facial visual words to exploit the spatial information, and learning temporal information in an incremental way. Experimental results illustrate that the proposed method can recognize identity online with high accuracy, and distinguish changes of identities, which is very desirable in real applications. In future work, we will extend our method to videos taken under more challenging conditions.

Acknowledgement. This work is funded by the National Basic Research Program of China (No. 2010CB327902), the National Natural Science Foundation of China (No. 61005016, No. 61061130560), the National High-tech R&D Program of China (2011AA010502), the Open Projects Program of National Laboratory of Pattern Recognition, and the Fundamental Research Funds for the Central Universities.

References

1. Liu, L., Wang, Y., Tan, T.: Online appearance model learning for video-based face recognition. In: Proc. CVPR, pp. 1–7 (2007)
2. Mian, A.: Online learning from local features for video-based face recognition. PR 44(5), 1068–1075 (2011)
3. Liu, X., Cheng, T.: Video-based face recognition using adaptive hidden markov models. In: Proc. CVPR, pp. 340–345 (2003)
4. Lee, K., Ho, J., Yang, M., Kriegman, D.: Video-based face recognition using probabilistic appearance manifolds. In: Proc. CVPR, pp. 313–320 (2003)
5. Gou, G., Shen, R., Wang, Y., Basu, A.: Temporal-spatial face recognition using multi-atlas and markov process model. In: Proc. ICME, pp. 1–4 (2011)
6. Viola, P., Jones, M.: Rapid object detection using a boosted cascade of simple features. In: Proc. CVPR, Intel, Microprocessor Research Labs, p. 511 (2001)
7. Carnegie, R.C.: Mean-shift blob tracking through scale space. In: Proc. CVPR, pp. 234–240 (2003)
8. Schneider, J., Borlund, P.: Matrix comparison, part 1: Motivation and important issues for measuring the resemblance between proximity measures or ordination results. JASIST 58(11), 1586–1595 (2007)
9. Grauman, K., Darrell, T.: The pyramid match kernel: Discriminative classification with sets of image features. In: Proc. CVPR, pp. 1458–1465 (2005)
10. Lowe, D.: Distinctive image features from scale-invariant keypoints. IJCV 60(2), 91–110 (2004)
11. Ahonen, T., Matas, J., He, C., Pietikäinen, M.: Rotation Invariant Image Description with Local Binary Pattern Histogram Fourier Features. In: Salberg, A.-B., Hardeberg, J.Y., Jenssen, R. (eds.) SCIA 2009. LNCS, vol. 5575, pp. 61–70. Springer, Heidelberg (2009)
12. Kim, M., Kumar, S., Pavlovic, V., Rowley, H.: Face tracking and recognition with visual constraints in real-world videos. In: Proc. CVPR, pp. 1–8. IEEE (2008)

Evaluation of Audio Quality Requirements over Extended Periods of Time Using Long Duration Audiovisual Content

Adam Borowiak, Ulrich Reiter, and U. Peter Svensson

Centre for Quantifiable Quality of Service in Communication Systems (Q2S),
Norwegian University of Science and Technology (NTNU)
Trondheim, Norway
{adam.borowiak,reiter}@q2s.ntnu.no, svensson@iet.ntnu.no

Abstract. Using our novel methodology for quality evaluation of long duration multimedia content, the effect of the time dimension on quality ratings and user responses was investigated. We were particularly interested in checking how audio artifacts related to different compression rates influence participants' reactions to quality changes over extended periods of time. By employing the mixed-effects ANOVA model we have revealed dependencies between time periods and a lack of such between the subjects. It turned out that participants' quality expectations are rather constant throughout the entire duration of the clip, which also holds for subjects' reaction time to quality degradations. Furthermore, it has been shown that the test persons were substantially more sensitive to quality changes when they were able to influence the quality themselves.

Keywords: Subjective audiovisual quality assessment; audio quality; quality of experience (QoE).

1 Introduction

Traditional techniques for quality assessment are mainly designed for short clips and do not take into account temporal variations of the quality. The clips are usually viewed in randomized order and with constant quality throughout their entire (and short) duration. After the stimulus has been presented, the quality rating is requested from the assessors, most often on a 5-point MOS scale. In such a situation, assessors are not really involved in the audio-video presentation, focusing rather on the evaluation task itself. This is fairly uncommon in a natural viewing environment, where a stimulus usually is of longer duration (e.g. full movie) and where visibility of the distortion, and hence perception of the quality, varies as a function of time and scene content [1], [2]. For such situations, non-intrusive, continuous measurement methods which allow for evaluation of long duration test material seem to be more suited, as they promise results more closely related to real-world viewing scenarios.

To cope with some of the above requirements, the Single Stimulus Continuous Quality Evaluation (SSCQE) method has been developed and incorporated into ITU

W. Lin et al. (Eds.): PCM 2012, LNCS 7674, pp. 10–20, 2012.

recommendation BT.500-7 [3] in 1996. The SSCQE allows for continuous evaluation of presented material (up to 30 min long) by using a slider to indicate the perceived quality. The slider represents a simple scale (typically from 0-100) and can be adjusted any time the user chooses to. It has been reported that the SSCQE is too demanding for assessors performing a real evaluation task and that continuous operation of the slider can be distracting [4]. Moreover, the method is designed only for quality assessment of video material where accompanying audio might be introduced. This means that suitability of this method for audio quality evaluation solely or with accompanying picture has – to the best of our knowledge – not been considered. In spite of these facts, the SSCQE remains the only internationally accepted recommendation for quality assessment of long duration audiovisual content. The lack of alternative methodologies which would allow to overcome the mentioned limitations of existing recommendations significantly slows down progress in this field. Therefore, in [5] we have proposed a new methodology which can be used for continuous examination of quality variations in audio, video or audiovisual stimuli over extended periods of time.

The objective of the study described in this paper is to apply and further investigate our methodology for quality evaluation of long duration audiovisual content. The suitability of the method for quality assessment of video (with accompanying, undistorted sound track) has been demonstrated in [5] and [6]. In this paper, we consider the reverse situation where audio quality (with accompanying, undistorted video) is evaluated.

The paper is organized as follows. Section 2 briefly summarizes the methodology used for this study. The experimental setup in terms of test material, participants as well as test conditions and procedures is discussed in section 3. In Section 4, the effect of different compression ratios of the audio stream on perceived quality is investigated. Finally, the conclusions are presented in Section 5.

2   Method Description

In [5] we have proposed a novel methodology which represents a different approach towards continuous quality evaluation of long duration material.

Instead of measuring the quality by using traditional Mean Opinion Score (MOS) based approaches, the method allows participants to select the most appreciated quality themselves. In case quality degradation occurs subjects have the possibility to adjust the quality to a desired level by using a rotary controller (e.g. scroll wheel, knob, etc.). The optimal (possibly the highest) quality level can be achieved solely by appropriate adjustment based on perceptual appreciation of what is seen or heard. There is no need for assessors to translate their sensations into a value on a numerical scale, thus avoiding most of the typical problems associated with MOS related concepts [7]. During the assessment task, automatic quality alterations are introduced at random or periodically and stepwise (e.g., the degradation procedure begins every third minute and subsequently, the quality level decreases every ten seconds). The participant's response (movement of the controller) to a quality change stops the automatic degradation procedure and provides him/her with full control over the quality adjustment. Turning the knob clockwise increases the quality level of the displayed material up to the point where the highest quality is attained. Rotating the device further clockwise introduces a gradual decrease in quality. This is in a way a penalty introduced when the maximum quality level is being surpassed. The process is reversible and by rotating the knob in the opposite direction the subject can return to the highest quality level (or decrease the quality level, if the maximum quality level has not been surpassed). A number of stimuli with different quality levels are produced beforehand, and for each of them a numerical value is allocated internally (e.g. lowest quality- 0, best- 10). Rotation of the knob selects between them. Users' responses are collected automatically by the system, at a time resolution of one millisecond and with values which lie within the range of the corresponding quality levels. A more detailed explanation of the operation principles of this method can be found in [5].

3   Subjective Test Setup and Procedures

A 32 minutes and 2 seconds extract from the third episode of the *BBC* nature documentary series titled *Life* was used in the test. The duration of the clip was selected with respect to the experimental design while still maintaining a logical structure with a beginning and end. The auditory part of the material contained speech, background music, nature sounds, and also dynamic, action-type music. The visual part was full of different shots and camera angles, including slow motion as well as action scenes with fine details, close-ups and movement. A high quality version was extracted from a Bluray disc edition and served as a starting point for further processing. The original audio track (DTS, 5.1ch, 16 bit/48 kHz, 1536 kbps) was downsampled to 44.1 kHz and downmixed to two channels PCM format (CD quality). Subsequently, the prepared audio stream was encoded as mp3 with L.A.M.E. encoder [8] at 11 different bitrates (32, 48, 56, 64, 80, 96, 112, 128, 160, 192 and 320 kb/s) with VBR off. The compression rates were selected according to results from a pilot test. The volume level of all audio quality levels was normalized (unweighted level) to maintain loudness consistency among them. The original video clip (1080p version) was decoded to the YUV format (preserving the quality and resolution) and used for video playback. Upon playback, both modalities were in synch at all times. The test conditions are summarized in Table 1.

Table 1. Test conditions

Clip duration	32min 2 sec
Audio properties	2ch, 16 bit/44.1 kHz
Audio compression rates (kbps)	32, 48, 56, 64, 80, 96, 112, 128, 160, 192 and 320
Video properties	HD 1080p (1920x1080), 25fps
Video color scheme	16bit YUV 4:2:0

Twenty participants, fourteen males and six females, took part in the experiment and received a cinema ticket for their participation. The participants' mean age was 31 years (age range 22 – 61 years). Ten out of twenty subjects had participated in earlier video quality assessments using the same testing methodology. 19 participants reported to have normal hearing and 1 subject reported a doubt with respect to that before the start of the main task. With regards to the purpose of the experiment, results provided by this person were excluded from further data analysis.

Participants received written and oral instructions prior to the experiment. The main part of the testing procedure was preceded by a training session which consisted of a ten minutes long clip selected to span the same quality range as the test clip. During the training, subjects had time to familiarize themselves with the test methodology, the sensitivity of the rotary knob device and also with the different levels of audio distortion. Questions were allowed throughout the whole training session.

In the main section of the experiment an over 30 minute long audiovisual clip was evaluated (as described above). The assessors were asked to react to audio quality changes only in case it was really audible for them. The first three minutes were used to familiarize participants with the reference sound quality (320kbps). Thereafter, an automatic degradation process was introduced every 3 minutes with the quality levels further decreasing every 10 seconds. The subjects were advised that the first degradation procedure would start at 1 to 5 minutes into the clip. Right after the main task participants were asked several questions regarding the easiness of the task, positive/negative aspects, difficulties (if any), and their overall experience regarding the methodology used for this test. Subjects were also asked about their interest in the presented material.

The experiment took place in a room designed to provide high quality listening and viewing conditions according to ITU recommendations BP.500-12, P.911 and BS.1116 [9], [10] and [11]. Two Dynaudio BM6A active loudspeakers were used for sound reproduction and a Pioneer PDP-5000EX plasma screen served as a display for video content. A USB control knob (PowerMate made by Griffin Technology) was used to instantaneously adjust the audio quality level in case of perceived degradation. To avoid too slow or too sudden changes, the sensitivity of the knob was set according to users' feedback from the previous experiment. Consequently, a 90 degree rotation was required to switch between adjacent levels but this was unknown to the participants. The total duration of the experiment ranged between 50 and 55 minutes and only one participant was performing the test at a time. Subjects were sitting in a cinema-style seat with a pull-out tray, which was used as a stand for the controller.

4   Results and Discussion

As mentioned previously, the test started with the maximum audio quality which was expected to last for the first three minutes, until the first degradation process had begun. One would expect a lack of subjects' responses (no movement of the knob) during this period, which turned out not to be the case (see Fig. 1, where the values decreasing from 10 during the first 3 minutes indicate that assessors were decreasing the quality by themselves). One of the reasons for such a situation is the users' reaction to the noises created by the nature scenes (e.g. an arctic wind). Those noises caused the impression of audio quality degradation despite the fact that compression artifacts were not present. Trying to improve the quality of the sound by rotating the knob clockwise, participants started to decrease it. The second reason for this phenomenon might be related to some subjects being overly eager to use the controller during the first minutes of the test.

After this period of time participants were quite consistent in their choices and occurring variations are most probably related to particular scenes which represent different audio attributes. Looking at Fig. 1 we can notice little variation in the means of users' responses during the last minutes of the main test. This is related to a specific type of audio material appearing at this particular time - mainly speech without background music. Subjects reported that it was easier for them to detect distortions at higher quality levels while speech was present. This is in accordance with results presented in [12]. Moreover, some of the test-persons declared that accompanying, high quality video diminished the effect of audio quality degradation, making them more tolerant to lower bitrates (cross-modal masking effect).

Fig. 1 suggests that the average participant would be satisfied with a quality level between 4 and 7, which corresponds to compression rates between 80 and 128 kbit/s. The overall mean value (6.16) implies that quality level 6 (112 kbit/s) would be satisfactory for most of the participants throughout the entire duration of the clip.

To better understand the above considerations and also explore our knowledge about users' responses to quality changes a statistical analysis was employed.

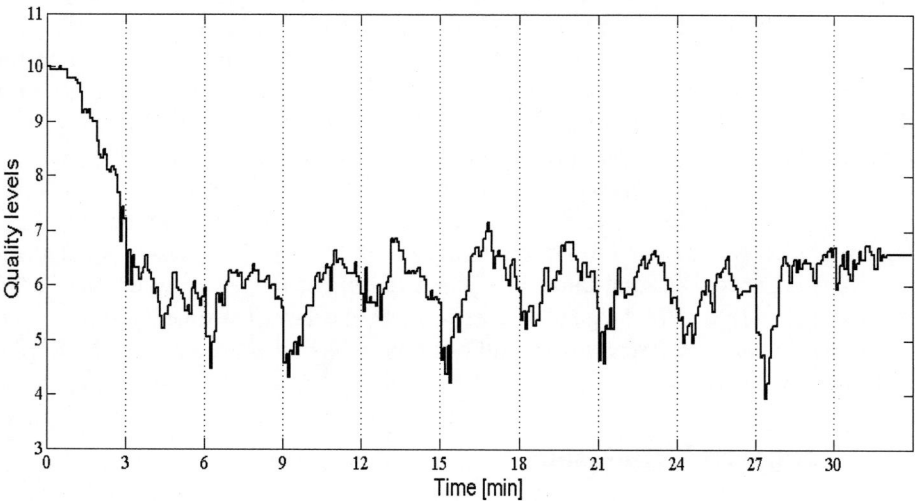

Fig. 1. Results showing averaged responses of all participants with respect to variations in the sound quality of the audiovisual clip

Three subsets of data were created to proceed with further data examination. These subsets included:

a) average quality level of the last minute of each 3 min time slot (this represents established/stationary quality preferences of the subjects)
b) response time to the automatic quality degradation right after the start of each 3 min time slot
c) quality level at the time when a user reacted to quality change

Due to the fact that the first three minutes were designed only to make participants familiar with the top quality the results for this time section were excluded from further analysis. The final size of the data matrix for each of the subsets was 19x9, where 9 corresponds to the number of three-minute time sections (without the first one) and 19 to the number of participants that were included.

The Analysis of Variance (ANOVA) was used as a tool to reveal dependencies between periods of time from one to another automatic degradation procedure (3 min time slots) and participants' reactions to quality variations. With ANOVA, the variability of scores between conditions and within conditions is analyzed and compared. This helps to find out if the independent variable has a significant effect on the dependent variable.

For validity of the results the data was checked for normality and homogeneity of variance across time slots as well as across users. All data sets showed close to normal distribution and close to homogeneous variance. A mixed-effects model of ANOVA with participants representing random-effect type factor and time slots representing fixed-effect type factor was used. Such a model can help to better understand which factor is responsible for most of the variation in the data and also compare the main effect of each of them. To justify a claim of a statistically significant effect the 0.05 level of significance was used.

Detailed results of the ANOVA test conducted on the subset data a) are presented in Table 2 and in Fig. 2. We can see that dissimilarities between mean quality expectations between users are statistically highly significant (F = 6.374; $p < 0.005$) and that variations in mean quality among participants are quite big (see Sum of Squares of User in the ANOVA table). This might be due to differences between the ways assessors were using the knob for the adjustment of quality or due to individual dissimilarities in hearing acuity or different interpretation of the instructions. On the other hand it can be noticed that such a phenomenon is not present if time sections are

Table 2. Results of ANOVA for data subset a)

Source	Df	Sum of Squares	Mean Square	F	P
User	18	356,049	19,781	6,374	0,000
Time slot	8	3,914	0,489	0,158	0,996
Error	143	443,768	3,103		
Total	169	803,731			

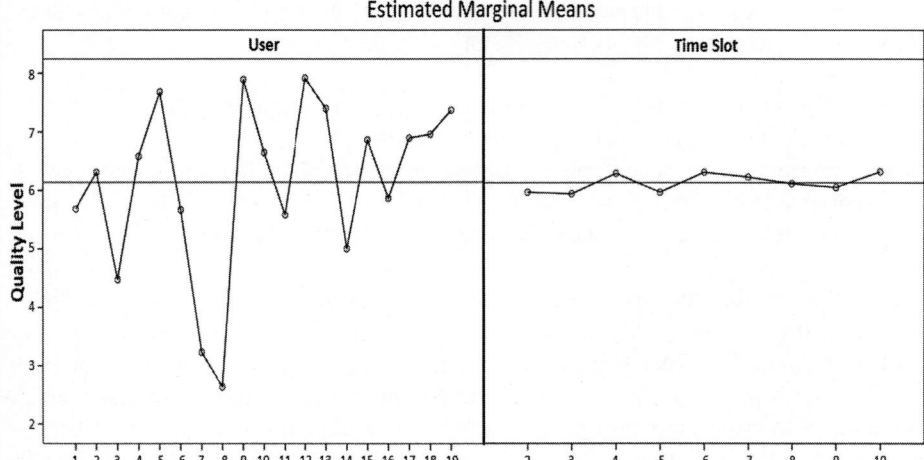

Fig. 2. Main effects plot for quality levels averaged over the last minute of each three minutes time interval (data subset a)

considered. In the statistical sense the differences between mean quality expectations between the time sections are not significant (F = 0.158; $p > 0.05$) which denotes that subjects were quite consistent in their choices throughout most of the clip's duration. This follows the pattern from a previous study on video quality assessment using the same method [6].

We were also curious to know if differences between the users depended on the level of the time section factor and vice versa. No such interaction between these two factors has been found. For data subset b), Table 3 shows that differences between mean reaction times between users are statistically significant (F = 3.042; $p < 0.005$). Participants were reacting to the automatic quality changes differently, starting usually from different quality levels.

This fact explains such big variations in mean reaction times between participants. Contrary to the between-user factor, no significant dissimilarities in reaction time to quality changes across time sections have been found (F = 0.826; $p > 0.05$). The mean time until people reacted to gradual quality decreases was roughly 24 seconds which corresponds to a 3 level drop in quality before the test-subject reacted.

From Fig. 3 we can see the distribution of means of reaction time with respect to users and time slots. It can be noticed that the variation due to time intervals is much smaller than the variation due to users' differences.

Table 3. Results of ANOVA for data subset b)

Source	Df	Sum of Squares	Mean Square	F	p
User	18	1,640E10	9,113E8	3,042	0,000
Time slot	8	1,980E9	2,476E8	0,826	0,581
Error	137	4,104E10	2,996E8		
Total	163	5,942E10			

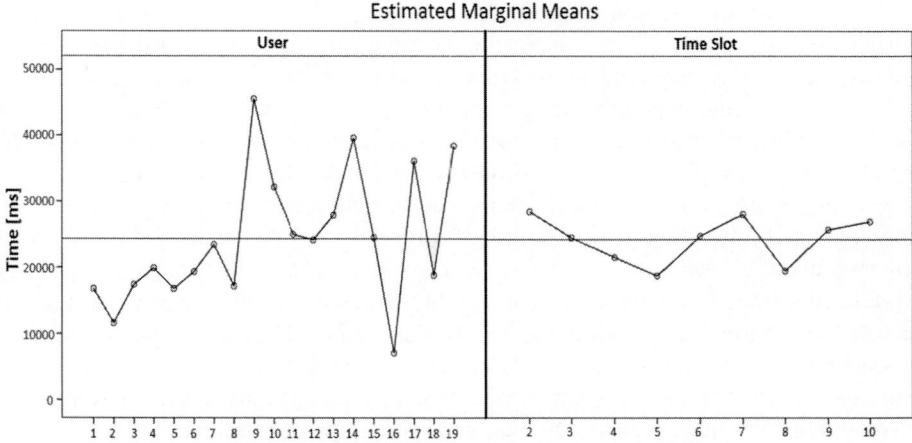

Fig. 3. Main effects plot for reaction time (data subset b)

Similar results were obtained for the data subset c) (see Table 4 and Fig. 4).

Table 4. Results of ANOVA for data subset c)

Source	Df	Sum of Squares	Mean Square	F	P
User	18	382,436	21,246	6,177	0,000
Time slot	8	30,367	3,796	1,104	0, 365
Error	137	471,230	3,440		
Total	163	884,033			

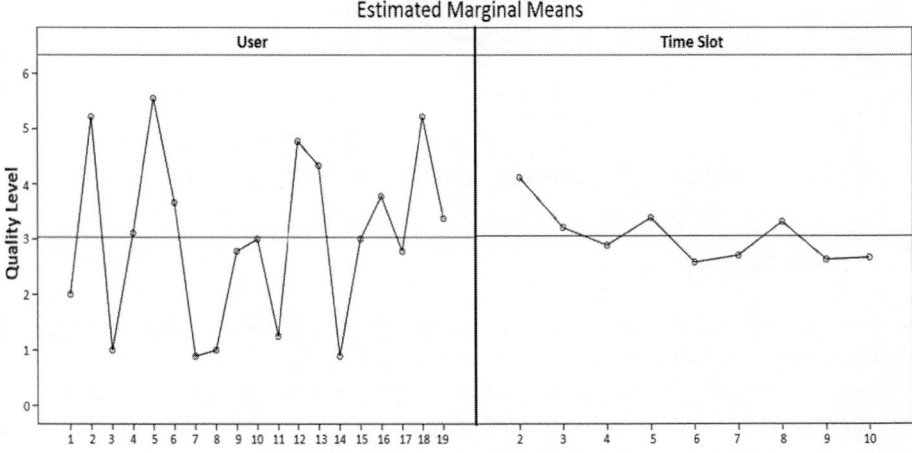

Fig. 4. Main effects plot for quality levels at time when a user reacted to quality change (data subset c)

Fig. 5 shows the relation between the average quality values set by participants during the last minute of each three minute time interval (AQL), and the average quality values corresponding to the time at which participants detected a change (QLRT). One could notice that except for the very beginning the difference between these two plots with respect to quality levels is relatively constant and on average equal to three levels. The smaller difference occurring in the beginning might be related to the bigger attention participants paid during the first minutes. However, as observed in Table 4, there was no significant effect of this tendency. The above suggests that it is easier for a person to distinguish between neighboring quality levels while concentrated on the task (e.g. quality adjustment) than when the change happens at random and is independent of his/her actions (e.g. automatic degradation procedure). In addition, the performance of those test-subjects who had participated in the previous experiment was checked against those for whom the methodology was new. It turned out that this learning process did not affect the users' performance; no significant difference was found between these two groups. This might imply that the method is quite intuitive and easy to follow from the very first time it is used.

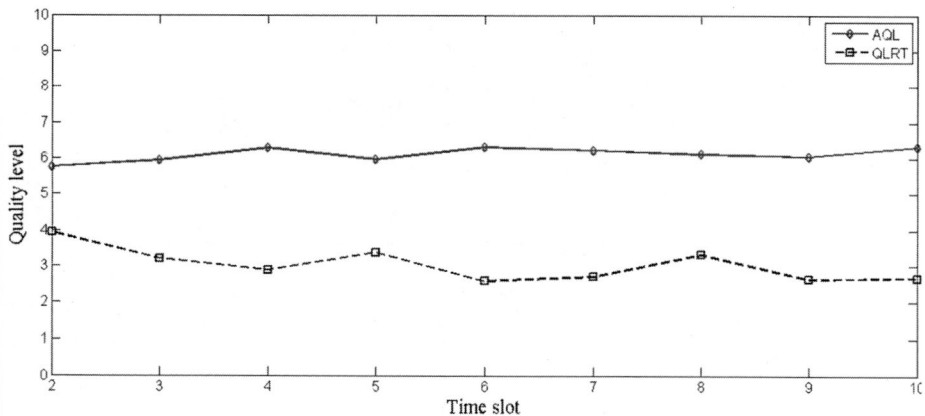

Fig. 5. Comparison of sensitivity to quality changes under different conditions

5   Conclusions

In this work the experimental setup and results of a long duration audiovisual content audio quality experiment are presented. It has been found that participants' preferences regarding audio quality are relatively constant with respect to time. A mixed-effects ANOVA model was used to gain insight into the relationship between means of specific factors. It turned out that the time factor does not influence quality ratings, whereas the between-user factor does. Similar conclusions can be drawn with respect to the response time to automatic quality changes. The between-user factor is responsible for most of the variations in the data, and the dissimilarities among participants (whether related to selected quality level or reaction time) are statistically significant. Furthermore, it has been shown that subjects are substantially more sensitive to quality changes when they themselves are in control of the quality adjustment process, than when the quality degradation process is controlled externally. We can see that the time dimension does not influence the audio quality expectation, which is contrary to what could be expected. The outcome might be different for much longer duration stimuli (e.g. full length movie), but this needs to be studied.

In addition, the suitability of our method for quality assessment of long duration audio streams (with accompanying, high quality video) has been demonstrated. The results uncover time/quality related dependencies and expand our knowledge of users' response to quality changes over extended periods of time.

In future studies, we will investigate the impact of audiovisual distortions (audio and video artifacts introduced simultaneously or in the same experiment) on participants' judgments in a similar setup, using the same methodology. Different content and content of much longer duration will also be examined.

The diversity of artifacts occurring during streaming transmission of audio, video or audiovisual material, e.g. degradations caused by packet loss, might be considered at a later time.

Acknowledgments. This study was performed within the PERCEVAL project, funded by The Research Council of Norway under project number 193034/S10.

References

1. Lodge, N.K., Wood, D.: Subjectively Optimizing Low Bit-Rate Television. In: Proceedings of the IEEE International Broadcasting Convention, IBC 1994, Amsterdam, pp. 333–339 (1994)
2. Aldridge, R., Davidoff, J., Ghanbari, M., Hands, D., Pearson, D.: Measurement of Scene-dependent Quality Variations in Digitally Coded Television Pictures. In: IEEE Proceedings Vision, Image and Signal Processing, vol. 142(3), pp. 149–154 (1995)
3. ITU-R Recommendation BT.500-7: Methodology for the Subjective Assessment of the Quality of Television Pictures. International Telecommunication Union, Geneva (1996)
4. Bouch, A., Sasse, M.A.: The Case for Predictable Media Quality in Networked Multimedia Applications. In: Proceedings of ACM/SPIE Multimedia Computing and Networking (MMCN 2000), San Jose, pp. 188–195 (2000)
5. Borowiak, A., Reiter, U., Svensson, U.P.: Quality Evaluation of Long Duration Audiovisual Content. In: The 9th Annual IEEE Consumer Communications and Networking Conference – Special Session on Quality of Experience (QoE) for Multimedia Communications, Las Vegas, pp. 353–357 (2012)
6. Borowiak, A., Reiter, U., Tomic, O.: Measuring the Quality of Long Duration AV Content – Analysis of Test Subject/Time Interval Dependencies. In: EuroITV 2012 – Adjunct Proceedings, Berlin, pp. 266–269 (2012)
7. Chen, K.T., Wu, C.C., Chang, Y.C., Lei, C.L.: A Crowdsourceable QoE Evaluation Framework for Multimedia Content. In: Proceedings of the 17th ACM International Conference on Multimedia, New York, pp. 491–500 (2009)

8. L.A.M.E (Lame Ain't an MP3 Encoder) - The Hydrogenaudio recommended MP3 encoder, http://lame.sourceforge.net
9. ITU-R Recommendation BS.1116 (rev. 1): Methods for the Subjective Assessment of Small Impairments in Audio Systems Including Multichannel Sound Systems. International Telecommunication Union, Geneva (1997)
10. ITU-R, Methodology for the Subjective Assessment of the Quality of Television Pictures BT.500-12, International Telecommunication Union (2009)
11. ITU-T, Subjective Audiovisual Quality Assessment Methods for Multimedia Applications P.911, International Telecommunication Union (1998)
12. Huber, R., Kollmeier, B.: PEMO-Q—A New Method for Objective Audio Quality Assessment Using a Model of Auditory Perception. IEEE Transactions on Audio Speech and Language Processing (2006)

Hashing with Cauchy Graph

Liang Tao and Horace H.S. Ip

Centre for Innovative Applications of Internet and Multimedia Technologies
(AIMtech), Department of Computer Science, City University of Hong Kong,
Kowloon, Hong Kong
liangtao3@student.cityu.edu.hk, cship@cityu.edu.hk

Abstract. Approximate nearest neighbor search within large scale image datasets strongly demands efficient and effective algorithms. One promising strategy is to compute compact bits string via the hashing scheme as representation of data examples, which can dramatically reduce query time and storage requirements. In this paper, we propose a novel Cauchy graph-based hashing algorithm for the first time, which can capture more local topology semantics than Laplacian embedding. In particular, greater similarities are achieved through Cauchy embedding mapped from the pairs of smaller distance over the original data space. Then regularized kernel least-squares, with its closed form solution, is applied to efficiently learn hash functions. The experimental evaluations over several noted image retrieval benchmarks, MNIST, CIFAR-10 and USPS, demonstrate that performance of the proposed hashing algorithm is quite comparable with the state-of-the-art hashing techniques in searching semantic similar neighbors, especially in quite short length hash codes, such as those of only 4, 6, and 8 bits.

1 Introduction

Owing to fast growth of digital cameras and varieties of image-oriented applications as well as websites over the Internet, different categories of images or pictures are effortlessly created, and are easily accessible. This leads to existence of a huge amount of online images. Further, these large numbers of image corpora pose a considerable challenge to image understanding research [1], in particular the issue of image similarity. Presently, numerous online image applications require short time and less memory for image retrieval. Thus the image hashing approach is one of the most promising solutions that creates short length bits string with enough semantics to address current problems of computing similarity between images.

The major goal of similarity search is looking for nearest neighbors. Earlier state-of-the-art tree-based techniques, such as R-tree and KD-tree, are widely applied to find approximate nearest neighbors, but they cannot gain efficiency and effectiveness in high dimensional large-scale image corpus, and tree-based search algorithms do not guarantee the linear time complexity of scanning [2]. Nevertheless, most of visual descriptors, like GIST and SIFT, are high dimensional vectors and, in consequence, tree-based partition approaches are not preferable

W. Lin et al. (Eds.): PCM 2012, LNCS 7674, pp. 21–32, 2012.

in content based image retrieval. Therefore, hashing-based approaches are put forward to address the matter of such high dimensional data so as to compute approximate nearest neighbors with short time and high accuracy via short binary codes [3].

Generally, existing hashing approaches may be grouped into two categories: data-independent and data-dependent techniques. Early methods mainly focus on data-independent scheme, and one of the widely known data-oblivious algorithms is Locality Sensitive Hashing (LSH) [2] that employs random projections to build hashing functions and often require long length hash bits to obtain high precision. The on-going LSH-related methods, for instance kernerlized LSH [4], and metric learning-based (Mahalanobis distance function) LSH [5], are extended to different sorts of distance metrics.

In contrast, the latest algorithm aspires to develop data-related hashing methods that usually yield more compact binary codes with sufficient information, since the data-dependent mode relies on data distribution. There are remarkable instances in data-dependent algorithms, for example, semi-supervised hashing [6], spectral hashing [7], hashing with graphs [8] and semantic hashing [9]. Interestingly, there is another novel spherical hashing [10] whose hashing functions are hypersphere-based instead of existing hyperplane-based hashing functions. All these methods can be generally split into three groups: supervised, unsupervised, and semi-supervised approach.

In supervised learning hashing, the most recent supervised hashing with kernels [11] utilizes coder inner product trick to build compact optimization, but it also involves computing quite difficult optimization. Not surprisingly, lower training cost with higher quality results of supervised learning hashing algorithm remains unobtainable yet. Supervised hashing approaches, meanwhile, are generally slower than unsupervised methods and they can easily lead to undesirable over-fitting due to small labeled training examples. In addition, one typical algorithm in semi-supervised Hashing is [6] whose formulation is stated as minimizing empirical error on the labeled data while adding an information theoretic regularizer over both labeled and unlabeled data.

In unsupervised learning, one of the popular and effective models is spectral hashing (SH) [7] that not only preserves the data sample similarity but also keeps the hash codes uncorrelated and balanced. In other words, different bits in codewords are independent of each other and each bit in codewords has the same 50% probability of being -1 or 1. Further, [8] employs Anchor graph [12] to construct approximate neighborhood graph whose similarities between a pair of data samples are measured with respect to a small number of anchors, and then apply the similar optimized formulation of spectral hashing for hash codes generation. Our algorithm being fully unsupervised, we chiefly consider several of these above unsupervised methods as comparisons in our experiments (see Sect. 4.1).

Importantly, unlike spectral hashing related hashing algorithms, our method utilizes Cauchy graph embedding (see Sect. 3.1) for the first time, which captures more semantics in intrinsic local topology than Laplacian graph embedding employed in spectral hashing. Further, unlike previous approaches, the kernel regularized least-squares (see Sect. 3.2) is applied to learn hash functions. Evaluations over three well-known large scale image datasets, USPS, MNIST and CIFAR-10, show that our proposed method is considerably comparable with the state-of-arts unsupervised hashing algorithms in accuracy of nearest neighbors searching, particularly in short length bits string.

2   Related Work

The principal goal of binary hashing is to map the original data points $\mathcal{X} = \{x_1, \ldots, x_n\} \in \mathbb{R}^{D \times n}$ subsuming n D-dimensional points to a Hamming metric space $\mathcal{H} = (h_1, \ldots, h_n) \in \mathbb{R}^{K \times n}$ such that the similarly/dissimilarity in the original space are kept in the Hamming space. Clearly, hashing codes are extremely fast to perform similarity/dissimilarity computation [13], since the given dataset is highly compressed, and then all the encoded data can be easily loaded into memory. Thus the Hamming distance between codewords can be efficiently computed by using XOR bit operation.

K hash functions create K bits length Hamming codes $\mathcal{Y} \in \mathcal{H}^{K \times n}$, and the k-th hash function is defined as $h_k(x) = sign(f(x)) = sign(w_k^\top x + b_k)$. Based on the $h_k(x) \in \{-1, +1\}$, the hash bit can be given by $y_k(x) = (1 + h_k(x))/2$ so as to satisfy $y_k(x) \in \{0, 1\}$. Intuitively, different methods of computing hashing codewords and choosing $f(\cdot)$ give rise to various hashing algorithms.

2.1   Laplacian Graph Embedding and Spectral Hashing

Spectral Hashing (SH) [7] was put forward to obtain compact binary codes for approximate nearest neighbors (ANN). Not only does it preserve labeled data similarity, but it requires the hash string to be uncorrelated and balanced respectively. These two requirements are defined by the following constraints. Strictly, the optimization function is built as follows:

$$\min \sum_{ij} sim(x_i, x_j) \| \mathcal{H}(x_i) - \mathcal{H}(x_j) \|^2 \tag{1}$$

$$\text{s.t.} : h_k(x_i) \in \{-1, +1\}$$

$$\sum_i h_k(x_i) = 0, k = 1, \ldots, K$$

$$\sum_i h_k(x_i) h_l(x_i) = 0, \text{ for } k \neq l,$$

where $H(x) = \{h_k(x), k = \{1, \ldots, K\}\}$ is Hashing codewords. It is difficult to directly find the optimal solution since the above optimization is equivalent to the problem of balanced graph partition that is NP-hard problem. For this reason, (1) can be solved using spectral analysis through relaxing the discrete constraint to continuous. It is generally considered that Laplacian embedding [14] has the intrinsic local structure perseverng property, i.e. , the data example with its nearest neighbors in the original space are embedded nearby in the embedding space, while data examples with minor similarities are embedded with large distances between them in the embedding space. By substituting Laplacian graph embedding for $sim(x_i, x_j)$, (1) can be rewritten as: $\min trace(\mathcal{H}(D - W)\mathcal{H}^T)$, in which $D(i,i) = \sum_j W(i,j)$, thus (1) is a standard generalized eigenvalue problem whose solutions are simply the K eigenvectors of $D - W$ associated with minimal eigenvalues. Graph Laplacian actually often fails to preserve local intrinsic structure [15] as we expected, Cauchy graph embedding (CGE) , however, lays heavy emphasis on smaller distance pairs in the original dataset $\mathcal{X}$ with larger similarities w_{ij} in the embedding space. Hence, CGE is a reasonable enough method for Hamming embedding (see Sect. 3.1).

3   Hashing with Cauchy Graph Embedding (HCGE)

Inspired by Cauchy Graph Embedding (CGE) [15] whose formulation is roughly similar to the usual Cauchy distribution $f(x) = 1/(x^2 + \sigma^2)$, we propose a novel image hashing algorithm based on CGE in this paper. There are two steps in HCGE to learn hash functions. First, hashing codewords $\mathcal{H}$ are obtained by employing CGE ,which differs fundamentally from Spectral Hashing [7] and Self-taught hashing (STH) [16] as both SH and STH apply spectral clustering. Second, the kernel least-squares with L2-norm regularization term is employed to compute linear Hash function, unlike the second step of STH that adopts SVM to learn hashing functions which require much time for SVM training and introduce some noise in this procedure as well . Moreover, the proposed algorithm is apparently dissimilar to CHMIS-AW [17] whose method couples Laplacian embedding with least-squares.

3.1   Local Topology Structure Preservation via Cauchy Graph Embedding

Cauchy Graph Embedding [15] emphasizes the smaller distance pairs (x_i, x_j) with larger similarities w_{ij}, while Laplacian embedding attaches more importance on larger distance pairs with smaller similarities. Clearly, Cauchy embedding focuses on preserving local topology structure that is sufficient to build the objective function so as to achieve more reasonable short length of hash bits string in semantic hashing algorithms. Meanwhile, the evaluations show highly competitive performance of CGE as well (see Sect. 4).

Given the K-dimensional embedded Hamming space $\mathcal{H} = (\boldsymbol{h}_1, \ldots, \boldsymbol{h}_n) \in \mathbb{R}^{K \times n}$, the optimization formulation can be defined as below.

$$\max_{\mathcal{H}} \mathcal{Q} = \sum_{i,j} \sum_{k=1}^{K} \frac{w_{ij}}{\|\boldsymbol{h}_k(x_i) - \boldsymbol{h}_k(x_j)\|^2 + \sigma^2} \tag{2}$$

$$\text{subject to:} \quad h_k(x_i) \in \{-1, +1\},$$

$$\text{Balance constraint:} \quad \mathcal{H} \cdot \boldsymbol{e} = 0,$$

$$\text{Independence constraint:} \quad \tfrac{1}{n}\mathcal{H} \cdot \mathcal{H}^T = \boldsymbol{I}.$$

Equation (2) is quite different from Spectral Hashing [7] algorithm that is one of the most popular unsupervised hashing algorithms, as (2) places strong emphasis on local topology structure information. In other words, the larger w_{ij} is, the more similar the pairs $(x_i \; x_j)$ are. Therefore, larger w_{ij} ensures the smaller Hamming distance between x_i and x_j, i.e., the first term $\sum_{k=1}^{K} \|\boldsymbol{h}_k(x_i) - \boldsymbol{h}_k(x_j)\|^2$ in the denominator of (2).

By contrast, Laplacian Graph Embedding is exploited in (1) of Spectral Hashing, where large distances between pairs $\|\mathcal{H}(x_i) - \mathcal{H}(x_j)\|^2$ make significant contribution to the objective function, as seen in the (1) – that is to say, spectral hashing de-emphasizes the intrinsic local structure information.

Through the comparison between the formulations of Cauchy graph embedding Hashing (2) and Spectral Hashing (1), this proposed HCGE algorithm is found to be more meaningful than the Laplacian embedding Hashing methods. It also makes much more sense in non-linear low-dimensional Hamming space mapped from real high-dimensional world data.

Nevertheless, how to select thresholds so as to satisfy good semantic hashing would be a natural question. As pointed out by [6], good semantic hashing algorithms need to be entropy maximization. In other words, maximum entropy leads to hashing codes that follow the uniform distribution in Hamming space so that the image corpus is uniformly mapped to Hamming space. Conversely, if the entropy over the image dataset is small, it means that the image corpus are mapped to small number of hashing codes in Hamming space, thus the generated hashing buckets are so inefficient that they increase the probability of hashing collisions. In this way, to meet the criterion of entropy maximization, the thresholds are set to be the median value (denoted as m_k) for the k-th Hash codes. From these analyses, it can be clearly illustrated that entropy maximization is exactly equivalent to balanced constraint in (2).

As a sequel, we first need to relax the discrete constraints $h_k(x_i) \in \{-1, +1\}$ to continuous. Second, with the optimization (2) tackled by Algo. 1, the continuous Hashing codewords can be acquired. Then, we discretize these Hashing codewords to binary hashing bits string by applying median values as thresholds.

3.2   Learning to Hash Functions with Kernel Least-Squares

In Sect. 3.1, the optimal Hamming space $\mathcal{H}$ is obtained, which preserves the similarities in original data space. However, the Hashing codes in Hamming space cannot be directly extended to the query examples. This issue is closely associated with out-of-sample-extension problem in manifold learning. It is true that we may use the Nyström method [18] and Spectral Hashing [7] to generalize the hashing codes for the query samples, but these approaches actually are as time-consuming as doing nearest neighbor search and dependent on rigorous assumption of data distribution. Hence we first propose kernel least-squares to learn to Hash functions, and the linear hash function is represented as $f(\boldsymbol{x_q}) = \sum_{i=1}^{K} \sum_{j=1}^{n} \mathcal{W}_{ij}{}^T \kappa(\boldsymbol{x_j}, \boldsymbol{x_q}) + \boldsymbol{b}$, in which $\mathcal{W} \in \mathbb{R}^{s \times K}$, and $\boldsymbol{b} = [b_1, \ldots, b_K]^T$. The concrete formulation is given by

---

Algorithm 1. Hashing with Cauchy Graph Embedding Training

1: **INPUT:** A data set $\mathcal{X} = \{x_i \in \mathbb{R}^D\}_{i=1}^n$, and length of hash bits string is K.
2: **OUTPUT:** The hashing codewords $\mathcal{H}$ for data samples $\mathcal{X}$.

3: **Initialization:**
4: $\mathcal{H} \longleftarrow$ Laplacian Embedding outcome as a warming start or random matrix $\mathcal{H}$
5: $\mathcal{W} \longleftarrow$ Adjacency matrix of the k nearest neighbours graph for the given image corpus
6: $\Omega = \{\mathcal{H} \in \mathbb{R}^{K \times n} : \mathcal{H}e = 0\}$
7: the iteration number $T = 0$
8: **repeat**
9:     Compute $\mathcal{H}^{(k+1)} \longleftarrow \Pi_\Omega(\mathcal{H}^{(k)} - \eta_t \nabla \mathcal{Q}(\mathcal{H}^{(k)}))$,

$$\text{where } \nabla \mathcal{Q}(\mathcal{H}) = \nabla \mathcal{Q}(\mathcal{H})_{\cdot i} + \lambda (\mathcal{H}\mathcal{H}^T - nI)\mathcal{H},$$

$$\text{in which } \nabla \mathcal{Q}(\mathcal{H})_{\cdot i} = -4 \cdot \sum_{j=1}^n \frac{w_{ij}}{(\sum_{k=1}^K \|\boldsymbol{h}_k(x_i) - \boldsymbol{h}_k(x_j)\|^2 + \sigma^2)^2} \cdot \begin{bmatrix} h_1(x_i) - h_1(x_j) \\ \vdots \\ h_K(x_i) - h_K(x_j) \end{bmatrix}.$$

10:     $T \longleftarrow T + 1$
11: **until** convergence: $\|\mathcal{Q}(\mathcal{H}^{(k+1)}) - \mathcal{Q}(\mathcal{H}^{(k)})\|_F^2 \le \epsilon \|\mathcal{Q}(\mathcal{H}^{(k)})\|_F^2$

12: **Hashing Codes Generation for Training dataset** $\mathcal{H} = \{\boldsymbol{h}_1, \ldots, \boldsymbol{h}_n\}$, and $\mathcal{H} \in \{+1, -1\}^{K \times n}$:
13: **for** $k = 1 : K$ **do**
14:     Obtaining the median value m_k for the k-th Hash codes $\boldsymbol{h}_p$, where $p \in \{1, \ldots, n\}$
15:     Generating the binary k-th hashing codes via $\boldsymbol{h}_p^{(k)} = 1$ if $h_p^{(k)} > m_k$, and returns -1 otherwise
16: **end for**

$$\min_{\mathcal{W}} L = \frac{1}{2} \|\mathcal{H}^T - \mathcal{K}\tilde{\mathcal{W}}\|_F^2 + \frac{\lambda}{2} \|\tilde{\mathcal{W}}\|_F^2, \tag{3}$$

where $\mathcal{H}$ is Hamming codes space

$$\mathcal{K} = \begin{bmatrix} 1 & \kappa(\boldsymbol{x_1}, \boldsymbol{x_1}) & \cdots & \kappa(\boldsymbol{x_1}, \boldsymbol{x_s}) \\ \vdots & \vdots & \vdots & \vdots \\ 1 & \kappa(\boldsymbol{x_n}, \boldsymbol{x_1}) & \cdots & \kappa(\boldsymbol{x_n}, \boldsymbol{x_s}) \end{bmatrix}, \mathcal{W} = \begin{bmatrix} w_{11} & \cdots & w_{1K} \\ \vdots & \vdots & \vdots \\ w_{s1} & \cdots & w_{sK} \end{bmatrix}, \text{ and } \tilde{\mathcal{W}} = \begin{bmatrix} \boldsymbol{b}^T \\ \mathcal{W} \end{bmatrix}.$$

Clearly, the first term in (3) is a loss function that measures the similarity between the outputs of hashing functions and the hashing codes obtained in Sect. 3.1, and the second term $\|\mathcal{W}\|^2$ is to avoid overfitting. λ is a trade-off parameters that can balance the loss function and the regularization term. Therefore, the optimal solution of above regularized kernel least squares (3) can be obtained by $\tilde{\mathcal{W}} = (\lambda I + \mathcal{K}^T \mathcal{K})^{-1} \mathcal{K}^T \mathcal{H}^T$.

3.3 Analysis

Combined with the above two stages, the whole flowchart of Hashing algorithm with Cauchy Graph Embedding is summarized in the following Algo. 2. For Algo. 1, the training procedure is always performed offline. Consequently, the process of prediction is our major concern that conducts dot products and sum aggregations between weight matrix $\tilde{\mathcal{W}}$ and κ. A few hundred data samples can be randomly and uniformly chosen as support samples from the training dataset in order to efficiently compute kernel matrix $\mathcal{K}$. However, note that the prediction can be done in constant time when we apply regularized least-squares, which usually generates high quality hashing functions as well (see Sect. 4.2).

Algorithm 2. Hashing with Cauchy Graph Embedding Predicting

1: **INPUT:**Binary Hashing codes for training examples $\mathcal{H}$ obtained from Algo. 1.
2: **OUTPUT:** The hashing function weight matrix $\tilde{\mathcal{W}}$ and the binary hashing codes for query example $\boldsymbol{x_q}$

3: Calculate $\mathcal{M} = (\lambda I + \mathcal{K}^T \mathcal{K})^{-1} \mathcal{K}^T$
4: Solve $\tilde{\mathcal{W}} = \mathcal{M} \mathcal{H}^T$
5: Calculate the regression output value by $f(\boldsymbol{x_q}) = \tilde{\mathcal{W}}^T \boldsymbol{\kappa}$, in which $\boldsymbol{\kappa} = [1, \kappa(\boldsymbol{x_1}, \boldsymbol{x_q}), \ldots, \kappa(\boldsymbol{x_s}, \boldsymbol{x_q})]^T$. For example, the number of random support samples could be 200, i.e. $s = 200$.

6: **Binary Hashing Codes Generation for query example $\boldsymbol{x_q}$,**
   $\boldsymbol{h} = f(\boldsymbol{x_q}) \in \{+1, -1\}^{K \times 1}$:
7: **for** $k = 1 : K$ **do**
8:    Creating the binary k-th hashing codes via $\boldsymbol{h_p}^{(k)} = (\boldsymbol{h_p}^{(k)} > m_k)$, in which m_k is the median value of the k-th Hash codes $\boldsymbol{h}$
9: **end for**

---

4   Experiments

The experiments are conducted on three popular image benchmarks, CIFAR-10[1], MNIST[2] and USPS[3]. The CIFAR-10 dataset is labeled subsets of 80 million tiny images dataset. It is composed of 60K 32×32 color images in 10 classes, including airplane, automobile, bird and so on, i.e., each class contains 6k sample. We randomly select 20K images as training images and the other 1K as testing queries. All these images are represented by 512-dimensional GIST feature descriptors [19]. Additionally, from the MNIST dataset which is made up of 784-dimensional, we uniformly and randomly choose 30K training samples and 1K

---

[1] http://www.cs.toronto.edu/~kriz/cifar.html
[2] http://yann.lecun.com/exdb/mnist/
[3] http://www.cs.nyu.edu/~roweis/data.html

test data points. As well, the whole 10K 256-dimensional 8-bit grayscale images in the USPS dataset are employed in the training procedure,together with 1K as testing samples. Both MNIST and USPS datasets are handwritten digits from '0' to '9'.

4.1   Comparison Methods and Evaluation Protocols

To validate how Cauchy embedding may capture more local topology semantics than Laplacian embedding, in particular with respect to small length hash codes, our proposed unsupervised HCGE algorithm is evaluated by mainly drawing comparisons with spectral hashing [7] from various measurements that is the best-known representative of unsupervised hashing methods based on Laplacian embedding. In hashing experiments, two practical evaluation procedures [6,8,11] - that is, Hash lookup and Hamming ranking, are commonly applied from short hashing codes length, i.e. 4, to 48 bits length in this paper. Specifically, hamming ranking means that, according to Hamming distance, all the data points are ranked and the desired neighbors are returned from the top of ranked list. It apparently relates to hash quality and its time complexity is linear. Second, Hash lookup indicates that a lookup table is built by utilizing the hashing codewords, and it stresses search speed. Hash lookup often fails owing to sparse Hamming space, and as a consequence the strategy is that neighbors with Hamming radius r of the query are returned and Hash lookup time complexity is constant time.

   For each dataset, we simply adopt least-squares with L2 regularization for the fast prediction process, and do not tune any parameters to an optimal value, such as η, σ and λ in Algo. 1. Further, we employ two different metrics: the precision for the top 50 and 100 retrieved images, and the precision for the images within the Hamming distance radius $r = 1$ and $r = 2$, as illustrated in Fig.1. Notably, the failure to look for any hash table for a test query is treated as zero precision that is rather different from spectral hashing [7], as spectral hashing ignores the failed queries in computing the mean average precision over all test samples. Moreover, we report the precision-recall curves based on the different length of hash codewords. In order to draw them, we vary Hamming radius from 0 to 19 while fixing the number of hashing bits, such as 6 and 8 bits, as depicted in Fig. 2. The final outcome, namely precision and recall, is the average results over all of the testing queries. Here the precision and recall in our experiments are defined as follows:

$$precision = \frac{\text{\# of retrieved relevant images}}{\text{\# of all retrieved images}}, \quad recall = \frac{\text{\# of retrieved relevant images}}{\text{\# of all relevant images}}.$$

4.2   Results and Discussions

To begin with, we evaluate the performance of mean average precision over the three image datasets by varying the length of hashing bits in $\{4, 6, 8, 10, 12, 14, 16\}$, since we need to validate the effectiveness and efficiency of HCGE via such smaller length hashing bits. If these short length hash bits gain better precision than spectral hashing algorithm as explained in Sect. 2.1 , we may consider, to some degree, HCGE obtains more local topology semantics. As displayed in Fig. 1, the smaller hashing bits, i.e., $\{4, 6, 8, 10, 12\}$, acquire better mean average precision than spectral hashing over all three image dataset. Nevertheless, it is worth noting that the HCGE performance, both Hamming distance within 1 and 2, has slightly dropped when the hashing bits length reaches $\{14, 16\}$. These comparison results reasonably confirm that HCGE captures more semantics with smaller length hashing strings. By fixing the number of hashing strings from 4 to 10, the evaluations of

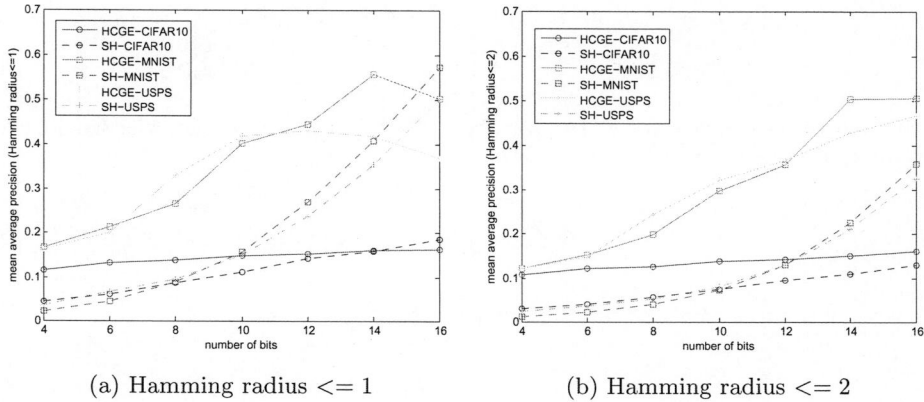

(a) Hamming radius $<= 1$ (b) Hamming radius $<= 2$

Fig. 1. Mean average precision within Hamming radius 1 and 2. HCGE gains its superior performance over the three datasets, MNIST, CIFAR-10, and USPS, especially in such small length of hash codes, namely 4, 6, and 8.

precision and recall curves over MNIST and USPS are described in Fig. 2a and Fig. 2b respectively. It is evident that among these datasets, HCGE delivers its better performance than the spectral hashing within short number of hashing bits. Additionally, as seen in Fig. 3, we compute the average precision for the top 50 and 100 retrieved samples of each test query. Concretely, we increase the Hamming radius until the number of retrieved examples is at least 50 and 100, then re-sort these candidate samples according to the original order in the training dataset. Additionally, the qualitative comparison result is presented in Fig. 4. In the upper two rows, the topmost 25-neighbor results in MNIST are obtained by SH and HCGE respectively, when only 6 hash bits are used. Likewise, the two rows of retrieval outcomes in the middle and bottom are from USPS and CIFAR-10 respectively when 8 binary bits are fixed. From these extensive comparisons among various number of bits, HCGE achieves competitive advantages by virtue of its reasonable property of local underlying structure semantic preserving, especially within such short length of hash bits.

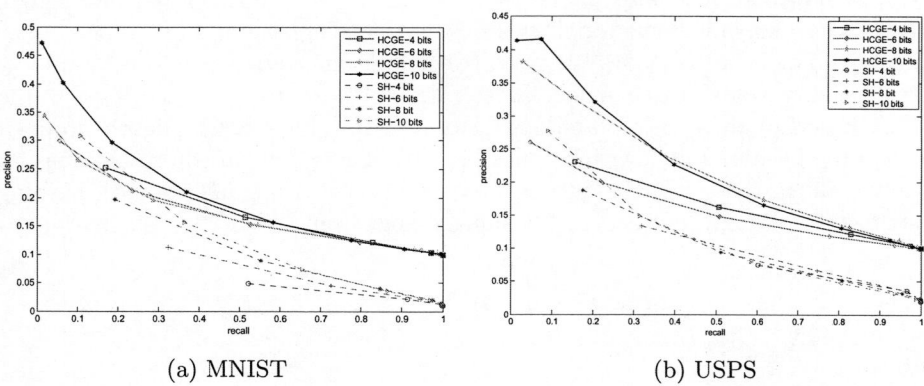

(a) MNIST

(b) USPS

Fig. 2. Precision and Recall Curve over the MNIST and USPS dataset, with fixed hash code length in $\{4, 6, 8, 10\}$

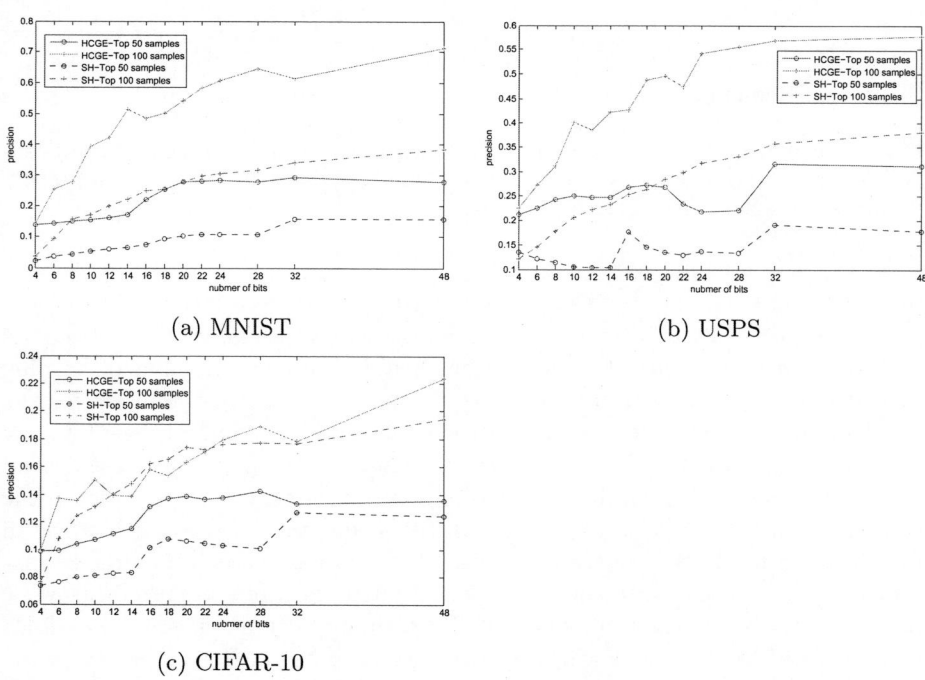

(a) MNIST

(b) USPS

(c) CIFAR-10

Fig. 3. Precision outcome for the top 50 and 100 returned samples. It is clear that HCGE achieves the stronger performance among the three different datasets.

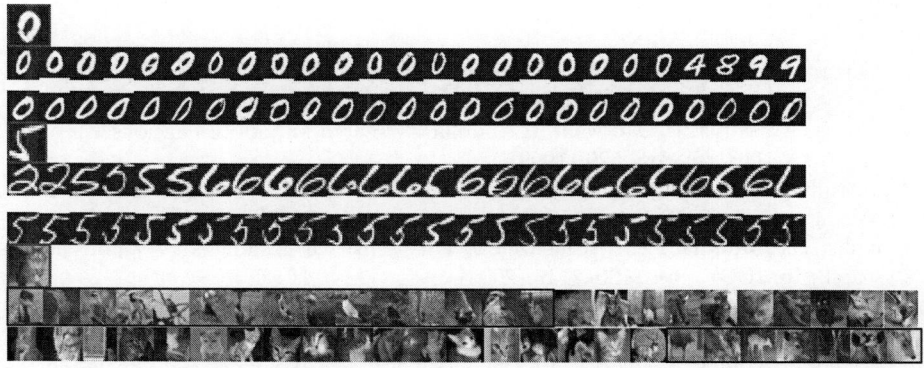

Fig. 4. Top 25 retrieved neighbors of two query digits and one cat query image marked by three red squares. It is apparent that the retrieval quality of HCGE (the 2nd, 4th and 6th rows) are better than SH (the 1st, 3rd, 5th rows) within the same short length binary bits, i.e., 6 and 8. Note that the unrelated retrieved images in CIFAR-10 are marked by blue rectangles.

5   Future Work and Conclusion

In this paper, we employ two independent steps to learn hashing functions. A natural question would be, however, could we well combine the aforementioned two steps to the one whole optimization? Then one acceptable alternative of the objective function will be changed to :

$$\max_{\mathcal{H},\tilde{W}} \mathcal{Q} = C_1 \sum_{i,j} \sum_{k=1}^{K} \frac{w_{ij}}{\left\| \boldsymbol{h}_k(x_i) - \boldsymbol{h}_k(x_j) \right\|^2 + \sigma^2} - (C_2 \|\mathcal{H}^T - \mathcal{K}\tilde{\mathcal{W}}\|_F^2) \quad (4)$$

Clearly, (4) involves the complicated optimization problem that needs to be handled in the future. Besides the joint optimization, sparse kernel least-squares could be adopted for the sake of fast and efficient prediction.

Given the speedy approximate similarity retrieval, semantic hashing is one successful technique that represents samples as very short binary strings so as to tremendously decrease the storage space and accelerate the search speed. The proposed HCGE algorithm incorporates Cauchy embedding into hashing for the first time and extensive evaluations obviously reveal its competitive advantages against the prior hashing approaches based on Laplacian embedding, in particular within remarkable small length binary bits.

Acknowledgments. Liang Tao would like to thank Xin Shu and Prof. Yinglin Wang at Shanghai Jiao Tong University for fruitful discussions and also gratefully thank anonymous reviewers for their critical comments.

References

1. Datta, R., Joshi, D., Li, J., Wang, J.Z.: Image retrieval: Ideas, influences, and trends of the new age. ACM Computing Surveys (April 2008)
2. Gionis, A., Indyk, P., Motwani, R.: Similarity search in high dimensions via hashing. In: VLDB, pp. 518–529 (1999)
3. Torralba, A., Fergus, R., Weiss, Y.: Small codes and large image databases for recognition. In: CVPR (2008)
4. Kulis, B., Grauman, K.: Kernelized locality-sensitive hashing for scalable image search. In: ICCV, pp. 2130–2137 (2009)
5. Kulis, B., Jain, P., Grauman, K.: Fast similarity search for learned metrics. IEEE Trans. Pattern Anal. Mach. Intell. 31(12), 2143–2157 (2009)
6. Wang, J., Kumar, S., Chang, S.F.: Semi-supervised hashing for large scale search. IEEE Transactions on Pattern Analysis and Machine Intelligence (2012)
7. Weiss, Y., Torralba, A., Fergus, R.: Spectral hashing. In: NIPS, pp. 1753–1760 (2008)
8. Liu, W., Wang, J., Kumar, S., Chang, S.F.: Hashing with graphs. In: Getoor, L., Scheffer, T. (eds.) Proceedings of the 28th International Conference on Machine Learning, ICML 2011. ACM, New York (2011)
9. Salakhutdinov, R., Hinton, G.E.: Semantic hashing. Int. J. Approx. Reasoning 50(7), 969–978 (2009)
10. Heo, J.P., Lee, Y., He, J., Chang, S.F., Yoon-eui, S.: Spherical hashing. In: Proceedings of IEEE Conference on Computer Vision and Pattern Recognition, CVPR (2012)
11. Liu, W., Wang, J., Ji, R., Jiang, Y.G., Chang, S.F.: Supervised hashing with kernels. In: Proceedings of IEEE Conference on Computer Vision and Pattern Recognition, CVPR (2012)
12. Liu, W., He, J., Chang, S.F.: Large graph construction for scalable semi-supervised learning. In: Proceedings of the 27th International Conference on Machine Learning, ICML 2010, pp. 679–686 (2010)
13. Stein, B.: Principles of hash-based text retrieval. In: SIGIR, pp. 527–534 (2007)
14. Yan, S., Xu, D., Zhang, B., Zhang, H., Yang, Q., Lin, S.: Graph embedding and extensions: A general framework for dimensionality reduction. IEEE Trans. Pattern Anal. Mach. Intell. 29(1), 40–51 (2007)
15. Luo, D., Ding, C.H.Q., Nie, F., Huang, H.: Cauchy graph embedding. In: ICML, pp. 553–560 (2011)
16. Zhang, D., Wang, J., Cai, D., Lu, J.: Self-taught hashing for fast similarity search. In: SIGIR, pp. 18–25 (2010)
17. Zhang, D., Wang, F., Si, L.: Composite hashing with multiple information sources. In: SIGIR, pp. 225–234 (2011)
18. Bengio, Y., Delalleau, O., Roux, N.L., Paiement, J.F., Vincent, P., Ouimet, M.: Learning eigenfunctions links spectral embedding and kernel pca. Neural Computation 16(10), 2197–2219 (2004)
19. Oliva, A., Torralba, A.: Modeling the shape of the scene: A holistic representation of the spatial envelope. International Journal of Computer Vision 42(3), 145–175 (2001)

Multimedia Event Detection Using Segment-Based Approach for Motion Feature

Sang Phan[1], Thanh Duc Ngo[1], Vu Lam[2], Son Tran[2], Duy-Dinh Le[4],
Duc Anh Duong[3], and Shin'ichi Satoh[4]

[1] The Graduate University for Advanced Studies, Tokyo, Japan
[2] University of Science, VNU-HCM, Vietnam
[3] University of Information Technology, VNU-HCM, Vietnam
[4] National Institute of Informatics, Tokyo, Japan
{plsang,ndthanh,ledduy,satoh}@nii.ac.jp,
{lqvu,ttson}@fit.hcmus.edu.vn, ducda@uit.edu.vn

Abstract. Detecting event in multimedia video has become a popular research topic. One of the most important clues to determine an event in video is its motion features. Currently, motion features are often extracted from the whole video using dense sampling strategy. However, this extraction method is computationally prohibitive when it comes to large scale video dataset. Moreover, video length may be very different, which makes it unreliable to compare the feature between videos. In this paper, we propose to use segment-based approach to extract motion feature. Basically, original videos are quantized into fixed-length segments for both training and testing, while still keep evaluation at video-level. Our approach has achieved promising results when applying for dense trajectory motion feature on TRECVID 2010 Multimedia Event Detection (MED) dataset. Combining with global and local features, our event detection system has comparable performance with other state-of-the-art MED systems, while the computational cost is significantly reduced.

Keywords: multimedia event detection, segment-based, keyframe-based, dense trajectory.

1 Introduction

Multimedia Event Detection (MED) is a challenging task in TRECVID. Given a collection of test videos and a list of test events, the task is to indicate whether each of the test events is present in each of the test videos or not. The aim of MED is to develop systems that can automatically find video clips containing any event of interest, assuming only a limited amount of training exemplars are given. The ultimate goal of this task is to build a system that could quickly and accurately search for ad hoc events.

The need for such MED systems is rising because the mass number of videos are produced every day. For example, there are more than 3 millions hours of video are uploaded and over 3 billion hours of video are watched each month on

W. Lin et al. (Eds.): PCM 2012, LNCS 7674, pp. 33–44, 2012.

YouTube[1], the most popular video sharing website. What is needed are tools for automatically process the video content and look for the presence of a complex event in such unconstrained capturing videos. Automatic detection of complex events has great potential for many applications, such as web video indexing and retrieval, consumer content management, etc. In practice, a football viewer may want to watch goal scenes in a long football video, a housewife may need to search for videos to teach her how to make a cake, a houseman may look for how to repair an appliance, etc.

However, detecting event in multimedia video is a challenging task due to large content variation. The video content is extremely diverse even for the same event. Moreover, there are many events are being tested: 3 events in MED 2010, 10 test events in MED 2011 and 20 test events in MED 2012. Each event may contain a large number of objects with some specific actions in a particular setting. Furthermore, multimedia videos are typically recorded under uncontrolled conditions such as different lighting, viewpoints, occlusions, and complicated camera motions, etc. Therefore, it is very hard for modelling and detecting of multimedia events.

The most successful way to build an MED system is combining multiple features, i.e. incorporating both audio and visual features to boost the performance of the event detection system [1–4]. However, performance of these features, especially motion features, is still limited on such a realistic video dataset like MED. The main reason is that we have to deal with uncontrolled capturing videos, as mentioned above. In addition to that, the video length is also very different (even from videos of the same event) and the clues to determine an event may appear within a small segment of the whole video. Thus, it is unreliable when comparing the representation of two videos because it may contain unrelated information.

In our MED system, we propose to use segment-based approach to lessen the impact of video length to the detection performance. More specifically, first we do statistics on the training dataset and calculate the mean length of all videos. Then we subdivide the video into fixed-length parts based on the calculated mean length above. These parts are referred to segments in our experiments. After that, we do all annotation, training and testing at segment-level. Finally, for evaluation, we empirically choose score of a video is the largest score of its segments. We compare performance of the new segment-based approach with the adaptive keyframe-based approach, where experiments for motion feature are done on fixed-length volumes around the keyframe extraction points. We also compare performance of our event detection system with other state-of-the-art MED systems by combining motion feature with global and local feature.

The rest of the paper is organized as follows. Section 2 introduces the related work. Section 3 gives an overview of dense trajectory motion feature and our segment-based approach. Experimental setup including introduction to the benchmark dataset and the evaluation method are presented in Section 4. Then, in Section 5, we present and analyze our experimental results. Finally, Section 6 concludes the paper with discussions of future work.

---

[1] http://www.youtube.com/t/press_statistics

2   Related Work

Start challenging from TRECVID 2010[2], Multimedia Event Detection has drawn attention of many researchers. There are 7 teams participated in the debut challenge and 19 teams participated one year after that (TRECVID MED 2011). Many MED system have been built and different strategies have been employed for the event detection system.

In TRECVID 2010, Columbia University (CU) team won the best MED system. Their success has a great influence to later MED systems. In their paper [1], they answered two important questions: (1) What kind of feature is more effective for multimedia event detection? (2) Are features from different feature modalities (e.g., audio and visual) complementary for event detection? In order to answer the first question, different kinds of feature have been studied: SIFT [5] for image feature, STIP [6] for motion feature and MFCC (Mel-frequency cepstral coefficients) for audio feature. In general, STIP motion feature is the best single feature for MED. However, in order to achieve better results, the system should combine strong complementary features from multiple modalities (both visual and audio).

IBM team [2] won the runner-up MED system in TRECVID 2010. They incorporated information from a wide range of static and dynamic visual features to build the baseline detection system. For static features, they used local SIFT [5], GIST [7] descriptors and various global features such as Color Histogram, Color Correlogram, Color Moments, Wavelet Texture, etc. For dynamic feature, they used STIP [6] feature with HOG/HOF [8] descriptor.

The Nikon MED 2010 system [3] is also a remarkable system by its simple but effective solution. They built an MED system based on the assumption that a small number of images in a given video contains enough information for event detection. Thus, they reduce the event detection task to the classification problem for a set of images, called keyframe. However, the keyframe extraction is based on a scene cut detection technique which is less reliable in realistic videos. Moreover, the scene length is not consistent, which may affect the detection performance.

The system of BBN Viser [4] achieved the best performance in TRECVID MED 2011. Their success confirmed the effectiveness of multiple modalities approach for multimedia event detection. In this work, they further investigated the performance of appearance features (e.g. SIFT [5]), color feature (e.g. RGB-SIFT [9]), and motion (e.g. STIP [6]), and also MFCC based audio features. Different kind of fusion strategies have been explored, from which the novel nonparametric fusion strategy based on video specific weighted average fusion has shown promising results.

In general, most teams utilized the multiple modalities approach to build their baseline detection systems. For motion features, they employed the popular STIP proposed by Laptev in [6]. Other systems also took into account HOG3D [10] and MoSIFT [11] motion feature. All these systems employed video-based

---

[2] www.nist.gov/itl/iad/mig/med10.cfm

approach for motion features, i.e. motion features are extracted from the whole video, which is very expensive in terms of computation time and storage cost. As a result, these systems rigorously rely on high-performance computers. The IBM's MED system [2] also applied the video-based approach but video was downsampled to five frames per seconds.

Different from other systems, we use segment-based approach for motion features. To the best of our knowledge, no MED system has employed this approach in their system. To prove the efficiency of our proposed approach, we evaluate its performance with dense trajectory motion feature, which is recently proposed by Wang in [12]. Dense trajectory has achieved state-of-the-art performance in various video dataset, including challenging dataset like Youtube Action[3] and UCF Sports[4]. Regarding to feature representation technique, we use the popular "bag-of-words" (BOW) model in [13]. For classification, we utilize the Support Vector Machine (SVM) classifier for training and testing. Finally, a simple non-weighted late fusion technique is adopted for combining multiple results.

3   Dense Trajectory and Segment-Based Approach

In this section, we introduce the dense trajectory motion feature proposed by Wang in [12]. We briefly review the trajectory extraction and description method. Detailed calculation for all related feature descriptors, especially for Motion Boundary Histogram, is also presented. Our segment-based approach for motion feature is introduced at the end of this section.

3.1   Dense Trajectory

Trajectories are obtained by tracking densely sampled points using optical flow fields. First, feature points are sampled on a grid with step size of 5 pixels and at multiple scales spaced by a factor of $1/\sqrt{2}$. Then feature points are tracked in each scale separately. Each point $P_t = (x_t, y_t)$ at frame t is tracked to the next frame $t+1$ by median filtering in a dense optical flow field $\omega = (u_t, v_t)$:

$$P_{t+1} = (x_{t+1}, y_{t+1}) = (x_t, y_t) + (M * \omega)|_{(\bar{x}_t, \bar{y}_t)}, \qquad (1)$$

where M is the median filter, and $(\bar{x}_t, \bar{y}_t)$ is the rounded position of (x_t, y_t).

Trajectory Descriptor (TD): The Trajectory Descriptor is the most simple one for representing an extracted trajectory. It is defined based on the displacement vectors. Given a trajectory of length L, its shape is described by a sequence $S = (\Delta P_t , ..., \Delta P_{t+L-1})$, where $\Delta P_t = P_{t+1} - P_t = (x_{t+1} - x_t, y_{t+1} - y_t)$. The resulting vector is then normalized by the sum of the magnitudes of the displacement vectors:

$$S' = \frac{(\Delta P_t, ..., \Delta P_{t+L-1})}{\sum_{j=t}^{t+L-1} \|\Delta P_j\|} \qquad (2)$$

---

[3] http://www.cs.ucf.edu/~liujg/YouTube_Action_dataset.html
[4] http://www.cs.ucf.edu/vision/public_html

Trajectory-Aligned Descriptors: More complex descriptors can be computed within a space-time volume around the trajectory. The size of the volume is NxN spatial pixels and L temporal frames. This volume is further divided into a grid of size n_σ x n_σ x n_τ to encode spatial-temporal information between features. The default setting for these parameters are N = 32 pixels, L = 15 frames, $n_\sigma = 2$, $n_\tau = 3$. The features are calculated and aggregated in each region separately. Finally, feature in all regions are concatenated to form a single representation for the trajectory. Following this design, three kinds of descriptors have been employed for representing trajectory:

1. Histogram of Oriented Gradient (HOG): The HOG descriptor is proposed by Dalal et al. in [14] for object detection. It captures appearance information within a tiled window of size NxN. At each pixel, the image gradient vector is calculated and converted to an angle in full orientation (360°). Based on this angle, that pixel is voted into its corresponding orientation bin, weighted by the magnitude of the gradient vector. For default setting, orientations are quantized into 8 bins for computing histogram. Once the histogram is computed, it is normalized with its L_2 norm.
2. Histogram of Optical Flow (HOF): The HOF descriptor is used by Laptev [8] in conjunction with HOG descriptor for human action recognition. The method to compute HOF is similar to HOG, but differs in that HOF is computed in the optical flow image. Thus it can capture the local motion information. By default, HOF are computed with 8 orientation bins and an additional zero bin (i.e., in total 9 bins). Just like HOG, HOF descriptor is also normalized with its L_2 norm.
3. Motion Boundary Histogram (MBH): The MBH descriptor is also proposed by Dalal et al. [15] for human detection, where derivatives are computed separately for the horizontal and vertical components of the optical flow I_ω = (I_x, I_y). Spatial derivatives are computed for each component of the optical flow field I_x and I_y independently. After that, orientation information is quantized into histogram, similarly to the HOG descriptor (8-bin histogram for each component). Finally, these two histograms are normalized separately with the L_2 norm and concatenated together to form the final representation. Since MBH represents the gradient of the optical flow, constant motion information is suppressed and only information about changes in the flow field (i.e., motion boundaries) is kept.

3.2   Segment-Based Approach for Motion Feature

For dense trajectory motion feature, we consider two approaches for feature extraction and representation: (1) the adaptive keyframe-based and (2) the proposed segment-based. The adaptive keyframe-based is used to make the system compatible with the keyframe sampling strategy for testing global and local feature in our previous study. In this approach, trajectories are extracted densely within a temporal volume of trajectory length (e.g. 15 frames) starting from the keyframe extraction point. By doing this, we can naturally incorporate static visual feature with motion information at a specific keyframe. On the other hand, in the second approach, the video is subdivided into fixed length segments, based on the mean video length in the development dataset. After that, dense trajectory features are extracted from the whole segment. From the raw trajectory features, a "bag-of-words" approach can be employed to generate the final representation for each segment (See Fig. 1).

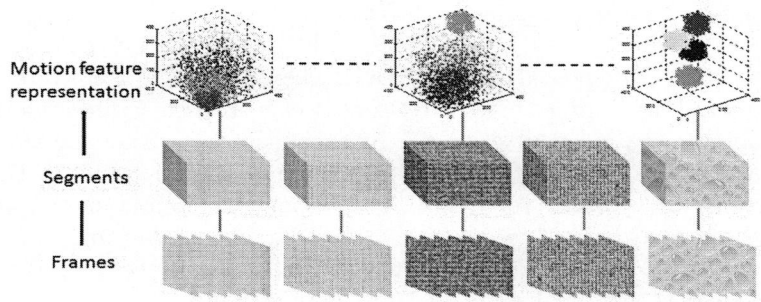

Fig. 1. Segment-based approach for motion features

Essentially, segment-based approach differs from the adaptive keyframe-based approach in three aspects: (1) trajectory features are extracted from a denser volume; (2) motion features captured in the a whole segment are more reliable (regularly, motion information at a specific keyframe is either constant or nonconsistent); and (3) combining segment-based motion features with static visual features must be done at video-level, while for the former approach, it can be done at keyframe-level.

There are some reasons that we didn't employ video-based approach. At first, it is computationally prohibitive in small computer systems. Loading and saving for a whole video may take a long time. Especially, if a data compression technique is applied to save the storage cost, it even put more computational burden because of I/O processing cost and excessive memory usage. To this end, the segment-based approach is the most efficient. Moreover, we believe that segment-based approach is also more effective compared to video-based. Our assumption is that the clues to determine an event is more likely to appear within a small segment rather than the whole video. Thus, using segment-based reduces capturing unrelated information in the final representation.

4   Experimental Setup

4.1   Datasets

All experiments reported in this paper are done on the MED 2010 video dataset. This dataset contains 3468 videos, including 1744 videos for training and 1724

Table 1. Statistics on MED'10 dataset

	Devel videos	Test videos
Min	10s	10s
Mean	116s	121s
Variance	141s	203s
Sum	201604s (56h)	209127s (58h)

videos for testing, with totally more than 100 video hours. In TRECVID MED 2010, there are totally 3 events classes: assembling a shelter, batting a run in and making a cake. An event kit is provided for each event giving definition and illustration of that event. Table 1 shows some statistics of the video duration in MED'10 dataset. Based on the mean length of all videos in the development dataset, we choose the segment length of 115 seconds for our segment-based experiments.

4.2   Evaluation Method

Evaluation of Motion Feature: Figure 2 shows our evaluation framework for motion features. We do experiment for both the adaptive keyframe-based and the proposed segment-based. To extract dense trajectory feature, we use the library published online by the author[5]. To save computing time, the source code is customized to make it resample points for tracking after every 15 frames. Other parameters are set to default. Due to the large number of features produced by dense sampling strategy, we employ the "bag-of-words" approach to generate features for keyframes/segments. At first, we randomly select 1,000,000 keypoints for clustering to form a codebook of 1000 visual codewords. After that, the frequency histogram of visual words is computed over keyframes/segments to generate the final feature vector. To improve the performance of the "bag-of-words" approach, we also adopt the soft assignment weighting scheme which was initially proposed by Jiang in [16].

Once all features are extracted, we use the popular Support Vector Machine (SVM) for classification. Concretely, we use the LibSVM library available online[6] and adopt the one-vs.-rest scheme for multi-class classification. To prepare data for the classifier, we annotate data as below: all keyframes/segments of positive videos are considered as positive samples; remaining keyframes/segments (in the development set) are chosen for negative samples. For testing purpose, we also use LibSVM to predict score of keyframes/segments in each testing video. The score of a video is defined as the largest score among its keyframes/segments. This score indicates how likely a video belongs to an event class.

---

[5] http://lear.inrialpes.fr/people/wang/dense_trajectories
[6] http://www.csie.ntu.edu.tw/~cjlin/libsvm/

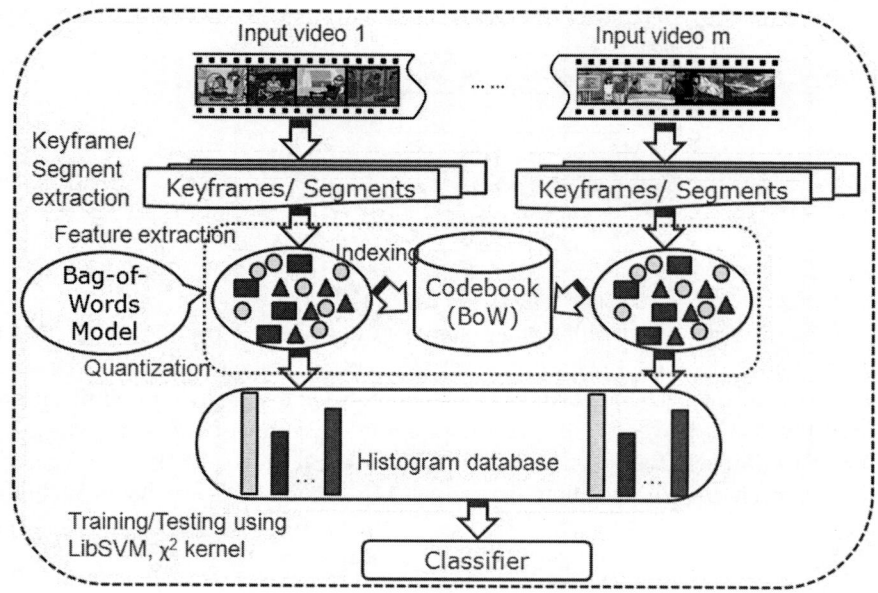

Fig. 2. Evaluation framework for our baseline MED system

Evaluation of Our Baseline MED System: To make our MED system comparable with state-of-the-art MED systems, we also adopt a multiple modalities approach. More specifically, we integrate global and local feature into our MED system and evaluate the performance along with the motion feature. We empirically choose four types of global features, namely Color Histogram, Color Moment, Edge Oriented Histogram and Local Binary Pattern. These features capture various kinds of global information including color, texture, edge, etc. According to our previous study, these global features are the most effective and stable for different image classification tasks. For local feature, we use the popular SIFT feature, proposed by Lowe in [5]. SIFT is best known for its invariant characteristics to rotation, shift and scale. Combining with the dense sampling strategy, SIFT is very powerful for image classification tasks. We also employ the "bag-of-words" approach to reduce the computation time while still keep the retrieval power of SIFT feature. Moreover, following Jiang's experimental setup in [17], we use 4 spatial layouts including 1x1, 2x2, 1x3 and 3x1 (colxrow) to encode spatial information for bag-of-words features. As for training and testing, we integrate these steps into our evaluation framework (See Fig. 2).

Finally, in order to combine multiple features for exploring event detection performance, we adopt the late fusion strategy. More concretely, after having scores of keyframes/segments for each feature, we calculate the average score for each keyframe/segment over all combined features. We consider the average score as the score of the fusion run and use it for evaluation.

5   Experimental Results

This section presents experimental results of dense trajectory feature for three events on the MED'10 dataset. We also report the performance of our baseline event detection system (combining global, local and motion features) in this section. All experiments are performed on our multi-processors computer, consisting 24 Intel(R) Xeon(R) CPU X7460 2.66GHz processors with totally more than 120GB RAM. All results are reported in terms of Mean Average Precision (MAP). From the final score of each video in the test set, we calculate MAP using the TRECVID evaluation tool[7]. The best performing feature is highlighted in bold for each event.

Table 2. Performance of dense trajectory feature on MED'10 dataset

Event/MAP	Adaptive Keyframe-based				Segment-based
	TD	HOG	HOF	MBH	MBH
assembling a shelter	0.2091	0.2575	0.2440	0.3579	**0.4246**
batting a run in	0.1404	0.2929	0.3640	0.4734	**0.7137**
making a cake	0.1033	0.0922	0.0896	0.1687	**0.2685**
all	0.1510	0.2142	0.2325	0.3333	**0.4686**

Result of Motion Feature: Table 2 shows the results of dense trajectory feature with different kinds of descriptors for both the adaptive keyframe-based and segment-based approach. The MBH descriptor is best single descriptor for dense trajectory feature. Its performance when using segment-based approach is significantly increased (nearly 15%) compared to the previous keyframe-based approach. The computation time when using adaptive keyframe-based is about 10 days. However, it took us more than one month to finish our segment-based experiment just for MBH feature descriptor.

Result of Our Baseline MED System: In Table 3, we show the performance of our baseline event detection system (in the second column). For each kind of feature, we choose to show our best run. Obviously, these features are complementary to each other. For example, while the MAP for detecting "assembling a shelter" event is quite low when using global and local features, it is improved more than 15% when using motion feature.

We also compare our results with the performance of top MED'10 systems: the best system by Columbia University [1] and the runner-up system by IBM [2]. For Columbia University's MED system, we choose the run using local SIFT feature, the run using STIP motion feature and their combined run (visual features only).

---

[7] http://www-nlpir.nist.gov/projects/trecvid/trecvid.tools/

Table 3. Comparison of our baseline system with top performance MED'10 systems

Event/ MAP	Our MED system				IBM [2]	Colombia University [1]		
	Global feature (1)	Local feature (SIFT) (2)	Motion feature (MBH) (3)	Fusion of (1),(2),(3)	Best result (GIST + SIFT + STIP)	Local feature (SIFT) (1)	Motion feature (STIP) (2)	Fusion of (1),(2)
assembling a shelter	0.2279	0.2714	**0.4246**	0.3295	N/A	0.353	0.468	**0.508**
batting a run in	0.7689	0.7257	0.7137	**0.7928**	N/A	0.787	0.719	**0.796**
making a cake	0.3459	0.4200	0.2675	**0.4316**	N/A	0.396	0.476	**0.476**
all	0.4476	0.4724	0.4686	**0.5180**	**0.46**	0.512	0.554	**0.593**

For IBM's MED system, we only have the overall performance of their best run (combing GIST, SIFT and STIP) [2]. Obviously, our single MBH feature already has comparable result with IBM's best result. However, although our combined run has significantly improved the overall performance, it is still lower than Columbia University's results. The reason is maybe our system is not well-optimized and we are still using a light-weight configuration for dense trajectory feature (i.e. resampling for tracking after every 15 frames instead of 1 frame by default).

Regarding to computation time for motion features, it is obvious that our system has lower cost than CU's and IBM's system. They both use STIP to capture motion feature. Our internal experiment showed that extracting STIP is approximately twice times longer than extracting dense trajectory feature on the same video. Moreover, we are using a light-weight configuration for dense trajectory feature. The computational cost for static features is assumingly equivalent among all systems and much more lower than that of motion features. Therefore, we conclude that our MED system is more efficient than others while still has state-of-the-art performance.

6   Summary and Conclusion

In this paper, we proposed to use segment-based approach for extracting motion feature. We evaluated our approach for the dense trajectory motion feature on MED 2010 dataset. To have insightful comparison, we also evaluated the performance of global and local feature. So far, the result of segment-based approach for motion feature is really promising: (1) it has much better performance compared to the adaptive keyframe-based approach for motion feature; (2) it has comparable performance with local feature and slightly better than global feature;

(3) when combining with global and local feature, it achieves state-of-the-art performance while still more efficient than other top MED systems.

Through this study, we also confirm that the multiple modalities approach for multimedia event detection is really useful. The combined run of global, local and motion feature can now serve as a baseline MED system for the community for further improvement. At the moment, we only use late fusion with equal weights for combining multiple features. We believe that the baseline system can be further improved by adopting a weighted fusion strategy, where weights are learnt from the development dataset.

In this work, we haven't done experiments on the MED 2011 dataset, which contains more than 1400 hours video. We also haven't compared performance of our segment-based approach with the video-based approach. However, a comprehensive comparison of these approaches can help build a better baseline system. Therefore, we suggest to further investigate on the impact different extraction strategies to the performance of the event detection system, including segment-based, video-based and approaches based on shot boundary detection, etc. To make more convincing conclusions, the comparison should be experimented on the MED 2011 dataset as well.

References

1. Jiang, Y.G., Zeng, X., Ye, G., Bhattacharya, S., Ellis, D., Shah, M., Chang, S.F.: Columbia-ucf trecvid2010 multimedia event detection: Combining multiple modalities, contextual concepts, and temporal matching. In: NIST TRECVID Workshop, Gaithersburg, MD (November 2010)
2. Hill, M., Hua, G., Natsev, A., Smith, J.R., Xie, L., Huang, B., Merler, M., Ouyang, H., Zhou, M.: Ibm research trecvid-2010 video copy detection and multimedia event detection system. In: NIST TRECVID Workshop, Gaithersburg, MD (November 2010)
3. Matsuo, T., Nakajima, S.: Nikon multimedia event detection system. In: NIST TRECVID Workshop, Gaithersburg, MD (November 2010)
4. Natarajan, P., Manohar, V., Wu, S., Tsakalidis, S., Vitaladevuni, S.N., Zhuang, X., Prasad, R., Ye, G., Liu, D.: Bbn viser trecvid 2011 multimedia event detection system. In: NIST TRECVID Workshop, Gaithersburg, MD (December 2011)
5. Lowe, D.G.: Distinctive image features from scale-invariant keypoints. International Journal of Computer Vision 60(2), 91–110 (2004)
6. Laptev, I.: On space-time interest points. International Journal of Computer Vision 64(2-3), 107–123 (2005)
7. Oliva, A., Torralba, A.: Modeling the shape of the scene: A holistic representation of the spatial envelope. International Journal of Computer Vision 42(3), 145–175 (2001)
8. Laptev, I., Marszałek, M., Schmid, C., Rozenfeld, B.: Learning realistic human actions from movies. In: Conference on Computer Vision & Pattern Recognition (June 2008)
9. van de Sande, K.E.A., Gevers, T., Snoek, C.G.M.: Evaluating color descriptors for object and scene recognition. IEEE Transactions on Pattern Analysis and Machine Intelligence 32, 1582–1596 (2010)

10. Kläser, A., Marszałek, M., Schmid, C.: A spatio-temporal descriptor based on 3d-gradients. In: British Machine Vision Conference, pp. 995–1004 (September 2008)
11. Chen, M., Hauptmann, A.: Mosift: Recognizing human actions in surveillance videos. In: Computer Science Department, CMU-CS-09-161 (2009)
12. Wang, H., Kläser, A., Schmid, C., Liu, C.L.: Action Recognition by Dense Trajectories. In: IEEE Conference on Computer Vision & Pattern Recognition, Colorado Springs, United States, pp. 3169–3176 (June 2011)
13. Csurka, G., Dance, C.R., Fan, L., Willamowski, J., Bray, C.: Visual categorization with bags of keypoints. In: Workshop on Statistical Learning in Computer Vision, ECCV, pp. 1–22 (2004)
14. Dalal, N., Triggs, B.: Histograms of oriented gradients for human detection. In: International Conference on Computer Vision & Pattern Recognition, INRIA Rhône-Alpes, ZIRST-655, av. de l'Europe, Montbonnot-38334, vol. 2, pp. 886–893 (June 2005)
15. Dalal, N., Triggs, B., Schmid, C.: Human Detection Using Oriented Histograms of Flow and Appearance. In: Leonardis, A., Bischof, H., Pinz, A. (eds.) ECCV 2006. LNCS, vol. 3952, pp. 428–441. Springer, Heidelberg (2006)
16. Jiang, Y.G., Ngo, C.W., Yang, J.: Towards optimal bag-of-features for object categorization and semantic video retrieval. In: Proceedings of the 6th ACM International Conference on Image and Video Retrieval, pp. 494–501 (2007)
17. Jiang, Y.G., Yang, J., Ngo, C.W., Hauptmann, A.G.: Representations of keypoint-based semantic concept detection: A comprehensive study. IEEE Transactions on Multimedia 12, 42–53 (2010)

Robust Feature Bundling

Stefan Romberg*, Moritz August, Christian X. Ries, and Rainer Lienhart

Multimedia Computing and Computer Vision Lab, Augsburg University
{romberg,ries,lienhart}@informatik.uni-augsburg.de
http://www.multimedia-computing.de

Abstract. In this work we present a feature bundling technique that aggregates individual local features with features from their spatial neighborhood into bundles. The resulting bundles carry more information of the underlying image content than single visual words. As in practice an exact search for such bundles is infeasible, we employ a robust approximate similarity search with min-hashing in order to retrieve images containing similar bundles.

We demonstrate the benefits of these bundles for small object retrieval, i.e. logo recognition, and generic image retrieval. Multiple bundling strategies are explored and thoroughly evaluated on three different datasets.

1 Introduction

In computer vision, the bag-of-visual words approach has been very popular in recent years. Hereby, an image is described by multiple local features; their high-dimensional descriptor vectors are clustered and quantized to a single integer number - called visual word - that represents the cluster center. An image is then usually modeled as an unordered collection of word occurrences, the so-called bag-of-words. This description provides an enormous data reduction compared to the original descriptor vectors. Its benefits are a fixed-size image description, robustness to occlusion and viewpoint changes and eventually simplicity, i.e. small computational complexity.

In this work we describe a novel approach that builds on visual words and aggregates spatially close visual words into bundles. Such bundles are more distinctive than individual visual words alone, i.e. objects and image regions are described with more expressiveness. We propose a robust method for approximate similarity search for such bundles, with performance close to the standard bag-of-words method, but with higher precision and much lower response ratio, i.e. less false positives.

Two different bundling strategies are evaluated thoroughly on three different dataset and compared to bag-of-words retrieval and two recent min-hashing approaches. We show that the retrieval using feature bundles yields similar performance as standard bag-of-words retrieval and outperforms two other min-hash-based approaches while providing a response ratio as low as the latter.

---

* This project is funded by Deutsche Forschungsgesellschaft (DFG).

W. Lin et al. (Eds.): PCM 2012, LNCS 7674, pp. 45–56, 2012.

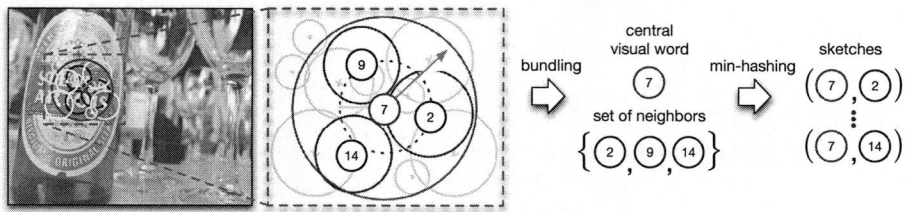

Fig. 1. Feature bundles: The neighborhood around a local feature, the *central feature* (red), is described by a feature bundle. Features that are too far away or on scales too different from that of the central feature are ignored during the bundling (yellow). The features included in such a bundle (blue) are represented as set of visual word occurrences and indexed by min-hashing (see Section 4).

2 Motivation

It has been observed several times that the retrieval performance of bag-of-word-based methods improves much more by reducing the number of mismatching visual words, e.g. by large vocabularies or Hamming Embedding [5], than by reducing quantization artifacts. In other words, the precision of the visual description seems to be more important than its recall, because low recall may be recovered by doing a second retrieval round, i.e. by query expansion.

Inspired by this observation our contribution is a feature bundling technique that builds on bag-of-words but does not describe each visual word individually but rather aggregates the spatial neighboring visual words into feature bundles. We propose an efficient indexing and search technique for such bundles based on min-hashing, that allows for similarity search without requiring exact matching.

As illustrated in Figure 1 on the left, we combine a visual word with its spatially neighboring visual words into a bundle in order to obtain a more expressive description of the respective image region.

Such bundles carry more information than individual visual words. Thus, we expect that more false positives are suppressed during the retrieval and the returned result set is much smaller and cleaner, compared to traditional bag-of-words. Small result sets are beneficial because expensive post-retrieval steps only need to be applied to a small number of images.

3 Related Work

As the core of our approach is based on min-hashing, we briefly highlight the related work on min-hashing relevant in the context of our approach.

Min-hashing (mH). Min-Hashing is a locality-sensitive hashing technique that is suitable for approximate similarity search of sparse sets. Originally developed for detection of duplicate text documents, it was adopted for near-duplicate image detection [3] and extended to the approximation of weighted set overlap as well as histogram intersection [4]. In each of these settings an image is modeled as a sparse set of visual word occurrences. As the average number of visual words per image is much smaller than the vocabulary size for large vocabularies, the resulting feature histograms are sparse and are converted to binary histograms or simply sets representing whether a visual word is present or not.

If one were able to do a linear search over all sets in a database one might define a threshold on the overlap $ovr(I_1, I_2)$ between such sets I_1 and I_2. This is equivalent to a threshold on the Jaccard similarity and determines whether these two sets are identical or "matching". However, as the linear search is infeasible in practice the min-hashing scheme provides an efficient way to index these sets based on this overlap criterion.

Given the set of l visual words $I = \{v_0, ..., v_{l-1}\}$ of an image, the min-hash function is defined as

$$mh(I) = \underset{v_i \in I}{\arg\min} \ h(v_i) \tag{1}$$

where h is a hash function that maps each visual word v_i to a random value from a uniform distribution. Thus, the min-hash mh itself is a visual word, namely that word that yields the minimum hash value (hence the name min-hash). The probability that a min-hash function mh will have the same value for two different sets I_1 and I_2 is equal to the set overlap:

$$P(mh(I_1) = mh(I_2)) = ovr(I_1, I_2) = \frac{|I_1 \cap I_2|}{|I_1 \cup I_2|} \tag{2}$$

Note that, an individual min-hash value not only represents a randomly drawn word that is part of the set, but each min-hash also implicitly "describes" the words that are *not* present and would have generated a smaller hash - because otherwise it would have been a different min-hash value.

The approximate search for similar sets is then performed by finding sets that share min-hashes. As single min-hashes alone yield true matches as well as many false positives or random collisions, multiple min-hashes are grouped into k-tuples, called *sketches*. This aggregation increases precision drastically. To improve recall, this process is repeated n times and independently drawn min-hashes are grouped into n tuples of length k. The probability that two different sets have at least one of these n sketches in common is then given by

$$P(collision) = 1 - (1 - ovr(I_1, I_2)^k)^n \tag{3}$$

This probability function depends on the set overlap and in practice the overlap between non-near-duplicate images that still show the same object is very close to 0. In fact, the average overlap for a large number of partial near-duplicate images was reported to be 0.019 in [6]. This makes clear that for applications which target the retrieval of partial-near-duplicates e.g. visually similar objects rather than full-near-duplicates, the most important part of that probability function is the behavior very close to 0.

The indexing of sets and the approximate search are then performed as follows: To index sets their corresponding sketches are inserted into hash-tables (by hashing the sketches itself into hash keys), which turn the (exact) search for a part of the set (the sketch) into simple lookups. To retrieve similar sets for a query set, one simply computes the corresponding sketches and searches for these sets in the database, that have one or more sketches in common with the query. This is performed by doing lookups of each query sketch and determining whether this sketch is present in the hash table, which we denote as "collision" in the following. The lookups can be done efficiently in constant time as hash table offer access in amortized $\mathcal{O}(1)$. If there is a query sketch of size k that collides with a sketch in the hash table, then the similarity of their originating sets is > 0, because at least k of the min-hash functions agreed. To avoid collisions resulting from unrelated min-hash functions, the sketches are put into separate hash tables, i.e. the k-th sketch is inserted into the k-th hash table.

Geometric min-hashing (GmH). A conceptually similar approach to ours is geometric min-hashing [2]. However, its statistical pre-conditions for the hashing of sparse sets are totally different to our setting. There are two major differences: (1) GmH samples several central features by min-hash functions from all over the image. Thus, neither all nor even most features are guaranteed to be included in the image description. (2) Given a central feature (randomly drawn by a hash function) the local neighborhood of such feature is described by a single sketch. In summary, this makes GmH very memory efficient, but not suitable for generic image retrieval because of bad recall. Consequently, the authors use it to quickly retrieve images from a large database in order to build initial clusters of highly similar images [2][1]. These clusters are then used as "seeds"; each of the contained image is used as query for a traditional image search to find more cluster members that could not be retrieved by GmH.

Partition min-hashing (PmH). In [6] a scheme is introduced that divides the image into several partitions. Unlike the global min-hashing (mH), min-hashes and sketches are computed for all partitions independently. The search then proceeds by determining the sketch collisions for each of the partitions. As the partitions may overlap and are processed step by step this scheme is conceptually similar to a sliding window search. The authors show that this scheme has identical collision probabilities for sketches as mH in the worst case, but better recall and precision if the duplicate image region only covers a small area. Furthermore PmH is significantly faster than mH. We include PmH in our evaluation and find that it performs not significantly better than mH on our dataset.

4   Feature Bundles

We build our bundling technique on min-hash mainly for two reasons: (1) Feature bundles can be naturally represented as sparse sets and (2) min-hash does not imply a strict ordering or a hard matching criterion. This requirement is not met by local feature bundles. Due to image noise, viewpoint and lighting changes, the individual local features, their detections, and their quantizations are unstable and vary across images. Even among two very similar images, it is extremely unlikely that they share identical bundles. We therefore utilize the min-hashing scheme as a robust description of local feature bundles because it allows to search for similar (not identical) bundles.

We consider the proposed bundling technique an efficient search method for similar images with higher memory requirements than pure near-duplicate search methods, but similar to that of bag-of-words. Its performance is close to bag-of-words, but with much lower response ratio and therefore higher precision.

4.1 Bundle Min-Hashing

The idea of our bundling technique is simple: We describe the neighborhoods around local features by bundles which simply aggregate the visual word labels of the corresponding visual features. The bundling starts by selecting *central features*, i.e. all features in an image with a sufficient number of local features in their neighborhood. Analogous to the feature histogram of a full image, the small neighborhood surrounding each central feature represents a "micro-bag-of-words". Such a bag-of-words vector will be extremely sparse because only a fraction of all features in the image is present in that particular neighborhood. Since the features of a bundle are spatially close to each other, they are likely to describe the same object or a region of interest.

More specifically, given a feature $\mathbf{x}_i$ its corresponding feature bundle $b(\mathbf{x}_i)$ is then defined as the set of spatially close features for a given feature $\mathbf{x}_i$:

$$b(\mathbf{x_i}) = \{\mathbf{x}_j | \mathbf{x}_j \in N(\mathbf{x}_i)\} \tag{4}$$

where $N(\mathbf{x}_i)$ is the *neighborhood* of feature $\mathbf{x}_i$ for which we propose two different definitions in the following section. We further assume that for all features $\mathbf{x}_i$ in an image the descriptor vectors have been quantized to the corresponding visual words $v_i = q(\mathbf{x}_i)$.

The bundle $b(\mathbf{x}_i)$ is then represented by the corresponding set of visual words of all features included in that bundle:

$$W_i(b(\mathbf{x}_i)) = \{ q(\mathbf{x}_j) \mid \mathbf{x}_j \in b(\mathbf{x}_i)\} \tag{5}$$

The resulting set W_i is then subsequently indexed by min-hashing which samples min-hashes based on the corresponding hash functions from this set and indexes them as sketches.

In extensive experiments we observed the following: First, sketches of size ≥ 3 do not work very well, therefore we perform all our experiments with sketches of size 2. Second, we found that the overall performance increases drastically if the first sketch element is not determined by min-hash but rather set to the visual word of the central feature itself. That is, for each bundle the n-th sketch is given as 2-tuple

$$(v_i, \; mh_n(W_i(b(\mathbf{x}_i))) \,) \tag{6}$$

where v_i denotes the visual word label of the central feature and mh_n denotes the min-hash returned by the n-th min-hash function from the set of all visual words W_i present in bundle $b(\mathbf{x_i})$. The full process is also illustrated in Figure 1.

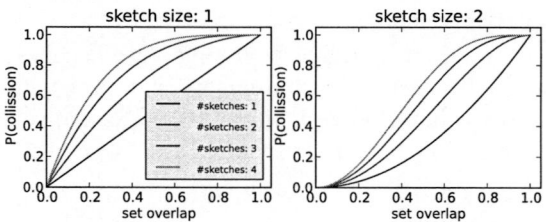

Fig. 2. Collision probabilities given the set overlap between bundles. Left: Collision probability for a single min-hash. Right: Sketches of size 2.

In Figure 2 the collision probabilities of sketches of size 1 (a single min-hash) and size 2 given 1 to 4 sketches are shown. One can see that even two bundles with an overlap of only 0.2, have a 0.5 chance to have one of 4 sketches colliding. This means, while there are multiple feature bundles that need to be described, each with several sketches, only very few sketches are needed per bundle to achieve a high probability to retrieve similar sets. This keeps the memory requirements for the indexing low. Further redundancy is added as images contain multiple bundles that may overlap. If some bundles do not match (collide) across images, there is the chance that other bundles in the same images collide. Throughout our experiments we therefore describe each feature bundle by 4 sketches, limiting the overall memory requirement to at most 4 times the storage of bag-of-words.

4.2   Bundling Strategies

In this section we introduce two strategies to select the features around a central feature which are then combined into a feature bundle. Each feature $\mathbf{x}_i$ in an image that has at least 2 features in its neighborhood $N(\mathbf{x}_i)$ is used to compute a feature bundle. Features with less or no neighbors are ignored.

Strategy 1: Bundles of Equal Area. The first bundling strategy is based on the intuition that features which are spatially close to each other might describe the same object. That is, given a central feature we bundle it with its direct spatial neighbors. We do not induce any further constraints except requiring that all features of a bundle must be on a similar scale. This is in line with the observation that true feature correspondences are often the same scale [5]. Thus, each feature that is closer to a given central feature $\mathbf{x}_i$ than a given cut-off radius is included in the respective bundle $b(\mathbf{x}_i)$:

$$N_{md}(\mathbf{x}_i) = \{\mathbf{x}_j \mid \|\mathbf{p}_i - \mathbf{p}_j\| \leq s_i \cdot r_{max}, \ s_{min} \cdot s_i \leq s_j \leq s_{max} \cdot s_i\} \qquad (7)$$

Here, $\mathbf{p}_i$ denotes the location of the feature in the 2-D image plane and s_i denotes the corresponding scale determined by the interest point detector. The scale is linked with the patch size that is described by the descriptor. For simplicity we assume that s_i denotes the radius of the patch in pixels. Only those neighboring features are included in the bundle which are closer to the central feature than the maximum distance r_{max} relative to the scale i.e. patch size of the central feature s_i. The minimum and maximum scales s_{min} and s_{max} control the scales considered for determining the neighborhood relative to the scale of the central feature. Figure 1 shows the bundling criterion for $r_{max} = 0.5$ (dashed gray circle), $s_{min} = 0.25$ and $s_{max} = 1.0$.

Strategy 2: Bundles of Equal Size. In this strategy, the neighborhood of a bundle is not determined by the size or scale of the central feature. Instead, the neighborhood is chosen such that it includes exactly the m visual words which are closest to the respective central feature and on a scale in between s_{min} and s_{max} relative to the scale of the central feature.

This definition is based on the assumption that image regions showing the same content in different images will yield roughly the same number of feature detections. Most importantly, this neighborhood definition has the major advantage that all bundles are of equal size, i.e. the overlap between these bundles will be easily comparable. The redundancy and the robustness of the min-hash-based search for bundles deals with missing or additionally included outlier features and still retrieves similar bundles.

4.3   Ranking and Filtering

As mentioned above, we use min-hashing in order to find images which share similar bundles with the query image. Once these images are determined, they may be ranked by their similarity to the query image. In preliminary experiments we evaluated several ways to compute a similarity score between query and retrieved images, based on the number of sketch collisions or number of matching bundles, either as absolute value or normalized in various ways. It turns out that the simple absolute count of sketch collisions was always on par with more complex similarity measures.

However, a ranking based on the cosine similarity between the full bag-of-words histogram of the query image and retrieved images still performs significantly better than a ranking based on the sketch collision counts only. Thus, in our experiments we rank all retrieval results by the cosine similarity between the bag-of-words histograms describing the full image that have been obtained with the same vocabulary size as used for bundling.

In other words, the retrieval by feature bundles is effectively a filtering step: The bundles are used to quickly fetch a small set of images that are very likely relevant. Subsequently, these images are then ranked by the cosine similarity. The small response ratio of the retrieval with bundles is a major benefit: Small result sets may be processed quickly even with more elaborate re-ranking methods.

5   Experiments

For all of our experiments we used SIFT descriptors as visual features computed from interest points found by the Difference-of-Gaussian (DoG) detector.

To quantize the descriptor vectors to visual words we use approximate k-means which employs the same k-means iterations as standard k-means but replaces the exact distance computations by approximated ones. Here, we use a forest of 8 randomized kd-trees to index the visual word centers [7]. This kd-forest then allows to perform approximate nearest neighbor search to find the nearest cluster for a descriptor vector both during clustering as well as when quantizing descriptor vectors to single visual words. To avoid overfitting, the clustering was performed with data from the training and validation set of FlickrLogos-32 only.

5.1   Dataset and Evaluation Method

We evaluate our approach on three different datasets: FlickrLogos-32 [10], Uk-Bench [8] and Oxford [9]. We use the FlickrLogos-32 dataset to perform parameter sweeps and optimization of our approach and compare the performance of some selected well-performing configurations to several baselines. Then the bundling is evaluated with unchanged configurations - without further tuning - on both the UkBench and the Oxford dataset to demonstrate how this technique generalizes.

As a retrieval system should have both good precision and good recall, we measure the retrieval performance as the mean average precision (mAP) which describes the area under the precision recall curve. It characterizes both aspects; a system will only gain high mAP scores if both precision and recall are high.

The response ratio (RR) is then used to measure the efficiency of the retrieval. It describes the number of retrieved images in relation to the database size. The higher the response ratio the more images are in the result set, which is usually post-processed or verified by computationally expensive methods. A low response ratio will therefore increase the overall efficiency of the search.

The retrieval on the UkBench dataset is measured by the average top 4 score (Top4), defined as the average number of correctly retrieved images among the top 4 results. A perfect retrieval would retrieve 4 correct top-ranked images and therefore yield a score of 4.0. We also report this score where appropriate.

5.2   FlickrLogos-32

The first dataset we use is FlickrLogos-32 (FlickrLogos) which is a recently published dataset consisting of 32 classes of brand logos [10]. Compared to other well-known datasets suited for image retrieval, e.g. Oxford, images of a similar class in FlickrLogos-32 share much smaller visually similar regions. For instance, the average object size of the 55 query images (derived from groundtruth annotation) of the Oxford dataset is 38% of the total area of the image (median: 28%) while the average object size in the test set of the FlickrLogos dataset

Table 1. Retrieval results on the FlickrLogos dataset obtained with min-hash (left) and Partition min-hash (right). $100K/1M$: visual vocabulary size, k: sketch size, n: number of sketches, p number of partitions, np: number of sketches per partition. The overlap of the p partitions was 0.5 in all Partition min-hash runs.

Min-hash	mAP	Top4	RR	Partition min-hash	mAP	Top4	RR
100K k: 2 n: 128	0.072	1.56	0.0155	100K k: 2, p: 4, np: 256	0.243	2.47	0.0675
100K k: 2 n: 256	0.113	1.97	0.0303	100K k: 2, p: 16, np: 64	0.235	2.44	0.0457
100K k: 2 n: 512	0.178	1.32	0.0553	100K k: 2, p: 64, np: 8	0.150	2.23	0.0327
100K k: 2 n: 1024	0.256	2.49	0.1011	100K k: 2, p: 64, np: 16	0.221	2.44	0.0623
1M k: 2 n: 128	0.036	0.96	0.0007	1M k: 2, p: 4, np: 256	0.150	2.30	0.0037
1M k: 2 n: 256	0.059	1.37	0.0012	1M k: 2, p: 16, np: 64	0.152	2.41	0.0037
1M k: 2 n: 512	0.098	1.78	0.0020	1M k: 2, p: 64, np: 8	0.108	2.09	0.004
1M k: 2 n: 1024	0.142	2.17	0.0036	1M k: 2, p: 64, np: 16	0.167	2.54	0.0077

is 9% (median: 5%) of the whole image. As the retrieval of the Oxford building is sometimes coined "object retrieval", the retrieval task on the FlickrLogos dataset can be truly considered "small object retrieval".

The dataset is split into three disjunct subsets. For each logo class, we have 10 train images, 30 validation images, and 30 test images - each containing at least one instance of the respective logo. For both validation and test set the dataset also provides a set of 3000 negative (non-logo) images downloaded from Flickr by the query terms "building, ""friends", "nature" and "people". This dataset of logos is interesting for both retrieval and classification since it features logos which can be considered as rigid objects with approximate 2-D planar surface visible from a single viewpoint only. The difficulty arises from the great variance of object sizes, from tiny logos in the background to image-filling views.

Our evaluation protocol is as follows: All images in the training and validation set, including those that do not contain any logo are indexed by the respective method (In total: 4280 images). These 960 images in the test set which do show a logo (given by the ground truth) are then used as queries to determine the most similar images from the training and validation set. The respective retrieval results are then ranked by the cosine similarity (see Section 4.3).

We evaluate the retrieval performance of all approaches for varying vocabulary sizes. As we are especially interested in the impact of extremely large visual vocabularies on the overall performance, we vary the vocabulary sizes from 10,000 (10K) to 4,000,000 (4M) words for all of our experiments.

Min-Hash and Partition Min-Hash. We compare the performance of our approach to the performance of the standard min-hashing approach (mH) as well as our Partition min-hash (PmH) implementation. These approaches are specifically meant for near-duplicate and partial-near-duplicate image search. This comparison shows how these methods perform for small object search on the FlickrLogos dataset when used with typical parameters.

Table 1 lists the obtained results for typical parameter constellations. From the results it can be seen that both min-hash and Partition min-hash show reasonable

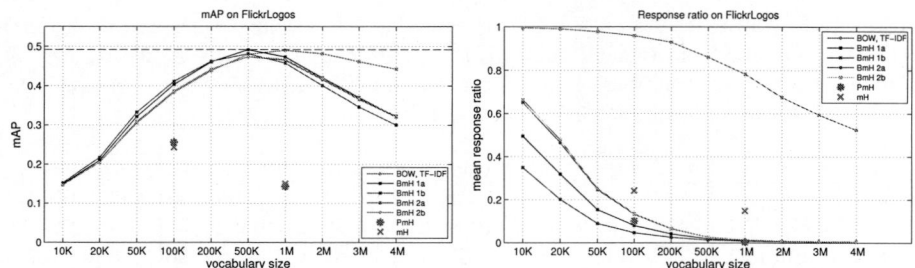

Fig. 3. Retrieval results on the FlickrLogos-32 dataset: The performance of the bundles is on par with the bag-of-words model (left) but the response ratio is an order of magnitude lower (right)

Table 2. Selected bundle configurations

Name	Bundling	r	s_{min}	s_{max}	Name	Bundling	m	s_{min}	s_{max}
BmH 1a	Strategy 1	1.0	0.5	1.0	BmH 2a	Strategy 2	4	0.7	1.42
BmH 1b	Strategy 1	1.5	0.7	1.42	BmH 2b	Strategy 2	6	0.7	1.42

performance at retrieving the top-most similar images but vary greatly in their mAP. In the following experiments, we compare the results for the arguably best parameter settings, i.e. 1024 sketches for min-hash and 256 sketches with 4 partitions for PmH, to our approach and the bag-of-words baseline.

Bag-of-Words and Feature Bundles. We evaluate the performance of both of our bundling strategies with regards to mAP and response ratio and compare it to a retrieval with bag-of-words and tf-idf weighting, as described e.g. in [9]. Figure 3 shows the obtained results on the FlickrLogos dataset for 10 different vocabularies. One can clearly see that the bag-of-words with tf-idf weighting has its peak at a vocabulary of 1 million words, which confirms that large vocabularies are beneficial for image search [9].

In order to find the best bundle configurations we have done an extensive parameter sweep on the parameters of the bundle configuration. Due to limited space, we cannot show a detailed evaluation for each of these parameters. Therefore we report the performance of 4 selected well-performing bundle configurations (two for each bundling strategy) shown in Table 2.

As can be seen clearly in our figures, the two different bundling strategies (denoted as BmH1 and BmH2) perform equally well. Similar to bag-of-words they profit from large vocabularies, but the peak is at $500K$ words. More importantly, the bundles are on par with bag-of-words, but have an order of magnitude lower response ratio as can be seen in Figure 3 on the right.

Note that we rank the result set with the same metric for all approaches, i.e. by the cosine similarity as determined by the bag-of-words model. As the bundling is by definition only able to find correspondences between images that share visual words, the result set of the retrieval by feature bundles is a true subset of the result set obtained with bag-of-words retrieval. This clearly demonstrates

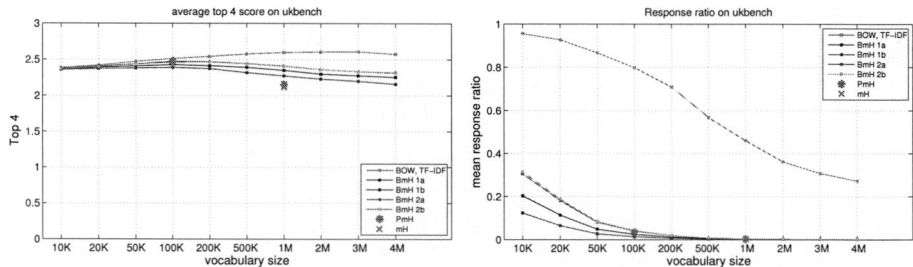

Fig. 4. Results on the UkBench dataset: The bundles yield an average top 4 score similar to bag-of-words as well as min-hashing and partition min-hash

the discriminative power of feature bundles for efficient filtering before more expensive post-retrieval steps are applied to the result set.

5.3 UkBench

We report the average top 4 score obtained on the UkBench dataset [8] (see Figure 4) to show the performance of feature bundles on a pure near-duplicate retrieval task. We do not optimize the bundle configurations specifically for this dataset. Instead, we show the performances for the bundle configurations as in Table 2, since we want to demonstrate how the bundle configurations obtained on the FlickrLogos dataset generalize on another dataset. From the results it can be seen that the retrieval precision of the bundling is similar or better than that of min-hashing and partition min-hashing and slightly lower than that of bag-of-words. Again, the response ratio is much lower and expresses the efficiency with which near-duplicates are retrieved.

5.4 Oxford Buildings

Finally, we also compare the performance of the feature bundles with bag-of-words retrieval, min-hash and partition min-hash on the Oxford buildings dataset [9]. This dataset contains 5063 images of 11 buildings from Oxford as well as various distractor images. It is known for its difficulty to discriminate very similar building facades from each other and is one of the most well-known datasets for image retrieval.

Again, we use the previously obtained bundle configurations and just report the retrieval performance as obtained with the evaluation protocol of the Oxford dataset. Figure 5 shows the results. One can observe that bag-of-words performs best, while the bundles are worse yet outperform mH and PmH. Interestingly, the bundles outperform the bag-of-words retrieval if the database is increased by adding 100,000 distractor images downloaded from Flickr. In that case one can observe a performance drop of both bag-of-words and feature bundles (see curve BOF, TF-IDF, 100k in Figure 5), but the bundles retain their extremely low response ratio. This demonstrates that bundling spatially related features suppresses false positives.

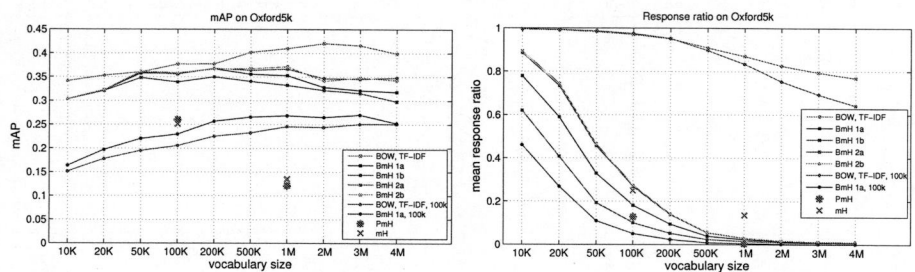

Fig. 5. Retrieval results on the Oxford dataset

6   Conclusion

In this work we introduced a robust technique for efficient indexing and search of feature bundles. Each bundle carries the information of individual visual words and their surrounding neighborhood. We showed that the bundles have a performance on par with bag-of-words models but with significant lower false positives, i.e. the result set is reduced by an order of magnitude. This makes much more complex and expensive post-retrieval operations on the small result set feasible.

References

1. Chum, O., Matas, J.: Large-scale discovery of spatially related images. PAMI, 371–377 (2010)
2. Chum, O., Perdoch, M., Matas, J.: Geometric min-Hashing: Finding a (thick) needle in a haystack. In: Proc. CVPR (2009)
3. Chum, O., Philbin, J., Isard, M.: Scalable near identical image and shot detection. In: Proc. CIVR (2007)
4. Chum, O., Philbin, J., Zisserman, A.: Near duplicate image detection: min-hash and tf-idf weighting. In: Proc. BMVC (2008)
5. Jégou, H., Douze, M., Schmid, C.: Improving Bag-of-Features for Large Scale Image Search. IJCV 87(3), 316–336 (2009)
6. Lee, D.C., Ke, Q., Isard, M.: Partition Min-Hash for Partial Duplicate Image Discovery. In: Daniilidis, K., Maragos, P., Paragios, N. (eds.) ECCV 2010, Part I. LNCS, vol. 6311, pp. 648–662. Springer, Heidelberg (2010)
7. Muja, M., Lowe, D.: Fast Approximate Nearest Neighbors with Automatic Algorithm Configuration. In: Proc. VISAPP (2009)
8. Nistér, D., Stewénius, H.: Scalable Recognition with a Vocabulary Tree. In: Proc. CVPR (2006)
9. Philbin, J., Chum, O., Isard, M., Sivic, J., Zisserman, A.: Object retrieval with large vocabularies and fast spatial matching. In: Proc. CVPR (2007)
10. Romberg, S., Garcia Pueyo, L., Lienhart, R., van Zwol, R.: Scalable Logo Recognition in Real-World Images. In: Proc. ICMR (2011)

Colorization for Gray Scale Facial Image by Locality-Constrained Linear Coding

Yang Liang, Mingli Song, Jiajun Bu, and Chun Chen

Zhejiang Provincial Key Laboratory of Service Robot
College of Computer Science, Zhejiang University
{liangyang,brooksong,bjj,chenc}@zju.edu.cn

Abstract. Colorization for gray scale facial image is an important technique in various practical applications. However, the methods that have been proposed are essentially semi-automatic. In this paper, we present a new probabilistic framework based on Maximum A Posteriori (MAP) estimation to automatically transform the given gray scale facial image to corresponding color one. Firstly, the input image is divided into several patches and non-parametric Markov random field (MRF) is employed to formulate the global energy. Secondly, Locality-constrained Linear Coding (LLC) is employed to learn the color distribution for each patch. At the same time, the simulated annealing algorithm is employed to iteratively update the patches chosen by LLC to optimize the MRF by decreasing global energy cost. The experimental results demonstrate that the proposed framework is effective to colorize the gray scale facial images to corresponding color ones.

Keywords: Colorization, MAP, MRF, LLC.

1 Introduction

Human face conveys lots of information such as identity, appearance, etc. during social communication or in security systems. However, sometimes only gray scale images or portraits can be obtained whose facial details like skin color, lip luster, etc. are lost. For example, because of the quality of surveillance cameras or storage space restriction, only gray scale images may be obtained. The same for archeologists, they may only obtain historical gray scale images. So colorization for gray scale facial image is useful.

In 1970 Wilson Markle[1] introduced the term colorization to describe the computer assisted process of adding color to a gray scale image. Several approaches have been presented towards successful image colorization. In general, the existing colorization approaches can be classified into two groups, one is example-based method and the other is optimization-based method.

The example-based method colorizes the gray scale image by choosing a similar image as a reference, and transferring its colors to the input gray scale image[2][3]. Welsh in [2] transfers the entire color mood by matching the luminance and texture of the example image to the target gray scale image pixel by

W. Lin et al. (Eds.): PCM 2012, LNCS 7674, pp. 57–67, 2012.

pixel. But it always fails on those images that are hardly segmented by luminance or texture. Kekre and Thepade in [3] searches the reference color image for the same palette of a certain scale pixel window by matching the luminance values of reference color image to target gray scale image. However, a suitable reference color image whose color mood and composition are required to be similar to the target gray scale image may take effort to find and it may fail on those images that are hardly segmented by luminance or texture.

The optimization-based method colorizes the image based on the color label priors offered by users [4][5][6]. Levin in [4] proposes a premise that neighboring pixels will have similar colors if they have similar intensities and Levin formalizes the premise as an optimization problem using a quadratic cost function based on a few color labels figured by users. The method can produce comparatively better colorized image than the techniques of former group without precise image segmentation, but it still needs user interactions to confirm several color labels for different color regions and dramatically depends on the accuracy of the color labels as prior.

Obviously, all those mentioned colorization techniques require human interactions to confirm either the color mood from a reference image or the color labels for different color regions, thus they are essentially semi-automatic. Aiming at this drawback, in this paper we propose an automatic colorization technique without any human interaction.

To automatically colorize a gray scale facial image, a natural idea is to reverse the conversion of color to gray. A lot of recent work[7][8][9] focus on how to keep information as much as possible during color image to gray scale conversion, and several of them achieve remarkable results, such as spatial color to gray for preserving chrominance edge information by Raja[7], and salience preserving color to gray method by Amy A. Gooch[8], etc.

However, all those conversion methods above do not consider inverse process, i.e. gray scale to color, and conversion from color to gray is usually irreversible because the data dimension is reduced from 3 to 1 with huge information lost. Thus converting a gray scale image to color one is essentially the problem of recovering data from deficient data sample and the recovery problem can be formulated as a probability to measure the recovery quality. Hence, our approach is driven by predicting the color of the gray scale images based on MAP framework, and our goal is to maximize the probability of the prediction. Furthermore, for facial images a certain local geometrical configuration can be found to enhance the recovery results.

To guarantee that the colorized facial image is acceptable, three criteria are proposed as follows:

- **Identity invariant:** the recovered color face should look like the given gray face.
- **Global constraint:** the common facial features should be kept during recovery process, which means the skin color, lip luster or other components' color should be natural.

– **Local constraint:** the shapes of facial components like eyes, nose, lip, etc. cannot be changed or dim.

To ensure that the prediction meets global constraint, a probabilistic framework launched by MAP is devised. And to keep the contours of facial components for local constraint, 1st order MRF based on a patch system is employed while LLC is introduced to fit the non-linear relation in the high dimensional data space. Thus when the global and local constraints are satisfied, naturally the identity invariant will be met.

Specifically, for predicting the color of a gray scale facial image, firstly the image is divided into several patches and the global energy is formulated based on the probabilistic framework. Then each gray scale patch is encoded by the locality-constrained linear subspace which is learnt dynamically through the training set, and eventually a colorized facial image is obtained via minimizing the global energy iteratively. Experimental results demonstrate that the proposed probabilistic framework is effective to colorize the gray scale facial images to corresponding color ones.

The remainder of the paper is organized as follows: Section 2 analyzes the colorization problem and presents our new approach; Section 3 describes how to predict candidate color patches and Section 4 presents a global optimization algorithm to decrease the Markov network's energy cost; Section 5 presents experiments results; Finally Section 6 summarizes our approach and lists our future works.

2   Problem Statement and Motivation

Generally, the RGB datum Cl of one color pixel can be denoted as a vector $[r, g, b]$ and converting it to gray value Gr can be formulated as follows:

$$Gr = Cl * g$$

where $g = [0.299, 0.587, 0.114]^T$. Let $F^c \in R^{m \times 3n}$ denote the color facial image with the resolution of $m \times n$ pixels, and the RGB values of each pixel are arrayed by the order $[r, g, b]$. Let $F^g \in R^{m \times n}$ denote the corresponding gray scale facial image, then F^g can be obtained by the matrix operation as follows:

$$F^g = F^c G \tag{1}$$

where G is the gray conversion matrix whose form is as follows:

$$G = \begin{bmatrix} g & \cdots & 0 \\ \vdots & \ddots & \vdots \\ 0 & \cdots & g \end{bmatrix}$$

To obtain a gray scale facial image from a color one by (1) is straightforward but the inverse process is apparently uncertain, with uncountable $F^c s$ satisfying the equation. Thus to solve the inverse problem, we should find the optimal one to maximize the posterior probability $P(F^c|F^g)$ based on the maximum a posteriori (MAP) criterion. Bayesian rule for the optimization problem is:

$$F^{c^*} = \arg\max_{F^c} P(F^c|F^g)$$
$$= \arg\max_{F^c} \frac{P(F^g|F^c)P(F^c)}{P(F^g)} \quad (2)$$

Since F^g is an observed value and $P(F^g)$ is a prior that can be considered as a constant, thus (2) can be written as:

$$F^{c^*} = \arg\max_{F^c} P(F^g|F^c)P(F^c) \quad (3)$$

For an automatic approach to convert gray to color, we introduce a patch based system. (3) can be rewritten as:

$$F^{c^*} = \arg\max_{\{p_1^c,p_2^c,\cdots p_n^c\}} \prod_{i=1}^n P(p_i^g|p_i^c)P(p_1^c,p_2^c,\cdots p_n^c) \quad (4)$$

where p_i denotes the *ith* patch on the face and the superscript (c,g) denotes whether it is color or gray.

Hence, the conversion problem can be decomposed as two parts:

1. $\prod_{i=1}^n P(p_i^g|p_i^c)$, each item is the probability that the observed gray value p_i^g is conditional on a predicted color value p_i^c as a local constraint. And the confidence of the predicted color is measured via comparing the ground truth p_i^g and the prediction $p_i^c * G$. Hence each item can be calculated as:

$$P(p_i^g|p_i^c) \propto \exp\left(\varPhi(p_i^g, p_i^c * G)\right) \quad (5)$$

where $\varPhi(.,.)$ is a estimation function to measure the similarity. So the local constraint can be formulated as:

$$P(F^g|F^c) \sim \exp\left(\sum_{i=1}^n \varPhi(p_i^g, p_i^c * G)\right) \quad (6)$$

2. $P(p_1^c, p_2^c, \cdots p_n^c,)$, the item can be considered as 1st-order Markov random field (MRF) that controls the smoothness of predicted patches as a global constraint. Thus it can be evaluated as follows:

$$P(p_1^c, p_2^c, \cdots p_n^c,) \sim \exp\left(\sum_{i=1}^n \sum_{j=1}^4 \varPhi(\partial p_i^c, \partial p_{ij}^c)\right) \quad (7)$$

where ∂p_i^c is the overlapped region of the patch and ∂p_{ij}^c is the overlapped part of neighborhood patch. Generally each patch is overlapped with four neighborhood patches.

To sum up all the above, the MAP problem can be formulated as follows:

$$\arg\max_{F^c} P(F^g|F^c)P(F^c) = \tag{8}$$

$$\arg\max_{w_i} \exp\left(\sum_{i=1}^{n}\left(\Phi(p_i^g, p_i^c * G) + \lambda\sum_{j=1}^{4}\Phi(\partial p_i^c, \partial p_{ij}^c)\right)\right)$$

where λ is a constant that controls the contribution of the smoothness item. Hence, our goal is to minimize the energy function U as follows:

$$U = \sum_{i=1}^{n}\left(\Phi(p_i^g, p_i^c * G) + \lambda\sum_{j=1}^{4}\Phi(\partial p_i^c, \partial p_{ij}^c)\right) \tag{9}$$

The optimization for the energy function U in (9) can be decomposed into two steps. Firstly, predict the low inner energy candidate corresponding color patches p_i^c for the given gray scale patches p_i^g. Secondly, with the candidate color patches, minimize the global energy function U.

3   Predicting Candidate Color Patches Based on LLC

When convert color image to gray, the data dimension is reduced from 3 to 1 with huge information lost. So converting a gray scale image to color one is essentially the problem of recovering data from deficient data sample. The color data of training samples with its corresponding gray data is already known, naturally the relation of the two data spaces is expected for recovering the color information for the given gray scale facial image. In addition, facial images have a certain local geometrical configuration, and the locality is essential for linear extraction from high-dimensional manifold as mentioned in LCC algorithm [10]. Hence, Locality-constrained Linear Coding strategy is employed to capture the nonlinear relationship between gray scale image and color image space. Also we assume the small image patches in the gray scale images and color images from manifold with similar local geometry in two different image spaces. So the gray and color data will share the same coordinate in the LLC.

Let S_i^c denote the linear space for the ith color patch and introduce a linear coordinate system to localize each data, as follows:

$$p_i^c = S_i^c W_i \tag{10}$$
$$p_i^g = S_i^c W_i G \tag{11}$$

where $W_i = [w_{i1}, w_{i2}, \cdots w_{il}]^T$ is the coordinate in S_i^c.

Given an input patch p_i^g with data distribution view, the condition of all the data samples is not necessarily known to localize p_i^c and for generality a subspace is expected to descript the distribution which contains p_i^c. Moreover human faces have strong configuration and lead to obvious locality. Thus S_i^c can be simplified as a locality-constrained subspace $D_i^{'c}$ which excludes some redundant data samples and preserves those samples are close to the p_i^g in Euclidian distance. Formally the $D_i^{'c}$ can be formed as a matrix as follows:

$$D_i^{'c} = [d_{i1}^c, d_{i2}^c, \cdots d_{im}^c]$$

where each column $d_{i.}^c$ is one of the m closest training patches. And (11) can be rewritten as:

$$p_i^g = D_i^{'c} W_i G \tag{12}$$

Solving (12) analytically to obtain a coordinate is almost non-sense because if no constraints applied on W_i, uncertain number of W_i would satisfy the equation and confuse the data position in the subspace. Inspired by LLC [12] , a locality penalty item that participates in the coordinate computation is added as follows:

$$W_i^* = \arg\min_{W_i} \left(\left\| p_i^g - D_i^c W_i G \right\|^2 + \gamma \sum_{j=1}^l Dist_i * w_{ij} \right)$$
$$s.t. \sum_{j=1}^l w_{ij} = 1$$

where $Dist_i = \exp\left(\frac{\left\| p_i^g - d_{ij}^c \right\|^2}{\sigma} \right)$. And Jinjun Wang proposes an approximated solution in [12] as follows:

$$W_i^* = Norm\left(C_i + \gamma * diag\left(\exp\left(\frac{\left\| p_i^g - d_{ij}^c \right\|^2}{\sigma} \right) \right) \right)$$

where $C_i = (D_i^c G - 1 p_i^g)(D_i^c G - 1 p_i^g)^T$ denotes the covariance matrix.

4   Optimizing the Global Energy

To minimize the energy function (9) of the patch system, the simulated annealing method is employed and each patch is treated as a node. For computing the independent energy of a node, (9) can be decomposed and the energy function of each node can be formulated as follows:

$$U_i = \Phi(p_i^g, D_i^{'c} W_i G) + \lambda \sum_{j=1}^4 \Phi(\partial p_i^c, \partial p_{ij}^c) \tag{13}$$

Without generality, the estimation function $\Phi(.,.)$ can be specialized as Euclidean distance because the L^2 norm is a reliable measure for the comparison of image patches and reflects the similarity well, supported by Efros and Leung [13]. And practically, such a huge subspace with all the m closest training samples does not participate in the coordinate computation, but randomly select l bases from $D_i^{'c}$ and form several $D_i^c s$. Then estimate whether the coordinate in its corresponding subspace D_i^c decrease the node energy, and the details are described in Algorithm 1.

Algorithm 1. Simulated Annealing

---

1. Initialization:

   Select $\{d_{ij}^c \mid \|p_i^g - d_{ij}^c G\|^2 < \epsilon\}$ to form $D_i^{'c}$

   Randomly select l bases from $D_i^{'c}$ to form D_i^c

   Calculate W_i for each patch and the global energy U

   Set Loop $= 0$

2. **for** $i = 1 : n$ **do**

   Randomly select l bases from $D_i^{'c}$ to form D_i^c

   Calculate W_i^* by the algorithms discussed in section 3

   Calculate $\Delta t_i = U_i^* - U_i$

   if $\Delta t_i < 0$, Accept current W_i^*

   else Accept current W_i^* by probability $\exp\left(-|\frac{\Delta t_i}{U}|\right)$

   end

3. Check the optimization condition

   if $U < \epsilon$ or $Loop > max$, Accept the current $W_i s$

   else Loop++ and go to 2 Calculate the color of each patch based the related W_i

---

5   Experimental Results

1000 color facial images are collected from Internet to form the training dataset. The dataset contains different race facial images having different skin color, such as yellow, white and black. All these face images are roughly aligned by AAM, and then cropped to the size of 128×96 pixels. Some examples are given in Figure 1. The patches in MRF are of size 7×7 pixels with 2 pixels overlapped. 100 outside color facial images are chosen as test cases, which are converted to gray scale images firstly.

Fig. 1. Example training color facial images and corresponding gray images in our experiments

In this experiments, 120 patches from training data that are closest to p_i^g are selected to form $D_i^{'c}$, and set l to be 40 in the initialization step. We compare our method with Sparse Coding(SC) [11] which is popular in rapid linear coding system for capturing salient patterns of local descriptors.

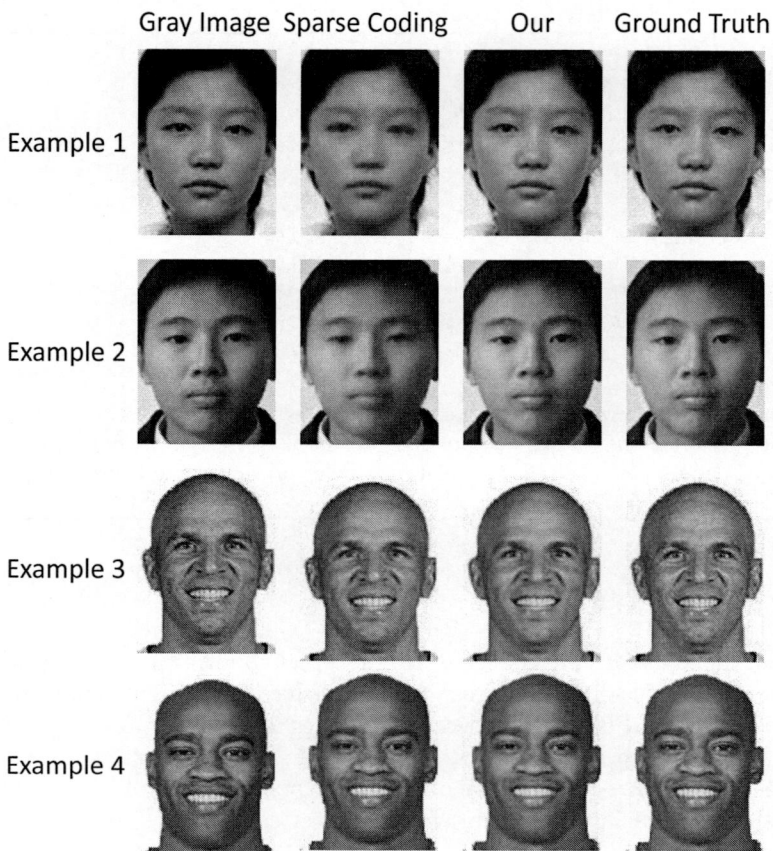

Fig. 2. Comparison our method with SC: The first column shows the input gray scale facial images. The 2nd and 3th columns are corresponding to results generated by SC and our method respectively. And the 4th column shows the ground-truth.

The results are shown in Figure 2. Through the colorized images, we can find that our probabilistic framework with LLC outperforms sparse coding. The framework with LLC can colorize gray scale images with clear edges and natural skin color, while those output images recovered by sparse coding have blurry edges and lose a lot details such as the skin luster, the color of lips and eye white, etc.

The global reconstruction error rate is measured by the follow equation:

$$Er = \frac{||I_c^* - I_c||^2}{||I_c||^2}$$

where I_c^* is the colorized image and I_c is the ground truth. The error rate of examples in Figure 2 is shown as Table 1. The error rate of Sparse Coding is about twice of our method.

Table 1. Global reconstruction error rate of different methods

Error rate	Example 1	Example 2	Example 3	Example 4
Sparse Coding	0.0562	0.0538	0.0691	0.0523
Our	0.0235	0.0232	0.0309	0.0279

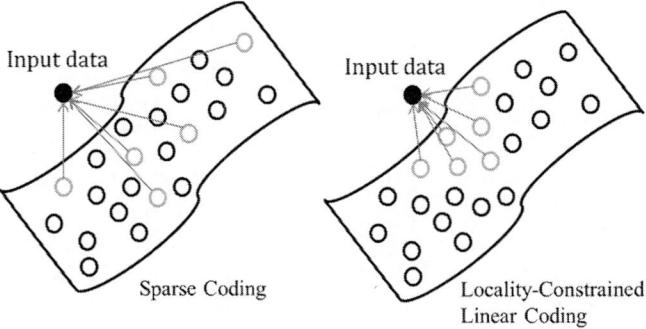

Fig. 3. Comparison between Sparse Coding and LLC. The selected bases for representation are highlighted in orange.

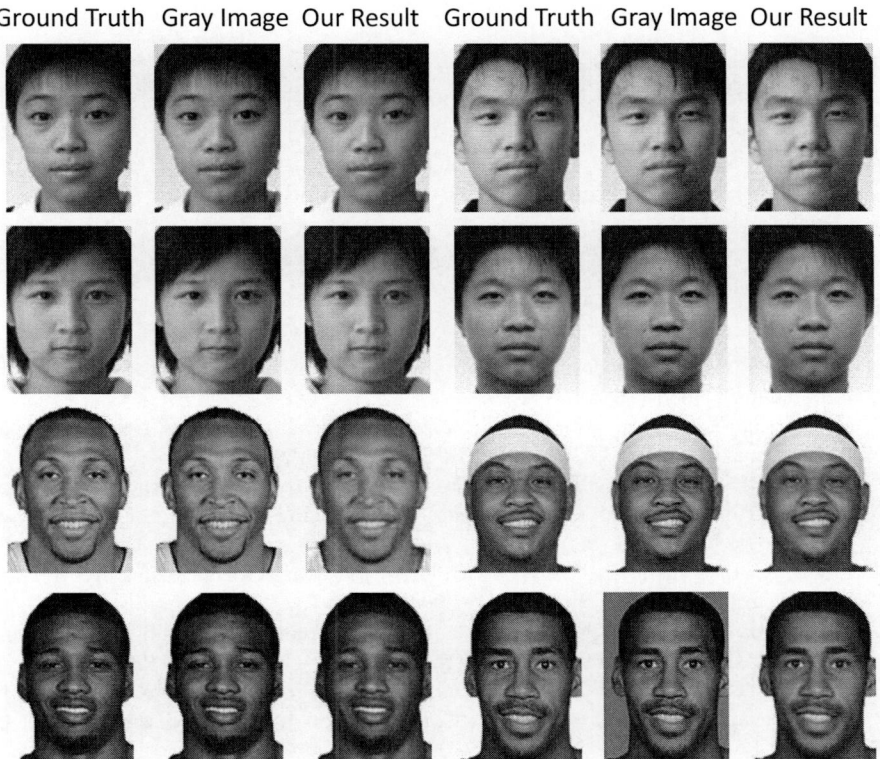

Fig. 4. More results from the proposed approach

Figure 3 shows the difference between Sparse Coding and LLC. The bases selected by Sparse Coding for encoded patches often distribute throughout the training data. While the bases selected by LLC are explicitly encouraged to be local to the encoded patches. And this locality property is more in line with the distribution of the facial image data space than sparsity.

To further validate the proposed approach, we show some more results from our approach in Figure 4.

6 Conclusion and Future Work

In this paper we present a new probabilistic framework based on MAP estimation to automatically colorize gray scale facial images. A non-parametric Markov random field (MRF) based on a patch system is constructed for the problem. And simulated annealing algorithm is employed to iteratively update the patches chosen by LLC to optimize the MRF by decreasing global energy cost. The experimental results show that the proposed framework with LLC is effective to colorize the gray scale facial images to corresponding color ones. In this paper only frontally captured images are tested. In the future we will extend our approach to break the pose limitation and try to apply it on more practical applications.

Acknowledgment. This work is supported by National Natural Science Foundation of China (61170142), National Key Technology R&D Program (2011BAG05B04),the Zhejiang Province Key S&T Innovation Group Project (2009R50009), and the Fundamental Research Funds for the Central Universities(2012FZA5017).

References

1. Markle, W.: The development and application of colorization. SMPTE Journal 93(7), 632–635 (1984)
2. Welsh, T., Ashikhmin, M., Mueller, K.: Transferring Color to Greyscale Images. ACM Transactions on Graphics 21(3), 277–280 (2002)
3. Kekre, H.B., Thepade, S.D.: Color Traits Transfer to Grayscale Images. In: Proc. of IEEE First International Conference on Emerging Trends in Engineering and Technology, pp. 82–85 (2008)
4. Levin, A., Lischinski, D., Weiss, Y.: Colorization using Optimization. ACM Transactions on Graphics 23(3), 689–694 (2004)
5. Yatziv, L., Sapiro, G.: Fast Image and Video Colorization Using Chrominance Blending. IEEE Transactions on Image Processing 15(5), 1120–1129 (2006)
6. Horiuchi, T., Hirano, S.: Colorization algorithm for grayscale image by propagating seed pixels. In: IEEE International Conference on Image Processing, vol. 1, pp. 457–460 (2003)
7. Bala, R., Eschbach, R.: Spatial Color-to-Grayscale Transform Preserving Chrominance Edge Information. In: 14th Color Imaging Conference: Color, Science, Systems and Applications, pp. 82–86 (2004)

8. Gooch, A.A., Olsen, S.C., Tumblin, J., Gooch, B.: Color2gray: salience-preserving color removal. ACM Transactions on Graphics 24(3), 634–639 (2005)

9. Smith, K., Landes, P.-E., Thollot, J., Myszkowski, K.: Apparent Greyscale: A Simple and Fast Conversion to Perceptually Accurate Images and Video. Computer Graphics Forum (Proc. of EUROGRAPHICS) 27(2), 193–200 (2008)

10. Yu, K., Zhang, T., Gong, Y.: Nonlinear Learning using Local Coordinate Coding. In: Advances in Neural Information Processing Systems, vol. 22, pp. 2223–2231 (2009)

11. Lee, H., Battle, A., Raina, R., Ng, A.: Efficient sparse coding algorithms. In: Advances in Neural Information Processing Systems, vol. 19, p. 801 (2007)

12. Wang, J., Yang, J., Yu, K., Lv, F., Huang, T., Gong, Y.: Locality-constrained Linear Coding for Image Classification. In: IEEE Conference on Computer Vision and Pattern Recognition (CVPR), p. 3306 (2010)

13. Efros, A.A., Leung, T.K.: Texture Synthesis by Non-parametric Sampling. In: Proceedings of the Seventh IEEE International Conference on Computer Vision, vol. 2, p. 1033 (1999)

14. Farkas, L.G.: Anthropometry of the Head and Face. Raven Press, Hewlett (1994)

15. Fortune, S.: Numerical Stability of Algorithms for 2D Delaunay Triangulations. In: Proceedings of the Eighth Annual Symposium on Computational Geometry, vol. 1(2), pp. 192–213 (1992)

New Eye Contact Correction Using Radial Basis Function for Wide Baseline Videoconference System

Xiaozhou Zhou and Pierre Boulanger

Department of Computing Science, University of Alberta
Edmonton, Alberta, Canada, T6G1K7
{xzhou3,pierreb}@ualberta.ca

Abstract. In this paper, we introduce a novel eye contact correction method for videoconference systems with wide baseline. In this system, assistant cameras are installed on each side of the monitor to help capture the views from left side and right side. A pattern with random dots and Radial Basis Function (RBF) interpolation are used to help create precise disparity maps that is then used for re-projection. The interpolated views show a smooth transit among cameras on two sides. The experimental results also demonstrate that the proposed method could be extended to produce more robust and accurate disparity maps than most of the existing algorithms from regular stereo images.

Keywords: eye contact correction, immersive videoconference, computer vision, stereo, radial basis function interpolation

1   Introduction

Videoconference system has been a hot research topic in recent years as it creates a true sense of immersion/presence between each participant by keeping eye contact and displaying participants at their real scale. It has been widely used in business, education, and personal entertainment and has been commercialized by numerous companies such as SONY, CISCO systems, and DVE. The key element of immersive videoconference systems is to maintain the correct eye contact as it carries non-verbal clues that are essential for emotional communications. In commercial systems, eye contact is approximated by using large semi-transparent beam splitter that allows to project an image of the remote participant as well as to capture the local participant image using a video camera aiming directly at the center of the screen. These systems are very expensive and require complex hardware and software setups. A low cost solution digitizes the participants by locating a group of cameras around the display screen and calculates a disparity map from those cameras using stereo matching algorithms. Once the disparity map is achieved, in order to compensate for eye contact, virtual images are generated from the viewpoint of the participant's gaze direction.

In most cases, in order to create a good disparity map, the cameras must be located very close to decrease the occlusions. For eye contact correction applications, a pair of cameras (or a camera array) is usually mounted on the top and bottom, or the left and right side of the screen [1]-[4].   Figure 1 shows an example of the camera setting and procedure of the work of Ott *et al.* [1].

W. Lin et al. (Eds.): PCM 2012, LNCS 7674, pp. 68–79, 2012.
© Springer-Verlag Berlin Heidelberg 2012

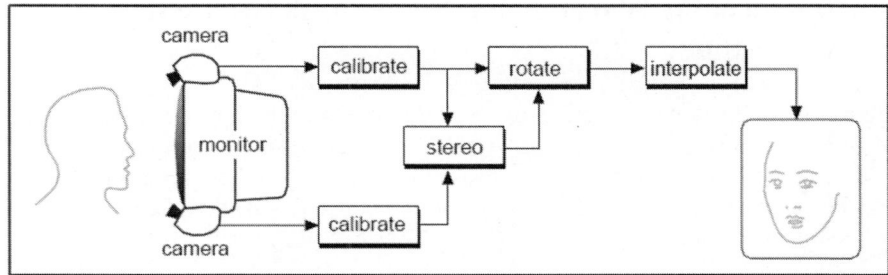

Fig. 1. The Tele-presence system of Ott *et al.* [1]

However, as the size of the display screens becomes larger and larger, the image taken by a pair of cameras shares little correspondence information, such as illustrated in Figure 2. Two cameras are set on the left and right side. The left camera can only take the left face and small part of right face while for the right camera, it takes the whole right face and a small part of left face. Even we apply a stereo matching algorithm to these images, only a few corresponding pixels could be found. The disparity map is far away from dense enough to generate new images from any virtual viewpoint.

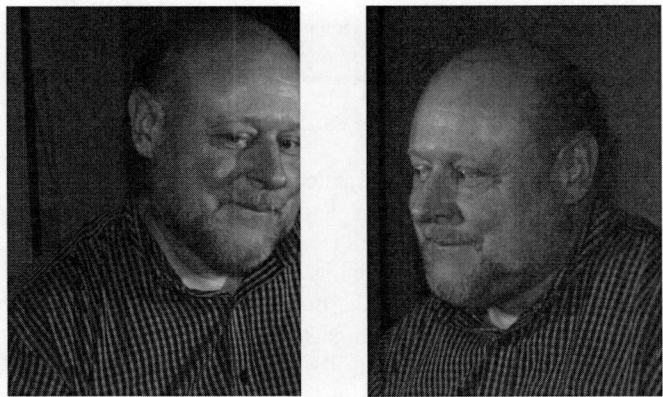

Fig. 2. Image taken by cameras in wide baseline

Therefore, in this paper, we propose a new videoconference system which could deal with the wide baseline problem and provides correct eye contact as well. Parts of the scene are collected by each set of cameras and gather at the location pointed out by users. Since the solution is based on the quality of the disparity map, we also propose a method to increase the precision by RBF interpolation.

The rest of this paper is organized as follows. Section 2 and 3 introduce the designed system and how it works. Section 4 explains the extension of the proposed method to general stereo matching. Experimental results in Section 5 show strong performance on both videoconference images and Middlebury datasets. Section 6 concludes the entire paper.

2   Design of the Wide Baseline System with Eye Contact Correction

Figure 3 is an illustration of our proposed system. On each side of the monitor (left and right), there is a set of cameras: two IR camera and one color camera. Two IR cameras are set very close to produce dense disparity map and color camera provides the color information.   The left and right side calculate the 3D world coordinates and their colors independently.

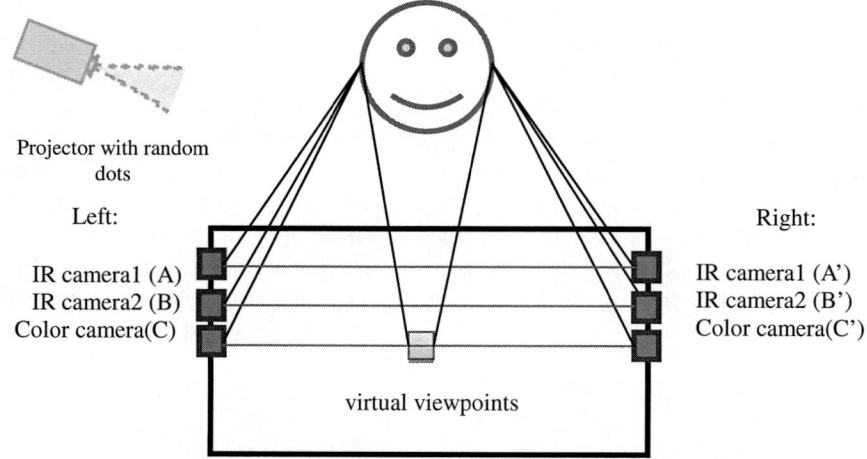

Projector with random
dots

Left:

IR camera1 (A)
IR camera2 (B)
Color camera(C)

Right:

IR camera1 (A')
IR camera2 (B')
Color camera(C')

virtual viewpoints

Fig. 3. The videoconference system for wide baseline

An IR pattern with random dots is projected to the scene to help derive the disparities in low texture areas, such as the skins and clothes. Because the IR pattern is only visible to the IR camera, one color camera is set to record the colors of the scene.

The images from new virtual viewpoints could be generated by two ways: re-projection or interpolation. In case that the projection matrix of the new virtual viewpoints is known, each 3D point is projected directly through projection matrix: $[x, y]' = P[X, Y, Z]'$, where $[X, Y, Z]'$ is the world coordinates of a point, P is the projection matrix, and $[x, y]'$ is the new image coordinates of the point $[X, Y, Z]'$. In case that the projection matrix of the new viewpoint is unknown, the new image could be generated by interpolation. The final image is a blending of the images re-projected or interpolated from the left and right side. Details will be discussed in the next section.

3   Stereo Matching Based on RBF for Videoconference Images

Simply speaking, there are two tasks for each set of cameras: generate disparity map and assign colors to pixels in the disparity map. Disparity maps are usually calculated by stereo matching algorithms which can be classified into two categories: local and global [5]. According to the evaluation on Middlebury test bed[6], the best results are plane-fitting based algorithms [7]-[12], which assume that the scenes could be modeled by a set

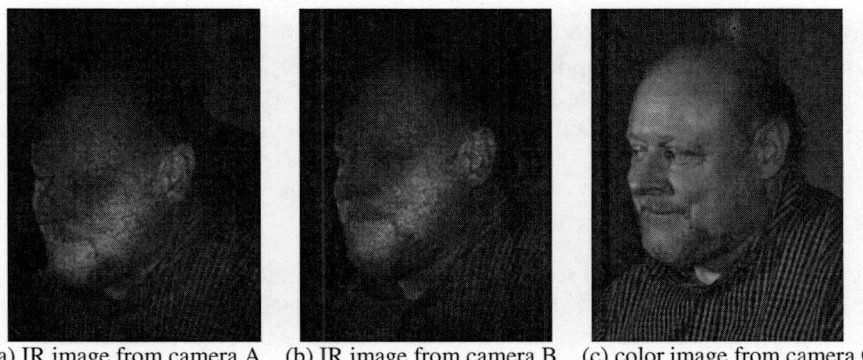

(a) IR image from camera A   (b) IR image from camera B   (c) color image from camera C

Fig. 4. Videoconference image with random dots

of planes and large disparity discontinuities only happen at the boundaries of homogenous color segments.   Over-segmentation is used to find all potential disparity discontinuities and disparities within in a segment are the same. However, plane-fitting based algorithms may fail when the images cannot be segmented properly.

Figure 4 is an example of images taken by the three cameras. The random dots add texture to low texture areas, but ruin the original texture to be processed by segmentation. We found that the head, neck and the upper torso have no sharp disparity changes, thus the whole foreground in Figure 4(a) or (b) could be covered by one surface which is easily obtained from foreground extraction. Therefore, we present a RBF interpolation based method in this paper to address this issue.

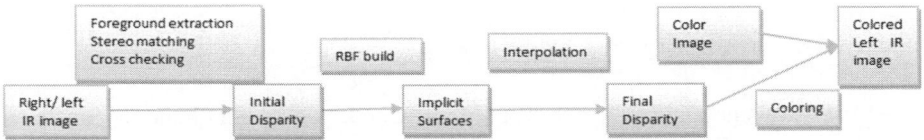

Fig. 5. Flow chart of the proposed method for videoconference system on each side

Figure 5 is the flow chart which explains how the system creates disparity map and assigns colors to each pixel in the disparity map on each side. The green boxes represent inputs, outputs and blue boxes mean the intermediate results. The orange boxes are operations performed on image, forwards to the direction of the arrows. The main steps are concluded as:

3.1   Foreground Extraction, Stereo Matching and Cross-Checking

Since the background in our system will be replaced by a uniform virtual scene, we only care about the disparity of the foreground which is extracted by subtracting a pre-shot background. The window based stereo matching algorithm is used to generate the initial disparity map from two rectified IR images. Equation (1) is an example of using Sum of Absolute Differences (SAD) as the matching function:

$$c(x,y,d) = \sum_{i=-m}^{m}\sum_{j=-n}^{n}|I_L(x+i,y+j) - I_R(x+i-d,y+j)|, \quad (1)$$

where (x, y) is the image coordinates, $(2m + 1) * (2n + 1)$ is the window size and d is the disparity. $I(\ )$ represents the color of a pixel. Then, the correct disparities are filtered by cross-checking [15] to guarantee the precision of parameter calculation of Equation (2). Occlusions and mismatches pixels (outliers) are marked as black in the initial disparity map.

3.2   RBF Build and Interpolation

The disparity map looks dense in a 2D image, but it becomes sparse in the 3D space. RBF interpolation is one of the global spatial interpolation techniques which work quite well for scattered point clouds and hence it has been widely used in 3D modeling [13][14] and face modeling [17].

RBF interpolation fits a radial basis function to each individual point so that there is no constraint on the complexity of the surface it can represent. The interpolations function is defined as:

$$f(x) = p(x) + \sum_{i=1}^{n} \lambda_i \phi(|x - x_i|) \ . \tag{2}$$

x_i is the image coordinates (x, y) and $f(x)$ is the disparity value of pixel x. Let's define $\{x_i\}_{i=1}^{n}$ to be a sample set of pixels with correct disparity values. $|x - x_i|$ is the Euclidean distance between x and x_i. $p(x)$ is a linear polynomial term in the form of $ax + by + c$, where a, b, and c are coefficients. $\phi(r)$ is a radial basis function. Any symmetric function with single positive variable (the distance from the origin) could be used as the radial basis function, such as the *inverse multiquadric* used in this paper. Namely:

$$\phi(r) = (r^2 + c^2)^{-1/2} , \tag{3}$$

where c^2 is a smoothness term. Normally, n samples could only build n functions, but there are $n + 3$ parameters in Equation (2). The problem cannot be solved without the following constraints:

$$\sum_{i=1}^{n} \lambda_i = \sum_{i=1}^{n} \lambda_i x_i = \sum_{i=1}^{n} \lambda_i y_i. \tag{4}$$

Then, Equations (2) and (4) can be combined as: $AX = B$ and solved linearly where the matrices A, X and B are defined as:

$$\begin{bmatrix} \phi_1 & \phi_2 & ... & \phi_n & x_1 & y_1 & 1 \\ \phi_1 & \phi_2 & ... & \phi_n & x_2 & y_2 & 1 \\ & & ... & & & & \\ & & ... & & & & \\ \phi_1 & \phi_2 & ... & \phi_n & x_n & y_n & 1 \\ x_1 & x_2 & ... & x_n & 0 & 0 & 0 \\ y_1 & y_2 & ... & y_n & 0 & 0 & 0 \\ 1 & 1 & ... & 1 & 0 & 0 & 0 \end{bmatrix} \begin{bmatrix} \lambda_1 \\ \lambda_2 \\ . \\ . \\ \lambda_n \\ a \\ b \\ c \end{bmatrix} = \begin{bmatrix} f_1 \\ f_2 \\ . \\ . \\ f_n \\ 0 \\ 0 \\ 0 \end{bmatrix} \ . \tag{5}$$

The parameters in Equation (2) are determined by solving Equation (5) and the disparity value d of a new point is calculated by giving its coordinates (x, y).

RBF interpolation is an over-fitting problem as it exactly passes through every sample. Noises must be reduced since they will disturb the parameter estimation significantly.

Based on all the pixels with correct disparity, we solve the $n + 3$ parameters of Equation (2) and then apply Equation (2) to calculate all missing disparities. After this step, each pixel in the foreground is with a valid disparity.

3.3   Pixel Coloring and Re-projection

Take the case of the left part for example. Each pixel pair (x, y) and $(x - d, y)$ corresponds to a point in a 3D world with coordinates (X, Y, Z) which can be computed by triangulation.   Since in our system the color images are acquired from a different camera rather than the IR cameras, coordinates of corresponding pixel in the color image is calculated by:

$$\begin{bmatrix} x_c \\ y_c \end{bmatrix} = P_c [R_c | T_c] \begin{bmatrix} X \\ Y \\ Z \end{bmatrix}, \tag{6}$$

where P_c, R_c, and T_c are projection matrix, rotation matrix and translation matrix of the color camera respectively, which are determined from a camera calibration procedure performed previously. With the coordinates of 3D points and the calibration parameters, we could fake another color image by projecting the 3D points to the position of color camera on the right side. The disparities of the corresponding pixels in the rectified left real color image and right fake color image are used to interpolate a virtual image I_L' presenting the left scene.

The final image I is a blending of two re-projected or interpolated images I_L' and I_R' from left and right respectively. Pixels marked as *null* means this pixel is not colored.

$$I(x, y) = \begin{cases} I_L', \ if I_L'! = null \ \&\& \ I_R' = null \\ I_R', if I_L' = null \ \&\& \ I_R'! = null \\ \frac{I_L' + I_R'}{2}, if \ I_L'! = null \ \&\& \ I_R' = \ ! null \\ 0, \ if \ I_L' = null \ \&\& \ I_R' = null \end{cases} \tag{7}$$

4   Extensions for Regular Stereo Images

The proposed method is inspired by the problem in videoconference images, but can be extended for general stereo matching. Araujo *et al.* and Carr *et al.* did similar work to fill up the gaps on depth map using RBF [18][19], but just simply train one group of RBF parameters on all the pixels in the image. We find in our experiments that RBF interpolation is not good at filling the gaps across several discontinuous data ranges. Artifacts come out near the discrete border areas. That is the reason they failed to produce impressive disparity maps [18]. For general stereo matching, the key of the extension is how to define the least number of non-overlapped surfaces (disparities are continuous on each surface) that could cover the whole scene and how to

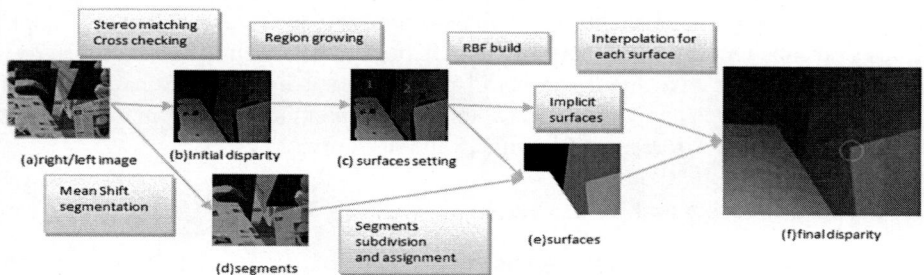

Fig. 6. Flow chart of the proposed method for general stereo matching

assign each pixel to a certain surface. Each surface is going to train its own RBF parameters. Three steps are designed to handle this: mean-shift segmentation, surface setting and segments assignment (Figure 6).

1) Mean-Shift Segmentation: The reference image is segmented using a mean-shift algorithm [16], but no need for over-segmentation.

2) Surface Setting: Surfaces could be fast extracted from the initial disparity map (from Section 3.1). Since interpolation has a bias on creating a smooth transition of data, sharp disparity discontinuities are not expected on a surface. Thus, improved region growing is designed to do this task. The improved region growing performs in this way: Once we find an "unvisited" pixel i, mark it as "visited" and check its neighbor pixels in the 3-by-3 block. If the absolute difference of i and a neighbor pixel j is less than a pre-set threshold, then pixel j is marked as "visited" and becomes the center. The algorithm then continues to check pixel j's neighbor pixels. The growing process stops when the absolute differences of a pixel with all its neighbor pixels are greater than the threshold and one surface is found. The algorithm then finds the next pixel marked as "unvisited" and repeats the growing to look for the next surface, until all the pixels are marked as "visited". Figure 7 is a recursive implementation of improved region grow we described. The disparities in a final surface may range in a wide space, but change smoothly.

```
For each pixel in the image: mark visit[p] as "unvisited"
For each black pixel in the image: mark visit [p] as "visited"
For each pixel in the image
    If visit[i] is "unvisited"
    RegionGrow (i)
    {
        mark visit[i] as "visited"
        for each pixel j in the 3-by-3 neighbor of i
            if (visit[j] equals to 0) and (|disparity[i]-disparity[j]| < threshold)
                RegionGrow(j)
    }
```

Fig. 7. Pseudo code of improved region grow

Since the occlusions usually happen because of large disparity discontinuity, the black color creates an artificial large discontinuity to stop growing. This threshold is the other defense to separate two surfaces on large disparity discontinuity if they are connected in space.

3) Segments Assistant Pixel Assignment: In this step, surfaces extracted from "surface setting" are spread to include those pixels with unknown disparities. Overlapping the segmented color image and surfaces detected, we can see there are four kinds segments: (1) A segment totally belongs to one surface; (2) A segment partially belongs to a surface; (3) A segment spans multiple surfaces. (4) A segment does not overlap with any surface. The segment is assigned to that surface in the first two cases. For the third case, the segment is then further sub-divided into several segments: segments on surfaces are assigned to those surfaces respectively while segments in the occlusions (floating segments) are assigned to the surface around and with the lowest average disparity. The segments in the case (4) are treated as floating segments. Floating segments are usually small areas. This is the reason why the over-segmentation is not preferred. So far, all the pixels in the image have been assigned to a unique surface.

4) RBF Interpolation: At last, the "RBF build and interpolation" step in Section 3.2 is applied to each surface independently to infer the missing disparities.

5   Experimental Results

We test our proposed method on both videoconference images and standard stereo images in this section. SAD is used as the matching cost for initial disparity map. The window size is 25 and the threshold in improved region grow is 10 for all the experiments.

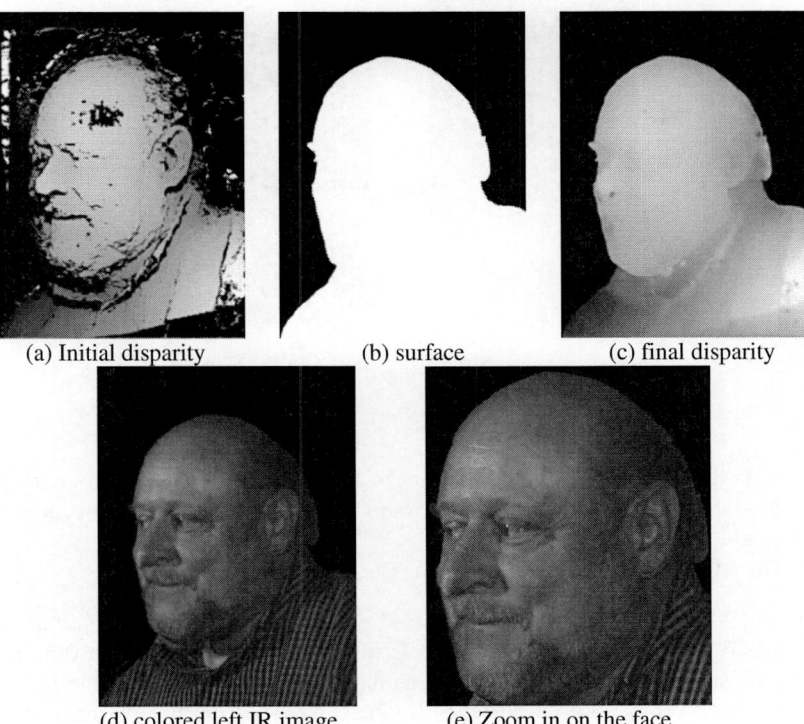

(a) Initial disparity   (b) surface   (c) final disparity

(d) colored left IR image   (e) Zoom in on the face

Fig. 8. Results of videoconference image

5.1   Tests for Videoconference Images

Videoconference images for test are shown in Figure 4. In Figure 8, (a) is the initial disparity derived from the Figure 4(a) and (b). Outliers are marked in black. The dense of disparity map is greatly enhanced by those random dots. Figure 8(b) is the surface representing the foreground area and (c) is the final foreground disparity map after the interpolation and Figure 8(d) is Figure 4(a) after coloring. (d) is visually flawless even after a zoom in shown in Figure 8(e).

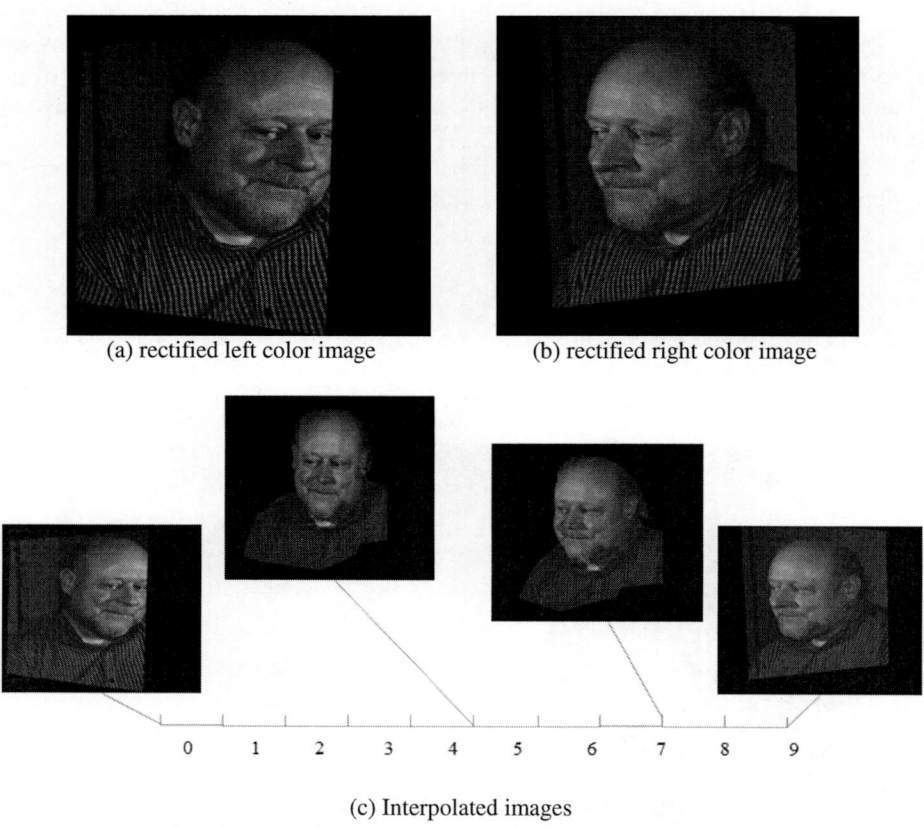

(a) rectified left color image   (b) rectified right color image

(c) Interpolated images

Fig. 9. Interpolation along the baseline of two color cameras

Figure 9 shows a series of virtual images interpolated by two color images. The images are interpolated along the line between two color cameras, but not limited.

5.2   Tests for Regular Stereo Images

We use the Middlebury dataset to test the extension and compare our method to others. Figure 6 is one example - "Venus". Errors may happen when the floating segments are assigned to the wrong surface, as indicated by the yellow circle in the final disparity. The "venus" uses 4 surfaces (indicated by red digital numbers in (c)) to cover the scene. Figure 10 and 11 are more example- "baby" and "teddy", which need 4 and 6 surfaces.

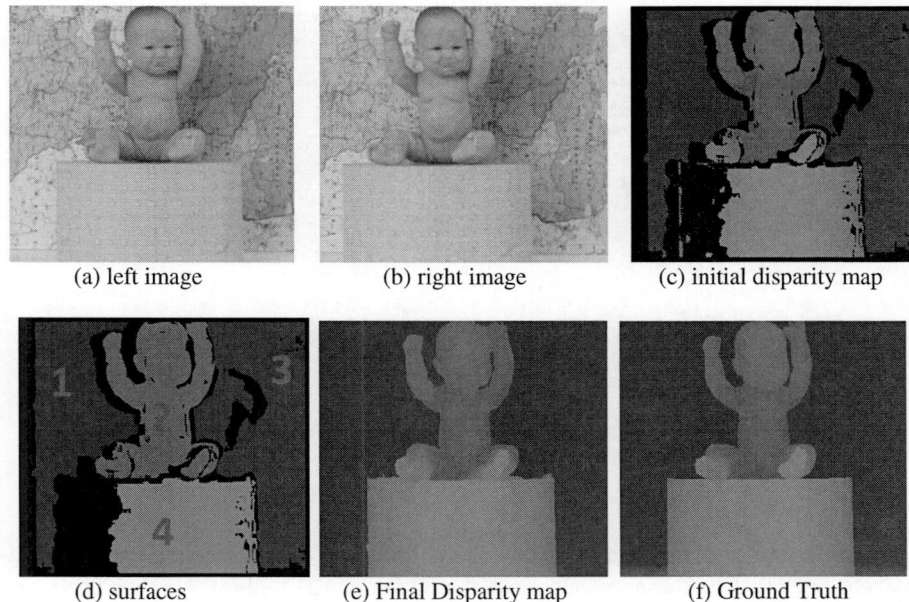

(a) left image   (b) right image   (c) initial disparity map

(d) surfaces   (e) Final Disparity map   (f) Ground Truth

Fig. 10. Disparity result of baby

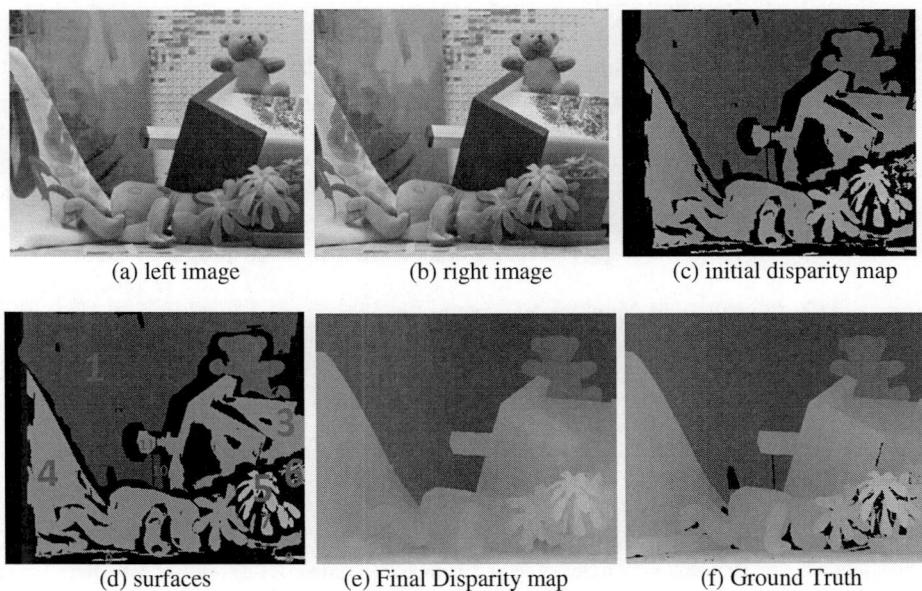

(a) left image   (b) right image   (c) initial disparity map

(d) surfaces   (e) Final Disparity map   (f) Ground Truth

Fig. 11. Disparity result of teddy

Error Threshold = 1		Sort by nonocc ▼			Sort by all ▼			Sort by disc ▼						
Algorithm	Avg. Rank ▼	Tsukuba ground truth			Venus ground truth			Teddy ground truth			Cones ground truth			Average Percent Bad Pixels
		nonocc ▼	all ▼	disc ▼	nonocc ▼	all ▼	disc ▼	nonocc ▼	all ▼	disc ▼	nonocc ▼	all ▼	disc ▼	
ADCensus [94]	7.0	1.07 14	1.48 11	5.73 16	0.09 2	0.25 8	1.15 3	4.10 5	6.22 3	10.9 6	2.42 6	7.25 6	6.95 6	3.97
CoopRegion [41]	8.6	0.87 3	1.16 1	4.61 2	0.11 4	0.21 4	1.54 7	5.16 16	8.31 12	13.0 12	2.79 16	7.18 5	8.01 21	4.41
AdaptingBP [17]	8.8	1.11 17	1.37 6	5.79 17	0.10 3	0.21 5	1.44 5	4.22 7	7.06 7	11.8 8	2.48 7	7.92 12	7.32 11	4.23
RVbased [116]	11.2	0.95 8	1.42 9	4.98 7	0.11 6	0.29 12	1.07 1	5.98 21	11.6 30	15.4 28	2.35 3	7.61 7	6.81 5	4.88
DoubleBP [35]	11.8	0.88 5	1.29 3	4.76 5	0.13 9	0.45 21	1.87 13	3.53 4	8.30 11	9.63 3	2.90 20	8.78 29	7.79 18	4.19
RDP [102]	12.3	0.97 9	1.39 7	5.00 8	0.21 24	0.38 18	1.89 14	4.84 9	9.94 19	12.6 10	2.53 8	7.69 9	7.38 12	4.57
OutlierConf [42]	12.6	0.88 4	1.43 10	4.74 4	0.18 17	0.26 10	2.40 23	5.01 11	9.12 16	12.8 11	2.78 15	8.57 23	6.99 7	4.60
YOUR METHOD	13.3	1.33 35	1.56 13	6.02 22	0.13 8	0.17 2	1.84 11	5.09 14	6.36 4	13.4 18	2.92 22	6.77 3	7.15 9	4.40
SubPixDoubleBP [30]	17.1	1.24 25	1.76 29	5.98 21	0.12 7	0.46 23	1.74 10	3.45 3	8.38 13	10.0 4	2.93 23	8.73 27	7.91 20	4.39
SurfaceStereo [79]	17.6	1.28 30	1.65 20	6.78 36	0.19 19	0.28 11	2.61 31	3.12 2	5.10 1	8.65 1	2.89 19	7.95 14	8.26 27	4.06

Fig. 12. The Evaluation results on Middlebury

We also evaluate our method using the Middlebury test bed [6] for quantitative analysis (Figure 12). Our approach ranks the 8th out of 123, only worse than one plane fitting based method- CoopRegion [11]. This is because the proposed method has no strict constraint about the disparity distribution of a surface, which makes it more flexible for surface selection and has stronger capacity of error tolerance.

6   Conclusion and Future Work

This paper presents a solution to wide baseline videoconference system. Two IR camera and one color camera are installed on each side of the monitor to capture the whole scene. RBF interpolation works on the initial disparity map to fill up the missing disparities. The reconstructed 3D points could be re-projected to any location on the screen to correct the eye contact. The way how to generate the disparity map on each side could also be applied to general stereo matching after defining the numbers of RBF surfaces. The impressive results demonstrate that the proposed method can generate correct virtual views with vivid eye contact and works well for general stereo images in both visual and quantitative aspects.

References

1. Ott, M., Lewis, J., Cox, I.: Teleconferencing Eye Contact Using a Virtual Camera. In: INTERCHI, pp. 119–110 (1993)
2. Lei, B.J., Hendriks, E.A.: Real-time Multi-step View Reconstruction for a Virtual Teleconference System. Journal on Applied Signal Processing 2002, 1067–1087 (2002)
3. Schreer, O., Hendriks, E., Schraagen, J., Stone, J., Trucco, E., Jewell, M.: Virtual Team User Environment – A Key Application in Telecommunication. In: Proceeding of eBusiness and eWork, Prague, pp. 916–923 (2002)
4. Baker, H.H., Tanguay, D., Sobel, I., Gelb, D., Goss, M.E., Culbertson, W.B., Malzbender, T.: The Coliseum Immersive Teleconferencing System. In: Proceedings of International Workshop on Immersive Telepresence (2002)

5. Scharstein, D., Szeliski, R.: A Taxonomy and Evaluation of Dense Two-Frame Stereo Correspondence Algorithms. International Journal of Computer Vision 47(1), 7–42 (2002)
6. http://vision.middlebury.edu/stereo/eval/
7. Tao, H., Sawhney, H.S., Kumar, R.: A Global Matching Framework for Stereo Computation. In: Proceedings of ICCV, vol. 1, pp. 532–539 (2001)
8. Hong, L., Chen, G.: Segment-based Stereo Matching Using Graph Cuts. In: Proceedings of CVPR, pp. 74–81 (2004)
9. Chen, Y., Quan, L.: Region – Based Progressive Stereo Matching. In: Proceedings of CVPR, pp. 106–113 (2004)
10. Klaus, A., Sormann, M., Karner, K.: Segment-based Stereo Matching using Belief Propagation and a Self-adapting Dissimilarity Measure. In: Proceedings of CVPR, pp. 15–18 (2006)
11. Wang, Z., Zheng, Z.: A Region based Stereo Matching Algorithm using Cooperation optimization. In: Proceedings of International Conference on Pattern Recognition, pp. 1–8 (2008)
12. Yang, Q., Wang, L., Yang, R., Stewenius, H., Nister, D.: Stereo Matching with Color-weighted Correlation, Hierarchical Belief Propagation and Occlusion Handling. In: Proceedings of International Conference on Pattern Recognition, pp. 347–354 (2006)
13. Carr, J.C., Beatson, R.K., Cherrie, J.B., Mitchell, T.J., Fright, W.R., McCallum, B.C., Evans, T.R.: Reconstruction and Representation of 3D Objects with Radial Basis Functions. In: Proceesings of ACM SIGGRAPH, pp. 67–76 (2001)
14. Labatut, P., Pons, J.P., Keriven, R.: Robust and Efficient Surface Reconstruction from Range Data. Computer Graphics Forum, 2275–2290 (2009)
15. Fua, P.: A parallel stereo algorithm that produces dense depth maps and preserves image features. Machine Vision and Applications 6(1), 35–49 (1993)
16. Comaniciu, D., Meer, P.: Robust Analysis of Feature Spaces: Color Image Segmentation. In: Proceedings of CVPR, pp. 750–755 (1997)
17. Min, K., Chun, J.: Image-Based 3D Face Modeling from Stereo Images. In: Gavrilova, M.L., Gervasi, O., Kumar, V., Tan, C.J.K., Taniar, D., Laganá, A., Mun, Y., Choo, H. (eds.) ICCSA 2006. LNCS, vol. 3980, pp. 410–419. Springer, Heidelberg (2006)
18. de Araujo, A.D.G., Doria Neto, A.D., de Medeiros Martins, A.: Stereo Map Surface Calculus Optimization Using Radial Basis Functions Neural Network Interpolation. In: Leung, C.S., Lee, M., Chan, J.H. (eds.) ICONIP 2009, Part I. LNCS, vol. 5863, pp. 229–236. Springer, Heidelberg (2009)
19. Carr, J.C., Fright, W.R., Beatson, R.K.: Surface Interpolation with Radial Basis Functions for Medical Imaging. IEEE Transactions on Medical Imaging 16, 96–107 (1997)

An Integrated Hole-Filling Algorithm for View Synthesis

Wenxin Yu, Weichen Wang, Zhengyan Guo, and Satoshi Goto

Graduate school of Information, Production and Systems,
Waseda University, Fukuoka, 808-0135 Japan
{yuwenxin,wangweichen}@fuji.waseda.jp,
ocean.milo@ruri.waseda.jp,
goto@waseda.jp

Abstract. Multi-view video can provide users a 3-D and virtual reality perception by its multiple viewing angles. In recent years, the depth image-based rendering (DIBR) is generally used to synthesize virtual view images in free viewpoint television (FTV) and three-dimensional (3-D) video. In order to conceal the zero-region more accurately and improve the quality of virtual view synthesized frame, an integrated Hole-filling Algorithm for View Synthesis is proposed in this paper. It contains five parts: the different regions distinguishing algorithm, foreground and background boundary detection, the texture image isophotes detection, the textural and structural isophotes prediction algorithm, the in-painting algorithm with gradient priority order. Based on the texture isophotes prediction with geometrical principle and the in-painting algorithm with gradient priority order, the boundary information of the foreground is much clearer and the texture information in the zero-region can be concealed much more accurately than the previous work. The vision quality mainly depends on the distortion of the structural information. Through the experimental results, the proposed algorithm not only improves the objective quality of the virtual image, but also improves the subjective quality of the virtual image a lot, and the human vision quality is also improved obviously based on the subjective results. Especially, it ensures the boundary contours of the foreground objects and the textural and the structural information.

Keywords: DIBR, Virtual view, Hole-filling, In-painting.

1   Introduction

In recent years, the 3-D products become more and more popular in people's daily life. In most traditional three-dimensional multi-media systems, only one pre-determined viewpoint of the images and the videos can be sawn by the observers. If the viewpoint is changed, the realistic 3-D impression will became much weaker and the quality of the 3-D video will be worse. In order to increase the viewpoints for the observers and make the sight more comfortable, the free viewpoint television (FTV) [1] [2] [3] is introduced. The interest in free viewpoint television is constantly increasing in recent years. Auto-stereoscopic displays provide a 3-D impression to an observer without the need to wear additional glasses [4], and the observers can enjoy the realistic 3-D impression in some

W. Lin et al. (Eds.): PCM 2012, LNCS 7674, pp. 80–92, 2012.
© Springer-Verlag Berlin Heidelberg 2012

different viewpoints. Such a display shows a number of slightly different views at the same time. To simultaneously deliver so many views, extremely large bandwidth is required in this kind of cases.

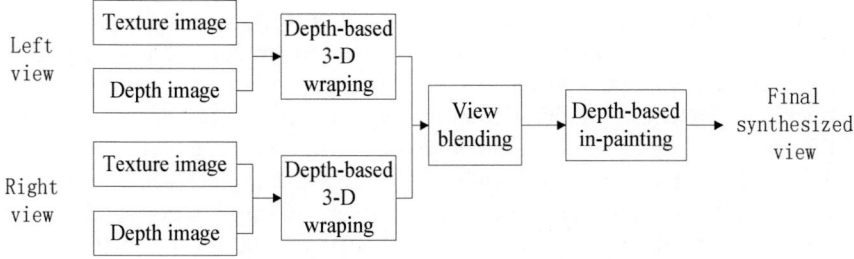

Fig. 1. Depth image-based virtual view synthesis

Therefore the view synthesis [5] is introduced to solve this kind of problems, and the depth-based virtual view synthesis process is shown in Fig.1. Depth-image-based rendering (DIBR) is a technology for synthesizing novel realistic images at a slightly different view perspective, using a textured image and its associated depth values. It is used to generate additional virtual views of a real-world scene from images or videos and associated per-pixel depth information. The 3-D warping is a key technique in the depth-image-based rendering (DIBR), and its general concept is shown in Fig.2. In 3-D warping, pixels in a reference image are back-projected to 3-D spaces, and then re-projected onto the target viewpoint. An inherent problem of the view synthesis concept is the fact that image information which is occluded in the original view may become visible in the "virtual" image. Then some holes will appear in the virtual image, and they can be also called zero-region. The information of the occluded region in the original image is lost in the virtual image and need to be concealed. Therefore the hole-filling technique is required and the in-painting is the most popular method for hole-filling problems.

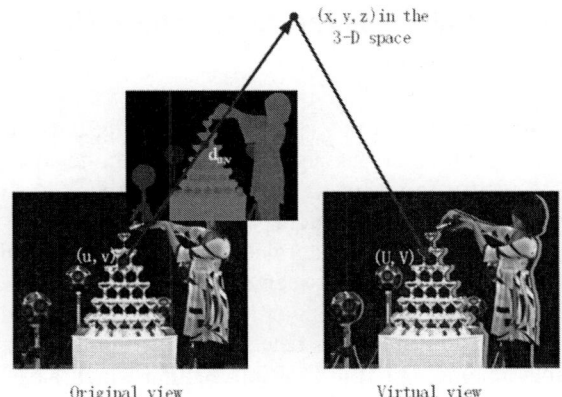

Fig. 2. General concept of 3-D warping

Some works [6] [7] have been done in this field. A simple approach repeats the last valid background sample line-wise into the zero-region. VSRS (View Synthesis Reference Software) also provides a solution, and it will make the boundary of the foreground objects to be blurred. But the structural information is very important in the 3-D cases. Criminisi et al. noted that exemplar-based texture synthesis contains the essential process required to replicate both texture and structure. The Criminisi's In-painting Algorithm conceals the zero-region with a priority order based on the texture and structure information. But this kind of priority order is not enough for the prediction of the texture and structure information with long term trend. Therefore this Integrated Hole-filling Algorithm for View Synthesis is proposed. It includes five parts: the different regions distinguishing algorithm, foreground and background boundary detection, the textural and structural isophotes detection, the texture image isophotes prediction algorithm, the in-painting algorithm with gradient priority order. The isophote is the boundary between two regions in different layers or two regions with much different lum and chroma information, and it intersects with the zero-region from the background side. The proposed method ensures the boundary of the foreground objects by distinguishing the different layers with depth information, predicts the textural and structural information in the zero-region by using the geometry principle, and paints the zero-region as a priority order based on the gradient information. The textural and structural information is very important in the 3-D cases, and it will affect the 3-D impression a lot in human vision. So the proposal will not only improve the objective quality of the synthesized virtual view, but also improve the subjective quality of the synthesized virtual view and improve the 3-D performance in human vision. Besides the multi-viewpoints cases, the proposed method can also be used in the conversion cases from 2-D video to 3-D video.

The rest of this paper is organized as follow. The architecture of the proposed integrated hole-filling algorithm for view synthesis is presented in Section 2. The details of the proposed method are described in Section 3. The experimental result is shown in the Section 4. And the Section 5 gives the conclusion.

2   The Architecture of the Integrated Hole-Filling Algorithm for View Synthesis

The architecture of the proposed process is shown in Fig.3. It starts with a different layers distinguishing algorithm. This algorithm divides the texture image into several layers based on the depth information. It can distinguish the foreground information and the corresponding background information.

The next step is foreground and background boundary detection algorithm. It is used to ensure the boundary information between the foreground objects and the zero-region clearly and decide the primary in-painting order in the background side.

The textural and structural isophotes detection is the third step. It is mainly used to find out the visible textural and structural information which have a stable long term trend next to the zero-region in the background side. The textural and structural lines are called isophotes, and they are used to predict the obvious textural and structural information in the zero-region.

The forth parts is the isophotes prediction algorithm. The prediction process is based on the geometry principle. The detected textural and structural information in the third parts will be fitted by different curves, and the function of the curves is used to predict the tendency of the textural and structural information. Up to now, the zero-region has already been divided into several parts by the predicted textural and structural information.

The last step is the in-painting algorithm with gradient priority order. Based on the primary in-painting order which has been decided in the second parts, it introduces an advanced priority order with the gradient information. It searches and compares the information of the boundary between the zero-region and the background, paints the position which has the highest priority and updates the boundary information. This process should be iterated until there is no suitable position which is satisfied

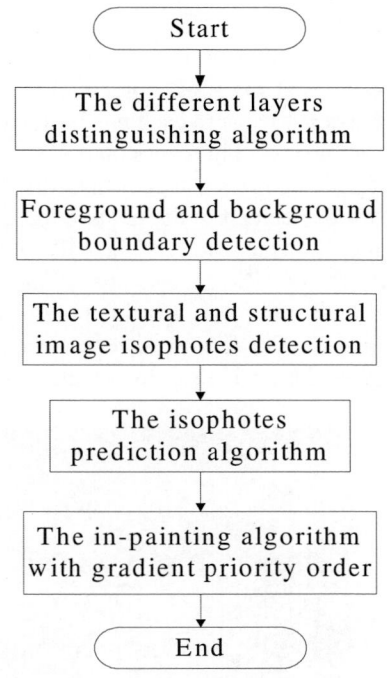

Fig. 3. The architecture of the proposed method

the priority condition. After these parts, there are still some little holes in the virtual image. Then the average in-painting which uses the average value of the neighbor pixels is used to fill this kind of the holes.

3   The Details of the Proposed Algorithm

3.1   The Different Layers Distinguishing Algorithm

This algorithm distinguishes the different layers based on the depth information. It decides the relative foreground layer and background layer in the texture image and it is the important basic for the next steps. The accuracy of the result will affect the hole-filling result directly.

Some of the previous works also check the foreground layer and background layer at first, such as VSRS. But they all only check one pair of the points which are on the both sides between the nonzero-region and the zero-region at the same horizontal level to decide the relative foreground and background. The most of the depth map is generated by the depth camera, and they are not very accurate. So if only check one pair of the points, it will cause some errors when the depth information has some artefacts.

The illustration of the proposed distinguishing algorithm is shown in Fig.4. One pair of patches which includes both nonzero-region and zero-region on the boundary of the holes at the same horizontal level in the depth image is got at first. Then the average depth value in each patch should be got and compare them.

There are two kinds of situations in the comparing result. The first one: If one of the depth value much bigger than the other one, the layer which contains the bigger one will be decided as the relative foreground layer in the texture image and the layer which contains the smaller one will be decided as the relative background layer in the texture image. The second one: If the average depth values of the two patches are almost the same, it means this hole is occurred by the 3-D warping process and the inaccurate depth information. The both sides of the holes will be decided as the background layer in this kind of situation.

Depth image   Texture image

Fig. 4. Illustration for the distinguishing process

The two patches comparing process is much more stable than the two points comparing process, and can provide much more accurate different layers decision.

3.2 Foreground and Background Boundary Detection

Based on the first step, the boundary of the different layers can be detected and recorded, and this information between the zero-region and the different layers should be separated into two kinds. The first one is the relative foreground boundary information and the other one is the relative background boundary information. The two kinds of the information is detected and recorded as shown in Fig.5. The relative foreground boundary information is used to ensure that the in-painting process will not make the boundary of the foreground objects blurred. This problem is existent in a lot of previous works. In the previous in-painting process, it paints the zero-region, and makes the boundary of the foreground objects blurred at the same time. The textural and structural information is very important in this kind of virtual view in-painting cases. If the boundary becomes blurred, the final 3-D impression will be affected a lot, even if the objective quality is improved. The relative background boundary information is used as a primary in-painting priority order and also is the important basic information for the next step textural and structural isophotes detection.

Background boundary   Foreground boundary

Fig. 5. The result of the boundary detection

3.3   The Textural and Structural Isophotes Detection

In this part, the Canny edge detection algorithm is used to get all of the edge information from the gray picture of the texture image. The gray picture is got at first. Then based on this picture, a binary edge map is calculated by the Canny edge detection algorithm.

The detection flow is shown in the Fig.6. It works based on the boundary information of relative background and the binary edge map. Check every point as point Q on the binary boundary map at first. If the point Q is on the boundary map and P is on the edge map, check the distance between Q and P. If the distance is smaller than $\triangle$ ($\triangle$ is the threshold to control the continuity of the detected isophotes), record the point P as the first point of the detected isophote L_i ($i = 0, 1, 2$ $\cdots$, n). Then check the neighbor points P' of the P. If P' on the edge map and the distance between Q and P' bigger than the distance between Q and P, records P' into the detected isophote L_i. The detection process should be iterated again and again until all of the isophotes have been found out. Then the textural and structural isophotes detection result can be got as shown in the Fig.7.

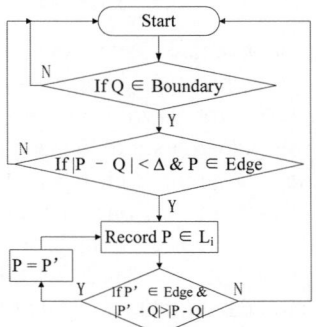

Fig. 6. The detection flow

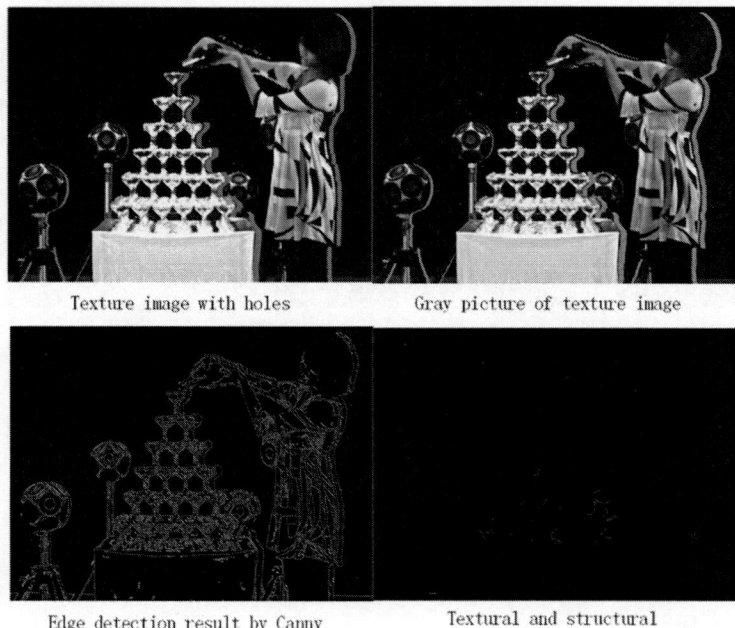

Fig. 7. The steps and the result of the textural and structural detection

3.4   The Isophotes Prediction Algorithm

Based on the result of the previous step, the textural and structural isophotes can be predicted in this part. The proposed algorithm uses curve functions to fit the existent isophotes, and predict the unknown isophotes in the zero-region with these curve functions.

The curve fitting and prediction is shown in Fig.8. In proposed method, the follow is used to fit the different isophotes.

$$(X - a)^2 + (Y - b)^2 = r^2$$

Three points on the existent isophote are used to solve the quadratic equation and get the values of the constant a, b, r, then use the equation to predict next point on the isophote in the zero-region. The point A is always the first point of the isophote line, the point C is always the newest added point of the isophote line and the point B is the midpoint of the isophote line. The point B changes when the point C was updated. This process should be repeated after added one point into the existent isophote.

The basic idea in this part is to predict the textural and structural isophotes which have the stable long term trend. If the curves which need to be fitted are very complex, they will be considered unstable and unpredictable. Therefore only the quadratic equation is enough to describe the tendency of the existent isophotes.

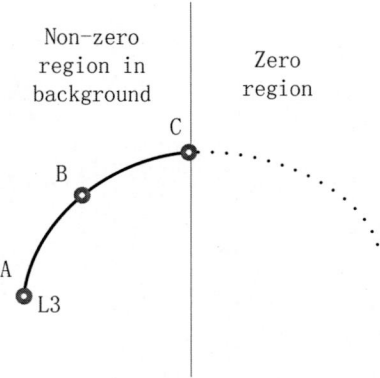

Fig. 8. Illustration of curve fitting and prediction

A threshold T is set for some special cases. If radius r > T, then the radius will be considered infinite and isophote will be considered as a beeline. In this kind of situation, the equation Y = aX + b is used to predict all points of this isophote in the zero region.

There is another special situation is that two predicted isophotes have an intersection in the zero-region. The solution is shown in **Fig.9**. When the prediction of the isophote L_1 is finished, this isophote should be recorded without filling it with the texture pixels. Until the prediction of the next isophote L_2 was finished, L_1 and L_2 have a point of intersection P. Then set P as the end of these two isophotes. If L_1 and L_2 have no point of intersection, then fill the L_1 with the texture pixels and record the L_2 as the new L_1, and repeat the previous process with the next new L_2.

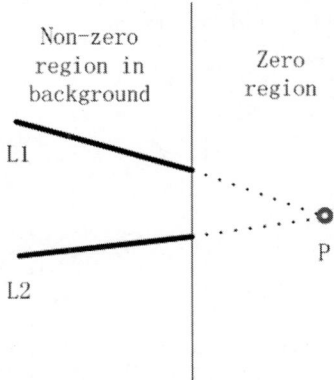

Fig. 9. Illustration of the intersection decision

3.5 The In-Painting Algorithm with Gradient Priority Order

Up to now, following the prediction process, the zero-region has already been divided into several pieces. The prediction process and result is shown in the Fig.10. Then the in-painting algorithm with gradient priority order is introduced.

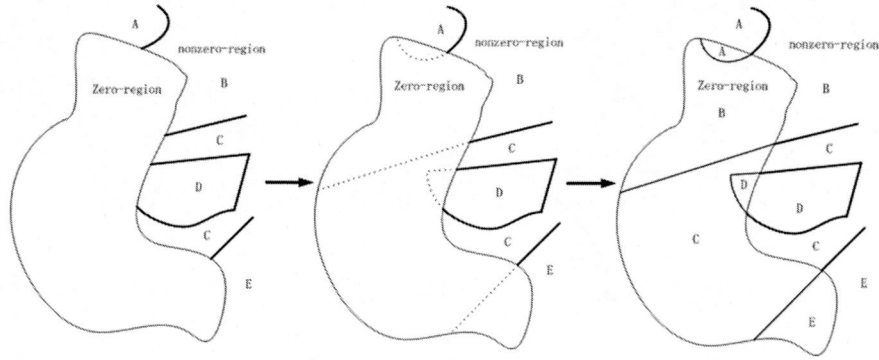

Before isophotes prediction   Predicting isophotes   After isophotes prediction

Fig. 10. The illustration of the prediction process

As shown in Fig.11, P is the current pixel on the boundary between the zero-region and the background, P1, P2, P3, P4 are the four neighbour pixels, G is the length of the gradient and α is the direction of the gradient. If the neighbour pixel is in zero-region, the value of the neighbour point is set to zero. The boundary map of the relative background layer should be search at first and calculated the length and the direction of the gradient of each pixel on the boundary map. The point which have longest length of the gradient and have a neighbour point in the zero-region on the direction of the gradient will be chosen as the predicting source. After filling the predict point in the zero-region, this point should be added into the predicting chosen candidates. The process is iterated until there is no suitable pixel left. In the choosing process, eight neighbour pixels can be the filling candidates for the current pixel. So the direction of the gradient should be separated to 8 different directions, and the separated result is shown in Fig.12.

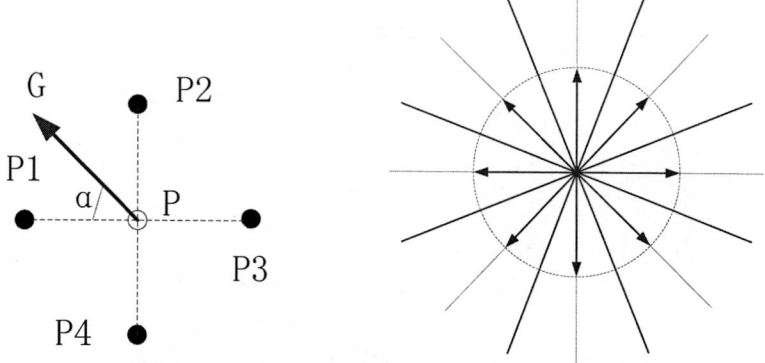

Fig. 11. The illustration of the gradient   **Fig. 12.** The illustration of the filling direction

The length of the gradient and the direction of the gradient are calculated based on the gray picture of the texture image and as the following equations:

$$
\begin{cases}
dx = V_{P3} - V_{P1} & (1) \\
dy = V_{P2} - V_{P4} & (2) \\
G = \sqrt{dx^2 + dy^2} & (3) \\
\alpha = \tan^{-1}(dy/dx) & (4)
\end{cases}
$$

V is the value of the pixels in the gray picture of the texture image.

4   The Experimental Results

The experiment is done with the Champagne_tower sequence based on the VSRS 3.5. The view 39 is the real view and the view 40 is the synthesized virtual view, and the comparison result is shown in Table.1. The PSNR can be considered as the objective quality evaluation criteria and the SSIM can be considered as the objective quality evaluation criteria. The PSNR is improved 0.2425 dB and the SSIM is improved 0.005 in the comparison result between VSRS and proposed algorithm, and the PSNR is improved 0.1664 dB and the SSIM is almost the same in the comparison result between line-wise approach and the proposed method. Through this comparison, the proposed algorithm not only improves the objective quality of the virtual view, but also improves the subjective quality of the virtual view.

Table 1. The experimental comparison result

Champagne_tower	VSRS		Line-wise approach		Proposed algorithm	
	PSNR(dB)	SSIM	PSNR(dB)	SSIM	PSNR(dB)	SSIM
39 to 40	28.7144	0.9429	28.7905	0.9434	28.9569	0.9434

 1. VSRS   2. Line-wise approach with boundary ensuring

Fig. 13. The details comparison result

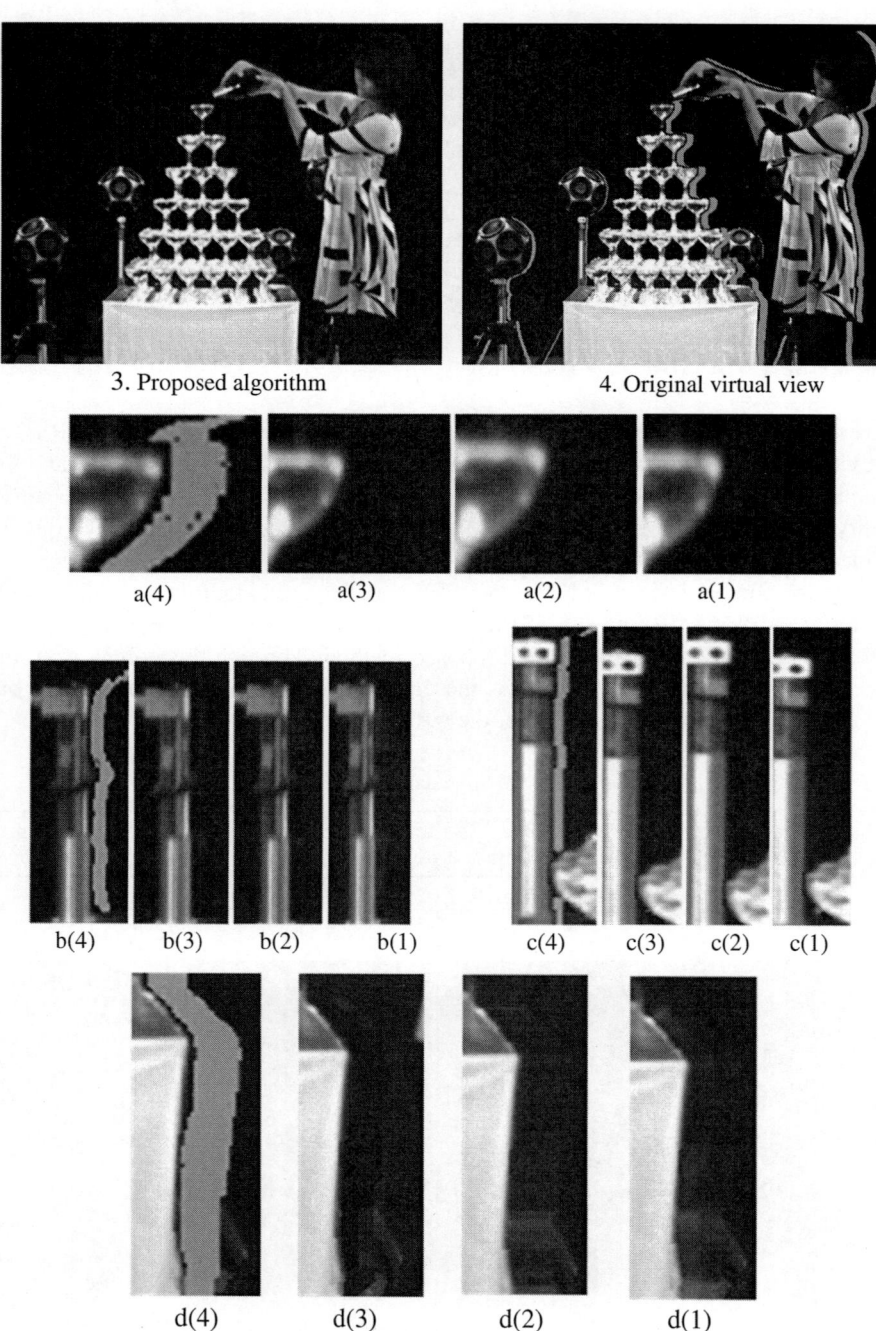

3. Proposed algorithm

4. Original virtual view

a(4)   a(3)   a(2)   a(1)

b(4)   b(3)   b(2)   b(1)   c(4)   c(3)   c(2)   c(1)

d(4)   d(3)   d(2)   d(1)

Fig.13. *(continued)*

Table 2. Some more experimental results

Sequence name	position	VSRS		Line-wise approach		Proposed algorithm	
		PSNR(dB)	SSIM	PSNR(dB)	SSIM	PSNR(dB)	SSIM
Champagne_tower	39 to 40	28.7144	0.9429	28.7905	0.9434	28.9569	0.9434
Mobile	3 to 4	32.5907	0.9790	33.0770	0.9819	33.1972	0.9822
Beer garden	5 to 6	22.1965	0.7085	21.2598	0.7063	23.6481	0.7128

The details and human vision comparison result is shown in Fig.13. The first result is obtained by VSRS, the second one is obtained by line-wise approach with the boundary ensuring principle, the third one is obtained by the proposed algorithm and the fourth one is the original virtual view for comparison. Through the a, b, c, d partial cases, it is obvious that the proposed algorithm can get better boundary contours of the foreground objects and can get more accurate background information in-painting result. Some result is given in Table.2. In the 3-D cases, the textural and the structural information are very important. Therefore the proposed algorithm performs much better performance than the previous work.

5   Conclusion

The proposed integrated hole-filling algorithm for view synthesis includes five parts: the different regions distinguishing algorithm, foreground and background boundary detection, the texture image isophotes detection, the textural and structural isophotes prediction algorithm, the in-painting algorithm with gradient priority order.

Through the experimental result, the objective quality and the subjective quality are also improved a lot with the proposed algorithm. Through the details comparison, the proposed algorithm can ensure the boundary contours of the foreground objects and the structural information much more clearly than the previous work.

Acknowledgment. This research is partly supported by Grants-in-Aid for Scientific Research <KAKENHI>, by "Ambient SoC Global COE Program of Waseda University" of the Ministry of Education, Culture, Sports, Science and Technology, Japan, and by the Core Research for Evolution Science and Technology (CREST) project of Japan Science and Technology Agency.

References

1. Smolic, A., Mueller, K., Merkle, P., Fehn, C., Kauff, P., Eisert, P., Wiegand, T.: 3D Video and Free Viewpoint Video – Technologies, Applications and MPEG Standards. In: Proc. of ICME 2006, pp. 2161–2164 (July 2006)
2. Tanimoto, M.: Overview of free viewpoint television. Proc. of Signal Processing: Image Communication 21, 454–461 (2006)
3. Kubota, A., Smolic, A., Magnor, M., Tanimoto, M., Chen, T., Zhang, C.: Multiview Imaging and 3DTV. IEEE Signal Processing Magazine 24(6), 10–21 (2007)

4. Konrad, J., Halle, M.: 3-D Displays and Signal Processing – An Answer to 3-D Ills? IEEE Signal Processing Magazine 24(6) (November 2007)
5. Kauff, P., Atzpadin, N., Fehn, C., Müller, M., Schreer, O., Smolic, A., Tanger, R.: Depth Map Creation and Image Based Rendering for Advanced 3DTV Services Providing Interoperability and Scalability. Signal Processing: Image Communication. Special Issue on 3DTV (February 2007)
6. Criminisi, A., Perez, P., Toyama, K.: Region filling and object removal by exemplar-based image inpainting. IEEE Transactions on Image Processing 13(9), 1200–1212 (2004)
7. Müller, K., Smolic, A., Dix, K., Merkle, P., Kauf, P., Wiegand, T.: View synthesis for advanced 3-D video systems. EURASIP J. Image Video Process. 2008, Art. ID 438148 (2008)

A Real-Time On-Chip Algorithm
for IMU-Based Gait Measurement

Shenggao Zhu, Hugh Anderson, and Ye Wang

School of Computing, National University of Singapore, Singapore
{zhusheng,hugh,wangye}@comp.nus.edu.sg

Abstract. This paper presents a real-time and on-chip gait measurement algorithm used in our Gait Measurement System (GMS). Our GMS is a small foot-mounted device based on an Inertial Measurement Unit (IMU), which contains an accelerometer and a gyroscope. The GMS can compute spatio-temporal gait parameters in real-time and transmit them to a remote receiver. Measured gait parameters include cadence, velocity, stride length, swing/stance ratio and so on. The algorithm is optimized to run in a ATmega328 microprocessor with only 2kB data memory. During a walking session, each stride is recognized instantaneously, and the stride length and other parameters are computed at the same time. Although inexpensive components are utilized, the algorithm achieves high accuracy, with an average stride length error smaller than 3%, and error in total walking distance less than 2%.

Keywords: Gait Measurement, Algorithm, IMU, Real-Time, On-Chip.

1   Introduction

The primary motivation for our gait measurement system (GMS) was in the Healthcare field, in clinical therapy and rehabilitation of people suffering from walking difficulties, such as Parkinson's disease (PD) patients and stroke victims. Many of their symptoms may be hard to treat, or even have no cure, and physiotherapy is commonly used to improve the patients' quality of life. For clinical use and rehabilitation, inertial measurement units (IMUs) have been widely utilized in various assistive and/or monitoring systems. Researchers have already developed IMU-based devices for detection and prevention of Freezing of Gait (FOG) symptoms of PD patients [1], fall detection [2], and general gait parameters measurement [3,4].

A specific music therapy method for these patients is known as Rhythmic Auditory Stimulation or RAS [5]. To facilitate and automate the music therapy procedures, our research group is developing a RAS-based gait training system, which has two subsystems. One is a gait measurement subsystem to detect the walking cadence in real-time. Another subsystem is the tempo-based music search engine, which can retrieve a proper song whose tempo is related to the patient's target walking cadence [6]. Patients can follow the rhythm of the selected songs while having gait training. Our IMU-based GMS is a small

W. Lin et al. (Eds.): PCM 2012, LNCS 7674, pp. 93–104, 2012.

foot-mounted device to measure cadence and other gait parameters, as well as assess the patient's improvement over time. The components of our GMS proto- type include an ATmega328 based microcontroller board (Arduino Pro Mini), an IMU, a radio frequency module (RFM12B), and a 3.7 volt Lithium-ion battery. The IMU is a combo board of a 3-axis accelerometer (ADXL345) and a 3-axis gyroscope (ITG-3200). The whole device measures $34mm \times 18mm \times 11mm$ in size and weighs 9g (battery included).

Recently there have been intensive investigations into sensor-based gait mea- surement as well as dead reckoning [7]. However, some gait measurement ap- proaches rely on the sensor fusion of IMU and other sensors, like a magnetome- ter [8] or Foot Force Sensor (force sensitive resistors) [3]. Other IMU-based ap- proaches require remote computers to calculate gait parameters [9,10]. Another study does use on-chip computing [4], but only the frequency domain algorithm is used, and it cannot measure velocity or stride length, which are important parameters for gait analysis. By contrast, our GMS only uses simple and cheap inertial sensors, and performs on-chip gait analysis in real-time. A wireless com- munication interface is also integrated into the GMS to work with applications in remote computers or mobile devices like smart phones. Therefor our GMS can operate in both indoor and outdoor scenarios with relatively level ground, such as a corridor or a level park road. This is much more convenient than the traditional machine vision based gait measurement.

Algorithms for IMU-based gait measurement can be generally grouped into three categories: abstraction model, gait model and direct integration. Abstrac- tion model based algorithms do not study the specific walking biomechanics, but use neural networks and machine learning methods to abstract and estimate the walking patterns [11]. Algorithms using gait models make use of the derived kinematic information from some predefined models, such as modeling two legs as the two sides of an isosceles triangle during walking [12]. However, the accu- racy of both methods is limited because they rely on models which vary between people. The resultant training or setup phase for these models can take a long time, rendering systems based on these algorithms less convenient to use.

Algorithms based on direct integration are relatively accurate and simple. The main idea is to measure walking acceleration through inertial sensors, so that the velocity and stride length can be derived by single and double integration of acceleration [3,7,9,13]. This kind of algorithms need to handle noises and sensor drifts carefully, using methods like zero velocity update (ZUPT) [10]. As reported in literature, the best accuracy result achieved with relatively expensive sensors is about 2% error in walking displacement [7,9,10].

In our GMS, the algorithm is also based on direct integration. The detailed data processing procedures will be described in this paper. Although our GMS prototype is built up with cheap components, the average stride length error is smaller than 3%, and the error of total walking distance measurement is less than 2%. These accuracy results are comparable with those achieved by the use of expensive sensors.

2   Stride Cycle Detection

2.1   Data Preprocessing

The inertial coordinate system XYZ of a foot-mounted IMU is represented in Fig. 1. The GMS is carefully attached to the heel or shoe so that the IMU's yz-plane stays approximately parallel to the user's forward direction during the walking session. In practice, this condition is easy to ensure. The algorithm assumes that people walk on relatively level ground, in both outdoor and indoor scenarios. Therefore, we can use acceleration in y-axis (a_y) and z-axis (a_z) as well as angular rate around x-axis (ω_x) to fully describe the foot motion. We need to calculate the horizontal acceleration (a_h) and perpendicular acceleration (a_p) in the global reference frame. The raw sensor data of an example walking session are shown in Fig. 2. As can be seen from the figure, a_y, a_z and ω_x are the three most significant signals among all the six sensor readings. In the following data processing, only these three signals are used.

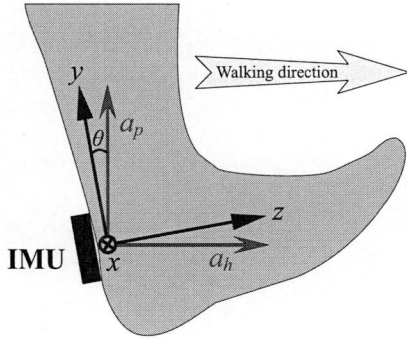

Fig. 1. Illustration of the IMU coordinate system XYZ and the walking direction

After the GMS is assembled, the IMU sensors must be calibrated once, recording the zero offset and sensitivity of each axis. For the accelerometer, the calibration is straightforward by using gravitational acceleration g. For each axis, we measure $+1$ g and -1 g values V_{1g} and V_{-1g}. Thus the acceleration sensitivity S_a and zero offset V_{offset} can be obtained by (1)

$$\begin{cases} S_a = (V_{1g} - V_{-1g})/(2g), \\ V_{offset} = (V_{1g} + V_{-1g})/2. \end{cases} \tag{1}$$

For the gyroscope, the zero offset is simply the data output when the hardware is stationary. The sensitivity of the gyroscope is determined by rotating the gyroscope about each axis through a range of constant angular rates. In our case, we found the sensitivity recorded in the gyroscope specification sheet was accurate, so there was no need for calibrating the sensitivity of the gyroscope.

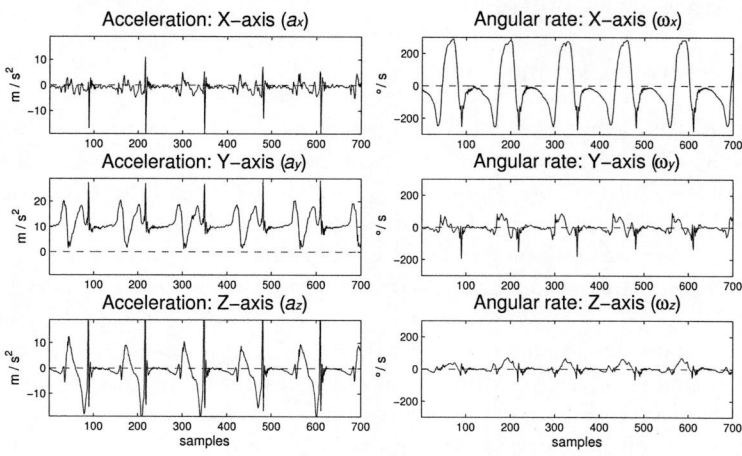

Fig. 2. IMU sensor outputs during walking gait

After the sensors are properly calibrated, the raw sensor readings (V_{raw}) can be correctly converted to signals (V_{signal}) in units of m/s^2 (accelerometer) or °/s (gyroscope), as expressed by (2).

$$V_{signal} = (V_{raw} - V_{offset})/Sensitivity. \tag{2}$$

Once the sensor data are collected and calibrated, we need to filter out the noise. Usually the walking frequency is lower than 2 Hz, thus we can set the stop frequency of the low-pass filter at 5 ∼ 10 Hz.

2.2   Stride Cycle Detection

People's walking motion is a series of alternate *stances* and *swings*, separated by the Toe-off and Heel-strike points (Fig. 3). In order to conduct in-depth and real-time gait analysis, each stride cycle should be recognized and extracted from the continuous walking data. According to a widely accepted "zero velocity assumption" [14], there is a certain *zero point* during the stance phase where the acceleration, velocity and angular rate of a foot-mounted IMU can all be regarded as zero. This is especially the case when the IMU is attached to the heel. In our GMS model, a complete stride is defined as the interval between two successive zero points.

Our real-time algorithm realizes intelligent stride cycle detection through a series of time-varying thresholds combined with a sliding window technique. Since the toe-off and heel-strike points correspond to sharp fluctuations of foot movement, they are identified by the negative impulses of the angular rate waveform, as shown in Fig. 4. A toe-off point (point A in Fig. 4) is confirmed only if the following three conditions are satisfied: (1) point A is the local minimum of ω_x and smaller than a certain low threshold; (2) a local maximum point B after

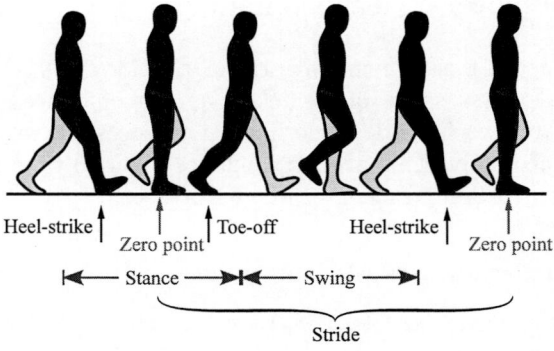

Fig. 3. Illustration of the gait phase and characteristic points (right foot)

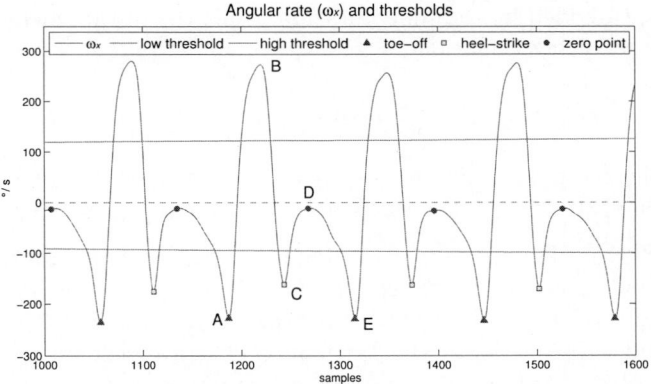

Fig. 4. Stride cycle detection based on angular rate

point A is bigger than a certain high threshold; and (3) both point A and B are within a sliding window with a size of about half a stride cycle. Similarly, a heel-strike point C is verified after the thresholds and sliding window conditions are met. During the process, the thresholds and window size are dynamically changed according to the waveform of ω_x, so that the algorithm can fit different walking patterns automatically.

The interval between heel-strike point C and toe-off point E is the stance phase. During the middle part of stance, the angular rate is relatively close to zero, indicating very slow foot movement. Therefore we define zero point as the vertex (point D) during stance phase, which is generally the closest point to zero. By identifying these characteristic points, we can recognize the swing and stance phases as well as every stride cycle, and this lays the foundation for further gait parameters analysis.

3   Gait Parameters Measurement

In our gait parameters measurement algorithm, a stride cycle is the fundamental unit for analysis, and a series of stride cycles can be processed one by one, independently. After each stride cycle has been processed, related parameters are updated immediately. This property enables our real-time implementation of the algorithm on a limited memory microprocessor.

3.1   Temporal Parameters Measurement

With the correct stride cycle detection, we can easily obtain the following temporal gait parameters.

1. Cadence: Cadence means the number of steps per minute. This is an essential gait parameter for many applications, such as cadence-based music retrieval and recommendation. The average cadence of a walking session can be computed as the total steps divided by the time duration, while the instantaneous cadence is given by the following Equation

$$c = 60 \cdot \frac{f}{n} \cdot 2, \tag{3}$$

where f is the sensor sampling frequency and n is the number of sample points within the current stride (one stride consists of two sequential steps).

2. Swing/Stance Ratio: By recognizing the toe-off and heel-strike points, we can collect and compare the swing time (T_{sw}) and the stance time (T_{st}). The swing/stance ratio (SSR) is defined as $SSR = T_{sw}/T_{st}$. Since the T_{sw} of one foot is related with the T_{st} of another foot, SSR can reflect the gait symmetry of two feet to some extent. This parameter may be used to assess the walking ability of a particular person over time.

As our group is cooperating with a local hospital, we have also observed that many patients have difficulty in holding gait balance: because of physical impairment or lack of confidence, they tend to put more weight of the body on one foot than on another, leading to asymmetric gait patterns. When a patient with gait imbalance walks in a straight line, the stride length of both feet should be close, but usually one leg would move faster than another. To assess the gait balance, we can compare the velocities of both feet, or the SSRs; the closer they are, the more balanced the gait is.

3.2   IMU Orientation Angle

In order to obtain horizontal acceleration (a_h), we need to project the measured acceleration in the IMU's coordinate system to a global reference frame, and thus the IMU's orientation angle θ (the angle between the IMU's y-axis and the a_p direction, as illustrated in Fig.1) has to be calculated first. The IMU orientation angle is a core parameter for gait analysis, and its accuracy has a considerable effect on the velocity and stride length.

Based on the "zero velocity assumption", we assume that the foot has no movement at zero points, so that only the gravitational acceleration is measured by the accelerometer. Therefore we can estimate the IMU's initial orientation angle θ_0 by (4)

$$\theta_0 = \arctan(\frac{a_{z0}}{a_{y0}}), \tag{4}$$

where a_{y0} and a_{z0} are the y-axis and z-axis acceleration at zero point, respectively. Many papers assume that θ_0 is also zero if the device is properly attached [9]. However, this will introduce a further measurement error.

During the walk, the IMU rotates about the x-axis. The total rotation angle $\theta_1(t)$ is the integral of angular rate ω_x over time:

$$\theta_1(t) = \int_0^t \omega_x d\tau. \tag{5}$$

Hence the IMU's instantaneous orientation angle is $\theta(t) = \theta_0 + \theta_1(t)$.

Assume that $\theta(t)$ has a value of θ_{end} at the end of a stride (which is also a zero point). θ_{end} is most likely different from θ_0' calculated by (4) at the beginning of the next stride, which will lead to a gap in the $\theta(t)$ waveform. This integration drift is usually caused by noise in the gyroscope output combined with accumulating numerical integration errors. To compensate for this drift, we developed a linear de-drift method, which resets θ_{end} to θ_0' and adjusts other intermediate $\theta(t)$ values linearly. The new values after de-drift are computed as

$$\theta_d(t) = \theta(t) + \frac{t}{T}(\theta_0' - \theta_{end}), \tag{6}$$

where T is the total time duration of the stride.

We choose the "linear" adjustment because integration is a linear transformation and we assume that the accumulated rate of errors is an approximately constant value. The orientation angle after de-drift is smooth throughout, as shown in Fig. 5.

3.3   Spatial Parameters Measurement

After obtaining the IMU's orientation angle, the following gait parameters can be derived from the sensor data.

1. Velocity. Given the accelerometer readings in y-axis (a_y) and z-axis (a_z), the IMU's horizontal acceleration (a_h) and perpendicular acceleration (a_p) are calculated by (7)

$$\begin{bmatrix} a_h \\ a_p \end{bmatrix} = \begin{bmatrix} -\sin(\theta) & \cos(\theta) \\ \cos(\theta) & \sin(\theta) \end{bmatrix} \begin{bmatrix} a_y \\ a_z \end{bmatrix} - \begin{bmatrix} 0 \\ g \end{bmatrix}, \tag{7}$$

in which g is the gravitational acceleration. In our GMS model, we assume people walk on level ground, and thus the horizontal acceleration and velocity are the

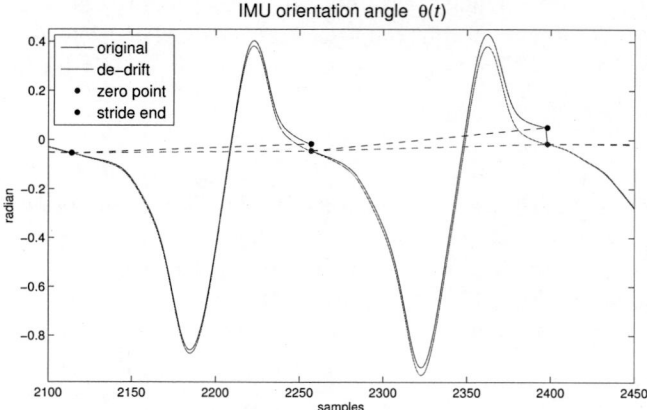

Fig. 5. Linear de-drift for IMU orientation angle

most significant. Since the initial velocity at the beginning of a stride is zero, the horizontal velocity $v(t)$ is the single integral of a_h.

$$v(t) = \int_0^t a_h d\tau. \tag{8}$$

Similarly, a linear de-drift method is performed on $v(t)$ which resets its value at the end of the stride to zero.

2. Stride Length: Stride length is the integral of velocity over the period of a stride cycle, given by

$$s = \int_0^T v(t)dt. \tag{9}$$

The derived horizontal acceleration, velocity and stride length are presented in Fig. 6. The stride length ground-truth (actual values) collected by camera are included to compare with the estimated values. The total walking distance is the sum of all stride lengths in a walking session. An important aspect affecting stride length measurement is the selection of the starting point and ending point of the stride cycle, or the zero points. One improper zero point may affect its adjacent stride lengths, but has less effect on the total walking distance. This is the reason why the error (2% in relative percentage) of walking distance is usually smaller than that of stride length (3%).

3. Stride Regularity: We use the percentage of the standard deviation of stride length in relation to the average stride length to represent the stride regularity of a walking session. A small stride regularity indicates a stable, regular walking pattern.

Other useful statistics (e.g., averages, maximums) can be derived from the above calculated parameters.

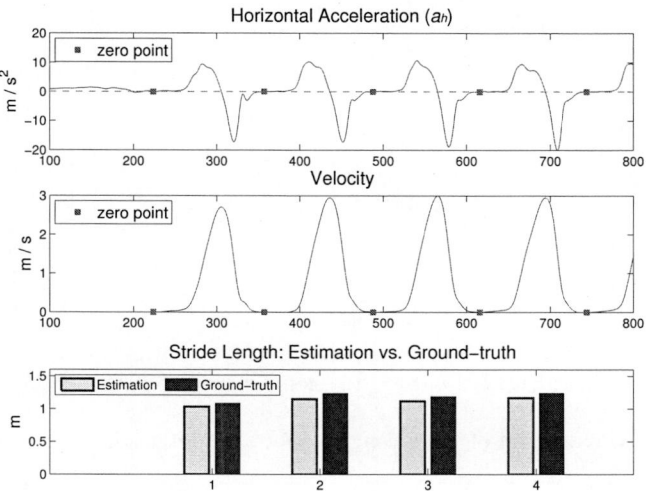

Fig. 6. Spatial parameters measurement: acceleration, velocity and stride length

3.4   Error Model

Although sensor calibration and de-drift methods are used, the stride length computed by the above algorithm tends to be smaller than the ground-truth (See the examples in Fig. 6). We closely observed the walking process, and confirmed that the bottom of the foot has zero velocity during the period around zero point. However, the IMU's velocity at zero point is slightly higher than zero because the IMU has a distance from the ground and can rotate slowly as the heel bends forward. As a result, resetting the velocity to zero finally leads to an underestimated stride length.

In order to compensate for this measurement error, we use a simple linear regression to model the relationship between estimated stride length and the ground-truth (Fig. 7). In the experiments, we collected a series of strides with different walking speed and stride lengths. The total stride count is 701 (346 for training and 355 for testing). Based on the regression result, we adjust the originally estimated stride length by (10).

$$S_{adjusted} = 0.99 * S_{estimated} + 0.08. \qquad (10)$$

The mean value, standard deviation (STD) and root mean squared error $(RMSE = \sqrt{\sum(V_{measurement} - V_{ground-truth})^2 / N})$ are used to assess the stride length before and after adjustment, as shown in Table 1. In the training set, the originally computed stride length has a mean error of 7 cm (6%), and its RMSE is 7.8 cm. After adjustment by (10), the RMSE is reduced to 3 cm. The testing strides also have similar improvement after adjustment, and finally achieve high accuracy.

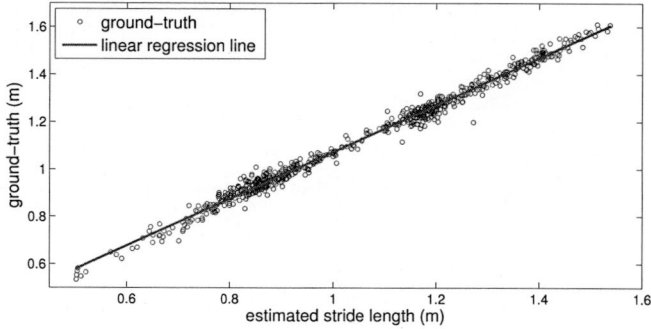

Fig. 7. Linear regression for stride length

Table 1. Comparison of stride length before and after adjustment (unit: m)

		Mean	STD	RMSE
Training strides (346)	ground-truth	1.13	0.20	/
	estimated	1.06	0.20	0.078
	adjusted	1.13	0.20	0.022
Testing strides (355)	ground-truth	1.11	0.24	/
	estimated	1.04	0.24	0.074
	adjusted	1.11	0.23	0.025

4   Experiments and Results

To evaluate the performance of the GMS measurement algorithm, walking experiments were conducted on five subjects (2 female and 3 male, all in their twenties). All subjects were healthy and had no gait abnormalities. Subjects were asked to walk along a 20-meter-long corridor with the GMS attached to the left heel. The corridor floor was marked to collect ground-truth by camera.

We designed four different walking patterns according to the walking speed: Slow, Normal, Fast and Mixed. The Mixed pattern was a combination of the first three patterns in which the walking speed varied among different strides. For each pattern, 10 walking sessions were completed and all the subjects were involved. No significant differences were found among subjects.

The mean value, RMSE and %RMSE (the ratio of RMSE to the average of ground-truth) are used to assess the accuracy of measured parameters like stride length and total walking distance of each session. Detailed experimental results are listed in Table 2 (cadence, velocity and swing/stance ratio are all average values).

In all the experiments, every stride cycle was recognized correctly. Compared with the Mixed pattern, the other three patterns had more stable gait (as can be seen from the stride regularity), and accordingly achieved higher accuracy in stride length and walking distance measurement. In general, we can conclude that the stride length error is less than 3%, and walking distance error less than 2%. These accuracy results are sufficient for many common applications.

Table 2. Experiment results

	Slow	Normal	Fast	Mixed
Sessions	10	10	10	10
Total strides	209	159	137	196
Cadence (step/min)	66	90	103	78
Velocity (m/s)	0.52	0.92	1.23	0.65
Swing/stance ratio	0.61	0.75	0.83	0.61
Stride regularity	5.7%	4.7%	5.8%	20.6%
Stride length — Mean(m)	0.94	1.23	1.43	1.01
Stride length — RMSE(m)	0.022	0.024	0.022	0.027
Stride length — %RMSE	2.3%	1.9%	1.6%	2.7%
Walking distance — Mean(m)	19.6	19.5	19.6	19.8
Walking distance — RMSE(m)	0.17	0.11	0.14	0.32
Walking distance — %RMSE	0.8%	0.5%	0.7%	1.6%

5   Conclusion and Future Work

We have presented the gait measurement algorithm for our small and low cost GMS. It has two important features: (1) real-time computation, which is critical for many context-aware and healthcare related applications; and (2) low complexity and memory usage, so that it can be implemented in a small microprocessor of an embedded system. In practice the GMS achieved accurate measurements, with an average stride length error smaller than 3%, and error in total walking distance less than 2%, which is comparable to systems based on much more expensive components. Other measurements such as gait cadence and stride regularity are also captured, useful in a clinical environment.

A companion paper [15] describes our efforts to reduce the current consumption of the GMS to a level which allows for months of continuous usage. We are working on improving the algorithm so that the GMS can work accurately with any orientation mounted on the foot (at the moment it must be mounted with a particular orientation). We are cooperating with a local hospital and will use this GMS with patients to evaluate the effectiveness of the system.

Acknowledgements. The work was supported by Singaporean MOE grant R-252-000-463-112. We thank the anonymous reviewers for their constructive comments.

References

1. Bachlin, M., Plotnik, M., Roggen, D., Maidan, I., Hausdorff, J., Giladi, N., Troster, G.: Wearable Assistant for Parkinson's Disease Patients With the Freezing of Gait Symptom. IEEE Transactions on Information Technology in Biomedicine 14(2), 436–446 (2010)

2. Lee, Y., Kim, J., Son, M., Lee, M.: Implementation of Accelerometer Sensor Module and Fall Detection Monitoring System based on Wireless Sensor Network. In: 29th Annual International Conference of the IEEE Engineering in Medicine and Biology Society, EMBS 2007, pp. 2315–2318 (August 2007)
3. Bamberg, S., Benbasat, A., Scarborough, D., Krebs, D., Paradiso, J.: Gait Analysis Using a Shoe-Integrated Wireless Sensor System. IEEE Transactions on Information Technology in Biomedicine 12(4), 413–423 (2008)
4. Yang, C.C., Hsu, Y.L., Shih, K.S., Lu, J.M., Chan, L.: Real-time gait cycle parameters recognition using a wearable motion detector. In: 2011 International Conference on System Science and Engineering, ICSSE, pp. 498–502 (June 2011)
5. Thaut, M.H., McIntosh, G.C., Rice, R.R., Miller, R.A., Rathbun, J., Brault, J.M.: Rhythmic auditory stimulation in gait training for Parkinson's disease patients. Movement Disorders 11(2), 193–200 (1996)
6. Li, Z., Xiang, Q., Hockman, J., Yang, J., Yi, Y., Fujinaga, I., Wang, Y.: A music search engine for therapeutic gait training. In: Proceedings of the International Conference on Multimedia, MM 2010, pp. 627–630. ACM, New York (2010)
7. Ojeda, L., Borenstein, J.: Non-GPS navigation for security personnel and first responders. Journal of Navigation 60(3), 391–407 (2007)
8. Facchinetti, T., Savioli, A., Goldoni, E.: Design and development of a real-time embedded inertial measurement unit. In: Proceedings of the 2010 ACM Symposium on Applied Computing, SAC 2010, pp. 491–495. ACM, New York (2010)
9. Li, Q., Young, M., Naing, V., Donelan, J.: Walking speed estimation using a shank-mounted inertial measurement unit. Journal of Biomechanics 43(8), 1640–1643 (2010)
10. Sabatini, A., Martelloni, C., Scapellato, S., Cavallo, F.: Assessment of walking features from foot inertial sensing. IEEE Transactions on Biomedical Engineering 52(3), 486–494 (2005)
11. Song, Y., Shin, S., Kim, S., Lee, D., Lee, K.: Speed Estimation From a Tri-axial Accelerometer Using Neural Networks. In: 29th Annual International Conference of the IEEE Engineering in Medicine and Biology Society, EMBS 2007, pp. 3224–3227 (August 2007)
12. Miyazaki, S.: Long-term unrestrained measurement of stride length and walking velocity utilizing a piezoelectric gyroscope. IEEE Transactions on Biomedical Engineering 44(8), 753–759 (1997)
13. Alvarez, J., Gonzalez, R., Alvarez, D., Lopez, A., Rodriguez-Uria, J.: Multisensor Approach to Walking Distance Estimation with Foot Inertial Sensing. In: 29th Annual International Conference of the IEEE Engineering in Medicine and Biology Society, EMBS 2007, pp. 5719–5722 (August 2007)
14. Peruzzi, A., Croce, U.D., Cereatti, A.: Estimation of stride length in level walking using an inertial measurement unit attached to the foot: A validation of the zero velocity assumption during stance. Journal of Biomechanics 44(10), 1991–1994 (2011)
15. Zhu, S., Anderson, H., Wang, Y.: Reducing the Power Consumption of an IMU-Based Gait Measurement System. In: Weisi, L., Dong, X., Anthony, H., Jianxin, W., Ying, H., Jianfei, C., Mohan, K., Ming-Ting, S. (eds.) PCM 2012. LNCS, vol. 7674, pp. 105–116. Springer, Heidelberg (2012)

Reducing the Power Consumption
of an IMU-Based Gait Measurement System

Shenggao Zhu, Hugh Anderson, and Ye Wang

School of Computing, National University of Singapore, Singapore
{zhusheng,hugh,wangye}@comp.nus.edu.sg

Abstract. This paper presents our approach to reducing the power consumption in our Gait Measurement System (GMS), which is the foundation for various monitoring and assistive systems. Our GMS is a small foot-mounted device based on an Inertial Measurement Unit (IMU), containing an accelerometer and a gyroscope. It can compute gait parameters in real-time, including cadence, velocity and stride length, before transmitting them to a nearby receiver via a radio frequency (RF) module. Our power saving strategy exploits the cooperation between both hardware and software. By realizing on-chip computing, reducing RF usage and enabling sleep mode, the GMS's current consumption was dramatically reduced. In active mode, the GMS consumes about 2.1mA, while in standby mode, the current is only 20μA. Powered by a small rechargeable 110mAh battery, we expect the GMS to last for months of normal usage without recharging; a duration necessary for our intended applications in e-health.

Keywords: Low Power, Gait Measurement, IMU, On-chip.

1 Introduction

Gait measurement techniques aiming to estimate various spatio-temporal walking parameters (e.g., cadence and stride length) are the foundation for numerous monitoring and assistive systems. From a technological perspective, there are three kinds of approaches: machine vision based, floor sensor based and wearable sensor based [1]. The machine vision approach has been used to monitor and track whole body movement, including highly accurate gait parameters. The floor sensor based approach is also widely applied, wherein a series of pressure sensors are placed on the floor or integrated into a mat, such that gait information is collected when people walk across. Both machine vision and floor sensor based approaches are restricted to use in a controlled environment; the gait measurement must be conducted at a specific time or location, only where the video or sensor mats are available.

By contrast, the wearable sensor based approach can move with the subject. Inertial Measurement Units (IMUs) for motion analysis have become relatively accurate and inexpensive. An IMU usually contains an accelerometer and/or a gyroscope and perhaps a magnetometer, each recording along 3 (x,y,z) axes.

W. Lin et al. (Eds.): PCM 2012, LNCS 7674, pp. 105–116, 2012.
© Springer-Verlag Berlin Heidelberg 2012

The units are attached to the human body (e.g., on the waist, shank or foot) to track motion. Since the units are becoming less expensive, they are finding applications in many fields, where previously you would not have considered using them. For example, by analyzing people's specific walking patterns, gait recognition can achieve very high accuracy in human identification [2]. IMU-based navigation system can be used in combination with GPS to improve accuracy [3], or in situations where GPS is not available [4]. Many context-aware applications use inertial sensors to detect whether the person is stationary, walking or running [5].

Our interest in IMU technology is in the Healthcare field, particularly with people suffering from walking difficulties, such as Parkinson's disease (PD) patients and stroke victims. Apart from the obvious use in measuring gait and recording the improvement over time, we have a specific application in a music therapy technique known as Rhythmic Auditory Stimulation (RAS), which offers an alternative treatment method for PD and stroke patients [6]. To facilitate and automate the music therapy procedures, our research group is developing a RAS-based gait training system, which involves a gait detection sensor and a tempo-based music search engine [7]. When the patients are having gait training, they can follow the rhythm of a selected song whose tempo is related to the patients' walking cadence. Therefore the convenient and real-time gait measurement is a fundamental part for our system.

Power saving is an important problem for practical applications, especially for mobile devices. However, few studies investigate the power consumption of an IMU-based Gait Measurement System (GMS). In our context, it is important to make a GMS that can be used in the field for a long time without maintenance. A related work is the Kalman Filter based power optimization [8], but it is in a quite different scenario.

In this paper, we describe the design and optimizations we used to reduce power consumption in our IMU-based Gait Measurement System. Our GMS measures a range of spatio-temporal gait parameters to assess in detail a patient's walking ability, for use in a clinical environment. In the future, it could also be integrated with other context-aware applications.

Our GMS is a tiny, low-cost and very power-efficient device with the capability of real-time on-chip gait parameters calculation, including cadence, velocity, stride length and so on. Although our GMS is built up with very inexpensive components, the average stride length measurement error is smaller than 3%, and the error of total walking distance measurement is less than 2%. These accuracy results are comparable with those obtained from expensive sensors as reported in literature [4,9,10]. By realizing on-chip computing, reducing RF usage and enabling sleep mode, the GMS's current consumption drops greatly. In active mode, when the patient is walking, the GMS consumes about 2.1mA, while in standby mode, when the patient is stationary, the current is only about 20μA. We expect the unit to last for months of normal usage without recharging, powered by a small rechargeable 110mAh battery. If the unit needs to be recharged it can be connected to a USB port and recharged in an hour or so.

The remainder of the paper is organized as follows. In Section 2, we present an overview of the GMS prototype, and briefly describe the gait parameters measurement. In Section 3, we introduce three versions of GMS with different power-saving strategies, and compare their power efficiency by experiments. Conclusions and future work are provided in Section 4.

2 System Overview

2.1 Prototype Architecture

The GMS prototype consists of an ATmega328 based microcontroller board (Arduino Pro Mini), an IMU, a RF module (RFM12B), and a 3.7 volt Lithium-ion battery. The IMU is a combo board with 6 degrees of freedom (DOF): a 3-axis accelerometer (ADXL345) and a 3-axis gyroscope (ITG-3200). Figure 1 shows these components, communicating over a shared communication link.

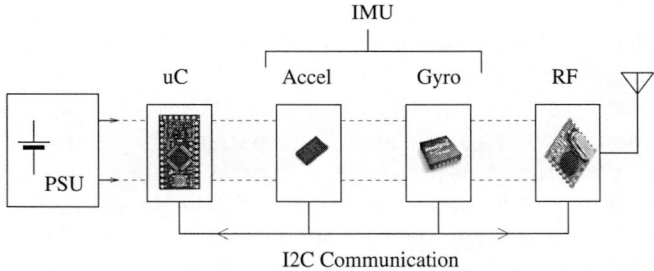

Fig. 1. Block diagram showing the power conditioning and charging circuitry (PSU), microcontroller (uC), accelerometer, gyro, and RF module

The prototype uses I^2C for communication between the microcontroller, the IMU and the RF module. The RFM12B 868MHz RF module provides a bidirectional data service at over 100kb/s over 100 metres (outside), and has an ultra-low power standby mode. We have experimented with techniques to use redundancy to recover from errors in transmission, and have found the unit reliable in our context.

The configuration of the IMU in the prototype is listed in Table 1.

Table 1. Accelerometer and gyroscope configurations

	Accelerometer	Gyroscope
Range	±16 g	±2000 °/s
Resolution	13 bits	16 bits
Sensitivity	256 LSBs / g	14.375 LSBs / °/s
Sampling Rate	100 Hz	100 Hz

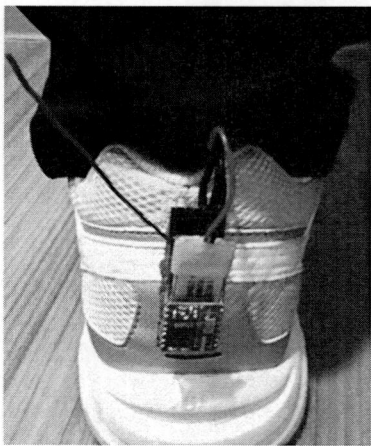

Fig. 2. The GMS prototype attached to a shoe

The complete system measures 34mm×18mm×11mm in size and weighs 9g (battery included). It is shown in use, attached to a shoe in Fig. 2.

After the GMS is assembled, the IMU sensors must be calibrated once, recording the offset and precision of each axis. These parameters are used by the on-chip software, and affect the measurement accuracy. When using the GMS, it is attached to the heel (on the sock, shoe or directly on the calcaneus). The GMS automatically detects if the patient is walking, and if so, calculates and records accumulated gait information. The calculated gait parameters for each stride are sent to a receiver via the RF module. If the patient is stationary, the system goes to sleep, drawing very little current, but waking up from time to time to see if the foot has moved.

2.2   Gait Measurement

We attach the GMS to the heel as shown in Fig. 3. Since we are primarily interested in the patient's horizontal movement, we calculate the horizontal acceleration (a_h) and perpendicular acceleration (a_p), using the measurements of acceleration in the y- and z-axes and the angular rate in x-axis (see Fig. 4).

The specific algorithms used for gait parameters measurement are described in detail in the paper [11]. We assume that at the beginning and the end of each stride, the velocity and acceleration of foot-mounted IMU are both zero, which we call *zero points* [12]. Each stride is detected by using a series of time-varying thresholds and sliding windows based on characteristic points such as the toe-off and heel-strike points (Fig. 4).

The following gait parameters can be derived from this collected sensor data:

1. **Cadence**: The number of steps per minute. It is computed by recognizing each stride in real-time.

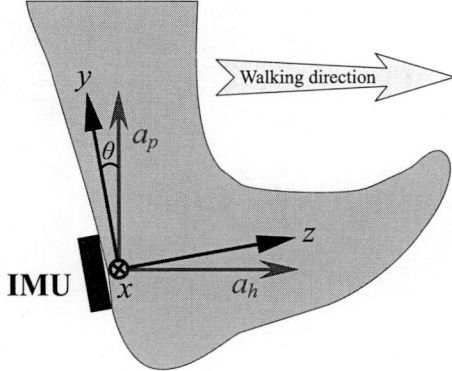

Fig. 3. Illustration of the IMU coordinate system XYZ and the walking direction

2. **Velocity**: The velocity is based on the integration of horizontal acceleration.
3. **Stride Length**: The integral of velocity over the period of the stride cycle.
4. **Swing/Stance Ratio**: The ratio of swing time (from toe-off to heel-strike) to stance time (from heel-strike to toe-off).
5. **Stride Regularity**: The percentage of the standard deviation of stride length in relation to the average stride length in a walking session.

Other useful data (e.g., averages, maximums) can be derived from the above five parameters.

An important element of our system is that our algorithms compute the above gait parameters, in real time, in the microprocessor. This is done by treating each stride as a separate computation, so that the system only needs to keep a small amount of historical data in the limited-memory microprocessor [11].

3   Power Saving Approaches

The prototype GMS is powered by a 110mAh 3.7v Lithium-ion battery. Our main goal is to reduce the power consumption and thus prolong the battery life. In this section we will describe and compare different power saving approaches and the results.

3.1   Approaches Summary

We used three power saving approaches: (1) use low power consumption components; (2) optimize the algorithm and reduce computational workload; and (3) put the components into sleep mode as often as possible.

When initially selecting components to build up a GMS with the desired functions, we considered the following features: size, accuracy, cost and power consumption. We had several false starts to the GMS development. At first we tried the combination of an accelerometer and magnetometer for stride length

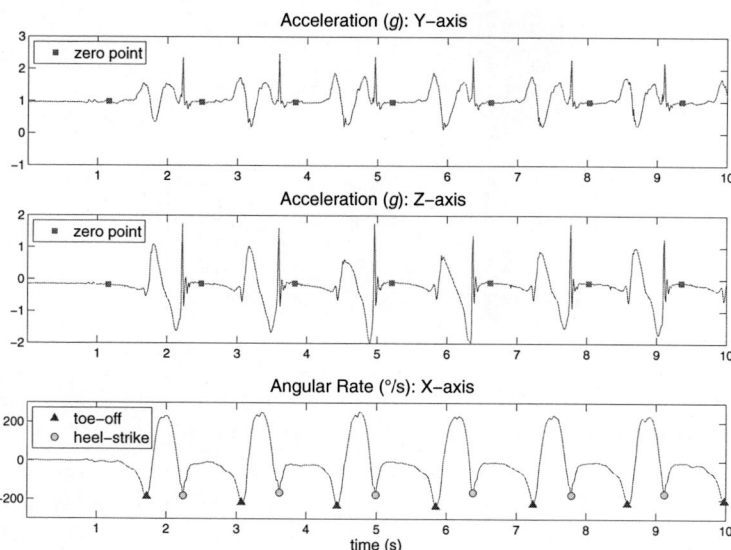

Fig. 4. An example of gait data: acceleration in y- and z-axes and angular rate in x-axis. Sampling rate is 100Hz. Zero points as well as toe-off and heel-strike points are marked on the waveforms.

measurement, because the magnetometer was cheaper and more power efficient than a gyroscope. However, the magnetometer alone was not enough to measure the GMS's exact orientation (and hence stride length). We finally chose an IMU with an accelerometer and a gyroscope.

When we investigated in more detail the power consumption of the individual components in the unit, we found that the current consumption of the regulator on the Arduino board alone was about 80μA. Therefore, we replaced the original regulator with a low-dropout (LDO) low-quiescent current regulator (MCP1703), and managed to reduce the current consumption to 5μA.

In many off-line processing applications, sensor data is sent to a remote computer through a wireless transmission. Usually data packet loss during transmission is inevitable. To reduce measurement error, packet loss must be properly handled. Sending redundant packets may be able to recover the lost data, but it also increases the transmission workload. Another common approach is using interpolation to reconstruct the missing data points. A more elegant solution is to implement on-chip computing, which can completely avoid the sensor data loss problem and simultaneously reduce the power consumption caused by wireless transmission.

Based on the the last two approaches mentioned above, we implemented three versions of the GMS with different configurations. Depending on whether the GMS is moving or not, we divide the GMS's working modes into active mode and standby mode. We measured the average current consumption of each mode,

Table 2. Summary of three versions of GMS

	version 1	version 2	version 3
Sleep Mode	Off	On	On
On-chip Computing	No	No	Yes
RF Usage	High	High	Low
Active Current	11.7mA	10.3mA	2.1mA
Standby Current	11.7mA	20μA	20μA
Active Battery Life	9.4 hours	10.7 hours	2.2 days
Standby Battery Life	9.4 hours	7.6 months	7.6 months

and then estimated the respective battery life of a 110mAh battery. Table 2 summarizes the main features of each version:

3.2 Naive Version (v1)

This is a naive version that only handles the sensor data collection, before transmitting all the sensor data to a remote computer where the gait analysis is conducted. The sampling rate is about 100Hz, so the period between two samples is close to 10 milliseconds. In each period, the GMS reads from the sensors, packetizes the sensor readings together and sends this packet to the receiver via the RF module. Then the GMS waits until new sensor data is available. The receiver is connected to a computer through a USB port, and the sensor data is processed by MATLAB in real-time. To improve measurement accuracy, data loss during transmission is recovered by sending redundant packets. In this version the GMS does not differentiate between active and standby modes, so the current consumption is the same in each case.

To calculate the current consumption, we added a 2Ω resistor in series with the power supply, and measured the voltage across the resistor. The power consumption (waveform of the resistor voltage) is shown in Fig. 5.

In each period, the maximum voltage is 40mV, so the corresponding current is 20mA. This high current consumption occurs during the RF transmission, which has a duty cycle of about 0.45. During the waiting time between RF transmissions the current drops to 5mA. The average current in one period is about 11.7mA. Powered by the 110mAh battery, we estimate that the GMS should work continuously for 9.4 hours. This estimate is consistent with earlier measurements of 5 hours continuous use, when the RF was operated with a duty cycle of 0.9.

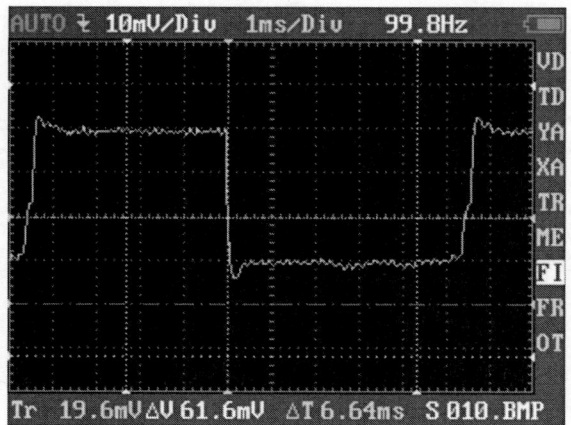

Fig. 5. Power consumption (v1). The green line is the voltage waveform, and the red dashed line is the zero voltage reference.

3.3   Sleep Version (v2)

In this version, to reduce power consumption, we put the unused components into sleep mode whenever possible.

Firstly, the microprocessor goes into sleep immediately after the corresponding data processing. When new sensor data is available, the accelerometer will trigger an interrupt to wake up the microprocessor. As such, the microprocessor is able to sleep about 6 milliseconds during the 10-millisecond interval between two sensor readings.

Secondly, since among the 3-axes gyroscope sensors, only the x-axis sensor is used in the prototype, the other two axes sensors are put into standby mode, reducing the gyroscope consumption from about 6.5mA to 2.2mA.

Thirdly, the RF module also goes to sleep after each data transmission.

Finally, the GMS can detect whether it is moving or stationary, and has different strategies for active mode and standby mode. In active mode, if there is no movement detected for a sufficient period of time (e.g., 30 seconds), the GMS will switch to standby mode. In standby mode, all components (microprocessor, accelerometer, gyroscope and RF module) are in sleep. A watchdog timer wakes up the microprocessor and accelerometer every 0.5 seconds, to check if the GMS is moving.

Table 3 gives a comparison of the components' typical current consumption in normal operating mode and sleep mode.

The GMS's power consumption for version 2 in active mode is shown in Fig. 6.

In version 2, the current during RF transmission and sensor reading stays the same with version 1 (20mA and 5mA respectively), but when the microprocessor goes into sleep, the current is only 2mA. In active mode, the average current is

Table 3. Typical current comparison

	Operating Mode	Sleep Mode
Microprocessor	5.2mA	4.2µA
Accelerometer	140µA	0.1µA
Gyroscope	6.5mA	5µA
RF module	16mA	0.3µA

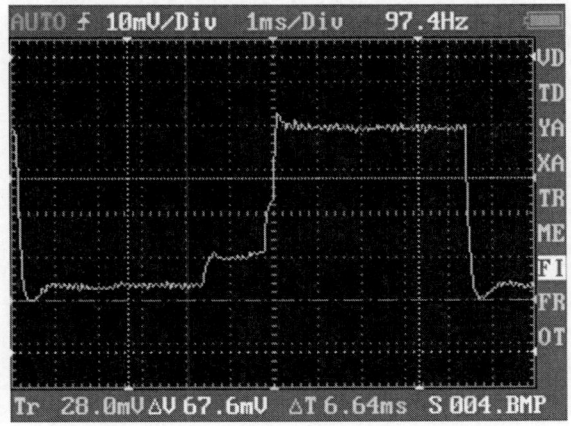

Fig. 6. Power consumption in Active mode (v2)

about 10.3mA, which means the battery can last 10.7 hours, slightly longer than that of version 1.

In standby mode, the GMS's current consumption drops to 12µA for most of the time, as shown in Fig. 7. Every 0.5 second, the microprocessor and accelerometer are awoken by the watchdog timer. Because of the accelerometer's wake-up delay, the GMS waits (in sleep) for another 13 milliseconds before reading the accelerometer to determine if it is moving again (thus there are two positive impulses in the waveform).

The average current consumption in standby mode is about 20µA, and the battery life can be as long as 7.6 months. When not using the GMS, we can simply put it away without unplugging the battery. This makes it possible to encapsulate the whole GMS (battery included) into a small box for easy and convenient deployment, and reduces the need to charge the battery between visits to the clinic.

3.4 On-Chip Version (v3)

We observed the highest current consumption during RF transmission. In order to reduce the RF usage and save more power, we developed a new version based on version 2, which implemented on-chip data processing. All the desired gait parameters are computed by the microprocessor and then sent directly to the

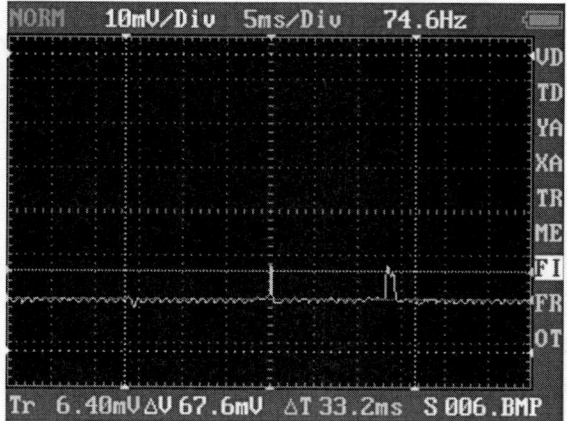

Fig. 7. Power consumption in Standby mode

receiver. In this way, we only need to transmit data for once during each stride (which usually takes longer than one second). By avoiding sending raw sensor data, the total RF transmission time is reduced to one 4.5mS transmission per stride, a duty cycle of less than 0.005.

The biggest difficulty in implementing the on-chip algorithm was the limited RAM (2kB) and computing capability of the ATmega328 microcontroller. The limits meant it was impossible to store large amounts of sensor data in buffers for later analysis, as MATLAB did. In addition, the least possible floating-point numbers and operations should be used while maintaining computing accuracy, due to the microprocessor's low speed with floating-point computation.

Thus in this version we re-designed the data structure and algorithm to strike an appropriate balance between accuracy and simplicity. In the real-time algorithm, each time after reading from the IMU sensors, these readings are processed immediately to recognize the stride cycle and compute gait parameters simultaneously. Thus there is no computation latency because once a stride is completed, it is recognized and all relevant parameters are computed. This turns out to be useful for quick responses to changes in a person's walking patterns. Our current program uses only 1kB of RAM for the computation.

The power consumption in active mode for version 3 is shown in Fig. 8.

As we can see from the waveform, the main current consumption is during sensor reading and data processing (approximately 5mA). Since there is no need for data transmission in every 10mS period, the microprocessor can sleep for a longer time. Even with data transmission in every stride, the average current consumption in active mode is 2.1mA, with a corresponding battery life of 2.2 days. In standby mode, the GMS's behavior is the same with that of version 2 (Fig. 7), and we again estimate the battery would last 7.6 months.

Version 3 is the final version of our GMS prototype. By using these power saving approaches, we decreased the average GMS power consumption to a

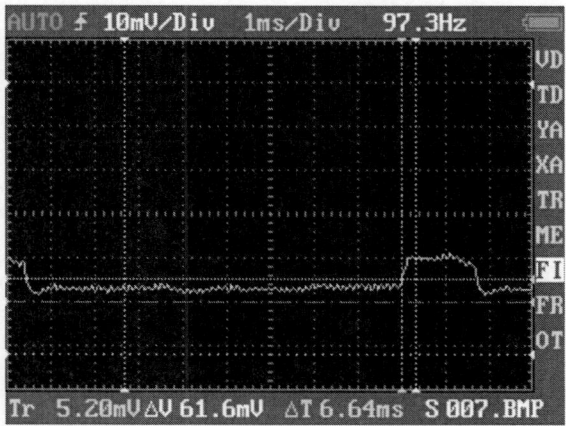

Fig. 8. Power consumption in Active mode (v3)

manageable level. With days of active battery life and months of standby battery life, our GMS can be conveniently operated and widely applied in various situations.

4   Conclusion and Future Work

We have presented a low power gait measurement system, including the prototype architecture and a range of power-saving approaches. The GMS can perform on-chip gait parameters calculation in real-time, and is expected to last for months of normal usage without recharging when powered by a 110mAh battery. Through the experiment results of our GMS prototype, this paper is intended to shed some light on the power saving problem of IMU-based systems, which is an important topic in healthcare. Since our GMS can measure various gait parameters and has a wireless communication interface, it can be easily integrated into other applications.

In our future work, we will design our own printed circuit board (PCB) instead of using the Arduino board. More efforts will be made towards reducing the size of the GMS to encapsulate it into a convenient wearable device. We are cooperating with a local hospital and will use this GMS with patients.

Acknowledgements. The work was supported by Singaporean MOE grant R-252-000-463-112. We thank the anonymous reviewers for their constructive comments.

References

1. Derawi, M.O.: Accelerometer-Based Gait Analysis, A survey. In: Norwegian Information Security Conference, NISK 2010, pp. 33–44 (2010)

2. Bours, P., Shrestha, R.: Eigensteps: A giant leap for gait recognition. In: 2010 2nd International Workshop on Security and Communication Networks, IWSCN, pp. 1–6 (May 2010)

3. Kim, S.B., Lee, S.Y., Choi, J.H., Choi, K.H., Jang, B.T.: A bimodal approach for GPS and IMU integration for land vehicle applications. In: 2003 IEEE 58th Vehicular Technology Conference, VTC 2003-Fall, vol. 4, pp. 2750–2753 (October 2003)

4. Ojeda, L., Borenstein, J.: Non-GPS navigation for security personnel and first responders. Journal of Navigation 60(3), 391–407 (2007)

5. Beach, A., Gartrell, M., Xing, X., Han, R., Lv, Q., Mishra, S., Seada, K.: Fusing mobile, sensor, and social data to fully enable context-aware computing. In: Proceedings of the Eleventh Workshop on Mobile Computing Systems and Applications, HotMobile 2010, pp. 60–65. ACM, New York (2010)

6. Thaut, M.H., McIntosh, G.C., Rice, R.R., Miller, R.A., Rathbun, J., Brault, J.M.: Rhythmic auditory stimulation in gait training for Parkinson's disease patients. Movement Disorders 11(2), 193–200 (1996)

7. Li, Z., Xiang, Q., Hockman, J., Yang, J., Yi, Y., Fujinaga, I., Wang, Y.: A music search engine for therapeutic gait training. In: Proceedings of the International Conference on Multimedia, MM 2010, pp. 627–630. ACM, New York (2010)

8. Udaya Shankar, P.S., Raveendranathan, N., Gans, N.R., Jafari, R.: Towards power optimized kalman filter for gait assessment using wearable sensors. In: Wireless Health 2010, WH 2010, pp. 137–144. ACM, New York (2010)

9. Sabatini, A., Martelloni, C., Scapellato, S., Cavallo, F.: Assessment of walking features from foot inertial sensing. IEEE Transactions on Biomedical Engineering 52(3), 486–494 (2005)

10. Li, Q., Young, M., Naing, V., Donelan, J.: Walking speed estimation using a shank-mounted inertial measurement unit. Journal of Biomechanics 43(8), 1640–1643 (2010)

11. Zhu, S., Anderson, H., Wang, Y.: A Real-Time On-Chip Algorithm for IMU-Based Gait Measurement. In: Weisi, L., Dong, X., Anthony, H., Jianxin, W., Ying, H., Jianfei, C., Mohan, K., Ming-Ting, S. (eds.) PCM 2012. LNCS, vol. 7674, pp. 93–104. Springer, Heidelberg (2012)

12. Peruzzi, A., Croce, U.D., Cereatti, A.: Estimation of stride length in level walking using an inertial measurement unit attached to the foot: A validation of the zero velocity assumption during stance. Journal of Biomechanics 44(10), 1991–1994 (2011)

SSIM-Based End-to-End Distortion Modeling for H.264 Video Coding*

Yuxia Wang, Yuan Zhang, Rui Lu, and Pamela C. Cosman*

[1] Communication University of China, Beijing, 100024, China
[2] University of California, San Diego, CA, 92093-0407, USA

Abstract. The estimation of end-to-end distortion plays a key role in error-resilient video coding and perceptual quality control. The traditional end-to-end distortion estimation methods are mainly based on the MSE or MAD values, which sometimes poorly reflect subjective perception. This paper proposes a novel method to model the end-to-end quality degradation based on the SSIM index. Using factors extracted from the encoder, we build the models by considering the source distortion, the error-propagated distortion and the error-concealment distortion. These models can be used in joint source-channel coding with rate-distortion optimization as well as error-resilient video coding based on perception.

Keywords: end-to-end distortion, error propagation, quality evaluation, GLM, SSIM.

1 Introduction

When compressed videos are transmitted through error-prone networks, the video quality at the receiver side can be highly affected by packet losses in addition to compression artifacts. In a packet-loss environment, transmitting the hybrid-coded video such as H.264 often suffers from error propagation, which may lead to the well-known drifting phenomenon [1]. Fortunately, estimating the end-to-end distortion in the error-resilient coding of the encoder can help to control the errors.

A generalized end-to-end approach has been proposed for video communication over packet-switched networks [2], in which a set of global distortion metrics were derived in terms of MAD. Further, a recursive optimal per-pixel estimate (ROPE) algorithm was proposed to estimate the end-to-end distortion at the pixel level [3]. Zhang et al. [4] proposed a concise and efficient end-to-end distortion model, in which the overall distortion is categorized into source, error-propagated and error-concealment distortion items.

All the previous models calculate the distortions based on MSE or MAD. However, sometimes these objective measurements poorly reflect perceptual quality, especially for error-concealed videos. Recently, many objective metrics were

---

* This reserch has been supported in part by National Natural Science Foundation of China: 61001177.

W. Lin et al. (Eds.): PCM 2012, LNCS 7674, pp. 117–128, 2012.

proved effective for video quality evaluation, such as SSIM [5], JND [6] and VQM [7] etc. Due to the accuracy of these full-reference metrics, many new methods of quality evaluation or prediction are proposed based on them in terms of different applications. In particular, a theoretical framework for end-to-end video quality prediction for MPEG sequences based on the SSIM index was proposed in [8]. The temporal variations of video quality also have different effects on global video quality, which is explored using the PSNR and the SSIM indices in [9]. A network-based model for video packet importance based on the VQM index is proposed in [10], which considers the effects of both compression artifacts and packet losses. Some rate-distortion (R-D) optimized techniques for video coding have been proposed based on the SSIM metric recently [11, 12], yet the channel distortion is not considered.

SSIM is widely considered to be more reasonable in measuring the perceptual visual quality than the MSE. We aim to apply the SSIM measurement in the error-resilient video coding. The challenge is how to estimate the SSIM index at the encoder side without the decoded lossy video. In this paper, we propose a model to predict the end-to-end perceptual quality degradation for compressed videos transmitted in an error-prone environment. We explore the relationship between the errors in the pixel domain and the visual quality degradation at the decoder side, and then predict the perceptual quality scores (SSIM) based on factors extracted from the encoder. We consider the quality scores at the macroblock (MB) level so that the perceptual quality of each MB can be improved accurately.

The organization of this paper is as follows. Section 2 describes the idea of the end-to-end distortion estimation at the MB level, based on the algorithm of the SSIM index. In Section 3, the test sequences and coding configuration are given, and a new method to model the end-to-end quality degradation of H.264 videos at the MB level is proposed. Section 4 presents the final models, followed by the analysis and validation of the experiments. Section 5 concludes the paper.

2   End-to-End Quality Evaluation at the MB Level

Based on the previous method [4], we take the end-to-end distortion as the comprehensive effect of the source distortion, the error propagation distortion and the error-concealment distortion, in which the estimate of pixel distortion is derived by simulating the decoding process multiple times in the encoder. The problem is that MSE or MAD value is not always consistent with the perceptual quality degradation.

Wang et al. proposed the SSIM index [5] to measure the subjective similarity between the original and distorted images. The SSIM index for a still image is derived based on similarities of local luminance, contrast and structure between a reference image and a distorted image :

$$SSIM(x,y) = \frac{(2\mu_x\mu_y + C_1)(2\sigma_{xy} + C_2)}{(\mu_x^2 + \mu_y^2 + C_1)(\sigma_x^2 + \sigma_y^2 + C_2)} \qquad (1)$$

where μ_x and μ_y are the means of the luminance values of the original block x and the reconstructed block y, and σ_x and σ_y are the standard deviations. σ_{xy} is the cross correlation, and C_1 and C_2 are constants used to avoid instability when the means and variances are close to zero. In implementation, a sliding window moves pixel by pixel horizontally and vertically through all the rows and columns of the image until the bottom-right corner is reached. The SSIM index of the whole image is obtained by averaging the local SSIM indices calculated using a sliding window of 11×11 .

To calculate the SSIM quality score for each MB, we have conducted the experiment with different window sizes and different block sizes. The statistics show that a 11×11 sliding window within a MB balances the subjective perception and computational complexity very well. The values of SSIM are in the range $[0, 1]$, where 0 corresponds to the worst quality, and 1 is the best quality. Considering the influence of the chroma, the final SSIM index is obtained by formula (2):

$$SSIM = 0.8SSIM_Y + 0.1SSIM_{CR} + 0.1SSIM_{CB} \qquad (2)$$

Where $SSIM_Y$ denotes the SSIM index values of the luminance component, $SSIM_{CR}$ and $SSIM_{CB}$ denote the SSIM values of the color components.

3   End-to-End Distortion Modeling

3.1   Test Sequences and Coding

The SSIM-based end-to-end distortion is modeled based on six coded video sequences (Foreman, News, Akyio, Coastguard, Hall and Mobile) which are selected according to various levels of detail and motion types. To cover various source distortions, we encode each sequence with six different QP values (20, 24, 28, 32, 36, 40). H.264 JM10.2 is adopted as the encoder, with the coding conditions shown in Table 1.

Table 1. Coding and sequence parameters

	settings
Spatial resolution	QCIF(176*144)
Duration (frames)	100
Compression standard	H.264
GOP structure	IPPP...
Frame rate	30
QP values	20, 24, 28, 32, 36, 40
Rate control	off
Packet losses	0.03, 0.05, 0.1, 0.2
Concealment	frame copy

To explore the effect of packet losses on the quality of decoded videos, we randomly drop packets from each sequence until the target packet loss rate is obtained. We assume the packets of the first frame are conveyed reliably. For each packet loss rate, each H.264 stream will be decoded as 30 sequences for 30 realizations of the lossy channel. The mean of the quality scores of the 30 sequences is calculated to build the model.

3.2   Modeling Approach

In order to predict the MB-level SSIM scores of the videos, we use a generalized linear model (GLM) [13], which can be represented as:

$$g(p) = \gamma + \sum_{j=1}^{P} x_j \beta_j \tag{3}$$

where $g(.)$ is the link function which is chosen depending on the distribution. The parameter p is modeled as a function of P factors (x_j), which denotes the SSIM score we are trying to predict. γ is the constant term, and $\beta_1, \beta_2, \ldots \beta_P$ are the coefficients of the factors. The coefficients and the constant term are usually unknown and need to be estimated from the data. Given N observations, one can fit models using up to N parameters. The simplest model (Null model) has only one parameter: the constant γ. On the other hand, a full model can have as many factors as observations.

Five factors are extracted from each MB of each frame at the encoder side:

(1) D_s: the estimated source distortion of each encoded MB.

(2) D_{ep}: the estimated error-propagated distortion of each MB from the reference frame.

(3) D_{ec}: the error-concealment distortion for each MB.

(4) $Qstep$: the quantization step (six values) for each sequence.

(5) PLR: the setting of packet loss rate (four values) for each sequence.

D_s, D_{ep} and D_{ec} are calculated based on the method in [4], and the last two items can be recursively calculated after a frame has been encoded. As discussed in the literature, the estimation algorithm of D_{ec} depends on the method of error concealment at the decoder side. To reduce the computation complexity, here we use the method of frame copy as referred in the JM decoder. The overall end-to-end distortion of a block can be taken as the sum of that from each pixel. We extend the block size from 4×4 to 16×16 by summation, as we aim at predicting the video quality at the MB level.

Figure 1 gives the distributions of the first three factors and the SSIM scores for the sequence Foreman when PLR equals 20%. Similar distributions are obtained for other conditions of all the sequences. We use "log" as the link function in model building based on the approximately Poisson distribution of SSIM scores in Figure 1, where the expression of the equation is

$$g(p) = \log(p) \tag{4}$$

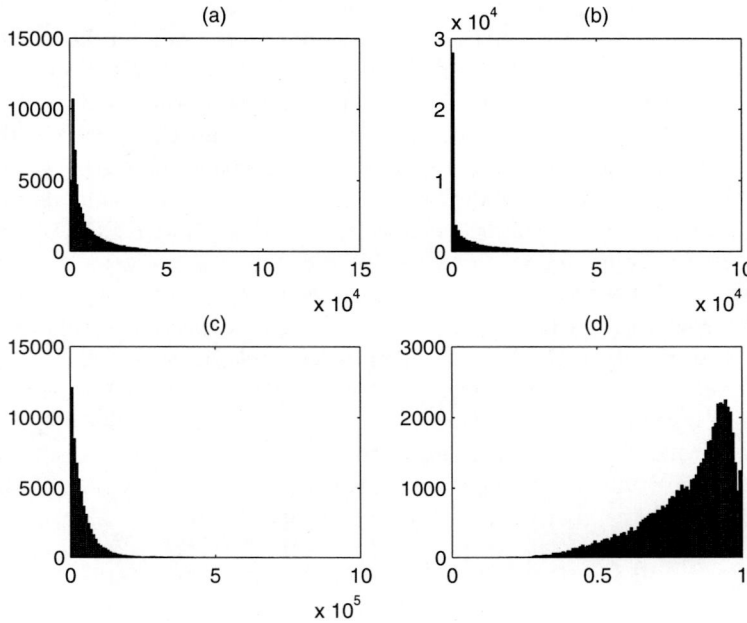

Fig. 1. The histogram distributions of (a) D_s (b) D_{ep} (c) D_{ec} (d) SSIM scores

Four-fold cross-validation is used to determine a model of the right size. In cross-validation, the data set is divided into four parts. Then three parts are used to train the model, and the resulting model is tested on the fourth part which was left out of the training. This process is repeated four times, with a different part left out each time. Factors are added into a model in order of importance. The MATLAB function "sequentialfs" is used, which performs sequential feature selection. It selects factors by sorting the importance from all the factors, based on the mean squared error between predicted values and actual values. The selection proceeds until there is no improvement in prediction.

4   Experiment Results

4.1   Final Models and the Analysis

As the first exploration, we would like to see if the end-to-end estimation function in [4] is still valid for SSIM scores instead of MSE. So D_s, D_{ep}, D_{ec} and PLR are selected as the factors, and the interaction terms are also added in model-building. With six sequences of 100 frames (99 P frames), we set six QP values and four $PLRs$ as shown in Table 1. There are 99 MBs per frame. We extract the factors for each MB, so there are more than 1 million data totally ($N = 6 \times 6 \times 4 \times 99 \times 99 = 1411344$). We randomly select one-tenth of the data to build the models in case of overtraining.

Figure 2 shows on the y-axis the correlation between the SSIM scores predicted by our model and the actual SSIM scores. Here each actual SSIM score is the mean of thirty SSIM scores from the thirty lossy channels given a certain PLR. The number of factors included in the model is on the x-axis, in order of importance. Table 2 gives the factors in order of importance. We can see that D_s is the most important factor which makes the correlation increase significantly. It is reasonable that the source distortion due to quantization is the main cause for quality degradation of the decoded video. $PLR*D_s$ and $PLR*D_{ec}$ are also useful factors in the model with negative coefficients, which means larger values lead to lower SSIM scores and worse quality of the MBs. The impact of packet losses will grow bigger with the increasing PLR as expected. Unlike the conclusion in the literature [4], D_{ep} is not an important factor and is excluded in the final model. The reason is that for an intra MB or a skip MB, there is no distortion of error propagation from quantization during encoding, D_{ep} will be zero, as a refreshed value. While the distortion from packet loss results in the main quality degradation, and the recursive estimating calculation of D_{ec} has reflected the quality impairment of the error propagation.

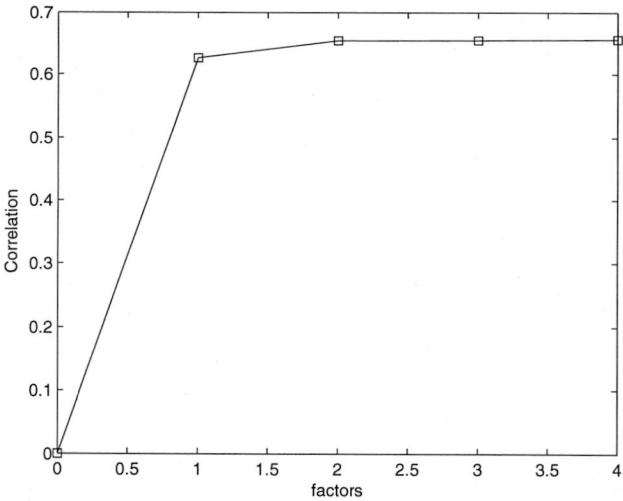

Fig. 2. Correlation between predicted scores and actual SSIM

The first model is built for all MBs, including intra, inter and skip ones. However, the characteristics of the three types of MBs are quite different. As concluded in paper [14], the $SSIM - Qstep$ relation model of I frames in H.264 can be modeled accurately with a linear function. That means the SSIM score of an intra MB can be predicted simply using one factor: $Qstep$. Therefore, we carry out this experiment only for Inter MBs. Since $Qstep$ can reflect the source

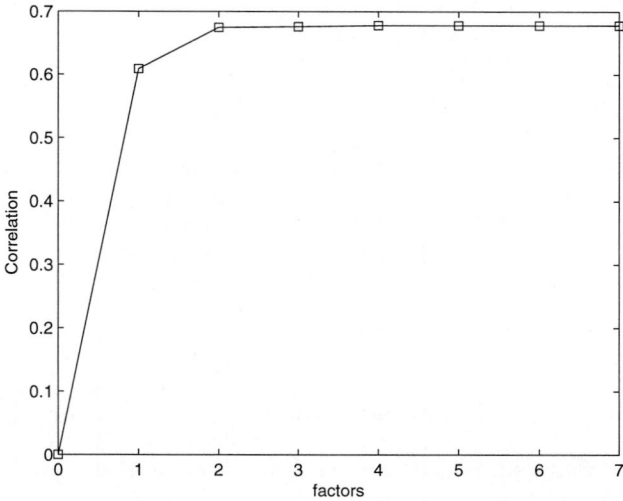

Fig. 3. Correlation between predicted scores of the new model and actual SSIM

distortion as a known parameter in the encoder, we replace D_s with $Qstep$ to build the new model. Figure 3 gives, on the y-axis, the correlation between the predicted SSIM scores and the actual SSIM scores. Table 3 gives the factors and corresponding coefficients in order of importance. We can see that $Qstep$ plays a key role in this model presenting the same impact as D_s. PLR^*D_{ec} is the second important factor having a similar effect as in the first model. D_{ep} is also included with the negative coefficient, which means there is the distortion of error propagation from quantization error for an inter MB besides the error-propagated distortion from packet losses. With these factors ($Qstep$, D_{ec}, D_{ep} and PLR), this model gives a better predictive result with lower computational complexity. Also we can simplify this model further by excluding the last five factors since the improvement on the correlation is not evident.

Table 2. Factors in order of importance for Model-ALL

Order	Factors	Coefficients
Intercept 1		-7.54e-002
1	D_s	-4.27e-006
2	PLR^*D_s	-5.19e-006
3	PLR^*D_{ec}	-1.78e-006
4	D_{ec}	3.13e-007

Table 3. Factors in order of importance for Model-INTER

Order	Factors	Coefficients
Intercept 1		4.28e-001
1	$Qstep$	-5.10e-001
2	PLR^*D_{ec}	-8.85e-006
3	D_{ep}	-1.78e-006
4	PLR^*Qstep	-4.22e-001
5	PLR	2.98e-001
6	D_{ec}	1.24e-007
7	PLR^*D_{ep}	3.38e-006

4.2   Validation of the Proposed Models

To validate the proposed models, we perform the experiment with another two sequences: Suzie and Container, which are not included in the model-building process. The videos are encoded by randomly setting a coding parameter QP with JM10.2 encoder. Similarly, given a PLR, a compressed stream suffering from packet losses by 30 channels is decoded as 30 lossy videos. Figure 4 shows the decoded videos from one channel. The actual SSIM score of each MB from the video is calculated by averaging the 30 lossy versions from 30 channel realizations. On the other hand, using the proposed model (Model-ALL), we can predict the SSIM score of the same MB by means of the effective factors as shown in Table 2.

Figures 5 and 6 show the estimated and the actual SSIM scores for video Suzie when QP is 40 and PLR is 5%. Figures 7 and 8 give the comparison for video Container when QP is 36 and PLR is 20%. To demonstrate the varying SSIM scores clearly, we randomly pick two segments of 200 MBs (about 2-frame-length for QCIF format). We can see that there are good correlations between the estimated SSIM scores by our models and the actual SSIM scores for both videos. Note that the distributions of the SSIM scores change with the different

Fig. 4. The decoded lossy videos: Suzie and Container

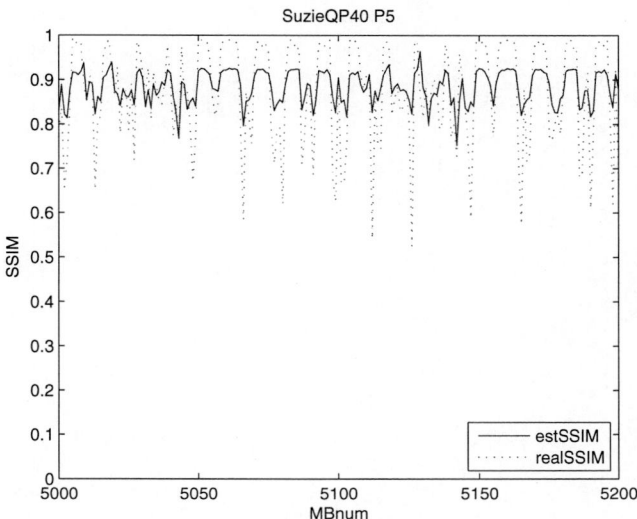

Fig. 5. The estimated SSIM scores vs. the actual SSIM scores of 200 MBs for video Suzie

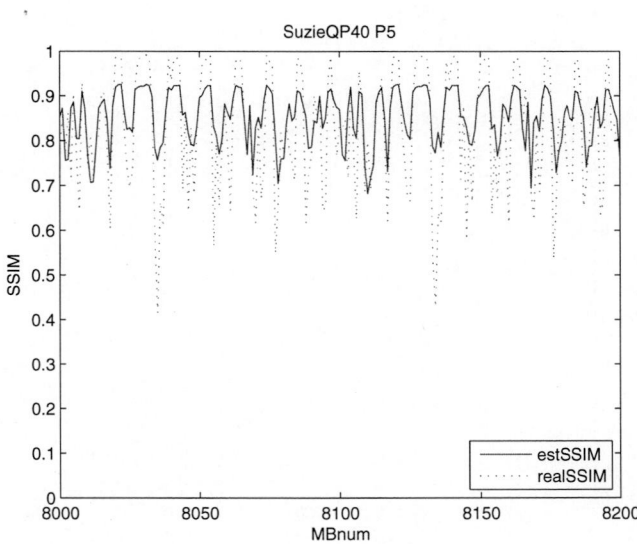

Fig. 6. The estimated SSIM scores vs. the actual SSIM scores of another 200 MBs for video Suzie

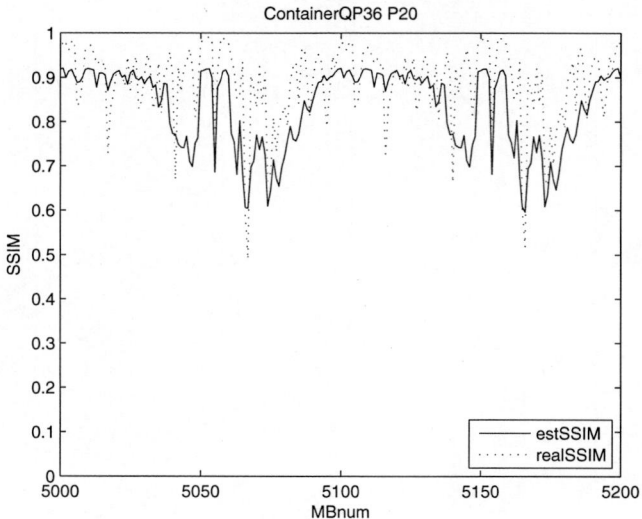

Fig. 7. The estimated SSIM scores vs. the actual SSIM scores of 200 MBs for video Container

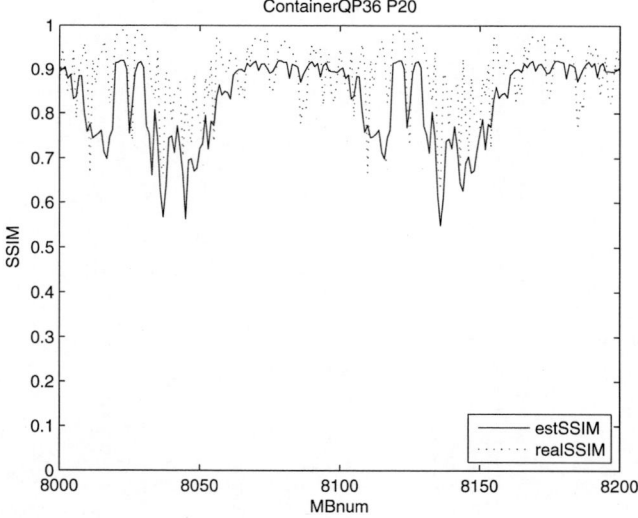

Fig. 8. The estimated SSIM scores vs. the actual SSIM scores of another 200 MBs for video Container

video contents as expected. For Suzie, the motion is well-distributed in the whole frame, so the quality scores fluctuate in a certain range, quite regularly. The quality scores change with an approximate period of 11 MBs, that means the quality change of each horizontal row of MBs is quite similar as expected. While there are some evident drops for the quality scores of Container as shown in Figures 7 and 8. There is a periodicity about 100 MBs for these scores besides the slight local fluctuations. The reason is that, given a certain QP and one *PLR*, the quality degradation of videos happens mainly in the regions with more details or large motion, i.e. the moving ship in this picture. Thus the MBs in this region get lower scores while the MBs of other regions (like water surface) get higher scores. Similar results can be achieved for other settings of QP and *PLR*. In short, the proposed model can predict the end-to-end distortion of the videos well. Although the estimated SSIM scores can not reach the peak or valley points of the actual scores, as shown in Figures 5 and 6, the variation trend is very similar. That means the dynamic range of SSIM values is compressed to some extent. However, our model is supposed to be used in joint source-channel rate-distortion optimization and error-resilient video coding. On this condition, we consider the relative quality of a MB given different coding modes, rather than the absolute scores. So the model is valid to predict and control the video quality at the MB level.

5   Conclusion

A novel method of modeling the end-to-end video quality degradation at the MB-level has been proposed in this paper. Considering the varying QP values and multiple packet loss rates, we have built GLM models to predict the perceptual quality degradation of H.264 videos based on the SSIM index. The source distortion, the error-propagated distortion and the error concealment distortion contribute to the actual quality degradation at the decoder side, especially for inter MBs. By estimating these distortions in the encoder, given a certain packet loss rate, we can predict the end-to-end quality using our models. The experiment results show that the proposed models give a good performance on perceptual video quality estimation. These models can be used to improve the perceptual quality of videos in joint source-channel rate-distortion optimization and error-resilient coding.

References

1. Stuhlmuller, K., Farber, N., Link, M., Girod, B.: Analysis of video transmission over lossy channels. IEEE J. Select. Areas Commun. 18, 1012–1032 (2000)
2. Wu, D., Hou, Y.T., Li, B., Zhu, W., Zhang, Y.-Q., Chao, H.J.: An end-to-end approach for optimal mode selection in Internet video communication: theory and application. IEEE J. Select. Areas Commun. 18(6), 977–995 (2000)
3. Zhang, R., Regunathan, S.L., Rose, K.: Video coding with optimal inter/intra-mode switching for packet loss resilience. IEEE J. Select. Areas Commun. 18(6), 966–976 (2000)

4. Zhang, Y., Gao, W., Lu, Y., Huang, Q., Zhao, D.: Joint source-channel rate-distortion optimization for H.264 video coding over error-prone networks. IEEE Trans. on Multimedia 9(3), 445–454 (2007)
5. Wang, Z., Bovik, A.C., Sheikh, H.R., Simoncelli, E.P.: Image Quality Assessment: From Error Visibility to Structural Similarity. IEEE Trans. Image Processing 13(4), 600–612 (2004)
6. ATIS: Objective Perceptual Video Quality Measurement Using a JND Based Full Reference Technique. Alliance for Telecommunications Industry Solutions Technical Report, T1.TR. 75-2001 (2001)
7. Pinson, M., Wolf, S.: A new standardized method for objectively measuring video quality. IEEE Trans. on Broadcasting 50(3), 312–322 (2004)
8. Koumaras, H., Kourtis, A., Lin, C.-H., Shieh, C.-K.: A Theoretical Framework for End-to-End Video Quality Prediction of MPEG-based Sequences. In: Proc. 3rd Int'l Conf. on Networking and Services, Athens, Greece (2007)
9. Yim, C., Bovik, A.C.: Evaluation of temporal variation of video quality in packet loss networks. Signal Processing: Image Communication, 24–38 (2011)
10. Wang, Y., Lin, T.-L., Cosman, P.: Network-based model for video packet importance considering both compression artifacts and packet losses. In: IEEE Globecom 2010 (2010)
11. Ou, T.-S., Huang, Y.-H., Chen, H.H.: SSIM-Based Perceptual Rate Control for Video Coding. IEEE Trans. on Circuits and Systems for Video Technology 21(5) (2011)
12. Wang, S., Rehman, A., Wang, Z., Ma, S., Gao, W.: Rate-SSIM Optimization For Video Coding. In: IEEE International Conference on Acoustics, Speech and Signal Processing, ICASSP (2011)
13. McCullagh, P., Nelder, J.A.: Generalized Linear Models, 2nd edn. Chapman and Hall (1989)
14. Cui, Z., Zhu, X.: Subjective Quality Optimized Intra Mode Selection for H.264 I Frame Coding Based on SSIM. In: The Sixth International Conference on Image and Graphics (2011)

A Videoconferencing-Oriented Hybrid-Domain H.264/SVC to H.264/AVC Spatial Transcoder

Lei Sun[1], Zhenyu Liu[2], and Takeshi Ikenaga[1]

[1] Graduate School of Information, Production and Systems,
Waseda University, Kitakyushu-shi, 808-0135 Japan
[2] Tsinghua National Laboratory for Information Science and Technology,
Tsinghua University, Beijing, 100084 China
sunlei@ruri.waseda.jp, liuzhenyu73@mail.tsinghua.edu.cn,
ikenaga@waseda.jp

Abstract. As an extension of H.264/AVC, Scalable Video Coding (SVC) provides the ability to adapt to heterogeneous requirements. However, transcoding between SVC and AVC becomes necessary due to the existence of legacy AVC-based systems. The straightforward full re-encoding method requires great computational cost, and fast SVC-to-AVC spatial transcoding techniques have not been thoroughly investigated yet. This paper proposes a low-complexity SVC-to-AVC spatial transcoder in hybrid domain (pixel domain & transform domain) with drift compensation. In the pixel-domain transcoding, a fast re-encoding method is proposed based on mode mapping and MV refinement. In the transform-domain transcoding, the quantized transform coefficients together with motion data are reused directly to avoid re-quantization loss. At last, the drift problem in proposed transcoder is solved. Simulation results show that proposed transcoder achieves averagely 96.4% time reduction compared with the full re-encoding method, and outperforms the reference methods in coding efficiency.

Keywords: SVC-to-AVC transcoding, spatial scalability, hybrid-domain, drift compensation, videoconferencing.

1 Introduction

With the intention of providing scalability to adapt to diverse network environments, SVC enables transmission of a single bitstream containing multiple subset bitstreams, which are organized in layered structure efficiently and can be extracted adaptively according to different requirements [1, 2]. SVC provides mainly three scalabilities, i.e., spatial, temporal and quality scalabilities. Performance evaluations are described in literatures [3–5].

SVC is expected to be a perfect solution for videoconferencing [6]. Unlike the traditional transcoding-based system, SVC-based system only requires lightweight operations for bitstream adaptation. However, legacy AVC-based systems are also potential participants in a future videoconferencing scenario. SVC provides an AVC-compatible base layer which can be decoded by AVC decoder. But AVC

W. Lin et al. (Eds.): PCM 2012, LNCS 7674, pp. 129–141, 2012.

decoder cannot decode the enhancement layers which provide higher resolution or quality. Thus, transcoding is needed because higher resolution and quality are desired in videoconferencing.

SVC provides a special encoder-side configuration for SVC-to-AVC rewriting [9], which requires the encoding process modification at the sender side. It is an additional functionality during bitstream generation, rather than a transcoder. If the sender side uses normal configuration without this functionality, rewriting cannot be applied. Besides, it only supports quality scalability.

A straightforward transcoding solution is the full re-encoding method. It fully decodes the input bitstream and then re-encodes the decoded pictures, consuming intensive computations. Basic transcoding approaches as explained in [7, 8] mainly fall into two categories, i.e., pixel-domain and transform-domain transcoding. The pixel-domain approaches carry out the main transcoding operations on decoded pictures while the transform-domain approaches operates directly on transform coefficients. The transform-domain transcoding achieves more time reduction, but less coding efficiency than the pixel-domain transcoding due to the well-known drift problem.

Representative works on SVC/AVC transcoding support the SVC scalability in terms of temporal [10], quality [11] and spatial [12, 13]. For SVC-to-AVC spatial transcoding, a pixel-domain fast mode decision method is proposed in [13]. The original motion data from the input SVC bitstream are utilized to speed up the AVC encoder mode decision process. Macroblocks (MBs) are classified into three types and treated with different mode-mapping strategies. Only the deduced modes need to be estimated, and the reference pictures & motion vectors (MV) are reused. This work achieves averagely 94.4% time reduction and slightly higher coding efficiency compared with the full re-encoding method.

This paper proposes a hybrid-domain SVC-to-AVC spatial transcoding architecture by utilizing both pixel-domain and transform-domain methods. The input SVC MBs are processed according to their mode types. Part of them are suitable for pixel-domain processing, and the others are suitable for transform-domain processing. Proposed transcoding architecture causes the "drift" problem. It is analyzed and solved by compensation techniques.

The rest of this paper is organized as follows. Section 2 describes the SVC inter-layer predictions and concludes the MB types in SVC. Section 3 explains the details of proposed hybrid-domain transcoding methods, and the resulted drift problem is solved in Section 4. Section 5 shows the overall transcoding structure with drift compensation. Simulation results are given in Section 6, and conclusions are drawn in Section 7.

2 Scalable Video Coding

2.1 Inter-layer Predictions

SVC adopts a layered coding structure. In spatial scalability, each layer corresponds to one particular resolution. The layer with smallest resolution is called "base layer", and the rest layers are called "enhancement layers". The coding tools within each layer is identical to AVC, but a new tool named "inter-layer prediction" is introduced between layers. The inter-layer predictions try to reduce the higher-layer bit-rate by exploring the lower-layer information. There are three kinds of inter-layer predictions, i.e., inter-layer intra, residual and motion predictions. These inter-layer predictions will be denoted as IL_Intra, IL_Residual and IL_Motion predictions hereafter.

IL_Intra prediction predicts the enhancement-layer (EL) input picture using the upsampled lower-layer reconstructed picture. The lower layer is usually called the "reference layer (RL)". IL_Intra prediction only occurs when the co-located position in RL is coded with conventional AVC INTRA mode (see [14]). The RL is encoded first, and then the RL reconstructed picture is upsampled and used as the predictor for EL input picture. The residual is transmitted after transform, quantization and entropy coding.

IL_Residual prediction tries to predict the first residual data generated by normal INTER prediction. The upsampled RL reconstructed residual is used as the predictor. The resulted second residual is transmitted after transform, quantization and entropy coding.

IL_Motion prediction tries to reduce the size of motion data for INTER coded MBs, such as coding mode and MV. The upsampled RL mode and MV is utilized to predict the EL motion data. Two types of motion prediction exist. When the syntax element "base_mode_flag" equals 1, the enhancement layer doesn't need to transmit any mode or motion vector information. They are proportionally deduced by the reference layer motion data while decoding. When the syntax elements "base_mode_flag" equals 0 and "motion_prediction_flag" equals 1, motion data is still transmitted except that MV is predicted by upsampled RL MV instead of neighboring MV.

The IL_Intra prediction is independent from the conventional AVC INTRA or INTER modes, while the IL_Residual and IL_Motion predictions are additional refinements based on conventional INTER mode.

2.2 Coding Modes in SVC

Besides the inter-layer predictions explained in previous section, SVC also inherits the conventional AVC modes (INTRA and INTER). The conventional INTRA coded MBs and INTER coded MBs without inter-layer prediction are classified into "AVC type". The IL_Intra coded MBs and INTER coded MBs with IL_Residual or IL_Motion prediction are classified into "SVC-type". It is

Table 1. MB classification

AVC type	SVC type
INTRA INTER without ILP	IL_Intra INTER with IL_Residual INTER with IL_Motion

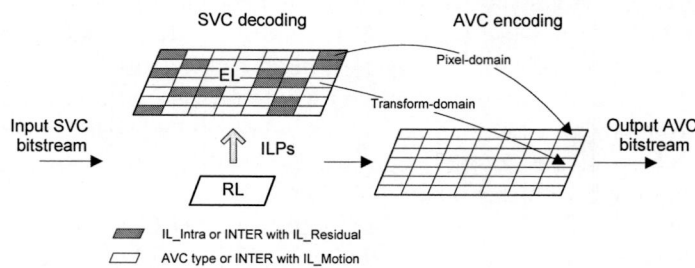

Fig. 1. Transcoding in combined pixel domain and transform domain

also possible that IL_Residual and IL_Motion predictions both exist for an IN-TER MB. In such case, the MB is considered as IL_Residual. Table 1 shows the classification intuitively.

3 Hybrid-Domain SVC-to-AVC Transcoding

3.1 Hybrid-Domain Transcoding

As mentioned in the Introduction section, the transcoding domains mainly include the pixel domain and the transform domain. The pixel-domain transcoding performs main operations after inverse transform and before forward transform. The full re-encoding method is a special case of the pixel-domain transcoding. The transform domain performs main operations on transform coefficients directly, without inverse transforming them.

In this paper, we propose a hybrid-domain transcoding architecture by combining the pixel-domain and transform-domain transcoding. As shown in Figure 1, the AVC-type MBs and INTER with IL_Motion MBs are processed in transform domain. The residual generation of these MBs in SVC encoding is identical to AVC encoding, since the basic coding tools are the same and no additional operation on residual is taken. Therefore the residual in the form of quantized transform coefficients can be reused without even re-quantization. Thus the residual quality is well preserved and transcoding time is reduced. On the contrary, the residuals of IL_Intra and INTER with IL_Residual MBs are generated in a different way from AVC encoding. The residuals in the form of transform coefficients cannot be reused. These kinds of MBs are processed in the pixel domain. Details are explained in following subsections.

3.2 Pixel-Domain Transcoding

As shown in Figure 1, if the input SVC MB is coded with IL_Intra mode or INTER mode with IL_Residual prediction (the shadowed MBs), a mode mapping based pixel-domain fast re-encoding method is applied.

For the IL_Intra predicted MB, the RL mode of co-located position must be INTRA. The IL_Intra prediction directly uses the RL reconstructed MB for prediction, implying a high correlation between EL and RL. IL_Intra prediction is a special coding mode in SVC, which is independent from conventional INTER or INTRA modes. No INTER partition or INTRA prediction direction information is transmitted in EL except a signal which means that IL_Intra prediction is used. In our transcoder, the RL INTRA prediction partition along with the INTRA prediction direction are reused as the AVC encoding mode.

For the IL_Residual predicted MB, the mode mapping depends on whether IL_Motion prediction is used. If IL_Motion prediction is not used, mode & MV information is transmitted in the EL. RL also transmits mode & MV information which is independent from the EL. The EL mode together with the up-sampled RL mode are provided as candidate modes for AVC encoding. Through rate-distortion optimization, better one will be selected as the final mode. If IL_Motion prediction is used and base_mode_flag equals 1, the EL transmits no mode information. The EL INTER partition and MVs are reconstructed from the RL, i.e., upsampled RL partition and MVs. The upsampled INTER mode are selected as the AVC encoding mode. Besides, if base_mode_flag equals 0 (and motion_prediction_flag equals 1), independent modes are transmitted in both EL and RL while MVs are predicted from upsampled RL MVs. In such case, both modes are provided as candidate modes and the MVs are reconstructed.

To verify the effectiveness of proposed mode mapping method, we examined the accuracy ratio as shown in Figure 2. The full re-encoding method is selected as the ground truth. If the deduced mode is the same as the mode encoded by the full re-encoding method, it is considered accurate. The average accuracy for IL_Intra and IL_Residual are 79% and 86% respectively.

Through experiments we find that if the MVs are reused as it is for IL_Residual MBs, the coding efficiency drops a lot. Instead of using the MVs directly, a further motion search is applied after the mode mapping. As shown in Figure 3, the endpoint of the input SVC MV is set as the center of the refined search area, and the search range is greatly reduced. In our experiments, the refined search range is selected as [-2,+2] for both horizontal and vertical directions.

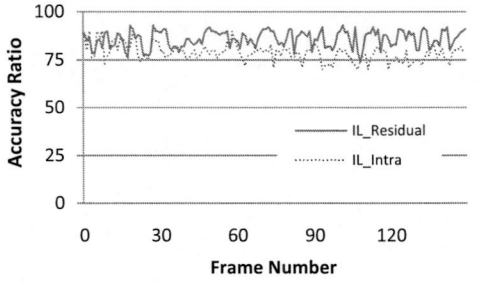
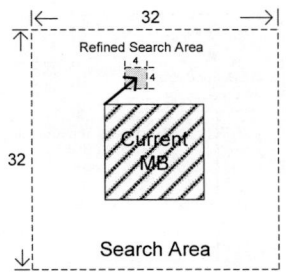

Fig. 2. Accuracy ratio for mode mapping (akiyo sequence, 2 spatial layers, 150 frames)

Fig. 3. MV refinement

The overall pixel-domain transcoding scheme is shown in Figure 4. The previously described mode mapping methods are first applied according to the MB type. Then for IL_Residual predicted MBs, the MV refinement scheme is applied.

3.3 Transform-Domain Transcoding

In Figure 1, if the MBs are coded with AVC-type modes or INTER mode with IL_Motion prediction (the unshadowed MBs), the SVC MB data including residual, mode and MV are copied into the the AVC MB. SVC headers are extracted and parsed into AVC format. The residual is copied in the form of quantized transform coefficients. Figure 5 shows the transcoding path in the transform domain, where "Ref." stands for the reference picture buffer. The quantized residual and motion data are extracted after entropy decoding in SVC decoding. They are copied into AVC encoding at the position before entropy coding. Thus, there is no quality loss for the residual data since it is not re-quantized. The operations between point **a** and point **b** are not performed. Thus transcoding time is greatly reduced. The SVC decoding path is still remained for two reasons. First, it is needed to decode other MB which uses this MB as a reference in SVC decoding. Second, the decoded MB is stored into the AVC reference picture buffer for predictions in AVC encoding since in transform domain there is no reconstruction loop any more.

4 Drift Compensation

4.1 Drift Analysis

In the transcoding field, "drift" refers to the continuous quality degradation through P pictures. It is often caused by mismatched prediction signals between encoder and decoder, and this mismatch is usually caused by lack or modification of the motion compensation (MC) loop at the encoder. The errors are accumulated through INTER predictions, resulting the "drift".

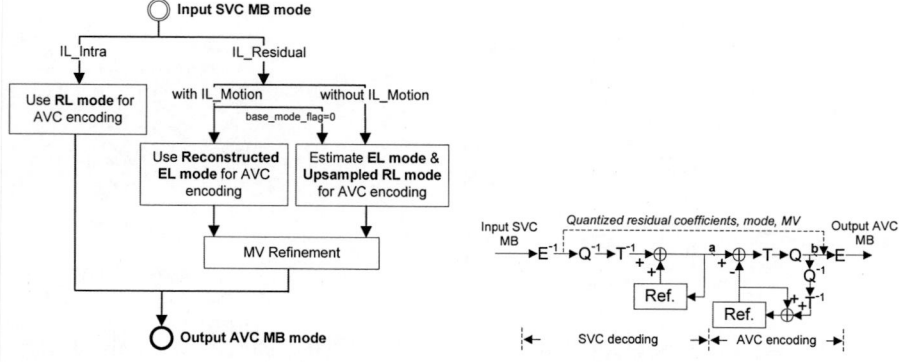

Fig. 4. Pixel-domain transcoding   **Fig. 5.** Transform domain transcoding

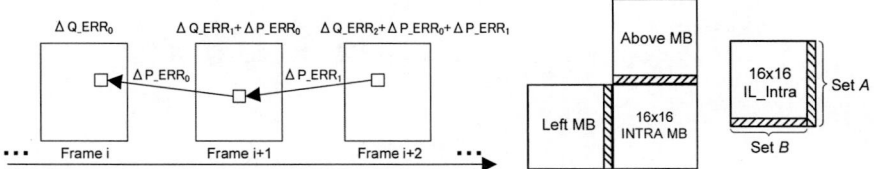

Fig. 6. Drift problem in proposed transcoder   **Fig. 7.** Prediction pixels

In motion-compensated video coding, the MB is predicted by a similar MB, as shown in Equation (1). The resulted residual is then quantized and transmitted. At the decoder side, the de-quantized residual signal is added back to the prediction, as shown in Equation (2). Here only the lossy quantization operations are shown. The coding error is calculated as Equation (3)-(5), where ΔQ_ERR and ΔP_ERR represent quantization error and prediction error.

$$Orignal\_MB = Residual + Prediction \tag{1}$$

$$Decoded\_MB = Q^{-1}[Q(Residual)] + Prediction' \tag{2}$$

$$Orignal\_MB - Decoded\_MB = \Delta Q\_ERR + \Delta P\_ERR \tag{3}$$

$$\Delta Q\_ERR = Residual - Q^{-1}[Q(Residual)] \tag{4}$$

$$\Delta P\_ERR = Prediction - Prediction' \tag{5}$$

In pure pixel-domain transcoding with synchronized MC loops, *Prediction* is exactly the same as *Prediction'*. However, in proposed transcoder, MC loop is removed for transform-domain transcoding. The residual is not re-quantized so that quantization error is eliminated. But the reference MB is supposed to be the decoded MB (left "Ref" in Figure 5), which is not guaranteed to be available at the receiver side. If this reference MB is re-encoded in the pixel domain during transcoding, mismatch occurs and results in prediction error.

Our proposed transcoder decreases the quantization error but introduces the prediction error. Prediction error can be accumulated through INTER predictions, as shown in Figure 6. The accumulated prediction errors cause great distortion and even visual artifacts through continuous P frames.

4.2   Drift Compensation in I frame

I frame includes two types of modes, i.e., IL_Intra and (conventional) INTRA. The INTRA MBs processed in transform domain is the source of the drift. In this section, a prediction-pixel based RDO (PPRDO) method is proposed for IL_Intra MBs in I frame, to improve the accuracy of INTRA MBs. Instead of using the conventional RDO metric, we propose a weighted metric to consider the importance of pixels used for predictions of following INTRA MBs.

The shadowed pixels in the left figure of Figure 7 show the neighboring pixels used for INTRA prediction, and the right figure shows the 31 pixels in an MB

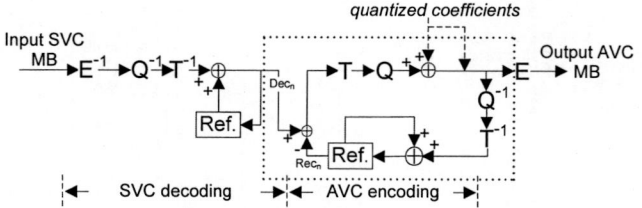

Fig. 8. Error Compensation

which might be used for predictions of following MBs. The RD cost is calculated as shown in Equations (6)-(8). The set A in Equation (6) and set B in Equation (7) represent the indexes of right-most column pixels and the rest 15 bottom-line pixels in the right figure of Figure 7. Equation (8) calculates the RD cost by combining the overall distortion with prediction-pixel distortion.

$$A = \{15 + j * 16 | j = 0, 1, ..., 15\} \tag{6}$$

$$B = \{16 * 15 + k - 1 | k = 1, ..., 15\} \tag{7}$$

$$RD\_COST = (1 - \phi) * Dist(all\ pixels) + \phi * s * Dist(A \cup B) + \lambda * R \tag{8}$$

Here $Dist(X)$ calculates the distortion for pixels in set X. ϕ denotes the weight ratio of prediction pixels and the value of ϕ is in the range of [0,1]. Via comprehensive experiments, we set ϕ to a fixed value: 0.5, which generally achieves good results. s is a scaling factor due to the unequal pixel numbers of all_pixel set (16x16) and $A \cup B$ set (31), which is set to 8 ($\approx$ 16x16/31). λ is the Lagrangian parameter and R is the number of bits for current MB, same as the standard.

In the proposed transcoder, RD_COST in Equation (8) is used as the RD optimization criterion for IL_Intra MBs in I frame. The coding efficiency of these MBs may drop a little. But the following conventional INTRA MBs will have higher quality, and hence decrease the drift.

4.3   Drift Compensation in P frame

In P frame there are three kinds of modes using INTER prediction which causes drift, i.e., INTER without ILP, INTER with IL_Residual and INTER with IL_Motion. For these MBs an error compensation (EC) method is proposed.

The dotted rectangular part in Figure 8 illustrates the error compensation method. This process is performed after AVC encoding. The input signal "quantized coefficients" is either generated by pixel-domain re-encoding or copied from the input SVC bitstream. Firstly the reconstruction MB Rec_n is calculated. Dec_n represents the decoded MB by SVC decoding. Then the accumulated error is calculated by Equation (9). The resulted error is transformed, quantized and added back to the quantized coefficients.

$$E_n = Dec_n - Rec_n \tag{9}$$

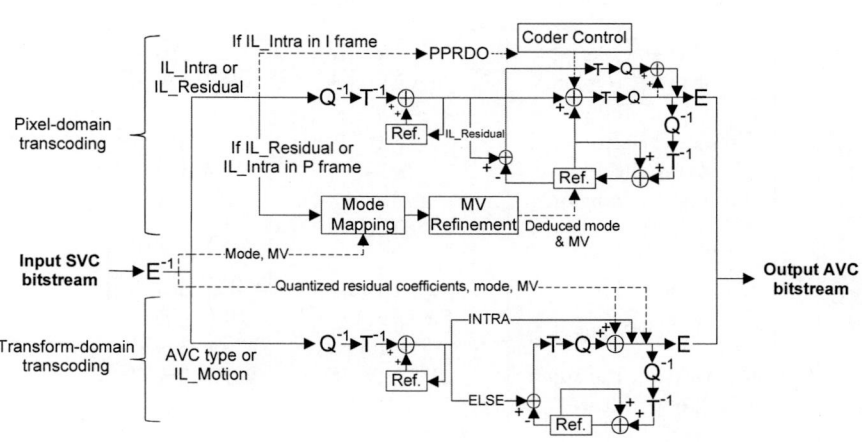

Fig. 9. Overall transcoding architecture

5   Overall Transcoding Architecture

Figure 9 shows the overall proposed transcoding architecture. The upper part shows the pixel-domain transcoding, and the lower part shows the transform-domain transcoding as described in Section 3. The drift compensation methods explained in Section 4 are also integrated. The dashed line stands for data transfer, and the PPRDO criterion is considered a kind of data transfer here.

6   Simulation Results

In this section, the proposed transcoder is applied to representative sequences and the results are shown. Software implementation is based on the SVC reference software JSVM (Joint Scalable Video Model). Eight sequences are examined with 2-layer dyadic spatial scalability. For each sequence 150 frames are tested. In our experiments, the QPs (quantization parameters) for input SVC encoder and transcoder are set to same values, which are selected as 20, 24, 28 and 32. The main parameters are shown in Table 2. All experiments are performed on an Intel Core 2 (2.67GHz) computer with 2.0GB RAM.

Table 3 shows the time saving of reference work [13] and the proposed transcoder, compared with the re-encoding method. The speed-up compared with the re-encoding method and [13] are 28 times and 2 times averagely. For CIF sequences, the processing speed is almost real-time based on our pure software implementation. Besides, the upper four sequences in Table 3 are videoconferencing-like sequences which are simple and slow. The other four sequences are complex and fast sequences. The proposed transcoder gains more time saving for the upper four sequences than the lower four sequences. It saves averagely 98.1% time for the upper sequences, 3.4% larger than the lower four

Table 2. Experimental configurations

Parameters	SVC encoding	AVC encoding
Software Version	JSVM 9.18	JSVM 9.18
AVCMode	0	1
FramesToBeEncoded	150	150
SymbolMode	CABAC	CABAC
Enable8x8Transform	disabled	disabled
CodingStructure	IPPP	IPPP
NumRefFrames	5	5
SearchMode	4 (FastSearch)	4 (FastSearch)
SearchRange	16 for CIF/QCIF, 32 for the rest	16 for CIF, 32 for the rest
Quantization Parameter	20/24/28/32	20/24/28/32
Loop Filter	enabled	enabled
NumLayers	2 (scaling factor = 2)	-
Inter-layer Prediction	2 (adaptive)	-
AVCRewriteFlag	0 (disabled)	-

Table 3. Time saving comparison. ("360p": 640x360)

Sequence	Re-encoding Time (s)	Reference [13]		Proposed transcoder	
		Time (s)	Time saving	Time (s)	Time saving
akiyo (cif+qcif)	163.2	8.6	94.7%	2.1	98.7%
panzoom2 (cif+qcif)	181.7	13.4	92.6%	4.4	97.6%
vidyo1 (720p+"360p")	1626.2	110.6	93.2%	29.3	98.2%
vidyo3 (720p+"360p")	1645.4	85.6	94.8%	33.0	98.0%
bus (cif+qcif)	197.3	15.6	92.1%	12.2	93.8%
football (cif+qcif)	206.9	19.4	90.6%	11.6	94.4%
flower_garden (vga+qvga)	619.3	55.7	91.0%	21.7	96.5%
cheer_leaders (vga+qvga)	766.7	74.4	90.3%	46.8	93.9%
Average	-	-	92.4%	-	96.4%

Criterions - C1: BDBR (%), C2: BDPSNR (dB), C3: Δ time(%)

sequences. Our proposed transcoder is expected to be suitable for videoconferencing applications.

To illustrate the coding efficiency, RD curves are shown in Figure 10. The results of four methods are shown, i.e., direct encoding, proposed transcoder, reference work [13] and the re-encoding method. All the PSNR calculation is using the original sequence (at the sender side) as the calculation reference. The "direct encoding" method means to transmit the original encoded sequence directly without transcoding, which would not be feasible if the receiver doesn't support SVC decoding. The other three methods are real solutions for SVC-to-AVC spatial transcoding. Figure 10 shows the comparison. The direct encoding method achieves the highest coding efficiency than the other three methods, since it is the ideal case. The re-encoding method achieves the worst coding efficiency. The gap between ideal direct encoding method and the re-encoding method is

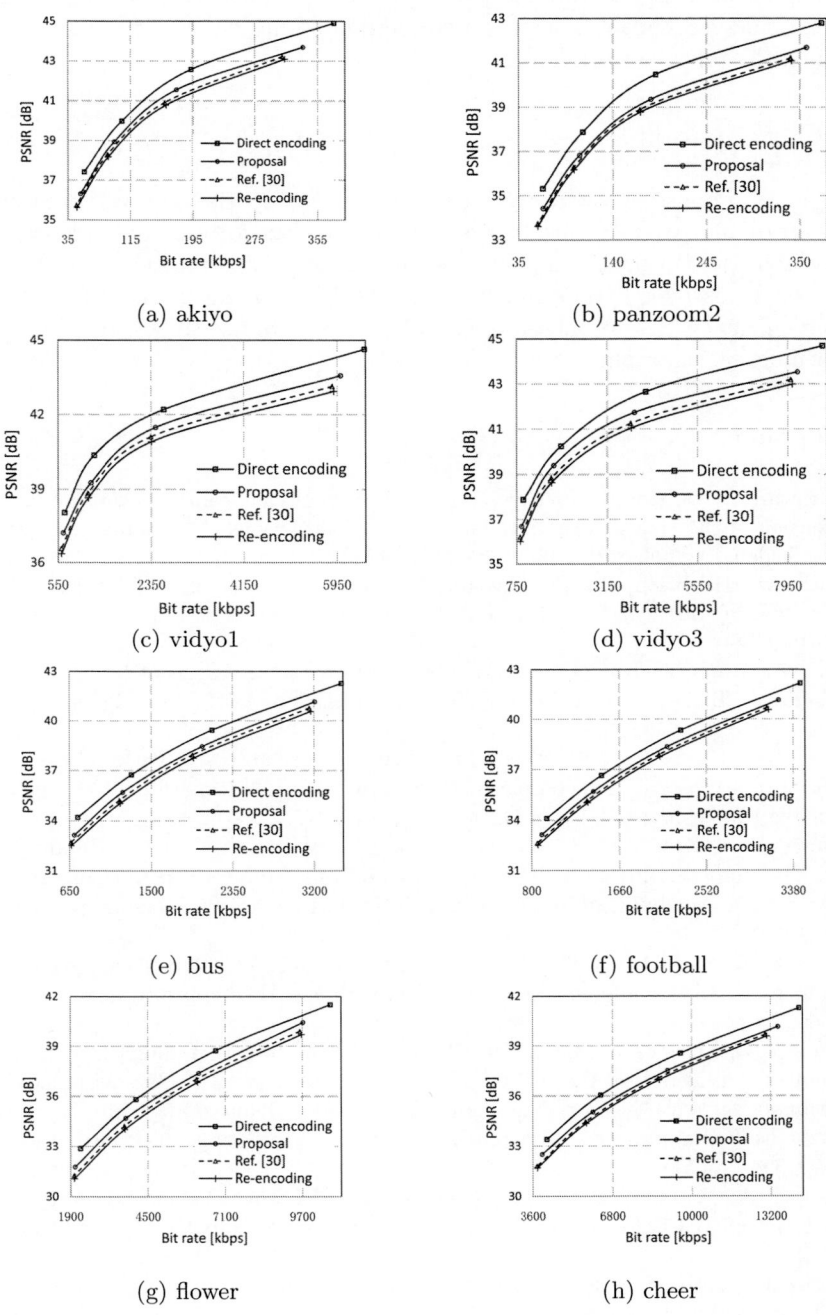

Fig. 10. RD curves comparison

about 1-2 dB. Reference work [13] is slightly better than the re-encoding method, about 0.1-0.2 dB higher. The proposed method additionally gains about 0.1-0.5 dB than the referece work [13].

7   Conclusions

This paper proposes a low-complexity SVC-to-AVC spatial transcoder based on a hybrid-domain architecture. Pixel-domain and transform-domain transcoding are combined with drift compensation techniques. Experiments show that the proposed transcoder speeds up 28 times the re-encoding method with higher coding efficiency. The proposed transcoder is expected to play a role in hybrid videoconferencing applications.

References

1. Schwarz, H., Marpe, D., Wiegand, T.: Overview of the Scalable Video Coding Extension of the H.264/AVC Standard. IEEE Transactions on Circuits and Systems for Video Technology 17(9), 1103–1120 (2007)
2. Schwarz, H., Wien, M.: The Scalable Video Coding Extension of the H.264/AVC Standard (Standards in a Nutshell). IEEE Signal Processing Magazine 25(2), 135–141 (2008)
3. Li, X., Amon, P., Hutter, A., Kaup, A.: Performance Analysis of Inter-Layer Prediction in Scalable Video Coding Extension of H.264/AVC. IEEE Transactions on Broadcasting 57(1), 66–74 (2011)
4. Oelbaum, T., Schwarz, H., Wien, M., Wiegand, T.: Subjective Performance Evaluation of the SVC Extension of H.264/AVC. In: IEEE International Conference on Image Processing, ICIP, San Diego, pp. 2772–2775 (2008)
5. Jang, E.D., Kim, J.G., Thang, T.C., Kang, J.W.: Adaptation of Scalable Video Coding to packet loss and its performance analysis. In: International Conference on Advanced Communication Technology, ICACT, Phoenix Park, vol. 1, pp. 696–700 (2010)
6. Davis, A.W.: A Ready Marcket: Introducing H.264-SVC (Next-Generation Technology for Videoconferencing Over IP Networks), a Wainhouse Research whitepaper (2006)
7. Vetro, A., Christopoulos, C., Sun, H.: Video Transcoding Architectures and Techniques: An Overview. IEEE Signal Processing Magazine 20(2), 18–29 (2003)
8. Ahmad, I., Wei, X., Sun, Y., Zhang, Y.Q.: Video Transcoding: An Overview of Various Techniques and Research Issues. IEEE Transactions on Multimedia 7(5), 793–804 (2005)
9. Segall, A., Zhao, J.: Bit-stream rewriting for SVC-to-AVC conversion. In: IEEE International Conference on Image Processing, ICIP, San Diego, pp. 2776–2779 (2008)
10. Garrido-Cantos, R., De Cock, J., Luis Martinez, J., Van Leuven, S., Cuenca, P.: Motion-based Temporal Transcoding from H.264/AVC-to-SVC in Baseline Profile. IEEE Transactions on Consumer Electronics 57(1), 239–246 (2011)
11. De Cock, J., Notebaert, S., Lambert, P., Van de Walle, R.: Architectures for Fast Transcoding of H.264/AVC to Quality-Scalable SVC Streams. IEEE Transactions on Multimedia 11(7), 1209–1224 (2009)

12. Sachdeva, R., Johar, S., Piccinelli, E.: Adding SVC Spatial Scalability to Existing H.264/AVC Video. In: IEEE/ACIS International Conference on Computer and Information Science, ICIS, Shanghai, pp. 1090–1095 (2009)
13. Liu, H., Wang, Y., Chen, Y., Li, H.: Spatial transcoding from Scalable Video Coding to H.264/AVC. In: IEEE International Conference on Multimedia and Expo., ICME, New York, pp. 29–32 (2009)
14. Schwarz, H., Hinz, T., Marpe, D., Wiegand, T.: Constrained Inter-layer Prediction for Single-loop Decoding in Spatial Scalability. In: IEEE International Conference on Image Processing, ICIP, Italy, vol. 2, pp. 870–873 (2005)

Robust Noise Estimation
Based on Noise Injection

Chongwu Tang, Xiaokang Yang, and Guangtao Zhai

Shanghai Key Labs of Digital Media Processing and Communication,
Shanghai Jiao Tong University, Shanghai, China
{tangcw,xkyang,zhaiguangtao}@sjtu.edu.cn

Abstract. Noise estimation is an important premise for image denoising and the related research therefore has drawn increasing attention and interest. Recent studies show that the distribution mode of local variances in natural image can be used as a simple yet efficacious estimator of the additive noise variance, no matter what distribution the noise follows. However, this type of method has the limitation that the target image must have a sufficiently large area with low pixel value variations. Furthermore, this type of noise estimator almost always lead to overestimation without taking into account the mode of local variance distribution of the noise-free image in textural regions. To improve the accuracy of distribution-mode analysis type of noise estimation and to resolve the problem of overestimation, we propose a novel algorithm using a cascade of wavelet sub-band estimation and noise-injection based rectification. The proposed algorithm reduces the detrimental influence of textural image area, and therefore alleviating overestimation of the noise variance. Extensive experiments and comparative study show the reliability and superiority the proposed method over some existing competitors.

Keywords: noise estimation, mode, wavelet transform, noise injection.

1   Introduction and Related Works

Noise reduction is an essential step for many image processing and pattern recognition tasks. Most of existing denoisers depend on prior knowledge of noise. Studies show that performance of state-of-the-art image denoising algorithms can drop dramatically given the wrong estimate of noise variation. As an consequence, an effective noise estimation method is of both theoretical and practical importance to nowadays image processing/analysis algorithms and systems.

Since noise estimation from a degraded image should be a blind process, the only prior information of the noise we can assume is the distribution type, such as additive White Gaussian Noise. Early attempts of image noise estimation date back to Gonzalez, who proposed a noise estimation method based on noisy pixel sampling from smooth regions of the noise-free image [1]. This pioneering method is simple but clearly of low accuracy. Later some more sophisticated statistical

W. Lin et al. (Eds.): PCM 2012, LNCS 7674, pp. 142–152, 2012.

type of algorithms were proposed, which can be classified into spatial domain algorithms and transform domain algorithms. The spatial domain algorithms are mostly based on the statistics of image local variances, which usually involve the following steps: First, suppress the original image contents to prevent over-estimation [2]; Second, extract the mask of edges from the suppressed image to further reduce the influence of the original image structure; Third, calculate local variances of the remaining content and use histogram statistics method to generate an estimation of noise variance. Beyond these basic steps, some variations and improvements were also proposed. In [2], Rank *et al.* first used a cascade of two 1-D difference operators to filter the noisy image, then computed the histogram of local variances by dividing the remained image into some sub-regions, and the noise variance can be estimated by averaging the weighted histogram. In [3,4,5], Laplacian filtering and Sobel edge extraction were used to get the edge mask. Block based local variances were calculated and the maximum or mean of the variances was taken as the estimator. Amer and Dubois further proposed a structure-oriented method to enhance the robustness of noise estimation for images with large texture areas [6]. In [7], noise level was estimated from the gradients of smooth or small texture regions for each intensity interval. Despite of the low computational complexity, those spatial domain methods usually cannot avoid the influence of original image structures and therefore have low accuracy. Moreover, image texture and structure cannot be satisfactorily detected under high noise level.

Transform domain noise estimation algorithms were proposed along with the development of multi-resolution analysis and wavelet theory. Since the high-frequency wavelet sub-band contains a great part of noise information, and the unitary wavelet transform basis will not alter the statistical property of the noise in sub-bands, Donoho *et al.* proposed in [9] a robust noise level estimator which is the median absolute value of wavelet coefficients at the highest resolution:

$$\hat{\sigma}_n = \frac{median(|y(i)|)}{0.6745}, \ y(i) \in HH_i \tag{1}$$

Though being widely used, the estimator in Eq. (1) tends to overestimate the noise variance when the SNR in the wavelet components is high. In [8], Stefano *et al.* proposed nonlinear statistical noise estimation functions and designed a set of training based in wavelet domain. Zlokolica *et al.* proposed a wavelet based method for spatial-temporal noise estimation by analyzing the distributions of spatial and temporal gradients which were determined from the finest scale of the spatial and temporal wavelet transform [10]. Recently, Liu *et al.* proposed a framework for automatic color noise estimation from a single image using piecewise smooth image models [11]. A novel continuous function describing the relationship between noise level and image brightness was proposed and an upper bound of the noise level was estimated by fitting a lower envelope to the standard deviations of per-segment image variances. These algorithms have good performance at the expense of higher computation complexity.

Another widely used noise estimation method is matching moment [12]. The 2nd and 4th moments of the noisy image are used for noise variance estimation. This method performs well in low level noise conditions, but tends to underestimate for lower noise level. All the aforementioned exiting algorithms have their own limitations of low estimation accuracy or high computational complexity. Towards a fast and reliable estimator for additive noise, Fernández et al. presented a novel approach based on distribution of local sample statistics [13]. The mode of the local variance distribution can be used as a fairly good estimator of the variance of additive noise, despite of noise's distribution. According to their works, the image to deal with must has a sufficiently great proportion of low-variability areas so as to validate the local hypothesis of "constant plus noise", i.e. the mode of the local variance distribution is approximately zero. When additive noise is injected, the mode is right shifted for an amount corresponding to noise variance. This "constant plus noise" assumption, though turned out to be valid for many real world images, may not hold well for images with plenty of textures. Furthermore, the estimator almost always lead to overestimation because the mode of local variance of the noise-free image is not taken into account. For textural images, the extent of overestimation will be even larger. To solve this problem, Lukin et al. adopted a pre-segmentation step to extract the homogeneous areas of the textural image, and the mode of local variance of these areas can improve the estimation accuracy considerably [14]. However, the unsupervised variational classification method they adopted in [14] had a high computation complexity that is not suitable for real-time applications.

Since the level of noise varies from one iteration to another in the recursive filtering scheme in some image restoration algorithms, it is always beneficial to have an effective and robust noise estimation algorithm. In this paper, we present a wavelet sub-band and noise injection based two-step scheme to estimate the variance of additive noise. The first step is to suppress the impact of noise-free image structures, in which we extract the high frequency wavelet sub-band of the image and then apply the mode estimator to get a preliminary estimation of noise variance. Second, we introduce a rectify procedure to tackle with the problem of overestimation. A test noise of known variance is injected into the original noisy image to produce a test "noisy image" that will undergo the same estimation procedure in the first step and generate a rectify value, which will then be used to improve the preliminary estimation. This rectify step effectively alleviates the overestimation, especially for the textural images. Extensive comparative study show the superiority and robustness of our proposed algorithm compared with it in [13].

The rest of the paper is organized as follows. In Section 2, we analyze the noise estimation problem and then introduce the wavelet transform and noise injection based estimation algorithm. Experiments and comparisons are presented and discussed in Section 3. Finally, concluding remarks are given in Section 4.

2 Wavelet Transform and Noise Injection Based Noise Estimation

2.1 The Local Variance Distribution and Mode Estimator

Consider an additive noise model

$$y = x + n \tag{2}$$

where y, x, n represent the noisy image, original image and noise signal, respectively. Note that the original image and noise are always independent, the local variance of noisy image can be written as

$$\sigma_{y_{loc}}^2 = \sigma_{x_{loc}}^2 + \sigma_n^2 \tag{3}$$

let $\sigma_{y_{loc}}^2$ and $\sigma_{x_{loc}}^2$ be local variance of noisy image and original image. According to the hypothesis in [13], the local areas should have relatively low variance for many natural images, i.e. the distribution of $\sigma_{x_{loc}}^2$ has a very large peak and a mode close to zero. Consequently, the mode of $\sigma_{y_{loc}}^2$ can be a reasonable estimator towards noise variance σ_n^2. Figure 1 illustrates the mode estimation of noise variance, from which we can see the local variance distribution of noisy image are just right-shift versions of original image's, and the shift amount is equal to σ_n^2, approximately.

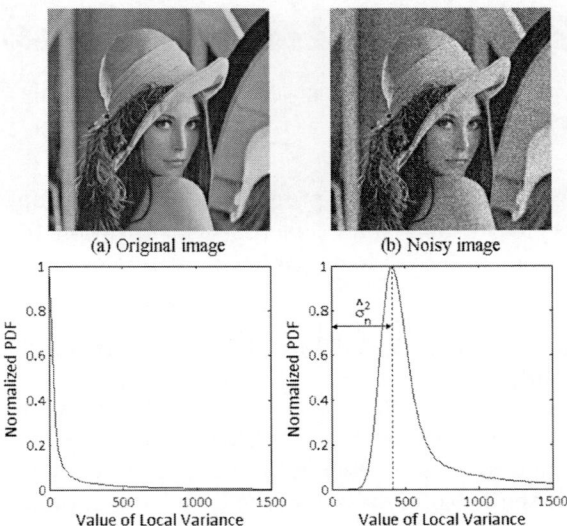

Fig. 1. Mode estimation of noise variance. (a) is the original image Lena, (b) is the noisy image with 0 mean and $\sigma_n^2 = 400$. Sub-figures in the bottom row are the distributions of their local variances, respectively. The local variances are sampled by a point-wise manner, using a 7×7 window. For easy to see, the distributions are normalized to $[0, 1]$.

However, the hypothesis mentioned above is found to be fallible in some situations. Textural images such as fingerprint image and some natural images with complex scenes are not kurtotic enough near their local variances. Figure 2 gives some examples of these images, and the distribution of their local variances are shown in the top row of Figure 3. The texture-rich property of these images makes the modes of their local variance distribution far from zero and even multi-modal. The local variances are sampled using windows of different sizes. Larger sample window tends to contain more textural parts of the images, the distribution of larger sample window are less kurtotic as it shows in non-textural images. Moreover, though the mode of original image's local variance distribution is minor, it will still lead to overestimation if used straightforwardly. In [13], Fernández *et al.* gave a rectification step of mode estimator through investigating statistical model of sample variance:

$$\hat{\sigma}_n^2 = \frac{N-1}{N-3} mode\{\sigma_{y_{loc}}^2\} \tag{4}$$

where N is the number of samples. If N is too large, the rectification can be neglected.

Fig. 2. Textural images. From left to right: FINGERPRINT; CANYON; RAFTING; RACING.

Based on the analysis above, we propose a novel algorithm which integrate texture suppression and noise injection based rectification to tackle with the aforementioned problems of mode estimator in subsection 2.2 and 2.3.

2.2 Preliminary Estimation: Mode Estimator in High-Frequency Wavelet Sub-band

In this subsection, we introduce the preliminary estimation step based on wavelet transform. The high-frequency (HF) wavelet sub-band of the noisy image contains majority of the noise information while abandoning most original image structures. As a result, the local variance of the HF sub-band will be low and distributes around the value of noise variance, i.e. the mode estimator in HF sub-band will be a better indicator of the noise variance compared with the result calculated straightforwardly from the local variance distribution of original noisy image. Figure 3 is the comparisons of local variance distribution from original images (as illustrated in Figure 1) and their HF wavelet sub-bands, where

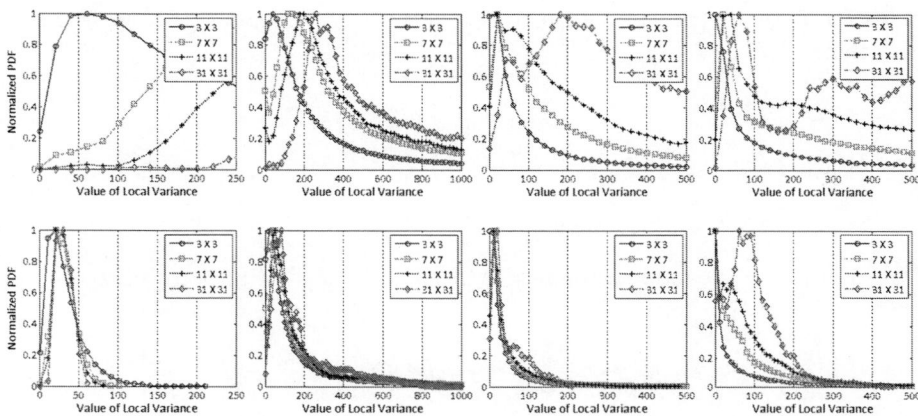

Fig. 3. Comparisons of local variances' normalized PDF between original images and their HF sub-bands. Top row: local variances distribution of original images. Bottom row: local variances distribution of CD sub-bands. Sampled by point-wise manner, using 3×3, 7×7, 11×11, 31×31 windows.

we can find that for textural images, the local variance of HF sub-band obeys the hypothesis better, no matter which size of window used for sampling.

Consequently, We apply 1-level wavelet transform on the noisy image to get the HF sub-band. The horizontal detail sub-band CH and vertical detail sub-band CV are found to be sensitive to directional edges and are not ideal for noise estimation. Therefore the diagonal detail sub-band CD should be chosen as the optimal HF substitute of the original noisy image. In our application, $db1$ wavelet basis is used because it is unitary so as to preserve the noise variance in the transform domain. Then preliminary estimation of noise variance can be calculated on CD sub-band using Eq. (4).

2.3   Advanced Estimation: Noise Injection Based Rectification

To tackle with the intrinsic problem of overestimation for the mode estimator, we propose a noise injection based rectification method for an advanced estimation. It is clear that there is a relationship between the extent of overestimation and the original image structures, as indicated by Figure 3. Larger variation of the local variance will result in larger mode of the distribution and subsequently a higher level of overestimation. Fortunately, the preliminary estimation result can be used to acquire the rectification value because overestimation are inherent in the preliminary results.

Here we use the preliminary estimation of noise variance $\hat{\sigma}^2_{n-pre}$ as the test noise variance $\sigma^2_{n\_test}$ and generate a test noise matrix according to the size of original noisy image, with 0 mean and variance equals to $\sigma^2_{n\_test}$. Because the mode estimator is irrelevant to any specific distribution of the noise, a simple

Gaussian noise matrix can be generated as the n_{test}. Then the test noisy image is obtained by:

$$y_{test} = y + n_{test} \tag{5}$$

Theoretically, we have:

$$\sigma^2_{y_{test}} = \sigma^2_y + \sigma^2_{n\_test} \tag{6}$$

But in practice, the mode estimator of local variance distribution will lead to an overestimation, i.e.

$$mode\{\sigma^2_{y_{test\_loc}}\} > mode\{\sigma^2_{y_{loc}}\} + \sigma^2_{n\_test} \tag{7}$$

The margin between left-hand and right-hand of the inequality can be attributed to the overestimated quantity brought in by the structures of noise-free image. So that the rectify value of advanced estimation can be calculate by:

$$\begin{aligned}
Q_{rec} &= mode\{\sigma^2_{y_{test\_loc}}\} - mode\{\sigma^2_{y_{loc}}\} - \sigma^2_{n\_test} \\
&\approx mode\{\sigma^2_{y_{test\_loc}}\} - 2 \times \sigma^2_{n\_test} \\
&= mode\{\sigma^2_{y_{test\_loc}}\} - 2 \times \hat{\sigma}^2_{n\_pre}
\end{aligned} \tag{8}$$

For the same purpose as in preliminary estimation, we also extract the HF wavelet sub-band of test noisy image to calculate $mode\{\sigma^2_{y_{test\_loc}}\}$. Using Eq. (8) we can obtain the rectified value easily. However, in practice, the generated test noise matrix may contain negative elements that will counteract with the noise in the original noisy image and compromise our whole noise estimation algorithm. To avoid this difficulty, we add an extra constraint: on the one hand, the rectification process would be canceled if we get a negative Q_{rec} from Eq. (8); on the other hand, the aforementioned processes of noise generation, injection and rectify value determination should be implemented for several times and the mean value $\overline{Q_{rec}}$ is computed as a more reasonable approximation to Q_{rec}.

The advanced estimation step is given by Eq. (9), and the two-step estimation scheme is illustrated in Figure 4. The experimental results are to be presented in section 3.

$$\hat{\sigma}^2_{n\_adv} = \hat{\sigma}^2_{n\_pre} - \overline{Q_{rec}} \tag{9}$$

3 Experimental Results

We first focus on noise estimation of textural images such as illustrated in Figure 1. To test our algorithm and compare it with the straightforward mode estimation method thoroughly, the white Gaussian noise is added to the images with a large standard deviation range of $[1, 50]$. We compare our algorithm with the work in [13] and the widely used matching moment, results are shown in Table 1,

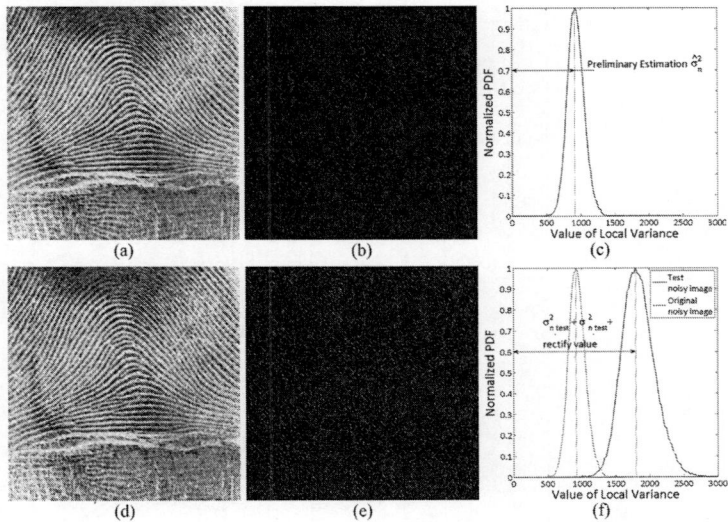

Fig. 4. Wavelet transform and noise injection based noise estimation. (a) Original noisy image. (b) HF wavelet sub-band of (a). (c) Normalized local variance distribution of (b). (d) Test noisy image. (e) HF wavelet sub-band of (d). (f) Normalized local variance distribution of (e). The wavelet sub-bands have been scaled for more visible and orderly layout.

where ***Para.*** is the noise parameter used to generate the noise matrix, σ_n is the real noise standard deviation calculate from the noise matrix. $\hat{\sigma}_n$, $\hat{\sigma}_n^F$ and $\hat{\sigma}_n^M$ represent estimations of our algorithm, Fernández's method and matching moment, respectively. We calculate the absolute difference (MAD) and relative error rates for each image and provide the mean values of them over the noise levels. The best results are emphasized in boldface. The data indicate that the proposed algorithm outperforms the competitor with remarkably large margin, especially for test image FINGERPRINT. Here we calculate the relative error using Eq. (10):

$$e_r = \frac{|\hat{\sigma}_n - \sigma_n|}{\sigma_n} \times 100\% \tag{10}$$

When the textural parts in image are relatively strong, i.e. the noise level is low, the noise overestimation is inevitable and this will reduce the estimation accuracy. It is noted that when neglecting the lowest 2 noise levels, accuracy of our proposed algorithm will be even higher. Note that the estimation results of the lowest 3 noise levels for CANYON depart from the real value tremendously, so we abandon them when calculating MAD and relative error rates to show the superiority of our algorithm in strong noise conditions.

Moreover, we conducted experiments on the 24 lossless true color images of the Kodak image set [15]. These images have different textural levels and are ideal to verify the robustness of our proposed algorithm. We also test the algorithm with white Gaussian noise over the noise standard deviation range of [1, 50], and the

Table 1. Estimation Results of Textural Images.

Para.	σ_n	FINGERPRINT			σ_n	CANYON			σ_n	RAFTING			σ_n	RACING		
		$\hat{\sigma}_n$	$\hat{\sigma}_n^F$	$\hat{\sigma}_n^M$		$\hat{\sigma}_n$	$\hat{\sigma}_n^F$	$\hat{\sigma}_n^M$		$\hat{\sigma}_n$	$\hat{\sigma}_n^F$	$\hat{\sigma}_n^M$		$\hat{\sigma}_n$	$\hat{\sigma}_n^F$	$\hat{\sigma}_n^M$
1	1.0000	4.4256	20.7123	15.4796	1.0000	7.1414	13.6382	0.8076	0.9992	2.7478	4.3589	1.1101	0.9996	1.7321	5.6569	1.1902
3	3.0030	5.1336	20.8087	16.2250	3.0000	7.3485	13.8924	2.2225	2.9962	4.3895	5.5678	2.1565	2.9955	3.1623	5.6569	2.0571
5	5.0079	6.7082	20.9523	17.2643	4.9902	8.2189	14.8661	3.9324	5.0034	5.7446	7.0112	4.0151	5.0003	4.5519	7.2801	3.7913
10	9.9988	11.4455	25.0400	20.6921	10.0070	12.4097	16.6433	8.6876	10.0000	10.5357	12.5698	8.9301	9.9978	10.9329	11.3137	8.8929
15	15.0046	16.0312	27.2213	24.5962	15.0123	16.5002	20.9523	13.9423	14.9931	15.2769	16.7929	13.9702	15.0103	15.8230	16.2481	13.9619
20	20.0316	20.2731	29.1204	28.7683	20.0135	21.3112	24.4131	18.5898	20.0282	20.0117	22.2486	18.6312	20.0121	21.4709	21.5870	18.6716
25	24.9678	25.2108	33.1964	33.2090	25.0558	26.7548	28.8964	24.0130	25.0256	25.4406	26.8887	24.1262	25.0094	25.6721	27.6225	23.7261
30	29.9903	29.9892	38.5746	37.4062	30.0030	31.7872	33.3167	28.9268	30.0192	29.6862	31.4960	29.1012	29.9677	30.6541	31.3369	28.7121
35	35.0674	34.8999	49.5782	41.9756	35.0321	34.9862	38.0657	33.3496	35.0354	35.2102	36.0139	33.3367	35.0640	35.6052	37.1618	33.5281
40	39.9985	39.3902	51.3517	46.4241	39.9835	41.4496	42.9185	38.2392	39.9757	39.7386	42.1307	38.2085	40.0141	39.8571	43.1393	38.5778
45	44.9393	44.5707	51.4393	51.0399	45.0038	46.1376	48.0254	42.8671	45.0505	45.0365	46.5403	42.8861	45.0703	44.4349	48.1871	42.7531
50	49.9884	49.6323	60.8851	55.9044	49.9941	50.5660	52.0960	48.0798	49.9441	49.8465	51.3907	48.0877	49.9446	50.9375	52.8015	47.9909
MAD		**0.9763**	12.4903	9.1656		**1.3255**	5.7170	1.4900		**0.4992**	1.9940	1.2217		**0.6858**	2.4088	1.2939
$\bar{e}_r$		**39.54%**	277.28%	205.53%		6.74%	167.21%	**5.88%**		20.64%	44.79%	8.96%		**10.01%**	55.92%	10.45%

Table 2. Estimation Results of Kodak Image Databases

σ_n	$\hat{\sigma}_n$	$\hat{\sigma}_n^F$	$\hat{\sigma}_n^M$
1	1.7540±1.2234	2.6321±2.5600	1.0628±0.1245
3	3.4316±0.9508	4.0992±2.1840	2.1494±0.1020
5	5.3352±0.7245	5.9691±1.9877	3.9088±0.0833
10	10.3215±0.5401	10.7894±1.3535	8.8369±0.0725
15	15.2793±0.4114	15.8181±1.1590	13.9417±0.0646
20	20.2235±0.5186	20.8008±0.9295	18.7312±0.0966
25	25.1946±0.5250	25.8619±0.9067	23.9610±0.2170
30	30.1941±0.5493	30.8858±0.8233	28.8603±0.1863
35	34.9871±0.3807	35.9303±0.7909	33.5304±0.1185
40	40.0014±0.6156	41.0565±0.9039	38.2685±0.3612
45	44.9028±0.5991	45.8470±0.9603	42.7197±0.1813
50	49.8829±0.6806	50.7836±0.8004	48.0210±0.1479
MAD	**0.2469**	0.9561	1.2612
$\bar{e}_r$	**8.72%**	20.98%	8.92%

comparisons are made as before, just as tabulated in Table 2. We can see from the two tables that our method has an prominent improvement compared with the other two methods both in single image and database. All the experiments are performed using MATLAB R2010a on a 2.93 GHz Intel Core2 PC.

4   Conclusion

We report that the low-variability hypothesis for local variance distribution may not hold well for images with strong textural areas, therefore the mode estimator will not be appropriate for representing noise variance in noise estimation, and the intrinsic overestimation is inevitable. We further propose a wavelet transform and noise injection rectification based two-step estimation scheme, which suppresses the influence of image structures and amends the overestimation effectively. Experimental results and comparative study show the improved effectiveness and robustness of the proposed algorithm over a large range of noise level as compared to straightforward mode estimation.

Acknowledgments. This paper was supported by National Nature Science Foundation of China (NSFC) (61025005, 60932006, 61001145, 61102098), Science and Technology Commission of Shanghai Municipality (STCSM) (12DZ2272600), Specialized Research Fund for the Doctoral Program of Higher Education (SRFDP) (20090073110022), China Postdoctoral Science Foundation (CPSF) (2010 0480603), Shanghai Postdoctoral Science Foundation (11R21414200), 111 Project (B07022).

References

1. Gonzalez, R.C., Woods, R.E.: Image restoration and reconstruction, 3rd edn. Digital Image Processing, Pearson Education, Inc., New Jersey (2008)

 2. Rank, K., Lendl, M., Unbehauen, R.: Estimation of image noise variance. In: IEE Proceedings on Vision, Image and Signal Processing, vol. 146, pp. 80–84 (1999)
 3. Immerkær, J.: Fast Noise Variance Estimation. Computer Vision and Image Understanding 64(2), 300–302 (1996)
 4. Tai, S.C., Yang, S.M.: A Fast Method for Image Noise Estimation Using Laplacian Operator and Adaptive Edge Detection. In: Proceedings of 3rd International Symposium on Communications, Control and Signal Processing, ISCCSP, pp. 1077–1081 (2008)
 5. Corner, B., Narayanan, R., Reichenbach, S.: Noise estimation in remote sensing imagery using data masking. International Journal of Remote Sensing 24(4), 689–702 (2003)
 6. Amer, A., Dubois, E.: Fast and Reliable Structure-Oriented Video Noise Estimation. IEEE Transactions on Circuits and Systems for Video Technology 15(1) (2005)
 7. Förstner, W.: Image Preprocessing for Feature Extraction in Digital Intensity, Color and Range Images. Lecture Notes on Earth Sciences. Springer (1998)
 8. Stefano, A.D., White, P.R., Collis, W.B.: Training Methods for Image Noise Level Estimation on Wavelet Components. EURASIP Journal on Applied Signal Processing 16, 2400–2407 (2004)
 9. Donoho, D.L., Johnstone, I.L.: Adapting to Unknown Smoothness via Wavelet Shrinkage. Journal of the American Statistical Association 90(12), 1200–1224 (1995)
10. Zlokolica, V., Pižurica, A., Philips, W.: Noise Estimation for Video Processing Based on Spatio-Temporal Gradients. IEEE Signal Processing Letters 13(6) (2006)
11. Liu, C., Szeliski, R., Kang, S.B., Zitnick, C.L., Freeman, W.T.: Automatic estimation and removal of noise from a single image. IEEE Transactions on Pattern Analysis and Machine Intelligence 30(2), 299–314 (2008)
12. Trees, H.L.V.: Detection, Estimation, and Modulation Theory, Part I. John Wiley & Son, New York (2001)
13. Fernández, S.A., Ferrero, G.V.S., Fernández, M.M., López, C.A.: Automatic Noise Estimation in Images Using Local Statistics. Additive and Multiplicative Cases. Image and Vision Computing 27, 756–770 (2009)
14. Lukin, V.V., Abramov, S.K., Vozel, B., Uss, M., Chehdi, K.: Performance Analysis of Segmentation-Based Method for Blind Evaluation of Additive Noise in Images. In: Proceedings of International Kharkov Symposium on Physics and Engineering of Microwaves, Millimeter and Submillimeter Waves, MSMW, pp. 1–3 (2010)
15. Kodak: Kodak Lossless True Color Image Suite, http://r0k.us/graphics/kodak/

Image Quality Assessment
Based on Improved Structural SIMilarity⋆

Jinjian Wu, Fei Qi, and Guangming Shi

School of Electronic Engineering, Xidian University,
Xi'an, Shaanxi, 710071, P.R. China
jinjian.wu@mail.xidian.edu.cn,
fred.qi@ieee.org,
gmshi@xidian.edu.cn

Abstract. In this paper, we propose a novel image quality assessment (IQA) based on an Improved Structural SIMilarity (ISSIM) which considers the spatial distributions of image structures. The existing structural similarity (SSIM) metric, which measures structure loss based on statistical moments, i.e., the mean and variance, represents mainly the luminance change of pixels rather than describing the spatial distribution. However, the human visual system (HVS) is highly adapted to extract structures with regular spatial distributions. In this paper, we employ a self-similarity based procedure to describe the spatial distribution of image structures. Then, combining with the statistical characters, we improve the structural similarity based quality metric. Furthermore, considering the viewing condition, we extend the ISSIM metric to the multi-scale space. Experimental results demonstrate the proposed IQA metric is more consistent with the human perception than the SSIM metric.

Keywords: Image Quality Assessment, Structural Similarity, Statistical Character, Spatial distribution, Self-Similarity.

1   Introduction

As a mathematical technology of the human behaviors in image quality evaluation, objective image quality assessment (IQA) metric has been widely used in various image processing application, e.g., compression, transmission and restoration [4]. The simplest and most common quality metrics are the mean square error (MSE) and the peak signal-to-noise ratio (PSNR), which directly compute the differences between the reference and distorted images. But both metrics do NOT accord with the human visual perception well, since the signal error is not equivalent to the degradation of visual quality in the human visual system (HVS).

⋆ This work is supported by Natural Science Foundation of China under Grant NO. 60805012, 61033004, 61070138, 61227004, and 61003148.

W. Lin et al. (Eds.): PCM 2012, LNCS 7674, pp. 153–163, 2012.
© Springer-Verlag Berlin Heidelberg 2012

Considering the perceptual characteristic of the HVS, Wang et al. introduced a structural similarity (SSIM) based quality metric [8]. The SSIM metric is under the assumption that the HVS is highly adapted to extract structural information from an input scene. In the SSIM metric, the image structure is represented by statistical characters, e.g., the mean and variance, and image quality is measured based on the similarity between these statistical characters. This metric imitates the human perception on image structure and returns a better assessment result (be more consistent with the HVS) than MSE and PSNR. Furthermore, Wang et al. improved the SSIM metric by taking the variations of the viewing conditions into account, and introduced a multi-scale structural similarity (MS-SSIM) based quality metric [10]. As an extension of the single-scale SSIM metric, the MS-SSIM metric further promotes the performance on image quality assessment. In [3], Li and Bovik segmented the image into three types of region, i.e., plain, edge, and texture, and gave different weights to the quality results (evaluated by the SSIM metric) of these regions. In addition, the edge structure represents the major information for visual perception and plays a crucial role in the recognition for image content [1][5]. And therefore, Liu et al. [5] improved the SSIM metric by considering the edge similarity.

Though the SSIM and MS-SSIM metrics achieve great success in subjective quality assessment, their statistic based structural descriptors, i.e., mean, variance, and covariance, are too rough to represent the complex image structure [3]. For example, the statistical variance mainly represents the luminance difference but gives little information about the spatial distribution of image structure. The HVS is not only sensitive to the luminance difference but also to the spatial distribution [11] of image structure. Therefore, a more precise structural descriptor, which can effectively represent the spatial structure, is required for much accurate quality assessment.

In this paper, we introduce a novel structure descriptor to improve the structural similarity based quality metric. Since the image structure is determined by the arrangements of and relations among pixels [11], a self-similarity based procedure, which is a valid representation of the relationship among pixels, is adopted to describe the spatial distribution of image structures. At the meanwhile, the statistical characters, which mainly represent the luminance change, is adopted to describe the luminance difference of image structures. Employing both statistical character and self-similarity to represent the luminance change and spatial distribution of the structure, respectively, a much precise structure descriptor is constructed. Then, with the novel structural descriptor, we improve the quality assessment between the reference and distorted images, which we call improved structural similarity (ISSIM) based quality metric. Furthermore, considering the variations of the viewing conditions, we extend the ISSIM metric into multi-scale space and introduce a multi-scale ISSIM (MS-ISSIM) metric. Experimental results demonstrate that the ISSIM/MS-ISSIM metric outperforms the SSIM/MS-SSIM metric.

The rest part of this paper is organized as follows. In section 2, we propose a novel IQA metric following the introduction of a precise structural descriptor based on the self-similarity of image content. Performance of the proposed ISSIM metric is evaluated with several experiments on the TID2008 database [6] in Section 3. Conclusions and discussions are given in Section 4.

2 Structural Descriptor and Quality Metric

In this section, we firstly analyze the spatial distribution of structure based on self-similarity procedure. Then combining with statistical character, a much precise structural descriptor is proposed. Finally, with the novel structural descriptor, an improved structural similarity based quality metric is introduced.

2.1 Self-similarity and Structural Descriptor

The structural information represents the primary visual contents of the input scene, and the HVS is highly sensitive to it [8]. As Fig. 1 shows, the two original images, (a) and (c), are composed of two types of pixels. Pixels in the two images are regularly and irregularly arranged, respectively. Since the spatial distributions of pixels in the two images are different, they present different structures. When contaminated by the same Gaussian white noise, as shown in Fig. 1(b) and (d), the two images have different quality degradations.

The statistical character cannot represent precisely the spatial distributions of the structure though it is effective to describe the rough features of the structure. As the two original images, shown by Fig. 1(a) and (c), are composed with the same amount of black and white pixels, they have the same statistical values. According to the SSIM metric, the two original images are with similar structural descriptors [8]. As a result, when the two original images are contaminated by the same noise, they will acquire the same quality values based on the SSIM metric. Obviously, this result does not accord with the human perception, since the HVS is much more sensitive to noise in Fig. 1(b) which has regular structures than in Fig. 1(d) which has irregular structures. Therefore, a more precise structural descriptor is required for accurate image quality assessment.

The structure appears as the relations among pixels [11]. As shown in Fig. 1(a), pixels in this regular image are strongly correlated with their surroundings and present self-repeating structures. The HVS is highly adapted to extract the homogeneous structures, and easily find out the distortion according to the comparison among them. However, the spatial distribution of pixels in an irregular image, as shown in Fig. 1(c), is disordered, the HVS is unable to accurately predict the structure and becomes insensitive to the distortion in it. Therefore, the regularity of the structure directly determines the sensitiveness of noise, and we need to consider the regularity for structural description.

Self-similarity, which describes the intrinsic relations among pixels, is an effective description of structural regularity [2]. An image with regular structure appears strong self-similarity, e.g., Fig. 1 (a), while an irregular image presents dissimilar structures, e.g., Fig. 1 (c). In this paper, we adopt self-similarity to represent the spatial distribution of the structure.

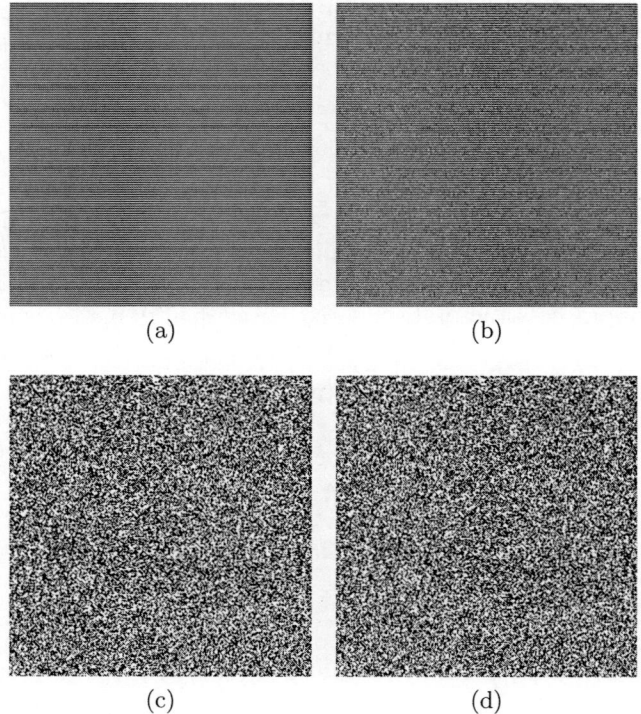

(a)   (b)

(c)   (d)

Fig. 1. Image structures have significant effects to visual quality assessment. (a) and (c) are the original images, which are composed of two types of pixels (black and white). (b) and (d) are distorted images contaminated by a same noise. Though (a) and (c) are with the same mean and variance, their structural characters are very different. The HVS is much more sensitive to the noise in (b) than that in (d).

Considering both the statistical character and self-similarity, which respectively represent the luminance difference and the spatial distribution, we introduce a precise structural descriptor. Let X be the reference image, and $\Omega(x)$ be a local region of a pixel $x \in X$. The self-similarity of a pixel x is measured by the similarity coefficients between pixel x and its surrounding, denoted by $\{d_1(x), \cdots, d_N(x)\}$. The similarity coefficient between the central pixel x and its ith neighbor y_i, with $i = 1, \cdots, N$, is computed as [11],

$$d_i(x) = \exp\left(-\frac{\|F(x) - F(y_i)\|_2^2}{2h_x^2}\right),\qquad(1)$$

where $F(x)$ and $F(y_i)$ denote the vectors formed by concatenating all columns in $\Omega(x)$ and $\Omega(y_i)$, and h_x is defined as [11],

$$h_x = \begin{cases} \sigma_0 & \text{if } \sigma_x \le \sigma_0 \\ \sigma_0(\frac{\sigma_0}{\sigma_x})^{0.5} & \text{else} \end{cases},\qquad(2)$$

where σ_x is the variance of the local region $\Omega(x)$, and σ_0 is the mean variance value of the image.

2.2 Improved Structural Similarity Based Quality Metric

With the precise structure descriptor, we propose an improved structural similarity based quality metric. The SSIM metric compute the similarity on three statistical components, which are luminance similarity, contrast similarity, and structural similarity [8]. Let X' be the distorted image of X, for any two pixels $x \in X$ and $x' \in X'$, the SSIM metric is as follows [8],

$$l(x, x') = \frac{2\mu_x\mu_{x'} + C_1}{\mu_x^2 + \mu_{x'}^2 + C_1}, \tag{3}$$

$$c(x, x') = \frac{2\sigma_x\sigma_{x'} + C_2}{\sigma_x^2 + \sigma_{x'}^2 + C_2}, \tag{4}$$

$$s(x, x') = \frac{\sigma_{xx'} + C_3}{\sigma_x\sigma_{x'} + C_3}, \tag{5}$$

$$\text{SSIM}(x, x') = l(x, x')\, c(x, x')\, s(x, x'), \tag{6}$$

where μ_x and $\mu_{x'}$ are the means of the local patches, which are with a size of 11×11, centered at x and x', respectively, σ_x and $\sigma_{x'}$ are the standard variance, $\sigma_{xx'}$ is the covariance of the two patches, C_1, C_2 and C_3 are small constants to make sure the denominator not being zero (Please refer to [8] for more details about the SSIM metric).

As it can be seen that (6) is based on the statistical characters, and cannot effectively represent the changes in the spatial distribution of image structures. Here, we compute the similarity of the spatial distribution based on the similar coefficients provided in (1). The similarity of the spatial distribution between the reference image X and the distorted image X' is computed as,

$$\text{SD}(x, x') = \frac{1}{N} \sum_{i=1}^{N} \frac{2d_i(x)d_i(x') + C_4}{d_i^2(x) + d_i^2(x') + C_4}, \tag{7}$$

where $C_4 = (K_1L)^2$, L is the gray level of the image and $K_1 = 0.01$ (similar as in [8]).

Combining (6) and (7), the ISSIM metric is acquired,

$$\text{ISSIM}(x, x') = \alpha\,\text{SSIM}(x, x') + \beta\,\text{SD}(x, x'), \tag{8}$$

where α and β are the relative importance of the two parts, and in this paper, we simply set $\alpha = \beta = 0.5$.

In addition, considering the viewing conditions, we extend the ISSIM metric into multi-scale and introduce a multi-scale ISSIM (MS-ISSIM) based quality metric. We downsample the original images into multi levels and operate the ISSIM metric on each one,

$$\text{MS-ISSIM}(x, x') = \prod_{l=1}^{M} \text{ISSIM}_l^{\gamma(l)}(x, x') \tag{9}$$

where M is the highest level. In this paper, we set $M = 5$ and γ to be 0.0448, 0.2856, 0.3001, 0.2363, and 0.1333 from $l = 1$ to $l = M$, respectively, according to [10].

3   Experimental Results and Discussion

In this section, we firstly analyze the effectiveness of the proposed metric on images with representative structures. Then we verify the proposed metric by comparing with the SSIM/MS-SSIM metric on the TID2008 [6]. The TID2008 database contains 1700 distorted images, which are generated from 25 reference images with 17 type of distortions at 4 different noise levels. Its corresponding Mean Opinion Score (MOS) is obtained through a complicated result, which is achieved by more than 800 experiments with a large number of observers from three countries (Finland, Italy, and Ukraine).

The proposed metric is based on a more precise structural descriptor than that in the SSIM metric. With the precise structural descriptor, the character of the image can be further analyzed. For a clear view, a part of one reference image from the TID2008 database, which is composed of 12 types of structures, is chosen, as shown in Fig. 2 (a). And Fig. 2 (b) is its corresponding white noise contaminated image. Though under the same noise, these patches with different structures present different visual quality degradations. Intuitively, the HVS is highly sensitive to the distortions on these patches with regular structures. And therefore, the more regular the patch is, the more seriously its quality degrades. For example, the right four patches are with highly self-similar structures and the noise in them is easy to be sensed, while the two patches in the fourth column are less self-similar than their nearby patches and are much robust to noise.

The evaluation results from the SSIM metric (The SSIM code is downloaded from Wang's homepage) and the ISSIM metric on contaminated image are shown in Fig. 2 (c) and (d), respectively. In Fig. 2(c), it can be seen that the results on the right 6 patches are almost the same, which is against the perception of the HVS. The output of the ISSIM metric presents different assessment result on these 6 patches. As shown in Fig. 2 (d), patches with regular structures (i.e., the right 4 patches) have more quality loss than these irregular ones (the two patches in the fourth column). Therefore, the output of the ISSIM metric is more consistent with the human visual perception than the SSIM metric.

For further analyzing the performance of the proposed algorithm against the SSIM metric, two natural images are chosen for comparison. The experimental results are shown in Fig. 3, which indicates that the structural degradations of the two contaminated images are limited, and their subjective qualities, where Fig. 3(a) is MOS=4.943 and Fig. 3(b) is MOS=5.032, are very near. Since the SSIM metric only adopts the statistical character for structural analysis, as shown in Fig. 3(c), the quality degradation on the smooth region is overestimated. As a result, according to the SSIM metric, the quality of Fig. 3(a) with SSIM=0.655 is far worse than that of Fig. 3(b) with SSIM=0.909, because the former possesses a large smooth region while the latter has a smaller smooth area.

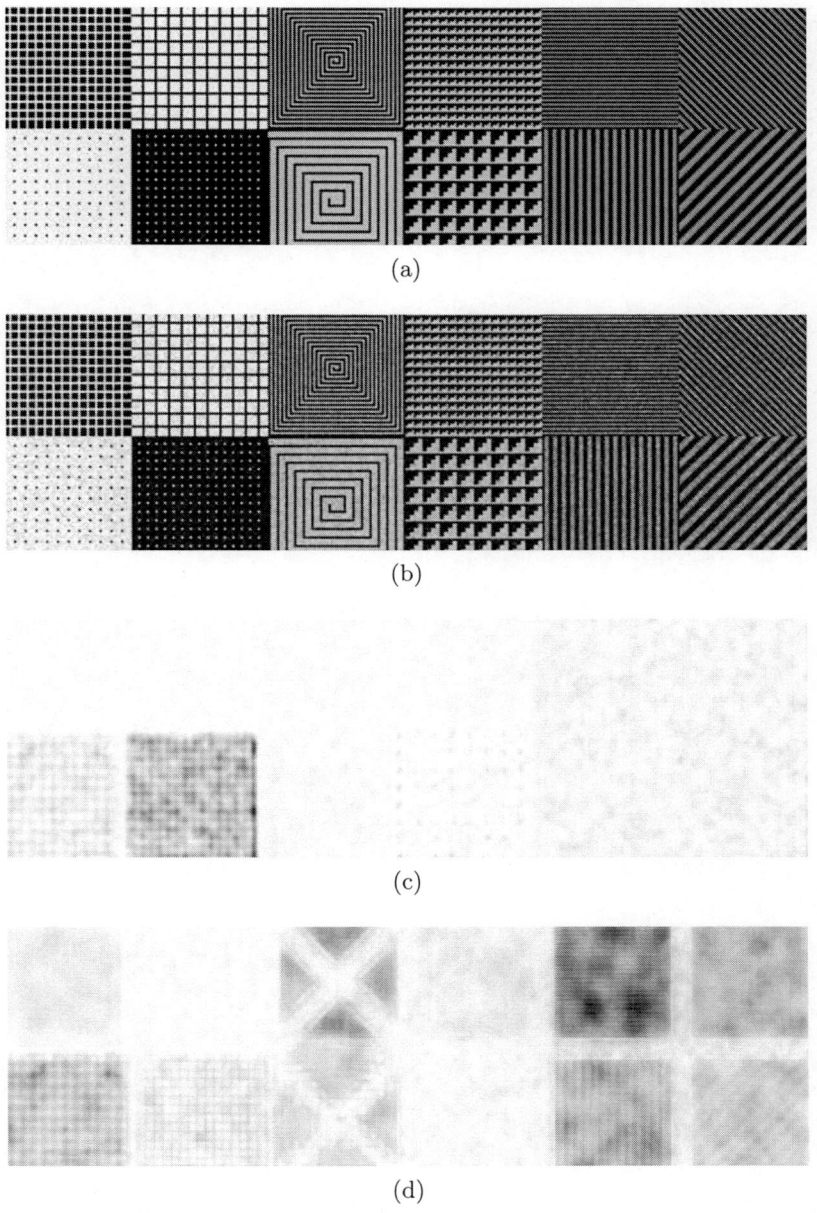

Fig. 2. IQA results comparison on a concept image. (a) Reference image. (b) distorted image. (c) SSIM based IQA result. (d) ISSIM based IQA result.

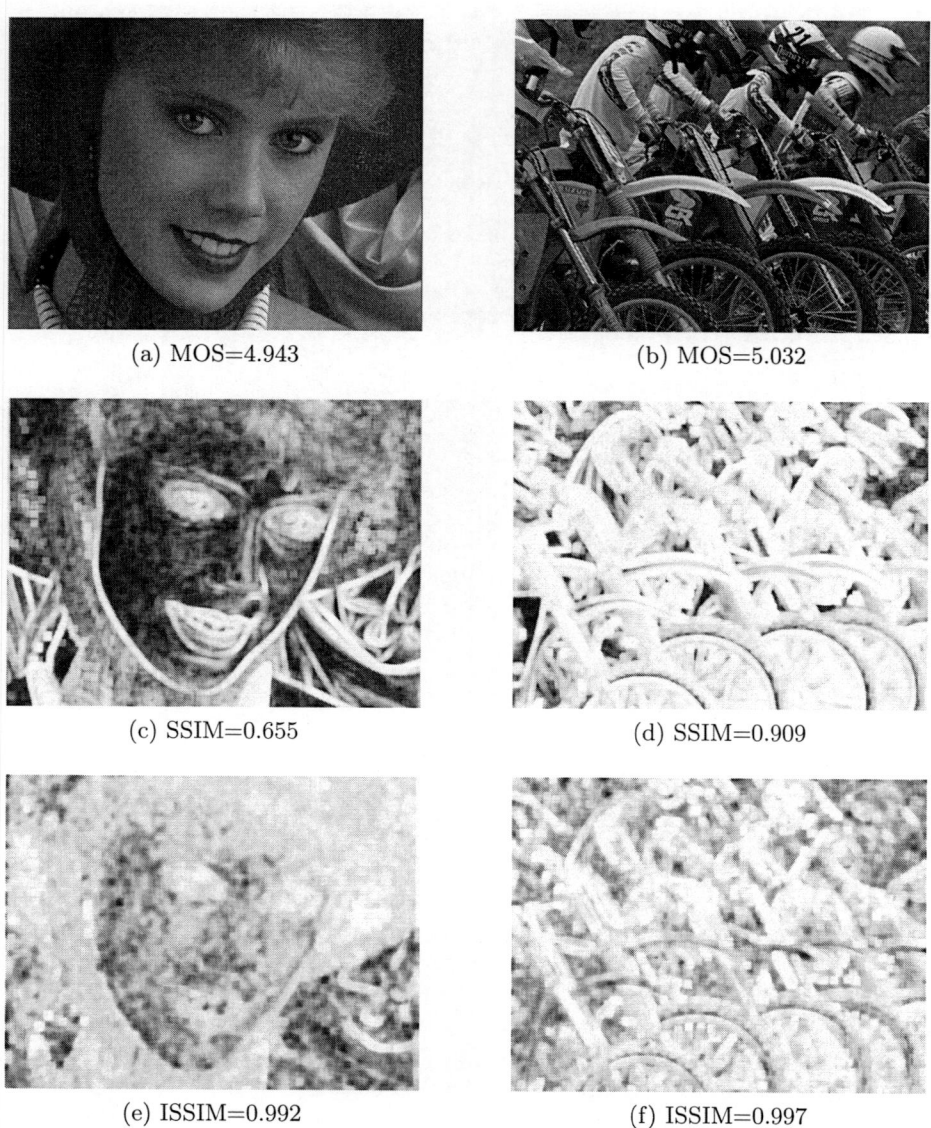

(a) MOS=4.943

(b) MOS=5.032

(c) SSIM=0.655

(d) SSIM=0.909

(e) ISSIM=0.992

(f) ISSIM=0.997

Fig. 3. IQA results comparison on natural images. (a) and (b) White noise contaminated images. (c) and (d) Outputs of the SSIM metric. (e) and (f) Outputs of the ISSIM metric. The subjective qualities (represented by MOS values) are very similar and the ISSIM metric coincides with this, while the SSIM metric shows that (a) is far worse than (b).

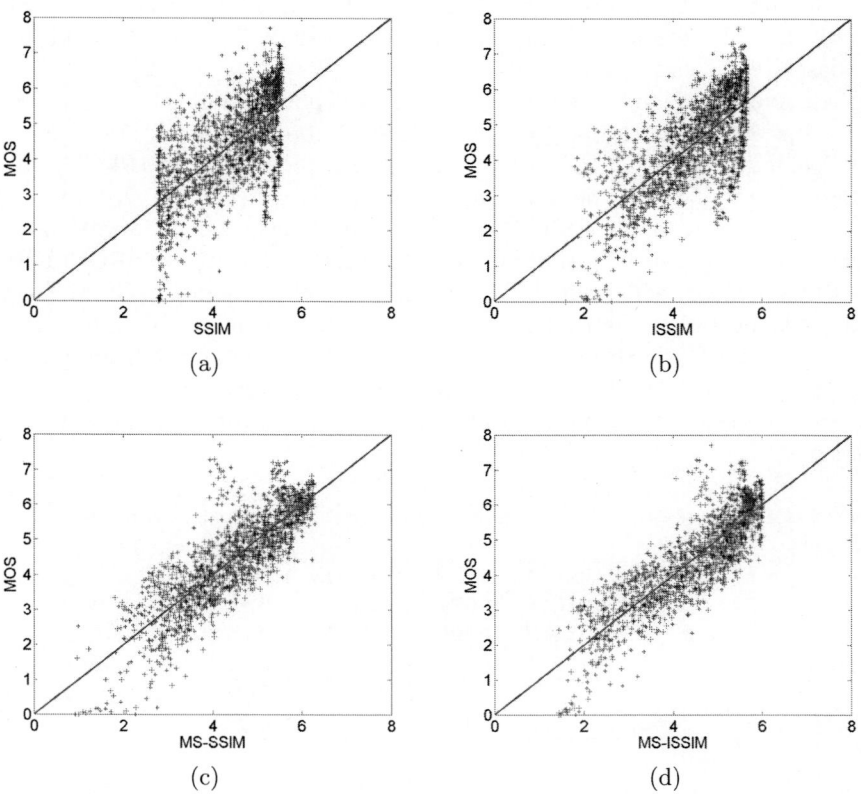

Fig. 4. Scatter plots of subject scores vs. the computational scores (mapping scores of the SSIM, ISSIM, MS-SSIM, and MS-ISSIM) for the TID2008 database

Though the luminance difference of the smooth region has been changed under the distortion, the self-similarity is almost unchanged and the structure degradation is small according to the HVS. With the ISSIM metric, the structural similarity is computed on both the luminance change and spatial distribution. The outputs of the ISSIM metric on the two images, Fig. 3(a) with ISSIM=0.992 and Fig. 3(b) with ISSIM=0.997, are much similar. Therefore, the ISSIM metric performs more consistently with the HVS than the SSIM metric does.

For a comprehensive analysis, we make a comparison between the SSIM metric and the ISSIM metric over the whole TID2008 database. To evaluate the performance of the two metrics on a common space during our experiment, we firstly employed a five-parameter mapping function [7] to nonlinearly regress the computational quality scores S_0,

$$S_r = \beta_1 \left(\frac{1}{2} - \frac{1}{1 + \exp(\beta_2(S_0 - \beta_3))} \right) + \beta_4 \, S_0 + \beta_5, \tag{10}$$

where β_j, $j = 1, \cdots, 5$, are the parameters to be fitted. The scatter plots of the computational score from the four metrics, i.e., SSIM, ISSIM, MS-SSIM, and MS-ISSIM, versus the mean opinion score (MOS) on the whole TID2008 database are shown in Fig. 4.

Then, five criteria are adopted [9] for result evaluation. The criteria are Spearman Rank-order Correlation Coefficient (SRCC), Kendall Rank-order Correlation Coefficient (KRCC), Pearson Linear Correlation Coefficient (PLCC), Mean Absolute Error (MAE), and Root Mean-Squared Error (RMSE). A better IQA metric should have higher SRCC, KRCC, and PLCC, while lower MAE and RMSE values. As listed in Table 1, the ISSIM metric has higher SRCC, KRCC and PLCC values, and lower MAE and RMSE values than the SSIM metric. Therefore, the ISSIM metric has an obvious improvement to the SSIM metric. Meanwhile, the MS-ISSIM metric also performs better on all the five evaluation criteria than the MS-SSIM metric, which further confirms that the proposed structural descriptor is more accurate and effective than that employed by the SSIM metric.

Table 1. Performance comparisons of image quality assessment algorithms on TID2008 database

Criteria	SSIM	ISSIM	MS-SSIM	MS-ISSIM
SRCC	0.641	**0.677**	0.850	**0.867**
KRCC	0.467	**0.499**	0.657	**0.673**
PLCC	0.643	**0.705**	0.782	**0.806**
MAE	0.831	**0.771**	0.669	**0.630**
RMSE	1.027	**0.951**	0.836	**0.794**

4   Conclusion

In this paper, an improved structural similarity based image quality assessment is proposed. Existing statistical characters based structural descriptor mainly represents the luminance change of the structure while cannot effectively represent the spatial distribution. Since the HVS is highly sensitive to the spatial distribution of image structures, we adopted self-similarity to describe structural character in detail. And then, combining both the luminance change and spatial distribution of the structure, an accurate structural descriptor is introduced. According to the novel structural descriptor, we improve the structural similarity based image quality assessment and introduce an ISSIM metric. Moreover, we extend the ISSIM metric into multi-scale space and deduce a MS-ISSIM based quality metric. Experimental results demonstrate the ISSIM/MS-ISSIM metric outperforms the SSIM/MS-SSIM metric.

References

1. Chen, G., Yang, C., Po, L., Xie, S.: Edge-Based structural similarity for image quality assessment. In: Proceedings of the 2006 IEEE International Conference on Acoustics, Speech and Signal Processing, ICASSP 2006, vol. 2, p. II (May 2006)

2. Katkovnik, V., Foi, A., Egiazarian, K., Astola, J.: From local kernel to nonlocal Multiple-Model image denoising. Int. J. Computer Vision 86, 1–32 (2009)
3. Li, C., Bovik, A.C.: Three-component weighted structural similarity index, pp. 72420Q-1–72420Q-9. SPIE (2009)
4. Lin, W., Kuo, C.J.: Perceptual visual quality metrics: A survey. J. Visual Communication and Image Representation 22(4), 297–312 (2011)
5. Liu, A., Lin, W., Narwaria, M.: Image quality assessment based on gradient similarity. IEEE Transactions on Image Processing: A Publication of the IEEE Signal Processing Society 21(4), 1500–1512 (2012)
6. Ponomarenko, N., Lukin, V., Zelensky, A., Egiazarian, K., Carli, M., Battisti, F.: Tid2008 - a database for evaluation of full-reference visual quality assessment metrics. Advances of Modern Radioelectronics 10, 30–45 (2009)
7. Video Quality Expert Group (VQEG): Final report from the video quality experts group on the validation of objective models of video quality assessment ii (2003), http://www.vqeg.org/
8. Wang, Z., Bovik, A., Sheikh, H., Simoncelli, E.: Image quality assessment: from error visibility to structural similarity. IEEE Transactions on Image Processing 13(4), 600–612 (2004)
9. Wang, Z., Li, Q.: Information content weighting for perceptual image quality assessment. IEEE Transactions on Image Processing 20(5), 1185–1198 (2011)
10. Wang, Z., Simoncelli, E., Bovik, A.: Multiscale structural similarity for image quality assessment. In: Conference Record of the Thirty-Seventh Asilomar Conference on Signals, Systems and Computers, vol. 2, pp. 1398–1402 (2003)
11. Wu, J., Qi, F., Shi, G.: Self-similarity based structural regularity for just noticeable difference estimation. Journal of Visual Communication and Image Representation 23(6), 845–852 (2012)

Multi-hypothesis Temporal Prediction Using Template Matching Prediction and Block Motion Compensation for High Efficiency Video Coding

Chun-Chi Chen[1], Wen-Hsiao Peng[1], and Shih-Chun Chou[2]

[1] Department of Computer Science,
National Chiao Tung University, Hsinchu, Taiwan
[2] The Innovative DigiTech-Enabled Applications & Services Institute,
Institute of Information Industry, Taipei, Taiwan
cheerchen.cs98g@g2.nctu.edu.tw, wpeng@cs.nctu.edu.tw, benchou@iii.org.tw

Abstract. This paper introduces a multi-hypothesis temporal prediction technique that combines two motion vectors (MVs) derived respectively from template and block matching for overlapped block motion compensation (OBMC). It achieves similar prediction performance to bi-prediction while only one MV has to be sent. Based on two signal models, the template MV is shown to approximate the pixel true motion around the template centroid. We then find another MV to best complement the template MV from both deterministic and statistical viewpoints, the latter leading to the search of its optimal sampling location in the motion field. The result is a search criterion with OBMC window functions forming a geometry-like motion partitioning. To compromise between performance and complexity, generalizations to adaptive template design, multi-hypothesis prediction and motion merging are made. Extensive experiments conducted with the HM-3.0 software confirm the effectiveness of the proposed schemes.

Keywords: Bi-prediction, OBMC, Template Matching.

1 Introduction

A key issue in video coders with motion-compensated prediction is how to trade off effectively between the accuracy of the motion field representation and the required overhead. Often a rough representation of the motion field is sufficient to provide good temporal prediction in terms of rate-distortion (R-D) performance. Obvious evidences are the frequent occurrence of large motion partitions and of SKIP mode. Accordingly, many literatures related to the decoder-side motion vector derivation (DMVD) techniques are proposed, hoping to leverage the ever-increasing processing capability of the decoder to save motion overhead.

Template matching prediction (TMP) [1] is a well-known DMVD technique. It estimates the motion vector (MV) of a target block by minimizing the matching

W. Lin et al. (Eds.): PCM 2012, LNCS 7674, pp. 164–175, 2012.

error over the reconstructed pixels in the template region, which is inverse-L-shaped and sitting on the top and to the left of the target block. Based on the concept, many of its variants have been proposed. Coding the target block at a lower spatial resolution followed by an interpolation was found more R-D efficient in flat areas, where TMP does not always guarantee to find a physically meaningful MV [2]. Even in non-flat areas, the template MV is merely a rough estimate of the target block's motion. Hence, the multi-hypothesis prediction becomes popular to improve TMP [3]. Other alternatives include higher weight to pixels spatially closer to the target block when calculating the template matching error [4], and adapting the template shape and location to local signal characteristics [5].

Another school of thought follows multi-hypothesis TMP, but one of the hypotheses is sent as a coded MV. Apparently, how to optimize this MV is the key to its effectiveness. It is obtained by carrying out block matching as for BMC and then used as an initial estimate to confine template matching search [6]. However, this scheme is not guaranteed a minimal prediction residual, for it neglects the combined effect of involved predictors. To overcome this problem, our prior works [7] proceed in reverse order, resulting in less residual than TMP and BMC. Because the scheme is achieved with two hypotheses, it is viewed as a particular bi-prediction featuring only one coded MV.

The critical step of the above bi-prediction is the combination of predictors. A simple way is to compute their average [8]. In this paper, we approach the problem from a theoretical perspective, assuming the use of the more general weighting scheme of *overlapped block motion compensation* (OBMC) [9]. Based on the underpinnings of [10] and [11], we show that the template MV is close to the true motion of a pixel near the top-left corner of the target block. A similar argument is then utilized to convert the problem of finding a MV to best complement the template MV into the search for a certain pixel whose true motion will be served as the output, wherein the criterion is such that the mean-square prediction error over the target block will be minimized when applying these motion samples for OBMC.

Experiments based on the HM-3.0 software and common test conditions [12] confirm our bi-prediction to be effective. Several variants, which implement adaptive template switching with multi-hypothesis prediction or extend the notion to Motion Merging [13], were studied to trade off between performance and complexity. The best of them achieves 2.1-2.9% BD-rate savings at a cost of 34% and 44% increases respectively in encoding and decoding times. Replacing template matching by motion merging brings down the time increases to 19% and 3%, respectively, with BD-rate reductions dropping to 1.3-1.9% as a result. While this is by no means an ideal operating point, our work shows the potential of having the encoder and decoder work jointly to deliver better results.

The rest of this paper is organized as follows: Section II analyzes TMP in a motion sampling framework. Within the framework, Section III formulates the optimal combination of TMP and BMC based on OBMC. Section IV evaluates the performance and complexity of the bi-prediction scheme and its variants. Section V concludes this paper.

2   Template Matching Prediction

In this section, TMP is studied to 1) reveal the factors that determine its prediction performance and 2) to understand its relationship to BMC.

2.1   Review of Signal Models

To analyze the residual of BMC, Tao *et al.* [10] modeled the *autocorrelation* functions of the intensity and motion fields by

$$E[I_k(\mathbf{s}_1)I_k(\mathbf{s}_2)] = \max\left(0, \sigma_I^2 \left(1 - \frac{||\mathbf{s}_1 - \mathbf{s}_2||_2^2}{K}\right)\right) \tag{1a}$$

$$E[v_x(\mathbf{s}_1)v_x(\mathbf{s}_2)] = E[v_y(\mathbf{s}_1)v_y(\mathbf{s}_2)] = \sigma_m^2 \rho_m^{||\mathbf{s}_1 - \mathbf{s}_2||_1}, \tag{1b}$$

respectively, where $I_k(\mathbf{s})$ represents the intensity value of pixel $\mathbf{s} = (x(\mathbf{s}), y(\mathbf{s}))$ of frame k; $\mathbf{v}(\mathbf{s}) = (v_x(\mathbf{s}), v_y(\mathbf{s}))$ denotes its true MV[1]; and $\{\sigma_I^2, K\}$ and $\{\sigma_m^2, \rho_m\}$ are parameters related to their respective variances and correlation coefficients. Equations (1a) and (1b) suggest that the intensity and motion correlations between any two pixels decrease with the distance in between them.

Similarly, in [11], Zheng *et al.* introduced a motion model assuming that the difference between the true MVs of any two pixels obeys the *normal* distribution:

$$v_x(\mathbf{s}_1) - v_x(\mathbf{s}_2) \text{ or } v_y(\mathbf{s}_1) - v_y(\mathbf{s}_2) \sim \mathcal{N}(0, \alpha\hat{r}^2(\mathbf{s}_1, \mathbf{s}_2)), \tag{2}$$

where α is a constant indicating the degree of motion variation in the horizontal or vertical direction, and $r(\mathbf{s}_1, \mathbf{s}_2) = ||\mathbf{s}_1 - \mathbf{s}_2||_2$ is the ℓ^2 distance between pixels $\mathbf{s}_1$ and $\mathbf{s}_2$. The "hat" in (2) indicates that its value will be clipped when exceeding a maximum threshold, which is essential for the model to be proper [14]. Equation (2) leads to the following *autocorrelation* function:

$$E[v_x(\mathbf{s}_1)v_x(\mathbf{s}_2)] = E[v_y(\mathbf{s}_1)v_y(\mathbf{s}_2)] = \sigma_m^2 - \frac{\alpha}{2}\hat{r}^2(\mathbf{s}_1, \mathbf{s}_2), \tag{3}$$

assuming the motion field is (wide-sense) stationary and zero-mean.

With these models, a closed-form expression for the mean-sqaure prediction error, $E[d^2(\mathbf{s}; \mathbf{v}(\mathbf{q}))]$ where $d(\mathbf{s}; \mathbf{v}(\mathbf{q})) \equiv I_k(\mathbf{s}) - I_{k-1}(\mathbf{s} + \mathbf{v}(\mathbf{q}))$, of pixel $\mathbf{s}$ based on the true MV of pixel $\mathbf{q}$ can be obtained. This result is useful for analyzing various prediction schemes, as we shall see later. In [10], the derivation is done by a direct application of (1a) and (1b) in evaluating $E[(I_{k-1}(\mathbf{s} + \mathbf{v}(\mathbf{s})) - I_{k-1}(\mathbf{s} + \mathbf{v}(\mathbf{q})))^2]$, where, under the constant intensity assumption, $I_{k-1}(\mathbf{s} + \mathbf{v}(\mathbf{s}))$ has been substituted for $I_k(\mathbf{s})$. This gives

$$E[d^2(\mathbf{s}; \mathbf{v}(\mathbf{q}))] = \frac{8\sigma_I^2 \sigma_m^2}{K}\left(1 - \rho_m^{||\mathbf{s} - \mathbf{q}||_1}\right). \tag{4}$$

---

[1] Under the constant intensity assumption, $I_k(\mathbf{s}) = I_{k-1}(\mathbf{s} + \mathbf{v}(\mathbf{s}))$ with $I_{k-1}(\mathbf{s})$ being the reference frame of $I_k(\mathbf{s})$.

Zheng *et al.* [11] take a different approach to find $E[d^2(\mathbf{s}; \mathbf{v}(\mathbf{q}))]$, without the need of an intensity model. They approximate the prediction error by Taylor expansion, $d(\mathbf{s}; \mathbf{v}(\mathbf{q})) \approx I'^{(x)}_{k-1}(\mathbf{s} + \mathbf{v}(\mathbf{q}))(v_x(\mathbf{s}) - v_x(\mathbf{q})) + I'^{(y)}_{k-1}(\mathbf{s} + \mathbf{v}(\mathbf{q}))(v_y(\mathbf{s}) - v_y(\mathbf{q}))$, take expectation of the square of both sides, and assume the x, y components of $I'_{k-1}(\mathbf{s} + \mathbf{v}(\mathbf{q}))$ and $(\mathbf{v}(\mathbf{s}) - \mathbf{v}(\mathbf{q}))$ are all independent of each other, to get

$$E[d^2(\mathbf{s}; \mathbf{v}(\mathbf{q}))] \cong \epsilon \tilde{r}^2(\mathbf{s}, \mathbf{q}) \cong \epsilon \|\mathbf{s} - \mathbf{q}\|_2^2, \tag{5}$$

where (2) is put into use and $\epsilon = \alpha E[(I'^{(x)}_{k-1}(\mathbf{s} + \mathbf{v}(\mathbf{q})))^2 + (I'^{(y)}_{k-1}(\mathbf{s} + \mathbf{v}(\mathbf{q})))^2]$.
  According to (4) and (5), several parallels between them can be drawn:

  – The minimum of $E[d^2(\mathbf{s}; \mathbf{v}(\mathbf{q}))]$ is reached when pixel $\mathbf{q}$ coincides with pixel $\mathbf{s}$, which is obvious from the constant intensity assumption.
  – The value of $E[d^2(\mathbf{s}; \mathbf{v}(\mathbf{q}))]$ increases when pixel $\mathbf{q}$ is further away from pixel $\mathbf{s}$ and converges to a value proportional to $8\sigma_I^2 \sigma_m^2 / K$ or ϵ, both have to do with the joint randomness of the motion and intensity fields.
  – The shape of $E[d^2(\mathbf{s}; \mathbf{v}(\mathbf{q}))]$, when viewed as a surface in the three-dimensional space constituted by $E[d^2(\mathbf{s}; \mathbf{v}(\mathbf{q}))]$ and the x, y components of $(\mathbf{s} - \mathbf{q})$, is mainly affected by the motion model.

2.2   Sampling the Motion Field

With (5), a block MV, $\mathbf{v}_b$, found from least-squares-based block matching was shown in [11] to approximate the true motion associated with the block center, $\mathbf{v}(\mathbf{s}_c)$, in the sense that the sum of prediction error variances over the target block is minimized when $\mathbf{v}_b$ is chosen to be $\mathbf{v}(\mathbf{s}_c)$:

$$\mathbf{s}_c = \arg\min_{\mathbf{q}} \sum_{\mathbf{s} \in \mathcal{B}} E[d^2(\mathbf{s}; \mathbf{v}(\mathbf{q}))] = \left(\frac{1}{|\mathcal{B}|} \sum_{\mathbf{s} \in \mathcal{B}} x(\mathbf{s}), \frac{1}{|\mathcal{B}|} \sum_{\mathbf{s} \in \mathcal{B}} y(\mathbf{s}) \right), \tag{6}$$

where $\mathcal{B}$ is a set consisting of coordinates of every pixel in the block. This can be easily verified by substituting (5) in (6) and setting the derivatives with respect to the x, y components of $\mathbf{q}$ equal to zero. A similar result is also observed with (4).[2] Together these observations leads to an insightful interpretation of BMC: *its operation may be viewed as a two-step process in which block-based motion estimation acts as a motion sampler taking samples at block centers while block-based motion compensation reconstructs the motion field by interpolating between motion samples using the nearest-neighbor rule* .
  Following the same line of derivation with $\mathcal{B}$ replaced by $\mathcal{T}$ and using (5), we have $\mathbf{s}_t = \left(\sum_{\mathbf{s} \in \mathcal{T}} x(\mathbf{s})/|\mathcal{T}|, \sum_{\mathbf{s} \in \mathcal{T}} y(\mathbf{s})/|\mathcal{T}| \right)$. Repeating the same computation with (4) gives a somewhat different result, but the trend remains similar. Table 1 shows the locations of $\mathbf{s}_t$. As can be seen, 1) the difference between $\mathbf{v}_t$ and $\mathbf{v}_b$ can be view as their sampling locations in the motion field and 2) a change to the template configuration amounts to a variation of $\mathbf{v}_t$'s sampling location.

---

[2] The optimal $\mathbf{q}$ in (6) cannot be found by differentation because of the ℓ_1 norm. We thus search exhaustively among all possible locations in quarter-pel precision.

Table 1. Sampling Locations of $\mathbf{v}_t$ for Various Template Configurations

Block	$\mathbf{s}_c$ (Block Center)	$W_t = 2$ Tao	$W_t = 2$ Zheng	$W_t = 4$ Tao	$W_t = 4$ Zheng	$W_t = 8$ Tao	$W_t = 8$ Zheng
4×4	(1.5,1.5)	(-1,-1)	(-0.25,-0.25)	(-1,-2)	(-1.25,-1.25)	(-3,-3)	(-3, -3)
8×8	(3.5,3.5)	(-1,-1)	(0.75, 0.75)	(-1,-1)	(0,0)	(-2,-3)	(-1.75,-1.75)
16×16	(7.5,7.5)	(-1,-1)	(2.75, 2.75)	(-1,-1)	(2,2)	(-2,-2)	(0.25,0.25)

(0,0) – the position of the top-left most pixel in the block $\mathcal{B}$.
W_t – the thickness of the template.

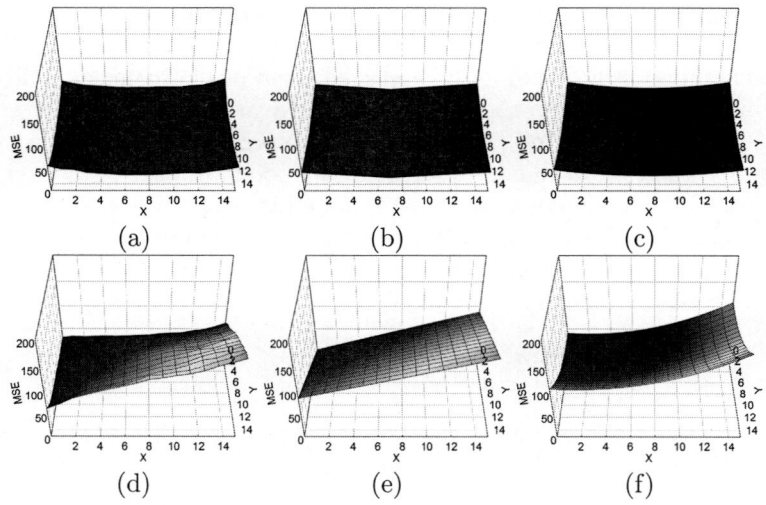

Fig. 1. Mean-square prediction error surfaces of block $\mathcal{B}$ produced with (a) BMC and (d) TMP. The second and third columns show the error surfaces predicted by Tao and Zheng's models, respectively. (BasketballDrill, $W_b = H_b = 16$, $W_t = 4$)

2.3   Prediction Error Surfaces of BMC and TMP

With the background developed so far, we are now ready to proceed with exploring the distribution of prediction error variance over the target block $\mathcal{B}$, termed the *prediction error surface*, for BMC and TMP. To do so, $\mathbf{v}_b$ and $\mathbf{v}_t$ are modeled by $\mathbf{v}(\mathbf{s}_c)$ and $\mathbf{v}(\mathbf{s}_t)$, respectively, and substituted for $\mathbf{v}(\mathbf{q})$ in (4) or (5) to compute the error variance for every pixel $\mathbf{s}$ in $\mathcal{B}$. The results are visualized in Fig. 1 and compared with empirical surfaces that have been generated through real encoding.

The error surfaces of BMC, predicted respectively by the models, are convex shapes, whose minimum occur at the block center; in other words, the error variance tends to be smaller around the center and larger at block boundaries, which is understandable if we recall that $\mathbf{v}_b$ approximates $\mathbf{v}(\mathbf{s}_c)$. Following the same argument, the residual of TMP has a larger variance at the bottom-right quarter of the target block, because $\mathbf{v}_t$, when viewed as $\mathbf{v}(\mathbf{s}_t)$, generally has a weaker correlation to pixels' true motion there. Comparing these results with their empirical counterparts confirms the accuracy of our theoretical predictions.

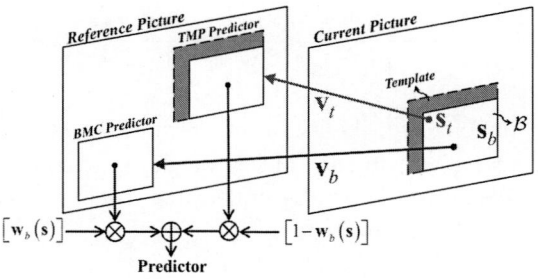

Fig. 2. Concept of bi-prediction combining TMP and BMC

3   Bi-prediction Combining TMP and BMC

3.1   Problem Formulation

The fact that in this application, $\mathbf{v}_t$ cannot be specified discretionarily by the encoder poses the key question of what is then the most appropriate choice for $\mathbf{v}_b$ and the OBMC weights which, along with the given $\mathbf{v}_t$, would minimize the residual for every block. Obviously, we cannot afford to specify a unique set of OBMC weights for each block, so the same weights must be shared among different blocks. Such restriction leads us to the following problem formulation:

$$\underset{\mathbf{v}_{b,i}, w_b(\widetilde{\mathbf{s}}), w_t(\widetilde{\mathbf{s}})}{\text{minimize}} \xi = \sum_{i \in \mathcal{I}} \sum_{\mathbf{s} \in \mathcal{B}_i} \left(I_k(\mathbf{s}) - w_t(\widetilde{\mathbf{s}}) I_{k-1}(\mathbf{s} + \mathbf{v}_{t,i}) - w_b(\widetilde{\mathbf{s}}) I_{k-1}(\mathbf{s} + \mathbf{v}_{b,i}) \right)^2$$

$$\text{subject to } w_t(\widetilde{\mathbf{s}}) + w_b(\widetilde{\mathbf{s}}) = 1, \text{ for all } \widetilde{\mathbf{s}} \tag{7}$$

where $\mathbf{s} = (x(\mathbf{s}), y(\mathbf{s}))$ is a pixel position relative to the top-left corner of a picture, with $\widetilde{\mathbf{s}} = (x(\widetilde{\mathbf{s}}), y(\widetilde{\mathbf{s}}))$ being its relative coordinates within a prediction block; $\{\mathcal{B}_i\}_{i \in \mathcal{I}}$ denotes a set of those blocks in a picture adopting this prediction scheme; and $w_t(\widetilde{\mathbf{s}})$ and $w_b(\widetilde{\mathbf{s}})$ are OBMC weights associated with the template and block MVs, respectively. Note that an unconstrained equivalent of (7) can be obtained by substituting $1 - w_b(\widetilde{\mathbf{s}})$ for $w_t(\widetilde{\mathbf{s}})$, leaving unknown only the block MVs, $\{\mathbf{v}_{b,i}\}_{i \in \mathcal{I}}$, and the corresponding OBMC weights, $w_b(\widetilde{\mathbf{s}})$.

3.2   Iterative Least-Squares (LS) Solution

The problem in (7) can be solved iteratively. Using an initial guess, called $w_b^{(0)}(\widetilde{\mathbf{s}})$, we can find a motion vector $\mathbf{v}_{b,i}^{(0)}$ for each prediction block $\mathcal{B}_i$, $i \in \mathcal{I}$, with the following search criterion

$$\mathbf{v}_{b,i}^{(0)} = \arg \min_{\mathbf{v}_{b,i}} \sum_{\mathbf{s} \in \mathcal{B}_i} \left(I_k(\mathbf{s}) - (1 - w_b^{(0)}(\widetilde{\mathbf{s}})) I_{k-1}(\mathbf{s} + \mathbf{v}_{t,i}^{(0)}) - w_b^{(0)}(\widetilde{\mathbf{s}}) I_{k-1}(\mathbf{s} + \mathbf{v}_{b,i}) \right)^2,$$

$$\tag{8}$$

where $\mathbf{v}_{t,i}^{(0)}$ is computed right before the search of $\mathbf{v}_{b,i}^{(0)}$ by performing TMP. Conditioned on the resulting $\mathbf{v}_{b,i}^{(0)}$ and $\mathbf{v}_{t,i}^{(0)}$, $w_b(\widetilde{\mathbf{s}})$ is refined subsequently as follows for every distinct $\widetilde{\mathbf{s}}$:

$$w_b^{(1)}(\tilde{\mathbf{s}}) = \frac{\sum_{i \in \mathcal{I}} \left(I_k(\mathbf{s}_i) - I_{k-1}(\mathbf{s}_i + \mathbf{v}_{t,i}^{(0)})\right)\left(I_{k-1}(\mathbf{s}_i + \mathbf{v}_{b,i}^{(0)}) - I_{k-1}(\mathbf{s}_i + \mathbf{v}_{t,i}^{(0)})\right)}{\sum_{i \in \mathcal{I}} \left(I_{k-1}(\mathbf{s}_i + \mathbf{v}_{b,i}^{(0)}) - I_{k-1}(\mathbf{s}_i + \mathbf{v}_{t,i}^{(0)})\right)^2}, \quad (9)$$

where $\mathbf{s}_i$ is a pixel in $\mathcal{B}_i$. Then, the iteration continues by substituting the newly obtained $w_b^{(1)}(\tilde{\mathbf{s}})$ for $w_b^{(0)}(\tilde{\mathbf{s}})$ in (8). This procedure, although straightforward, is less instructive. We do not know the underlying mechanism that gives rise to the solution, nor can we explain it.

3.3   Least Mean-Square (LMS) Solution

To gain more insights into the result, we transform the problem of minimizing the sum, ξ, of squared prediction errors into that of minimizing its expected value, $E[\xi]$, so that the aforementioned motion sampling concept and the signal models can come into play. Assuming that the intensity and motion fields are stationary, the new objective becomes

$$\underset{w_b(\tilde{\mathbf{s}}),\mathbf{s}_b}{\text{minimize}} \sum_{\mathbf{s} \in \mathcal{B}} E\left[\left(I_k(\mathbf{s}) - (1 - w_b(\tilde{\mathbf{s}})) I_{k-1}(\mathbf{s} + \mathbf{v}(\mathbf{s}_t)) - w_b(\tilde{\mathbf{s}}) I_{k-1}(\mathbf{s} + \mathbf{v}(\mathbf{s}_b))\right)^2\right].$$
$$(10)$$

Obviously, for (10) to be minimized, the optimal $w_b(\tilde{\mathbf{s}})$ must satisfy, for all $\mathbf{s} \in \mathcal{B}$,

$$w_b(\tilde{\mathbf{s}}) = \frac{E[d(\mathbf{s}; \mathbf{v}(\mathbf{s}_t))(d(\mathbf{s}; \mathbf{v}(\mathbf{s}_t)) - d(\mathbf{s}; \mathbf{v}(\mathbf{s}_b)))]}{E[(d(\mathbf{s}; \mathbf{v}(\mathbf{s}_t)) - d(\mathbf{s}; \mathbf{v}(\mathbf{s}_b)))^2]}, \quad (11)$$

where $d(\mathbf{s}; \mathbf{v}(\mathbf{q})) = I_k(\mathbf{s}) - I_{k-1}(\mathbf{s} + \mathbf{v}(\mathbf{q}))$, $\mathbf{q} = \mathbf{s}_t$ or $\mathbf{s}_b$. Recall that from Table 1, $\mathbf{s}_t$ is known once the template shape and signal model are selected. Then, substituting (11) into (10), the summation is seen to be a function of $E\left[d(\mathbf{s}; \mathbf{v}(\mathbf{s}_t))^2\right]$, $E\left[d(\mathbf{s}; \mathbf{v}(\mathbf{s}_b))^2\right]$ and $E\left[d(\mathbf{s}; \mathbf{v}(\mathbf{s}_t))d(\mathbf{s}; \mathbf{v}(\mathbf{s}_b))\right]$, and $\mathbf{s}_b$ is the last term to be solved. Depending on which signal model is in use, the optimal $\mathbf{s}_b$ can be derived as

$$\mathbf{s}_b^* = \arg\min_{\mathbf{s}_b} \sum_{\mathbf{s} \in \mathcal{B}} \frac{8\sigma_I^2 \sigma_m^2}{K} \left(1 - \rho_m^{||\mathbf{s}-\mathbf{s}_t||_1} - \frac{\left(1 - \rho_m^{||\mathbf{s}-\mathbf{s}_b||_1} - 1 + \rho_m^{||\mathbf{s}_t-\mathbf{s}_b||_1} + 1 - \rho_m^{||\mathbf{s}_t-\mathbf{s}_b||_1}\right)^2}{4\left(1 - \rho_m^{||\mathbf{s}_t-\mathbf{s}_b||_1}\right)}\right)$$
$$(12)$$

with Tao's model or

$$\mathbf{s}_b^* = \arg\min_{\mathbf{s}_b} \sum_{\mathbf{s} \in \mathcal{B}} \epsilon \left(\hat{r}^2(\mathbf{s}, \mathbf{s}_t) - \frac{(\hat{r}^2(\mathbf{s}, \mathbf{s}_t) - \hat{r}^2(\mathbf{s}, \mathbf{s}_b) + \hat{r}^2(\mathbf{s}_t, \mathbf{s}_b))^2}{4\hat{r}^2(\mathbf{s}_t, \mathbf{s}_b)}\right) \quad (13)$$

with Zheng's model. In particular, both equations suggest that there is no closed-form expression for $\mathbf{s}_b^*$–i.e., it has to be sought numerically.

Fig. 3 plots the sum of prediction error variances over the target block $\mathcal{B}$ as a function of $\mathbf{s}_b$'s position, with $(0,0)$ being the position of the top-left pixel in $\mathcal{B}$. The sum reaches the minimum when $\mathbf{s}_b^*$ sits in the bottom-right quarter (see Table 2 for $\mathbf{s}_b^*$). As was noted before, TMP is less efficient in predicting pixels in the bottom-right area. It is natural to expect the block MV to be so sampled as to compensate for its inefficiency. Once $\mathbf{s}_b^*$ is known, the corresponding $w_b(\tilde{\mathbf{s}})$ is immediately obvious by (11) (See Fig. 4).

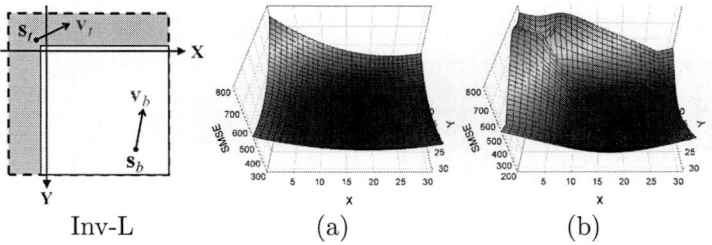

Fig. 3. Error surfaces showing how the sum of prediction error variances over the target block varies with the location of s_b: (a) Tao's and (b) Zheng's models

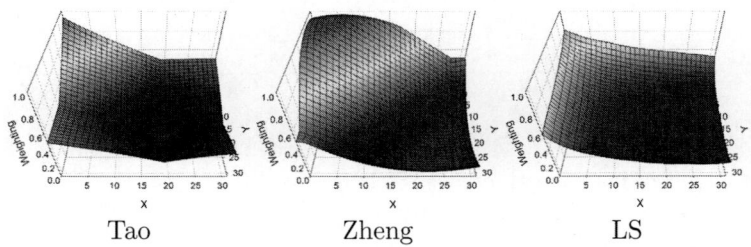

Fig. 4. Comparison of window functions, $w_t(\tilde{s})$

4   Experimental Results

Experiments are carried out using the HM-3.0 software and common test conditions [12] to measure the coding performance of the proposed scheme (referred hereafter to as the TB-mode). A flag is sent for each non-skipped, 2Nx2N Prediction Unit (PU) to implement TB-mode as a switchable coding option. The search range for TMP is ±4 pixels and $W_t = 4$. The OBMC weights for the LS solution are computed offline based on a separate set of training sequences, while the model parameters for the LMS solutions are selected empirically.[3]

4.1   Coding Performance

Table 3 shows the coding results of the LS and LMS solutions. In particular, three heuristic variants of the TB-mode, demonstrating the effects when v_b is estimated independently or dependently of v_t and/or when a simple averaging of predictors is used in place of OBMC, are tested (Section ♯2). These simple heuristics perform worse than the LS and LMS solutions (Section ♯1); the straightforward approach (TB, 1/2), which simply averages the template and block predictors, even incurs 0.1% BD-rate increase. Incorporating OBMC (TB, LS) seems more beneficial than optimizing the block MV (TB, 1/2, ME opt.). But, neither approach comes close to the LS and LMS schemes, which deliver

---

[3] For Tao's model, $\rho_m = 0.95$; for Zheng's model, the clipping threshold is set equal to $(2N)^2/2$ with $2N$ denoting the width, or height, of the target PU.

Table 2. Sampling Locations of s_b^* for Various Template Configurations

		$W_t = 2$		$W_t = 4$		$W_t = 8$	
Block	s_c (Block Center)	Tao	Zheng	Tao	Zheng	Tao	Zheng
4×4	(1.5, 1.5)	(2, 2)	(2, 2)	(2, 2)	(1.5, 1.5)	(2, 2)	(1.5, 1.5)
8×8	(3.5, 3.5)	(5, 5)	(4.5, 4.5)	(5, 5)	(4.5, 4.5)	(4, 4)	(4, 4)
16×16	(7.5, 7.5)	(10, 10)	(9.5, 9.5)	(10, 10)	(9.5, 9.5)	(10, 10)	(9, 9)

Table 3. Comparisons of TB-modes and TMP

Sec	Mode	Weighting	ME Opt.	RAHE	RALC	LBHE	LBLC	Avg.	Enc.	Dec.
♯1	TB	LS	o	-0.7	-0.5	-0.8	-0.9	-0.7	106%	121%
	TB	LMS-Tao	o	-0.7	-0.5	-0.7	-0.9	-0.7	106%	121%
	TB	LMS-Zheng	o	-0.7	-0.5	-0.8	-0.8	-0.7	106%	116%
♯2	TB	1/2		0.0	0.0	0.1	0.2	0.1	103%	109%
	TB	LS		-0.3	-0.2	-0.3	-0.3	-0.3	103%	116%
	TB	1/2	o	-0.1	0.0	-0.1	-0.3	-0.1	105%	122%

Note – Negative values mean a rate reduction while positive values indicate a rate inflation.

0.7% in BD-rate reduction. All the schemes have almost the same level of encoding and decoding time increases. Their impact on encoding time (a 3-6% increase) is relatively modest, but the decoding time increase is still considerable (9-25%), mainly casued by performing TMP.

4.2   Adaptive Template Switching

The coding performance of the TB-mode can improve at the cost of extra signaling overhead and computation. For instance, the encoder can switch between different template designs (see Fig. 5) to better adapt to time-varying signal characteristics. Of course, besides signaling the choice of template, the OBMC weights and block MV also need to be optimized by the same procedure described in Section 3. From Table 4, this scheme further improves the rate saving by 0.4-0.6%, adding up to an average BD-rate saving of 1.2%, while elevating the encoding and decoding time ratios to 114% and 119%, respectively, due to extra computation needed for mode decision.

4.3   Multi-hypothesis Extension

The results given above have been generated by limiting the hypothesis number to two. Considering a three-hypothesis case, two block MVs, $\mathbf{v}_{b1}$ and $\mathbf{v}_{b2}$, and their associated OBMC weights, $w_{b1}(\tilde{\mathbf{s}})$ and $w_{b2}(\tilde{\mathbf{s}})$, has to be determined. More unknowns are to be solved, which largely complicates the iteration process of the LS solution, so we resort to the LMS approach. In analogy with (10), the objective is to find two pixels, $\mathbf{s}_{b1}$ and $\mathbf{s}_{b2}$, in the target block $\mathcal{B}$ that minimize:

$$\xi = \sum_{s \in \mathcal{B}} E\left[\left(\begin{array}{c} I_k(\mathbf{s}) - w_t(\tilde{\mathbf{s}})I_{k-1}(\mathbf{s}+\mathbf{v}(\mathbf{s}_t)) - w_{b1}(\tilde{\mathbf{s}})I_{k-1}\left(\mathbf{s}+\mathbf{v}(\mathbf{s}_{b1})\right) \\ -w_{b2}(\tilde{\mathbf{s}})I_{k-1}\left(\mathbf{s}+\mathbf{v}(\mathbf{s}_{b1})\right) \end{array}\right)^2\right], \quad (14)$$

where $\mathbf{v}_t$, $\mathbf{v}_{b1}$ and $\mathbf{v}_{b2}$ are modeled, respectively, by $\mathbf{v}(\mathbf{s}_t)$, $\mathbf{v}(\mathbf{s}_{b1})$ and $\mathbf{v}(\mathbf{s}_{b2})$ with $\mathbf{s}_t$ as a priori, and $w_t(\tilde{\mathbf{s}}) = 1 - w_{b1}(\tilde{\mathbf{s}}) - w_{b2}(\tilde{\mathbf{s}})$. Proceeding in much the same

Table 4. Comparisons of TB-modes with Fixed or Variable Template Pattern

	RAHE	RALC	LBHE	LBLC	Avg.	Enc.	Dec.
(a) Fixed Template Pattern (Inverse-L)	-0.7	-0.5	-0.7	-0.9	-0.7	106%	121%
(b) Variable Template Pattern	-1.1	-0.9	-1.1	-1.5	-1.2	114%	119%

Note – The results shown are with Tao's model and 2 hypotheses.

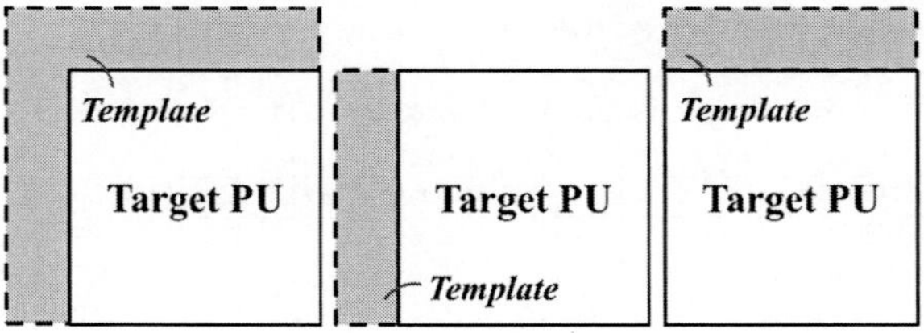

Fig. 5. Adaptive template switching

way as in [14], we can solve for the solution, $\mathbf{s}_{b1}^*$ and $\mathbf{s}_{b2}^*$, by evaluating ξ for all permissible values of $\mathbf{s}_{b1}, \mathbf{s}_{b2} \in \mathcal{B}$, which involves only the second-order moments of $d(\mathbf{s}; \mathbf{v}(\mathbf{s}_t))$, $d(\mathbf{s}; \mathbf{v}(\mathbf{s}_{b1}))$, $d(\mathbf{s}; \mathbf{v}(\mathbf{s}_{b2}))$.[4] Using the result, $\mathbf{v}_{b1}$ and $\mathbf{v}_{b2}$ are then estimated by *divide-and-conquer*, with $\mathbf{v}_{b1}$ first found by

$$\mathbf{v}_{b1}^* = \arg\min_{\mathbf{v}_{b1}} \sum_{\mathbf{s} \in \mathcal{B}} \left(I_k(\mathbf{s}) - (1 - w_{b1}^*(\widetilde{\mathbf{s}}; \mathbf{s}_t, \mathbf{s}_{b1}^*)) I_{k-1}(\mathbf{s} + \mathbf{v}_t) - w_{b1}^*(\widetilde{\mathbf{s}}; \mathbf{s}_t, \mathbf{s}_{b1}^*) I_{k-1}(\mathbf{s} + \mathbf{v}_{b1}) \right)^2$$

(15)

and utilized subsequently alone with $\mathbf{v}_t$ to find $\mathbf{v}_{b2}$ as follows:

$$\mathbf{v}_{b2}^* = \arg\min_{\mathbf{v}_{b2}} \sum_{\mathbf{s} \in \mathcal{B}} \left(\begin{array}{l} I_k(\mathbf{s}) - (1 - w_{b1}^*(\widetilde{\mathbf{s}}; \mathbf{s}_t, \mathbf{s}_{b1}^*, \mathbf{s}_{b2}^*) - w_{b2}^*(\widetilde{\mathbf{s}}; \mathbf{s}_t, \mathbf{s}_{b1}^*, \mathbf{s}_{b2}^*)) I_{k-1}(\mathbf{s} + \mathbf{v}_t) \\ -w_{b1}^*(\widetilde{\mathbf{s}}; \mathbf{s}_t, \mathbf{s}_{b1}^*, \mathbf{s}_{b2}^*) I_{k-1}(\mathbf{s} + \mathbf{v}_{b1}^*) - w_{b2}^*(\widetilde{\mathbf{s}}; \mathbf{s}_t, \mathbf{s}_{b1}^*, \mathbf{s}_{b2}^*) I_{k-1}(\mathbf{s} + \mathbf{v}_{b2}) \end{array} \right)^2,$$

(16)

where the $w_{b1}^*(\widetilde{\mathbf{s}})$ and $w_{b2}^*(\widetilde{\mathbf{s}})$ are augmented with the sampling points $(\mathbf{s}_t, \mathbf{s}_{b1}^*$ or $\mathbf{s}_{b2}^*)$ from which they are computed.[5]

We also preserve the flexibility of TB-mode to switch between two- and three-hypothesis cases, in order to be R-D effective. However, the $\mathbf{s}_{b1}^*$ in (14) is generally not equal to $\mathbf{s}_b^*$ in (10), resulting in three times of motion search respectively for $\mathbf{v}_b^*$, $\mathbf{v}_{b1}^*$, and $\mathbf{v}_{b2}^*$. To reduce the complexity, we simply let $\mathbf{s}_{b1}^* = \mathbf{s}_{b2}^* = \mathbf{s}_b^*$, resulting in $w_{b1}^*(\widetilde{\mathbf{s}})$ and $w_{b2}^*(\widetilde{\mathbf{s}})$ equal to $\frac{1}{2}w_b^*(\widetilde{\mathbf{s}})$. Hence, there is no need to find $\mathbf{v}_{b1}^*$ since its result is exactly identical to $\mathbf{v}_b^*$.

Table 5 compares the results of TB-modes with varying the numbers of hypothesis. Note that the notation, taking Experiment (b) as an example, (1 $\mathbf{v}_t$ + 2 $\mathbf{v}_b$'s) means that the encoder can choose adaptively the TB-mode with (1 $\mathbf{v}_t$ + 1 $\mathbf{v}_b$) or (1 $\mathbf{v}_t$ + 2 $\mathbf{v}_b$'s). In (b) and (e), there is almost no difference, in terms of BD-rate savaings, between the heuristic and theoretically optimal approaches. Only 0.1-0.2% rate saving in the low-delay conditions is obtained from the optimal approach, while increasing the encoding time by 10% which is nearly unacceptable. Hence, we adopt the heuristic approach for the later experiments.

---

[4] Refer to (6) and (11) in [14] for evaluating ξ, $w_t(\widetilde{\mathbf{s}})$, $w_{b1}(\widetilde{\mathbf{s}})$, $w_{b2}(\widetilde{\mathbf{s}})$.

[5] $\mathbf{s}_{b2}^*$, $w_{b1}^*(\widetilde{\mathbf{s}}; \mathbf{s}_t, \mathbf{s}_{b1}^*)$ in (15) is generally *not* equal to $w_{b1}^*(\widetilde{\mathbf{s}}; \mathbf{s}_t, \mathbf{s}_{b1}^*, \mathbf{s}_{b2}^*)$ in (16).

Table 5. Comparisons of TB-modes with Multi-hypothesis Prediction

Hypotheses	Heuristic	RAHE	RALC	LBHE	LBLC	Avg.	Enc.	Dec.
(a) 2 $(1\ \mathbf{v}_t + 1\ \mathbf{v}_b)$		-1.1	-0.9	-1.1	-1.5	-1.2	114%	119%
(b) 3 $(1\ \mathbf{v}_t + 2\ \mathbf{v}_b\text{'s})$	o	-1.6	-1.6	-1.7	-2.2	-1.8	119%	125%
(c) 3 $(2\ \mathbf{v}_t\text{'s} + 1\ \mathbf{v}_b)$		-1.6	-1.4	-2.0	-2.4	-1.8	118%	143%
(d) 4 $(2\ \mathbf{v}_t\text{'s} + 2\ \mathbf{v}_b\text{'s})$	o	-2.0	-1.9	-2.2	-2.7	-2.2	122%	147%
(e) 3 $(1\ \mathbf{v}_t + 2\ \mathbf{v}_b\text{'s})$		-1.6	-1.5	-1.8	-2.4	-1.8	129%	125%

Note – The results shown are with adaptive template switching.

Table 6. Comparisons of TB-modes with Motion Merging

Hypotheses	RAHE	RALC	LBHE	LBLC	Avg.	Enc.	Dec.
(a) 2 $(1\ \mathrm{MRG}\ \mathbf{v}_t + 1\ \mathbf{v}_b)$	-0.7	-0.5	-0.9	-0.8	-0.7	106%	101%
(b) 3 $(1\ \mathrm{MRG}\ \mathbf{v}_t + 2\ \mathbf{v}_b\text{'s})$	-0.9	-0.8	-1.2	-1.3	-1.1	110%	102%
(c) 3 $(2\ \mathrm{MRG}\ \mathbf{v}_t\text{'s} + 1\ \mathbf{v}_b)$	-0.9	-0.7	-1.2	-1.2	-1.0	108%	102%
(d) 4 $(2\ \mathrm{MRG}\ \mathbf{v}_t\text{'s} + 2\ \mathbf{v}_b\text{'s})$	-1.1	-1.0	-1.3	-1.5	-1.2	109%	103%

From the table (a-d), increasing the maximum hypothesis number from 2 to 4 almost doubles the rate saving in every test condition, achieving an average BD-rate reduction of 2.2%, and the increase of decoding time is about 30% higher than the $(1\ \mathbf{v}_t + 1\ \mathbf{v}_b)$. As it stands, the setting $(1\ \mathbf{v}_t + 2\ \mathbf{v}_b\text{'s})$ seems to offer a better compromise between performance and complexity, with a comparable encoding/decoding time increase to $(1\ \mathbf{v}_t + 1\ \mathbf{v}_b)$, yet a moderate rate saving (1.8%, on average). The same observation does not apply to the other 3-hypothesis scheme, $(2\ \mathbf{v}_t\text{'s} + 1\ \mathbf{v}_b)$, which differs in using more $\mathbf{v}_t$'s. For this reason, its decoding time increase is as considerable as $(2\ \mathbf{v}_t\text{'s} + 2\ \mathbf{v}_b\text{'s})$.

4.4   Generalization to Motion Merging

The idea of Motion Merging [13] is to send few bits to reuse MV(s) from a previously decoded neighboring PU as $\mathbf{v}_t$. It is similar to treating the motion sample taken at the center of the referred PU as $\mathbf{v}_t$, in which case selecting adaptively from a range of candidate PUs is assimilated to switching between different template designs. In this analogy, we simply apply the previous OBMC windows to the present case, and the weight values are rounded to power-of-two numbers with 3-bit integer precision for simplification. Comparing Table 6 with Table 5, the performance declines 0.5-1.0% across different experiments, but also much lower encoding and decoding time increases. The high complexity associated with TMP can be thus resolved. Performance loss may be inevitable; it however can be mitigated without significantly complicating the decoder.

5   Conclusion

We proposed a bi-prediction scheme combining BMC and TMP predictors through OBMC. First, TMP is examined in the context of motion field sampling and showed that the template MV may be viewed as the pixel true motion around the template centroid. Following a similar argument, we formulated the problem of finding an MV to best complement the template MV as the search of its sampling location in the motion field. This formulation allows solving the problem analytically and leading to useful insights into the solution. We found that when sampled optimally, this MV, along with the template MV, forms a geometry-like motion partitioning. The notion of our scheme is capable of tremendous generalization. The template pattern need not be fixed, the number of hypotheses can be extended over two, and TMP can be replaced with other DMVD techniques, such as Motion Merging. Experimental results confirm our scheme to be effective.

Acknowledgements. This study is conducted under the "Project Digital Convergence Service Open Platform" of the Institute for Information Industry which is subsidized by the Ministry of Economy Affairs of the Republic of China.

References

1. Kamp, S., et al.: Decoder Side Motion Vector Derivation for Inter Frame Video Coding. In: Proc. Int'l Conf. on Image Processing (2008)
2. Suzuki, Y., et al.: Block-based reduced resolution inter frame coding with template matching prediction. In: Proc. Int'l Conf. on Image Processing (2006)
3. Kamp, S., et al.: Multihypothesis prediction using decoder side motion vector derivation in inter frame video coding. Visual Comm. and Image Processing (2009)
4. Huang, Y.W., et al.: TE1: Decoder-side motion vector derivation with switchable template matching. Doc. JCTVC-B076 (2011)
5. Lin, S., et al.: TE1: Huawei report on DMVD improvements (joint document with Peking University). Doc. JCTVC-B037 (2010)
6. Suzuki, Y., Boon, C.S.: An improved low delay inter frame coding using template matching averaging. In: Proc. Picture Coding Symposium (2010)
7. Lee, C.L., et al.: Bi-prediction Combining Template and Block Motion Compensations. In: Proc. Int'l Conf. on Image Processing (2011)
8. Wang, R., et al.: Combining Template Matching and Block Motion Compensation for Video Coding. In: Proc. Int'l Symp. on Intelligent Signal Processing and Communication Systems (2010)
9. Orchard, M.T., Sullivan, G.J.: Overlapped block motion compensation: An estimation-theoretic approach. IEEE Trans. on Image Processing 3(5), 693–699 (1994)
10. Tao, B., Orchard, M.T.: A parametric solution for optimal overlapped block motion compensation. IEEE Trans. on Image Processing 10(3), 341–350 (2001)
11. Zheng, W., et al.: Analysis of space-dependent characteristics of motion-compensated frame differences based on a statistical motion distribution model. IEEE Trans. on Image Processing 11(4), 377–386 (2002)
12. Bossen, F.: Common test conditions and software reference configurations. Doc. JCTVC-E700 (2011)
13. Winken, M., et al.: Description of Video Coding Technology Proposal by Fraunhofer HHI. Doc. JCTVC-A116 (2010)
14. Chen, Y.W., Peng, W.H.: Parametric OBMC for Pixel-Adaptive Temporal Prediction on Irregular Motion Sampling Grids. IEEE Trans. on Circuits and Systems for Video Technology 22(1), 113–127 (2012)

Leveraging Exemplar and Saliency Model for Image Search Reranking

Hong Lu*, Kai Chen, Guobao Jiang, Renzhong Wei, and Xiangyang Xue

Shanghai Key Lab of Intelligent Information Processing
School of Computer Science
Fudan University, Shanghai, China
honglu@fudan.edu.cn

Abstract. In this paper, we propose to rerank the image retrieval results using a novel method which can be fitted to both objects classes and scenes classes. We first introduce the two methods: Exemplar model and Saliency Map (SM). Exemplar model is a top-down method which considers region of interest (ROI) of images from the same class containing lots of similar discriminative local features. These discriminative local features can be trained as the model of the specific class and to rerank the retrieved images by their similarities with the trained model of the query class. On the other hand, SM is a bottom-up method which uses winner-take-all and inhibition-of-return mechanisms to draw different locations in descending saliency order, and the images can be reranked by their salient scores. In experimental results, we observe that Exemplar Model performs well in object classes and SM performs well in scene classes for these two methods focus on different aspects to rerank images. Then we propose a method named ExSM which combines the advantage of Exemplar model and SM. ExSM inherits the superiority of Exemplar model in object classes and SM in scene classes and outperforms both of them in general.

Keywords: Image Reranking, Exemplar model, Saliency Map, ExSM method, Flickr.

1 Introduction

Nowadays, more and more images are generated, distributed, and made available all over the world. Specifically, statistical information on 18th March, 2012 shows that Flickr has reached 60 billion images with tags and Facebook has more than 1000 billion images already. Therefore, how to effectively and efficiently annotate, classify, and retrieve images becomes more and more important.

Most web image search engines return the rank list according to the related textual information. Although the text-based ranking method can be used to rank the images effectively in most situations, it does not take fully advantage of the visual information of images. Figure 1 shows the result of the keyword "tiger" we search in a popular image search engine, which shows the weakness of the image search engine just uses the technique of text retrieval for image searching. It can be observed that the result

---

* Corresponding author.

W. Lin et al. (Eds.): PCM 2012, LNCS 7674, pp. 176–185, 2012.
© Springer-Verlag Berlin Heidelberg 2012

Fig. 1. Returned image list with search keyword "tiger" in a popular image search engine. From the list, we can observe that the butterfly with tiger stripes, "tiger shark", and "tiger tank" are not the images we want. But just because the surrounding texts have "tiger", they are included in the retrieved result.

contains some images that are not tiger but the surrounding texts contains "tiger". So how to mine the visual information like color, shape, texture of images and make the returned list more accurately becomes an interesting research topic.

The existing visual search reranking methods can be classified as follows. Graph-based method [1–6] can effectively search images for Web-scale search engine and has therefore received increased attention. Firstly, it treats each image as a node and builds a graph on them. An edge is defined between two images if they are visual neighbors of each other and the edges are weighted by the visual similarities between the images. Then, reranking can be formulated, such as random walk over the graph [1–5] or an energy minimization problem [6]. PageRank method [7] is similar to the random walk in some aspect. The PageRank algorithm is used to rank the importance of each node according to the number of edges linking to it. Classification model [8–12] chooses some pseudo-relevant images from the initial search result. These pseudo-relevant/-irrelevant images are then regarded as training data for a classifier or a ranking model to be learnt and to be built. Clustering method [13] groups the images returned from initial ranking list into several clusters. Then the reranking result is generated by ordering the clusters according to the cluster conditional probability and then by ordering the samples within a cluster based on their cluster membership value.

The image annotation, classification, and retrieval methods are normally based on the global features, i.e. to extract features from the whole image. However, for some classes such as "cow", "cat", etc., the features extracted from the whole image may contain the information from the background part. So how to extract the salient features and interesting region becomes important.

There are some methods about how to detect salient region or region of interest (ROI). Specifically, in [14, 15], low-level visual features such as color, intensity, and orientation are extracted at different scales to form the saliency maps (SMs). And the SMs from different feature channels are combined to form the final SM. These methods are in the manner of bottom-up. The others are top-down methods [16, 17]. These methods consider the images and the class they belonging to form the vocabulary and find the representative words to represent the class. Specifically, local features such as SIFT of points from images of all classes are clustered to form the vocabulary of images. Then the images belonging to one specific class are used to select the words for discriminating the class. Finally, the points having same words with the top selected words are used to form the bounding box of ROI of one class appearing in the image. Then not only the image low level visual features are used, but also the class information is used.

Considering the different aspects that Exemplar model and SM focus on, we propose a method that combines the advantages of them. The method performs well in not only object classes but also scene classes. It is a method combining top-down and bottom-up information.

The paper is organized as follows. Section 2 describes the method to detect discriminative and salient features and how to combine them for image reranking. Section 3 gives experimental details. And we conclude our work in Section 4.

2   Reranking Method

2.1   Preparation

In the training phase, there are N images in each class in the initial retrieved results. We assume that top n images are positive samples, and uses other sampled images from the list as negative ones. Then we use a training model to learn among these training images to build each class model. Finally, rerank the first obtained retrieval results based on the model.

2.2   Exemplar Based Model

Exemplar model [16] is first proposed by Chum and Zisserman to detect the objects in images in VOC Challenge. In the training phase, it uses SIFT of points from images of all classes to build a vocabulary of size L. Then it selects l words from the vocabulary to build each class model. These l words are selected based on the criterion that they have high occurrence rate in the images from one class. After that, the points having same words with the top selected words are used to form the first bounding box of the class instance in one image. Considering the scale, translation change problems, the discriminative words are re-extracted from the translated and enlarged bounding box based on the initialized bounding box. Then we can get the W discriminative words in each class model, and we use these discriminative words as our new class model to make our model more accurate. In the reranking phase, we also select discriminative words for each class based on the initial ranking results. Then we use the following formulation to calculate the score of each image for the query class.

$$S_{Ex} = \sum_{i=1}^{W} (e(w_i) * n(w_i)). \tag{1}$$

where $e(w_i)$ represents the value of w_i appearing in the trained vocabulary, $n(w_i)$ the number of the w_i in the test image, and W is the the number of visual words appearing in the model. Last, we sort them from high to low to get the new rank list.

2.3   Saliency Map Based Model

We employ Saliency Map (SM) [18] to rerank the images as a bottom-up method. In the training phase, we first obtain the SM image with each pixel having saliency value computed based on summed color, intensity, orientation saliency values on the retrieved image. Then we set a threshold τ to get the salient pixels. If the SM value ($s(w_i)$) of the pixel is higher than τ, we consider it as a salient pixel and extract SIFT on these points, then do k-means clustering on all salient pixels to form the model for a specific class. In the reranking phase, we do the same procedure to each image in the returned list. Then we compute the sum of the salient pixel values for the image, where the salient pixel also appears in its model. Finally, we sort images by their scores from high to low as the new rank list. The score formulation is given as following:

$$\mathrm{S_{SM}} = \sum_{i=1}^{W} (s(w_i) * m(w_i)), \text{if } s(w_i) > \tau. \tag{2}$$

where $m(w_i)$ represents the number of w_i in the test image.

2.4   Combination of Exemplar Model and SM

Based on the property of Exemplar model, it detects discriminative words in the images and build the model to evaluate the image. Thus it performs well in the object classes because of the same object has lots of same visual words, and for scene images like "wedding" which differ a lot, the method cannot perform well. While SM method which detects the salient pixels in the images, for scene images it can perform better than Exemplar model. According to the above analysis, we propose a method which combines the properties of Exemplar model and SM Model (ExSM) and can perform well in both object and scene images. The formulation can be derived as follows:

$$\begin{aligned}
\mathrm{S_{ExSM}} &\propto p(w|SM, Ex) \\
&\propto p(SM, Ex|w)p(w) \\
&\propto p(SM|Ex, w)p(Ex|w)p(w)
\end{aligned} \tag{3}$$

where $p(w)$ represents the probability of visual word w. Since SM and Exemplar model focus on different aspects of the images, we assume $p(SM)$ is independent of $p(Ex)$, Then $p(SM|Ex, w)$ can be rewritten as $p(SM|w)$, and the derivation can be written as:

$$\mathrm{S_{ExSM}} \propto p(SM|w)p(Ex|w)p(w) \tag{4}$$

In this derivation, we assume the words that appears highly in both Exemplar model and SM can be recognized as discriminative and salient words in the images. Then the $p(SM|w)$ and $p(Ex|w)$ can be multiplied as a weight factor for w.

The above derivation can be written as the following formulation:

$$\mathrm{S_{ExSM}} = \sum_{i=1}^{W} (e(w_i) * p(Ex|w_i) * s(w_i) * p(SM|w_i)) \tag{5}$$

where $p(Ex|w_i)$ is the probability when the w_i appears that it belongs to Exemplar model, and the same to $p(SM|w_i)$, $e(w_i)$ is the value in Exemplar model of w_i, $s(w_i)$ is the value in SM model. This formulation explains that when both $p(Ex|w_i)$ and $p(SM|w_i)$ are all high that the S_{ExSM} will be high. So only $p(Ex|w_i)$ or $p(SM|w_i)$ can not help a lot. From the formulation, we can see that it can overcome the weakness of Exemplar and Saliency model. The key points only appear in one model which are not recognized as the key points of ExSM, and the key points appearing in both models are key points in ExSM.

3   Experiments

3.1   Experiment Setting and Performance Evaluation

We search some keywords [1] in Flickr and obtain first ranking results used for reranking. These keywords include object classes such as aeroplane, cat, car, etc., and scene classes such as America, China, wedding, etc. The initial ranking list returned by Flickr is mostly according to the popularity of the image which reflects the users' preference. In our database, each class contains 100 images. We assume top results are mostly related to the topic, so training positive images of the specific class are selected from top 20 images in the list.

We use Normalized Discounted Cumulative Gain (NDCG), which is a measure of effectiveness of a Web search engine algorithm or related applications, often used in information retrieval. Using a graded relevance scale of documents in a search engine result set, NDCG measures the usefulness, or gain, of a document based on its position in the result list. The gain is accumulated from the top of the result list to the bottom with the gain of each result discounted at lower ranks. Given a ranking list, the NDCG score at position n is defined as,

$$\text{NDCG}_n = Z_n \sum_{i=1}^{n} \frac{2^{r_i} - 1}{\log_2(1 + i)}. \tag{6}$$

where r_i is the relevance score of ith image, Z_n is the normalization factor which is used to guarantee the best ranking list's $NDCG_n$ is 1, and the score is the higher the better.

3.2   Experimental Results and Analysis

Figure 2 shows the key points in images by Exemplar model, SM, and ExSM model. For the "bottle" image shown in Figure 2(b), the key points are mostly distributed in the dark background. Since the dark color are more salient than the bottle color, SM recognizes the background as the salient region. On the contrary, for the "bottle" image in Figure 2(a), we can observe that most key points are on the bottle. Since the Exemplar

---

[1] Aeroplane, America, apple, architecture, Australia, beach, bicycle, bird, boat, bottle, bus, car, cat, chair, China, city, cow, dining table, dog, eiffel tower, Europe, horse, London, motorbike, person, potted plant, rainbow, sea, sheep, sofa, sun, train, tv, Venus planet, wedding.

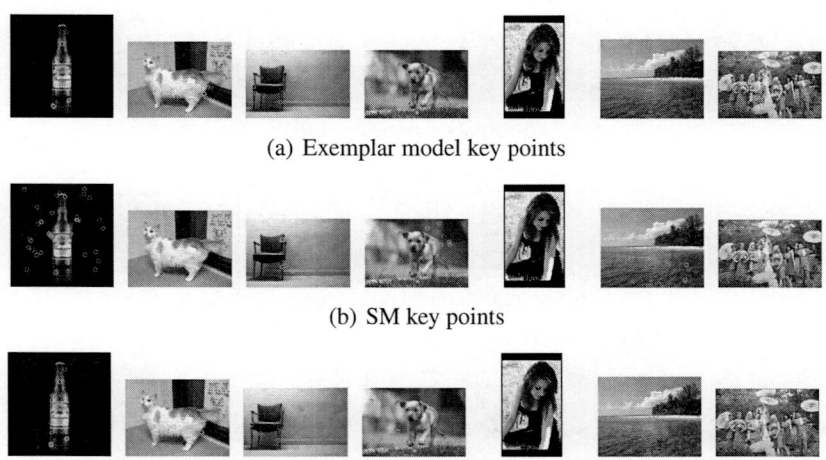

Fig. 2. The key points on images of seven different classes: object (bottle, cat, chair, dog, person) and scene (sea, wedding) returned by Exemplar model, SM, and ExSM

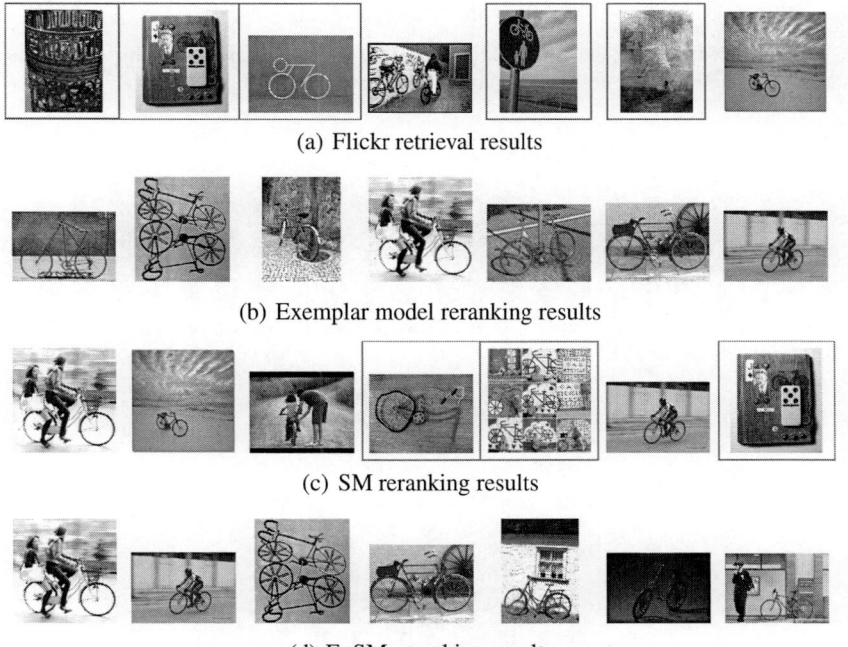

Fig. 3. Top 7 "bicycle" images of Flickr retrieval results, reranking results by using Exemplar model, SM, and ExSM

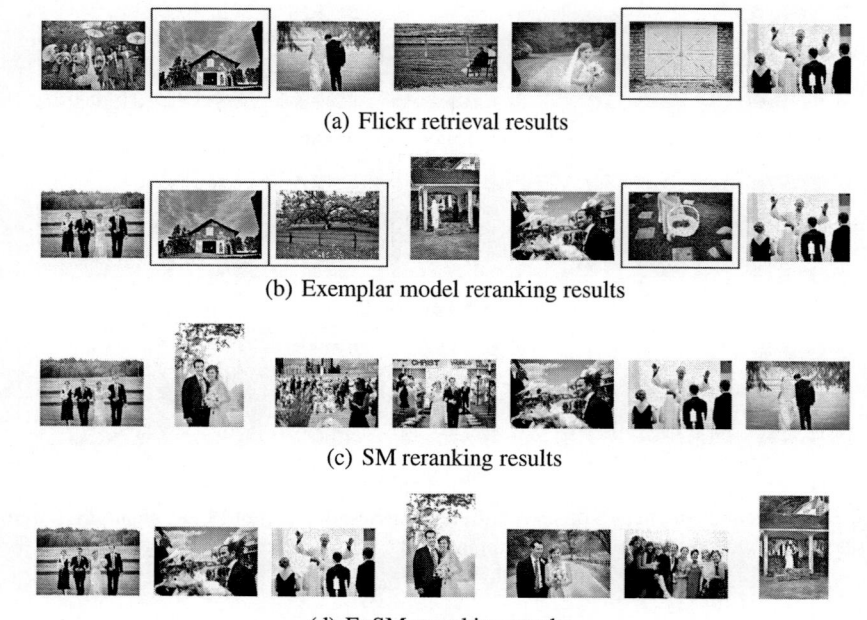

(a) Flickr retrieval results

(b) Exemplar model reranking results

(c) SM reranking results

(d) ExSM reranking results

Fig. 4. Top 7 "wedding" images of Flickr retrieval results, reranking results by using Exemplar model, SM, and ExSM

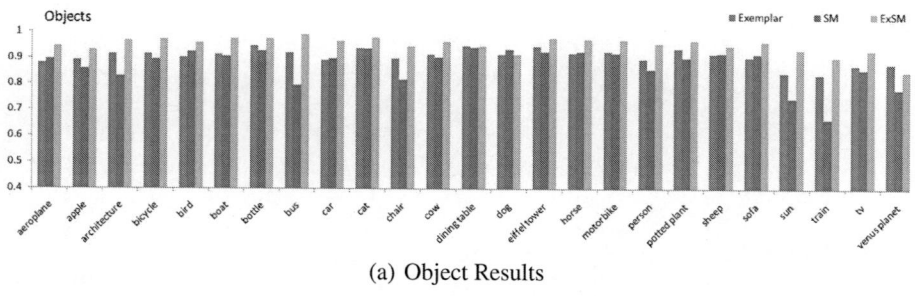

(a) Object Results

(b) Scene Results

Fig. 5. Performance of the reranking methods

model extracts the discriminative features belonging to one specific class, it can resolve the background problem. So we can see that the key points in ExSM model which combines Exemplar model and SM get better result than SM. For the other object class images, we can also observe the same results. But for last three scene images (i.e. sea, and wedding), SM performs better than Exemplar model, and ExSM can perform better than Exemplar model due to it combines the results of SM. So, the combination with SM and Examplar model can overcome the shortage of using one method alone. So we think the ExSM is fitted to rerank both objects and scenes. Figure 2(c) shows the key points of ExSM model that combines the advantages of Exemplar model and SM. It performs well not only in object but also scene images. Key points mostly appear in both Exemplar and SM model. Some key points appear only in SM or Exemplar just appear little in ExSM model.

Figure 3 and Figure 4 show the retrieval results of "bicycle" and "wedding" returned by Flickr respectively. In these two different classes, we can observe clearly that Exemplar model performs well in object class of "bicycle" and SM performs better in scene class of "wedding". In the initial retrieval results by Flickr, there are still some images with red rectangle which are not relevant to the keywords in Figure 3(a) and Figure 4(a). In Figure 3, reranking results returned by SM and Exemplar model all improve the original result, but Exemplar model obviously outperforms SM. And for ExSM, the result is still very well. We can observe that the positive images are arranged on the top and some negative images in SM result are listed bottom in its top list, which are labeled using a red rectangle in the list. As a comparison, in Figure 4, where SM performs better than Exemplar model in the "wedding" images. We can obverse there are three negative images in Figure 4(b). In contrast, the top images of Figure 4(c) are all positive ones. And still, ExSM also performs well in the scene classes.

Figure 5 shows the NDCG results of the three methods. From this diagram, we can observe that Exemplar model and SM all improve the results of original search results returned by Flickr. But they perform different in object and scene images. Specifically, Exemplar model performs better than SM for most objects, while SM performs better than Exemplar model for scenes.

Table 1 illustrates the mean and standard deviation of NDCG results for Exemplar model, SM and ExSM methods. Specifically, μ_{all} is mean NDCG for all classes, μ_{obj} for object classes, and μ_{sce} for scene classes. And the same is for the standard deviation σ.

Table 1. The mean and standard deviation of image reranking performance by using Exemplar model, SM and ExSM methods

	μ_{all}	μ_{obj}	μ_{sce}	σ_{all}	σ_{obj}	σ_{sce}
Exemplar	0.857	**0.939**	0.775	0.091	**0.028**	0.067
SM	0.872	0.836	**0.908**	0.065	0.067	**0.056**
ExSM	**0.946**	**0.951**	**0.941**	**0.047**	**0.024**	**0.054**

It can also be observed from Table 1 that Exemplar model performs better than SM on object classes, i.e. larger mean value and smaller standard variation value, and SM performs better for scene classes. Furthermore, combination of Exemplar model and SM Model helps to detect the key points which are both discriminant in Exemplar model and salient in SM, and can obtain improved reranking performance.

4   Conclusions

We propose in this paper a reranking to combine the properties of Exemplar model and SM. Specifically, the key points and words extracted by the method are both discriminative and salient to the retrieved object and scene classes. Experimental results show that Exemplar model based method performs better for object classes, and SM based method performs better for scene classes. Furthermore, the combination of the two methods can obtain improved performance for both object and scene classes.

Acknowledgements. This work is supported in part by 973 Program (Project No. 2010CB327900), Natural Science Foundation of China (No. 61170094), Shanghai Committee of Science and Technology, China (No. 11ZR1403400), and National High Technology Research and Development Program of China (No. 2011AA100701).

References

1. Hsu, W.H., Kennedy, L.S., Chang, S.F.: Reranking Methods for Visual Search. IEEE Multi-Media 14(3), 14–22 (2007)
2. Yan, R., Hauptmann, A.G.: Co-retrieval: a boosted reranking approach for video retrieval. IEE Proceedings - Vision, Image and Signal Processing 152(6), 888–895 (2005)
3. Tan, H.-K., Ngo, C.-W., Wu, X.: Modeling video hyperlinks with hypergraph for web video reranking. In: Proceeding of the 16th ACM International Conference on Multimedia, pp. 659–662. ACM, New York (2008)
4. Hsu, W.H., Kennedy, L.S., Chang, S.-F.: Video search reranking through random walk over document-level context graph. In: Proceedings of the 15th International Conference on Multimedia, pp. 971–980. ACM, New York (2007)
5. Jing, Y., Baluja, S.: VisualRank: Applying PageRank to Large-Scale Image Search. IEEE Transactions on Pattern Analysis and Machine Intelligence 30, 1877–1890 (2008)
6. Tian, X., Yang, L., Wang, J., Yang, Y., Wu, X., Hua, X.S.: Bayesian video search reranking. In: ACM Multimedia Conference, pp. 131–140 (2008)
7. Jing, Y., Baluja, S.: Pagerank for product image search. In: Proceeding of the 17th International Conference on World Wide Web, pp. 307–316. ACM, New York (2008)
8. Schroff, F., Criminisi, A., Zisserman, A.: Harvesting image databases from the web. In: IEEE 11th International Conference on Computer Vision, pp. 1–8 (2007)
9. Yang, L., Hanjalic, A.: Supervised reranking for web image search. In: Proceedings of the International Conference on Multimedia, pp. 183–192. ACM, New York (2010)
10. Liu, Y., Mei, T., Hua, X.-S., Tang, J., Wu, X., Li, S.: Learning to video search rerank via pseudo preference feedback. In: IEEE International Conference on Multimedia and Expo (23, 2008)
11. Yan, R., Hauptmann, E., Jin, R.: Multimedia search with pseudo-relevance feedback. In: Intl Conf. on Image and Video Retrieval, pp. 238–247 (2003)
12. Yang, Y.-H., Hsu, W.H.: Video search reranking via online ordinal reranking. In: IEEE International Conference on Multimedia and Expo, pp. 285–288 (2008)

13. van Leuken, R.H., Garcia, L., Olivares, X., van Zwol, R.: Visual diversification of image search results. In: Proceedings of the 18th International Conference on World Wide Web, pp. 341–350. ACM, New York (2009)
14. Elazary, L., Itti, L.: Interesting objects are visually salient. Journal of Vision 8(3), 1–15 (2008)
15. Itti, L., Koch, C., Niebur, E.: A model of saliency-based visual attention for rapid scene analysis. TPAMI 20(11), 1254–1259 (1998)
16. Chum, O., Zisserman, A.: An exemplar model for learning object classes. In: CVPR (2007)
17. Wei, R., Lu, H., Zheng, Y., Cen, L., Jin, C., Xue, X., Wu, W.: How context helps: A discriminative codeword selection method for object detection. In: 17th IEEE International Conference on Image Processing, pp. 3905–3908 (2010)
18. Harel, J., Koch, C., Perona, P.: Graph-based visual saliency. In: Advances in Neural Information Processing Systems 19, pp. 545–552. MIT Press (2007)

Real-Time Markerless Hand Gesture Recognition with Depth Camera

Shuxin Qin, Xiaoyang Zhu, Haitao Yu, Shuiying Ge,
Yiping Yang, and Yongshi Jiang

The Integrated Information System Research Center,
Institute of Automation, Chinese Academy of Sciences
Beijing, China

Abstract. This paper presents a novel method for markerless hand gesture recognition with a recently developed depth sensor. The proposed method encompasses a collection of techniques that enable the modeling and recognition of hand gestures. Hand detection and location are processed with the depth information acquired from a depth sensor. Then, the hand is robustly segmented in cluttered background without any marker around using only depth information. A convex shape decomposition method based on Radius Morse function is proposed for hand shape decomposition in real time. Hand palm and fingertips are recognized based on the hand shape decomposition and hand features. A prototype implementation of the developed system operates on 640x480 live video with both depth image and color image in real time on a conventional processor. Representative experimental results prove the accuracy, efficiency and robustness of our method.

1 Introduction

Hand gesture recognition is a challenging problem. Real time hand gesture recognition affords users the ability to interact with computers in more natural and intuitive ways. So, it is fully used in virtual reality and computer games [1]. Conventional hand gesture recognition systems detect and segment hands based on the methods including using color gloves [2], and skin color detection [3][4][5][6][7], both of which have advantages and drawbacks. These methods are vision-based and far from satisfactory for real-time applications in varied environments. Other hand gesture recognition systems detect and segment hands using marker-aided methods [2][8]. These methods are inconvenient because people must wear something before experiencing.

The key problem in gesture interaction is how to make hand gesture understood by computers. Extra instruments or sensors, such as data gloves, might be very easy to collect hand state information. However, these equipments are expensive and inconvenient to users. So, markerless and vision based hand gesture interaction has many appealing advantages.

W. Lin et al. (Eds.): PCM 2012, LNCS 7674, pp. 186–197, 2012.

1.1   Scale-Space Feature Based Detection

Since Lindberg published his work on scale-space framework for geometric features detection [9], scale-space feature detection has been widely applied in object recognition, image processing and registering etc. Bretzner and Fang use scale-space feature detection to detect blob and ridge structures of hand [5][10][11]. Both of them define palm and fingers as blob and ridges. However, the scale space feature detection is time-consuming for real-time applications. What's more, it is not robust in cluttered background because shapes that are similar with palm and fingers in background will affect the detection results. Although Fang improves the detectors to reduce the computation cost for real-time hand gesture recognition, the accuracy of the recognition is decreased [11].

1.2   Color Based Segmentation

Many researchers work on the color based skin segmentation [4][5][6]. Lee uses skin color segmentation for hand AR(Augmented Reality) [4], which requires a high accuracy of hand contour. He uses a skin color based classifier with an adaptively learned skin color histogram. However, this method needs a lot of training samples and results in a poor performance in robustness to lighting variations. Argyros selects a suitable color space to reduce the effect caused by background and illumination [6]. What's more, a technique is proposed that permits the avoidance of much of the burden involved in the process of generating training data in his work [6]. But this method is also easy to affect by non-hand skin area and skin-like object surface.

1.3   Depth Based Gesture Recognition

In order to avoid the problems described above, depth image based gesture interactions are studied and developed [8][12][13][14][15]. Thanks to the recent development of inexpensive depth cameras, such as Kinect sensor, new opportunities for gesture recognition emerge. Although there are many recent successful applications for human body tracking [14] and face recognition [15], it is still an challenge to use the low-resolution depth map for hand gesture recognition. A robust hand gesture recognition system using Kinect depth map is developed [8] and used in some applications successfully. However, the user need to wear a black belt on the gesturing hand's wrist, which is inconvenient for users. Another research on 3D tracking of hand articulations using Kinect [13] presents a good work on modeling a hand, but they segment the hand using skin color method, which can be easily confused by face, bared arm and skin-liked objects. Real-time human pose recognition from single depth images [14] is proposed. They present a new method to predict 3D positions of body joints from a single depth image with training data, which proves the practical applicability of depth information. Another type of tracking and recognition method is based on time-of-flight (ToF) camera. By employing a ToF camera, a system, which is capable of reliably recognizing gestures at the finger level in real-time, is constructed

[16]. A method for human full-body pose estimation from ToF camera images is presented in [17]. Their method can track various full-body movements, including self-occlusions and estimate 3D full-body poses with a high accuracy. However, the method based on ToF camera is hard to provide an accurate result on hand gesture recognition because of its low-resolution depth images. The original depth data from depth sensor, such as Kinect, contains a numerous occlusions and uncovered areas because of the device and environments. So, some studies try to inpaint a low-resolution depth map to obtain an applicable depth map for some recognition work [18][19]. Their work solve the problem on some level but the processing procedure is time-consuming if a better result is required. Thus, it's hard to use a time-consuming method in a real-time system.

1.4 Proposed Approach

This paper presents a novel method that segments hand precisely only based on depth information without marker. With the help of depth map inpainting and filtering, an ideal hand contour is available in real-time. With the hand contour, a new robust hand recognition method is proposed. Our hand recognition method is based on approximate convex shape decomposition [20] which is very useful in some graphics and vision tasks. The method is smart designed for real-time applications compared with the conventional convex shape decomposition which is time-consuming. Applying this shape decomposition method, the hand is decomposed to palm and fingers, which are useful for gesture recognition. Fingertips are detected using a smart method with the fingers acquired by the decomposition. Thus, the most important information from the candidate hand gesture is detected and obtained as we want. A simple hand gesture dataset is collected to test the efficiency and accuracy of our method. The results reveal that the employed method is very efficient, computationally. The rest of the paper is organized as follows. Section 2 presents the hand detection and segmentation. Section 3 provides the hand shape decomposition and fingertip detection. Section 4 provides experiments and test results of the hand shape decomposition and the hand gesture recognition. Section 5 presents the main conclusions of this work as well as extensions that are under investigation.

2   Hand Detection and Segmentation

2.1   Hand Detection

Hand detection is the first step of hand gesture recognition, so it is the basis of the subsequent steps. There are many methods for only detection the hand on the image. Different from the conventional color based hand detection, we choose the depth map as the input information, which is obtained from Kinect sensor. As for hand interaction, the user need to make sure that the hand is facing the sensor and without any obstacles between the hand and sensor. Thus, by thresholding from the nearest depth position with a certain gap a rough hand region can be easily detected, as shown in Fig. 1(a) and Fig. 1(b).

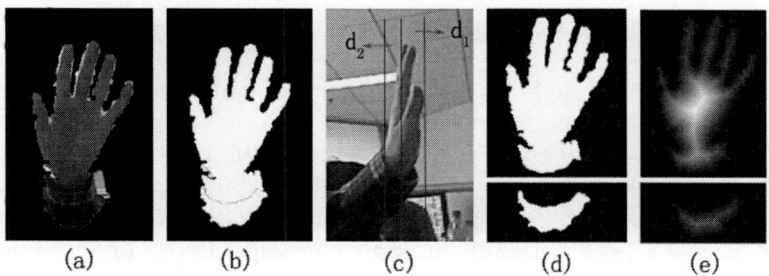

Fig. 1. (a) The rough hand region; (b) The binary rough hand region; (c) The segmentation gap(d_1 and d_2); (d) The binary rough hand region and wrist region; (e) Distance Transform of (d).

2.2 Hand Segmentation

As for Fig. 1(b), wrist is included in the rough hand region, which makes the hand recognition difficult. So, a smart method is proposed as shown in Fig. 1(c). First, we choose a gap d_1 to segment a rough hand region. Then, we use another gap d_2 to segment the region which stands for wrist. The two regions segmented are shown in Fig. 1(d) and Fig. 1(e) presents the results of the Fig. 1(d) after Distance Transform respectively. We choose the maximum distance point of each Distance Transform result as the center of the region that is shown in Fig. 2(a) as c_0 and c_1. We define $R_{in}(x, y)$ and $R_{out}(x, y)$ as the input and output regions of hand; define $l(x, y, d)$ as the cut line function where d is the distance of c_0 to this line. So, the accurate hand region is computed employing the following rule:

$$R_{out}(x, y) = l(x, y, d) < 0 \cap R_{in}(x, y) \qquad (1)$$

Because our hand detection and segmentation method is based on depth map obtained from Kinect sensor, the hand region on the binary hand region map may be have holes and cracks, which will seriously affect the accuracy of hand shape decomposition. Although some inpainting and filtering methods [19][21][22] are able to get better results, the algorithms are too complex to be used in real-time applications. We choose the simple morphological operations to obtain an applicable result.

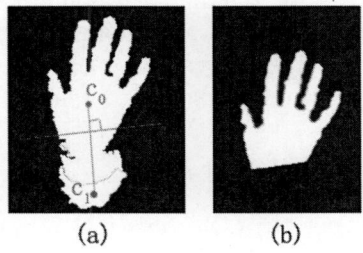

Fig. 2. (a) Hand center c_0 and wrist center c_1; (b) Hand region after cut

3   Hand Shape Decomposition

As we know, shape decomposition is very useful in shape analysis, shape matching, topology extraction, collision detection and other geometric processing methods employing divide-and-conquer strategies [20]. Lien and Amato propose methods to decompose polygons into approximately convex parts [23]. However, their methods usually result in smaller number of parts. Mi and DeCarlo present methods to decompose shapes taking into account relativity to determine part boundaries [24]. However, their methods are complicated and time-consuming.

We now present our main idea about hand shape decomposition. Our method is inspired by the convex shape decomposition idea [8][20], which employs the Reeb graph and Morse functions to compute candidate cuts. However, their algorithms compute multiple Morse functions from a number of directions, which is inefficient. As proposed in [20], each decomposed part may not be strictly convex, thus a parameter ε which indicates the convex tolerance of the decomposed parts is defined. Formally, for a shape S, $R(S, \varepsilon)$ is defined as a decomposition that the concavity of every decomposed part is no more than ε. So, $R(S, \varepsilon) = \cup_{i=1}^{n} P_i$, $\forall_{i \neq j} P_i \cap P_j = \emptyset$ and $\forall_{i \leqslant n} Concavity(P_i) \leqslant \varepsilon$, where n is the number of decomposed parts, P_i is a decomposed part and the degree of its concavity is denoted by $Concavity(P_i)$ which is proposed in [20].

As is described in [20], the $Concavity(P_i)$ is measured by projecting the shape contour in multiple Morse functions, which is obtained by changing the projecting direction. As shown in Fig. 3(a) and [20], Morse function $f : M \rightarrow S$, is constructed using the Height Function, and the Reeb graph [25] is determined by the changes in the number of connected components of f^{-1}. In Fig. 3(b) the Reeb graph has three nodes, which reflects partial topological information of the shape in Fig. 3(a). However, multiple Morse functions must be computed because the topological information of the shapes is assumed to be unknown to users. This is similar to brute force computing. In order to better use this method on hand shape decomposition, a new Morse function is proposed as shown in Fig. 4(a). The new Morse function f is constructed as follows: for every point p in this object, $f(p)$ is the distance between the point p and the central point o, thus called Radius Function. Same as the Height based Morse function, the Reeb graph is shown in Fig. 4(b). The radius based Morse function is efficient in hand shape decomposition because only one Morse function is computed for the decomposition when the central point o is specified. The feasibility of radius based Morse function is based on the topological information of the hand, which is already known to users. As we know, the topological structure of a hand can be defined as a palm and some fingers which are outward around the palm. Moreover, the angles of any two fingers are less than π.

3.1   Candidate Cuts and Cost of Cuts

In order to solve the problem $\forall_{i \leqslant n} Concavity(P_i) \leqslant \varepsilon$, candidate cuts that can separate a shape S with $Concavity(S_i) > \varepsilon$, can be found. The way to find a shape S_i with $Concavity(S_i) > \varepsilon$ is to use the Reeb graph constructed from

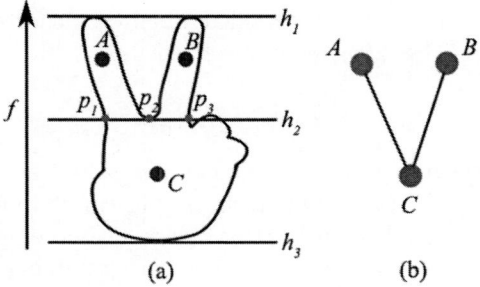

Fig. 3. (a) Height based Morse function of a hand gesture; (b) The Reeb Graph

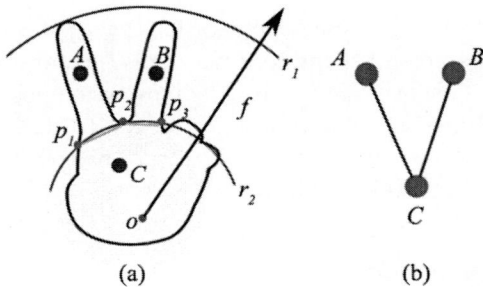

Fig. 4. (a) Radius based Morse function of a hand gesture; (b) The Reeb Graph

Radius based Morse function f. The cuts between adjacent nodes of the Reeb graph are all candidate cuts. All the n candidate cuts of a shape S form a candidate cut set, denoted by $C\,(S) = \{cut_1, \cdots, cut_n\}$. The final decomposition consists of a subset of $C\,(S)$, denoted by $I\,(S) \subseteq C\,(S)$. A binary variable is assigned to each cut_i in $C\,(S)$, as is shown:

$$x_i = \begin{cases} 1 & cut_i \in I\,(S) \\ 0 & cut_i \notin I\,(S) \end{cases} \tag{2}$$

Thus $\mathbf{x} = (x_1, x_2, \cdots, x_n)^{\mathrm{T}}$ is a binary vector indicating the selectivity of cuts from $C\,(S)$. Each is assigned a value to weight the cost of the cut, denoted by $w\,(cut_i)$. Define $\mathbf{w} = (w\,(cut_1), w\,(cut_2), \cdots, w\,(cut_n))^{\mathrm{T}}$, thus a decomposition problem is translated in to a integer linear programming and we use the same method proposed in [20] to solve the programming problem:

$$\min \mathbf{w}^{\mathrm{T}}\mathbf{x} \qquad x_i \in \{0, 1\} \tag{3}$$

For a given cut cut_i, $w\,(cut_i)$ is defined as function (4):

$$w\,(cut_i) = \frac{length\,(cut_i)}{dist\,(cut_i, o) - r} \tag{4}$$

where $length\,(cut_i)$ is the length of cut_i, $dist\,(cut_i, o)$ is the distance between central point o and cut_i, r is the palm radius calculated by Distance Transform of the shape. The central point o is specified when the accurate hand region is segmented. As shown in Fig. 2(a), c_0, c_1 are two centers. Thus o is calculated as following:

$$\mathbf{c_0 o} = \lambda \cdot \mathbf{c_0 c_1} \qquad 0 < \lambda < 1 \qquad (5)$$

Thus, the overall procedure of our method is descripted as: compute central point o; compute Morse function and Reeb Graph; compute candidate cut set $C(S)$; for each cut_i in $C(S)$, compute $w(cut_i)$, check whether cut_i intersect with already checked cuts and finally solve the linear programming problem (3).

3.2 Results of Hand Shape Decomposition

To test the result of hand shape segmentation, two parameters ε and λ are specified. ε is the threshold of shape concavity, λ is the parameter to specify the central point o. Fig. 5 shows the results of shape decomposition with different central point and shape concavity. In Fig. 5, (b), (c), (d) use the same threshold of shape concavity $\varepsilon = 10$, and (e) $\varepsilon = 4$. When given proper parameters, usable results are shown in Fig. 6(c), in which the palm and fingers are well splitted.

3.3 Fingertips Detection

Fingertips are detected from the result of the hand shape decomposition. From the shape decomposition the fingers and palm are easy to find. The decomposed shape with hand center is a palm shape and others are finger shapes. For a finger shape S, there is a corresponding cut denoted as cut_i. The fingertip point P_{tip} is defined as:

$$P_{tip} = \{P_j | \max \, dist \, (cut_i, P_j), P_j \in S\} \qquad (6)$$

which means that the fingertip is the point on the finger shape with the maximum distance against the cut line. The validity of this method is based on the convexity of the finger shape and the topological structure of a hand. The fingertips detection results are shown in Fig. 7, where the red contours are the recognized hand shape contours, the green circles are the hand palm centers and the black circles stand for the detected fingertips in each hand shape.

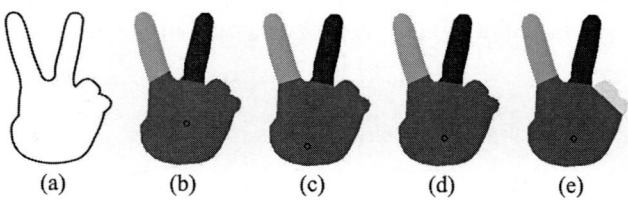

$$\text{(a)} \qquad \text{(b)} \qquad \text{(c)} \qquad \text{(d)} \qquad \text{(e)}$$

Fig. 5. Shape decomposition results. (a) The original shape contour. (b), (c), (d), (e) Decomposition results where the black circle stand for Morse function center.

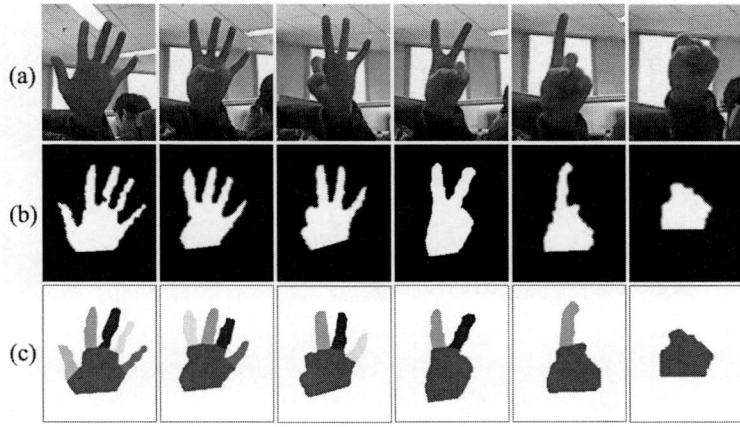

Fig. 6. Hand shape decomposition. (a) The original hand images. (b) The binary hand maps obtained by hand segmentation. (c) Hand shape decomposition results.

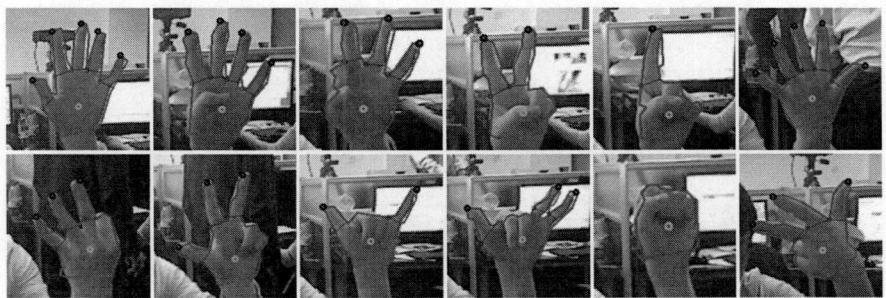

Fig. 7. Fingertips detection results

Each of the fingers has unique functional significance. From the thumb on the radial side to the ulnar side of the hand, the fingers are in this order: Thumb, Index finger, Middle finger, Ring finger, Little finger. With the fingertips detection above, the number of fingers is easy to obtain. If the number of fingers is 5, we only need to find the Thumb or Little finger. But it's hard to recognize the significance of each finger because some of the hand gesture shapes are approximately symmetric as shown in Fig. 8. They are ambiguous to specify. Although it is difficult to specify each of the fingers in some of the hand gesture shapes, it is easy to distinguish them from each other's when using each gesture shape as a whole. So, the number and positions of fingers should be taken into consideration when defining hand gestures in order to avoid ambiguity.

4   Experiments

We use a Kinect sensor as the depth maps collecting device and all the experiments operate in real-time on a conventional processor. With the information

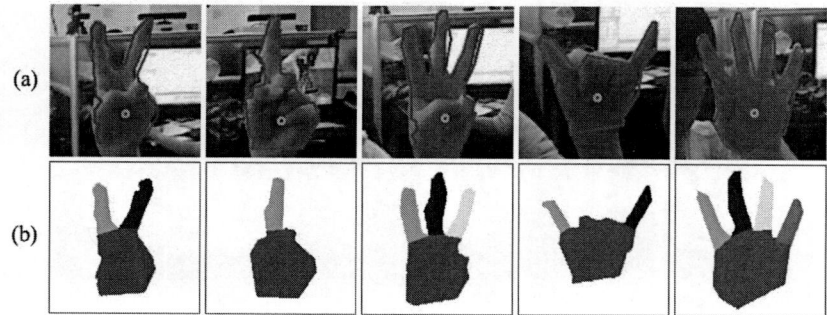

Fig. 8. (a) Original hand gesture shapes and contours; (b) Symmetric decomposed shapes according to (a) respectively

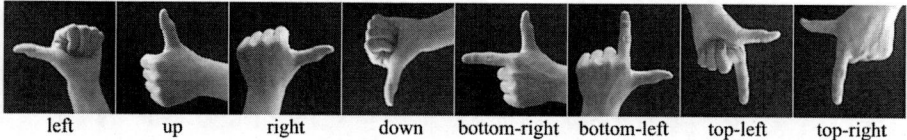

left   up   right   down   bottom-right   bottom-left   top-left   top-right

Fig. 9. Gesture definition

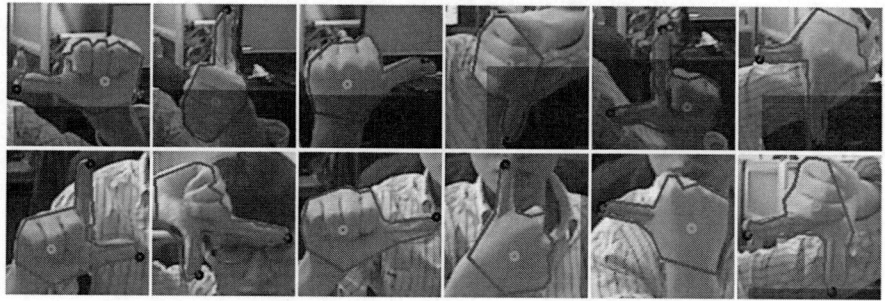

Fig. 10. Sample results for gesture recognition

of the hand gesture shapes described above, it's easy to define a simple hand gesture dataset to test our method. A simple dataset which use the number of fingers of a hand to present the number is defined, as shown in Fig. 6. What's more, other hand gestures can be designed easily with the help of shape decomposition results and fingertips information obtained using our method. We defined another dataset as shown in Fig. 9. The four directions are presented by Thumb and the four corners of a rectangle are defined by the corners composed of Thumb and Index finger.

To assess the performance of this combined method, more than 2000 frames were recorded in experiments. The experiments are performed in cluttered background by different users. A few sample results are shown in Fig. 10. Table 1

Table 1. Recognition results of the gestures

Gesture	left	up	right	down	bottom-right	bottom-left	top-left	top-right
Total	215	233	242	236	262	271	277	282
Correct	203	213	227	218	237	254	245	243
Accuracy	0.944	0.914	0.938	0.924	0.905	0.937	0.884	0.865

Table 2. Comparison of the our method with the methods in [8]

Method	Accuracy	Running Time
Thresholding Decomposition + FEMD in [8]	90.6%	0.5004s
Near-convex Decomposition + FEMD in [8]	93.9%	4.0012s
Our method	91.2%	0.046s

shows results of the gesture experiments. The average accuracy of recognition in this experiment is about 0.912. The low accuracy of the gesture top-left and top right is caused by the difficulty of posing these gestures. Compared with [8], our method is much more efficient in real-time applications, which is shown in Table 2.

5   Conclusions and Future Work

We present a new measure for markerless hand gesture recognition with depth camera. A novel hand shape segmentation is prepared for accurate hand shape decomposition. In order to decompose hand shape in real-time applications, a new hand shape decomposition method based on Radius Morse function is presented. Fingertips are easy to detected using the hand shape decomposition information. Extensive experiments demonstrate the accuracy, efficiency and robustness of our method. For future work, we will study on the hand tracking the dynamic hand gesture recognition using depth camera. Also, Two-handed static and dynamic gesture multimodal interaction is thus a promising area for future research.

References

1. Wachs, J., Kölsch, M., Stern, H., Edan, Y.: Vision-based hand-gesture applications. Communications of the ACM 54(2), 60–71 (2011)
2. Wang, R., Popović, J.: Real-time hand-tracking with a color glove. ACM Transactions on Graphics (TOG) 28(3) (2009)
3. Lee, T., Hollerer, T.: Handy AR: Markerless inspection of augmented reality objects using fingertip tracking. In: 11th IEEE International Symposium on Wearable Computers, pp. 83–90. IEEE (2007)
4. Lee, T., Hollerer, T.: Multithreaded hybrid feature tracking for markerless augmented reality. IEEE Transactions on Visualization and Computer Graphics 15(3), 355–368 (2009)

5. Bretzner, L., Laptev, I., Lindeberg, T.: Hand gesture recognition using multi-scale colour features, hierarchical models and particle filtering. In: Fifth IEEE International Conference on Automatic Face and Gesture Recognition, pp. 423–428. IEEE (2002)

6. Argyros, A.A., Lourakis, M.I.A.: Real-Time Tracking of Multiple Skin-Colored Objects with a Possibly Moving Camera. In: Pajdla, T., Matas, J. (eds.) ECCV 2004, Part III. LNCS, vol. 3023, pp. 368–379. Springer, Heidelberg (2004)

7. Argyros, A.A., Lourakis, M.I.A.: Vision-Based Interpretation of Hand Gestures for Remote Control of a Computer Mouse. In: Huang, T.S., Sebe, N., Lew, M., Pavlović, V., Kölsch, M., Galata, A., Kisačanin, B. (eds.) HCI/ECCV 2006. LNCS, vol. 3979, pp. 40–51. Springer, Heidelberg (2006)

8. Ren, Z., Yuan, J., Zhang, Z.: Robust hand gesture recognition based on finger-earth mover's distance with a commodity depth camera. In: Proceedings of the 19th ACM International Conference on Multimedia, pp. 1093–1096. ACM (2011)

9. Lindeberg, T.: Feature detection with automatic scale selection. International Journal of Computer Vision 30(2), 79–116 (1998)

10. Fang, Y., Cheng, J., Wang, K., Lu, H.: Hand gesture recognition using fast multi-scale analysis. In: Fourth International Conference on Image and Graphics, ICIG 2007, pp. 694–698. IEEE (2007)

11. Fang, Y., Wang, K., Cheng, J., Lu, H.: A real-time hand gesture recognition method. In: IEEE International Conference on Multimedia and Expo, pp. 995–998. IEEE (2007)

12. Liu, X., Fujimura, K.: Hand gesture recognition using depth data. In: Sixth IEEE International Conference on Automatic Face and Gesture Recognition, pp. 529–534. IEEE (2004)

13. Oikonomidis, I., Kyriazis, N., Argyros, A.: Efficient model-based 3D tracking of hand articulations using kinect. In: Procs. of BMVC, Dundee, UK, August 29-September 10 (2011) [547]

14. Shotton, J., Fitzgibbon, A., Cook, M., Sharp, T., Finocchio, M., Moore, R., Kipman, A., Blake, A.: Real-time human pose recognition in parts from single depth images. In: IEEE Conference on Computer Vision and Pattern Recognition, CVPR, vol. 2, pp. 1297–1304 (2011)

15. Cai, Q., Gallup, D., Zhang, C., Zhang, Z.: 3D Deformable Face Tracking with a Commodity Depth Camera. In: Daniilidis, K., Maragos, P., Paragios, N. (eds.) ECCV 2010, Part III. LNCS, vol. 6313, pp. 229–242. Springer, Heidelberg (2010)

16. Hackenberg, G., McCall, R., Broll, W.: Lightweight palm and finger tracking for real-time 3D gesture control. In: IEEE Virtual Reality Conference, VR, pp. 19–26. IEEE (2011)

17. Schwarz, L., Mkhitaryan, A., Mateus, D., Navab, N.: Estimating human 3D pose from time-of-flight images based on geodesic distances and optical flow. In: IEEE International Conference on Automatic Face & Gesture Recognition and Workshops, FG 2011, pp. 700–706. IEEE (2011)

18. Zhu, J., Wang, L., Yang, R., Davis, J.: Fusion of time-of-flight depth and stereo for high accuracy depth maps. In: IEEE Conference on Computer Vision and Pattern Recognition, pp. 1–8. IEEE (2008)

19. Daribo, I., Saito, H.: A novel inpainting-based layered depth video for 3DTV. IEEE Transactions on Broadcasting (99), 533–541 (2011)

20. Liu, H., Liu, W., Latecki, L.: Convex shape decomposition. In: IEEE Conference on Computer Vision and Pattern Recognition, CVPR, pp. 97–104. IEEE (2010)

21. Telea, A.: An image inpainting technique based on the fast marching method. Journal of Graphics Tools 9(1), 23–34 (2004)

22. Kopf, J., Cohen, M., Lischinski, D., Uyttendaele, M.: Joint bilateral upsampling. ACM Transactions on Graphics 26(3) (2007)
23. Lien, J., Amato, N.: Approximate convex decomposition of polygons. Computational Geometry 35(1), 100–123 (2006)
24. Mi, X., DeCarlo, D.: Separating parts from 2D shapes using relatability. In: IEEE 11th International Conference on Computer Vision, pp. 1–8. IEEE (2007)
25. Cole-McLaughlin, K., Edelsbrunner, H., Harer, J., Natarajan, V., Pascucci, V.: Loops in reeb graphs of 2-manifolds. In: Proceedings of the Nineteenth Annual Symposium on Computational Geometry, pp. 344–350. ACM (2003)

Social Tag Enrichment via Automatic Abstract Tag Refinement

Zhaoqiang Xia[1], Jinye Peng[1], Xiaoyi Feng[1], and Jianping Fan[2]

[1] School of Electronics and Information, Northwestern Polytechnical University,
Xi'an 710029, China
[2] School of Electronics and Information, Northwest University, Xi'an 710069, China
xiazhaoqiang@gmail.com

Abstract. Collaborative image tagging systems, such as Flickr, are very attractive for supporting keyword-based image retrieval, but some social tags of these collaboratively-tagged social images might be imprecise. Some people may use general or high-level words (i.e., abstract tags) to tag their images for saving time and effort, thus such general or high-level tags are too abstract to describe the visual content of social images precisely. As a result, users may not be able to find what they need when they use the specific keywords for query specification. To tackle this problem of abstract tags, a concept ontology is constructed for detecting the abstract tags from large-scale social images. The co-occurrence contexts of social tags and k-NN algorithm with Gaussian Weight are used to find the most specific tags which can signify out the abstract tags. In addition, all the relevant keywords, which are corresponded with intermediate nodes between the high-level concepts (abstract tags) and object classes (most specific tags) on our concept ontology, are added to enrich the lists of social tags, so that users can have more choices to select various keywords for query specification. We have tested our proposed algorithms on two data sets with different images.

Keywords: tag refinement, tag enrichment, concept ontology, co-occurrence contexts, abstract tags.

1 Introduction

Large-scale social medias and their associated personal terms or social tags are more and more popular on the Internet. Collaborative image tagging system, such as Flickr[1], is now a popular way to obtain large set of tagged images easily by relying on the collaborative effort of a large population of Internet users. When users share their images, they would give some tags to describe the content of the corresponding images. With the exponential growth of these social medias, social tagging seems to be the natural way for people to classify and search images on the Internet. Collaborative image tagging has become very popular for people to share, tag and search social images because: (a) keywords are more

---

[1] http://www.flickr.com/

W. Lin et al. (Eds.): PCM 2012, LNCS 7674, pp. 198–209, 2012.

coral,**animal**   sand,**vehicle**

Fig. 1. Examples of abstract tags: images have multiple tags from users and labels with larger font size are the abstract tags

intuitive for most users to specify their images precisely; and (b) automatic image annotation is still imperfect and error-prone due to the semantic gap.

In a collaborative image tagging system, users can tag their images according to their social or cultural backgrounds, personal expertise and perception. We call such collaboratively-tagged social images as *weakly-tagged social images* because there may have huge uncertainty on the relationships between the semantics of social images and their social tags, e.g., individuals may have an incentive to tag their images with terms that are easy for them to remember later, and it is impossible to use a complex, hierarchical, controlled vocabulary for social image tagging. Without controlling the word vocabulary, supporting keyword-based retrieval of large-scale social images may seriously suffer from the problem of *abstract tag*: some abstract tags, which correspond to high-level image concepts rather than more specific real-world object classes, are used for social image tagging and users cannot find the relevant social images when they use more specific object tags rather than abstract tags for query formulation.

In this paper, we focus on the problem how to identify the abstract tags from the tag lists and find most specific tags for these abstract tags which can be used to enrich the tag lists. For example, the tags of social images may be like in Fig. 1. The words "animal" and "vehicle" can be used to describe the content of two images, however, they are too general for the content. For the specific query formulation, it is more appropriate to add the words "fish, sea-fish" and "car, off-road vehicles" to refine and enrich the list of social tags. The replaced words can enrich the list of social tags for image content description. Our assumption is that some users may always like to use abstract tags to tag the images. Thus it is very attractive to develop new algorithms for abstract tag refinement and enrichment.

The abstract tags, which correspond to high-level image concepts rather than more specific real-world object classes, may not be able to find the relevant image regions from the social images. As a result, we cannot assign such abstract tags into the most relevant image regions. To enrich the social tags for social image indexing and retrieval, it is very important to refine the abstract tags into the most relevant object tags. Our abstract tag refinement algorithm consists of two key components: (a) automatic abstract tag identification via searching from a concept ontology; and (b) abstract tag refinement, e.g., determining the most relevant object tags.

Our algorithm for abstract tags refinement and enrichment consists of 3 key components as shown in Fig. 2: (a) using a concept ontology to determine

Fig. 2. The framework of our algorithm for abstract tag refinement and enrichment

whether a given social tag is abstract tag or not; (b) incorporating the concept ontology and the co-occurrence contexts of social tags to narrow the search scope of finding the most specific object tags, where k-NN algorithm with Gaussian Weight is used to determine the most specific object tags; and (c) enriching the lists of social tags by adding the text terms for interpreting the intermediate nodes between the nodes of abstract tags and the nodes for most specific object tags on our concept ontology.

The rest of this paper is organized as follows. Section 2 reviews the related work briefly; Section 3 presents our work on concept ontology construction; Section 4 introduces our work on calculating the co-occurrence contexts for narrowing the search scope; Section 5 presents the algorithm for tag enrichment; Section 6 introduces our experimental results for algorithm evaluation; Section 7 introduces the conclusion and future work.

2   Related Work

Some related works have been done to remove the noisy tags and enrich the tags of images from collaborative tagging systems [1,4,6,7,16,17]. Fan *et al.* [4] develop a new framework to build up image database automatically from collaborative image tagging system, and the tags which are synonymous or polysemous or even spam are cleaned through cross-modal tag cleansing and junk image filtering. Tang *et al.* [16] propose sparse graph-based semi-supervised learning approach to deal with the noisy tags. Liu *et al.* [6] develop a retagging scheme to refine and enrich the tags. Bucak *et al.* [1] utilize multi-label learning algorithm for building up the image classifiers with some missing tags. Yang *et al.* [17] propose a new scheme to detect the regions of tags in images and add six properties of each tag to enrich the tags of images. These works focus on refining the inaccurate tags (i.e., irrelevant tags) other than the abstract tags.

Some pioneering works have been done to utilize the specify domain knowledge to build up the concept ontology. A concept ontology for multimedia domain has been built up for bridging the semantic gap, applied to the high-level feature detection task of TRECVID [12]. Lu *et al.* [9] propose a framework to automatically develop a lexicon of high-level concepts with the small semantic gap, but this lexicon could not represent the relationship between concepts because of its flat structure. Some more general ontologies have been developed until now. For example, WordNet [11] is the most popular one which ImageNet organized images as, and the basic unit of WordNet is the synsets (synonym sets) other than single keyword which users like to use.

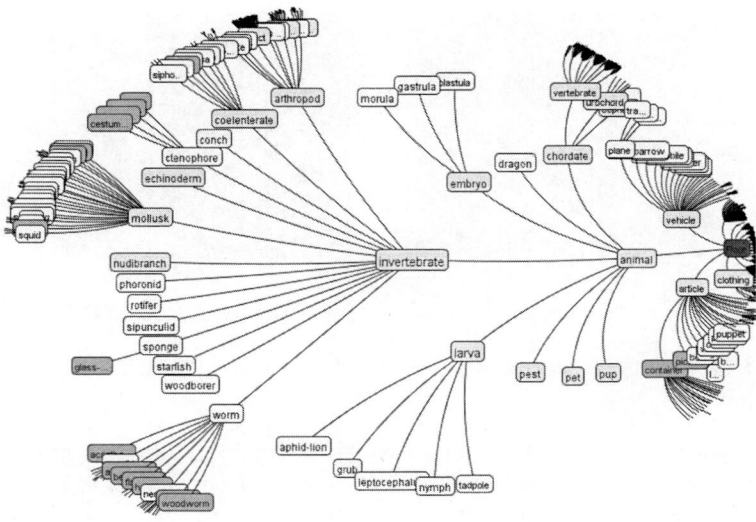

Fig. 3. The concept ontology designed for tags with different semantic levels (Different colors indicate the different gradations of tags: abstract or non-abstract)

3 Ontology Construction

Although using synsets defined by WordNet[2] is more precise than using a single word or phrase for concept interpretation, users in a collaborative image tagging system may not use such complex synsets to tag social images. Motivated by this observation, a concept ontology is constructed for organizing large amounts of most popular real-world image concepts which are used to interpret most popular real-world object categories of large-scale social images. In this paper, we have extracted more than 20,000 synsets from ImageNet[3] and simplified these synsets into 3645 image concepts according to their utility and feasibility in large-scale social images.

As shown in Fig. 3, all the concepts are organized as an ontology tree where each node represents one concept (tag). This ontology can cover most popular social tags in collaborative image tagging systems. The structure of concepts in our ontology is designed based on the "IS-A" relation of concepts, which is most comprehensive and useful. Our concept ontology consists of 3645 concept nodes with 7 semantic levels. In collaborative image tagging, those social tags, which are used to interpret the concepts on the high-level nodes of concept ontology, would be treated as the abstract tag. By searching our concept ontology, we can automatically determine whether a given social tag is abstract tag or not. To achieve this target, these concepts are divided into 17 categories on the topside level, such as *"animal"*, *"plant"* and so on, and all 7 semantic levels are divided

[2] http://wordnet.princeton.edu/
[3] http://www.image-net.org/

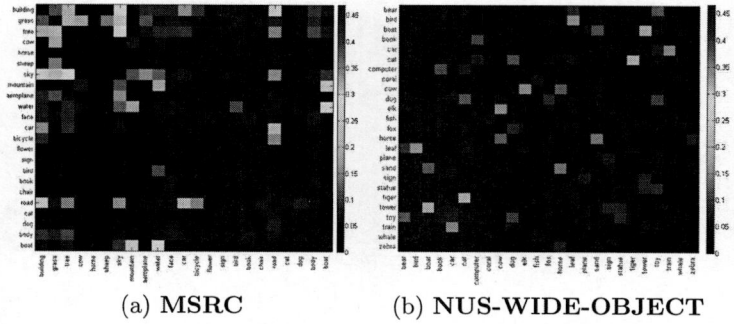

(a) **MSRC**   (b) **NUS-WIDE-OBJECT**

Fig. 4. Context matrix of MSRC and NUS-WIDE-OBJECT data set

into 3 gradations [13,14]: **abstract gradation, basic gradation and specific gradation**. The basic gradation and specific gradation constitute non-abstract gradation. Each node utilizes one attribute to represent the semantic gradation of concepts. Illustrated in Fig. 3, the nodes with green color are the abstract concepts in the common sense while the yellow ones and blue ones, which are separately the basic concepts and specific concepts, are non-abstract tags.

After building up the ontology, the tags of images which are abstract could be decided easily though the ontology with 3 gradations. Detecting out the abstract tags from large-scale images is just through traversing the ontology tree until finding the node and judging the tags' attribute whether it is abstract or not. At the same time, the searching range of most specific tag can be narrowed to the sub-nodes of this abstract tag. The subsequent searching steps are limited in the tree with the abstract tag as the root node.

4   Co-occurrence Context

For large-scale images, it is computationally expensive to find most specific tags to replace abstract tags using k-NN algorithm directly. It is desirable to narrow the search range before using the k-NN algorithm. The replacing manipulation has been limited to the sub-nodes of abstract tags after the ontology has been built up. In general, tags occurred in the same image may have closer relationship than those don't co-occur. If an abstract tag has been detected out, the most specific tag for the abstract tag should occur in the tag sets that co-occur with other tags in the same image with this abstract tag. Starting from these observations, the co-occurrence context of abstract tags can play an important role of narrowing the search range to discover the replaced tags.

Co-occurrence matrix are often computed based on the whole data set and represent the relationship of concepts using concept pairs. The co-occurrence probability of two concepts is defined as

$$O(i,j) = \begin{cases} \frac{\sum_{t\in\Phi}\mathcal{I}_{ij}(t)}{\sum_{t\in\Phi}\mathcal{I}_i(t)+\sum_{t\in\Phi}\mathcal{I}_j(t)} & if\ i\neq j \\ \frac{\sum_{t\in\Phi}\mathcal{I}_{ij}(t)}{\mathcal{N}_\Phi} & if\ i=j \end{cases} \qquad (1)$$

$\mathcal{I}_i(t)$ and $\mathcal{I}_j(t)$ are the indicator function which indicates the presence or absence of concept(tag) i and j in the image t. $\mathcal{I}_{ij}(t)$ indicates whether both the concepts i and j would appear in the image t. An entry $O(i,j)$ in the co-occurrence matrix represents the frequency of concept i co-occurred with another concept j in an image database. Φ represents the whole image set and $\mathcal{N}_\Phi$ is the number of images in the image data set. The diagonal entries correspond with the frequency of concepts in the image set. Figure 4 illustrates the context matrix based on the MSRC and NUS-WIDE-OBJECT data set respectively.

If the context matrix of concepts for an image set had been computed, the context concepts of tags which co-occur with the abstract tag in the same image can be found out by utilizing the context matrix. The algorithm would look up the context matrix using the method given below

$$C_t = \{j|\ O(t_i, j) > 0, j \neq t_i, j \in \Phi_T, t_i \in \Phi_t\} \tag{2}$$

C_t represents the search range of most specific tags for the abstract tag t in the tag sets of images, it equals to the context of tags co-occurred with the abstract tag in the same image. Φ_T is the collection of tags occurred in the annotations of images. Φ_t is the set of tags co-occurred with the abstract tag t. t_i is one element of set Φ_t. Thus the image sets including the most specific tag is narrowed to the images set $\Omega_t = \{I|t_I \in C_t\}$.

5   Abstract Tag Refinement

After determining the search range Ω_t for the abstract tag t, k-NN algorithm with Gaussian Weight based on the similarity between images is utilized to get the most k relevant images of image I_t with the abstract tag t in the whole images set Ω_t and statistic the frequency of tags in the most k relevant images.

5.1   Image Similarity Characterization

To measure the relevance of images more effectively, both global and local visual features are extracted for image content representation in our framework. In this paper, the following visual features are extracted to describe the different aspects of images: (a) 32-bin RGB color histogram to characterize the global color content of images [3]; (b) 32-dimensional cascade vector of means and variances from the responses of Gabor filters to characterize the global texture of images [10]; (c) a number of salient points and their SIFT descriptors to characterize the local gray-scale variation of the underlying salient image components [8]. However, these features of images may be heterogeneous in the high-dimensional feature space and they need different metrics to characterize the similarity of different features. Thus it is not effective enough to use only one single type of metrics to characterize the diverse visual similarity between images precisely.

Based on these observations above, three high-dimensional visual features are first extracted and mapped into different feature spaces and each feature space is used to characterize one certain type of visual properties of images. Kernel can be used to compute the similarity of high-dimensional feature space without too much computational complexity. So suitable base kernels for each feature subset are designed to characterize image similarity. The base kernel for color histogram and texture feature is adopted based on the χ^2 kernel function. Given two feature vector u and v, the χ^2 kernel is defined below

$$\chi^2 = \frac{1}{2} \sum_{i=1}^{D} \frac{(u_i - v_i)^2}{u_i + v_i} \tag{3}$$

D is the dimension of color or texture feature vector. The u_i and v_i is the ith dimension of feature vector u and v. Then the kernel function $k(u,v)$ for color and texture feature is defined as

$$K(u,v) = e^{-\chi^2(u,v)/\sigma_c} \tag{4}$$

σ_c is the mean value of the χ^2 distance between all the images pairs in the search range Ω_t.

For different images, the number of salient SIFT points in the images is different from each other. So the χ^2 kernel is not very suitable to characterize the similarity of points set in image pairs. The EMD (earth mover's distance) can be used to compute the distance of image pairs with different SIFT points. For two images, R and S are used to represent their salient points, M_R and N_S are used to represent the number of points in set R and S. Earth mover's distance is given below

$$D(R,S) = \frac{\sum_{i=1}^{M_R} \sum_{j=1}^{N_S} \omega_{ij} d(r_i, s_j)}{\sum_{i=1}^{M_R} \sum_{j=1}^{N_S} \omega_{ij}} \tag{5}$$

ω_{ij} is the factor to be determined by solving a linear programming problem [15]. $d(r_i, s_j)$ is the Euclidean distance between two points r_i and s_j. Then the kernel function for SIFT feature is defined as

$$K(R,S) = e^{-D(R,S)/\sigma} \tag{6}$$

σ is the mean value of $D(R,S)$ within the image pairs in the search range Ω_t.

At last the optimal kernel for feature subset can be approximated by using a linear combination of these base kernels with different weights and these weights can be determined by cross validation. For the images occurred in the search scope Ω_t, the diverse visual similarity between images are characterized more precisely by using a mixture-of-kernels:

$$k(u,v) = \sum_{l=1}^{\tau} \beta_l k_l(u,v), \quad \sum_{l=1}^{\tau} \beta_l = 1 \tag{7}$$

where τ is the number of base image kernels, $\beta_l \geq 0$ is the weight for the lth base image kernel $k_l(u,v)$. In this paper, τ is set to two because there are two base kernel functions.

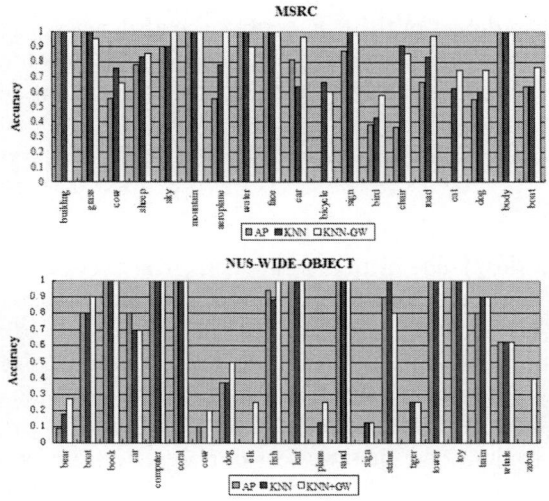

Fig. 5. Refinement accuracy on hte MSRC and NUS-WIDE-OBJECT data set

5.2   Tag Refinement and Enrichment

Utilizing mixture-of-kernels to compute the similarity between images with the abstract tag and other images in the search range, we can rank the images according to their similarity to the image with abstract tags. The images with most specific concept should occur on the top of image ranking because the images containing the most specific tag are more similar with this image than others. Therefore, we could take top k images of ranking results to count frequency of each concepts. The most relevant k images of the image I_t can be selected out as follows

$$\arg \max_{i,N_i=K}\{ \ k(u_{I_i}, v_{I_t}) \ \}, \quad I_i \in \Omega_t \tag{8}$$

I_i is the image in the search range Ω_t. u_{I_i} and v_{I_t} represent the feature vector of the image I_i and I_t.

Actually, the ranking results with different similarity have different importance. The images which are closer to the image I_t with abstract tag t in the feature space are more important than others. In other words, the images with abstract tag may probabilistically have the same category as the images close to them. Based on this observation, the Gaussian weights are added to describe the importance of ranking results. The frequency and weights are combined as:

$$C_i = \sum_{j=1,j\in i}^{K} w_j, \quad w_j = e^{-\frac{j^2}{2K^2}} \tag{9}$$

C_i is the count of concept i in the top k images. Taking the number and its weights into consider, we can achieve more precise results for finding out the abstract tag. At last, the concept occurred in the most images are taken as the most specific tag to refine the abstract tag.

After that, we can detect out the path from the abstract tag node to the most specific tag node in the ontology and all the nodes on the path can be added to enrich the tag lists because each tag in the path can certainly characterize the content of images.

6   Experiments

To measure the performance of tags refinement, the accuracy of detecting out the most specific tag for abstract tag is used to characterize the performance of our method. This accuracy is defined as the number of correct specific tag divided by the number of all the specific tags for abstract tag. Although our algorithm can run on the image sets downloading images from any collaborative on-line tagging systems, it is hard to get the ground-truth of large-scale images for the algorithm evaluation. Thus we test our algorithm on two data sets with ground-truth.

To evaluate our algorithm precisely, two different levels of databases are used to verify effectiveness of our method. MSRC[4] data set has very precise ground-truth but a small amount of images, while NUS-WIDE[2] has enough images but the ground-truth are imprecise. These two data sets can construct a complementarity group for precise algorithm evaluation. On the other hand, both of them have the ground-truth created by hand-labeling and have the similar tags just like those in the collaborative tagging systems. The difference between these two data sets and collaborative tagging systems is that the tags of collaborative tagging systems are more imprecise and don't have the ground-truth by the hand-labeling. Thus we can modify some tags of images from these two image sets to get some abstract tags simulating the real-world images of collaborative tagging systems.

Table 1. Average accuracy on two databases using different methods and features

	AP	k-NN	KNN-GW	COLOR	GARBOR	SIFT
MSRC	68.8%	82.1%	**87.1%**	78.4%	57.1%	70.0%
NUS	59.2%	61.7%	**67.4%**	63.8%	61.4%	56.3%

In our experiments, we use the AP(Affinity Propagation) clustering[5] and k-NN algorithm as our baseline methods and compare the k-NN with Gaussian weight(abbreviated as KNN-GW) to the AP and k-NN methods on the two image databases above. The images which are similar to the image with abstract tag can be obtained from the images in the cluster of it though AP clustering, while the k-NN algorithm can acquire the similar images of the image with abstract tag directly though the distance or similarity between the image pairs.

---

[4] http://research.microsoft.com/en-us/projects/msrammdata/

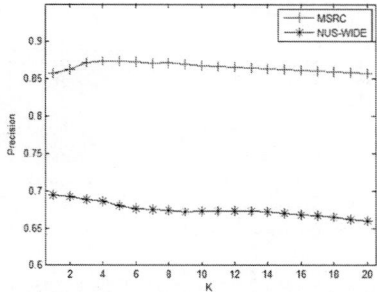

Fig. 6. The average accuracy of different k on the k-NN with Gaussian Weight

In Table 1(first 3 columns), the average refinement accuracy of three algorithms are showed on both MSRC and NUS-WIDE data sets. The results of three algorithms on MSRC are better than the NUS-WIDE. There may be two reasons for this result: (a)the content of images in MSRC data set is less diverse than those in NUS-WIDE data set. The images from NUS-WIDE are downloaded from Flickr, so these images are taken from multi-view and heterogeneous environment and the content of these images are more sophisticated; (b)the ground-truth of MSRC is absolutely accurate as this data set has pixel-wise ground-truth in each image. The ground truth of NUS-WIDE is still annotated manually by persons from different backgrounds and some tags are imprecise because large scale images need to be tagged.

The results of our experiments with three algorithms on these two image sets in details are shown in Fig. 5. On these two image sets, k-NN with Gaussian weight can achieve better results than other two methods on most tags(concepts). AP clustering method don't find similar images taken this image with abstract tag as the centroid of cluster, and k-NN only considers the numbers of similar images, which k-NN may make good performance on some concepts and worse on other concepts. Because of this, k-NN with Gaussian Weight can achieve better uniform results than others.

To observe the effectiveness of different features mixture, we compare the average accuracy of different features on two data sets relatively. The results of compare are shown in Table 1(last 4 columns). Observed From the results, the color feature has achieved the best performance between the features. However, none of these individual features are better than the mixture. This shows that the features can complement each other and make the results better.

As shown in Fig. 6, the accuracy of refinement would be influenced by the value of k in k-NN algorithm with Gaussian Weight. The accuracy would have some changes when k is small, however, the accuracy becomes stable with the increasing of k because the ratio of noisy images similar with each category is fixed when the selected images are more and more with larger k. Actually, the stable accuracy reflect the NUS-WIDE image set are more noisy than the MSRC image set.

Table 2. The results of tag enrichment

Images				
Abstract tag	sand, vehicle	sand, horse, animal	cat, mammal	sign, construction
Enrichment tag	sand,vehicle,train	sand,horse,animal chordate,mammal cow	cat,mammal,dog	sign,construction tower
Images				
Abstract tag	grass, animal	grass, sky, plant	sky, grass, vehicle	water,boat,sky construction
Enrichment tag	grass,animal chordate,mammal cow	grass,sky,plant,tree	sky,grass,vehicle plane,aeroplane	water,boat,sky construction mountain

At last, we show some results of our enrichment experiments on the MSRC and NUS-WIDE data set in Table 2. The results show the enrichment of tags can make the tag lists of images richer. The enrichment can contain the intermediate nodes between the high level of tags and specific level of tags. So we can get more keywords to help social image retrieval.

7 Conclusion and Future Work

In this paper, we propose a framework to detect out abstract tags of images and enrich them. The large-scale ontology is developed to determine whether a tag is abstract or not. After the abstract tag has been detected, we use the ontology and context matrix to narrow the search range of finding the most specific tag and then k-NN with Gaussian Weight are taken to find the most specific tag with the mixture of features. At last, the nodes between the abstract tag and specific tag are added into the tag lists to enrich the tags of images.

In the future, we would seek for more effective feature combination to characterize the content of social images and similarity between image pairs. We may utilize the relationship between the tags and the regions to solve the problem of diversity between different objects if tags have been assigned to the regions.

Acknowledgment. This work is supported by the doctorate foundation of Northwestern Polytechnical University (No: CX201113) and National Science Foundation of China (under Grant No.61075014 and 60875016).

References

1. Bucak, S., Jin, R., Jain, A.: Multi-label learning with incomplete class assignments. In: IEEE Conference on Computer Vision and Pattern Recognition, CVPR, pp. 2801–2808 (2011)
2. Chua, T., Tang, J., Hong, R., Li, H., Luo, Z., Zheng, Y.: Nus-wide: A real-world web image database from national university of singapore. In: Proceeding of the ACM International Conference on Image and Video Retrieval, p. 48 (2009)
3. Deng, Y., Manjunath, B., Kenney, C., Moore, M., Shin, H.: An efficient color representation for image retrieval. IEEE Transactions on Image Processing 10(1), 140–147 (2001)
4. Fan, J., Shen, Y., Zhou, N., Gao, Y.: Harvesting large-scale weakly-tagged image databases from the web. In: IEEE CVPR, pp. 802–809 (2010)
5. Frey, B., Dueck, D.: Clustering by passing messages between data points. Science 315(5814), 972 (2007)
6. Liu, D., Hua, X., Wang, M., Zhang, H.: Image retagging. In: Proceedings of the International Conference on Multimedia, pp. 491–500 (2010)
7. Liu, D., Hua, X., Zhang, H.: Content-based tag processing for internet social images. Multimedia Tools and Applications 51(2), 723–738 (2011)
8. Lowe, D.: Distinctive image features from scale-invariant keypoints. International Journal of Computer Vision 60(2), 91–110 (2004)
9. Lu, Y., Zhang, L., Tian, Q., Ma, W.: What are the high-level concepts with small semantic gaps? In: IEEE Conference on Computer Vision and Pattern Recognition, pp. 1–8 (2008)
10. Ma, W., Manjunath, B.: Texture features and learning similarity. In: IEEE Computer Society Conference on Computer Vision and Pattern Recognition, pp. 425–430 (1996)
11. Miller, G.: Wordnet: a lexical database for English. Communications of the ACM 38(11), 39–41 (1995)
12. Naphade, M., Smith, J., Tesic, J., Chang, S., Hsu, W., Kennedy, L., Hauptmann, A., Curtis, J.: Large-scale concept ontology for multimedia. IEEE Multimedia 13(3), 86–91 (2006)
13. Rorissa, A.: User-generated descriptions of individual images versus labels of groups of images: A comparison using basic level theory. Information Processing & Management 44(5), 1741–1753 (2008)
14. Rosch, E.: Principles of categorization. In: Concepts: Core Readings, pp. 189–206 (1999)
15. Rubner, Y., Tomasi, C., Guibas, L.: A metric for distributions with applications to image databases. In: IEEE Sixth International Conference on Computer Vision, pp. 59–66 (1998)
16. Tang, J., Yan, S., Hong, R., Qi, G., Chua, T.: Inferring semantic concepts from community-contributed images and noisy tags. In: Proceedings of the 17th ACM International Conference on Multimedia, pp. 223–232. ACM (2009)
17. Yang, K., Hua, X., Wang, M., Zhang, H.: Tag tagging: Towards more descriptive keywords of image content. IEEE Transactions on Multimedia (99), 1 (2011)

"...It's Orange and Small, and White Stripes..."[*]
Augmented-Reality System for Fish Species Identification in Aquariums

Charles-Henri Quivy and Itsuo Kumazawa

Department of Information Processing, Tokyo Institute of Technology
Nagatsuta-cho, Midori-ku, Yokohama, Kanagawa, Japan

Abstract. This paper presents an original Augmented-Reality system to automatically identify aquarium fish species, providing a rich multimedia experience to customers. Our goal is to replace the signs placed near tanks in aquariums with a smartphone application based on image-processing. Our system is grounded on the Active Appearance Model for fish texture sampling. This paper also introduces a novel AAM matching function that measures the superimposition degree of the AAM instance edges and the targets' edges. The newly defined function significantly improves the AAM matching performance on textureless targets without modifying the computational cost. We evaluate our identification algorithm quantitatively on a comprehensive synthetic data set of static images, whereas we evaluate the usability of our AR system in real conditions qualitatively. It yields a 94% correct-identification rate on 15 species and runs up to 15 frames per second on an iPod Touch 4G, ensuring a satisfying user experience.

Keywords: Active Appearance Model, Fish Species Identification, Augmented Reality, Edge extraction, CLAHE.

1 Introduction

Automatic Fish Species Identification (AFSI) has been investigated for a few decades, mainly for industrial purposes [1,2], automatic ecological monitoring [3] and as a part of knowledge systems [4,5]. AFSI usually involves fish localization and fish species classification. To our knowledge, the former is performed by means of movement detection [3], or pattern detection [6]. The latter is based on shape information extracted from the result of the previous step, on generative shape or texture models [7,1,8], or on template matching [2].

In this paper, we propose to replace the signs placed near aquarium tanks with an Augmented-Reality (AR) system that identifies fish species in real-time on the videos taken by customers with their smartphones. Its main advantage is the possibility for visitors to get interactively rich information on the species they may find in aquariums. Furthermore, unlike the existing standard interactive systems based on static cameras inside tanks which require considerable financial investment by aquariums–set up and regular clean up due to underwater conditions–our system is cost-effective and portable.

---

[*] The guessing game (Dory and Marlin), *Finding Nemo*, 2003.

W. Lin et al. (Eds.): PCM 2012, LNCS 7674, pp. 210–221, 2012.
© Springer-Verlag Berlin Heidelberg 2012

Since the goal of our AR system is to identify fish species that customers are not familiar with, we have decided to skip the detection step and to replace it with a point-and-identify interface. As regards the identification algorithm, color-based techniques are not considered since color is not a discriminative parameter for fish species classification. Instead, we consider "appearance" information, using a generative technique for fish texture segmentation–the Active Appearance Model (AAM)– that has proved effective in a related study [8], and a Linear Discriminant Analysis (LDA) applied to the sampled textures for the classification.

Contributions. In this paper, we define a new objective function for AAM matching that guarantees better segmentation on textureless targets. Not only do we keep texture information for the matching of AAMs, but we also make use of edge information directly during the matching procedure–unlike related studies that modified the texture representation of the AAM. The new function is defined as the weighted sum of the standard texture-reconstruction error and the length of the targets'edges that lie under the AAM instance edges. This leads to an increase of the identification rate by 10 to 20% for textureless targets.

Outline. Our paper is structured as follows. Firstly, we introduce the Active Appearance Model algorithm and the works related to the AAM matching function robustness. Secondly, we present an overview of the system. More specifically, after introducing the constraints related to fish species identification and AR, we describe the segmentation and identification techniques. Thirdly, we introduce our new method, the Direct-Edge enhanced AAM (DEAAM). Fourthly, we present the data sets used to train and evaluate the DEAAM, as well as the experimental results. Finally, we discuss the system's implementation on a low-end device and envisage future work in this field.

2   Related Works

2.1   Active Appearance Model

The Active Appearance Model (AAM) is a linear morphable model based on shape and texture information [9]. The following paragraphs describe the fundamental theory of the AAM and some of its extensions.

Model Training. As this paper is not aimed at bringing improvements to the model itself, the training procedure is mentioned as a reminder. First, M landmarks are manually selected for each image i of a training data set, $i = 1 \rightarrow N$. We define shape vectors X_i as : $X_i = {}^t \left(x_1 \cdots x_M \; y_1 \cdots y_M \right)$–where $\{x_j, y_j\}$ are the coordinates of the jth landmark in the ith image frame–and the shape vector set X as: $X = \{X_1, X_2, \cdots, X_N\}$. We compute a compact generative shape model by applying Principal Component Analysis (PCA) to the normalized shape data set. Shape vectors generation follows the equation 1, where X_G is the generated shape, X_0 is the mean shape, λ_X is the parameter that controls shape generation, and Φ_X is the matrix that describes shape variation modes.

$$X_G = X_0 + \Phi_X . \lambda_X \tag{1}$$

Each image i is warped so that X_i matches X_0, and sampled into T_i. We create the texture vector set T as $T = \{T_1, T_2, \cdots, T_N\}$, and apply PCA to the normalized texture data set to create a compact generative texture model that follows Equation 2, where T_G is the generated texture, T_0 is the mean texture vector, λ_T is the parameter that controls texture generation, and Φ_T is the matrix that describes texture variation modes.

$$T_G = T_0 + \Phi_T.\lambda_T \tag{2}$$

Finally, for each image i of the data set, we compute the corresponding parameters λ_X and λ_T that we normalize and concatenate together, and apply PCA to the combined shape and texture parameters data set. This leads to the combined generative model ruled by equation 3, where C represents combined shape and texture, λ_C is the parameter that controls the generation of shapes and textures and Φ_C is the matrix that describes combined variation modes:

$$C = \Phi_C.\lambda_C \tag{3}$$

Model Matching. Let I be an unseen image to which we match an AAM. We define the pose parameter λ_P as the concatenation of t_x, t_y (translation), Θ_α (vertical out-of-plane angle), Θ_β (horizontal out-of-plane angle), Θ_γ (in-plane angle) and s (scale). We also define

$$w : (x, y, \lambda_C, \lambda_P) \rightarrow (x', y') \tag{4}$$

as the warping function from X_0 to X_G followed by pose transformations.

Matching an AAM to I consists in evaluating $\{\lambda_C, \lambda_P\}$ so that the generated texture T_G be as close as possible to T_S, the normalized texture sampled in the generated shape to which are applied pose transformations. Hence, matching an AAM consists in minimizing the function $f(I, \lambda_C, \lambda_P) = ||T_G - T_S||_2$, where $||.||_2$ is the Euclidean distance and T_S is a function of I, λ_C and λ_P. In our paper, this minimization is based on the Nelder-Mead Simplex (NMS) algorithm, similarly to [10,8].

2.2   Active Appearance Model for FSI

To our knowledge, two papers deal with fish texture sampling using the AAM. This was first proposed by Larsen *et al.* [1], who train a model from three species, and evaluate the confusion matrix of a Linear Discriminant Analysis (LDA) conducted on the two dimensional representation of combined shapes and textures. The authors reach a 76% correct identification at best (*i.e.* on validation). The Unified AAM was then proposed by Quivy and Kumazawa for computational cost reduction [8]. These authors state that training manually one model from different species leads to a loss of information, owing to the difficulty of selecting landmarks on species-specific texture patterns. For this reason, they propose to merge N species-specific AAMs into one model by means of triangulations and bilinear interpolations. The UAAM is evaluated against a set of standard AAMs, and yields up to 84% of correct identification. It also turns out that it performs faster than the brute force search on the set of AAMs it is made of.

2.3 State-of-the-Art Improvements

In real-life applications, the robustness of the AAM matching function is a problem of concern, as the model is sensitive to illumination variations [11] and to pose initialization. Texture-based and shape-based solutions have been proposed thus far. The following techniques can be found: increase of the number of texture bands [11], selection of an appropriate texture representation (CLAHE histogram equalization followed by distance transform [12], hill representation[11], smoothed gradient based features[13]), addition of neighboring regions of objects of interest into the texture model [14] and driving the AAM with the active contour algorithm [15]. Most of the above techniques are said–by their respective authors–to be more robust to initial displacement or to illumination variations than the original AAM. However, most of those algorithms are built on the assumption that edges are stable in the data set (*i.e.* can be detected properly and appear at the same place on all images). This condition is not fulfilled in the case of fish Active Appearance Models, mostly due to fish fins and underwater conditions, as illustrated in Fig. 1. We evaluate the CLAHE preprocessing algorithm in Sect. 5.

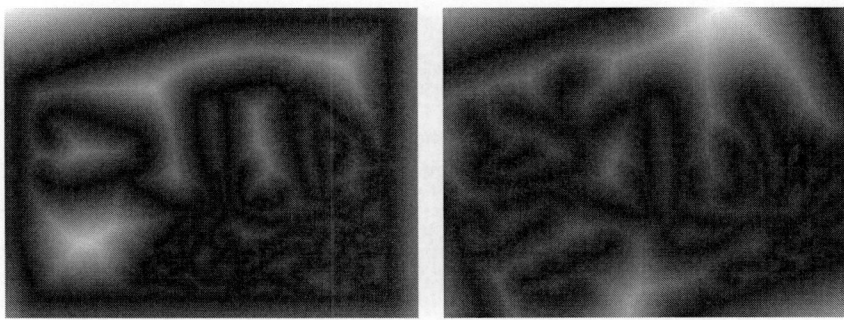

Fig. 1. Distance transform applied to two different images of the same species: non-extracted edges create artifacts on distance-transformed images

3 Overview of the AR System

The proposed AR system is based on image processing *only*: it captures video streams from smartphone camera sensors, identifies the species of the targets visible on images, and, once a species has been identified, displays an image of a fish of the same species–which allows the user to check the result before getting more information. Figure 2 presents two screenshots of the AR system. The following subsections describe the different components of the AR system.

3.1 Prerequisites and Interfaces

In this paper, we assume that target fish swim sideways from visitors' angle.

In the case of slowly moving species, we suppose users can center the fish on their smartphone screen and track targets this way. It leads to the *real-time interface*, which

Fig. 2. Screenshots of the AR system implemented on an iPod Touch 4G. The segmentation result is superimposed on the target, and an image of the identified species is displayed in the top left corner.

displays–in real-time–a picture of the species superimposed to the input video stream. On the contrary, in the case of fast moving species, we assume users cannot track targets, which leads to a "scanning" interface: the video stream is stopped once a species is identified.

3.2   Segmentation and Identification Algorithms

Most video systems follow the common scheme: detection, segmentation, followed by identification, where the identification results are highly related to the quality of the segmentation. As regards our AR system, on the one hand, dealing with a moving camera makes the use of movement detection techniques challenging or impossible: background-subtraction techniques cannot be used, and we do not recommend optical-flow based techniques, as fish may move too quickly to fulfill the low-displacement requirement. On the other hand, pattern recognition techniques based on Haar-like features [6] are class-specific, not robust to pose variations, and the training of the standard algorithm is stated to be time-inefficient [16]. Hence, as explained in the previous Sect., the user is asked to detect targets himself. It leads to the bypass of the detection step, and to the direct segmentation of targets. Unconstrained external conditions make the segmentation step difficult, because separating the targets from backgrounds cluttered with plants, sand, or other animals is not trivial. As we intend to implement our identification algorithm on low-end/cheap hardware, we select an algorithm known to be computationally inexpensive, and that has proved to perform well on fish texture segmentation: the Active Appearance Model.

We train a set of N species-specific Active Appearance Models. During the identification step, we use a hierarchical approach for the selection of the best model. Given $g < N$ the number of generations for the hierarchical process, we initialize a set S of N NMS, one per species-specific AAM. For each generation, we run a few steps of all the NMS algorithm included in S, and remove the worst one(s)–in terms of best-vertice matching accuracy–from the set S. Usually, $g = N - 1$.

Concerning the identification technique itself, we assess two classification techniques for Fish Species Identification: Best Matching Model (BMM) and Linear Discriminant Analysis (LDA). The BMM technique assumes that the species of the target corresponds to the remaining NMS's AAM-species, whereas the LDA algorithm is preceded by the use of the Unified Active Appearance Model for texture sampling after segmentation.

The two proposed classification techniques suffer from one major limitation: the matching quality of species-specific AAM mainly depends on the target's texture-pattern and its associated feature points (see Subsection 2.1). During the matching of a textureless AAM (*i.e.* few inside landmarks), the evaluation of pose parameters is prone to errors due to convergence issues, leading to false results for the identification algorithms.

4   Direct-Edge Enhanced-AAM

In this section, we introduce an original technique to improve the segmentation of textureless species, leading to better identification rates. Unlike related works (see Section 2), we do not include shape information in the model because it adds artificial variance into the data set, mainly due to edge noise, as presented in Fig. 1 for the distance transform. Instead, we propose to make use of edge information directly during the optimization process. We define the following variables.

1. J as the RGB images delivered by the smartphone camera,
2. The 2-channel input images I as the concatenation of:
   - I_1, greyscale conversion of J to which we apply CLAHE histogram equalization.
   - I_2, distance-transformed image of I_1 (canny edge extraction, median filter followed by distance transform).
3. The Direct-Edge function g as:

$$g(I_2, \lambda_C, \lambda_P) = \sum_{k=0}^{m} I_2(w(x_k, y_k, \lambda_C, \lambda_P))) \tag{5}$$

where $\{x_k, y_k\}$ are the coordinates of pixels belonging to the contour of the mean shape X_0.

In order to match species-specific AAMs to input images, we minimize both f (see Section 2.1) and g by using a multi-objective optimization technique. Although Multi-Objective Genetic Algorithms (MOGA) are well-studied techniques, we focus on the plain-aggregating approach [17]. Indeed, MOGA require a large initial population, and are best suited for off-line applications. Moreover, if edges are correctly extracted, the minimization of f should naturally lead to the minimization of g (see Fig. 3). Hence, we minimize h defined as:

$$h(I, \lambda_C, \lambda_P) = (1 - \alpha) \cdot f(I_1, \lambda_C, \lambda_P) + \alpha \cdot g(I_2, \lambda_C, \lambda_P) \tag{6}$$

We set $\alpha \ll 0.5$ because g is designed to strengthen the global minimum of f without introducing significant local minima.

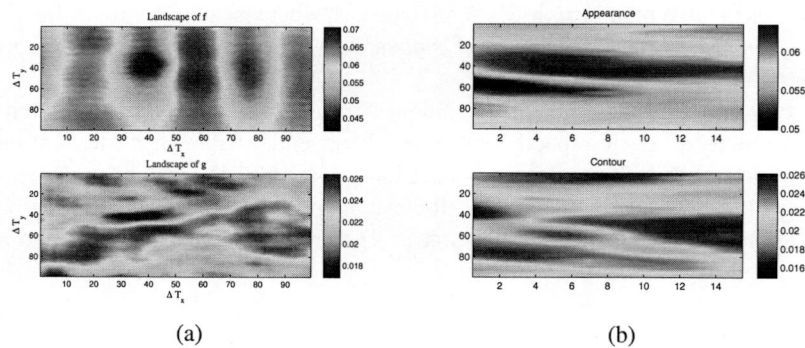

Fig. 3. Landscape of f and g functions. 3(a) presents the variation of translation parameters only, while 3(b) shows the landscape of f and g when we vary the scale and the in-plane rotation parameters only. One can notice on 3(a) that f presents one local minimum owing to the stripe pattern of the fish while g does not present such local minimum. Furthermore, g brings out more precision in terms of Δt_y. The same pattern can be observed on 3(b).

5   Experiments

After introducing the training and testing data sets, we focus on the quantitative evaluation of the Direct-Edge enhanced objective function (in terms of accuracy, we assume the performance of the whole system equals that of the identification algorithm). The usability of the system is discussed in Sect. 6.

5.1   Data Sets

Evaluating our system requires creating a comprehensive testing data set of fish images. Other AAM applications, such as facial expression identification, are evaluated either against open-source databases (*e.g.* the PIE data set [18]), or against data sets built thanks to the cooperation of testing subjects. The lack of open-source databases, as well as the impossibility to control illumination conditions or the pose of testing subjects in the fish species identification area have led us to propose a new data set, mostly made of synthetic images.

Real-life Images (training). We captured fish images at the Enoshima Aquarium (Kanagawa prefecture, Japan), focusing on the following 15 species–all present in the same tank–to which we give a specific ID number to make the presentation of results clearer: Chromis Atripectoralis (ID 1), Premnas Biaculeatus (ID 2), Pseudanthias Bicolor (ID 3), Amphiprion Clarkii (ID 4), Pomacentrus Coelestis (ID 5), Chrysiptera Cyanea (ID 6), Zebrasoma Flavescens (ID 7), Amphiprion Frenatus (ID 8), Sphaeramia Nematoptera (ID 9), Amphiprion Perideraion (ID 10), Amphiprion Sandaracinos (ID 11), Gnathanodon Speciosus (ID 12), Pseudanthias Squamipinnis (ID 13), Microcanthinae Strigatus (ID 14), and Abudefduf Vaigiensis (ID 15). We used a Sony Reflex α100 and an iPod touch 4G for video and image capture. All targets were centered on the images resized to 320×240 pixels. As the number of available pictures per species depends on

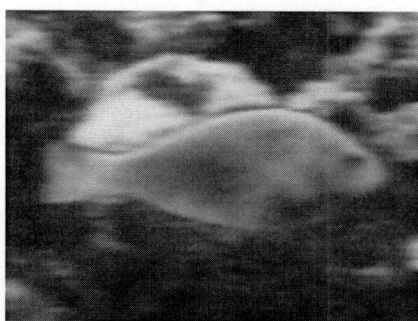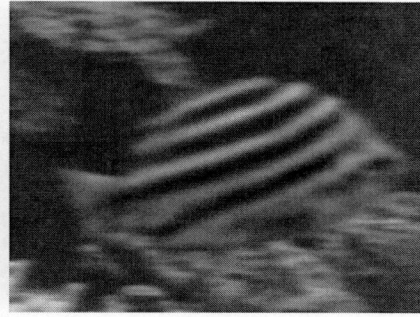

Fig. 4. Synthetic testing images

parameters such as moving speed or water flow, it is difficult to get an even number of images for different species. Hence, the number of training images was set to the lowest common denominator: 25 images for each species-specific AAM training.

Synthetic Images (testing). We manually created a data set of $S = 10$ real-life background images, generate $R = 15$ fish images for each species by making use of the appropriate AAM (built without zero-mean and unit-variance texture normalization in order to get photo-realistic results), composed fish images with each background image, and filtered the resulting images (Gaussian blur and motion blur). In order to simulate the approximate centering of targets in the center of smartphone screens and the out-of-plane angles between the target and the camera sensor plane, we added uniform noise to each of the pose parameters, given the following ranges: $\Delta t_x = \Delta t_y = \pm 5$ pixels, $\Delta\Theta_\alpha = 0° \pm 15°$, $\Delta\Theta_\beta = 0° \pm 15°$, $\Delta\Theta_\gamma = 0° \pm 10°$, $Scale: \pm 10\%$.

In total, we got 300 testing images per species (Gaussian blurred and motion blurred images). Figure 4 presents two images generated by following the above steps.

5.2   Experimental Conditions and Results

For evaluation purposes, we only consider left-to-right orientation.

The evaluation of the system is performed in terms of identification results (for both the BMM and the LDA algorithms) and distance between pose parameters of converged AAMs and ground truth. We retain 95% of variance during the species-specific AAMs training. $\Delta t_x, \Delta t_y, \Delta\Theta_\alpha, \Delta\Theta_\beta, \Delta\Theta_\gamma, \Delta s$ represent the range of pose-parameter variations for the initialization of the NMSs. We set up the number of generations to 7, and the number of NMS iterations per generation to 15.

First, we evaluate the pre-processing algorithm proposed in [12]. Results are presented in Table 1. As stated in Section 2.3, the identification rates greatly vary according to the species. Thus, we do not evaluate the DEAAM against the improvement (that underperforms the standard AAM for some species), but against the standard AAM objective function. Then, we perform validation on the training data set in order to make sure the DEAAM outperforms the standard AAM: we initialize the NMSs using the different sets of pose parameters presented in Fig. 5, and vary the α parameter from 0 (*i.e.*

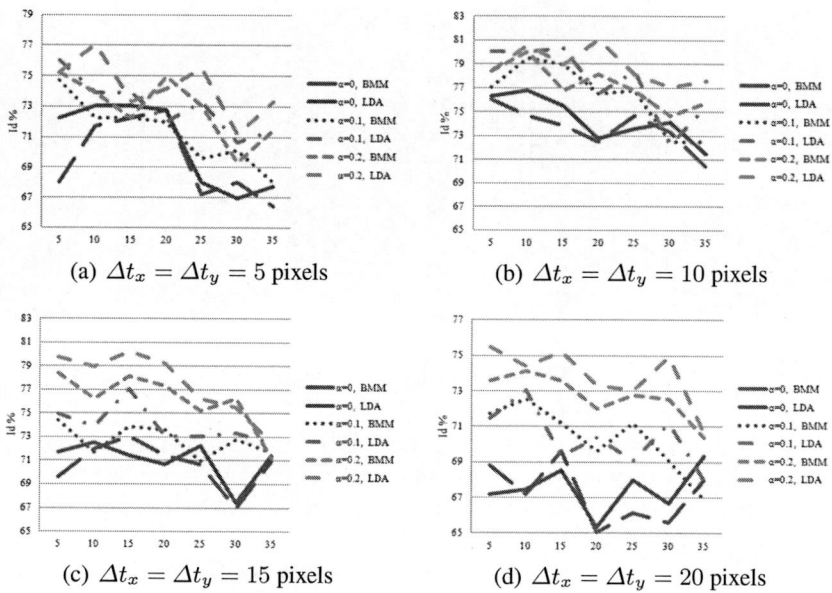

(a) $\Delta t_x = \Delta t_y = 5$ pixels

(b) $\Delta t_x = \Delta t_y = 10$ pixels

(c) $\Delta t_x = \Delta t_y = 15$ pixels

(d) $\Delta t_x = \Delta t_y = 20$ pixels

Fig. 5. Validation of h (see Sect. 4) for $\alpha = 0$, $\alpha = 0.1$ and $\alpha = 0.2$. X-axis represents the range of $\Delta\Theta_\alpha$ and $\Delta\Theta_\beta$ for the initialization of the optimization algorithm, and Y-axis represents identification rates. For all the validation experiments, we set $\Delta s = \pm 10\%$ and $\Delta\Theta_\gamma = \pm 10$ degrees. The DE-enhanced objective function outperforms the standard approach by 8%. The four sub-figures present variations of the identification rates depending on the range of Δt_x and Δt_y for the initialization of the search algorithm.

Table 1. *Validation* results per species using the improvement proposed in [12]. We use the BMM classification technique to compare the *texture reconstruction* performance of AAMs without introducing bias. We set $\Delta t_x = \Delta t_y = \pm 10$ pixels, $\Delta\Theta_\alpha = \pm 20°$, $\Delta\Theta_\beta = \pm 20°$, $\Delta\Theta_\gamma = \pm 15°$ and $\Delta s = \pm 10\%$. This table proves that including edge information in the model does improve the AAM matching for some textureless species, such as ID 6, or ID 11, but underperforms the standard technique in the general case, due to edge-extraction failures.

Species	1	2	3	4	5	6	7	8	9	10	11	12	13	14	15
Standard AAM, in %	96	56	36	100	96	68	48	64	100	28	36	88	88	96	100
CLAHE preprocessing, in %	56	88	16	80	20	88	48	68	64	36	72	24	16	15	15

standard objective function) to 0.2. Finally, our system is evaluated against the synthetic data set, using the following parameters: $\Delta t_x = \Delta t_y = \pm 5$ pixels, $\Delta\Theta_\alpha = \pm 15°$, $\Delta\Theta_\beta = \pm 15°$, $\Delta\Theta_\gamma = \pm 10°$ and $\Delta s = \pm 10\%$.

Results obtained with the LDA algorithm are presented in Tables 2 and 3. Table 2 shows the DE-enhanced objective function leads to a 10%–or more–increase of correct-identification rate for the textureless species 3, 6, 7, 10 and 11, and yields 87% (BMM) and 94% (LDA) correct-identification results on average. However, if the evaluation of our technique on real-life images was possible, the performance rate would probably

Table 2. Comparison of correct-identification rates between the standard and the DE-enhanced ($\alpha = 0.2$) objective functions applied to synthetic images (Gaussian and motion blurred images), obtained using the LDA classification technique. Both functions perform correctly on textured species, while the DE-enhanced objective function outperforms the standard one on all the textureless species.

Species	1	2	3	4	5	6	7	8	9	10	11	12	13	14	15
$\alpha = 0$, in %	96.5	99.5	59	100	98	67	73.5	94.5	99.5	78.5	76	100	98	95.5	100
$\alpha = 0.2$, in %	99.5	100	73	100	99	74	91.5	97	99.5	91	91	100	98	97	100

Table 3. Comparison of the evaluation of pose parameters between f ($\alpha = 0$) and h ($\alpha = 0.2$), computed on the Gaussian blurred images (15×150 images). δt_x and δt_y are expressed in pixels, $\delta\Theta_\alpha$, $\delta\Theta_\beta$ and $\delta\Theta_\gamma$ in degrees, and δs in percent.

(a) Mean error

	δt_x	δt_y	$\delta\Theta_\alpha$	$\delta\Theta_\beta$	$\delta\Theta_\gamma$	δs
$\alpha = 0$	3.33	3.12	11.29	10.93	3.78	2.12
$\alpha = 0.2$	2.61	2.71	9.87	9.44	1.30	0.87

(b) Error deviation

	δt_x	δt_y	$\delta\Theta_\alpha$	$\delta\Theta_\beta$	$\delta\Theta_\gamma$	δs
$\alpha = 0$	2.66	2.72	9.04	7.82	5.71	2.13
$\alpha = 0.2$	1.59	1.91	7.61	7.35	3.17	1.10

be lower than the results stated above. Table 3 presents the distance and deviation between pose parameters of converged AAMs and ground truths (justifying the need for a synthetic data set). It proved h leads to more precise AAMs matching.

6 Implementation

We implement our AR system on the Apple iPod touch 4G. The objective function introduced in Sect. 4 is implemented using the iOS vDSP library, barycentric coordinates are computed offline for computational efficiency, as presented in [19], and the grayscale conversion of input frames is implemented using the NEON instruction set [20]. As a result, the computational time of the grayscale conversion is negligible, and one objective function computation takes about 1 ms for 64×64 pixels model textures and 3 shape and texture variation modes (0.75 ms for texture warping, 0.05 ms for model computation and 0,1 ms for error computation). Concerning the implementation of the optimization procedure, as the system input is a video stream (contrary to images used for the Direct-Edge AAM evaluation), we spread the 15 species-specific AAMs matching on 15 consecutive frames. The maximum number of objective function evaluations is set to 60, leading to 15 frames per seconds (fps) for the CPU implementation. Thus, in terms of user interface, the *maximum* delay required to identify one target is one second. We can consider this is fast enough to provide a good user interface.

7 Conclusion

In this paper, we propose a new Augmented-Reality system that successfully identifies up to 15 fish species in real-time, yielding a 94% correct identification. Moreover, we introduce a new Active Appearance Model objective function that allows better matching

for textureless targets and a new testing data set for the evaluation of fish species identification algorithms. Future work will be devoted to 3D model computation (mainly to
improve the matching of AAMs for fish displaying large out-of-plane angles), Direct-
Edge function improvements in terms of local minima, and multi-objective algorithms
evaluation for the Direct-Edge enhanced objective function minimization. Finally, increasing the number of species the system can identify has been partly addressed in a
related study [8]–the Unified Active Appearance Model–and is to be implemented in
the future.

Acknowledgments. We would like to thank Japan's Ministry of Education, Culture,
Sports, Science and Technology (MEXT) for its financial support. We are also grateful
to Dr. Takeshima and Dr. Sakiyama of the Enoshima Aquarium for their advice and for
their collaboration in capturing training data.

References

1. Larsen, R., Olafsdottir, H., Ersbøll, B.K.: Shape and Texture Based Classification of Fish
   Species. In: Salberg, A.-B., Hardeberg, J.Y., Jenssen, R. (eds.) SCIA 2009. LNCS, vol. 5575,
   pp. 745–749. Springer, Heidelberg (2009)
2. Rova, A., Mori, G., Dill, L.M.: One fish, two fish, butterfish, trumpeter: Recognizing fish
   in underwater video. In: IAPR Conference on Machine Vision Applications, pp. 404–407
   (2007)
3. Spampinato, C., Giordano, D., Salvo, R.D., Heh Chen-burger, Y., Fisher, R.B., Nadarajan, G.:
   Automatic fish classification for underwater species behavior understanding. In: Proceedings
   of the First ACM International Workshop on Analysis and Retrieval of Tracked Events and
   Motion in Imagery Streams, ARTEMIS 2010, pp. 45–50 (2010)
4. Semani, D., Bouwmans, T., Frelicot, C., Courtellemont, P.: Automatic fish recognition in
   interactive live videos. In: International Workshop on Interactive Video between Research
   and Industrial Applications, IVRCIA, vol. XIV, pp. 94–99 (2002)
5. Semani, D., Saint-Jean, C., Frélicot, C., Bouwmans, T., Courtellemont, P.: Alive Fishes
   Species Characterization from Video Sequences. In: Caelli, T.M., Amin, A., Duin, R.P.W.,
   Kamel, M.S., de Ridder, D. (eds.) SSPR&SPR 2002. LNCS, vol. 2396, pp. 689–698.
   Springer, Heidelberg (2002)
6. Benson, B., Cho, J., Goshorn, D., Kastne, R.: Field programmable gate array based fish
   detection using haar classifiers. American Academy of Underwater Science (2009)
7. Tillett, R., Mcfarlane, N., Lines, J.: Estimating dimensions of free-swimming fish using 3d
   point distribution models. Computer Vision and Image Understanding 79, 123–141 (2000)
8. Quivy, C.H., Kumazawa, I.: Normalization of active appearance models for fish species identification. In: ISRN Signal Processing, vol. 2011 (2011)
9. Cootes, T.F., Edwards, G.J., Taylor, C.J.: Active appearance models. IEEE Trans. Pattern
   Anal. Mach. Intell. 23, 681–685 (2001)
10. Aidarous, Y., Séguier, R.: Fast Simplex Optimization for Active Appearance Model. In:
    Wada, T., Huang, F., Lin, S. (eds.) PSIVT 2009. LNCS, vol. 5414, pp. 106–117. Springer,
    Heidelberg (2009)
11. Kahraman, F., Gökmen, M.: Illumination Invariant Face Alignment Using Multi-band Active
    Appearance Model. In: Pal, S.K., Bandyopadhyay, S., Biswas, S. (eds.) PReMI 2005. LNCS,
    vol. 3776, pp. 118–127. Springer, Heidelberg (2005)

12. Le Gallou, S., Breton, G., Garcia, C., Séguier, R.: Distance maps: A robust illumination preprocessing for active appearance models. In: First International Conference on Computer Vision Theory and Applications, VISAPP 2006, vol. 02, pp. 35–40 (2006)

13. Kittipanya-ngam, P., Cootes, T.: The effect of texture representations on AAM performance. In: Proceedings of the 18th International Conference on Pattern Recognition, vol. 02, pp. 328–331 (2006)

14. Stegmann, M.B.: Master's thesis, active appearance models: Theory, extensions and cases (2000)

15. Sung, J., Kim, D.: A background robust active appearance model using active contour technique. Pattern Recognition 40, 108–120 (2007)

16. Pham, M.T., Cham, T.J.: Fast training and selection of haar features using statistics in boosting-based face detection. In: IEEE 11th International Conference on Computer Vision, pp. 1–7 (2007)

17. Konak, A., Coit, D.W., Smith, A.E.: Multi-objective optimization using genetic algorithms: A tutorial. Reliability Engineering & System Safety 91, 992–1007 (2006)

18. Face recognition homepage (September 2011),
    http://www.face-rec.org/databases/ (last accessed November 13, 2011)

19. Ahlberg, J.: Real-time facial feature tracking using an active model with fast image warping. In: International Workshop on Very Low Bitrate Video, pp. 39–43 (2001)

20. A very fast bgra to grayscale conversion on iphone (February 2011),
    http://computer-vision-talks.com/ (last accessed October 27, 2011)

An Adaptive Non Reference Anchor Array Framework for Distant Speech Recognition

Arpit Shukla, Karan Nathwani, and Rajesh M. Hegde

Department of Electrical Engineering,
Indian Institute of Technology Kanpur
rhegde@iitk.ac.in
http://202.3.77.107/mips/

Abstract. Distant speech recognition over microphone arrays is challenging, especially in multi source environments. In this paper, a non reference anchor array (NRA) framework for distant speech recognition is proposed. The NRA framework uses a non reference anchor array to capture the interfering speech sources, in addition to the primary array that captures the speech source of interest. The framework uses a linearly constrained minimum variance beam former (LC-MV) beam former such that the signal coming from the look direction is preserved while rejecting correlated interferences coming from the same direction as the source of interest. The performance of the proposed method discussed herein is evaluated by conducting experiments on clean speech acquisition from distant microphones and also on distant speech recognition on the TIMIT and MONC databases. Experimental results obtained from the proposed method indicate a reasonable improvement over correlation, subspace and standard minimum variance beam forming methods.

1 Introduction

Single channel speech enhancement methods suffer from speech distortion [1]. This speech distortion problem also occurred in single microphone array [2] [1]. In a microphone array, a set of microphones placed so as to acquire the spatial information present in signal. The geometry of microphone array also affects their performance and its knowledge is required for source localization. Apart from linear and circular arrays, complex 3D arrays are also used [3] [4].

Multi channel methods based on beam forming are able to spatially filter signals from non look directions very effectively. A minimum variance (MV) beam former [5] rejects interferences effectively compared to fixed delay sum beam formers. However, the performance of the MV beam forming method is limited in the presence of correlated interference and under direction of arrival (DOA) estimation errors. Methods like quadratically constrained MV beam forming [6], robust MV beam forming [7] have been proposed to address these issues. Techniques like the LC-MV beam former [8] with a null constraint have also been used to effectively cancel the interfering source. In this paper, a non-reference anchor (NRA) array framework is proposed to enable the LC-MV beam forming

W. Lin et al. (Eds.): PCM 2012, LNCS 7674, pp. 222–231, 2012.

method to filter noise coming from the same direction as the signal of interest (SOI). The paper is organized as follows. Section 2, describes the incorporation of the LC-MV beam forming method into the proposed non reference anchor array (NRA) framework. In Section 3, the performance of the proposed method is evaluated by conducting experiments on distant speech recognition on the TIMIT and the MONC database.

2   A Non Reference Anchor Array Framework Incorporating an Adaptive LC-MV Beam Former

In the proposed non reference anchor array (NRA) framework, an auxiliary array is used to capture the noise sources, in addition to the primary array that captures the signal of interest. Such a NRA framework is illustrated in Figure 1. This framework enables the subtraction of the interfering sources from a combi-

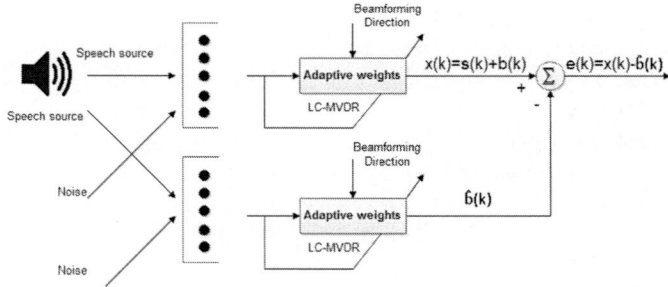

Fig. 1. Incorporating the adaptive LC-MV beam former into the non reference anchor array framework with the primary array (top) and non reference array (bottom)

nation of SOI and interfering sources in an adaptive fashion, when the LC-MV beam forming is incorporated into it. Let $\theta_1, \theta_2, ..., \theta_m$ represent the DOA of the interfering speech sources on which the null constraint is enforced. The signal of interest is assumed to have a DOA of θ_0. If the desired weight vector of the LC-MV beam former [8] is represented by $\boldsymbol{w_d}$, then

$$P_B = S^H w_d \tag{1}$$

Finally, the LC-MV beam former is realized by solving for $\boldsymbol{w_d}$ in Equation 1. $\boldsymbol{S}^H$ is conjugate transpose of steering matrix $\boldsymbol{S}$. $\boldsymbol{S}^H$ is not necessarily a square matrix therefore a pseudo-inverse or least-square solution for $\mathbf{w}_d$ can be obtained in such cases. The above solution yields weights that exhibit very low gain along the directions $\theta_1, ..., \theta_m$. The computational requirement can be reduced, if necessary by choosing less number of sensors. However, this means selecting a lesser number of weights will results in less degree of freedom available for the

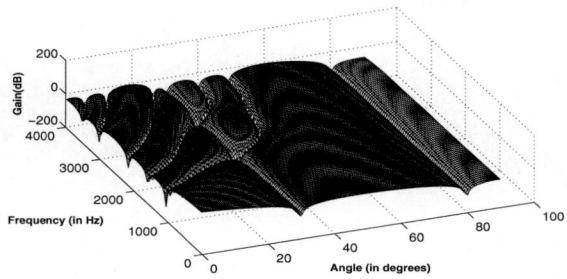

Fig. 2. Beampattern of LC-MV beamformer for two interfering source signals with a five element ULA

solution of Equation 1. The results of beam pattern analysis for the proposed method are illustrated in Figure 2. A speech signal with DOA of $\theta_0 = 60°$ is taken as the signal of interest. Speech signals with DOA of $\theta_1 = 30°$ and $\theta_2 = 60°$ are taken as interfering sources. Weights $\mathbf{w}_1$ obtained from Equation 1 using least-square solution can cancel the noise for interfering signals from two different DOAs. It can be seen that the designed beam former enforces good attenuation at DOAs of the interfering sources, while maintaining unity gain in the look direction. For each individual beam former (primary and non reference), the weights can be represented by

$$\mathbf{W} = [\mathbf{w}_0, \mathbf{w}_1, \cdots, \mathbf{w}_{L-1}]^\mathrm{T} \tag{2}$$

These weights are updated in an adaptive manner. Hence the the estimated signal is computed as

$$\hat{b}(\mathrm{k}) = \mathbf{W}^\mathrm{T}\mathbf{g} \tag{3}$$

where g_k is the array output at time k and is given by

$$\mathbf{g}(k) = [g_1, g_2 , \cdots , g_{L-1}]^\mathrm{T} \tag{4}$$

From Figure 1, if the LC-MV beam former is designed for a look direction of the SOI, then the primary array output is given by

$$x(k) = s(k) + b(k) \tag{5}$$

If the non reference array is designed for a DOA corresponding to the interference, it will reject the SOI and give an estimate of $b(k)$. Due to the time taken by the signal for reaching the auxiliary microphone array, the noise modeled by the auxiliary array is a time-shifted estimate of $b(k)$. If $\hat{b}(k)$ is the time shifted estimate of noise, then the differential output of the primary array (PMA) and auxiliary array (AMA) is given by

$$e(k) = s(k) + b(k) - \hat{b}(k) \tag{6}$$

Assuming $\hat{b}(\mathrm{k})$ is a good approximation for $b(k)$, the desired SOI is given by

$$d(k) = s(k) + b(k) - \hat{b}(k) \tag{7}$$

In the case of multiple interfering sources, the weight vector can be obtained by multiplying the beam patterns with the nulls at those particular DOA values. The corresponding weight vector can then be evaluated from the beam pattern obtained. In order to illustrate the effectiveness of the NRA array framework for clean speech acquisition from distant microphones, a DOA of 40° is considered for the SOI which is assumed to impinge on the primary array. Noise at 25 dB is generated such that 60 % of the noise arrives from the same direction of the SOI and 20% of the noise arrives from two different directions of 10° and 80° respectively. The results are illustrated as spectrograms in Figure 3. It can be

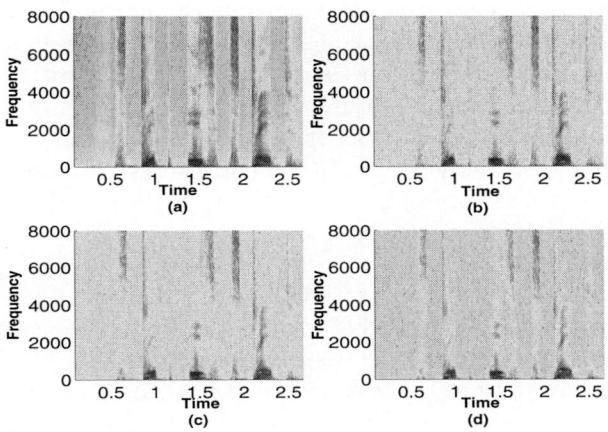

Fig. 3. Spectrograms for (a) clean speech signal, (b) Noisy speech signal, (c) Standard MV beam former with a NRA array & (d) Adaptive LC-MV beam former with a NRA array

noted that the proposed NRA framework with adaptive LC-MV beam former is reasonably better than the standard MV beam former. This can be attributed to the presence of correlated noise as discussed earlier.

3   Performance Evaluation

The performance of the proposed adaptive LC-MV beam forming method in a non-reference anchor (NRA) array framework is evaluated by conducting large vocabulary speech recognition (speaker dependent) experiments on the spatialized version of the TIMIT [9] database. TIMIT contains broadband recordings of 630 speakers of eight major dialects of American English, each reading ten phonetically rich sentences. The TIMIT corpus includes time-aligned orthographic, phonetic and word transcriptions as well as a 16-bit, 16kHz speech waveform file for each utterance. In the lab experiments, speech of 12 different speakers was taken into consideration. Digit recognition experiments are also conducted

on the MONC database [10]. Both sets of experiments were conducted using the
NRA framework on an inexpensive cell phone. Anchoring of the non-reference
array plays an important role in the performance of the proposed method. A
general strategy for determining the location of non-reference anchor array on a
cell phone is first described.

3.1   Determining the Anchor Location of Non Reference Array

Optimal placement of the non reference array requires that it captures a very
small component from the signal of interest. An optimal location for the non
reference array is somewhere close to the PMA with the signal of interest having
a different DOA with respect to the primary and the non reference array. It must
also be ensured that the noise source has the same DOA at both the arrays. The
experimental setup for clean speech acquisition and distant speech recognition is
shown in Figure 4. Here SS represents source for signal of interest. NS1, NS2 and
NS3 represent three noise sources. The location of source for signal of interest,
i.e. SS is at radial distance 0.6m from the mic 3 in PMA and subtends at an
angle of 60° with respect to the x-axis. Noise sources NS1, NS2 and NS3 (Figure
4) are each at distance of 7m from the central mic in PMA and subtends at an
angle of 80°, 40° and 10° respectively.

In Figure 5, AMA1 and PMA are in line with respect to the signal source.
So in this case, AMA1 will have contribution from the signal source and will
lead to distortion of the actual signal of interest. At the same time, the location
of AMA should not be very close to the noise source because the DOA of the
noise source at AMA and PMA will be different. In Figure 5, AMA3 represents
this situation. An optimal location of AMA is therefore close to the PMA placed
such that the signal of interest has different DOA at PMA & AMA and noise
source has the same DOA at PMA & AMA. AMA2 in the Figure 5 represents
such a location in 2-D. A detailed analysis regarding the placement can be done
by using the correlation plot of the signal received at AMA and PMA as shown
in Figure 6.

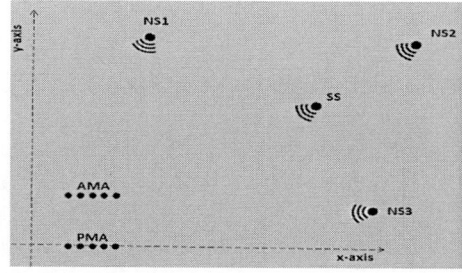

Fig. 4. Figure illustrating the projection of experimental setup on X-Y plane (not to
scale)

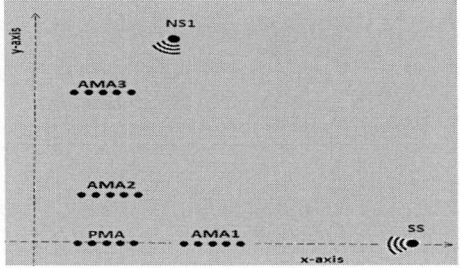

Fig. 5. Figure illustration for the optimal placement of AMA

3.2   Experimental Conditions

A simple way of determining it mathematically is to use the correlation between the signal received at the primary and the non reference array over each frame in the speech signal. The index, where the correlation function takes a maximum value represents the anchor location of the non reference array. Figure 6 illustrates the normalized correlation plots for the cases, where among the arrays (primary array or NRA) one is fixed and the other is moved. From the Figure 6 (a), it can be observed that as the noise source moves away from the both the PMA and AMA, the correlation improves. This can be explained by the fact that as the noise source is moved farther, the DOA for PMA and AMA gets closer and closer.

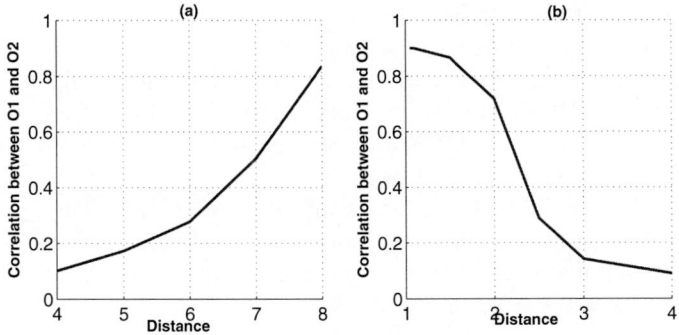

Fig. 6. Plots illustrating normalized correlation between the primary array output (O1) & non reference array output (O2). (a) Non reference array location (M2) is fixed and (b) Primary array location (M1) is fixed.

From the Figure 6 (b), it can be observed that as the distance between the AMA and PMA is increased, correlation decreases due to the different DOA of noise at both the arrays. The experiments on distant speech recognition were carried out by mounting the primary and the auxiliary microphone arrays on a cell phone. Based on the correlation function analysis, we found that, we should place PMA in front end of the cell phone and AMA at the rear end of the cell phone.

3.3   Experimental Results

The performance of the adaptive LC-MV beamforming method is observed in terms of word error rate (WER), and is compared with other conventional beam forming methods. Experiments are conducted using several methods using a Close Talking Microphone (CTM), Using a single distant microphone (SM), MV beam former using a NRA array (MV-NRA), LC-MV beam former using a NRA array (LCMV-NRA), Standard minimum variance beam forming (MV), MUSIC and the GCC-PHAT methods. For the MUSIC and GCC-PHAT methods, filter and sum (FS) beam formers are used in the recognition process which are trained using the obtained DOA. Experiments are also conducted for different spatial distributions of noise. In order to quantify the spatial distribution of noise coming from various directions, two measures are defined. The Alignment factor (A_f) is defined as below :

$$\text{Alignment Factor, } A_f \ = \ \frac{\text{Noise energy from DOA of SOI}}{\text{Total noise energy}}$$

The Split factor (S_f) defined as the Number of noise sources with DOA different from the direction of SOI. Experiments were conducted for several values of A_f and S_f.

- Condition 1 : DOA of SOI is taken as 40°. 90 % of the noise energy is incident from direction of SOI whereas 10 % of the noise energy is incident from DOA of 80°. Therefore, Condition 1 has $A_f = 0.9$ and $S_f = 1$.
- Condition 2 : DOA of SOI is taken as 40°. 60 % of the noise energy is incident from direction of SOI. 20 % of the noise energy is incident from DOA of 10° and the remaining 20 % of the noise energy is incident from 80°. Therefore, Condition 2 has $A_f = 0.6$ and $S_f = 2$.
- Condition 3 : DOA of SOI is taken as 40°. 30 % of the noise energy is incident from direction of SOI. 40 % of the noise energy is incident from DOA of 10° and the remaining 30 % of the noise energy is incident from 80°. Therefore, Condition 3 has $A_f = 0.3$ and $S_f = 2$.

The experimental results for the TIMIT data are listed in Table 1, Table 3 and Table 5 for Condition 1, Condition 2 and Condition 3 respectively. Similar results on digit recognition on the MONC database are listed in Table 2, Table 4 and Table 6. From the experiments on the TIMIT data, it can be observed that for lower SNR values, the performance of MV-NRA and LCMV-NRA improves emphasizing the significance of the NRA array.

Experimental results on the MONC data indicate that the WER of both MV-NRA and LCMV-NRA increases with an increase in S_f and decrease in A_f. The difference in WER also increases possibly due to a small finite correlation between the SOI and the interfering source.

Table 1. Comparison of Word Error Rate (WER) for the TIMIT Database (SNR is in dB) for A_f=0.9 and S_f=1 (Conditon 1)

Signal	Clean	SNR=25	SNR=20	SNR=15
CTM	26.58	37.87	51.55	67.24
SM	25.42	39.81	54.78	68.82
MV-NRA	23.19	28.73	35.42	40.16
LCMV-NRA	23.19	26.24	33.61	37.62
MV	23.19	36.06	50.94	65.86
MUSIC	35.65	50.19	66.85	83.86
GCC-PHAT	51.64	57.84	64.26	84.82

Table 2. Comparison of Word Error Rate (WER) on MONC Database (SNR is in dB) for A_f=0.9 and S_f=1 (Conditon 1)

Signal	Clean	SNR=25	SNR=20	SNR=15
CTM	2.89	20.91	31.65	48.57
SM	4.69	31.65	36.07	52.84
MV-NRA	3.53	5.74	16.72	25.77
LCMV-NRA	3.53	4.79	13.75	21.49
MV	3.53	18.68	32.06	46.29
MUSIC	18.22	35.03	55.81	68.33
GCC-PHAT	21.28	44.59	67.17	77.87

Table 3. Comparison of Word Error Rate (WER) for the TIMIT Database (SNR is in dB) for A_f=0.6 and S_f=2 (Conditon 2)

Signal	Clean	SNR=25	SNR=20	SNR=15
CTM	26.58	37.87	51.55	67.24
SM	25.42	39.81	54.78	68.82
MV-NRA	23.19	36.08	43.13	50.45
LCMV-NRA	23.19	33.69	40.96	45.88
MV	23.19	42.29	49.33	61.11
MUSIC	35.65	50.61	63.09	79.66
GCC-PHAT	51.64	56.72	65.85	81.38

Table 4. Comparison of Word Error Rate (WER) on MONC Database (SNR is in dB) for A_f=0.6 and S_f=2 (Conditon 2)

Signal	Clean	SNR=25	SNR=20	SNR=15
CTM	2.89	20.91	31.65	48.57
SM	4.69	21.73	36.07	52.84
MV-NRA	3.53	9.67	20.54	31.88
LCMV-NRA	3.53	7.59	16.81	26.80
MV	3.53	15.44	30.02	41.89
MUSIC	18.22	33.40	57.13	64.74
GCC-PHAT	21.28	40.70	66.49	77.27

Table 5. Comparison of Word Error Rate (WER) for the TIMIT Database (SNR is in dB) for A_f=0.3 and S_f=2 (Conditon 3)

Signal	Clean	SNR=25	SNR=20	SNR=15
CTM	26.58	37.87	51.55	67.24
SM	25.42	39.81	54.78	68.82
MV-NRA	23.19	39.97	47.26	57.64
LCMV-NRA	23.19	35.15	43.77	50.83
MV	23.19	41.09	49.20	58.97
MUSIC	35.65	49.59	66.32	80.25
GCC-PHAT	51.64	58.92	65.78	84.27

Table 6. Comparison of Word Error Rate (WER) on MONC Database (SNR is in dB) for A_f=0.3 and S_f=2 (Conditon 3)

Signal	Clean	SNR=25	SNR=20	SNR=15
CTM	2.89	20.91	31.65	48.57
SM	4.69	21.73	36.07	52.84
MV-NRA	3.53	13.60	27.81	40.63
LCMV-NRA	3.53	9.35	21.56	32.96
MV	3.53	14.39	31.24	40.92
MUSIC	18.22	38.39	59.33	62.12
GCC-PHAT	21.28	41.28	65.50	74.37

4   Conclusion

This paper discusses the significance of a linearly constrained MV beam former with NRA framework which can cancel interference more effectively compared with conventional MV beam formers. This method is able to minimize the effects of correlated interferences coming from the direction of the signal of interest, when used in a non reference anchor array framework. Experiments on clean speech acquisition from microphone arrays and on distant speech recognition indicate that this method performs reasonably better than conventional MV beam forming methods. Although the proposed method has been compared to conventional and modified versions of MV beam forming, the method needs to be evaluated thoroughly against multi channel Wiener filtering methods and under reverberant conditions.

Acknowledgements. This work was supported by the BITCOE IIT Kanpur.

References

1. Chen, J., Benesty, J., Huang, Y., Doclo, S.: New insights into the noise reduction wiener filter. IEEE Transactions on Audio, Speech, and Language Processing 14(4), 1218–1234 (2006)
2. Chen, J., Benesty, J., Huang, Y.A.: On the optimal linear filtering techniques for noise reduction. Speech Communication 49(4), 305–316 (2007)
3. Meyer, J., Elko, G.: Spherical microphone arrays for 3d sound recording. In: Audio Signal Processing for Next-Generation Multimedia Communication Systems, pp. 67–89 (2004)
4. Meyer, J., Elko, G.: A highly scalable spherical microphone array based on an orthonormal decomposition of the soundfield. In: 2002 IEEE International Conference on Acoustics, Speech, and Signal Processing, ICASSP, vol. 2, p. II-1781. IEEE (2002)
5. Capon, J.: High-resolution frequency-wavenumber spectrum analysis. Proceedings of the IEEE 57(8), 1408–1418 (1969)
6. Zhang, W., Rao, B.D.: Robust broadband beamformer with diagonally loaded constraint matrix and its application to speech recognition. In: Proceedings of the 2006 IEEE International Conference on Acoustics, Speech and Signal Processing, ICASSP 2006, vol. 1, p. I. IEEE (2006)
7. Li, J., Stoica, P., Wang, Z.: On robust capon beamforming and diagonal loading. IEEE Transactions on Signal Processing 51(7), 1702–1715 (2003)
8. Van Trees, H.L.: Optimum Array Processing. Wiley-Interscience (2002)
9. Zue, V., Seneff, S., Glass, J.: Speech database development at mit: Timit and beyond. Speech Communication 9(4), 351–356 (1990)
10. Levi, A.: Multi Channel Overlapping Numbers Corpus distribution, Linguistic Data Consortium (2003), http://cslu.cse.ogi.edu/corpora/

Real-Time Macroblock Level Bits Allocation for Depth Maps in 3-D Video Coding*

Jimin Xiao[1,2], Tammam Tillo[2], and Hui Yuan[3]

[1] Department of Electrical Engineering and Electronics,
University of Liverpool, Liverpool, UK
[2] Department of Electrical & Electronic Engineering,
Xi'an Jiaotong-Liverpool University, Suzhou, China
jimin.xiao@liverpool.ac.uk, tammam.tillo@xjtlu.edu.cn
[3] School of Information Science and Engineering, Shandong University, Jinan, China

Abstract. In the texture-plus-depth 3-D video format, the texture videos and depth maps will affect the quality of the synthesized views, this makes bits allocation for the depth maps indispensable. The existing bits allocation approaches are either inaccurate or requiring pre-encoding and analyzing in temporal dimension, making them unsuitable for the real-time applications. Motivated by the fact that different regions of the depth maps have different impacts on the synthesized image quality, a real-time macroblock level bits allocation approach is proposed, where different macroblocks of the depth maps are encoded with different quantization parameters and coding modes. As the bits allocation granularity is fine, the R-D performance of the proposed approach outperforms other bits allocation approaches significantly, while no additional pre-encoding delay is caused. Specifically, it can save more than 10% overall bit rate comparing with Morvan's full search approach, while maintaining the same synthesized view quality.

Keywords: 3-D video coding, bits allocation, macroblock level, real-time, R-D optimization.

1 Introduction

The texture-plus-depth format has been chosen as the format for 3-D scene representation in the free viewpoint video (FVV) working group in MPEG. In this format, the depth maps are always used together with the associated texture videos, and both the texture video and the depth map quality will affect the synthesized view quality. Thus, one fundamental problem needs to be addressed is how to allocate bit rate for the depth maps. A heuristic approach with fixed ratio (5:1) bits allocation between texture videos and depth maps was used

---

* This work was supported by the National Natural Science Foundation of China (No.60972085, N0.61210006), Xi'an Jiaotong-Liverpool University Research Development Fund (RDF-11-01-11), and it was also supported partially by China Postdoctoral Science Foundation funded project (2011M501131) and Independent Innovation Foundation of Shandong University (2011GN061).

W. Lin et al. (Eds.): PCM 2012, LNCS 7674, pp. 232–240, 2012.
© Springer-Verlag Berlin Heidelberg 2012

in [2]. Later, Morvan [3] proposed a full search algorithm to find the optimal quantization parameter (QP) pair for texture videos and depth maps. In [4], Liu proposed a distortion model to estimate the distortion of the synthesized views without the need of comparing the synthesized view with its corresponding real view. A fast bits allocation algorithm was proposed in [5] to reduce the complexity, where the allocation performance is comparable with that of [4]. In recent work [6], a region-based view synthesis distortion estimation approach and a general R-D property estimation model is proposed, the reported results in [6] show that it can provide better R-D performance than [4] with lower computational cost. There are, however, some major issues in all the above mentioned bits allocation approaches, one is that [3–5] need to pre-encode and analyze a certain number of frames of the encoded video sequence, which makes them not suitable for the real-time 3-D streaming applications; another is that the granularity of bits allocation in [3–6] is frame level, which means that the same QP is used for the whole frame. In the 3-D scenes, the importance of different regions in the same depth map is usually different, and the same level of depth map distortion in different regions may lead to different level of rendering view distortion. To address these two issues, a Real-Time Macroblock (MB) level Bits Allocation (RT-MBA) approach for depth maps is proposed in this paper, where different amount of bit rate is allocated to different regions of the depth maps. The allocation is based on the texture video QP and other texture video characteristics and using the synthesized view R-D optimization.

The rest of the paper is organized as follows. The proposed approach is presented in Section 2. In Section 3 experimental results validating the proposed approach are given. Finally, conclusions are drawn in Section 4.

2   Proposed Real-Time Macroblock Level Bits Allocation Approach

2.1   Distortion Model for Synthesized View

In order to optimally allocate the bits for the depth maps, the distortion model for the synthesized view will be required. Given that the proposed RT-MBA approach aims to do bits allocation at MB level, then the distortion modeling unit should not be larger than one MB. The synthesized view distortion will be estimated without comparing the virtual view with its corresponding real view, as in [1, 4, 5], because in practical applications, the existence of the real view is not guaranteed. Based on the above requirements, we select the synthesized view distortion model presented in [1], where the distortion is modeled at pixel level, and it mimics the view synthesizing process with sub-pixel interpolation.

The distortion of the synthesized view will be the sum of squared distance (SSD) between two versions of the synthesized view; the first version, denoted by $V_{x',y'}$, is synthesized from the original texture videos and the depth maps; whereas the other is generated from the compressed version of the decoded texture videos and their associated depth maps, denoted by $\tilde{V}_{x',y'}$. The SSD in this case is:

$$SSD_V = \sum_{(x',y')} \left| V_{x',y'} - \tilde{V}_{x',y'} \right|^2$$

$$= \sum_{(x,y)} \left| f_w(C, D_{x,y}) - f_w(\tilde{C}, \tilde{D}_{x,y}) \right|^2 \tag{1}$$

where C and D indicate the original color video and the depth map, respectively; whereas $\tilde{C}$ and $\tilde{D}$ denote the decoded color video and depth map, respectively; (x',y') is warped pixel position for the synthesized view V corresponding to (x,y) in C and D by the predefined warping function, f_w, and (x,y) is the pixel inside the current non-synthesized macroblock B. As in [1], the Equation (1) can be further simplified as $SSD_V = E_t + E_d$, with $E_t = \sum_{(x,y)} \left| f_w(C, D_{x,y}) - f_w(\tilde{C}, D_{x,y}) \right|^2$, denoting the distortion caused by the compression of the texture videos, and $E_d = \sum_{(x,y)} \left| f_w(\tilde{C}, D_{x,y}) - f_w(\tilde{C}, \tilde{D}_{x,y}) \right|^2$, denoting the distortion caused by the compression of the depth maps.

In the 1-D parallel camera setting configuration, the 3-D configuration used in this paper, the synthesized view distortion that caused by the depth maps can be further approximated as [1]:

$$E_d \approx \sum_{(x,y)} \left| \tilde{C}_{x,y} - \tilde{C}_{x-\Delta p(x,y),y} \right|^2 \tag{2}$$

where Δp denotes the translational horizontal rendering position error. It is already proven that it is proportional to depth map error:

$$\Delta p(x, y) = \alpha \cdot (D_{x,y} - \tilde{D}_{x,y}) \tag{3}$$

where α is a proportional coefficient determined by the following equation:

$$\alpha = \frac{f \cdot L}{255} \left(\frac{1}{Z_{near}} - \frac{1}{Z_{far}} \right) \tag{4}$$

with f being the focal length, L being the baseline between the current and the rendered view, Z_{near} and Z_{far} being the values of the nearest and farthest depth of the scene, respectively. Finally, the value of E_d can be approximated as [1]:

$$E_d \approx \sum_{(x,y)} \frac{|\Delta p(x,y)|}{2} \left(\left| \tilde{C}_{x,y} - \tilde{C}_{x-1,y} \right| + \left| \tilde{C}_{x,y} - \tilde{C}_{x+1,y} \right| \right) \tag{5}$$

2.2   Optimal Bits Allocation for the Depth Maps

In the proposed RT-MBA approach, we optimally allocate bit rate for the depth maps at MB level. To find the optimal bits allocation, the following constrained minimization is formulated.

$$\begin{cases} \min SSD_V \\ \text{subject to } R_t + R_d = R_B \end{cases} \tag{6}$$

where R_t and R_d denote the amount of bits used to encode the MB's texture and depth map, respectively; R_B is the total number of bits dedicated for both texture and the depth map for the current MB B. Therefore, this problem can be solved by means of the standard Lagrangian approach by minimizing the cost function:

$$J = SSD_V + \lambda(R_t + R_d) \tag{7}$$

where λ is the Lagrangian multiplier. Imposing $\Delta J = 0$ we get:

$$\frac{\partial J}{\partial R_t} = \frac{\partial E_t}{\partial R_t} + \lambda = 0 \tag{8}$$

$$\frac{\partial J}{\partial R_d} = \frac{\partial E_d}{\partial R_d} + \lambda = 0 \tag{9}$$

By combining (8) and (9) we can conclude that in order to minimize J the following condition must be satisfied:

$$\frac{\partial E_d}{\partial R_d} = \frac{\partial E_t}{\partial R_t} = -\lambda \tag{10}$$

It is important to note that the slope of the distortion of the texture versus its bit rate is equal to the slope of the depth distortion versus its bit rate. This slope is λ, the Lagrangian multiplier, and for H.264/AVC it is given by

$$\lambda = 0.85 \cdot 2^{(QP_t - 12)/3} \tag{11}$$

with QP_t being the quantization parameter of the texture videos. Combining Formula (10) and (11), we can get

$$\frac{\partial E_d}{\partial R_d} = -\lambda = -0.85 \cdot 2^{(QP_t - 12)/3} \tag{12}$$

This means that for a fixed QP_t for the texture video, we need to find a combination of QP and coding mode for the depth map that satisfies the Equation (12). Therefore, finding the optimal allocation of the bit rate for the depth map requires the QP value and the coding mode that minimize the cost function J'

$$J' = E_d + 0.85 \cdot 2^{(QP_t - 12)/3} \cdot R_d \tag{13}$$

Based on this, the optimal encoding option for the depth maps, O^* could be denoted as follows:

$$O^* = \arg\min_{o \in \Gamma} J' \tag{14}$$

where the possible candidates of QP (QP_d) and encoding mode (m) pairs are $\Gamma = \{(QP_d, m) \mid QP_t - T \leq QP_d \leq QP_t + T, m \in MODE\}$, with T being the searching range of the QP for the depth map ($T = 14$ is used this article), and $MODE$ being all the available prediction coding modes for the current type of slice. Typically, decreasing the texture QP also requires decreasing the depth map QP, this is reasonable as high quality texture videos also require high quality depth maps to achieve high overall R-D performance, whereas for low quality texture videos, providing high quality depth maps may not synthesize to high quality virtual views. For this reason, QP_t is set to be at the middle point of the searching range. Thus, the full search algorithm becomes trying all the QP and coding mode pairs, and select the pair that leads to minimal J', and using this QP and coding mode could lead to optimal bits allocation for the depth map.

2.3   Fast Algorithm for QP and Coding Mode Selection

The number of possible QP and coding mode combinations is large, which means the computational complexity of the full search algorithm is high. Nevertheless, it is observed that the optimal coding modes for adjacent QPs are highly correlated. In other words, the selected coding modes for QP_d and $QP_d \pm 1$ are with high probability the same. Inspired by this observation, the number of tested QP and coding mode pairs will be reduced. To do this, firstly, we down-sample the possible QP range, which means that the new QP candidates for depth maps become $\mathcal{Z}_{QP} = \{QP_i, i = 1, 2, 3...\}$. The down-sampling process could be uniform or nonuniform, in this article, for simplicity, uniform down-sampling is used so as to have five QPs to test, which means $\mathcal{Z}_{QP} = \{QP_t - T, QP_t - T/2, QP_t, QP_t + T/2, QP_t + T\}$. After down-sampling, for each QP_i the R-D optimization is carried out. In order to demonstrate the simplified algorithm, let us assume that the optimal coding mode is M_i for QP_i. Secondly, each M_i will be compared with the following one, $i.e.$, M_{i+1}, for $i = 1, 2, 3, 4$. For example, if $M_i = M_{i+1}$, for all the $\{QP_d | QP_i < QP_d < QP_{i+1}\}$, the only available coding mode is M_i; whereas if $M_i \neq M_{i+1}$, the possible coding modes could be either M_i or M_{i+1}. Finally, for the refined set of QP and coding mode pairs, the one that leads to the minimal J' will be used to encode the current MB's depth map. It is also observed that the reduction of the computational complexity is not obtained by sacrificing the overall bits allocation performance. Experiments have been carried out using both full search algorithm and the fast algorithm, the performance gap is less than 0.05 dB, therefore, in the following part, the fast algorithm is applied instead of the full search RT-MBA algorithm.

3   Experimental Results

In the experiments, we use the video sequences: BookArrival, Kendo, Pantomine, Newspaper, Poznan Street and Ballet, and the detailed test setting is listed in Table 1. The proposed algorithm is implemented based on H.264/AVC reference software JM 14.0 [7], and View Synthesis Reference Software [8] is used for view synthesis.

In the first set of experiments, we compared the R-D performance of the proposed bits allocation algorithm with fixed ratio 5 : 1 bits allocation method

Table 1. The experimental environments for the simulations

Sequences	BookArrival	Newspaper	Kendo	Pantomine	PoznanStreet	Ballet
Resolution	1024 × 768	1024 × 768	1024 × 768	1280 × 960	1920 × 1088	1024 × 768
GOP size	8	15	15	15	12	8
Frame	1-60	1-60	1-60	1-60	151-210	1-60
Intra period	8	15	15	15	12	8
View No. (I-P)	10-8	2-4	1-3	39-41	3-5	0-2
Frame rate	16.7	30	30	30	25	15

and full search algorithm [3]. The results of bits allocation schemes in [4–6] are not reported, because as reported in [5, 6], these methods are less performing than [3] in terms of the R-D performance. The R-D curves of different bits allocation algorithms are reported in Figure 1. Comparing the proposed RT-MBA approach with Morvan's full search algorithm, it is noted that to get the same synthesized view quality, 10% to 20% overall bit rate is saved for the video sequences BookArrival, Kendo, Pantomine and Newspaper and PoznanStreet, whereas more than 40% overall bit rate can be saved for the Ballet sequence. This is because for the Ballet sequence, the quality of the depth map has a big impact on the synthesized view, and it requires more bit rate than the texture videos in order to get the best R-D performance. This is the reason for which Ballet has more gain than the other sequences, for which the depth maps only account for about 20% of the texture bit rate.

In Table 2, we compare the R-D performance of the proposed RT-MBA approach with Byung's algorithm [1]. Three separable methods have been proposed in Byung's article [1], it is important to note that the second and third methods can also be jointly applied with the proposed RT-MBA approach, so we compare the RT-MBA approach with the first method of [1], which is the main contribution of Byung's article, without using the second and third methods. In Byung's Method, the coding mode of each MB's depth map is optimally selected based on the new synthesized view distortion model, while the QP value for the whole depth map is fixed, which is pre-assigned. Thus, Byung's algorithm does not have the functionality of optimal bits allocation for the depth maps.

To have a fair comparison between the RT-MBA approach and Byung's algorithm, the same QP is used for the texture videos, while for the depth maps, firstly we encode the depth maps with the proposed RT-MBA approach, then for depth coding of Byung's algorithm, we use the QP parameter, which generates more bits than the proposed RT-MBA approach. This procedure ensures fair comparison by favoring Byung's algorithm. Nevertheless, as reported in Table 2, in spite of the fact that RT-MBA approach has 6.88% less bits for the depth maps, the average synthesized view PSNR is 0.40 dB higher than Byung's method. This results serve to demonstrate the importance of using different QPs for the different regions of the depth maps.

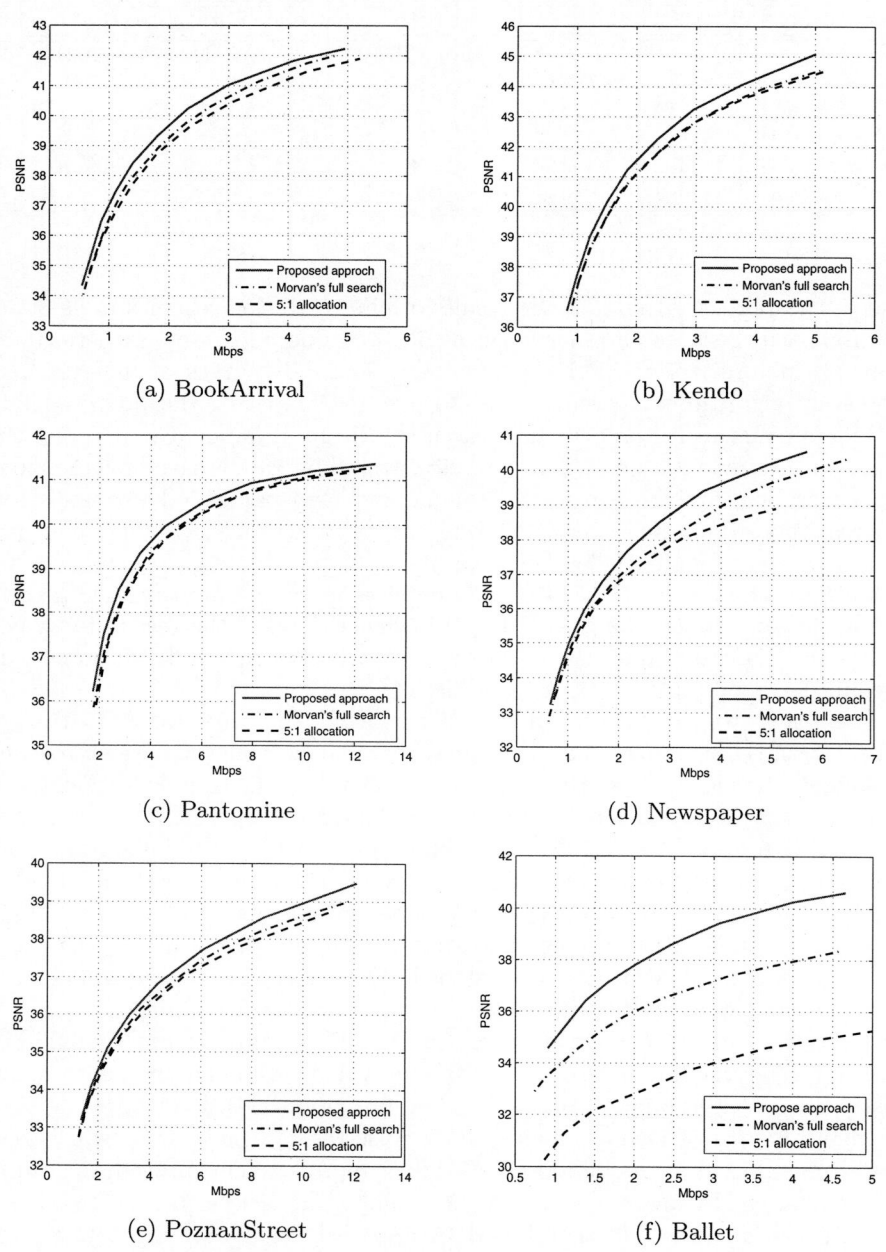

(a) BookArrival

(b) Kendo

(c) Pantomine

(d) Newspaper

(e) PoznanStreet

(f) Ballet

Fig. 1. R-D performance of different bits allocation algorithms; (a) BookArrival, (b) Kendo, (c) Pantomine, (d) Newspaper, (e) PoznanStreet, (f) Ballet

Table 2. Performance comparison between the proposed RT-MBA approach and Byung's approach (Method-1) [1]

video sequence	texture QP	bit rate of RT-MBA (Kbps)	bit rate of Byung's (Kbps)	RT-MBA PSNR (dB)	Byung PSNR (dB)
BookArrival	24	560.96 (−8.78%)	614.96	41.84 (0.37)	41.47
	28	367.71 (−1.50%)	373.33	40.24 (0.57)	39.81
	32	242.15 (−6.67%)	259.48	38.41 (0.30)	38.11
Kendo	24	764.18 (−5.65%)	809.99	45.09 (0.40)	44.69
	28	458.10 (−1.05%)	463.00	43.24 (0.13)	43.11
	32	283.03 (−3.48%)	293.25	41.23 (0.06)	41.17
Pantomine	26	2121.50 (−8.33%)	2314.36	41.21 (0.02)	41.19
	30	1057.25 (−10.14%)	1176.60	40.51 (0.03)	40.48
	34	498.87 (−12.96%)	573.18	39.35 (0.06)	39.29
Newspaper	24	1257.58 (−3.47%)	1302.81	40.17 (0.25)	39.82
	28	709.16 (−7.27%)	764.81	38.52 (0.29)	38.23
	32	400.06 (−6.45%)	427.65	36.79 (0.13)	36.66
PoznanStreet	26	3002.80 (−8.26%)	3273.48	39.49 (0.36)	39.13
	30	1560.74 (−13.61%)	1806.64	37.71 (0.18)	37.53
	34	806.50 (−0.64%)	811.72	36.00 (0.15)	35.85
Ballet	24	2233.47 (−3.72%)	2319.85	40.26 (1.77)	38.49
	28	1542.16 (−7.06%)	1659.33	38.59 (1.14)	37.45
	32	1102.65 (−2.04%)	1125.72	37.13 (1.09)	36.04
Average	–	1053.8 (−6.88%)	1131.7	39.76 (0.40)	39.36

4   Conclusions

In this paper, a bits allocation scheme for the depth maps in the texture-plus-depth format has been proposed. The proposed scheme allocates the bit rate resource in real-time fashion. Moreover, the resource allocation granularity is at MB level, which makes the proposed allocation scheme quite accurate. Experimental results have demonstrated that R-D performance of the proposed scheme is higher than Morvan's full search approach and Byung's approach.

References

1. Oh, B.T., Lee, J., Sik Park, D.: Depth map coding based on synthesized view distortion function. IEEE Journal of Selected Topics in Signal Processing 5(7), 1344–1352 (2011)
2. Fehn, C.: Depth-image-based rendering (DIBR), compression and transmission for a new approach on 3-D-TV. In: Proc. SPIE, Stereoscopic Image Process. Render., vol. 5291, pp. 93–104 (January 2004)
3. Morvan, Y., Farin, D., de With, P.H.N.: Joint depth/texture bit-allocation for multi-view video compression. In: Picture Coding Symposium (PCS), pp. 265–268 (2007)
4. Liu, Y., Huang, Q., Ma, S., Zhao, D., Gao, W.: Joint video/depth rate allocation for 3-D video coding based on view synthesis distortion model. Signal Process.: Image Commun. 24(8), 666–681 (2009)
5. Yuan, H., Chang, Y., Huo, J., Yang, F., Lu, Z.: Model-based joint bit allocation between texture videos and depth maps for 3-d video coding. IEEE Transactions on Circuits and Systems for Video Technology 21(4), 485–497 (2011)
6. Wang, Q., Ji, X., Dai, Q., Zhang, N.: Free Viewpoint Video Coding with Rate-Distortion Analysis. Accpeted in IEEE Transactions on Circuits and Systems for Video Technology
7. HHI Fraunhofer Institute, H.264/AVC Reference Software,
   http://iphome.hhi.de/suehring/tml/download/
8. MPEG-3-DV View Synthesis Reference Software,
   http://wg11.sc29.org/svn/repos/MPEG-4/test/trunk/3D/view.synthesis

Least Square Based View Synthesis Prediction
for Multi-view Video Coding

Jinhui Hu, Ruimin Hu, Zhongyuan Wang, Mang Duan, Rui Zhong, and Zhen Han

National Engineering Research Center for Multimedia Software, School of Computer,
Wuhan University, Wuhan, 430072, China
{cn.hjh,hanzhen_2003}@hotmail.com,
{hrm1964,wzy_hope}@163.com, duanmang1989@sina.com

Abstract. In the applications of Free View TV, pre-estimated depth information is available to synthesize the intermediate views as well as to assist texture video coding. Existing view synthesis prediction schemes generate virtual view picture only from interview pictures. However, there are many types of signal mismatches caused by depth errors, camera heterogeneity or illumination difference across views, and these mismatches decrease the prediction capability of virtual view picture. In this paper, we propose a least square based view synthesis prediction method to enhance the prediction capability of virtual view picture. This method integrates least square estimation with backward warping to synthesize the virtual view picture, which not only utilizes the adjacent views information but also the temporal information. Experiments show that the proposed method reduces the bitrate by up to 23% relative to the multi-view video coding standard, and about 16% relative to the conventional view synthesis prediction method.

Keywords: Free view TV, Multi-view video coding, View synthesis, Least-square.

1 Introduction

The first generation of 3D display terminal is based on the stereo format, which provides only two views, one for the left eye and one for the right eye. This means that stereo-based displays require the viewer either to sit within a narrow area or to wear special glasses. Although, current stereo-based systems can provide high quality 3D video, such constraints on the viewing style disturb the comfort and naturalness experienced by the viewer. Recent progress in depth map research has led to the rapid development of a new 3D display terminal called Free View TV.

Free View TV shows different stereo video in each direction, it can provide free view navigation of the scene to users and special glasses are not required. In order to support a wide viewing angle and smooth motion parallax, this display requires a large number of views be provided. Depth map information would help synthesizing intermediate views to simulate a seamless transition from one view to the other. However, the presence of multiple cameras results in a significant increase in the data amount. This acts as a motivation for researching more advanced compression

W. Lin et al. (Eds.): PCM 2012, LNCS 7674, pp. 241–250, 2012.

algorithms. One straight forward approach is to utilize the latest multi-view video coding international standard Multi-view Video Coding (MVC) to compress the different texture views. However, on the one hand, the translational motion model used in MVC is not sufficient enough to remove the interview redundancies due to the position of the objects with respect to the different cameras [1]. On the other hand, this scheme ignores the relationship between texture view and the corresponding depth map.

Hence, in 2006, Martinian et al. first proposed a depth assisted prediction method called view synthesis prediction (VSP) to improve the interview prediction efficiency[1]. The basic idea of this method is to create a virtual view of current view via 3D warping which can be used as an additional reference picture during the prediction process. Compared to the disparity compensated prediction, VSP can finely compensate scene geometry. In 2008, Oh et al. utilized the VSP technique to compress the multi-view depth data [2]. Furthermore, in 2009, Sehoon et al. proposed a rate distortion optimized framework that incorporates view synthesis for improved prediction in multi-view video coding [3]. In order to improve the disparity vectors prediction, in 2010, Iyer et al. adopted a backward warping based VSP and proposed a 3D warping based disparity vectors prediction method [4]. In 2011, Shinya et al. utilized the virtual view frame to complete the backward motion and disparity estimation [5].

However, the existing VSP techniques merely use the adjacent views information to synthesize the virtual view, because of the inaccurate depth information, camera heterogeneity and the non-Lambert reflection of the object, the quality or prediction capability of virtual view is limited. Therefore, it is difficult for existing VSP techniques to reduce the bitrate drastically.

In VSP technique, the virtual view is not to be used for display but to be used for prediction. Hence, we propose a new technique to enhance the prediction capability of VSP by improving the process of virtual view synthesis. This method not only utilizes the adjacent views information but also the temporal information to create the virtual view. The rest of this paper is organized as follows: In section 2, we describe view synthesis prediction and analyze the problem existing in this technique. The proposed method is elaborated on section 3. Section 4 introduces the experiment that was conducted and its results, and Section 5 concludes this paper.

2   View Synthesis Prediction

View synthesis prediction (VSP) generates an inter-view predictor of image signals for efficient multi-view video coding. VSP has such strong geometric compensation ability that it is possible to offer more accurate prediction than block based disparity compensated prediction. The crucial part of VSP is to synthesize the virtual view. Each pixel in the reference pictures is pixel-wise warped by using scene depth information and camera parameters. The depth-based warping (3D warping) process consists of the inverse projection of pixels, the re-projection of 3D points reconstructed by the inverse projection and pixel intensity assignment. Eq.1 and Eq.2 define the inverse projection and the re-projection, respectively, Eq.3 defines the pixel value assignment.

$$[u,v,w] = R(c) \cdot A^{-1}(c) \cdot [x,y,1] \cdot D[c,t,x,y] + T(c) \tag{1}$$

$$[x',y',z'] = A(c') \cdot R^{-1}(c') \cdot \{[u,v,w] - T(c')\} \tag{2}$$

$$P_{syn}(x'/z', y'/z', 1) = P_{ref}(x,y,1) \tag{3}$$

In Eq.1 and Eq.2, A, R, and T denote the intrinsic matrix, rotation matrix, and translation vector of the camera, respectively. c and t denote the reference view number and the temporal number in a view, respectively. While $[x,y,1]$ are the pixel coordinates in the reference view P_{ref}, and $[x',y',z']$ are the pixel coordinates in synthesized view P_{syn}. $[u,v,w]$ refers to the world coordinates. Finally, to obtain a pixel location, the synthesized view coordinates are converted to homogeneous form $(x'/z', y'/z', 1)$. Eq.3 shows the intensity of pixel located in the synthesized view is copied from the pixel located in reference view. If more than one reference view is available, the weighted average is used as the pixel intensity in the synthesized view.

In addition, the warping direction includes forward warping and backward warping. In forward warping, for any given point in a reference view picture, we find a corresponding point in virtual view picture and intensity value of the point in virtual view picture is copied from the intensity of the given point in the reference view picture. Whereas in backward warping, for any given point in virtual view picture, we find a corresponding point in reference view picture and intensity value of the point in reference view picture is assigned to the intensity given point in virtual view picture. In [4], the analysis indicated that backward warping results in better view synthesis quality with lesser complexity as compared to forward warping. In this paper, we adopt backward warping in view synthesis.

Although virtual view pictures have good subjective quality, there are a lot of mismatch between real view pictures and virtual view pictures. Firstly, Eq.1 shows that the depth information is an important cue to locate the projected pixel position, but in actuality, the imprecise of the depth information caused by depth estimation or compression errors result in the offset between projected pixel position and real pixel position [6]. Another problem of the signal mismatch is caused by camera heterogeneity and the non-Lambert reflection of objects. Furthermore, because virtual view pixels are copied from the reference, in practical FTV capture scene, color and illumination mismatches between interviews also cause the difference between virtual view and real view. It may be possible to compensate such differences by using additional information [7-8], but at the cost of increased bitrate. The existing VSP techniques merely use the adjacent views information to synthesize the virtual view, which restrict the better prediction capability of virtual view due to these mismatches.

Therefore, we propose a least square based view synthesis prediction method to enhance the virtual view prediction capability. In multi-view video coding process, for B or P view, when the virtual view picture is preparing to be synthesized for the current picture, the virtual view picture of previous decoded picture has been obtained and used for prediction. Following the idea of Wiener Filter, the previous decoded picture is assumed to be the "noiseless" signals, and the corresponding virtual view picture is assumed to be the "noisy" signals. The filter coefficients could be obtained by least square estimation. And then, we could apply the filter coefficients to the synthesis process of current virtual view picture.

3 The Proposed Method

As already described, existing VSP techniques fail to generate high quality prediction pictures due to their inability to compensate the signal mismatches, such as the pixel offset caused by depth errors. For backward warping, the essence is to find the projected pixel located in the reference view picture, and then the intensity value of the projected pixel is assigned to the given point in the synthesized view picture. Due to the depth errors or camera heterogeneity, each given point in synthesized view picture may not exactly find the correct projected position in the reference view picture. However, we assume that each given point in the synthesized view picture will be similar to the surrounding pixels around the projected position in the reference view picture. Hence, instead of copying the intensity value of the projected position directly, we obtain the intensity value of each pixel in the synthesized view picture by a linear estimation of these surrounding pixels around the projected position, which could be formulated as a least square problem. We also combine this process into the view synthesis.

3.1 Least Square Based Backward Warping

This least square based backward warping scheme is implemented in a pixel-wise fashion. For each position in the virtual view picture, the scheme identifies its projected position and the neighbors within a window. The pixel in projected position and its neighbors are used to linearly estimate the value of the virtual view picture

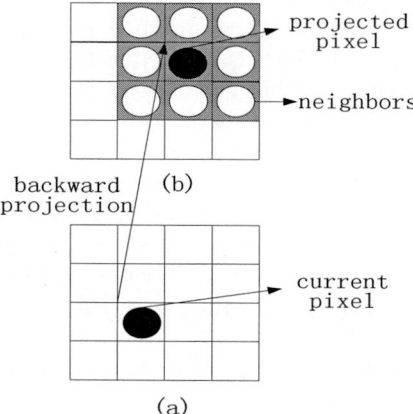

Fig. 1. Backward coordinates projection. (a) current virtual view picture, (b) reference view picture

pixel. For a current pixel $P_{syn}(\vec{n}_1)$ in virtual view picture, the position of projected pixel $P_{ref}(\vec{m}_1)$ can be obtained through Eq.1 and Eq.2, N neighbors of $P_{ref}(\vec{m}_1)$ also can be obtained within a region. In this paper, we define a 3×3 region and N is 8. Fig.1 gives an example which includes the projected pixel and its neighbors. The black spot in (a) denotes the current pixel position in virtual view picture, and this spot is backward projected to the black spot in (b), while the eight white hollow spots in (b) are the neighbors.

Therefore, after backward coordinates projection, for a pixel position in virtual view picture, its intensity value could be obtained by a linear estimating of those pixels in pre-defined region, which is given by Eq.4.

$$P_{syn}(\vec{n}_1) = \sum_{k=1}^{N+1} \alpha_k P_{ref}(\vec{m}_k) \tag{4}$$

Where $\vec{n}_1$ represents the pixel coordinates $(x'/z', y'/z', 1)$ in virtual view picture, while $\vec{m}_k$ represents the projected pixel coordinates and its neighbors. In Eq.4, the estimation coefficients $\vec{a}$ should be adaptively updated within different regions. One way of adapting $\vec{a}$ is to follow Wiener's classical idea of minimizing the mean square error within a local training window M:

$$MSE = \sum_{\vec{n}_1 \in M} [P_{syn}(\vec{n}_1) - \sum_{k=1}^{N+1} \alpha_k P_{ref}(\vec{m}_k)]^2 \tag{5}$$

Supposing there are M samples in the training window M. We can write all samples in the training window into an M×1 vector $\vec{y}$, If we put the projected position pixel and its N neighbors for each training sample into a 1×(N+1) row vector, then all training samples generate a covariance matrix C between the pixels in the training window with size of M×(N+1), The derivation of locally optimal estimation coefficients $\vec{a}$ is formulated into the least square problem:

$$\vec{\alpha} = \arg\min_{\vec{\alpha}} MSE = \arg\min_{\vec{\alpha}} \left\| \vec{y}_{M\times1} - C_{M\times(N+1)} \vec{\alpha}_{(N+1)\times1} \right\|^2 \tag{6}$$

When the training window size M is larger than the filter support size N+1, the above problem is over-determined and admits the following close-form solution:

$$\vec{\alpha} = (C^T C)^{-1} C^T \vec{y} \tag{7}$$

3.2   The Selection for Training Window

In this paper, we use the previous decoded picture to train the prediction coefficients. The training window is selected as follow:

$$W(T_1, T_1) = [-T_1, T_1] \times [-T_1, T_1] \tag{8}$$

Where T1 is the spatial window size, in our experiment, T1 is 3. So the size of the training window is 7×7. In addition, because the virtual view picture of the previous decoded picture has been obtained, for a training sample, its prediction pixels are the pixels around the corresponding position in the virtual picture. The selection is illustrated in Fig. 2. The black spot in (b) located in the corresponding position of black spot in (d).

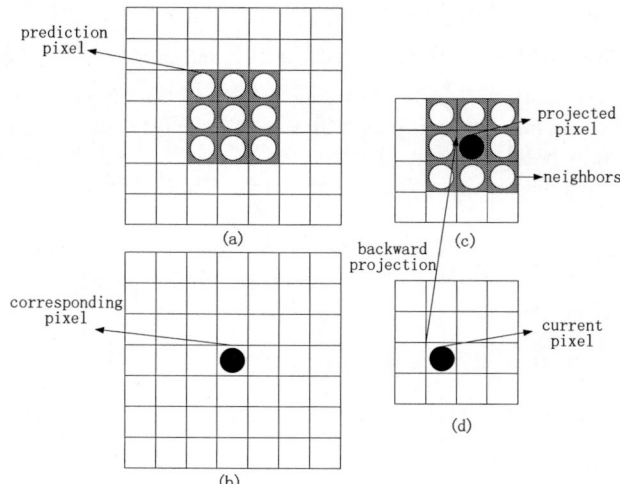

Fig. 2. The selection for training window. (a) previous virtual view picture, (b) training window in previous decoded picture, (c)current virtual view picture, (d) reference view picture

3.3   The Final Virtual View Generation

For P-views, we apply the least square based backward warping on the one reference view to synthesize the virtual view, while for B-views, we apply the least square based backward warping on the two reference views respectively, and the weighted average is used to combine the two synthesized virtual view. Furthermore, after the least square based back warping process, there are some regions marked as holes due to dis-occlusion. We use the inpainting algorithm [9] to fill in these holes.

3.4   The Reference Lists Management

For the anchor pictures of P-views, only LIST_0 is used for prediction, we add virtual view picture to the end of the list directly. For the non-anchor pictures of P-views, both LIST_0 and LIST_1 are used for hierarchy B coding, hence we replace the first backward temporal reference picture in LIST_0 with virtual view picture, while the first forward temporal reference picture in LIST_1 is replaced with the virtual view picture. For the anchor pictures of B-views, we add virtual view picture to the end of the LIST_0 and LIST_1 directly, for the non-anchor pictures of B-views, the reference lists management is the same as P-views.

4   Experimental Results

We implemented the proposed method on the MVC reference software JMVC6.0 [10]. Experiments were conducted on 'Ballet' and 'Breakdance' MSR test sequences [11] since reasonable depth information was available. The selected sequences were of spatial resolution 1024x768 and frame rate 15 fps. In total, 3 consecutive views (3-4-5) with 49 temporal frames per view were coded. GOP length was chosen as 8.

CAVLC was chosen for entropy coding. I-B-P kind of coding structure was used in view direction & hierarchical B structure was used in temporal direction. Interview prediction was enabled for both anchor and non-anchor pictures. The experiment was repeated for 4 different texture quantization parameters (QP) 22, 27, 32 and 37 while keeping the depth QP constant at 22. VSP was enabled for P-view and B-view. Because the existing VSP method proposed in [4] utilized backward warping to synthesize the virtual view, we selected it as the anchor method.

Table 1. Performance of our method and anchor compared to MVC

Sequences	QP	JMVC PSNR (Y) (dB)	JMVC Bitrate (Kbps)	Anchor BDPSNR (dB)	Anchor BDBR (%)	Proposed BDPSNR (dB)	Proposed BDBR (%)
Break-dancers	22	40.82	3738.05	0.11	-6.6	0.33	-19.44
	27	39.12	1082.66				
	32	37.82	433.76				
	37	36.33	242.66				
Ballet	22	41.88	1225.80	0.17	-7.25	0.56	-23.72
	27	40.73	469.70				
	32	39.02	253.72				
	37	36.99	155.44				
Newspaper	22	40.82	3738.05	0.24	-6.79	0.61	-16.10
	27	39.12	1082.66				
	32	37.81	433.76				
	37	36.33	242.65				
Lovebird1	22	43.10	1984.63	0.30	-8.06	0.54	-14.13
	27	40.06	846.60				
	32	36.76	366.67				
	37	33.95	171.21				
Average				0.21	-7.18	0.51	-18.35

Table 1 shows the bitrate reductions and PSNR gains of proposal and anchor relative to MVC in the Bjøntegaard measure [12]. As can be seen, the proposed method shows more improvements than anchor method. The better case, for the ballet sequence, is the bitrate reduction of more than 23% relative to MVC and about 16% relative to anchor method. The average bitrate reduction for the two sequences was around 21% against MVC and about 15% against anchor. These correspond to average PSNR gains of 0.45dB and 0.31dB, respectively. Fig.3 shows the resulting rate distortion curves. The "MVC" curves plot the coding results for the international standard MVC. The "anchor" curves show the coding performance for the existing VSP [4]. The "Proposed" curves are for the proposed method. This also indicates that our method could achieve better coding performance.

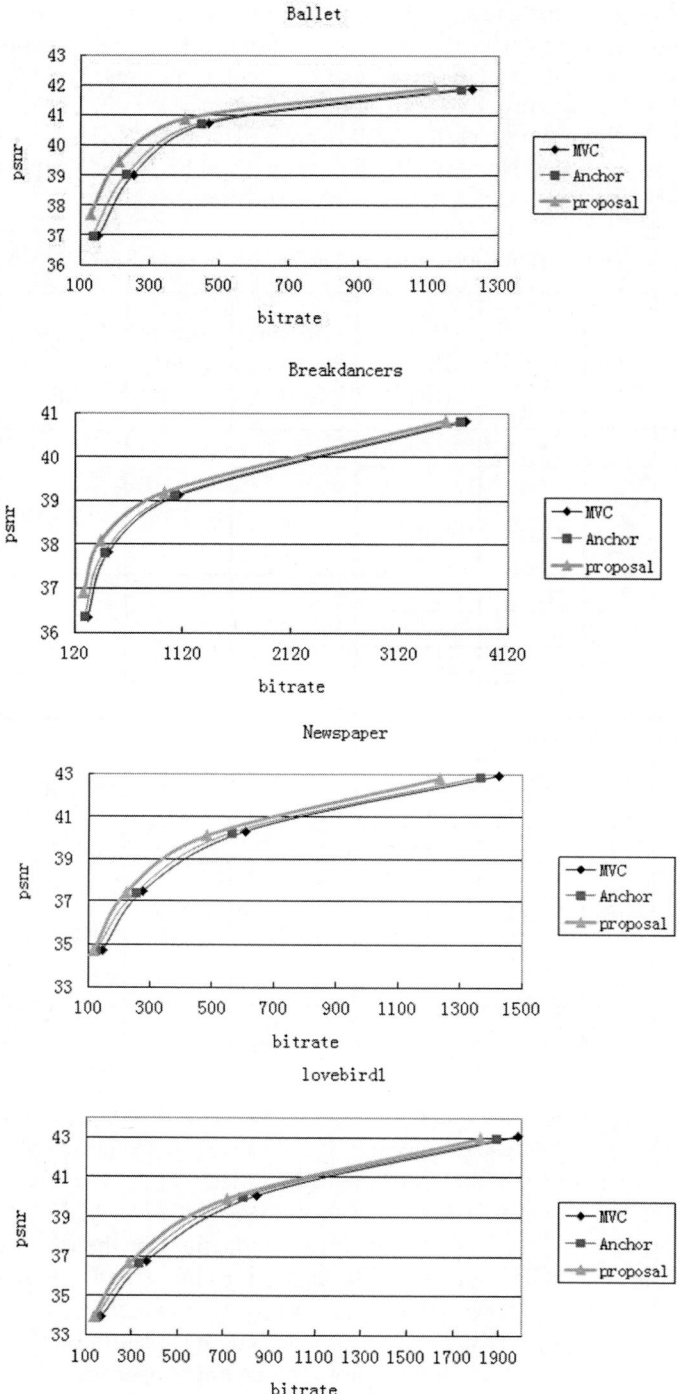

Fig. 3. Overall RD performance

The experiment results prove that the proposed method could enhance the predication capability to a certain degree by adaptively adjusting the view synthesis process according to previous information. However, the computational complexity of view synthesis is significantly increased due to least square process. In addition, the coding gains at high bitrate are lower than at low bitrate. The future work would be to reduce the complexity by efficient liner regression model and fast mode decision. Furthermore, the improvement of coding performance at high bitrate will also be considered.

5   Conclusion

The inaccurate depth information, camera heterogeneity and the non-Lambert reflection of objects restrict the coding efficiency improvement of the existing VSP techniques. In order to enhance the performance of view synthesis prediction for multi-view video coding, the least square based backward warping is designed to synthesize the virtual view, which enhance the predication capability by adaptively adjusting the view synthesis process according to previous information. Experiments show that it is possible to achieve bitrates reductions about 21 % on average for 2 sequences relative to the MVC and about 15% relative to existing VSP method.

Acknowledgments. The research was supported by the major national science and technology special projects (2010ZX03004-003-03), the National Basic Research Program of China (973 Program) (2009CB320906), the National Natural Science Foundation of China (60832002, 60970160, 61070080, 61003184, 61271256), 2011 Academic Scholarship for Doctoral Candidates of Wuhan University.

References

1. Martinian, E., Behrens, A., Xin, J., Vetro, A.: View synthesis for multiview video compression. In: Proceedings of the Picture Coding Symposium, PCS, Beijing, China (2006)
2. Na, S.-T., Oh, K.-J., Ho, Y.-S.: Joint coding of multi-view video and corresponding depth map. In: Proceedings of the International Conference on Image Processing, ICIP, San Diego, USA (2008)
3. Yea, S., Vetro, A.: View synthesis prediction for multiview video coding. Signal Processing: Image Communication 24(1), 89–100 (2009)
4. Iyer, K.N., Maiti, K., Navathe, B., Kannan, H., Sharma, A.: Multiview video coding using depth based 3D warping. In: Proceedings of the International Conference on Multimedia and Expo, ICME, Singapore (2010)
5. Shimizu, S., Kimata, H., Sugimoto, S., Matsuura, N.: Decoder side macroblock information derivation for efficient multiview video plus depth map coding. In: Proceedings of the 3DTV Conference, Turkey (2011)
6. Kim, W.-S., Ortega, A.: Depth map distortion analysis for view rendering and depth coding. In: Proceedings of the International Conference on Image Processing, ICIP, Cairo, Egypt (2009)
7. Yamamoto, K., Kitahara, M., Kimata, H.: Multiview video voding using view interpolation and color correction. IEEE Transaction on Circuits and Systems for Video Technology 17(1), 1436–1449 (2007)

8. Hur, J.-H., Cho, S., Lee, Y.-L.: Adaptive local illumination change compensation method for H.264/AVC-based Multiview Video Coding. IEEE Transaction on Circuits and Systems for Video Technology 17(11), 1496–1505 (2007)
9. Telea, A.: An Image Inpainting Technique Based on the Fast Marching Method. Journal of Graphics Tools 9(1), 25–36 (2004)
10. Chen, Y., Pandit, P., Yea, S., Lim, C.S.: Draft Reference Software for MVC. Joint Video-Team (JVT) of ISO/IEC MPEG & ITU-T VCEG, ISO/IEC JTC1/SC29/WG11 and ITU-T SG16 Q.6, Doc. JVT-AE207, London (2009)
11. Zitnick, C.L., Kang, S.B., Uyttendaele, M., Winder, S., Szeliski, R.: High-qulity Video View Interpolation using a Layered Representation. In: Proc. of ACM SIGGRAPH, pp. 600–608 (August 2004)
12. Bjøntegaard, G.: Calculation of average PSNR differences between RD-curves. VCEG Doc. VCEG-M33 (April 2001)

Zoomable Video Playback
on Mobile Devices by Selective Decoding

Feipeng Liu and Wei Tsang Ooi

Department of Computer Science,
National University of Singapore,
13 Computing Drive, Singapore 117417
liuf0005@gmail.com, ooiwt@comp.nus.edu.sg

Abstract. Modern mobile devices support multi-touch gestures that allow users to naturally zoom into and pan around Web pages, photos, and videos. When users zoom into a video, only part of the region in the video frames are displayed. Ideally, only the regions that the user is viewing are decoded, reducing the computation time (hence increasing the playback frame rate) and power consumption. We call this *selective decoding*. We have implemented a system consisting of an offline analyzer and a mobile video player that implements selective decoding in MPEG-4 Part 2 Simple Profile codec. The analyzer traces various dependency relationships among macroblocks of a given video and produces a meta-data file. The mobile video player supports zoom and pan gestures, and uses the meta-data to trace the macroblocks that are needed to decode the RoI. The player uses a modified decoding process to decode macroblocks selectively based on the trace. Our experiments show that selective decoding can improve playback frame rate by up to 193.3% and reduce energy consumption by up to 64.5%.

Keywords: selective decoding, zoomable video, energy saving, Region of Interest playback.

1   Introduction

Due to constraint in the physical form of a mobile device, the display on mobile devices is limited in physical size despite increases in display resolution. To overcome the limited screen size, zoom and pan gestures have been widely adopted to help users to view photos, maps, and Web pages. Recent research indicates zoom and pan are helpful for users when watching videos [1]. When a video is zoomed into, only part of the video is displayed. The visible part is referred to as Region-of-Interest (RoI). A simple approach to display the RoI is to decode the entire frame, crop the RoI, and scale the RoI for display. This approach is inefficient since the entire video frame is decoded but only part of it is needed for display. This observation presents an opportunity to achieve more efficient video playback on mobile devices.

W. Lin et al. (Eds.): PCM 2012, LNCS 7674, pp. 251–262, 2012.
© Springer-Verlag Berlin Heidelberg 2012

We propose a software approach named *selective decoding* that improves the efficiency of zoomable video playback. As its name suggests, this approach decodes video selectively based on the RoI captured from user interactions. With the improved efficiency, this approach can improve the playback frame rate and reduce the energy consumption.

Our work is based on MPEG4 Part 2 Simple Profile (SP) codec. This approach, however, should be applicable for other Discrete Cosine Transform (DCT) based video codec. We focus our work on the decoder side of the codec in the local playback context, but the principles and techniques could be extended to encoder and video streaming.

The selective decoding approach pre-processes the video to obtain the dependencies among the macroblocks in the video. The dependencies are stored in a meta-data file that is placed along the video. During playback, the video decoder reads the meta-data file along with the video, and computes a bitmask based on the dependencies for every frame on the fly, where the selected macroblocks are marked as '1' and others are marked as '0'. The modified decoder then decodes the selected macroblocks according to the bitmask. In this manner, the macroblocks that are necessary and sufficient to render the RoI are decoded.

The key contributions in our research are as follows. First, we designed a selective decoding process that decodes user specified RoI efficiently. Secondly, we implemented the selective decoding process as a zoomable video player on Android to demonstrate its practical usage. Finally, we experimentally evaluated the frame rate and energy consumption benefits of selective decoding over standard decoding.

The rest of this paper is organized as follows. Section 2 reviews related works. Section 3 analyzes the dependencies in detail and discusses the offline computation of selective decoding. Online computation is covered in Section 4, including the selective mask generation and modified decoder. The implementation of the proposed approach is described in Section 5. We evaluate selective decoding in Section 6 and finally conclude at Section 7.

2   Related Work

Encoding support for zoomable video were explored by several research groups. Mavlankar et al. studied the optimal slice size for zoomable video in a network streaming context [2]. Feng et al. presented how to produce a video stream with RoI cropping support by constraining the video compression process [3].

Other related work exists on zoomable video in the context of video streaming, each with its own focus. Utilizing zoomable video to save bandwidth by refining the encoding process is studied by Ngo et al.[4]; Zoomable video on peer-to-peer streaming is explored by Mavlankar et al.[5]; RoI prediction and tracking for streaming zoomable video has also been examined [6–8]; multiple RoIs support is investigated by Bae et al.[9].

A recent work that is close to ours is the work by Liu et al. [10]. They proposed a partial decoding scheme for H.264 decoder, decoding I-frames fully and

P-frames partially. In partial decoding, they decode all macroblocks within a fixed distance away from the RoI. Their approach does not ensure that all RoI macroblocks are decoded correctly because RoI macroblocks can depend on a macroblock outside the partial decoding area. In contrast, our approach analyze the motion vectors so that all macroblocks are decoded correct and only relevant macroblocks are decoded.

3   Offline Computation

In this section, we elaborate on the pre-processing stage of our selective decoding approach. In this stage, we analyze the dependencies among the macroblocks in the video and store some of the dependency information in a meta-data file to reduce the dependency during decoding. Since it is essential to understand various dependencies in order to comprehend offline computation, we first explain the types of dependencies that exist in MPEG4 SP coding. For all subsequent discussions in this paper, we assume the video is in YCbCr420 color space, which means a macroblock contains four luminance blocks and two chrominance blocks.

3.1   Dependencies

Two categories of dependencies can be identified, namely intra-frame dependency and inter-frame dependency. Dependencies are the reason why some macroblocks outside of RoI need to be decoded. By saving certain information, we can reduce the dependencies and improve the efficiency of selective decoding. Below we analyze the dependencies and introduce the methods to reduce the dependencies..

Intra-frame Dependency. Intra-frame dependency refers to the dependencies among macroblocks within a single frame. There are two sources of intra-frame dependency, including DC&AC Prediction and MV coding.

DC&AC Prediction is performed for I-macroblock when the header field short_video_header is set to '0'. It consists of two steps, namely reference block selection and prediction decoding. The reference block selection step can be illustrated by Fig. 1.

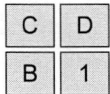

Fig. 1. DC&AC Prediction Reference Block Selection

There are two candidate reference blocks for each block, the immediate left block and the immediate upper block. In addition, the upper left block is also needed in order to determine the reference block. To determine the reference block for block 1 in Fig. 1, the following rule is applied,

```
if (|F(B)[0][0] - F(C)[0][0]| < |F(C)[0][0] - F(D)[0][0]|)
   predict from block D
else
   predict from block B
```

F(B)[0][0], F(C)[0][0] and F(D)[0][0] refer to inverse quantized DC value of block B, C and D respectively. This rule implies that a block is dependent on three neighboring blocks during the reference block selection process. In prediction decoding, however, the block depends only on the selected reference block.

To reduce the dependencies during the reference block selection process, we store a single bit to indicate the reference block, with '0' indicating up and '1' referring to left. Storing this meta-data reduces the dependency for a block from three to one during decoding.

Since MV of P-frame is differentially coded, it serves as another source of intra-frame dependency. At motion decoding, the decoder recovers the MV values based on the decoded base values and residue values obtained from neighboring macroblocks. In our selective decoding implementation, we store the MVs to trace the inter-frame dependency, which is discussed next. Therefore the MVs can be read directly by decoder and no MV prediction decoding is needed. Thus the dependency due to MV prediction decoding is eliminated completely.

Inter-frame Dependency. Inter-frame dependency refers to the dependencies among macroblocks at different frames, which is caused by motion compensation coding. In MPEG4 SP, motion compensation decoding only occurs at P-macroblock of P-frame. The inter-frame dependency is illustrated as Fig. 2.

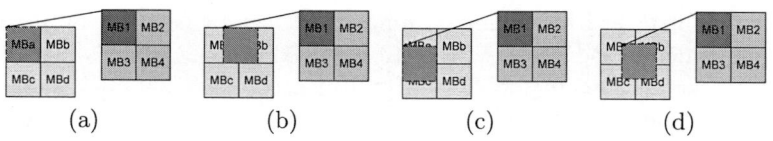

(a)   (b)   (c)   (d)

Fig. 2. Different Cases of Motion Compensation Decoding

Motion compensation decoding is performed on MB1 of the current frame, with reference to a region of a previous frame. The number of dependent macroblocks depends on whether the reference region aligns with the macroblock boundary. As shown in Fig. 2, MB1 depends on one macroblock at (a), two macroblocks at (b) and (c), and four macroblocks at (d).

Khiem etc. proposed an approach to reduce dependency due to motion compensation [4]. We adopted their technique in this research. Using the case in Fig. 2(d) as an example, the approach is illustrated Fig. 3.

MB1 at Frame 1 depends on four macroblocks at Frame 2. MBa at Frame 2 depends on another four macroblocks at Frame 3. Dependency can be reduced

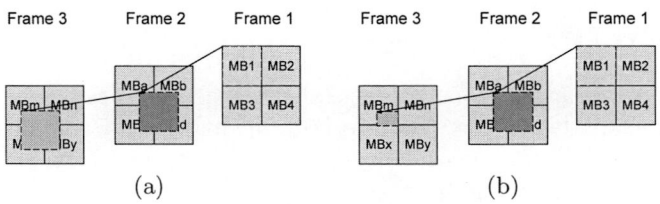

Fig. 3. Dependency Analysis for Motion Compensation

by tracing it at pixel level. The dependency between Frame 1 and Frame 2 remains the same. But we do not really need all pixels at Frame 2 MBa. The region needed at MBa depends on only part of MBm at Frame 3. Therefore, the dependency for MBa between Frame 2 and 3 are reduced from four to one in this example.

3.2 Dependency Files

The offline computation partially decodes a video and records down the dependency information into a set of meta-data files named *dependency files*. The dependency files are generated for each Group of VOP (GOP). For every GOP, the dependency files include the following,

1. GOP record file: it contains the start and end frame numbers of a GOP.
2. MB start and end position file: it stores the macroblock start and end bit positions in the video bitstream for every MB of all frames in a GOP. The positions are needed for the decoder to seek the bits for a MB.
3. DC&AC prediction direction file: it contains the DC&AC prediction direction. A single bit is used to store the direction for each block. The direction is read directly by the decoder to avoid decoding the macroblocks used in DC&AC prediction reference selection but not in actual prediction decoding. The direction is also used to trace the intra frame dependency.
4. MV file: it records the MV values for every macroblock of each P-frame in the GOP and the number of bits for MVs. The selective decoder reads the MV from this file and skip the encoded bits. This file not only eliminates the MV decoding dependency, but also allows the online computation to trace the inter-frame dependency.

We modified the standard MPEG4 SP decoder to partially decode a video in order to generate the above files.

4   Online Computation

Offline computation is done once and the dependency files are saved. Every time the video is played, the selective decoder loads the dependency files, computes a selective mask for each frame, and decodes according to the mask.

4.1   Selective Mask Computation

Selective mask indicates the macroblocks that the decoder needs to decode as '1' and the rest as '0'. It considers both inter-frame and intra-frame dependencies. Note that the inter-frame dependency has to be computed first. If intra-frame dependency is computed first, when computing inter-frame dependency, the computation will select some new P-macroblocks and I-macroblocks. Not computing the intra-frame dependency for the newly selected I-macroblocks would lead to decoding errors at these I-macroblocks. The error will subsequently affect the motion compensation decoding at other macroblocks using these I-macroblocks as reference. In contrast, if inter-frame dependency is computed first, the intra-frame computation will select only I-macroblocks because DC&AC prediction coding only applies to I-macroblock. Since inter-frame dependency does not apply to I-macroblocks, the newly selected I-macroblocks will not introduce errors.

Inter-frame Dependency Computation. Inter-frame dependency is caused by motion compensation decoding. A MPEG4 SP GOP consists of an I frame followed by a sequence of P frames. The P-macroblocks of every P frame are motion compensated with reference to macroblocks of its previous frame. Thus, every P frame is dependent on its previous frame. Therefore we compute the inter-frame dependency from last frame back to the first frame of the GOP. The dependencies are shown as Fig. 4(a).

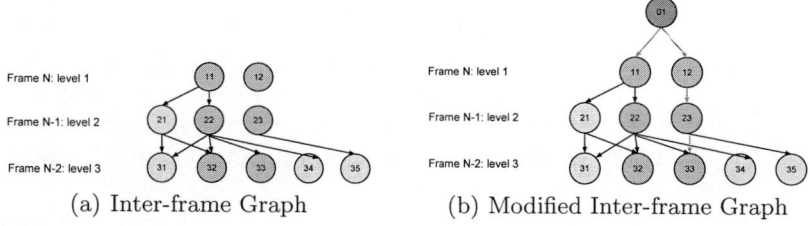

(a) Inter-frame Graph   (b) Modified Inter-frame Graph

Fig. 4. Inter-frame Dependency Abstraction

Suppose frame N is the last frame of the GOP, the figure shows the dependencies in three frames. The macroblocks and the dependencies form a graph. By adding a pseudo root node and edges connecting the RoI macroblocks, the graph is transformed to a weakly connected directed acyclic graph shown as Fig. 4(b). With this modification, the graph traversal algorithm Depth-First Traversal (DFT) or Breadth-First Traversal (BFT) can be applied. The macroblocks that are visited by the graph traversal are selected, while the rest are not needed.

Intra-frame Dependency Computation. Similar to Inter-frame dependency, intra-frame dependency computation is abstracted as a graph traversal problem.

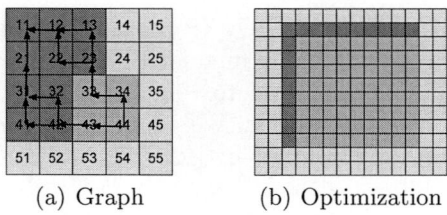

(a) Graph   (b) Optimization

Fig. 5. Intra-frame Dependency and the Optimization

In Fig. 5(a), macroblock 33, 34, 43 and 44 are RoI macroblocks. The dependency graph due to DC&AC prediction coding is depicted. Because the dependency direction is always pointing up or left, the graph rooted at a macroblock is always formed by one of the graphs rooted at the first row and first column macroblocks of the RoI and some macroblocks within the RoI. Therefore, an optimization is to apply graph traversal algorithms only on the macroblocks at upper and left edges of the RoI, and select all macroblocks within RoI. This is illustrated as Fig. 5(b).

4.2   Select the Bits

In order to decode selectively, a mechanism is needed for the decoder to select the bits for selected macroblocks. Two approaches can be used to select the bits, namely bitstream reconstruction and bit seeking. In bitstream reconstruction, a new video bitstream is constructed according to the selective masks and the macroblock start and end positions. The newly constructed bitstream consists of only the macroblocks selected in selective masks. At bit seeking approach, we instruct the decoder to seek to the start position of next selected macroblock at decoding. The second approach avoids the additional memory allocation for the new bitstream therefore it is the preferred approach in our work.

5   Implementation

We implemented the techniques and processes described in previous sections on Android platform as a zoomable video player. The architecture of the player is depicted in Fig. 6.

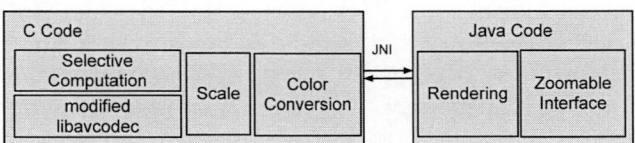

Fig. 6. Zoomable Video Player Implementation

We modified the open source MPEG4 SP codec from libavcodec of ffmpeg 0.7 [11] and added the selective decoding functions. At the time of implementation, the ffmpeg codec was not optimized to run on Android platform, especially the scale and color conversion process. We adopted the code from another two open source projects: scaling from libyuv [12] and color conversion from Google Chromimum project [13].

We implemented the rendering and zoomable interface in Java with Android SDK. The gesture detector detects a user's pinch or pan gesture, and translates the gesture detected as zoom scale and pan scale. We then compute a RoI from these scales based on what user can see on the phone screen.

6   Evaluation

The purpose of selective decoding is to achieve more efficient zoomable video playback. We evaluate the efficiency of selective decoding from two aspects, video playback frame rate and energy consumption.

We used a Samsung Galaxy S2 phone for experiment. The device has a dual core processor of 1200 MHz clock rate each and 1024 MB RAM; it runs Android 2.3.6. Two videos of 1080p are used for evaluation. The first one is a five minute recording of a university lecture. The lecturer is the only person moving around, so there is little motion in the video. The second video captures a scene of a few toys rotating constantly, therefore contains a large amount of motion. The video is about 15 seconds. We refer the lecture recording video as video A and the toy rotation video as video B.

6.1   Frame Rate

Selective video playback frame rate is affected by both RoI size and position. We designed experiments to examine the influence of each.

Different RoI Positions. Different regions of a video frame may contain different amount of motions and dependencies, therefore the RoI position can affect the amount of processing at decoding and subsequently the video playback frame rate. We fix the RoI size, and then move the RoI from the upper left corner to the lower right of the video frame. The tests are repeated for three different RoI sizes, with the RoI width and height set as 50%, 70%, and 90% of the original video's width and height.

In Fig. 7, each 3D surface indicates the frame rate for a RoI size. The intersection in a surface indicates the start position of a particular RoI size.

Looking at each 3D surface, the frame rate tends to decrease when the RoI starting width and/or starting height increases. The frame rate decreases because the intra-frame dependencies increase towards the lower right, and more dependencies cause more macroblocks to be selected and decoded. There are, however, exceptions to this decrease trend, which are probably caused by different amount of motions at different RoI positions. Compare different 3D interfaces

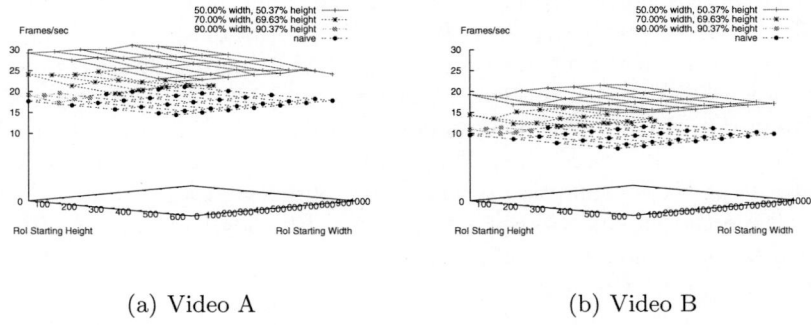

(a) Video A   (b) Video B

Fig. 7. Frame Rate with 90%, 70%, and 50% of RoI at Different Positions

at a single figure, it is clear that the RoI size has a more significant effect than RoI position and selective decoding outperforms standard decoding. Compare Fig. 7(a) with (b), the frame rate for video A is higher than video B. This result is expected because video A has less amount of motion than video B.

Different RoI Size. Previous experiment already reveals that RoI size has significant influence on video playback frame rate. This experiment examines the affection of RoI size further. We position the RoI at the center of the video frame and vary the RoI height and width from 10% to 100% of original video height and width.

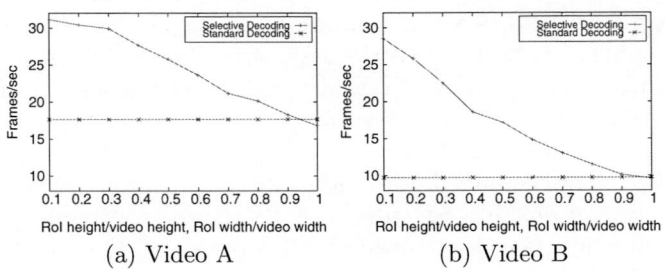

(a) Video A   (b) Video B

Fig. 8. Frame Rate with 10% to 100% RoI Centered

Looking at either Fig. 8(a) or (b), frame rate decreases as RoI size increases. Selective decoding achieves higher frame rate at RoI size smaller than 90%. At 10% RoI, the frame rate is improved by 76.3% and 193.3% for video A and B respectively. The curves at different figures differ due to different amount of motion at center of the video frame.

6.2   Energy Consumption

Energy consumption is the other important aspect of our evaluation. Two experiments are done with different focuses.

PowerTutor Measurements. Battery energy is mainly consumed by display and CPU at video playback. PowerTutor [14], an Android power measurement tool, is capable of measuring power consumed by different hardware components for a user specified app. In this experiment, we vary RoI size from 10% to 100%. The frame rate is controlled so that both selective decoding and standard decoding always play at same rate. This control is essential for a fair comparison because the power consumption is dependent on display time.

For display measurements, we found selective decoding and standard decoding consume almost same amount of energy. However, this is not the case for CPU power consumption, which is shown as Fig. 9.

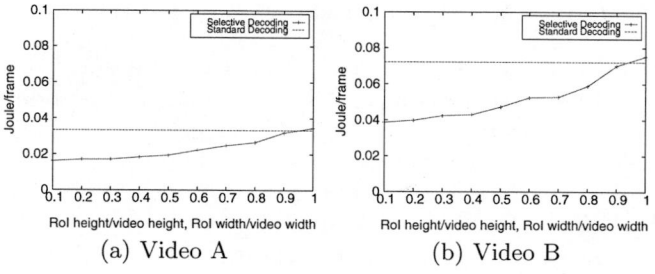

(a) Video A   (b) Video B

Fig. 9. CPU Power Consumption Per Frame

Looking at each figure individually, CPU power consumption per frame at selective decoding increases when RoI size increases. At RoI size 90% or less, selective decoding consumes less CPU energy than standard decoding. Compare Fig. 9(a) with (b), video playback for heavy motion video tends to consume more power because of more motion compensation decoding.

Power Drain Experiment. PowerTutor measurements show selective decoding can save energy, mainly by reducing CPU power consumption. However, PowerTutor measurement is obtained through offline-training models [14] and may not be accurate for all phones. We designed another experiment to measure the power consumption.

In this experiment, we place RoI at the video frame center and play the video repeatedly with constant frame rate. Based on the processing power and video, we set the frame rate for two videos as 15 FPS and 8FPS respectively. The percentage of power drained is recorded for comparison. Before each test, we fully charge the phone battery to 100% and disable all background activities including Wi-Fi, Bluetooth, GPS, etc.

Looking at each figure individually, selective decoding consumes less power. At 10% RoI size, the battery consumption is reduced by 61.1% and 64.5%.

In summary, selective decoding proves to be efficient in terms of playback frame rate and battery energy consumption when RoI size is below certain threshold.

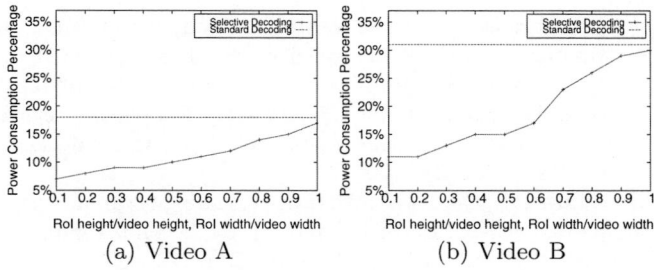

(a) Video A   (b) Video B

Fig. 10. Percentage of Power Drained

7   Conclusion and Future Work

We designed a software approach named selective decoding to reduce the battery power consumption and increase the frame rate for zoomable video playback on mobile devices. Selective decoding is based on analyzing and tracing various intra- and inter-frame dependencies among macroblocks. By doing so, we compute a selective mask which indicates the macroblocks needed to present a clear scene in a user requested RoI and the modified decoder can then decode selectively according to the mask.

Selective decoding illustrates the idea of achieving more efficient zoomable video playback by tracing the dependencies among macroblocks. There are many possible future work can be done. Firstly, the dependency file storage overhead is large. The size of dependency files for video A is about five times the original video size, while the size for video B is 96% of original video size. Because the two videos have same resolution but different bit rates, and dependency file size is dependent on video resolution rather than bit rate, the difference of dependency file size overhead is obvious. We store the dependency information as plain values in binary format. Better storage scheme and compression can be applied to reduce storage overhead. Secondly, the dependency file generation could be done online, which requires optimizing the process and integrating it with selective mask computation. Thirdly, expanding selective decoding to encoder may bring some benefits. The encoder can generate dependency files and control the amount of dependencies among macroblocks. Lastly, selective decoding at decoder may help to improve the existing research on zoomable in network streaming context, which deals with encoders mostly.

Acknowledgement. This research is conducted under the NExT Search Center, supported by the Singapore National Research Foundation and the Interactive Digital Media R&D Program Office of Media Development Authority under research grant WBS:R-252-300-001-490.

References

1. Khiem, N.Q.M., Ravindra, G., Ooi, W.T.: Towards understanding user tolerance to network latency in zoomable video streaming. In: Proceedings of the 19th ACM International Conference on Multimedia, MM 2011, pp. 977–980. ACM, New York (2011)

2. Mavlankar, A., Baccichet, P., Varodayan, D., Girod, B.: Optimal slice size for streaming regions of high resolution video with virtual pan/tilt/zoom functionality. In: Proc. of 15th European Signal Processing Conference, EUSIPCO (2007)
3. Feng, W.C., Dang, T., Kassebaum, J., Bauman, T.: Supporting region-of-interest cropping through constrained compression. ACM Trans. Multimedia Comput. Commun. Appl. 7(3), 17:1–17:16 (2011)
4. Ngo, K.Q.M., Guntur, R., Ooi, W.T.: Adaptive encoding of zoomable video streams based on user access pattern. In: Proceedings of the Second Annual ACM Conference on Multimedia Systems, MMSys 2011, pp. 211–222. ACM, New York (2011)
5. Mavlankar, A., Noh, J., Baccichet, P., Girod, B.: Peer-to-peer multicast live video streaming with interactive virtual pan/tilt/zoom functionality. In: Proc. of IEEE International Conference on Image Processing, ICIP
6. Mavlankar, A., Varodayan, D., Girod, B.: Region-of-interest prediction for interactively streaming regions of high resolution video. In: Proc. International Packet Video Workshop (2007)
7. Shimoga, K.B.: Region-of-interest based video image transcoding for heterogenous client displays. In: Packet Video 2002 (2002)
8. Fan, X., Xie, X., Qin Zhou, H., Ying Ma, W.: Looking into video frames on small displays. In: Proc. of ACM Multimedia 2003, pp. 247–250. Press (2003)
9. Bae, T.M., Thang, T.C., Kim, D.Y., Ro, Y.M., Kang, J.W., Kim, J.G.: Multiple region-of-interest support in scalable video coding. ETRI Journal, 239–242 (2006)
10. Liu, C., Jin, X., Zhang, T., Goto, S.: Partial decoding scheme for H.264/AVC decoder. In: 2010 International Symposium on Intelligent Signal Processing and Communication Systems, ISPACS, pp. 1–4 (December 2010)
11. ffmpeg: Ffmpeg (May 2012),
    http://ffmpeg.org/index.html
12. libyuv: libyuv (May 2012),
    http://code.google.com/p/libyuv/
13. chromium: chromium (May 2012),
    http://code.google.com/p/chromium/issues/detail?id=71403
14. Zhang, L., Tiwana, B., Qian, Z., Wang, Z., Dick, R.P., Mao, Z.M., Yang, L.: Accurate online power estimation and automatic battery behavior based power model generation for smartphones. In: Proceedings of the Eighth IEEE/ACM/IFIP International Conference on Hardware/Software Codesign and System Synthesis, CODES/ISSS 2010, pp. 105–114. ACM, New York (2010)

SSIM-Based Error Resilient Video Coding over Packet-Switched Networks

Lei Zhang, Qiang Peng, and Xiao Wu

Southwest Jiaotong University, Chengdu, China
swjtu_zl@yahoo.cn, {qpeng,wuxiao}@home.swjtu.edu.cn

Abstract. The visual quality is a critical factor of compressed videos for error-prone transmission. This paper proposes a structural similarity (SSIM) based error resilient video coding scheme to improve the visual quality of compressed videos for transmission over packet-switched networks. In the proposed scheme, a SSIM-based end-to-end distortion model is developed to estimate the perceptual distortion for spatial and temporal error propagation. Based on the model, an optimal mode selection strategy is presented to improve the rate-distortion performance. Experiments show that the proposed scheme significantly improves the visual quality for H.264/AVC video coding over packet-switched networks.

Keywords: Error resilience, structural similarity, rate distortion optimization.

1 Introduction

Due to the limited bandwidth of the network channels, most video coding standards use the transform coding and motion compensated prediction to achieve high compression. However, the motion compensated prediction creates strong spatial-temporal dependency in video frames, which is very sensitive to the transmission errors. In packet-switched networks, packets may be discarded due to buffer overflow, or may be considered lost due to long queuing delays. Thus, transmitting the highly compressed video streams over packet-switched networks may suffer from spatial-temporal error propagation and lead to severe quality degradation at the decoder side. Therefore, error resilient video coding is a crucial requirement to protect compressed videos from packet loss.

As most compressed videos are represented to human users, the problem of error resilient video coding can be defined as follows: given the transmission conditions, such as bit-rate and packet-loss ratio, how to minimize the perceptual distortion at the receiver

$$\min \sum_{i=1}^{N} D_i \qquad s.t. \quad \sum_{i=1}^{N} R_i \leq R_T \quad and \quad p \tag{1}$$

W. Lin et al. (Eds.): PCM 2012, LNCS 7674, pp. 263–272, 2012.
© Springer-Verlag Berlin Heidelberg 2012

where D_i and R_i denote the perceptual distortion and bit-rate of coding block i in a coding order while N is the number of the coding blocks. R_T is the target bit-rate. p is the packet loss rate. Note that we assume the packet loss ratio is available at the encoder throughout this paper. This can be either specified as part of the initial negotiations, or adaptively calculated from information provided by the transmission protocol [1].

To solve this problem, two major issues have to be addressed. The first issue is to establish an efficient model to estimate the perceptual distortion of decoded videos. The second one is to incorporate the distortion estimation model into the rate-distortion (RD) based video codec, which aims to minimize the perceptual distortion of decoded videos by optimizing the coding options.

For the first issue, many schemes utilize the end-to-end distortion model to provide joint source-channel distortion estimation [1-4]. However, these models are derived in terms of mean squared error (MSE), which has been criticized for not correlating well with perceptual characteristics. On the other hand, some approaches estimate the visual quality based on the region of interest (ROI) [5-6]. However, ROI based approaches cannot provide accurate distortion estimation, and ROI determination may be difficult for most videos, especially for videos with natural scenes. Therefore, it is expected that perception-based end-to-end distortion model could be derived to provide more general and accurate distortion estimation. For the second issue, unlike the traditional error resilient video coding, the relationship between the bit-rate and the perceptual distortion is not easy to model. Recently, a number of perception-based RD optimization schemes have been proposed for error-free environment [7-8]. However, perception-based RD optimization for lossy transmission remains an unfilled blank.

In this paper, we adopt the well-known structural similarity (SSIM) index [9] as the distortion metric and present a SSIM-based error resilient video coding scheme. Firstly, a SSIM-based end-to-end distortion model is developed to estimate the perceptual distortion of decoded video. Secondly, SSIM-based mode selection strategy is presented to maximize the visual quality of decoded videos for the given transmission conditions. Better preserving the structural information of the decoded videos, the proposed scheme can achieve significant visual quality improvement for H.264/AVC video coding over packet-switched networks.

The remaining of the paper is organized as follows. Section 2 provides the SSIM-based end-to-end distortion model. Section 3 describes the optimal mode selection strategy based on the end-to-end distortion model. Section 4 provides the simulation results and Section 5 concludes the paper.

2   SSIM-Based End-to-End Distortion Model

2.1   Problem and Motivation

The traditional end-to-end distortion model recursively computes the overall decoder distortion due to the quantization, spatial-temporal error propagation, and error concealment. For a given packet loss rate p, the end-to-end expected distortion of pixel i in the n_{th} frame is

$$d_n^i = E\{[f_n^i - \tilde{f}_n^i]^2\}$$

$$\approx (1-p) \cdot (f_n^i - \hat{f}_n^i)^2 + (1-p) \cdot E\{[\hat{f}_n^i - \tilde{f}_n^i]^2\} + p \cdot (f_n^i - \hat{c}_n^i)^2 + p \cdot E\{[\hat{c}_n^i - \tilde{c}_n^i]^2\} \tag{2}$$

$$= (1-p) \cdot d_Q^i(n) + p \cdot d_C^i(n) + (1-p) \cdot d_{P\_f}^i(n) + p \cdot d_{P\_c}^i(n)$$

where f_n^i is the original value. $\hat{f}_n^i$ and $\tilde{f}_n^i$ are the corresponding reconstruction value at the encoder and decoder, respectively. $\tilde{c}_n^i$ is the error concealment value at the decoder. d_Q denotes the quantization distortion. d_C represents the error concealment distortion. d_{P_f} and d_{P_C} are the error propagation distortion from the reference frames and concealment frames, respectively.

With such an end-to-end distortion model, the complex error propagation in the video decoding loop has to be modeled with joint source-channel distortion analysis. However, it is to be noted that the above end-to-end distortion model cannot estimate well the visual quality in consistent with human visual system (HVS). Firstly, identical MSE values may amount to different levels of perceptual distortion. Secondly, the same transmission error propagated to different video contents may result in different perceptual distortions. Therefore, in the following section, we will develop a perception-based end-to-end distortion model to provide better estimation of overall perceptual distortion.

2.2   SSIM-Based End-to-End Distortion Estimation

To estimate the expected perceptual distortion of decoded videos, we adopt SSIM as the distortion metric due to its good trade off among accuracy, simplicity and efficiency. Moreover, we use expected decoded image instead of expected distortion to describe the error propagation, which works as follows:

Let b_n^i denote the original block i in the frame n. $\hat{b}_n^i$ and $\tilde{b}_n^i$ be the corresponding reconstruction block at the encoder and decoder, respectively. In inter-mode, $\hat{b}_r^j$ denote the motion prediction block of b_n^i at the encoder and $\tilde{b}_r^j$ be the corresponding motion prediction block at the decoder. The prediction error is $e_n^i = b_n^i - \hat{b}_r^j$ and its reconstruction value is denoted by $\hat{e}_n^i$. In intra-mode, the original value of the block is directly coded and transmitted, we treat $\tilde{b}_n^i = \hat{e}_n^i$ as a special case $\tilde{b}_r^j = 0$. If the block is lost, the decoder conceals the error using the block i in the frame $n-1$, in this case $\tilde{b}_n^i = \tilde{b}_{n-1}^i$. For a given packet loss rate p, the SSIM based end-to-end distortion can be expressed as

$$d_{SSIM}(n,i) = 1 - SSIM(b_n^i, \tilde{b}_n^i) \tag{3}$$

with

$$\tilde{b}_n^i = (1-p) \cdot E[\tilde{b}_r^j + \hat{e}_n^i] + p \cdot E[\tilde{b}_{n-1}^i]$$

$$= (1-p) \cdot \hat{b}_n^i + p \cdot \hat{b}_{n-1}^i + (1-p) \cdot E(\tilde{b}_r^j - \hat{b}_r^j) + p \cdot E(\tilde{b}_{n-1}^i - \hat{b}_{n-1}^i) \qquad (4)$$

$$= (1-p) \cdot \hat{b}_n^i + p \cdot \hat{b}_{n-1}^i + (1-p) \cdot B_{P\_f} + p \cdot B_{P\_c}$$

where B_{P_f} denotes the error propagation in the reference block and B_{P_c} denotes the error propagation in the conceal block. Finally, we use the Equation (5) to recursively describe the error propagation B_P for a given block x in the frame y as

$$B_P(y, x) = E(\tilde{b}_y^x - \hat{b}_y^x)$$

$$= p \cdot \hat{b}_{y-1}^x + (1-p) \cdot B_{P\_f} + p \cdot B_{P\_c} \qquad (5)$$

When the reference or conceal block is coded with the intra-mode, there is no error-propagation need to be considered. It can be seen that the proposed model provides a simple and general solution to estimate the content-based perceptual distortion. However, the calculation of SSIM and the decoding operation for each reconstruction block make an increase of computational cost.

3   SSIM-Based Error Resilient Video Coding

After obtaining the end-to-end perceptual distortion estimation, we incorporate it into the RD optimized error resilience to solve the minimization problem in Equation (1) for H.264/AVC video coding. Since the decoding of an intra-coding block does not need the information from its previous frames, it is widely recognized that intra-coding is an important tool for mitigating the effects of packet loss. However, intra-coding typically requires a higher bit rate than inter-coding. Thus, the optimization problem in Equation (1) can be converted to the problem of mode selection between intra-coding and inter-coding as follows

$$\min\{J(mode)\} = \min\{D_{SSIM}(mode \mid p, QP) + \lambda_{SSIM} \cdot R(mode \mid QP)\} \qquad (6)$$

where D_{SSIM} and R denote the expected perceptual distortion and bit-rate of current coding block. $mode$ denotes either an intra-coding or an inter-coding. QP is the quantization parameter, which is determined by the target bit-rate. λ_{SSIM} is the Lagrange multiplier, which is a critical parameter needs to be determine for the trade-off between overall perceptual distortion and bit-rate.

Different from the MSE-based approach in the error-free environment, a new Lagrange multiplier should be determined due to the overall perceptual distortion and bit-rate. According to [1, 7, 10], a new Lagrange multiplier λ_{SSIM} for the error-prone environment is approximately obtained by

$$\lambda_{SSIM} = \omega \cdot (-\frac{\beta}{R_T}) \cdot \overline{D'_{SSIM}} \qquad (7)$$

with

$$\omega = 2^{(QP-\overline{QP})/3} \qquad (8)$$

where $\overline{D'_{SSIM}}$ denotes the average distortion of previous coding units without the transmission error. R_T is the target bit-rate and β is a negative constant. With extensive simulations, we construct a experimental look-up table for use as $-\beta/R_T$. $\overline{QP}$ is the average quantization parameter of previous coding units and ω is used to adjust the percentage of intra-coding macroblocks.

Thus, the new Lagrange multiplier λ_{SSIM} is dependent on the video content, which needs to be updated after each encoding frame. Fig.1 presents the relationship between the Lagrange multiplier λ_{SSIM} and the target bit-rate for different test sequences in the error-free environment. It can be seen that λ_{SSIM} is diverse for different test sequences due to varying relationship of perceptual distortion and bit-rate.

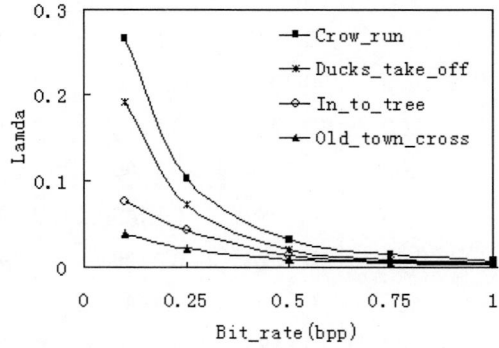

Fig. 1. Relationship between the λ_{SSIM} and target bit-rate

4   Experimental Results

To verify the performance of the proposed approach, four HD sequences (640×360): 'Crow_run', 'In_to_tree', 'Ducks_take_off' and 'Old_town_cross' [11] are tested in the experiments. The proposed scheme is integrated into the standard H.264/AVC test model JM9.8. The first 100 frames of these sequences are coded. The first frame is coded as intra-frame (I frame) and the rest frames are coded as inter-frames (P frames). The frames are subject to random packet loss. According to the Internet error pattern tested by VCEG [12], the test sequences are encoded in 10% and 20% packet-loss ratio, respectively. The experiments are repeated 30 times and the distortion results are averaged, which are used as the actual distortion.

4.1   Evaluation of RD Performance

We compare the performance of the proposed SSIM-based perceptual error-resilient video coding with the MSE-based error-resilient video coding. The results with different bit-rates and packet-loss ratios for all four sequences are listed in Table 1. The initial QP is equal to 28 and 36. The "SER" shows the coding results of proposed SSIM-based error-resilient video coding and the "MER" denotes the coding performance of MSE-based error-resilient video coding. Fig. 2 (a) and (b) demonstrate the Rate-SSIM curves of two video sequences, respectively.

For all sequences, the proposed scheme achieves better visual quality than 'MER'. The average gain of SSIM is 0.021. The proposed scheme is more effective with high packet-loss ratio or at low bit-rate. Especially for the 'Ducks_take_off' sequence at 0.4Mbps with 10% packet-loss ratio, a high SSIM gain of 0.0495 can be obtained. Note that the proposed method does not optimize the mode selection against objective quality, thus PSNR may decrease, compared with the conventional error-resilient video coding.

Table 1. Simulation results with different packet-loss ratios and bit-rates

Sequence (Packet loss ratio)	Bit-rate (Mbps)	SSIM		PSNR(dB)	
		MER	SER	MER	SER
Crow_run (20%)	2.00	0.7945	**0.8097**	27.08	27.42
	1.00	0.7023	**0.7276**	24.54	24.18
Crow_run (10%)	2.00	0.8078	**0.8213**	27.42	27.66
	1.00	0.7064	**0.7306**	24.63	24.22
Ducks_take_off (20%)	1.50	0.7989	**0.8145**	27.80	27.63
	0.40	0.5674	**0.6120**	23.93	23.38
Ducks_take_off (10%)	1.50	0.8107	**0.8203**	28.07	27.80
	0.40	0.5685	**0.6180**	23.93	23.42
In_to_tree (20%)	1.00	0.8417	**0.8581**	34.19	34.47
	0.50	0.7894	**0.8176**	32.22	31.76
In_to_tree (10%)	1.00	0.8599	**0.8667**	34.95	34.22
	0.50	0.8057	**0.8337**	32.77	32.55
Old_town_cross (20%)	0.75	0.8801	**0.8867**	32.18	32.80
	0.15	0.7088	**0.7297**	26.87	26.73
Old_town_cross (10%)	1.00	0.9039	**0.9095**	33.40	34.15
	0.15	0.7117	**0.7312**	26.93	26.76

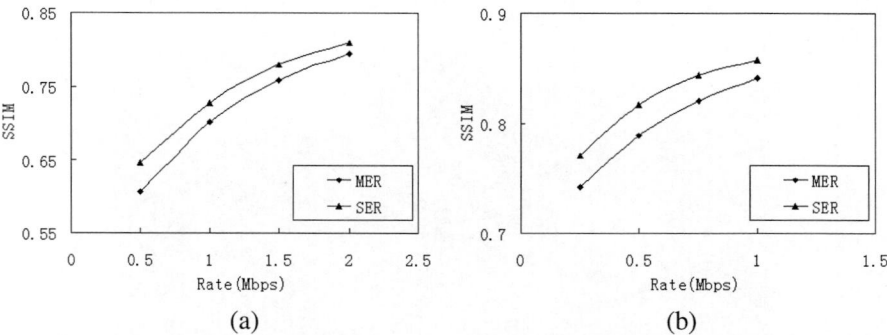

Fig. 2. Overall Rate-SSIM performance: (a) 'Crow_run' with 10% packet-loss; (b) 'In_to_tree' with 20% packet-loss.

Table 2 shows the average percentage of intra-coding macroblocks (MBs) for all four sequences with different bit-rates and packet-loss ratios. It can be seen that, for those sequences in which more distortion can be tolerated, such as 'In_to_tree' and 'Old_town_cross', less intra-coding mode are selected using the SSIM-based perceptual error-resilient video coding.

Table 2. Average percentage of intra-coding MBs

Sequence	Bit-rate (Mbps)	Packet loss: 20%		Packet loss: 10%	
		MER	SER	MER	SER
Crow_run	2.00	0.45	0.34	0.38	0.27
	1.00	0.41	0.40	0.37	0.37
Ducks_take_off	1.50	0.46	0.49	0.36	0.41
	0.40	0.35	0.37	0.32	0.36
In_to_tree	1.00	0.31	0.17	0.25	0.12
	0.50	0.26	0.19	0.22	0.14
Old_town_cross	0.75	0.17	0.11	0.12	0.07
	0.15	0.12	0.14	0.11	0.13

4.2   Evaluation of Subjective Quality

Finally, a comparison on visual quality of the reconstructed images by different error resilient video coding is shown in Fig. 3 and Fig. 4. For the similar bit-rate, the proposed scheme based on SSIM provides better visual quality because more information and details have been protected from the transmission errors. On the other hand, the conventional scheme based on MSE suffers from larger perceptual distortion.

(a)

(b)

(c)

Fig. 3. 78th frame of 'crow_run' encoded at 2Mbps with 20% packet-loss: (a) Original frame; (b) MER (SSIM: 0.786); (c) SER (SSIM: 0.805).

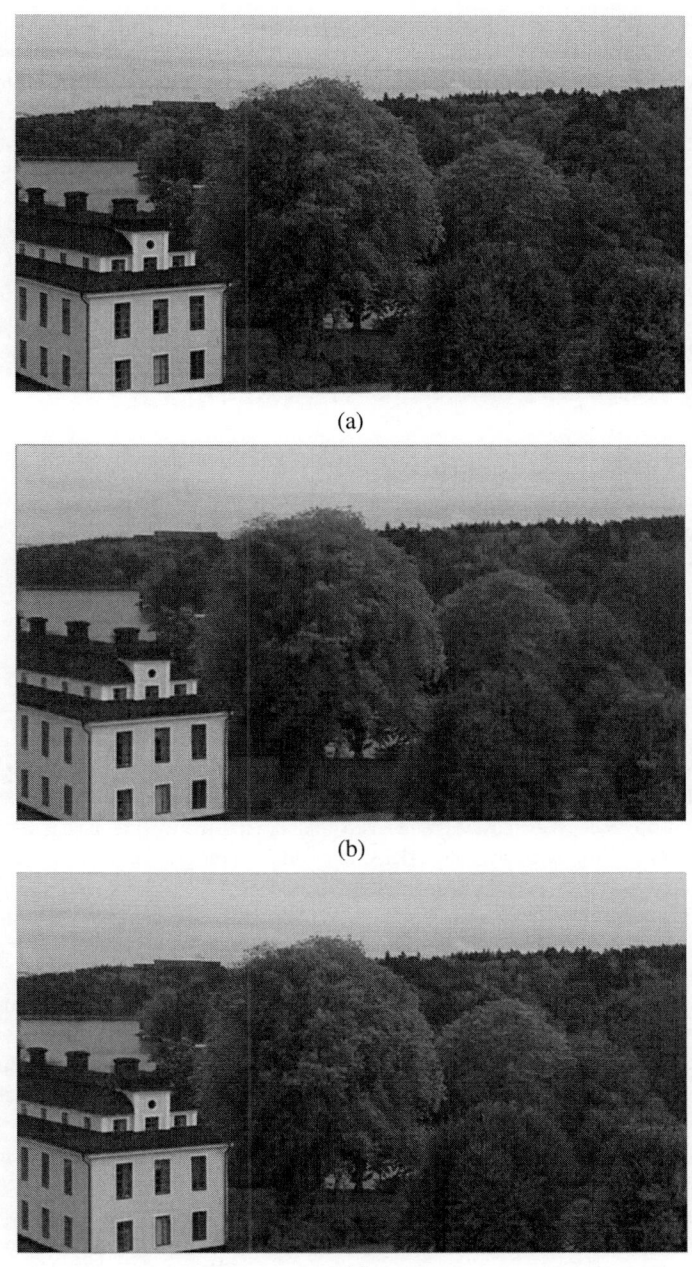

(a)

(b)

(c)

Fig. 4. 96th frame of 'in_to_tree' encoded at 1Mbps with 10% packet-loss: (a) Original frame; (b) MER (SSIM: 0.810); (c) SER (SSIM: 0.823).

5 Discussion

In this paper, we propose a SSIM-based perceptual error resilient video coding for H.264/AVC over packet-switched networks. With the SSIM-based end-to-end distortion, a new RD optimized error resilient video coding scheme is presented and the rate-SSIM performance is improved significant. Our future work on the perceptual error resilience will focus on the accuracy of Lagrange multiplier and optimized bit allocation.

Acknowledgments. This work described in this paper was supported by the NSFC (Grant No. 60972111, 61036008, 61071184), Research Funds for the Doctoral Program of Higher Education of China (No. 20100184120009, 20120184110001), Program for Sichuan Provincial Science Fund for Distinguished Young Scholars (No. 2012JQ0029), and the Fundamental Research Funds for the Central Universities (Project no. SWJTU09CX032, SWJTU10CX08, SWJTU11ZT08).

References

1. Zhang, R., Regunathan, S.L., Rose, K.: Video coding with optimal inter/intra-mode switching for packet loss resilience. IEEE Journal on Selected Areas in Communications 18, 966–976 (2000)
2. He, Z.H., Cai, J.F., Chen, C.W.: Joint source channel rate-distortion analysis for adaptive mode selection and rate control in wireless video coding. IEEE Transaction on Circuits System Video Technology 12, 511–523 (2002)
3. Wang, Y., Wu, Z.Y., Boyce, J.M.: Modeling of transmission-loss-induced distortion in decoded video. IEEE Transaction on Circuits System Video Technology 16, 716–732 (2006)
4. Zhou, Y., Hou, C.P., Xiang, W., Wu, F.: Channel distortion modeling for multi-view video transmission over packet-switched networks. IEEE Transaction on Circuits System Video Technology 21, 1679–1692 (2011)
5. Xue, Z., Loo, K.K., Cosmas, J., Tun, M., Yip, P.Y.: Error-resilient scheme for wavelet video coding using automatic ROI detection and Wyner-Ziv coding over packet erasure channel. IEEE Transaction on Broadcasting 56, 481–493 (2010)
6. Dissanayake, M.B., Worrall, S., Fernando, W.A.C.: Error resilience for multi-view video using redundant macroblock coding. In: IEEE International Conference on Industrial and Information Systems, ICIIS, pp. 472–476. IEEE Press, New York (2011)
7. Ou, T.S., Huang, Y.H., Chen, H.H.: SSIM-based perceptual rate control for video coding. IEEE Transaction on Circuits System Video Technology 21, 682–691 (2011)
8. Wang, S.Q., Rehman, A., Wang, Z., Ma, S., Gao, W.: SSIM-motivated rate distortion optimization for video coding. IEEE Transaction on Circuits System Video Technology 22, 516–529 (2012)
9. Wang, Z., Bovik, A.C., Sheikh, H.R., Simoncelli, E.P.: Image quality assessment: From error visibility to structural similarity. IEEE Transaction on Image Processing 13, 600–612 (2004)
10. Wiegand, T., Girod, B.: Lagrange multiplier selection in hybrid video coder control. In: IEEE International Conference on Image Processing, ICIP, pp. 542–545. IEEE Press, New York (2001)
11. Xiph.org Video Test Media, http://media.xiph.org/video/derf/
12. Wenger, S.: Error Patterns for Internet Experiments,
    ftp://ftp.imtc-files.org/jvt-experts/9910_Red/Q15-I16r1.zip

De-blocking Filter Design for HEVC and H.264/AVC

Muchen Li, Jinjia Zhou, Dajiang Zhou, Xiao Peng, and Satoshi Goto

The Graduate School of Information, Production and Systems, Waseda University
Muchen.li@toki.waseda.jp

Abstract. As the successor of H.264/AVC, HEVC inherits the basic property of H.264/AVC and gives some new features. This paper introduces a novel dual-standard de-blocking filter architecture which could support both of the HEVC and H.264/AVC standards. It takes 48 clock cycles for H.264/AVC and 24 cycles for HEVC for every 16×16 block. The proposed unified-cross based processing order greatly reduces the design complexity. The proposed architecture occupies 43.3k equivalent gate count at frequency of 200MHz in SMIC 65nm library, which could satisfy the throughput requirement of quad-full high definition (QFHD) on 60fps for H.264/AVC and super hi-vision (SHV) on 60fps for HEVC. In addition, the total power consumption could be reduced by 37.8% in skipping mode when the edges need not be filtered.

Keywords: HEVC, H.264/AVC, De-blocking filter, dual-standard, Low Power, SHV, HD.

1 Introduction

Digital video compression technology has been developed enormously in the last twenty years. H.264/AVC is currently the most powerful video coding tool and has been deployed widely in various applications [1] [2] [3]. With raising pursuit of visual effects, the high efficiency video coding (HEVC) is proposed for high resolution video applications. HEVC aims to substantially reduce bitrate by half with comparable image quality compared to AVC High Profile [4] [5] [6]

Since the devices and media content with current popular H.264/AVC standard would not be replaced immediately. It is necessary to design a universal decoder which is capable of supporting H.264/AVC and HEVC, rather than the individual designs dedicated to each standard, which will lead to high power and unworthy hardware cost. Consequently, the dual-standard architecture for de-blocking filter, which is an important part in video codec, is a critical problem in this topic.

Due to the high adaptability and the small 4×4 processing block, the de-blocking filtering of H.264/AVC becomes computational intensive process which simply accounts for one-third of the computational complexity of the whole decoder [7]. These demanding properties make it difficult and challenging to design an efficient de-blocking filter, especially for the high definition video applications. There are many works focus on the efficient de-blocking design in [8] [9] [10] [11]. In order to achieve real time performance for larger frame dimensions videos, HEVC significantly reduces the complexity of it, which mainly from the use of larger processing unit.

W. Lin et al. (Eds.): PCM 2012, LNCS 7674, pp. 273–284, 2012.
© Springer-Verlag Berlin Heidelberg 2012

The filtering is just performed on the edges of 8×8 sample grids. Furthermore, the novel processing order of HEVC de-blocking reduces the data dependency and increase the parallelism. The horizontal filtering and vertical filtering could be performed parallel respectively, which is not available for H.264/AVC [13].

The rest of this paper is organized as follows. Section 2 introduces and compares the de-blocking filter algorithm defined in HEVC and H.264/AVC standard. Section 3 presents the system architecture and function module design. In Section 4, the implementation results and power analysis discussion are addressed. Finally, section 5 draws the conclusion.

2   Deblocking Filter Algorithm in HEVC

This section mainly states the critical difference between HEVC and H.264/AVC based on the latest HEVC work draft 6 [14] and HM-6.0 rc1 [15]. The filtering decision which is related to the design is also stated.

2.1   LCU-Based Process

In HEVC, coding tree blocks (CTB) which is also called large coding unit (LCU) is the basic processing unit. The LCU size varies from 8×8 to 64×64. De-blocking filtering is performed based on LCU with the raster scan order, showed in Fig.1. Following the quad-tree structure, each LCU could be further split into coding units (CUs) in flexible size not less than 8×8. Fig.1 also shows an example of quad-tree structure of 64×64 LCU. All the edges in 8×8 block will be checked and the de-blocking filter will be applied to the PU edges and TU edges except the edges at the picture or slice boundary, where the de-blocking filtering is disabled.

Raster Scan order for frame   Z Scan order for LCU

Fig. 1. Raster Scan and Z Scan order

2.2   Parallel De-Blocking

HEVC has already adopted the frame-based filtering process proposed by Sony Corporation [14]. On this condition, the horizontal filtering is performed firstly to all the LCUs in the processing picture, and then the vertical filtering is performed to all the LCUs later, which is also called frame-based processing. In H.264/AVC, the de-blocking process of both directions for current MB should be completed before moving to the next MB.

HEVC de-blocking filter are performed on 8×8 blocks. For each minimum vertical or horizontal edge, 4 pixels on each side will be involved and finally at most 3 pixels will be modified. The edges in the same direction of one LCU are independent. For example, as showed in Fig.2, V11 and V12 in current LCU is independent.

The use of larger de-blocking block and the frame based filtering order removes the data dependency between the edges in one direction. In other words, the vertical filtering or horizontal filtering could be parallelized fully. This is why the HEVC de-blocking is also called parallel de-blocking.

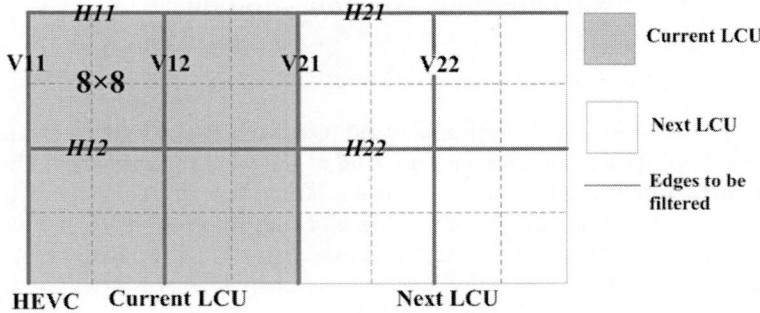

Fig. 2. Data dependency of HEVC

2.3   Filtering Decision and Calculation

Filtering decision for an edge includes two Levels: the first is whether the filtering is applied; the second is how strong the filtering is applied.

Fig.3 depicts an example of vertical edge and pixel samples.

Boundary strength (Bs) is one of the parameters that determine how strong the filtering is applied. The Bs value varies from 0~2 according to the coding information of the blocks in both sides [15]. Compare to the BS values varies from 0~4 in H.264 [7], the Bs calculation for HEVC is much simpler [14]. For chrominance component, when Bs is not equal to 2, the edge should not be filtered. For luminance, there are two cases that the filtering will not be applied. The First is Bs=0. The second is Bs is non-zero and condition (3) is not satisfied. β is QP-dependent parameter [7]. These skipping cases are corresponding to the skipping mode in the hardware implementation which could greatly reduce dynamic power.

After the filtering is determined, strong filtering or weak filtering will be conditionally applied [14].

$$d_0 = \left| p2_0 - 2p1_0 + p0_0 \right| + \left| q2_0 - 2q1_0 + q0_0 \right| \tag{1}$$

$$d_3 = \left| p2_3 - 2p1_3 + p0_3 \right| + \left| q2_3 - 2q1_3 + q0_3 \right| \tag{2}$$

$$d_0 + d_3 < \beta \tag{3}$$

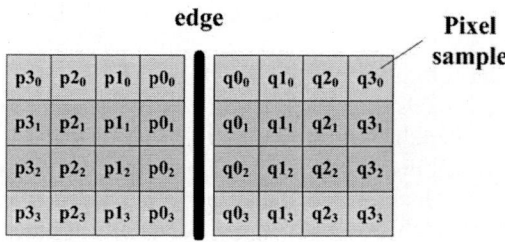

Fig. 3. Filtering decision example for HEVC

3   System Architecture and Function Module

3.1   Unified-Cross Based Processing Order

As described in last section 2, the frame-based processing is not suitable for hardware implementation. Because the intermediate data of the whole frames should be stored after horizontal filtering and reused in vertical filtering. It needs too many registers.

However, CU size is variable but the de-blocking filter in HEVC is always implemented on 8×8 blocks.   The most reasonable design is LCU based, because LCU size is relatively fixed and it could be backward compatible to H.264/AVC.

Since the algorithm is frame based, there are some problems for the LCU-based implementation. Fig.4 gives an example of LCU-based processing

To obey the basic processing order of HEVC, the right most horizontal edges in the current LCU could not be processed before the left most vertical edges of next LCU is processed. As showed in Fig.4, the filtering on, edge 21, 22 should be processed after edge 17, 18, 19, 20. From the time slot, it is easy to find that the filtering for #n+1, #n, #n-1 LCU is not sequential but alternative, which introduce 3 drawbacks.

1. The control of the filtering is complexity and the hardware cost in control part is large. Usually, the control part cost is larger than the filtering computation part, so the control complexity is very important for the hardware design.
2. The filtering of one LCU involves the data from upper, left and right neighboring LCUs. The cost of buffers or memory accesses will be increased.
3. There is a latency in the process of current LCU,   in other words, the filtering of current LCU could not completed before the data of next LCU is available. It will decrease performance of the whole decoding system.

A novel processing order is proposed. Fig.5 shows that we choose the different blocks to combine a processing unit called unified-cross unit which is different from LCU. This unit is symmetric, and the edges need to filtered are arranged in several crosses. It is easy to find that the unified-cross units are independent with each other. By further analysis, we found that the crosses in this unit are also independent with each other. If we take a cross as a basic processing unit, the filtering of the whole larger unit is a simple loop of the filtering based on crosses. The processing order for the unified-cross unit is shown in Fig.6. Comparing with the LCU-based processing, the cross-based processing can greatly reduce the cost in control module and buffers.

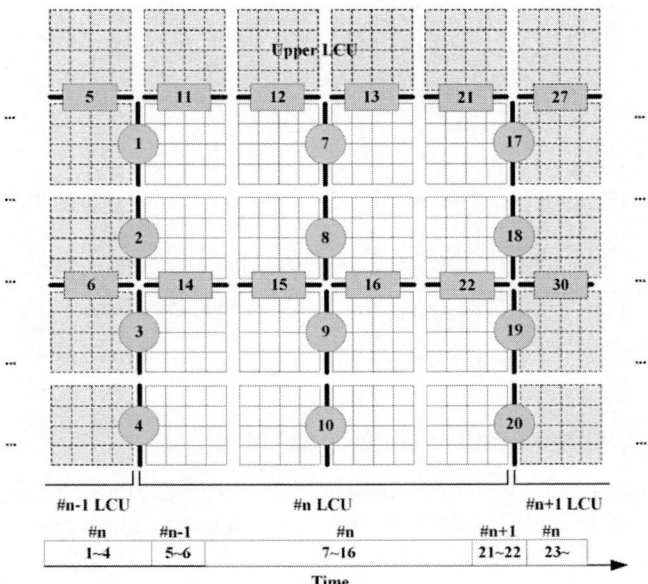

Fig. 4. LCU-based processing

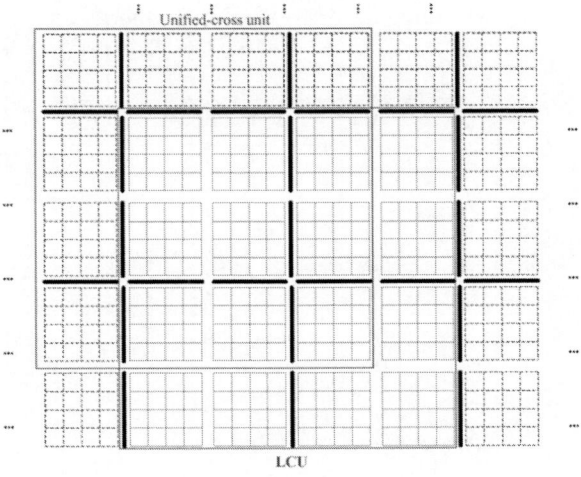

Fig. 5. Unified-cross unit

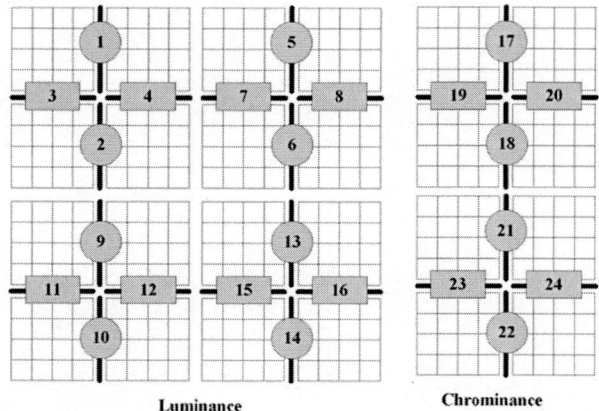

Fig. 6. Unified-cross based processing

3.2 System Architecture for De-Blocking Filter

Fig. 7 shows the block diagram of the whole de-blocking filter. The proposed architecture of HEVC-H.264/AVC de-blocking filter architecture mainly includes 3 parts.

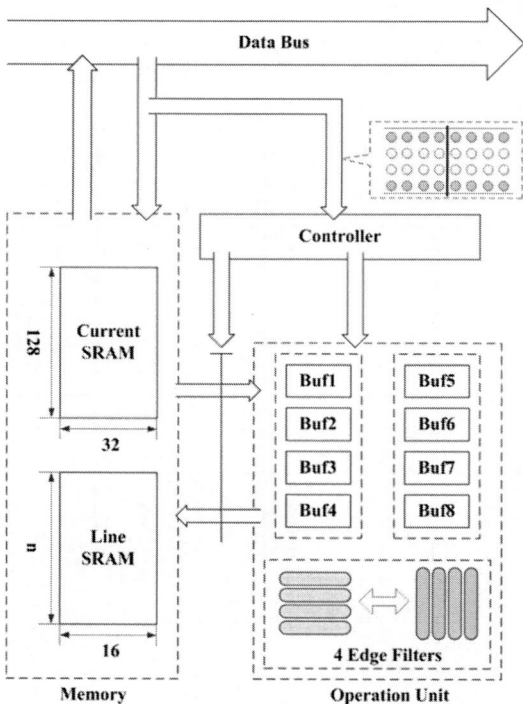

Fig. 7. Block diagram of dual-standard architecture

The Memory part contains two kinds of memory: the dual-port Current SRAM is used to store the data fetched from the main data bus, arrange the final filtered results in proper sequence and output the results to the data bus; the Line SRAM is used to store the lowermost blocks in current LCU which would be used in lower LCU some LCUs later. The words of this line SRAM is determined by the frame width [8]. The temporal data of the cross-based processing is just stored in buffer and updated in 4 clock cycles.

The controller is used to control the order of the filtering, especially for the skipping mode. As described in section 2, when the skipping cases are detected, the controller will disable the operation unit by clock gating. At the same time, the memory accesses between the memory and operation unit are also canceled.

The operation unit contains 4 edge filters which are used for vertical and horizontal edges as demands. The 8 buffers in operation unit are all made up of registers, each of which could store 16 pixels. Which are used to store the temporal data Filtering order for HEVC and H.264/AVC

3.3   Filtering Order of HEVC and H.264

The Unified-cross based processing is used in conjunction with an efficient and suitable memory organization.

As shown in the Fig. 8(a), for a unified-cross unit, the first line of 4×4 blocks are accessed from the Line SRAM and the other is read from Current SRAM. The 4×4 blocks besides a vertical are stored in the same address of the current SRAM. By this memory arrange, the cross-based filtering could be performed

As shown in the Fig.8 (b), the first two steps are reading data from memory to filter edge 1 and 2. Each step needs to deal with 32 pixels, and then the width of memory should be 32×8=256 bit (assuming one pixel is represented by 8 bits). The temporal results of step 1 and step 2 are stored in buffers. Step 3 and step 4 are fetching data from the proper buffers and writing the results to memory. Since the temporal data are stored in buffers, the memory accesses of data bus and memory accesses of operation unit could overlap accurately for dual-port SRAM.

Fig. 9 shows the filtering order and buffer arrangement for H.264/AVC. Because of the dependency of edges between MBs, the leftmost 4 blocks from the previous MB are stored in buffer 5 to 8 for luminance case. Generally this proposed filtering order is based on the principle that the occupied buffer should be released as quickly as possible since the cost of buffer is expensive. Also, it should guarantee that the rightmost 4 blocks should be stored in buffer 5 to 8 for the next MB. As shown in Fig. 9, it takes 32 clock cycles to finish luminance filtering and 8 clock cycles to finish chrominance filtering. Thus, a 16×16 MB in H.264/AVC takes 48 clock cycles on average.

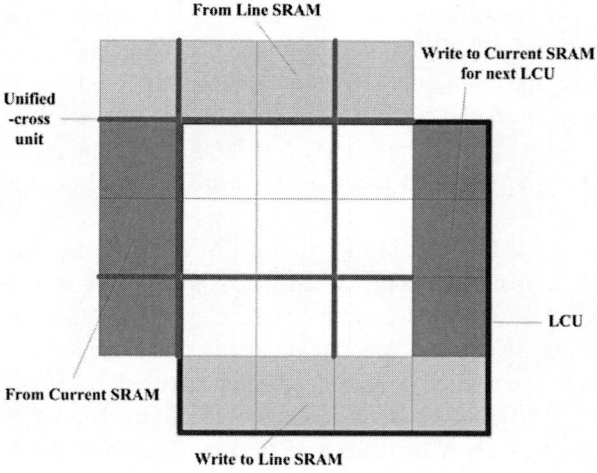

(a) Memory organization

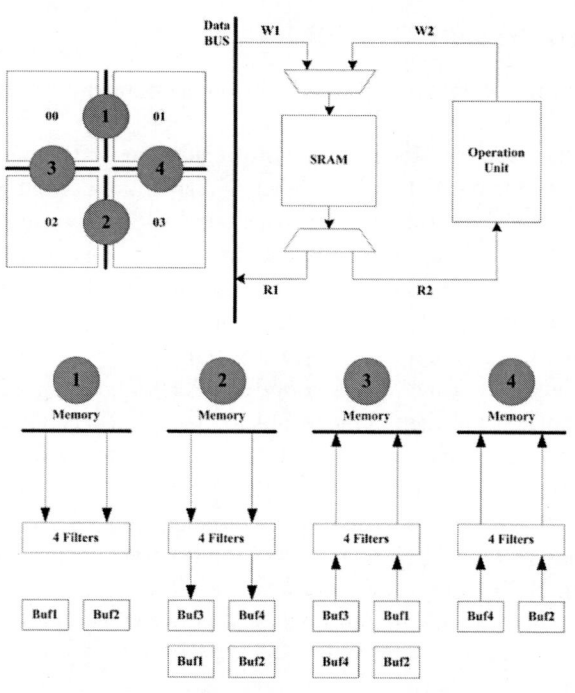

MEM_W: Memory write

MEM_R: Memory read

W1: Memory write from Data Bus
W2: Memory write from operation unit
R1: Memory read to Data Bus
R2: Memory read to operation unit

(b) Filtering order of a cross.

Fig. 8. Memory organization and filtering order for HEVC

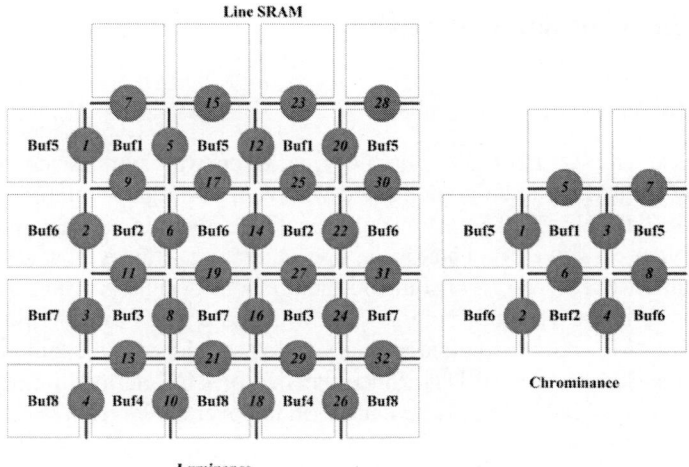

Fig. 9. Filtering order for H.264/AVC

3.4   Hardware Reusing Design

In the proposed reconfigurable de-blocking filter architecture, luminance and chrominance are calculated serially. It means that the filter should be designed to satisfy 4 kinds of filtering functions including not only the HEVC and H.264/AVC but also the luminance and chrominance. According to the calculation equations listed in the two standards [7] [14], some of the computation components could be reused. Fig. 10 shows the architecture of the integrated filter which depicts some major reusing functions. As a result in the implementation, this hardware reusing could save 30% gate count.

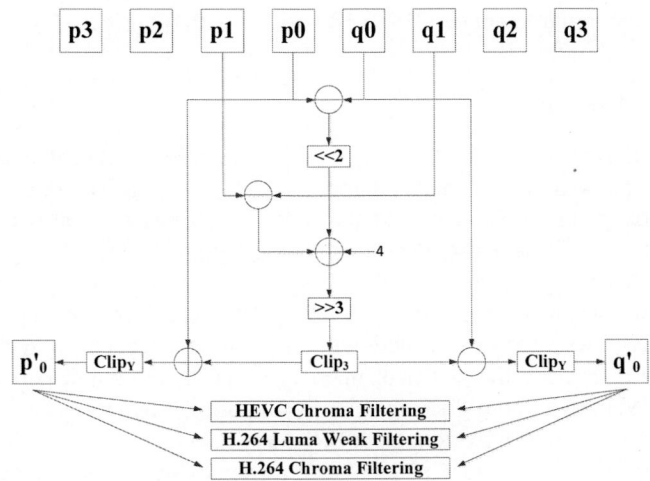

Fig. 10. Example of filtering reuse

4   Implementation and Analysis

4.1   Synthesis Result

The proposed HEVC-H.264/AVC de-blocking filter was synthesized with SMIC 65nm 1.08V library. It can be implemented with equivalent gate count of 43.3k at the frequency of 200MHz. To the best of our knowledge, there is no implementation for HEVC de-blocking filter available in the open literature. However, since our design can also support H.264/AVC, we compare the previous designs in Table 1. As shown in Table 1, our design uses much bigger SRAM than the previous designs. The reason is that this SRAM is not the internal memory which should store the temporal data for filters like the designs in [10] [11]. Since the size of LCU defined in HEVC varies from 8 to 64, two 128×128 SRAM here are used to cover the larger size case.

Table 1. Comparison of de-blocking filter

	[10]	[11]	This work
Support standard	H.264/AVC	H.264/AVC	H.264/AVC/HEVC
Cycles/16x16block	48-100	48	24/48
Gates Count	17.1K	30.2K	43.3K
Process	130nm	130nm	65nm
Edge Filter Number	2	4	4
Internal SRAM	2p 28×32×2	2p 24×64	2p 128×128×2
Line Buffer	External	External	External

Under this condition, the 4 extra buffers are added for H.264/AVC's leftmost blocks and other temporal results. Considering this design can also support HEVC standard, it is a reasonable cost.

On throughput, our proposed architecture needs 24 clock cycles for 16x16 block for HEVC standard. The Thus, it realizes 2.13×10^9 pixels per second which could easily satisfy the requirement of SHV (7680×4320) with 60fps case [16].

4.2   Power Analysis

As described in section 2, when Bs is 0 or other skip case   is detected, the controller would enable the skipping mode. In skipping mode, the edge filters could be terminated by clock gating technique, and the memory accesses are also eliminated by skipping controller. Table 1 lists the percentage of skipped edges during the software based experiments of 4 sequences.

The power analysis is also carried out in the VCS and Power Compiler after synthesis. Fig. 11 shows the power reduction on the case of sequence (3) in Table 2.

As shown in Fig. 11, the power of memory access is the major part of the whole architecture. Although about 86% edges are skipped, the memory writing from data bus to SRAM and memory reading from SRAM to data bus are not be skipped. Thus, the power reduction of memory is 43%. The power reduction from clock gating for filters is 26.4%. In total power, the clock gating only contribute 8.4% reduction, and the final power could be reduced by 37.8%.

Table 2. Proportion of skipped edges

Sequence	Luma			Chroma
	Total Skip	Bs=0	Bs!=0&(3)not satisfied	Bs!=2
(1)RaceHorses	74.39%	47.61%	26.78%	76.64%
(2)BasketballPass	87.52%	77.88%	9.64%	88.22%
(3)BQMall	86.38%	74.81%	11.57%	87.09%
(4)vidyo1	89.39%	87.30%	2.09%	91.08%

(Gop = IPPP   QP = 27   LCU = 64×64   with HM 5.0)

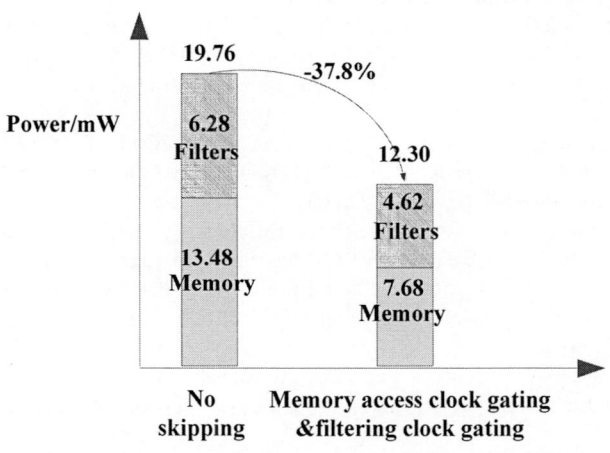

Fig. 11. Power analysis of skipping mode

5   Conclusion

This paper introduces a novel dual-stamdard de-blocking filter architecture which could support both of the HEVC and H.264/AVC standards. For H.264/AVC standard, it takes 32 clock cycles for luminance part and 16 clock cycles for chrominance part in one 16×16 macro-block. For the HEVC standard, the proposed unified-cross based processing greatly reduces the design complexity. As a result, 16×16 coding unit needs 16 and 8 clock cycles for luminance case and chrominance case respectively. In the implementation, the proposed design occupies 43.3k equivalent gate count at frequency of 200MHz in SMIC 65nm library, which could easily satisfy the throughput requirement of super hi-vision (SHV). In addition, the total power consumption could be reduced by 37.8% in skipping mode when the edges need not be filtered.

References

1. Draft ITU-T recommendation and final draft international standard of joint video specification (ITU-T Rec. H.264/ISO/IEC 14 496-10 AVC. Joint Video Team (JVT) of ISO/IEC MPEG and ITU-T VCEG, JVTG050 (2003)

2. Wiegand, T., et al.: Overview of the H.264/AVC video coding standard. IEEE Trans. Circuits Syst. Video Technol. 13(7), 560–576 (2003)
3. http://www.engadget.com/2011/11/13/2012-london-olymipics-super-hi-vision-broadcast-coming-to-se/
4. http://www.itu.int/en/ITU-T/studygroups/com16/video/Pages/jctvc.aspx
5. Li, B., Sullivan, G.J., Xu, J.: Comparison of Compression Performance of HEVC Working Draft 5 with AVC High Profile. JCTVC-H0360, JCTVC 8th Meeting, San José, CA, USA, February 1-10 (2012)
6. Kossentini, F., Mahdi, N., Guermazi, H., et al.: Informal Subjective Quality Comparison of Compression Performance of HEVC Working Draft 5 with AVC High Profile. JCTVC-H0562 JCTVC 8th Meeting: San José, CA, USA, February 1-10 (2012)
7. List, P., Joch, A., Lainema, J., Bjøntegaard, G., Karczewicz, M.: Adaptive deblocking filter. IEEE Trans. on Circuits and Syst. for Video Tech. 13(7), 614–619 (2003)
8. Xu, K., Choy, C.S.: A five-stage pipeline, 204 cycles/MB, single-port SRAM-based deblocking filter for H.264/AVC. IEEE Transactions on Circuits and Systems 18(3), 363–374 (2008)
9. Tobajas, F., Callicó, G.M., Pérez, P.A., de Armas, V., Sarmiento, R.: An Efficient Double-Filter Hardware Architecture for H.264/AVC De-blocking Filtering. IEEE Transactions on Consumer Electronics 54(1) (February 2008)
10. Lin, Y.-C., et al.: A Two-Result-per-Cycle De-blocking Filter Architecture for QFHD H.264/AVC Decoder. IEEE Trans. on VLSI Systems 17(6) (June 2009)
11. Zhou, D., Zhou, J., Zhu, J., Goto, S.: A48 Cycles/MB H.264/AVC De-blocking Filter Architecture for Ultra High Definition Applications. IEICE Trans. Fundamentals E92-A(12) (December 2009)
12. McCann, K., Han, W.-J., Kim, I.: Samsung's Response to the Call for Proposals on Video Compression Technology. JCTVC-A124, JCTVC 1st Meeting: Dresden, DE, April 15-23 (2010)
13. Ugur, K., Andersson, K., Fuldseth, A., et al.: High Performance, Low Complexity Video Coding and the Emerging HEVC Standard. IEEE Trans. on Circuits and Systems for Video Technology 20(12) (December 2010)
14. Bross, B., Hhi, F., Han, W., et al.: High efficiency video coding (HEVC) text specification draft 6. JCTVC-H1003, JCTVC 7th Meeting: Geneva, CH, November 21-30 (2011)
15. https://hevc.hhi.fraunhofer.de/svn/svn_HEVCSoftware/tags/
16. Zhou, D., Zhou, J., Zhu, J., Liu, P., Goto, S.: A 2Gpixel/s H.264/AVC HP/MVC Video Decoder Chip for Super Hi-Vision and 3DTV/FTV Applications. ISSCC Dig. Tech. Papers, pp. 224–225 (2012)

A Local Texture-Constrained Super-Resolution Method

Qingjie Liu, Yunhong Wang, and Zhaoxiang Zhang

IRIP Lab., Beijing Key Laboratory of Digital Media,
School of Computer Science and Engineering, Beihang Univ., 100191 Beijing, China
liuqingjie@cse.buaa.edu.cn, {yhwang,zxzhang}@buaa.edu.cn

Abstract. This paper proposes a local texture constrained super-resolution method for the reconstruction of high-resolution image. Through the learned low/high-resolution patches from training images, the intended high resolution patches are reconstructed using neighbor embedding method. The major contributions of this paper are: 1) Local Binary Pattern (LBP) is adopted to classify the patches into different categories, only those patches who have the same pattern with the input patches are used as candidates; 2) Structural SIMilarity (SSIM) metric which can find the patches with texture most similar to the input is used to search the k most suitable patches in the corresponding category. Experiments show that LBP index can provide proper candidate patches and SSIM metric is better than other metric in finding the most texture similarity patches.

Keywords: image super-resolution, LBP, neighbor embedding, SSIM.

1 Introduction

Learning based single image super-resolution (SR), also known as "image hallucination" or "example-based super-resolution", has been very popular in recent years. This method was first introduced by W.Freeman [1], and later was studied widely by many other researchers [2–7].

These methods learn relationships between low-resolution (LR) and high-resolution (HR) patch pairs from a set of training images, then applied on a LR image patch to synthesize its most likely HR version. To recover a high quality HR image, the key issue is applying a good prior or constraint on recovering HR image patch. Sun et al. [5] proposed a context-constrained hallucination approach for image SR. This approach introduces reasonable high frequency details into the HR results by utilizing a patch-selection process. HaCohen et al. [6], who were inspired by the recent progress in example-based texture synthesis, proposed another textural constraint method called "texture hallucination". This method succeeds in reproducing finer details in various regions However, non-exist textures are also produced due to the texture synthesis process, sometimes the appearance is not realistic.

Based on the hypothesis that small patches in the low- and corresponding high-resolution images share similar local manifold structure, Chang et al. [2]

W. Lin et al. (Eds.): PCM 2012, LNCS 7674, pp. 285–293, 2012.
© Springer-Verlag Berlin Heidelberg 2012

proposed SR method through neighbor embedding, in which a HR patch can be reconstructed by weighted linear combination of its neighbors. The weights are learned from the known low resolution images. However, the consistency between these two manifolds does not always hold. This results in unrealistic jaggy or ringing artifacts. And, because there is no effective constraints or priors on the construction process, the performance is sensitive to the choice of the training images, so the results are not stable.

In this paper, we present a method which is effective in finding the optimal candidates in searching process. We use Local Binary Patterns (LBP) [8] combining with a structure sensitive metric called structural similarity (SSIM) [9] to enforce the texture constraint. In our method, LBP, which has been found to be a powerful feature for texture classification, is used as a constraint to classify the training patches into different categories. k best matching texture similar patches are retrieved by SSIM. Finally, HR patches are constructed through neighbor embedding [2].

The remainder of this paper is organized as follows: In Section 2, we will present our local texture constrained SR algorithm in detail. Experimental results will be demonstrated in Section 3. Finally, this paper is concluded in Section 4.

2   Local Texture Constrained SR Algorithm

2.1   Patches Classification by LBP

Most of the example-based SR algorithms search the similar patches directly in the entire training database, which is inefficient and may not find optimal similar patches. Some researchers try to solve this problem by searching the similar patches in the subset of the database. In [5] and [6], image segmentation is employed to segment the training images into different segments according to the textural similarity. Patches similar to the input LR patch are searched in the corresponding segment. In this subsection, we utilize LBP to classify the training patches into different categories.

The original LBP operator forms labels for the image pixels by thresholding the 3×3 neighborhood of each pixel with the center value and considering the result as a binary number. The LBP operator was extended to many versions by using neighborhood of different sizes. To simplify, in this paper we only use the basic 3×3 LBP operator. An example of LBP computation can be seen in Fig. 1 inside the dotted line.

In the training phase, patches are classified into different subset by their LBP number, as shown in Fig. 1. It is reasonable to classify the training set into subsets based on their textural similarity, since only those similar to the input patch are useful in HR patch generation process.

2.2   Structural Similar Patches Search

We now discuss the metric method of finding texturally similar patches from the training database. The simplest and most widely used metric method in

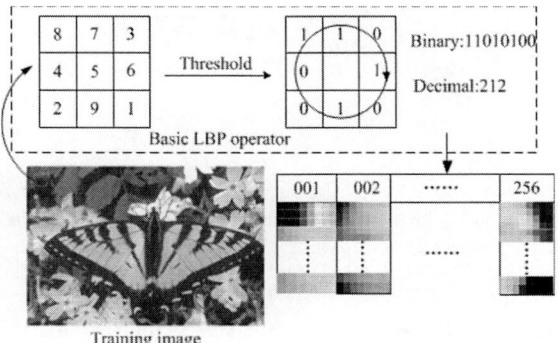

Fig. 1. Basic LBP computation is used as texture similar measurement to classify the patches into different categories

the searching process is Eucliden Distance, which is defined in Cartesian Coordinates. However, small patches in the low and high-resolution images tend to form manifolds, Eucliden Distance may fail in finding appropriate nearest neighbors in manifold, as illustrated in Fig. 2 (c). So, how to find the best candidate patches is critical. In the following we will introduce a new structure similar metric.

In this paper, we use structural similarity measurement [9] defined as follows to measure the similarity between two patches v_1 and v_2:

$$\text{SSIM}(v_1, v_2) = \frac{(2\mu_1\mu_2 + C_1)(2\sigma_{1,2} + C_2)}{(\mu_1^2 + \mu_2^2 + C_1)(\sigma_1^2 + \sigma_2^2 + C_2)} \tag{1}$$

where (μ_1, σ_1^2) and (μ_2, σ_2^2) are the means and variance of v_1 and v_2; $\sigma_{1,2}$ is the covariance of v_1 and v_2; C_1 and C_2 are two variables to stabilize the division with weak denominator:

$$C_1 = (K_1 L)^2 \quad C_2 = (K_2 L)^2$$

where K_1 and K_2 are two constants far smaller than 1, in this paper we choose $K_1 = 0.01$, $K_2 = 0.03$; L is the dynamic range of pixel values (255 for gray scale images.)

The value of SSIM is a number range from -1 to 1. As two patches are getting more similar, the result is approaching to 1, and value 1 is reachable only in the case of two patches are identical. Fig. 2 shows results of patch retrieval, it should be noted that, the intended patches are searched in the database trained by one image. As we can see, the patches found by SSIM metric is much similar to the query patch than the results searched by Eucliden Distance.

2.3   HR Patch Generation

It is widely accepted that LR patches and corresponding HR patches may share the similar intrinsic local manifold structure [2]. Under this assumption, HR

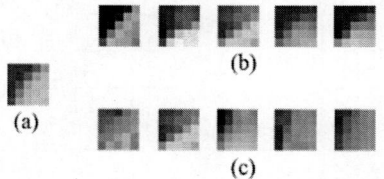

Fig. 2. Search results using two different metrics, (a) is a query patch; (b) 5 nearest neighbors with SSIM metric; (c) 5 nearest neighbors using Eucliden Distance

image patches can be reconstructed using the principle of local linear embedding [2]. In the following, we will give a brief introduction on neighbor embedding.

For each patch v_l in the input LR image I_l, we seek k nearest neighbors in the corresponding sub-database using SSIM metric. We denote $p_l^i (i = 1...k)$ as k LR neighbor patches; v_h is the unknown desired path in HR image I_h. Then the patch v_l can be represented by the linear combination of its neighbors:

$$v_l = \sum_{i=1}^{k} \omega_i p_l^i + \varepsilon_l \tag{2}$$

where, ω_i is the weight for p_l^i, and subject to constrains $\sum_{i=1}^{k} \omega_i = 1$; ε_l is the error vector. Specifically, the optimal weight vector ω is achieved by minimizing the reconstruction error vector as follows:

$$\varepsilon_l = \| v_l - \sum_{i=1}^{k} \omega_i p_l^i \|^2 \tag{3}$$

To solve ω, let's define a Gram matrix $\mathbf{G}$ for v_l as:

$$\mathbf{G} = (v_l \mathbf{1}^T - \mathbf{P})^T (v_l \mathbf{1}^T - \mathbf{P}); \tag{4}$$

where $\mathbf{1}$ is a column vector with all entries equaling to one, and $\mathbf{P}$ is a d×k matrix with its columns being the neighbors of v_l. ω can be solved efficiently by solve the linear system of equations $\mathbf{G}\omega = \mathbf{1}$, then normalize the weights so $\sum_{i=1}^{k} \omega_i = 1$. Finally, the desired HR path v_h can be constructed as follows:

$$v_h = \sum_{i=1}^{k} \omega_i p_h^i \tag{5}$$

Other methods to solve ω can be found in [2].

Then the HR patches are stitched together using a one-pass algorithm [1] to enforce the compatibility between adjacent patches. The patches are processed in raster-scan order in the image, from left-top to right-bottom. Fig. 3 illustrates reconstruction results using neighbor embedding by two different metric methods, Fig. 3(c) shows the reconstruction error. It can be observed that our method gives much better result.

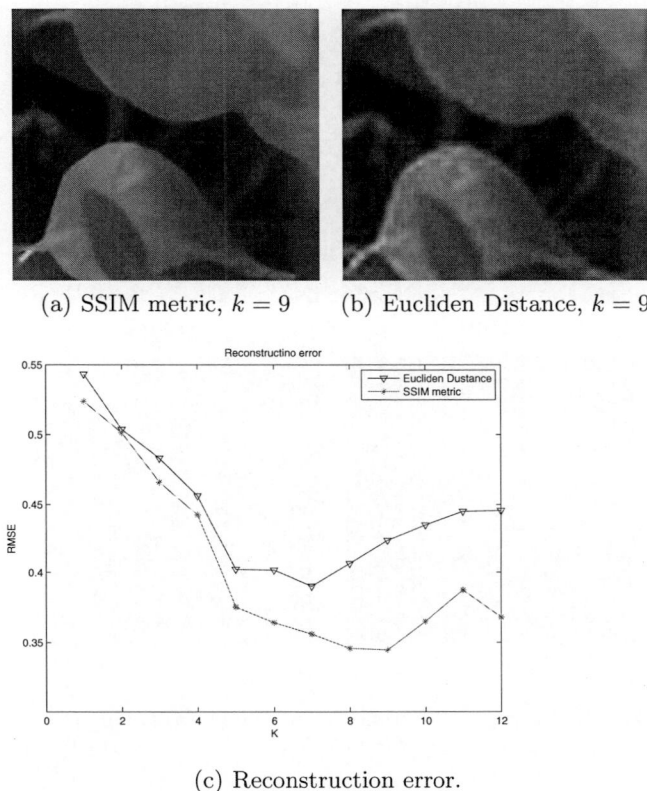

(a) SSIM metric, $k = 9$ (b) Eucliden Distance, $k = 9$

(c) Reconstruction error.

Fig. 3. Super resolution with 4×. (a) is result using SSIM metric, and (b) is by Eucliden Distance. (c) is the reconstruction error of these two cases.

3 Experiments

3.1 Feature Representation

In example-based SR algorithm, feature representation is very important. Many literatures employ first-order and second-order gradients of the luminance as feature [2, 3]. In this paper we combine first-order gradient and high-pass component of the image as the feature for LR patch. The first-order gradient preserves the sketch of the image, and high-pass component contains high frequency information. We simply use the following 1-D filters to extract the first-order derivatives of the image:

$$F_1 = [-1, 0, 1], \quad F_2 = F_1^T \tag{6}$$

where " T " means transpose. And high-pass component of an image can be obtain as follows:

$$H_I = I - \mathcal{U}(\mathcal{D}(I * G_\sigma)) * G_\sigma \tag{7}$$

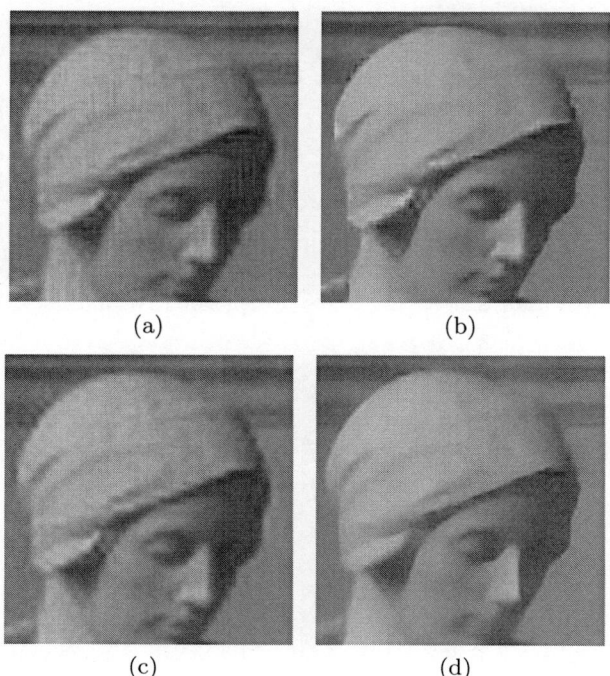

Fig. 4. Super resolution with 4× by different methods. (a) Chang et al. 's method [2];
(b) Glasner et al.'s method [4]; (c) Yang et al.'s method [3]; and (d) is our method.

where $\mathcal{U}$ is up-sampling operator, $\mathcal{D}$ is down-sampling operator, G_σ is a Gaussian
filter at scale σ, and $*$ is convolution operator. By concatenating first-order
gradient and high-pass component, we therefore form the new feature vectors.

3.2   Experimental Results

We use 32 natural images collected from internet as our training data. In the
training step, the LR images are derived from these images by blurring with a
Gaussian filter (standard variance $\sigma = 0.8$) and then down-sampling 4 times.
We use uniform pattern of LBP as our classify criterion. Then these LR and

Table 1. Performance assessments for images (4× up scale)

Image	RMSE				SSIM			
	Chang's.	Glasner's.	Yang's	Proposed	Chang's.	Glasner's.	Yang's.	Proposed
statue	25.44	21.27	28.82	19.18	0.892	0.917	0.922	0.934
koala	29.31	24.62	27.38	24.23	0.854	0.926	0.911	0.921
butterfly	31.25	23.62	25.24	22.36	0.879	0.915	0.904	0.927

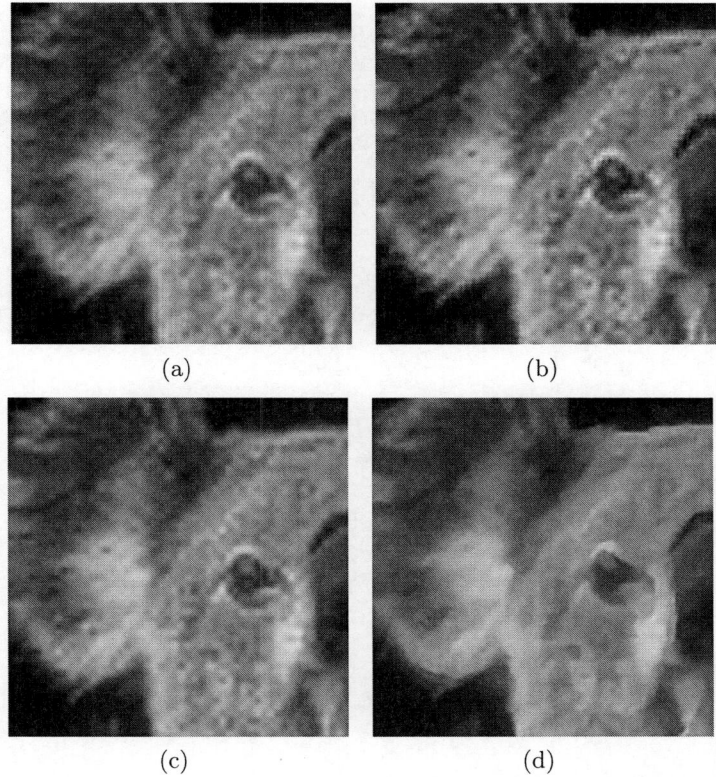

Fig. 5. Images magnified by a factor of 4. (a) Chang et al.'s method [2]; (b) Glasner et al.'s method [4]; (c) Yang et al.'s method [3] and (d) is result of our method.

HR patch pairs are classified into 59 categories according to the LBP number of the LR patches. The LR patch size is 3×3, the corresponding HR patch size is $3f \times 3f - 1$.

In the searching process phase, we firstly search the similar patch in the down sampled version of the input image, if enough patches are found, the desired HR patch are synthesized using HR version of these patches. Otherwise, searching will be implemented in the trained dictionary. To reduce outlier, every patch is normalized by its similar score. Note that human eyes are more sensitive to the luminance of the image, for color image, we convert it to YCbCr color space, and apply our algorithm only on luma component, and the chroma component CbCr are simply up-sampled by bicubic interpolation.

We compare our method with three state-of-the-art example-based methods: original neighbor embedding method of [2], sparse reconstruction method in [3] and Glasner et al.'s method [4], as shown in Fig. 4 and Fig. 6. Because Glasner do not release their source code, we use a third part implementation on the web[1].

---

[1] http://www.stanford.edu/class/ee368/Project_11/index.html

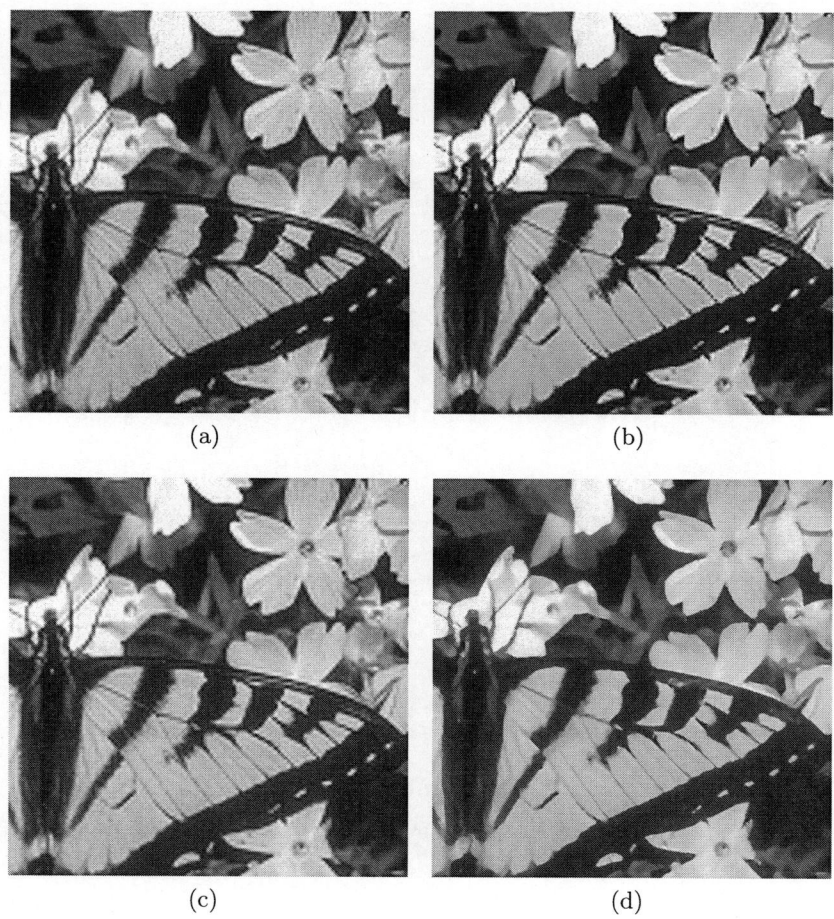

Fig. 6. Images magnified by a factor of 4. (a) Chang et al.'s method [2]; (b) Glasner et al.'s method [4]; (c) Yang et al.'s method [3] and (d) is result of our method.

Table 1 lists that our method achieves highest SSIM and lowest root mean square error. Compared to Chang et al.'s method, our method improves the results by using LBP and SSIM. In addition, our method out perform sparse reconstruction method in [3] and Glasner et al.'s method [4]. In Fig. 4, Yang et al.'s method has artifacts and rings along the edges. Glasner et al.'s method is better than other two methods, as it has fewer artifacts, but still it can be observed that artifacts exist in the head of Fig. 4 (b). Nevertheless, our results lack of textures in the SR images, as it can be seen in Fig. 6 (d), koala face tends to smoothness because of normalization of the patches.

4   Conclusions

In this paper, we present a novel single image super-resolution method. In the method, we employ a new combination of feature for both sketch and high frequency preservation. Patches extracted from training images are divided into different subset by LBP for guiding the neighbor search, this strategy is efficiently in searching process under a great number of training patches. A novel structural similarity metric called SSIM is adopted to measure the similarity of two patches in searching process. Experiments show that the proposed method performs better in preserving sharp edges. However, there are lack of texture in the resulted HR images, work will be done to improve the reconstruction quality.

Acknowledgment. This work is funded by the National Basic Research Program of China (No. 2010CB327902), the National Natural Science Foundation of China (No. 61005016, No. 61061130560), the National High-tech R&D Program of China (2011AA010502), the Open Projects Program of National Laboratory of Pattern Recognition, and the Fundamental Research Funds for the Central Universities.

References

1. Freeman, W.T., Jones, T.R., Pasztor, E.C.: Example-based super-resolution. IEEE Comput. Graph. Appl. 22, 56–65 (2002)
2. Chang, H., Yeung, D.Y., Xiong, Y.: Super-resolution through neighbor embedding. In: CVPR, vol. I, pp. 275–282 (2004)
3. Yang, J., Wright, J., Huang, T.S., Ma, Y.: Image super-resolution as sparse representation of raw image patches. In: CVPR (2008)
4. Glasner, D., Bagon, S., Irani, M.: Super-resolution from a single image. In: ICCV (2009)
5. Sun, J., Zhu, J., Tappen, M.: Context-constrained hallucination for image super-resolution. In: CVPR (2010)
6. HaCohen, Y., Fattal, R., Lischinski, D.: Image upsampling via texture hallucination. In: ICCP (2010)
7. Chan, T.M., Zhang, J., Pu, J., Huang, H.: Neighbor embedding based super-resolution algorithm through edge detection and feature selection. Pattern Recogn. Lett. 30, 494–502 (2009)
8. Ojala, T., Pietikäinen, M., Mäenpää, T.: Multiresolution gray-scale and rotation invariant texture classification with local binary patterns. IEEE Transactions on Pattern Analysis and Machine Intelligence 24(7), 971–987 (2002)
9. Wang, Z., Bovik, A.C., Sheikh, H.R., Simoncelli, E.P.: Image quality assessment: From error visibility to structural similarity. IEEE Transactions on Image Processing 13(4), 600–612 (2004)

Top-Down Saliency by Multi-scale Contextual Pooling

Yuanyuan Qiu[1,2], Jun Zhu[1,2], Rui Zhang[1,2,*], and Jun Huang[3]

[1] Institute of Image Communication and Network Engineering,
Shanghai Jiao Tong University, Shanghai, P.R. China
[2] Shanghai Key Laboratory of Digital Media Processing and Transmission
qyy.laura@gmail.com, {junnyzhu,zhang_rui}@sjtu.edu.cn
[3] Shanghai Advanced Research Institute, Chinese Academy of Sciences
huangj@sari.ac.cn

Abstract. Goal-driven top-down mechanism plays an important role in the case of object detection and recognition. In this paper, we propose a top-down computational model for goal-driven saliency detection based on a coding-based classification framework. It consists of four successive steps: feature extraction, descriptor coding, local pooling and saliency prediction. In the step of local pooling, we investigate the effect of multi-scale contextual information for saliency detection and find that there exists an optimal contextual scale to achieve the patch-level feature presentation. On basis of this observation, we propose an approach for automatic scale selection in saliency prediction step. The experimental results demonstrate that our method can effectively improve the performance of goal-driven saliency detection as well as related object detection.

Keywords: Top-down Saliency, Goal-driven Visual Attention, Multi-scale.

1 Introduction

Visual saliency plays an important role in many computer vision and multimedia applications such as object recognition and detection, automatic image cropping, adaptive compression of image/video and image retrieval. So far, the mechanism of saliency detection has been extensively studied and could be generally divided into two categories: bottom-up mechanism and top-down mechanism. Bottom-up mechanism is data-driven and independent of the goal while top-down mechanism is task-dependent and goal-driven. Many bottom-up computational models have contributed to saliency detection [1-4]. As one of the classic model, Itti *et al.* [1]propose a visual attention model combining feature channels of color, intensity, and orientation based on center-surround contrast. Hou X. *et al.* [3] propose a phased-based saliency detection method. Cheng M. *et al.* [2] advance a regional color contrast based saliency extraction algorithm.

Although these bottom-up methods may detect salient regions in a fast manner, they ignore any knowledge of target and distracted background which is important in object detection and recognition. The influencing factors of the top-down mechanism include the task to be performed, the prior knowledge of feature distribution on target,

---

* Corresponding author.

W. Lin et al. (Eds.): PCM 2012, LNCS 7674, pp. 294–305, 2012.
© Springer-Verlag Berlin Heidelberg 2012

and the context of the visual scene and so on. Most existing top-down methods exploit the prior knowledge of the feature distribution of images and learn the weight vector based on different principles [5-7]. Olivia *et al.* [8] integrate the top-down information from visual context to facilitate the task of object detection. The contextual information plays an important role in saliency detection.   The principle of maximizing the signal-to-noise ratio of target object and its background is exploited in [5]. In [6], the weight is considered to be the ratio of the mean target saliency and mean background saliency. In [7], a conditional random field is learned to extract the salient object more accurately. Gao D. *et al.* [9] put forward a saliency detection model based on information maximization principles.

In this paper, we focus on goal-driven saliency detection and apply it to object detection. To exploit the knowledge of target, a top-down computational model is presented on saliency detection, motivated by the state-of-the-art coding-based image classification approaches [11]. We formulate top-down saliency detection as a binary classification problem, in which our model is learned to separate the target stimuli of goal object from background regions. In general, our approach consists of four successive steps: *feature extraction, descriptor coding, local pooling and saliency predication*. Particularly, in the key step of local pooling, we investigate the role of pooling code responses with various neighborhood scales for utilizing contextual information, and propose a simple method to select optimal contextual scale. The experimental results on a car dataset and a plane dataset demonstrate that our method can effectively improve the performance on saliency detection of the goal object as well as corresponding object detection application.

The contributions of this paper are summarized as follows:

- A top-down computational model is presented on goal-driven saliency detection, based on the coding-based classification framework.
- We empirically observe that pooling with contextual information in multi-scale spatial neighborhood can make for saliency detection.
- A scale selection algorithm is proposed to select the optimal scale automatically.

The rest of this paper is organized as follows: Section 2 outlines the saliency detection framework proposed in the paper. Section 3 elaborates the local pooling and scale selection algorithms. In section 4, we construct experiments to evaluate our model and compare it with other saliency detection methods. Finally, the conclusion is presented in section 5.

2   Top-Down Saliency Detection Framework

In this section, we briefly introduce the framework of our computational model, and then discuss the significance on goal-driven saliency detection. As illustrated in Fig. 1, it consists of the following four successive steps:

1. Feature extraction

For an image I, we densely sample local patches (interest points) on a regular grid. Then, each patch is represented by a feature descriptor $d \in \mathbb{R}^D$. In this paper, we use SIFT descriptor [10] which is invariant to luminance, rotation and scale changes to some extent.

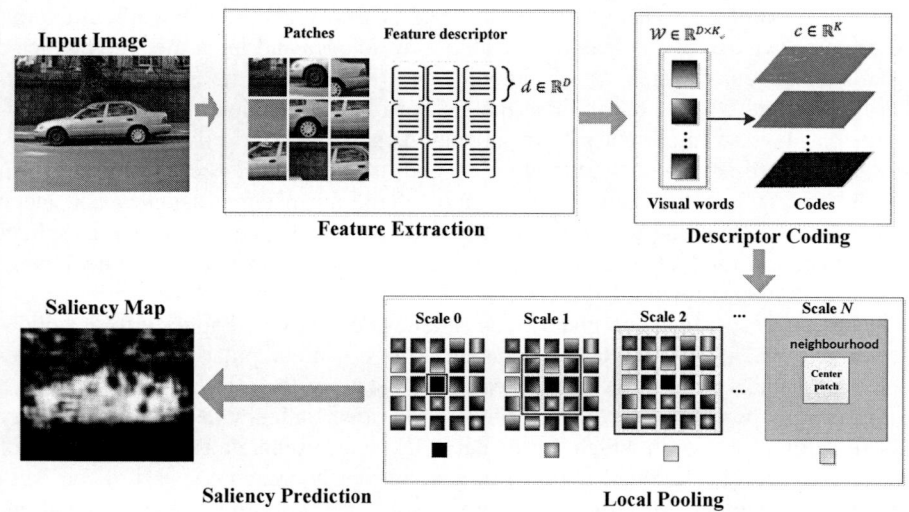

Fig. 1. A brief, concise overview of our framework

2. Descriptor coding

Given a visual vocabulary $\mathcal{W} \in \mathbb{R}^{D \times K}$, each descriptor of an image patch is non-linearly mapped to a high-level dimensional code vector. We use locality-constrained linear coding (LLC) [11] to transform the feature descriptor to a sparse code, which pursues the optimum reconstruction from its nearest visual words bases. After the coding step, each patch is represented by a K-dimensional code $c \in \mathbb{R}^K$. This coding step can facilitate the learning of non-linear relationship between the target variable and its feature descriptor representation[12].

3. Local pooling

For each local patch, the code only describes the information of itself. However, contextual information is proven to be significant in saliency detection literatures [8, 13]. As shown in Fig. 1, the code of a single patch and the neighboring ones are aggregated to form a K-dimensional feature vector $f \in \mathbb{R}^K$. Through this local pooling step, contextual information is induced for representing the central patch, producing a robust feature representation on saliency prediction. In section 3, we will discuss the significance of local pooling with multi-scale context in detail.

4. Saliency prediction

On basis of the feature representation after local pooling step, we construct a probabilistic model to predict the saliency for each patch. Let s_x denotes the saliency value of the target at location x for image I. Formally, it is defined by a log-linear model as follows:

$$s_x = p(target|f_x) \propto e^{<\sigma, f_x>} \qquad (1)$$

where f_x refers to the pooled feature vector at location x and σ denotes model parameter. The saliency of the target is represented through a normalized probability $p(target|f_x)$, and σ is learned based on training images.

Concretely, we collect the positive patches from regions of the target and negative ones from the background regions on training images. Then the model parameter, which can be deemed as the weights of the bins on pooled feature vector, is learned through a binary-class linear SVM [14] in this paper. After that, the saliency for each densely sampled patch is predicted by Eq. (1). As a result, the saliency map is composed of the saliency values on all patches in sampling grid. If we sample patches by the space of every pixel, we can construct a full resolution saliency map w.r.t. original image.

In summary, our saliency detection framework is derived from the coding-based classification framework. However, it is different from image classification in the steps of pooling and saliency prediction. To form a patch-level feature representation, the local pooling step in our framework operates on a local region around the central patch rather than the whole image domain in image classification framework. In the saliency prediction step, we learn our model for predicting probabilistic saliency valued from [0, 1] instead of a discrete valued label used in image classification.

3   Local Pooling with Multi-scale Context

In this section, we first elaborate the local pooling operation in detail, and then discuss the significance of multi-scale context for saliency detection.

3.1   The Local Pooling Operation

After descriptor coding step, the codes only represent information for the encoded patches themselves, without any contextual information from their neighborhood ones. To take advantage of contextual information, we obtain the patch-level feature representation for a patch by applying max pooling operation over the codes of itself as well as its neighboring ones. Particularly, as described below, we consider pooling with contextual information at multiple scales.

As can be seen in the Fig. 1, we define a set of contextual patches at scale n by $\Omega_n = \left\{ c_i^{(n)} | i = 1, 2, \cdots, 8n \right\}$, where $c_i^{(n)} = (c_{i,1}^{(n)}, c_{i,2}^{(n)}, \cdots, c_{i,K}^{(n)})$ denotes the ith surrounding patch at scale n w.r.t. the central one. For instance, the contextual patch set of scale 1 involves 8 adjacent patches w.r.t. the central one, while scale 2 corresponds to the set of 16 patches one more round outward. Besides, we also introduce two additional scale 0 and ∞ as special cases: the surrounding patch set of scale 0, denoted by Ω_0, includes only the code of central patch itself, and the infinite scale patch set Ω_∞ actually corresponds to all the patches over the whole image domain. Thus, through the local pooling operation with multi-scale context, the resultant feature vector $f^{(n)} = (f_1^{(n)}, f_2^{(n)}, \cdots, f_K^{(n)})$ for the central patch is given by

$$f_k^{(n)} = \max_j \; c_{j,k} ,$$

$$\text{(2)}$$

$$s.t. \quad c_j \in \Omega_0 \cup \Omega_1 \cup \cdots \cup \Omega_n , \forall \, k = 1,2,\cdots,K$$

where $f_k^{(n)}$ and $c_{j,k}$ refers to the kth component of the pooled representation $f^{(n)}$ and code vector c_j respectively.

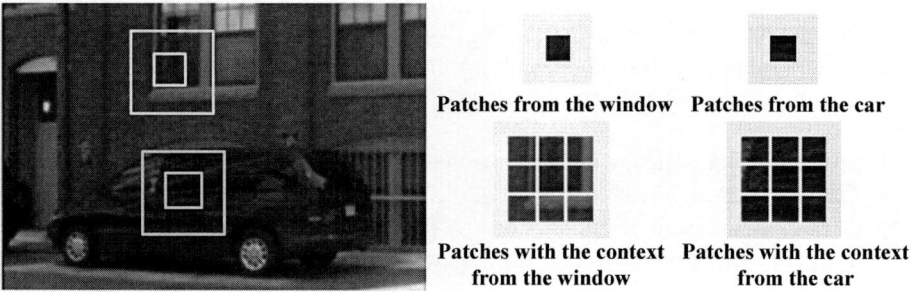

Fig. 2. Illustration of the importance of the context (Best viewed in color)

3.2   The Effect of Neighborhood Scale on Local Pooling

In this subsection, we investigate the effect of contextual scale in local pooling operation. As illustrated in [15], significant features will be highlighted at appropriate scales. When the contextual scale becomes smaller, the visual ambiguity between the positive patches and negative ones increases so that discrimination will be more difficult. Fig. 2 illustrates an intuitive example on the significance of multi-scale contextual information. On the basis of the central patch itself, it is difficult to distinguish the glass window patch from the car and that from the building because of their large inter-class similarity on visual appearance. However, when we consider surrounding contextual patches, the ambiguity will be eliminated to a great extent.

In Fig. 3, we compare the empirical distribution of extracted saliency value between positive and negative patches for different scale values. As can be seen, the separation appears to be more remarkable when the contextual scale becomes larger. It suggests that pooling with multi-scale context generally makes for discrimination and corresponding saliency detection for the target. Fig. 4 illustrates the saliency map extracted by different contextual scales.

However, the effect of discrimination does not improve as the scale increases infinitely. Supposing the special case of scale $n = \infty$, the pooled feature representation for every patch is actually the same with each other and equal to the one representing the information of whole image. As a result, there is not any discriminativity at all between the positive patches and negative ones. Therefore, we hypothesize that the ambiguity after local pooling will not continue to decrease anymore and begin to rise when the contextual scale increases to a certain degree. This motivates our scale selection approach: we adopt Kullback-Leibler Divergence (KLD) between the predicted saliency and ground-truth one as the measurement to evaluate the quality of contextual scale. Given the learned model, the KLD of each candidate scale is evaluated on the training samples. The scale of smallest KLD is selected as the optimal one. Then for each patch we pool its feature representation with the optimal scale to generate saliency map. The calculation of KLD will be introduced in section 4.3.

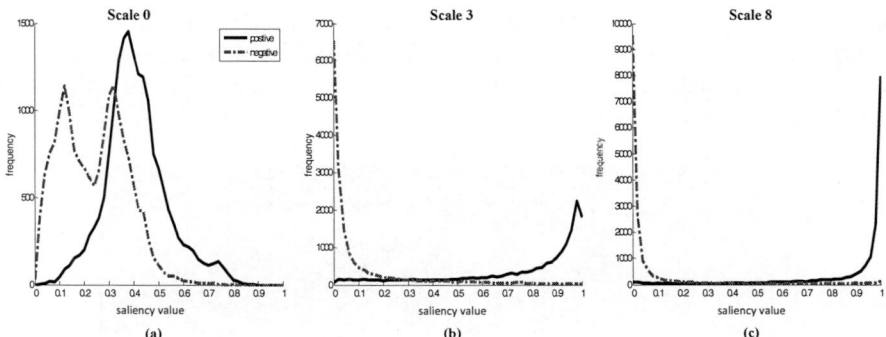

Fig. 3. Discriminativity vs. Contextual Scale

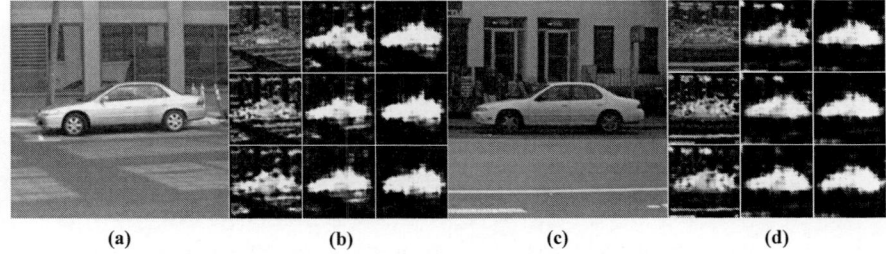

Fig. 4. Goal-specific saliency maps at multi-scales: (a)(c) original images (b)(d) saliency maps at several scales, from top to down, left to right corresponds to scale 0~8 respectively

4   Experiments

In this section, we evaluate the proposed method through a series of experiments on two datasets, and show quantitative and qualitative results on goal-driven saliency detection as well as related object detection application.

4.1   Image Dataset

In experiment, we test our approach on two datasets (i.e., the Car Dataset[1] and the Plane Dataset[2]). For each image, there is a pixel-wise binary label map as ground

---

[1] http://lear.inrialpes.fr/data
[2] http://labelme.csail.mit.edu/

truth, where the intensity value 1 indicates that it is a pixel of target and 0 corresponds to a background pixel. Fig. 5 illustrates several examples of original images and their ground-truth label maps from these datasets. In Fig. 5(a), we can see that some ground-truth maps of the Car Dataset are not labeled accurately enough in the cases of occlusion. Thus, we choose clear and accurately labeled images from the original dataset and create a subset, some example images from which are illustrated in Fig. 5(b). For simplicity, we call the original dataset and new subset by Car Dataset $\mathcal{A}$ and Car Dataset $\mathcal{B}$, respectively. Car Dataset $\mathcal{A}$ contains 474 images in total while Car Dataset $\mathcal{B}$ includes 172 images. Fig. 5(c) shows some examples from the Plane Dataset, which contains 173 images in total.

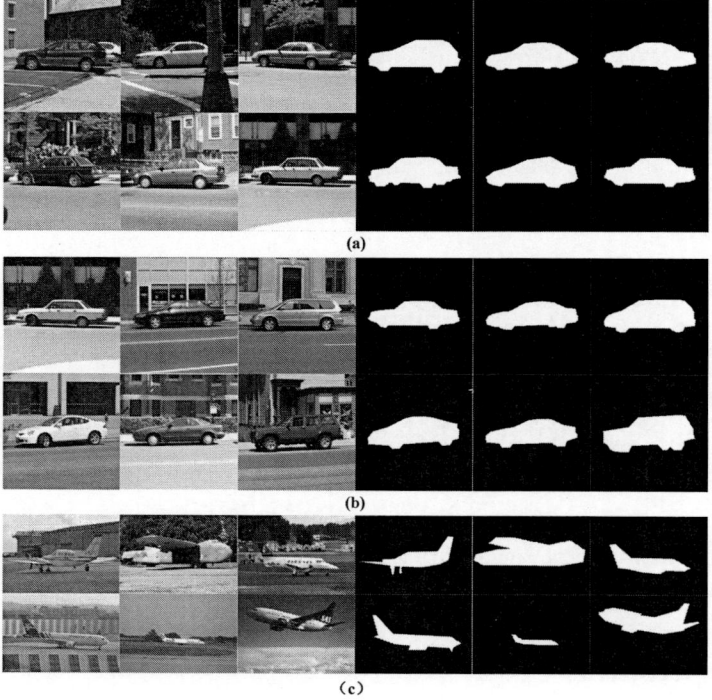

Fig. 5. Example images and ground truth maps from (a) Car Dataset $\mathcal{A}$, (b) Car Dataset $\mathcal{B}$ and (c) Plane Dataset

4.2 Experiment Setup

In the step of feature extraction, the SIFT feature descriptors are extracted from densely sampled 16×16 pixel patches, on a grid with the space of 3 pixels. In the descriptor coding step, a visual vocabulary of 1024 visual words is adopted in experiments, which is constructed by K-means clustering on the descriptor samples collected from training images. The parameter setting of LLC coding is consistent with [11]. In local pooling step, we use the candidate contextual scales from 0 to 8. In the step of saliency prediction, for each dataset, we randomly select about 40% images for training and the rest ones for testing. In the training stage, we collect the positive patches from the regions of target according to the ground-truth label map, and construct the set of negative patches from the background regions. Then, we learn the model by using the patches sampled from various candidate scales. As the saliency map is not full resolution w.r.t the original image, we resize the saliency map to the size of original image using bilinear interpolation.

4.3   Evaluation

In order to quantitatively evaluate the performance of our method, we adopt the KLD as the measurement for assessing the quality of predicted saliency map, and use the P-R curve as the evaluation criterion in corresponding object detection application.

1. The Kullback-Leibler Divergence

The KLD is non-negative similarity metric for comparing two probability distributions. Let $S = \{s_x\}$ and $G = \{g_x\}$ respectively denote the predicted saliency map and ground-truth label map, where s_x and g_x refer to saliency value and binary ground-truth label for the location x accordingly. The KLD is computed by

$$D_{KL}(G||S) = -\frac{1}{N}\Sigma_x\left(1_{\{g_x=1\}}(x)logs_x + 1_{\{g_x=-1\}}(x)log(1-s_x)\right) \tag{3}$$

where $1_{\{g_x=1\}}(x)$ equals 1 for a pixel of target and 0 for a background pixel. N denotes the total number of patches sampled from this image. As the predicted saliency map approximates the ground-truth label map, it will obtain a smaller value of KLD. If the saliency map and ground truth map are the same, the KLD is zero.

2. Precision vs. Recall Curve

For the evaluation criterion on object detection, we define precision and recall following [7]:

$$precision = \frac{\Sigma_x g_x s_x}{\Sigma_x s_x}, recall = \frac{\Sigma_x g_x s_x}{\Sigma_x g_x} \tag{4}$$

Thus, a Precision vs. Recall (P-R) curve can be obtained by varying different threshold from 0 to 1.

4.4   Experimental Results

4.4.1   Quantitative Results

At first, we evaluate our saliency detection results with multi-scale context based on KLD metric. Furthermore, we compare our saliency methods with other saliency detection methods in literatures (i.e. FT[4], LC[16], HC[2], RC[2], and SR[3]) based on

KLD and P-R curve. Table 1 shows the KLD for different contextual scales. From the table, we can observe that there exists an optimal scale for local pooling. Table 2 shows the KLD computed on saliency maps by different methods. In Car Dataset $\mathcal{A}$ and Car Dataset $\mathcal{B}$, our approach can produce the saliency maps more close to the ground truth maps than other methods. Fig. 6 illustrates the resultant P-R curves compared with other saliency detection methods. It is shown that our method outperforms other state-of-the-art methods in object detection application.

Table 1. KLD at multiscales

Scale	0	1	2	3	4	5	6	7	8
Car $\mathcal{A}$	0.462	0.441	**0.437**	0.437	0.440	0.448	0.475	0.483	0.521
Car $\mathcal{B}$	0.409	0.350	0.315	0.287	0.270	0.250	**0.241**	0.243	0.257
Plane	0.166	**0.148**	0.161	0.184	0.218	0.253	0.291	0.321	0.341

Table 2. KLD for different saliency detection methods

method	SR	LC	FT	HC	RC	**Our**
Car $\mathcal{A}$	0.759	0.815	0.594	0.906	0.442	**0.437**
Car $\mathcal{B}$	0.553	0.627	0.504	0.783	0.418	**0.241**
Plane	0.418	0.178	**0.104**	0.449	0.243	0.148

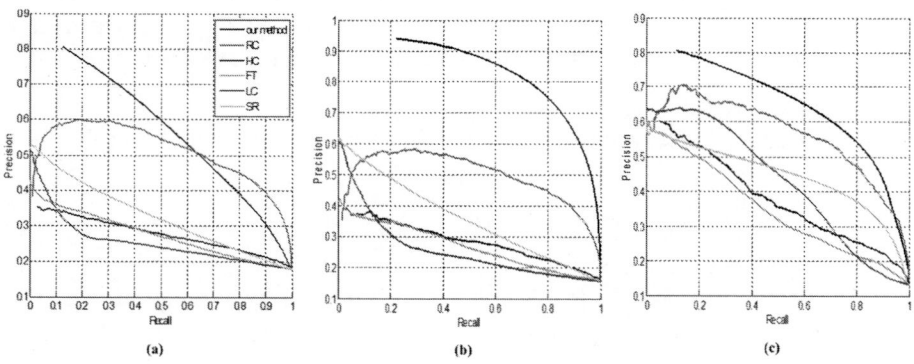

       (a)   (b)   (c)

Fig. 6. P-R curves for naive threshold of saliency maps on (a) Car Dataset $\mathcal{A}$, (b) Car Dataset $\mathcal{B}$ and (c) Plane Dataset. Our method is compared with FT,LC, HC, RC, SR[3].

4.4.2   Qualitative Results

Corresponding to Fig. 6, the qualitative results for comparison are shown in Fig. 7. It is clear that our approach suppresses the background and highlights the target at the

---

[3] We have used the code of M.M. Cheng in [2].

same time, while other saliency detection methods only highlight the salient locations. As other saliency detection methods are based on the low-level contrast, some bright colored objects are considered as salient independent of the target. The results of object detection by extracted saliency maps are shown in Fig. 8. It illustrates that our approach can predict the goal-specific locations accurately. In Fig. 8, we could also observe that combining the context information in local pooling step improves the detection results considerably.

(a)   (b)   (c)   (d)   (e)   (f)   (g)   (h)

Fig. 7. Qualitative comparison of saliency detection, the top part is based on car dataset and the bottom part is based on the plane dataset. From left to right: (a)original images (b)~(g)saliency maps produced by our method, FT, LC, HC, RC, SR (h)ground truth map. For better visualization, our saliency map is smoothed with Gaussian filter.

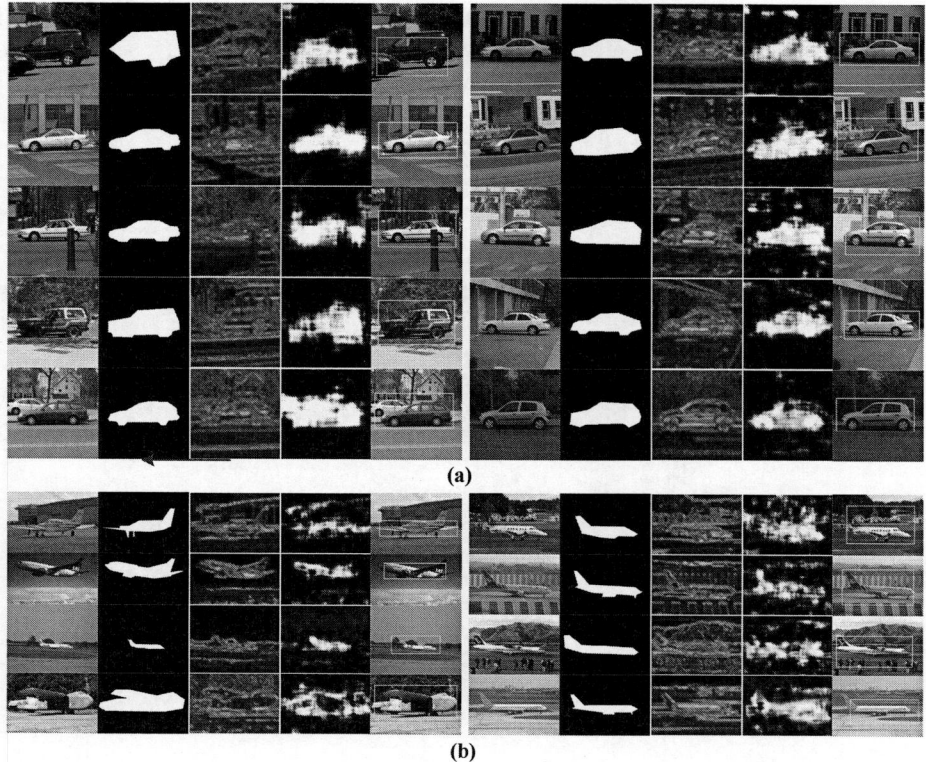

Fig. 8. Some results based on our model (a) car dataset: the left panel is from Car Dataset $\mathcal{A}$ and the right panel is from Car Dataset $\mathcal{B}$ (b) plane dataset; for each panel, from left to right are original images, ground truth maps, saliency map at scale 0, saliency map at the optimal scale, detection results based on saliency maps (Best viewed in color and magnification).

5   Conclusions

This paper proposes a top-down saliency detection model derived from the coding-based classification framework, in which the saliency is defined as the probability of goal given its visual features. Multi-scale contextual information is integrated in the pooling step and a simple scale selection algorithm based on KLD is proposed in saliency prediction step. It should be noted that multi-scale context is an important, but implicit part of the saliency detection problem. Combining the context information at multi-scales improves the experimental results significantly. The experimental results demonstrate that the proposed model achieves better performance than other saliency detection models for goal-specific saliency detection. On the future work, we consider integrating bottom-up color attention with the model to utilize more visual cues for saliency detection.

Acknowledgements. This work is funded by the Project NSFC 61071155, 973 National Program 2010CB731401, 2010CB731406 and STCSM 12DZ2272600.

References

1. Itti, L., Koch, C., Niebur, E.: A model of saliency-based visual attention for rapid scene analysis. IEEE Transactions on Pattern Analysis and Machine Intelligence 20, 1254–1259 (1998)
2. Cheng, M.M., Zhang, G.X., Mitra, N.J., Huang, X.L., Hu, S.M.: Global Contrast based Salient Region Detection. In: 2011 IEEE Conference on Computer Vision and Pattern Recognition, pp. 409–416 (2011)
3. Xiaodi, H., Liqing, Z.: Saliency Detection: A Spectral Residual Approach. In: 2007 IEEE Conference on Computer Vision and Pattern Recognition, pp. 2280–2287 (2007)
4. Achanta, R., Hemami, S., Estrada, F., Susstrunk, S.: Frequency-tuned Salient Region Detection. In: 2009 IEEE Conference on Computer Vision and Pattern Recognition, vol. 1-4, pp. 1597–1604. IEEE, New York (2009)
5. Navalpakkam, V., Itti, L.: An Integrated Model of Top-Down and Bottom-Up Attention for Optimizing Detection Speed. In: 2006 IEEE Computer Society Conference on Computer Vision and Pattern Recognition, pp. 2049–2056 (2006)
6. Frintrop, S., Backer, G., Rome, E.: Goal-Directed Search with a Top-Down Modulated Computational Attention System. In: Kropatsch, W.G., Sablatnig, R., Hanbury, A. (eds.) DAGM 2005. LNCS, vol. 3663, pp. 117–124. Springer, Heidelberg (2005)
7. Tie, L., Zejian, Y., Jian, S., Jingdong, W., Nanning, Z., Xiaoou, T., Heung-Yeung, S.: Learning to detect a salient object. IEEE Transactions on Pattern Analysis and Machine Intelligence 33(2), 353–367 (2011)
8. Oliva, A., Torralba, A., Castelhano, M.S., Henderson, J.M.: Top-down control of visual attention in object detection. In: 2003 International Conference on Image Processing, pp. 253–256 (2003)
9. Gao, D., Han, S., Vasconcelos, N.: Discriminant Saliency, the Detection of Suspicious Coincidences, and Applications to Visual Recognition. IEEE Transactions on Pattern Analysis and Machine Intelligence 31, 989–1005 (2009)
10. Lowe, D.G.: Distinctive image features from scale-invariant keypoints. International Journal of Computer Vision 60, 91–110 (2004)
11. Jinjun, W., Jianchao, Y., Kai, Y., Fengjun, L., Huang, T., Yihong, G.: Locality-constrained linear coding for image classification. In: 2010 IEEE Conference on Computer Vision and Pattern Recognition, pp. 3360–3367 (2010)
12. Yu, K., Zhang, T., Gong, Y.: Nonlinear learning using local coordinate coding. In: Advances in Neural Information Processing Systems, pp. 2223–2231 (2009)
13. Torralba, A., Oliva, A., Castelhano, M.S., Henderson, J.M.: Contextual guidance of eye movements and attention in real-world scenes: The role of global features in object search. Psychol. Rev. 113, 766–786 (2006)
14. Chang, C.C., Lin, C.J.: LIBSVM: a library for support vector machines. ACM Transactions on Intelligent Systems and Technology (TIST) 2, 27 (2011)
15. Lee, Y.B., Lee, S.: Robust Face Detection Based on Knowledge-Directed Specification of Bottom-Up Saliency. Etri Journal 33, 600–610 (2011)
16. Zhai, Y., Shah, M.: Visual attention detection in video sequences using spatiotemporal cues, pp. 815–824. ACM (2006)

A Robust Watermarking Scheme Based on Dual Quantization of Wavelet Significant Difference

Bin Ma[1], Yunhong Wang[1], Chunlei Li[2], Zhaoxiang Zhang[1], and Di Huang[1]

[1] Laboratory of Intelligent Recognition and Image Processing (IRIP),
School of Computer Science and Engineering, Beihang University, Beijing, China
[2] School of Electronic and Information Engineering,
Zhongyuan University of Technology, Zhengzhou, China

Abstract. This paper proposes a blind robust watermarking algorithm based on the quantization of significant DWT coefficients. Low frequent wavelet coefficients of the host image are randomly permutated into subgroups firstly. To guarantee watermark robustness while preserving good fidelity, watermarking modifications are distributed on the maximum positive and minimum negative coefficients of each group which preserve the most significant local amplitudes. The difference between two largest positive (or smallest negative) coefficients is quantized to an even or odd multiple of a quantization step parameter Q according to the watermark bit to be embedded. The blind watermark extraction could be straightforwardly achieved by checking the parity of the quotient between significant differences and Q. Comparison experiments with existing methods demonstrate the superiority of our scheme on robustness against content-preserving operations and incidental distortions such as JPEG compression, Gaussian noise.

Keywords: Biometric authentication, digital watermarking, DWT, QIM.

1 Introduction

With the rapid promotion of multimedia and Internet techniques, copyright protection and source authenticity of digital images have become increasingly critical. As an emerging security tool, robust digital watermarking resolves these problems by imperceptibly embedding secret information, i.e. watermark, into host media in such a way that it is still retrievable even in degraded copies. Generally, in order to make the watermark robust against incidental or malicious signal processing, the modification should be distributed on perceptually significant elements of the host image. Therefore among the existing methods, DWT based techniques have attracted relatively high interest and achieve better results, due to the advantages in characterizing human vision system and capturing local significant details [1] [2] [3].

Recently, Lin *et al.* [4] propose a blind robust watermarking scheme based on the quantization of the significant difference between wavelet coefficients (SDQ).

W. Lin et al. (Eds.): PCM 2012, LNCS 7674, pp. 306–314, 2012.

Their results demonstrate better robustness to a wide variety of signal processing attacks than existing work. Generally, the SDQ method randomly sorts adjacent wavelet coefficients into groups and quantizes the difference between two largest coefficients of one group to larger than a threshold or equal to zero for embedding watermark bit one or zero. Meerwald *et al.* [5] point out one security defect of SDQ and suggest randomly grouping non-adjacent coefficients in the preprocessing step. You *et al.* [3] propose a non-tensor based wavelet transform and introduce SDQ to the new domain as a promoted application. However, few attentions have been paid to the intrinsic drawbacks of SDQ embedding strategy, which limits the performance and applicability of the algorithm.

In this paper, we analyze the quantization based strategy of SDQ method and summarize its defects into three main aspects: 1) Singular distortions might arise due to the operation of equalizing the largest and the second largest value for embedding watermark symbol zero. 2) Negative coefficients which also preserve significant amplitudes are not employed for embedding. 3) The adaptive detection threshold is sensitive to the component of watermark sequence and the characteristics of host image. We propose a significant difference QIM (SD-QIM) based method to tackle with these problems. The improvements are twofold: 1) the QIM based approach can efficiently restrain watermark distortion and perform reliable extraction under various attack conditions. 2) Dual quantization of both positive and negative significant differences can exploit more large-magnitude coefficients for embedding and thus achieves better robustness and feature adaptivity.

2   Significant Difference Quantization Based Watermarking

The SDQ method [4] performs a three-level DWT decomposition and selects the LH3 subband for watermark embedding. The adjacent coefficients are firstly grouped into blocks of a predefined size (seven as suggested in [4]), and a secret key is then utilized to randomly select N_w blocks for embedding where N_w is the number of watermark bits.

For each block Λ_i, $i \in [1, N_w]$, its significant difference value, namely the difference between the largest and second largest coefficient $max_i - sec_i$, is modulated according to the watermark bit to be embedded. Concretely, if the watermark bit for embedding is 1, max_i is quantized to max_i' as:

$$max_i' = \begin{cases} max_i + T, & \text{if } (max_i - sec_i) < \tau \\ max_i, & \text{otherwise} \end{cases} \qquad (1)$$

where $\tau = \max(\varepsilon, T)$, ε denotes the average significant difference of all N_w blocks and T is the parameter controlling the embedding strength. Otherwise, if the watermark bit is 0, the corresponding max_i is quantized as:

$$max_i' = sec_i \qquad (2)$$

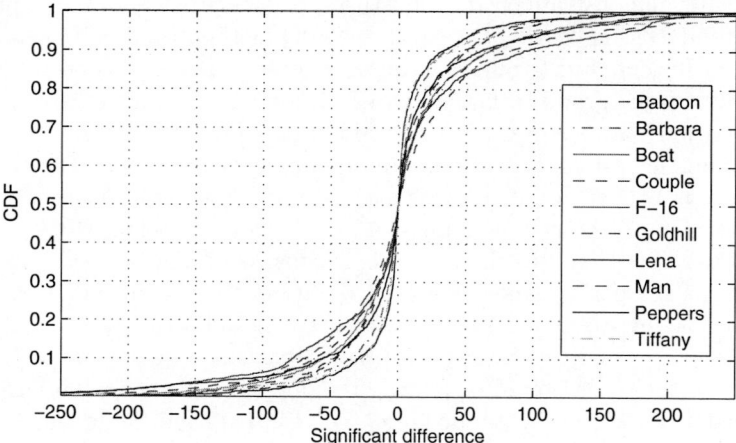

Fig. 1. The significant difference CDF of some natural images

For watermark extraction, Lin *et al.* define an adaptive threshold y as:

$$y = \left\lfloor \frac{1}{N_w \times \alpha} \sum_{i=1}^{N_w \times \alpha} \varphi_i \right\rfloor \tag{3}$$

where $\varphi_1 \leq \varphi_2 \leq ... \leq \varphi_{N_w}$ are the ordered significant differences of the received image, and $\alpha \in [0, 1]$ is a trade-off parameter depending on the ratio between two watermark symbols. Subsequently, in order to extract watermark information bits w_i, the retrieved significant difference is compared to the threshold y:

$$w_i = \begin{cases} 1, & \text{if } (max'_i - sec'_i) \leq y \\ 0, & \text{otherwise} \end{cases} \tag{4}$$

3 Quantization Index Modulation of Significant Difference

While maintaining a relative large capacity with the subgroup-based embedding strategy, the SDQ method demonstrates better robustness against various signal processing attacks than existing work [4]. Nevertheless, we argue that three deficiencies of SDQ are not well addressed.

1) For the coefficient blocks embedded with watermark symbol 0, the significant differences are directly modulated to zero regardless of their magnitudes or T (see Eq. (2)). Consequently, singular distortions are probably emerged in blocks with large significant differences, which is beyond the control of embedding strength parameter.

2) SDQ only employs positive maximum of one block for watermark embedding. However, in Fig. 1 we could observe that the absolute magnitudes of

positive and negative significant differences demonstrate a similar distribution. We state that further employing these negative maxima for watermarking could efficiently increase watermark robustness along with the adaptability to local image feature.

3) The adaptive extraction threshold y is sensitive to the content of watermark sequences (i.e., the ratio between watermark symbols 0 and 1) as well as the characteristic of host images and various attack conditions.

In this paper, we propose a quantization index modulation (QIM) [6] based simple yet efficient blind watermarking scheme to tackle with the above withdraws of SDQ and achieve further improvements. Details of the proposed watermarking method are presented in the following subsections.

3.1   Watermark Embedding

The intrinsic reason for SDQ to generate uncontrollable great distortions is equalizing the local largest coefficient to the second largest coefficient. Therefore, in order to restrain the distortion introduced by watermarking, we adopt the QIM [6] strategy to limit the modifications within one quantization cell. Concretely, for the embedding of one watermark bit 0 or 1, the significant difference is modulated to even or odd multiple of a quantization step Q, instead of larger than T or equal to 0.

Let Δ_i denote the original significant difference value of block i, and w_i the corresponding watermark bit, the embedding procedure could be achieved by the following equations:

$$\Delta'_i = \text{round}\left(\frac{\Delta_i + w_i Q}{2Q}\right) \cdot 2Q - w_i Q \qquad (5)$$

$$max'_i = max_i + (\Delta'_i - \Delta_i) \qquad (6)$$

where Δ'_i denotes the quantized significant difference and max'_i indicates the modulated maxima. It is evident that the upper bound of the modification on local maxima is Q, therefore the distortion could be well restricted by changing its value. Larger value of Q indicates better robustness but lower fidelity. Besides, to further conceal the embedding locations for higher security, the preshuffle operation suggested in [5] is also performed in the proposed method. The whole embedding progress could be summarized as follows:

1) *Wavelet decomposition*: Apply three-level wavelet decomposition to the host image and select LH3 and HL3 sub-bands for embedding.

2) *Coefficients grouping*: Randomly shuffle the coefficients according to a secret key K, and subsequently group non-overlapped coefficients into blocks with the pre-defined size (28 is adopted here). Due to the employment of one more subband and the negative coefficients, SD-QIM could quadruple the block size of SDQ while maintaining the same capacity, and thus have a larger probability to capture significant coefficients.

3) *Watermark embedding*: To embed the watermark bits, compute the significant difference of corresponding block and quantize the largest value according to Eq. (5) and (6). A similar progress is then repeated for embedding the rest watermark bits on negative coefficients.

4) *Inverse transforming*: Recover the watermarked coefficients to original positions, and apply inverse wavelet transform to obtain the watermarked image.

3.2   Watermark Extraction

Different from the SDQ method, which chooses the adaptive threshold according to the components of watermark sequence and image conditions [4], the blind extraction of the proposed method could be performed in a straightforward manner. With the quantization step parameter Q and the secret key K, the watermark extraction progress could be summarized as follows:

1) *Wavelet decomposition*: Decompose the image with three-level wavelet transform and select LH3 along with HL3 subband for watermark extraction.

2) *Coefficients grouping*: Shuffle the subband coefficients with the secret key K, and group non-overlapped coefficients into blocks. Localize the blocks assigned for watermark bits.

3) *Watermark bits extraction*: For each watermark bit $w_i, i \in [1, N_w]$, compute the corresponding significant difference $\hat{\Delta}_i$ and decode the information as:

$$\hat{w}_i = \mathrm{mod}\left(\mathrm{round}\left(\frac{\hat{\Delta}'_i}{Q}\right), 2\right) \qquad (7)$$

4   Experimental Results and Analysis

In this section, we use twenty gray scale images of size 512×512 from the USC-SIPI database [7] and perform various attacks on the watermarked image sets to evaluate watermarking performance. For making fair comparisons with SDQ and other classical watermarking methods [2][4][8], random sequences of the same length $N_w = 512$ with equal ratio of watermark symbol 0 and 1 are employed as watermarks. The normalized cross correlation (NC) between the extracted watermark and the original watermark is adopted to evaluate the quality of retrieved watermarks.

4.1   Fidelity

Generally, larger value of T and Q should indicate higher robustness and lower fidelity for SDQ and SD-QIM. As demonstrated in Table 1, with a large variation of T, the PSNR of SDQ stabilizes at the average value of about 41 dB but shows large variance for each fixed parameter.

This implies that the fidelity of SDQ method depends more on image characteristics rather than embedding parameter. The phenomenon could be ascribed

Table 1. PSNR (dB) of SDQ and SD-QIM with various parameters

	10	20	30	40
T	41.7 ± 7.34	41.4 ± 6.56	41.0 ± 5.35	40.6 ± 4.20
Q	59.0 ± 0.03	53.3 ± 0.02	49.8 ± 0.02	47.4 ± 0.03

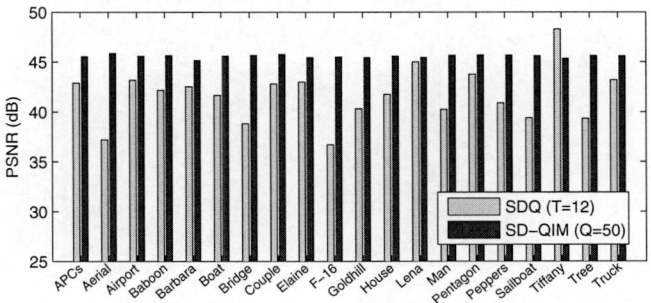

Fig. 2. PSNR of the watermarked images

to that Eq. (2) directly quantizes the significant difference to zero regardless of T. Therefore, images with larger significant differences are more likely to suffer great distortions from this operation (e.g., F-16). Contrarily, SD-QIM illustrates good error controllability due to the relatively rigorous restrain of quantization step. For subsequent comparisons, the parameters of SDQ and SD-QIM are set to $T = 12$ and $Q = 50$ respectively to maintain an acceptable similar fidelity (about 45 dB on Lena). Further, the PSNR of all images are exhibits in Fig. 2. It should be noted that the fluctuation of SDQ's result for different images just confirms our previous analysis.

Fig. 3 demonstrates the watermarked Lena images and the spacial watermark distribution of SDQ and SD-QIM. With a similar fixed PSNR, the two water-marked images have approximately the same pixel-wise mean square distance to the original image. However, as the watermark distribution map exhibits, SDQ mainly concentrates extremely large manipulations on a few significant coefficients. Companionably, owing to the QIM embedding strategy and the further employment of negative wavelet coefficients, the modifications of SD-QIM are well-distributed along the perceptual significant components (such as contours) of the host image.

4.2   Robustness to JPEG Compression and Gaussian Noise

We next compare the robustness against JPEG compression with other methods based on Lena image. The NC values between watermarks extracted from compressed Lena image and original watermark are exhibited in Table 2. The image quality metrics (PSNR in dB) and NC values of other methods are collected

Fig. 3. Watermarked Lena images and the spacial distribution of watermarks (top: SDQ 44.25dB, bottom: SD-QIM 45.45dB)

from the original papers. It could be observed that while keeping the highest fidelity, SD-QIM demonstrates the best robustness and could accurately extract nearly all 512 bits even when the quality factor is decreased to 30.

Table 2. Comparisons of robustness to JPEG compression on Lena image

	10	20	30	40	70	90
Wang [2] (38.20 dB)	–	–	0.15	0.23	0.57	1.00
Byun [8] (41.95 dB)	0.49	0.60	0.77	0.81	0.94	0.99
Lin　[4] (44.25 dB)	0.41	0.68	0.87	0.95	1.00	1.00
Proposed(45.45 dB)	0.44	0.91	0.99	1.00	1.00	1.00

We next evaluate watermark robustness on the USC-SIPI data set. JPEG and Gaussian noise as two typical distortions during everyday utilization and transmission are selected for comparing SDQ and SD-QIM. From Fig. 4(a) we could observe that, the extraction accuracy of SDQ is very sensitive to the choice of parameter $\alpha \in [0, 1]$: While the NC values of extracted watermark increase with α at extremely low image quality (JPEG quality factor = 10), $\alpha = 0.8$ achieves the best overall performance. This means the optimal α depends on the condition of watermarked image sets (i.e. distortion kind and degrees) which is hard to estimate in real applications.

Normally distributed Gaussian noise with zero mean and standard deviation σ is added to the watermarked images. The experiment is repeated for different σ. The results summarized in Fig. 4(b) imply similar conclusions with the JPEG compression case. Only with $\alpha = 1$, the SDQ method slightly outperforms SD-QIM at the extremely noisy condition (PSNR $\approx$ 22.21dB) whereas this parameter is hardly suitable for watermark extraction under other conditions.

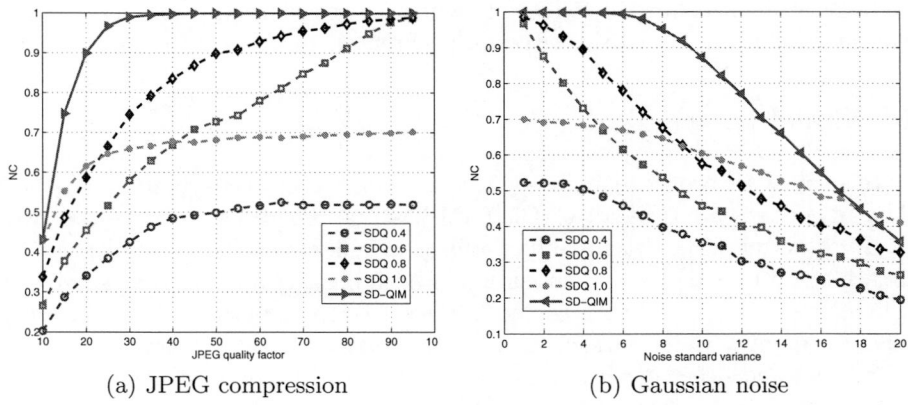

(a) JPEG compression   (b) Gaussian noise

Fig. 4. Comparison of watermark robustness. The watermarks of SDQ method are extracted with different parameters: $\alpha = 0.4$, 0.6, 0.8 and 1.

4.3 Robustness to Miscellaneous Attacks

As previously demonstrated, the performance of SDQ is quite sensitive to the choice of extracting parameter and the fixed value suggested by [4] can hardly adapt various distortion conditions. In our subsequential experiments, the results of SDQ are obtained by traversing the value of α within $[0, 1]$ with an incremental of 0.05, and select the best extraction performance of SDQ to compare with SD-QIM. Concretely, for the *Resize* attack, the watermarked images are downsampled by a scale factor and afterward interpolated to original resolution for watermark extraction. The comparison results are demonstrated in Table 3.

According to the analysis of Kundur [1], for watermark information with the length of 512 bits, even when the NC value is decreased to 0.23, the watermark can still be regarded as valid only with a false positive rate of 10^{-7}. Therefore, it could be concluded that both SDQ and SD-QIM can resist median filter with mask size up to 5×5, salt & pepper noise with the ratio of 3%. And SD-QIM outperforms SDQ with approximately 5 to 10 percent under other attacks.

Table 3. Comparison with SDQ on other attacks

	Median filter		Salt noise		Resize	Gauss
	3×3	5×5	1%	3%	0.5	filter
SDQ [4]	0.71	0.40	0.52	0.29	0.81	0.92
SD-QIM	0.83	0.38	0.68	0.26	0.94	0.96

Since SD-QIM is designed to survive content-preserving operations and incidental distortions, there is no specific synchronization or redundancy mechanisms. Consequently, geometric attacks such as rotation will cause similar problems as in [4]. However, note that as a coefficient quantization strategy, SD-QIM could be straightforward introduced to any other transform domain (e.g., Radon, Fourier-Mellin) in order to meet certain characteristics.

5   Conclusions

In this paper, we proposed an SD-QIM based blind robust watermarking method. The advantages are twofold: 1) The QIM based approach can take good control of the watermark distortion while performing reliable extraction under various attack conditions. 2) Dual quantization of both positive and negative significant differences can employ more coefficients with large amplitudes for embedding, which promotes watermark robustness and adaptiveness. Comparison results with SDQ and other conventional watermarking methods prove that SD-QIM could provide better robustness toward a large variety of attacks while keeping relative high fidelity and capacity. In the future work, adaptive quantization step, distortion compensation and other variants of QIM could be applied for further improvements.

Acknowledgement. This work is funded by the National Basic Research Program of China (No. 2010CB327902), the National Natural Science Foundation of China (No. 61202499, No. 60873158, No. 61005016, No. 61061130560), the National High-tech R&D Program of China (2011AA010502), the Open Projects Program of National Laboratory of Pattern Recognition, and the Fundamental Research Funds for the Central Universities.

References

1. Kundur, D., Hatzinakos, D.: Digital watermarking using multiresolution wavelet decomposition. In: Proc. ICASSP, pp. 2969–2972 (1998)
2. Wang, S., Lin, Y.: Wavelet tree quantization for copyright protection watermarking. IEEE Trans. Image Processing 13(2), 154–165 (2004)
3. You, X., Du, L., Cheung, Y., Chen, Q.: A blind watermarking scheme using new nontensor product wavelet filter banks. IEEE Trans. Image Processing 19(12), 3271–3284 (2010)
4. Lin, W., Horng, S., Kao, T., Fan, P., Lee, C., Pan, Y.: An efficient watermarking method based on significant difference of wavelet coefficient quantization. IEEE Trans. Multimedia 10(5), 746–757 (2008)
5. Meerwald, P., Koidl, C., Uhl, A.: Attack on "watermarking method based on significant difference of wavelet coefficient quantization". IEEE Trans. Multimedia 11(5), 1037–1041 (2009)
6. Chen, B., Wornell, G.: Quantization index modulation: A class of provably good methods for digital watermarking and information embedding. IEEE Trans. Information Theory 47(4), 1423–1443 (2001)
7. The USI-SIPI image database, vol. 3, http://sipi.usc.edu/database
8. Byun, K., Lee, S., Kim, H.: A watermarking method using quantization and statistical characteristics of wavelet transform. In: Proc. PDCAT 2005, pp. 689–693 (2005)

Robust Image Content Authentication
Using Perceptual Hashing and Watermarking

Li Weng[1], Rony Darazi[2], Bart Preneel[1], Benoît Macq[2], and Ann Dooms[3,*]

[1] Katholieke Universiteit Leuven
[2] Université catholique de Louvain
[3] Vrije Universiteit Brussel

Abstract. Perceptual hashing is a promising tool for multimedia content authentication. Digital watermarking is a convenient way of data hiding. By combining the two, we get a more efficient and versatile solution. In a typical scenario, multimedia data is sent from a server to a client. The corresponding hash value is embedded in the data. The data might undergo incidental distortion and malicious modification. In order to verify the authenticity of the received content, the client can compute a hash value from the received data, and compare it with the hash value extracted from the data. The advantage is that no extra communication is required – the original hash value is always available and synchronized. However, on the other hand, image quality can be degraded due to watermark embedding. There is interesting interaction between hashing and watermarking. We investigate this issue by proposing a content authentication system. The hash algorithm and the watermarking algorithm are designed to have minimal interference. This is achieved by doing hashing and watermarking in different wavelet subbands. Through extensive experiments we show that the parameters of the watermarking algorithm have significant influence to the authentication performance. This work gives useful insights into the research and practice in this field.

1   Introduction

Multimedia is an important element of digital life. Recent technology development has made it easy to produce and distribute multimedia content.

---

* This work was supported in part by the Research Council K.U.Leuven: GOA TENSE (GOA/11/007), by the IAP programme P6/26 BCRYPT of the Belgian State (Belgian Science Policy), by the European Commission through the ICT programme under contract ICT-2007-216676 ECRYPT II, and by the IBBT/AQUA project with the involved companies. IBBT (Interdisciplinary Institute for BroadBand Technology, Gaston Crommenlaan 8, Ghent) is a research institute founded in 2004 by the Flemish Government and the involved institutions. Additional support was provided by the FWO (Fonds Wetenschappelijk Onderzoek) within the project G.0206.08 "Perceptual Hashing and Semi-fragile Watermarking" and G.0213.11N "Watermarking, Encryption and Transcoding", and by the Post-Doctoral Fellowship of Peter Schelkens.

W. Lin et al. (Eds.): PCM 2012, LNCS 7674, pp. 315–326, 2012.
© Springer-Verlag Berlin Heidelberg 2012

While there is abundant media content distributed in a large scale system, an important issue is *trustworthiness protection*. Since software for editing digital content is easily accessible, modified or synthesized content often appears. Unless one knows the original content, it is difficult to find out whether the content has been professionally modified.

In this work, we focus on the trustworthiness protection of images and video. In a heterogeneous network, there are servers, clients, and intermediate nodes with different computing capabilities. Clients receive multimedia data from servers through intermediate nodes that form a distribution chain. The distribution chain is not perfectly reliable, due to the following issues:

- *Incidental distortion* – the content may undergo re-encoding, e.g. a format change or re-compression, since it is necessary to adjust the data stream according to the client's capability and the network condition. Properties, such as resolution, contrast, etc., may change.
- *Malicious modification* – there might be malicious nodes that modify or replace the content.

In such a circumstance, an important question of the client is *whether the received content is authentic.*

The above problem is easy when the original content is available for comparison, but in practice it is usually not the case. When the original content is not available, a possible solution is to generate a *hash value* on the server side and send it securely to the client side. The hash value is a compact abstract of the content. A client can re-generate a hash value from the received content, and compare it with the original hash value. If they match, the content is considered as authentic. Conventionally, there exist cryptographic hash algorithms for data authentication, such as MD5, SHA-1 [1]. However, they are not suitable for multimedia data, because they are extremely sensitive and do not tolerate any change of the data. In order to correctly authenticate the content even when it has undergone some incidental distortion, the hash value must possess some *robustness*. Therefore, a new generation of hash algorithms has emerged in the multimedia domain, called robust or perceptual hash (PH) algorithms [2].

Perceptual hash algorithms enable robust content authentication, whereas sometimes it is not easy to setup a secure channel for transmitting hash values. Therefore, a more convenient approach comes fourth – instead of sending through a secure channel, we can deliver the hash value by imperceptibly embedding it into the content itself using robust digital watermarking techniques. The new approach *avoids extra communication, and ensures that the original hash value is always available and synchronized.* The authentication procedure is simple: a client extracts the original hash value from the watermarked data, and compares it with the re-computed hash value. Such a system was envisioned by Fridrich and Goljan in [3,4]. They motivated the usefulness of content-dependent watermarks and designed a robust hash algorithm. However, so far there is no practical design and in-depth study on a complete content authentication system based on perceptual hashing and robust watermarking.

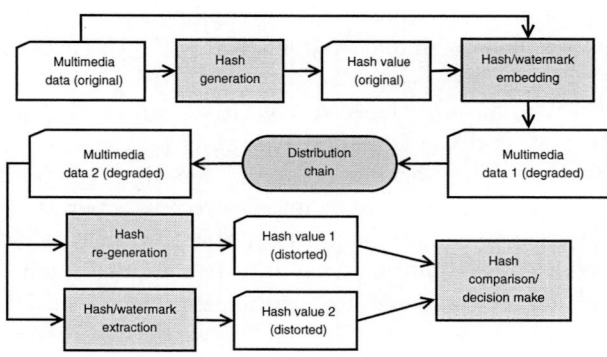

Fig. 1. Diagram of image content authentication

In this work, we propose a novel content authentication system by combining perceptual hashing and robust watermarking. We use the hash algorithm to essentially achieve content authentication, and focus on the authentication performance under the influence of watermarking. We define the overall system performance as the authentication performance and the image quality loss by watermarking. The proposed system is extensively tested and exhibit good performance. The results justify the validity of the design and serve as a reference for research and practice in this field.

2   System Requirement and Overview

The content authentication system includes an image hash algorithm and a watermarking algorithm. They have their own requirements, but also interact. The schematic diagram of content authentication is shown in Fig. 1.

2.1   The Image Hash System

A perceptual hash value must fairly represent the corresponding content. The hash algorithm should possess the following properties:

- *Compactness* – a hash value is compact;
- *Robustness* – hash computation is insensitive to a certain level of distortion to the input image;
- *Discriminability* – perceptually different content results in significantly different hash values;
- *Key dependence* – hash generation depends on a key.

We define perceptually similar images as images generated by certain incidental distortion. If two images are not perceptually similar, they are considered as perceptually different. In the content authentication scenario, the distance d between two hash values is compared with a threshold T. The decision is made from two hypotheses: 1) $\mathbb{H}_0$ – the images correspond to different content; 2) $\mathbb{H}_1$ – the images correspond to similar content. If $d \leq T$, we choose $\mathbb{H}_1$; otherwise we choose $\mathbb{H}_0$.

The overall performance of the hash algorithm can be characterized by the true positive rate P_d and the false positive rate P_f. A good algorithm should suppress the false positive rate while maintaining a high true positive rate. The relationship between P_d and P_f is known as the receiver operating characteristic (ROC) curve. In order to choose the most suitable threshold value, we also need to take into account of the false negative rate P_m. By definition, $P_m = 1 - P_d$. Actually P_f and P_m are contradicting requirements. Different applications give their own bias towards P_f or P_m. By default, we choose the equal error rate (EER) point, where $P_f = P_m$, as the working point.

2.2   The Watermarking System

The watermarking scheme, as a method for data hiding, generally concerns the following issues:

- *Payload capacity* – the scheme can carry a certain amount of information;
- *Robustness* – the scheme should withstand certain distortion to the image;
- *Perceptual quality* – the watermark has little impact on the image quality;
- *Key dependence* – the algorithm depends on a key.

The performance of a watermarking scheme depends on the embedding strength and the size of the payload.

In this work, we use the quantization index modulation (QIM) [5]. It is very robust to noise. In addition to the high capacity-robustness trade-offs, QIM methods are simple and have a small computational cost. Watermark detection in QIM is performed without access to the original data or the original watermark.

2.3   Performance Evaluation

The overall performance is a balance between the authentication performance under incidental distortion and the quality loss due to watermarking. Typically, the watermark embedding also brings distortion to the original image, so it might affect the re-computation of the hash value. This interference, denoted as I_{wh}, must be small.

Besides, the parameters of the two algorithms also influence each other's performance. For example, increasing the hash size typically increases the discrimination performance, but also increases the payload and decreases the robustness of the watermark. Increasing the watermark embedding strength may increase I_{wh}, but on the other hand achieves better robustness of the watermark.

Therefore, the design of such a system involves the interaction between the two components. We need to optimize the authentication performance and the perceptual quality. In practice, we can fix one of them and try to get the best performance for the other.

3 The Proposed Scheme

In the proposed scheme, the adopted watermarking algorithm is the spread transform dither modulation (STDM), a variant of QIM. It exhibits robustness to requantization and meanwhile maintains low complexity. Instead of quantizing the host signal x itself, the quantization occurs entirely in the projection of the host signal x onto a randomly generated vector p, which depends on a secret key K_w. Consequently, the embedding of each information bit occurs in the projection of the host signal x by quantizing it with a uniform, scalar, dithered quantizer [5]. In this method, each bit of the watermark message is spread into n samples instead of one sample.

Consider a host signal $\mathbf{x} = [x_1, x_2, ..., x_N]^T$ of length N. We break the whole signal into segments with equal length n, and embed one bit into each segment $\mathbf{x_i}$ ($i = 1, 2, \cdots, \lfloor N/n \rfloor$). This bit is spread in the projection of the segment onto a random vector $\mathbf{p}$. The watermarked signal is:

$$\mathbf{y_i} = \mathbf{x_i} + (Q_m(\mathbf{x_i}^T \mathbf{p}) - \mathbf{x_i}^T \mathbf{p})\mathbf{p} , \qquad m \in \{0, 1\}, \tag{1}$$

where Q_m is a quantizer with quantization step Δ. The STDM decoder makes a decision based on the projection of the channel output $\mathbf{y_i}$ onto the spreading vector $\mathbf{p}$. The detection can be performed with a minimum distance decoder:

$$\hat{m} = arg \min_{m \in \{0,1\}} |\mathbf{y_i}^T \mathbf{p} - Q_m(\mathbf{y_i}^T \mathbf{p})| . \tag{2}$$

The watermarking space is the two-dimensional discrete wavelet transform space. We use the biorthogonal 4.4 wavelet. The embedding happens on the third decomposition level of luminance component using the horizontal and vertical (LH and HL) subbands.

Regarding perceptual hashing, we need a hash algorithm which is representative, light-weight, and has moderate performance. Additionally, it is easily configurable and compatible with the watermarking algorithm. Based on these considerations, we design an image hash algorithm which also works in the wavelet domain. The advantage of using the same domain as the watermarking algorithm is that the influence of watermark embedding to the hash recomputation I_{wh} can be minimized by doing watermarking and hashing in different wavelet subbands. The algorithm generates an L_h-bit PH value which depends on a secret key K_h. It has the following steps:

1. Convert the input image to gray-scale and proportionally resize it to make the maximum dimension equal to 512 pixels;
2. Compute X so that level X has more than L_h wavelet coefficients;
3. Two-dimensional wavelet transform until level X;
4. Apply a two-dimensional discrete cosine transform (DCT) to the approximate (LL) subband;
5. Extract the sign bits of the first L_h DCT coefficients using a zigzag scan, excluding the DC;

6. Concatenate all the extracted bits and perform a random permutation according to K_h.

When two hash values are compared, the bit error rate (BER), i.e., the normalized Hamming distance, is used as the distance metric.

Since the hash generation happens in the approximation subband and the watermark embedding happens in the detail subbands, *hash re-computation is almost not affected by watermark insertion.*

4 Experiment Results

The system performance depends on the parameters of both algorithms. In this work, we investigate how the watermarking algorithm affects the content authentication performance. We fix the hash size to 128 bits, and vary the watermarking parameters n and Δ, i.e., the length of the spreading vector and the quantization step. The following values are used:

- n – 16, 32, 64, 128, 256;
- Δ – 40, 60, 80, 100, 120, 160, 200, 240.

For each combination of n and Δ, we evaluate the content authentication performance by three tests:

- *Robustness test* – hash values of original images and their distorted versions are compared;
- *Discrimination test* – hash values of different images are compared;
- *Hypothesis test* - the false positive rate and and false negative rate are computed for all thresholds.

A database of 100 images is used. They are natural scene photos of different genres such as architecture, art, humanoids, landscape, objects, vehicles, etc. In the robustness test, distorted versions are generated for each original image. Five kinds of incidental distortion are simulated. Additionally, we also simulate malicious modification by block tampering – an image block is replaced with a different block randomly chosen in the same image. The size of a block is 1/64 of the image area. The distortions are listed in Table 1. Ideally, our system should be able to distinguish incidental and malicious distortion.

There are 100 original images and 4200 distorted images. Hash values are generated for all of them. Note that a hash value of an original image is generated by the following procedure: 1)embedding the original hash value into the image; 2) distort the image; 3) extract the watermark. The hypothesis test is done by pair-wise comparing all the hash values (excluding those by block tampering since they are not considered as authentic). There are 4300 runs of hash generation and $\binom{3600}{2} = 6,478,200$ hash comparisons for each $\{n, \Delta\}$ pair.

The content authentication performance is represented by the EER, i.e., P_f or P_m when they are equal. Different EER values w.r.t different $\{n, \Delta\}$ combinations are listed in Table 2. A lower value means better performance.

Table 1. List of legitimate and malicious distortion

Distortion	Parameter range (step)
AWGN	PSNR 20 – 50 dB (5)
JPEG compression	Quality factor (QF) 10 – 70 (10)
Gaussian filtering	Window size 7 – 19 (2)
Sharpening	Strength 0.1 – 0.7 (0.1)
Gamma correction	Gamma 0.5 – 1.7 (0.2)
Block tampering	No. of blocks 1 – 7 (1)

Table 2. EER values for different $\{n, \Delta\}$ combinations

$n \backslash \Delta$	40	60	80	100	120	160	200	240
16	.0633	.0244	.0067	.0061	.0044	.0021	.0019	.0010
32	.0888	.0494	.0113	.0065	.0061	.0041	.0028	.0020
64	.1312	.0804	.0508	.0181	.0092	.0044	.0032	.0022
128	.2248	.1066	.0639	.0507	.0480	.0123	.0047	.0046
256	.3656	.2327	.1303	.0809	.0613	.0508	.0264	.0174

The image quality loss can be measured by comparing the images before and after watermark embedding. Three quality metrics are considered here: the peak signal-to-noise ratio (PSNR), the signal-to-noise ratio (SNR), and the structural similarity (SSIM) [6]. The average results are listed in Table 3, 4, and 5 respectively. A higher value means better perceptual quality. Based on the above results, there are two observations:

1. The authentication performance increases with smaller n and larger Δ;
2. The image quality loss increases with smaller n and larger Δ.

Implicitly, there is a third relationship on watermarking:

3. The security of watermarking decreases with smaller n and larger Δ.

This is because a longer spreading vector is in general more difficult to discover; on the other hand, when the quantization is stronger, the watermark pattern becomes more noticeable to an attacker.

In practice, a user can first choose an acceptable image quality level and a watermarking security level, then he can find the corresponding authentication

Table 3. Average PSNR (dB) values for different $\{n, \Delta\}$ combinations

$n \backslash \Delta$	40	60	80	100	120	160	200	240
16	53.10	49.94	47.68	45.90	44.43	42.10	40.28	38.78
32	56.28	52.79	50.62	48.92	47.50	45.23	43.44	41.97
64	60.89	56.07	53.55	51.82	50.45	48.25	46.53	45.10
128	69.00	61.16	57.62	55.47	53.95	51.71	50.03	48.64
256	84.71	70.26	64.46	61.23	59.11	56.36	54.51	53.11

Table 4. Average SNR (dB) values for different $\{n, \Delta\}$ combinations

$n\backslash\Delta$	40	60	80	100	120	160	200	240
16	46.34	43.18	40.92	39.14	37.67	35.34	33.51	32.02
32	49.51	46.03	43.86	42.15	40.74	38.47	36.68	35.21
64	54.13	49.31	46.79	45.06	43.68	41.49	39.77	38.34
128	62.24	54.40	50.86	48.71	47.19	44.95	43.27	41.88
256	77.95	63.50	57.70	54.47	52.35	49.60	47.75	46.35

Table 5. Average SSIM values for different $\{n, \Delta\}$ combinations

$n\backslash\Delta$	40	60	80	100	120	160	200	240
16	.9976	.9953	.9923	.9888	.9847	.9750	.9635	.9507
32	.9988	.9974	.9959	.9941	.9920	.9869	.9808	.9739
64	.9996	.9988	.9978	.9968	.9958	.9932	.9901	.9866
128	.9999	.9996	.9991	.9986	.9980	.9968	.9954	.9937
256	1.000	.9999	.9998	.9996	.9994	.9988	.9982	.9976

performance, or vice versa. For example, we can choose $n = 64$, $\Delta = 120$ to get a PSNR around 50 dB in Table 3. The corresponding EER is $P_f = P_m = 0.0092$ in Table 2. The detailed authentication performance results are presented below.

In order to evaluate the robustness of watermark embedding, we compare the original hash value with the extracted one after distortion. The average results are listed in Table 6. One can see that in most cases the original hash value has a tiny difference from the extracted one. Therefore, the watermarking part works properly. On the other hand, we also need to evaluate the influence of watermark embedding on hash re-computation I_{wh}. We compare the re-computed hash values with and without watermarking, and list the average distances (BERs) in Table 7. The results show that the influence is quite small. This is expected, because hashing and watermarking are carried out in different wavelet subbands.

Table 8 shows the robustness test results. Among the incidental distortion, except for JPEG 10 and gamma correction 0.5, the average hash distances are all quite small (less than 0.1). They indicate strong resistance to incidental distortion. Regarding malicious distortion, note that besides AWGN 20 dB, JPEG 10, and gamma correction 0.5, the rest of incidental distortion results smaller hash distances than the distances by tampering two or more blocks. Therefore, the current configuration is able to distinguish incidental and malicious distortion in most cases. If better distinction is required, one may use a larger hash size.

Figure 2 shows the actual distribution of hash distances in the discrimination test. They are derived from 6415200 hash comparisons between different images. The hash values are assumed to be independent of each other. Ideally, the distribution of the normalized Hamming distances is binomial with $p = 0.5$ and $N = 128$. The empirical distribution has a standard deviation 0.0519, with a mean of 0.4957. Most hash distances for different images are close to 0.5, which is close to the ideal situation. Since the standard deviation of a binomial distribution is given by $\sigma = \sqrt{p(1-p)/N}$, the distribution of hash distances

Table 6. Robustness of watermark embedding for $\{n = 64, \Delta = 120\}$. Original hash values are compared with extracted ones.

AWGN	20	25	30	35	40	45	50
Mean BER	.069	.000	0	0	0	0	0
JPEG	10	20	30	40	50	60	70
Mean BER	.283	.007	.007	.017	.072	.000	.000
Gaussian filt.	7	9	11	13	15	17	19
Mean BER	0	0	0	0	0	0	0
Sharpening	0.1	0.2	0.3	0.4	0.5	0.6	0.7
Mean BER	.021	.020	.020	.019	.019	.019	.019
Gamma corr.	0.5	0.7	0.9	1.1	1.3	1.5	1.7
Mean BER	.068	.032	0	0	.001	.005	.013
Block tampering	1	2	3	4	5	6	7
Mean BER	0	0	0	.001	.001	.002	.002

Table 7. Influence of watermark embedding on hash re-computation for $\{n = 64, \Delta = 120\}$. The re-computed hash values with and without watermarking are compared.

AWGN	20	25	30	35	40	45	50
Mean BER	.013	.008	.005	.003	.001	.001	.001
JPEG	10	20	30	40	50	60	70
Mean BER	.001	.001	.002	.002	.001	.002	.002
Gaussian filt.	7	9	11	13	15	17	19
Mean BER	.001	.001	.001	.001	.001	.001	.001
Sharpening	0.1	0.2	0.3	0.4	0.5	0.6	0.7
Mean BER	.001	.001	.001	.001	.001	.001	.001
Gamma corr.	0.5	0.7	0.9	1.1	1.3	1.5	1.7
Mean BER	.002	.002	.001	.001	.001	.001	.001
Block tampering	1	2	3	4	5	6	7
Mean BER	.143	.005	.004	.005	.006	.005	.005

corresponds to a binomial process with $N = 92$ and $p = 0.5$, whose theoretical distribution is plotted by a solid line in Fig. 2. One can see that the theoretical distribution approximately fits the actual data. Therefore, 92 out of 128 (72%) hash bits are independent and unpredictable. The probability that two random image blocks have the same hash value is about 2^{-92}. If a lower collision rate is required, one could use a larger hash size.

Figure 3 and 4 show the hypothesis test results. A state-of-the-art algorithm [7] is implemented as a baseline for performance comparison. This scheme was shown in [7] to outperform Fridrich's scheme [3]. We configure it to have the same hash size (128 bits) as the proposed scheme, and test it in the same way. One can see efficient trade-offs between the false positive rate and the false negative rate from the figures. Some typical values of the ROC curve are listed in Table 9.

Table 8. Robustness test for $\{n = 64, \Delta = 120\}$

AWGN	20	25	30	35	40	45	50
Mean BER	.082	.009	.006	.003	.002	.002	.001
JPEG	10	20	30	40	50	60	70
Mean BER	.290	.013	.013	.022	.073	.003	.003
Gaussian filt.	7	9	11	13	15	17	19
Mean BER	.003	.003	.003	.003	.003	.003	.003
Sharpening	0.1	0.2	0.3	0.4	0.5	0.6	0.7
Mean BER	.045	.045	.044	.044	.043	.044	.043
Gamma corr.	0.5	0.7	0.9	1.1	1.3	1.5	1.7
Mean BER	.119	.062	.012	.011	.030	.050	.074
Block tampering	1	2	3	4	5	6	7
Mean BER	.047	.081	.101	.166	.181	.192	.196

Table 9. Typical values of the ROC curves for the proposed scheme $\{n = 64, \Delta = 120\}$ and the baseline scheme [7]

P_f	P_d	
	proposed	baseline
10^{-1}	0.996	0.977
10^{-2}	0.990	0.945
10^{-3}	0.982	0.814
10^{-4}	0.974	0.366
10^{-5}	0.973	...
10^{-6}	0.972	...
10^{-7}	0.912	...

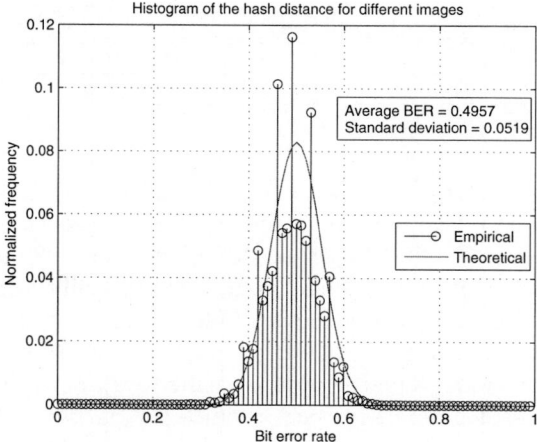

Fig. 2. BER Histogram for different images for $\{n = 64, \Delta = 120\}$

Our scheme can achieve a true positive rate above 0.9 while maintains a false positive rate below 10^{-7}. These results prove that the proposed system works properly and significantly outperforms the baseline algorithm.

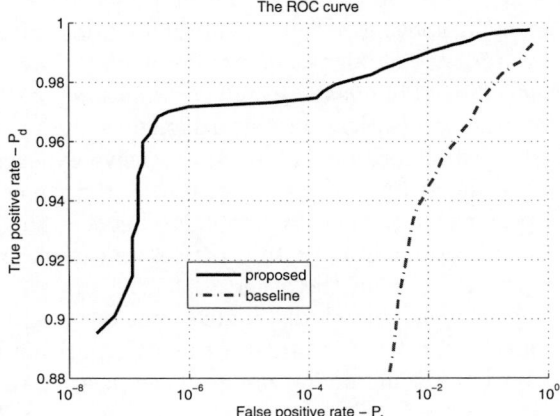

Fig. 3. The ROC curves for the proposed scheme $\{n = 64, \Delta = 120\}$ and the baseline scheme [7]

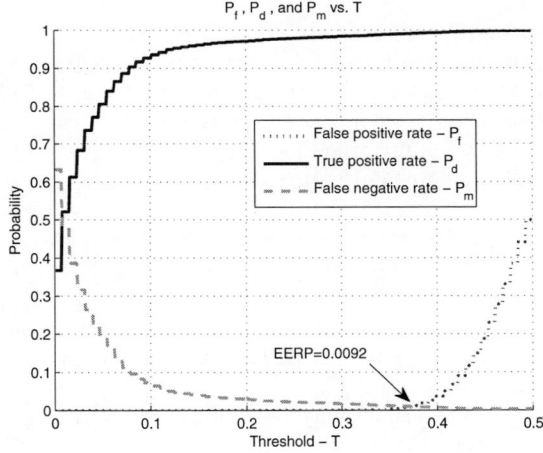

Fig. 4. Hypothesis test results for $\{n = 64, \Delta = 120\}$

5   Conclusion

Robust hashing is a promising solution to the multimedia content authentication problem. It can be used together with digital watermarking techniques. Instead of being transmitted separately, hash values can be embedded in the corresponding multimedia data. The advantage is that no extra communication is required – the original hash value is always available and synchronized. This makes robust hashing a more versatile solution. However, on the other hand, image quality can be degraded due to watermark embedding.

There is interesting interaction between hashing and watermarking. We investigate this issue by proposing a content authentication system. The hash algorithm and the watermarking algorithm are designed to have minimal interference. This is achieved by doing hashing and watermarking in different wavelet subbands. We define the authentication performance as the receiver operating characteristics of the hash algorithm. Through extensive experiments we show that the parameters of the watermarking algorithm have significant influence to the authentication performance. There is a trade-off between the authentication performance and the perceptual quality. In practice, we can fix one of them and try to get the best performance for the other.

The proposed algorithm is able to distinguish incidental and malicious distortion. It significantly outperforms a state-of-the-art algorithm by achieving a true positive rate above 0.9 while maintaining a false positive rate below 10^{-7}. Our work gives useful insights into the research and practice in this field.

References

1. Schneier, B.: Applied Cryptography: Protocols, Algorithms, and Source Code in C, 2nd edn. John Wiley & Sons (1996)
2. Swaminathan, A., Mao, Y., Wu, M.: Robust and secure image hashing. IEEE Transactions on Information Forensics and Security 1(2), 215–230 (2006)
3. Fridrich, J.: Robust bit extraction from images. In: Proc. of IEEE International Conference on Multimedia Computing and Systems, vol. 2, pp. 536–540 (1999)
4. Fridrich, J., Goljan, M.: Robust hash functions for digital watermarking. In: Proc. of International Conference on Information Technology: Coding and Computing, pp. 178–183 (2000)
5. Chen, B., Wornell, G.: Quantization index modulation: a class of provably good methods for digital watermarking and information embedding. IEEE Transactions on Information Theory 47(4), 1423–1443 (2001)
6. Wang, Z., Bovik, A., Sheikh, H., Simoncelli, E.: Image quality assessment: From error visibility to structural similarity. IEEE Transactions on Image Processing 13(4), 600–612 (2004)
7. Khelifi, F., Jiang, J.: Perceptual image hashing based on virtual watermark detection. IEEE Transactions on Image Processing 19(4), 981–994 (2010)

A Secure Semi-fragile Self-recoverable Watermarking Algorithm Using Group-Based Wavelet Quantization

Chunlei Li[1,2], Bin Ma[1], Yunhong Wang[1], Di Huang[1,*], and Zhaoxiang Zhang[1]

[1] Image Processing and Intelligent Recognition Laboratory (IRIP), School of Computer Science and Engineering, Beihang University, Beijing, China, 100191
[2] School of Electronic and Information Engineering, Zhongyuan University of Technology, ZhengZhou 450007, China

Abstract. In this paper, we propose a secure semi-fragile self-recoverable watermarking algorithm using group-based wavelet quantization. The image is split into image blocks with size 16×16. A 5-bit authentication watermark is generated from the first-order statical moments of each image block, and embedded into the mid-frequency bands of another image block by our proposed group-based wavelet quantization method. Security is enhanced by randomly permutating coefficients among a group. Robustness is improved by embedding watermark in largest coefficient inside a sub-group based on significant difference parity quantization (SDPQ) method. Moreover, all adjacent blocks of the test block and its mapping block are taken into account to improve localization accuracy. Experimental comparisons with existing techniques highlight the effectiveness of the proposed watermarking approach.

Keywords: semi-fragile, self-recoverable, tamper detection, incidental manipulation.

1 Introduction

Nowadays, the integrity and authenticity of digital content is of great threat with the emergence of digital image editing software. Authentication watermarking techniques provide a possible solution to prove tampering of the digital content. Based on the functionality, existing techniques can be categorized as fragile and semi-fragile watermarking. Compared with fragile watermarking, semi-fragile watermarking techniques have recently attracted much attention since they are robust to content-preserving manipulations such as JPEG compression and channel AWGN (Additive White Gaussian Noise), but fragile to malicious attacks like image cropping. Besides tamper proofing for authentication of the image, semi-fragile self-recoverable watermarking techniques were further developed to recover the tampered region [1].

---

* Corresponding author.

W. Lin et al. (Eds.): PCM 2012, LNCS 7674, pp. 327–336, 2012.

In [2, 3, 4], the wavelet-based semi-fragile watermarking schemes are developed to concisely determine the regions where the integrity fails. In addition, another watermark is embedded to perform self-recovery in case of malicious attack. However, the authentication watermarks are generated and embedded independent of the host image, it is vulnerable to vector quantization (VQ) attack [5] and collage attack [6]; Moreover, to recover the tampered region, the recovery data except the authentication data is required in these schemes, and it increases the amount of the embedding watermarks. Thus, the robustness of these methods is relatively low. Li et al. [7] applied discrete wavelet transform (DWT) technique into each image block with size 8×8, and then generated 12-bit watermark from the low-frequency coefficient of one image block. In the end, three copies of 12-bit watermark are hidden in the mid-frequency components of the other three image blocks. However, the proposed method did not present a efficient method to precisely localize the tampered block, and one image block with size 8×8 needs to be embedded into 36-bit watermark, the robustness of the method is very low. In [8], the proposed method is block-wise, the watermarking of one block is closely related to all the blocks surrounding it. However, a close relationship between uncorrelated blocks may come at the cost of reduced error localization properties and introduce confusion for the consequent authentication process.

In this paper, we propose a novel self-recoverable semi-fragile watermarking scheme based on group-based wavelet quantization. A 5-bit authentication watermarks are generated from the first-order statical moment for each image block, and embedded into the mid-frequency bands of another image block by our proposed group-based wavelet quantization method. Security is enhanced by randomly permutating coefficients among a group. Robustness is improved by embedding watermark in largest coefficient inside a sub-group based on significant difference parity quantization (SDPQ) method. Moreover, all adjacent blocks of the test block and its mapping block are taken into account to improve localization accuracy.

2   Semi-fragile Self-recoverable Watermarking

The proposed watermarking scheme consists of three parts including watermark generation and embedding, tamper detection, tampered region recovery.

2.1   Watermark Generation and Embedding

Our method is block-wise, the generated watermark from an image block is embedded into another image block for content authentication and self-recovery. The generated watermark needs to tolerate incidental manipulation, for each image block, we calculate its first-order statistical moment, and use its 5 most significant bits (MSBs) as authentication watermark. Meanwhile, the embedded watermark also should be robust to incidental manipulation, therefore, the size of the embedded image block should be large for robustly embedding the 5-bit watermark, whereas it will reduce the localization accuracy of the method.

Considering the tradeoff between robustness and localization accuracy, 16×16 image block size is an optimal choice. The watermark generation and embedding algorithm is described as follows.

1) Partition the host image X into blocks $X_i(i = 1, 2, \cdots, N_b)$ with size 16×16, where N_b is the number of image block. Set the 3 least significant bits (LSB) as zeros. Then, calculate the first-order statistical moment of $\overline{X_i}$. It can be represented as $m_i = \frac{1}{m \times n} \sum (\overline{X_i})$, where $m \times n$ is the size of image block.

2) Covert m_i to an 8-bit binary sequence. And select its 5 most significant bits (MSBs) as watermarks $B_{ij}(i = 1, 2, \cdots, N_b, j = 1, 2, \cdots, 5)$. In order to improve the security of the proposed method, these information bits are encrypted using secret key k_1, and the encrypting process can be described as follows.

$$W_{i,j} = B_{ij} \oplus S_{ij} \tag{1}$$

where S_{ij} is a random binary sequence generated by k_1.

3) Embed the generated watermark based on a block-chain structure [9]. The generated watermark $W_{P(i)}$ from image block $X_{P(i)}$ is embedded into its next block $X_{P(i+1)}$, where P is a random position sequence generated by secret key k_2. And generated watermark from image block $W_{P(i+1)}$ is embedded into its next block $X_{P(i+2)}$, and so on.

In order to improve the robustness and security of our method, we propose a group-based wavelet quantization method for embedding 5-bit watermark generated from an image block into the mid-frequency of its next image block, as shown in Fig.1. And it is described as follows.

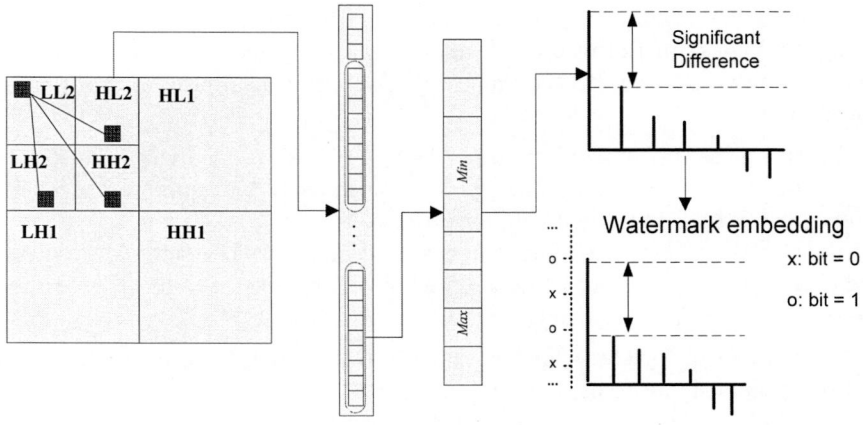

Fig. 1. Illustration of watermark bits embedding

1) Perform two level wavelet decompositions. Each image block with size 16×16 has three groups of mid-frequency coefficients, including LH2, HL2, and HH2, in which the size of each group is 4×4.

2) Convert three groups of mid-frequency coefficients with size 4×4 into a 16-dimension sequence, respectively. Then concatenate them into a single sequence with 48 coefficients.

3) In order to enhance the security of the system against local attacks, the sequence S is permuted as PS using secret key k_3.

4) Split PS into five sub-groups, noted as $PS = \{PS_k, k = 1, 2, \cdots, 5\}$. For each sub-group, we embed one watermark bit in the largest coefficient based on significant difference parity quantization (SDPQ) method.

For each sub-group $PS_k, k \in [1, 5]$, the significant difference, which refers to the difference of the largest and second largest value $max_k - sec_k$ is modulated according to the watermark bit to be embedded. To embed watermark bit 0 or 1, the significant difference is modulated to even or odd multiple of a quantization step Q, as shown in Fig 1. Let Δ_k denote the original significant difference value of group k, and w_k the corresponding watermark bit, the embedding procedure could be achieved by the following equations:

$$\Delta'_k = 2Q \cdot \left[\frac{\Delta + w_k Q}{2Q}\right] - w_k Q \tag{2}$$

$$max'_k = max_k + (\Delta'_k - \Delta_k) \tag{3}$$

where $[\cdot]$ is the round operator, Δ'_k denotes the quantized significant difference and max'_k is the modulated maximum. Evidently, the upper bound of the modification on local maximum is Q, and the trade-off between fidelity and robustness could be controlled by changing its value.

2.2   Tamper Detection

The block-chain embedding strategy will cause false detection [9]. In our method, all adjacent blocks of the test block and its mapping block are taken into account to improve localization accuracy. And the verification process contains the following steps.

1) Partition the test image Y into blocks $Y_i(i = 1, 2, \cdots, N_b)$ with size 16×16. For each image block, the 5-bit encrypted watermark W_i^* is generated according to step 1 and step 2 in the embedding process.

2) Extract the 5-bit embedding watermark W_i' from each image block. Watermark extraction process can be considered as the inverse process of watermark embedding, and it is described as follows.

– Perform 2-level wavelet transform for the test image. Each image block has three groups of mid-frequency coefficients with size 4×4, including LH2, HL2, and HH2. Convert them into a 48-dimension vector. Shuffle the sub-band coefficients using the secret key k_3, and regroup non-overlapped coefficients into five sub-groups.

– For each coefficient sub-group $k \in [1, 5]$, compute the significant difference $\hat{\Delta}_k$, and decode the watermark bit $\hat{w}_k$ as

$$\hat{\Delta}_k = \text{mod}\{[\frac{\hat{\Delta}_k}{Q}], 2\} \tag{4}$$

Then, for test image block Y_i which has five sub-group coefficients, a 5-bit watermark W'_i is extracted.

3) Generate random position sequence P by secret key k_2. For each test image block $Y_{P(i)}$, we compare the watermark $W^*_{P(i)}$ generated from $Y_{P(i)}$ with the watermark $W'_{P(i+1)}$ extracted from $Y_{P(i)}$, and get a detection indicators.

$$D_{P(i)} = \begin{cases} 1, & if\, W^*_{P(i)} = W'_{P(i+1)} \\ 0, & \text{otherwise} \end{cases} \tag{5}$$

The block $Y_{P(i)}$ is inconsistent if $D_{P(i)}=1$; otherwise, it is consistent. Then a tamper detection mask D is generated.

4) Optimize D using 8-neighborhood characterization. The optimization equation is written as follows.

$$T_{P(i)} = \begin{cases} 1, & if\, (D^1_{P(i)} = 1)\&(m^8_{I(i)} \geq m^8_{P(i+1)}) \\ 0, & \text{otherwise} \end{cases} \tag{6}$$

where $m^8_{P(i)}$ is the number of "1" in the 8-neighborhood of $D_{P(i)}$. As shown in Eq.(6), the inconsistent block is marked as tampered if the block-neighborhood characterization is more than or equal to that of its mapping block. Otherwise, the inconsistent block is genuine.

5) Count the number of the blocks in their 8-neighborhood where $T_{P(i)} = 1$, if the number is larger than or equal to 4, then indicating the block is tampered.

$$TDM_{P(i)} = \begin{cases} 1, & \sum N_8(T_{P(i)}) \geq 4 \\ 0, & \text{otherwise} \end{cases} \tag{7}$$

where $\sum N_8(T_{P(i)})$ denotes the number of inconsistent blocks in the 9-neighborhood of $T_{P(i)}$. Consisting of $TDM_{P(i)}$, the final detection masks TDM is generated.

2.3   Tampered Image Recovery

After tamper detection, all image blocks are marked as valid or invalid. The invalid blocks can be recovered using the following process.

1) According to verification results, image blocks are classified into two categories: valid blocks and invalid blocks.

2) For test image block $Y_{P(i)}$, if the image block is marked as valid, we calculate its first-order statical moment. Otherwise, we verify its mapping block $Y_{P(i+1)}$. If the mapping image block is valid, we extract the watermark $W_{P(i+1)'}$ from its mid-frequency coefficients, and decrypt it using secret k_1. Then we convert it into an integer, and multiply it by eight to get the recovered first-order statical moment. If the mapping block is also invalid, the recovered first-order statical moment is set to 128. Finally, we obtain the recovered thumbnail $\overline{Y}^*_{I(i)}$, and up-scale it to the size of the test image.

3   Experimental Results

In the following, we present the effect of watermarks, tamper localization , tamper detection under incidental manipulation, and tampered image recovery to validate the effectiveness of our proposed method.

3.1   Analysis of Watermarks

A set of images are chosen in our experiments, which comprises 10 images of size 512×512, such as 'Lena', 'Baboon', 'Couple', 'Peppers', et al.. Table 1 shows the average quality metric based on Peak Signal to Noise Ratio (PSNR), for different quantization steps, while embedding the watermark. By increasing quantization step, imperceptibility decreases and robustness increases. Therefore, a trade-off is made while selecting the suitable quantization step. In this paper, we select quantization step as 40 while the PSNR is above 40dB.

Table 1. Quantization step and PSNR

Q steps	10	20	30	40	50	60
PSNR(dB)	52.7	46.3	42.8	40.2	38.3	36.7

3.2   Tamper Localization

In order to quantitatively evaluate the tamper localization accuracy, two measures are adopted: false detection probabilities P_{fd} and false alarm probabilities P_{fa}. False detection is the tampered image blocks which are falsely marked as valid, and false alarm is the valid blocks which are falsely marked as invalid. Suppose the proportion of the tampered region a is in [0.01, 0.6] with the interval of 0.01; for each a, we randomly carry on region tampering 20 times, and get the average value for P_{fd} and P_{fa}, the results are exhibited in Fig. 2. From Fig.2(a), we can see that the three methods can localize the tampered region with low false detection probability. Fig.2(b) shows that the method in [2] has ideal false detection probability which always approximately equals zero, however this method is block-independent, thus it is vulnerable to vector quantization (VQ) attack [5] and collage attack [6]. The method in [4] only can localize the small region tamper, even if the tamper ratio is up to 10%, the false alarm probability is close to 38.5%, and it cannot be tolerated. Our method has relatively low false alarm probability, even if the tamper ratio is up to 60%, P_{fa} is only 24.8%, moreover, the block-chain dependent embedding strategy makes our method invulnerable to VQ attack and collage attack. In order to further validate the performance of our method, we present a tampered 'apple' image and its detection result using the three methods in Fig.3. The three methods can localize the tampered region. The detected tampered area using our method is larger than the other two methods, the reason lies in the image block size is 16×16 in our method, however, the other two methods is 4×4.

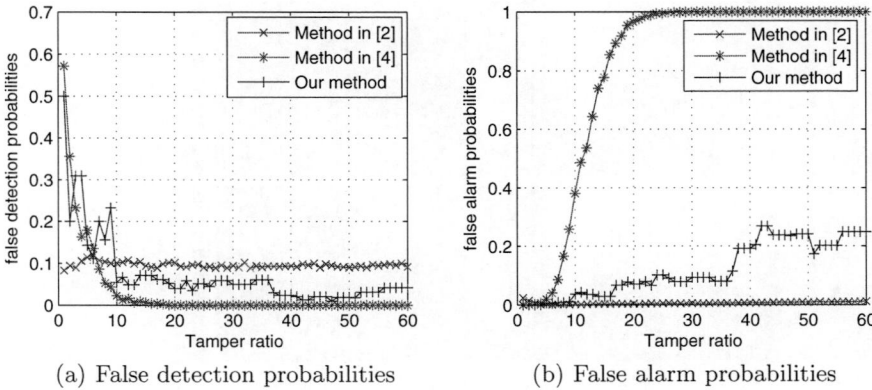

(a) False detection probabilities   (b) False alarm probabilities

Fig. 2. Tamper detection probability

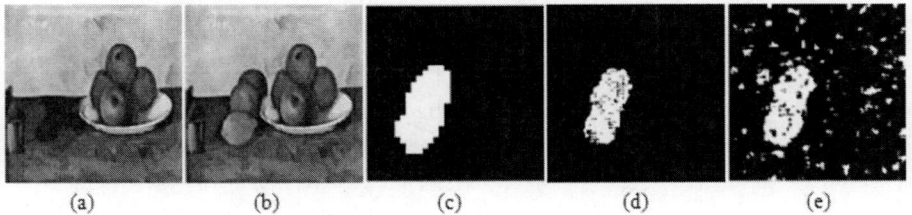

Fig. 3. (a) Watermarked image; (b) Tampered image; (c) Our method; (d) Method in [2]; (e) Method in [4]

3.3 Tamper Detection under Incidental Manipulation

In this section, we evaluate the temper detection performance under incidental manipulation. To fairly compare our method with the other two methods, in the experiments, the images are all watermarked to the same PSNR value, about 40 dB. In the first and second row of Fig.4, we apply incidental manipulation on the watermarked images using JPEG compression (quality factor is 90) and Gaussian noise (standard deviation is 5), respectively, and it is shown in Fig.4(a); Fig.4(b) is the tampered image; Fig.4(c) is the detection result by our method; Fig.4(d) is the detection result by [2]; Fig.4(e) is the detection result by [4]. From Fig.4, we can conclude that our method can localize the tamper region under incidental manipulation. The method in [2] almost localizes the tamper region under JPEG compression (quality factor is 90), but it is vulnerable to Gaussian noise (standard deviation is 5). However, the method in [4] could hardly work under the two incidental manipulations.

3.4 Tampered Image Recovery

In the following, we will verify the performance of recovery. Fig.5 depicts the detection result and recovery of our method when the image suffers from malicious

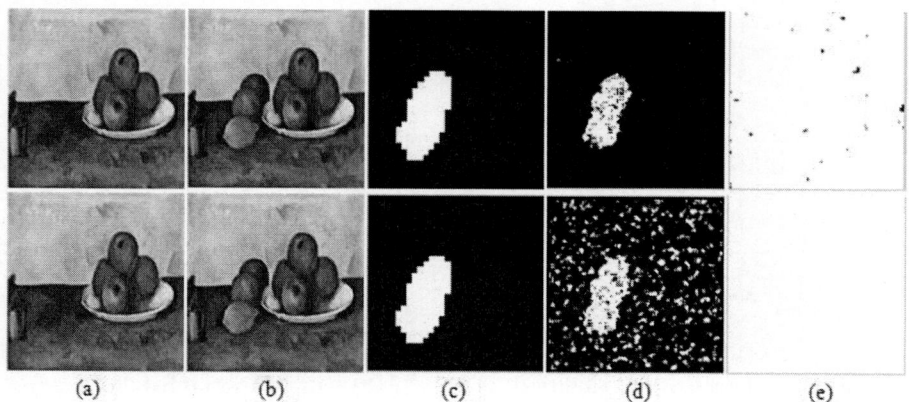

(a)   (b)   (c)   (d)   (e)

Fig. 4. Tamper detection under incidental manipulation: first row is under JPEG compression, second row is under Gaussian noise. (a) Watermarked image; (b) Tampered image; (c) Our method; (d) Method in [2]; (e) Method in [4].

attack and incidental attack. Fig.5(a) is the detection result for tampered image as shown in Fig.4(b), Fig.5(b) is the recovered image; Fig.5(c) and Fig.5(e) are the detection result under JPEG compression (quality factor is 70) and Gaussian noise (standard deviation is 5), respectively. And the corresponding recovered images are shown in Fig.5(d) and Fig.5(f). Fig.5 illustrates that our method can recover the host image when suffering from malicious tamper and incidental manipulations. Moreover, we compare the PSNR of the recovered tampered region using our method with the methods in [2] and [4] when the tamper ratio is 5%, and it is shown in Fig.6. Fig.6(a) demonstrates the recovered result under gaussian noise using different deviation from 0 to 8 with interval 2. We can see that the PSNR of the methods in [2] and [4] is higher than our method when the deviation is 0, but it decreases very quickly with the increment of deviation. However, the PSNR of our method nearly keep unchanged even if the deviation is up to 6. When the watermarked image suffers from JPEG compression using different quality factor from 100 to 60, the recovered result of our method is also superior to the method in [2] and [4].

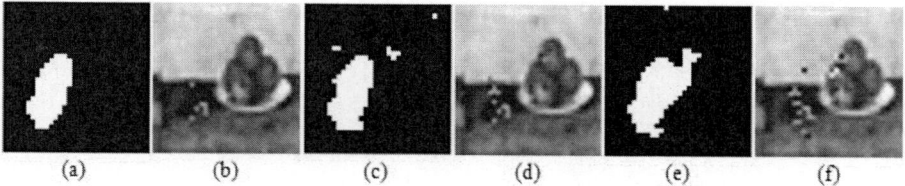

(a)   (b)   (c)   (d)   (e)   (f)

Fig. 5. Tamper recovery under incidental manipulation. (a), (b): detection result and recovery; (c), (d): detection and recovery under JPEG compression; (e), (f): detection and recovery under Gaussian noise.

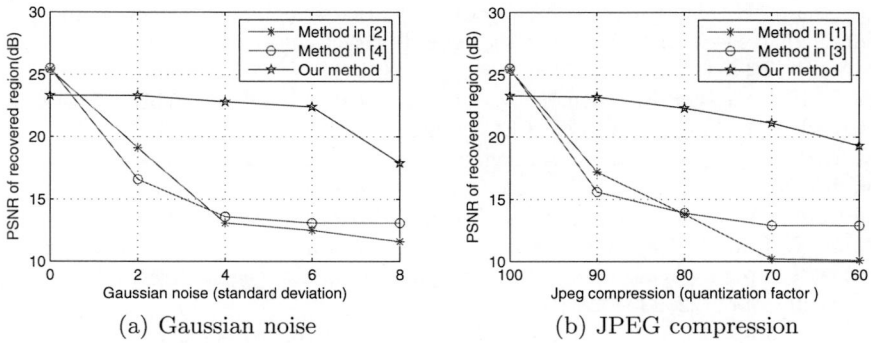

(a) Gaussian noise   (b) JPEG compression

Fig. 6. Recovered result under incidental manipulation

4 Conclusions

In this paper, we propose a novel self-recoverable semi-fragile watermarking scheme based on significant difference parity quantization. The main features of the method are summarized below: 1) The generated authentication watermarks are also used as information watermarks, which reduces the amount of the embedding watermarks; 2) The embedding block-chain is generated by a chaotic map, which makes it difficult to obtain the information of the block-mapping sequence and therefore improves the security of the proposed method; 3) Moreover, Security is enhanced by randomly permuting coefficients among a group. Experimental comparisons with existing approaches validate the usefulness of the proposed self-recoverable semi-fragile watermarking approach. Especially, in our method, we can precisely localize the tampered region even if the tamper ratio is large. And it is robust to incidental manipulation.

Acknowledgement. This work is funded by the National Basic Research Program of China (No. 2010CB327902), the National Natural Science Foundation of China (No. 61202499, 61202237, No. 61005016, No. 61061130560), the National High-tech R&D Program of China (2011AA010502), the Open Projects Program of National Laboratory of Pattern Recognition, and the Fundamental Research Funds for the Central Universities.

References

1. Li, C.T., Si, H.: Wavelet-based fragile watermarking scheme for image authentication. Journal of Electronic Imaging 16(1), 013009 (2007)
2. Tsai, M.-J., Chih-Chien: Authentication and recovery for wavelet-based semifragile watermarking. Optical Engineering 47(6), 067005, 1–9 (2008)
3. Chamlawi, R., Khan, A., Usman, I.: Authentication and recovery of images using multiple watermarks. Computers and Electrical Engineering 36, 578–584 (2010)
4. Chamlawi, R., Khan, A.: Digital image authentication and recovery: Employing integer transform based information embedding and extraction. Information Sciences 180, 4909–4928 (2010)

5. Holliman, M., Memon, N.: Counterfeiting attacks on oblivious blockwise independent invisible watermarking schemes. IEEE Transactions on Image Processing 3(10), 432–441 (2000)
6. Fridrich, J., Goljan, M., Memon, N.: Cryptanalysis of the yeungmintzer fragile watermarking technique. Journal of Electronic Imaging 11(4), 262–274 (2002)
7. Li, K.F., Chen, T.S., Wu, S.C.: Image tamper detection and recovery system based on discrete wavelet transformation. In: Proceedings of the International Conference on Communications, Computers, and Signal Processing, vol. 1 (2001)
8. Zhua, X., Hob, A.T.S., Marziliano, P.: A new semi-fragile image watermarking with robust tampering restoration using irregular sampling. Signal Processing: Image Communication 22, 515–528 (2007)
9. He, J., Zhang, J.S., Tai, H.M.: Block-chain based watermarking scheme with superior localization. In: IHW, pp. 147–160 (2008)

Towards Independent Color Space Selection
for Human Skin Detection

Tao Xu, Yunhong Wang, and Zhaoxiang Zhang

Laboratory of Intelligent Recognition and Image Processing,
Beijing Key Laboratory of Digital Media, Beihang University, Beijing, China
xutao@cse.buaa.edu.cn, {yhwang,zxzhang}@buaa.edu.cn

Abstract. Skin color detection plays an important role in video based applications. Without considering the selection of suitable color space, a novel skin color detection method is proposed based on the flexible neural tree, which can identify the important components of color spaces automatically. With large training data sets, our method builds a flexible neural tree structure and optimizes its parameters using Genetic Programming and Particle Swarm Optimization algorithms. In experiments, features comprised of all channels extracted from RGB, YCbCr and HSV color spaces are used for the constructing and evaluating of the novel skin color model, in which six most important components, i.e., R, G, B, Y, Cr and S are selected for testing. Furthermore, our method achieves higher accuracy and lower false positive rate than state of the art methods on Compaq and ECU data set.

Keywords: skin detection, color space, flexible neural tree, skin classification.

1 Introduction

Skin color is a powerful and robust cue for face detection, localization and tracking. Other real time applications, like hand gesture analysis, can also benefit from automatic detection of skin color. Human skin has very consistent colors distinct from the colors of many other objects, which leads a number of pixel-based skin detection methods arising in the past few years.

The objective of pixel-wise skin detection is to build a decision rule that classifies each pixel as skin or non-skin individually. The choice of suitable color space and skin color classification techniques are two important issues in skin color detection, and a few papers have presented comprehensive studies[1,2,3]. Ref. [4] presented proof and experiments to show that the separability of the skin and non-skin classes is independent of the color space chosen. However, comparative studies and investigations of the effect of color space choice[5,6] have shown that the choice of color space not only affect the performance of skin detection, but also determines how effectively we can model the skin color distribution. As another issue, skin classification techniques can be roughly divided into three steams: fixed threshold methods, parametric methods and non-parametric methods. Mixtures of Gaussian model and elliptic boundary method[2] model the skin distribution with parameters, which have better generalization than fixed threshold methods; Bayesian classifier[7] is one of the non-parametric methods, which

W. Lin et al. (Eds.): PCM 2012, LNCS 7674, pp. 337–346, 2012.

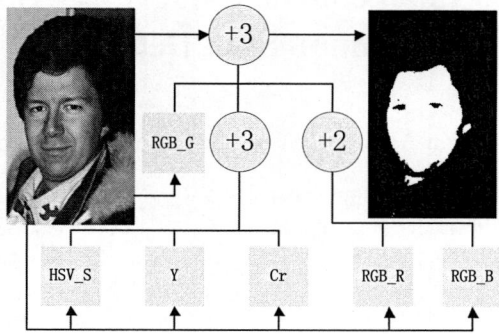

Fig. 1. The skin color model based on flexible neural tree. The model allows over-layer connections, can automatically select the input features, give higher accuracy and lower false positive rate for pixel-wise skin color detection.

usually need many storage spaces. Algorithms in machine learning, such as Mutilayer Perceptron(MLP), have also been investigated for pixel-wise skin color detection[3].

Although existing methods have good performance on skin color detection, there are problems that are not concluded: (1) The optimal color space for skin color detection is not determined. Performance of skin color detection is strongly affected by the choice of color space. A suitable color space should be determined before modeling the skin color distribution, in which exhaustive experiments would be involved; (2) Methods with higher accuracy also have higher false positive rate(FPR). In this paper, a novel pixel-wise skin color detection methods is proposed based on the flexible neural tree(FNT)[8,9](see Fig. 1), which has two contributions: (1) FNT based skin color model allows input variable's selection. The choice of color space is not a problem here, because the model can automatically select the suitable and important color channels from various color representations; (2) In the training stage, individuals with simplicity structure and similar accuracy model will be selected and reserved, which makes our method giving higher accuracy and lower FPR compared with state of the art methods.

2   FNT Based Skin Color Model

Addressing the problem of existing mentioned above, FNT based skin color model is proposed. For skin color detection, the FNT model enable automatic components selection of color spaces and better performance of skin pixel classification.

2.1   Flexible Neural Tree

Flexible neural tree is a special multi-layer feed forward network[8], allows over-layer connections, input variables selection and different activation functions for different nodes. A flexible neural tree can be generated by function set F and terminal instruction set T, which are described as follows:

$$S = F \cup T = \{+_2, +_3, ..., +_N\} \cup \{x_1, ..., x_n\} \tag{1}$$

Function set F contains multi-category non-leaf nodes named flexible neurons. $+_i(i = 1, 2, 3, ..., N)$ means instructions of non-leaf nodes that taking i inputs. The terminal instruction set T with elements $x_1, x_2, ..., x_n$ are instructions of leaf nodes taking no other arguments. A general flexible neuron operator is illustrated in Fig. 2(a).

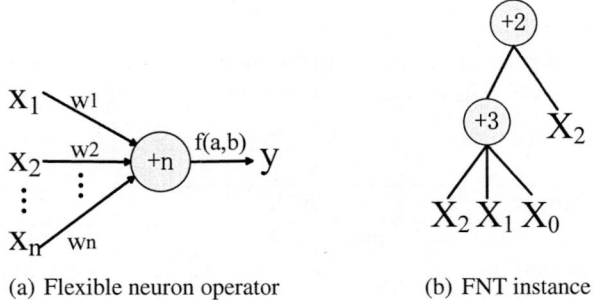

(a) Flexible neuron operator   (b) FNT instance

Fig. 2. The flexible neuron and an instance of flexible neural tree

Given predefined model structure M_i, which has function set F_i and terminal instruction set T_i, the hierarchical structure and parameters of FNT model can be evolved and optimized using Genetic Programming algorithm(GP) [10] and Particle Swarm optimization algorithm(PSO)[11], respectively. Fig. 2(b) shows a trained FNT model with function set $F = \{+_2, +_3\}$ and terminal instruction set $T = \{x_1, x_2, x_3\}$ (similar to $M1$ model in Table. 1).

In the stage of FNT modeling, random structures and corresponding parameters are evolved and optimized recursively, until a satisfactory solution is found or a time limit is reached. If Gaussian activation function(Equ. 2) is used, the two adjustable parameters a_i and b_i will be randomly created as flexible activation function parameters.

$$f(a_i, b_i, x) = e^{-((x-a_i)/b_i)^2} \tag{2}$$

The overall output of FNT model is the total excitation of the root flexible neuron(i.e., $+_2$ node in Fig. 2(b)).The excitation of $+_n$ is $net_n = \sum_{j=1}^{n} w_j \cdot x_j$, where $x_j(j = 1, 2, ..., n)$ are the input features to node $+_n$. Combined with Equation. 2, the output of the node $+_n$ is calculated by,

$$out_n = f(a_n, b_n, net_n) = e^{-((net_n-a_n)/b_n)^2} \tag{3}$$

The overall output of FNT model can be computed from left to right by depth-first method recursively.

2.2   Structure Optimization with GP

There are three important issues for FNT based skin color modeling: optimization of structure, optimization of parameters, and general learning procedure. In initialization, feature f comprised of x_i is viewed as input, written as $f = \{x_1, x_2, ..., x_n\}$, where n is the number of samples. x_i denotes the vector $(x_{i1}, x_{i2}, ..., x_{ij})^T$, where j is number of channels of all color spaces. To find the optimal model, the root mean squared error(RMSE),

$$RMSE = \sqrt{\frac{\sum_{i=1}^{N}(x_i - \hat{x}_i)}{N}} \quad (4)$$

is employed as fitness function, where the x_i denotes the actual skin data, $\hat{x}_i$ is the output of the skin model. The procedure of structure optimization with GP is illustrated in Algorithm. 1.

Algorithm 1. Structure optimization with GP

Data: M=Population Size; N=Maximum of Run
Result: Optimal Structure
Run = 0;
for *i=1* **to** *N* **do**
    Gen = 0;
    Generate initial population randomly;
    while *not reach terminate condition for Run* **do**
        Evaluate fitness of each individual;
        for *j=1* **to** *M* **do**
            Op = select genetic Operator;
            switch *Op* **do**
                case *neural tree mutation operators*
                    do as Ref. [8];
                otherwise
                    do as standard GP[10];
                endsw
            endsw
            Gen = Gen+1;
        end
        designate result for run;
        Run = Run + 1;
    end
end

Optimization using Genetic Programming starts with an initial population composed of F set and T set(see Tab. 1). After execution of each individual program in the population, the fitness function provided in Equ. 4, will be used to measure how well it performs the task of each individual program. Genetic operations, such as crossover, mutation and reproduction, are applied to individuals that are probabilistically selected from the population based on fitness. In the flexible neural tree structure, the leaf node can be a neural sub-tree or a terminal neuron. The crossover operator would select two neural sub-trees randomly and select one non-terminal node in the hidden layer for each neural tree randomly, and then swap the selected subtree with a pre-defined probability. Additional neural tree mutation variation operators are defined in Ref. [8].

After the genetic operations are performed on the current population, the new generation replaces the current population. The run of genetic programming terminates when the termination criterion is satisfied.

2.3   Parameter Optimization with PSO

In the construction of FNT based skin model via Algorithm. 1, its parameters, i.e., the weights $\{w_j\}$ and adjustable parameters a_i and b_i, will be optimized using PSO algorithm[11]. Let $\mathbf{f} : \mathbb{R}^n \to \mathbb{R}$ be the fitness function, and $\mathbf{S}$ be the number of particles in the swarm, each having a position $\mathbf{x_i} \in \mathbb{R}^n$ in the searching space and a velocity $\mathbf{v_i} \in \mathbb{R}^n$. The goal is to find a solution $\mathbf{a}$ for which $f(a) \leq f(b)$ for all $\mathbf{b}$ in the search space. The details of parameter optimization are depicted in Algorithm. 2.

Algorithm 2. Parameter optimization using PSO algorithm

Data: w_i, a_i and b_i
Result: Best solution $\mathbf{g}$
foreach *particle $i = 1, ...S$* **do**
    Initialize the particle's position x_i with w_i ;
    Initialize the particle's best known position: $p_i \leftarrow x_i$;
    if $f(p_i) < f(g)$ **then**
        | update the swarm's best known position: $g \leftarrow p_i$;
    end
    Initialize the particle's velocity: v_i ;
end
repeat
    foreach *particle $i = 1, ..., S$* **do**
        foreach *dimension $d = 1, ..., n$* **do**
            | Pick random numbers:$r_p, r_g \sim U(0, 1)$;
            | Update the particle's velocity as Equation.5 ;
        end
        Update the particle's position as Equation.6 ;
        if $f(x_i) < f(p_i)$ **then**
            Update the particle's best known position: $p_i \leftarrow x_i$;
            if $f(P_i) < f(p_g)$ **then**
                | Update the swarm's best known position: $g \leftarrow p_i$;
            end
        end
    end
until *Maximum iterations or minimum error criteria*;

The population of particles $\{w_j\}$, a_i and b_i is randomly generated initially. Each particle keeps track of its own best position in vector $\mathbf{p_i}$. The best position among all the particles is kept track of as $\mathbf{p_g}$. At each step t, by using the individual best position, $\mathbf{p_i}$, and the global best position, $\mathbf{p_g(t)}$, a new velocity for particle i is updated by,

$$\mathbf{v_i}(t+1) = \mathbf{v_i}(t) + c_1\phi_1(\mathbf{p_i}(t) - \mathbf{x_i}(\mathbf{t})) + c_2\phi_2(\mathbf{p_g}(t) - \mathbf{x_i}(\mathbf{t})) \tag{5}$$

where c_1 and c_2 are parameters selected by the practitioner. ϕ_1 and ϕ_2 are uniformly distributed random numbers in [0,1]. Based on the updated velocities, each particle changes its position according to the following equation:

$$\mathbf{x_i}(t+1) = \mathbf{x_i}(t) + \mathbf{v_i}(t+1) \tag{6}$$

2.4   General Learning Algorithm

With predefined F set and T set, a FNT based skin color model M can be created and evolved via a general learning algorithm, which is combined the structure optimization(Algorithm. 1) and parameter optimization(Algorithm. 2).

Algorithm 3. General Learning algorithm

Require: Function set F and features f(as T set)
Ensure: Optimal model M
  1: Initialization. Create an initial population randomly, set initial values of parameters used in GP and PSO algorithms;
  2: Structure optimization. Optimal structure will be achieved by the natural tree variation operators as described in Section 2.2 with GP algorithm;
  3: If a better structure is found, then go to step (4), otherwise go to step (2);
  4: Parameter optimization. The architecture of FNT is fixed in this step, the parameters (weights and adjustable parameters) encoded in the best tree formulate a particle;
  5: If the maximum number of the local search is reached, or no better parameter vector is found for a significantly long time then go to step (6); otherwise go to step (4);
  6: If satisfactory solution is found, then the algorithm is stopped; otherwise go to step (2);
  7: **return** Optimal FNT based skin model.

For FNT based skin color model, the nature of model construction procedure allows the model to identify important input features that is computationally efficient and effective. The mechanisms of feature selection in the model constructing procedure is illustrated as follows:

1. The components in $x_i f$ are selected to formulate the FNT based skin model with same probabilities;
2. The components which have more contributions to the objective function will be enhanced and have high opportunity to survive in the next generation by a evolutionary procedure;
3. The evolutionary operators i.e., crossover and mutation, provide a input selection method by which the FNT should select appropriate variables automatically;
4. return selected features.

3   Experiments

In experiments, Compaq[7] and ECU[6] data sets are used for the training and testing of FNT based skin color detection method. The two data sets consist of original color images and ground-truth images, which ensure diversity in terms of the background, lighting conditions and skin types. We randomly select 2,000 images for training and testing from each data set.

(a) Sample images in Compaq set   (b) Sample images in ECU set

Fig. 3. Example images in data set. Skin images with ground truth of Compaq data set are shown in (a), and (b) shows color images with corresponding skin segmented regions in ECU data set.

Some example images in Compaq and ECU data set are shown in Fig. 3. Skin pixels are taken from skin segmented images in Compaq and ECU sets. Non-skin pixels are taken from non-skin images in Compaq and the complements of skin segmented images in ECU, respectively. In testing, the skin segmented images are compared pixel-wise with the corresponding ground truth images. No extra steps are used. The performance of our methods and other methods are measured in terms of true positive rate(TPR), false detection rate(FPR) and accuracy(Acc).

For the purpose of pixel based skin color detection, three most popular color spaces RGB, YCbCr and HSV are selected for our experiments. For each pixel in each color space, a feature vector can be created by combined all the three channels in each color space. The amount of data for the training and testing of our methods is over 17GB in Compaq data set and ECU data set. We construct five FNT based skin color models with a different number of features and instruction set, as shown in Table.1. Three types of feature vector are constructed: (1) 3f: combined R, G and B channels of RGB color space; (2) 6f: Y, Cb, and Cr channels of YCbCr color space are added to 3f; (3) 9f: H, S, V of HSV color space are added to 6f.

Table 1. Different FNT based Skin Color Models

Model	F-Set	T-Set	Features
M1	$\{+_2, +_3\}$	$\{x_1, x_2, x_3\}$	3f
M2	$\{+_2, +_3\}$	$\{x_1, x_2, ..., x_9\}$	9f
M3	$\{+_2, +_3, ...+_6\}$	$\{x_1, x_2, x_3\}$	3f
M4	$\{+_2, +_3, ...+_6\}$	$\{x_1, x_2, ..., x_6\}$	6f
M5	$\{+_2, +_3, ...+_6\}$	$\{x_1, x_2, ..., x_9\}$	9f

With a subset data(30% of Compaq data set), these five models were trained and tested. As shown in Table.2, accuracy of each FNT based skin color model is greater than 93% and FPR is lower than 6%. $M2$ model has the better performance in terms of trade-off between accuracy and FPR, which will be used in the comparison with state of the art methods. Fig.1 shows the framework of FNT based skin color model with $M2$ model after being trained using Compaq data set.

Table 2. Comparison of Five FNT based Skin Color Models

	M1	M2	M3	M4	M5
TPR	96.86%	94.97%	96.37%	93.96%	93.39%
FPR	5.70%	2.60%	5.99%	4.06%	2.32%
Acc	95.59%	96.18%	95.19%	94.95%	95.53%

Histogram based Bayes Classifier(HB), Gaussian Mixture model(GMM) , Elliptic Boundary Model(EB) and Multi-layer Perceptron Classifier(MLP) are selected for experiments, which have good performance in reported works. The parameters of HB and MLP are trained using our training data, and GMM, EB use parameters published by Jones[7] and Lee[12]. For the MLP classifier, we trained the network using Levenberg-Marquardt algorithm and Back Propagation algorithm. Different network size and activation functions were investigated, and the best network was reserved.

Table 3. Comparison Of Skin Color Classifiers

	HB	GMM	EB	MLP	Proposed
TPR^1	91.47%	89.12%	84.68%	90.12%	90.87%
FPR^1	10.19%	10.80%	19.52%	12.24%	6.16%
Acc^1	90.17%	89.18%	81.38%	89.57%	92.27%
TPR^2	83.27%	80.83%	90.43%	88.91%	86.78%
FPR^2	10.29%	15.75%	24.05%	13.70%	9.71%
Acc^2	88.47%	83.59%	78.73%	87.63%	90.79%

[1] for Compaq data set.
[2] for ECU data set.

As shown in Table.3, without extra pre-processing and post-processing, our method shows state of the art performance in accuracy and TPR, which achieves an TPR of 90.87% and accuracy of 92.27% for Compaq data set, TPR of 86.78% and accuracy of 90.79% for ECU data set. Furthermore, the FPR of 6.16% for Compaq data set and 9.71% for ECU data set is lower than other methods, which will provide detailed skin color detection. Because the training data and testing data are randomly selected for experiments, the results of other methods do not re-appear as reported in previous works, but the same data sets used for training and testing is guaranteed.

Some skin color detection results are shown in Fig.4. The first row (a) in Fig.4 shows the original color images. The ground-truth image and results of skin color classifiers are illustrated in row (b) through (g). Compared with he ground-truth image, our method classifies the skin pixel and non-skin pixel more correctly with lower false positive detection than other methods.

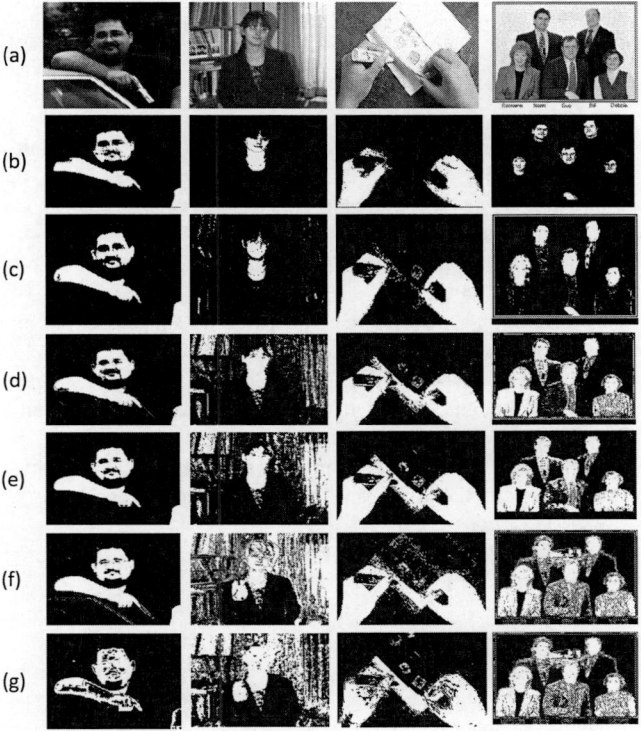

Fig. 4. Sample results of skin classifiers. The original image and its ground-truth is shown in row(a) and (b). The detection results of our method(c), HB(d), GMM(e), MLP(f) and EB(g) are depicted in bottom rows.

4   Conclusions

In this paper, we have introduced a novel human skin detection method based on the flexible neural tree for pixel-wise skin color detection. Without considering the selection of suitable color spaces, the proposed method selects important components of color spaces automatically. Our method presents a solution of the choice of color spaces. Furthermore, FNT based skin detection method achieves higher accuracy and lower false positive rate compared with state of the art methods. In the training stage, the individuals which have simple structures and similar model accuracy will be selected, which makes the structure of our model is generally simpler. The optimized hybrid tree structure guarantees state of the art performance in skin pixel classification but has shortage of time consuming for the optimization of structure and parameters. It is not a problem with high-performance computers and parallel algorithm, which will be the next part of our work.

Acknowledgment. This work is funded by the National Basic Research Program of China (No. 2010CB327902), the National Natural Science Foundation of China (No. 61005016, No. 61061130560), the National High-tech R&D Program of China (2011AA010502), the Open Projects Program of National Laboratory of Pattern Recognition, and the Fundamental Research Funds for the Central Universities.

References

1. Vezhnevets, V., Sazonov, V., Andreeva, A.: A survey on pixel-based skin color detection techniques. Cybernetics 85(1), 85–92 (2003)
2. Kakumanu, P., Makrogiannis, S., Bourbakis, N.: A survey of skin-color modeling and detection methods. Pattern Recognition 40(3), 1106–1122 (2007)
3. Khan, R., Hanbury, A., Stöttinger, J., Bais, A.: Color based skin classification. Pattern Recognition Letters 33(2), 157–163 (2012)
4. Albiol, A., Torres, L., Delp, E.: Optimum color spaces for skin detection. In: Proceedings of the 2001 International Conference on Image Processing, vol. 1, pp. 122–124. IEEE (2001)
5. Chaves-González, J.M., Vega-Rodríguez, M.A., Gómez-Pulido, J.A., Sánchez-Pérez, J.M.: Detecting skin in face recognition systems: A colour spaces study. Digital Signal Processing 20(3), 806–823 (2010)
6. Phung, S., Bouzerdoum, A., Chai, D.: Skin segmentation using color pixel classification: Analysis and comparison. IEEE Transactions on Pattern Analysis and Machine Intelligence 27(1), 148–154 (2005)
7. Jones, M., Rehg, J.: Statistical color models with application to skin detection. International Journal of Computer Vision 46(1), 81–96 (2002)
8. Chen, Y., Yang, B., Abraham, A.: Flexible neural trees ensemble for stock index modeling. Neurocomputing 70(4-6), 697–703 (2007)
9. Chen, Y., Yang, B., Meng, Q.: Small-time scale network traffic prediction based on flexible neural tree. Applied Soft Computing 12, 276–279 (2011)
10. McKay, R., Hoai, N., Whigham, P., Shan, Y., O'Neill, M.: Grammar-based genetic programming: a survey. Genetic Programming and Evolvable Machines 11(3), 365–396 (2010)
11. Poli, R., Kennedy, J., Blackwell, T.: Particle swarm optimization. Swarm Intelligence 1(1), 33–57 (2007)
12. Lee, J., Yoo, S.: An elliptical boundary model for skin color detection. In: Proc. of the 2002 International Conference on Imaging Science, Systems, and Technology (2002)

A Novel Smart Multi-license Plate Recognition Method

Dawei Du[1], Honggang Qi[2], and Kui Fan[3]

[1] School of Energy Science and Engineering, University of Electronic Science
and Technology of China, 611731 Chengdu
[2] Graduate University of the Chilnese Academy of Science, 100049 Beijing
[3] Beijing Jiaotong University, 100044 Beijing, P.R. China
daviddo@yahoo.cn, hgqi@jdl.ac.cn, myfan07214033@sina.com

Abstract. This paper presents a Smart License Plate Recognition System (SLPRS) which employs a cascade scheme guaranteeing high accuracy and reliability. The system consists of three phases. First, the proposed pseudo-morphological closing operation algorithm is applied to extract license plate candidates based on contour image and the so-called license plate transition rule. Second, improved adaptive template-matching algorithm is used in character segmentation to obtain precise segmented characters by solving an optimization model. Finally we adopt pattern match method for recognition based on proper designed character templates. Compared to the traditional morphology method, connected component analysis and projection method, our method is lower computational, more accurate and parametric intelligent, which reaches the basic requirements of SLPRS. Experiments show that the system can recognize license plates in various sizes of images with different scenes without changing the parameters in the system.

Keywords: license plate recognition, pseudo-morphology close operation, adaptive template-matching.

1 Introduction

The License Plate Recognition System (LPRS) is widely applied in intelligent transport technologies such as vehicle related crimes, traffic surveillance, etc. And the high-definition (HD) video introduced in surveillance field is very helpful for the development of high-performance LPRS. Usually the system is mainly composed of three sub-technologies: license plate localization, character segmentation and character recognition, and many different approaches have been proposed. We first review some significant works from previous literature as follows.

For localization, Kasaei et al. [1] presented a real time and robust method of license plate detection based on the morphology. Giannoukos et al. [2] reported an adaptive sliding concentric windows algorithm leading to a successful location rate of 98.3%. In [3], a match filter was designed to detect candidate regions as plate in consideration of edge and color information. For segmentation, projections and binary algorithms are the most common and simplest methods [4].

W. Lin et al. (Eds.): PCM 2012, LNCS 7674, pp. 347–358, 2012.

Jiao *et al.* [5] developed a connected component model to solve this problem. Franc and Hlavac [6] established hidden Markov chains model to segment character for noisy low-resolution images. For recognition, some works used multi-layer neural networks in [7]. Furthermore, Viand *et al.* [8] designed some SVM-based recognizers for Farsi license plates with recognition rate of more than 95%. In addition, Chen *et al.* [9] proposed a two-stage hybrid recognition system based on feature salience theory to achieve robust performance.

Although many LPRS technologies are proposed, some challenges, such as complex background, various scenarios and even execution efficiency, are still the obstacles of LPR. Thus, in this paper, we consider the necessary features of images or videos for Smart License Plate Recognition System (SLPRS) are that (1) the system can be used in all kinds of scenes with handling the detection and recognition task for single-license plate or multi-license plates; (2) the system can modulate parameters adaptively based on scenarios, and less or no manual parameters will be better; (3) the system is with the memory as small as possible and runs fast with high recognition accuracy.

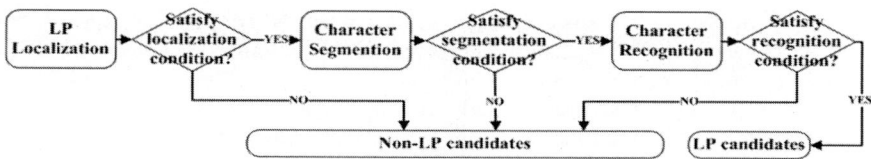

Fig. 1. System Structure

Similar to the majority of LPR techniques, the proposed SLPRS is divided into three modules. The emphasis is on the improvement of the first two ones. In this paper we adopt a classical cascade scheme as shown in Fig. 1. In the license plate (LP) localization module, several possible candidates are collected and only the candidates satisfying the localization condition will be input into the next module, i.e. character segmentation module. The segmentation module can also generate several candidate segmentation results based on our algorithms to select the most reliable one as the input of the recognition module according to the segmentation condition. Among the three modules, any sample which does not satisfy the corresponding condition is discarded as Non-LP candidates immediately otherwise reserved as LP candidates. Here are the conditions:

- Localization condition: if the width and height of the extracted region is less than the minimum size considered as a real license plate, then this region is look as Non-LP candidate.
- Segmentation condition: if any segmentation result cannot be obtained from the current candidate LP region, it is a Non-LP candidate.
- Recognition condition: if all the samples in the candidate region cannot be recog-nized as real characters, it is a Non-LP candidate.

The cascade conditions scheme guarantees high accuracy and reliability. Although our methods are applied in Chinese plate in this paper, but they can be applied in other kinds of plates after changing some parameters, and our primary contributions are unique as:

– According to extracted contour image, a pseudo-morphological closing operation algorithm is proposed to obtain all the LP regions based on the so-called LP transition rule, more accurately and lower computationally than the traditional common morphology method and the connected component analysis (CCA), especially speeding up the execution process in HD images.
– According to prior knowledge of the LP formats, an improved adaptive template-matching algorithm is developed to segment every character precisely for further character recognition because of the design of flexible template to cover the characters, and all the parameters are configured automatically.

2   License Plate Localization

Based on the assumption that texture of LP region is of dense edges compared to the ones of other regions, our localization method consists of two steps: edge detection where skeletonization algorithm is employed for extracting image contours in order to highlight the dense edges in LP regions, as well as the pseudo-morphological closing operation algorithm which is proposed to extract candidate rectangles.

2.1   Edge Detection and Skeletonization

The LP regions on a contrasting background obviously have abundant edge transitions. The vertical transitions of characters in LP have great regularity, and are significantly different from the ones of other textures. Thus, we can conclude the so-called LP transition rule illuminated in Fig. 2: first, the horizontal distance between black and white transition points in the character area of LP should be in a certain not too big interval, while is not like this in other regions; second, compared to other regions, character area should be full of transition points.

According to the above rule, the proposed localization method is based on binary contour image. Among all the edge detection methods and thinning algorithms to extract contour image, we select the simple vertical Sobel operator and the classical fast Zhang's parallel algorithm [10] to extract the contours of image, in consideration of the tradeoff between complexity and performance.

2.2   Pseudo-morphological Closing Operation Algorithm

In previous works [1], [5], the morphological operation such as close operation is usually used to highlight the texture of interesting after edge detection, and then extract LP regions based on CCA. However, the traditional methods have

Fig. 2. Contour Image of LP Region. Vertically, in Region A, the other texture area, the horizontal distance between black and white transition points is so big that does not meet the rule. While in Region B and C, the character area in LP, the distance is in a suitable small interval. Horizontally, Region D, the non-character area, just has just few transition points, reversely, Region E, the character area, has so many ones.

some drawbacks: the morphological operation demands well-designed templates, which may not be the same in different scenarios and different sizes of images. Therefore, this will lead to how to design good templates; the calculation of close operation is relatively long because of twice convolution operations used for the whole image, even longer in the HD image with large size of template; to obtain the sizes and positions of LP candidates, CCA has to be used even though this method is troublesome when considering how to find the most suitable rectangles to express the LP candidates from irregular shapes.

To solve the above problem, we propose a pseudo-morphological closing operation algorithm, including *pseudo-dilation operation* and *pseudo-erosion operation*, which is lower computational, more accurate and parametric intelligent compared to the traditional methods. Our algorithm consists of three steps: Firstly, based on the LP transition rule, the *Feature Matrix* describing the rule will be calculated; secondly, *pseudo-dilation operation* is executed so that the coarse regions of LP candidates are collected; thirdly, based on the image called *pseudo-dilation map*, *pseudo-erosion operation* is realized to obtain sizes and positions of LP candidates.

Calculation of Feature Matrix. The diagram of the whole algorithm for calculating the Feature Matrix is illustrated in Fig. 3. Co is the coordinate matrix for recording all the coordinates of transition points between contours and blanks, and calculated first. By scanning every element $I(i, j)$ in the contour image, we can obtain the coordinates as follow

$$Co(r, c) = j \quad \text{if } |I(i, j + 1) - I(i, j)| = 1 \tag{1}$$

where $Co(r, c)$ means the cth coordinate of transition point in the rth row. Subsequently, Cv and Cd will be calculated. Cv is the histogram of transition points standing for maximum number of transition points in a row, and Cd is the distance matrix for recording all the distances between two adjacent transition points in a row.

Scanning every element of Cv, if the value of the element is greater than Vn, the current row is selected as the *interesting row*. Vn is the acceptable threshold number for vertical transition points in a row, determined by the average value

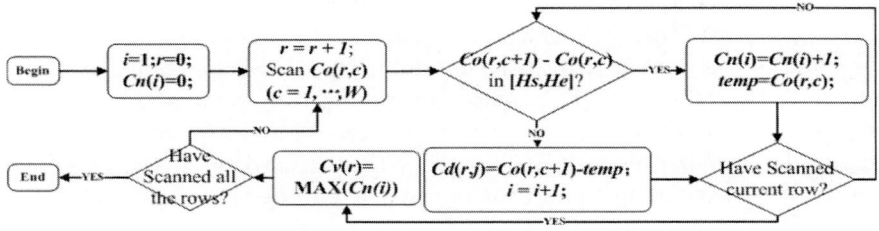

Fig. 3. Calculation of Feature Matrix. H and W are the height and width of the source image. Cn is the vector standing for the number of vertical transition points in a row, and Hs and He is the upper and lower bound for horizontal distance between two adjacent transition points in a row, respectively.

of Cv as in (2), where the max operator ensures the threshold is not so small that the whole computation increases too much.

$$Vn = \max(\frac{1}{H}\sum_{r=1}^{H} Cv(r), m) \tag{2}$$

Finally, the number of continuous interesting rows is counted, and these rows are regarded as the *candidate strip* whose width is equal to the one of the whole image if the number is in the interval $[Vs, Ve]$, where Vs and Ve is the minimum and maximum threshold for continuous rows of the acceptable number of vertical transition points respectively, in other words, the minimum and maximum possible height of LP we consider ($Vs = 0.05 \times H$, $Ve = 0.2 \times H$ in this paper). Given the source image as in Fig. 4(a), we can determine the candidate strip cut by Vn. In the further calculation we will ignore other rows (black rows in Fig. 4(b)) except the *candidate strip* for simplification.

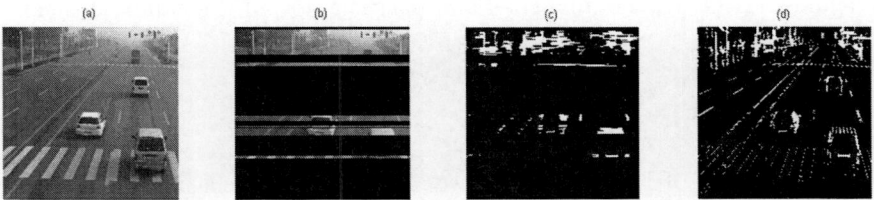

Fig. 4. (a)Source Image(b)Candidate Strip(c)Pseudo-dilation Map(d)Morphological Close Operation

Pseudo-dilation Operation. At first, we create a new image with the same size of the whole image as the *pseudo-dilation map* to display the coarse shapes of LP and build it like that: scanning all the elements $Co(r, c)$, if $Co(r, c + 1) - Co(r, c) \in [Hs, He]$, we let $map(r, j) = 1$ where $j \in [Co(r, c), Co(r, c + 1)]$ and define these pixels as real white points (RWP), or let $map(r, j) = 0$ otherwise. Thus filling in the small blanks between the transition points in Co, the areas with dense adjacent transition points are effectively connected, and looks like rough regions of LP candidates with burrs and small hollows shown in Fig. 4(c). Compared to Fig. 4(d) shown the result of morphological close operation by the template with size of 5×10, it is obviously observed that our method gives better results because of less interference block (less RWP in non-LP regions) and less computation (saving at least 50% average time according to the experiment because of ignoring almost half rows of the image from Fig. 4(b)).

Pseudo-erosion Operation. *Pseudo-erosion operation* can obtain the sizes and positions for LP candidates. Since the LP region is full of RWP, an appropriate rectangle with the maximum number of RWP will be found by sliding searching method. A pseudo-template is designed for sliding searching and its size is changing with certain condition. And the process is shown as bellows:

- Based on the *pseudo-dilation map*, every *candidate strip* is projected vertically to count RWP. Then we pick the region as candidate whose every column sum of RWP is greater than the threshold Hn (1/3 of the height of candidate strip is used in this paper). Thus the height and width of a LP candidate, that is, zH_0 and zW_0, are easily obtained.
- Given the aspect ratio of current candidate $\lambda_0 = zW_0/zH_0$, if $\lambda_0 \geq \lambda$ (the parameter stands for the maximum aspect ratio according to the format of Chinese LP, $\lambda = 5.8$ in experiment), we updata zW such that $zW = \lambda \times zH_0$ so that the new aspect ratio is equal to λ. Thus the size of current pseudo-template is $zH_0 \times zW$. Then we find the zone with the maximum number of RWP, that is, R_{sum}, by sliding window method horizontally based on the template and obtain its left and right bound of LP candidate. If $\lambda_0 < \lambda$, then $zW = zW_0$, this update step will be ignored before we calculate R_{sum}.
- Finally, we updata zH such that $zH = R_{sum}/zW$, and find the new zone with the maximum number of RWP by new-size($zH \times zW$) template vertically similarly. Then we can obtain its top and bottom bound. By twice sliding searching, the final sizes and positions for all the candidates can be determined.

3   Character Segmentation

After localization of LP candidates, we should segment character individually to identify them, and the common methods are projection [2], [4] and CCA method [5]. However, the character region may have so adhesive and partially hid because of inappropriate binarization so that it is hard for the CCA method to collect proper character regions; on the other hand, the projection method is not strong for character segmentation in some cases because of deformation and interference in different situations without some pre-designed fussy conditions.

In order to overcome the drawbacks above, we propose an improved adaptive template-matching method, which consists of two steps: firstly, based on local binarization method, the vertical projection calculated for binary image of the LP region can create some feature sets including segmentation line clusters (SL)

and accumulative segmentation line clusters (AL); secondly, based on the feature sets, different adaptive templates for different plate formats are designed to obtain the optimal segmentation result in view of our evaluation criterion. And the advantages of our method are flexible size of template to match characters and few constraints to describe and find out the most possible result.

3.1   Vertical Projection Based on Local Binarization Method

Since the image is often affected by uneven illumination, it is difficult for global binarization methods to extract important details only by global threshold. However, local binarization methods can solve the problem effectively by exacting local thresholds. The *Niblack* method gives the best effect among a variety of binarization methods in [11]. Given the binary image of LP region, we can calculate SL and AL based on the vertical projection Pv in (3), where BOOL operation judges whether the element belongs to the set.

$$\begin{cases} SL = \{i | Pv(i) \leq \min(\alpha \times zH, Pv(i-1), Pv(i+1)\} \\ AL = \{j | j = \sum_{i=1}^{j} BOOL(i \in SL)\} \end{cases} \quad (3)$$

where α is the adjustment value, which should not be so small that real segmentation lines are omitted and so large that false ones are identified. SL is the set of all possible coordinates or indexes for segmenting all the characters and AL is the set of accumulative number of segmentation lines up to current index.

3.2   Improved Adaptive Template-Matching Method

With SL and AL, we can implement an adaptive template-matching method. The adaptive rectangular segmentation box (RSB) is designed to match the LP region, ensuring that the vertical box lines can exactly pass through the valley between two characters. Then the optimal location of RSB can be found based on minimum distance principle. The template vector p illustrating the location of RSB is shown in Fig. 5, where the bottom index is the horizontal coordinate for the corresponding line. In other words, all the box lines of the template vector $p(i)$ should coincide or almost coincide with some lines in SL (*Principle 1*). On the other hand, the number of segmentation lines in a box should be less than a threshold so that the optimal result will not converge at the area full of segmentation lines but no characters (*Principle 2*).

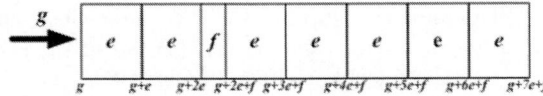

Fig. 5. Adaptive Rectangular Segmentation Box for Blue Plate

For the most common blue plate in China, $RSB = (e, f, g)$ is shown in Fig. 5, where e is the width of a single character, f is the bigger gap between the second and third character, and g is the horizontal offset of the license plate. Thus, the segmentation problem can convert into an optimization model. The goal of the model should be to describe the most perfect valley where has the minimum gap for the distance between box lines from template vector and their nearest segmentation lines from SL, so the goal combines the sum of binary projection value at all the box lines $Pr(p(i))$ and the gap d as in (4), where the exponential term means d is the priority.

$$\min \sum_{i=1}^{N} Pr(p(i)) \times 10^d \qquad (4)$$

$$\begin{cases} d \leq 3 & (a) \\ p(N) \leq zW & (b) \\ AL(p(3)) - AL(p(2)) \leq e/2 & (c) \\ AL(p(2)) - AL(p(1)) \leq e/2 & (d) \\ \min|p(i) - SL(j)| \leq d & (e) \\ N - C \leq 2 & (f) \end{cases} \qquad (5)$$

Then we propose six constraints in (5) for the goal: Constraint (a) means the maximum value of d can not exceed its threshold; Constraint (b) means sliding RSB should not overflow the right bound of the LP area; Constraint (c)(d) implement *Principle 2*; Constraint (e) implements *Principle 1*, where ($i = 1, ..., N$); Constraint (f) means that C, the number of boxes satisfying Constraint (b)(c)(d)(e) simultaneously, is almost the number of all the box (at least $N - 2$), which relaxes *Principle 1* not to miss right segmentation results. The detailed implementation for our model is illustrated in Fig. 6.

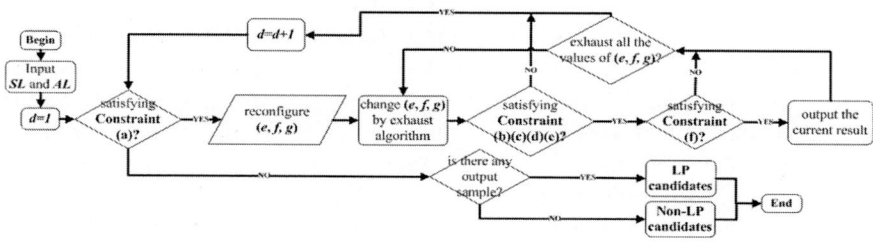

Fig. 6. Flow Chart for Improved Adaptive Template-matching Method. To release the model, we try different parameters (e, f, g) to match these constraints by brute-force method and then find the minimum value of goal (4) for all the results on the same minimum d. According to the priori knowledge of Chinese license plate, the standard width of single character is about half of the height of LP, so $e \in [\lfloor 0.4 \times zH \rfloor, \lfloor 0.65 \times zH \rfloor]$ based on our experiment; the standard aspect ratio of single character is 0.37, so $f \in [\lfloor 0.3 \times e \rfloor, \lfloor 0.45 \times e \rfloor]$; the standard aspect ratio of whole plate is 3.14, g should reach 1/3 width of LP region according to λ, that is, $g \in [0, \lfloor zW/3 \rfloor]$.

3.3   Horizontal Skew Correction and Precise Segmentation

Because of the design of the template with margin or image distortion, the left and right sides, or the top and bottom sides of characters region may remain blank, rivets and noise, even a certain degree horizontal skew. Thus the following step shows to correct the skew and remove the useless space.

After scanning all the pixels in character region and finding the top and the bottom coordinates of each character, we propose a kind of the least squares model to calculate the skew slope to make appropriate adjustment based on the bottom points of characters. The model consists of two parallel lines in the top and bottom of the character area, and the bottom one is determined by the least squares method, while the top one can be inferred by the average character height mH. Thus we can compensate and adjust the angle. The model is shown in Fig. 7, where mH should be calculated without outlier point A.

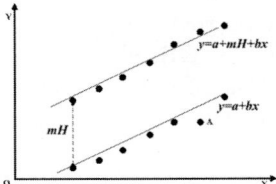

Fig. 7. Least Squares Model for Horizontal Skew Correction

According to vector Hp standing for the number of horizontal transition points and vector Hc standing for horizontal projection, the two vectors' thresholds are determined in (6) to remove the rivets or noise when the corresponding value of the two vectors is less than its threshold.

$$\begin{cases} cT = \sum Hc(i)/(\beta \times mH) \\ pT = \sum Hp(i)/(\beta \times mH) \end{cases} \tag{6}$$

where β is the constant to control the cutting level. Then scanning the left and right sides of every character region, the blank pixel columns can be removed to obtain precise segmented characters easily.

4   Character Recognition

Based on the obtained character samples with precise segmentation after previous two modules, we can easily adopt template match method for identifying Chinese character, alphabet and number recognition. We use three kinds of proper templates for 31 Chinese characters, 24 letters and 10 numbers. Although this method is used in binary images less computationally, we find that properly built templates obtain better results for gray images. In recognition process, it is more than 90% of time consumed for the computation of the cross-correlation between the various templates and the sample. However, we define the standard size for identifying the single character in this paper is 32×16 shown in Fig. 8, which is a small size, so the problem of computational time can be overcome.

Fig. 8. Some Templates

5 Experimental Results

We build a mixed LP database to test the efficiency of the proposed system. The database has nearly 9000 images with four kinds of image sizes from 768×576 to 1628×1236. The images are acquired from the real toll stations at different lighting condition (daytime, nighttime) with different kinds of vehicles (van, truck and car). Our method is realized by C++ code whose performance is carried out on Pentinum IV 3.0 GHz. Based on the experimental results in Table 1, the computational time of our method in four sets varies from about 40 ms to 230 ms according to the sizes of images, and the average successful rate is 92.07%. In the table, first, compared to the previous localization method (morphology & CCA), current localization method costs less time and reaches the same successful detection rate. Second, compared to the previous recognition method (projection & pattern matching), current recognition method reaches better successful recognition rate and costs almost the same time. In summary, the key is our methods extract LP regions and characters more precisely and process just about half of the image by selecting the possible image rows in the view of our LP transition rule.

Table 1. Experimental Results on Four Sets

Database Size	Image Number	Current Localization	Current Recognition	Previous Localization	Previous Recognition
Daytime Set1 (768×576)	82 images (1 plate)	31 ms (99.71%)	8 ms (95.12%)	47 ms (99.71%)	8 ms (91.46%)
Nighttime Set2 (1628×1236)	356 images (1–2 plates)	187 ms (98.59%)	11 ms (96.91%)	343 ms (98.59%)	11 ms (93.91%)
Daytime Set3 (1232×504)	8451 images (1–4 plates)	62 ms (99.62%)	22 ms (93.10%)	109 ms (98.42%)	23 ms (89.25%)
Day and Night Set4 (1600×1200)	100 images (1–4 plates)	171 ms (94.55%)	49 ms (90.07%)	328 ms (92.78%)	48 ms (85.44%)

From the accuracy on four sets, we can see our method is effective in several situations. Some detected LP regions of the four datasets and precise segmented characters are shown in Fig. 9 and Fig. 10, where the red rectangles and white lines show the results intuitively.

Fig. 9. Examples of Localization Results

Fig. 10. Examples of Segmentation and Recognition Results

6   Conclusion

This paper proposes a Smart License Plate Recognition System, and builds a robust cascade scheme for it. Our focus is on the improvement of localization and segmentation method. The localization algorithm needs to extract contour image at first and then obtain all the LP candidates with few adaptive parameters by the pseudo-morphological closing operation algorithm. In segmentation module, we develop an improved adaptive template-matching method to find the optimal segmentation result. To get more precise segmented characters, we propose the horizontal skew correction for LP regions, and remove the useless gaps and noises around the characters. After that the character samples are compared with pre-defined templates for recognizing Chinese characters, letters and numbers. The experimental results show that our method is both low complexity and high accuracy.

Acknowledgements. This work was supported in part by National Natural Science Foundation of China: 61001108, in part by National Natural Science Foundation of China: 61070116.

References

1. Kasaei, S.H., Kasaei, S.M., Kasaei, S.A.: New Morphology Based Method for Robust Iranian Car Plate Detection and Recognition. International Journal of Computer Theory and Engineering 2, 264–268 (2010)
2. Giannoukos, I., Anagnostopoulos, C., Loumos, V., Kayafas, E.: A Operator context scanning to support high segmentation rates for real time license plate recognition. Pattern Recognition 43, 3866–3878 (2010)
3. Abolghasemi, V., Ahmadyfard, A.: An edge-based color-aided method for license plate detection. Image and Vision Computing 27, 1134–1142 (2009)
4. Ho, W.Y., Pun, C.M.: A Macao License Plate Recognition System Based on Edge and Projection Analysis. In: IEEE Int. Conf. on Industrial Informatics, vol. 3512, pp. 67–72 (2010)
5. Jiao, J., Ye, Q., Huang, Q.: A configurable method for multi-style license plate recognition. Pattern Recognition 42, 358–369 (2009)
6. Franc, V., Hlaváč, V.: License Plate Character Segmentation Using Hidden Markov Chains. In: Kropatsch, W.G., Sablatnig, R., Hanbury, A. (eds.) DAGM 2005. LNCS, vol. 3663, pp. 385–392. Springer, Heidelberg (2005)
7. Broumandnia, A., Fathy, M.: Application of pattern recognition for Farsi license plate recognition. In: Proc. Int. Conf. GVIP, Cairo, Egypt (2005)
8. Viand, A.S., Seyedjavadi, S.H., Rahmani, A.M.: Enhancing Automatic Speed Estimation Systems Performance Using Support Vector Machines. In: IEEE Int. Conf. on ICCP, pp. 185–188 (2009)
9. Chen, Z.X., Liu, C.Y., Chang, F.L., Wang, G.Y.: Automatic license plate location and recognition based on feature salience. IEEE Trans. on Vehicular Technology 58, 3781–3785 (2009)
10. Zhang, T.Y., Suen, C.Y.: A fast parallel algorithm for thinning digital patterns. Comm. ACM 27, 236–239 (1984)
11. Trier, O.D., Jain, A.K.: Goal-directed evaluation of binarization methods. IEEE Trans. on PAMI 17, 1191–1201 (1995)

Persistent Object Tracking in Road Panoramic Videos

Yuan Zhou, Zhong Zhou[*], Ke Chen, and Wei Wu

State Key Laboratory of Virtual Reality Technology and Systems, Beihang University
School of Computer Science and Engineering, Beihang University
Beijing 100191, P.R. China
zz@vrlab.buaa.edu.cn

Abstract. Panorama has the full directional view of the scene and can provide an object vision persistently from its emerging to vanishing except occlusion. Though, traditional tracking algorithms are apt to fail since the object may change its appearance or even disappear occasionally during its display lifetime. A persistent object tracking algorithm for static objects in panoramic videos is proposed in this paper. It creates several auxiliary trackers to guide the tracking. Once the object is obscured or deformed, the auxiliary trackers are engaged in estimating the position of the main tracker. Even though the appearance of the object changes a lot, its position still could be estimated with help of the auxiliary trackers. Experiment results illustrated that this algorithm provides a real-time tracking effectively on signs in road panoramic videos. This algorithm is easy to perform and especially valuable for road sign labeling and management.

Keywords: persistent, object tracking, panoramic video, auxiliary tracker.

1   Introduction

Object tracking has a variety of vision applications such as surveillance, video classification or labeling and traffic monitoring. Object tracking across multiple camera views has been regarded with high priority in many fields since single camera has limited field of view. Panoramic video has a stitched full directional view, and has a persistent vision of a target from its emerging to disappearing except occlusion. A panoramic camera is designed for video surveillance vehicle to monitor pedestrians [1]. Cylindrical panoramic images are easy to be mapped to a plane and then pursue regular object tracking algorithms for videos. A detection and tracking algorithm for human [2] utilizes a combination of frame differencing, face detection and adaptive color blob tracking to detect and track people in cylindrical panoramic videos. Spherical panorama videos have more distortion in images, and they can be transformed to cubic panorama. The cubic panorama can pursue regular tracking in each side image, but need an expansion for continuous tracking when the object goes through faces [3]. Fig. 1 shows one cubic panoramic frame.

---

[*] Corresponding author.

W. Lin et al. (Eds.): PCM 2012, LNCS 7674, pp. 359–368, 2012.

Fig. 1. Cubic panoramic frame

A noticeable phenomenon for multiple camera surveillance is that the appearance of the object may change a lot with the change of the camera on it although it still exists in the stitched panorama frame. Recently some algorithms have been proposed to deal with the problem of appearance change during tracking. Ross et al. proposed incremental learning for visual tracking which is robust to changes in pose, scale, and illumination [4]. Han et al. present a probabilistic sensor fusion technique which shows robustness to severe occlusion, clutter, and sensor failures [5]. W. Du et al. integrated multiple cues, edge, and color in a probabilistic framework [6], and B. Stenger et al. fuse multiple observation models with parallel and cascaded evaluation [7]. Kwon et al. proposed a visual tracking de-composition scheme for the efficient design of observation and motion models as well as trackers [8]. Although these tracking algorithms perform well for the change of the object appearance, they are not applicable to the occasional disappearance of the target object. There is also a huge literature on the subject which uses modern particular filtering approaches. Okuma et al. develop a boosted particle filter that combines detection and tracking [9]. Yin et al. treat tracking as a numerical optimization problem and switch from local to global mode seeking after an occlusion in attempt to detect the position of the object [10]. These methods are used to predict the location of the object in the next frame, which is quite useful in case of short, transient occlusion. For long period occlusions the prediction of these filtering methods will degrade because the tracked object is more probable to move in a way that is not modeled by the filter [11].

Traditional tracking algorithms are apt to fail since the object zone may not only change the appearance but also even be minimized during its display lifetime. It's challenging to make a persistent tracking from an object's emerging to vanishing, regardless of appearance change or even occasional disappearance. The persistent tracking is very important for road sign labeling or management. To the best of our knowledge, little work has been done on persistent tracking in panoramic videos.

We propose an easy-to-perform tracking algorithm in this paper. It doesn't need any 3D calculation or depth analysis, and works on the videos directly. The main contribution of this paper is to create several auxiliary trackers to guide the object tracking in cubic panoramic videos. The auxiliary trackers are preserved to guide the tracking when the main tracker loses the target. Even when the target object disappears for some time, its position still can be estimated with the help of the auxiliary trackers.

2   Motivation and Main Idea

Cubic panoramic video consists of six side images which can be expanded for continuous tracking. Besides the deformation and discontinuity at the boundaries [3], the appearance of an object may change a lot with the change of the camera monitoring it. In fact, road panoramic videos cannot always provide adequate visual size for object observation because of the relative movement.

To illustrate the appearance change of a target object, we count the pixels of the target and calculate the average YUV values in the sign zone. Fig. 2 shows the appearance changing of a road sign in the frame sequence. Furthermore, Fig. 3 shows the number of pixels of the traffic sign in each frame. The pixels diminish in the first 50 frames, reach the minimum at the 50th frame and then increase gradually. When the number of pixels is very few, traditional tracking cannot work. And they cannot be found back since the videos now cover its back instead of front side i.e. the other reason for the failure of directly tracking is the sudden change in the color of the target zone. Fig. 4 shows the average YUV values of the sign in each frame. The change of the color is discontinuous and sharp breaks occur from the 40th frame to the 60th. These two factors make it impossible to track the target directly only with their textures.

Fig. 2. The appearance of a road sign in different frames

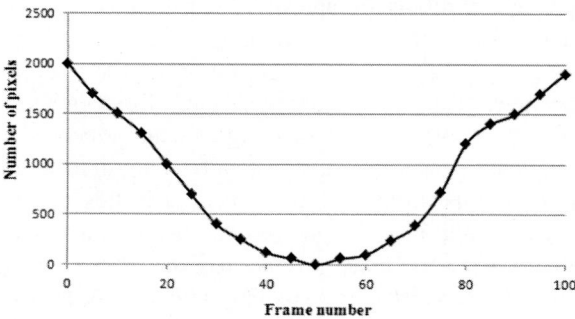

Fig. 3. The number of pixels of the traffic sign in each frame

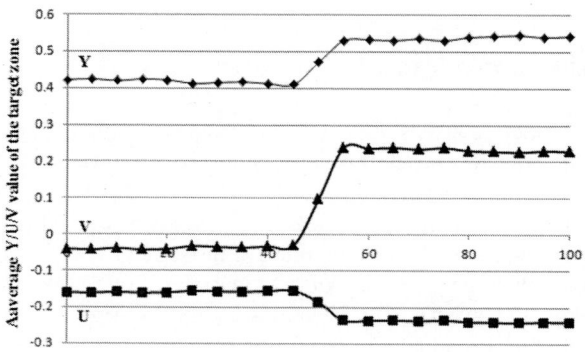

Fig. 4. Average Y/U/V value of the pixels in the target zone

In fact, static objects like traffic signs or trees in close proximity to the camera usually will have similar motion due to resolution limitation. Therefore, the position of the object can be estimated by other ones. We propose to create a main tracker and several auxiliary trackers which can guide the tracking. On the one hand, the main tracker uses a tradition tracking algorithm to track the target object. On the other hand, the auxiliary trackers are composed of dozens of blocks whose motion vectors are the same to the target. The motion vector of each block can be computed by block-matching motion estimation (BMME) because BMME is similar to a rough optical flow and its computation is much lower [12]. When the main tracker loses the target, the auxiliary trackers will help estimate the position of the target. With these auxiliary trackers, the proposed algorithm can track a target object persistently regardless of the appearance change or even occasional disappearance.

The method is very easy to perform. Since nearly all the videos will be encoded before storage or transportation, the motion vectors could be obtained directly. Therefore road signs could be recognized and tracked after block motion estimation in the encoding process, or a real-time object tracking could be applied accompanying the video decoding.

3   Auxiliary Trackers

Auxiliary trackers are created when the observation of the target object is adequate. They will be utilized to estimate the position of the target object when the target is deformed or occluded. We divide every road panoramic video frame into blocks of size 16*16 and compute every motion vector for each block between two adjacent frames and compute the average motion vector $\overline{MV}$ of the target object. Fortunately, the motion vectors can be obtained directly from the video encoding/decoding process.

For simplicity, an auxiliary tracker S is defined as a rectangle area. Suppose that S has n blocks in total in which m ones' motion vectors are $\overline{MV}$. For robustness, S must satisfy two criterion functions J_1 and J_2 as follows:

$$J_1 = n \geq n_0$$
$$J_2 = m/n \geq p_0$$

$$(1)$$

where n_0 and p_0 are two empirical values which indicate the size and reliability restriction respectively.

According the criterion functions J_1 and J_2, we cluster those blocks whose motion vectors are the same as that of the target. Let $B=\{B_1,B_2,...,B_N\}$ be the blocks whose motion vectors are $\overline{MV}$ and $R=\phi$ be the initial set of clusters. The details of the clustering algorithm are described as follows:

1. Initialize the first classification $R_1 = \{B_1\}$, add R_1 to R and remove B_1 from B.
2. Suppose there have been K classifications R_1, R_2, ..., R_K in the frame image. Choose the next element B_i ($1 \leq i \leq N$) of B. For each cluster R_k in R, extend R_k exactly enough to cover B_i, count the m and n in the extended area and compute the criterion J_2.
3. If R_k satisfies J_2, then assign B_i to R_k and remove B_i from B. If B_i satisfies more than one classification, B_i is supposed to be put into the classification which has the biggest result of J_2 after including B_i.
4. If B_i is not assigned to any clusters R, a new cluster $R_{K+1} = \{B_i\}$ is added to R and remove B_i from B.
5. Repeat the process from (2) to (4), until B is empty.
6. For each classification R_k in R, compute J_1 and if it doesn't satisfy J_1, remove it from R.

Those classifications remained in R are the candidate areas for auxiliary trackers. We build a MAX-HEAP with elements of the candidate areas and sort them by frequency of occurrence in the frame sequence. Candidate areas with high frequency of occurrence are chosen as the auxiliary trackers with priority.

When the observation of the tracked target is adequate for the main tracker, we should identify which two selected candidate areas in adjacent frames are actually of the same one. When the main tracker becomes invalid, we stop matching the same candidate area and start to track the candidate areas existed in the MAX-HEAP. Candidate areas appearing in every frame are selected as the auxiliary trackers. The process of auxiliary trackers selection is illustrated in Fig. 5 where (a) is the initial image. The blocks with the same MV to the target area's are showed in Fig.5(b). Then the blocks are clustered into several classifications in green rectangles as candidate areas in Fig.5(c), and three are selected as auxiliary trackers in red rectangles as Fig.5(d) in the end.

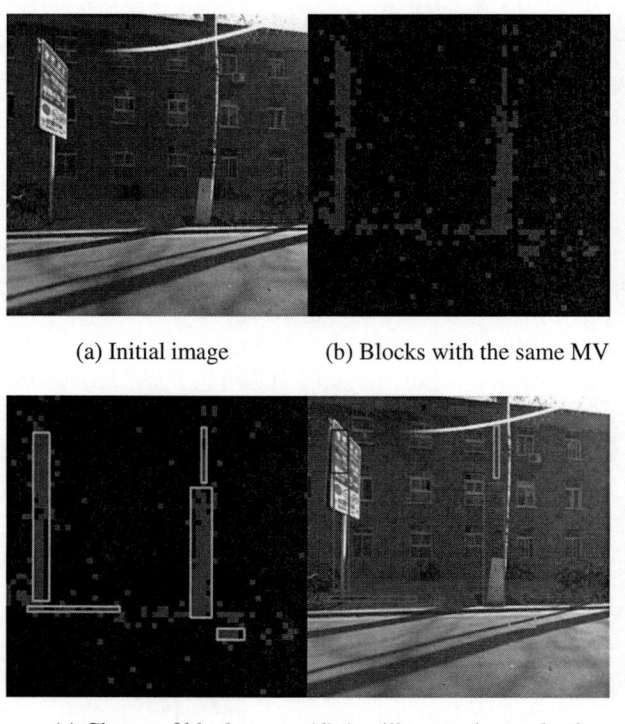

(a) Initial image   (b) Blocks with the same MV

(c) Cluster of blocks   (d) Auxiliary trackers selection

Fig. 5. Process of selecting auxiliary trackers (green: candidate areas; red: selected auxiliary trackers)

4   Persistent Tracking

The Background Eliminated Mean-Shift algorithm is chosen as the tracking method for the main tracker, and the observation of the main tracker I_k in frame k is defined by the sum of back projection value of each pixel in the tracked area. We set the original observation of tracked object as I_0, the center of the tracked object as P_0. Starting from the second frame, we compute the observation changing rate d_k in frame k by I_k/I_0. When d_k is bigger than 0.5, the main tracker is supposed to be in the adequate-observation state. In this state we directly use the main tracker's tracking result as the final position P_k of the tracked object, i.e. $P_k = M_k$, where M_k is the center of the main tracker. At the same time, we compute the relevant distance $L_{k,i}$ between every auxiliary tracker and main tracker by:

$$L_{k,i} = M_k - S_{k,i} \tag{2}$$

where $S_{k,i}$ denotes the center of the i-th auxiliary tracker in the k-th frame. If the value of d_k is between 0.5 and 0.1, the main tracker is supposed to be in the semi-adequate-observation state. In this state, we stop computing the relevant distance, and calculate the final tracking position P_k as a weighted value with the following formula:

$$P_k = M_k d_k + \frac{1}{n} \sum_{i=1}^{n} \left(S_{k,i} + L_{k-1,i} \right) \left(1 - d_k \right) \tag{3}$$

In formula 3, results from both the main tracker and the auxiliary trackers are taken into consideration. When $d_k < 0.1$, the main tracker is supposed to be in the lack-observation state. In this state, we abandon the main tracker's tracking result and directly use the auxiliary trackers to determine the final position P_k:

$$P_k = \frac{1}{n} \sum_{i=1}^{n} \left(S_{k,i} + L_{k-1,i} \right) \tag{4}$$

For each frame during this state, the color histograms of the tracking area of the present frame are compared with the previous one by the following formula:

$$Match\left(h(k-1), h(k) \right) = \sum_{i}^{n} \left| b_{k,i} - b_{k-1,i} \right| \tag{5}$$

where $h(k)$ is the histogram of the k-th frame, $b_{k,i}$ is the i-th bin of the $h(k)$. When the value of function $Match()$ is close to 0, we estimate that the observation of the main tracker recovers. Then the main tracker is set to the adequate-observation state, and as before, we directly use the main tracker's tracking result as the final position P_k of the tracked object, i.e. $P_k = M_k$.

The tracking need to stop in conditions below including 1) the main tracker goes into the central zone of the back image of cubic panorama, eg. 20% central window; 2) the target object covers a small zone, eg. 5*5 pixels; 3) all the auxiliary trackers become invalid and the main tracker still doesn't recovers. Thresholds can be set according to the requirements.

5   Experiment Evaluation

The panoramic videos used in our experiments are captured by Pointgrey Ladybug3 panoramic device in university campus, high ways etc. with the frame rate 15fps. The resolution of the panoramic video is 3000*1500, and each side image in cubic format is 512*512. During the whole tracking process, side images are expanded so that the traversing between side images is avoided. This will bring some distortion to the boundaries of the side images but don't affect the proposed methods.

The starting of our work comes from the application requirements of road sign labeling and management by the high way management bureau of ShanXi province, China. Two examples of road sign tracking are demonstrated in Fig. 6 and Fig. 7. Each one shows three critical frames of the tracking process as (a) - (c) together with the comparison of the sign's front and back views in (d).

We can see that the sign's front view and back view have different texture in Fig. 6. There are more complex background and illumination in Fig. 7, which bring more difficulties for regular tracking. The blue and red rectangles in the figures denote the main and auxiliary trackers, and the yellow one is the final tracking zone. The two examples show that our method can perform well in these conditions.

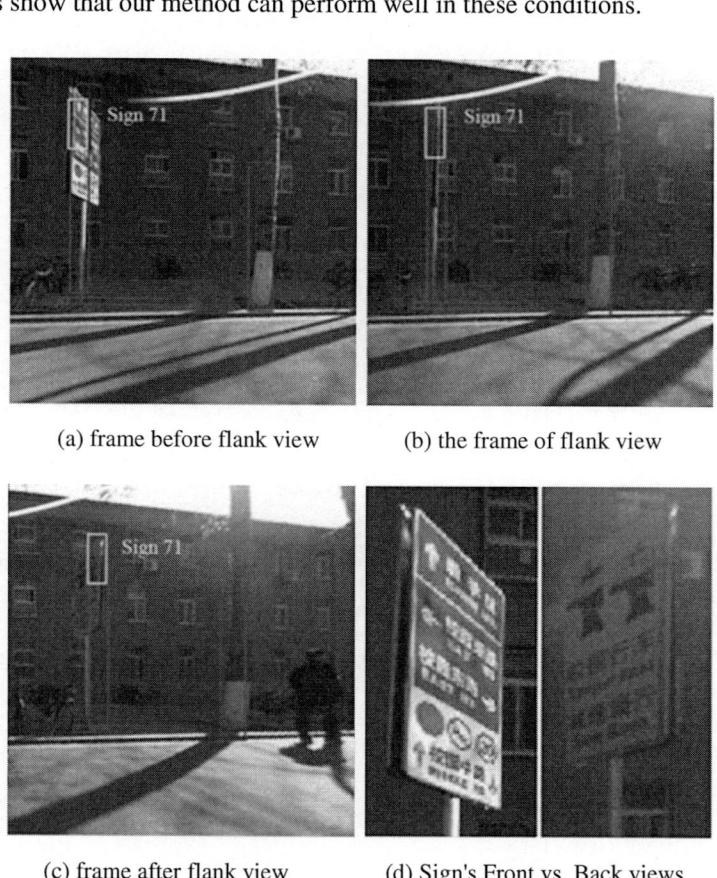

(a) frame before flank view   (b) the frame of flank view

(c) frame after flank view   (d) Sign's Front vs. Back views

Fig. 6. Example 1 of road sign tracking

(a) frame before flank view   (b) the frame of flank view

(c) frame after flank view   (d) Sign's Front vs. Back views

Fig. 7. Example 2 of road sign tracking (yellow: final tracking zone)

The performance experiment is conducted in a laptop with CPU Intel core2 duo 2.0GHz and 1G memory. The motion vectors can be provided as a given condition by the video. The algorithm mainly includes two parts, the block clustering and tracking of the main tracker. Table 1 gives the time cost in videos of different scenes. It's sufficient for real-time tracking in panoramic videos. The algorithm could be further optimized with parallel programming.

Table 1. Time cost in videos of different scenes (ms)

Sequences	Clustering for Auxiliary Trackers	Mean-shift Tracking for Main tracker	Total
Campus	23	12	35
Street	30	13	43
High Way	12	12	24

6   Conclusion

An algorithm of persistent object tracking in road panoramic videos has been proposed in this paper. This algorithm could track static objects from its emerging to vanishing regardless of their appearance change or occasional disappearance, which preserves several auxiliary trackers to guide the tracking. Experimental results show that the method is effective in static object tracking such as road signs in panoramic videos. This algorithm could use the motion vectors in video coding and is very easy to perform. It's especially valuable for road sign labeling and management.

However, current tracking zone is only one of the clusters of the same MVs. Due to the noises or errors in motion estimation, the final zone isn't exactly consistent to the target boundaries. Further improvement could be made if the similar MVs are clustered.

Acknowledgement. This work is supported by the National 863 Program of China under Grant No.2012AA011801, the Natural Science Foundation of China under Grant No.61170188, and the National 973 Program of China under Grant No. 2009CB320805.

References

1. Yuan, P.-H., Yang, K.-F., Tsai, W.-H.: Real-Time Security Monitoring Around a Video Surveillance Vehicle With a Pair of Two-Camera Omni-Imaging Devices. Vehicular Technology, 3603–3614 (October 2011)
2. Koch, A., Dipanda, A., Bourgeois-Republique, C.: 3D Panoramic Reconstruction with an Uncalibrated System of Stereovision Using Evolutionary Algorithms. In: Signal Image Technology & Internet Based Systems, SITIS (2008)
3. Zhou, Z., Niu, B., et al.: Static Object Tracking in Road Panoramic Videos. In: International Symposium on Multimedia, ISM (2010)
4. Ross, D.A., Lim, J., Lin, R., Yang, M.: Incremental learning for robust visual tracking. International Journal of Computer Vision, IJCV 77, 125–141 (2008)
5. Han, B., Joo, S., Davis, L.S.: Probabilistic fusion tracking using mixture kernel-based Bayesian filtering. In: International Conference on Computer Vision, ICCV (2007)
6. Du, W., Piater, J.: A Probabilistic Approach to Integrating Multiple Cues in Visual Tracking. In: Forsyth, D., Torr, P., Zisserman, A. (eds.) ECCV 2008, Part II. LNCS, vol. 5303, pp. 225–238. Springer, Heidelberg (2008)
7. Stenger, B., Woodley, T., Cipolla, R.: Learning to track with multiple observers. In: Computer Vision and Pattern Recognition, CVPR (2009)
8. Kwon, J., Lee, K.M.: Visual tracking decomposition. In: Computer Vision and Pattern Recognition, CVPR (2010)
9. Okuma, K., Taleghani, A., de Freitas, N., Little, J.J., Lowe, D.G.: A Boosted Particle Filter: Multitarget Detection and Tracking. In: Pajdla, T., Matas, J(G.) (eds.) ECCV 2004, Part I. LNCS, vol. 3021, pp. 28–39. Springer, Heidelberg (2004)
10. Yin, Z., Collins, R.: Object tracking and detection after occlusion via numerical hybrid local and global mode seeking. In: Computer Vision and Pattern Recognition, CVPR (2008)
11. Abramson, H., Avidan, S.: Tracking through scattered occlusion. In: Computer Vision and Pattern Recognition Workshops, CVPRW (2011)
12. Sun, D., Roth, S., Black, M.J.: Secrets of Optical Flow Estimation and Their Principles. In: Computer Vision and Pattern Recognition, CVPR (2010)

Active Learning for Transferrable Object Classification in Cross-View Traffic Scene Surveillance

Zhaoxiang Zhang, Jun Tang, Yuhang Zhao, Yunhong Wang, and Jianyun Liu

Laboratory of Intelligent Recognition and Image Processing,
Beijing Key Laboratory of Digital Media, Beihang University, Beijing, China

Abstract. We discuss the problem of object classification in cross-view traffic scene surveillance videos in this paper. To classify moving objects in traffic scene videos into pedestrian, bicycle and variety of vehicles, an effective intelligent classification framework has been proposed which takes advantage of a transfer machine learning method to bridge the gap between source scene data and target scene data. The transfer learning algorithm makes one classifier adaptive to perspective changes instead of training two different classifiers for corresponding perspectives. The samples transferred from source scene database have saved much manual labeling work on target scene database. In this paper, we propose an active transfer learning method to decrease manual labeling work further for target scene traffic object classification. Redundant experiments are conducted and experimental results demonstrate the effectiveness and convenience of our approach.

Keywords: Active Transfer Learning, Object Classification, Visual Surveillance.

1 Introduction

Since public security is paid more and more attention to in modern society, surveillance systems are everywhere to see especially in traffic occasions. The process of intelligent society construction put forward the requirement that intelligent surveillance system should be able to interpret what's going on in the monitored sites automatically and immediately. Object classification is a key step for such an intelligent surveillance system. It is a bridge between low level video processing and high level semantic interpretation. In a traffic scene, as long as the intelligent system "knows" which kind of the object travelling through the scene is, it will be able to judge whether or not this object is a law-breaker. For instance, a pedestrian who's walking across an closed expressway is a law-breaker. Meanwhile, the result of object classification may help improve the performance of low level video processing as kind of a feedback.

The accomplishment of object classification in traffic scene surveillance videos faces some basic obstacles such as low resolution of the video frame, perspective

W. Lin et al. (Eds.): PCM 2012, LNCS 7674, pp. 369–377, 2012.

distortions, real-time running and so on. Since the amount of useful information is limited by the capacity of traffic scene cameras, object appearances vary a lot due to perspective changes and the complexity of object classification algorithms is limited by real-time requirement, much work has been done to improve the performance of object classifier.

The easiest way to be thought of to classify objects into predefined types is that we distinguish different types of objects by their geometrical features. Brown et. al.[1] use simple shape features and motion features to achieve narrow view field object classification. Area, compactness, bounding box, aspect ratio, speed, motion direction and trajectories are all taken advantage of. However, these information suffers projective distortion of traffic scene surveillance camera so as to make the classification model not as intelligent as we expect. Then more powerful features consist of more information are proposed to improve the performance of object classification. Compared to simple geometric features, distinctive image texture feature descriptors are robust to noise and these transformations are calculated for object classification. SIFT feature, LBP feature, Wavelet feature and HOG feature have been widely used in computer vision and pattern recognition area.

In terms of learning strategy, both discriminant model and generative model are very popular. SVM has been used with HOG feature descriptor in object classification applications in [2]. Viola et. al. proposed a well-worked framework to finish automatic feature selection and object classification tasks by Boosting. In [3], HMM and Graph Models which are generative have been adopted to recognize objects in surveillance videos. However, before an intelligent system can work, large database of samples has to be built and labeled for classification model training. This manual work is time-consuming. Jianyun Liu et al. [4] proposed a transfer learning method used in multi-view moving objects classification. Their idea comes from [5]. The TrAdaBoost machine learning algorithm bridges the gap between source scene data and target scene data. Massive labeling work for target scene is avoided since the knowledge in source scene is fully used.

much source scene data   little target scene data   classification in target scene

Fig. 1. Active transfer learning

In this paper, we propose an active learning method based on transfer learning. Samples in training database are no longer treated by the same weight, which means more effective and efficient instances for training are selected by active learning strategy. Due to more important knowledge offered to object classification models, manual labeling work will be decreased further. In addition, the SIFT feature is also tried in our object classification framework which turns out more efficient than HOG feature.

The remainder of the paper is organized as follows. In section 2, we will briefly introduce the preprocessing part of our classification system. Object detection and feature extraction are included. In section 3, the active transfer learning method are presented. In section 4, experimental results and analysis are described. Finally, we draw our conclusions in section 5.

2 Preprocessing

The task of preprocessing is to find objects of interest and to extract features from objects in traffic scene object classification. In our system, object detection is achieved by combining background subtraction and edge detection. As long as ROIs of moving objects are acquired, we extract both HOG feature and SIFT feature so as to get convenient representations for classification model.

2.1 Object Detection

The first step of object detection is background substraction. Gaussian Mixture Model(GMM) is a popular model for background substraction and motion detection. In our system, an improved GMM [6] is applied to handle fast illumination changes and shadows. The difference between live image and background image shows where moving objects are. However, one object has a great chance being divided into several separated blobs.

Then the second step, edge detection, is used to match separated blobs to what moving objects actually are. Since pixel values of object edges in the images usually vary fiercely in a local area, which means points of edges have large values of gradient, we use an operator proposed by Canny which is highly effective for edge detection to calculate gradients. The formula is given below:

$$EB_{i,j}^t = \begin{cases} 1, & \sum_{k=0}^{N-1} E_{i,j}^{t-k} > T_e N \\ \\ 0, & \text{otherwise} \end{cases} \tag{1}$$

$$ME_{i,j}^t = E_{i,j}^t - EB_{i,j}^t \tag{2}$$

$E_{i,j}^t$ represents edge image of tth frame, $EB_{i,j}^t$ represents edge background of tth frame, N and T_e are frame number and static edge threshold, $ME_{i,j}^t$ represents motion edge of tth frame.

When result images of background substraction and edge detection are combined, every blob is an object matching the real one which has at least one edge path go through itself. We use a flood filled based method to group fragments of objects.

2.2   Feature Extraction

The first feature we extract for object classification is Histogram of Oriented Gradients(HOG) which proves to describe the appearance and shape of objects very well. We calculate the HOG feature of each blob to represent the detected objects. Literally, the basic idea of HOG is to divide every image into small cells, and calculate the gradient value and orientation of every pixel in the cell. These gradient vectors are then divided into small predefined bins and contribute to the histogram of the closest bin. After every pixel is handled by its weight, the histogram of each cell is normalized by calculating the intensity across other region around, which makes the descriptor robust to illumination changes and bias. To meet real-time demand, we apply a fast algorithm to calculate HOG descriptors in our traffic object classification system. Integral image is an efficient tool for HOG feature computation. We calculate the integral image for each orientation as kind of a preprocess of HOG descriptor calculation. Then this integral image can be applied during the iteration repeatedly and the performance of our object classification system will be improved to a large extent.

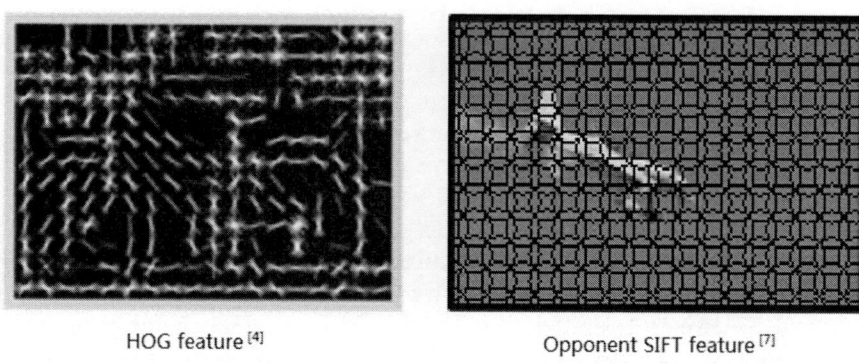

HOG feature [4]   Opponent SIFT feature [7]

Fig. 2. Feature extraction

The second feature is SIFT. The SIFT descriptor proposed by Lowe describes the local shape of a region using edge orientation histograms. Under light intensity changes, the gradient direction and the relative gradient magnitude remain the same. In this paper, we use an OpponentSIFT [7] descriptor to add color information to SIFT feature. It describes all the channels in the opponent color space using SIFT descriptors. The information in the third channel is equal to the intensity information, while the first and the second describe the color information in the image. The intensity information of OpponentSIFT is mainly used in our object classification system. However, when the classifier distinguishes between car and taxi, color information is made use of. Considering the numbers of dense sampled OpponentSIFT descriptors are not the same in different ROIs of objects, we use a visual codebook [7] to cluster descriptors and formalize the representations of objects.

3 Active Transfer Learning

Traditional supervised machine learning methods take advantage of labeled data to train models. We call these labeled data knowledge, which means as soon as a classifier was trained by corresponding labeled data, it digests the knowledge. The performance of the classifier depends on the knowledge which it knows. However, these labeled instances are randomly acquired. Aim at one specific classification model, randomly obtained samples are not highly efficient for its build. As the manual work of labeling samples is very costly, more effective samples should be labeled first.

So we proposed an active learning method based on Transfer Learning [4] to automatically select effective and efficient samples for training. Assuming that if a sample is more possible to change the structure of the classification model after the training, it will be chosen prior to other samples. While the outstanding samples are selected, manual work will be done to label them. This procedure ensure the optimal knowledge absorbability and decrease further the manual work to build a classifier working in target scene.

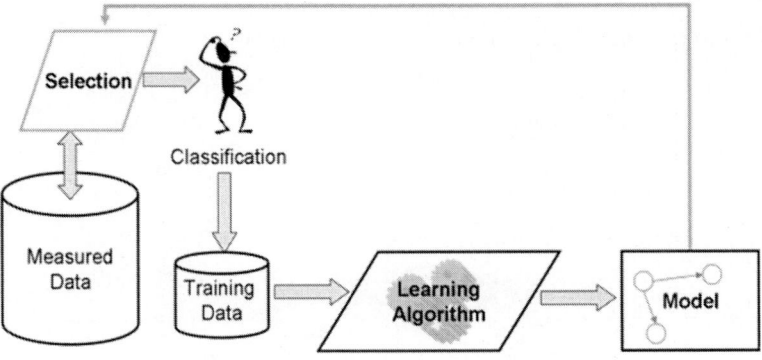

Fig. 3. Active learning

Now we introduce the algorithm of Active TrAdaBoost. Let X_s be the set of source scene feature instances, X_t be the set of target scene feature instances, Y = 0, 1 be the set of category labels and T = <X, Y>be the training data set . $c(x)$ returns sthe label of the data instance x.

Algorithm 1. ATA(Active TrAdaBoost)

Require:

    A labeled data sets T_s, the unlabeled data set S, a base learning algorithm Learner and number of active selected samples per round K.

1: Initialize the initial weight vector, that $\omega^1 = (\omega_1^1, ... \omega_{n+m}^1)$;

2: Make train data set $T = T_s$, train the Learner to acquire the first classifier: $h_0 : X \to Y$;

3: **for** $t = 1$ to N **do**

4:    Call classifier h_{t-1}, classify the instances in data set S and calculate posterior probabilities;

5:    According to information entropy, get the uncertainties of each instance;

6:    Rank instances by their uncertainties, top K instances are added into T_a and elements in T_a are labeled by manual work;

7:    $T = T \cup T_a, S = S - T_a$;

8:    Initialize weight vector for top K instances: $\omega_{n+m+1}^t = \sum\limits_{i=1}^{n+m} \dfrac{\omega_i^t}{n}$;

9:    $m = m + 1$;

10:    Set $p^t = \dfrac{\omega^t}{\sum\limits_{i=1}^{n+m} \omega_i^t}$;

11:    Call Learner, get a hypothesis $h_t : X \to Y$, providing the combined training set T, distribution p^t and the unlabeled data set S;

12:    Calculate the error of h_t on T_s under the function: $\sigma_t = \sum\limits_{i=n+1}^{n+m} \dfrac{\omega_i^t |h_t(x_i) - c(x_i)|}{\sum\limits_{i=n+1}^{n+m} \omega_i^t}$;

13:    Set $\beta_t = \dfrac{\sigma_t}{1-\sigma_t}$ and $\beta = \dfrac{1}{1+\sqrt{2 \ln \frac{n}{N}}}$;

14:    Update the new weight vector under the function:

$$\omega_i^t = \begin{cases} \omega_i^t \beta^{|h_t(x_i)-c(x_i)|}, & 1 \leq i \leq n \\ \omega_i^t \beta_t^{-|h_t(x_i)-c(x_i)|}, & n+1 \leq i \leq n+m \end{cases};$$

15: **end for**

16: Output the final hypothesis

$$h_f(x) = \begin{cases} 1, & \prod_{t=\lceil \frac{N}{2} \rceil}^{N} \beta_t^{-h_t(x)} \geq \prod_{t=\lceil \frac{N}{2} \rceil}^{N} \beta_t^{-\frac{1}{2}} \\ 0, & \text{otherwise} \end{cases}$$

Different from TrAdaBoost algorithm [4] whose target scene samples are randomly selected, training instances are actively chosen by the classifier itself. Notice that K is the number of samples active selected from unlabeled data set S by our algorithm which is going to be added to training data set T in every round of iteration.

4   Experimental Results and Analysis

We collected traffic surveillance videos for the evaluation of our cross-view object classification system. Pairs of traffic surveillance videos are shot from two different perspectives in the same site, which we call them source scene and target scene respectively. Moving traffic objects are detected to build our training database. Fig. 4 shows part of the collected database.

Target Scene   Source Scene

Fig. 4. Part of the training database

In our system, objects in traffic surveillance videos are predefined as five different types: pedestrian, bicycle, sedan, van and taxi. After moving objects in the videos are detected, they are labeled manually. Then HOG feature vectors and Bags of SIFT Words vectors are extracted from moving objects. So far, training and test data $T = <FeatureVector, Label>$ has been prepared for our experiments on Active Transfer Learning algorithm. T_s represents source scene data and T_t represents target scene data.

The SVM Light [8] is adopted as our basic weak classifier. Then TrAdaBoost and ATA machine learning method are used to strengthen the basic classifier. In each experiment, the ratio between T_t elements and T_s elements is from 0.01 to 0.5.

Table 1. Accuracies when the ratio is 0.5

	HOG Basic SVM	HOG TrAdaBoost	HOG ATA	SIFT ATA
ped vs bicycle	90.50%	90.77%	96.87%	99.23%
bicycle vs sedan	93.00%	93.15%	100%	100%
sedan vs ped	97.44%	99.00%	100%	100%
taxi vs sedan	95.90%	96.00%	100%	100%
sedan vs van	90.59%	90.57%	97.71%	99.20%

Then we take a look at table 1 which shows the accuracies of five different two-type classifications when the ratio between target scene samples and source scene samples is 0.5. We can find that all four classifiers perform well with this training set. However, when the ratio decreases down to 0.01, the advantage of machine learning method is showed in table 2. The ideas of fully making use of source scene data and treating samples differently take effect. So we need only small amount of newly labeled target scene data to obtain satisfying classification.

Table 2. Accuracies when the ratio is 0.5

	HOG Basic SVM	HOG TrAdaBoost	HOG ATA	SIFT ATA
ped vs bicycle	90.50%	90.77%	96.87%	99.23%
bicycle vs sedan	93.00%	93.15%	100%	100%
sedan vs ped	97.44%	99.00%	100%	100%
taxi vs sedan	95.90%	96.00%	100%	100%
sedan vs van	90.59%	90.57%	97.71%	99.20%

Fig. 5 shows some of our experiment results. Taken classifying sedan and bicycle as an example, we can see that with samples of target scene database increases, classifiers trained by different machine learning methods perform better in target scene. Obviously, ATA algorithm improve weak classifiers in a more efficient way than TrAdaBoost algorithm thanks to its active selection of target scene instances. Moreover, we can see in Fig. 5 that SIFT feature bears perspective distortion better than HOG feature since with the same ATA learning method, performance of classifier using SIFT feature is superior when the ratio between target scene and source scene is small.

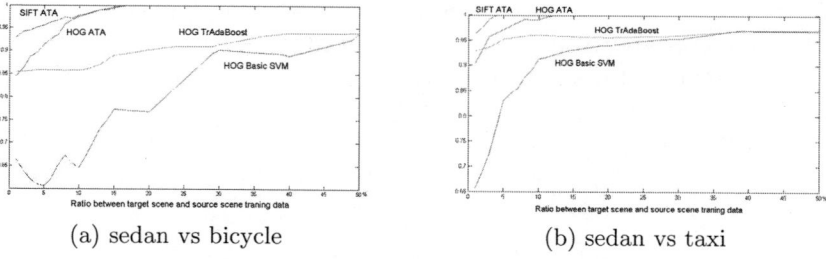

(a) sedan vs bicycle   (b) sedan vs taxi

Fig. 5. Accuracies of classification

But in Fig. 5(b) we can find that the performance of classifier is not always better since the scale of target scene data increases. The performance of classifier using HOG feature which is trained by TrAdaBoost algorithm turns bad when the ratio between target scene and source scene training data goes up to 0.24 from 0.09. This is an overfitting phenomenon which means the classifier is over trained. In addition, notice that Fig. 5(b) shows the result of classifying sedan and taxi, the accuracy of the classifier using Opponent SIFT boosted by ATA algorithm reach 1 soon. Since the color difference is large between sedan and taxi, we contribute this good performance to the advantage of Opponent SIFT which contains color information.

5   Conclusions

In this paper, we modify the transfer learning method by adding active learning to it. ATA, short for Active TrAdaBoost, does not only fully take advantage of source scene data, but also makes use of target scene data highly efficient. The experiment results demonstrate that classifier trained by ATA performs better than that trained by TrAdaBoost with the same number of newly labeled target scene instances. Also, the SIFT feature which tolerates perspective distortion better, cooperates with ATA better than the HOG feature. As a result, more manual labeling work is saved with our classification system than traditional transfer learning framework.

Acknowledgement. This work is funded by the National Basic Research Program of China (No. 2010CB327902), the National Natural Science Foundation of China (No. 61005016, No. 61061130560), the Fundamental Research Funds for the Central Universities, National High-tech R&D Program of China (2011AA010502), and the Open Projects Program of National Laboratory of Pattern Recognition.

References

1. Brown, L.M.: View independant vehicle/person classification. In: Proc. of the ACM 2nd International Workshop on Video Surveillence and Sensor Networks (2004)
2. Han, F., Shan, Y., Cekander, R., Sawhney, H.S., Kumar, R.: A two-stage approach to people and vehicle detection with hog-based svm. In: Performance Metrics for Intelligent Systems 2006 Workshop (2006)
3. Munoz, D., Bagnell, J., Vandapel, N., Hebert, M.: Contextual classification with functional max-margin markov networks. In: IEEE Computer Society Conference on Computer Vision and Pattern Recognition (2009)
4. Liu, J., Wang, Y., Zhang, Z., Mo, Y.: Multi-view Moving Objects Classification via Transfer Learning. In: Asian Conference on Pattern Recognition (2011)
5. Blitzer, J., McDonald, R., Pereira, F.: Domain adaptation with structural correspondence learning. In: Proceedings of the 2006 Conference on Empirical Methods in Natural Language Processing, EMNLP 2006, pp. 120–128 (2006)
6. Liu, Z., Huang, K., Tan, T., Wang, L.: Cast shadow removal with gmm for surface reflectance component. In: International Conference on Pattern Recognition, vol. 1, pp. 727–730 (2006)
7. van de Sande, K.E.A., Gevers, T., Snoek, C.G.M.: Evaluating Color Descriptors for Object and Scene Recognition. Transactions on Pattern Analysis and Machine Intelligence (2009)
8. Joachims, T.: Learning to Classify Text Using Support Vector Machines. In: Methods, Theroy and Algorithms (2002)

Laplacian-Based Feature Preserving Mesh Simplification

Lin Zhang, Zhen Ma, Zhong Zhou*, and Wei Wu

State Key Laboratory of Virtual Reality Technology and Systems, Beihang University
Beijing 100191, P.R. China
zz@vrlab.buaa.edu.cn

Abstract. We introduce a novel approach for feature preserving mesh simplification based on vertex Laplacians, specifically, the uniformly weighted Laplacian. Our approach is unique in three aspects: 1) a Laplacian based shape descriptor to quantize the local geometric feature sensitivity; 2) a Laplacian weighted cost function that is capable of providing different retaining rates of the geometric features; and 3) an optimal clustering technique which combines K-means and the Laplacian based shape descriptor to implement vertex classification. During simplification, the Laplacian based shape descriptors are firstly computed, and then a chosen error function to be optimized is penalized by our Laplacian weighted cost function, leading it to feature preserving. By applying the clustering technique, different simplification operators may be applied to different vertex groups for different purposes. Different error functions have been implemented to demonstrate the effectiveness, applicability and flexibility of the approach. Experiments conducted on various models including those of natural objects and CAD ones, show superior results.

Keywords: Mesh simplification, Laplace operator, Feature preservation, Feature detection.

1 Introduction and Related Work

Simplification of geometric models has become a hot topic today due to the rapid development of 3D scanning and acquisition technology. The acquired complex polygonal meshes face challenges in rendering, processing, and so on. Hence, after acquisition of geometric data, a simplification step is necessary, and its output should be a faithful approximation of the input. Generally, human vision is more sensitive to fine detail features and distinct sharp parts. Those detail features are usually visually meaningful fine scale components of a natural object, and typically require fine meshes to represent them well. This paper focuses on how to preserve these detail features during mesh simplification.

In the past decades, a fair amount of research on simplification techniques has been developed. In most existing simplification algorithms, edge collapse [1], which simplifies models by iteratively contracting edges has been adopted

---

* Corresponding author.

W. Lin et al. (Eds.): PCM 2012, LNCS 7674, pp. 378–389, 2012.
© Springer-Verlag Berlin Heidelberg 2012

to provide it with precise results and high performance. Among numerous edge collapse algorithms, quadric error metric (QEM) [2], which estimates the error introduced by a pair collapse as the distance from a vertex to a quadratic surface, is the one with high performance but usually with the most precise results.

In order to preserve detail features of models during simplification, varieties of feature preserving mesh simplification algorithms have been proposed. One approach is to introduce new error arguments by geometric feature extraction. According to this viewpoint, algorithms based on QEM were introduced to avoid smearing out of real important features, such as [3,4,5]. The main difference between these algorithms lies in how they expands the quadric error matric with feature detection. Wang et al. [6] proposed a simplification algorithm based on feature extraction with the average curvature estimation to triangle mesh. Some direct methods such as [7] are proposed to control the relative importance of different surface regions by a user-guided approach. Rather than optimizing a piecewise-linear approximant of an original surface, [8] proposed an efficient variational approach which simplify models by mutual and repeated error-driven optimizations of a partition and a set of local proxies.

Most of the methods mentioned above do not provide users with different retaining rates of the geometric meaningful features. Vertex curvatures are widely used in these methods for feature detection, but computation of curvatures is obviously not cheap. The main contribution of this paper is to detect geometric features with a Laplacian based shape descriptor and to preserve the geometry feature with a Laplacian weighted cost function. Moreover, our approach is capable of providing different retaining rates of the geometric features. To the best of our knowledge, few works have been done before on feature preserving mesh simplification using the uniform Laplacian operator.

2   Uniform Laplacian Operator

Before describing the uniform Laplacian operator, we introduce notations. The surface mesh is represented as a graph $S = (V, E)$, with vertices V and edges E, where $V = [\mathbf{v}_1^T, \mathbf{v}_2^T, ..., \mathbf{v}_n^T]^T$, $\mathbf{v}_i = [v_{ix}, v_{iy}, v_{iz}]^T \in \mathbb{R}^3$. If two distinct vertices $\mathbf{v}_i$ and $\mathbf{v}_j$ are linked by an edge $\mathbf{e}_{ij} = \mathbf{v}_j - \mathbf{v}_i$ then we denote $j \in \mathcal{N}(i)$. The normal of vertex $\mathbf{v}_i$ is denoted as $\mathbf{n}_i$. Furthermore, δ_i is the Laplacian of $\mathbf{v}_i$, the result of applying the discrete Laplace operator to $\mathbf{v}_i$, i.e.

$$\delta_i = \sum_{j \in \mathcal{N}(i)} w_{ij}(\mathbf{v}_j - \mathbf{v}_i) = \left[\sum_{j \in \mathcal{N}(i)} w_{ij}\mathbf{v}_j \right] - \mathbf{v}_i, \tag{1}$$

where $\sum_{j \in \mathcal{N}(i)} w_{ij} = 1$, and the choice of weights

$$w_{ij} = \frac{\xi_{ij}}{\sum_{k \in \mathcal{N}(i)} \xi_{ik}} \tag{2}$$

defines the nature of δ_i. One popular choice is $\xi_{ij} = 1$, which defines the uniform weights, i.e. the umbrella operator.

The umbrella operator of $\mathbf{v}_i$ points to the centroid of its neighboring vertices. When the umbrella operator is applied to the mesh, it smears out the real important features of the mesh, which named shrinking. Different from many works that try to avoid the shrinking problem, we utilize it and introduce an normal-dependent umbrella operator to quantize geometric sensitivity. The operator will be described and discussed in the next section.

However, the umbrella operator suffers from the problem of large inaccuracies for irregular meshes, which prevents us from using it for feature detection directly. It is a linear from implying the assumption that the mesh has edges of length 1 and all the angles between two adjacent edges around a vertex should be equal. This is obviously not true in actual meshes, which leads to inadequacy of the umbrella operator. Fig. 1(b) shows such a behavior, when the umbrella operator is applied, border lines are strangely distorted into curves. To deal with the problem caused by different length of edges, [9] presented a scale-dependent umbrella operator. Besides, [10] presented the mean curvature normal which compensates both for unequal edge lengths and for unequal face angles. However, they suffers from a difficulty in dealing with arbitrary surfaces, such as quad meshes. For more details refer to [11].

3   Normal-Dependent Umbrella Operator

To improve inaccuracies of the umbrella operator, we introduce the normal-dependent umbrella operator using the following formula:

$$\widetilde{\delta}_i = \left[\sum_{j \in \mathcal{N}(i)} \frac{1}{|\mathcal{N}(i)|} (\mathbf{v}_j - \mathbf{v}_i)\mathbf{n}_i \right] \cdot \mathbf{n}_i, \tag{3}$$

where $|\mathcal{N}(i)|$ is the number of neighbors of vertex $\mathbf{v}_i$.

Note that when all edges are of size 1, and all the angles between two adjacent edges around a vertex are equal, $\widetilde{\delta}_i$ reduces to the umbrella operator. Fig. 1(e) shows an example of it for a triangle mesh vertex and its neighbors.

Fig. 1 demonstrates the normal-dependent umbrella operator performs more stable for an actual mesh than the original and scale-dependent ones, particularly for sharp features such as lines and corners, meaning that it quantizes the local geometric feature sensitivity precious more precisely. Moreover, the normal-dependent umbrella operator is actually the projection of the umbrella operator along the normal $\mathbf{n}_i$, which does not limit the umbrella operator to triangulated surface, and it is also computationally fast. Our Laplacian based shape descriptor which will be introduced later is based on it.

4   Mesh Simplification

In this section, the overall pipeline of the approach is first described. Laplacian based shape descriptor is then discussed in detail, followed by the Laplacian weighted cost function. Finally an optimal clustering technique to implement vertex classification is discussed.

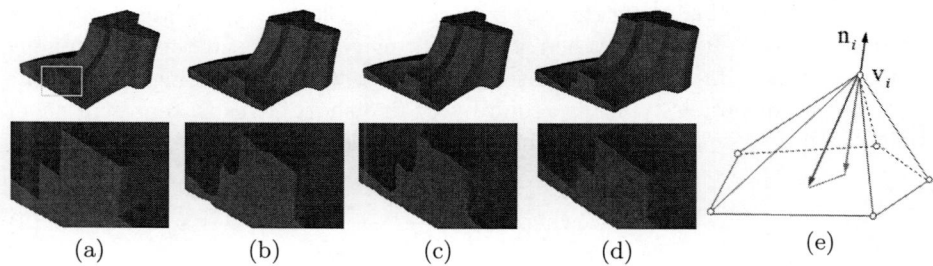

(a)   (b)   (c)   (d)   (e)

Fig. 1. (a) Original Fandisk model; (b), (c), (d) are smoothed results by applying umbrella operator, scale-dependent, and normal-dependent umbrella operator; (e) uniform (red) and normal-dependent (green) umbrella operator vectors for a vertex $\mathbf{v}_i$ and its 1-ring neighbours, as well as the vertex normal $\mathbf{n}_i$. While the other two operators distort lines and corners, the normal-dependent one does not.

4.1   Algorithm Description

Our simplification approach is based on two steps (see Fig. 2):

   A Laplacian based feature detection and vertex classification: geometry features are first detected by calculating the Laplacian based shape descriptor, and then an optimal clustering algorithm can be applied to divide vertices into clusters, particularly for the CAD models.

   A Laplacian-weighted simplification: a chosen error function to be optimized is penalized by the Laplacian weighted cost function while leading to a feature preserving simplification.

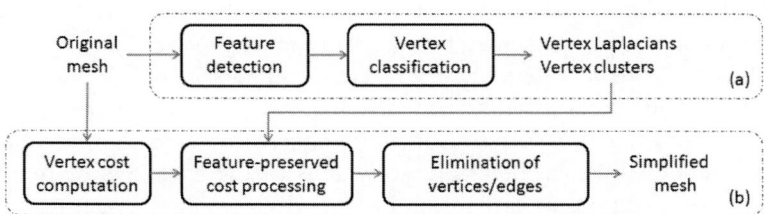

Fig. 2. Two steps of the approach. (a) Laplacian based feature detection and vertex classification; (b) Laplacian-weighted simplification.

4.2   Laplacian Based Shape Descriptor

We use the normal-dependent umbrella operator to detect geometric features. For each vertex $\mathbf{v}_i$, the length of its normal-dependent umbrella operator vector

$$|\widetilde{\delta}_i| = \frac{1}{|\mathcal{N}(i)|} \left[\sum_{j \in \mathcal{N}(i)} (\mathbf{v}_j - \mathbf{v}_i) \right] \cdot \mathbf{n}_i \tag{4}$$

is the projection of δ_i along the vertex normal $\mathbf{n}_i$. Clearly, $|\widetilde{\delta}_i|$ is larger at crease vertices than at flat ones. When $\mathbf{v}_i$ and its neighbors are in the same plane, $|\widetilde{\delta}_i|$ goes to zero. In addition, as discussed before, visually meaningful fine scale components or details typically require very fine short edges to represent them well, we thus score the geometric importance at vertex $\mathbf{v}_i$ as

$$l_i = \frac{|\widetilde{\delta}_i|}{c_i}, \text{ where } c_i = \frac{1}{|\mathcal{N}(i)|} \sum_{j \in \mathcal{N}(i)} |\mathbf{e}_{ij}|. \tag{5}$$

In the remainder of this paper, we will denote this Laplacian based shape descriptor as the *Laplacian descriptor*. By computing l_i for each vertex $\mathbf{v}_i$, a quantitative 1D data array $L \in \mathbb{R}^{1 \times n}$ is then generated as $L = [l_1, l_2, ..., l_n]$. Consequently, vertices with small l_i are those non-feature vertices of meshes, and vertices with large l_i are those meaningful feature details.

Fig. 3 shows the Laplacian descriptor and its comparison with popular curvatures. As we can see in Fig. 3(b) and Fig. 3(d), Laplacian descriptors of meaningful geometric feature vertices are larger than those of the non-feature vertices in flat regions. Fig. 3(e) and Fig. 3(f) shows comparison of Laplacian descriptors and curvatures. In Fig. 3(e) and Fig. 3(f), to enable a better visual comparison, vertices are firstly sorted in ascending order by their values of features descriptors, and then are plotted along the horizontal axis. In general, vertices in same region (e.g., flat surface, border line) should have similar values of shape descriptors. Take the Fandisk model in Fig. 3(a) as an example, vertices of it can be roughly clustered into several small groups, such as flat surface vertices, curved surface vertices, border vertices, and so on. Therefore, feature descriptors should also have such characteristic of clustering. As can be seen in Fig. 3(e), both the Laplacian descriptor and the mean curvature has obvious grouping results (staircase curve), meaning that they are more precise than the other two.

Fig. 4(a) is a partial enlarged view of Laplacian descriptors in Fig. 3(e), and is roughly divided into several segments. Fig. 4(b) is the 3D plot of vertices corresponding to Fig. 4(a). Each segment demonstrates a small group of vertices with the similar Laplacian descriptors, demonstrating that it is more accurate than the smooth curvature estimation in [6] and Gaussian curvature.

4.3   Laplacian Weighted Cost Function

Since the Laplacian descriptor l_i gives the geometric importance for vertex $\mathbf{v}_i$, we use it to guide an existing simplification method for a feature preserved simplification. Given a chosen cost function $g()$, such as QEM or shortest edge length, we apply the Laplacian weighted cost function that we design below.

$$f(\mathbf{v}_i) = g(\mathbf{v}_i)e^{\lambda l_i} \tag{6}$$

where λ is a scale factor and all l_i are linearly rescaled into range [0,1]. By changing the value of λ, we can get different retaining rate of the geometric features.

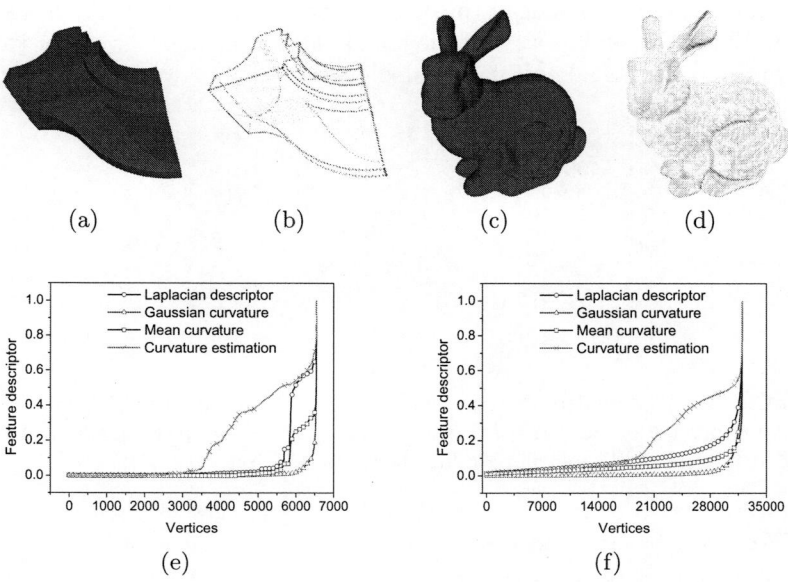

Fig. 3. Feature descriptor. (a), (c) input models; (b), (d) 3D plot of Laplacian descriptors; (e), (f) comparison of Laplacian descriptors and curvatures.

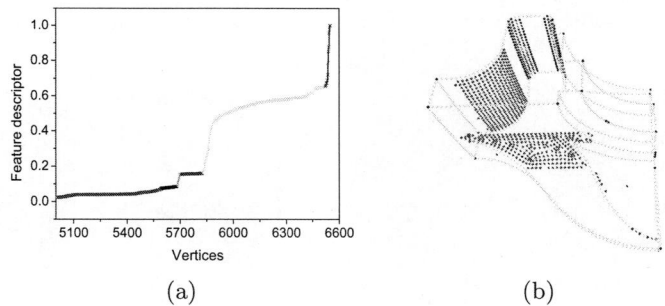

Fig. 4. (a) a partial enlarged color view of Laplacian descriptors in Fig. 3(f); (b) 3D plot of vertices corresponding to (a)

For ease of explanation, we take the shortest edge first algorithm as an example. It first computes cost for each vertex $\mathbf{v}_i$ as

$$g(\mathbf{v}_i) = min(|\mathbf{e}_{ij}|), \text{ where } j \in \mathcal{N}(i), \tag{7}$$

then the order of collapses is built on the basis of $g(\mathbf{v}_i)$. This straightforward algorithm can not preserve geometric features during simplification. Nevertheless, we can now improve it to a feature preserving simplification algorithm by simply applying Equation 6 on $g(\mathbf{v}_i)$, see Fig. 5. Most of the edge contraction algorithms, which can not lead to a feature preserving simplification, can also be improved in the similar way. In the remainder of this paper, we refer to those improved algorithms as Laplacian guided ones.

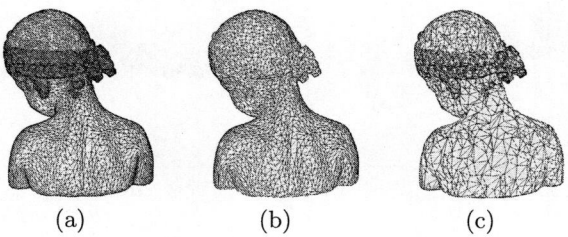

(a)   (b)   (c)

Fig. 5. Compare the guided shortest edge first altorithm with the original ($\lambda = 10$). (a) original girl model (30k tri.); (b) result of the original shortest edge first algorithm (11k tri.); (c) result of Laplacian-guided shortest edge first (11k tri.).

4.4   Vertex Classification

In many cases, one simple simplification algorithm cannot generate a satisfactory reconstruction. Fig. 6 demonstrates such an example. This suggests that different methods may best be applied for different purposes. Vertex classification is thus a good way to go further. For example, if we classify vertices into two non-feature and feature groups, we may apply different simplification operators with different parameter selections to pursue a better reconstruction.

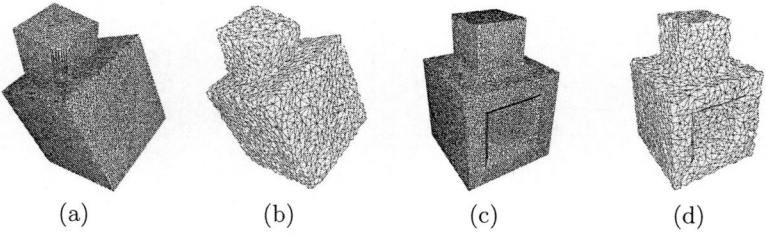

(a)   (b)   (c)   (d)

Fig. 6. Boundaries are distorted when the shortest edge first algorithm is applied to models. (a) original Mech A (30k tri.); (b) simplified Mech A (5k tri.); (c) original Mech B (30k tri.); (d) simplified Mech B (5k tri.).

Vertices of the mesh are classified by their Laplacian descriptors. The clustering is done via the K-means algorithm [12], allowing to divide vertices into k groups. Given the Laplacian descriptor array L, we first seek a partition $L_1, L_2, ..., L_k$ to minimize the objective function

$$\sum_{j=1}^{k} \sum_{l_i \in L_j} |l_i - \mu_j|, \tag{8}$$

where L_j is a set of vertices in the j-th cluster and $\mu_j = mean(\sum_{l_i \in L_j} l_i)$ is the center point over the j-th cluster. In current context, vertices are divided into two clusters, feature and non-feature (see Fig. 7). Vertex classification is usually useful for a CAD model but not for a natural object such as Bunny in Fig. 3(c). However, this statistical information maybe still be useful in other contexts.

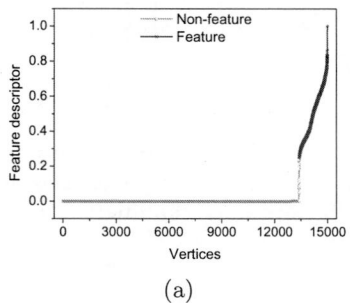
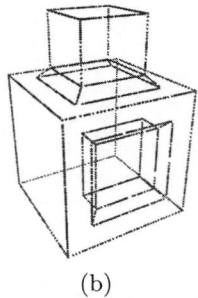

(a)   (b)

Fig. 7. (a) two clusters by K-means on Laplacian descriptors of model in Fig. 3(a); (b) 3D plot of feature vertices based on clusters in (a).

Fig. 7 demonstrates that our method yields rather pleasing results in terms of vertex clustering. But due to the diversities and complexity of different models, we may not get exact vertex classification even when the more advanced clustering techniques are employed. Some feature vertices might be wrongly grouped into non-feature cluster. Therefore, a post-clustering procedure is needed. Notice that boundary vertices for a CAD model should have at least two neighboring feature vertices. By making good use of this property, we apply the clustering and refinement procedure as below (see Fig. 8 for the result).

1) Compute the Laplacian descriptor array L.
2) Clustering: Apply the K-means clustering on L.
3) Refinement: If there exist vertices in the feature cluster which have less than two feature neighbors, send the vertex in the non-feature group whose Laplacian descriptor is the biggest into the feature cluster.
4) Repeat step 3 until each vertex in the feature cluster has more than two feature neighbors, or the approach reach a certain threshold.

There has been a considerable research work on boundary detection relevant to the problem of CAD mesh segmentation, but the main goal of the refinement approach here is to show the advantage of using the Laplacian descriptor array $\tilde{L}$, and we do not pretend in this paper to contribute in the field of CAD mesh segmentation. To conduct a perfect boundary making of a complex model such as Fandisk model in Fig. 3(a), more advanced classification refinement techniques are certainly needed, for instance, contour tracking in [13].

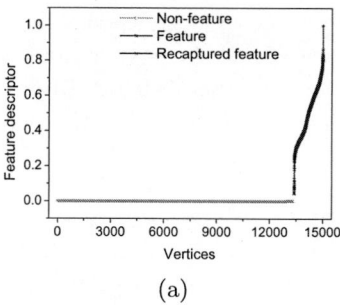
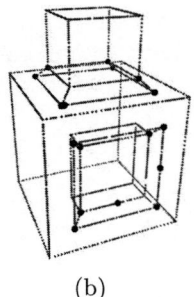

(a)   (b)

Fig. 8. Clustering refinement of example in Fig. 7. (a) recapturing potential feature vertices back into the feature cluster with the classification refinement procedure; (b) 3D plot of feature vertices where blue dots mark the recaptured vertices.

Since vertices are divided into to two clusters, we can now improve the boundary distorting problem in Fig. 6(b) and Fig. 6(d). For each boundary vertex, we compute its cost $g(\mathbf{v}_i)$ by finding the shortest edge only between its feature neighbors instead of Equ. 7. The improved results are shown in Fig. 9.

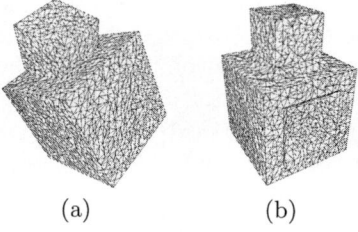

(a)   (b)

Fig. 9. Improve the shortest edge first algorithm by using different cost functions based on vertex classification. (a) improved result of Fig. 6(b); (b) improved result of Fig. 6(d).

5   Case Study

All tested algorithms here are integrated into the same testing framework written by Somers. Fig. 1 demonstrates that the normal-dependent umbrella operator performs precisely on practical irregular meshes. Figs. 3 and 4 demonstrate that the Laplacian shape descriptor produces rather pleasing results. Fig. 10 demonstrates the successful extension of it to non-manifold and quad meshes. Table 1 summarizes the running time of computing the Laplacian shape descriptor array L, comparing with curvature-based methods on a PC with Intel Duo 3.30GHz processor and 4GB memory. Due to the fast normal-dependent umbrella operator, our algorithm is much more faster than the mean curvature. The mean curvature estimation method proposed in [6] costs the similar time with ours.

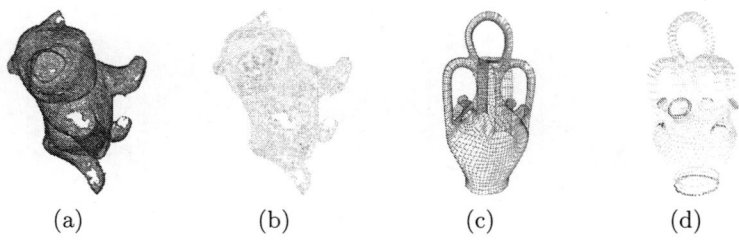

(a)   (b)   (c)   (d)

Fig. 10. (a) non-manifold cinghiale; (b) 3D plot of Laplacian descriptors of (a); (c) quad mesh; (d) 3D plot of Laplacian descriptors of (c)

Table 1. Time Comparison of feature detection (in s)

Model	Vertices	Faces	Laplacian operator	Mean Curvature	Curvature Estimation
Cow	2903	5804	0.004	0.009	0.006
Fandisk	6551	13098	0.009	0.021	0.012
Mech A	14999	29994	0.027	0.081	0.038
Mech B	15000	29996	0.026	0.08	0.03
Girl	15516	31028	0.028	0.122	0.043
Bunny	34834	69451	0.065	0.469	0.118

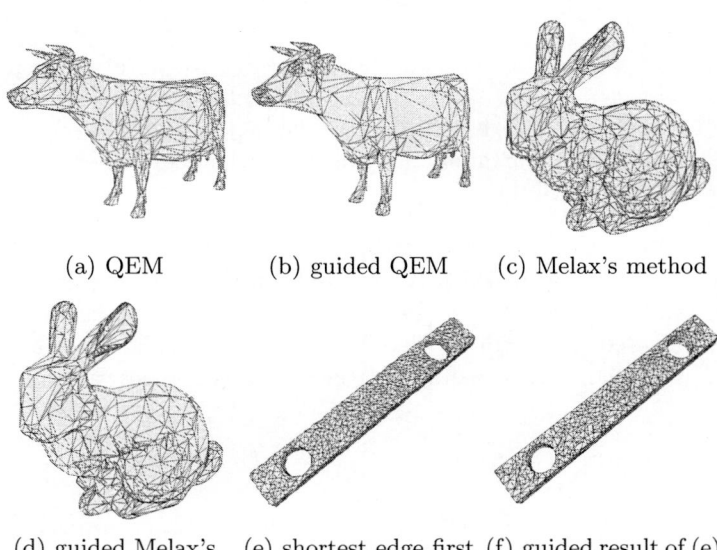

(a) QEM   (b) guided QEM   (c) Melax's method

(d) guided Melax's   (e) shortest edge first   (f) guided result of (e)

Fig. 11. Experiments on different error functions. (a),(b) Cow (5804 tri. to 2052 tri.); (c),(d) Bunny (69451 tri. to 4081 tri.); (e),(f) Mech (15k tri. to 4k tri.).

Figs. 5 and 11 show some example implementations of our Laplacian-based approach and demonstrate that it can improve different error functions to feature preserving. All test models has distinct feature regions including creases, corners and boundaries, those results demonstrate how important geometric structures are preserved in the output. Fig. 12 demonstrates that our method is capable of providing different retaining rates of the geometric features by only changing

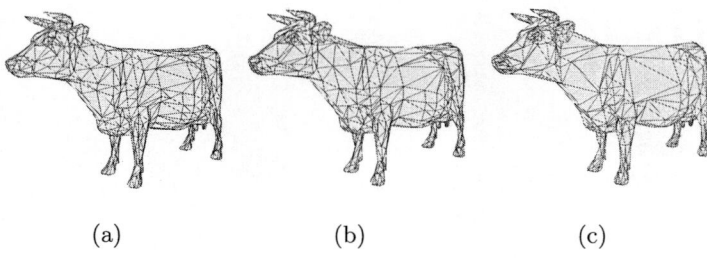

(a)   (b)   (c)

Fig. 12. Simplified Cow models from guided QEM algorithm with different retaining rate of features (all 3k tri. to 2k tri.). (a) $\lambda = 1$; (b) $\lambda = 10$; (c) $\lambda = 50$.

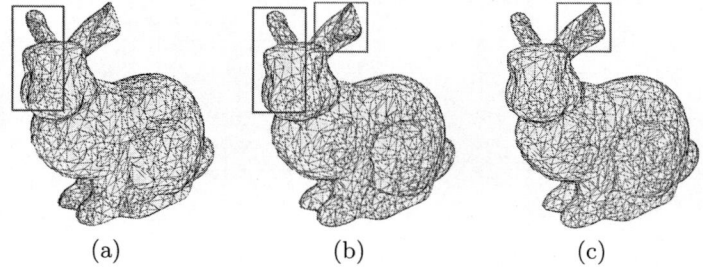

(a)   (b)   (c)

Fig. 13. Contrast with Curvature Estimation [6] and Curvature-weighted QEM [4] (35k tri. to 6924 tri.). (a) curvature estimation; (b) Laplacian guided QEM ($\lambda = 10$); (c) curvature-weighted QEM.

the value of scale factor λ, which is very useful in practical application. Fig. 13 shows the comparison results for the Bunny model. Both Laplacian guided and curvature-weighted algorithm preserve better feature details than the curvature estimation algorithm, because of their accuracy in shape description.

6   Conclusion

We have presented a new feature preserved simplification approach. Geometry features are first detected using a Laplacian based shape descriptor. An optional clustering technique which combines K-means and vertex Laplacians is developed to implement vertex classification, different simplification and refinement operators can then be applied on different vertex groups for different purposes. Moreover, we introduce a Laplacian weighted cost function which is capable of providing different retaining rates of the geometric features. In addition, our approach may be applied on different error functions, leading them to feature preserving. The Laplacian based shape descriptor could be easily extended to handle arbitrary mesh topology. Due to advantages of it, our method is computationally efficient and can be easily implemented. Experimental results demonstrate that our algorithm has strong applicability and yields superior results.

Acknowledgments. This work is supported by the National 863 Program of China under Grant No.2012AA011803, the Natural Science Foundation of China under Grant No.61170188, and the National 973 Program of China under Grant No. 2009CB320805.

References

1. Hoppe, H., DeRose, T., Duchamp, T., McDonald, J., Stuetzle, W.: Mesh optimization. In: Proceeding of SIGGRAPH 1993, pp. 19–26 (1993)
2. Garland, M., Heckbert, P.: Surface Simplification Using Quadric Error Metrics. In: Proceeding of SIGGRAPH 1997, pp. 209–216 (1997)
3. Wei, J., Lou, Y.: Feature Preserving Mesh Simplification Using Feature Sensitive Metric. Journal of Computer Science and Technology 25, 595–605 (2010)
4. Li, L., He, M., Wang, P.: Mesh Simplification Algorithm Based on Absolute Curvature-weighted Quadric Error Metrics. In: 5th IEEE Conference on Industrial Electronics and Applications, ICIEA, pp. 399–403 (2010)
5. Jong, B.S., Teng, J.L., Yang, W.H.: An efficient and low-error mesh simplification method based on torsion detection. The Visual Computer 22, 56–67 (2005)
6. Wang, J., Wang, L.R., Li, J.Z., Hagiwara, I.: A feature preserved mesh simplification algorithm. Journal of Engineering and Computer Innovations 6, 98–105 (2011)
7. Kho, Y., Garland, M.: User-guided simplification. In: Proceedings of ACM Symposium on Interactive 3D Graphics, pp. 123–126 (2003)
8. Cohen-Steiner, D., Alliez, P., Desbrun, M.: Variational shape approximation. In: Proceedings of ACM SIGGRAPH, pp. 905–914 (2004)
9. Fujiwara, K.: Eigenvalues of laplacians on a closed riemannian manifold and its nets. In: Proceedings of AMS, vol. 123, pp. 2585–2594 (1995)
10. Meyer, M., Desbrun, M., Schröder, P., Barr, A.H.: Discrete differential-geometry operators for triangulated 2-manifolds. In: Proceedings of VisMath, Berlin, Germany (2002)
11. Sorkine, O.: Differential Representations for Mesh Processing. Computer Graphics Forum 25(4), 789–807 (2006)
12. Gersho, A., Gray, R.: Vector quantization and signal compression. Kluwer, Boston (1992)
13. Lavoué, G., Dupont, F., Baskurt, A.: A new CAD mesh segmentation method, based on curvature tensor analysis. Computer-Aided Design, 975–987 (2005)

An Image Splicing Detection
Based on Interpolation Analysis

Rimba W. Ciptasari[1,2], Kyung-Hyune Rhee[3], and Kouichi Sakurai[1]

[1] Graduate School of Information Science and Electrical Engineering,
Department of Informatics, Kyushu University, Fukuoka, Japan
[2] Faculty of Informatics, Telkom Institute of Technology, Bandung, Indonesia
[3] Department of IT Convergence and Application Engineering, Pukyong National
University, 599-1, Daeyeon 3-Dong, Nam-Gu, Busan 608-737, Korea

Abstract. With the advent of low-cost and high-resolution digital cameras and sophisticated editing software, it is becoming increasingly easier to tamper with the digital image. A common form of manipulation is to combine parts of the image fragment into another different image to remove objects from the image. Inspired by the digital image correlation concept, we exploit the peak of cross-correlation function to automatically detect the splicing artifacts in any fragment of an image. We show the efficacy of the proposed scheme on revealing the source of spliced regions. We make the first concrete technique towards appropriate tools which are necessary for rendering digital forgeries.

Keywords: Image splicing, digital image correlation, edge detection, membership function, interpolation.

1 Introduction

1.1 Background

Nowadays, powerful technologies, such as Photoshop, are available in processing and editing digital images. As a consequence, the creation of photograph manipulation is relatively easy task by using those technologies.

There are three main categories of image manipulation: copy/move, enhancement, and composite. Image enhancement comprises change of the color of object, blurring out the object, or change of the weather condition. Copy/move contains copying region of the original image and pasting it into other area of the original image. Image composite involves combining two or more image regions to create a new image. This kind of manipulation is often referred to as image splicing in which we focus on. In addition, image splicing is conducted without further post-processing such as smoothing of boundaries among different regions. Since the artifacts introduced by image splicing are almost imperceptible, image splicing detection remains a challenging task.

W. Lin et al. (Eds.): PCM 2012, LNCS 7674, pp. 390–401, 2012.
© Springer-Verlag Berlin Heidelberg 2012

1.2 Related Work

Farid [1] stated that in digital forensics, explicit knowledge of the original signal is not assumed. This situation is contrast to digital watermarking and authentication. Further, Ng et al. [2] mentioned such case as passive-blind image forensics or passive detection. A number of passive detections focused on pixel-based have been developed over the past several years. Popescu and Farid [3] exploited expectation/maximization (EM) algorithm to detect re-sampling's lattice of the original image. Unlike Popescu and Farid [3], Prasad and Ramakrishnan [4] have a propensity to investigate the properties of a re-sampled discrete sequence and proposed deterministic techniques to detect re-sampling. *Ye et al.* [5] investigated blocking artifacts introduced during JPEG compression. The inconsistencies caused by compression could be used as evidence of image integrity. Pan and Lyu [6] exploited scale invariant feature transform (SIFT) algorithm to develop a duplicated region detection which is robust to typical image transforms.

Other approaches to detect tampered image are based on machine learning framework. Farid and Lyu [7] built a classification scheme to differentiate between natural image and tampered image. *Ng et al.* [8] improved the performance of bicoherence features [1] to detect spliced image. *Avcibas et al.* [9] constructed a classifier by employing image quality metrics as the essential features. The rationale of using this metrics is to examine different quality aspects of an image impacted during manipulations. *Bayram et al.* [10] exploited the feature correlations between bit planes and binary texture characteristics within the bit planes. *Chen et al.* [11] extracted the image features by calculating the moment of wavelet characteristics function and phase congruency. *Dong et al.* [12] analyzed the spliced artifact on image run-length representation and edge statistics. *Sutthiwan et al.* [13] employed support vector machine (SVM) to train image features as well. The image model is based on Markovian Rake Transform (MRT) on image luminance.

1.3 Challenge Issue

We classify all aforementioned outstanding work into two types of problem: duplicated region, and image tampering detection. In the former case, since the duplicated regions are taken from other region(s) of the same image, one only need the given targeted image, as reported in [6],[14]. For the latter case, we classify the approach into two categories: approximation-based, and machine learning-based approach. Akin to duplicated region problem, approximation-based approaches [3],[4],[5] also require a single image only to evaluate its authenticity. Unlike approximation-based, machine learning-based approach requires as many as possible images in the dataset in order to have an adequate various tampering pattern. These schemes, however, are computationally inefficient. In addition, most previous researches cannot precisely decide from which the spliced/tampered regions is derived. They are only able to determine whether the given image is tampered without further justification.

Inspired by Ng [15], it is more reasonable to exploit only similar images to assess an image authenticity. Despite image tampering is often imperceptible, it introduces specific correlations. When it is detected, it can be used as evidence of digital tampering. Motivated by Liu and Iskander [16], we formulate a tampered image problem as measuring the displacement occurred between given and reference images, which is conducted by investigating their correlations. Thus, the challenge issue lies on how to incorporate and describe the form of these correlations to assess the authenticity of an image.

1.4   Contribution

We propose a novel scheme for spliced image detection which involves only the images that are similar, in terms of color, texture, or shape, to the targeted image as depicted in Fig 1. To retrieve these similar images, we directly employ a content-based image retrieval (CBIR) technique. CBIR is a popular scheme in image retrieval, we do not need discuss in detail in this article since it is beyond the scope of our research. In order to have a meaningful scheme, we assume that these similar images are definitely authentic ones. Further, based on its results, we select only the representative images as references. On the other side, given a targeted image, an edge detector is employed to detect edge pixels expected to contain any spliced artifacts. Assume that spliced regions introduce discontinuity in their intensities. To find accurately the spliced artifacts, we exploit an interpolation technique to reconstruct the gray-value at the both-side locations nearby the detected edge pixels. By utilizing membership functions, the error rate of the intensities' reconstruction is used to determine whether the artifacts fall into spliced candidates. Afterward, the peaks of correlation coefficient of spliced region candidates are computed throughout reference images.

We fundamentally adopt digital image correlation (DIC) concept to investigate the authenticity of an image. DIC is a classic pattern recognition technique to obtain information by measuring deformation and motion of rigid body.

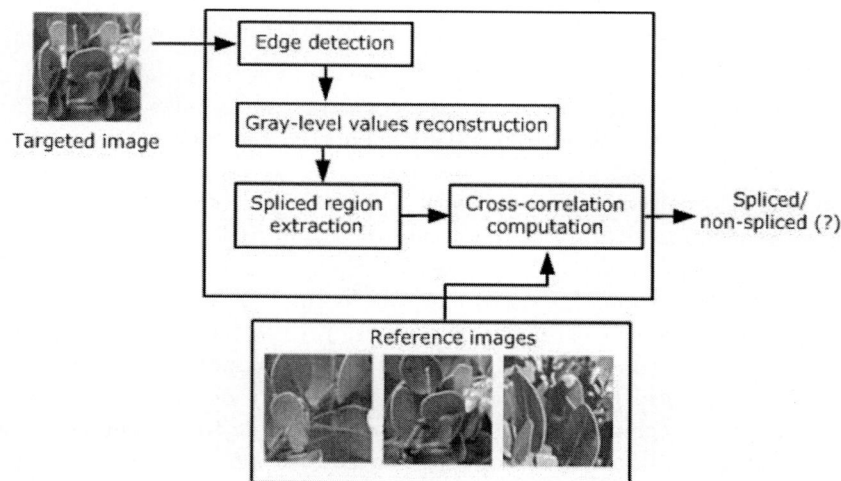

Fig. 1. General scheme of tampered image detection

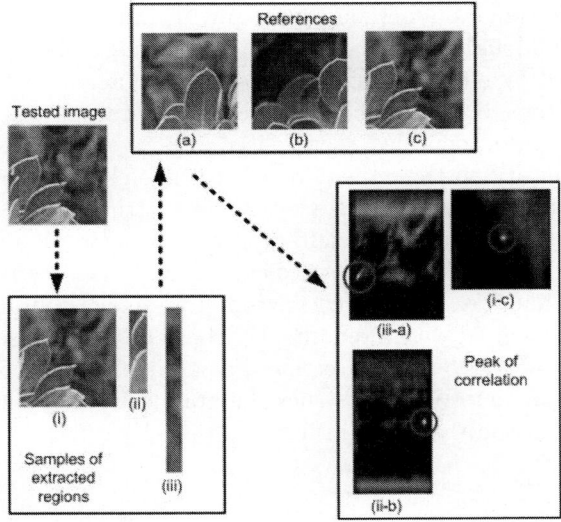

Fig. 2. Illustration of image authenticity evaluation

DIC is based on correlation function to locate the best matching position of two images thus predicting movements [16]. Thereby, investigating the peak of cross-correlation is the core point of our scheme.

Figure 2 is a description of our basic idea to determine an image's authenticity. Given a tested image and N reference images that are similar to a tested image. Assume the tested image is a spliced one, and its spliced regions can completely be extracted. By locating the peaks of cross-correlation coefficient in reference images, it can be used as evidence of tampering. The peak of cross-correlation of each image (i), (ii), and (iii) are discovered in one of the reference images, respectively (the brightest point in image (i-c), (ii-b), and (iii-a)). It reflects that the targeted image contains other image regions and the image is considered as a spliced image.

Let us assume that an extracted region is not the spliced one. Even if there is no truly corresponding entity in the reference images, there are high possibilities of some peaks of correlation coefficient. Based on this condition, we define the following definition.

Definition 1 (suspected spliced-image). Suppose there are n extracted regions $A= \{a_1, a_2, \cdots, a_n\}$ derived from a given image I, and m reference images $B=\{b_1, b_2, \cdots, b_m\}$. Assume that there exists at least one a_i such that $a_i \subseteq b_j$ for $i=1, \cdots, n$ and $j=1, \cdots, m$. Then, image I is said to be a suspected spliced-image.

2 Spliced Image Detection Methods

2.1 Interpolation-Based Approach

Several kinds of interpolation formula are used throughout the literature, such as the bilinear interpolation method, the polynomial interpolation method and the bicubic spline interpolation method. In the present work, the bilinear interpolation method is used and can be expressed as linear interpolation in x-direction, and then, proceed by interpolating in the y-direction again.

We consider the spliced artifact is introduced as line or edge features. Suppose an edge has been identified. The spliced region may be viewed as an area in which the intensity on the either side of the edge changes abruptly. To confirm the occurrence of this inconsistency, we reconstruct the intensity levels at areas on both side of the edge (i.e. left/right or top/bottom), and calculate the prediction error by subtracting the predicted intensity values from its original values. Figure 3 illustrates a zoomed section of an image containing a straight edge segment highlighted with a red line. We consider the edge segments are detected in horizontal and vertical direction. Each blue dot corresponds to a pixel along the edge segment. We reconstruct the gray-level value on two locations, e.g. the edge pixels and the pixels in between the edge pixel.

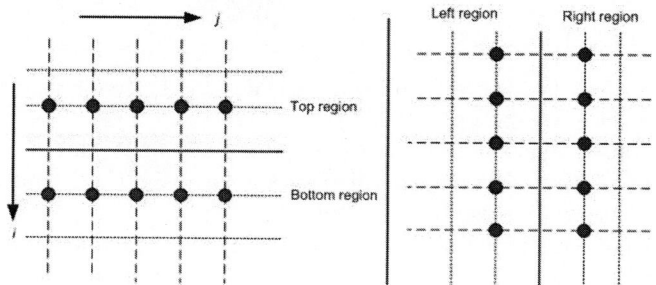

Fig. 3. The left column shows an edge detected and its adjacent pixels in horizontal direction and the right column is an edge introduced in vertical direction.

2.2   Spliced Region Identification

We define a spliced image as an image derived by combining image portions from different images without further post-processing such as smoothing of boundaries among different portions. Of course, the artifacts introduced by the splicing process may be almost imperceptible.

Given a targeted image, $I_t(x,y)$ for $x = 0, 1, ..., M$ - 1 and $y = 0, 1,..., N$ - 1. Our objective is to obtain one or more spliced region candidates derived from $I_t(x,y)$ in which their peaks will be investigated throughout reference images. In doing so, edge detection is firstly exploited to detect the spliced artifacts. In case of spliced artifact detection, Roberts cross operator performs better than that of Canny, Prewit, or Sobel; thus it is used in the current work. It implements masks of size 2×2 with a diagonal preference.

Let us denote $I_e(x,y)$, where the component of $I_e(x,y)$ is in $\{0,1\}$, is the resulting of edge-detected image. We then construct two edge matrices E_h and E_v to be a $m \times n$, $n=3$, $m \in [0, L\text{-}1]$, where L is the number of detected edges. E_h and E_v respectively contains detected edges in both horizontal and vertical direction whose $(i,1)^{th}$, $(i,2)^{th}$, and $(i,3)^{th}$ entries represents the row/column index, onset of an edge, and the number of edge pixels, correspondingly.

It is expected that the spliced portions will demonstrate their prediction error in large difference, thus making the splicing detection more efficient. Thus, we conduct interpolation on detected edges as described in the preceding section. Then, we compute the residual error prediction. As a result, there are two residual matrices, MSE_p and MSE_{ratio}. On the next section, these error prediction values are evaluated using membership functions to classify whether the edges on both E_h and E_v fall into spliced artifacts.

Once the spliced artifacts identified, we obtain two candidates spliced region. To verify the spliced condition, the peak of correlation between each candidate spliced region and reference images is computed. Throughout, we use the normalized correlation coefficient (NCC) as a measure of similarity. The NCC between two images f and t is given as follows:

$$\varsigma(u,v) = \frac{\sum_{x,y} \left[f(x,y) - \overline{f}_{u,v}\right]\left[t(x-u,y-v) - \overline{t}\right]}{\sqrt{\sum_{x,y}\left[f(x,y) - \overline{f}_{u,v}\right]^2 \sum_{x,y}\left[t(x-u,y-v) - \overline{t}\right]^2}} \qquad (1)$$

where f is the reference image , $\overline{t}$ is the mean of the spliced region, and $\overline{f}$ is the mean of $f(x,y)$ in the region under the spliced region. The correlation coefficient ς is in the range $[0,1]$, with larger value indicating higher level of similarity. ς close to -1 means the matching entities are inverse of each other, ς close to 1 refers to matching entities are exactly the same, and $\varsigma=0$ is an indication of no relationship between the matching entities. As previously mentioned, the peak of correlation function may occur among non-corresponding entities in the reference images. Therefore, it is necessary to determine a threshold τ for coefficient ς above which the splicing is accepted.

2.3   Statistics-Based Approach

Fundamentally, it is somewhat difficult to precisely identify the spliced region. The spliced artifacts are often introduced hardly noticeable. This issue tends to fall into uncertainty problems. Further, as motivated by Ye et al in [17], we consider that exploiting membership function is the most adequate in representing uncertainty in measurement.

In order to identify the spliced region, a single prediction error, an acceptable prediction error ratio, and a number of occurrence are respectively investigated for verification. The following are the rules constructed based on the observations:

Rule 1: The candidate spliced region should have an extreme prediction error and large deviation, whereas the prediction error of a non-tampered region is in average value.

Rule 2: The spliced region candidate should have a prediction error ratio in an extreme value and have large deviation, whereas the ratio of a non-tampered region is in small value.

Rule 3: The spliced region candidate should have an extreme occurrence and large deviation, whereas the non-tampered region occurs in an average amount.

We use sigmoid and Gaussian membership functions to calculate the degree of membership for each rule. Degree of rule 1 is defined as:

$$\mu_1^E = \begin{cases} 1 & \text{if } e \geq \gamma_{mse}, \\ \dfrac{1}{1+exp\left(-\dfrac{(e-\gamma_{mse})^2}{(e-\alpha_{mse})\sigma_{mse}^2}\right)} & \text{otherwise} \end{cases} \tag{2}$$

where e is a *mean squared error* (MSE) of MSE_p, γ_{mse} is a maximum acceptable value of MSE, α_{mse} is a minimum acceptable value of MSE, and σ_{mse}^2 refers to a standard deviation. The following is degree of non-tampered region formulated by using Gaussian function.

$$\mu_1^{av} = exp\left(-\frac{\left(e-\overline{E}\right)^2}{e.\sigma_{mse}^2}\right) \tag{3}$$

where $\overline{E}$ is an average of acceptable MSE.
   Degree of rule 2 is devised as:

$$\mu_2^E = \begin{cases} 1 & \text{if } r \geq \gamma_{ratio}, \\ \dfrac{1}{1+exp\left(-\dfrac{(r-\gamma_{ratio})^2}{(r-\alpha_{ratio})\sigma_{ratio}^2}\right)} & \text{otherwise} \end{cases} \tag{4}$$

where r is the MSE ratio of MSE_{ratio}, γ_r is a maximum acceptable value of MSE ratio, α_r is a minimum acceptable value of MSE ratio, and σ_r^2 refers to standard deviation. The following is degree of non-tampered region:

$$\mu_2^{av} = exp\left(-\frac{\left(r-\overline{R}\right)^2}{r.\sigma_{ratio}^2}\right) \tag{5}$$

where $\overline{R}$ is an average of acceptable MSE ratio.
   Degree of rule 3 is expressed as:

$$\mu_3^E = \begin{cases} 1 & \text{if } oc \geq \gamma_{occ}, \\ \dfrac{1}{1+exp\left(-\dfrac{(oc-\gamma_{occ})^2}{(oc-\alpha_{occ})\sigma_{occ}^2}\right)} & \text{otherwise} \end{cases} \tag{6}$$

where oc is the number of occurrence of an extracted edge pixel, γ_{oc} is a maximum acceptable value of occurrence, α_{oc} is a minimum acceptable value of occurrence, and σ_{oc}^2 refers to standard deviation. The following is degree of non-tampered region:

$$\mu_3^{av} = exp\left(-\frac{\left(oc-\overline{OC}\right)^2}{oc.\sigma_{occ}^2}\right) \tag{7}$$

where $\overline{OC}$ is an average of acceptable occurrence. Then, these rules are combined to calculate degree of authenticity and spliced:

$$\begin{cases} D_S = max\left\{\mu_1^E, \mu_2^E, \mu_3^E\right\} \\ D_A = max\left\{min\left(1 - \mu_1^E, 1 - \mu_2^E, 1 - \mu_3^E\right), min\left(\mu_1^{av}, \mu_2^{av}, \mu_3^{av}\right)\right\} \end{cases} \quad (8)$$

where D_S is the degree of spliced, and D_A is the degree of authenticity. If $D_S > D_A$, then the region is identified as a spliced one; otherwise it is considered as non-spliced region.

We observe that spliced features tend to exhibit an outlier value over others. Thus, to determine those γ_s and α_s values, we calculate an outlier and set up the values ranged in outlier areas. Let Q1, Q2, and Q3 be quartile, *interquartile range* (IQR) is computed as Q3-Q1. Then, outliers are values that are:

$$\begin{cases} 1.5\,(IQR) > Q3 \\ 1.5\,(IQR) < Q1 \end{cases}. \quad (9)$$

3   Experimental Results

We are finally ready to present some experiments with our proposed scheme to validate our work on a set of generated forgery images with spliced regions.

3.1   Synthesized Spliced Images

Spliced images are generated based on uncompressed BMP grayscale images of size 128×128 pixels provided by Columbia DVMM Research Lab [18]. It consists of 933 authentic and 912 spliced image blocks. Each class is divided into five categories, i.e. smooth, texture, smooth-smooth, smooth-texture, and texture-texture. However, all spliced region on provided images are roughly derived from the image itself. To adjust with our problem statement,we have to construct different spliced image dataset. We collect 218 authentic from provided images and construct 218 spliced images based on authentic ones. For each authentic image, we first retrieve the similar images resulted from Content-Based Image Retrieval (CBIR) system, and select them as references. Then, we randomly choose the region from references for splicing. To yield an unnoticeable artifact, the size of spliced region is arbitrary. Seven examples from total 218 spliced images are shown in Fig 4.

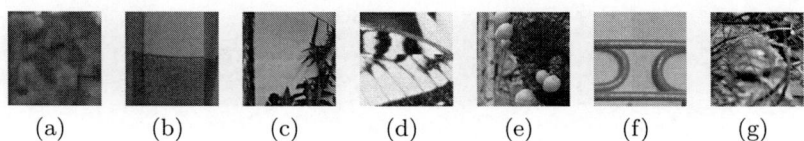

   (a)   (b)   (c)   (d)   (e)   (f)   (g)

Fig. 4. Seven examples of synthesized spliced images used in our experiments. The first five images consist of one spliced region (a)-(e), and the last two images have two spliced regions (f)-(g).

3.2   Spliced Image Identification

Consider the following four categories: True positives (TP) are examples correctly identified as spliced images. False positive (FP) refers to non-spliced examples incorrectly identified as spliced images. True negative (TN) corresponds to non-spliced examples correctly identified as a non-spliced image. Finally, False negative (FN) refers to spliced examples incorrectly identified as non-spliced images. We define the True Positive Rate (TPR) as the fraction of spliced images that are correctly identified, i.e. TPR= TP/(TP+FN), and False Positive Rate (FPR) as the fraction of non-spliced images that are misclassified as spliced images, i.e. FPR=FP/(FP+TN). We do not compare the performance by using the proposed scheme with that reported in [7,8,9,11,13] because we exploit a completely different scheme.

We evaluate the images, either spliced or authentic images, into three categories: smooth, texture, and smooth-texture. The total number of samples used in experiment is 435 images. The parameters are configured as follows: we set up experimentally the parameter γ_{mse} and α_{mse} to be 6581.31 and 3023, respectively. In terms of ratio, the parameter γ_r and α_r is correspondingly set to be 120 and 44. And, we let respectively γ_{oc} and α_{oc} be 25 and 15 for occurrence. These parameters are investigated by using (9). The threshold τ is set to 0.7213.

Figure 5 is an example of detection result of a given spliced image. The spliced region is located on top region of the targeted image. Then it is followed by three reference images selected from CBIR results. By exploiting (8), the spliced artifact is identified. Since we cannot differentiate which region is the non-spliced and which one is the spliced one, we extract these both regions. Once the extracted spliced region is obtained, we compute its correlation to each of reference images. The resulting peak values corresponding to the three reference images are respectively 0.9483, 0.6106, and 0.6599. The peak of correlation with respect to the first reference image is depicted in the last figure. Thus, we can conclude that the given image is a spliced one in which its portion is derived from the first reference image by investigating its peak of correlation value.

The resulting ROC curve in various types is shown in Fig 6. For images with smooth type, an average of 86.25% of the spliced images are detected with an average of 0.2 false positives. For images with texture type, an average of 87.18% of the spliced images are detected with an average of 0.22 false positives. For smooth-texture type, an average of 83.33% of the spliced images are detected with an average of 0.12 false positives.

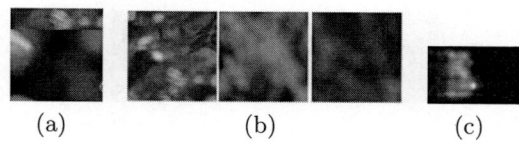

(a)   (b)   (c)

Fig. 5. (a) A targeted image, (b) reference images , and (c) the peak of correlation corresponds to the spliced region candidate. The resulting peak value ς is equal to 0.9483 that corresponds to the first reference image, while the other two peak values are under the threshold τ.

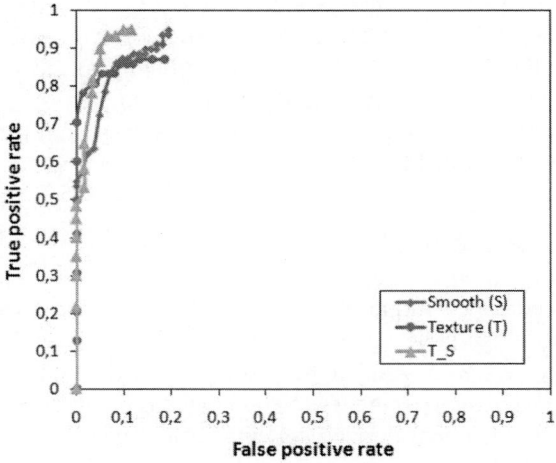

Fig. 6. ROC curve of various image types. It confirms that the proposed scheme performs well for smooth-texture type.

Our scheme principally relies on how accurate the detector algorithm identifies the spliced artifacts. The high values of false positive are mostly affected by undetected edges or inaccurate extraction. We observe that Robert's detector utilizes 2-D mask with a diagonal preference which means that diagonal edge direction is of interest. Thus, images that occur with various directions in intensity are likely undetectable.

3.3   Spliced Region Identification Accurateness

Definition 2 (suspicious region). Suppose the synthesized and extracted spliced region are $S(m,n)$ and $E(x,y)$, respectively, where $m=0,1,\ldots, M - 1$, $n=0, 1,\ldots, N - 1$, $x=0, 1,\ldots, X - 1$, and $y=0,1,\ldots, Y$-1. Assume that $S(m,n)$ includes $E(x,y)$ where $X{\leq}M$ and $Y{\leq}N$. $E(x,y)$ is said to be suspicious region if its correlation coefficient with $S(m,n)$ is above specific threshold τ.

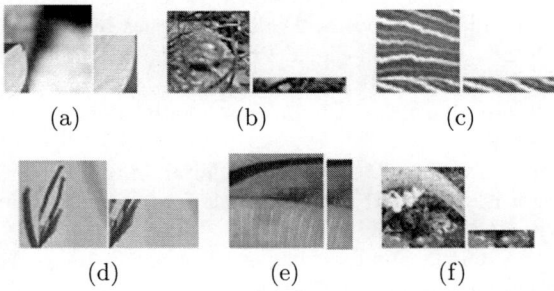

Fig. 7. Examples of synthesized spliced images and its corresponding extracted regions subjected to suspicious regions (a-c) and inaccurate region (d-f)

The number of extracted spliced-region achieves 88.53% (193 of 218 spliced images). Based on Definition 2, the number of relatively accurate spliced region approximately achieves 92.75% (179 of 193 spliced images). If the spliced artifacts have reasonably similar intensity to the authentic image, all the statistics values tend to fall into authentic one. The examples of both accurate and inaccurate spliced region are given in Fig 7.

4   Concluding Remark

We have described a technique with a different point of view for detecting a common form of image splicing. The main technique adopts image correlation concept to locate the source of spliced portions. Central design of the technique is to exploit only the correlated images to the targeted one rather than various image scenes. Results from synthesized splicing experiments state that the scheme can detect most splicing artifacts, with relatively few false positives. We have also shown that the technique can reveal the source of splicing when the spliced occurred. The proposed technique can be widely applied to image forensics.

Acknowledgments. The first author is partially supported by Doctor Course Scholarship and Grant of Graduate School of ISEE of Kyushu University for Supporting Students' Overseas Traveling. Moreover, research support for the first author is fully provided by the Directorate General of Higher Education, Ministry of National Education, Indonesia. The second author acknowledges support provided by Grant NRF-2011-013-D00121 from the National Research Foundation of Korea.

References

1. Farid, H.: Detecting Digital Forgeries Using Bispectral Analysis. Technical Report AIM-1657, AI Lab, Massachusetts Institute of Technology (1999)
2. Ng, T.T., Chang, S.F., Lin, C.Y., Sun, Q.: Passive-blind Image Forensics. In: Zeng, W., Yu, H., Lin, C.Y. (eds.) Multimedia Security Technologies for Digital Rights, ch. 15, pp. 383–412. Academic Press, Missouri (2006)
3. Popescu, A.C., Farid, H.: Exposing Digital Forgeries by Detecting Traces of Resampling. IEEE Transaction on Signal Processing 53(2), 758–767 (2005)
4. Prasad, S., Ramakrishnan, K.R.: On Resampling Detection and its Application to Detect Image Tampering. In: IEEE International Conference on Multimedia and Expo, ICME (2006)
5. Ye, S., Sun, Q., Chang, E.C.: Detecting Digital Image Forgeries by Measuring Inconsistencies of Blocking Artifact. In: IEEE International Conference on Multimedia and Expo, ICME (2007)
6. Pan, X., Lyu, S.: Region Duplication Detection using Image Feature Matching. IEEE Transaction on Information Forensics and Security 5(4), 857–867 (2010)
7. Farid, H., Lyu, S.: Higher-order Wavelet Statistics and their Application to Digital Forensics. In: IEEE Workshop on Statistical Analysis in Computer Vision (in Conjunction with CVPR) (2003)

8. Ng, T.T., Chang, S.F., Sun, Q.: Blind Detection of Photomontage using Higher Order Statistics. In: IEEE International Symposium on Circuits and Systems, vol. 5, pp. 688–691 (2004)
9. Avcibas, I., Bayram, S., Memon, N., Sankur, B., Ramkumar, M.: A Classifier Design for Detecting Image Manipulations. In: IEEE International Conference on Image Processing, ICIP (2004)
10. Bayram, S., Avcibas, I., Sankur, B., Memon, N.: Image Manipulation Detection. Journal of Electronic Imaging 15(4), 041102 (2006)
11. Chen, W., Shi, Y.Q., Su, W.: Image Splicing Detection using 2-D Phase Congruency and Statistical Moments of Characteristic Function. In: Society of Photo-Optical Instrumentation Engineers (SPIE) Conference Series, vol. 6505, art. No. 65050R. SPIE, Washington (2007)
12. Dong, J., Wang, W., Tan, T., Shi, Y.Q.: Run-Length and Edge Statistics Based Approach for Image Splicing Detection. In: Kim, H.-J., Katzenbeisser, S., Ho, A.T.S. (eds.) IWDW 2008. LNCS, vol. 5450, pp. 76–87. Springer, Heidelberg (2009)
13. Sutthiwan, P., Shi, Y.Q., Zhao, H., Ng, T.T., Su, W.: Markovian Rake Transform for Digital Image Tampering Detection. In: Shi, Y.Q., Emmanuel, S., Kankanhalli, M.S., Chang, S.-F., Radhakrishnan, R., Ma, F., Zhao, L. (eds.) Transactions on DHMS VI. LNCS, vol. 6730, pp. 1–17. Springer, Heidelberg (2011)
14. Wang, W., Farid, H.: Exposing digital forgeries in video by detecting duplication. In: Proceeding ACM Workshop on MMSec, Dallas, TX (2007)
15. Ng, T.T.: Statistical and Geometric Methods for Passive-blind Image Forensics. Ph.D. Dissertation, Columbia University (2007)
16. Liu, J., Iskander, M.: Digital Image Correlation. In: Iskander, M. (ed.) Modeling with Transparent Soils, SSGG, pp. 137–164. Springer, Heidelberg (2010)
17. Ye, S.M., Sun, Q.B., Chang, E.C.: Error resilient content-based image authentication over wireless channel. In: IEEE Int. Symp. Circuits and Systems, ISCAS, Kobe, Japan, pp. 2707–2710 (2005)
18. Ng, T.T., Chang, S., Sun, Q.: A data set of authentic and spliced image blocks. In: ADVENT Technical Report 203-2004-3. Columbia University (June 2004), http://www.ee.columbia.edu/trustfoto

A Multimodal Approach for Online Estimation of Subtle Facial Expression

Xiaohong Xiang and Mohan S. Kankanhalli

School Of Computing,National University Of Singapore,
Singapore, 117417
{xiangxiaohong,mohan}@comp.nus.edu.sg

Abstract. Recognizing subtle emotional expression of human is a challenging and interesting problem in the field of human computer interaction. Multimodality is a prospective way to help solve this problem. Therefore, in this paper, we first take advantage of a novel "sparse representation" approach to compute the matching degree of current facial expression to each basic emotion class. Concurrently, we also use an eye tracker to obtain the instant pupillary response, which gives us clues to the subtle emotion. We combine the results of facial expression and pupillary information, take into account the previous emotional state to classify the current subtle emotional expression. Finally, a Markov Model is used to compute a directed graph to model the changes of human's emotion. The experimental results show that: First, the sparse representation has a good classification rate on facial expression; Second, the fusion of facial expression, pupillary size and previous emotional state is a promising strategy for analyzing subtle expression.

Keywords: subtle facial expression, eye pupil, online.

1 Introduction

Human Centered Computing is an emerging field which aims to provide natural ways for humans to use computers as aids. It is argued that for the computer to be able to interact with humans, it needs to have the communication skills of humans. One of these skills is the ability to understand the emotional state of people. In humans, emotion fundamentally involves "physiological arousal, expressive behaviors, and conscious experience" [12]. Facial expression is the most expressive way humans display their emotions. Therefore, extracting and validating emotional cues through analysis of users' facial expressions is of high importance for improving the level of interaction in man machine communication systems.

A facial expression results from one or more motions or positions of the muscles of the face [2]. These movements, including both global motions like head rotation and local motions like eye or mouth movements, all convey the emotional state of the individual to observers. Ekman [2] found six classical categories, referred to as the universal emotions: happiness, sadness, surprise, fear, anger, and disgust. However, humans rarely display those emotions in a clear unambiguous

W. Lin et al. (Eds.): PCM 2012, LNCS 7674, pp. 402–413, 2012.

manner [4]. Subtle facial expressions are more often involuntary as expressions are closely related to emotion. It is nearly impossible to avoid expressions for certain emotions, even when it would be strongly desirable to do so. In other words, there always exist some subtle cues, no matter how unnoticed they are. The current existing approaches to measure facial expression are categorized into three characteristics [18]: the location of facial actions, the intensity of facial actions, and the dynamics of facial actions. However, it is difficult to acquire these three characteristics of subtle facial expression. Additionally, in fact that people do not always portray extreme facial expressions in normal situations. Therefore, there is an urgent need for effective computational methods for analyzing subtle facial expression which are brief, precise and appropriate for an online system.

The idea that the eyes are clues to emotions - "windows of the soul," as the French poet Guillaume de Salluste wrote - is almost commonplace in literature and everyday language [1]. A person's eyes can reveal much about how they are feeling, or what they are thinking. For example, the blink rate can show how nervous or at ease a person may be, and even the stress levels the person is feeling [6]. Among these eyes' responses, pupillary response is a physiological response that varies the size of the pupil, either resulting in constriction or dilation (expansion), via activation or deactivation of the iris dilator muscle. There are a variety of causes to result in changes on pupil's size, such as an involuntary reflex reaction to exposure or inexposure to light, and interest in the subject of attention. Specifically, dilated pupils indicate greater affection or attraction, while constricted pupils send a colder signal [1]. Thus, the pupillary dilation and constriction of eyes is a significant cue to convey some messages of emotion to observers. Moreover, the pupillary reaction is involuntary which can not be faked [11]. Therefore, taking advantage of eye pupil data into analyzing subtle expression is preferred. We find that the concurrent use of multiple modalities: facial expression and eye pupil data is a viable strategy.

In this paper, we propose an approach for online estimation of subtle expression exploiting multiple modalities: facial expression, pupil size and previous emotional state. The whole framework of our approach is shown in Fig 1. In this paper, our key contributions are:

- A novel sparsity-based and multimodalities method is proposed to analyze the subtle expressions of human. Compared to existing approaches of analyzing the subtle expression, our method is relatively simpler and faster.
- A novel concept to model person's emotion changes is proposed. This provides us a predictive estimation about the probabilities of transition among individual's emotions in the future research on analyzing individual's emotion.
- To the best of our knowledge, our paper is the first work to fuse facial expression, pupillary emotional response and previous emotion for analyzing the current emotional state of human.

This paper is organized as follows. Section 2 reviews the related work to serve as a preamble, and Section 3 describes the proposed methodology. Section 4 presents the experimental results of the proposed methodology, and finally, conclusions are drawn in Section 5.

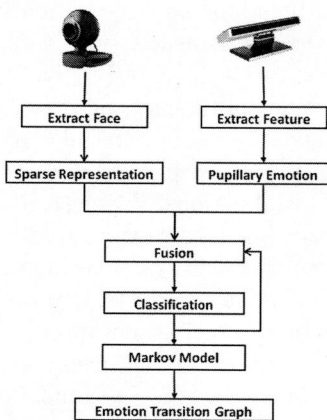

Fig. 1. The overall framework of our proposed approach

2 Related Work

2.1 Facial Expression Recognition

Many researchers have focused on facial expression recognition, and proposed a variety of methods to recognize human's facial expression. Cohn et al. [3] used a hierarchical optical flow method to automatically track feature points, and different discriminant functions in each facial region. Cohen et al. [10] proposed two approaches: Tree-Augmented-Naive Bayesian and multilevel Hidden Markov models to classify the facial expressions from the static and dynamic orientations respectively. Song et al. [15] exploited proposed a novel method based on Helmholtz-Hodge vector field decomposition to model subtle facial expressions. Park and Kim [18] used motion magnification to transform subtle expression into corresponding exaggerated ones. Pai and Chang [21] presented a novel facial expression recognition scheme based on extension theory. Sandbach et al. [23] proposed a method that exploited 3D motion-based features between frames of 3D facial geometry sequences for dynamic facial expression recognition. Ying et al. [20] proposed a new approach for facial expression recognition (FER) based on fusion of sparse representation. As far as we know, few researchers have focused on detecting subtle facial expressions, and they all are offline implementations.

2.2 Multimodal Human's Emotion Analysis

The research in analysis of human's emotion has seen a shift towards multi-modal analysis. Zeng et al. [13] presented their effort towards audio-visual HCI-related affect recognition, and used a voting method to combine the classification outputs from face and prosody modalities. Gunes and Piccardi [14] presented an approach to automatic visual emotion recognition from two modalities: expressive face and body gesture. Caridakis et al. [17] presented a multimodal approach for the recognition of eight emotions that integrated information from facial expressions, body movement and gestures and speech. Nicolaou et al. [22] proposed a method for continuous prediction of spontaneous affect from multiple cues and modalities in Valence-Arousal Space.

The emotion of people can be reflected by many channels: facial expression, body language, physiological signal, etc. As discussed above, the eyes also create the obvious and immediate cues that lead to the formation of impressions [16]. To the best of our knowledge, no earlier work has taken taken into account the eye pupillary response information to help infer the human's emotion state in facial expression analysis, especially used it as an aid to help analyze the subtle expressions.

3   Methodology

3.1   Modeling The Changes of Human's Emotion

Six basic emotion classes - happiness, sadness, surprise, fear, anger, and disgust - has been categorized by Ekman [2]. A person's emotional state can vary between these six basic emotions in time. However, we try to answer the question: is the probability of change from one emotional state to any other emotional state in a natural situation the same? Specifically, we also ask do people change from "happy" emotional state to the other extreme, "sad" emotional state suddenly? Is this a common case? And if it occurs often, what is the probability? Therefore, we propose a model to compute and represent these probabilities of transitions. In addition, we argue that the transition probabilities for different people are different. In order to solve this problem, we make the following assumptions:

- People can switch their emotions only among seven emotions: neutral, happiness, sadness, surprise, fear, anger, and disgust.
- There is only environmental (external) stimulation (ignoring biochemical (internal) stimulation), which means that if and only if there is an environmental stimulus, the switch of emotions occurs.
- People are initially in 'neutral' state.
- The switch of emotions is not sudden, that is, the current emotion is related to the emotion state at previous instant time.

Markov chain is the simplest model which is a stochastic model that assumes the Markov property, namely that, given the present state, the future and past states are independent. It models the state of a system with a random variable that changes through time. Fig 2 gives an example of Markov Chain. Therefore, the Markov chain is very suitable for modeling our problem.

Specifically, the seven emotional states are referred as the state space S. The switch of human's emotion has become the transition among emotional states in S along with time - t. Therefore, the transition probability of each pair is calculated by eq. (1).

$$P(s_i \rightarrow s_j) = \frac{\|s_i \rightarrow s_j\|}{\|s_i\|}, i, j \in 0, 1, 2, 3, 4, 5, 6 \tag{1}$$

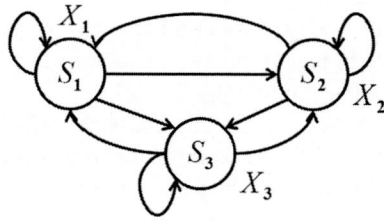

Fig. 2. A Markov Chain with 3 states (labeled S_1, S_2, S_3)

Here, s_i represents the i-th emotion. "$s_i \rightarrow s_j$" represents the event that the occurrence of emotional state s_j is following emotional state s_i (i.e, the switch from emotion s_i to emotion s_j); "$\|s_i \rightarrow s_j\|$" means the times of occurrence of the event - $s_i \rightarrow s_j$; "$\|s_i\|$" is the times of occurrence of s_i in entire sequence.

Therefore, based on the collection of prior knowledge of emotion switches, we use the equation (1) to compute the model graph. Finally, one directed graph for group and one special personal directed graph for each subject are created respectively.

3.2   Subtle Expression Analysis

Sparse Representation. The main idea of "sparse representation" is that the recognition of facial expression is converted to the reconstruction of a sparse signal. To quote Patterns [7], "When it comes to expressing emotions, members of widely different cultures have much in common,..., Such findings imply that beneath all the cultural complexity of mankind, there is a core of basic emotional expression that is understood all over the world." For a photograph of facial expression, the interpretations of different cultures people are in accord. We assume that there exists a common pattern for each facial expression to display expression separately. However, which and how the low dimensional features of a facial expression images are the most relevant for recognition? It is difficult to give a specific emotional pattern in terms of age, skin color, etc. Fortunately, sparse representation can overcome this problem as long as there are sufficient and overcomplete samples. Given a set of representative facial expression images for each emotion class can be found as the basic expression patterns of that emotion class, each facial expression image coming from that emotion class can be represented as a linear combination of the basic expression patterns.

We denote by $y \in \Re^D$ test facial expression image with i-th emotion, and $\{y_i^1, \cdots, y_i^k\}$ the k basic expression pattern images of i-th emotion space. Then the y can be represented by eq. (2).

$$y = y_i^1 \alpha_1 + y_i^2 \alpha_2 + \cdots + y_i^k \alpha_k$$
$$\doteq A_i \overrightarrow{\beta}_i, \quad \overrightarrow{\beta}_i \in \Re^k \tag{2}$$

$$\text{Where,} \quad A_i = [y_i^1, y_i^2, ..., y_i^k] \tag{3}$$
$$\beta_i = [\alpha_1, \alpha_2, ..., \alpha_k]^T \tag{4}$$

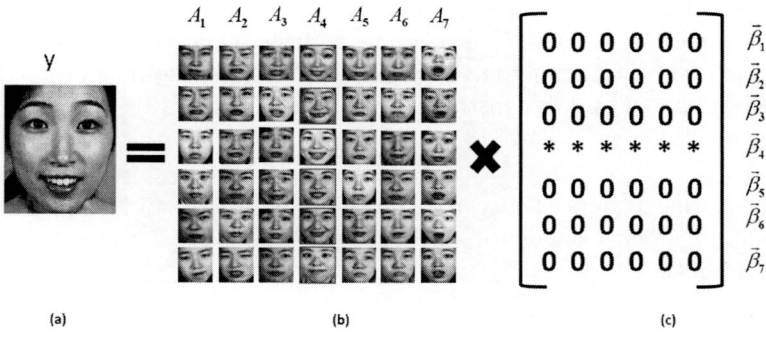

Fig. 3. One intuitive example for sparse representation of facial expression in the ideal situation. Fig 3(a): test 'happy' facial expression image; Fig 3 (b): one example of sample matrix A. Each column is corresponding to one emotion basis. From the top to bottom, the emotions of rows are anger, disgust, fear, happy, neutral, sad and surprise respectively. Fig 3 (c): sparse solution. In order to view conveniently, the sparse solution which should be a column vector is organized as a matrix, and each entry in it corresponds to the sample in Fig 3 (b). ('*' represents the nonzero value, and 'x' represents the product of matrices); All these facial expression images are from JAFFE database [5].

Here, we have to point out that for each emotion class, k can vary. If we suppose that a given test expression image of face can only be represented by those basic expression pattern images from the same emotion space-i, that is, only $\overrightarrow{\beta}_i$ is not zero vector. We can use the eq. (5) to summarize it. In addition, we provide an intuitive example about this concept as Fig 3.

$$y = A_1 \overrightarrow{\beta}_1 + A_2 \overrightarrow{\beta}_2 + \cdots + A_n \overrightarrow{\beta}_n = Ax \qquad (5)$$

$$\text{where,} \quad A = [A_1, \ldots, A_{i-1}, A_i, A_{i+1}, \ldots, A_n] \qquad (6)$$

$$x = [\overrightarrow{\beta}_1, \ldots, \overrightarrow{\beta}_{i-1}, \overrightarrow{\beta}_i, \overrightarrow{\beta}_{i+1}, \ldots, \overrightarrow{\beta}_n]^T$$
$$= [0 \ldots 0 * 0 \ldots 0]^T \in \Re^{nk} \qquad (7)$$

A is called the 'sample matrix', each column is a expression pattern, and the solution $x \in \Re^N$, $N = n \times k$, should be a sparse vector: $n-1$ of its entries should be zero, except for the ones associated with the correct emotion. '*' represents the nonzero entries $\overrightarrow{\beta}_i$. We can obtain solution x by solving the linear equation $y = Ax$ using Eq:

$$\ell^1 : x = \arg\min_x \|x\|_1, \ \text{subject to} \ y = Ax \qquad (8)$$

Ideally, the nonzero entries in x will be related to the columns of corresponding sample matrix A, and we can easily do the classification. However, noise and modeling error will result in separating the sparse entries into multiple classes. Thus, considering the global sparse representation, we classify test facial expression image based on how well the sparse entries associated with the patterns of each emotion space. Furthermore, for each emotion, we can construct a temporary image to represent it based on the sparse solution. Specifically, we define a new function δ_i that: for $x \in \Re^N$, $\delta_i(x) \in \Re^N$ is a new vector whose nonzero entries correspond to the coefficients belonging to i-th class in x. The temporary image for i-th facial expression denoted by I_i is constructed using the equation (9).

$$I_i = A * \delta_i \tag{9}$$

In addition, the difference between original feature image y and temporary image I_i is named 'Sparse Confidence' denoted by SC_i. Finally, we use the following eq. (10) to obtain it.

$$SC_i = \|y - I_i\|_2 \tag{10}$$

Eyes' Pupillary Response. As mentioned in previous section, combining different informative cues to analyze humans' subtle emotion is preferred, since humans rarely display extreme facial expressions on their faces. "eye tracking and pupil size variation can provide useful cues to discriminate emotional states" [11]. So taking advantage of eye tracking and pupil size into analyzing humans' emotion is a possible way. On the other hand, Hess [1] argue that "dilation and constriction of pupils reflect not only changes in light intensity but also ongoing mental activity" and extreme dilation to interesting or pleasing stimuli and extreme constriction to unpleasant or distasteful material. When people receive stimuli, the pupil size will change: dilation or constriction along with the changes of stimuli. And one key point or fact is that people can not control their pupillary response. Thus, the pupil size can provide a more reliable cue for analyzing human emotional state even when people try to hide or control their expression such as facial expression. On the other hand, there is considerable variation in the maximum pupil size in any human age group [8]. Therefore, it is not reasonable to use a single and fixed value to represent the pupil size of all people. The definition of dilation or constriction of pupil of each person also should be different.

Algorithm 1. The Overall Algorithm For Recognition Of Subtle Expression

1. **INPUT:**
   - 'Sparse Confidence' values - SCs
   - Previous emotional state - E_0
   - The current pupil emotion - E_p
2. SWITCH (E_p)
   - CASE NEUTRAL:
     E_c = 'neutral'
   - CASE DILATION:
     E = the set of positive stimuli, GOTO (3).
   - CASE CONSTRICTION:
     E = the set of negative stimuli, GOTO (3).
3. IF $E_0 \in E : E_c = E_0$
   ELSE GOTO (4).
4. $E_c = \arg\min(SCs)$ *in* E.
5. **OUTPUT:** E_c

$$\begin{cases} Neutral & |\Lambda - \mu| \leq 2\sigma \\ Dilation & \Lambda - \mu > 2\sigma \\ Constriction & \mu - \Lambda > 2\sigma \end{cases} \tag{11}$$

We use the equation (11) to quantitatively define the dilation and constriction of pupil size for individuals. μ and σ represent the mean and standard variation of individual pupil size in neutral stimuli respectively, and Λ represent the instant pupil size of a person.

Recognition of Emotion. Based on the 'Sparse Confidence' values (SCs) computed by eq. (10), we take into account the pupillary cue and the previous emotional state using the decision-level fusion. The overall algorithm is summarized in Algorithm (1). Finally, the result E_c of classification of emotion is fed into the Markov Chain to update the personal directed graph of transition among seven emotions. Upon obtaining sufficient individual data of emotion changes, the personal directed graph is closer to the approximate of 'real' transition directed graph.

4 Experimental Results

4.1 Modeling Human's Emotion Changes

In order to compute the group graph of average transition probabilities between seven basic emotions: happy, sad, fear, anger, surprise, disgust and neutral, we invite 10 people as our subjects (five males and five females). We download about 55 videos from Youtube and Tudou. We downloaded videos as we were unable to find any standard dataset of videos for emotion recognition. We assign an emotion label to a video, only if three participants all choose that emotion label. Finally, 27 videos have been selected and each emotion class has three videos. We concatenate these videos into one long video of 23 mins and 14 seconds. The ten participants were seated in front of a common camera of a solution of 640 x 480 and required to show their facial expressions in a natural way. An emotion

Table 1. The transition probability matrices for group and one person respectively. 'EM' = emotion, 'NE' = neutral, 'HA' = happy, 'SU' = surprise, 'AN' = anger, 'DI' = disgust, 'FE' = fear, and 'SA' = sad. Each element $p_{i,j}$ represents the transition probability from ith emotion to jth emotion. Here, all values are $100 * $ probability.

EM	NE	HA	SU	AN	DI	FE	SA
NE	75.58	0.30	0.53	9.73	1.29	0.53	12.03
HA	0.13	91.95	1.49	1.34	0.89	3.09	1.11
SU	0.39	1.19	89.16	0.28	0.34	1.53	7.10
AN	8.79	2.00	0.48	71.14	6.45	0.95	10.18
DI	1.69	1.71	0.73	8.09	82.34	0.94	4.49
FE	1.67	13.44	6.57	2.99	2.33	64.53	8.47
SA	4.06	0.67	4.43	3.71	1.27	1.13	84.72

application which is developed by Sebe group [9] is used to record their emotions along with time. The classification obtained from the emotion application is manually verified to eliminate the classification error by the application. The collection of data is fed into our Markov Model to compute a group directed graph model representing the average transition probabilities among seven basic emotions as shown in Table 1 and one personal directed graph model for each subject by the method we propose.

4.2   Sparse Representation in Analyzing Facial Expression

We use the Japanese Female Facial Expression (JAFFE) Database [5] to do the experiments of sparse representation of facial expressions. Because the choice of sample matrix is still a challenge in compressive sampling area [19], random generation is one way to choose the basic expression pattern images from database for us. Therefore, we totally generate 250 sample matrices, and 16000 experiments have been done based on different sparse level parameter in sparse representation. Of course, these sample matrices have overlap. For each emotion, we find the largest classification rate, and they are organized in a confusion matrix as shown in table 2.

From table 2, we can see that based on different sample matrices, all of the best classification rates for each emotion are over 85% in person-independent experiment. Moreover, the classification rates of 'anger' and 'fear' for person-independent are even over 90%. Specially, the results on the recognition of emotions: Fear, Surprise, Disgust, Anger has the best performance in person-independent experiments of facial expression recognition with JAFFE database. These results convince us that the sparse representation of facial expression would have higher performance on larger database for some other 'optimal' sample matrices.

4.3   Experimental Results for Subtle Facial Expression Analysis

For our experiment to determine subtle expression, we use the videos mentioned in the previous section. These videos have been classified under different emotional tags: happy, sad, surprise, anger, fear, disgust and neutral. We try to use those videos to stimulate the subject's emotion. Here, we have to point out that it must be the first time for the subject to watch these videos, so that their responses are direct, reliable and authentic, required for testing our approach.

Table 2. Person-independent confusion matrix for classifying facial expressions using sparse representation

Emotion	Happy	Surprise	Sad	Anger	Disgust	Fear	Neutral
Happy	**83.87**	57.14	58.07	60.00	65.52	62.50	56.67
Surprise	41.94	**89.29**	32.26	33.33	34.48	40.63	36.67
Sad	61.29	53.57	**83.87**	66.67	65.52	62.50	53.33
Anger	67.74	32.14	38.71	**90.00**	44.83	56.25	16.67
Disgust	12.90	25.00	9.68	20.00	**89.66**	15.63	36.67
Fear	25.81	32.14	32.26	43.33	48.78	**93.75**	26.67
Neutral	64.52	28.57	51.61	50.00	37.93	56.25	**86.67**

The camera we use in the experiment is a common camera of 640 x 480 solution. The eye-tracker we use is the product of SMI group. The eye-tracker uses 250 Hz to capture the diameters of pupils.

We design two experiments for different goals. In the first experiment, the subject is required to be seated in front of the camera and eye-tracker to watch the videos from each of the emotional tags and display their natural emotions. When the subject finishes watching one video, she is also required to state her emotional state when she is watching that video. If and only if the emotion declared by the subject is in accord with the video's emotion, then the corresponding experimental results can be used. This is because different people display different emotions for the same video. Thus, this step is to make sure the experimental results are reliable. After that, the experimental results corresponding to exaggerated facial expressions are eliminated since we aim to test the classification rate of subtle facial expression. In the second experiment, the subject is required to display wrong facial expression, that is, the emotional expressions on face are not the 'real' emotions she is feeling. Finally, the experimental results of two experiments are shown in the table 3. From the table 3, we can see that the ability to tell the 'real' emotion of humans reaches 0.9158 by our approach. On the other hand, all of the recognitions of 'surprise', and 'neutral' subtle facial expressions are over 90%. Compared to the results in table 2, the performances of recognizing 'surprise', and 'neutral' emotions get improvements with the help of eye pupil information. The detected images of other emotions after we eliminate the expressive images are very rare, so the results of these emotions are not listed in this table.

Table 3. The experimental results for the proposed subtle facial expression recognition method. $N_{detected}$ represents the total number of captured subtle facial expression images. $N_{correct}$ represents the number of subtle expression images which are recognized correctly. EP_2 represents the second experiment that tests the ability to tell the 'real' emotion.

Emotion	Happy	Surprise	Neutral	EP_2
$N_{detected}$	50	51	103	95
$N_{correct}$	13	50	95	87
Rate	26.00	98.04	92.00	91.58

5   Conclusions

In this paper, we propose a multimodal approach for online estimation of subtle facial expression. A novel sparsity-based facial expression analysis is proposed to recognize the facial expressions. To the best of our knowledge, our paper is the first work to fuse the facial expression, pupil size and previous emotional state to classify the subtle facial expressions. Additionally, we propose a novel concept to model the transition probabilities among the seven emotions. The establishment of the model can provide a predictive estimation about switch of emotions, which is good for the future research of individuals' emotion changes. The experimental results show that: first, the sparse representation has a good classification rate on facial expression. Second, the fusion of facial expression, pupil size and previous emotional state is a promising strategy for analyzing subtle expressions.

In the future, we will aim to find a better sample matrix which may provide higher classification performance. We will further study the relationship between pupil size and emotion, and hope to propose a better method to fuse pupil emotional information into analyzing subtle facial expression. Furthermore, we will establish a public database which includes the facial expression and the corresponding pupil information.

Acknowledgments. This research was done for CSIDM Project No. CSIDM-200801 partially funded by a grant from the National Research Foundation (NRF) administered by the Media Development Authority (MDA) of Singapore. We would like to thank Skanda Muralidhar for his help in improving the presentation of this paper.

References

1. Hess, E.H.: Attitude and pupil size. Scientific American (1965)
2. Ekman, P., Friesen, W.: Facial Action Coding System: A Technique for the Measurement of Facial Movement, Palo Alto (1978)
3. Cohn, J.F., Zlochower, A.J., Lien, J.J., Kanade, T.: Feature-point tracking by optical flow discriminates subtledifferences in facial expression. In: Proceedings of IEEE International Conference on Automatic Face and Gesture Recognition, pp. 396–401 (1998)
4. Kaiser, S., Wehrle, T., Schmidt, S.: Emotional Episodes, Facial Expressions, and Reported Feelings in Human-Computer Interactions. In: Proceedings of Xth Conference of the International Society for Research on Emotions (1998)
5. Lyons, M., Akamatsu, S., Kamachi, M., Gyoba, J.: Coding facial expressions with gabor wavelets. In: Proceedings of IEEE International Conference on Automatic Face and Gesture Recognition, pp. 200–205 (1998)
6. Tsubota, K.: Blink of an Eye. Newsweek, PE 134 (1999)
7. Patterns, I.S.: The classification of smile patterns. J. Can. Dent. Assoc. (1999)
8. Atchison, D.A., Smith, G.: Optics of the human eye. Butterworth-Heinemann, Oxford (2000)
9. Sebe, N., Lew, M.S., Cohen, I., Garg, A., Huang, T.S.: Emotion recognition using a cauchy naive bayes classifier. In: Proceedings of the International Conference on Pattern Recognition, vol. 1, pp. 17–20 (2002)
10. Cohen, I., Sebe, N., Garg, A., Chen, L.S., Huang, T.S.: Facial expression recognition from video sequences: Temporal and static modeling. Computer Vision and Image Understanding 91(1-2), 160–187 (2003)
11. Partala, T., Surakka, V.: Pupil size variation as an indication of affective processing. International Journal of Human-Computer Studies 59, 185–198 (2003)
12. Myers, D.: Theories of Emotion. Psychology, 7th edn. (2004)

13. Zeng, Z., Tu, J., Liu, M., Zhang, T., Rizzolo, N., Zhang, Z., Huang, T.S., Roth, D., Levinson, S.: Bimodal HCI-related affect recognition. In: Proceedings of the 6th International Conference on Multimodal Interfaces, pp. 137–143 (2004)
14. Gunes, H., Piccardi, M.: Fusing Face and Body Display for Bi-modal Emotion Recognition: Single Frame Analysis and Multi-frame Post Integration. In: Tao, J., Tan, T., Picard, R.W. (eds.) ACII 2005. LNCS, vol. 3784, pp. 102–111. Springer, Heidelberg (2005)
15. Song, M., Wang, H., Bu, J., Chen, C., Liu, Z.: Subtle facial expression modeling with vector field decomposition. In: Proceedings of IEEE International Conference on Image Processing, pp. 2101–2104 (2006)
16. Freitas-Magalhães, A.: The Psychology of Emotions: The allure of human face. University Fernando Pessoa Press, Oporto (2007)
17. Caridakis, G., Castellano, G., Kessous, L., Raouzaiou, A., Malatesta, L., Asteriadis, S., Karpouzis, K.: Multimodal Emotion Recognition from Expressive Faces, Body Gestures and Speech. In: Boukis, C., Pnevmatikakis, A., Polymenakos, L. (eds.) Artificial Intelligence and Innovations: From Theory to Applications. IFIP, vol. 247, pp. 375–388. Springer, Boston (2007)
18. Park, S., Kim, D.: Subtle facial expression recognition using motion magnification. Pattern Recognition Letters 30(7), 708–716 (2009)
19. Needell, D., Tropp, J.A.: CoSaMP: Iterative signal recovery from incomplete and inaccurate samples. Applied and Computational Harmonic Analysis 26(3), 301–321 (2009)
20. Ying, Z.-L., Wang, Z.-W., Huang, M.-W.: Facial Expression Recognition Based on Fusion of Sparse Representation. In: Huang, D.-S., Zhang, X., Reyes García, C.A., Zhang, L. (eds.) ICIC 2010. LNCS, vol. 6216, pp. 457–464. Springer, Heidelberg (2010)
21. Pai, N.S., Chang, S.P.: An embedded system for real-time facial expression recognition based on the extension theory. Computers & Mathematics with Applications 61(8), 2101–2106 (2011)
22. Nicolaou, M.A., Gunes, H., Pantic, M.: Continuous Prediction of Spontaneous Affect from Multiple Cues and Modalities in Valence-Arousal Space. IEEE Transactions on Affective Computing, 92–105 (2011)
23. Sandbach, G., Zafeiriou, S., Pantic, M., Rueckert, D.: Recognition of 3D Facial Expression Dynamics. Image and Vision Computing (2012)

Just Noticeable Difference
for 3D Images with Depth Saliency

Rui Zhong, Ruimin Hu, Yi Shi, Zhongyuan Wang, Zhen Han, Lu Liu, and Jinhui Hu

National Engineering Research Center for Multimedia Software,
School of Computer, Wuhan University, Wuhan, 430072, China
zhongrui0824@126.com, {hrm1964,wzy_hope}@163.com

Abstract. The just noticeable difference (JND) threshold of images in essence depends on the inconsistent human visual sensitivity for different stimulus. As the key difference between 2D and 3D visual perception, the depth saliency will adjust the eyes' sensitivity to the image content significantly. This paper carves out a 3D image JND model that integrates depth saliency as the main influence factor to simulate the human vision more accurately. The depth saliency is first calculated by integrating multiple depth perceptual stimuli such as intensity and depth contrast. Then the final JND values are computed on different 3D image areas according to the influence of different depth saliency. The experiment result demonstrates that the proposed model in this paper could tolerant more additional noise in the original image while still keeping the similar subject quality with the corresponding models.

Keywords: Just noticeable difference (JND), stereoscopic multi-view image, human vision sensitivity, depth saliency, depth contrast.

1 Introduction

In recent years, 3D TV and movies provide people favorable immersion and visual experience, meanwhile some technical challenges have been introduced such as compression and storage problems of the rapidly increasing multi-view video data. A lot of well-performed compression algorithms for 3D video data have been proposed based on exploiting the statistic features of the 3D video. However, the coding performance is improved by increasing the computational complexity, and it eventually makes the traditional encoding technologies face a bottleneck. Human perception shouldn't be ignored during conventional algorithms design. It's well known that as the final receiver of the stereoscopic scene, human eyes could only detect the image variations above a specified visual threshold. By removing the visual perception redundancies of stereoscopic images, encoding algorithms could achieve remarkable progress.

At present a few 3D image just noticeable difference models have been developed to measure the accurate visual perception redundancy. But physical and psychological characteristics that affect the JND model of stereoscopic images are not taken into consideration. A depth JND model is addressed firstly in ICIP2010, which illustrates the reason why human being isn't sensitive to the varied depth perception with the

W. Lin et al. (Eds.): PCM 2012, LNCS 7674, pp. 414–423, 2012.
© Springer-Verlag Berlin Heidelberg 2012

different depth values [1]. But with the development of 3D image processing technologies, the depth JND model which only measures the depth perception difference couldn't meet the mass requirements. It's essential to build the 3D image JND model for the purpose of describing the total stereoscopic perception. In 2011, Zhao proposed a binocular JND (BJND) model to illustrate the basic binocular vision properties concerning the asymmetric noises in paired stereoscopic images [2]. With the formal psychophysical experiment, the paper presented the first binocular JND model considering the luminance adaption and contrast masking. The experiment result demonstrated that the JND value could be obtained accurately. However, the model was constructed with the assumption that disparity equals zero. Thereby the model isn't applicable for the normal binocular stereo image with nonzero disparity. In VCIP 2011, a joint JND (JJND) model is proposed based on the idea that occlusion region often appears at the edges of objects with different depths, which brings human stronger depth perception [3]. It solved the problem caused by zero disparity, and measured the sensitivity difference of the occlusion and non-occlusion regions separately. This procedure makes it more accurate for human vision perception. However it is worth noting that the just noticeable difference threshold in essence depends on the inconsistent human visual sensitivity for different stimulus [4]. For 3D images, it can hardly measure the visual sensitivity precisely by also considering the depth intensity simply. It's significant to explore the main features such as depth intensity and depth contrast which influence the human vision perception during building the 3D image JND model.

In pixel domain, the JND threshold of 2D images depends on the vision sensitivity to stimulus of the luminance adaptation and contrast masking [4]. The depth perception is an important different factor to influence the perception of 3D images when comparing with the 2D image perception. In this paper, the stereo image saliency is related to depth saliency decided by depth characters, such as depth intensity and depth contrast. For instance, it's more attractive for human eye to look at the pop-out part of a stereo image, the part with inconsecutive depth or with higher depth contrast. As mentioned above, visual saliency could adjust the vision sensitivity which affects just noticeable difference value directly [5]. This paper proposes a 3D image JND model based on the above idea. In this proposed model, the depth saliency is first calculated by integrating multiple depth perceptual stimuli such as intensity and depth contrast [7]. Then the final JND values are computed on different 3D image areas according to the influence of different depth saliency. The more of depth saliency a pixel is, the less of the corresponding JND threshold it has, and vice visa. The experiment result demonstrates that the proposed model fits the human subjective perception more accurately.

To sum up, the psychological and physiological characteristics of stereo perception are not taken into consideration in present JND modeling of the stereo image. This paper presents a new JND model for stereo image based on depth saliency which affects human vision sensitivity. The rest of this letter is organized as follows. The second part will introduce and analyze the depth saliency model for stereo image, the third part will demonstrate the stereo image JND model based on depth saliency and why this model performs better than the previous JND model. The fourth part is the experiment result as well as the analysis of the result. The last part is the conclusion.

2   Depth Saliency Model Building

The attention degree of video content is calculated through simulating the human visual perception mechanism in the traditional 2D video saliency model. The depth perception is the prominent difference between 3D perception and 2D perception. And the significant influences of the depth characteristics on saliency are as follows: 1) generally speaking, the pop-out region of 3D image are interesting to people while the attention degree to concave region is relatively weaker; 2) the part with inconsecutive depth or with higher depth contrast is more attractive for human eye, and these regions provide better vision sensitivity. This part utilizes the depth saliency model [7] to get the depth saliency map, which is of the same size as the original image. And each pixel of the map corresponds to the depth attention degree of corresponding pixel. As shown in figure 1, the first step is to calculate the depth from the disparity map. And then the depth intensity and depth contrast are weighed to get the final depth saliency map.

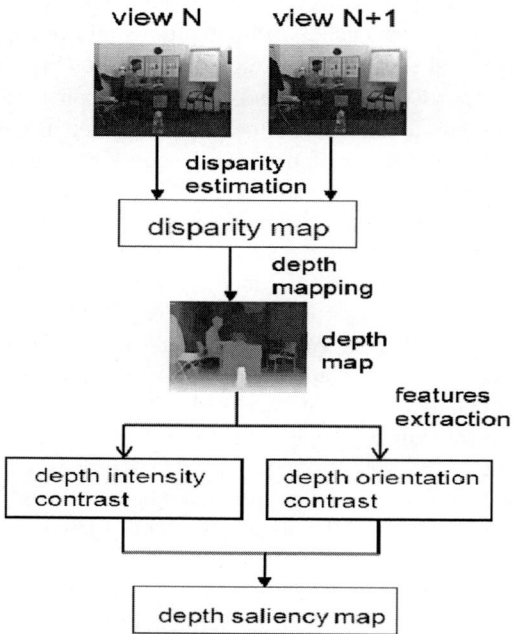

Fig. 1. Solution procedures of depth saliency map

In this section, a stereo matching algorithm based on color segmentation is utilized to calculate the disparity map which presents relative depth in two view video. The disparity means the horizon disparity, while the vertical disparity equals zero. The next step is to translate the disparity map into depth map.

$$Z = \frac{B \cdot F}{disp}, disp \neq 0 \tag{1}$$

Where F represents the focal length of the camera, B is the baseline distance between the adjacent cameras, $disp$ indicates disparity of the object corresponding in the neighbor view video, and Z is the depth value which presents the distance from object to camera in the scene.

The depth saliency could be calculated from the depth map given by equation (1). The intersection of the two cameras creates a zero disparity plane, and this zero disparity is the default screen for the 3DTV. The pop-out objects correspond to the negative disparity, and the concave objects have the positive disparity. Depth value is inversely proportional to disparity value. Then depth value is quantized as an 8bit value, where 0 means the farthest object and 255 expresses the nearest object. The saliency degree will decrease with the distance of objects monotonically, which indicates the nearer of the objects the more sensitivity of the human vision perception. Thereby the depth value is mapped to the range between a minimum and maximum value [8] through the non-linear quantization.

$$v = \left\lfloor 255 \cdot \frac{z^n}{z} \cdot \frac{z^f - z}{z^f - z^n} + 0.5 \right\rfloor \tag{2}$$

Where $\lfloor a \rfloor$ indicates the integer less than or equals to a, z^f and z^n represent the farthest and nearest depth value, $z^f = Bf / \min\{disp\}$ and $z^n = Bf / \max\{disp\}$. $v(x, y)$ presents the non-linear mapping space of depth value. Recent research denotes that the pop-out part of a stereo image and the part with inconsecutive depth or with higher depth contrast are more attractive for human eye. The depth contrast map is determined by the absolute center-surround difference (CSD) [6] between different depth intensity channels as illustrated in the equation (3).

$$F_D = N \left(\oplus_{c=2}^4 \oplus_{s=c+3}^{c+4} N \left(|v(c) \ominus v(s)| \right) \right) \tag{3}$$

Where $\ominus$ means across-scale difference between two maps, and $\oplus$ is across-scale addition. The final feature map is established by fusing the depth contrast and orientation contrast in this section. The orientation feature is derived from the depth intensity through oriented Gabor filters. Furthermore, it is denoted as $O(\sigma, \theta)$, where $\sigma \in [0 \cdots 8]$ indicates image scale at the different pyramids level, and $\theta \in \{0, \pi/4, \pi/2, 3\pi/4\}$ is the orientation. This paper obtains the depth orientation map F_O from the absolute center-surround difference (CSD) between different depth orientation channels by

$$F_O = \frac{1}{4} \sum_{\theta \in \{0, \pi/4, \pi/2, 3\pi/4\}} N \left(\oplus_{c=2}^4 \oplus_{s=c+3}^{c+4} N \left(|O(c, \theta) \ominus O(s, \theta)| \right) \right) \tag{4}$$

Where $N(\cdot)$ normalizes the values into a fixed range. The depth contrast and depth orientation maps listed in the above equations are summed into the final saliency map averagely.

$$S_D = \frac{1}{2}(N(\mathrm{F}_O) + N(\mathrm{F}_D)) \tag{5}$$

3   Proposed 3D JND Method

In this paper, we build the 3D image JND model in pixel domain. As mentioned above, depth saliency is a direct factor that will affect human vision sensitivity to the image content [5]. The JND threshold in pixel domain is decided by the human vision sensitivity to stimuli, e.g. the region with less attention could conceal more noise [4]. The existing 3D image JND models overlook the influence of saliency, which makes it hard to stimulate the human vision mechanism accurately.

To overcome this problem, this section will calculate the 3D image JND model on different image regions with different depth saliency which is given in section 2. Due to the selectivity mechanism of human eyes, different regions of the image will correspond to different visual attention degree [6]. It's worth noting that depth emphasizes the difference between 3D and 2D perception. Being different from 2D JND models, depth saliency is adopted as the main additional factor for the final 3D JND model.

In conventional 2D image JND model proposed by Yang [9], the luminance adaptation and the contrast masking are weighted non-linearly and summed to obtain the JND values. Here, the luminance adaptation describes the visibility threshold to the background luminance, and it obeys the Weber law. The contrast masking factor illustrates that the visibility of a spatial object will be reduced with the presence of another neighboring object.

$$JND_{2d}(x,y) = LA(x,y) + CM(x,y) - C^{LC}(x,y) \cdot \min\{LA(x,y), CM(x,y)\} \tag{6}$$

Where $JND_{2d}(x,y)$ presents the 2D image JND value, $LA(x,y)$ and $CM(x,y)$ are the visibility thresholds from luminance adaptation and contrast masking respectively, $C^{LC}(x,y)$ exhibits the overlapping effect between the effect factors and $0 < C^{LC}(x,y) \leq 1$. These factors of the 2D JND could also   work in 3D image JND. Furthermore, depth saliency is combined into the 3D JND model. Specifically, the formula is illustrated in equation (7):

$$JND_{ds}(x,y) = \alpha \times JND_{2d}(x,y) \times \beta^{N(S_D(x,y))}, \beta \in (0,1) \tag{7}$$

Where (x,y) represents the location of a pixel in an image. $JND_{ds}(x,y)$ indicates the final 3D image JND value, $JND_{2d}(\mathrm{x},\mathrm{y})$ presents the basic JND value given in (6). According to the sample data, it can be observed that the relationship between saliency degree and 3D JND value meet exponential function. β is the bottom number, it's set as 0.15 empirically. The exponent $S_D(x, y)$ corresponds to the depth saliency of a pixel in a 3D image from arbitrary view. $N(\cdot)$ normalizes the value into a fixed range. α is a scale factor set as 1.397 constantly.

4   Overall Experimental Results

The JND model which can tolerate more additional noise without sacrificing the subjective image quality is a better model [10]. Therefore, to evaluate the JND model accurately, it's necessary to measure the objective and subjective quality of the noise injected image. The objective PSNR is used to calculate the mount of noise added into the images. And a formal experiment that is carried out to verify the subjective quality is described as follows.

Table 1. Five-grade impairment scale

5	imperceptible
4	perceptible, but not annoying
3	slightly annoying
2	annoying
1	very annoying

Table 2. Subjective and objective results comparison

3D sequences	Yang's PSNR (dB)	Yang's MOS	[3]'s PSNR (dB)	[3]'s MOS	Ours' PSNR (dB)	Ours' MOS
Poznan_carpark	30.52	4.1	29.42	3.8	27.65	4.3
Poznan_street	33.15	4.3	32.18	4.4	30.29	4.5
Poznan_hall	31.3	4.8	30.2	4.9	28.43	4.9
Leavinglaptop	29.91	4.6	29.06	4.7	27.04	4.3
Doorflower	30.22	4.5	29.4	4.4	27.35	4.6
Altmoabit	30.93	4.9	29.41	4.9	28.07	4.6
average	31	4.5	29.95	4.5	28.14	4.5

In this section, the overall performance of the proposed scheme is compared with the NAMM pixel domain JND model and [3]'s model. The multi-view video sequences provided by HHI and Poznan University are chosen as the test material. Altmobie, Doorflowers and Leavinglaptop are with resolution 1024*768[11]. Moreover the sequences named as Poznan_carpark, Poznan_Hall and Poznan_Street are with the HD resolution of 1920*1080[12]. Twenty testers participated in the scoring of the noisy image. The display screen is the TCL TD-42F 3D auto-stereoscopic TV with a display resolution of 1080P. It supports up to 8 views as the input video signals and then displays a synthetic high definition stereoscopic image as the output on the screen.

The additional noise the amount of which was obtained by the JND model proposed by Yang, [3] and this paper was inserted into 8 views input images respectively. And the noisy input images were fused into the output stereoscopic images which displayed on 3D screen. The subjective viewing tests named as "Double Stimulus Impairment Scale methods" which is recommended by ITU-R BT.500-11 standard [13] were used to ensure the experiments formal and objective. The five-grade impairment scale was used to score for the processing 3D images, as illustrated in table 1. In DSIS(Double Stimulus Impairment Scale) method, an original 3D image was displayed first, followed by an impaired image processed by the JND models for assessors.

The assessors scored for the second image according to the subjective quality of the first image in their mind. However, the assessor couldn't distinguish which impairment images were processed by Yang, [3] or our model. A session would not last more than half an hour, including the explanations and preliminaries.

After the subjective test, the subjective scores are statistically analyzed by calculating the mean MOS scores, the number are listed in the third and fifth columns of table 2. The MOS scores could measure the satisfaction of the human perception decided by the amount of the noise obtained through the JND models. Moreover, the comparison of the original images (the sequences named Poznan_hall and Leavinglaptop) and the impaired ones processed by Yang's , [3]'s and the proposed JND models are shown in figure 2.

From the subjective results given in fig. 2, we could observe that 2D image from our 3D JND model achieve the similar quality with the 2D image from Yang's and [3]'s model successfully. However, the display limitation makes it hard to give the 3D JND images in figure. The MOS scores in table 2 are for 3D noise injected images which displayed in auto-stereo TV. The same MOS scores of Poznan_hall and Leavinglaptop demonstrate that the 3D images from our JND model are also at the same perceptual qualities with 3D images processed by other two JND models.

Meanwhile, the objective quality is evaluated by PSNR values, the PSNR of the noisy images produced by Yang's, [3]'s and ours' model are provided in the second, fourth and sixth columns of table 2. While calculating the PSNR value, the original image is used as reference image. Through comparing the 2D impaired images processed by the two JND models, the attention regions will have better subjective performance while the non-attention parts have a little worse subjective quality. This phenomenon is more apparent in the sequence Leavinglaptop provided by HHI. However, the similar MOS scores of 3D images imply the similar subjective quality between the proposed model and reference models. The PSNR of the images processed by the proposed model is 1.81dB lower than [3]'s model as well as 2.84dB lower than Yang's model averagely. It means that the more noise could be added into images guided by the proposed model. Therefore, for 3D images, the proposed model could explore more vision redundancies while keep the 3D images at the similar subjective performance level.

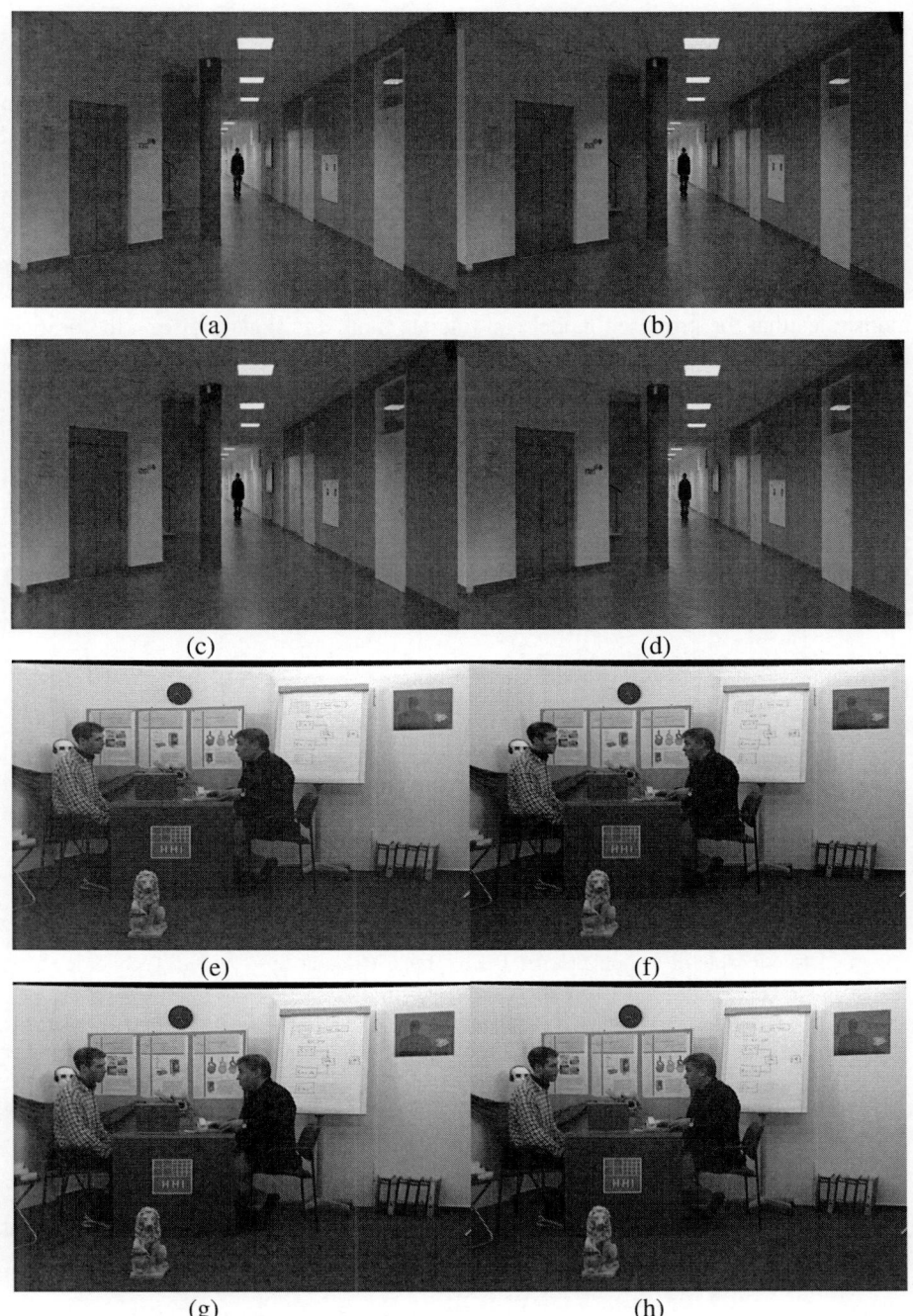

Fig. 2. Comparison images with different JND models. (a).original Poznan_hall image. (b).proposed model with Poznan_hall. (c).model [3] Poznan_hall. (d).model [9] with Poznan_hall.   (e).original Leavinglaptop image. (f) proposed model with Leavinglaptop. (g). model [3] Leavinglaptop. (h). model [9] with Leavinglaptop.

5   Conclusion

In this paper, the main problem we want to tackle is how to simulate the human vision sensitivity accurately while building the stereo image JND model. And our proposed JND model integrates depth saliency as the main influence factor for human vision sensitivity. The 3D JND model also takes the vision effect of the conventional 2D JND model as the available part. Moreover, this model emphasizes the depth saliency which affects the vision sensitivity, i.e. the image region with smaller depth saliency value will correspond to higher JND value, and vice visa. The experiment result demonstrates that the proposed model can tolerate more additional noise in the original image while keeping the similar subjective quality. This result also indicates that more redundancies can be removed from the compressed image without the degradation of the subjective quality, which proves the accurate of the proposed model.

Acknowledgments. The research was supported by the major national science and technology special projects (2010ZX03004-003-03), the National Basic Research Program of China (973 Program) (2009CB320906), the National Natural Science Foundation of China (60832002, 60970160, 61070080, 61003184, 61271256), 2011 Academic Scholarship for Doctoral Candidates of Wuhan University.

References

1. De Silva, D.V.S.X., Fernando, W.A.C.: Just noticeable difference in depth model for stereoscopic 3D displays. In: IEEE ICME 2010, pp. 1219–1224 (July 2010)
2. Zhao, Y., Yu, L.: Binocular just noticeable-difference model for stereoscopic images. IEEE Signal Processing Letters 18(1), 19–22 (2011)
3. Li, X., Wang, Y., Zhao, D.: Joint just noticeable difference model based on depth perception for stereoscopic images. In: IEEE VCIP, pp. 1–4 (November 2011)
4. Chou, C.-H., Li, Y.-C.: A perceptually tuned sub-band image coder based on the measure of just-noticeable-distortion profile. IEEE Trans. Circuits Syst. Video Technology 5(6), 467–476 (1995)
5. Niu, Y., Kyan, M.: A visual saliency modulated just noticeable distortion profile for image watermarking. In: European Signal Processing Conference, pp. 2039–2043 (September 2011)
6. Itti, L., Koch, C., Niebur, E.: A model of saliency-based visual attention for rapid scene analysis. IEEE Transactions on Pattern Analysis and Machine Intelligence 20(11), 1254–1259 (1998)
7. Zhang, Y., Jiang, G.: Stereoscopic visual attention-based regional bit allocation optimization for multi-view video coding. EURASIP Journal on Advances in Signal Processing 2010, 24 pages (2010)
8. Tanimoto, M., Fujii, T., Suzuki, K.: Improvement of depth map estimation and view synthesis. ISO/IECJTC1/SC29/WG11, M15090, Antalya, Turkey (January 2008)
9. Yang, X.K., Yao, S.S.: Just noticeable distortion model and its applications in video coding. Signal Processing: Image Commun. 20(7), 662–680 (2005)

10. Liu, A., Lin, W., Paul, M., Deng, C., Zhang, F.: Just noticeable difference for image with decomposition model for separating edge and texture regions. IEEE Trans. Circuits and Systems for Video Technology 20(11), 1648–1652 (2010)
11. Müller, K.: HHI Test Material for 3D Video. ISO/IECJTC1/SC29/WG11, M15413 (April 2008)
12. Stankiewicz, O., Wegner, K.: Poznan Multi-view Video Test Sequences and Camera Parameters. ISO/IECJTC1/SC29/WG11, M17050 (October 2009)
13. Methodology for the Subjective Assessment of the Quality of Television Pictures. ITU, Document ITU-R BT.500-11, Geneva, Switzerland (2002)

Improving Image Distance Metric Learning by Embedding Semantic Relations

Fang Wang[1,2], Shuqiang Jiang[1,2], Luis Herranz[1,2], and Qingming Huang[1,2,3]

[1] Key Lab of Intell. Info. Process,
Chinese Academy of Sciences, Beijing 100190, China
[2] Institute of Computing Technology,
Chinese Academy of Sciences, Beijing 100190, China
[3] Graduate University of Chinese Academy of Sciences, Beijing 100049, China
{wangfang,sqjiang,qmhuang}@jdl.ac.cn,
luis.herranz@vipl.ict.ac.cn

Abstract. Learning a proper distance metric is crucial for many computer vision and image classification applications. Neighborhood Components Analysis (NCA) is an effective distance metric learning method which maximizes the kNN leave-out-one score on the training data by considering visual similarity between images. However, only using visual similarity to learn image distances could not satisfactorily cope with the diversity and complexity of a large number of real images with many concepts. To overcome this problem, integrating concrete semantic relations of images into the distance metric learning procedure can be a useful solution. This can more accurately model the image similarities and better reflect the perception of human in the classification system. In this paper, we propose Semantic NCA (SNCA), a novel approach which integrates semantic similarity into NCA, where neighborhood relations between images in the training dataset are measured by both visual characteristics and their concept relations. We evaluated several semantic similarity measures based on the WordNet tree. Experimental results show that the proposed approach improves the performance compared to the traditional distance metric learning methods.

Keywords: Metric Learning, kNN, Image Classification, NCA, Semantic Relations.

1 Introduction

A simple method to classify a data point is by comparing it with its neighbors. The k-Nearest Neighbor (kNN) rule[1] classifies each point using the majority class of its k nearest (most similar) neighbors in the training set. Recently, there has been an increasing interest in non-parametric kNN for image classification[2], with a competitive classification performance compared to other parametric classification methods.

Distance metric learning plays an important role in computer vision, machine learning and multimedia retrieval. In particular, due to the very nature

W. Lin et al. (Eds.): PCM 2012, LNCS 7674, pp. 424–434, 2012.

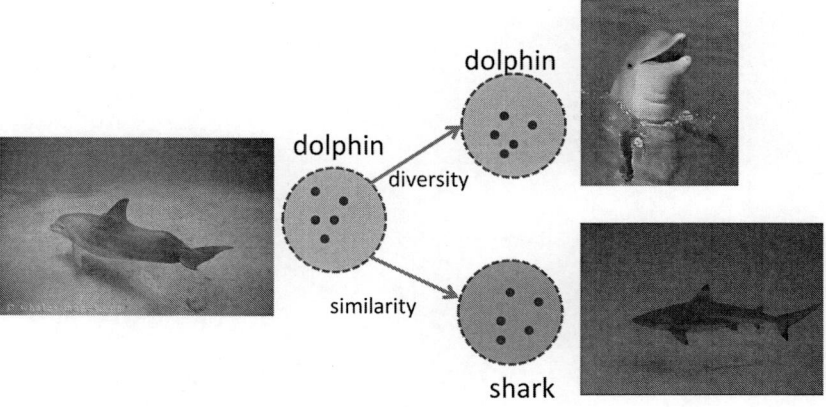

Fig. 1. Intra-class diversity and inter-class similarity

of kNN classification, an appropriate distance metric is critical to improve the kNN classification performance[3]. In image classification, most distance metric learning approaches try to employ the information contained in visual features and class labels, so that an appropriate Mahalanobis distance metrics are obtained to achieve better classification performance. The Mahalanobis distance is usually characterized by a positive semidefinite (PSD) matrix, which depends on the training data, and its estimation is the objective of distance metric learning. A variety of distance metric learning methods have been proposed in the literature[4,5,6,7,8,3,9,10,11,12,13], such as Neighborhood Components Analysis (NCA)[10], Large Margin Nearest Neighbor (LMNN)[6], Maximally Collapsing Metric Learning (MCML)[5] and Information-Theoretic Metric Learning (ITML)[8] and so on. NCA tries to maximize the probability of each sample assigned to those of same class using the visual information in each class label. The nearest neighborhood relation between two images in NCA is characterized by their visual similarity. A prevalent idea in metric learning is that points in the same class is made to be near to each other, however those points belonging to different concepts are pushed away and MCML explicitly constructs a convex optimization building on the basis of the idea. The same idea is applied in LMNN based on the large margin framework.

However, in conventional distance metric learning methods, semantic relations between concepts are not taken into account. These solutions may suffer from the following limitations:

1) First, using only low level visual features could not appropriately model the intra-class diversity and inter-class similarity. In a large scale scenario, each class contains a large number of images, which leads to very heterogeneous classes, with diverse shapes and visual characteristics. Besides, the number of concepts may be large, and discriminating between the distributions of the different concepts can be very complex, as images belonging to different classes may be visually similar. So these facts pose a tremendous challenge for measuring image similarity using only visual features. For instance, in Fig. 1 two images with

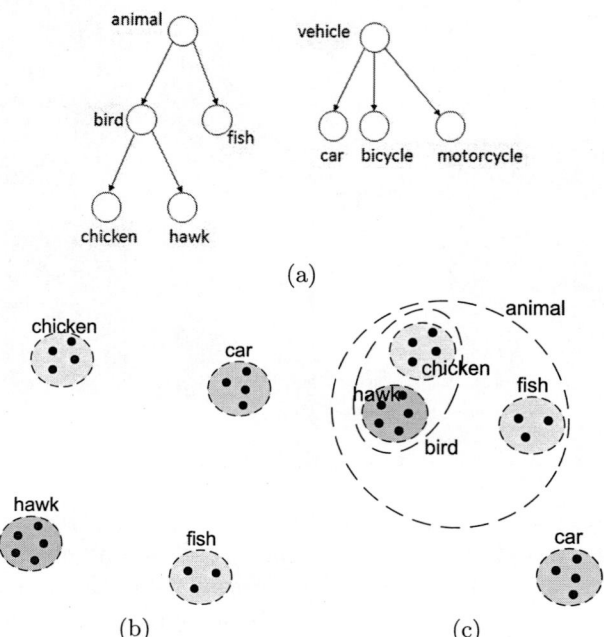

Fig. 2. Semantic information and the transformed space in kNN: a) tree with related concepts, b) distribution in the transformed space considering only visual similarity, and c) distribution in the transformed space considering visual and semantic similarity.

the same label *dolphin* have wide visual differences in shape, color and texture (i.e. intra-class visual diversity). At the same time, another image with the label *shark* is visually similar to one of the *dolphin* images (i.e. inter-class visual similarity).

2) Second, using only low level visual features could not satisfactorily reflect humans' real perception on image similarity. As the final objective of distance metric learning is to obtain a metric which better reproduces human perception, ignoring the semantic relations of concepts may not well satisfy this requirement. However, this kind of information can better reveal more meaningful high level similarities between images[14]. For instance, as shown in Fig. 2a, the concepts of *chicken* and *hawk* should be closer between them than to the concept *car*, as both are related to the concepts *animal* and *bird*. Data points are projected in such a way that they are optimized for classification according to the given training class labels, as shown in Fig. 2b. However, using semantic relations, the projection can reflect a more semantically meaningful structure (see Fig. 2c). A kNN classifier can also benefit from this projection, as related classes are closer than non-related.

Motivated by the above observations, in this paper we study the integration of semantic similarity in distance metric learning in the case of NCA and propose Semantic NCA (SNCA). In order to learn a more suitable matrix A to improve the performance of kNN, the nearest neighborhood relation between two images is characterized by their visual similarity as well as the semantic relationship between their class labels, using an appropriate semantic measure based on the WordNet database[15]. Following the NCA formulation, the probability that a data point selects another point as its neighbor in the transformed space is measured based on both visual similarity and semantic correlation. As the performance of the proposed approach highly depends on the way in which semantic similarity is measured, we also study several semantic metrics based on the WordNet database.

The rest of this paper is organized as follows. The proposed Semantic NCA method is described in Section 2. Section 3 introduces the semantic similarity measures between concepts. Experimental evaluation is detailed in Section 4. The last section draws the conclusions.

2   Semantic Neighborhood Component Analysis

In this section, we first introduce the distance metric problem and the NCA framework for kNN multi-class image classification. Then, we integrate semantic similarity into this framework, resulting in the proposed Semantic NCA (SNCA) algorithm.

2.1   Distance Metric Learning

Suppose that we have a training dataset $C = \{x_1, x_2, \cdots, x_N\}$ with N images, where x_i represents the feature vector of the element i in the dataset. The element i belongs to a class with the label y_i. Given two elements i and j, the (squared) Mahalanobis distance between their feature vectors is calculated as:

$$d^2(x_i, x_j) = (x_i - x_j)^T M (x_i - x_j) \tag{1}$$

where M is the PSD matrix ($M \geq 0$) we want to learn. As the classification procedure is based on neighbors, an optimal M should have the following property: data points belonging to the same class should have a low distance and data points belonging to different classes are separated as much as possible (see Fig. 2b).

Using $M = A^T A$, then Eq. (1) can be also rewritten as:

$$d^2(x_i, x_j) = (x_i - x_j)^T A^T A (x_i - x_j) \tag{2}$$

Following this transformation, the distance between two points is calculated as the Euclidean distance between the projected points Ax_i and Ax_j. Thus, the Mahalanobis distance is transformed to Euclidean distance via the matrix A.

2.2   Including Semantic Similarity in NCA

In NCA[10], the objective is to learn a metric A maximizing the classification performance for future test images in a kNN multi-class image classifier. However, the only available resource is the training dataset C. NCA applies the leave-one-out (LOO) rule to maximize the performance to obtain A. During the learning stage, the assignment of neighbors is stochastic, which means that an element j is selected as a neighbor of another element i with certain probability $p_{ij}^{(NCA)}$. Thus, it is not certain whether j is considered as a neighbor of i or not. Such certainty would correspond to $p_{ij} = 1$ and $p_{ij} = 0$, respectively. A higher value of $p_{ij}^{(NCA)}$ shows that the two closer points are more likely to be neighbors. Therefore the similarity between i and j is calculated as[10] :

$$I^{(NCA)}(i,j) = v(\boldsymbol{x_i}, \boldsymbol{x_j}) = \exp\left(-d^2(\boldsymbol{x_i}, \boldsymbol{x_j})\right) = \exp(-\|A\boldsymbol{x_i} - A\boldsymbol{x_j}\|^2) \quad (3)$$

where $v(\boldsymbol{x_i}, \boldsymbol{x_j})$ is the visual similarity between two elements via their feature vectors $\boldsymbol{x_i}$ and $\boldsymbol{x_j}$. An important characteristic of NCA is the description of neighborhood relations using a stochastic assignment rule in the LOO-kNN framework. When dealing with images, visual features are used to measure neighborhood relation between two points. However, visual features are not the only information available in a supervised classification system, such as kNN. As high-level textual descriptions of the content of images, class labels should not be ignored as they can help to better describe the relation between two images.

Fig. 1 illustrates both visual and semantic description of images. In the examples, each image is described by two parts, including visual feature $\boldsymbol{x_i}$ and textual label y_i. In general, y is the class label which is closely related to classification. For a given pair of images i and j, their visual similarity is measured using the feature vectors as $v(\boldsymbol{x_i}, \boldsymbol{x_j})$. In SNCA we also use the semantic similarity $s(i,j)$ between concepts, in order to obtain a classification system being more consistent with human cognition. Thus, not including the semantic component in neighborhood relations can prevent NCA from using important information which could help to improve the classification performance.

Therefore, we compute the similarity between two images i and j using both visual and semantic similarity as:

$$I^{(SNCA)}(i,j) = v(\boldsymbol{x_i}, \boldsymbol{x_j}) s(i,j) = \exp(-\|A\boldsymbol{x_i} - A\boldsymbol{x_j}\|^2) s(i,j) \quad (4)$$

Comparing Eq. (3) and (4), this new similarity between two images also depends on semantic information. In order to be consistent with the definition of probability, we normalize the previous expression. Then the probability $p_{ij}^{(SNCA)}$ including both visual and semantic similarity can be rewritten as:

$$p_{ij}^{(SNCA)} = \begin{cases} \frac{1}{\Omega} I_{ij}^{(SNCA)}(\boldsymbol{x_i}, \boldsymbol{x_j}) = \frac{s(i,j)\exp(-\|A\boldsymbol{x_i} - A\boldsymbol{x_j}\|^2)}{\Sigma_{k \neq i} s(i,k)\exp(-\|A\boldsymbol{x_i} - A\boldsymbol{x_k}\|^2)}, & i \neq j \\ 0 & i = j \end{cases} \quad (5)$$

which denotes the probability that a point i selects another point j as its neighbor given their visual features and corresponding concept relation.

The objective is to try to find a projection which maximizes the probability that points with the same label are neighbors in projected space. For that purpose, we use the objective function proposed in [10], which maximizes the LOO score of the of all data points in the training set C:

$$g^{(SNCA)}(A) = \sum_{i=1}^{N} \log p_i^{(SNCA)} = \sum_{i=1}^{N} \log \sum_{j \in C_i} p_{ij}^{(SNCA)} \qquad (6)$$

where C_i is a set of all points which have the same class label to point i. In Eq. (6) the only factor involving semantic correlation is $s(i,j)$, with the matrix A remaining independent. Thus we can compute the gradient of $g^{(SNCA)}(A)$ as:

$$\frac{\partial g^{(SNCA)}(A)}{\partial A} = 2A \sum_{i=1}^{N} \left(\sum_{k=1}^{N} p_{ik}^{(SNCA)} x_{ik} x_{ik}^T - \frac{\sum_{j \in C_i} p_{ij}^{(SNCA)} x_{ij} x_{ij}^T}{\sum_{j \in C_i} p_{ij}^{(SNCA)}} \right) \qquad (7)$$

where x_{ij} means $x_i - x_j$.

The same optimization method used in NCA can still be used to estimate A, while we also take advantage of semantic similarity. After obtaining A, the input data can be projected in the transformed space, in which conventional kNN classification can be performed.

3   Semantic Similarity between Concepts

In this paper, semantic similarity is measured based on WordNet[15]. In the experiment we tested four different measures: node count (*path*), Resnik (*res*)[16], Leacock and Chodorow (*lch*)[17], and the least common subsumer measure[18] (*LCS*). Except for *LCS*, the other three measures can be found in the JAVA WordNet Similarity (JWS) package[19] which implements several widely used semantic similarity measures between concepts in WordNet. Table 1 details how these measures are computed.

In WordNet[15], each concept is represented as a node in the tree taxonomy, with the term synonym set (synset). We denote depth(i) as the length of the path from root to node i. The most common subsumer CS(i,j) is the most specific concept which is a common ancestor of the concepts i and j. The information content IC(i) of a node i is computed as described in [16].

4   Experimental Results

4.1   Dataset and Feature Representation

We evaluate the proposed method over the Caltech256[20] and ImageNet[21] datasets. We selected a total of 4546 images from the Caltech256 dataset covering 40 subconcepts of the concept *animal* (Caltech40). For the second dataset ImageNet20 we selected 20 concepts covering subconcepts of the broad concepts *animal*, *vegetable*, *flower* and *vehicle*, represented by about 21100 images from

Table 1. Concept semantic similarity measures used in the experiments

Measure	Formulation	Description
path	$s_{path}(i,j) = \frac{1}{\min(depth(i),depth(j))}$	The reciprocal of the number of nodes along the shortest path between i and j
res	$s_{res}(i,j) = \text{IC}(\text{CS}(i,j))$	$\text{CS}(i,j)$ is the least common subsumer of node i and j, $\text{IC}(i)$ is the information content of node i
lch	$s_{lch}(i,j) = -\log(L/2D)$	L is the length of the shortest path between i and j and D is the maximum depth of the taxonomy
LCS	$s_{\mathcal{LCS}}(i,j) = \frac{depth(\text{CS}(i,j))}{\max(depth(i),depth(j))}$	The length of the least common subsumer node normalized by the longest branch

Table 2. Comparison of the classification accuracy of NCA, LMNN and SNCA with different semantic measures in Caltech40

Accuracy(%)	Caltech40			
Method	color		GIST	
	$k=20$	$k=40$	$k=20$	$k=40$
kNN	9.78	10.43	13.48	14.72
NCA	11.40	11.27	20.37	19.71
LMNN	10.26	10.92	13.83	13.70
SNCA (*path*)	**12.23**	11.75	18.56	18.16
SNCA (*res*)	11.71	**12.01**	21.56	20.28
SNCA (*lch*)	12.01	11.79	20.11	20.24
SNCA (*LCS*)	11.93	11.79	**22.18**	**20.86**

the ImageNet dataset. For each concept approximately half of the images were used for training and the remaining were considered as test images.

We used color histograms in the HSV space (16x4x4 bins) and GIST[22] to represent the images in the visual feature space.

4.2 Results and Analysis

In the first experiment, we studied the classification accuracy of SNCA, NCA, LMNN and basic kNN over both datasets, with different values of k. SNCA uses *path, res, lch, LCS* as semantic similarity measures. The dimensionality is reduced using PCA to 80 dimensions for both color and GIST feature, in order to accelerate the classification process.

Table 2 shows the classification accuracy in Caltech40. For both features, the best performance is obtained using SNCA with different semantic metrics, as shown in Table 2. However, the classification accuracy using color features is still very limited. Using GIST features, it improves considerably. In both cases SNCA has better performance than NCA and LMNN for most of the semantic measures. In general the classification accuracy is reasonably high, considering that the dataset

Table 3. Comparison of the classification accuracy of NCA, LMNN and SNCA with different semantic measures in ImageNet20

Accuracy(%)	ImageNet20			
Method	color		GIST	
	$k = 20$	$k = 40$	$k = 20$	$k = 40$
kNN	31.46	30.13	38.36	37.93
NCA	33.47	33.75	41.05	40.97
LMNN	33.75	33.63	41.72	41.22
SNCA (path)	32.99	34.03	41.26	41.09
SNCA (res)	34.59	34.84	42.16	41.20
SNCA (lch)	**34.63**	33.83	42.34	41.93
SNCA (LCS)	34.07	**34.88**	**42.69**	**42.22**

Table 4. Comparison of the five most frequently predicted concepts using instances of the *cormorant* concept as test images in Caltech40. F: frequency, SS: semantic similarity using *LCS* metric.

Method								
NCA			SNCA (LCS)			SNCA (res)		
Concept	F (%)	SS (%)	Concept	F (%)	SS (%)	Concept	F (%)	SS (%)
penguin	16.98	84.62	*cormorant*	15.09	100	*cormorant*	18.87	100
gorilla	13.21	53.33	*penguin*	15.09	84.62	*hummingbird*	11.32	69.23
hummingbird	11.32	69.23	*horse*	9.43	57.14	*penguin*	11.32	84.62
cormorant	9.43	100	*hummingbird*	9.43	69.23	*gorilla*	9.43	53.33
horse	7.55	57.14	*gorilla*	7.55	53.33	*horse*	9.43	57.14

has forty concepts. Particularly, SNCA improves the accuracy of conventional NCA. The classification accuracy over ImageNet20 is shown in Table 3. The performance of SNCA is better than NCA with *res, lch, LCS* measures using the color feature. In the case of the GIST feature, we can observe that NCA has a worse performance than LMNN. However, the performance of NCA is significantly improved by integrating semantic information, resulting in a better accuracy than LMNN. Thus, integrating semantic information in NCA helps to better discriminate between images, and a better performance can be achieved.

However, the improvement of SNCA is still limited. Even though the number of concepts considered in the experiment is high compared to other datasets used in the evaluation of distance metric learning methods[6], this number still falls short to fully exploit semantic relations in the WordNet hierarchy, especially in ImageNet20 where the concepts were selected randomly among all the concepts in ImageNet. Although the effect in small datasets with few concepts is still unsatisfactory, such kind of semantic relations may be significant in large datasets with high diversity. Thus, most distance learning methods using only visual similarity may have good performance when dealing with specialized datasets with relatively few and narrow concepts (e.g. faces, letters, plants)[6], but may fail when they are used in scenarios with larger datasets, as they may not be able to cope with all the variability in the dataset.

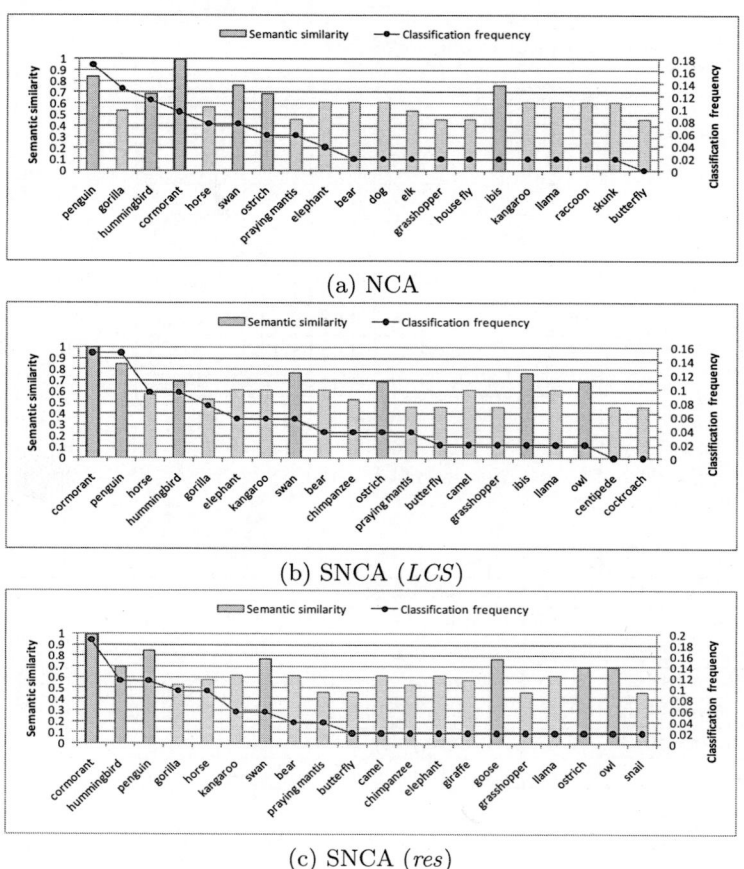

(a) NCA

(b) SNCA (*LCS*)

(c) SNCA (*res*)

Fig. 3. Most frequently predicted concepts (top 20) using instances of the *cormorant* concept as test images in Caltech40: a) NCA, b) SNCA (*LCS*) and, c) SNCA (*res*). Frequency and semantic similarity (using *LCS* metric) between the true and the predicted concepts are shown combined in each figure (better viewed in color).

Apart from improving the classification accuracy of the classifier, another objective of this work is to project concepts in a more semantically meaningful structure, in which semantically related concepts are projected closer. In order to illustrate how the resulting space using SNCA can be more suitable, Fig. 3 shows an example in which instances of the concept *cormorant* are classified using both NCA and SNCA (using both *LCS* and *res* metrics) in Caltech40, with the GIST feature and $k = 20$. The figure shows the 20 most frequently predicted concepts for each of the methods. The classifier did not assign any test image to any of the remaining concepts, so we did not include them in the figure. These concepts are shown in the horizontal axis sorted in descending order by frequency. In the same plot, the semantic similarity between the true and the predicted concept is also shown. In this case, to measure semantic similarity we used the *LCS* metric, as it is bounded between 0 and 1. For better visualization, concepts are represented in different colors depending on the type of animal (*bird, mammal, amphibian, invertebrate, reptile* or *fish*), and the concept *cormorant* is emphasized. Similarly, Table 4 shows the numerical results for the five most predicted concepts.

A first observation is that in NCA the correct concept is only the forth most predicted result, being *penguin* the most predicted one with a much higher frequency, which is still a kind of *bird*. However, the second most predicted concept is *gorilla*, which is a kind of *mammal*, thus less semantically related to the correct concept. However, in this case SNCA can return a more reasonable predictions, in which *cormorant* is the most predicted concept, and also with higher accuracy, especially using the *res* metric. Besides, in both cases the most confusing results are also kinds of *bird*. However, in this example even using semantic relations the result is still limited, as the input image is often confused with some kind of mammals (e.g. *horse* and *gorilla* in the top five) with relatively high frequency. One reason may be that the similarities between *cormorant* and other birds and between *cormorant* and mammals are not very different, so the semantic relations may not be fully exploited.

5   Conclusion

In this paper, we explored the integration of semantic relations into an image classification system via distance metric learning. Thus, a distance metric learning method using both semantic and visual similarities can project the input data to a space with a more meaningful structure. This observation motivates the proposed SNCA method, which has been studied with different semantic similarity measures and datasets, improving the classification performance. Although the improvement is still limited in these datasets, we expect that the gain can be higher in large scale scenarios, in which the number of concepts is high and their semantic relations can be fully exploited. The proposed framework to integrate semantic similarity in metric learning is generic, so we expect that it can be extended to other learning methods.

Acknowledgement. This work was supported in part by National Basic Research Program of China (973 Program):2012CB316400, in part by National Natural Science Foundation of China: 61070108,61025011, and 61150110480, in part by Chinese Academy of Sciences Fellowships for Young International Scientists: 2011Y1GB05

References

1. Cover, T.M., Hart, P.E.: Nearest neighbor pattern classification. IEEE Transactions on Information Theory 13(1), 21–27 (1967)
2. Boiman, O., Shechtman, E., Irani, M.: In defense of nearest-neighbor based image classification. In: Proc. of IEEE Conf. Computer Vision and Pattern Recognition, pp. 1–8 (2008)

3. Shen, C., Kim, J., Wang, L.: A scalable dual approach to semidefinite metric learning. In: Proc. of IEEE Computer Vision and Pattern Recognition, pp. 2601–2608 (2011)

4. Singh-Miller, N., Collins, M., Hazen, T.J.: Dimensionality reduction for speech recognition using neighborhood components analysis. In: INTERSPEECH 2007, pp. 1158–1161 (2007)

5. Globerson, A., Roweis, S.: Metric learning by collapsing classes. In: Proc. of the Conference on Advances in Neural Information Processing Systems (2006)

6. Weinberger, K.Q., Saul, L.K.: Distance metric learning for large margin nearest neighbor classification. Journal of Machine Learning Research 10, 207–244 (2009)

7. Wang, Z., Hu, Y., Chia, L.-T.: Image-to-Class Distance Metric Learning for Image Classification. In: Daniilidis, K., Maragos, P., Paragios, N. (eds.) ECCV 2010, Part I. LNCS, vol. 6311, pp. 706–719. Springer, Heidelberg (2010)

8. Davis, J., Kulis, B., Sra, S., Dhillon, I.: Information-theoretic metric learning. In: Proc. of the International Conference on Machine Learning, pp. 209–216. ACM, New York (2007)

9. Bronstein, M.M., Bronstein, A.M.: Data fusion through cross-modality metric learning using similarity-sensitive hashing. In: Proc. IEEE Conf. Computer Vision and Pattern Recognition, pp. 3594–3601 (2010)

10. Goldberger, J., Roweis, S., Hinton, G., Salakhutdinov, R.: Neighbourhood components analysis. In: Proc. of the Conference on Advances in Neural Information Processing Systems (2005)

11. Sugiyama, M.: Dimensionality reduction of multimodal labeled data by local fisher discriminant analysis. Journal of Machine Learning Research 8, 1027–1061

12. Xing, E.P., Ng, A.Y., Jordan, M.I., Russell, S.: Distance metric learning, with application to clustering with side-information. In: Proc. of the Conference on Advances in Neural Information Processing Systems, vol. 40 (2003)

13. Hwang, S.J., Grauman, K., Sha, F.: Learning a tree of metrics with disjoint visual features. In: Proc. of the Conference on Advances in Neural Information Processing Systems (2011)

14. Li, L., Jiang, S., Huang, Q.: Learning hierarchical semantic description via mixed-norm regularization for image understanding. IEEE Transactions on Multimedia 14 (2012)

15. Fellbaum, C.: WordNet: An electronic lexical Database (1998)

16. Resnik, P.: Using information content to evaluate semantic similarity. In: Proc. of the International Joint Conference on Artificial Intelligence, pp. 448–453 (1995)

17. Leacock, C., Chodorow, M.: Combining local context and WordNet similarity for word sense identification. In: WordNet: An Electronic Lexical Database. MIT Press (1998)

18. Fergus, R., Bernal, H., Weiss, Y., Torralba, A.: Semantic Label Sharing for Learning with Many Categories. In: Daniilidis, K., Maragos, P., Paragios, N. (eds.) ECCV 2010, Part I. LNCS, vol. 6311, pp. 762–775. Springer, Heidelberg (2010)

19. Hope, D.: Java WordNet similarity (2008), http://www.sussex.ac.uk/Users/drh21

20. Griffin, G., Holub, A., Perona, P.: Caltech-256 object category dataset. Tech. Rep. 7694, California Institute of Technology (2007)

21. Deng, J., Dong, W., Socher, R., Jia Li, L., Li, K., Fei-Fei, L.: ImageNet: a large scale hierarchical image database. In: Proc. of IEEE Computer Vision and Pattern Recognition, pp. 248–255 (2009)

22. Oliva, A., Torralba, A.: Modeling the shape of the scene: A holistic representation of the spatial envelope. International Journal of Computer Vision 42, 145–175 (2001)

Pose Estimation with Motionlet LLC Coding

Li Sun, Mingli Song, Jiajun Bu, and Chun Chen

Zhejiang Provincial Key Laboratory of Service Robot,
College of Computer Science, Zhejiang University
{lsun,brooksong,bjj,chenc}@zju.edu.cn

Abstract. 3D human pose estimation is a challenging but important research topic with abundant applications. As for discriminative human pose estimation, the main goal is to learn a nonlinear mapping from image descriptors to 3D human pose configurations, which is difficult due to the high-dimensionality of human pose space and the multimodality of the distribution. To address these problems, we propose a novel motionlet LLC coding on a discriminative framework. A motionlet consists of training examples covering a local area in terms of image space, pose space and time stream. We first group most informative and helpful training examples into motionlets, then perform LLC Coding to learn the nonlinear mapping and get candidate poses, and finally choose the most appropriate pose as the result estimate. To further eliminate ambiguities and improve robustness, we extend our framework to incorporate multiviews. We conduct qualitative evaluation on our Taichi data set and quantitative evaluation on HumanEva data set, which show that our approach has gained the-state-of-the-art performance and significant improvement against previous approaches.

Keywords: human pose estimation, multimodality, multiview, motionlet, LLC coding.

1 Introduction

3D human pose estimation from images is a challenging but important research topic with applications in many areas including Human-Computer Interaction, robotics, surveillance, computer graphics and sport science. Recent approaches to 3D human pose estimation can be roughly classified into two categories, generative and discriminative. Generative approaches explicitly model human body appearance and kinematic constraints and usually concentrate on development of efficient inference methods that are able to handle the high dimensionality of human pose. Discriminative approaches directly learn the mapping from image space to pose space.

Discriminative approaches are popular due to their flexibility of choosing image descriptors, easy adaptation to different learning methods, no need for initialization, and most importantly, the ability of fast inference in real-world databases. The main goal of discriminative 3D human pose estimation is to

W. Lin et al. (Eds.): PCM 2012, LNCS 7674, pp. 435–443, 2012.

learn a nonlinear mapping from image descriptors to 3D human pose configurations. This is challenging due to high-dimensionality and multimodality of the mapping. Moreover, the mapping is highly noisy because of image ambiguities and subject variations.

In this paper we present a novel discriminative framework that can learn a complex mapping from image descriptors to 3D human pose configurations. We propose a local online approach to select most informative and helpful training examples for the query frame, and then group them into motionlets. As depicted by fig. 1, every motionlet consists of training examples that covers a local area with respect to image space, pose space and time stream. The concept of motionlets is a natural embodiment of the local motion similarity of human motion, which is the basis assumption of discriminative human pose estimation. We take advantage of Locality-constrained Linear Coding (LLC) algorithm [7] to reconstruct 3D human poses using motionlets as codebooks. LLC offers an efficient local smooth sparse projection of an image descriptor into its local-coordinate system with good reconstruction. Each motionlet contributes a candidate pose. We handle the problem of multimodality through selecting the most appropriate pose from these candidate poses. To further eliminate inference ambiguities, we extend our framework to incorporate multiviews and retain an accurate and robust inference from image descriptors to 3D human poses.

We review related work in the next section, and then present our online framework of motionlet LLC coding. We define local neighborhoods for a query frame, and then show that multimodality of the mapping is mainly caused by the multiple instances of motionlets. We demonstrate how to choose from candidate poses recovered by LLC coding and how to incorporate multiviews into our framework.

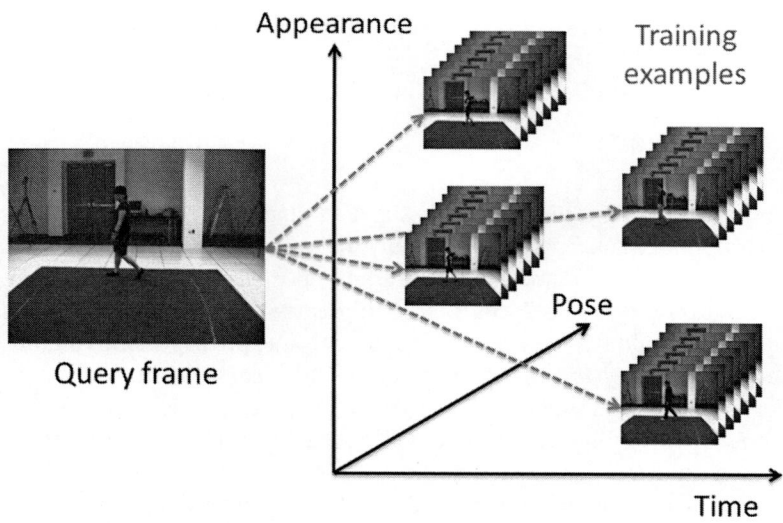

Fig. 1. Motionlets for a query frame. Each motionlet consists of training examples that cover a local region in terms of appearance space, pose space and time stream.

Finally, we show qualitative results on our Taichi data set and quantitative results on the HumanEva-I data set [15].

2   Related Work

Discriminative approaches to human pose estimation provide fast inference because they directly learn the mapping from image descriptors to human pose configurations, avoiding heavy likelihood inference. There are various image descriptors that can be flexibly incorporated into discriminative human pose estimation. These image descriptors are usually based on silhouettes [3,6], gradients [2,11], or edges [1,10,14,18], with different computation complexity, descriptor dimensionality, robustness against clutter, discriminating power and generalization ability. Notably, many of these image descriptors requires accurate location of the subject or background segmentation. As a consequence, the result of segmentation has substantial influence on the performance of a pose estimation algorithm. Alternatively, hierarchical multi-level image descriptors such as HMAX [8,13], spatial pyramids [8], and vocabulary trees [8] can be used with no need for localization or segmentation. In this work, we choose HMAX [8,13] as image descriptor to ensure stable performance.

In the existing literature, various methods can be adopted to learn the mapping from image descriptors to human pose configurations, ranging from nearest-neighbor retrieval [14] and manifold embedding [3,8] to linear/nonlinear regression [21]and probabilistic mixture of predictors [17,9]. As we mentioned in the introduction, discriminative approaches have to model multimodality of the high-dimensional nonlinear appearance-to-pose mapping. Usually, multimodality of the mapping is represented by mixture of models, such as Bayesian mixture of experts (BME) [17,9], mixture of probabilistic PCA [5], and mixture of multi-layer perceptrons [12]. In [19,22,4], mixture of local gaussian process experts was used, where multimodality was handled by expert selection. Different from previous strategies, we propose to model multimodality of the mapping by motionlets, each of which contains training examples that covers a local area with respect to image space, pose space and time stream. As will be shown in following section, the main cause of multimodality of the appearance-to-pose mapping is that there usually exist multiple instances of motionlets for the query frame. Our solution directly and efficiently deal with the multimodality by selecting candidate poses contributed by these motionlets.

Recently, Local Coordinate Coding (LCC) has demonstrated promising results on learning the local geometry of data points [20]. As a variant of LCC, Locality-constrained Linear Coding [7] offers an efficient local smooth sparse projection of an image descriptor into its local-coordinate system with good reconstruction. In our discriminative pose estimation framework, we take advantage of LLC to reconstruct 3D human poses for the query frame using motionlets as codebooks.

3   Motionlet LLC Coding for Human Pose Estimation

3.1   Local Motion Similarity

There are three aspects of human motion that should be taken into consideration for human pose estimation: appearance, pose, and time. One key property of human motion is local motion similarity with respect to appearance, pose and time, which is the basis assumption of all discriminative human pose estimation methods. From this point of view, the improved accuracy and efficiency of recent local approaches [19,22,4] should be owed to their effective and efficient use of local motion similarity of human motion.

An embodiment of local motion similarity is showed by fig. 2. Local motion similarity is represented by the similarity among training/validate frames within an local region in terms of image space, pose space and time stream, which is reflected by dark strips along inclined downward 45 degrees in the affinity matrices for HMAX image descriptors and pose vectors. Note that several dark strips along inclined upward 45 degrees appear in the affinity matrices for HMAX image descriptors, which are caused by ambiguities of HMAX image descriptors. We believe that it is interesting to develop a criterion of good image descriptors for discriminative human pose estimation based on this observation. Intuitively speaking, the more the affinity matrix for image descriptors resembles the corresponding affinity matrix for pose vectors in appearance, the better are the image descriptors for pose estimation. We leave it here for future study.

3.2   Motionlets for Human Pose Estimation

The concept of motionlets for human pose estimation is a natural embodiment of local motion similarity of human motion. We now formulate the definition of motionlets in the context of discriminative human pose estimation.

Let $X = (F, P)$ be a training sequence, where $F = [f_1, f_2, \cdots, f_N]$ consists of image descriptors (e.g. HMAX) of the image sequence of length N, and $P = [p_1, p_2, \cdots, p_N]$ contains corresponding ground truth poses. Given a query frame with its image descriptor f_q, there exists one or more motionlets, denoted by $M = M_1, \cdots, M_T$ where $T \geq 1$. As shown by fig. 1, each motionlet covers a local region of training examples in terms of appearance space, pose space and time stream, which is given by

$$M_i = (F_i, P_i), i \in \{1, \cdots, T\} \tag{1}$$
$$F_i = [f_{a_i}, \cdots, f_{b_i}]$$
$$P_i = [p_{a_i}, \cdots, p_{b_i}].$$

a_i and b_i are head index and tail index of the motionlet respectively, which should hold the following conditions, a) $a_i < b_i$, $a_i, b_i \in \{1, 2, \cdots, N\}$; b) $\forall j \in \{a_i, \cdots, b_i\}$, $d(f_q, f_j) < \delta$; c) $a_i < 1 \parallel d(f_q, f_{a_i-1}) > \delta$; and d) $b_i > N \parallel d(f_q, f_{b_i+1}) > \delta$, where d is a distance function and δ is a threshold determining how close the image descriptors of the motionlet are with that of the query frame. Here we use Euclidean distance.

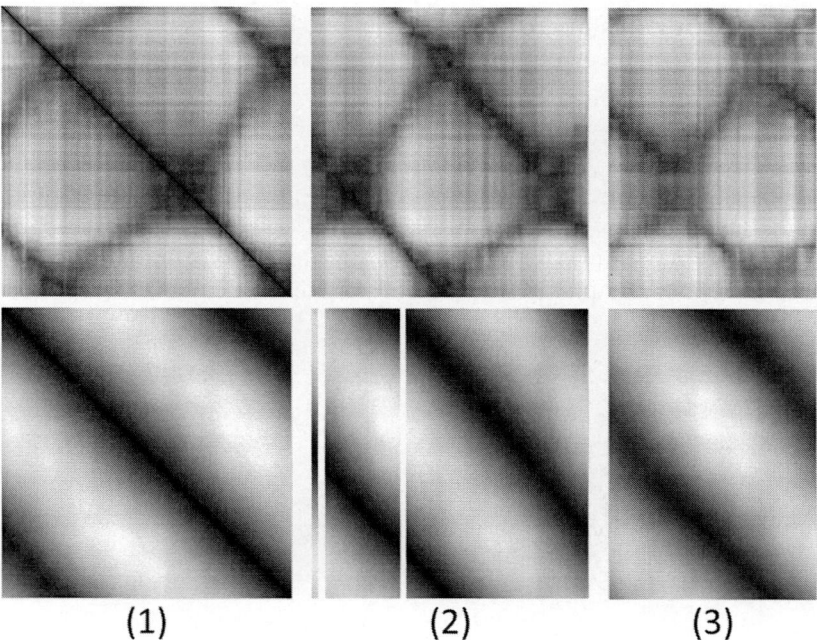

(1)   **(2)**   **(3)**

Fig. 2. Affinity matrices for camera 1 of (1) subject 1 training walking sequence, (2) subject 1 training walking sequence v.s. validate walking sequence, and (3) subject 1 training walking sequence v.s. subject 2 training walking sequence of HumanEva-I data set. First row shows affinity matrices of HMAX image descriptors,and second row shows affinity matrices of ground truth poses represented as vectors. Dark values stand for small distances. The white bar in the middle column of second row is caused by absence of mocap data in subject 1 validate walking sequence.

Combining the definition of motionlets and local motion similarity of human motion, it's easy to understand that there are usually multiple motionlets for a query frame. This is because there usually several training sequences, each of which usually contains several motionlets for the query frame. As mentioned in the introduction, the multiple instances of motionlets is the main cause of multimodality of the mapping in discriminative human pose estimation. By making use of the concept of motionlets, multimodality of the mapping can be handled more directly.

3.3   Motionlet LLC Coding

In our local discriminative framework of human pose estimation, Local Coordinate Coding (LCC) is adopted to reconstruct 3D human poses for the query frame using motionlets as codebooks. Let $M' = \{M'_1, M'_2, \cdots, M'_{T'}\}$, where $M'_i = (F'_i, P'_i)$ and $i \in \{1, \cdots, T'\}$, be all the motionlets for the query frame from training sequences. A series of LLC coding coefficients of f_q, denoted by $C_M = \{c_1, \cdots, c_{T'}\}$, are computed by performing LLC coding on the image descriptor f_q with each of the motionlets as codebook. Then the reconstructed image descriptors and corresponding 3D human poses are given by

$$F_M = \{f'_1, \cdots, f'_{T'}\}, \ f'_i = F'_i c_i \tag{2}$$
$$P_M = \{p'_1, \cdots, p'_{T'}\}, \ p'_i = P'_i c_i, \tag{3}$$

where $i \in \{1, \cdots, T'\}$.

Now P_M contains candidate poses, each of which is contributed by one of the motionlets. The most appropriate candidate pose is selected as result estimate given by

$$p^* = p'_\theta \tag{4}$$
$$\theta = \arg \min_i [d(f_q, f'_i) + \lambda dist(f_q, F'_i)],$$

where λ is relative weight of the image descriptor distance term over the image descriptor reconstruction error term and the distance between a image descriptor and those of a motionlet is defined by

$$dist(f, F') = \min_{f_i \in F'} d(f, f_i). \tag{5}$$

This is much like a Nearest-Neighbor strategy. One may deem that the image descriptor reconstruction error term is positively correlated with the image descriptor distance term and one of them can be omitted. But in fact there exist cases where the former is relatively small with the latter being relatively big and vice versa.

At this end, we can inference 3D human pose from monocular image sequences. The following text will show how to exploit multiview image sequences to achieve more accurate and robust human pose estimation.

3.4   Multiview Integration

For monocular human pose estimation, there are considerable ambiguities in the mapping from image space to pose space, not mentioning the ambiguities caused by image descriptors (e.g. dark strips along inclined upward 45 degrees in the affinity matrices for HMAX image descriptors shown by the first row of Fig. 2). To account for these inference ambiguities, we extend our framework to incorporate multiviews.

When multiview sequences are available, we first estimate 3D human pose from each single view. This provides several candidate poses, each of which corresponds with one view. Again, candidate pose selection is applied to get final estimate. Unlike the method in [11] combining all views into one descriptor, our method is more robust against estimation failure occurs in one of the views, while in [11] the occurrence of inaccurate background segmentations in one or more views will always generate bad estimation result.

4   Experimental Evaluation

4.1   Taichi Data Set

In this experiment, we evaluate our method qualitatively on our Taichi data set. For the Taichi data set, we collect monocular image sequences of a subject exercising Taichi with synchronized ground truth pose captured by two Microsoft Kinect sensors. 3D pose is represented as a vector of 20 concatenated 3D joint positions and is estimated from HMAX image descriptors. Fig. 3 depicts serval test frames of Taichi data set and their corresponding estimated 3D human poses. Note that in some cases it's hard to distinguish arms from torso due to very dark clothes and self occlusion, but our method can accurately infers 3D poses under such condition.

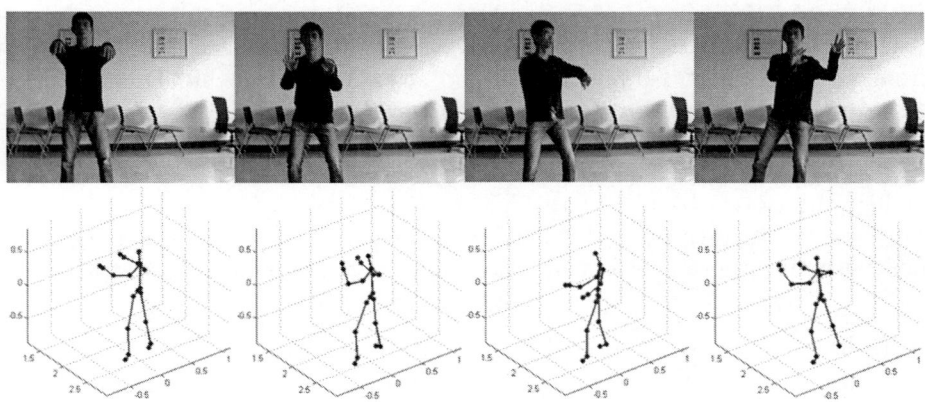

Fig. 3. Qualitative results from monocular 3D human pose estimation of our proposed method on our Taichi data set

4.2   HumanEva-I Data Set

To quantitatively evaluate our method, we also conduct experiments on the HumanEva-I data set [15]. The HumanEva-I data set contains multiview video sequences that are synchronized with 3D body poses obtained from a motion capture system. The database contains sequences of different subjects performing several predefined actions (e.g. walking, jogging, gesturing, etc.), which are originally partitioned into training, validation, and testing sets. In this experiment, we use the original training and validation sets as training set and the original testing set for testing. Again, 3D body pose is represented by joint positions and HMAX image descriptors are used. Except for monocular pose recovery, we also evaluate our 3D human pose estimation method with multiviews incorporated on the data set.

We report mean 3D difference errors between estimated joint positions and ground truth joint positions in mm, relative to the pelvis (torsoDistal) joint. In the experiments, we remove frames with invalid ground truth poses from

Table 1. Quantitative results on HumanEva-I data set: Mean 3D error in mm for HumanEva-I testing set of 3 subjects performing various actions, evaluated with a single view (C1) and multiviews (C1,BW1-BW4).

Action	Subject1		Subject2		Subject3	
	Single-View	Multiview	Single-View	Multiview	Single-View	Multiview
Walking	43.80(19.84)	34.89(10.56)	53.66(35.39)	40.44(22.66)	50.80(40.33)	36.54(20.96)
Jog	70.70(37.35)	50.90(18.16)	51.59(27.06)	35.55(10.95)	61.10(31.45)	43.30(18.86)
Throw/Catch			81.69(34.23)	61.75(25.38)		
Gestures	26.40(4.69)	22.14(4.71)	95.96(34.50)	68.05(15.89)	73.70(16.91)	54.96(7.56)
Box	92.64(28.01)	64.88(12.42)	110.98(43.73)	87.25(31.36)	121.50(68.64)	81.79(20.45)
Average	49.90(33.00)	37.76(19.20)	77.57(41.57)	57.68(28.52)	79.59(53.01)	55.77(25.29)

the training set[1]. With ground truth poses of testing set withheld, we use the on-line evaluation system of HumanEva project [16]. The results are reported in Tab. 1. Note that training sequences and testing sequences are originally from different sequences, but our method accurately infers the 3D body poses even though the poses and appearances in training and testing data might have been relatively different. In the single-view case, the errors are relative big. This might be due to the lack of discriminating power of HMAX descriptors and ambiguities caused by them (see Fig. 2). Compared to the results of Poppe's work [11] where foreground HOG is used as image descriptors, our method with multiviews incorporated offers more accurate and robust human pose estimation.

5   Conclusions

In this paper we presented a local online framework for 3D human pose estimation, which is able to learn a complex, high-dimensional, and multimodal nonlinear mapping from image descriptors to 3D human poses. We have formulated the concept of motionlets and showed that multimodality of the mapping is mainly caused by the multiple instances of motionlets for each query frame. We directly handle multimodality of the mapping by first group most informative and helpful training examples into motionlets, then perform LLC Coding to learn the nonlinear mapping and get candidate poses, and finally choose the most appropriate pose as the result estimate. To improve accuracy and robustness, we extend our framework to incorporate multiviews. We conducted the experiments on our Taichi data set and the real HumanEva-I data set to evaluate our proposed method qualitatively and quantitatively, and achieved accurate results. In future work, we plan to develop a method to assess image descriptors and to find good image descriptors for discriminative human pose estimation.

Acknowledgments. This work is supported by National Natural Science Foundation of China(61170142), National Key Technology R&D Program

---

[1] Most of the ground truth poses of Subject1 Throw/Catch sequence are invalid and those of Subject3 are unavailable.

(2011BAG05B04), the Zhejiang Province Key S&T Innovation Group Project (2009R50009), and the Fundamental Research Funds for the Central Universities(2012FZA5017).

References

1. Agarwal, A., Triggs, B.: A Local Basis Representation for Estimating Human Pose from Cluttered Images. In: Narayanan, P.J., Nayar, S.K., Shum, H.-Y. (eds.) ACCV 2006, Part I. LNCS, vol. 3851, pp. 50–59. Springer, Heidelberg (2006)
2. Bo, L., Sminchisescu, C.: Twin gaussian processes for structured prediction. IJCV (2010)
3. Elgammal, A., Lee, C.-S.: Nonlinear manifold learning for dynamic shape and dynamic appearance. CVIU 106(1), 31–46 (2007)
4. Fergie, M., Galata, A.: Local Gaussian processes for pose recognition from noisy inputs. In: BMVC (2010)
5. Grauman, K., Shakhnarovich, G., Darell, T.: Inferring 3D structure with a statistical image-based shape model. In: ICCV (2003)
6. Howe, N.R.: Silhouette lookup for monocular 3D pose tracking. Image and Vision Computing 25(3), 331–341 (2007)
7. Wang, J., Yang, J., Yu, K., Lv, F., Huang, T., Gong, Y.: Locality-constrained Linear Coding for image classification. In: CVPR (2010)
8. Kanaujia, A., Sminchisescu, C., Metaxas, D.: Semi-supervised hierarchical models for 3D human pose reconstruction. In: CVPR (2007)
9. Ning, H., Wei, X., Gong, Y., Huang, T.: Discriminative learning of visual words for 3D human pose estimation. In: CVPR (2008)
10. Ong, E.-J., Micilotta, A.S., Bowden, R., Hilton, A.: Viewpoint invariant exemplar-based 3D human tracking. CVIU 104(23), 178–189 (2006)
11. Poppe, R.W.: Evaluating example-based pose estimation: Experiments on the Humaneva sets. Tech. Report TR-CTIT-07-72, University of Twente (2007)
12. Rosales, R., Sclaroff, S.: Learning body pose via specialized maps. In: NIPS (2002)
13. Serre, T., Wolf, L., Poggion, T.: Object recognition with features inspired by visual cortex. In: CVPR (2005)
14. Shakhnarovich, G., Viola, P.A., Darrel, T.: Fast pose estimation with parameter-sensitive hashing. In: ICCV (2003)
15. Sigal, L., Black, M.: Humaneva: Synchronized video and motion capture dataset for evaluation of articulated human motion. Tech. Report CS-06-08, Brown University (2006)
16. HumanEva project, http://vision.cs.brown.edu/humaneva/
17. Sminchisescu, C., Kanaujia, A., Li, Z., Metaxas, D.: Discriminative density propagation for 3D human motion estimation. In: CVPR (2005)
18. Sminchisescu, C., Kanaujia, A., Metaxas, D.: Learning joint top-down and bottom-up processes for 3D visual inference. In: CVPR (2006)
19. Urtasun, R., Darrel, T.: Local probabilistic regression for activity-indenpendent human pose inference. In: CVPR (2008)
20. Yu, K., Zhang, T., Gong, Y.: Nonlinear learning using local coordinate coding. In: NIPS (2009)
21. Zhao, X., Ning, H., Liu, Y., Huang, T.: Discriminative estimation of 3D human pose using Gaussian processes. In: CVPR (2008)
22. Zhao, X., Fu, Y., Liu, Y.: Temporal-Spatial Local Gaussian Process Experts for Human Pose Estimation. In: Zha, H., Taniguchi, R.-I., Maybank, S. (eds.) ACCV 2009, Part I. LNCS, vol. 5994, pp. 364–373. Springer, Heidelberg (2010)

Transfer Discriminant-Analysis of Canonical Correlations for View-Transfer Action Recognition

Xinxiao Wu, Cuiwei Liu, and Yunde Jia

Beijing Laboratory of Intelligent Information Technology,
School of Computer Science, Beijing Institute of Technology,
Beijing, 100081 ,China
{wuxinxiao,liucuiwei,jiayunde}@bit.edu.cn

Abstract. A novel transfer learning approach, referred to as Transfer Discriminant-Analysis of Canonical Correlations (Transfer DCC), is proposed to recognize human actions from one view (target view) via the discriminative model learned from another view (source view). To cope with the considerable change between feature distributions of source view and target view, Transfer DCC includes an effective nonparametric criterion in the discriminative function to minimize the mismatch between data distributions of these two views. We utilize the canonical correlation between the means of samples from source view and target view to measure the data distribution distance between the two views. Consequently, Transfer DCC learns an optimal projection matrix by simultaneously maximizing the canonical correlation of mean samples from source view and target view, maximizing the canonical correlations of within-class samples and minimizing the canonical correlations of between-class samples. Moreover, we propose a Weighted Canonical Correlations scheme to fuse the multi-class canonical correlations from multiple source views according to their corresponding weights for recognition in the target view. Experiments on the IXMAS multi-view dataset demonstrate the effectiveness of our method.

Keywords: Transfer discriminative learning, canonical correlation analysis, view-transfer action recognition.

1 Introduction

Automatic human action recognition from different views has become an essential research topic in computer vision for its wide real-world applications such as video surveillance, human-action interaction and video retrieval. Due to the changing positions of cameras and self-occlusions between different body parts, the appearance of actions may drastically vary from one view to another. Therefore, cross-view action recognition poses substantial challenges for computer vision algorithms.

One strategy [1, 2] is to learn a separate action model for each view, however, it is difficult to collect sufficient labeled samples for each view to cover all the

W. Lin et al. (Eds.): PCM 2012, LNCS 7674, pp. 444–454, 2012.

action categories. Another alternative resorts to 3D reconstruction from multiple views [3, 4] or epipolar geometry reasoning [5, 6]. These methods require calibration setup of multiple cameras or reliable point correspondences, which limits their applicability in practice. Other methods [7, 8] exploit the view-invariant descriptor for recognition. Recently, transfer-learning based approaches [9–11] for cross-view action recognition have received considerable attention in computer vision. This emerging family of methods transfers the feature representation or action models learned on one or more views (source views) to another different view (target view) by exploring the statistical connections between source view and target view without inferring camera geometry or 3D construction from multiple cameras.

In transfer learning, the feature distributions of samples from source view and target view change tremendously, so training with samples from the source view may degrade the performance in the target view. Therefore, it is crucial to reduce the difference between the data distributions of source view and target view. We propose a new transfer learning approach, called Transfer Discriminant-Analysis of Canonical Correlations (Transfer DCC), to handle the considerable inconsistency between data distributions of source view and target view. Our method extends the Discriminant-Analysis of Canonical Correlations (DCC) [12] method to include a nonparametric criterion for comparing data distributions based on the canonical correlation between the means of samples from two views in the projected discriminative data space. Consequently, in Transfer DCC, the optimal discriminative function is proposed to project both source-view and target-view samples, so that the canonical correlation of between-view mean samples is maximized while the canonical correlations of within-class samples and between-class samples are respectively maximized and minimized in the projected data space. In order to further improve the recognition performance, we additionally present a Weighted Canonical Correlations scheme to effectively and flexibly fuse the multi-class canonical correlations from multiple source views according to their corresponding weights to generate the multi-class canonical correlation in the target view. The estimation of the combination weights is formulated under a multi-task learning framework and the learned weight value describes how contributive the canonical correlation of the corresponding class from the corresponding view is to the action prediction in the target view.

2   Related Work

The methods most closely related to our approach are that of [9–11]. Farhadi *et al* [9] used maximum margin clustering to generate the splits in the source view and then transferred the split values to the target view to learn the split-based features in the target view. Their work requires feature-to-feature correspondence at the frame-level to train a classifier. Liu *et al* [10] proposed a bipartite-graph-based approach to learn bilingual-words from source view and target view vocabularies, and then transferred action models between two views via the bag-of-bilingual-words model. This method relies on simultaneous observations of the same action instance from multiple views. In contrast, our method requires neither the feature-to-feature correspondence nor the video-to-video correspondence, which significantly relaxes the requirements on the training data. Li *et al* [11] proposed "virtual views" to connect action descriptors from source view and target view. Each virtual view is associated with a linear transformation of the action descriptor, and the sequence of transformed descriptors can be used to compare actions from different views. From a different perspective, our method simply reduces the inconsistency of data distributions between source view and target view to improve the discrimination in target view, without assuming the continuous transformation of action descriptors between two views.

Our work is also relevant to transfer learning [13] which retains previous knowledge learned from one or multiple existing domains to improve learning in the new domains of interest. In recent years, transfer learning has been successfully applied in many real-world applications such as image and video classification [14–18]. In this paper, we apply the proposed transfer learning method to the view-transfer action recognition. Based on different definitions of the knowledge to be transferred, our method can be categorized into the feature-representation-transfer, which finds a "good" projected feature space that reduces difference between source and target domains. Based on different situations between source and target domains, our method belongs to the transductive transfer, in which the source and target tasks are the same while the source and target domains are different.

3   Transfer DCC Learning Framework

Each action sample is represented by an orthogonal linear subspace of an image set (i.e., sequential images) and the similarity between two actions is defined by the canonical correlation of the corresponding two subspaces. We do not take into account the temporal dynamics of an action and in some cases several principal images even a single image is sufficient to recognize what a person is doing.

Given a large number of labeled samples from the source view, a small (even no) number of labeled samples from the target view, and some unlabeled samples from the target view, we propose Transfer DCC to find a discriminative space (represented by a projection matrix T) where the canonical correlation of mean samples from source view and target view is maximized while the canonical correlations of within-class samples and between-class samples from all the labeled training samples are maximized and minimized, respectively. Then, the similarity between two actions is measured by the canonical correlation between the two image sets projected by the projection matrix T.

3.1   Brief Review of DCC

Discriminant-Analysis of Canonical Correlations (DCC) [12] introduces a linear discriminative function to maximize canonical correlations of within-class sets and minimize canonical correlations of between-class sets. Assume m image sets are given as $\{X_1, X_2, ..., X_m\}$, where X_i represents a matrix with each column describing an image. X_i belongs to one action class denoted by C_i. A d-dimensional linear subspace of X_i is represented by an orthonormal basis matrix $P_i \in R^{D \times d}$ s.t. $X_i X_i^T = P_i \Lambda_i P_i^T$, where Λ_i is the d largest eigenvalues, P_i is the corresponding eigenvectors, and D is the dimension of image descriptor. The discriminative projection matrix $T = [t_1, t_2, ..., t_n] \in R^{D \times n}$ is defined by $T : X_i \rightarrow Y_i = T^T X_i$, where $n \leq D$ and $|t_i| = 1$, to make the projected image sets more discriminative using canonical correlations. Orthonormal basis matrices of the subspaces of the projected data are given by $Y_i Y_i^T = (T^T X_i)(T^T X_i)^T = (T^T P_i)\Lambda_i(T^T P_i)^T$. The matrix P_i is normalized to P_i' so that the columns of $T^T P_i'$ are orthonormal. By the SVD computation $(T^T P_i')^T (T^T P_j') = Q_{ij}\Lambda Q_{ji}^T$, the similarity of two projected data sets is defined as the sum of canonical correlations $F_{ij} = \max_{Q_{ij}, Q_{ji}} \mathrm{tr}\{T^T P_j' Q_{ji} Q_{ij}^T P_i'^T T\}$. T is determined to maximize the similarities of any pair of within-class sets and minimize the similarities of pair-wise sets of different classes by

$$T = \arg \max_T \frac{E_w(T)}{E_b(T)}, \tag{1}$$

where $E_w(T) = \sum_{i=1}^{m} \sum_{k \in W_i} F_{ik}$ and $E_b(T) = \sum_{i=1}^{m} \sum_{l \in B_i} F_{il}$. The two index sets $W_i = \{j | C_j = C_i\}$ and $B_i = \{j | C_j \neq C_i\}$, respectively, denote the within-class and between-class sets for a given set of class C_i.

3.2   View Transfer via Minimizing Data Distribution Mismatch

The conventional DCC method assumes that the training and test data are drawn from the same data distribution. However, for view-transfer action recognition, the training and test samples from different views have different data distribution properties (such as mean, intra-class and inter-class variance). So we extend DCC to handle the problem of reducing the mismatch between the data distributions of source view and target view. An effective nonparametric criterion is integrated into the discriminative function in Eq.(1) to compare data distributions by the canonical correlation between the means of image sets from source view and target view in the projected data space. Then the learning framework of Transfer DCC is formulated as:

$$T = \arg \max_T \frac{E_w(T) + \alpha E_r(T)}{E_b(T)}, \tag{2}$$

where $E_r(T)$ is the canonical correlation of between-view mean samples from source view and target view, and defined on all the training samples from source view and target view in the projected data space. α is the tradeoff parameter to balance the data distribution difference between these two views and the discriminative criterion defined on all the labeled training data.

Let $D^s = \{X_i^s\}_{i=1}^N$ be the source-view training dataset, where X_i^s is i-th training sample (i.e., an image set) from the source view. Let $D^t = D_l^t \bigcup D_u^t$ be the target-view training dataset, where $D_l^t = \{X_{l,i}^t\}_{i=1}^M$ and $D_u^t = \{X_{u,i}^t\}_{i=1}^K$ denote the labeled and unlabeled training data from the target view, respectively. $E_r(\mathrm{T})$ in Eq.(2) can be rewritten as:

$$E_r(\mathrm{T}) = \max_{Q_{st}, Q_{ts}} \mathrm{tr}\{\mathrm{T}^T \mathrm{P}'_s Q_{st} Q_{ts}^T \mathrm{P}'^T_t \mathrm{T}\}, \qquad (3)$$

where P'_s is the normalized orthonormal basis matrix of the mean of source-view training data $\overline{\mathrm{X}}^s = \frac{1}{N}\sum_{i=1}^N \mathrm{X}^s_i$. P'_t is the normalized orthonormal basis matrix of the mean of target-view training data $\overline{\mathrm{X}}^t = \frac{1}{M+K}(\sum_{i=1}^M \mathrm{X}^t_{l,i} + \sum_{i=1}^K \mathrm{X}^t_{u,i})$. Q_{st} and Q_{ts} are defined by the SVD computation $(\mathrm{T}^T \mathrm{P}'_s)^T(\mathrm{T}^T \mathrm{P}'_t) = Q_{st}\Lambda Q_{ts}^T$. $E_r(\mathrm{T})$ evaluates the data distribution variations between source view and target view, thus we attempt to maximize $E_r(\mathrm{T})$ to reduce the between-view difference.

By the linear algebra $\mathrm{T}^T \mathrm{P}'_j Q_{ji} Q_{ij}^T \mathrm{P}'^T_i \mathrm{T} = \mathrm{I} - \mathrm{T}^T(\mathrm{P}'_j Q_{ji} - \mathrm{P}'_i Q_{ij})(\mathrm{P}'_j Q_{ji} - \mathrm{P}'_i Q_{ij})^T \mathrm{T}/2$, we can rewrite the objective function in Eq.(2) as

$$\mathrm{T} = \arg\max_{\mathrm{T}} \frac{\mathrm{tr}(\mathrm{T}^T S_b \mathrm{T})}{\mathrm{tr}(\mathrm{T}^T(S_w + \alpha S_r)\mathrm{T})}, \qquad (4)$$

where $S_r = (\mathrm{P}'_s Q_{st} - \mathrm{P}'_t Q_{ts})(\mathrm{P}'_s Q_{st} - \mathrm{P}'_t Q_{ts})^T$, $S_b = \sum_{i=1}^{N+M}\sum_{l \in B_i}(\mathrm{P}'_l Q_{li} - \mathrm{P}'_i Q_{il})(\mathrm{P}'_l Q_{li} - \mathrm{P}'_i Q_{il})^T$, $S_w = \sum_{i=1}^{N+M}\sum_{k \in W_i}(\mathrm{P}'_k Q_{ki} - \mathrm{P}'_i Q_{ik})(\mathrm{P}'_k Q_{ki} - \mathrm{P}'_i Q_{ik})^T$, $B_i = \{j | C_j \neq C_i\}$ and $W_i = \{j | C_j = C_i\}$. Finally, the optimal T is computed by the eigen-decomposition of $(S_w + \alpha S_r)^{-1}S_b$.

3.3 Learning Algorithm

Similar to DCC, we use an iterative optimization algorithm to find the optimized projection matrix T. With the identity matrix I as the initial value of T, the detailed algorithm of Transfer DCC is listed in Algorithm 1. Once the optimal T is found, a comparison of any two actions is achieved by projecting them via T and then computing the canonical correlation.

4 Weighted Canonical Correlations for Multiple View Fusion

Since single source view may provide partial action knowledge, it is beneficial to combine the action knowledge transferred from multiple source views to improve the recognition performance in the target view. We propose a new Weighted Canonical Correlations method to effectively fuse multi-class canonical correlations from multiple source views into the multi-class canonical correlations of the target view for recognition.

We define the canonical correlation between the target-view sample X^t and the j-th action class from the h-th source view as $a_{jh} = \max_k Similar(\mathrm{X}^t, \mathrm{X}_k)$, where X_k represents the labeled training samples of the j-th action class from both h-th source view and target view. $Similar(\mathrm{X}^t, \mathrm{X}_k)$ denotes the canonical correlation between X^t and X_k by projecting them via the projection matrix

---

Algorithm 1. Transfer Discriminant-Analysis of Canonical Correlations

Input: N labeled training samples $\{X_i^s\}_{i=1}^N$ from the source view

M labeled training samples $\{X_{l,i}^t\}_{i=1}^M$ from the target view

K unlabeled training samples $\{X_{u,i}^t\}_{i=1}^K$ from the target view

Output: Projection matrix $T \in R^{D \times n}$.

Initialize: $T = I$.

1. Compute the mean of source-view samples by $\overline{X}^s = \frac{1}{N}\sum_{i=1}^N X_i^s$.

2. Compute the mean of target-view samples by $\overline{X}^t = \frac{1}{M+K}(\sum_{i=1}^M X_{l,i}^t + \sum_{i=1}^K X_{u,i}^t)$.

3. Compute the orthonormal basis matrices P_i, P_s, P_t of X_i, $\overline{X}^s$, $\overline{X}^t$ by $XX^T = P\Lambda P^T$, $P \in R^{D \times n}$.

4. **Do iterate the following:**

5.   Normalize P_i, P_s, P_t to P_i', P_s', P_t' by QR-decomposition: $T^TP = \Phi\Delta$, $P' = P\Delta^{-1}$.

6.   For every pair P_i', P_j' from the labeled training dataset, do SVD: $(T^TP_i')^T(T^TP_j') = Q_{ij}\Lambda Q_{ji}^T$.

7.   For P_s', P_t', do SVD: $(T^TP_s')^T(T^TP_t') = Q_{st}\Lambda Q_{ts}^T$.

8.   Compute S_r, S_b, S_w.(See Eq.(4))

9.   Compute eigenvectors $\{t_i\}_{i=1}^n$ of $(S_w + \alpha S_r)^{-1}S_b$.

10. **End**

11. $T = [t_1, t_2, ..., t_n] \in R^{D \times n}$.

T_h learned from the h-th source view. Then the combined canonical correlation between X^t and the j-th action class from V source views is given by $g_j = \mathbf{w}_j^T\mathbf{d}_j$, where $\mathbf{w}_j = [w_{j1}, w_{j2}, ..., w_{jV}]^T \in R^{V \times 1}$ is the weight vector of the j-th action class canonical correlations from V source views. $\mathbf{d}_j = [a_{j1}, a_{j2}, ..., a_{jV}]^T \in R^{V \times 1}$ is the j-th class canonical correlation vector from V source views. Actually, g_j can be considered as the final decision value of X^t belonging to the j-th action class. Thus it is essential to estimate the combination weights $\mathbf{W} = [\mathbf{w}_1, \mathbf{w}_2, ..., \mathbf{w}_C] \in R^{V \times C}$ with C the number of action classes.

Let $Y_i = [y_{i1}, y_{i2}, ..., y_{iC}]^T \in R^{C \times 1}$ be the multi-class label of the i-th training sample $X_{l,i}^t$ from the target view, where y_{ij} represents the j-th class label of $X_{l,i}^t$. If $X_{l,i}^t$ belongs to the C-th action class, then $y_{iC} = 1$ and $y_{ij} = 0$, $\forall j \neq C$. Let $\mathbf{d}_{ji} \in R^{V \times 1}$ be the j-th class canonical correlation vector from V source views of $X_{l,i}^t$, we aim to find the optimized $\mathbf{W}$ via the following formulation:

$$\mathbf{W} = \arg\min_{\mathbf{w}_j} \sum_{j=1}^C \sum_{i=1}^M L(y_{ij}, \langle \mathbf{w}_j, \mathbf{d}_{ji} \rangle) + \gamma \sum_{j=1}^C \langle \mathbf{w}_j, \mathbf{w}_j \rangle, \qquad (5)$$

where $\gamma > 0$ is a regularization parameter. The first term $\sum_{j=1}^C \sum_{i=1}^M L(y_{ij}, \langle \mathbf{w}_j, \mathbf{d}_{ji} \rangle)$ in Eq.(5) is the average of the error cross the classes, measured according to a prescribed loss function L which is a square loss in this paper. The second term $\gamma \sum_{j=1}^C \langle \mathbf{w}_j, \mathbf{w}_j \rangle$ is the average of the 2-norm regularization problem cross the classes. This minimization is a convex problem and can be carried out independently cross the classes. In our implement, the Matlab code for the multi-task feature learning proposed in [19] is utilized to solve the optimization problem in Eq.(5).

5   Experiments

5.1   Dataset and Experimental Setup

We evaluate the performance of our method on the IXMAS multi-view dataset [3] which consists of 11 complete action classes. Each action is executed three times by 12 subjects and recorded by five cameras observing the subjects from very different perspectives with the frame rate of 23fps and the frame size of 390×291 pixels. The body position and orientation are freely decided by different subjects. An action video is represented by an image set of sequential frames and each frame is described by the extracted body region which is normalized to the size of 80×40 pixels. The dimension of the linear subspace of each image set is around 10 to represent 98% data energy of the set. Figure 1 shows some action examples from five views.

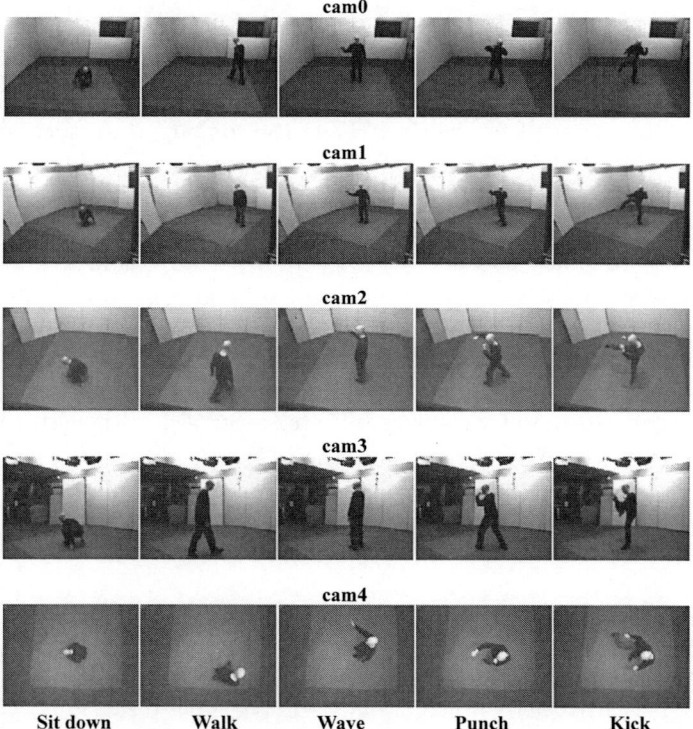

Fig. 1. Samples frames from action videos on the IXMAS multi-view dataset

5.2   Pairwise View-Transfer Recognition

To verify the effectiveness of Transfer DCC across pairwise views, we look into the recognition performances of all possible pairwise combinations. The leave-one-subject-out cross validation strategy (i.e., 12-fold cross validation) is employed. Specifically, for each time, we use videos of one subject from the target view for testing and the remaining videos (i.e., videos of the rest 11 subjects) from the target view as well as all the videos from the source view are utilized as training data. For the training data, only a small number of samples from the target view and all the samples from the source view are labeled.

We compare Transfer DCC with the baseline DCC [12]. For both these two methods, 1-Nearest Neighbors (1NN) is employed for classification. Table 1 demonstrates the recognition results of Transfer DCC and DCC with the fraction of labeled samples from the target view of 0, 1/11, 2/11 and 3/11. From Table 1, we have the following observations: 1) TDCC is better than DCC in terms of recognition accuracy over almost all the cases, which clearly demonstrates that TDCC can successfully deal with the view-transfer recognition by minimizing the data distribution difference between source view and target view. 2) Only in a few cases (e.g., the source view is C1 and the target view is C4 with the fraction of the labeled target-view samples of 0), TDCC works worse than DCC. The possible explanation is that the data distribution difference between C1 and C4 is so large that the transferred information degrades the performance. In the future, we will investigate how to avoid such negative transfer problem. 3) With the increment of the labeled samples from the target view, the performances of both DCC and TDCC significantly improve because of the increasing supervision information from the target view. It is interesting to note that the proposed TDCC provides more discrimination than DCC even when no target labels are available (i.e., the fraction is 0).

5.3   Multiple View-Transfer Recognition

We select one view as the target view and use the other four views as source views to exploit the benefits of combining multiple source views for target recognition. Multi-class canonical correlations from the four source-target pairs are fused via the proposed Weighted Canonical Correlation (WCC) method. To verify the effectiveness of the combination weights of multi-class canonical correlations from multiple source views, we also try a fusion method that uses equal combination weights of canonical correlations (ECC, i.e., $\mathbf{W} = I$) for comparison. Table 2 shows the comparison results between ECC and WCC in the Transfer DCC learning framework. In this experiment, the fraction of the labeled training data from target view is set to 3/11. As shown in Table 2, it is interesting to notice that TDCC-WCC outperforms TDCC-ECC, which obviously demonstrates the effectiveness of our fusion method. By comparing Table 2 to Table 1, it is also interesting to observe that for most target views, the fusion of multiple source views achieves better results than each single source view because of the limited discriminative ability of one single view. Figure 2 demonstrates the recognition accuracy of each action class.

Table 1. Pairwise view-transfer recognition accuracies (%) using Transfer DCC (TDCC) and DCC with the fraction of labeled samples from the target view of 0, 1/11, 2/11 and 3/11. The rows and columns correspond to the training and test views, respectively. "C0", "C1", "C2", "C3" and "C4" represent the five camera views.

(a) fraction=0

	C0	C1	C2	C3	C4
C0		36.4 / 40.2	29.6 / 34.9	22.0 / 28.8	6.8 / 9.1
C1	37.1 / 40.2		42.2 / 44.7	25.0 / 24.2	9.9 / 7.6
C2	30.3 / 37.1	43.2 / 50.8		32.6 / 38.6	10.6 / 15.2
C3	23.5 / 28.8	31.1 / 35.6	35.6 / 44.7		7.6 / 14.4
C4	9.1 / 9.9	16.7 / 13.6	17.4 / 13.6	12.9 / 12.1	
Ave.	25.0 /29.0	31.9 / 35.1	31.2 / 34.5	23.1 / 25.9	8.7 / 11.6

(b) fraction=1/11

	C0	C1	C2	C3	C4
C0		42.4 / 48.5	45.6 / 57.0	53.8 / 47.7	22.7 / 34.1
C1	47.7 / 48.5		50.0 / 50.0	49.2 / 48.5	31.1 / 34.1
C2	39.4 / 47.0	50.0 / 53.8		50.8 / 54.6	28.0 / 31.8
C3	43.2 / 48.5	40.2 / 49.2	37.9 / 50.8		29.6 / 31.1
C4	35.6 / 41.7	41.7 / 46.2	29.6 / 37.9	51.5 / 50.8	
Ave.	41.5 / 46.4	43.6 / 49.4	40.8 / 48.9	51.3 / 50.4	27.9 / 32.8

(c) fraction=2/11

	C0	C1	C2	C3	C4
C0		44.7 / 54.6	49.2 / 52.3	52.3 / 52.3	32.6 / 40.9
C1	52.3 / 56.8		50.8 / 47.0	52.3 / 51.5	37.9 / 38.6
C2	47.0 / 50.8	50.8 / 59.9		51.5 / 54.6	37.1 / 37.1
C3	43.2 / 53.8	46.2 / 51.5	48.5 / 52.3		33.3 / 40.2
C4	43.9 / 49.2	37.9 / 45.5	36.4 / 43.9	50.8 / 50.8	
Ave.	46.6 / 52.7	44.9 / 52.9	46.2 / 48.9	51.7 / 52.3	35.2 / 39.2

(d) fraction=3/11

	C0	C1	C2	C3	C4
C0		48.5 / 59.1	48.5 / 52.3	56.1 / 57.6	34.9 / 44.7
C1	60.6 / 56.8		56.8 / 55.3	63.6 / 62.9	41.7 / 42.4
C2	51.5 / 56.8	53.8 / 60.6		53.0 / 60.6	42.4 / 40.9
C3	52.5 / 56.8	53.8 / 56.1	47.7 / 53.0		40.2 / 45.5
C4	48.5 / 55.3	53.0 / 50.8	37.9 / 41.7	56.1 / 53.8	
Ave.	53.3 / 56.4	52.3 / 56.7	47.7 / 50.6	57.4 / 58.7	39.8 / 43.4

Table 2. Multiple view-transfer recognition accuracies (%) on different methods

Methods	C0	C1	C2	C3	C4	Ave.
TDCC-ECC	59.1	62.1	54.6	60.6	47.7	56.8
TDCC-WCC	64.4	64.4	57.6	62.9	47.7	59.4

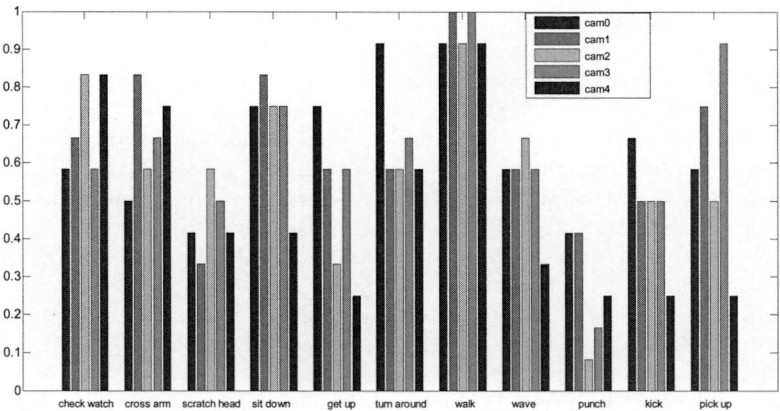

Fig. 2. Recognition results of multiple view-transfer on each action class. The horizontal and vertical axes indicate the action classes and recognition accuracies, respectively.

6   Conclusions

We have proposed a novel Transfer Discriminant-Analysis of Canonical Correlations (Transfer DCC) method for view-transfer action recognition. The data distribution inconsistency between source view and target view is minimized to improve the performance of the discriminative model for the target view when learned from the source view. Our method dose not require any corresponding action instances in the two views and operates under a weakly supervised or even non-supervised scheme. Moreover, a Weighted Canonical Correlations approach is presented to flexibly fuse multiple action predictions from multiple source views. Experiments have shown the effectiveness of our method. Future work includes extracting dynamic motion features for recognition since in this work each action is represented by an image set neglecting the temporal information of motion.

Acknowledgments. This work was supported by the Natural Science Foundation of China(NSFC) under Grant No. 90920009 and NSFC-Guangdong Joint Fund under Grant No. U1035004.

References

1. Wu, X., Xu, D., Duan, L., Luo, J.: Action recognition using context and appearance distribution features. In: Proc. CVPR, pp. 489–496 (2011)
2. Liu, J., Shah, M.: Learning human actions via information maximization. In: Proc. CVPR, pp. 1–8 (2008)
3. Weinland, D., Boyer, E., Ronfard, R.: Action recognition from arbitrary views using 3d exemplars. In: Proc. ICCV, pp. 1–7 (2007)
4. Yan, P., Khan, S., Sha, M.: Learning 4d action feature models for arbitrary view action recognition. In: Proc. CVPR, pp. 1–7 (2008)

5. Yilmaz, A., Shah, M.: Recognizing human actions in videos acquired by uncalibrated moving cameras. In: Proc. ICCV, pp. 150–157 (2005)
6. Shen, Y., Foroosh, H.: View-invariant action recognition using fundamental ratios. In: Proc. CVPR, pp. 1–6 (2008)
7. Junejo, I., Dexter, E., Laptev, I., Perez, P.: View-independent action recognition from temporal self-similarities. IEEE T-PAMI 33(1), 172–185 (2011)
8. Lewandowski, M., Makris, D., Nebel, J.-C.: View and Style-Independent Action Manifolds for Human Activity Recognition. In: Daniilidis, K., Maragos, P., Paragios, N. (eds.) ECCV 2010, Part VI. LNCS, vol. 6316, pp. 547–560. Springer, Heidelberg (2010)
9. Farhadi, A., Tabrizi, M.K.: Learning to Recognize Activities from the Wrong View Point. In: Forsyth, D., Torr, P., Zisserman, A. (eds.) ECCV 2008, Part I. LNCS, vol. 5302, pp. 154–166. Springer, Heidelberg (2008)
10. Liu, J., Shahz, M., Kuipersy, B., Savarese, S.: Cross-view action recognition via view knowledge transfer. In: Proc. CVPR, pp. 3209–3216 (2011)
11. Li, R., Zickler, T.: Discriminative virtual views for cross-view action recognition. In: Proc. CVPR (2012)
12. Kim, T., Kittler, J., Cipolla, R.: Discriminative learning and recognition of image set classes using canonical correlations. IEEE T-PAMI 29(6), 1005–1018 (2007)
13. Pan, S., Yang, Q.: A survey on transfer learning. IEEE T-KDE 22(10), 1345–1359 (2010)
14. Duan, L., Xu, D., Tsang, I., Luo, J.: Visual event recognition in videos by learning from web data. In: Proc. CVPR, pp. 1959–1966 (2010)
15. Kulis, B., Saenko, K., Darrell, T.: What you saw is not what you get: domain adaptation using asymmetric kernel transforms. In: Proc. CVPR, pp. 1785–1792 (2011)
16. Gopalan, R., Li, R., Chellappa, R.: Domain adaption for object recognition: an unsupervised approach. In: Proc. ICCV, pp. 999–1006 (2011)
17. Lampert, C.H., Krömer, O.: Weakly-Paired Maximum Covariance Analysis for Multimodal Dimensionality Reduction and Transfer Learning. In: Daniilidis, K., Maragos, P., Paragios, N. (eds.) ECCV 2010, Part II. LNCS, vol. 6312, pp. 566–579. Springer, Heidelberg (2010)
18. Jie, L., Tommasi, T., Caputo, B.: Multiclass transfer learning from unconstrained priors. In: Proc. ICCV, pp. 1863–1870 (2011)
19. Argyriou, A., Evgeniou, T., Pontil, M.: Convex multi-task feature learning. Machine Learning 73(3), 243–272 (2008)

Personalized Celebrity Video Search Based on Cross-Space Mining

Zhengyu Deng, Jitao Sang, and Changsheng Xu

Institute of Automation, Chinese Academy of Sciences,
100190 Beijing, China
{zydeng,jtsang,csxu}@nlpr.ia.ac.cn

Abstract. Online videos are becoming popular these days. Personalized search has been recognized as effective solution for user accessing desired information when facing a daunting volume of videos. Personalized query understanding serves as one of the most challenges in personalized search, which indicates that unique query has distributed meanings and produce different semantics for different users. Take query of celebrity as example, many celebrities are engaged in multiple fields and certain user may be just interested in the field of videos related to his/her own preference. In this paper, we address the challenge of personalized query understanding by focusing on the problem of personalized celebrity video search. An interest-popularity cross-space mining based method is proposed for solution. Specifically, celebrity popularity and user interest distributions are first learned by topic modeling from heterogeneous data of expert knowledge and user online activities, respectively. We then exploit topic-word distribution refinement to correlate the two heterogeneous topic spaces. Finally the candidate videos are re-ranked based on the derived interest-popularity correlations. Carefully designed experiments have demonstrated the effectiveness of the proposed method. The obtained ranking list is highly consistent with the test users' preferences.

1 Introduction

Nowadays, online video propagation has surged up to an unparalleled level. Within the vast video pool, the videos about celebrities appear highly frequently and are closely followed by the users because of the "Celebrity Effect". It's common that celebrities are engaged in multiple domains. Take David Beckham for example, he is famous for his specialty in soccer sports; but he is also active in the field of entertainment as a fashion expert. From the perspective of users, some Real Madrid fans may take interest in his soccer videos; whereas some like young ladies may adore his fashion style and search for entertainment videos; even some idolaters may prefer the videos that are related to his daily life. Therefore, when a user searches "Beckham", a real personalized search scheme should consider this phenomenon and rank the videos based on the user's specific interested area, i.e., Beckham's soccer games, fashion style or daily life.

The challenges of realizing such a personalized celebrity video search scheme lie in three aspects. (1) The various fields that certain celebrity gets involved in

W. Lin et al. (Eds.): PCM 2012, LNCS 7674, pp. 455–463, 2012.

is not always clear and needs to be explored. (2) Users seldom explicitly provide their interest profiles and the interest-oriented preferences are not available in topic level. (3) How to connect user interest with celebrity popularity is not trivial. Generally, user interest and celebrity popularity are extracted in different spaces from heterogeneous data sources. Therefore, how to explore the latent association of the two spaces is the key factor to solve the problem.

In this paper, we propose an Interest-Popularity Cross-space Mining based method to address the abovementioned challenges. For the celebrity side, celebrity popularity is explored by leveraging expert information, e.g., the corresponding wikipedia homepages. Standard topic modeling method of Latent Dirichlet Allocation (LDA) is adopted to extract the celebrity popularity distribution in abstract topic level. For the user side, since off-the-shelf user profile is unavailable or hardly informative, we exploit user interest based on his/her online activities, e.g., video sharing, social tagging. LDA is again utilized for user interest topic extraction. Given the derived heterogeneous popularity and interest spaces, we introduce a cross-space correlation method. Semantic and context intra-word relations are refined by random walk to bridge the interest and popularity spaces. The framework of our proposed approach is shown in Fig. 1. The inputs include the celebrities' Wikipedia profile and the users' uploaded and favorite videos with associated tags. The output is the generated video ranking list. The framework contains three components, namely interest and popularity space construction, cross-space correlation and video re-ranking. Video re-ranking is based on joint probability distribution of user, celebrity and videos in interest space. See section 3 for detailed elaboration. To summarize, the main contributions of this paper are as follows.

(1) We introduce the novel problem of personalized celebrity video search, by exploiting the user interest and celebrity popularity in topic level.

(2) We propose a cross-space correlation method to connect heterogeneous spaces, which serves as a feasible solution to other cross-domain problems.

(3) With celebrity as a special case of distributed query, we provide one of the first attempts to address the query understanding challenge in personalized search problem.

2   Related Work

In academic communities, some researchers attempt to employ clustering algorithms to assist video retrieval [10] [9]. For instance, Shepitsen et al. [10] clustered the social tags into several concepts and thereafter connected the user and item through those concepts. Some other researchers [6] [2] [5] [12] adopted a hierarchically-arranged collection of concepts or ontologies, in which each node of the ontologies represents a certain interest. For example, Leung and Lee [6] proposed a concept-based profiling strategy to represent users' preferences using weighted concept vectors. Evans et al. [2] defined user interest as a distribution over the category nodes of an ontology. Furthermore, some papers have reported to build up one united space for users and items [10] [3] [8] [9] [11]. Among them,

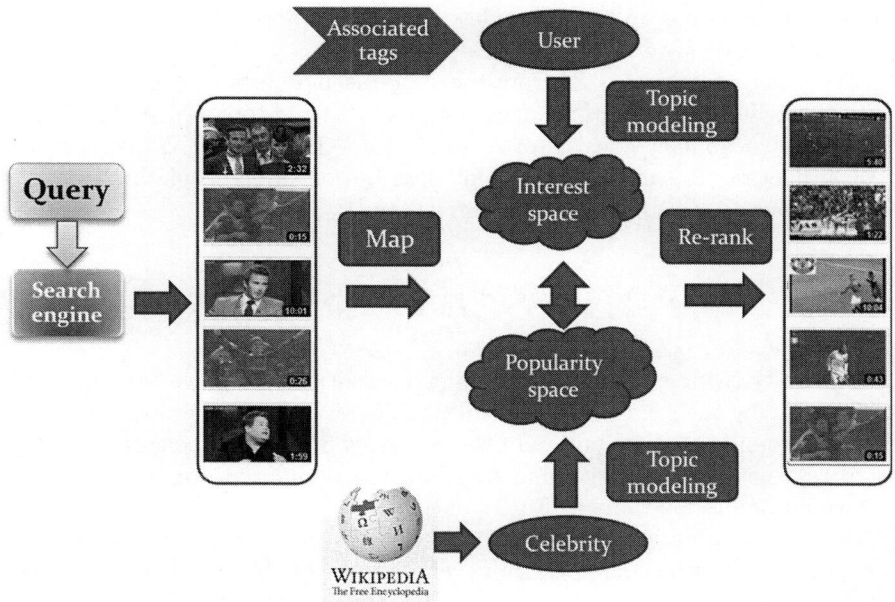

Fig. 1. The framework of our proposed approach

Xu et al. [11] proposed a topic-based personalized search scheme, which maps the sources (user profiles and web pages) onto a unified topic space and decide the ranking score both by the term similarity matching and the topic similarity matching in the unified space. However, these work considers users and items in the same topic space, which is not applicable in our scenario. Besides these works predetermine the subject of interests; hence they fail to represent user interest flexibly. Our work is the first to build up the interest and popularity spaces for user and celebrity separately and re-rank the videos based on the cross-space mining on the topic level.

3 Approach

3.1 Interest and Popularity Topic Spaces Construction

1) **Interest Space**. Generally speaking, users' registration information is useful to analyze their preferences. But it's not easy to aquire because of privacy problem. In comparison, users' active actions (like "upload" or "favor") on a video strongly indicate their attentions and preferences. And since these videos are easy to retrieve through video sharing websites, the users' profiles could be built up by extracting the tags and categories associated with those videos. However, the tags annotated by web users contain plenty of noises such as meaningless words or typos. To tackle this issue, we utilize WordNet to filter out the noises

and only keep noun tags which are the least noisy representations for users' interests. After building up users' profiles, LDA [1] is adopted to learn the latent topics for interest space.

LDA extracts topics ($z \in Z$) from the set of user profiles ($u \in U$) and generates two distributions: user-topic distribution $p(z|u)$ and topic-word distribution $p(w|z)$. The vocabulary consists of N words ($w \in W$). Denote α and β as the hyperparameters respectively. The joint distribution of the topic mixture θ, a set of K topics Z, and N words W, is given by [1]

$$p(\theta, Z, W | \alpha, \beta) = p(\theta | \alpha) \prod_{n=1}^{N} \sum_{i=1}^{K} p(z_i | \theta) p(w_n | z_i, \beta). \tag{1}$$

2) **Popularity Space.** Generally speaking, celebrities often have Wikipedia entries introducing their careers, achievements, life and many other aspects, which reflect the popularity distribution of the celebrity. So we use the entry information to represent the celebrity and build up the popularity space accordingly. The formulation is the same as Eq. 1.

After the probability distribution of a celebrity over the latent topics is obtained, the distribution could determine whether the celebrity is dominant in one or multiple domains. Apparently, if the probability distribution score is high in several latent topics, the celebrity may be engaged in multi-domains, vice versa. Therefore, we utilize entropy of information to differentiate celebrities. Given celebrity c, the entropy could be explicitly written as

$$H(c) = \sum_{i=1}^{L} p_c(x_i) \log \frac{1}{p_c(x_i)} = -\sum_{i=1}^{L} p_c(x_i) \log p_c(x_i) \tag{2}$$

where L is the number of the latent topics extracted by LDA and x_i ($i \in \{1, ..., L\}$) is the ith hidden topic. $p_c(x_i)$ is the probability of celebrity c on topic x_i. The bigger the value is, the more even the distribution will be, i.e., the more domains the celebrity is engaged in.

3.2   Cross-Space Correlation

After the latent topics of each space have been extracted via LDA, the two spaces could be inter-correlated by these topics. We have known that each topic contains a number of semantic words and there is a probabilistic distribution over them. Thus, we can compute the similarity between these topics by KL-divergence on these words. However, since the user and the celebrity are from heterogeneous spaces, the vocabulary of the interest space is not identical with that of the popularity space. Besides, when we extract latent topics using LDA, we have not considered the correlation between the semantic words, which are very important for information propagation, especially when the training data is very sparse. Therefore, we merge the two vocabularies together and set up an transition matrix by WordNet. After that, the random walk which has been widely applied in machine learning and information retrieval fields [4] [7], is utilized to update the probability distribution of topic-word.

We use s_{ij} to denote the similarity of word i and j, which is obtained from WordNet. Given a word graph composed of N words and each word is regarded as a node, the transition matrix is denoted by $\mathbf{P}_{N \times N}$. Its element p_{ij} indicates the probability of the transition from the node i to node j and is computed as $p_{ij} = s_{ij} / \sum_k s_{ik}$. Denote $r_k(i)$ as the relevance score of the node i at iteration k, the relevance scores of all the nodes in the graph at iteration k form a column vector $r_k = [r_k(i)]_{N \times 1}$. So the random walk process is formulated as

$$\mathbf{r}_k = \lambda \sum_i \mathbf{r}_{k-1} \mathbf{P} + (1 - \lambda) \mathbf{y} \tag{3}$$

where $\mathbf{y}$ is the initial probability distribution vector of the topic-word, and $\lambda \in (0, 1)$ is a weight parameter. The above process will make the similar words have the similar scores and strengthen the words that have many close neighbors. The iteration of Eq. 3 converges to a fixed point $\mathbf{r}_\pi = (1 - \lambda)(\mathbf{I} - \lambda \mathbf{P})^{-1} \mathbf{y}$ [7].

Random walk makes each topic has a probabilistic distribution over the whole vocabulary of words. Afterwards, KL-Divergence is utilized to connect user and celebrity at the topic level. Since KL-divergence is direction-related, the average value of the two directions is used here. Assume that z and x are topics from interest and popularity space respectively, the KL-Divergence between them is defined as

$$D_{KL}(z \parallel x) = \frac{1}{2}\left(\sum_i z(i) ln \frac{z(i)}{x(i)} + \sum_i x(i) ln \frac{x(i)}{z(i)}\right) \tag{4}$$

where $z(i)$ and $x(i)$ denote the distribution scores of topic z and x on word i. The similarity s_{zx} of topic z and x is defined as the inverse of KL-Divergence. $s_{zx} = 1/D_{KL}(z \parallel x)$

3.3   Video Re-ranking

In this section we will elaborate how to re-rank the video list based on the user-celebrity correlation. Given a user u, when u query certain celebrity c, we search c in video retrieval engine. Afterwards we re-rank the top-n videos by the correlation of interest-popularity space. Specifically, we first project the celebrity videos on the interest space (Notably, for the sake that we want to provide potential interesting videos to user, it's more reasonable to focus on interest space of users). Assume Φ is a $K \times M$ (K is the topic number of interest space. M is the dimension of the vocabulary of the semantic words) Markov matrix, each row of which denotes the probability distribution vector of a topic over each word in the vocabulary. For any video vector $v_{M \times 1}$, we project it to interest space as $v'_{K \times 1} = \Phi v$

For any celebrity video v, the relevance score is computed as

$$p(score \mid v, u, c)$$

$$= \sum_{i=1}^{K} p(z_i \mid v) p(z_i \mid u) p(z_i \mid c)$$

$$= \sum_{i=1}^{K} p(z_i \mid v) p(z_i \mid u) \sum_{j=1}^{L} p(x_j \mid c) p(z_i \mid x_j)$$

where L is the topic number of popularity space, z_i (x_j) is the ith (jth) topic of interest (popularity) space, $p(z_i \mid x_j)$ is approximated by KL-Divergence (see Eq. 4). After getting the score for each of celebrity videos, we re-rank the videos according to the scores and return a ranking list to the target user.

4   Experiments

4.1   Experimental Settings

We conduct our experiments on a dataset collected from YouTube. Firstly we pick up 330 most popular or powerful celebrities from Forbes[1]. Afterwards we shortlist 106 multi-domains engaged celebrities from them via information entropy (see Eq. 2). Then we extract top-200 related videos on the average for each celebrity from YouTube. At the same time, we collect 143 users from YouTube. The average number of videos uploaded or favored by these users is 205. For each user (denoted by u), some of the videos he/she uploaded or favored are related with certain celebrity (denoted by c) among the abovementioned 106 celebrities. Therefore, in our experiments, we assume that u will issue a query c and obtain a ranking list. Afterwards we count how many videos (not in the training dataset) in the target user's video list are recalled in the ranking list. In order to evaluate the performance of our approach, we compare with 1) the method that just learn a united topic space for users and celebrities and 2) non-personalized search. The performance assessment measure is F-score.

$$F - score = 2 \cdot \frac{Precision \cdot Recall}{Precision + Recall} \tag{5}$$

We empirically fix the hyperparameters according to the prior expectation about the data. The hyperparameter β controls the smoothing and sparsity of topic-word distribution. Small β encourages more words to have high probability in each topic. Enlightened by this, we empirically choose a relatively small value of $\beta = 0.1$. Similarly, α is fixed as 0.25.

---

[1] http://www.forbes.com/wealth/celebrities

4.2   Experiment Results

Parts of the discovered latent topics of interest and popularity spaces are displayed in Table 1, which confirms our hypothesis that the latent topics of user and celebrity could be well extracted via LDA. Besides, through the monitoring of the user and celebrity data, it is found that the learnt interest and popularity distributions for user and celebrity are well tallied with their profiles. Take Beckham as an example, his probability distributions on Topic 1, 4 and 7 are 0.49, 0.25 and 0.10 respectively, which correspond to the fields of sports, entertainment and daily-life, and is consistent with the actual situation. The key words of each topic are shown in Table 1.

Table 1. Parts of the Latent Topics

No	Interest Space	No	Popularity Space
2	movie disney film story	1	season game team sports
3	education book central	4	interview perform romance
5	music cover rock	7	family life dating ceremony
6	interview season party	9	film role series character
8	comedy funny humour	11	album released song awards

The comparison of average F-score at different depths is illustrated in Fig. 2 (the number of latent topics and the weight of random walk is tuned to its optimal value.). We can see that our approach outperforms other methods consistently. Additionally the influence of random walk is shown in Fig. 3. In this figure, the number of latent topics in interest space and popularity is fixed as 30, and the weight of random walk λ is within the range from 0 to 1 with the interval

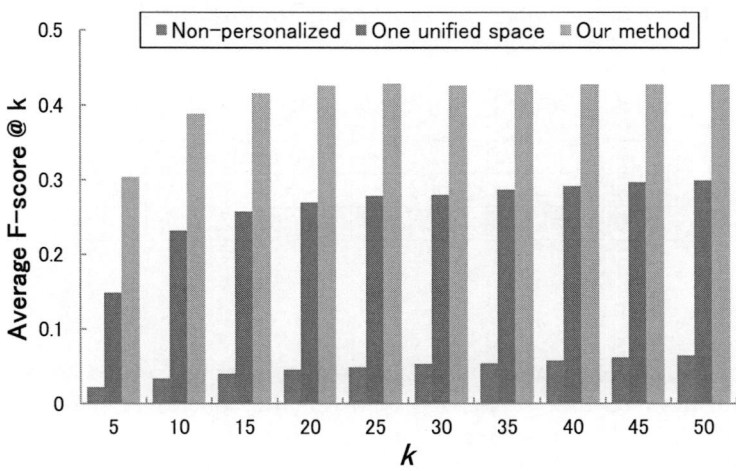

Fig. 2. Different approaches comparing with F-score.

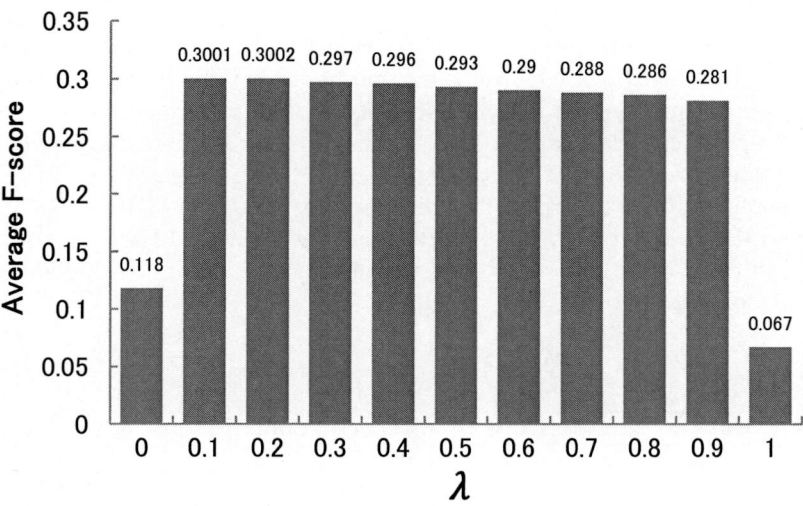

Fig. 3. The influence of random walk. The average F-score of top-50.

of 0.1. $\lambda = 0$ (see Eq. 3) means that there is no random walk applied; whereas $\lambda = 1$ means that the effect of initial value is ignored. It is shown from the figure that basically setting λ in (0.1, 0.9) is better than setting λ to 0 or 1. The former case means that the two spaces are linked directly and the connection would be minimized. The latter case means that the random walk takes fully effect, which makes the word distribution for each topic become identical, so the result is the least satisfactory. The optimal performance is achieved at around $\lambda = 0.2$. This result confirms the significance of random walk in updating the distribution of topic-word. On the other hand, the statistics on the tags of user and celebrity spaces shows an overlapping rate of around 70% (see Table 2), which in turn confirms the necessity to adopt random walk.

Table 2. Statistic of Semantic Words

-	Interest Space	Popularity Space	Total
No. of words	5602	5524	7980
% in total	70.2%	69.2%	-

5 Conclusions

In this paper, we have presented a cross-space mining method to exploit the correlation between user preferences and celebrity queries. Personalized video search is conducted by matching the user's interest distribution with distributed celebrity popularizes. Promising experimental results have demonstrated the effectiveness of our approach. In the future work, we will develop our current studies in the following direction. (1) Utilize visual information to facilitate the learning from interest space or popularity space. (2) Instead of returning a ranking list, we will try to visualize the search results into semantically consistent groups. (3) We will investigate the problem of personalized query understanding in more general personalized search applications.

Acknowledgment. This work was supported in part by National Program on Key Basic Research Project (973 Program, Project No. 2012CB316304) and the National Natural Science Foundation of China (Grant No.90920303, 61003161).

References

1. Blei, D., Ng, A., Jordan, M.: Latent dirichlet allocation. The Journal of Machine Learning Research 3, 993–1022 (2003)
2. Evans, A., Fernández, M., Vallet, D., Castells, P.: Adaptive multimedia access: from user needs to semantic personalisation. In: Proceedings of the 2006 IEEE International Symposium on Circuits and Systems, ISCAS 2006, 4 p. IEEE (2006)
3. Gauch, S., Chaffee, J., Pretschner, A.: Ontology-based personalized search and browsing. Web Intelligence and Agent Systems 1(3/4), 219–234 (2003)
4. Hsu, W., Kennedy, L., Chang, S.: Video search reranking through random walk over document-level context graph. In: Proceedings of the 15th International Conference on Multimedia, pp. 971–980. ACM (2007)
5. Kim, H., Chan, P.: Learning implicit user interest hierarchy for context in personalization. In: Proceedings of the 8th International Conference on Intelligent User Interfaces, pp. 101–108. ACM (2003)
6. Leung, K., Lee, D.: Deriving concept-based user profiles from search engine logs. IEEE Transactions on Knowledge and Data Engineering 22(7), 969–982 (2010)
7. Liu, D., Hua, X., Yang, L., Wang, M., Zhang, H.: Tag ranking. In: Proceedings of the 18th International Conference on World Wide Web, pp. 351–360. ACM (2009)
8. Liu, F., Yu, C., Meng, W.: Personalized web search for improving retrieval effectiveness. IEEE Transactions on Knowledge and Data Engineering 16(1), 28–40 (2004)
9. Ma, Z., Pant, G., Sheng, O.: Interest-based personalized search. ACM Transactions on Information Systems (TOIS) 25(1), 5 (2007)
10. Shepitsen, A., Gemmell, J., Mobasher, B., Burke, R.: Personalized recommendation in social tagging systems using hierarchical clustering. In: Proceedings of the 2008 ACM Conference on Recommender Systems, pp. 259–266. ACM (2008)
11. Xu, S., Bao, S., Fei, B., Su, Z., Yu, Y.: Exploring folksonomy for personalized search. In: Proceedings of the 31st Annual International ACM SIGIR Conference on Research and Development in Information Retrieval, pp. 155–162. ACM (2008)
12. Zhou, X., Wu, S., Li, Y., Xu, Y., Lau, R., Bruza, P.: Utilizing search intent in topic ontology-based user profile for web mining. In: IEEE/WIC/ACM International Conference on Web Intelligence, WI 2006, pp. 558–564. IEEE (2006)

Effective Comic-Like Representations with Embedded Regions of Interest

Luis Herranz, Huiying Liu, and Shuqiang Jiang

Key Lab of Intelligent Information Processing,
Institute of Computing Technology,
Chinese Academy of Sciences, Beijing 100190, China
luis.herranz@vipl.ict.ac.cn, {hyliu,sqjiang}@jdl.ac.cn

Abstract. Comic-like summaries exploit the narrative structure of comics to create intuitive and easily readable abstracts. However, real comics use complex composition techniques which are difficult to mimic in an unsupervised way as they involve high level semantic understanding. This paper explores the use of visual attention analysis and face detection to embed regions of interest in adjacent images, obtaining more compact yet informative representations. This paper also addresses the generation of the layout, which involves combinatorial optimization problems. In practice, using exhaustive search to solve the problem is not feasible due to the large number of images. A split and merge approach is proposed to effectively address the layout problem, thus the limitations of finding solutions in a wide range of row widths can be avoided. A user study conducted on several episodes of TV series confirmed the utility of the proposed approach.

Keywords: Comics, layout, visual attention, video summarizations, regions of interest.

1   Introduction

Comic strips have inspired works in video processing in which a video sequence is converted to a comic-like representation. Usually, people find in comic strips a friendly and intuitive format to present sequential visual information[8]. In addition, comics can be regarded as an extension of storyboards in which the size of the images can vary. In contrast to conventional storyboards, the narrative structure of comics is more complex and includes images with different sizes arranged in the layout according to their importance (layout problem). The related work can be roughly divided into two groups: movie to comic conversion and (large scale) comic-like summaries.

In the first group, video posters[11] and *movie2comics*[5] present video sequences as comic booklets, so the user can visualize the content as a comic book. Each page represents a shot or scene, with few images. As each page is independent of the rest, the layout problem can be solved easily.

In contrast, comic-like summaries try to provide the user with a compact and easily readable representation with the main information, so the user can get

W. Lin et al. (Eds.): PCM 2012, LNCS 7674, pp. 464–475, 2012.

a quick idea of the content of the underlying video sequence. In general, the presentation area is a limited resource which has to be optimized to present as much information as possible in a compact and useful way. Thus, the sequence is represented in few pages with a large number of images, each page representing the narrative of 10-30 minutes of video. Larger images highlight the main semantic information while smaller images provide complementary visual information. In contrast to the methods in the previous group, finding the optimal layout involves NP-hard combinatorial problems. The optimal solution can be found using exhaustive search, but it becomes unfeasible in practice after few images (20-30 images), due to the large search space. For this reason, the work in this group has been mainly focused on efficient suboptimal algorithms to solve the problem[10,4,2,1]. However, they often introduce layout artifacts and may not even guarantee a solution for a given size of the layout. In this paper we propose a suboptimal split and merge layout in which the layout is divided in sublayouts when the number of images is high. The problem of dividing layout into rows is also addressed.

The use of regions of interest (ROIs) has been also explored in comic-like representations[2,5], to save layout space while preserving the interesting regions, thus providing a more compact yet informative abstraction. However, not much attention has been given to composite panels, where some regions of interests are placed over another image. The problem of inserting the ROIs in a suitable location, without interfering with the background image and still following the comic style, has not been studied. In this paper we propose the use of saliency analysis to find low attentive regions where ROIs (faces in our case) can be placed without overlapping with relevant parts of the background image.

With these two contributions, we expect to obtain more natural and intuitive comic-like summaries. The rest of the paper is organized as follows. Section 2 gives an overview of the framework. The proposed methods to generate composite panels and the overall layout are described in Sections 3 and 4. Experimental evaluation and conclusions are presented in Sections 5 and 6.

2   Proposed Framework

Since the objective is to present as much information as possible but in a compact and pleasant format , the proposed system tries to discard redundant information and combine the rest in a meaningful and easily readable format. The proposed summarization process is depicted in Figure 1. There are three main stages: preprocessing, panel compostion and global layout generation. During the preprocessing stage, a set of keyframes is extracted from the video. In our case, we perform shot boundary detection and then sample a keyframe in the middle of each shot. The keyframes are clustered to remove redundancies, using the affinity propagation algorithm[3]. The keyframes are processed to obtain composite panels using visual attention analysis and face detection. The resulting panels are combined with other keyframes during the layout generation stage into the final comic-like summary, arranged according to predefined templates.

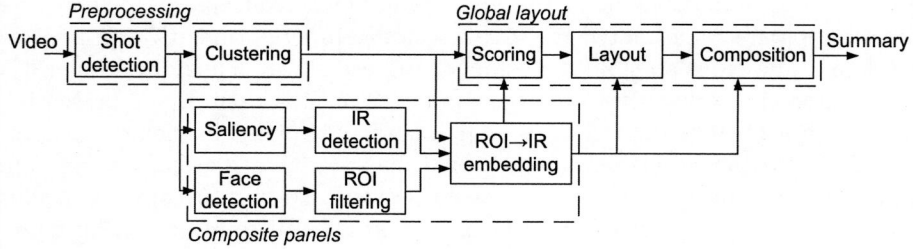

Fig. 1. Architecture of the proposed framework

3   Panel Templates

As in other previous works[11,4,2], the *panel* is the basic unit of the comic-like layout, consisting of several consecutive keyframes arranged in a certain spatial order consistent with the temporal order in the sequence, following the reading conventions of comic strips (for western comics, the order is left to right and then top down). In the proposed system, we denote the comic-like layout Y, which consists of a sequence of panel templates T. Thus, a panel $P = \{p, E\}$ is represented by the index p of the panel template T_p, and the set E with the indices of the keyframes that are scaled and placed in the corresponding locations, and the layout with M panels is represented as $Y = (p_1, p_2, \ldots, p_M)$. For this paper we use two different types of panel templates: basic and composite (see Figure 2).

3.1   Basic Templates

If we limit the possible image sizes to integer multiples of a basic size, and assume that a panel is not divisible vertically, for a given height there is only a certain number of possible combinations satisfying the reading rules. Thus each panel template is represented by a sequence of frame sizes $T = (\Omega_1, \Omega_2, \ldots)$, $\Omega_i \in \{1, 2, \ldots, h\}$. For instance for maximum panel height $h = 4$, there are only eight possible templates (shown in Figure 2a). They are represented as $T_1 = (1, 1, 1, 1)$, $T_2 = (2, 2)$, $T_3 = (2, 1, 1, 1, 1)$, $T_4 = (1, 1, 2, 1, 1)$, $T_5 = (1, 1, 1, 1, 2)$, $T_6 = (3, 1, 1, 1)$, $T_7 = (1, 1, 1, 1, 3)$ and $T_8 = (4)$. Given a panel template T we can also represent its width as $W(T)$ and the length (i.e. number of images) as $|T|$.

3.2   Composite Templates

In comic books, the artist often embeds small images (faces, close-ups) over a related image (in this paper we use the term *background image* to refer to that image), conveying more information than a single image. Thus, in this paper we also consider composite panels, in which several complementary ROIs from different frames are embedded in an adjacent background image. ROIs are usually

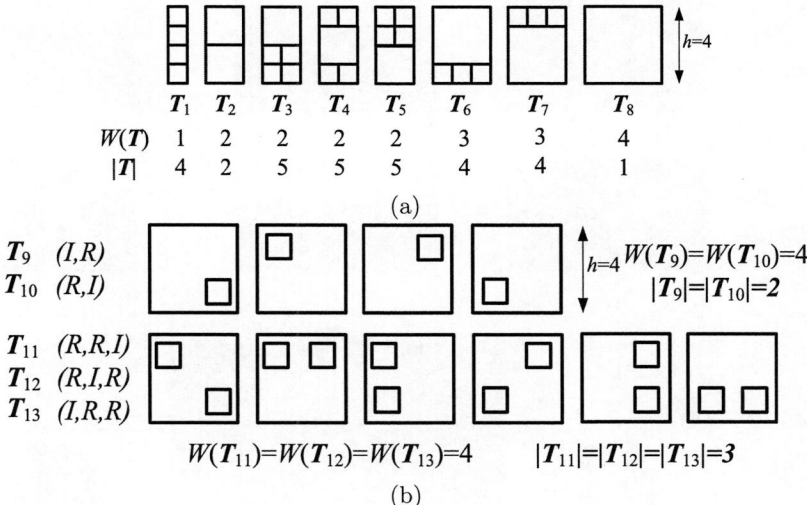

Fig. 2. Panel templates for $h = 4$: a) basic, b) composite panels (I: background image, R: ROI); the groups of templates (T_9 and T_{10}) and (T_{11}, T_{12} and T_{13}) differ in the relative temporal order of I and R, where arrows would be used in the final layout to indicate the temporal flow

embedded on a corner, as the important visual information in the background image is localized in the center of the frame. The composite templates used in the proposed system are shown in Figure 2b. The region of the background image in which a ROI is inserted is the insertion region (IR). For simplicity we only consider composite panels of size h, with a maximum of two IRs (and consequently a maximum of two ROIs), located in any of the corners of the background image. As the reading rules are not so obvious in the case of composite panels, arrows will be used in the final layout to guide the temporal flow of the story, as in real comics.

In Figure 2b we use a different notation, with the background image labeled with I and the ROI with R. Thus, depending on the relative temporal order of the background image and the frame from which the ROIs are extracted there are two possible combinations: $T_9 = (I, R)$ and $T_{10} = (R, I)$ with length $|T| = 2$, and three possible combinations with length three, as the maximum number of ROIs is two. Additionally, the location of the IRs must be also specified.

4   Panel Composition

When the artist creates a composite panel, it should be designed in such a way that the embedded region of interest does not interfere with the background image. Inspired by this idea, we propose an automatic method to insert ROIs into background images, resulting in a more compact combined representation (see Figure 3). ROIs are detected, cropped and inserted conveniently resized in suitable IRs of the background image.

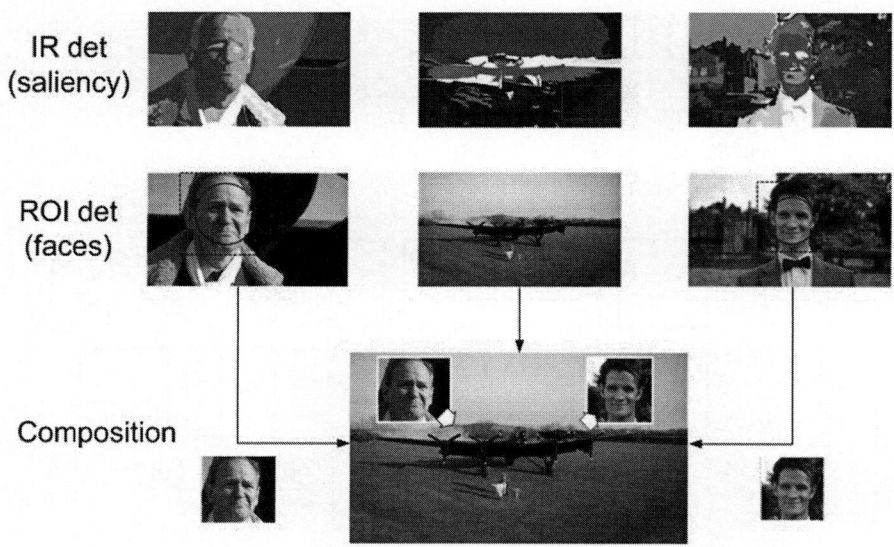

Fig. 3. Example of a composite panel

4.1   Region of Interest Detection

We only consider faces as ROIs, as they can be detected with reasonably accuracy and are meaningful from the panel composition point of view. We use the OpenCV face detection method, extending the detected region to cover the whole head and hair. When more than one face is detected, the bounding rectangle covering all the ROIs is selected as final ROI.

4.2   Insertion Region Detection

ROIs are embedded into uninformative regions of the background image where the saliency is low. The saliency map of an image is obtained using the static attention model proposed in [7], based on contrast and information density. Then, the saliency map is binarized using the Otsu method[9]. We check only the four corners for potential IRs, using integral images to evaluate the average saliency of potential rectangular windows (larger than a minimum size). If the combined saliency is low enough, the region is selected as an IR. Some rules are used to filter unsuitable IRs, such as discarding those which overlap with a ROI detected in the same frame.

4.3   Grouping and Composition

As a result of the previous detection stages, two curves $\eta_i \in \{0,1\}$ and $\mu_i \in \{0,1,2\}$ indicate the number of ROIs and IRs detected in the i-th keyframe,

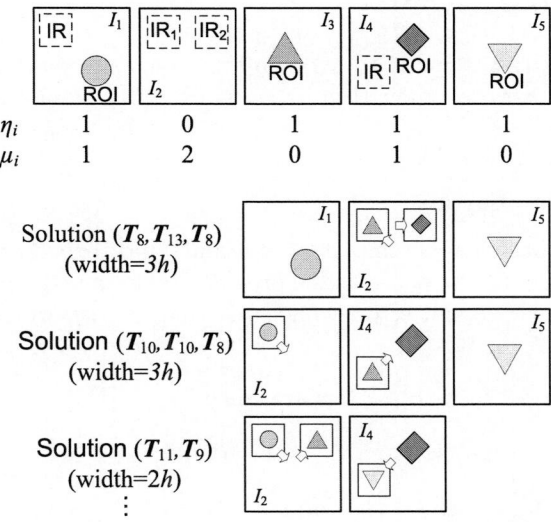

Fig. 4. Keyframe grouping in composite panels. Given the number of detected regions η_i and IR μ_i for each keyframe, some of them may be combined in composite panels.

respectively. All the possible ways to combine ROIs in adjacent IRs can be computed, by just evaluating η_i and μ_i for different windows. It can be posed as an optimization problem, and it can be solved by defining an objective function and using exhaustive search. All the combinations are evaluated and the one with optimal value is selected. The problem is illustrated in Figure 4, in which the objective is to minimize the total width of the resulting sequence (which is reasonable, as the objective is a compact representation). In this particular example, the third combination would be preferred, as it only has two composite panels, with information from five different keyframes. However, exhaustive search with a large number of images is unfeasible in practice due to the combinatorial nature of the problem.

We use a simple yet effective local search method to solve the problem in which the keyframes are processed sequentially from left to right. At each step, all the valid combinations are evaluated and a composite panel (or the individual image panel) is selected, based on the combination that contains more images (i.e. templates T_{11}, T_{12} and T_{13} have three images, so they are preferred over T_9 and T_{10}, with two images, and these over T_8).

To remove redundant keyframes, whenever a keyframe is included in a composite panel, either as a ROI or background image, the rest of the keyframes in the same cluster are discarded for further processing. We also check this condition in composite panels with two IRs, trying to avoid including the same face twice in the same panel. Hopefully, after this stage, the representation is much more compact, as we have already discarded redundant images and some of the remaining are combined in composite panels.

5   Comic-Like Layout

The objective of this stage is to arrange the composite panels and remaining images in a multirow layout with a given width W_{row}, and perhaps in several pages.

5.1   Single Row Layout

Given the set of basic panel templates, keyframes and their relevance, the single row layout problem can be posed as the problem of finding the optimal layout Y^* which minimizes the layout error, while satisfying the row width constraint[2]:

$$Y^* = \arg\min_{Y} \sum_{m=1}^{M} \varepsilon\left(P_m\right)$$

$$\text{subject to} \quad \sum_{m=1}^{M} W\left(P_m\right) = W_{row}$$

where $\varepsilon\left(P_m\right) = \sum_{i \in E_m} \left(C_i - \Omega_i\right)^2$ and $W\left(P_m\right) = |T_{p_m}|$ are the error and the width of the panel $P_m = \{p_m, E_m\}$. The score C_i represents the relevance of the i-th keyframe. At this stage we give the same score $C_i = h$ to all the keyframes (those not discarded). The exhaustive search algorithm explores all the possible combinations of basic panels making up valid layouts. The number of panels M is unknown until the optimal solution is found.

As the optimal solution is only feasible for a small number of images, the method in [2] uses a suboptimal left-to-right dynamic programming approach. But it does not guarantee an exact solution for a given row width (except by resizing the row image). Instead of using the left-to-right local approach, we use a top-down split and merge approach which tries to guarantee a solution (see Figure 5). We impose the restriction that composite panels cannot be downsized, as the embedded ROIs are already small images, so their size is kept always to h. Using them as fixed points, we divide the sequence of keyframes into K segments S_k, composed by the composite panels and panels keyframes located between two composite panels. Thus, only the layouts of these segments are computed, using the exhaustive search but in a reduced solution space. If a segment still has too many elements, it is further split in shorter sublayouts (in our case, up to 25 images each).

However, having few images in a sublayout has one limitation: it can only be solved for certain widths. Figure 6a shows the number of combinations satisfying given lengths for the case of 10 images, and Figure 6b represents the number of combinations as a function $g\left(N, W\right)$ of length N and width W. It is important to note that $g\left(N, W\right)$ is obtained empirically, not being a convex function and probably a close form does not exist. So traditional optimization techniques such as convex optimization or integer programming are not applicable. However, we noticed that the mean depends linearly on the length, so we can reasonably estimate the width of a sublayout as $\tilde{W}\left(N\right) = 2.34 + 1.39N$ (shown also in Figure 6), and then estimate a suitable row width as $\widetilde{W_{row}} = \sum_{k=1}^{K} \tilde{W}\left(|S_k|\right)$, where $|S_k|$ represents the number of images in the segment S_k.

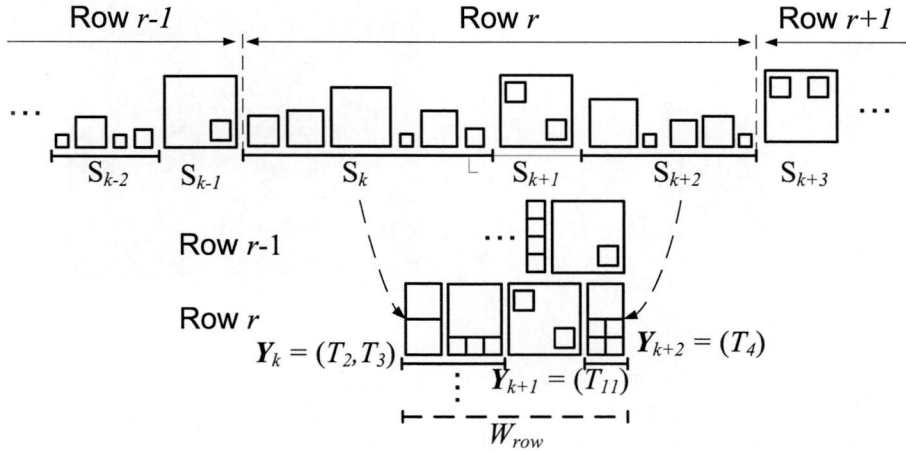

Fig. 5. Layout approach and related problems. A sequence of keyframes (with scores) and composite panels must be distributed first into different rows, and then the layout problem must be solved for each row

Once we have an estimation, we find the partition with most valid solutions, by solving the problem

$$Y^* = \arg \max_{(W_1, W_2, \cdots, W_K)} \sum_{k=1}^{K} g\left(|S_k|, W_k\right)$$

$$\text{subject to} \quad \sum_{k=1}^{K} W\left(|S_k|\right) = \widetilde{W_{row}}$$

$$g\left(|S_k|, W_k\right) > 0, 1 \leq k \leq K$$

It might happen that there still does not exist any valid solution. Fortunately, in our system we have the possibility of slightly changing the input data to accommodate it to the particular constraints, in order to find a valid solution. This is achieved by increasing the number of images in certain segments, so we can find a solution satisfying width $\widetilde{W_{row}}$. These extra images are selected from the keyframes discarded in the previous stage. We include keyframes with cluster labels different to the ones in the panel. They are given a lower score $C_i = 1$, as they are considered less important. Once we know that all the segments have at least one solution, the layout is computed independently for each of them.

5.2 Multirow Layout

The multirow problem is more complex and also involves multiple combinations which can be simplified considering each row as an independent subproblem. The method in [1] estimates the number of images of each row from the scores, but it does not guarantee a solution.

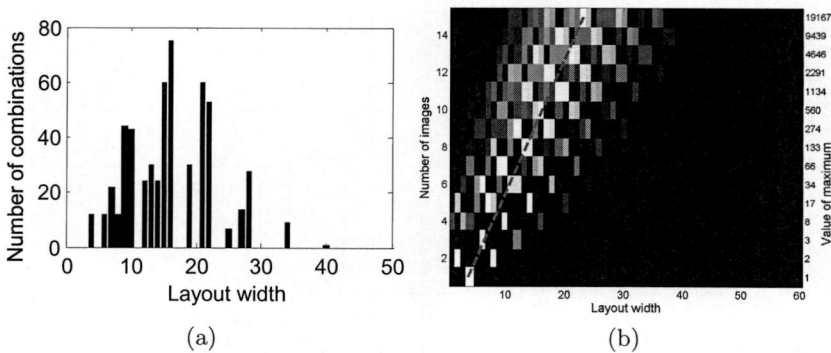

Fig. 6. Number of valid solutions for a), 10 images, b) different number of images, i.e. $g(N, W)$. Note that only certain combinations of number of images and row widths have valid solution. The mean of the distribution, used as an estimation of the layout width, is also shown.

We also separate the multirow problem into several single row problems, but with a different approach. Using the idea described in the previous section, we can estimate the accumulated width $\tilde{W}(K) = \sum_{k=1}^{K} W(|S_k|)$ for the first K segments. When $\tilde{W}(K)$ reaches W_{row}, we have a candidate row with K sublayouts. We first check whether an actual solution for W_{row} exists. If not, a discarded image of one sublayout is included and the row is checked again until a solution is found. Then, each row layout can be computed using the single row method. The process continues until all the sublayouts are distributed in rows. If the number of rows does not fit in one page, additional pages are created.

6   Experimental Results

We conducted a user study in the context of TV series. Episodes from the series *Friends, 7 vidas, The Good Wife, Fringe, Doctor Who* and *Los Protegidos* (22, 38, 42, 43, 58 and 81 minutes, respectively) were used as test set. We generated comic-like summaries using both the proposed method and the method in [2]. For the latter we used the same clustering as in the proposed method, and then the scoring function and layout algorithm proposed in [2]. Seven subjects participated in the study. The following questions (evaluation criteria):

- The summary contains the main information of the content (*informativeness*).
- The summary is redundant, given the length of the video (*redundancy*).
- The overall effect is appealing and interesting (*enjoyability*).

were posed to them, and they were asked to rate their level of agreement using a typical Likert scale[6], with 1 meaning *Disagreement* and 5 meaning *Agreement*. Episodes from the TV series *Friends, 7 vidas, The Good Wife, Fringe, Doctor Who* and *Los Protegidos* (22, 38, 42, 43, 58 and 81 minutes, respectively) were

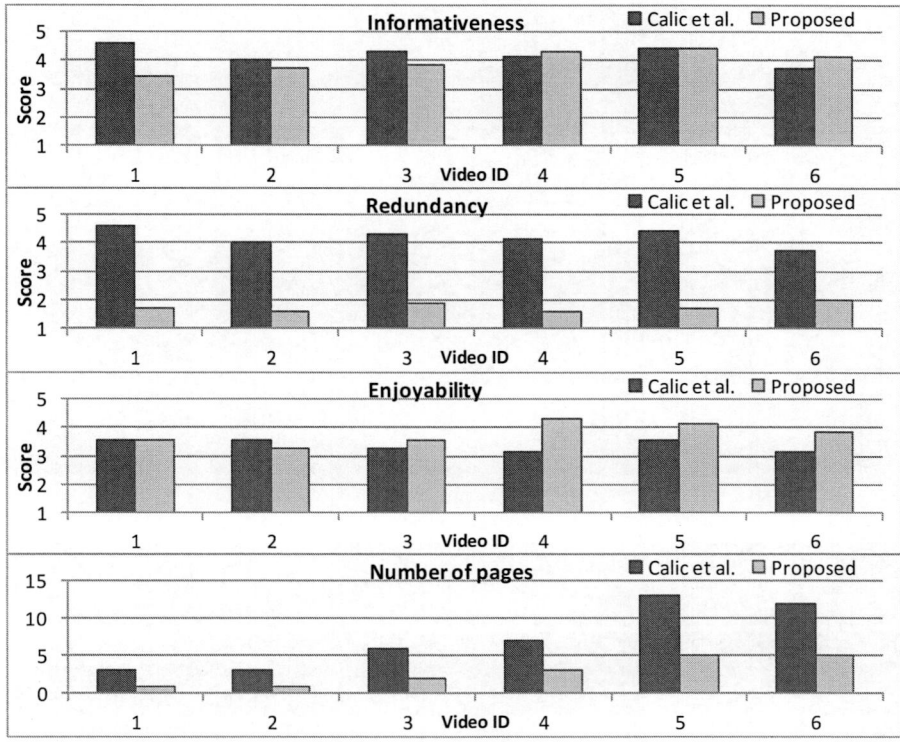

Fig. 7. User study results

used as test set. The results are shown in Figure 8, with the videos ordered by increasing duration.

Both methods are effective in covering the main information (*informativeness*), with a slight preference for [2] in shorter sequences and the proposed method in longer ones. However, the proposed method generates less redundant and much more compact summaries, as the *redundancy* score and the number of pages clearly show. The subjects also found the proposed abstractions more appealing and interesting (*enjoyability*), especially with longer videos.

An example of comic-like summary is shown in Figure 8a, with an excerpt of a five pages summary. The result is reasonably satisfactory, with most of the faces correctly detected and placed in non intrusive regions, and the overall layout resembling a long comic strip. However, there are still some limitations related with the accuracy of the detectors, which may find false ROIs (see last row first panel in Figure 8a). Problems derived from incorrect clustering may lead to cases in which two faces of the same person and the same scene are combined in the same panel, which is often redundant (see second row fifth panel in Figure 8a). These two problems can make the summary look unnatural. A summary of the same sequence using the method in [2] is shown in Figure 8b for comparison. This method tries to present all the keyframes, highlighting only few big ones

Fig. 8. Excerpts of comic-like summaries for $W_{row} = 20$: a) proposed method, b) Calic et al.[2]

and with the rest in smaller size. However, the resulting summary is still very redundant and requires 13 pages. Besides, in order to meet the row width, some rows are stretched, leading to distorted images.

7   Conclusions

We described an effective method to condense the visual information of long videos in just a few pages, in a friendly and easily readable comic-like style. The use of ROIs and more complex panels and composition techniques can be also useful to obtain more compact summaries. Additionally, an efficient and robust layout method is presented to address some limitations of previous methods in terms of existence of valid solutions for given row widths. Experimental results show reasonably satisfactory results and a good acceptance.

Acknowledgements. This work was supported in part by the National Basic Research Program of China (973 Program): 2012CB316400, in part by the National Natural Science Foundation of China: 61070108, and 61150110480, and in part by the Chinese Academy of Sciences Fellowships for Young International Scientists: 2011Y1GB05.

References

1. Calic, J., Campbell, N.W.: Compact visualisation of video summaries. EURASIP Journal on Advances in Signal Processing 2007(2), 14 pages (2007)
2. Calic, J., Gibson, D.P., Campbell, N.W.: Efficient layout of comic-like video summaries. IEEE Transactions on Circuits and Systems for Video Technology 17(7), 931–936 (2007)
3. Frey, B.J., Dueck, D.: Clustering by passing messages between data points. Science 315, 972–976 (2007)
4. Girgensohn, A.: A fast layout algorithm for visual video summaries. In: Proc. of International Conference on Multimedia and Expo, vol. 2, pp. 77–80 (2003)
5. Hong, R., Yuan, X.-T., Xu, M., Wang, M., Yan, S., Chua, T.-S.: Movie2comics: a feast of multimedia artwork. In: Proceedings of the ACM International Conference on Multimedia, pp. 611–614 (2010)
6. Likert, R.: A technique for the measurement of attitudes. Archives of Psychology 22(140), 1–55 (1932)
7. Liu, H., Jiang, S., Huang, Q., Xu, C.: A generic virtual content insertion system based on visual attention analysis. In: Proc. of the ACM International Conference on Multimedia, pp. 379–388 (2008)
8. McCloud, S.: Understanding Comics: The Invisible Art. HarperCollins (May 1994)
9. Otsu, N.: A threshold selection method from gray-level histograms. IEEE Transactions on Systems, Man and Cybernetics 9(1), 62–66 (1979)
10. Uchihashi, S., Foote, J., Girgensohn, A., Boreczky, J.: Video manga: generating semantically meaningful video summaries. In: Proc. of the ACM International Conference on Multimedia, pp. 383–392 (1999)
11. Yeung, M.M., Yeo, B.-L.: Video visualization for compact presentation and fast browsing of pictorial content. IEEE Transactions on Circuits and Systems for Video Technology 7(5), 771–785 (1997)

Kinect-Based Easy 3D Object Reconstruction

Di Xu[1], Jianfei Cai[2], Tat Jen Cham[2], Philip Fu[2], and Juyong Zhang[1]

[1] BeingThere Centre, Institute for Media Innovation,
Nanyang Technological University, Singapore
[2] School of Computer Engineering,
Nanyang Technological University, Singapore

Abstract. Inspired by the recently developed KinectFusion technique, which is able to reconstruct a 3D scene in real time through moving Kinect, we consider improving KinectFusion for 3D reconstruction of a real object. We make some adaptations to KinectFusion so as to identify the object-of-interest and separate the 3D object model from the entire 3D scene. Moreover, considering that the 3D object model generated by KinectFusion often contains some clearly visible outliers due to the noisy Kinect data, we propose a refinement scheme to remove the outliers. Our basic idea is to make use of the existing powerful 2D segmentation tool to refine the silhouette in each color image and then form visual hull via the refined dense silhouettes to improve the 3D object model. Experimental results show improved performance.

Keywords: 3D reconstruction, Kinect, 2D segmentation, visual hull.

1 Introduction

It is of great practical values to enable easy creation of 3D models of real objects. Main technologies have been developed towards this goal. Among them, the multi-view stereo (MVS) [1] is the most popular one, which builds 3D models of real objects from multi-view images. Despite the great advance, most of the MVS systems are still in the prototype level, limited to lab environment, not user-friendly, often require a few hours computation, and have some impractical assumptions such as assuming the silhouettes of the object are known.

In 2010, Microsoft has launched the Kinect sensor for game applications. Kinect is equipped with an infrared camera and a RGB camera. The infrared camera can generate the depth information easily by capturing the continuously-projected infrared structured light. With the assistance of this additional depth information, many challenging computer vision problems can now be simplified and tackled in an efficient manner.

Kinect has been used in 3D reconstruction recently [2–6]. In particular, in [2], multiple fixed kinects are used for fully dynamic real-time 3D scene capture for room-based telepresence systems. The depth data from each Kinect is being denoised first and then merged together weighted according to the angle and the distance to the camera. Although the 3D model of the entire scene can be

W. Lin et al. (Eds.): PCM 2012, LNCS 7674, pp. 476–483, 2012.
© Springer-Verlag Berlin Heidelberg 2012

generated in real time, the reconstruction is not of good quality. In [4], Cui and Stricker proposed a 3D object scanning scheme, where a Kinect is slowly moved around an object to capture different views. Super-resolution technique is applied to improve the quality of the raw data from Kinect. The method can achieve high-quality object reconstruction at the cost of high computation complexity and long processing time.

The recent developed KinectFusion [5] is a system for accurate real-time mapping of indoor scenes, using only a moving low-cost depth camera and commodity graphics hardware. The robustness of this system lies in that it fuses all of the depth data streamed from a Kinect sensor into a single global implicit surface model of the observed scene in real-time. Similar to other techniques, they first de-noise the input raw data with a bilateral filter and a multi-resolution method. Then the truncated signed distance function (TSDF) is used as the data structure for later processing. The global fusion of all depth maps is formed by the weighted average of all individual TSDFs. The resulted 3D model from Kinect-Fusion is of reasonable quality.

In this paper, we apply KinectFusion for easy 3D construction of real objects. First, considering that KinectFusion is designed for scene reconstruction, we make some adaptations to KinectFusion so as to identify the object-of-interest and separate the 3D object model from the entire 3D scene. Second, due to the noisy Kinect data, the 3D object model generated by KinectFusion often contains some clearly visible outliers. We propose a refinement scheme to remove the outliers. Our basic idea is to make use of the existing powerful 2D segmentation tool to refine the silhouette in each color image and then form visual hull via the refined dense silhouettes to improve the 3D object model. Experimental results show improved performance.

The rest of the paper is organized as follows. We describe the proposed system in Section 2. The experimental results are shown in Section 3. Finally, we conclude the paper in Section 4.

2 Proposed System

Fig. 1 shows the proposed easy 3D object reconstruction system. The primary inputs to the system are the color and depth videos captured by Kinect, and the output of the system is the reconstructed 3D model. In this first stage, considering the real-time 3D reconstruction capability of KinectFusion, we choose it to generate an initial 3D object model. Since Kinect data is very noisy and KinectFusion only makes use of the depth information, the reconstructed 3D object models is of limited quality and often contains clearly visible errors. Thus, in the second stage, we propose to obtain dense and accurate silhouettes in color images via a powerful 2D segmentation technique to remove the outliers in the initial 3D object model generated by KinectFusion. The second stage consists of three iterative steps: 3D to 2D projection, silhouette refinement by 2D cut, and

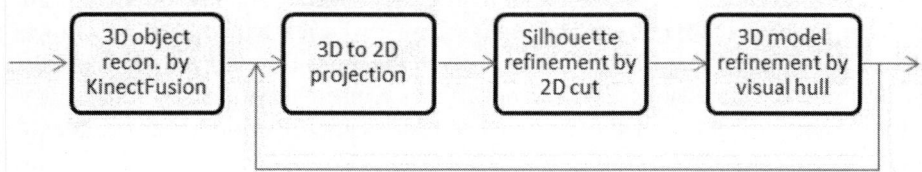

Fig. 1. The system diagram of the proposed easy 3D object reconstruction

3D model refinement by visual hull. The iteration is to ensure the 2D segmentation performed in each individual image are consistent and converged with the visual hull projections. In the following, we elaborate the two main stages in detail.

2.1   3D Object Reconstruction Using KinectFusion

KinectFusion in it original form cannot be directly used for 3D object reconstruction since it is designed for reconstructing the entire scene. One common solution is to assume that the object is always the closest one to the viewer and use some thresholding to separate its 3D construction from the background 3D reconstruction. However, in this way, the object is hard to be separated from its supporting entity since the object has to be place on top of an entity such as ground or table. In the KinectFusion paper [5], it suggests another solution, i.e. obtaining the 3D object model by subtracting the 3D reconstructions with and without the object. But no implementation detail is provided.

In this research, we follow the idea in [5] to generate an initial 3D object model. In particular, the object-of-interest is first placed in the scene and the user holding a Kinect scans the scene to obtain the entire 3D scene reconstruction using KinectFusion. Later, after some repeating scene scanning, the user removes the object from the scene and the final KinectFusion reconstruction is the 3D scene without the object. By subtracting the final 3D reconstruction from the initial one containing the 3D object, we obtain the 3D object model we want. Note that the scanning is a non-stop process till the end so as to ensure the same global coordination system between the two reconstructions and avoid the alignment problem. Fig.2 shows an example of the initial 3D object model generation.

2.2   3D Model Refinement via 2D Segmentation

The initial 3D object model obtained by KinectFusion often contains some outliers due to the noisy depth data. Thus, in this second stage, we make use some powerful 2D segmentation tool to generate dense silhouettes to help remove the outliers of the 3D model.

(a)   (b)

Fig. 2. An illustration of generating the initial 3D object model using KinectFusion. We produce the mesh of the whole scene on (a). After the Robot being removed, another 3D model is generated as in (b). By subtracting the model of (a) by that in (b), we can get the initial model of the robot.

Since the 2D object segmentation requires some initial contour, we first perform 3D-to-2D projection. The initial 3D mesh is projected to each of the 2D images using the corresponding projection matrices generated by KinectFusion, which results in a binary mask in each image. As expected, because of the inaccurate initial 3D model as well as the inaccurate projection matrices, the generated initial 2D contours typically suffers a segmentation error up to 20 pixels for an image with a size of 640x480. This can be observed in Fig. 3(c), where the boundary of the binary mask is not snapped with the silhouette of the object.

Therefore, next we apply our recently developed robust convex active contour tool [7] for the silhouette refinement. The tool has strong ability to evolve the initial contour to snap to the geometry features/edges in an image. Besides, it has fast processing speed since it can be solved by convex optimization. The convex active contour model can be expressed as

$$\min_{0 \le u \le 1} \left(\int_\Omega g_b |\nabla u| dx + \lambda_1 \int_\Omega h_r u dx \right), \tag{1}$$

where u is a function on image domain Ω and receives a value between 0 and 1 at each pixel location x in the image, function g_b is typically an edge detection function, and function h_r is a region function that measures the coherence of the inside and outside regions. (1) consists of two terms, where the first term is a boundary term and the second term is a region term. The boundary term favors the segmentation along the places that the edge detection function reaches minimum, i.e. detecting edges, and also favors the segmentation with smooth boundary curve. The region term ensures the segmentation complying with some region coherence criteria defined in function h_r.

In particular, for the initial binary mask obtained by 3D projection, it is reasonable to assume that the areas far away from the initial boundary are likely to be correctly classified. The area that are within a threshold of D pixels away from the initial boundary is treated as the unknown region. Each pixel is then given a probability, where the foreground and the background pixels are set to 1 and 0, respectively, and a pixel in the unknown region is given a probability value that is proportional to its distance away from the initial contour. In this way, we obtain an initial probability map $P(X)$ and we let $u(x) = P(x)$ in (1) for initialization. In addition, based on the foreground and background pixels, we also build up local foreground and background Gaussian Mixture Model (GMM) color models for each image. With the local GMM models, the region term h_r is then defined as

$$h_r(x) = \alpha(P_B(x) - P_F(x) + (1 - \alpha)(1 - 2P(x))), \tag{2}$$

where where $P_F(x)$ and $P_B(x)$ are the normalized foreground and background likelihoods respectively, and $\alpha \in [0, 1]$, is a tradeoff factor. The first term $(P_B(x) - P_F(x))$ in (2) ensures that the active contour evolves towards the one complying with the local GMM color models. The second term $(1 - 2P(x))$ in (2) prevents the refined contour drifting too far apart from the initial segmentation.

Once the optimization of the convex active contour model (1) is solved, we obtain the solution of $u(x)$, which represents the probability of a pixel x belonging to the foreground. By thresholding $u(x)$ against a threshold (typically, 0.5), we obtain a refined 2D segmentation. After that, a visual hull containing the object is generated from the dense refined silhouettes using the shape-from-silhouette method in [8]. The visual hull acts as a hard constraints on the initial 3D model. Any part outside the visual hull is deemed as background and thus cut away from the initial 3D model.

The last three steps of 3D-to-2D projection, 2D segmentation and visual hull are tightly coupled and they together form an iteration process. In each iteration, the refined silhouettes provide better visual hull to cut the 3D model and in return the refined 3D model produces better initial silhouette for the next-round 2D segmentation.

3   Experimental Results

We test our proposed system using two objects, i.e. a chair and a robot. In our experiment, one video clip usually contains hundreds of frames so that we are able to generate intensive silhouettes from those frames. Theoretically, the more silhouettes we use, the finer visual hull we can obtain. To avoid heavy computation, we uniformly sample the video frames and each final data set contains about 100 views of 640x480 color and depth images.

Fig. 3 shows the results of the chair example. It can be seen that the initial silhouette projected from the initial 3D model does not align with the chair boundary in the image. With our 2D segmentation technique, the chair's silhouette can be accurately refined. Moreover, the refined 3D object model is also of high quality. Fig.5 shows the 3D model of the final reconstructed chair from one view.

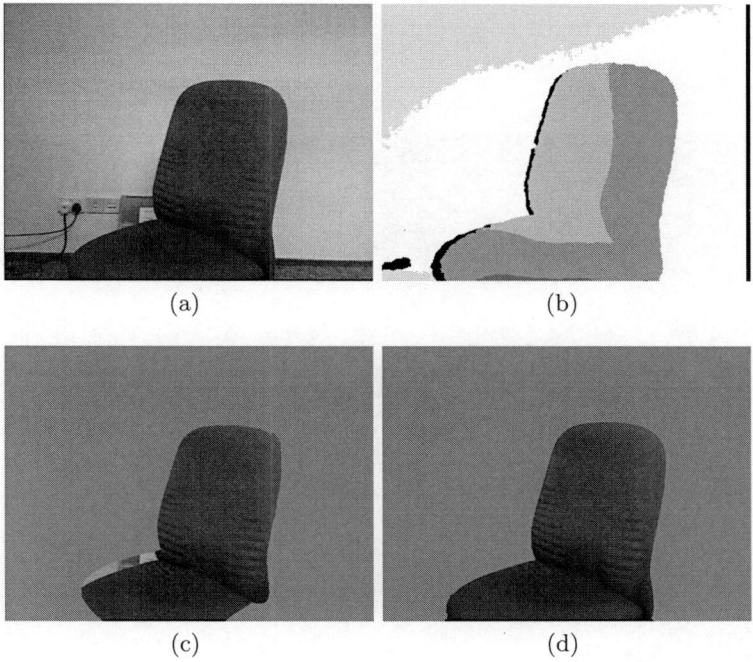

Fig. 3. The results of the chair example. (a) Original color image; (b) Original depth image; (c) Projected image from KinectFusion; (d) Refined image via 2D segmentation.

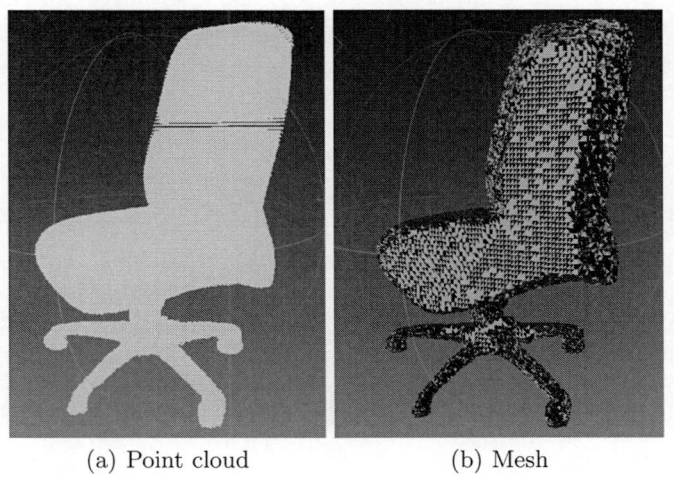

(a) Point cloud   (b) Mesh

Fig. 4. An illustration of the 3D reconstruction result of the chair.

The proposed system still has some limitation. Fig. 5 gives an example of reconstructing the robot. We can see that although our 2D segmentation tool improves the silhouette, there are still some clearly visible errors. This is mainly because the color of the object is similar to some of the background.

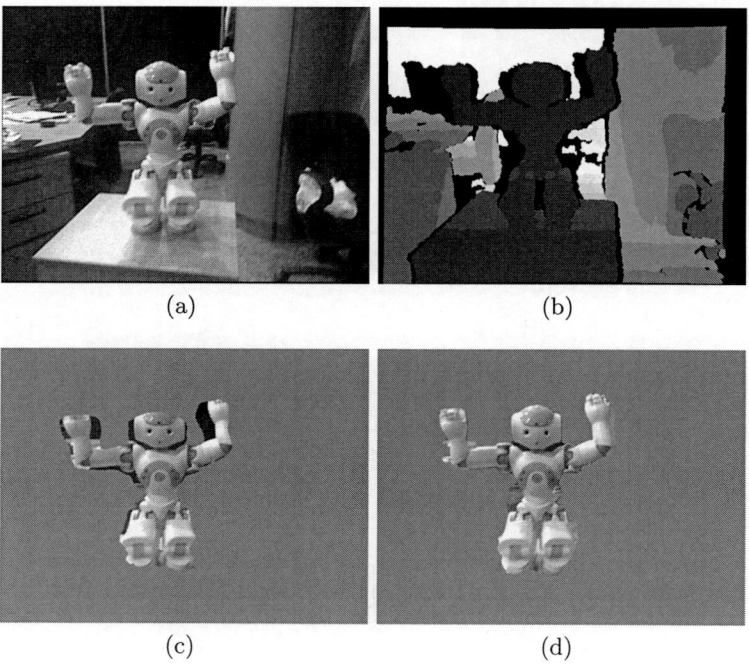

(a)   (b)

(c)   (d)

Fig. 5. The results of the robot example. (a) Original color image; (b) Original depth image; (c) Projected image from KinectFusion; (d) Refined image via 2D segmentation.

4   Conclusion

In this paper, we have proposed a system to easily reconstruct the 3D model of a real object. The system is a coherent integration of several modern techniques including KinectFusion, the convex active contour, and visual hull. The experimental results have demonstrated that the proposed system is a practical and effective tool that can refine the 3D object model generated by KinectFusion. The future work includes further improving the reconstruction quality and designing better schemes to fuse the depth and color information.

Acknowledgement. This research, which is carried out at BeingThere Centre, is supported by the Singapore National Research Foundation under its International Research Centre @ Singapore Funding Initiative and administered by the IDM Programme Office.

References

1. Seitz, S., Curless, B., Diebel, J., Scharstein, D., Szeliski, R.: A comparison and evaluation of multi-view stereo reconstruction algorithms. In: 2006 IEEE Computer Society Conference on Computer Vision and Pattern Recognition, vol. 1, pp. 519–528. IEEE (2006)
2. Maimone, A., Fuchs, H.: Encumbrance-free telepresence system with real-time 3d capture and display using commodity depth cameras. In: 2011 10th IEEE International Symposium on Mixed and Augmented Reality (ISMAR), pp. 137–146. IEEE (2011)
3. Kuster, C., et al.: Freecam: A hybrid camera system for interactive free-viewpoint video. In: Proceedings of Vision, Modeling, and Visualization, VMV (2011)
4. Cui, Y., Stricker, D.: 3d shape scanning with a kinect. In: ACM SIGGRAPH 2011 Posters, p. 57. ACM (2011)
5. Izadi, S., Kim, D., Hilliges, O., Molyneaux, D., Newcombe, R., Kohli, P., Shotton, J., Hodges, S., Freeman, D., Davison, A., et al.: Kinectfusion: real-time 3d reconstruction and interaction using a moving depth camera. In: Proceedings of the 24th Annual ACM Symposium on User Interface Software and Technology, pp. 559–568. ACM (2011)
6. Steinbrucker, F., Sturm, J., Cremers, D.: Real-time visual odometry from dense rgb-d images. In: 2011 IEEE International Conference on Computer Vision Workshops, ICCV Workshops, pp. 719–722. IEEE (2011)
7. Bresson, X., Esedoglu, S., Vandergheynst, P., Thiran, J., Osher, S.: Fast global minimization of the active contour/snake model. Journal of Mathematical Imaging and Vision 28, 151–167 (2007)
8. Laurentini, A.: The visual hull concept for silhouette-based image understanding. IEEE Transactions on Pattern Analysis and Machine Intelligence 16, 150–162 (1994)

Adaptive Rate-Distortion Prediction for Multiple Reference Selection and Inter-mode Decision*

Tiesong Zhao[1,2], Yun Zhang[1,2], Sam Kwong[2], Hanli Wang[3], and Qian Chen[1]

[1] Shenzhen Institute of Advanced Technology,
Chinese Academy of Sciences, Shenzhen, China
[2] Department of Computer Science, City University of Hong Kong, Hong Kong
[3] Key Laboratory of Embedded System and Service Computing,
Ministry of Education, Tongji University, Shanghai, China
{ztiesong2,cssamk}@cityu.edu.hk, {yun.zhang,qian.chen}@siat.ac.cn,
hanliwang@tongji.edu.cn

Abstract. To minimize Rate-Distortion (RD) cost in video coding, RD Optimization (RDO) technique is adopted, which also brings increasingly computational complexity in Motion Estimation (ME), multiple reference selection and mode decision. In this paper, a Gaussian model based adaptive RD cost prediction method is developed to jointly speed up multiple reference selection and inter-mode decision. Besides the ability of achieving good coding efficiency with much reduced computational power, our method is also with two major advantages. First, it can achieve robust performance, including computational complexity reduction and almost intact video quality, with a wide range of video sequences resolutions and even for various scene changes; second, it could be either individually used or combined with the other efficient mode decision algorithms, and in both cases, our method could achieve remarkable performance, which is revealed by exhaustive experimental results.

Keywords: Rate-Distortion estimation, early termination, video coding.

1 Introduction

To promote new video services such as Standard Definition (SD) and High Definition (HD) video storage and transmission, the international video coding

* This work was supported in part by the Hong Kong Research Grants Council General Research Fund, under Project 9041495 (CityU 115109) and City University of Hong Kong Grant 9610025, the National Natural Science Foundation of China under Grant 61070147/61102088, Basic Research Program of Shenzhen (JC2010052703), and the Program for Professor of Special Appointment (Eastern Scholar) at Shanghai Institutions of Higher Learning, the Program for New Century Excellent Talents in University of China under Grant NCET-10-0634, the Shanghai Pujiang Program under Grant 11PJ1409400, the National Natural Science Foundation of China under Grant 61102059, the Fundamental Research Funds for the Central Universities under Grant 0800219158.

W. Lin et al. (Eds.): PCM 2012, LNCS 7674, pp. 484–491, 2012.
© Springer-Verlag Berlin Heidelberg 2012

standard H.264 [2] adopts RDO [1] and many other techniques to achieve a higher compression ratio. However, the computational complexity is meanwhile dramatically increased, especially in the inter-mode decision and related multiple reference selection and ME modules, which limits realtime and mobile multimedia applications. Hence, there is a need to optimize the mode decision, multiple reference selection and ME processes so as to promote the computational efficiency in video coding.

To address the aforementioned problem, many Fast Mode Decision (FMD) algorithms has been proposed to optimize the inter-mode and intra-mode decision processes, such as [3,4], which utilize the features of the image or MacroBlock (MB) to skip redundant inter-modes. In [3], the homogeneous and stationary characteristics extracted from image textures are employed to skip unnecessary inter-modes. In [4], Liu *et al.* designed another FMD algorithm, in which the homogeneity of the encoding MB could be derived by checking INTER4×4 mode first, and after that some redundant inter-modes could be skipped. On the other hand, some algorithms focus on multiple reference selection and ME optimization. In [5], an algorithm called Early Mode Decision Termination (EMDT) was proposed, which is based on all-zero block detection and could be used independently or combined with other FMD algorithms. The RD cost information is also used for early termination of mode checking. In [6], unnecessary ME search points are skipped based on RD cost prediction, with an adaptive threshold. Besides, in [7], the RD cost from the reference frame is utilized for prediction; in [8], early termination thresholds are derived with RD costs of the neighboring MBs.However, these algorithms only predict the RD cost roughly with the predicted RD cost being not suitable for usage of early termination individually, limiting their applicability with other mode decision algorithms.

In order to improve the RD cost prediction performance, we propose another algorithm based on an adaptive Gaussian model. With the predicted RD cost, the inter-mode decision and multiple reference selection could be optimized to reduce redundant computations. Moreover, the proposed algorithm is general in the sense that it can be used not only individually but also with combination of other efficient algorithms for performance improvement. The rest of this paper is organized as follows. In Section 2, the proposed RD cost prediction method is discussed. Section 3 introduces a two-level early termination scheme with the predicted RD costs. Experimental results and conclusions are provided in Sections 4 and 5, respectively.

2 Adaptive RD Cost Prediction

In natural video sequences, strong correlations exist between neighboring blocks. Therefore, such a relationship is explored to model the RD costs of neighboring MBs. Let a MB located in the nth frame with its upper-left pixel at (x, y) be $MB(n, x, y)$, and $MB(k, i, j)$ be a neighboring MB, where $k = n + \Delta n$, $i = x + \Delta x$ and $j = y + \Delta y$. In Table 1, the mean absolute difference (MAD) between RD costs of $MB(n, x, y)$ and $MB(k, i, j)$ is listed for all neighboring MBs of the

Table 1. MAD between RD costs of neighboring MBs

$MB(k,i,j)$			MAD between RD costs		
index	Δn	Δx	Δy $Q_p = 24$	$Q_p = 32$	$Q_p = 40$
0	-1	-16	-16 574.5	714.8	1116.1
1	-1	-16	0 426.8	508.6	772.3
2	-1	-16	16 563.2	713.7	1142.8
3	-1	0	-16 524.2	646.3	1018.0
4	-1	0	0 324.2	342.2	454.7
5	-1	0	16 512.7	642.9	1019.6
6	-1	16	-16 549.5	689.3	1100.7
7	-1	16	0 419.0	505.1	773.6
8	-1	16	16 536.4	679.8	1068.4
9	0	-16	-16 512.8	686.2	1096.2
10	0	-16	0 326.4	444.2	708.4
11	0	0	-16 449.9	605.1	981.0
12	0	16	-16 483.8	657.2	1074.8
13	$-1'$	0	0 244.0	291.3	408.2

video sequence *Table Tennis* in Common Intermediate Format (CIF). Similar observations could be obtained from other Quantization Parameters (Q_ps) and other benchmark video sequences. Considering intra-modes have disparate RD cost features with inter-modes, and there is little time consumed on intra-modes, we only list the results for inter-modes.

In the last row of Table 1 another reference MB is introduced as $MB'(n-1,x,y)$, which represents the previous collocated MB of the same slice type. In many literatures such as [7], $MB(n-1,x,y)$ (indexed as 4 in Table 1), which may not be of the same slice type to $MB(n,x,y)$, is used for reference in mode and RD cost prediction. However, from the table, better performance could be obtained with $MB'(n-1,x,y)$ and thus the RD cost of $MB'(n-1,x,y)$ is used to predict the RD cost of $MB(n,x,y)$. The prediction error is:

$$\Delta C(n,x,y) = C(n,x,y) - C'(n-1,x,y), \tag{1}$$

where $C(n,x,y)$ and $C'(n-1,x,y)$ denote the RD costs of $MB(n,x,y)$ and $MB'(n-1,x,y)$, separately.

To improve the accuracy of RD cost prediction, RD cost of different modes are further studied. In H.264, intra-modes tend to have different RD costs from inter-modes; and among all inter-modes, SKIP/DIRECT mode always has a larger RD cost different with the other inter-modes [9]. Therefore, Eq. (1) is rewritten as:

$$\Delta C_M(n,x,y) = C_M(n,x,y) - C'(n-1,x,y), \tag{2}$$

where M denotes an inter-mode; $C_M(n,x,y)$ denotes the RD cost when encoding $MB(n,x,y)$ with mode M. Assume the best inter-mode of $MB'(n-1,x,y)$ is M_0,

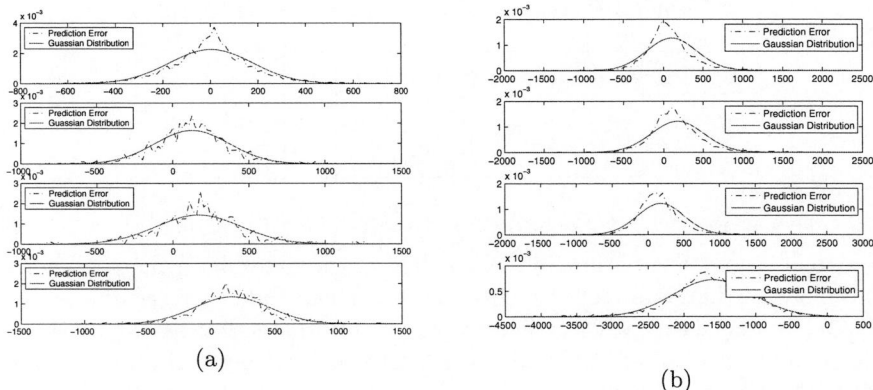

Fig. 1. RD cost prediction errors. (a) M_0=SKIP/DIRECT, values of M from top to bottom: SKIP/DIRECT, INTER16×16, INTER16×8 and P8×8; (b) M_0=INTER16×16, values of M from top to bottom: INTER16×16, INTER16×8, INTER8×16 and P8×8.

statistical results show that, for specific M_0 and M, $\Delta C_M(n,x,y)$ could be approximated by a Gaussian distribution. Two examples are given in Fig. 1, where the distribution of $\Delta C_M(n,x,y)$ in B slices when encoding *Mobile* (CIF, IBBP structure with $Qp = 28$) is given. Due to lack of space, simulation for the other sequences with the other Q_ps is not shown, in which similar results could be obtained.

In Fig 1, the approximated Gaussian curve is drawn for comparison. The two curves keep close to each other for different encoding modes. Therefore, we apply the Gaussian distribution $N(\mu(M_0,M),\sigma(M_0,M))$ to describe the distribution of prediction errors (where μ and σ denote the mean and standard deviation of Gaussian distribution), and the parameters are adjusted with an adaption rate γ. Considering different Gaussian distributions apply for different mode pairs (M_0,M), as shown in Fig. 1, we build different Gaussian models for them. For a specific mode pair (M_0,M), the corresponding Gaussian model is regulated only when the MB to be encoded, $MB(n,x,y)$, has the best inter-mode as M, and meanwhile, the best inter-mode of $MB'(n-1,x,y)$ is M_0. In this work, we set the initial $\mu(M_0,M)$ and $\sigma(M_0,M)$ as $\mu_0 = 0$ and $\sigma_0 = 0$, respectively. Assume that consequent MBs with the mode pair (M_0,M) are indexed with $k = 1,2,3,\cdots$ and the corresponding prediction error is ΔC_k, the model parameters μ_k and σ_k are updated as below.

1. For $k = 1$: $\mu_1 = \Delta C_1$, and $\sigma_1 = 0$;
2. For $k = 2$: $\mu_2 = (\mu_1 + \Delta C_2)/2$, and $\sigma_1 = \|\mu_1 - \Delta C_2\|/2$;
3. For $k > 2$: $\mu_k = (1 - \gamma)\mu_{k-1} + \gamma\Delta C_k$, and $\sigma_k = \sqrt{(1-\gamma)\sigma_{k-1}^2 + \gamma(\Delta C_k - \mu_{k-1})^2}$.

To adapt the model parameters for different types of texture, motion and scene change, we set $\gamma = 0.2$ based on exhaustive experiments. Then, for the following early termination, a predicted minimum RD cost of inter-modes is derived as:

Table 2. Percentage of the best reference indices

L_1 \ L_0	-1	0	1	2	3	4
-1	0.00	4.42	1.67	0.43	0.11	0.10
0	8.35	80.99	2.86	0.89	0.11	0.07

$$C_M(n, x, y) = C'(n - 1, x, y) + \mu(M_0, M) - \tau \cdot \sigma(M_0, M), \tag{3}$$

where τ is a constant parameter. A smaller τ would result in more early terminations and therefore more time saving, but meanwhile there would be more video performance loss; while larger τ would result in less time saving but better video performance. After trade-off, we set a typical value $\tau = 1.5$ in this work. Note that when the Gaussian model has not been built, that is, $\mu_0 = \sigma_0 = 0$, the predicted minimum RD cost for this mode pair (M_0, M) is initialized to be zero, and thus there is no early termination performed.

3   Two-Level Early Termination

With the predicted RD cost, early termination of mode decision and related ME could be employed. Before that, another encoding feature of H.264 should be noticed. In H.264, multiple reference frame ME is performed, however, experimental results show that ME in some reference slices is unnecessary and could be skipped. In Table 2, the percentage of the best reference indices for B slices in *Mobile* (QCIF, IBBP structure) is shown, where the number of reference frames is set to 5, L_0 and L_1 denote the forward and backward reference list. Note that the reference frame index "-1" means the corresponding reference list is not used, *e.g.* $L_0 = 0$ and $L_1 = -1$ indicate a block encoded only with the prediction from the first frame in L_0.

Two conclusions can be derived from Table 2. Firstly, almost all MBs (93.76%) are encoded as bi-prediction or single prediction with index 0 (the nearest reference frame). Secondly, farther reference frames tend to have lower chances to be the best, that means, farther reference frames usually result in larger RD costs. As a consequence, we could check the reference frame with index 0 first in each reference list, and then check the other frames consequently. If the RD cost of a reference frame is much larger than the minimum RD cost obtained so far, the RD costs of remaining frames might be even larger than it, therefore, these frames could be skipped for checking. For a block or sub-block being checked, we define an early termination condition $C_{idx} > \eta C_{list}$, where C_{idx} denotes the RD cost of the reference frame currently being checked, C_{list} denotes the minimum RD cost found so far in the list being checked, and η is a control parameter with the typical value of 1.05 in this work.

Based on the above analyses, we propose a two-level early termination strategy with RD cost prediction, that is, mode level and block level early termination. At the mode level, the sufficient condition for early termination is

$$C_{min} < C_M(n, x, y), \tag{4}$$

Table 3. Simulation results when used individually

Seq.	EMDT [5]			Proposed		
	TS	BDPSNR	BDBR	TS	BDPSNR	BDBR
City	10.33	-0.141	2.63	41.81	-0.023	0.46
Crew	13.28	-0.272	5.52	42.64	-0.021	0.40
QCIF-link	8.85	-0.093	1.83	32.35	-0.045	0.87
Salesman	23.58	-0.061	1.39	23.94	-0.035	0.83
Stefan	-1.65	-0.190	3.67	45.22	-0.048	0.91
CIF-link	8.43	-0.240	5.19	42.77	-0.019	0.40
Shields	19.71	-0.108	3.18	42.75	-0.036	1.12
Stockholm	21.02	-0.084	2.81	37.31	-0.029	1.27
SD-link	19.70	-0.343	10.62	40.57	-0.037	1.06
Bluesky	41.74	-0.484	10.65	46.01	-0.041	0.87
Rivebed	12.59	-0.404	10.84	40.67	-0.027	0.67
HD-link	35.75	-0.367	15.13	36.47	-0.026	1.00
Average	**17.78**	**-0.232**	**6.12**	**39.38**	**-0.032**	**0.82**

where M denotes the checking mode; C_{min} denotes the minimum RD cost among all checked modes; and $C_M(n, x, y)$ denotes the predicted RD cost for encoding $MB(n, x, y)$ with mode M as in Eq. (3). If the RD cost of the current mode is less than the predicted RD cost, the mode decision process could be early terminated.

At the block level, for a block or sub-block, all reference frames in both lists are checked one by one, and the sufficient condition for early termination is

$$C_{idx} > \eta C_{list} \ || \ C_{list} < \frac{C_M(n,x,y)}{block\_num}, \tag{5}$$

where $||$ represents the "or" condition; $block\_num$ represents the number of sub-blocks of the mode (e.g. there are two sub-blocks for INTER16×8 and four sub-blocks for P8×8). If the condition is satisfied, the mode decision for the current list could be early terminated. Especially, if the block is the last sub-block, and the sum of motion costs of all the sub-blocks is less than $C_M(n, x, y)$, the mode decision for the current list is early terminated too.

4   Experimental Results

To examine the encoding performance, the proposed algorithm is implemented into the H.264 reference software [10]. The encoding conditions are summarized as follows: 1) High profile is used with RDO being low complexity mode; 2) Two Group Of Picture (GOP) structures (IPPP and IBBP) and five Q_ps (24, 28, 32, 36 and 40) are tested; 3) For QCIF and CIF sequences, 300/298 frames are coded for IPPP/IBBP structure; for SD and HD sequences, 100/118 frames are coded for IPPP/IBBP structure; 4) The intra period is 10 and the IDR period is 0, the number of reference frame is 5; 5) Search range is 16, 32 and 64 pixels

Table 4. Simulation results when combined with [3]

Seq.	FMD[3]			Combined		
	TS	BDPSNR	BDBR	TS	BDPSNR	BDBR
City	29.87	-0.007	0.14	55.38	-0.020	0.39
Mobile	4.39	-0.004	0.08	39.65	-0.073	1.40
Garden	14.72	-0.008	0.15	52.78	-0.062	1.09
Salesman	33.97	-0.029	0.69	47.95	-0.064	1.53
Harbour	20.46	-0.010	0.26	52.55	-0.048	1.29
Parkrun	12.72	-0.026	0.61	52.06	-0.042	0.99
Average	**19.36**	**-0.014**	**0.32**	**50.06**	**-0.052**	**1.12**

for QCIF, CIF and SD/HD sequences, respectively; 6) The other parameters are set as defaults of the reference software. Three criteria are used for performance evaluation, as encoding Time Saving (TS) in percentage, Bjontegaard average peak signal to noise ratio decrease (BDPSNR) in dB and Bjontegaard average bit rate increase (BDBR) [11] for video performance in percentage.

For comparison, the proposed method is firstly implemented independently and compared with the EMDT algorithm [5], as shown in Table 3. Three QCIF sequences (City, Crew and QCIF-link, which comprises 75 frames of each of four QCIF sequences Foreman, Mobile, News and Silent), three CIF sequences (Salesman, Stefan and CIF-link, which comprises 75 frames of each of four CIF sequences Bus, Crew, Football and Mother), three SD sequences (Shields, Stockholm and SD-link, which comprises 50 frames of each of three SD sequences Crew, Harbour and Parkjoy) and three HD sequences (Bluesky, Riverbed and HD-link, which comprises 50 frames of each of three HD sequences Bluesky, Opening and Riverbed) are used to test the encoding performance with various textures and motions including scene change. From the table several conclusions can be drawn. Firstly, the time saving of the proposed scheme is significantly better than the compared algorithm, with the video performance almost intact to the original encoder. Secondly, the proposed approach could achieve acceptable time saving and video performance for all sequences with different textures, motions and resolutions while the compared algorithm dose not work well for fast-motion or complex-texture sequences (such as Stefan and Shileds) and SD/HD sequences. Thirdly, the proposed scheme is a self-adaptive RD cost estimation algorithm, and it can achieve both significant time saving and acceptable video performance at various types of scene change, which is superior to the compared algorithm.

To test the proposed scheme when combined with mode checking optimization algorithms, it is combined with the algorithm [3], named "FMD [3]" in Table 4, where the algorithm [3] is also implemented for comparison. Due to lack of space, only encoding results of two QCIF sequences (City and Mobile), two CIF sequences (Garden and Salesman) and two SD sequences (Harbour and Parkrun) are given. From Table 4, it could be noticed that combined with the proposed scheme, the mode checking optimization algorithm [3] could have significantly better time saving performance, while the video performance is more or less intact. Another remark could be derived from Table 3 and Table 4 is that, the proposed scheme could have better encoding performance for fast-motion or complex-texture video sequences, while most of FMD algorithms, such as [3], have better performance for slow-motion or simple-texture sequences. Therefore, combined with the proposed approach, these FMD algorithms could have robust performance for videos with different texture and motion features.

5 Conclusion

In this paper, a novel algorithm is proposed for multiple reference selection and inter-mode decision. With RD costs predicted from pre-coded MBs, a two-level early termination strategy is employed for encoding computations reduction. The proposed algorithm could achieve significantly better performance either individually or combined with the other FMD algorithms.

References

1. Sullivan, G., Wiegand, T.: Rate-Distortion Optimization for Video Compression. IEEE Signal Process. Mag. 15(6), 74–90 (1998)
2. ISO/IEC 14496-10:2005(E) ITU-T Rec. H.264(E): Advanced Video Coding for Generic Audiovisual Services (2005)
3. Wu, D., Pan, F., Lim, K.P., et al.: Fast Intermode Decision in H.264/AVC Video Coding. IEEE Trans. Circuits Syst. Video Technol. 15(7), 953–958 (2005)
4. Liu, Z., Shen, L., Zhang, Z.: An Efficient Intermode Decision Algorithm Based on Motion Homogeneity for H.264/AVC. IEEE Trans. Circuits Syst. Video Technol. 19(1), 128–132 (2009)
5. Wang, H., Kwong, S., Kok, C.-W.: An Efficient Mode Decision Algorithm for H.264/AVC Encoding Optimization. IEEE Trans. Multimedia 9(2), 882–888 (2007)
6. Lin, Y., Fink, T., Bellers, E.: Fast Mode Decision for H.264 Based on Rate-Distortion Cost Estimation. In: Proc. IEEE ICASSP 2007, pp. 1137–1140 (2007)
7. Kozu, H., Kuniyasu, H., Song, T., Shimamoto, T.: Spatial-temporal correlation based mode decision algorithm for H.264/AVC. In: Proc. IEEE ISCE 2009, pp. 647–650 (2009)
8. Shen, L., Liu, Z., An, P., Ma, R., Zhang, Z.: An Adaptive Early Termination of Mode Decision using Inter-layer Correlation in Scalable Video Coding. In: Proc. IEEE ICIP 2010, pp. 4229–4232 (2010)
9. Hu, S., Zhao, T., Wang, H., Kwong, S.: Fast Inter-Mode Decision Based on Rate-Distortion Cost Characteristics. In: Qiu, G., Lam, K.M., Kiya, H., Xue, X.-Y., Kuo, C.-C.J., Lew, M.S. (eds.) PCM 2010, Part II. LNCS, vol. 6298, pp. 145–155. Springer, Heidelberg (2010)
10. H.264/AVC Reference Softwares, http://iphome.hhi.de/suehring/tml/
11. Bjontegaard, G.: Calculation of Average PSNR Differences between RD-Curves, JVT Doc. VCEG-M33 (2001)

A New Rate-Quantization Model
for H.264/AVC Low-Delay Rate Control

Junhui Hou[1,2], Shuai Wan[2], Zhan Ma[3], Fuzheng Yang[4], and Lap-Pui Chau[1]

[1] School of Electrical and Electronics Engineering, Nanyang Technological University,
639798 Singapore
[2] School of Electronics and Information, Northwestern Polytechnical University,
Xi'an, 710072 China
[3] Dallas Technology Lab, Samsung, Richardson TX 75082, USA
[4] State Key Laboratory of ISN, Xidian Universtity, Xi'an, 710071 China
houj0001@e.ntu.edu.sg, swan@nwpu.edu.cn, zhan.ma@ieee.org,
fzhyang@mail.xidian.edu.cn, elpchau@ntu.edu.sg

Abstract. In this paper, we present a new rate-quantization (R-Q) model for H.264/AVC low-delay rate control. Our rate model is a power function of the quantization stepsize, which is derived through theoretical analysis assuming the Laplacian distributed source. Model parameters are content adaptive and updated frame by frame. Proposed R-Q model is implemented on H.264/AVC reference software JM17.2 to evaluate the performance, where accurate quantization stepsize is selected for each frame according to the target bit rate. As compared to the most recent published work [5] and well-known R-Q model adopted in JM [13], we have shown that almost 2x performance improvement in terms of the bits mismatch error.

Keywords: Rate-quantization model, H.264/AVC, low-delay rate control.

1 Introduction

In video encoding, a fundamental problem is how to select an appropriate quantization stepsize (QS) or equivalent quantization parameter (QP) to meet the bit rate constraint. Precise bit rate control is very important and critical for the encoder design, in particular for the real-time low-delay encoder rate control which is widely used in low-delay or ultra low-delay scenarios including video-conferencing, live video show and etc. Accurate rate-quantization (R-Q) model is high desired to solve this problem and such R-Q modeling problem has been extensively studied over decades. For instance, a well-known quadratic R-Q model is developed assuming the Laplacian distributed source [2] [3], with frame residual complexity dependent parameter to accurate capture the frame content variation. This model is adopted in MPEG-4 reference software to do encoder rate control and frame complexity is measured using the mean of the absolute of difference (MAD) for residual signal. In addition to MAD, other frame complexity measurements, such as variance of the difference (VOD) [5], sum of the

W. Lin et al. (Eds.): PCM 2012, LNCS 7674, pp. 492–500, 2012.

absolute of the transform difference (SATD) [6], are introduced to improve the
R-Q model for rate control. Meanwhile, a power function based R-Q model is
introduced in [8] [9] assuming the Cauchy distributed residual, where a gradient based frame complexity is used in [9] to enhance the bit prediction. Besides
these R-Q models, a ρ-domain rate model has been developed, where ρ indicates
the percentage of zero coefficients after quantization [10]. The ρ-domain model
turns out to be very accurate, however it does not give the explicit relationship
between bit rate and QS or QP.

In this paper, a new R-Q model is derived analytically based on the Laplacian
distributed residual source. To accurately capture the bit consumption for each
frame, frame residual complexity is measured by MAD and adjacent pixel correlation for residual block. Our proposed R-Q model has the power functional
form which is consistent with the work in [8]. We implement the proposed model
in rate control to measure its performance, where accurate quantization stepsize
for each frame is selected based on the proposed R-Q model according to the
target bit rate. Results show that our proposed R-Q model can reduce the bits
mismatch error up to 50% compared with the models proposed in [5] [13].

The remainder of this paper is organized as follows. The theoretical derivation
of the proposed model is given in Section 2. In Section 3, on-line model parameter
prediction and update are presented, while Section 4 shows the rate prediction
accuracy of our proposed model when performing rate control for H.264/AVC.
This paper closes with the conclusions given in Section 5.

2   Analytical Rate-Quantization Model

Assuming a $M \times M$ residual block $\mathbf{X}$ after prediction, the pixel values in $\mathbf{X}$ can
be captured by a Laplacian distribution with a zero mean and separable autocorrelation function [11]. In video encoder, $\mathbf{X}$ is further transformed (through
DCT or DCT-alike integer transform) for energy compaction. For example, in
H.264/AVC, after transform, we can have $\mathbf{Y} = (\mathbf{C}_f \mathbf{X} \mathbf{C}_f^T)$ [1] with $\mathbf{C}_f$ representing the forward transform. The variance of the transformed coefficients at
(u, v)-th position ($0 \leq u < M$, $0 \leq v < M$) in any frame, i.e., $\sigma_Y^2(u, v)$, can be
statistically expressed as [12]

$$\sigma_Y^2(u, v) = K(u, v)\sigma_X^2, \tag{1}$$

where σ_X^2 is the variance of $\mathbf{X}$. $K(u, v)$ is the (u, v)-th element of the 4×4^1
matrix $\mathbf{K}$, noted as

$$\mathbf{K} = \mathrm{diag}(\mathbf{C}_f \mathbf{P} \mathbf{C}_f^T)\mathrm{diag}(\mathbf{C}_f \mathbf{P} \mathbf{C}_f^T)^T, \tag{2}$$

Here $\mathrm{diag}(\mathbf{C}_f \mathbf{P} \mathbf{C}_f^T)$ is a column vector consisting of all the diagonal elements of
the input matrix $\mathbf{C}_f \mathbf{P} \mathbf{C}_f^T$. $\mathbf{P}$ in (2) is the correlation matrix defined as

---

[1] We assume the 4x4 block transform used in H.264 for theoretical analysis. 8x8 block
transform can be analyzed similarly.

$$\mathbf{P} = \begin{pmatrix} 1 & \zeta & \zeta^2 & \zeta^3 \\ \zeta & 1 & \zeta & \zeta^2 \\ \zeta^2 & \zeta & 1 & \zeta \\ \zeta^3 & \zeta^2 & \zeta & 1 \end{pmatrix} \tag{3}$$

where $|\zeta| \leq 1$ is the correlation coefficient between adjacent residual pixels. Moreover, for a Laplacian distributed random signal, σ_X can be approximated by the mean of the absolute difference for residual signal, i.e.,

$$\sigma_X = \sqrt{2} \cdot \text{MAD}. \tag{4}$$

Substituting (4) into (1), we can have

$$\sigma_Y = \sqrt{2K(u,v)} \cdot \text{MAD}. \tag{5}$$

As shown in [14], it has been demonstrated that the transformed coefficients at (u,v)-th can be also captured by a Laplacian distribution as

$$f_{Y(u,v)}(y) = \frac{\lambda(u,v)}{2} e^{-\lambda(u,v)|y|}, \tag{6}$$

where $\lambda(u,v)$ is the Laplacian distribution parameter, i.e.,

$$\lambda(u,v) = \frac{\sqrt{2}}{\sigma_Y(u,v)} = \frac{1}{\sqrt{K(u,v)} \cdot \text{MAD}}. \tag{7}$$

As we can see, transform coefficients distribution can be easily derived if ζ and MAD are known. Hence the bits consumption for encoding one frame can be accurately predicted.

Under the magnitude error criterion [15], the well-known R-D function for the coefficient at (u,v)-th is given by

$$R_{(u,v)}(D) = \begin{cases} \ln(\frac{1}{\lambda(u,v)D}) & 0 < D < \frac{1}{\lambda(u,v)} \\ 0 & D \geq \frac{1}{\lambda(u,v)}. \end{cases} \tag{8}$$

where $\lambda_{u,v}$ represents $\lambda(u,v)$ at (u,v)-th position. Eq. (8) can be expanded using Taylor series as

$$\begin{aligned} R_{(u,v)}(D) \\ = (\frac{1}{\lambda_{u,v}D} - 1) - \frac{1}{2!}(\frac{1}{\lambda_{u,v}D} - 1)^2 + R_3(D) \\ = -\frac{3}{2} + \frac{2}{\lambda_{u,v}}D^{-1} - \frac{1}{2(\lambda_{u,v})^2}D^{-2} + R_3(D), \end{aligned}$$

Since the magnitude error criterion is used as the distortion measure in Eq. (8), $D = q/4$ as shown in [16] with q standing for QS. Therefore, a R-Q model for the coefficients at (u,v) can be formulated (where the high-order terms is neglected) as follows:

$$R_{(u,v)}(q) = a_0 + \frac{a_1}{\lambda(u,v)}q^{-1} + \frac{a_2}{\lambda(u,v)^2}q^{-2}, \tag{9}$$

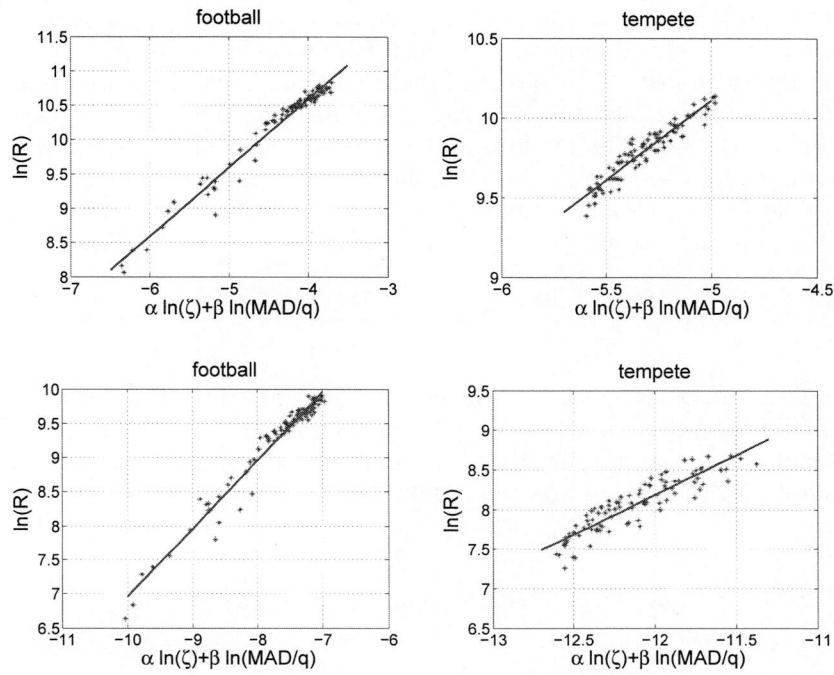

Fig. 1. Illustration of $\ln(R)$ versus ζ and MAD in scatter plots for different QPs. (The first row: QP=30; The second row:QP=36.)

with a_0, a_1 and a_2 as the model parameters.

Combining Eq. (7) into (9), it yields

$$R_{(u,v)}(q) = a_0 + a_1 \sqrt{K(u,v)}\mathrm{MAD} \cdot q^{-1} + a_2 K(u,v)\mathrm{MAD}^2 \cdot q^{-2}. \tag{10}$$

As a result, the total number of texture bits $R(q)$ for a frame is the sum of the bits distributed at each position, i.e.,

$$R(q) = \sum_{u=0}^{M-1} \sum_{v=0}^{M-1} (R_{(u,v)}(q)) = a_0 + a_1 \frac{\mathrm{MAD}}{q} \sum_{u=0}^{M-1} \sum_{v=0}^{M-1} \sqrt{K(u,v)}$$

$$+ a_2 (\frac{\mathrm{MAD}}{q})^2 \sum_{u=0}^{3} \sum_{v=0}^{3} K(u,v). \tag{11}$$

As aforementioned [(cp. (2) and (3)], it is noted that $\sqrt{K(u,v)}$ is a function of ζ. We define two functions, i.e., $f_1(\zeta)$ and $f_2(\zeta)$, denoting $\sum_{u=0}^{M-1} \sum_{v=0}^{M-1} \sqrt{K(u,v)}$ and $\sum_{u=0}^{M-1} \sum_{v=0}^{M-1} K(u,v)$, respectively. Hence, (11) can be rewritten as

$$R(q) = a_0 + a_1 \frac{\mathrm{MAD}}{q} f_1(\zeta) + a_2 (\frac{\mathrm{MAD}}{q})^2 f_2(\zeta). \tag{12}$$

It is noted that $R(q)$ is a polynomial function of the MAD/q. However, it is difficult to find a closed form for $f_1(\zeta)$ and $f_2(\zeta)$ so as to derive the close-form $R(q)$ analytically. Instead, we observed that the logarithm of the $R(q)$ is linearly related to the the logarithm of the MAD/q, as illustrated in Fig. 1. Such linearity is well preserved for different video contents coded with different QPs. To save the space, we only show two videos (Football as an example of motion intensive video while Tempete as an example of rich texture content) at two different QPs. Therefore, we can simplify the $R(q)$ model in (12) as

$$R(q) = C \times \zeta^\alpha \times (\frac{\mathrm{MAD}}{q})^\beta, \qquad (13)$$

where C, α and β are model parameters, which are refined using least square method (LSM) [18] after encoding one frame. ζ and MAD reflect the frame complexity. Note that the functional form of our proposed R-Q model is also consistent with the models presented in [8] [19].

3   Model Parameter Prediction and Update

3.1 ζ and MAD Prediction

In practice, the actual values of ζ and MAD are not available before finishing a frame encoding [13]. We adopt the linear prediction used in [13] to predict the MAD of current frame, i.e.,

$$\mathrm{MAD}_p[i] = Y_1[i] \times \mathrm{MAD}[i-1] + Y_0[i], \qquad (14)$$

where $\mathrm{MAD}_p[i]$ denotes the predicted MAD of the i-th frame, $\mathrm{MAD}[i-1]$ denotes the actual MAD after encoding the $(i-1)$-th frame, and $Y_1[i]$ and $Y_0[i]$ are the first-order and zero-order parameters of this linear prediction model, which would be updated after encoding every frame the same as in [13].

Let ζ_d be the correlation coefficient for direct residual signal, where direct residual signal is the co-located difference between current original frame and previous reconstructed frame. We have found that ζ_d always has the same trend as the ζ. Hence, we propose to predict ζ as follows:

$$\zeta_p[i] = \zeta[i-1] \cdot (1 + \omega \cdot \rho_\zeta[i]), \qquad (15)$$

where $\zeta_p[i]$ is the predicted autocorrelation coefficient of the i-th frame, $\zeta[i-1]$ is the actual autocorrelation coefficient of the $(i-1)$-th frame, $\omega = \zeta[i-1]/\zeta_d[i-1]$ and $\rho_\zeta = (\zeta_d[i]-\zeta_d[i-1])/\zeta_d[i-1]$. Table I shows the averaged prediction error for N coded frames, defined as $e_\zeta = \frac{1}{N} \sum_{i=1}^{N} |\zeta[i] - \zeta_p[i]|$. We also plot the predicted and actual values of ζ in Fig. 2 for Football and Silent. As demonstrated, (15) can predict the actual autocorrelation coefficient very well.

Table 1. Averaged prediction errors for ζ prediction

Sequence	Mother	Silent	Football	Foreman
e_ζ	0.0252	0.0906	0.0251	0.0624

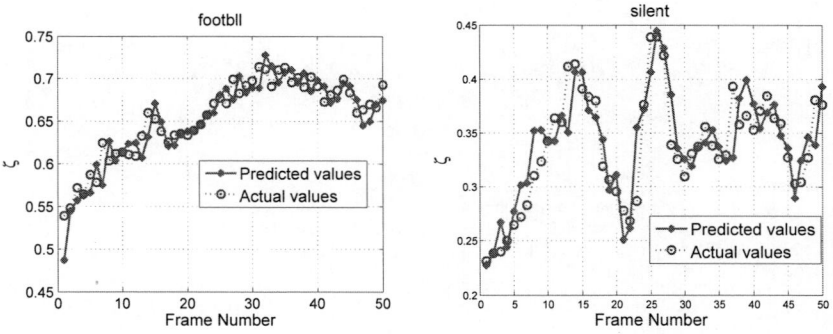

Fig. 2. Illustration of predicted and actual ζ for Football and Silent

3.2   Online Joint Update of C, α and β

C, α and β are updated before encoding the next frame using least mean square error (LMS) [18]. For instance, after coded the current frame, encoder collects the number of bits, MAD, ζ and QS to form $\mathbf{R} = [R_1, R_2, \ldots, R_n]^T$ and $\mathbf{V} = [V_1, V_2, \ldots, V_n]^T$ with $V_i = [1, \ln \zeta_i, \ln(\text{MAD} \cdot q_i^{-1})]$, $1 \leq i \leq n$. n denotes of the number of previously coded frame used for parameter updating. In our simulation, we set $n = 20$ as in [13], and parameters can be updated through

$$[\ln C, \alpha, \beta]^T = (\mathbf{R}^T\mathbf{R})^{-1}\mathbf{R}^T\mathbf{V}. \tag{16}$$

4   Experimental Results and Discussions

In this section, we present the experimental results of rate prediction accuracy for different R-Q models used in H.264/AVC rate control. Latest H.264/AVC reference software, i.e., JM17.2 [17] is used to do the benchmark with rate control enabled. The test sequences are chosen with different characteristics, i.e., "mother-daughter", "ice", "soccer", "city", and "crew" at CIF resolution and 30 frames per second. Each sequence is encoded with only first intra frame followed by all P-frames for low-delay encoding. Several typical target bit rates are simulated for verify the model accuracy. We compare the proposed R-Q model with the models described in [5] and [13]. In our experiment, constant target bits are set for each frame. Then, the first three frames of a sequence are coded with an initial QP, and the QP values of the following frames are determined

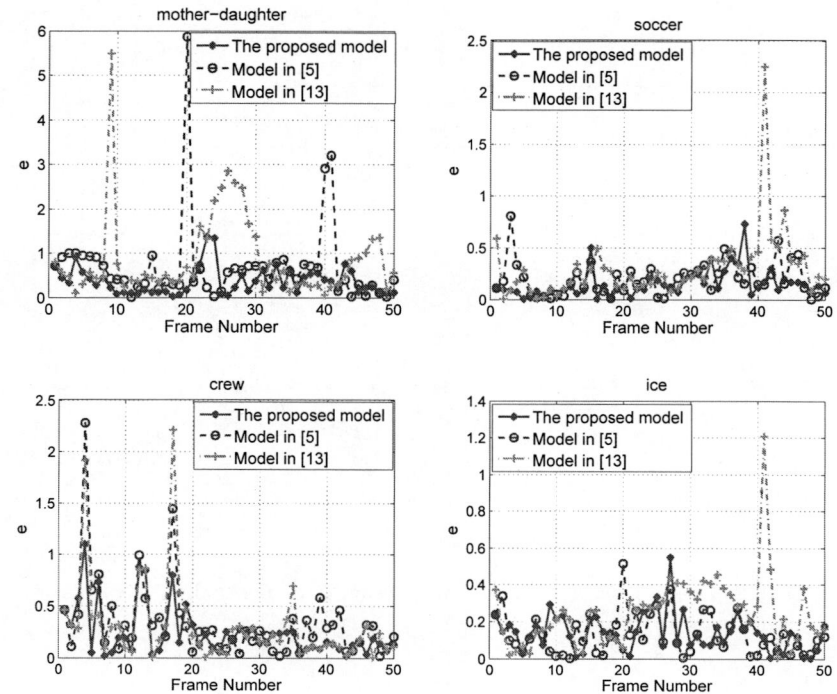

Fig. 3. The relative error between targeted bits and generated bits for each frame

based on the employed R-Q models. The average bits mismatch error between the target bits and the actual generated bits is used to evaluate the performance of R-Q models, defined as

$$e = \frac{1}{N} \sum_{i=1}^{N} \frac{|R_t(i) - R(i)|}{R_t(i)}$$

where $R_t(i)$ and $R(i)$ are the target and the actual coded bits in the i-th frame, respectively.

The average bits mismatch error are shown in Table II, from which it can be observed that the proposed R-Q model consistently outperforms the models in [5] and [13] with smaller rate prediction error. Apparently, the actual bits are more close to the target bits using the proposed model. The relative errors at frame encoding order are plotted in Fig. 3, which also shows that the maximum relative error is dramatically lower than previous works in addition to the smaller average relative error. Meanwhile, the complexity of the proposed method is similar to the schemes used for comparison because the same least square method is adopted to update model parameters for all three models.

Table 2. Averaged relative errors between target and actual bits

	R_t (kb/s)	e		
		Model in [13]	Model in [5]	Proposed
Mother	120	0.8108	0.7435	0.3348
	60	1.1270	0.8171	0.4475
	30	1.3214	1.1101	0.5212
Soccer	600	0.2210	0.1807	0.1289
	180	0.2851	0.1955	0.1477
	60	0.3537	0.2739	0.1537
City	600	0.1725	0.2448	0.1442
	240	0.3050	0.4129	0.1177
	60	0.2901	0.4418	0.1393
Crew	540	0.2502	0.2822	0.1820
	240	0.3537	0.4034	0.2867
	90	0.4906	0.4816	0.3522
Ice	600	0.1319	0.1213	0.0771
	180	0.2418	0.1749	0.1459
	60	0.2338	0.2002	0.1540
Ave.		0.4388	0.4069	**0.2221**

5   Conclusions

In this paper, a novel rate quantization (R-Q) model is proposed through theoretical derivation assuming the Laplacian distributed source. There are five model parameters in total with two content dependent parameters: one is the frame complexity measured by MAD while the other is the adjacent residual pixel correlation ζ. All these parameters are updated on-line frame by frame. For MAD and ζ, they are predicted using two simple prediction methods while other three parameters are updated using least square method. Experimental results have demonstrated that the proposed algorithm reduces the bit mismatch error by average 45%, 49% compared with the latest work [5] and default method adopted in the H.264/AVC reference software [13], respectively.

References

1. Malvar, H.S., Hallapuro, A., Karczewicz, M., Kerofsky, L.: Low-complexity transform and quantization in H.264/AVC. IEEE Trans. Circuits Syst. Video Technol. 13(7), 598–603 (2003)
2. Chiang, T., Zhang, Y.-Q.: A New Rate Control Scheme Using Quadratic Rate Distortion Model. IEEE Trans. Circuits Syst. Video Technol. 7(1), 246–250 (1997)

3. Lee, H.-J., Chiang, T., Zhang, Y.-Q.: Scalable rate control for MPEG-4 Video. IEEE Trans. Circuits Syst. Video Technol. 10(6), 878–894 (2000)
4. Wan, S., Izquierdo, E.: A new rate distortion model for rate control of video coding. In: Pro. of WIAMIS (2006)
5. Seo, C.-W., Kang, J.W., Han, J.-K., Nguyen, T.Q.: Efficient Bit Allocation and Rate Control Algorithms for Hierarchical Video Coding. IEEE Trans. Circuits Syst. Video Technol. 20(9), 1210–1223 (2010)
6. Kwon, D.-K., Shen, M.-Y., Kuo, C.-C.J.: Rate Control for H.264 Video With Enhanced Rate and Distortion Models. IEEE Trans. Circuits Syst. Video Technol. 17(5), 517–529 (2007)
7. Hu, S., Wang, H., Kwong, S., Zhao, T.: Frame level rate control for H.264/AVC with novel rate-quantizaion model. In: Pro. of ICME, pp. 226–231 (2010)
8. Karmaci, N., Altunbasak, Y., Mersereau, R.M.: Frame Bit allocation for the H.264/AVC video coder via Cauchy-density-based rate and distortion models. IEEE Trans. Circuits Syst. Video Technol. 15(8), 994–1006 (2005)
9. Jing, X., Chau, L.-P., Siu, W.-C.: Frame complexity-based rate-quantization model for H.264/AVC intraframe rate control. IEEE Signal Process. Lett. 15, 373–376 (2008)
10. He, Z., Mitra, S.K.: A unified rate-distortion analysis framework for transform coding. IEEE Trans. Circuits Syst. Video Technol. 11(12), 1221–1236 (2001)
11. Pao, I.-M., Sun, M.-T.: Modeling DCT coefficients for fast video encoding. IEEE Trans. Circuits Syst. Video Technol. 9(4), 608–616 (1999)
12. Jain, A.K.: Fundamentals of Digital Image Processing. Prentice-Hall, Englewood Cliffs (1989)
13. Li, Z.G., Pan, F., Lim, K.P., Feng, G., Lin, X., Rahardja, S.: Adaptive basic unit layer rate control for JVT, Doc. JVT-G012-rl, Thailand (2003)
14. Lam, E.Y., Goodman, J.W.: A Mathematical Analysis of the DCT Coefficient Distribution for Images. IEEE Trans. Image Process. 9(10), 1661–1666 (2000)
15. Berger, T.: Rate Distortion Theory, pp. 94–95. Prentice-Hall, Englewood Cliffs (1971)
16. Gish, H., Pierce, J.N.: Asymptotically efficient quantizing. IEEE Trans. Inform. Theory IT-14(5), 676–683 (1968)
17. H.264/14496-10 AVC Reference software JM17.2, http://iphome.hhi.de/suehring/tml/index.html
18. Nash, S.G., Sofer, A.: Linear and Nonlinear Programming. McGraw-Hill Companies, Inc., New York (1996)
19. Ding, W., Liu, B.: Rate control of MPEG video coding and recoding by rate-quantization modeling. IEEE Trans. Circuit and Sys. for Video Technology 6(2), 12–20 (1996)

Chaos-Based Selective Encryption
for AVS Video Coding Standard

Oi-Yan Lui, Ching-Hung Yuen, and Kwok-Wo Wong

Department of Electronic Engineering
City University of Hong Kong, 83 Tat Chee Avenue, Kowloon Tong
Hong Kong Special Administrative Region, China
{oiyanlui2,chyuen}@student.cityu.edu.hk, itkwwong@cityu.edu.hk

Abstract. A chaos-based selective encryption scheme implemented on the Audio Video Standard (AVS) is proposed. The scheme employs multiple Rényi chaotic maps to generate a pseudorandom bit sequence for the encryption of selected AVS syntax elements using cipher block chaining (CBC) mode. It maintains the bitstream format compliance while provides sufficient protection by destroying the commercial value of video clips reconstructed without the key. Moreover, the security analysis shows that the proposed algorithm is highly sensitive to the secret key and has good perceptual security.

Keywords: AVS, Chaos, Encryption, Video Coding.

1 Introduction

Recently, there is a drastic increase in the amount of multimedia applications and services due to the rapid growth of broadband communication. However, the risk of unauthorized access of the multimedia data is often ignored since most of the data are transmitted through public networks without encryption. Some venders try to deal with this problem simply by releasing low-quality video clips for attracting potential buyers to purchase the high-quality version. Thus, selective encryption is preferred as it only encrypts a portion of the significant information [2]. Once the encrypted part cannot be recovered properly, the quality of the reconstructed video drops dramatically and its commercial value is degraded.

Here, we propose a chaos-based selective encryption algorithm for the Audio Video Standard (AVS) compression scheme [10]. In our algorithm, several Rényi chaotic maps [1] are combined as a pseudorandom number generator (PRNG) to produce a keystream for the selective encryption of significant video data. The encryption algorithm operates alternatively with the original compression in the entropy coding stage to achieve joint compression and encryption.

The rest of this paper is organized as follows. A brief introduction of AVS and the Rényi chaotic map are given in the rest of Section 1. The proposed approach is

W. Lin et al. (Eds.): PCM 2012, LNCS 7674, pp. 501–512, 2012.

presented in Section 2. Simulation results are reported in Section 3. Finally, a conclusion is drawn in the last section.

1.1   Audio Video Standard (AVS)

AVS is a digital audio and video compression standard which is developed in 2002 by Science and Technology Department of National Information Industry Ministry, People's Republic of China [3]. This standard aims at high-definition quality multimedia broadcasting and applications with less complexity compared with the H.264 video compression standard [5][13]. In AVS, a video frame is divided into a number of 16x16-pixel blocks called macroblock (MB). Each MB is encoded by intra-predictive or inter-predictive coding.

Intra-predictive coding is designed to remove the spatial redundancy. It is processed on 8x8-pixel luminance or chrominance blocks. The block values are predicted from neighboring blocks in the same frame. There are 5 modes for the luminance blocks and 4 modes for the chrominance blocks. Unlike intra-predictive coding, inter-predictive coding eliminates the temporal redundancy. The prediction of the current block is based on the blocks from the previous coded frames.

The difference between the pixels in the source video frame and the predicted one is called the residual, which is the value to be encoded. The residuals are first processed by the transform coder where the Integer Cosine Transform (ICT) [4] is applied. The complexity is low since there are only addition and shift operations, without any multiplications. Then, the transformed residual blocks are quantized and undergo a zigzag scan. The 2D transformed residual blocks are converted into 1D Level-Run (L_i, R_i) pairs by Run-Length Coding. Since the Jizhun Profile is used, Context-based 2D Variable Length Coding (C2DVLC) [11] is adopted as the entropy coding scheme to encode the (L_i, R_i) pairs. Its block diagram is shown in Fig. 1. After the zigzag scan, the first (L_0, R_0) pair is coded by searching the C2DVLC tables and initialize $TableIndex_0$ to zero. For each C2DVLC table, there is a fixed range of values. If the value of the (L_i, R_i) pair fall into the range, the regular mode is used for encoding. Otherwise, the escape mode is chosen.

In regular mode, the (L_i, R_i) pair with positive Level magnitude is mapped to the positive *CodeNumber* by looking up the C2DVLC tables. Afterward, the positive *CodeNumber* is mapped to the unique Exp-Golomb codeword to form the encoded bitstream. The (L_i, R_i) pair with negative Level magnitude is coded like the positive ones but the value of *CodeNumber* is increased by 1. In escape mode, the (L_i, R_i) pair is coded separately by mapping to the Exp-Golomb codewords. Only the sign of R_i and the magnitude of L_i are chosen.

The update of $TableIndex_{i+1}$ for selecting the suitable C2DVLC table for the next (L_{i+1}, R_{i+1}) pair is necessary because of the adaptive property of C2DVLC. The table update is based on the maximum magnitude of the previous coded Level (L_{max}). After the entropy coding, the magnitude of L_i is used to update L_{max}. When the value of L_{max} is larger than $Threshold_j$ of the current C2DVLC table, $TableIndex_{i+1}$ is updated according to Equation (1).

$$TableIndex_{i+1} = j \quad if \quad (Threshold_{j+1} > L_{max} \geq Threshold_j) \tag{1}$$

The threshold values of the C2DVLC tables are given by Equation (2)

$$Threshold[0\ldots7] = \begin{cases} (0,1,2,3,5,8,11,\infty) & intra\_luminance \\ (0,1,2,3,4,7,10,\infty) & inter\_luminance \\ (0,1,2,3,5,\infty,\infty,\infty) & chrominance \end{cases} \tag{2}$$

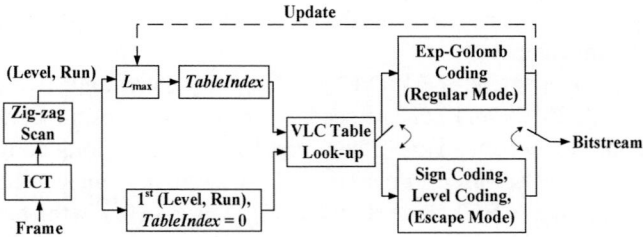

Fig. 1. C2DVLC of AVS

1.2 Chaos-Based Pseudorandom Number Generator Using Rényi Map

Chaotic systems have been widely used in cryptography in recent years because of their ergodicity properties and the high sensitivity to the initial conditions. Owing to the long computational time of the chaotic systems, most of the researchers solely applied them in text or image encryption [6][8][9][12] but not real-time video encryption. In [1], Addabbo *et al.* designed a family of maximum-period nonlinear congruential generators (NLCGs) based on the digitized Rényi map. NLCGs can be employed as PRNGs with a good randomness performance at a relatively low computational complexity.

The Rényi map can be implemented efficiently as it involves only a multiplication, an addition and two bit-shift operations. In order to achieve the maximal period of the PRNG, Addabbo *et al.* suggested some sets of parameters for bit-length smaller than or equal to 31. However, a bit-length of 31 is usually not sufficient for most of the applications. Thus, a 32-bit composite PRNG by combining two PRNGs is suggested. One of the PRNGs has a bit-length of 15 while the other has 17 bits. A constraint of this approach is that the bit-lengths of the two generators must be relatively prime to each other. Then the period of the composite PRNG is equal to the product of the individual generator period, i.e. $(2^{15}-1)(2^{17}-1) \approx 2^{32}$.

2   The Proposed Approach

To maintain the format compliance for all regular decoders to process the encrypted video clips without decoding error, there are some restrictions on the choice of parameters for encryption. In an (L_i, R_i) pair, the sign bit and the magnitude of L_i are decent for encryption. However, the magnitude of R_i is not appropriate because it may change the length of the encrypted bitstream. Since L_{max} is used to switch the C2DVLC tables for encoding the next (L_{i+1}, R_{i+1}) pair, only L_i and its corresponding encrypted L_i with the same range can be chosen [7].

In regular mode, only the magnitude and the sign of L_i are encrypted. The sign and the suffix of the Exp-Golomb codewords are encrypted using escape mode. In both modes, the parameters chosen for encryption must not violate the format compliance requirement. The value of intra predictive mode is also a suitable candidate for encryption since the number of bits used to represent it is fixed. Thus the format compliance can be maintained.

Based on [1], we extend the PRNG to 128-bit by combining five Rényi maps of bit-length 19, 23, 26, 29 and 31. The seeds of these five maps are denoted as s_{19}, s_{23}, s_{26}, s_{29}, s_{31} and they become part of the secret key. The pseudorandom bits generated from these five maps are used to mask the chosen syntax elements. In particular, the cipher block chaining (CBC) mode shown in Fig. 2 is adopted in the masking process.

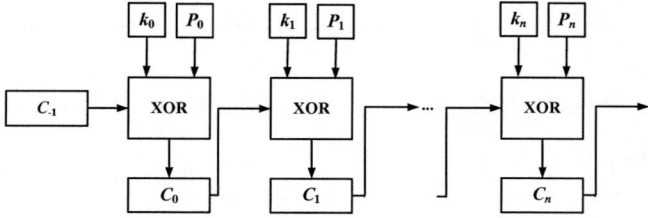

Fig. 2. The masking process in CBC mode

2.1   Encryption Procedures

Step 1: The five Rényi maps are iterated individually. The number of iterations for each map is governed by $\lceil 128/l \rceil$, where $l = 19, 23, 26, 29, 31$, respectively. After at least 128 pseudorandom bits have been generated from each map, they are bit-wisely XORed to form a 128-bit keystream block k_i. Since the cipher block chaining mode is used, k_i is first XORed with the 128-bit previous cipher block C_{i-1} to form a new 128-bit keystream block k'_i, as governed by Equation (3).

$$k'_i = k_i \oplus C_{i-1} \tag{3}$$

For the first plaintext block P_0, there is no previous ciphertext block and so C_{-1} is derived from the secret key.

Step 2: The chosen syntax element of m-bit long are masked by bit-wisely XOR with the first m bits of k'_i generated in Step 1. Afterward, m bits are shifted out from k'_i and the m-bit codeword is packed until the current 128-bit ciphertext (C_i) buffer is full. However, if the number of bits remaining in k'_i is not enough for masking the whole m-bit syntax element, this element will be divided into two parts. The first part is masked by the remaining bits in k'_i while the second part is masked by the front part of k'_{i+1} which is generated by XORing C_i with k_{i+1}. The resultant codeword of this syntax element is a concatenation of the two masked parts.

Step 3: The codeword of the chosen syntax element is packed back into the video stream for subsequent compression operations.

Step 4: Repeat Step 1 to Step 3 until the end of the video stream.

2.2   Decryption Procedures

The decryption procedures are similar to the encryption ones. Given the same initial conditions (secret keys and initial vector C_{-1}), the five Rényi maps at the decoding side are able to re-generate the identical 128-bit keystream block k_i and also k'_i. Then the encrypted important syntax elements are bit-wisely XOR with the masking stream to obtain the original syntax elements. After that, they are passed back to the original video bitstream before inverse quantization and inverse ICT. These processes repeat until the whole coded video stream has been decoded.

3   Simulation Results

The Rényi map is given by Equation (4) [1]

$$f(r) = r \times B + (\frac{r}{2^j}) \bmod 2^l \tag{4}$$

where r is a l-bit number obtained by iterating the map, B and j are the specific parameters chosen for the l-bit map, as suggested in Table 1 of [1]. The initial value of r is set by the corresponding seed s_l.

For the 19-bit Rényi map, s_{19} is selected as 0xF0001123 which is the secret key, B is 0x00022EF2, $j = 18$. For the 23-bit map, s_{23} is selected as 0xF0001123, B is 0x001CDB6C, $j = 21$. For the 26-bit map, the value of s_{26} is 0xF0001123, B is 0x00656096, $j = 25$. For the 29-bit map, s_{29} is set to 0xF0001123, B is 0x10000002, $j = 28$. For the 31-bit map, s_{31} is chosen as 0xF0001123, B is 0x40000800, $j = 20$. The proposed algorithm is implemented in C++ programming language running on a personal computer with an Intel Core i5 750 2.67GHz processor and 1.96GB memory.

In the implementation, we have used the AVS reference implementation model for processing the video sequences at CIF size (176×144 pixels). The video sequences "mobile", "foreman", "coastguard", "bus", "news" and "Stefan" are used as examples to show the performance of our algorithm.

3.1   Encryption Performance

In the proposed algorithm, Rényi map encryption and AVS based on C2DVLC compression are operated simultaneously. The first frames, decoded with the correct key, of 6 different video streams are shown in Fig. 3. Since AVS is a lossless compression scheme, our algorithm does not cause any degradation on the video quality after reconstructed using the correct key.

Fig. 3. The first frame, decoded with the correct key, of six different video clips (a) mobile, (b) foreman, (c) coastguard, (d) bus, (e) news, (f) Stefan

Then we change the sign bits and some pixel values of the video sequences in the encoding process. In the spatial domain, some important syntax elements are altered. The luminance (Y) and chrominance (U and V) are also changed in the temporal domain. Therefore, color distortion is clearly observed in Fig. 4, which shows the first frame, decoded without the key, of 6 different video streams encoded in I+P-frame mode with intra period 2 at quantization parameter (QP) value 28. Intra period 2 is adopted here for the purpose of clear presentation. It is evident that the commercial value of the video clips is completely ruined given that only trivial characters can be recognized and the colors of the reconstructed video are unnatural.

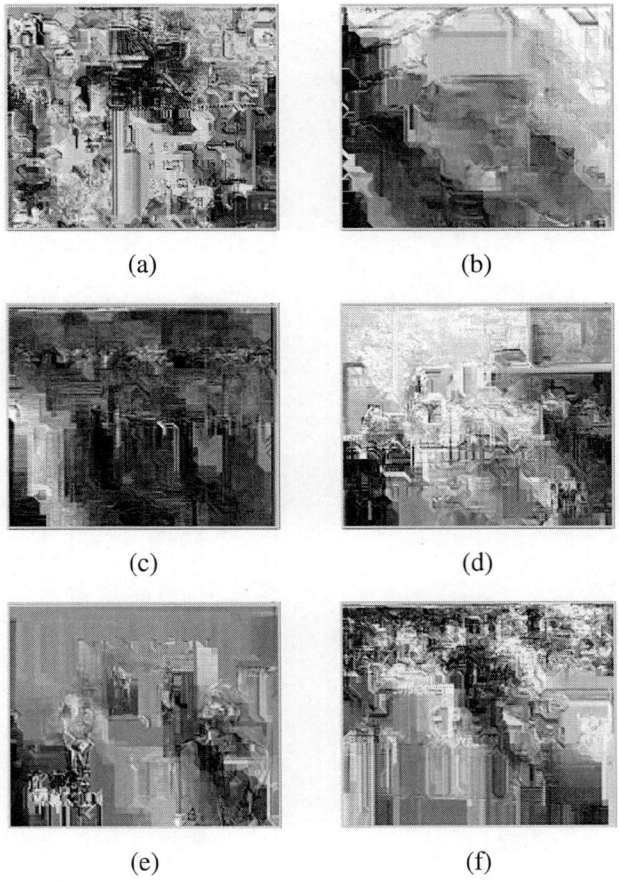

(a)   (b)

(c)   (d)

(e)   (f)

Fig. 4. The first frame, decoded without the key, of six different video clips (a) mobile, (b) foreman, (c) coastguard, (d) bus, (e) news, (f) Stefan

3.2   Reconstruction Quality

To clearly demonstrate the effectiveness of our scheme, Fig. 5 shows the first frame, decoded without the key, of the foreman video clip encoded in I-frame mode at different QP values. Only the object outlines can be identified without any detailed information.

The peak signal-to-noise ratio (PSNR) is employed as a performance index to evaluate the quality of the reconstructed video clips. Tables 1 and 2 list the PSNR of the I-frames and I+P-frames, respectively, of six standard video sequences at QP value 28 using the original algorithm without encryption (ORIG) and our selective encryption algorithm (SE). In Table 1, the average PSNR values of ORIG are 40.31dB, 43.09dB and 44.01dB for the Y, U, and V components, respectively. However, the corresponding values of our algorithm are only 8.81dB, 20.50dB and 22.13dB. In Table 2, the average PSNR values of ORIG for the Y, U and V components are 39.14dB, 43.19dB and 44.11dB, respectively. The proposed algorithm gives 8.45dB, 20.20dB and 21.04dB, respectively. These results show that our algorithm effectively lowers the PSNR values of the Y, U and V components for different types of video sequences.

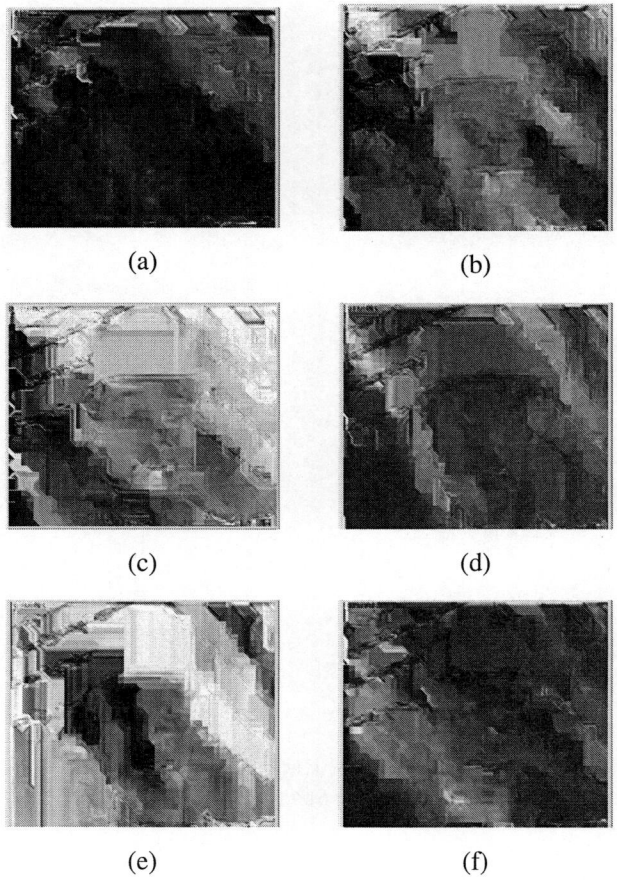

(a)   (b)

(c)   (d)

(e)   (f)

Fig. 5. The first frame, decoded without the key, of the foreman video clip at QP value (a) 12, (b) 20, (c) 28, (d) 36, (e) 44, (f) 52

Tables 3 and 4 show the PSNR results of the I-frames and I+P-frames, respectively, of the foreman video sequence at different QP values. The data list in both tables justify that our approach works well in diminishing the PSNR values of both the luminance and the chrominance components at various QP values. The luminance values drop to around 8dB while the chrominance values descend to nearly 24dB and 21dB. Thus the commercial value of the video clips is destroyed substantially.

Table 1. PSNR of I-frame without encryption (ORIG) and using our selective encryption (SE) at QP = 28

Sequence	PSNR Y (dB)		PSNR U (dB)		PSNR V (dB)	
	ORIG	SE	ORIG	SE	ORIG	SE
mobile	38.48	8.57	39.97	14.64	39.97	11.50
foreman	44.13	9.16	43.60	25.05	46.14	25.49
coastguard	38.78	10.46	46.13	21.92	47.24	29.15
bus	39.01	7.29	43.08	26.84	43.91	27.36
news	41.40	7.89	43.45	18.07	44.51	20.81
Stefan	40.04	9.48	42.32	16.49	42.30	18.48
average	40.31	8.81	43.09	20.50	44.01	22.13

Table 2. PSNR of I+P-frame at intra period 2 without encryption (ORIG) and using our selective encryption (SE) at QP = 28

Sequence	PSNR Y (dB)		PSNR U (dB)		PSNR V (dB)	
	ORIG	SE	ORIG	SE	ORIG	SE
mobile	37.78	8.79	40.17	14.33	40.15	10.38
foreman	39.78	8.45	43.72	24.41	46.23	23.51
coastguard	38.23	10.5	46.21	21.65	47.33	28.55
bus	38.47	6.55	43.19	27.23	44.04	26.21
news	41.17	6.72	43.52	17.07	44.59	18.79
Stefan	39.40	9.68	42.31	16.52	42.34	18.78
average	39.14	8.45	43.19	20.20	44.11	21.04

Table 3. PSNR of I-frame in the reconstructed foreman video clip without encryption (ORIG) and using our selective encryption (SE) approach at different QP values

QP	PSNR Y (dB)		PSNR U (dB)		PSNR V (dB)	
	ORIG	SE	ORIG	SE	ORIG	SE
12	49.69	6.89	50.58	25.20	51.31	19.07
20	44.70	6.08	47.02	25.49	48.89	23.64
28	44.13	9.16	43.60	25.05	46.14	25.49
36	36.09	7.59	40.74	23.05	43.00	16.34
44	32.59	10.15	38.68	19.57	40.14	21.00
52	29.33	8.24	37.57	20.62	38.25	17.18
average	39.42	8.02	43.03	23.16	44.62	20.45

Table 4. PSNR of I+P-frame in the reconstructed foreman video clip without encryption (ORIG) and using our selective encryption (SE) approach at different QP values

QP	PSNR Y (dB)		PSNR U (dB)		PSNR V (dB)	
	ORIG	SE	ORIG	SE	ORIG	SE
12	48.51	6.32	50.48	26.65	51.09	20.12
20	44.14	6.54	47.09	25.30	48.89	23.13
28	39.78	8.45	43.72	24.41	46.23	23.51
36	35.93	8.04	40.83	24.45	43.06	18.45
44	32.37	9.82	38.71	23.46	40.13	23.25
52	30.32	7.53	37.70	19.89	38.39	17.73
average	38.51	7.78	43.09	24.03	44.63	21.03

3.3   Security Analysis

The secret key used in the proposed scheme is composed of the five seeds of the Rényi maps. Each map is controlled by an individual secret key. The bit-lengths of the seeds are 19, 23, 26, 29 and 31, respectively. The total key length is $19+23+26+29+31 = 128$ bits. Therefore, our scheme can be considered as secure enough to resist attacks.

To test the key sensitivity for our algorithm, a bit in one of the five Rényi map keys is randomly selected and toggled. Then the bitstream is decoded using the modified key. The PSNRs of 10 decoded I-frames in the reconstructed foreman video sequence at different QP values are shown in Table 5. The results for 10 I+P-frames at intra period 2 are presented in Table 6. The data indicate that the PSNR values drop substantially when the key is slightly modified. For the luminance component (Y), all the PSNRs are lower than 10dB. They clearly show that our algorithm is highly sensitive to the secret keys.

Table 5. PSNR of I-frame in the reconstructed foreman video clip without encryption (ORIG) and using our selective encryption (SE) approach with a one-bit error key at different QP values

QP	PSNR Y (dB)		PSNR U (dB)		PSNR V (dB)	
	ORIG	SE	ORIG	SE	ORIG	SE
12	49.69	7.90	50.58	27.63	51.31	19.27
20	44.70	6.60	47.02	24.61	48.89	24.29
28	44.13	8.89	43.60	23.71	46.14	22.47
36	36.09	7.21	40.74	23.76	43.00	19.37
44	32.59	9.66	38.68	19.99	40.14	20.46
52	29.33	8.06	37.57	21.12	38.25	18.52
average	39.42	8.05	43.03	23.47	44.62	20.73

Table 6. PSNR of I+P-frame in the reconstructed foreman video clip without encryption (ORIG) and using our selective encryption (SE) approach with a one-bit error key at different QP values

	PSNR Y (dB)		*PSNR U (dB)*		*PSNR V (dB)*	
QP	*ORIG*	*SE*	*ORIG*	*SE*	*ORIG*	*SE*
12	48.51	7.50	50.48	26.53	51.09	18.20
20	44.14	7.96	47.09	26.65	48.89	22.71
28	39.78	9.24	43.72	24.31	46.23	22.82
36	35.93	7.41	40.83	24.51	43.06	19.37
44	32.37	8.68	38.71	20.07	40.13	21.27
52	30.32	7.43	37.70	20.13	38.39	21.26
average	38.51	8.04	43.09	23.70	44.63	20.94

4   Conclusion

A chaos-based selective encryption scheme for AVS video compression standard has been proposed. Five Rényi maps are employed to form a PRNG for masking the selected syntax elements. Simulation results show that without the exact key, the quality of the reconstructed video clips is very low, but will not cause decoding error. Therefore our approach provides protection to AVS video clips while maintains the format compliance property.

Acknowledgements. The work described in this paper was fully supported by a grant from City University of Hong Kong [Project No. 7008106].

References

1. Addabbo, T., Alioto, M., Fort, A., Pasini, A., Rocchi, S., Vignoli, V.: A class of maximum-period nonlinear congruential generators derived from the Rényi chaotic map. IEEE Trans. on Circuits and Syst.-I: Regular Papers 54, 816–828 (2007)
2. Cheng, H., Li, X.: Partial encryption of compressed images and videos. IEEE Trans. on Signal Process. 48, 2439–2451 (2000)
3. Fan, L., Ma, S., Wu, F.: Overview of AVS video standard. In: IEEE Int. Conf. on Multimedia and Expo (ICME), vol. 1, pp. 423–426 (2004)
4. Ma, S., Gao, W.: Low complexity integer transform and adaptive quantization optimization. J. Comput. Sci. Technol. 21, 354–359 (2006)
5. Puri, A., Chen, X., Luthra, A.: Video coding using the H.264/MPEG-4 AVC compression standard. Signal Process.: Image Commun. 19, 793–849 (2004)
6. Sam, I., Devaraj, P., Bhuvaneswaran, R.: A novel image cipher based on mixed transformed logistic maps. Multimedia Tools and Appl. 56, 315–330 (2010)
7. Shahid, Z., Chaumont, M., Puech, W.: Selective encryption of C2DVLC of AVS video coding standard for I & P frames. In: IEEE Int. Conf. on Multimedia and Expo (ICME), pp. 1655–1660 (2010)

8. Taneja, N., Raman, B., Gupta, I.: Chaos based cryptosystem for still visual data. To Appear in Multimedia Tools and Appl., doi 10.1007/s11042-011-0837-7
9. Ye, R.: A novel chaos-based image encryption scheme with an efficient permutation-diffusion mechanism. Optics Commun. 284, 5290–5298 (2011)
10. Yu, L., Chen, S., Wang, J.: Overview of AVS-video coding standard. Signal Process.: Image Commun. 24, 247–262 (2009)
11. Zhang, L., Wang, Q., Wang, N., Zhao, D., Wu, X., Gao, W.: Context-based entropy coding in AVS video coding standard. Signal Process.: Image Commun. 24, 263–276 (2009)
12. Zhu, C.X.: A novel image encryption scheme based on improved hyperchaotic sequences. Optics Commun. 285, 29–37 (2012)
13. Draft ITU-T recommendation and final draft international standard of joint video specification (ITU-T Rec. H.264/ISO/IEC 14496-10 AVC). Technical report, Joint Video Team (JVT), Doc. JVT-G050r1 (2003)

Q-CSLBP: Compression of CSLBP Descriptor

Junaid Baber[1], Shin'ichi Satoh[2], Nitin Afzulpurkar[1], and Maheen Bakhtyar[1]

[1] School of Engineering and Technology, Asian Institute of Technology, Thailand
{junaid.j.baber,nitin,maheen.bakhtyar}@ait.ac.th
[2] Multimedia Information Research Division, National Institute of Informatics, Japan
satoh@nii.ac.jp

Abstract. Center Symmetric-Local Binary Pattern (CSLBP) is textured based operator which is mostly used as keypoint descriptor, it is 256-length descriptor to represent single keypoint or affine patch. This operator is an extension of Local Binary Pattern (LBP) operator. The CSLBP descriptor is computationally simple, effective, and robust for various image transformations such as illumination change and image blurring. However, the space and time utilization of CSLBP can be improved by simple compression which can make CSLBP a smart selection for large databases and smart phones. In this paper, we propose simple compression of CSLBP without loss of its discriminative power. We reduce the descriptor length (dimensions) upto 50% without applying any dimensionality reduction techniques such as PCA or LDA. We evaluate our framework on state-of-the-art matching protocols and compare the effectiveness of proposed compressed descriptor (Q-CSLBP) with CSLBP, SIFT and PCA-SIFT.

1 Introduction

Representing the images by their local features for image indexing, searching, and efficient retrieval is widely used for many applications such as image copy detection, video copy detection, image classification, scene classification, and object detection/recognition. In first step, keypoints are detected from the images which should be repeatable and invariant to affine and other transformations such as scale change, rotation and image degradation. There are many keypoint detectors such as SIFT keypoints which are also known as Difference of Gaussian [1], Harries and Hessian keypoints [2]. In second step, these keypoints are presented by some robust local affine patch which should present the local structure or texture around the keypoint. Finally, distinctive and robust descriptors are computed over the local affine patch. Some of the famous descriptors in literature include SIFT [1], SURF [3], GLOH [4], and CSLBP [5].

An extensive evaluation of different descriptors is conducted by Mikolajczyk and Schmid [4], they show that the descriptor SIFT [1] has highest consistency against various transformations. Therefore, it is also considered the gold standard. The SIFT descriptor is the representation of gradient orientation histograms. To compute the SIFT descriptor of any keypoint, the patch around the

W. Lin et al. (Eds.): PCM 2012, LNCS 7674, pp. 513–521, 2012.
© Springer-Verlag Berlin Heidelberg 2012

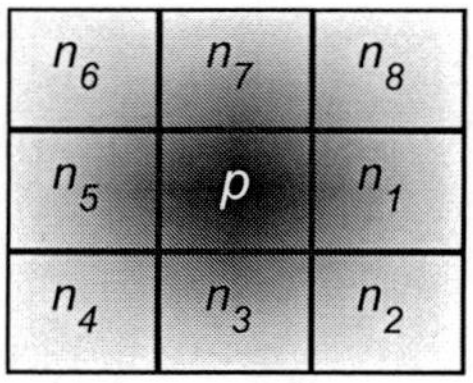

Fig. 1. Example of keypoint p with its $N = 8$ neighbor pixels at the radial distance $R = 1$. In case of LBP, each neighbor pixel is compared with p, whereas, in CSLBP comparison pairs are as follow: $(n_1, n_5), (n_2, n_6), (n_3, n_7), (n_4, n_8)$.

keypoint is divided into grid of 4×4. In each cell, the gradient magnitudes and orientations are computed for all pixels. The gradient orientation are quantized into 8 directions and the histograms of quantized orientations are computed. During the histograms computation, each sample added to histograms are weighted by their gradient magnitude and Gaussian weight. The main problem with SIFT is computational cost and complexity. The H. Marko et al [5] proposed texture based descriptor known as CSLBP. They argue that CSLBP is computationally fast and simple to compute. They also show that CSLBP descriptor has similar performance compared to SIFT under different transformations. As stated above, CSLBP represents single keypoint by 256-length vector. A single image might have thousands of keypoints, and storing the set of raw descriptors for a single image could require more storage than the image itself. This makes CSLBP difficult for, say, a movie studio to index the frames of its video collection for purposes of illegal copy detection. Therefore, it is necessary to have compact representation of descriptors. One possible way to reduce the dimensions is PCA as used for SIFT [6]. Some of the major limitations of PCA include off-line training, sensitive to training data, and poor performance in case of non-linear transformations [7].

In this paper, we propose simple but effective compression of CSLBP, we successfully reduced its dimensions without applying any dimensionality reduction techniques such as PCA or LDA. However, applying PCA to the descriptor makes it more robust as compared to the native descriptor. For example in case of SIFT, PCA-SIFT [6] performs better for image retrieval but computation time increases two folds due to off-line training. The main contribution of this paper is simple and effective compression of CSLBP descriptor which decreases the storage requirement and provide fast features matching. The rest of paper is organized as follow. Detail insight of CSLBP descriptor is given in Section 2. The compression technique is explained in Section 3. Experiments and results are discussed in Section 4 and 5. Finally, conclusion is presented in Section 6.

2   Center-Symmetric Local Binary Pattern

CSLBP is a texture based operator which is also used as descriptor. It is an extension of LBP. In LBP, each pixel value p is compared with its N neighbors

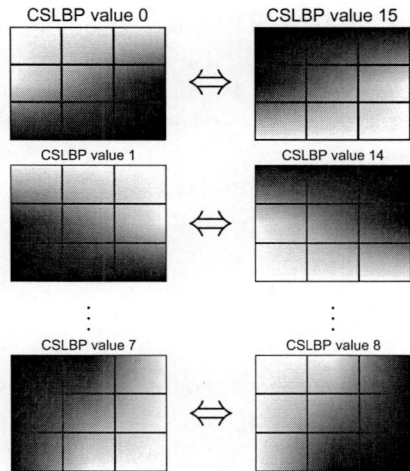

Fig. 2. Q-CSLBP: merging the symmetric patterns

with radial distance R. For every pixel p, there are N comparisons and the output for each pixel p is of N bits and that can be represented by decimal number:

$$LBP_{N,R}(p) \quad = \sum_{i=1}^{N} s(|n_i| - |p|)2^{i-1},$$

$$s(j) \quad = \begin{cases} 1 & j \geq 0 \\ 0 & \text{otherwise} \end{cases} \tag{1}$$

where $|p|$ is the pixel value and n_i are the neighbor pixels at the radial distance R. In practice, the values of N and R are 8 and 1, respectively. For given image or patch, the histogram of LBP is computed where the length of histogram is 2^N. The length of LBP histogram can be reduced by uniform patterns [8]. The LBP histogram is quite long and can not be efficiently used for region descriptor [5].

The CSLBP operator is quantized representation of LBP operator as described in Equation 1. In $CSLBP$, instead of comparing each neighbor with p, only center-symmetric neighbors are compared as shown in Figure 1:

$$CSLBP_{N,R,T}(p) \quad = \sum_{i=1}^{\frac{N}{2}} s(|n_i| - |n_{i+\frac{N}{2}}|)2^{i-1},$$

$$s(j) \quad = \begin{cases} 1 & j > T \\ 0 & \text{otherwise} \end{cases} \tag{2}$$

For given image or patch, the histogram of $CSLBP$ is computed, the length of histogram is $2^{\frac{N}{2}}$ which is quite short as compared to LBP. The suggested values for N, R and T are $8, 1, 0.01$, respectively.

To compute the $CSLBP$ descriptor, the given patch P is divided into spatial grid of $G_x \times G_y$, and the histogram of $CSLBP$ is computed in each cell. Finally, all histograms are concatenated to form the descriptor. The length of CSLBP descriptor is $G_x \times G_y \times 2^{\frac{N}{2}}$ which is quite often the double of SIFT descriptor. For our experiments, the values for $CSLBP_{N,R,T}$ are $CSLBP_{8,1,0.01}$, and optimal results are obtained keeping $G_x = 4$ and $G_y = 4$ which makes $CSLBP$ the length of 256. The vector obtained by concatenating the CSLBP histograms from all the cells is then normalized to unit length. After normalization, the values having long peaks are again thresholded by 0.2 to ensure that no value is greater then 0.2, as suggested by [5]. After thresholding with 0.2, the vector is renormalized to unit length.

3   CSLBP Compression

In CSLBP, for each pixel there are four comparisons between eight neighbors as shown in Figure 1. Based on eight neighbor texture, there are 16 unique patterns using Equation 2, these patterns are represented by decimal numbers from 0-15, and CSLBP histogram of these 16 patterns for all pixels are computed for given patch P. One possible way to reduce the dimensions is to use less number of bins instead 16. Analysis on co-occurrence distribution [9] of CSLBP patterns on VGG dataset (dataset explained in Experimental section) shows that the adjacent bins have high correlation. Therefore, information loss will be significant if dimensions are reduced by taking less number of bins.

The co-occurrence distribution also show that the symmetric patterns have less co-relation in image texture. Experiments show that merging of symmetric patterns is more effective, symmetric patterns can be obtained by flipping the comparison operator used in Equation 2, i.e., $j > T$. We examined many combinations to reduce the bins by merging the different patterns. However, maximum efficiency is achieved when symmetric patterns are merged, as shown in Figure 2. We simply merge two patterns obtained by flipping the comparison operator used in Equation 2. For example, given two points p_1, p_2 in region P, we get following CSLBP:

Example	Equation 2 with $j > T$	Flipped comparison $j < T$
15 255 150 / 100 P_1 50 / 75 100 5	CSLBP(p_1) = 0	CSLBP(p_1) = 15
50 25 120 / 100 P_2 150 / 190 85 250	CSLBP(p_2) = 15	CSLBP(p_2) = 0

The above example shows that two different patterns of same texture are obtained by flipping the comparison operator. In framework, $p1$ and $p2$ are treated as single pattern and their decimals are put into single bin. By merging the symmetric patterns and computing the histogram, 2^3 length histogram is obtained. Whereas, CSLBP is 2^4 length histogram. The compression of CSLBP descriptor is 50% without significant loss in discrimination power. The compressed CSLBP descriptor is called Q-CSLBP.

4 Experimental Evaluation

This section summarizes the experimental verification of CSLBP compression. The robustness of Q-CSLBP under different types of image transformations with different level of degradations is evaluated.

The dataset provided by Visual Geometry Group (VGG) is used, this is standard dataset and used by many researchers [4,5], dataset is available on-line[1]. The dataset contains different types of geometric and photometric transformations on different type of scenes, it contains illumination change (*leuven*), image blur (*bikes*), JPEG compression (*ubc*), zoom and rotate (*bark* and *boats*), and viewpoint change (*graffiti*), as shown in Figure 3. For each transformation, original image Q is provided with 5 gradual deformed images $\{L_1, L_2, \ldots, L_5\}$, image L_i has severe transformation compared to I_{i-1}. Therefore, performance of descriptors matching start decreasing as transformation get more severe. All the images in test dataset are related by a homography and provided by their fundamental matrix.

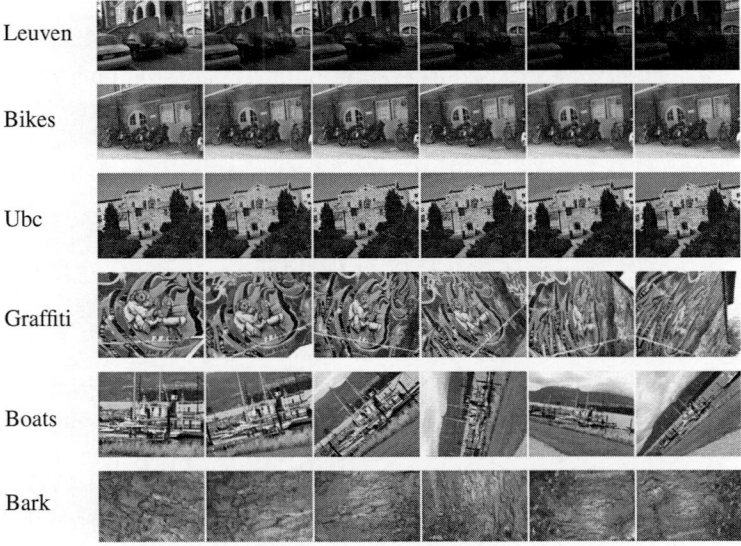

Fig. 3. Dataset used for features matching. First column from the left contains the query images, and rest all are gradual deformed transformations.

We used Harris Affine (HA) keypoints [2], these points have corner like structure with low localization error and higher repeatability compared to Difference

---

[1] http://www.robots.ox.ac.uk/~vgg/research/affine/

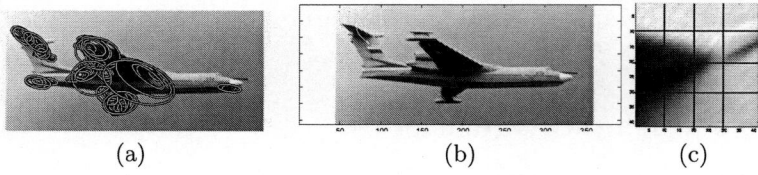

(a)   (b)   (c)

Fig. 4. Example of descriptor computation, (a) show the image with Harris affine keypoints, (b) shows one random elliptical keypoint, and (c) shows the normalized patch divided into 4×4 spatial grid.

of Gaussian (DOG) keypoints which is used by SIFT algorithm [2]. For HA keypoints, multi-scale harris detector is used, each point is represented by elliptical region, computed by second moment matrix [2]. The elliptical region is mapped to circular region, circular region is rotated in the direction of dominant gradient to make it rotation invariant [1]. For descriptor computation, the circular region is normalized to 41×41 pixels in Cartesian grid, and further divided into 4×4 cells [4,5], as shown in Figure 4. From each cell, histograms of CSLBP and Q-CSLBP are computed and merged to their single respective vectors. The descriptor length for CSLBP is 256 and Q-CSLBP is 128 only.

4.1   Evaluation Metrics

Recall Vs $1 - precision$ are used as evaluation metrics, as number of false point correspondences relative to total number of correspondences are efficiently expressed by $1 - precision$ [6], similar matrices are widely used for descriptors evaluation [4,5,6], $1 - precision$ and *recall* are determined as below:

$$recall = \frac{\text{number of } true \ positives}{\text{total } positives}$$
$$1 - precision = \frac{\text{number of } false \ negatives}{true \ positives + false \ negatives} \tag{3}$$

True positives and false negatives are determined with the overlap error [2,4], overlap error determines the efficiency of affine regions correspondences under homography (transformation). Details can be found in [2,4].

4.2   Descriptors Matching

We used nearest neighbor matching strategy between the descriptors. Let D_Q and D_R be the set of descriptors from image Q and R, where $R \in \{L_1, L_2, \ldots, L_5\}$, the point pair $(\mathbf{d}_i^Q, \mathbf{d}_j^R)$ is considered a match if following two conditions hold. The Euclidean distance E, where $E(\mathbf{d}_i^Q, \mathbf{d}_j^R) = \min_{d_k^R \in D_R} E(d_i^Q, d_k^R)$, and following inequality holds: $E(\mathbf{d}_i^Q, \mathbf{d}_j^R) \times T_m < \min_{\mathbf{d}_l^R \in D_R, l \neq j} E(\mathbf{d}_i^Q, \mathbf{d}_l^R)$ where T_m is threshold for consistent matching. The values of precision and recall are obtained by the changing the T_m.

Table 1. Mean Square Error of Q-CSLBP

Leuven	Bikes	Ubc	Graffiti	Bark	Boats
0.0004	0.0030	0.0023	0.0017	0.0001	0.0013

5   Results

In this section, we present the evaluation results of QCSLBP. For various transformations, CSLBP gives better performance compared to SIFT, the main limitation of CSLBP is its dimensions which is quite often the double of SIFT. All values in CSLBP descriptor are floating points that causes CSLBP to consume more memory then SIFT, and SIFT is also faster for features matching. The Q-CSLBP is a complimentary approach to CSLBP that has equal dimensions compared to SIFT, and the robustness is approximately similar to CSLBP.

5.1   Features Matching Performance

The proposed descriptor performs equivalently better on many challenging transformations. For each transformation, the query image Q is compared with remaining five degraded images $\{L_1, L_2, \ldots, L_5\}$. For various transformations, CSLBP performance is better then SIFT such as Illumination change, image blur, and JPEG compression. Whereas, for viewpoint change and rotation types of transformation, the CSLBP has approximately the same performance compared to SIFT as shown in Figure 5. The Q-CSLBP has similar performance compared to CSLBP. The Mean Square Error (MSE) after compression of CSLBP is very less as shown in Table 1, precision on different values of recall are calculated for both CSLBP and Q-CSLBP, and the average of their squared precision differences on different transformations are shown in Table 1.

For each transformation, matching performance of query image Q with L_1 and L_3 are reported, it can be seen that Q-CSLBP has approximately the same performance compared to CSLBP, SIFT and PCA-SIFT. In case of JPEG transformations, the performance is same on initial levels but get lower gradually. The performance of Q-CSLBP is better then PCA-SIFT for blur, illumination, viewpoint change, and rotation types of transformations.

Table 2. Memory required in Gigabytes to store 6.5×10^6 descriptors. The † indicates that the length of the descriptor is normalized to unit length.

CSLBP†	CSLBP	Q-CSLBP†	Q-CSLBP	SIFT†
12.4	1.6	6.2	0.8	6.2

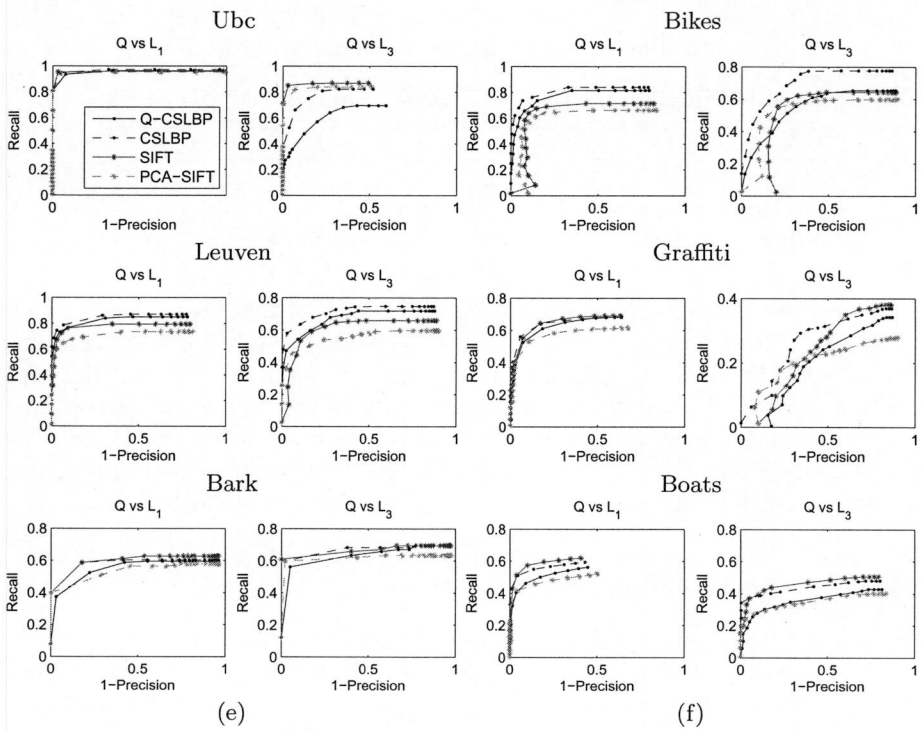

Fig. 5. Matching performance of Q-CSLBP compared to CSLBP, SIFT and PCA-SIFT. (a) is illumination transformation (b) is blur transformation, and (c) JPEG transformation.

5.2   Memory Consumption

Q-CSLBP is 128 length descriptor, it achieves significant gain in memory compared to CSLBP. The CSLBP descriptor requires 256×8 bytes to store one descriptor, whereas Q-CSLBP descriptor requires only 128 bytes of memory to store one descriptor. In case of Object Classes Challenge 2010 dataset[2] that have 11321 images and 6.5 million keypoints using Difference of Gaussian detectors. To store 6.5 million descriptors statistically, 12.4 GB memory is required by CSLBP descriptors, whereas only 0.8 GB memory required by Q-CSLBP descriptors as shown in Table 2.

6   Conclusion

We have proposed an efficient and simple compression of CSLBP without applying any dimensionality reduction techniques. We achieve similar performance with reduced dimensions. The Q-CSLBP outperforms SIFT and PCA-SIFT for

---

[2] http://pascallin.ecs.soton.ac.uk/challenges/VOC/

illumination and blur transformations. Due to the compact length of proposed descriptor, it is efficient for features matching and memory storage compared to CSLBP and SIFT. Since, Q-CSLBP is textured based descriptor, it can efficiently be used for smart phones and tablets.

Acknowledgments. We are thankful to National Institute of Informatics, Tokyo, for supporting the research. This research was partially supported by University of Balochistan. Junaid Baber is Ph.D student in Asian Institute of Technology, Thailand.

References

1. Lowe, D.G.: Distinctive image features from scale-invariant keypoints. IJCV (2004)
2. Mikolajczyk, K., Schmid, C.: Scale and affine invariant interest point detectors. IJCV (2004)
3. Bay, H., Ess, A., Tuytelaars, T., Van Gool, L.: Speeded-up robust features (surf). Comput. Vis. Image Underst. (2008)
4. Mikolajczyk, K., Schmid, C.: A performance evaluation of local descriptors. IEEE Transactions on PAMI (2005)
5. Heikkila, M., Pietikainen, M., Schmid, C.: Description of interest regions with local binary patterns. Pattern Recognition (2009)
6. Ke, Y., Sukthankar, R.: Pca-sift: A more distinctive representation for local image descriptors. In: Proc. CVPR, pp. 511–517 (2004)
7. Yamazaki, M., Fels, S.: Local image descriptors using supervised kernel ica. IEICE Transactions on Information and Systems, 1745–1751 (2009)
8. Mäenpää, T., Ojala, T., Pietikäinen, M., Maricor, S.: Robust texture classification by subsets of local binary patterns. In: ICPR (2000)
9. Haralick, R.M., Shanmugam, K., Dinstein, I.: Textural features for image classification. IEEE Transactions on Systems, Man and Cybernetics (1973)

Efficient Partial Decoding Scheme
for Intra Frame in H.264/AVC Stream

Dongming Zhang[1], Yongdong Zhang[1], Xiaoguang Gu[1,2], and Chao Zhou[1,2]

[1] Advanced Computing Research Laboratory,
Beijing Key Laboratory of Mobile Computing and Pervasive Device,
Institute of Computing Technology, Chinese Academy of Sciences
[2] Graduate University of Chinese Academy of Sciences
{dmzhang,zhyd,xggu,zhouchao}@ict.ac.cn

Abstract. Partial decoding is an effective way to improve the processing efficiency in many video applications such as video retrieval and mobile video display. But after many advanced prediction technology were introduced into video coding, partial decoding encountered many difficulties due to the strong data dependency of the high compressed stream.In this paper, one partial decoding scheme is presented, in which user can specify the region of interest(ROI) to be decoded. In particular, we focus on dealing with the decoding the specified region of the intra slice data in the H.264/AVC stream. To decode the ROI, we build one decoding dependency graph (DDG) to collect all necessary information during parsing the corresponding data. And then we reconstruct one macroblock(MB), or skip it, which depends on the MB's dependency state in the DDG. Furthermore, one simplified decoding dependency graph(SDDG) is proposed, in which less important dependency is removed from DDG to speed up decoding. One decoder with support DDG and SDDG is implemented and some typical video streams are used to evaluate the proposed decoding system. Experiments show that the proposed partial decoding scheme can save the decoding time efficiently with negligible decoded picture quality loss.

Keywords: video decoding, H.264,intra prediction, partial decoding.

1 Introduction

Nowadays, there are two trends in video coding domain. On the one hand, high-definition(HD) and super-high-definition(SHD) videos become more and more popular. A variety of digital video contents are available in 720p,1080p and even higher definitions. On the other hand, a lot of advanced encoding tools have been introduced into video coding to improve the compressive ratio and to enable the applicability of video compression to new real-time applications. But due to display capacity of terminals, it is impossible for many mobile terminals to achieve the HD/SHD video. A typical solution to display one HD video on mobile devices is to fully decode the HD video and downgrade the decoded video before display the video to the low resolution monitor. There are two typical ways

W. Lin et al. (Eds.): PCM 2012, LNCS 7674, pp. 522–533, 2012.

to downgrade the video, one is to down-sample the video to a low definition, the other is to choose one ROI of the video,such technology as smart-view.However such a method wastes lots of computing power and memory bandwidth because the video still needs to be fully decoded. The limited computation power is another problem concerned.On some handhold devices,low computation power may lead to intolerable latency when decoding full HD video and displaying frame by frame.Even if decoding is a piece of cake for increasing computation power of terminals, partial decoding is an effective way from viewpoint of energy saving issue.At the mean time, in many video applications,it is unnecessary or inefficient to decode stream fully. For example,in one video logo retrieval system,we only need to pay attention to the four corners of the image, while in one video copy detection system, the center window becomes the main focus. To save decoding time, even some works investigate the copy detection system in compressed video directly, such as literature [1].

The underlying methods to cover this kind of problem lie in video encoding stage. Among the methods, scalable video coding(SVC) is the most attractive one. SVC enables the transmission and decoding of partial bit streams to provide video services with lower temporal or spatial resolutions or reduced fidelity while retaining a reconstruction quality. SVC divides the video stream into different layers including base layer, enhanced layer, etc.. Thus decoder can choose decoding only the base layer or more layers.The Joint Video Team of the ITU-T VCEG and the ISO/IEC MPEG had also standardized a Scalable Video Coding (SVC) extension of the H.264/AVC standard [2]. This is a good idea, but its real application is severely restricted because SVC is very complex and the output stream consumes high disk storage.This is proved by the observation that among the distributed videos or movies on the Internet, we seldom found the SVC version.

Partial decoding is another effective way to decrease unnecessary time consuming. But it is becoming one difficult task due to video data dependency. In particular, with the emergence of the state-of-art video standards including MPEG4 and H.264/AVC,the data dependency is becoming more and more strong because advanced intra prediction and inter prediction are used. Objectively,multiple slices encoding structure,which is proposed for error concealment,can reduce data dependency.However its application is very limited due to the similar reason as SVC.

Liu,et al. presented a partial decoding scheme for H.264 based on ROI [3].In this work, a motion vector modification scheme was proposed to solve the missing reference MBs that are not decoded,whereas intra frames were decoded fully yet.

In this paper, we mainly focus on partial decoding of intra frames of standard H.264 video stream without SVC layers or multiple slices. One complex spatial prediction scheme has been adopted to remove spatial redundancy in H.264 [4],which leads to very strong data dependency in intra slice data ,and brings much difficulties to partial decoding.We investigate the dependency relation and propose one method to find all the dependent MBs corresponding to the specified MBs and construct DDG.Furthermore, SDDG is proposed to speed up the partial

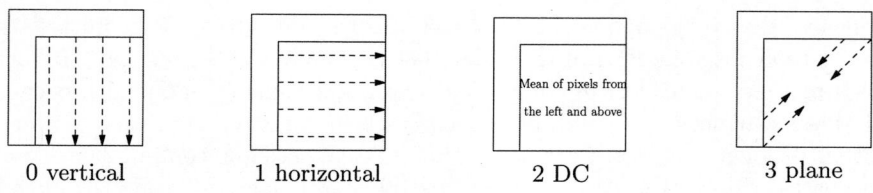

Fig. 1. Four-modes prediction in H.264

decoding. Based on DDG and SDDG, one decoder is implemented with support for partial decoding and it works well on the specified region.

The rest of this paper is organized as follows.In section 2, we analyze the dependency relation of intra prediction in H.264.Then we design one partial decoding scheme in section 3.In section 4, a speed-up partial decoding scheme is presented.In section 5, the experimental results and discussions are shown. Finally, the conclusion is given in section 6.

2   Analysis of Intra Prediction in H.264

To improve the prediction efficiency in intra frame encoding, a complex intra prediction scheme is introduced into H.264. Each prediction mode(PM) indicates different texture of image content.The intra prediction scheme can be divided into 2 types, i.e. four-modes prediction and nine-modes prediction [4].

2.1   Four-Modes Prediction

Four PMs(Fig. 1) are defined for intra predictions of luma block with size 16x16,in which vertical prediction needs the last row reconstructed pixels of the upper MB, horizontal prediction uses the most right column reconstructed pixels of the left MB and the other two modes(DC prediction and Plane prediction) reference both of them.So according to the positions of the referenced MBs, the intra PMs for 16x16 can be classified into 3 types respectively, only the left MB is referenced, only the upper MB is referenced and both of them are referenced together.

The same PMs are applied to chroma 4x4 block and the difference is the number of the referenced pixels in vertical or horizontal direction decreases to 1/4 for 4:2:0 chroma format.

2.2   Nine-Modes Prediction

H.264 permits less block size intra prediction. Dependent on the syntax element transform_8x8_mode_flag in picture parameter set, H.264 defines intra block prediction with size 8x8 and 4x4.Both of the two kinds of prediction use the same 9 modes.Here, we illustrate them using block 4x4 as example.

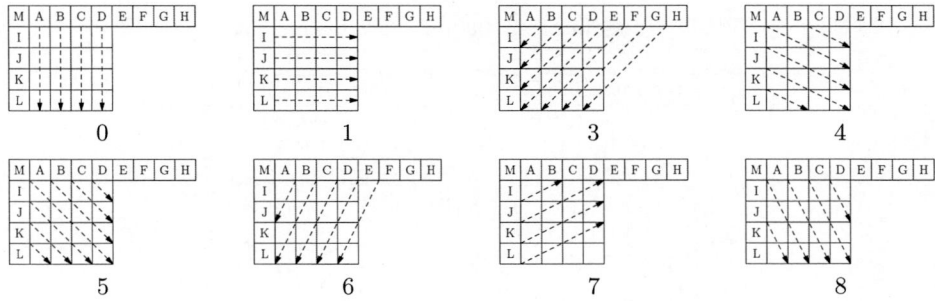

Fig. 2. 8 intra 4x4 directional prediction modes in H.264(0:VERT_PRED, 1:HOR_PRED,3:DIAG_DOWN_LEFT_PRED,4:HOR_DOWN_PRED,5:DIAG_DOWN_RIGHT_PRED, 6:VERT_LEFT_PRED,7:HOR_UP_PRED,8:VERC_RIGTH_PRED)

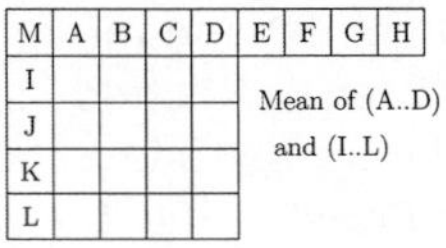

Fig. 3. DC prediction in H.264

For 4x4 luma block prediction, 9 PMs (8 directional PMs in Fig. 2 and DC PM in Fig. 3) are defined. According to which MBs are referenced, all the 9 intra predictions can be classified into 4 types.

– Only the neighbour left MB is referenced,
– Only the neighbour upper MB is reference,
– Both of the left and upper MBs are referenced together,
– The upright neighbour macroblock besides the left and upper is also referenced.

Here,we summarize the dependency in 4x4 luma block prediction in Table1 according to Fig. 2 and Fig. 3.

When the nine modes applies to luma block 8x8, the referenced pixels and prediction size becomes double.

In addition, for nine modes intra prediction, mode prediction may be used to improve coding efficiency.When the syntax element prev_intra4x4_pred_mode_flag or prev_intra8x8_pred_mode_flag in mb_pred layer is set to 1, the PM C of the current block is predicted using A and B, which are the PM of its upper and left blocks respectively.

3   The Proposed Partial Decoding Scheme

Intra prediction improves the encoding performance of intra frame significantly at the cost of high computation and strong data dependency. There are two kind

Table 1. 4x4 intra prediction and reference pixels

4x4 intra prediction	reference pixels
VERT_PRED	A,B,C,D
HOR_PRED	I,J,K,L
DC_PRED	A,B,C,D,I,J,K,L
DIAG_DOWN_LEFT_PRED	A,B,C,D,E,F,G,H
DIAG_DOWN_RIGHT_PRED	A,B,C,D,I,J,K,L,M
VERT_LEFT_PRED	A,B,C,D,I,J,K,M
HOR_DOWN_PRED	A,B,C,I,J,K,L,M
VERT_LEFT_PRED	A,B,C,D,E,F,G
HOR_UP	I,J,K,L

of dependent data,i.e. prediction modes and referenced pixels. To decode one MB
,its real PMs must be obtained from prediction using its neighbour blocks' PMs
if they are available,and then the pixels to be referenced and filtering equations
are chose via the decoded PM to predict its pixels. This brings many difficulties
for partial decoding.

3.1   Building Dependency Graph

According to the above analysis of intra prediction in H.264, decoding one MB
may use the left neighbour pixels or the upper ones,and even use the upright
ones in a few occasions. In essence, how many and which pixels are used as
reference depend on the intra PM of the current MB to be decoded. While the
referenced MBs may also depends on their neighbour MBs as well,therefore, to
find all the dependent MBs of one MB, all related MBs and their neighbours
should be checked iteratively until it comes to the picture or slice boundaries.

In addition, in H.264, chroma intra PM is chose according to RD cost independently from luma component, so dependent MBs for chroma component
decoding are different from luma one in many cases. Therefore, in principle the
dependency graph should be constructed respectively for luma and chroma,but
for efficiency in real algorithm implementation, the dependency graph is constructed in one scan and dependency states for luma and chroma are stored in
two different bits of the graph node state.

when certain region is specified to be decoded in one stream, the graph of
dependency MBs can be constructed according to the flowchart in Fig. 4. The
detailed steps are described as follows:

- calculate the maximum index($MaxIndex$) of the MBs in the specified region.
  $MaxIndex$ is the index of the most right-bottom MB of the region.Here the
  most common rectangle window is used to specify the region to be decoded,
  which can be defined by vector (y,x,h,w) on the MB basis,in which y is the
  vertical coordinate of the up-left MB, x is the horizontal coordinate of the
  up-left MB, w is the width of the region and h is the height. So $MaxIndex$

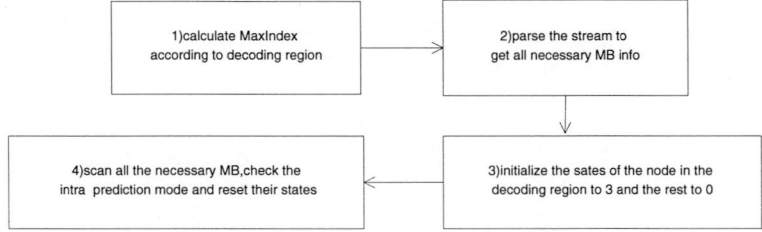

Fig. 4. Flowchart to construct the dependency graph

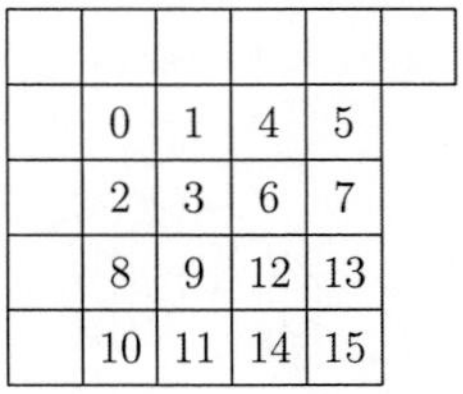

	0	1	4	5	
	2	3	6	7	
	8	9	12	13	
	10	11	14	15	

Fig. 5. Block dependency of Intra 4x4 in H.264

can be calculated according to the equation(1),in which $MBWidth$ is the picture width in MBs.

$$MaxIndex = (y + h - 1) * MBWidth + x + w - 1 \qquad (1)$$

- parse all the overhead information (MBType,CBP,PredMode, etc.) and residual information by entropy decoding for the MBs with index ranging from the 0 to the $MaxIndex$.
- allocate graph with $MaxIndex + 1$ nodes and each node represents one MB.Set the graph node state as 3 for the MBs within the specified region and the other nodes state as 0.set $idx = MaxIndex$
- find the dependent MBs of the MB with index equal to idx and store into the corresponding graph nodes according to the following steps:
(1)Check luma component, if it is encoded in intra16x16, array $state$ is set as follows:

  if PM is not vertical
  $state[index\_of\_left\_MB]| = 1$
  if PM is not horizontal
  $state[index\_of\_up\_MB]| = 1$

  otherwise, if it is encoded in intra4x4, array $state$ is set as follows:

  if PMs of block 0,2,8 and 10 in Fig.5 are not VERT_PRED
  $state[index\_of\_left\_MB]| = 1$
  if PMs of blocks 0,1,4 and 5 in Fig.5 are neither HOR_PRED or HOR_UP_PRED
  $state[index\_of\_up\_MB]| = 1$
  if PM of block 5 in Fig.5 is DIAG_DOWN_LEFT_PRED or

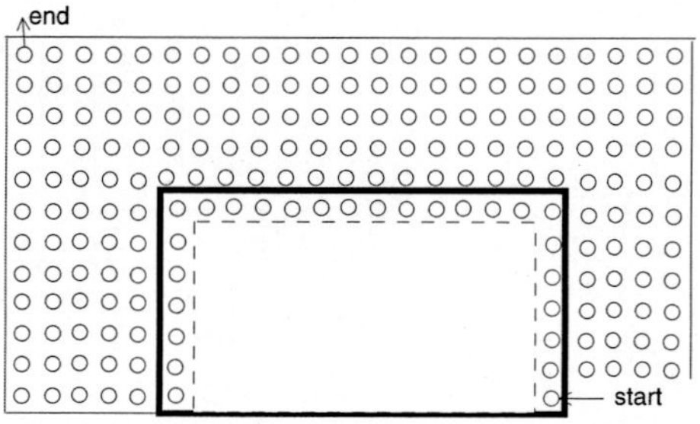

Fig. 6. Scan order for building decoding dependency graph,bold rectangle is the decoding region,circled MBs need to be checked in the order from bottom to top and from right to left

3	3	3	3	3	1	1	1	1	1	1	1	1	1	1	1	1	1	0	0	0	0
3	1	1	1	3	3	3	1	1	1	1	1	1	1	1	1	1	1	0	0	0	0
3	1	1	1	1	1	3	3	3	1	1	1	1	1	1	1	1	1	0	0	0	0
3	3	3	3	3	3	3	3	3	3	1	1	1	1	1	1	1	1	0	0	0	0
3	1	1	3	3	3	3	3	3	3	1	1	1	1	1	1	1	1	0	0	0	0
3	1	1	3	3	3	3	3	3	3	3	3	3	3	3	1	1	1	0	0	0	0
3	3	3	3	3	3	3	3	3	3	3	3	3	3	3	1	1	0	0	0	0	0
3	1	3	3	3	3	3	3	3	3	3	3	3	3	3	1	1	0	0	0	0	0
3	3	3	3	3	3	3	3	3	3	3	3	3	3	3	1	1	0	0	0	0	0
3	3	3	3	3	3	3	3	3	3	3	3	3	3	3	1	1	0	0	0	0	0
3	3	3	3	3	1	1	3	3	3	3	3	3	3	3	1	1	0	0	0	0	0
1	1	1	1	3	3	3	3	3	3	3	3	3	3	3	1	0	0	0	0	0	0
1	1	1	1	1	1	3	3	3	3	3	3	3	3	3	1	0	0	0	0	0	0
1	1	1	1	1	1	1	3	3	3	3	3	3	3	3							

Fig. 7. DDG for Foreman(CIF),frame no. 0,the decoding region is the rectangle(6,7,8,8) marked by dashed line

VERT_LEFT_PRED
$state[index_of_upright_MB]| = 1$

(2)Check chroma component, array *state* is set as follows:
if chroma PM is not vertical
$state[index_of_left_MB]| = 2$
if (chroma PM is not horizontal
$state[index_of_up_MB]| = 2$

– move to the next MB according to the scan order illustrated in Fig.6 and repeat the above step until all graph nodes are checked.

From the above process, building DDG only involves simple comparisons, 11 comparisons at most for one MB,so the overhead decoding time consumed is negligible. However, the partial decoding scheme will consumes more memory to buffer the parsed residual data than standard decoding, about 800 bytes for each dependent MB. An example of the built DDG for frame 0 of foreman sequence is showed in Fig. 7, in which the rectangle region labeled by dash line is the decoding region.In the graph, the MBs labeled "0" will not be decoded, the ones labeled "1" only needs to be decoded luma component, the ones labeled as"3" should be decoded fully. If the MBs is labeled "2",which does not exist in this graph, only its chroma component needs to be decoded .

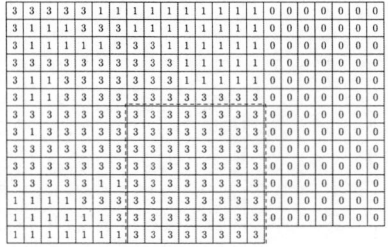

Fig. 8. SDDG for Foreman(CIF),frame 0,decoding region(6,7,8,8) is marked by dashed line

Though the above algorithm assumes the center windows as the region to be decoded, it also works on many other kind of decoding regions by changing the initial graph node state in the above 4th step.

3.2 Partial Decoding Based on DDG

After the dependency graph is built, all the dependent MBs need to be decoded for the specified region decoding are determined. Herein, we can reconstruct the MBs from the parsed MB overhead information and residual information beforehand. The decoding order is same as the standard decoder, but skipping the unreferenced luma, chroma blocks. In the built DDG, graph node may have state 0,1,2 or 3. If the node state is 0, the MB is skipped reconstructing; otherwise if it is 1, only luma component is constructed, only chroma component is reconstructed if it is 2 and the MB is reconstructed fully if it is 3.

4   Speed-Up Decoding

With the proposed decoding scheme described in the above section, the specified MB(s) can be safely decoded without any loss compared to standard decoding. In this section, we present one way to speed up partial decoding, in which some of the dependent MBs with little affection to the decoding pixels are removed so that the decoding path in DDG is shortened.

As showed in Fig. 5, when one MB is encoded in intra 4x4 mode, each 4x4 block choose the PM individually. However, it is impossible to choose mode 3(DIAG_DOWN_LEFT_PRED) or mode 6(VERT_PRED) for block 3,13 and 15 because their upright blocks are always unavailable. For the other blocks, if mode 3 or mode 6 is chose,the pixels referenced by Block 0,1 and 4 are inside the upper neighbour MB,the pixels referenced by block 2,6,8,9,12,10,11 and 14 are inside current MB to be decoded, and only the pixels referenced by block 5 belong to the neighbour upright MB. So the simple DDG is defined to remove upright MB dependency, an example of the built SDDG for frame 0 of foreman sequence is showed in Fig. 8.

Furthermore, when upright dependency is removed, some necessary modifications need to be made for the prediction for block 5 to reduce prediction error.

Table 2. Results for CIF with decoding region (6,7,8,8)

sequ-ence	luma DDG		luma SDDG			chroma	
	MB	ratio	MB	ratio	PSNR	MB	ratio
foreman	240	79.7	210	69.8	74.4	144	47.8
bus	208	69.1	200	66.4	84.3	162	53.8
city	221	73.4	210	69.8	82.5	196	65.1
crew	155	51.5	142	47.2	69.6	169	56.1
avg.	206	68.4	190	63.1	77.7	168	55.8

Table 3. Results for D1 with decoding region (12,14,15,16)

sequ-ence	luma DDG		luma SDDG			chroma	
	MB	ratio	MB	ratio	PSNR	MB	ratio
city	801	68.2	799	68.1	85.6	739	62.9
crew	498	42.4	492	41.9	78.2	765	65.2
harbour	660	56.2	629	53.6	90.3	737	62.8
ice	719	61.2	662	56.4	88.5	766	65.2
avg.	670	57.0	646	55.0	85.6	751	64.0

In our method, the upright block of block 5 is always forced to set as unavailable so that the corresponding pixel E,F,G and H are forced to set as D showed in sub-figure 3 and 6 in Fig. 2.

5   Experiments

According to the above proposed framework we implemented one H.264 decoder, in which two types of constructing dependency graph are embedded. In the experiments,we choose some typical test streams to test this decoder and evaluate the decoding performances using the two types of dependency graph. JM18 [5] is chose to produce test streams. The test sequences' chroma formats are all 4:2:0, and sequences include foreman(CIF),bus(CIF),city(CIF and D1),crew(CIF and D1),harbor(D1) and ice(D1) [6].Ten frames are encoded for each sequence.

Since the importance of center region of video in the real applications, the decoding region is specified in the center of frame, such as it is defined as (6,7,8,8) for CIF (352x288) video and (12,14,15,16) for D1(704x576). PSNR between the standard decoder and the one with SDDG is used to evaluate SDDG's influence on decoded image quality. PSNR is computed for luma component of the MBs in the specified region since whether DDG or SDDG is used does not affect the chroma component. Considering standard decoding can also be terminated beforehand at the bottom-right MB of the partial-decoding region, we calculate reconstructing MB ratio $ratio = MB/MaxIndex + 1$.

The experimental results for reconstructing ratio and PSNR for CIF and D1 are showed in Table 2 and Table 3 respectively. For standard decoder with last

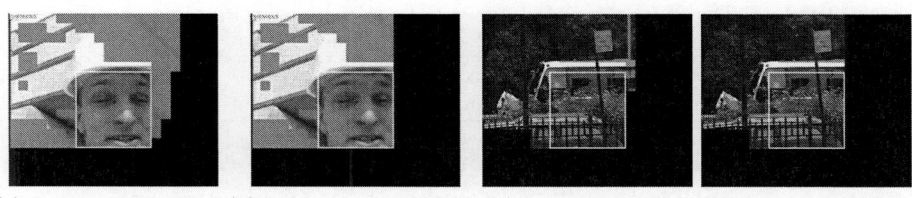

(a) foreman with DDG (b) foreman with SDDG   (c) bus with DDG   (d) bus with SDDG

Fig. 9. Decoded CIF video,white rectangle is decoding region(6,7,8,8)

(a) city with DDG   (b) city with SDDG   (c) crew with DDG   (d) crew with SDDG

Fig. 10. Decoded D1 video, decoding region(12,14,15,16) is marked by white rectangle

MB termination, the total number of MBs needed to be decoded in CIF video with decoding region $(6,7,8,8)$is $MaxIndex = 300$ and it is $MaxIndex = 1173$ for D1(704x576) with decoding region (12,14,15,16). The results show that DDG can reduce reconstructing about $1 - (luma\_DDG\_ratio * 2 + chroma\_ratio)/3 \approx$ 39% MBs, SDDG can reduce reconstructing about $1 - (luma\_SDDG\_ratio * 2 + chroma\_ratio)/3 \approx 41\%$ MBs.

The results also show PSNR between the quality using SDDG and DDG is very high,which proves that the simplifications to DDG is acceptable and the corresponding modifications to the intra predictions ensures the very little picture quality degradation.The stream ice(D1) is an exception, SDDG does not get any further speedup because there are not any MBs referencing neighbour upright MBs in the corresponding DDG. As a result, the average PSNR for D1 is calculated without ice. However partial decoding with SDDG may lead to error propagation in P or B frames, so we adopt it in the situations in which only I frames need to be decoded. Some decoded pictures for CIF and D1 are showed in Fig. 9 and Fig. 10 respectively. The MBs in the black regions are totally skipped decoding, and only chroma components of the MBs in the green region are skipped.

Skipping the decoding unnecessary MBs saves consumed time.To evaluate the speed-up ratio between the proposed partial decoding scheme and the standard decoding, we collect the real consumed decoding time of the 3 different partial decoders. The experiments are carried out on platform with Intel(R) Core(TM) i5 CPU@2.53GHz and 4GB DDRII.The results of CIF sequences are showed in Table 4 and the one of D1 sequences are showed in Table 5.Compared to decoder

Table 4. Decoding time comparisons of CIF sequences,in microsecond

sequ- ence	decoding with DDG	decoding with SDDG	decoding with termination
foreman	8.7	8.5	12.9
bus	13.9	11.2	15.8
city	11.0	10.3	13.6
crew	7.2	6.6	13.3

Table 5. Decoding time comparisons of D1 sequences,in microsecond

sequ- ence	decoding with DDG	decoding with SDDG	decoding with termination
city	34.7	31.9	44.5
crew	22.6	19.9	34.9
harbor	29.3	27.8	42.8
ice	22.5	20.1	32.8

with the last MB termination, the real average speed-up ratio of DDG and SDDG amount to 26.7%,34.2% in CIF sequence and 27.8%,33.9% in D1 sequence respectively.Why the speed-up ratio is less than the ratio of the skipped MBs without reconstructing? We think it is due to that the decoding time is consumed by stream parsing and reconstructing, while our scheme only speeds up the reconstructing. In theoretically, the area and position of the specified decoding region will significantly affect the speed-up ratio of the partial decoding scheme. To verify this, we carry out some experiments with different decoding regions on one HD sequence 720p5994_stockholm_ter(720p) [7].The details are listed in Table 6, from which we can observe that compared to the standard decoder with last MB termination, the partial decoding has the following traits:1)when decoding region lies in center it can obtain much speed-up .2) with the increasing of the percentage of the decoding region in the total frame, the speed-up ratio decreases.3)the further to the top-left MB in MB scan order, it obtains the more speed-up ratio.

Table 6. Partial decoding with different decoding regions of sequence 720p5994_stockholm_ter

decoding region	luma DDG		luma SDDG		chroma	
	MB	ratio	MB	ratio	MB	ratio
(0, 0,14,28)	392	100	392	100	392	100
(0,10,14,28)	532	49.4	532	49.4	532	49.4
(10, 0,14,28)	589	31.5	577	30.9	629	33.7
(10,10,14,28)	906	48.3	865	46.1	844	45.0
(10, 0,28,56)	2074	68.8	2074	68.8	2064	68.5
(0,10,28,56)	1858	83.5	1848	83.1	1824	82.0

6 Conclusion

This paper presents one partial decoding scheme for intra frame in H.264 video stream. When one region is specified to be decoded, the two kinds of decoding dependency graph,including DDG and SDDG, can be built according to the proposed steps. For common used center window decoding region, compared to standard decoder with the last MB termination, a decoder with DDG and SDDG can reduce decoding time about 26% and 34%.The additional memory size is about 800 bytes for one dependent MB.

And the proposed partial decoding scheme also works on MPEG4, in which intra prediction is carried out in DCT domain, and the difference lies on that the simpler dependency relation compared to H.264.

In the future work, we will improve this scheme and apply it to HEVC. This is one challenge task because there are more complicated dependency in the HEVC stream.

Acknowledgement. This work is supported by National Nature Science Foundation of China (61273247, 61271428,61272323), National Key Technology Research and Development Program of China(2012BAH06B01),and Co-building Program of Beijing Municipal Education.

References

1. Mezaris, V., Kompatsiaris, I., Boulgouris, N.V., Strintzis, M.G.: Real-time compressed-domain spatiotemporal segmentation and ontologies for video indexing and retrieval. IEEE Transactions on Circuits and Systems for Video Technology 14(5), 606–621 (2004)
2. Schwarz, H., Marpe, D., Wiegand, T.: Overview of the Scalable Video Coding Extension of the H.264/AVC Standard. IEEE Transactions on Circuits and Systems for Video Technology 17(9), 1103–1120 (2007)
3. Liu, C., Jin, X., Zhang, T.R., Goto, S.: Partial decoding scheme for H.264/AVC decoder. In: International Symposium on Intelligent Signal Processing and Communication Systems (2010)
4. Wiegand, T., Sullivan, G.J., Bjontegaard, G., Luthra, A.: Overview of the H.264/AVC Video Coding Standard. IEEE Transactions on Circuits and Systems for Video Technology 13(7), 560–576 (2003)
5. Joint Video Team (JVT) Reference Software,
   http://iphome.hhi.de/suehringltml/download/
6. Test Sequences,
   ftp://ftp.tnt.uni-hannover.de/pub/svc/testsequences/
7. HD Test Sequences,
   ftp://ftp.ldv.e-technik.tu-muenchen.de/pub/test_sequences/

Histopathology Image Streaming

Manoranjan Mohanty and Wei Tsang Ooi

Department of Computer Science, School of Computing
National University of Singapore, Singapore

Abstract. This paper proposes an image streaming framework to stream histopathology image of a patient over a lossy network. Firstly, the large histopathology image is divided into a number of fixed size tiles to facilitate ROI-based streaming. Secondly, each tile is compressed using a variant of WebP so that the size of the compressed data is 20% to 30% less than the size of the compressed data when the same tile is compressed using JPEG. Finally, a greedy packetization scheme is proposed to pack the inter-dependent macroblocks of any compressed tile so that the client is able to decode more number of macroblocks than the naive method at any intermediate stage of streaming.

Keywords: Histopathology Image, Predictive Image Compression, WebP, Packetization, CABAC, CAVLC.

1 Introduction

Advances in telecommunications, technologies in acquiring high quality digital images, and the benefits in remote diagnosis of medical images have made telepathology a popular choice to analyze a patient's histopathology image. The widespread use of this technique is due to two main advantages: *immediate response to emergency cases* and *cost-effectiveness*. Firstly, it offers the best available solution to attend *off the hour* emergency cases by obviating the presence of pathologists in the image acquisition premise and electronically transmitting the acquired image to a remote pathology laboratory [1]. Secondly, it provides a cost-effective alternative to hospitals of developed countries by outsourcing their medical images to developing countries [2].

In telepathology, a large histopathology image needs to be compressed before transmitting it to a remote pathology laboratory. Mainly, JPEG and JPEG2000 are used as the compression technique to compress the histopathology image [3] [4]. It has been, however, found that the size of a compressed file that is compressed using JPEG or JPEG2000 is 25%-34% more than the size of the same file when it is compressed using WebP [5] [6]. Our experiment on histopathology images also validated this claim as we found a WebP compressed histopathology image to be 20% − 30% smaller in size than the JPEG compressed image. Therefore, we believe that WebP can be a preferred compression technique for telepathology as it can reduce the transmission time of a histopathology image.

As a side effect, WebP, however, introduces extra levels of dependencies by predicting a macroblock from its neighboring macroblocks and by using the

W. Lin et al. (Eds.): PCM 2012, LNCS 7674, pp. 534–545, 2012.

context adaptive binary arithmetic coding (CABAC) as the entropy coder. These dependencies require that the macroblocks must be decoded in the same order in which they are encoded (i.e., FCFS order). As a result, macroblocks of WebP need to be packetized in the FCFS order before sending them over the Web. Therefore, WebP is not suitable to compress image that has to be streamed in a lossy network as the number of decoded macroblocks can be less than the number of received macroblocks at any intermediate stage of streaming [7].

This paper proposes a framework to stream histopathology image in a lossy network. Firstly, a histopathology image is divided into a number of fixed size tiles to provide ROI access to the remote pathologist. Secondly, each tile is compressed using a proposed variant of WebP called *modified*-WebP. Modified-WebP removes the FCFS inter-macroblock dependency by removing the dependency due to the CABAC entropy coding. Finally, a greedy packetization scheme, which extends the packetization scheme proposed by Cheng et al. [7], is used to pack macroblocks of the modified-WebP in such a way that the number of *undecodable* (received but cannot be decoded) macroblocks is minimized. Note that although WebP is considered as the compression technique, our framework can work with any other predictive image compression technique.

The rest of the paper is organized as follows. In Section 2, we review previous work related to both compression and streaming of pathology images. Section 3 gives an overview of WebP and discusses the data dependency it introduces. In Section 4, we discuss the proposed framework and in Section 5, we discuss the experimental results. Finally, Section 6 concludes our work.

2   Related Work

In this section, we first review the existing work related to compression of histopathology images and then discuss about Cheng et al.'s greedy packetization scheme that we extend in our framework.

Among lossless and lossy image compression techniques, lossy image compression technique is preferred to compress large histopathology images [3] [8]. Particularly, JPEG, lossy JPEG2000, and singular value decomposition (SVD) based compression techniques have been used for this purpose [9] [10]. It has been found that the size of an image compressed by a SVD-based compression technique is more than the size of the same image when it is compressed using either JPEG or JPEG2000 [9]. In comparison to WebP, both JPEG and JPEG2000, however, results 25%-34% more size in compressed data [5] [6]. Therefore, we believe that WebP can be preferred to compress a large histopathology image.

Cheng et al. proposed a greedy algorithmic to packetize inter-dependent vertex splits of a progressive mesh [7]. In their work, they proposed an analytical model to determine the dependency of each vertex split and a greedy algorithm to pack the vertex splits in a packet that is transmitted in a lossy network using UDP (with application-level retransmission of lost packets) as the transport protocol. Due to less inter-macroblock dependency, Cheng et al.'s scheme decodes more

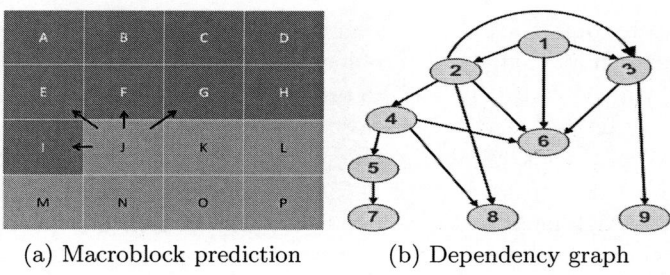

(a) Macroblock prediction   (b) Dependency graph

Fig. 1.

number of intermediate vertex splits than other known packetization schemes such as FCFS, breadth-first, and b-sub [7]. Their technique, however, is inefficient to packetize variable size inter-dependent elements such as WebP compressed macroblocks as it assumes that each element must be of equal size.

3 Data Dependency of WebP Compression

The WebP compression technique, which uses inter macroblock prediction and CABAC entropy coder to compress an image, introduces two levels of data dependencies between macroblocks. These dependencies can be unsuitable for image streaming as discussed below.

Similar to the video compression techniques such as H.264 and Google's VP8 video codec, WebP uses inter-macroblock prediction to encode a macroblock by predicting it from four of its neighboring macroblocks that have been encoded earlier [11]. For example, as shown in Fig. 1a, macroblock J can be predicted from macroblocks E, F, G and I. To predict a macroblock from its neighbors, WebP proposes 10 different schemes; neither of them needs all the four neighboring macroblocks to predict the macroblock. Two or more schemes, however, are often combined to obtain the best possible PSNR value from the compressed image [11]. As a result, a macroblock (i.e., child macroblock) may need at least one and at most all four of its neighboring macroblocks (i.e., parent macroblocks) for its prediction. This parent-child relationship among the macroblocks can be modeled as a direct acyclic graph $G = (V, E)$ known as the *dependency graph* (Fig. 1b). In this graph, each node represents one macroblock and each directed edge (u, v) represents the dependency of node v (child macroblock) on node u (parent macroblock). It is important to note that the child macroblock cannot be decoded unless all of its parent macroblocks are decoded earlier.

Unlike Huffman tree based entropy coders such as context adaptive variable length coding (CAVLC), codewords of a macroblock in CABAC shares a bit with the codeword of the macroblock that was entropy encoded immediately before it [12]. For example, if a macroblock B is CABAC entropy encoded immediately after the encoding of a macroblock A, then B may share a bit that is used to store codeword of A. Therefore, it is apparent that the decoding of macroblock B is dependent on the decoding of macroblock A as it cannot be decoded unless

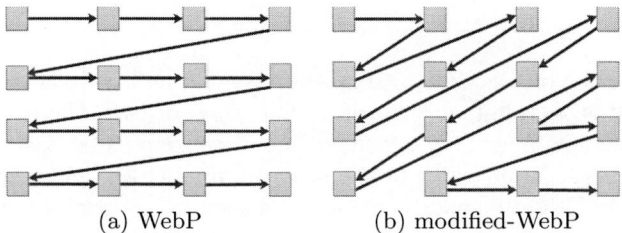

(a) WebP   (b) modified-WebP

Fig. 2. Order of macroblock (represented by square) decoding

the bit that macroblock B shares as well as the percentage of the share is known. Due to this restriction, the macroblocks of WebP need to be decoded in the same order in which they are encoded (i.e., FCFS order).

Among the two dependencies, the dependency due to the use of CABAC overshadows the dependency that is occurred by the use of inter-macroblock prediction as it requires that all the macroblocks which are encoded before macroblock B must also be decoded before the decoding of B. Therefore, the macroblocks of WebP can be decoded only by the raster scan order (Fig. 2a). Due to this strict restriction in decoding, the possibility of prioritizing the decoding of an important macroblock before a non-important macroblock is eliminated. As a result, in an image streaming framework that uses WebP to compress an image, the server need to send macroblocks that are not required by the viewer before sending a requested macroblock. Therefore, WebP becomes an unattractive option to compress an image that need to be streamed as it can both increase the viewing latency and require more network bandwidth by sending unwanted macroblocks. In other words, to be suitable for streaming, WebP must be modified to break the dependency that is induced by the CABAC entropy coder.

4   Proposed Framework

In this section, we propose our framework to stream histopathology image of an emergency patient from the host hospital (i.e., Server) to a remote pathology laboratory (i.e., Client) (Fig. 3). As shown in the figure, the server adopts a pipeline of three techniques to compress and transmit the histopathology image. Firstly, the image is divided into a number of fixed size tiles to provide ROI access. Secondly, each tile is independently encoded using a variant of the WebP compression technique. Finally, Cheng et al.'s packetization scheme is extended to smartly packetize encoded macroblocks of each tiles. Each packet is then transmitted to the client via a lossy network using UDP as the transport protocol. Unlike classical UDP, however, lost packets are retransmitted in our framework. In the client side, successfully received and decodable macroblocks are decoded and the part of the decoded image is shown to the viewer. In the following sections, we elaborate more about the proposed approach.

4.1   Tiling

In order to provide ROI access to the viewer, we divide the histopathology image into a number of rectangular size tiles. Dimension of each tile can be fixed by the hospital; in this paper, we have fixed the dimension to 64 × 64 macroblocks. Height of the last row or width of the last column of tiles, however, can be less than the regular height or width. Each tile is then independently encoded using modified-WebP that we propose in the next section.

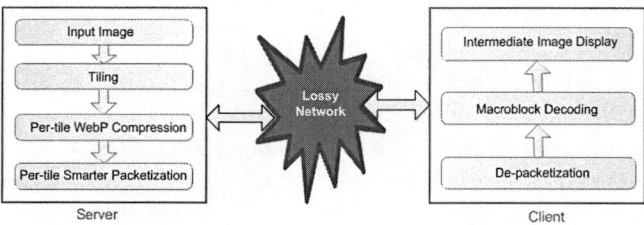

Fig. 3. Our streaming framework using modified-WebP and greedy packetization scheme

4.2   Modification of WebP

To make WebP suitable for compressing an image that need to be streamed, we propose to modify WebP by replacing the CABAC with CAVLC entropy coder; other steps of modified-WebP, however, are similar to the conventional WebP. As CAVLC uses universal look up tables that do not need fractional bits to encode a syntax element, the recursive dependency between macroblocks is eliminated. In addition, decoding of CAVLC is faster than CABAC as it uses look up tables in place of complex computations.

By eliminating the recursive dependency, the modified-WebP provides an option of decoding more than one macroblocks at any particular step of decoding. Therefore, it also provides more than one decoding order in which the macroblocks can be decoded. Figure 2b shows one such decoding order of the modified-WebP which is different than the conventional raster scan order. As discussed in the next section, this flexibility is important to stream images because it minimizes the effect of dependency between macroblocks and prioritizes the decoding of important macroblocks.

However, modified-WebP still has a level of parent-child dependency that results from the inter-macroblock prediction. Due to this dependency, in an intermediate stage of streaming, the number of decoded macroblocks can be different for different packetization schemes. Taking this into account, we propose a smarter greedy packetization scheme that offers the maximum number of decoded macroblocks in the intermediate stage of streaming.

4.3   Packetization

Due to the inter-macroblock dependency, the packets, which pack macroblocks of modified-WebP, can be interdependent with each other as the packets containing the parent macroblocks must be received before decoding of their child macroblock. For example, if server packs a parent macroblock in a packet X and its child in another packet Y, then packet Y is dependent on packet X as the client requires both packet X and packet Y to decode the child macroblock. As a result, if these inter-dependent packets are sent via a lossy network that uses UDP as the transport protocol, then the dependency among the packets can manipulate the number of macroblocks that can be decoded. For example, even if packet Y is received earlier than the lost packet X, the macroblocks packed in Y that are dependent on macroblocks packed in X cannot be decoded unless X is received by the client successfully. Note that due to the loss of X, not only the macroblocks packed in Y but also the macroblocks that are dependent on the undecoded macroblocks of Y cannot be decoded. Therefore, depending on the network parameters such as round trip time (RTT) (T_d), packet loss rate (p), and data send rate (R), the number of undecodable macroblocks can increase recursively.

This inter-packet dependency is similar to the inter-packet dependency that is resulted from the inter-dependent vertex splits of a progressive mesh as both of them produce similar type of dependency graphs. The inter-packet dependency resulted from vertex splits and its effect on the intermediate quality of a progressive mesh has been studied by Cheng et al. earlier [7]. According to them, among all possible ways of packing vertex splits, the one that results in the minimal packet dependency produces the best intermediate quality of the progressive mesh. Obtaining such an optimal solution, however, is infeasible as the problem has been proved to be NP-complete [13] . Therefore, a greedy packetization scheme that heuristically minimizes the inter-packet dependency has been proposed by Cheng et al. [7]. As this scheme has been extended to pack the macroblocks of modified-WebP, we summarize it in the following section.

Cheng et al.'s Packetization Scheme: Cheng et al.'s proposed packetization scheme has two main steps: first, an analytical model is proposed to calculate the degradation in quality of the mesh (i.e., *penalty*) due to deferment of the packing of any vertex split to a subsequent packet; and second, a greedy algorithm is proposed to pack vertex splits in a packet.

Penalty of a vertex split is calculated from two factors: priority of the vertex split and the difference in its expected decoding time if its packing is deferred to the next packet. Mathematically, δ_i, the penalty of a vertex split i is given by:

$$\delta_i = w_i(E[D_i^{next}] - E[D_i^{curr}]), \tag{1}$$

where, w_i is the priority of vertex split i; and $E[D_i^{curr}]$, $E[D_i^{next}]$ are the expected decoding time when vertex split i is packed in the current and in the next packet respectively. The detailed mathematical derivation of $E[D_i^{curr}]$ and $E[D_i^{next}]$ can be found in [7].

The greedy algorithm selects vertex splits to pack in a packet by iteratively picking them until the packet is empty or there is no more vertex split to select. At each step of the iteration, the algorithm picks a vertex split that is *packetable* (i.e., a vertex split which all parents have been picked) and that has the maximum penalty. After packing the vertex split, the set of packetable vertex splits is updated by including any child of the currently packed vertex split into it.

Algorithm 1. Greedy Packetization to Pack Macroblocks

for all node i whose parents are already packed **do**
  calculate its penalty δ_i if it is moved to the next packet;
  insert i into a maximum heap H with δ_i as key;
end for
while H is not empty and packet is not full **do**
  Pop j from H;
  if packing j into current packet do not oversize it (i.e., Algorithm 2 returns **true**) **then**
    Pack j into current packet;
    for all children k of j whose parents are already packed **do**
      calculate δ_k if k is moved to the next packet;
      insert k into H with δ_k as key;
    end for
  end if
end while

Algorithm 2. Checking if Macroblock j is Fits in the Current Packet

$T \leftarrow 0$;
for all macroblock m which has been already packed in the current packet **do**
  insert ID of m into a list L;
  $T \leftarrow T + \text{size of } m$;
end for
insert j of into L;
$T \leftarrow T + \text{size of } j$;
perform CAVLC entropy coding on L and assign the compressed size into W;
$T \leftarrow T + W$;
if $T \leq \text{MTU of packet}$ **then**
  return **true**;
else
  return **false**;
end if

Packetization Scheme for Modified WebP: Similar to Cheng et al.'s approach, our packetization scheme, which packs macroblocks of modified-WebP, consists of two main steps: the calculation of penalty and the greedy algorithm.

The penalty of all unpacked macroblocks are calculated using Eqn.(1). Unlike vertex splits, the size of macroblocks, however, can vary from each other. Therefore, size of a macroblock can be a factor in calculating its priority.

Due to two main reasons, Cheng et al.'s greedy algorithm cannot be used to pack macroblocks without modifying it. Firstly, Cheng et al.'s algorithm, which packs equal number of vertex splits in a packet, is inefficient to pack variable size macroblocks as a fixed number of macroblocks in a packet can result either an oversized packet or large packet overhead. Specifically, if the number of macroblocks is fixed to a large number, then it may result in an oversized packet. On the other hand, the choice of a smaller number can introduce more UDP packet overhead by requiring significantly more numbers of packets than the optimal. Secondly, unlike Cheng et al.'s algorithm, which does not consider packing the vertex split ID in a packet, the ID of each macroblock must be packed as it is required by the client during the time of decoding.

Based on the above observation, we propose a greedy packetization scheme that is outlined in Alg. 1. Our algorithm modifies Cheng et al.'s greedy algorithm in two ways. Firstly, we choose a macroblock having size less or equal to the size of the available free space in the current packet, which has all its parents packed earlier, and which has the highest penalty among all the macroblocks those can be packed in the current packet. Secondly, the ID of the selected macroblocks are also packed by compressing them using CAVLC entropy encoder. To facilitate CAVLC encoding, the selected macroblocks of a packet are arranged in a batch of 16 macroblocks as shown in Fig. 4.

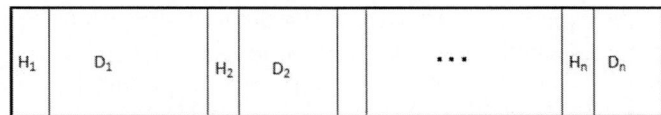

Fig. 4. m number of macroblocks arranged into n number of groups within a packet. First $(n-1)$ number of groups contain 16 number of macroblocks each and n_{th} group may contain less than equal to 16 macroblocks. H_i and D_i denote the optimized header (CAVLC compressed macroblock IDs) and compressed data of the ith group of macroblocks respectively.

5   Experimental Results

We implemented the proposed framework first by modifying Google's WebP to facilitate the modified-WebP and then by simulating the greedy packetization scheme in a notebook powered by *Intel Core 2 Duo 2.00 GHz processor* and four GB of RAM. The simulation is implemented on Ubuntu platform and using C as the programming language. We tested this experimental setup with two histopathology images: *ImageA* (Fig. 5b) and *ImageB* (Fig. 5a), which are divided into tiles of dimension 64×64 macroblocks each. The detailed specifications of these two images can be found from Table 1. When *ImageA* is streamed using the proposed framework, the part of the image that can be viewed by the

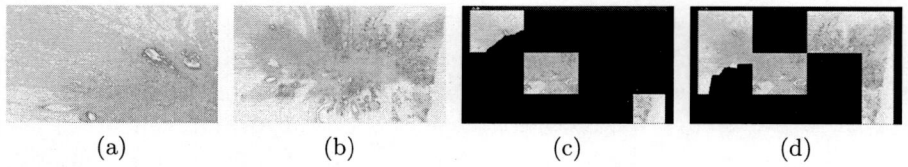

| (a) | (b) | (c) | (d) |

Fig. 5. (a) *ImageB*; (b) *ImageA*; (c) Decoding of *ImageA* at time t_1; and (d) Decoding of *ImageA* at time t_2 $(t_2 > t_1)$

Table 1. Specification of *ImageA* and *ImageB*

Name	Size	Dimension	No. of macroblocks	WebP Comp. Size	Modified WebP Comp. Size
ImageA	18.6 MB	3664 × 2763	39671	5.3 MB	5.4 MB
ImageB	38.2 MB	3795 × 3520	52360	5.6 MB	5.9 MB

client at different point of time are shown in Fig. 5c and Fig. 5d. Note that the order in which the tiles of the image are streamed for this experiment is dependent on a specific *ROI* request; this order can change with the client's *ROI* requirement.

Figures 6a to 6d compare the number of undecodable macroblocks of the FCFS packetization scheme that uses TCP as the transport protocol with the number of undecodable macroblocks of the greedy packetization scheme. As can be seen from the figures, irrespective of the network conditions, more number of received macroblocks are decoded by the greedy packetization as its inter-packet dependency is significantly less than the inter-packet dependency of the FCFS packetization. Moreover, with an increase in any one of the network parameters among R, p, and T_d, the number of undecodable macroblocks of FCFS increases more than that of greedy packetization. This behavior of the packetization schemes is due to either the increase in number of dependent macroblocks or the increase in the number of lost macroblocks. The number of dependent macroblocks is increased when either R or T_d is increased by keeping remaining two parameters as constants. Similarly, the number of lost macroblocks is increased when p is increased for unchanged R and T_d values. The number of macroblocks packed in a packet also plays a major role in the number of undecodable macroblocks as there is an increase in the number of dependent macroblocks with an increase in the number of macroblocks that can be packed in a packet. Due to this reason, *ImageB* has more number of undecodable macroblocks than *ImageA* in the initial stage of streaming (Fig. 6d).

Figure 7 shows the difference in the number of decoded macroblocks between the FCFS packetization scheme and the greedy packetization scheme. As can be verified from the figure, at any particular time t, the number of macroblocks decoded by the greedy scheme is more than the FCFS scheme. This advantage is achieved even though greedy scheme has an extra overhead that is incurred

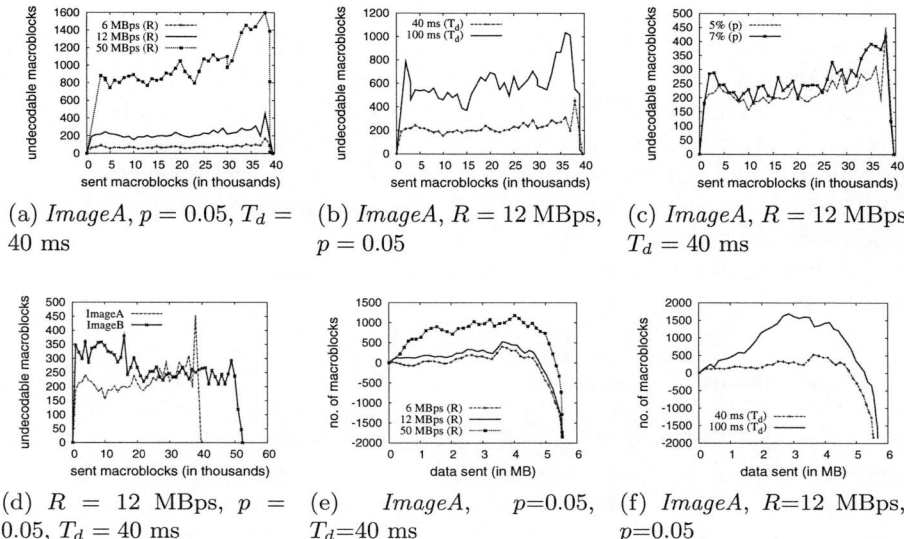

(a) *ImageA*, $p = 0.05$, $T_d = 40$ ms

(b) *ImageA*, $R = 12$ MBps, $p = 0.05$

(c) *ImageA*, $R = 12$ MBps, $T_d = 40$ ms

(d) $R = 12$ MBps, $p = 0.05$, $T_d = 40$ ms

(e) *ImageA*, $p=0.05$, $T_d=40$ ms

(f) *ImageA*, $R=12$ MBps, $p=0.05$

Fig. 6. (a) to (d) show the difference between number of undecodable macroblocks of FCFS packetization scheme with respect to greedy packetization scheme for different network parameters and images. For *ImageA*, (e) to (f) compare the number of macroblocks that are decoded by greedy packetization scheme with the number of macroblocks decoded by FCFS packetization scheme.

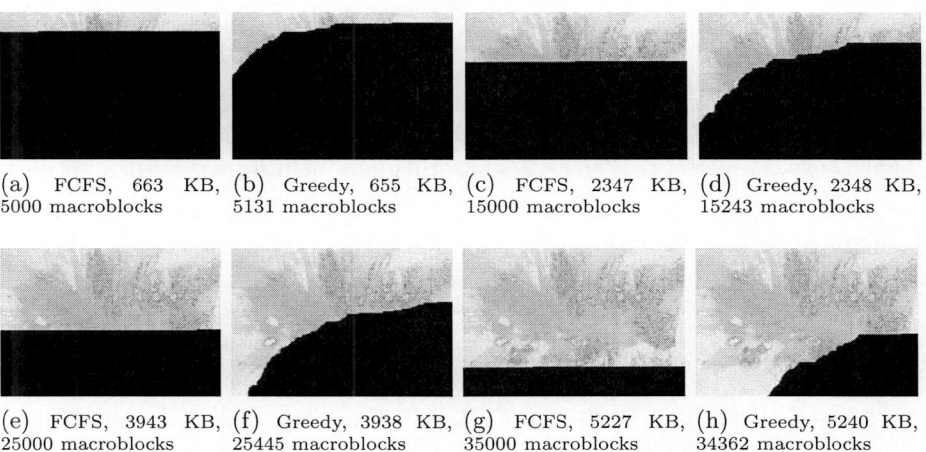

(a) FCFS, 663 KB, 5000 macroblocks

(b) Greedy, 655 KB, 5131 macroblocks

(c) FCFS, 2347 KB, 15000 macroblocks

(d) Greedy, 2348 KB, 15243 macroblocks

(e) FCFS, 3943 KB, 25000 macroblocks

(f) Greedy, 3938 KB, 25445 macroblocks

(g) FCFS, 5227 KB, 35000 macroblocks

(h) Greedy, 5240 KB, 34362 macroblocks

Fig. 7. At any time t, each pair ((a), (b)), ((c), (d)), ((e), (f)), and ((g), (h)) compares the number of macroblocks decoded by FCFS packetization scheme with the number of macroblocks decoded by greedy packetization scheme. The size of data that is sent by the server is given in KB.

by packing the ID of each macroblock in the payload of a packet. As shown in Fig. 6e and 6f, the number of macroblocks decoded by any one of these packetization schemes is mainly dependent on two factors: the inter-packet dependency and the number of macroblocks packed in a packet. Specifically, if greedy packs significantly less number of macroblocks than FCFS scheme, then the number of decoded macroblocks is also less. In all other cases, the greedy scheme decodes more number of macroblocks as it has less inter-packet dependency than FCFS. As can be seen in Fig. 6e and 6f, the difference of the number of decoded macroblocks between these two schemes increases with an increase in the inter-packet dependency that is caused by the increase in either R and T_d value respectively.

6   Conclusion

By using the prediction based compression technique such as WebP, this paper proposed a ROI-based image streaming framework to stream large histopathology images. Firstly, we observed that the FCFS inter-macroblock dependency introduced by WebP is not suitable to stream histopathology images as it cannot prioritize the decoding of an important macroblock. Hence, we modified WebP by using CAVLC in place of CABAC entropy coder. Secondly, we observed that the parent-child dependency that is part of the modified-WebP affects the number of decoded macroblocks at any intermediate stage of streaming. In addition, we also learnt that the intermediate quality of an image can vary with the order in which macroblocks are packed in a packet as the packing order can manipulate the inter-packet dependency. Hence, we proposed a greedy based packetization scheme that both minimizes the inter-packet dependency and prioritizes the picking of important macroblocks.

Acknowledgement. We would like to thank the ANR project MICO−Ref.ANR-10-TECS-015 and the MITOS dataset from the Pitié-Salpêtrière Hospital, Paris (http://ipal.cnrs.fr/ICPR2012/) for providing the histopathological images.

References

1. Leiserson, M.: The future of medical imaging. TuftScope: The J. of Health, Ethics, and Policy 9, 17–18 (2010)
2. Cheng, L.T., Ng, S.E.: Teleradiology in Singapore-taking stock and looking ahead. Ann. Acad. Med. Singapore 35, 552–556 (2006)
3. Tuominen, V.J., Isola, J.: Linking whole-slide microscope images with DICOM by using JPEG2000 interactive protocol. J. Digital Imaging 23, 454–462 (2010)
4. Krupinski, E.A.: Virtual slide telepathology workstation of the future: lessons learned from teleradiology. Human Pathology 40, 1100–1111 (2009)
5. Google Inc. WebP compression study. Draft 0.1 (May 2011),
   https://developers.google.com/speed/webp/docs/webp_study
6. Google Inc. Comparative study of WebP, JPEG, and JPEG2000 (August 2012),
   https://developers.google.com/speed/webp/docs/c_study

7. Cheng, W., Ooi, W.T., Mondet, S., Grigoras, R., Morin, G.: An analytical model for progressive mesh streaming. In: Proc. of the 15th Intl. Conf. on Multimedia, Augsburg, Germany, pp. 737–746 (September 2007)
8. Foran, D.J., Meer, P.P., Papathomas, T., Marsic, I.: Compression guidelines for diagnostic telepathology. IEEE Trans. Inf. Technol. Biomed. 9, 55–60 (1997)
9. Baeza, I., Verdoy, J.A., Villanueva-Oller, J., Villanueva, R.J.: ROI-based procedures for progressive transmission of digital images: A comparison. Mathematical and Computer Modelling 50, 849–859 (2009)
10. Devaraj, S.J., Ezra, K.: Current trends and future challenges in wireless telemedicine system. In: Intl. Conf. on Elect. Computer Techn., Coimbatore, India, pp. 417–421 (April 2011)
11. Google Inc. VP8 data format and decoding guide. RFC 6386 (November 2011), http://www.rfc-editor.org/rfc/rfc6386.txt
12. Marpe, D., Schwarz, H., Blättermann, G., Heising, G., Wieg, T.: Context-based adaptive binary arithmetic coding in the H.264/AVC video compression standard. IEEE Trans. Circuits Syst. Video Technol. 13, 620–636 (2003)
13. Gu, Y., Ooi, W.T.: Packetization of 3D progressive meshes for streaming over lossy networks. In: Proc. of the 14th Intl. Conf. on Computer Communications and Networks, San Diego, CA (October 2005)

Visual Saliency and Distortion Weighting Based Video Quality Assessment

Lin Zhu, Li Su, Qingming Huang, and Honggang Qi

Graduate University of Chinese Academy of Sciences, Beijing, China
{lzhu,lsu,qmhuang,hgqi}@jdl.ac.cn

Abstract. Video quality assessment (VQA) is very important in many video processing applications. For example, the rate-distortion (RD) optimization in video coding needs an efficient distortion metric to assess the RD cost of candidate coding parameters. However, most existing metrics employ little visual perceptual information, or some are too complex to meet real-time requirement. In this paper we propose a new model called saliency and distortion weighted structural similarity index with temporal pooling strategy (SDTW-SSIM). In the proposed model, spatial and temporal saliency is obtained from the referenced video. Besides, a distortion weighting map is employed to give a full description of visual attention. To better present the perceptual properties of videos, both frame and sequence level saliency features are taken into account. Experimental results show that, compared with state-of-the-art methods, the proposed method performs well on both computational efficiency and assessment accuracy.

Keywords: Video Quality Assessment, Visual Attention, Motion Estimation, Distortion Weighting, Structural Similarity.

1 Introduction

With the rapid development of multimedia technology, video service is getting more and more popular. Therefore, video quality measurement plays a fundamentally important role in video processing applications. A straightforward way of evaluating video quality is achieved by subjective testing [1]. However, it has to follow strict evaluation conditions, and is laborious and expensive. Thus, objective quality assessment metrics that can reflect the perceived video quality are necessary. For example, most recently video coding algorithms use the rate-distortion optimization (RDO) to remove the redundant information, during which, objective video quality is calculated to evaluate the video coding distortion.

Traditional distortion metrics usually calculate the video's mean squared error (MSE) or peak signal-to-noise ratio (PSNR), as a result often deviating from the human perceptual feelings. In order to automatically assess the quality of videos in a perceptually consistent manner, human visual system (HVS) has been introduced into this field by modeling its physiological and psychological features [2, 3]. Considering

W. Lin et al. (Eds.): PCM 2012, LNCS 7674, pp. 546–555, 2012.

that the HVS is an extremely complicated system and there still lacks full understanding of it currently, improving methods are required.

With the knowledge that natural image signals are highly structured, a measure of structural similarity (SSIM) [4] to approximate the perceived image quality has been employed, which outperforms many state-of-the-art perceptual image quality metrics. The visual information fidelity (VIF) [5], which is based on visual statistics, models images as realizations of Gaussian Scale Mixtures in the wavelet domain. Though VIF and several recently proposed methods deliver better consistency with perceptual image evaluations, such as the feature similarity (FSIM) index [6] and the information content weighted SSIM (IW-SSIM) index [7], the highly computational complexity prevents them from real-time video applications. A video SSIM (VSSIM) [8] metric has been proposed to measure the quality of the distorted video in three levels, namely the local region level, the frame level, and the sequence level. However, the motion information along temporal trajectory and visual attention of HVS has not been made full used. More recently, a motion-based video integrity evaluation (MOVIE) index [9] has been proposed. MOVIE is shown to match human visual perception of video quality quite closely, but it is complicated to meet real-time video assessment.

Visual attention (VA) [10] is one of the most essential visual phenomena of HVS, which shows that the salient regions in visual field are highly focused by human eyes. In [11], a saliency detection method is incorporated with several video quality metrics and could improve the evaluating accuracy. While, the saliency based weighting strategy is only executed in frame level. In practice, the sequence level pooling stage is often done in simplistic or ad-hoc ways. It lacks theoretical principles as the basis for the development of reliable computational models. On the other hand, the saliency map in [11] is only obtained from the referenced videos. The differences between original and reconstructed ones are ignored. An intuitive idea shows that more emphasis should be put at high distorted regions, which can be done by using non-uniform weighting approach [12].

In order to deal with the aforementioned issues, in this paper we propose a VA based video quality assessment (VQA) approach, as shown in Fig. 1. The proposed VA map combines both visual saliency and distortion attention information. And it is finally employed as weight through the frame and sequence level quality pooling procedure. Correspondingly, we call the metrics proposed in these two levels: saliency and distortion weighted SSIM (SDW-SSIM), and SDW-SSIM with temporal pooling strategy (SDTW-SSIM). In our method, block-based motion estimation (BME) is applied to provide the motion information for temporal analysis. By considering visual factors, the proposed metric performs more consistency with human visual perception, meanwhile, it is efficient enough to meet real-time applications.

The rest of the paper is organized as follows. Firstly, the proposed visual saliency detection methods in frame level and sequence level are depicted in Section 2. Then, in Section 3, pooling strategies considering distortion weighting are developed to obtain the VQA index. In Section 4, experimental results are presented and analyzed. Finally, the work is summarized in Section 5.

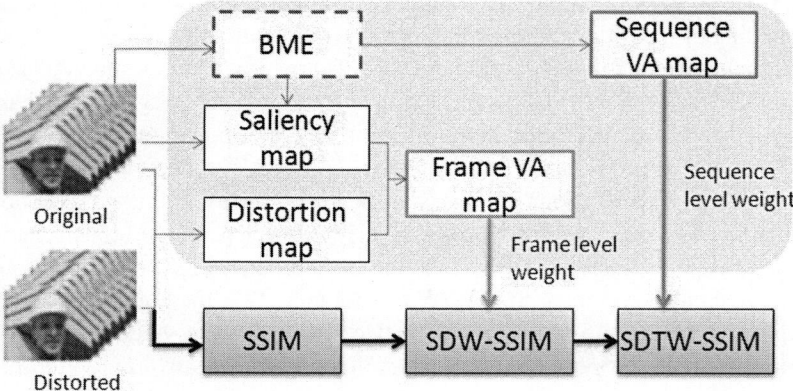

Fig. 1. Framework for the proposed VQA system

2   Spatial and Temporal Visual Saliency Analysis

2.1   Frame Level Saliency Map

Among existing saliency detecting methods, a Fourier transform based approach is proposed, which uses phase spectrum extracted from spectral domain to construct the corresponding salient areas in spatial domain [13]. Standing out from other models in computer vision, it is independent of prior knowledge and parameters and performs fast enough to meet real-time requirements. Furthermore, it can be extended from a two-dimensional Fourier transform to a quaternion Fourier transform (QFT) [14].

Firstly, each frame in the video sequence is represented as a quaternion image with four features. Different features affect the final saliency detection result [11, 13]. Here, we choose luminance, chrominance and motion information to construct the quaternion, considering that this kind of composition principle is similar to human visual perception process. Chrominance is represented by the H channel in HSV color space, and BME is applied to provide the motion information. Define the tth frame in a video sequence as $F(t)$, $t=1, 2, \ldots, N$, where N is the total frame number of the video. $I(t)$, $H(t)$ are the luminance and chrominance components of frame $F(t)$.

After performing BME approach on luminance channel for each frame $F(t)$, we get the horizontal and vertical motion vector $V_x(t)$, $V_y(t)$. Then, the new quaternion image can be conducted as

$$q(t) = I(t) + H(t)\mu_1 + V_x(t)\mu_2 + V_y(t)\mu_3 \tag{1}$$

where
$$\mu_i^2 = -1, \ i = 1, 2, 3$$
$$\mu_1 \perp \mu_2, \ \mu_2 \perp \mu_3, \ \mu_3 \perp \mu_1, \ \mu_3 = \mu_1\mu_2$$

According to the theory demonstrated in [13], the saliency map $SM(t)$ can be obtained through the following ways. Firstly, QFT is applied to get the frequency domain representation $Q(t)$ of the quaternion image $q(t)$. Then, in order to construct the saliency map, the inverse QFT is employed to the phase spectrum $p(t)$ extracted from $Q(t)$, i.e.

$$Q(t) = QFT(q(t)) \tag{2}$$

$$p(t) = P(Q(t)) \tag{3}$$

$$SM(t) = g(t) \cdot \| QFT^{-1}(e^{\mu \cdot p(t)}) \|^2 \tag{4}$$

where $g(t)$ is a Gaussian filter function, μ is a unit pure quaternion, and implementation details of QFT are available in [14].

This improved QFT method presents integrated saliency of intensity, color, and motion features. We choose to execute this method under the resolution of 64×64, and achieve a fast and visual friendly result.

2.2   Sequence Level Saliency Analysis

Most existing video saliency detection methods developed from image processing are lacking in temporal visual attention analysis. Considering that the changes of objects' moving speed are more likely to cause human concern, here we attempt to model this phenomenon as saliency along temporal trajectory.

Since time dimension features can be associated with moving information of objects in the scene, we use motion vectors as the modeling basis. We merge the previously obtained horizontal and vertical motion vectors into one component $V(t)$, we obtain

$$V(t) = \sqrt{V_x(t)^2 + V_y(t)^2} \tag{5}$$

With $V(t)$, the extent of changes between moving velocity in current frame and previous adjacent ones is calculated, and then the temporal salient degree $SV(t)$ is summed up as follows

$$SV(t) = \frac{1}{H \cdot W} \sum_{i=1}^{H} \sum_{j=1}^{W} | V_{ij}(t) - \frac{1}{3} \sum_{k=t-3}^{t-1} V_{ij}(k) | \tag{6}$$

where i and j denote the location of pixels, H and W are the height and width of the frame, respectively.

3   Pooling Strategy For VQA Index

3.1   Frame Level Pooling Strategy: SDW-SSIM

In section 2, saliency is obtained from the referenced videos only. Considering that HVS tends to pay more attention to the low quality region [12], here we employ distortion as another factor that affects VA. In this section, we incorporate the visual saliency map and distortion weight with SSIM metric in frame level.

For the distortion weight, here we use square error measure,

$$DM(t) = [I_r(t) - I_d(t)]^2 \qquad (7)$$

where $I_r(t)$ and $I_d(t)$ denote the referenced and distorted frame pixels in the luminance channel, respectively.

The frame quality index (FQI) at the tth frame is merged as follows,

$$FQI(t) = \frac{\sum_{i=1}^{H} \sum_{j=1}^{W} \left[SM_{ij}(t) \cdot DM_{ij}(t) \cdot SSIM_{ij}(t) \right]}{\sum_{i=1}^{H} \sum_{j=1}^{W} \left[SM_{ij}(t) \cdot DM_{ij}(t) \right]} \qquad (8)$$

Saliency map and distortion map are the two factors that are considered here as visual attention information. While in the saliency detection stage, luminance, color and motion information are included, distortion map stresses the corresponding distorted areas. All together, they are used to simulate the HVS observation mechanism. One advantage of the proposed frame level strategy is that it is sample and efficiency, making it appropriate for the RDO process of real-time video coding.

In order to give an intuitive perception of the frame level weighting scheme, here we present some saliency and distortion map detected from the referenced and distorted frames. As being seen from Fig. 2(c), the brighter areas show more significance for visual observation. Since the saliency detection procedure combines luminance, color and motion information, areas apt to catch VA in the referenced video are successfully detected. In order to make up the deficiency of saliency maps which is obtained from the referenced video only, the distortion maps provide information of the distorted video that is different from the referenced one. The corresponding distortion maps are shown in Fig. 2(d), in which, deeper distortion areas are brighter. Thus, the combination of these two points of view gives the VA a more comprehensive description in Fig. 2(e), and the following test demonstrates that the VA scheme proposed can significantly improve the performance of SSIM index.

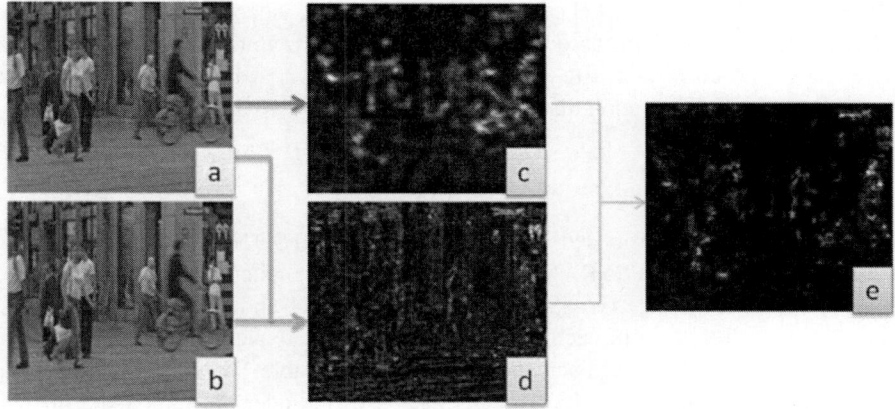

Fig. 2. (a) frame selected from the referenced video; (b) distorted frame; (c) saliency map; (d) distortion map; (e) VA map

3.2   Sequence Level Pooling Strategy: SDTW-SSIM

After each frame quality index have been generated with the saliency and distortion weighted method, the following stage is to pool the quality index sequences along time-domain to obtain the final VQA index. By taking into account temporal visual saliency in sequence level pooling, we obtain the proposed VQA metric SDTW-SSIM differently from the general mean value method.

The temporal salient degree $SV(t)$ is described in (6). The VQA index of the overall video is finally generated as

$$VQI = \sum_{i=1}^{N}[SV(t) \cdot FQI(t)] / \sum_{i=1}^{N} SV(t) \tag{9}$$

where N is the total frame number of the video. The introducing of this sequence level pooling strategy makes the objective VQAs more consistency with the characteristics of human visual process, thus, the performance of the VQAs can be improved.

4   Experiments

In this section, several VQAs together with the proposed SDW-SSIM method are tested on the LIVE VQA database [1]. First, three evaluation metrics are employed to compare the obtained objective assessment index with the subjective score provided within the database. Second, we present the time cost to make a comparison of the complexity between different metrics. Third, the scatter plot of the proposed method is compared with three other ones.

The LIVE VQA database [1] consists of 10 referenced videos of natural scenes and 150 distorted videos with the associated differential mean opinion score (DMOS). Each referenced video corresponds to 15 distorted ones with a wide range of distortions, created by using four common distortion types.

4.1 Performance Comparisons

The performance of the proposed method SDW-SSIM and SDTW-SSIM are compared with other VQAs. For PSNR, SSIM [4], VIF [5], weighted signal-to-noise ratio (WSNR) [15], FSIM [6], IW-SSIM [7], VS-SSIM [11] and SDW-SSIM, we first generate the quality index of each frame, and then make an average to obtain the final VQA index. The performance statistics of MOVIE in Table 1 is obtained from [16], which is also executed on the LIVE VQA database [1] under the same experimental conditions.

To evaluate the performance of the objective quality assessment models, we employ the metrics recommended in the VQEG Phase I FR-TV test [17]. Spearman rank-order correlation coefficient (SROCC) between the objective and subjective scores is presented as a measure of prediction monotonicity. After non-linear regression analysis, the Pearson linear correlation coefficient (LCC) and the root-mean-square error (RMSE) are calculated to measure the prediction accuracy. Higher LCC, SROCC and lower RMSE values indicate better evaluating performance.

Table 1. Performance comparisons

Algorithm	LCC	SROCC	RMSE
PSNR	0.5331	0.5032	9.2871
SSIM	0.5373	0.5184	9.2582
VIF	0.5869	0.5566	8.8878
WSNR	0.6783	0.6439	8.0658
FSIM	0.7238	0.7061	7.5739
IW-SSIM	0.7487	0.7411	7.2767
VS-SSIM	0.6101	0.5885	8.6976
MOVIE	0.8116	0.7890	-
SDW-SSIM	**0.7773**	**0.7630**	**6.9063**
SDTW-SSIM	**0.7868**	**0.7711**	**6.7756**

Table 1 shows, by employing visual saliency and distortion attention weighting with SSIM on the frame level pooling procedure only, the proposed SDW-SSIM metric shows reasonably good results compared with the other VQAs listed. Furthermore, SDTW-SSIM combines both frame and sequence level VA weight, and consequently provides even better performance. It still performs a slightly worse comparing with the MOVIE index. The time-consuming optical flow and complex HVS model have been used in the MOVIE index, as a result, making it too complicated to meet real-time requirement. While the statistical data of time cost in the following test shows that, the complexity of the proposed metric is quite acceptable.

4.2   Complexity Comparisons

In order to compare the complexity between different VQAs in practical applications, here, we also evaluate the running speed of some VQAs selected in Table 2. All these tests were run at Matlab R2010a software on Windows XP platform. Experimental environment is a DELL PC, with 2.00 GB memory. Because the released software of MOVIE index is a C++ implementation, the Matlab version is not available, so the MOVIE index is not listed in our test of this part. In Table 2, we record the time cost for different VQAs while evaluating the visual quality of the randomly selected video sequence pa3_25fps.yuv from LIVE VQA database [1].

Table 2. Time cost comparisons

Algorithm	Time(seconds)
PSNR	5.3
SSIM	45.5
VIF	861.8
WSNR	73.4
FSIM	477.3
IW-SSIM	408.9
VS-SSIM	180.9
SDTW-SSIM	184.2
SDTW-SSIM-noBME	**59.6**

Different from image applications, video processing is more sensitive to the complexity of the algorithm being used. The proposed SDTW-SSIM index also shows superiority in this respect as can be noticed from Table 2. Note that IW-SSIM and FSIM supply more flexibility than many VQAs listed in Table 1. However, the two schemes are more time-consuming. In addition, considering that BME module has been integrated into quite a few video processing systems already, for instance, the advanced video coding standard H.264, as a result, the actual time cost of SDTW-SSIM can be further reduced accordingly. The SDTW-SSIM-noBME in Table 2 represents the rest cost after removing the time used for the BME process. It shows that there is only a slight increase comparing with SSIM, while the evaluation performance of SSIM is much lower as can be seen from Table 1.

4.3   Scatter Plot Comparisons

For each scatter plot in Fig. 3, vertical and horizontal axes are for subjective and objective measurements, respectively. Each sample point represents one test video sequence. As being observed in Fig. 3, the sample points of the proposed SDTW-SSIM metric distribute more closely to the fitted line, which means it outperforms other VQAs. The same conclusion has been drawn from the above mentioned Table 1, the proposed metric has higher prediction monotonicity and accuracy.

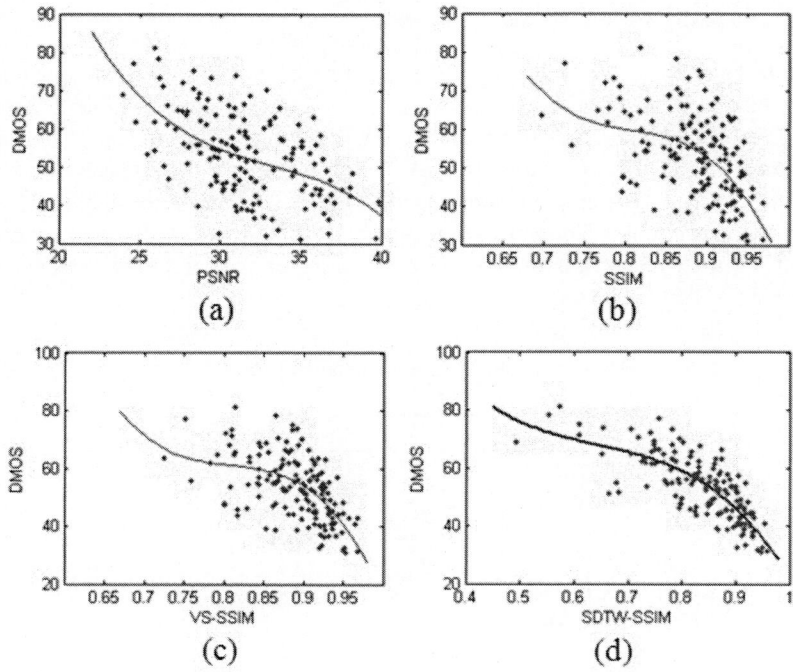

Fig. 3. Scatter plot comparison of different VQAs on LIVE VAQ database. (a) PSNR; (b) SSIM; (c) VS-SSIM; (d) SDTW-SSIM (proposed method)

Thus, from both the quantitative evaluation results and the scatter plots, the proposed SDTW-SSIM metric achieves rather good evaluation result. At the same time, the executing procedure is clear and with few parameters dependence and shows a meaningful balance between performance and efficiency. Since many video processing applications utilize a motion compensation scheme, the motion vectors can be reused while applying our saliency detection method, which reduces the consumption of time. In order to meet the requirement of real-time processing, here we only corporate the proposed VA weight with SSIM as a test. Moreover, the proposed model can be easily ported to other VQAs applications, such as FSIM, VIF and IW-SSIM.

5   Conclusions

In this paper, a visual saliency and distortion attention based perceptual VQA metric is proposed. The total algorithm is implemented in three stages. Firstly, each frame is evaluated by an SSIM index map. Secondly, spatial and temporal features of perceptual significance are modeled as visual saliency. Thirdly, in the pooling process, the visual saliency and distortion weight are combined with SSIM index to generate the final quality score. In order to obtain more consistent perception of human visual evaluation, the visual saliency detection and quality pooling stages are executed in both frame level and sequence level. Experimental results show that the proposed method is computationally efficient and performs well on the current widely used VQA database.

Acknowledgement. This work was supported in part by National Basic Research Program of China (973 Program): 2009CB320906, in part by National Natural Science Foundation of China: 61025011, 60833006, 61001177 and 61001108.

References

1. Seshadrinathan, K., Soundararajan, R., et al.: Study of Subjective and Objective Quality Assessment of Video. IEEE Trans. on Image Processing 19, 1427–1441 (2010)
2. Moorthy, A.K., Seshadrinathan, K., et al.: Wireless Video Quality Assessment A Study of Subjective Scores and Objective Algorithms. IEEE Trans. on Circuits Systems for Video Technology 20, 587–599 (2010)
3. Lin, W., Jay Kuo, C.-C.: Perceptual Visual Quality Metrics: A Survey. J. of Visual Communication and Image Representation 22, 297–312 (2011)
4. Wang, Z., Bovik, A.C., et al.: Image Quality Assessment: From Error Measurement to Structural Similarity. IEEE Trans. on Image Processing 13, 600–612 (2004)
5. Sheikh, H.R., Bovik, A.C.: Image Information and Visual Quality. IEEE Trans. on Image Processing 15, 430–444 (2006)
6. Zhang, L., Zhang, L., et al.: FSIM: A Feature Similarity Index for Image Quality Assessment. IEEE Trans. on Image Processing 20, 2378–2386 (2011)
7. Wang, Z., Li, Q.: Information Content Weighting for Perceptual Image Quality Assessment. IEEE Trans. on Image Processing 20, 1185–1198 (2011)
8. Wang, Z., Lu, L., et al.: Video Quality Assessment Based on Structural Distortion Measurement. Signal Processing: Image Communication 19, 121–132 (2004)
9. Seshadrinathan, K., Bovik, A.C.: Motion Tuned Spatio-temporal Quality Assessment of Natural Videos. IEEE Trans. on Image Processing 19, 335–350 (2010)
10. Engelke, U., Kaprykowsky, H., et al.: Visual Attention in Quality Assessment. IEEE Signal Processing Magazine 28, 50–59 (2011)
11. Ma, L., Li, S., et al.: Motion Trajectory Based Visual Saliency for Video Quality Assessment. In: IEEE International Conference on Image Processing, pp. 233–236 (2011)
12. Wang, Z., Shang, X.: Spatial Pooling Strategies for Perceptual Image Quality Assessment. In: IEEE International Conference on Image Processing, pp. 2945–2948 (2006)
13. Guo, C., Ma, Q., et al.: Spatio-temporal Saliency Detection Using Phase Spectrum of Quaternion Fourier Transform. In: IEEE Conference on Computer Vision and Pattern Recognition, pp. 1–8 (2008)
14. Ell, T.A., Sangwine, S.J.: Hypercomplex Fourier Transforms for Color Images. IEEE Trans. on Image Processing 16, 22–35 (2007)
15. Gaubatz, M., Hemami, S.S.: MeTriX MuX Visual Quality Assessment Package, http://foulard.ece.cornell.edu/gaubatz/metrix_mux
16. Moorthy, A.K., Bovik, A.C.: Efficient Video Quality Assessment Along Temporal Trajectories. IEEE Trans. on Circuits and Systems for Video Technology 20, 1653–1658 (2010)
17. VQEG: Final Report from the Video Quality Experts Group on the Validation of Objective Models of Video Quality Assessment (2000), http://www.vqeg.org/

A Resource Scheduling Approach
for Media Uploading in Video Data Center

Yihong Gao, Huadong Ma, and Haitao Zhang

Beijing Key Lab of Intelligent Telecomm. Software and Multimedia,
Beijing University of Posts and Telecomm., Beijing 100876, China
hii_gao@hotmail.com, mhd@bupt.edu.cn, zhht.83@gmail.com

Abstract. Currently, more and more Internet of Things (IoT) applications use Internet cameras to sense the physical world, and a large amount of streaming media data is uploaded onto video data center. Consequently, it brings much pressure on the media streams' caching and storage resources of data centers. For solving this problem, we propose a streaming media caching resource scheduling approach which gives full consideration on the resource constraints of cameras and the caching server instability. We adopt a server-slave model to manage the caching server cluster. The management server monitors the state of each slave caching server in real-time, and schedules the connecting requests of Internet cameras according to the stability of the distributed caching servers. Therefore, we can obtain the higher reliability for streaming media uploading and the better workload balance among the caching servers. Based on the proposed scheduling approach, we implement a distributed caching system for reliable video uploading in data center, and the experimental results validate the effectiveness of our approach.

Keywords: video data center, streaming media, distributed caching system, scheduling, uploading.

1 Introduction

More recently, the related technologies of data center and cloud computing have attracted much attention of researchers. Based on the large scale of data center clusters and the current Internet infrastructure, the various service-oriented computing models are widely used for mass data service [1], [2], [3], and many companies have established their massive multimedia services based on data center or cloud such as the Apple's icloud service, Facebook's video and picture share service and Google's picture retrieval service. On the other hand, some researchers consider the multimedia cloud computing or video data center [4], [5], [6], [7], [8].

With the development of IoT, more and more cameras are connected to Internet, and generate large amounts of streaming media data continuously. This uploaded streaming media data gives much pressure on the caching and storage resource of video data centers. However, the current work about data center

W. Lin et al. (Eds.): PCM 2012, LNCS 7674, pp. 556–567, 2012.

mainly focuses on the delivery service of massive streaming media from data centers to users [14], [15], [16], [17]. Many researchers present the architectures which mainly concern how the content in the server can be delivered efficiently to end users. Dai *et al.* focused on how caching servers can support a collaborative content delivery to serve mobile users[14]. Shuai *et al.* adopted a caching approach achieving high quality video playing on smart phones called MobiUP [15]. This method extracts some features from the video clips, which mainly are visual artifacts, as video stream's metadata. Metadata can help users obtain high-quality video clips and play real-time video on mobile devices. On the other hand, researchers also consider how to guarantee the content delivery quality. Jurca and Frossard presented a video stream transmission approach based on the multi-path transmission scheme [16]. This approach can obviously reduce the distortion of the data during video transmission. But the redundant uploading streaming data means that more workload needs to be added into the system. Fujimoto *et al.* used a novel backup strategy to guarantee high transmission quality [17]. The video streams in this strategy are divided into two parts: important ones and less important ones. They assumed that a single video stream cannot keep the integrity of the content in the network environment and the video quality are heavily damaged during transmitting process. Based on this assumption, the authors concluded that keeping important video streams with redundant streams would improve the service quality. In this work, the end users are several smart and powerful devices, and the objective is to supply a high quality and reliability content delivery from the data center to the end users.

In this paper, we consider a reverse streaming media transmission process with resource-limited end devices. Lots of distributed Internet cameras continuously upload video data to data center servers. In this situation, we point that the traditional streaming media distribution modes cannot be adopted, and a new streaming media collection mode needs to be studied for supporting system reliability and high quality connection. Actually, some early work has already considered the streaming media uploading service [11], [12], [13]. In these literatures, end users upload multimedia files and compete for a single server's caching service. Each uploading job has a deadline, the server determines the sequence of these jobs. Finally, the scheduler must guarantee that every jobs can be finished before the certain deadline. There is a presupposition in these literatures: continuous playback is not a required specification for the uploading system. However, in the Internet of Things (IoT) environments, massive resource-limited devices continuously generate data and usually do not support the data caching service. On the other hand, in the large scale data center, the server's reliability should be considered during uploading process for a better uploading quality.

The traditional read/write operation in data center usually needs the cooperation of servers and users. For example, if a user needs to write some files into a data center, it needs to write data in a block sequence and support data synchronization service at the same time. When some errors happen in the writing operation, the user needs to help the data center recover the missing data. However, this method is not suitable for resource-limited cameras which generate the continuous media stream with high speed and do not support the local storage. Most of the data centers usually treat the multimedia data as common data, and suppose users store the uploaded data locally. Actually, many sensing devices including Internet cameras do not have enough resources to run data caching policy. This means that the existing cameras do not have the capability of the cooperation with the data center and the data center do not guarantee reliable video uploading for cameras. When resource-limited cameras upload massive streaming media to the video data center, there are two issues we need to address:

- Continuous media streaming: Many video surveillance applications request 24 hours × 7 days service. This means that massive and continuous streams are sent to video data center and consume large amounts of resources.
- Limited resource: Data centers need the stable uploading data source. But the current widely used cameras cannot provide the caching resource required to stably upload data to data center.

To deal with the above issues, we deploy a distributed caching system between Internet cameras and data center storage resources. By using a resource scheduling approach for streaming media data, the caching service cluster can cache the cameras' video data and guarantee the request connection quality of resource-limited cameras. In addition, the workload balance strategy of the system resource is addressed while running the caching resource scheduling policy.

The contributions of this paper are as follow. First, for obtaining the high reliability of streaming media uploading, we design a distributed caching system which adopts a server-slaves model. The server called the management server takes in charge of monitoring slaves' state. The slaves called the caching servers take in charge of connecting with cameras and caching streaming media data. Then, based on this caching system, we propose a caching resource scheduling approach achieving the better connection quality of video transmission. We characterize the factors which impact the caching server's stability as the failure ratio of server and the resource utilization. Based on the stability of the distributed caching servers, the management server schedules the connecting requests from the Internet cameras to the caching servers. Therefore, our scheduling approach can guarantee the workload balance among the caching servers and improve the reliability of streaming media uploading. Finally, we evaluate the performance of our caching approach through our testbed, and the experimental results validate the effectiveness of our approach.

The rest of this paper is organized as follow. In section 2, we propose a caching resource scheduling approach for reliable streaming media uploading. We conduct some experiments to validate our scheduling approach in section 3. In section 4, we conclude the paper.

2 A Novel Streaming Media Caching Resource Scheduling Approach

2.1 Overview

The service objects of data centers are usually the smart end users. That is to say the end users upload their local data to data center and collaborate with data center for data transmission. However, with development of IoT, the range of the data center's end users is expanded. For example, for some intelligent surveillance applications, the video data center needs to be connected with massive resource-limited Internet cameras. When the video generated by these Internet cameras is transmitted to data centers, the continuous media streaming may lead to poor uploading quality. To deal with these problems, we design a system in which streaming media caching resources are deployed at service providers to support multi-camera connections. Using a cluster can ensure an efficient data caching service when it confront massive streaming media. Then we propose a caching resource scheduling approach based on the distributed system to guarantee high camera connection quality and the system's reliability. On the other hand, each server in the cluster has its own work state which can be described through the server's failure ratio and server's resources usage. Here, the failure ratio is the proportion of the failure tasks to the total tasks of a server. A task's failure can be caused by task's bad running environment factors and some other reasons. Since a general data center uses block as a storage unit, data center selects a list of servers for every block belonging to the same file. The task we mentioned in this paper means the video data center responses the camera's request, caches streaming media and sends media data to storage node. Because this kind of task does not analyze the media data, the resource usage of this task are mainly bandwidth. Considering some quality requirements, the cluster should try to schedule servers with good state to cache streaming media. If some server fails down, the system must schedule another server to serve the previously connected cameras. Based on the above considerations, we design a distributed caching system to achieve high connection quality of cameras.

The problem can be stated as follows: How the unstable caching servers in this cluster can guarantee a reliable streaming media caching service and in the meanwhile keep the caching system's workload balance. Considering server state, this paper gives a solution based on a caching resources' scheduling approach: the good servers and the general servers should cache more streaming than bad ones. We call a caching server good server with a low task running failure percentage and have a low resource usage. On the contrary, the bad caching server is with a high task running failure percentage and a high resource usage. The general ones are between good servers and bad servers. For a better management of the caching servers, a management server is necessary in this distributed system. The management server takes in charge of scheduling the connection requests from Internet cameras to caching servers based on servers' states. The distributed caching system is illustrated in Fig. 1. It is a server-slave based architecture of streaming media caching system. This caching system is constituted

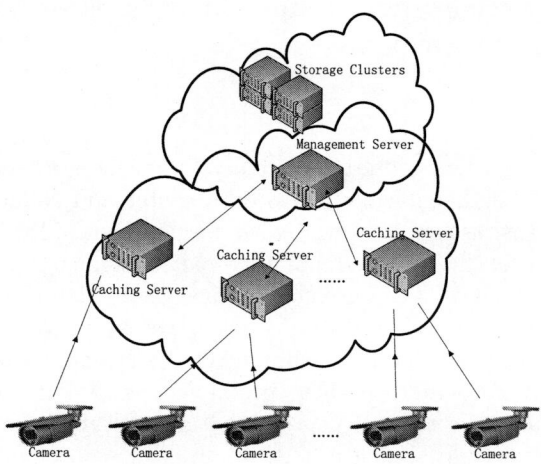

Fig. 1. Architecture of the caching system

by one manager server and many caching servers. Each caching server connects with several Internet cameras, and receives these camera media streams. At the meanwhile, every single caching server caches its own media streams and sends the caching data to the video data center. According to the management server's assignment which is based on each caching server's state, the new coming requests of the Internet cameras will be allocated to some of the caching servers in this system. The management server communicates with every caching servers, gets caching servers' states periodically and schedule the camera's connection requests. If a caching server stop reporting, the management server will consider this server fails down and will schedule another server to take over the failure server's caching work. A server's state weight will be used to measure the server's state. The management server manages all the caching servers in the cluster and calculates each server's state weight. Based on the servers' state weights, an appropriate strategy will be executed on the management server: Schedule a camera connection to a caching server or migrate a camera connection from one caching server to another. Fig. 2 shows the functional model of the system.

2.2   Work State Formulation

To schedule the cameras to a certain caching server, the management server need to know all the work states of caching servers. We propose a mathematic method to describe the working state of caching server. As mentioned before, the caching servers' resources which mainly comprise of servers' bandwidth and cache should be scheduled efficiently. And the server instability should be considered in the caching resource scheduling. The resource usage and the server instability should be qualified to help management server assign the caching resources. We use the server work state to measure the caching resource quality, we divide the server

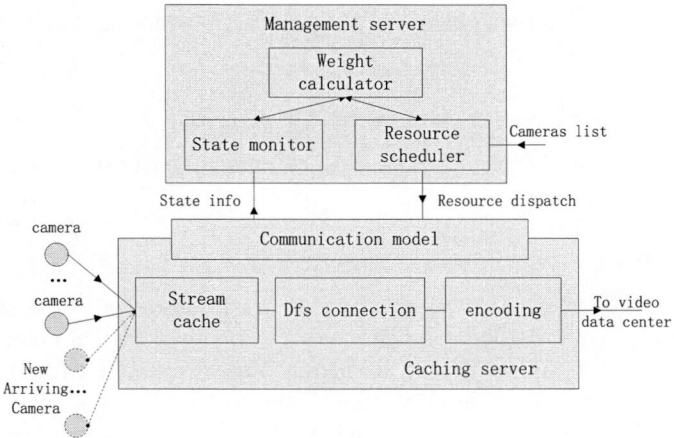

Fig. 2. Functional model of caching system

state into two parts: the server's stability and the server's resource usage. First, we use *failure ratio* α to describe the stability, which is given by

$$T_i = t_i + f_i, i \in (1, 2, \ldots, n). \tag{1}$$

$$\alpha_i = f_i/T_i, i \in (1, 2, \ldots, n). \tag{2}$$

where T_i is the number of tasks that have been finished by a caching server i. t_i is defined as the number of successful accomplished tasks on server i, and f_i is the number of failure tasks. α_i is the failure ratio of caching server i. n is the number of the caching servers. When a caching server restarts again, the failure ratio will be initialized to 0.

Second, we use the occupancy rate of the server resource to describe the *resource usage* β, which is given by

$$\beta_i = (r_1 + r_2 + \ldots + r_m)/R_i, i \in (1, 2, \ldots, n). \tag{3}$$

where β_i is the occupancy rate of caching server i. The whole resource of caching server i is quantified by R_i. $r_j, j \in (1, 2, \ldots, m)$ denotes the resource occupied by stream j which is cached by server i. And $\{r_1, r_2, \ldots, r_m\}$ is a vector that describes the resource occupying situation. In our experiments, $r_j, j \in (1, 2, \ldots, m)$ is mainly about a servers network bandwidth. Since we consider the cameras are homogeneous, the bandwidths of different cameras are nearly the same. And then we have the following equation

$$\beta_i = (r_1 + r_2 + \ldots + r_m)/R_i = m \times r_s/R_i, i \in (1, 2, \ldots, n). \tag{4}$$

where m is the number of streams of a caching server.

Finally, we define a value ω as a *server workload weight* to describe a caching servers work state. The weight of caching server i, which is denoted by ω_i, is given by

$$\omega_i = \alpha_i \times \beta_i = \alpha_i \times (r_1 + r_2 + \ldots + r_m)/R_i, i \in (1, 2, \ldots, n). \qquad (5)$$

and when the bandwidth occupied by each camera is nearly the same, ω is given by

$$\omega_i = \alpha_i \times \beta_i = \alpha_i \times m \times r_s/R_i, i \in (1, 2, \ldots, n). \qquad (6)$$

The above two equations can well describe the caching server's work state. Once a caching server is not at good condition or suffering overload, its weight is higher than the others. On the contrary, in this caching system, the lower a caching server's weight is, the better quality it has. The workload weight vector sorted in descending order can describe the global state of the distributed system. Then, by using this vector, the management server can decide which caching server can build up a connection with new coming camera. We will describe our resource scheduling policy in section 2.3.

2.3   Resource Scheduling Policy of Caching Servers

To schedule the caching resource in the proposed caching system efficiently, a resource scheduling policy of caching servers will be addressed. This policy has two parts: an assignment policy and a re-balance policy of caching resource. Both of the policies will use the server workload weight proposed above to schedule caching servers. In this paper, we assume all servers in cluster are with good condition at the start stage of the caching system running. The management server equally assigns cameras' connection requests to the caching servers. As the time goes by, the server's working state will be changed. And this is mainly caused by bandwidth consumption, certain task's failure, new tasks' adding, etc. In the caching server, all the storage resource can be used to cache streaming media. The number of cameras a server can connect with is depended on the server's bandwidth. The management server periodically calculate the workload weight vector $\hat{V} = \{\omega_1, \omega_2, \ldots, \omega_n\}$ of the caching servers. Based on the descending vector V sorted by $\hat{V}$, a scheduling decision will be made by management server.

When a new camera added in the assignment policy, the management server schedules low weight caching server i to cache the streaming media generated by that camera. When several caching servers have the same weight, the caching server with higher occupancy rate has the connection chance. That is to say the good condition server's bandwidth will be used first and then turn to allocate the higher failure ratio server's bandwidth. If the caching servers resource is exhausted, the management server does not allocate streams to it any more. And its weight item will be deleted from the vector V. This approach can achieve a high service quality.

However, the failing server and the new coming server will affect the actual running results and lead to workload imbalance. When the distributed caching system meet these conditions, a workload re-balance policy is needed. The re-balance policy concerns two aspects: failing server re-balance and new coming server re-balance. When some server in cluster fails down, the connected cameras need to be assigned to the other server. By periodically retrieving caching servers' state, the management server can find server failure and migrate non-connection cameras to other servers in time. And the server selection process is based on the caching server scheduling rules mentioned above.

On the other hand, with the cluster's scale expansion, the new coming servers will take part in the caching system. Workload imbalance will come out at that time. While the management server find a new caching server added in the cluster, an additional server re-balance policy will be triggered to migrate heavy workload from the bad server to the new server. For achieving a better quality of caching service, the distributed caching system should allocate streaming media's caching work to the servers whose work state is stable (lower failure ratio and lower bandwidth occupancy rate). According to such rules, when a new server are added into the cluster, the worse state servers' camera connections will be migrated to the new coming server until new server's resource run out. Considering this migration may lose critical video clips, the migration process should be performed at night or other time period in which less moving objects appear in the video.

3   Experimental Results

We evaluate our cache scheduling approach on a distributed caching system. We implement this distributed system based on Zookeeper [10] to coordinate servers in a cluster. Zookeeper is an open source centralized service that can enables highly reliable distributed coordination among servers in a cluster. In this cluster, znode servers, which are defined in Zookeeper, are classified into two classes: one is the management server and the others are the caching servers. We use Hadoop's HDFS as our data center's file system, which is an open source version of Google file system [18]. All the streaming media data cached in the caching servers will be stored in HDFS.

Two clusters are used in the experiments: a 5-server and a 10-server testbed on 4 physical servers. We deploy a group of virtual machines on the physical servers on the testbed. Each virtual machine has one 2.4GHz single-core CPU, 1GB DRAM and 60GB storage space. The OS installed on all virtual servers is Ubuntu 10.10. On the data center cluster, we use Hadoop 0.20.2 and Zookeeper 3.4.3 also. We use 55 Internet cameras to generate streaming media data. Each of the cameras has its IP and sends videos to the caching servers by HTTP protocol.

Workload Balance :
We first evaluate the performance of our scheduling approach on workload balance. We increase the number of connected cameras in caching system from 35 to 55. This shows the workload change of each server during the cameras adding process. Fig. 3 shows a workload experiment result. Each line in the figure represents the caching server's workload. The decimal of each line represents the

Table 1. 5-server testbed failure ratio

$server_i$	1	2	3	4	5
α_i	0.2	0.3	0.4	0.6	0.8

value of server failure ratio. Table 1 shows that the 5-server testbed's server id and its corresponding failure ratio. This cluster has one good server with failure ratio 0.2, two general servers whose failure ratio range from 0.3 to 0.6, and one bad server with failure ratio 0.8. Then we can conclude from the experimental result that a good server gets the most cameras and its upward trend is more obvious. The bad server's upward trend is relatively flat. This result also approve that the caching approach can guarantee system's stability requirement.

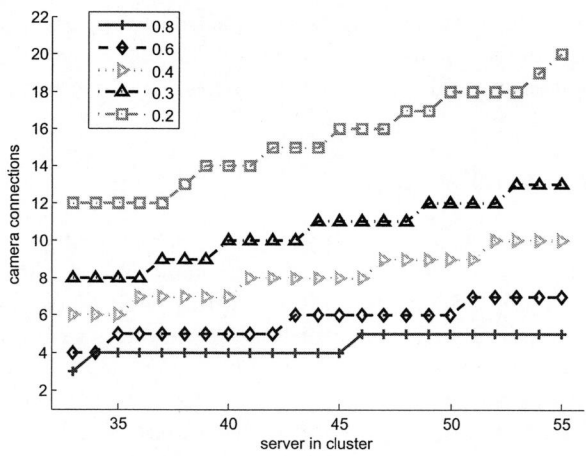

Fig. 3. Workload of caching servers in a 5-server cluster experiment

System Reliability :

In this subsection, we verify the reliability of our streaming media uploading approach. The experimental testbed is constituted by a 10-server cluster and 40 Internet cameras. We implement two caching strategies to compare caching system reliability in this cluster, one is the average allocation strategy which is a traditional resource scheduling strategy widely used in data centers and the other is our workload balance strategy. The average allocation strategy supposes that the cameras are equally allocated to each caching server without giving consideration on server's state. In this experiment, the scale of the system decreases from 10-server to 6-server, and the failure ratio of each server is shown in Table 2. We use the data storage percentage to evaluate system's camera connection quality and streaming media uploading reliability. The data storage percentage is

Table 2. 10-server testbed failure ratio

$server_i$	α_i	$server_i$	α_i
1	0.1	2	0.2
3	0.3	4	0.4
5	0.5	6	0.6
7	0.7	8	0.8
9	0.85	10	0.9

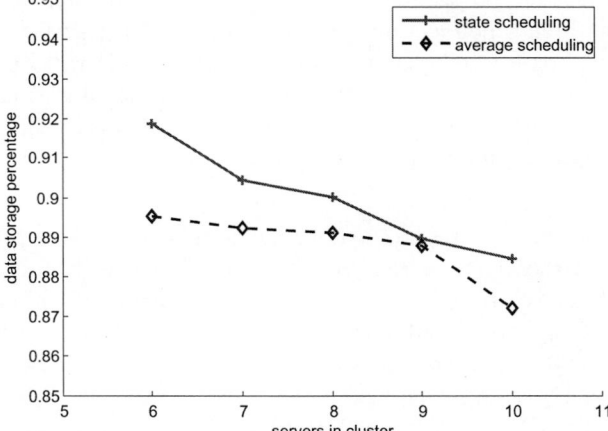

Fig. 4. Data storage percentage of caching system for different strategies in a 10-server testbed

given by the actual storage data in HDFS divided by total camera sending data. Fig. 4 respectively gives the experimental results in the cases of average allocation strategy and workload balance strategy. We observe that the average data storage percentage in both strategies are downward-sloping. Because we do not just add the good servers, some bad servers and general servers are added also. When the number of bad servers is reduced, for example in 6 servers cluster, the efficiency of the caching system is improved. In this experiment, the proposed workload balance strategy is always better than average allocation strategy on data storage, and this means more useful content will be stored in video data center.

Through conducting above two experiments, we show that the system can dynamically achieve a workload balance. The experimental results validate our caching resource scheduling approach can obtain high connection quality and system reliability too.

4   Conclusions

In this paper, we study the streaming media uploading problem in video data center. First, we design a distributed caching system which uses a server-slave model to obtain the high reliability of streaming media uploading. Second, through taking the caching server instability into account, a caching resource scheduling approach is proposed to achieve a better connection quality of video transmission. Our scheduling approach gives full consideration on the resource-limited cameras and the caching server instability. Third, some policies are presented in this scheduling approach to guarantee the workload balance among caching servers and improve the reliability of streaming media uploading. Finally, we evaluate the performance of our caching approach through the extensive experiments, and validate that the proposed caching scheduling approach can achieve the higher connection quality and the better system stability. For the future work, some intelligent video analysis functions will be added at the caching servers to reduce the system's response time to abnormal events. Online data analysis on the caching system can take advantage of the other idle resources, and can provide more useful IoT service.

Acknowledgment. The research reported in this paper is supported by the National Basic Research Program of China (973 Program) under grant No. 2011CB302701; The National Natural Science Foundation of China under Grant No. 60833009; China National Funds for Distinguished Young Scientists under Grant No. 60925010; The Co-sponsored Project of Beijing Committee of Education; Asia Foresight Program under NSFC Grant No. 61161140320; The Funds for Creative Research Groups of China under Grant No.61121001; The Program for Changjiang Scholars and Innovative Research Team in University under Grant No.IRT1049.

References

1. Armbrust, M., Fox, A., Griffith, R., Joseph, A.D., Katz, R., Konwinski, A., Lee, G., Patterson, D., Rabkin, A., Stoica, I., Zaharia, M.: Above the clouds: A Berkeley view of cloud computing, EECS Dept., Univ. California, Berkeley, No. UCB/EECS-2009-28 (2009), http://radlab.cs.berkeley.edu/
2. Buyya, R., Yeo, C.S., Venugopal, S.: Market-Oriented Cloud Computing: Vision, Hype, and Reality for Delivering IT Services as Computing Utilities. In: IEEE International Conference on High Performance Computing and Communications, pp. 5–13 (2008)
3. Buyya, R., Yeo, C.S., Venugopal, S., Broberg, J., Brandic, I.: Cloud computing and emerging IT platforms: Vision, hype, and reality for delivering computing as the 5th utility. Future Generation Computer Systems 25(6), 599–616 (2009)
4. Zhu, W., Luo, C., Wang, J., Li, S.: Multimedia Cloud Computing. IEEE Signal Processing Magazine 28(3), 59–69 (2011)
5. Reed, D.A., Gannon, D.B., Larus, J.R.: Imagining the Future: Thoughts on Computing. IEEE Computer Society 45(1), 25–30 (2012)

6. Wu, Y., Wu, C., Li, B., Qiu, X., Lau, F.C.M.: CloudMedia: When Cloud on Demand Meets Video on Demand. In: International Conference on Distributed Computing Systems, ICDCS, pp. 268–277 (2011)
7. Zhu, X., Pan, R., Dukkipati, N., Subramanian, V., Bonomi, F.: Layered Internet Video Engineering (LIVE): Network-Assisted Bandwidth Sharing and Transient Loss Protection for Scalable Video Streaming. In: INFOCOM, pp. 1–5 (2010)
8. Huang, Z., Mei, C., Li, L.E., Woo, T.: CloudStream: delivering high-quality streaming videos through a cloud-based SVC proxy. In: INFOCOM, pp. 201–205 (2011)
9. http://hadoop.apache.org/
10. http://zookeeper.apache.org/
11. Zhang, M., Wong, J., Tavanapong, W., Oh, J., de Groen, P.C.: Media uploading systems with hard deadlines. In: Proceedings of the IASTED International Conference on Internet and Multimedia Systems and Applications, pp. 305–310 (2004)
12. Zhang, M., Wong, J., Tavanapong, W.: Design and implementation of a media uploading system. Technical report. Department of Computer Science, Iowa State University (2005), http://archives.cs.iastate.edu/
13. Mu, Z., Johnny, W., Wallapak, T., Oh, J.: Deadline-constrained media uploading systems. Multimedia Tools and Applications 38(1), 51–74 (2008)
14. Dai, J., Li, B., Liu, F., Li, B., Liu, J.: Collaborative Caching for Video Streaming among Selfish Wireless Service Providers. In: Globecom, pp. 1–5 (2011)
15. Shuai, H., Yang, D., Cheng, W., Chen, M.: MobiUP: An Upsampling-Based System Architecture for High-Quality Video Streaming on Mobile Devices. IEEE Transactions on Multimedia 13(5), 1077–1091 (2011)
16. Jurca, D., Frossard, P.: Media Flow Rate Allocation in Multipath Networks. IEEE Transactions on Multimedia 9(6), 1227–1240 (2007)
17. Fujimoto, A., Hirota, Y., Tode, H., Murakami, K.: Parity Stream Construction Method Based on Estimated Utility for Multi-Server Video Streaming System. In: IEEE International Conference on Communications, ICC, pp. 1–5 (2011)
18. Ghemawat, S., Gobioff, H., Leung, S.: The Google file system. In: SOSP, pp. 29–43 (2003)

Fast Intra Prediction for High Efficiency Video Coding

Hao Zhang[1] and Zhan Ma[2]

[1] School of Information Science and Engineering
Central South University, Changsha, Hunan 410083 China
hao@csu.edu.cn
[2] Dallas Technology Lab
Samsung Electronics, Richardson, TX 75206 USA
zhan.ma@sta.samsung.com

Abstract. Emerging High Efficiency Video Coding (HEVC) video coding standard promises the significant compression performance improvement compared to the H.264/AVC. However it comes with the tremendous encoding complexity increase. Thus, it is very useful and necessary to develop fast algorithms for HEVC, so as to reduce the encoder complexity. In this paper, we propose a fast intra prediction scheme for HEVC to reduce the prediction mode search for each prediction unit. For all available test sequences provided by the JCT-VC, it demonstrates 38% encoding time reduction for *all intra* case with BD-RATE increase about 2.9%. Several sub-algorithms are developed and integrated for complexity reduction. First, we applied the Hadamard transform on 2:1 downsampled prediction residual to derive the sum of absolute Hadamard transformed difference (SATD) for rough mode decision, where a progressive search process is then used to reduce effective mode candidates for fully rate-distortion optimized quantization (RDOQ). Finally, an early termination based on SATD cost and mode distances is also included in RDOQ process to further complexity reduction. Extensive simulation results demonstrate that our proposed method is quite efficient for intra mode prediction speed-up. Our proposal is complementary to other separated works on fast coding unit, prediction unit, and transform unit decision. We expect more encoder complexity reduction by combing our solution and other fast algorithms.

Keywords: Fast Intra prediction, mode decision, High-efficiency video coding (HEVC).

1   Introduction

The emerging video coding standard HEVC [1], under the efforts of Joint Collaborative Team on Video Coding (JCT-VC), has achieved significant compression efficiency in comparison to the widely deployed H.264/AVC [2]. Although it is still under the block-based hybrid motion-compensation and transform coding

W. Lin et al. (Eds.): PCM 2012, LNCS 7674, pp. 568–577, 2012.

framework, HEVC is much more complex by introducing the recursive tree structure, large block transforms, advanced motion prediction, additional filtering operations and etc [1, 3, 4]. The *macroblock* concept has been extended by defining Coding Unit (CU), Prediction Unit (PU) and Transform Unit (TU). Starting from the largest CU (referred as LCU), each CU can be recursively split into multiple sub-CUs. Each leaf sub-CU can be further split into multiple PUs. For the intra case, both CU and PU are squared size with either one 2Nx2N block or 4 NxN sub-block after further splitting, $N \in [4, 8, 16, 32]$. Besides, recursive TU is also implemented on top of each PU for residual coding, which incurs more complexity requirement. Figure 1 gives the simple illustration for recursive CU, PU and TU adopted in HEVC. Please refer to [1] to more detailed description.

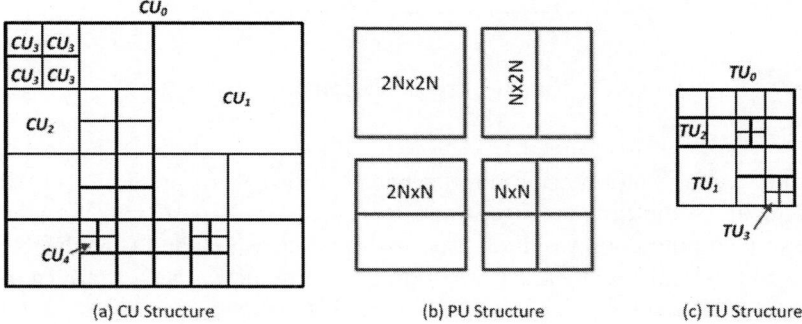

(a) CU Structure   (b) PU Structure   (c) TU Structure

Fig. 1. Recursive block structure for HEVC, where k indicates the depth for CU_k and TU_k

In addition to the complexity increase introduced by the recursive block structure of HEVC, the complexity is further augmented for intra prediction by using extended spatial prediction directions. As of the Draft 6 [1], there are 35 directional intra prediction candidates, where mode 0 is Planar mode, and mode 1 is DC mode, as shown in Figure 2. It requires unbearable computing resource to conduct full Rate-Distortion Optimized Quantization (RDOQ) for all these modes at different PU levels. In practise, a three-step mode decision process is adopted in the HEVC reference software HM [5]. First, a rough mode decision is performed to select a mode candidate set based on prediction residual SATD and estimated mode bits[1]. Reduced number of modes selected in the first stage are chosen for the normal computational intensive RDOQ to obtain the best prediction. Furthermore, recursive transforms are applied to the optimal mode from the first two stages for the residual coding to derive the final best coding mode. With such three-step encoding process optimization, overall intra coding complexity is partly reduced without noticeable quality loss. However, the complexity is still very high due to extensive modes search.

---

[1] In HM, 8x8 and 4x4 Hadamard transforms are applied.

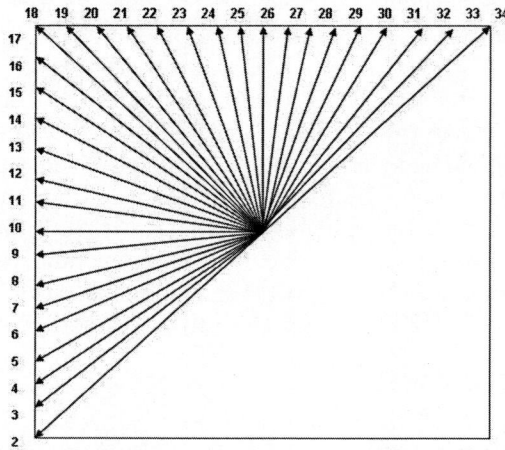

Fig. 2. Intra Prediction Modes

In this paper, we propose a novel scheme for fast intra prediction in HEVC, which includes multiple-stage optimization (i.e., Hadamard transform on 2:1 downsampled prediction residual, progressive mode search and early RDOQ termination), yielding significant intra coding time reduction at a sacrifice of negligible bit rate increase. The remainder of this paper is organized as follows. Section 2 gives a brief literature review of fast intra prediction methods developed for HEVC. Section 3 describes the proposed fast intra prediction mechanism. Section4 presents experimental results to demonstrate the effectiveness of the proposed solution. Finally, conclusion remarks and discussion are drawn in Section 5.

2   Fast Intra Mode Decision for HEVC: A Review

Fast intra mode decision (FIMD) has been extensively studied for H.264/AVC [6–17]. However, these algorithms can not be directly applied to HEVC due to quite different coding structures and prediction modes. Recently, a few fast intra mode decision (MD) algorithms are proposed for HEVC (some algorithms are proposed for both inter and intra MD). These works are briefed as follows.

In HEVC, residual quad-tree coding (RQT) is applied to further exploit the spatial correlation and improve the coding efficiency [1] by implementing recursive TU splitting. However, it demands significant computational overhead. Hence, Tan *et al.* proposed fast RQT algorithms for both intra and inter mode coding so as to reduce the complexity [18]. As reported using HM2.0, for all intra case, fast RQT saves 13% encoding time with 0.1% BD-Rate increase. For random access and low delay scenarios, proposed fast RQT algorithm reduces up to 9% encoding time at the expense of (up to) 0.3% BD-Rate performance degradation. Another RQT coding scheme is proposed by Teng *et al.* that replaces the original depth-first mode decision process by a Merge-and-Split decision process [19]. They propose to early terminate merge and split processes, i.e., when the current TU is a zero-block, no further split is performed any more. It reports almost 2x speedup for random access using High Efficiency configuration (for Class C and Class D non-HD sequences) on HM2.0, with negligible coding loss.

Meanwhile, Choi *et al.* have developed a tree pruning algorithm for fast coding unit decision, based on the observation that if the current CU chooses the SKIP mode as the best mode, then no further splitting is required [20]. This algorithm is implemented and reported on HM3.0 software, and claims 40% encoding time reduction. However, early SKIP mode decision does not apply to *all intra* case.

Zhao *et al.* studied the impact of the number of mode candidates after the rough mode decision [21]. Basically, proposed method tried to reduce the number of candidates for full RDOQ process. According to the experimental data, with a negligible loss of compression efficiency, it achieved 20% and 28% encoding time saving on average in High Efficiency and Low Complexity test conditions using HM1.0 reference software, respectively.

A gradient based FIMD is proposed by Jiang *et al.*, where gradient directions are calculated and histogram is generated, for CU size decision [22]. With this approach, 20% time savings on average is achieved with negligible loss of coding efficiency on HM4.0.

Shen *et al.* recently proposed a fast mode decision scheme based on Bayesian decision rule [23]. The split and non-split decision is made on the Bayesian risk, which can be calculated from the Lagrangian cost, the class-conditional probability density functions and priori probabilities. The feature vectors are calculated online while other parameters are calculated off-line. Random Access and Low Delay Configuration are used for simulations and on average 41.4% encoding time saving is reported.

Tian and Goto proposed a content adaptive FIMD based on texture complexity analysis and two mode filtering stages [24]. In the pre-stage, LCUs are firstly downsampled to 16x16 blocks, and texture complexity are calculated. The intuition is that when the complexity is less than some threshold, small PUs are not checked; otherwise large PUs are not checked. There are some other mechanisms to filter out small PUs when encoding the last 32x32, e.g., if the minimum PU sizes of its neighboring 32x32 CUs are the same (MxM), then the PUs sizes smaller than M will be skipped. The proposed algorithm achieves averagely 44.91% for 4kx2k sequences and 28.8% for 1080p sequences.

Most of the aforementioned algorithms are mainly focusing on early CU, or PU block size decision without requiring further split or merge process, while our scheme is developed to reduce the number of intra prediction modes at any

PU level. These algorithms are complementary to our proposal, which can be combined with our solution to achieve more speed up.

3   The Proposed Fast Intra Prediction Algorithm

Our proposed fast intra prediction method is composed of three major sub-algorithms, including Hadamard transform on 2:1 downsampled prediction residual, progressive mode search for rough mode decision and early RDOQ termination.

3.1   Hadamard Transform on Down-Sampled Residual

Given a NxN PU, its prediction residual is the difference between original signal and its predictor, noted as $r(i,j), i,j \in [0, N-1]$. We first apply the 2:1 down-sampling filter on residual signal using a very simple average operator as shown in Figure 3. On top of the down-sampled residual signal, we further perform the Hadamard transform to derive the corresponding SATD, where 4x4 and 2x2 block based Hadamard transforms are used instead of original 8x8 and 4x4 based transforms in HM. As we can see, for each available intra prediction modes, we will have different prediction residual as well as its SATD together with estimated mode bits consumption.

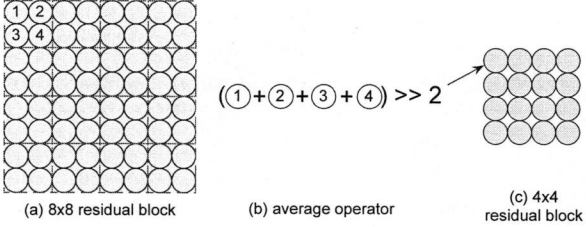

(a) 8x8 residual block   (b) average operator   (c) 4x4 residual block

Fig. 3. Illustration of simple averaging based downsampling on a 8x8 prediction residual block, other NxN blocks have the similar operation

3.2   Progressive Mode Search

Besides using Hadamard transform on down-sampled prediction residual, we also propose the *progressive mode search* for rough mode decision. Such idea is enlightened by the fast motion estimation (FME) process. For FME algorithms, such as three-step search or diamond search, locations with a large search range are examined first [25, 26]. When the best location at one step is found, it becomes the new search center for the next step. Usually the search range gets smaller at later steps and converges to the best location.

First, we define the difference between intra mode indices to represent distance between two modes. For instance, we call mode m_i is a d-distance neighbor of mode m_j if $|m_i - m_j| = d$. During the rough mode decision process, it checks equally spaced eight modes (i.e., two adjacent modes are of distance 4). For the best six modes (with least six SATD cost), check their adjacent modes that are of distance 2 with them. Last, check the adjacent modes of the best two modes that are of distance 1 with them as well as the selected modes from the above and left CUs. Each step, we maintain the ordered costs list and their corresponding intra prediction modes. It is very like the FME where the search range gradually decreased.

3.3 Early RDOQ Termination

After performing the rough mode decision, reduced number of prediction candidates, i.e., M modes with least costs, are categorized together as Ψ and go through the fully RDOQ process to decide the final best mode m_{opt}. Here, we propose an early RDOQ termination to further encoder time reduction. For each intra mode $m \in \Psi$, we derive its overall cost $J(m)$ as the combination of SATD cost ($C_{SATD}(m)$) and associated mode index bits consumption. Within Ψ, we can have the minimal J_{min} for a certain intra mode. Such mode is defined as *rough best mode* $m_{\text{opt\_rough}}$. If such *rough best mode* is Planar or DC mode, i.e., $m_{\text{opt\_rough}} = 0$ or 1, all other modes in Ψ will be skipped. Otherwise (i.e., $m_{\text{opt\_rough}} \neq 0$ or 1 , if $|m - m_{\text{opt\_rough}}| > 3$, such mode m is skipped also; Meanwhile, if $J(m) > \alpha J_{\text{min}}$, mode m will not be checked. In this paper, we have $\alpha = 1.2$. After such early termination procedure, all left modes will be checked by RDOQ.

3.4 Integrated Fast Intra Prediction and Illustrative Example

In this section, we integrate aforementioned sub-algorithms to form the proposed fast intra prediction method, as shown in Figure 4. Additionally, we also gives an illustrative example to clearly demonstrate this procedure.

1) Initially, S1 = {0, 1, 6, 10, 14, 18, 22, 26, 30, 34} are checked. Note that the distance between two modes are 4 except for mode 0 and 1. Suppose the best 6 modes as the result of this process are S2 = {0, 6, 10, 14, 18, 26}.
2) The 2-distance neighbors of mode 6, 10, 14, 18, 26 are {4, 8}, {8, 12},{12, 16},{16, 20},{24, 28}, respectively (we assume mode 0 and 1 do not have neighbors). The collection of 2-distance neighbors of S2 is S3 = {4, 8, 12, 16, 20, 24, 28}. Additionally, suppose the modes of upper and left PUs are S4 = {0, 4}. Check modes in S3 and S4.
3) Suppose the best 2 modes till now after checking S1, S2, S3, S4 are {4, 6}. The 1-distance neighbors of mode 4 and 6 are {3, 5}, {5, 7}, respectively. And hence S5 = {3, 5, 7} are checked.

```
for m = [0, 1, 2+4*i], 1≤i≤8
    // on down-sampled residual
    check J(m);
    Order J(m) in list Q;
end
// select best 6 modes from ordered Q
for m in Q₆
    if m ≠ 0, 1
        check J(m) for its 2-distance neighbors;
        update ordered Q;
    end
end
// check upper/left block mode
check J(m_upper) and J(m_left);
Update ordered Q;
// select best 2 modes from ordered Q
for m in Q₂
    if m ≠ 0, 1 check J(m) for its 1-distance neighbors;
        update ordered Q;
endend

// select candidates
Denote by n the number of modes in Q;
if 8x8, 4x4 prediction unit
    Select best min(n, 3) modes from Q as Ψ
else
    Select best min(n, 8) modes from Q as Ψ
end
```

(a) progressive rough
mode decision

```
for m in Ψ
    Find the m for corresponding minimal J
end

//pick the minimal J and its mode m_opt_rough
J_min = J(m_opt_rough);
α = 1.2;
if m_opt_rough = 0 , 1
    skip all other m;
else
    for m in Ψ
        if J(m) > α J_min
            skip mode m
        end
        if |m - m_opt_rough| > 3
            skip mode m;
        end
    end
end

// RDOQ for all left modes Ψ_new
// after early termination
for m in Ψ_new
    Find best mode m through RDOQ
end
```

(b) Early RDOQ
Termination

Fig. 4. Proposed Fast Intra Prediction Algorithm

4) Choose the best M modes as candidates for full RDOQ optimization after checking S1, S2, S3, S4, S5. If M = 3 and the best M modes till now is $\{4, 5, 6\}$. Suppose the minimum cost of these 3 modes is J_4, and if the cost of mode 5 is much larger than that of mode 4, i.e., $J_5 > \alpha J_4$, then mode 5 is not required to perform the full RD optimization. The same principle is followed for checking mode 6.

5) Follow the early termination process for the full RDOQ optimization as aforementioned. For those modes m which are not skipped, conventional RDOQ optimization is applied.

4   Experimental Results

This sections presents the experimental results with our proposed fast intra prediction, in comparison to the default HEVC encoding using HM6.0, following the common conditions defined in [27]. All intra encoder setting is simulated to demonstrate proposed algorithm. Class A (4Kx2K), B (1080p), C (WVGA), D (QWVGA) and E (720p) sequences are all used for performance verification. Results are shown in Table 1 with BD-Rate performance. In addition, Figure 5 illustrates four samples with their rate-distortion plots. On average, our proposed solution achieves 38% encoding time reduction for all intra coding with less than 3% BD-Rate increase.

Table 1. Coding efficiency and complexity reduction for proposed fast intra prediction on HM6.0

		Luma-Y	Chroma-U	Chroma-V
Class A	Traffic	2.5%	0.4%	0.4%
	PeopleOnStreet	2.8%	-0.4%	-0.2%
	Nebuta	0.8%	0.9%	0.6%
	SteamLocomotive	0.9%	0.5%	0.4%
Class B	Kimono	1.4%	0.4%	0.4%
	ParkScene	1.9%	-1.0%	-0.7%
	Cactus	2.6%	-0.1%	0.1%
	BasketballDrive	2.7%	0.0%	0.2%
	BQTerrace	2.3%	-0.7%	-1.3%
Class C	BasketballDrill	3.6%	0.3%	0.5%
	BQMall	3.9%	0.3%	0.4%
	PartyScene	3.7%	0.5%	0.5%
	RaceHorses	2.5%	0.1%	0.1%
Class D	BasketballPass	4.2%	1.0%	1.2%
	BQSquare	4.7%	0.7%	0.8%
	BlowingBubbles	4.4%	0.6%	0.4%
	RaceHorses	3.6%	0.9%	0.9%
Class E	FourPeople	3.4%	0.3%	0.3%
	Johnny	3.4%	0.5%	0.4%
	KristenAndSara	3.9%	0.8%	0.9%
	Overall	2.9%	0.5%	0.5%
	Enc Time[%]	62%		

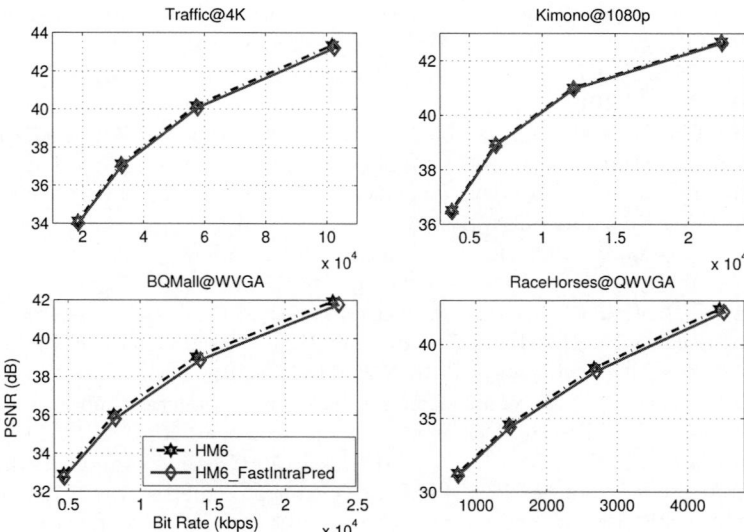

Fig. 5. Illustration of rate-distortion performance for proposed fast intra prediction

5   Conclusion

We propose a novel fast intra prediction approach in this paper. Compared with the reference software HM6.0, proposed algorithm leads to a great encoding speed improvement and negligible bitrate increment and PSNR loss. Our solution is trying to reduce the intra prediction modes at any PU level, therefore, other separated works as reviewed in Section 2 can be combined with our work to further boost the encoding speed. We also would like to open our source code [28] and welcome other researchers to use our code base for their research purpose. As the future study, we will work on inter mode prediction complexity reduction and present the combined fast intra/inter prediction for practical HEVC based video applications.

References

1. Bross, B., Han, W.-J., Ohm, J.-R., Sullivan, G., Wiegand, T.: High efficiency video coding (hevc) text specification draft 6. In: Doc. JCTVC-H1003_dK. Joint Collaborative Team on Video Coding (JCT-VC) of ITU-T SG16 WP3 and ISO/IEC JTC1/SC29/WG11 (2011)
2. Li, B., Sullivan, G.J., Xu, J.: Comparison of Compression Performance of HEVC Draft 6 with AVC High Profile. JCT-VC Doc. I0409r1 (2012)
3. Sullivan, G., Ohm, J.-R.: Recent developments in standardization of high efficiency video coding (HEVC). In: Proc. SPIE (2010)
4. Marpe, D., Schwarz, H., Bosse, S., Bross, B., Helle, P., Hinz, T., Kirchhoffer, H., Lakshman, H., Nguyen, T., Oudin, S., Siekmann, M., Suhring, K., Winken, M., Wiegand, T.: Video compression using nested quadtree structures, leaf merging and improved techniques for motion representation and entropy coding. IEEE Transactions on Circuits and Systems for Video Technology 20(10), 1676–1687 (2010)
5. Piao, Y., Min, J., Chen, J.: Encoder improvement of unified intra prediction. In: JCTVC-C207 (2010)
6. Pan, F., Lin, X., Rahardja, S., Lim, K.P., Li, Z.G., Wu, D., Wu, S.: Fast Mode Decision Algorithm for Intraprediction in H.264/AVC Video Coding. IEEE Transactions on Circuits and Systems for Video Technology 15(7), 813–822 (2005)
7. Kwon, S.-K., Punchihewa, A., Bailey, D., Kim, S.-W., Lee, J.: Adaptive simplification of prediction modes for H.264 intra-picture coding. IEEE Transactions on Circuits and Systems for Video Technology 58(1), 125–129 (2012)
8. Huang, Y.-H., Ou, T.-S., Chen, H.: Fast decision of block size, prediction mode, and intra block for H.264 intra prediction. IEEE Transactions on Circuits and Systems for Video Technology 20(8), 1122–1132 (2010)
9. Quan, D., Ho, Y.-S.: Categorization for fast intra prediction mode decision in H.264/AVC. IEEE Transactions on Consumer Electronics 56(2), 1049–1056 (2010)
10. Bharanitharan, K., Liu, B.-D., Yang, J.-F., Tsai, W.-C.: A low complexity detection of discrete cross differences for fast H.264/AVC intra prediction. IEEE Transactions on Circuits and Systems for Video Technology 10(7), 1250–1260 (2008)
11. Tseng, C.-H., Wang, H.-M., Yang, J.-F.: Enhanced intra-4 4 mode decision for H.264/AVC coders. IEEE Transactions on Circuits and Systems for Video Technology 16(8), 1127–1132 (2006)

12. Tsai, A.-C., Paul, A., Wang, J.-C., Yang, J.-F.: Intensity gradient technique for efficient intra-prediction in H.264/AVC. IEEE Transactions on Circuits and Systems for Video Technology 18(5), 694–698 (2008)
13. Zeng, H., Ma, K.-K., Cai, C.: Hierarchical intra mode decision for H.264/AVC. IEEE Transactions on Circuits and Systems for Video Technology 20(6), 907–912 (2010)
14. Kim, C., Shih, H.-H., Kuo, C.-C.J.: Fast H.264 intra-prediction mode selection using joint spatial and transform domain features. J. Vis. Commun. Image R. 17, 291–310 (2006)
15. Lee, J., Park, H.: A fast mode decision method based on motion cost and intra prediction cost for H.264/AVC. IEEE Transactions on Circuits and Systems for Video Technology 22(3), 393–402 (2012)
16. Kim, D.-Y., Han, K.-H., Lee, Y.-L.: Adaptive single-multiple prediction for H.264/AVC intra coding. IEEE Transactions on Circuits and Systems for Video Technology 20(4), 610–615 (2010)
17. Tsai, A.-C., Wang, J.-F., Yang, J.-F., Lin, W.-G.: Effective subblock-based and pixel-based fast direction detections for H.264 intra prediction. IEEE Transactions on Circuits and Systems for Video Technology 18(7), 975–982 (2008)
18. Tan, Y., Yeo, C., Tan, H., Li, Z.: On residual quad-tree coding in HEVC. In: IEEE International Workshop on Multimedia Signal Processing, MMSP (2011)
19. Teng, S.-W., Hang, H.-M., Chen, Y.-F.: Fast mode decision algorithm for residual quadtree coding in HEVC. In: The Visual Communications and Image Processing (VCIP) Conference (2011)
20. Choi, K., Jang, E.: Fast coding unit decision method based on coding tree pruning for high efficiency video coding. Opt. Eng. 51, 030502 (2012)
21. Zhao, L., Zhang, L., Ma, S., Zhao, D.: Fast mode decision algorithm for intra prediction in HEVC. In: The Visual Communications and Image Processing (VCIP) Conference (2011)
22. Jiang, W., Ma, H., Chen, Y.: Gradient based fast mode decision algorithm for intra prediction in HEVC. In: International Conference on Consumer Electronics, Communications and Networks, CECNet (2012)
23. Shen, X., Yu, L., Chen, J.: Fast coding unit size selection for HEVC based on bayesian decision rule. In: Picture Coding Symposium, PCS (2012)
24. Tian, G., Goto, S.: Content based hierarchical fast coding unit decision algorithm for HEVC. In: Picture Coding Symposium, PCS (2012)
25. Li, R., Zeng, B., Liou, M.: A new three-step search algorithm for block motion estimation. IEEE Transactions on Circuits and Systems for Video Technology 4(4), 438–442 (1994)
26. Zhu, S., Ma, K.: A new diamond search algorithm for fast block-matching motion estimation. IEEE Transactions on Image Processing 9(2), 287–290 (2000)
27. Bossen, F.: Common test conditions. JCT-VC Doc. I1100 (2012)
28. http://vision.poly.edu/~zma03/opensrc/sourceHM7.zip

A Low Complexity Multiplierless Transform Coding for HEVC[*]

Chunxiao Fan, Fu Li, Guangming Shi, Leilei Zhou, and Haizhou Yang

Key Laboratory of Intelligent Perception and Image Understanding (Chinese Ministry of Education), School of Electronic Engineering, Xidian University, Shaanxi, 710071, P.R. China
fuli@mail.xidian.edu.cn

Abstract. Transform coding with multiple blocks results in high complexity of HEVC. Butterfly combined with multipliers method provides an efficient implementation. However, the matrix multiplication is inevitable based on this method. In this paper, matrices and element decomposition are proposed to decompose the multiplication matrices into orthogonal matrices and general matrices with smaller elements. The number of different elements in these matrices can be reduced after decomposing, so that the multiplications can be reduced. Further, the decomposed elements become smaller and much closer to power of 2, which means we can use shifting and adding to achieve the multiplications conveniently. The proposed method is suitable for the hardware implementation.

Keywords: HEVC, Transform coding, DCT, DST, Multiplierless.

1 Introduction

With the development of image/video capture technologies, high definition (HD) video contents have been more and more practical in our daily life. However, the contradiction between the mass media data and the limited transmission channel drives us to develop a high efficient compression standard. In 2010, ISO/IEC and ITU-T joined together to call for the next-generation coding standard which has been known as the High Efficiency Video Coding (HEVC) [1].

The proposed standard is also made up of hybrid framework comparing with its former: prediction, transform and entropy coding [2]. There are three basic units in HEVC: coding unit (CU), prediction unit (PU) and transform unit (TU). CU is a basic coding unit which is similar to the macro block in H.264/AVC. In HEVC, the largest CU is 64×64 and the smallest CU is 8×8. PU is used for prediction. A CU can be recursively divided into four PUs. TU is defined for transform which comes from the further recursively spitting of PU. This splitting strategy establishes complex interactions among CU, PU and TU. Obviously, TU is with the largest scale in the three

---

[*] This work is supported by the NSFC (No. 61100155, 61033004, 61227004 and 61070138), the Fundamental Research Funds of the Central Universities of China (No. K50510020032).

W. Lin et al. (Eds.): PCM 2012, LNCS 7674, pp. 578–586, 2012.
© Springer-Verlag Berlin Heidelberg 2012

blocks. Meanwhile, the sizes of TU are variable from 4×4 to 32×32. Thus, designing a transform with low complexity for HEVC is desirable.

Several low complexity methods for video transform coding are introduced in recent years [3-5]. In [3], a low power and high speed DCT for image compression is proposed by optimizing 1D-DCT. A 16 points multiplierless 1-D DCT for HEVC standard is introduced in [4]. It is based on the replacement of multipliers with adders and shifters. [5] proposed an ICT (Integer Cosine Transform) algorithm to decompose the base matrices into several matrices which only contain smaller elements. However, most of these methods deal with the transform with stable block sizes or adopt the approximate transforms which result in low performance.

In this paper, we present a low complexity multiplierless transform coding for HEVC according to matrix and element decomposition. In order to remove the multipliers in transform coding, multiplication matrices are decomposed into orthogonal matrices and general matrices with smaller elements. The number of different elements in the decomposed matrices can be reduced after decomposing, so that the multiplications can be reduced. Meanwhile, the orthogonal matrix is made up of simple numbers. Most of the elements in the general matrix are closer to the power of 2. Thus the multipliers can be replaced by shifters and adders conveniently. The implementation results show that the proposed manner is suitable for hardware implementation.

The remainder of this paper is organized as follows: Section 2 gives the overview of the transform coding in HEVC. In Section 3, the low complexity multiplierless transform coding is proposed. The implementation results are illustrated in Section 4. We briefly conclude our work in Section 5.

2   Transform Coding in HEVC

As well known, two-dimensional (2-D) transform is fundamental to almost all video compression systems. The complexity of the 2-D transform can be reduced by using the row-column approach. This means it can be implemented by successive calling of 1-D transform with a transposition intermediately. The row-column approach is also adopted by HEVC. Thus, the design of a suitable 1-D transform is important.

In order to provide a closely performance to the Karhunen-Loeve transform (KLT), HEVC adopts two types of transform coding: DCT and DST. It supports 4×4, 8×8, 16×16, 32×32 DCT and 4×4 DST [6]. The 1-D DCT for each block is based on the butterfly combined with multipliers method, which can use fewer adders and multipliers [7]. However, with the property that the elements in base matrix are symmetric and elements in a smaller block are included in a larger one, even-odd method for the implementation of DCT transform is proposed [7-8]. Based on this method, 1-D DCT is implemented by the partial butterfly structure combined with matrix multiplications [8].

The butterfly structure can provide a high efficiency for the even order transform. The matrix multiplication structure performs a friendly implementation for the odd order transform. It can be achieved by the parallel processing with minimal dependency and control logic [8]. Thus, the partial butterfly combined with matrix multiplication method results in a high throughput. Meanwhile, the computing of the even order transform in a line of a block can re-use the circuit of the smaller block's transform. This means the larger block transform can share the same circuit with the smaller one. It can reduce the hardware utilization considerably. The detailed algorithm of the butterfly structure combined with matrix multiplication can be got from references [9].

3   Low Complexity Transform Coding

3.1   Motivation of the Proposed Method

In the partial butterfly combined with matrix multiplication approach, an 8×8 1-D transform needs 16 multipliers to get odd order results together in a line and re-use a 1-D 4×4 transform to get even order results in this line. 1-D 16×16 transform needs 64 multipliers to acquire odd order coefficients together in a line and multiplexes a 1-D 8×8 transform block for even order results in this line. Similarly, 1-D 32×32 block requires 256 multipliers to get odd order results together in a line and shares a 1-D 16×16 transform for the even order coefficients in the line. Obviously, there are many multipliers in transform that makes it becoming a bottleneck in HEVC considering the power consumption and the operation speed in VLSI design. Thus, reducing or replacing the multipliers is valuable.

As a classical fast algorithm for DCT transform based on the symmetry of the base matrix, butterfly structure has been proposed for many years. Actually, the nature of butterfly is decomposing the base matrix into several simple matrices by making use of the symmetry to reduce the number of adders and the multipliers. This reminds us that we can decompose a base matrix into several simple matrices. One of the matrices is also an orthogonal matrix with the elements made up of ± 1, 0 and ± 2 . The number of the different elements in the other matrices become fewer, the number of multiplications would be reduced. Besides, if we can guarantee, after decomposing, the elements in these matrices become smaller, they may more closer to power of 2 than the elements in the base matrix. This means replacing the multipliers by shifting and adding operations becomes possible. For example, an element a is 33, and its binary form is

$$a = (\underset{5}{1}0000\underset{0}{1})_2 \qquad (1)$$

The multiplication of $a \times N$ can be described as follows:

$$a \times N = N \ll 5 + N \qquad (2)$$

However, when the elements in base matrix are large, they may need much shifting and adding operation to accomplish multiplication. If the number of shifting and adding operation is different greatly among each element, these may cause imbalance of pipelines in hardware implementation. If we can decompose the original matrix into two matrices, the total operations of the shifting and adding could be divided into two stages. The imbalance can be released.

A modified integer cosine transform (MICT) by introducing the decomposition of the base matrix is proposed in [5]. The base matrix of MICT is get from the modification of the base matrix of IDCT according to the principle of symmetry. It makes every row of the base matrix in MICT orthogonal. So the MICT can be decomposed quite easily, and the elements in the base matrix can be represented by only 3 to 4 bits after decomposing. This decomposition method is feasible based on the condition that every row is orthogonal. However, the base matrix in HEVC is non-orthogonality. But the decomposition strategy provides an approach to us.

3.2 Proposed Algorithm for Matrix Decomposition

Based on the partial butterfly structure combined with matrix multiplication method, the (2N)×(2N) transform coding is implemented by calling of an N×N transform for odd order coefficients and using an N×N matrix multiplication for the even order coefficients. There are only N elements in the N×N multiplication matrix just with different orders and signs in each row considering the property of symmetry.

If we can decompose a matrix M into two matrices M_1 and M_2, M can be described as

$$M = M_1 \times M_2 \tag{3}$$

In this equation, there exists a sufficient condition:

$$\det(M) = \det(M_1) \times \det(M_2) \tag{4}$$

In view of the fact that the integer elements in M, M_1 and M_2 are very practical for DCT transform, $\det(M)$, $\det(M_1)$ and $\det(M_2)$ are also integers. According to equation (4), we can select a suitable $\det(M_1)$ and $\det(M_2)$ to decompose M quite easily. Here, we expect M_1 is made up of simple integers such as ± 1, 0, ± 2 because the multiplication can be implemented facilely by these integers. If M_1 has been decided, M_2 can be obtained as follows:

$$M_2 = M_1^{-1} \times M \tag{5}$$

In formula (5), if M_1 is a general matrix, the elements in M_1^{-1} may contain some decimals with long floating-points, which may lead M_2 including some non-integer elements. If every row in M_1 was orthogonal, every column in M_1^{-1} could be acquired conveniently, which can make insuring M_2 be an integer matrix become practicability.

Thus far, there are three conditions to decide the selection of matrix M_1: 1) the elements are made up of ± 1, 0, ± 2; 2) $\det(M_1)$; 3) orthogonal matrix. If M_1 with the low dimension, we can get it conveniently.

3.3   Proposed Algorithm for Element Decomposition

The matrix decomposition is shown in the subsection above. However, we can't guarantee to get the integer decomposition of M_1 and M_2 if M has high dimension. So, we propose a new algorithm which does not decompose the matrix, but only decompose the elements in the multiplication matrix.

As we have mentioned in subsection 3.2, there are N elements but with different signs and orders in each row. Therefore, we can decompose the N elements instead of the matrix decomposition. If these elements are decomposed by other smaller and fewer elements which are close to power of 2, the multiplication can be reduced and replaced. Suppose the N elements are a column vector L. The element decomposition is defined as follows:

$$L = P \times Q \tag{6}$$

where P is an N×N matrix, Q is a column vector. According to the purpose of element decomposition, Q must have smaller elements and some elements are same or equal to zero. This can reduce the number of multiplications. L has been known, Q can be obtained by

$$Q = P^{-1} \times L \tag{7}$$

This equation can be explained to find out an N points vector to make the projection of L on them are smaller. Obviously, one of the optimal solutions is acquired when the N points vector are orthogonal and have equal length.

From formula (6), we can get:

$$L^T \times L = Q^T \times P^T \times P \times Q \tag{8}$$

Considering the determinant, equation (8) can be described as follows:

$$\det(L^T \times L) = \det(Q^T \times P^T \times P \times Q) \tag{9}$$

L is a column vector, $\det(L^T \times L)$ is the L2-norm of L. Suppose $p_i (i=1...N)$ is the row of orthogonal matrix P and each p_i has the same length. $q_i (i=1...N)$ is the element in column vector Q. $P^T \times P$ is equal to an identity matrix multiplied by the length of p_i. Thus, from formula (9), we can obtain that:

$$length(L)^2 = length(Q)^2 \times length(p_i)^2 \tag{10}$$

According to formula (7) and (10), q_i can be acquired as follows:

$$q_i = p^{-1}_i \times L = p_i \,/\, length(p_i) \times L \tag{11}$$

where $p^{-1}_i (i=1...N)$ is one of the row in the inverse of P.

The procedure of the element decomposition is described as follows:

Step 1: Compute the length of L and decompose the square of it according to equation (10) to get the possible lengths of Q and p_i;

Step 2: Get the possible elements in p_i according to the length of it;

Step 3: According to equation (10) and the integer property of q_i, select some suitable p_i;

Step 4: Obtain an orthogonal matrix P with p_i;

Step 5: Get a suitable Q according to equation (11).

4   Implementation Results

As we have mentioned above, the matrix decomposition method is suitable for the multiplication matrix with low dimension, while the element decomposition is practical for the multiplication matrix with high dimension. In this paper, we decompose the base matrices in HEVC for testing. The 4×4 and 8×8 DCT transforms adopt the matrix decomposition. 16×16 and 32×32 DCT transforms use the element decomposition. 4×4 DST uses the element decomposition for its base matrix without the property of symmetry.

In 4×4 DCT of HEVC, the even order transforms in a line are acquired by shifting the results of the butterfly. The odd order transforms in it are obtained according to a 2×2 matrix multiplication. The 2×2 matrix can be decomposed as follows:

$$\begin{bmatrix} 83 & 36 \\ 36 & -83 \end{bmatrix} = \begin{bmatrix} 2 & -1 \\ -1 & -2 \end{bmatrix} \times \begin{bmatrix} 26 & 31 \\ -31 & 26 \end{bmatrix} \tag{12}$$

The even order results in a line of 8×8 DCT are achieved by calling of a 4×4 DCT. The odd order results of it are acquired by a 4×4 matrix multiplication. It can be decomposed as follows:

$$\begin{bmatrix} 89 & 75 & 50 & 18 \\ 75 & -18 & -89 & -50 \\ 50 & -89 & 18 & 75 \\ 18 & -50 & 75 & -89 \end{bmatrix} = \begin{bmatrix} -1 & 2 & & \\ & & -2 & -1 \\ & & -1 & 2 \\ -2 & -1 & & \end{bmatrix} \times \begin{bmatrix} -25 & 5 & -40 & 32 \\ 32 & 40 & 5 & 25 \\ -40 & 25 & 32 & 5 \\ 5 & -32 & 25 & 40 \end{bmatrix} \tag{13}$$

From equation (12) and (13), we can find that the multiplication matrix can be decomposed into an orthogonal matrix and a matrix with smaller elements. These elements are closer to the power of 2 than they are in the original multiplication matrix.

In 16×16 DCT of HEVC, the even order results in a line can be obtained according to share the 8×8 DCT. The odd order coefficients in a line are acquired by an 8×8 matrix multiplication. We decompose the 8 elements in this matrix by the element decomposition method. The decomposition result is shown as follows:

$$
\begin{bmatrix} 90 \\ 87 \\ 80 \\ 70 \\ 57 \\ 43 \\ 25 \\ 9 \end{bmatrix} = \begin{bmatrix} 2 & 2 & -1 & 2 & & & & \\ -2 & 2 & & & 1 & 2 & & \\ 1 & & 2 & & 2 & & 2 & \\ & & & & 2 & -1 & -2 & 2 \\ & 1 & 2 & -2 & & & & 2 \\ -2 & & & 2 & -2 & 1 & & \\ & & 2 & 1 & & & -2 & -2 \\ & 2 & & -2 & -2 & & & -1 \end{bmatrix} \times \begin{bmatrix} 0 \\ 33 \\ 18 \\ 21 \\ 21 \\ 0 \\ 1 \\ 15 \end{bmatrix} \tag{14}
$$

The even order results in a line of 32×32 DCT are achieved by calling of a 16×16 DCT. The odd order results of it are obtained by a 16×16 matrix multiplication. The 16 elements in this matrix can be decomposed as follows:

$$
\begin{bmatrix} 90 \\ 90 \\ 88 \\ 85 \\ 82 \\ 78 \\ 73 \\ 67 \\ 61 \\ 54 \\ 46 \\ 38 \\ 31 \\ 22 \\ 13 \\ 4 \end{bmatrix} = \begin{bmatrix} & & & & & 1 & 1 & & & & & & \\ & & & 1 & & & & 1 & & & & & \\ & & 1 & & & & & & 1 & & & & \\ & & & & 1 & 1 & & & & & & & \\ & 1 & & & & & & & & 1 & & & \\ 1 & & & & & & & & & 1 & & & \\ & & & 1 & & & & 1 & & & & & \\ & 1 & & & & & & & 1 & & & & \\ & 1 & & & & & & & & -1 & & & \\ 1 & & & & & & & & & -1 & & & \\ & 1 & & & & & & & -1 & & & & \\ & & 1 & & & & & -1 & & & & & \\ & & & 1 & & & -1 & & & & & & \\ & 1 & & & & & & -1 & & & & & \\ & & & 1 & -1 & & & & & & & & \\ & & & 1 & -1 & & & & & & & & \end{bmatrix} \times \begin{bmatrix} 1 & 1 & -1 & & & & & & \\ -1 & 1 & & 1 & & & & & \\ 1 & & 1 & 1 & & & & & \\ & & & & 1 & -1 & 1 & & \\ 1 & 1 & -1 & & & & & & \\ & & & 1 & 1 & & 1 & & \\ & & & -1 & & 1 & 1 & & \\ & & & 1 & 1 & -1 & & & \\ & & & & & 1 & 1 & 1 & \\ & & & & & & 1 & 1 & 1 \\ & & 1 & -1 & & & & & 1 \\ & & 1 & & & -1 & 1 & & \\ & & & -1 & 1 & & 1 & & \\ & & 1 & -1 & & & & 1 & \\ & & & 1 & -1 & 1 & & & \\ & & & -1 & 1 & 1 & & & \end{bmatrix} \times \begin{bmatrix} 22 \\ 62 \\ 18 \\ 24 \\ 22 \\ 12 \\ 53 \\ 18 \\ 34 \\ 9 \\ 0 \\ 9 \\ 18 \\ 9 \\ 9 \\ 12 \end{bmatrix} \tag{15}
$$

The elements in 4×4 DST can be processed by element decomposition method. The implementation results are shown as follows:

$$
\begin{bmatrix} 84 \\ 74 \\ 55 \\ 29 \end{bmatrix} = \begin{bmatrix} 1 & & & 1 \\ -1 & & & 1 \\ & 1 & 1 & \\ & -1 & 1 & \end{bmatrix} \times \begin{bmatrix} -1 & -1 & 1 & \\ -1 & 1 & & -1 \\ 1 & & 1 & -1 \\ & 1 & 1 & 1 \end{bmatrix} \times \begin{bmatrix} 8 \\ 29 \\ 42 \\ 8 \end{bmatrix} \tag{16}
$$

From equation (14) to equation (16), we can find that some elements become same or zero after the decomposition. This can reduce the number of multiplication considerably. Furthermore, these elements in the multiplication matrix can be replaced by adders and shifters conveniently because they are close to power of 2. Here, we notice that the element decomposition in equation (15) and equation (16) have two orthogonal matrices because the determinants of them can be decomposed into three numbers.

Either the matrix decomposition method or the element decomposition method, the elements in the decomposed matrix or the decomposed column vector are smaller than the elements in the original multiplication matrix. Table 1 shows the detailed translation of these elements in multiplication to shift and addition (subtraction can be achieved by addition). Obviously, the decomposed elements can be described by the shift and addition instead of the multiplication conveniently.

Table 2 shows the complexities of the transform for the odd order results in a line by original matrix multiplication and the decomposition method. After the decomposition, the number of multipliers is reduced. Furthermore, we can achieve the multipliless transform by shifting and adding operation. The number of the adders and shifters for variable blocks by multipliless method is also shown in Table 2. Obviously, all the multipliers are replaced by adders and shifters.

Table 1. Translation of the elements in multiplication to shift and addition

Transform	Coefficients	Shift-add(+: Sums / - : Subtractions)						
		64	32	16	8	4	2	1
		<<6	<<5	<<4	<<3	<<2	<<1	keep
4×4DCT	31		+					-
	26			+	+		+	
4×4DST	42		+		+		+	
	29		+				-	-
	8				+			
8×8DCT	40		+		+			
	32		+					
	25			+	+			+
	5					+		+
16×16DCT	33		+					+
	21			+		+		+
	18			+			+	
	15			+				-
	1							+
32×32DCT	62	+					-	
	53		+	+		+		+
	34		+				+	
	24			+	+			
	22			+		+	+	
	18			+			+	
	12				+	+		
	9				+			+

Table 2. Comparison the complexities

	original		Decomposed			Multipliless	
	multiply	add	multiply	shift	add	shift	add
4×4 DCT	4	2	4	2	4	10	10
4×4 DST	15	11	12	0	33	24	49
8×8 DCT	16	12	16	4	16	28	32
16×16 DCT	64	56	32	144	128	192	160
32×32 DCT	256	240	112	0	656	240	816

5 Conclusion

In this paper, we proposed a low complexity transform coding for HEVC. The multiplication matrices in the butterfly combined with multipliers method are decomposed by the matrices decomposition and element decomposition method. The multiplication matrices can be decomposed into orthogonal matrices and matrices with smaller elements. These elements can be replaced by shift and addition conveniently to achieve a multipliless transform for variable blocks in HEVC. The proposed method is suitable for the hardware implementation.

References

1. Joint Collaborative Team: Video Coding, Test Model Under Consideration. JCTVC-A205, Dresden, Germany, April 15-23 (2010)
2. Joint Collaborative Team: Video Coding, High Efficiency Video Coding (HEVC) text specification draft 6. JCTVC-H1003, Geneva, Switzerland, November 21-30 (2011)
3. Aakif, M., Belkouch, S., Chabini, N., Hassani, M.: Low Power and Fast DCT Architecture Using Multiplier-Less Method. In: Proc. IEEE on Faible Tension Faible Consommation, pp. 63–66. IEEE Press, Marrakech (2011)
4. Jose, C.S., Gustavo, W., Ruhan, C., Mateus, G., Julio, M., Luciano, A.: Low Cost and High Throughput Multiplierless Design of a 16 Point 1-D DCT of the New HEVC Video Coding Standard. In: 2012 VIII Southern Conference on Programmable Logic, pp. 1–6. IEEE Press, Bento Gonçalve (2012)
5. Dong, J., Ngan, K.N., Fong, C.K., Cham, W.K.: 2-D Order-16 Integer Transforms for HD Video Coding. IEEE Transactions on Circuits and Systems for Video Technology 19(10), 1462–1474 (2009)
6. Saxena, Fernandes: Mode dependent DCT/DST for intra prediction in block-based image/video coding. In: 2011 18th IEEE International Conference on Image Processing, pp. 1685–1688. IEEE Press, Brussels (2011)
7. Chen, W.H., Smith, C., Fralick, S.: A Fast Computational Algorithm for the Discrete Cosine Transform. IEEE Transactions on Communications 25(9), 1004–1009 (1977)
8. Gong, D., He, Y., Cao, Z.: New cost-effective VLSI implementation of a 2-D discrete cosine transform and its inverse. IEEE Transactions on Circuits and Systems for Video Technology 14(4), 405–415 (2004)
9. Fuldseth, A., Bjøntegaard, G., Sadafale, M., Budagavi, M.: Transform Design for HEVC with 16 Bit Intermediate Data Representation, JCTVC-E243, Geneva, Switzerland, March 16-23 (2011)

Efficient DSP Implementation of Fractional-Pixel Interpolation for AVS[*]

Zhigang Yang, Shuhong Jiao, and Lutao Liu

College of Information and Communication, Harbin Engineering University,
Harbin 150001, China
{zgyang,jiaoshuhong,liulutao}@hrbeu.edu.cn

Abstract. Fractional-pixel motion compensation can greatly improve the compressing efficiency in video coding, while quarter-pixel interpolation also leads to a significant increment in computational complexity. This paper presents some techniques for efficient implementation of quarter-pixel interpolation in AVS-P2 on a fix-point digital signal processor (DSP). Firstly, the whole interpolation process is divided into five sub-processes from the DSP-oriented viewpoint. Then highly parallel software pipelines are designed for each sub-process with elaborately balancing the resources on each side of the CPU data path. A task-level optimization strategy is also applied to arrange the software pipelines. Finally, the simulated results demonstrate that the execution time of interpolation can be greatly reduced by using this specific design.

Keywords: Interpolation, digital signal processors, AVS, video coding.

1 Introduction

The transform and motion compensation hybrid coding framework is commonly adopted in state-of-the-art video coding standards such as H.264 [1] and AVS [2]. The accuracy of motion compensation is a key technique in this coding scheme. As a real motion has arbitrary precision, enabling motion vectors to have fractional-pixel resolution can greatly improve the prediction accuracy. Half-pixel motion vector accuracy has already been used in prior standards like MPEG-2. Quarter-pixel interpolation is first found in MPEG-4 (Advanced Simple Profile) and then improved in the development process of modern standards H.264 and AVS. In H.264, a 6-tap filter is used for half-pixel interpolation. In AVS-P2, 4-tap filters are used for both half- and quarter-pixel interpolation.

Motion compensation with fractional-pixel accuracy can progressively reduce spatial redundancy as the level of fractional-pixel accuracy increases. Half-pixel motion vector resolution can provide a coding gain of about 2.7dB when compared to

---

[*] This work was supported in part by the National Natural Science Foundation of China under Grant Number 61201238 and 61201410, and the Fundamental Research Funds for the Central Universities under Grant Number HEUCFR1017.

integer-pixel resolution, and an additional coding gain of about 0.9dB can be obtained with quarter-pixel motion vector resolution [3]. Some adaptive interpolation techniques also studied to further improve the prediction efficiency [4][5].

However, fractional-pixel interpolation also leads to a significant increase in computational complexity. Some VLSI architectures have been presented to solve the problem. For example, R. Wang *et al.* proposed a parallel and pipeline architecture for the sub-pixel interpolation filter in H.264/AVC [6], and L. Lu. *et al.* presented a reconfigurable sub-pixel interpolation architecture for motion estimation [7]. While on DSP platform, the optimizing methods adopted in VLSI architectures are usually inefficient for DSP pipelines and always lead to worse DSP performance.

The purpose of this paper is to provide a DSP solution to accelerate the interpolation process for AVS-P2, mainly at the encoder side. The rest of this paper is organized as follows. In Section 2, the luma sample interpolation in AVS-P2 is briefly introduced. In Section 3, the luma interpolation process is divided into five software pipelines, and then instruction-level pipelines on the DSP platform are designed in detail. Software pipelines are also arranged from a task-level viewpoint. In Section 4, simulated results are demonstrated to show the effectiveness of the specific design. Finally Section 5 concludes the paper.

2   Luma Sample Interpolation

In Fig. 1, the positions labeled with upper-case letters represent luma samples at full sample locations and the positions labeled with lower-case letters represent luma samples at fractional sample locations. Given the luma samples 'A' to 'L' at full sample locations, the luma samples 'a' to 's' at fractional sample positions are derived by the following rules.

- The luma prediction value at half sample position labeled as 'b' shall be derived by applying a 4-tap filter with tap values (-1, 5, 5, -1) in the horizontal direction.
- The luma prediction values at half sample positions labeled as 'h' and 'j' shall be derived by applying a 4-tap filter with tap values (-1, 5, 5, -1) in the vertical direction.
- The luma prediction values at quarter sample positions labeled as 'a', 'c', 'i', and 'k', shall be derived by applying a 4-tap filter with tap values (1, 7, 7, 1) in the horizontal direction..
- The luma prediction values at quarter sample positions labeled as 'd', 'f', 'n', and 'q', shall be derived by applying a 4-tap filter with tap values (1, 7, 7, 1) in the vertical direction.
- The luma prediction values at quarter sample positions labeled as 'e', 'g', 'p', and 'r' shall be derived by averaging samples at full and half sample positions in the cross direction.

The detailed process for each fractional position is described in the AVS-P2 standard [2].

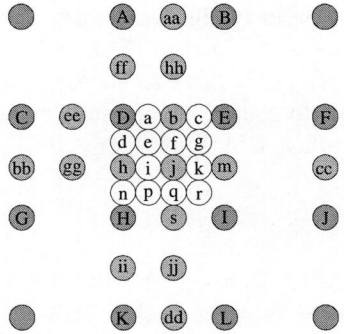

Fig. 1. Integer samples (upper-case letters) and fractional samples (lower-case letters) for quarter sample luma interpolation

3   DSP Pipeline Design

Our work is based on a very long instruction word (VLIW) fixed-point DSP, TI TMS320C6455 [8]. A brief introduction to the DSP instruction set and the CPU data paths would help to ease the understanding of the specific design.

3.1   DSP Architecture

DSP has a powerful instruction set. Many enhanced instructions in assembly language can deal with multiple data in parallel. Properly choosing the enhanced instructions can bring a great increment for pipeline efficiency. As shown in Fig. 2, the CPU in the DSP has two similar data paths (A/B), and each data path mainly consists of 32 register files and 4 functional units. More detailed information of this kind of DSP can be found in [9].

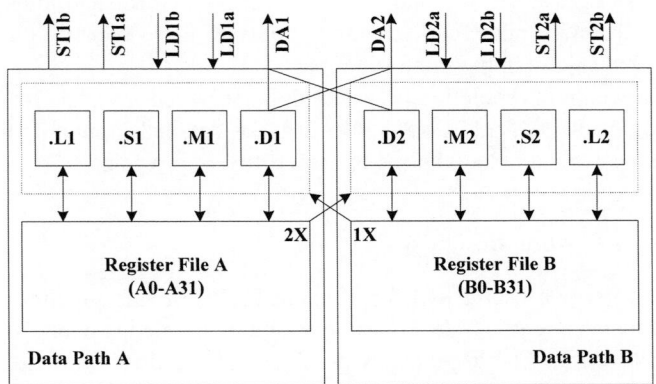

Fig. 2. CPU Data Paths

Parallelism is the key to extremely high performance. As for this architecture, high parallelism is achieved by software pipelines. There are total eight functional units in CPU, so in a single clock cycle, CPU can execute a maximum of eight instructions in parallel, reaching its peak performance. To design high parallel software pipelines is one of the most important parts in DSP applications.

3.2   Process Division

As shown in Fig. 1, half samples 'b' and 'h' are directly related with integer samples, while half sample 'j' is derived by 'b' or 'h'. Quarter samples closely depend on both integer and half samples. So it is not efficient to build up only one pipeline for the whole process. The whole process need to be divided into several parts and then pipelines are designed for each part.

Firstly, the samples from the same fractional position are stored together. So it turns to be sixteen images, including one integer-pixel image (at position "D"), three half-pixel images (at position "b", "h", and "j"), and twelve quarter-pixel images (at position "a", "c", "d", "e", "f", "g", "i", "k", "n", "p", "q", and "r"). The integer-pixel image is the original source data, and the rest fractional-pixel images are to be interpolated. In addition, one row of pixels is set as a macro process unit.

Then according to the fractional type (half / quarter), the interpolation filter direction (horizontal / vertical / cross), and data reuse strategy, the whole interpolation process is divided into seven sub-processes:

    (1) Half horizontal interpolation at position 'b';
    (2) Half vertical interpolation at positions 'h' and 'j';
    (3) Quarter horizontal interpolation at positions 'a' and 'c';
    (4) Quarter horizontal interpolation at positions 'i' and 'k';
    (5) Quarter vertical interpolation at positions 'd' and 'n';
    (6) Quarter vertical interpolation at positions 'f' and 'q';
    (7) Quarter cross interpolation at positions 'e', 'g', 'p' and 'r'.

Furthermore, sub-processes (3) and (4) are similar in form and function, so one pipeline with different inputs can separately apply to these two sub-processes. Sub-processes (5) and (6) are in the same situation.

Finally, the whole interpolation process can be achieved by total five pipelines, as summarized in Table 1. And Table 1 also lists the detailed input/output samples on both CPU data paths in the loop kernel of each software pipeline.

3.3   Software Pipeline Design

Dependency graph is a useful tool for efficient DSP software pipeline design. Each node in the dependency graph denotes an operand, and an edge connecting the nodes denotes an instruction. The dependency graph can also indicate how to allocate data paths. The basic rule of drawing a dependency graph is that all the resources on each side of CPU data path should be balanced.

Table 1. Loop kernel statistics of each software pipeline

idx	type/dir	pos	A side	B side	A side	B side
	Loop kernel		Input		Output	
1	HalfHor	b	8 integer samples	8 integer samples	8 half samples at 'b'	8 half samples at 'b'
2	HalfVet	h j	8*4 integer samples	8*4 half samples at 'b'	8 half samples at 'h'	8 half samples at 'j'
3	QuaHor	a c	8 integer samples	8 half samples at 'b'	8 qua samples at 'a'	8 qua samples at 'c'
		i k	8 half samples at 'h'	8 half samples at 'j'	8 qua samples at 'i'	8 qua samples at 'k'
4	QuaVet	d n	8*2 integer samples 4 half samples at 'h'	8*2 half samples at 'h' 4 half samples at 'h'	8 qua samples at 'd'	8 qua samples at 'n'
		f q	8*2 half samples at 'b' 4 half samples at 'j'	8*2 half samples at 'j' 4 half samples at 'j'	8 qua samples at 'f'	8 qua samples at 'q'
5	QuaCross	e g p r	8*2 integer samples	8 half samples at 'j'	8 qua samples at 'e' 8 qua samples at 'g'	8 qua samples at 'p' 8 qua samples at 'r'

For further explanation, we set half horizontal interpolation at position 'b' as an illustrative instance. The dependency graph of the luma sample interpolation at position 'b' is shown in Fig. 3, and the detailed process is described as follows.

Layer 1: Loading integer samples from the memory.
On A side, one LDNDW instructions is used to load eight input integer samples 2-9, stored in a 32-bit register pair "int_9876 : int_5432". The previous four samples are reserved from the last loop, stored in a 32-bit register "int1_10n1n2" On B side, the previous four samples stored in "int_9876' " are copied from A side, and other processes are similar.

Layer 2: Repacking integer samples.
On A side, the PACKLH2, SHRMB and SHLMB instructions are used to repack the loaded integer samples into different 4-sample (32-bit) registers, including "int_210n1", "int_3210", "int_4321", "int_6543", "int_7654", and "int_8765". On B side, the processes are similar.

Layer 3: Performing 4-tap filter.
On A side, the DOTPUS4 instruction is used to perform the 4-tap filter (-1, 5, 5, -1). The temporary results "half_0", "half_1", …, and "half_7" are stored in different 32-bit registers. On B side, the processes are similar.

Layer 4: Producing filtered results.
On A side, two 32-bit temporary values are packed into one 32-bit register by the PACK2 instruction, such as "half_10", "half_32", "half_54", and "half_76". Then the

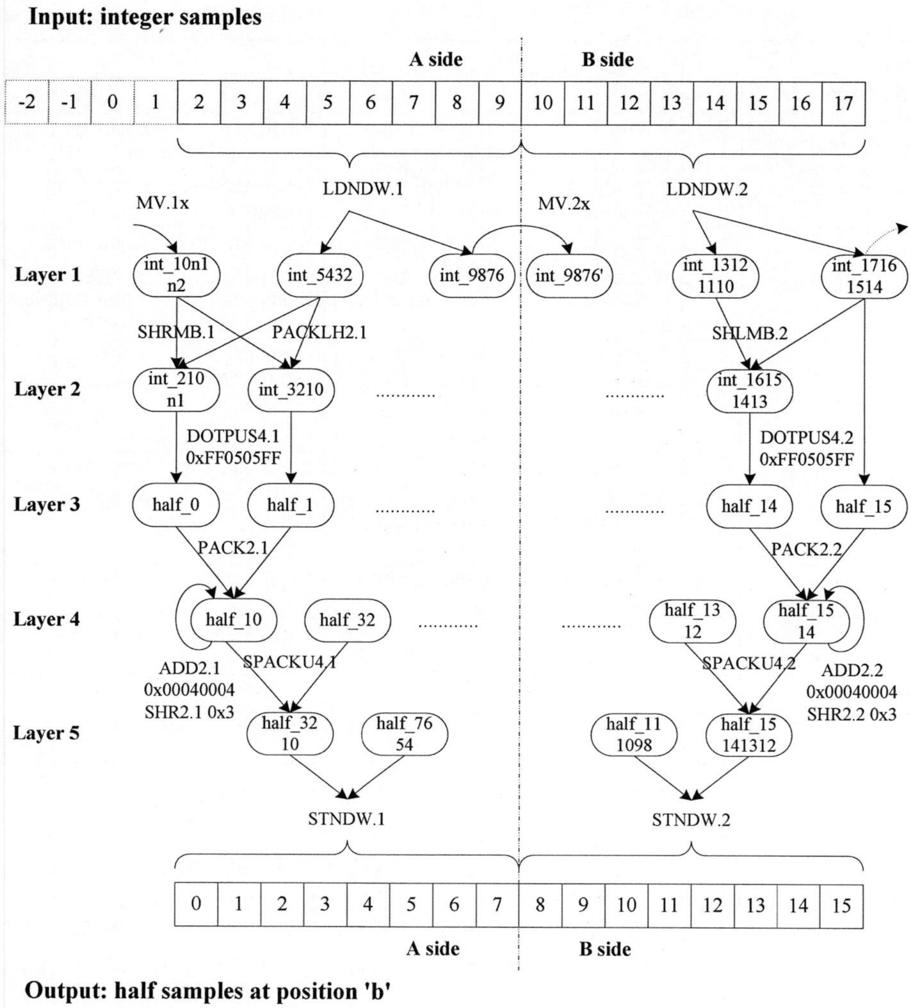

Input: integer samples

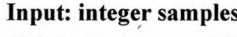

Fig. 3. Dependency graph of the luma sample interpolation at position 'b'. Note that the dependency graph corresponds to the loop kernel of the software pipeline, and some similar parts are omitted to make the whole graph clear, including the processing flows of packed values of 'half_32', 'half_1312', 'half_7654', and 'half_15141312'.

two packed 16-bit temporary values in one 32-bit register can be together bounded by the ADD2 and SHR2 instructions. On B side, the processes are similar.

Layer 5: Packing and saving half samples.

On A side, the SPACKPU4 instruction saturates four 16-bit values to four 8-bit values as final results. The STNDW instruction is used to store eight half samples "half_7654 : half_3210" into memory. On B side, the processes are similar.

Following the above guide line from the dependency graph, a pipeline has been built up for horizontal interpolation at position 'b'. Other software pipelines listed in Table 1 can also be achieved in the similar way.

3.4   Software Pipeline Arrangement

In the previous section, the luma interpolation process is accelerated from the aspect of instruction-level parallelism. While in this section, a task-level optimization strategy is to be applied.

As mentioned in Section 3.2, the samples from the same fractional position are stored together, contributing to sixteen separated images. Furthermore, each image is padded with extra 16 pixels on every side. Therefore, sixteen (16+720+16) * (16+576+16) images will be outputted when interpolating a 720*576 image. One row of pixels is set as a macro process unit, corresponding to one of the five software pipelines listed in Table 1.

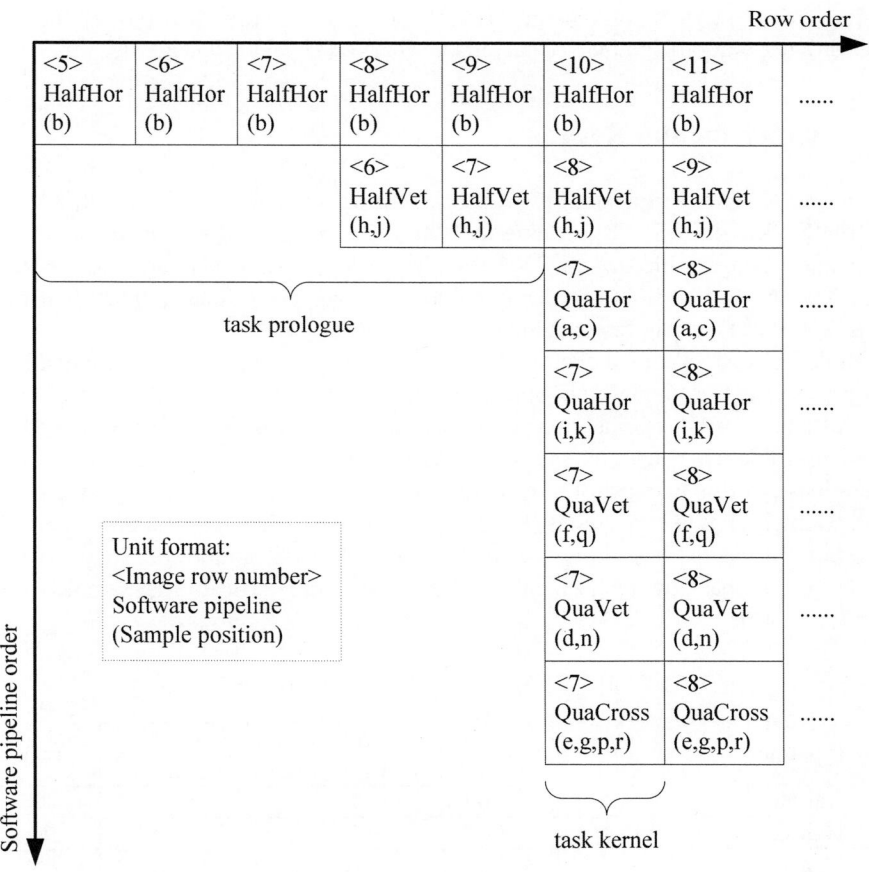

Fig. 4. Software pipeline arrangement

The software pipeline arrangement is shown in Fig. 4. The execution order is up-to-down (software pipeline order) and then left-to-right (row number order). In addition, quarter-sample interpolation is started from the 7th row of the padded image to ease the whole control and data transfer,.

The task prologue shown in Fig. 4 consists of software pipelines "HalfHor(b)" from 5th to 9th rows and "HalfVet(h,j)" from 6th to 7th rows. As shown in Fig. 1, four samples 'aa', 'b', 's', and 'dd' in the vertical direction should be calculated in advance to get the prediction values of half sample 'j'. So the software pipeline "HalfHor(b)" was firstly performed four times from the 5th to 8th rows before the software pipeline "HalfVet(h,j)" as shown in Fig. 4. In the same way, four samples 'b', 'j', 's', and 'jj' in the vertical direction should be calculated in advance to get the prediction values of quarter sample 'q', so the software pipeline "HalfVet(h,j)" was performed three times from the 6th to 8th rows before the software pipeline "QuaVet(f,q)" as shown in Fig. 4.

The task kernel shown in Fig. 4 consists of all the software pipelines listed in Table 1. The half horizontal interpolation pipeline "HalfHor()" is performed two rows ahead of the vertical interpolation pipeline "HalfVet()", and three rows ahead of all the other quarter interpolation pipelines "QuaHor()", "QuaVet()", and "QuaCross()".

4   Experimental Results

In the following experiments, SD (720*576) format sequence is tested with AVS-P2 on TMS320C6455 DSP [8] running at 1GHz. The image pad-size is 16 pixels. For each input image with size of 720*576, the output is sixteen images with size of (16+720+16) * (16+576+16), including one integer-pixel image, three half-pixel images, and twelve quarter-pixel images.

Table 2 lists the detailed cycle statistics of the software pipelines, corresponding to those in Table 1. Although the pipeline of quarter cross interpolation at position 'e', 'g', 'p' and 'r' produces the largest number of output samples (32 samples per loop, listed in Table 1), it has the shortest 5-cycle loop kernel. This is because its filter operations are simple, most of which are averaging two samples. The pipeline of half vertical interpolation at positions 'h' and 'j' has the longest 12-cycle loop kernel. This is because it has the largest number of input samples (64 samples per loop, listed in Table 1) and repacking the horizontal-order samples into vertical-order samples needs some extra time.

Table 2. Cycle Statistics of Each Software Pipeline

Pipeline	Loop Kernel	Loop Count	Prolog Epilog	Function Call	Total
HalfHor	8	46	34	6	408
HalfVet	12	94	7	6	1141
QuaHor	9	93	16	6	859
QuaVet	11	94	10	6	1050
QuaCross	5	93	14	6	485

Table 3 lists the overall interpolation time per image under different optimization strategies. Using the original C code without any optimization, the running time of interpolating a 720*576 image into sixteen (16+720+16) * (16+576+16) images is about 1720 ms. After enabling compiler optimization option -O3, the running time is shorten to 530 ms, which means that compiler optimization accelerates the interpolation process by a factor of about 3. After using some techniques, e.g. loop combination and DSP intrinsic instructions, the interpolation time is reduced to 130 ms. S. Hu *et al.* presented some optimization methods by using linear assembly and DMA, and the processing time is 18.2 ms [10]. According to Table 3, the overall interpolation time under the proposed optimization scheme is only 7.3 ms, the least among all strategies, further demonstrating the effectiveness of the specific design.

Table 3. Overall Interpolation Time Statistics under Different Optimization Strategies

	Optimization strategies	Time per image
1	Original C code, no optimization	1720 ms
2	Original C code, -O3 option	530 ms
3	Refined C code	130 ms
4	Linear assembly, DMA [10]	18.2 ms
5	Proposed	7.3 ms

5   Conclusions

This paper provides some optimization techniques to accelerate the quarter-pixel interpolation in AVS-P2 on a VLIW DSP platform. In order to design efficient software pipelines, the whole interpolation process is divided into five sub-processes according to the fractional type, filter direction, and data reuse rules. Then highly parallel software pipelines are achieved with carefully choosing instructions and elaborately balancing all the resources on each side of the CPU data path. Besides the instruction-level optimization, software pipelines are also arranged from a task-level viewpoint. Experimental results show that the proposed techniques can greatly reduce the execution time of interpolation.

References

1. Draft ITU-T recommendation and final draft international standard of joint video specification (ITU-T Rec. H.264/ISO/IEC 14 496-10 AVC). JVT of MPEG and VCEG, JVTG050 (2003)
2. Final draft of information technology – advanced coding of audio and video – part 2: video. AVS workgroup Doc. N1214, Shanghai, China (September 2005)
3. Hill, P.R., Chiew, T.K., Bull, D.R., Canagarajah, C.N.: Interpolation Free Subpixel Accuracy Motion Estimation. IEEE Transactions on Circuits and Systems for Video Technology 16(12), 1519–1526 (2006)
4. Vatis, Y., Ostermann, J.: Adaptive Interpolation Filter for H.264/AVC. IEEE Transactions on Circuits and Systems for Video Technology 19(2), 179–192 (2009)

5. Wedi, T.: Adaptive interpolation filters and high-resolution displacements for video coding. IEEE Transactions on Circuits and Systems for Video Technology 16(4), 484–491 (2006)
6. Wang, R., Li, M., Li, J., Zhang, Y.: High Throughput and Low Memory Access Sub-pixel Interpolation Architecture for H.264/AVC HDTV Decoder. IEEE Transactions on Consumer Electronics 51(3), 1006–1013 (2005)
7. Lu, L., McCanny, J.V., Sezer, S.: Subpixel Interpolation Architecture for Multistandard Video Motion Estimation. IEEE Transactions on Circuits and Systems for Video Technology 19(12), 1897–1901 (2009)
8. TMS320C6455 Fixed-Point Digital Signal Processor, SPRS276L, Texas Instruments (May 2005)
9. TMS320C64x/C64x+ DSP CPU and Instruction Set Reference Guide, SPRU732J, Texas Instruments (July 2010)
10. Hu, S., Zhang, X., Yang, Z.: Efficient Implementation of Interpolation for AVS. In: International Congress on Image and Signal Processing, pp. 133–138 (2008)

Audio-Based Copy Detection in the Large-Scale Internet Videos

Hongliang Bai[1], Lezi Wang[2], Chong Huang[2], Wei Liu[1], Chengbin Zeng[1],
and Yuan Dong[1,2]

[1] France Telecom Research & Development - Beijing, 100190, P.R. China
[2] Beijing University of Posts and Telecommunications,100876, P.R. China
{hongliang.bai,wei.liu,chengbin.zeng,yuan.dong}@orange.com,
{wanglezi.bupt,huangchong661100}@gmail.com

Abstract. With the large-scale internet video data explosion, the content-based copy detection (CCD) related application and research are significant and necessary. Beside the image-based CCD, the audio-based method has the advantage in its simpleness and efficiency. The article improves the recent methods on the audio-based copy detection. Three improvements are introduced in the study. Firstly, the CEPS-like feature is proposed to satisfy the different audio scale requirements in the feature extraction. Then, the flexible hash-based searching algorithm is presented to strengthen the querying robustness. Finally, the results-based fusion is introduced to take the advantages of the different features. The actual NDCR performances of the balanced profile vary in 0.223~0.460 in the TRECVID2011 copy detection database. The results outperform any single feature.

Keywords: CCD, CEPS-like, Flexible Searching, Fusion, TRECVID.

1 Introduction

With the growth of images and videos in the internet, the retrieving requirement from users has increased enormously. They can record videos or take photos by the mobile phones, video camcorders, or directly download from the video webs, and then distribute them with some modifications. More than 13 million hours of video were uploaded during 2010 and 35 hours of video are uploaded every minute, and YouTube reached over 700 billion playbacks in 2010 [5]. Among these huge volumes of images and videos, the large number of them are duplicate or near duplicate.

Based on a sample of 24 popular queries from YouTube, Google Video and Yahoo! Video, on average there are 27% redundant videos which are duplicate or nearly duplicate to the most popular version of a video in the search results [12]. Nearly 30% videos are duplicated in one-day Orangesport videos[1]. Users always feel frustrated when they see many duplicate sequences and don't find what

---

[1] http://sports.orange.fr/

W. Lin et al. (Eds.): PCM 2012, LNCS 7674, pp. 597–604, 2012.
© Springer-Verlag Berlin Heidelberg 2012

they are interested. So the copy detection is one of very important techniques to retrieve and delete the videos. It also can reduce the large disk storage for the video website.

The video and audio information can be used to implement the copy detection. The audio-based methods can well solve the difficulty, especially when the audio information is consistent with the variable video frames. The audio-based copy detection is to find the corresponding copy sequences of one query from the video database, and the query maybe have different compression style, and mix with speech. Usually, the framework is composed by preprocessing, feature extraction, searching engine and postprocessing.

For the feature extraction, a Weighted Audio Spectrum Flatness (WASF) is presented to extend the MPEG-7 descriptor-ASF by introducing human auditory system functions to weight audio data [1]. The feature is robust to several audio transformations, but tuning the parameters is one hard work. The HAAR filters are influenced by the training data [8]. Mel-Frequency Cepstral Coefficients (MFCC) is a feature used in the speech recognition and copy detection [7]. Energy Differences Feature (EDF) is widely used in [3,4,11], and the good performance is achieved in the large-scale video database. However, EDF can only consider one scale property of the frequency. For the video retrieving, the hash function [2] is used for the accurate searching with the higher efficiency. But, the hash-based searching can not deal with the near duplicate audio clips. Locality-Sensitive Hashing (LSH) [6] is not suitable in the low-dimensional audio feature space.

So three improvements have been introduced to solve the above problems in the study. The system framework is described in Section 2. The multi-scale audio feature extraction is proposed in Section 3. Section 4 presents the flexible Hash-based retrieval algorithm. The fusion of searching results is introduced in Section 5. Section 6 shows some experimental results as well as its limitation. Finally, the conclusions and future works are listed.

2   System Overview

In this section, the audio-based copy detection system framework is introduced in Fig. 1. Firstly, the querying audio signal is separated from the videos. Then the audio signal is processed by the Butterworth and Hamming window filtering. After the Fast Fourier Transform (FFT) analysis, the 17 sub frequent bands are selected in the mel-frequency space. 16-bit EDF and 16-bit CEPS-like feature are extracted respectively. The two types of features are used to query in the reference database. The different searching results from the above features are fusioned finally.

3   Feature Extraction

3.1   Butterworth and Hamming Window Filtering

In the reference video database from the internet, the audio' sampling rates vary in a large range. The first step is to normalize the sampling rates into a constant

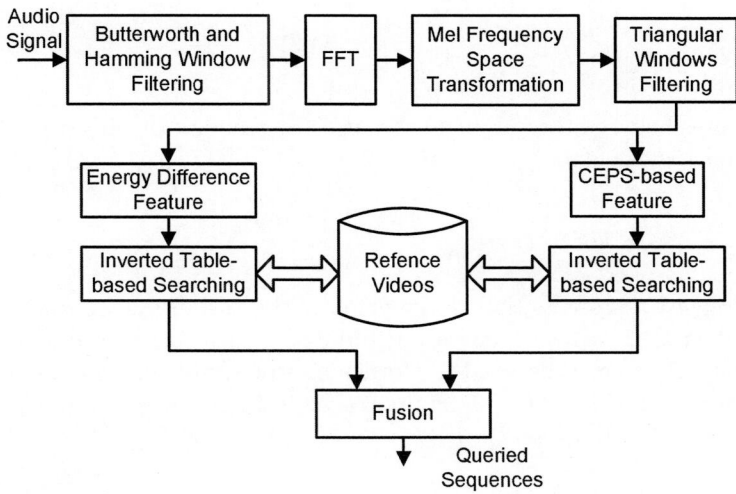

Fig. 1. Audio-based copy detection system framework

value F_N, here F_N is set 44100 Hz. Then the normalized signals S are lowpass filtered to 4000 Hz by a Butterworth filter. The magnitude-squared response of a N-order analog lowpass Butterworth filter is $|\mathbf{H}(j\Omega)|^2 = 1/(1 + (\Omega/\Omega_c)^{2N})$, where the cutoff frequency Ω_c is 3dB. Through the filter, the top 100 coefficients are used to convolve with S in the time domain.

Then the hamming window filtering is applied to every frame in order to keep the continuity of the first and the last points in the frame before FFT. The hamming window filtering is $\mathbf{H}(i) = 0.54 - 0.46 * \cos{(2\pi i/(N-1))}$, where N is the sample number in each frame and set 2048. The inter overlapping is 1024 samples $(23.2ms)$.

3.2   FFT and Mel-frequency Space Transformation

After the Hamming window filtering, the 1-D audio signals are transformed into 2-D spectrograms by FFT. The spectrum between 300 Hz and 4000 Hz is equally divided into 17 sub bands in the mel-frequency space. The mel-frequency can reflect similar effects in the human's subjective aural perception. The relation of the mel-frequency and natural frequency is $Mel(f) = 2595 * \log{(f/700 + 1)}$, where f is the natural frequency.

3.3   Energy Difference Feature

A triangular filtering is used in the magnitude frequency response to compute the energy of each sub band. The number of the filters is equal to that of the sub bands. The coefficients of the filter are defined by

$$w(n) = \begin{cases} \frac{2n}{N-1} & n = 0, 1, ..., \frac{N-1}{2} \\ 2 - \frac{2n}{N-1} & n = \frac{N-1}{2}, ..., N-1 \end{cases} \quad (1)$$

EDF features between the sub-bands are used to generate the fingerprint of each frame, which is calculated by Equation 2.

$$EF_n(m) = \begin{cases} 1 & EB_n(m) > EB_n(m+1) \\ 0 & otherwise \end{cases} \quad (2)$$

where $EB_n(m)$ represents the energy value of the n-th frame at the m-th sub-band, and $m \in [1 \cdots 16]$. The 15-bit and 32-bit fingerprints are used in [3,4] respectively. After considering the storage size of *short int* and robustness of the searching algorithm, the 16-bit fingerprint $EF_n(m)$ is selected. The feature is demonstrated in the Fig. 2(a).

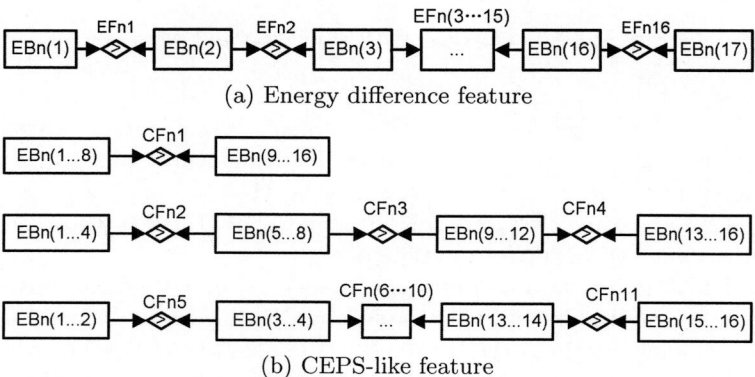

(a) Energy difference feature

(b) CEPS-like feature

Fig. 2. Extraction of two types of audio features, which describe the energy property of the different scales

3.4   CEPS-Like Feature

The cepstrum is the information about the rate of the change in the different spectrum bands and the result of taking Fourier Transform (FT) of the log spectrum. The EDF feature only considers the energy difference in the low level. The CEPS-like feature is proposed to combine the multi-scale energies into one feature.

In Fig.2(b), $CF_n(1)$ is the highest-scale feature, which used all information of 16 sub bands. $CF_n(2 \cdots 4)$ are in the second level and the difference of four adjacent sub bands. $CF_n(5 \cdots 11)$ are in the third level. $CF_n(12 \cdots 16)$ are the same with $EF_n(1), EF_n(4), EF_n(7), EF_n(10)$ and $EF_n(13)$ respectively. $EB_n(m_1 \cdots m_2)$ is the energy sum from the m_1-th sub band to the m_2-th sub band.

4   Flexible Hash-Based Searching

The hash-based searching is a very important and widely used technology. The searching performance is improved by two aspects: (1)one-bit modification in the hash matching. If the hamming distant of a querying and reference feature is one, they are regarded as a matching pair; (2)matching time can tolerate some time errors because of the frame losing or noise interference. The above algorithms can improve the searching flexibility.

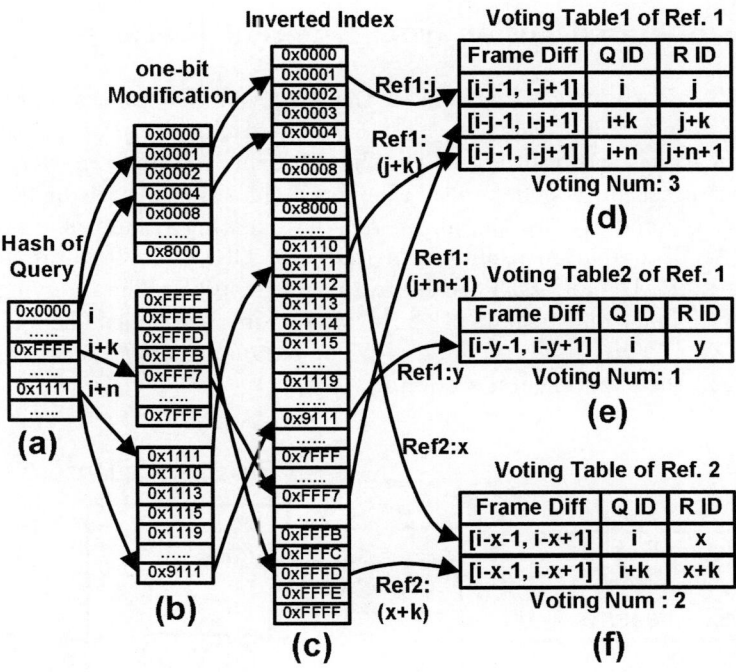

Fig. 3. Flexible hash-based searching with one-bit modification and time redundance

Fig. 3 demonstrates the audio fingerprint matching strategy. Fig. 3(a) shows the sequence of hash values in a querying clip. And Fig. 3(b) can make the hash matching more robust by modification of any one bit of a hash value. Seventeen different values are generated for a 16-bit feature. These modified hash values are matched with the ones from reference data in the inverted index table, shown in Fig. 3(c). The voting tables are used in references, which is related to the matched hash values from the inverted table. The voting number are the hitting values in some time difference between indexes of the matched reference and querying. The voting strategy is illustrated in Fig. 3(d)(e)(f). The largest voting results N_{vote}(Voting Number 3) occurs in Fig. 3(d). The time duration of the queried sequence is $[j, j + n + 1]$ in the reference database.

$$N_{vote} \triangleq \arg\max_{\tau} \sum_{r,q \in N} \delta(\tau - |r - q|) \tag{3}$$

where r and q are the time indexes of the matching sequence of the querying and reference. If N_{vote} is greater than the predefined threshold T, the queried reference sequences will be regarded as the querying results.

5   Result-Based Fusion from Different Features

The fusion algorithm can be used in the stages of the feature extraction or searching results. The fusion of the searching results are proposed from the different features, shown in Fig. 4. For the retrieving results from every feature, the higher precision is generated if the threshold T is set with higher values. In Fig. 4, G_1 and G_2 are the above reliable querying results, and G_3 is the logical "AND" operation results from EDF and CEPS-like features. Both the advantages of EDF and CEPS-like are taken in the G_3. The querying results are more reliable if the outputs of above two features are same. The final results are the logical "OR" of G_1, G_2 and G_3. The parameters TH_1 and TH_2 will be discussed in the experimental section.

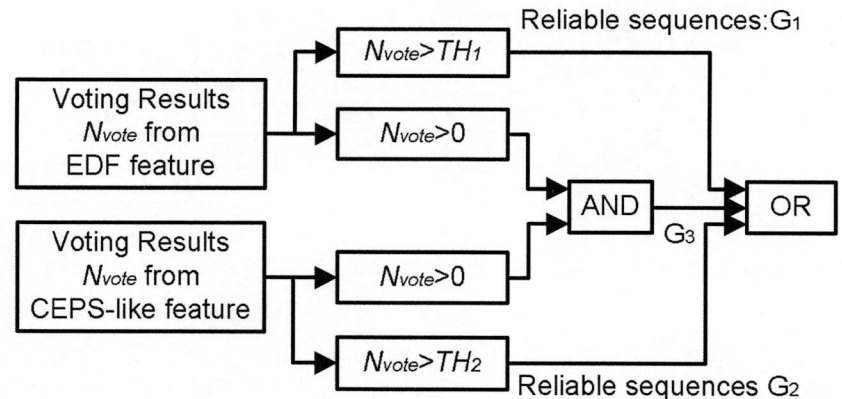

Fig. 4. Fusion of the searching results from EDF and CEPS-like features

6   Experiments

In this section, the experiments are conducted to demonstrate the effectiveness of the proposed method.

6.1   Database Description

TRECVID [10] has a well-known CCD task. The reference data is identical to 400 hours and 12000 files in the 2011 test and training data. Each query has 8-type video and 7-type audio transformations. In the audio-related task, the original audio clips are transformed into the following seven types, namely, ($T1$) do "nothing"; ($T2$) mp3 compression; ($T3$) mp3 compression and multiband companding; ($T4$) bandwidth limit and single-band companding; ($T5$) mix with speech; ($T6$) mix with speech, then multiband compress; ($T7$) bandpass filter, mix with speech, compress. Many evaluation metrics are used in the CCD task. Normalized Detection Cost Rate (NDCR) is defined in following

$$NDCR = P_{miss} + \beta.R_{FA} \tag{4}$$

where P_{miss} and R_{FA} are the conditional probability of a missed copy and the false alarm rate respectively, and β is profile related.

6.2   Parameter Selection and System Performance

In the audio-based copy detection system, the parameters TH_1 and TH_2 are main parameters, which can influence the system performance. After the parameters are trained from TRECVID CCD 2010 training and testing data, then they are used in the TRECVID CCD 2011 testing data. The performances of the balanced profile are shown in Table 1 after the different values has been selected. In the tables, EF-10 means the threshold TH_1 is set 10 for the EDF feature, and CF-15 means the threshold TH_2 is set 15 for the CEPS-like feature.

For the NDCR metric, the best performance of EDF-based querying is 0.338 in the transform $T1$, and that of CEPS-like-based querying is 0.576. After the fusion , the NDCR is improved to 0.233, which is better than any of features querying results. In the most complex transform $T7$, the performance is also improved from 0.577 and 0.515 to 0.323.

The comparison has also been done with other groups submitted into the TRECVID CCD 2011. Only INRIA-LEAR submitted their audio-only detection

Table 1. Actual NDCR of the different TH_1 and TH_2, and the fusion results from different features

	T1	T2	T3	T4	T5	T6	T7
EF-10	1.837	1.623	1.501	1.562	0.973	0.698	0.943
EF-22	**0.338**	**0.454**	**0.454**	**0.385**	**0.485**	**0.500**	**0.577**
EF-30	0.377	0.485	0.569	0.438	0.562	0.600	0.692
CF-15	2.709	2.319	1.501	1.982	0.767	0.561	0.675
CF-30	0.744	0.690	**0.730**	0.583	**0.515**	**0.608**	**0.515**
CF-40	**0.576**	**0.592**	0.822	**0.423**	**0.515**	0.669	0.638
FUSION	0.223	0.460	0.384	0.338	0.384	0.323	0.323
INRIA	0.634	0.520	0.507	0.520	0.540	0.642	0.455

results in Fig. 4. The INRIA-LEAR's descriptor is constructed by concatenating several filter banks[9]. From Table 1, our auido-based querying results outperform the INRIA-LEAR's. For example, in the *T1* case, our and INRIA-LEAR's actual NDCRs are 0.223 and 0.634, respectively.

From the experiments, after TH_1 and TH_2 are selected as 22 and 30, the best fusion results can be archived. From the above table, the worst performance occurred in the speech-related transformation because their frequencies focus on the higher frequency.

7   Conclusions and Future Works

In the copy detection system, the feature extraction and querying methods are the most important sections. The article focuses on the audio-based copy detection. In the feature extraction, the novel CEPS-like feature is proposed. The flexible hash-based searching algorithm can improve the querying performance. The querying results-based fusion is also presented. After the experiments are conducted, the proper parameters are selected and the fusion performance outperforms any feature. In the future, the speech mixture querying is our research topics.

References

1. Chen, J., Huang, T.: A Robust Feature Extraction Algorithm for Audio Fingerprinting. In: Huang, Y.-M.R., Xu, C., Cheng, K.-S., Yang, J.-F.K., Swamy, M.N.S., Li, S., Ding, J.-W. (eds.) PCM 2008. LNCS, vol. 5353, pp. 887–890. Springer, Heidelberg (2008)
2. Döhring, I., Lienhart, R.: Mining tv broadcasts for recurring video sequences. In: Conference on Image and Video Retrieval, CIVR, pp. 1–8 (2009)
3. Haitsma, J., Kalker, T.: A highly robust audio fingerprinting system. In: Music Information Retrieval, ISMIR (2002)
4. Heritier, M., Gupta, V., Gagnon, L., Cardinal, P.: Crim's content-based copy detection system for trecvid. In: Content-Based Multimedia Indexing, CBMI (2010)
5. http://www.youtube.com/t/press_statistics
6. Indyk, P., Motwani, R.: Approximate nearest neighbors: towards removing the curse of dimensionality. In: Symposium on Theory of Computing, STOC, pp. 604–613 (1998)
7. Jegou, H., Douze, M., Gravier, G., Schmid, C., Gros, P.: Inria lear-texmex: Video copy detection task (2010)
8. Ke, Y., Hoiem, D., Sukthankar, R.: Computer vision for music identification: Video demonstration. In: CVPR (2005)
9. Serra, J.: Identification of versions of the same musical composition by processing audio descriptions. Ph.D. thesis, Universitat Pompeu Fabra (2011)
10. Smeaton, A.F., Over, P., Kraaij, W.: Evaluation campaigns and trecvid. In: Multimedia Information Retrieval, MIR, pp. 321–330 (2006)
11. Ton, J.H., Kalker, T.: Robust audio hashing for content identification. In: Content-Based Multimedia Indexing, CBMI (2001)
12. Wu, X., Ngo, C., Hauptmann, A.G., Tan, H.: Real-time near-duplicate elimination for web video search with content and context. IEEE Tran. on Multimedia 11(2), 196–207 (2009)

Automatic User Preference Elicitation
for Music Recommendation

R. Srivastava[1], Sujoy Roy[2], Tan Dat Nguyen[3], and Shuicheng Yan[1]

[1] Dept. of Electrical and Computer Engineering, National University of Singapore
[2] Institute for Infocomm Research, Singapore
[3] Panasonic Singapore Laboratories

Abstract. Recommendation Systems involve effort from the user to elicit their preference for the item to be recommended. The contribution of this paper is in eliminating such effort by automatically assessing user's personality and using the personality scores for recommending music tracks to them. Automatic personality assessment is performed by automatically answering a personality questionnaire by observing user's audiovisual recordings. To obtain personality scores, traditionally the answers to the questionnaire are combined using a set of rules specific to the questionnaire to get personality scores. As a second contribution, an approach is proposed to automatically predict personality scores from answers to a questionnaire when the rules to combine the answers may not be known. Promising results on a dataset of 50 movie characters support the proposed approaches.

Keywords: Personality Assessment, Movie Analysis, Conditional Random Fields, Emotion Recognition.

1 Introduction

This paper investigates into minimizing the effort in eliciting user preference (referred to henceforth as *user effort*) in a typical recommendation system (RS). Typically, the user needs to give an initial input to the RS which can be in the form of rating a certain number of items or a query with the characteristics of the desired item before obtaining recommendations. However, studies [7] confirm that users can even compromise on RS accuracy to reduce the effort on their part. Although in minimizing elicitation effort, personality quizzes are found to be more effective as compared to rating items [3], but in certain scenarios, even the minimal user effort needed in personality-based RS may not be feasible.

Consider a *target scenario* of automatic music recommendation in response to user behavior captured in a video. The user may be talking to friends or watching TV which restrict him from filling up a personality questionnaire or rating songs. For a new user, his/her past preferences are also not available.

To deal with such situations, this paper presents an approach for automatically eliciting user preference by assessing their personality from videos. Specifically,

W. Lin et al. (Eds.): PCM 2012, LNCS 7674, pp. 605–615, 2012.

Table 1. The Big-Five dimensions (Dim.) along which personality is scored and the associated traits. O: Openness, C: Conscientiousness, E: Extraversion, A: Agreeableness, N: Neuroticism.

Dim.	Associated traits of someone scoring high in the factor
O.	Appreciation for arts, Imagination, Curiosity, Valuing intellectual matters
C.	Order, Dutifulness, Achievement striving, Self-discipline, Deliberation
E.	Warmth, Gregariousness, Activity, Excitement seeking, Positive emotions
A.	Trust, Altruism, Compliance, Modesty, Tender-mindedness
N.	Anxiety, Self-pity, Being self-conscious, Impulsiveness, Fluctuating moods

the procedure of filling up a personality questionnaire has been automated (Figure 1 and Sect. 3.2). The motivation behind using personality assessment comes from psychological findings which show significant correlations between human personality and music preferences [9] [10].

However, automated personality assessment in the target scenario mentioned above may contain challenges in the form of poor illumination, non-frontal faces, low resolution, background noise, low audibility, etc. Extracting dialogs using Automatic Speech Recognition (ASR) may not be very reliable in such situations.

To be able to handle the above mentioned difficulties, data from movies is chosen for evaluating the proposed method. While on one hand, movie data can be considered closer to real life, on the other hand it is also better recorded as compared to real life data. For example, in movies, most of the faces are frontal, audio quality is mostly clear and dialogs are available in the form of subtitles. Note that in real life one of the modalities (Speech acoustics, video and dialog) may not be available but in this work we assume their availability.

Once BFI answers are predicted, an important issue is scoring the questionnaire. A typical personality questionnaire is associated with manual rules used to compute a personality score. For example, BFI contains 10 questions for predicting personality scores along Big-5 dimensions of personality (Section 3.1). Each personality dimension is associated to 2 of the 10 questions based on extensive psychological studies. To score a dimension, the answers to the associated subset of questions are combined according to predefined rules.

For a personality based RS, designing an appropriate questionnaire and a set of rules that combines the answers to those questions in a non-trivial task. While more questions can help to get a better coverage, understanding interdependencies between questions to generate rules that can map to a personality score gets tougher. This work also looks into modelling the relationship between answers to the questionnaire and personality scores. This gives a flexibility to use any personality questionnaire without worrying about the rules for scoring it.

The part of automatic personality assessment using standard BFI scoring scheme has already been presented in [12]. *The contributions of this work are 1) Applying automatic personality assessment to elicit user preference for the task of music recommendation. This removes the effort for getting user preference; and 2) Extending automatic personality assessment in [12] by allowing the use*

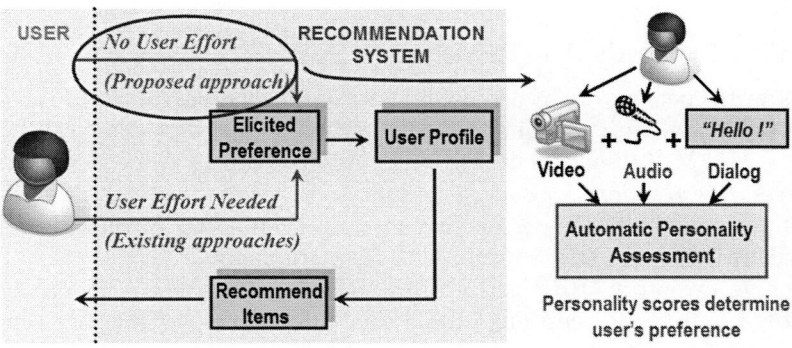

Fig. 1. Proposed method to automatically elicit user's preference for music recommendation

of any personality questionnaire for which the rules of combining their answers is not clear.

2   Related Works

The proposed work has three major aspects, 1) **Automatic** personality assessment, 2) **Music** recommendation , and 3) **Personality based** recommendation.

The works on automatic personality assessment such as [6] are not covered here since they use different approach for personality assessment as pointed in [12].

Most of the works on music recommendation (such as [1]) use collaborative filtering (CF) technique which estimates user's preference from his/her past choices. However, such CF based systems suffer with the difficulty in knowing the choice of a new user (The cold-start problem [11]). [4] use content-based approach for music recommendation which also requires an initial item search by the user. Personality based RS involve less user effort than the rating based systems [3]. However, even in such systems the user needs to fill up a questionnaire. Dunn et al. [2] suggest implicitly acquiring personality traits using the Implicit Adaptive Test (IAT) but there also user needs to complete a computer based exercise. A common limitation of the above-mentioned systems is in the user effort required to elicit their preferences which may not suit the target scenario.

The TWIN system[1] automatically extracts personality information from text and recommend hotels to users. However, personality traits are predicted directly from lexical features which may be less accurate than personality assessment by first answering a personality questionnaire [12].

In the proposed work, the user need not spend any extra effort to give his preference for music items.

---

[1] http://www.twin-persona.org/

3   Methodology

3.1   Five Factor Model (FFM)

In this work, personality of an individual is defined based on the Five Factor Model (FFM) [5] which is gaining popularity among psychologists [12]. According to the FFM, personality has five dimensions; namely *Openness, Conscientiousness, Extraversion, Agreeableness* and *Neuroticism* (Table 1). Traditionally, to evaluate an individual's personality, scores are computed for each of these five dimensions based on his/her response to a questionnaire.

Big Five Inventory (BFI) is one of the questionnaires whose shorter version (BFI-10) has only 10 questions (Table 2a.). BFI is used in this work because of its simplicity and reliability [8] in spite of having only 10 questions. BFI can be answered with five possible values; *Disagree Strongly (1), Disagree a little (2), Neither agree nor disagree (3), Agree a little (4)* and *Agree Strongly (5)*. Personality scores; computed using the BFI scoring scheme (Section 4.3); can take 5 possible values from 1 (weakness) to 5 (dominance) indicating the degree of presence of that personality trait.

3.2   Predicting Answers to BFI

For personality assessment, predicting personality scores by first answering BFI is found to be more accurate as compared to directly predicting the scores from the features [12]. To predict answers to BFI from movie shots, multimodal features are chosen based on their relationship with personality traits as established by psychological studies. Chosen features are mentioned below. For details on feature extraction and predicting BFI answers, please refer to [12].

1. Whether the character speaks in the shot or not.

2. Probabilities of character expressing each of the seven emotions (*Anger (An), Disgust (Di), Fear (Fe), Happiness (Ha), Sadness (Sa), Surprise (Su), Neutral (Ne)*) in the shot.

3. Time taken by the character to speak the dialog related to the shot.

4. Number of words in the dialog.

5. Dialog Polarity: Whether the dialog has positive or negative connotation.

6. Number of persons in the scene containing the shot.

7. Mean, minimum, maximum and relative entropy of the acoustic pitch, spectral energy, and the first and second formant frequencies for the audio signal for the shot.

Answers to the BFI are predicted using a regression model based on sparse and low rank transformation. Available data is divided into training and testing sets (Section 4.1). Let the number of training clips be N_{tr} and the number of features be N_f. Let Z ($10 \times N_{tr}$ matrix) contain the ground truth of the 10 answers for all the training clips, F_{tr} ($N_f \times N_{tr}$ matrix) store the features extracted for all the training clips and W be the parameters of the regression model. The problem of estimating W from the training samples can be formulated as,

$$\min_{W} \left\{ \frac{1}{2} \|Z - W F_{tr}\|_F^2 + \lambda_1 \|W\|_* + \lambda_2 \|W\|_1 \right\}. \tag{1}$$

Here $\|.\|_F$, $\|.\|_*$ and $\|.\|_1$ represent Frobenius norm, nuclear norm and ℓ_1 norm respectively. λ_1 and λ_2 are the regularization parameters. Predictions on test data are obtained as $Z_{tes} = W F_{tes}$ and are rounded to the nearest whole number. Here F_{tes} is the feature matrix for the test data. For details on solution of (1), refer to [12].

3.3 Conditional Random Field Model to Predict Personality Scores

In computing personality scores from questionnaires, the complex interrelationships between the questions need to be considered. Also, deciphering the relationship between questions and personality dimensions needs thorough psychological studies. Formulating a scoring scheme can be very difficult for a large questionnaire. This work proposes to use Conditional Random Fields (CRF) for learning the scoring scheme. CRFs are discriminative undirected probabilistic graphical models which can be used as classifiers for temporal data. A major advantage of CRF is that its prediction is unaffected by complex interdependencies between features. Consequently, predicted BFI answers (Section 3.2) for the training data are used as features to train CRF.

Learnt CRF predicts the probabilities of each possible value of the personality score (1 to 5) for each clip of the character. clips of a character have been used in the form of a temporal sequence with the order of the clips determined based on the order of their appearance in the movie. Using clips in this way can be justified by the observation that personality in a particular clip is closely related to the adjacent clips. Figure 2 shows the variation of personality scores (ground truth) across the Big-5 dimensions for the character *Jack Dawson* in the movie *Titanic*. Note that the clips with insufficient information about a personality dimension have been excluded from the plot. It is observed from the plot for Neuroticism that scores for the neighbouring clips are mostly similar and their variation follows a trend of going from low to high. These temporal relationships between adjacent clips are captured using CRF.

3.4 Personality Based Music Recommendation

At this point, the personality scores of characters for each clip are available. Considering characters as real life persons, music can be recommended to them based on the computed personality scores. Relationship between user personality and music preference is established using a supervised approach. Music preference of the character in a test clip is assumed to be the same as the character in the training set with personality scores most similar to the test character.

Since each score has 5 dimensions, it can be plotted in a 5 dimensional space. Once the personality scores of all the training samples are plotted , the personality score of the test clip is projected into in this 5-dimensional space. The nearest neighbour of the projected test score is estimated using Euclidean distance. If the nearest neighbour has the music recommendation 'jazz' associated with it,

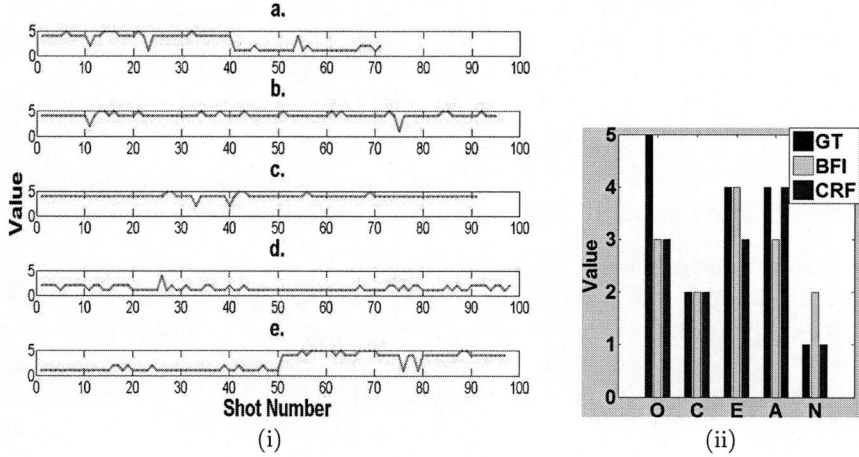

Fig. 2. (i) Variation of personality scores for the character Jack Dawson in *Titanic*. a. Openness, b. Conscientiousness, c. Extraversion, d. Agreeableness, e. Neuroticism. Apart from few outliers, the scores are temporally related supporting the use of CRF. (ii) Predicted personality scores for a sample clip of Jack. Predictions using the proposed method (CRF) are comparable to the traditional method (BFI). GT stands for Ground Truth.

the character in the test clip is recommended 'jazz' music. The music recommendations for the training set clips are obtained by manual labelling (Section 4.1). Experimental details are presented in Sect. 4.4.

4   Experiments

4.1   Dataset

For experimental evaluation, the following two datasets were used.

1. Videos for Personality Assessment. Due to the non-availability of a suitable dataset to evaluate the approach for automatic personality assessment, we collected a dataset consists of video recordings (3907 clips) of 50 characters from 6 movies belonging to different genres[2]. Characters speaking at least 30 dialogs in the entire movie are selected. Dialogs are extracted from the movie subtitles. To establish the ground truth for emotion of the clip, 10 volunteers labeled each clip of the relevant character with one of the seven emotions, i.e., *Anger, Disgust, Fear, Happiness, Sadness, Surprise* and *Neutral*. Besides annotating emotions, personality scores (whole numbers from 1 to 5) are given for each personality dimension and BFI is answered for each clip of the relevant characters. If the information about a personality dimension in a clip is insufficient, the score for that dimension is given

---

[2] Comedy: Evan Almighty, Adventure: Meet Dave, Titanic, Drama: The Prestige, Fantasy: Bedtime stories and Action: You don't mess with the Zohan.

a value 3. In addition to the clip level annotation, annotation at the movie level are made in which volunteers are asked to answer BFI questions and give personality scores to the relevant characters based on the full movie.

It was observed that volunteers preferred to give labels of 2 to 4 rather than giving extreme labels of 1 and 5 in answering BFI. This resulted in the labels 1 and/or 5 missing for a few answers. Considering this, annotations were scaled such that annotation for each answer ranges from 1 to 5 over all characters. Same scaling was applied for personality scores.

Training and Testing Data: Experimental data is divided into 4 parts such that each part consists of approximately 25% of characters and 4-fold cross validation is performed. The test data is selected uniformly from all movie genres.

For evaluating music recommendation performance, volunteers also recommended 30 music tracks for each clip. From the tracks which are recommended by more than 5 volunteers (out of 10) 10 are selected as the ground truth recommendations for that clip.

2. Music Tracks for Recommendation. The dataset from which recommendations are made to the user consists of 1000 audio tracks in .wav format each of 30 seconds duration. 10 genres, *blues, classical, country, disco, hiphop, jazz, metal, pop, reggae* and *rock* are covered each containing 100 tracks [13]. For our experiments, we chose only 10 songs per genre.

4.2 Predicting Answers from Multimodal Features

Kernel Regression model (Section 3.2) is used for predicting answers to BFI from the multimodal features. Regularization parameters λ_1 and λ_2 are set as 2 and 16 respectively based on cross-validation performed on training data [12]. Average results of predicting answers over 4 runs is presented in Table 1b. For each run, accuracies obtained are mean accuracies of predicting each answer over all the tested clips. Note that results differ from those presented in [12] because of the scaling applied to ground truth labels (Section 4.1).

4.3 Predicting Scores from Answers

For predicting personality scores, a CRF model is trained using the scaled conjugate gradient algorithm implemented in Kevin Murphy's CRF toolbox[3]. The parameters selected for training CRFs are: regularizer weight $\alpha = 1$ and maximum iterations = 200. Note that the clips with personality values labeled as 3 are excluded from training data since they lack sufficient information about the personality trait.

The output of the CRF is the personality scores for each clip of the characters. The prediction is in the form of probabilities corresponding to the 4 values for the score (Value of 3 being excluded). The value with the highest probability is taken as the predicted score if it exceeds a threshold θ. If none of the probabilities exceed θ, predicted score is 3.

---

[3] http://www.cs.ubc.ca/murphyk/Software/CRF/crf.html.

Table 2. a. Big Five Inventory-10 (BFI-10). **b.** Personality assessment accuracy. O: Openness, C: Conscientiousness, E:Extraversion, A: Agreeableness, N: Neuroticism. BFI: BFI-scoring scheme, CRF: Proposed approach.

Instruction: How well do the following statements describe the character's personality? You see the character as someone who ...	Accuracy (clip-level) (%)
1... is reserved	87.3
2... is generally trusting	73.9
3... tends to be lazy	94.9
4... is relaxed, handles stress well	61.1
5... has few artistic interests	94.5
6... is outgoing, sociable	75.1
7... tends to find fault with others	70.8
8... does a thorough job	82.8
9... gets nervous easily	80.4
10... has an active imagination	87.7
Avg. Accuracy	80.9

a.

Trait	Accuracies	
	BFI	CRF
O.	84.2	84.4
C.	80.8	85.9
E.	69.6	73.1
A.	59.4	62.1
N.	57.1	63.4
Avg.	70.2	**73.8**

b.

A comparison is also made with standard BFI scoring scheme to predict clip-level personality scores from answers. Under this scheme, answers obtained for each of the 10 questions are mapped onto personality scores along 5 dimensions. The questions associated with each of the 5 factors are Extraversion: 1R, 6; Agreeableness: 2, 7R; Conscientiousness: 3R, 8; Neuroticism: 4R, 9; Openness: 5R, 10. Here suffix 'R' to a question number indicates that the answer (in the range of 1 to 5) for this question will be reverse scored i.e. subtracted from 6 before calculating the score. Next, for each of the Big 5 factors, the values of questions associated with that factor are averaged to get a score in the range of 1 to 5. The scores are rounded to whole numbers.

Figure 2 shows the predicted personality scores for a sample clip of Jack using both BFI and CRF. Predictions using CRF are close to that using BFI scoring since difference between the two predictions is never more than one unit for all the dimensions. As compared to the ground truth, CRF predicts 3 dimensions accurately as compared to 2 dimensions of BFI resulting in an accuracy of 60% for CRF and 40% for BFI for this clip. The prediction performances of CRF and BFI averaged over all test clips is reported in Table 2 (clip-level). CRF is found to perform better than BFI for all the Big-5 dimensions.

4.4   Music Recommendation

In each run of the 4-fold cross validation (Section 4.1), having obtained the personality score for a character in a test clip, 10 music clips are recommended to him/her as mentioned in Sect. 3.4. For evaluating recommendation performance, 10 volunteers were asked to label each recommendation as good or bad.

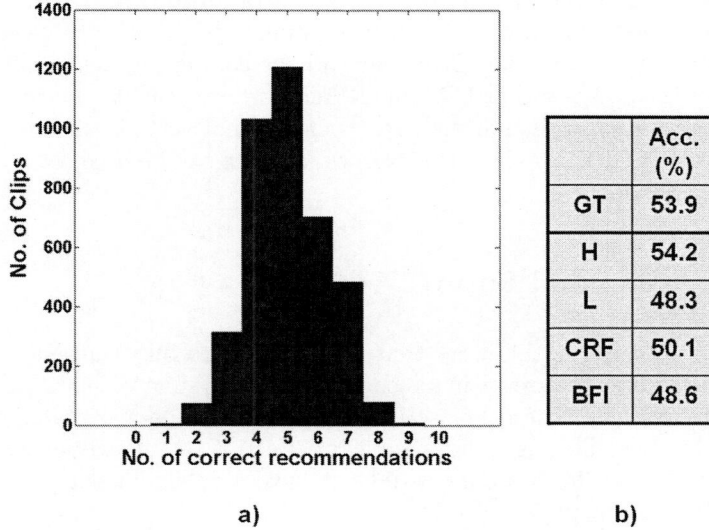

	Acc. (%)
GT	53.9
H	54.2
L	48.3
CRF	50.1
BFI	48.6

a)   b)

Fig. 3. a) Recommendation results. b) A comparison of recommendation accuracies when different methods were used for personality assessment. GT: Using Ground Truth of personality assessment, H or L: Using clips with high (H) or low (L) accuracy in personality assessment, CRF: Proposed method, BFI: Using BFI scoring scheme (Section 4.3).

Majority voting was used to decide the assigned label. The fraction of good recommendations out of the 10 recommendations (precision) is used as the accuracy measure.

Figure 3a. shows a distribution of the number of clips vs. the number of correct recommendations. It is observed that most of the clips (63.5%) had 5 or more correct recommendations. The overall recommendation accuracy was found to be 50.1%. The personality based system in [3] achieved an accuracy of 54.9%. One possible reason for the reduced accuracy is the error in personality assessment as evident from the comparison with recommendation accuracy using the ground truth personality labels (Figure 3b.).

Additionally results are presented separately for clips with high ($\geq 80\%$) and low ($\leq 60\%$) accuracy in personality assessment corresponding to H and L respectively (Figure 3b.). Note that only a fraction of all the clips are used for these two cases. GT corresponds to the results when ground truth of personality scores were used. CRF and BFI refer to the proposed method and using BFI scoring scheme (Section 4.3). Note that for personality assessment task the prediction accuracy for a clip is the fraction of personality traits correctly predicted for that clip (Section 4.3). Results show that error in personality prediction reduces the prediction accuracy (from 53.9% for GT to 50.1% for CRF) but it may be acceptable considering the significant reduction in user effort.

Effectiveness of CRF Modelling for Recommendation Task. Effectiveness of CRF modelling (Section 3.3) was evaluated by comparing recommendation results obtained using CRF and BFI for computing personality scores. Results in Fig. 3b. show that CRF modelling performs slightly better than the BFI scoring scheme. Although the improvement is not very significant, it is relevant since using CRF, any personality questionnaire can be used for personality assessment (Section 1).

5   Conclusion and Future Work

It has been observed in this work that it is possible to fully automate the process of eliciting user preference in a recommendation system without a significant decrease in accuracy. The decrease in accuracy should be acceptable since the reduction in user effort is quite significant (Section 1). It was observed that automating personality assessment did not have very significant effect on recommendation accuracy.

There are a few limitations of the proposed approach regarding collecting the relevant data. Movies are still in a controlled environment and a real world data can better test the approach. Future work involves experimenting on real life character as it will also help to evaluate user satisfaction for the recommendation task.

Moreover, BFI is a short questionnaire and future work involves studying the effectiveness of the proposed learning scheme on other questionnaires especially when CRF modelling can be an alternative to questionnaire specific scoring schemes. There is a large room for improvement of recommendation accuracy as in some cases the user may also wish to spend some effort to get better recommendations.

References

1. Chen, H.C., Chen, A.L.P.: A Music Recommendation System Based on Music and User Grouping. J. Intell. Inf. Syst. 24(2/3), 113–132 (2005)
2. Dunn, G., Wiersema, J., Ham, J., Aroyo, L.: Evaluating Interface Variants on Personality Acquisition for Recommender Systems. In: Houben, G.-J., McCalla, G., Pianesi, F., Zancanaro, M. (eds.) UMAP 2009. LNCS, vol. 5535, pp. 259–270. Springer, Heidelberg (2009)
3. Hu, R., Pu, P.: Acceptance issues of personality-based recommender systems. In: The 3rd ACM Conference on Recommender Systems, RecSys (2009)
4. Logan, B.: Music recommendation from song sets. In: Proc. ISMIR (2004)
5. McCrae, R., John, O.: An introduction to the five-factor model and its applications. J. Pers. 60(2), 175–215 (1992)
6. Mohammadi, G., Vinciarelli, A., Mortillaro, M.: The voice of personality: mapping nonverbal vocal behavior into trait attributions. In: Proc. 2nd International Workshop on Social Signal Processing (2010)
7. Pu, P., Chen, L., Hu, R.: Evaluating recommender systems from the user's perspective: survey of the state of the art. User Model. User-Adap., 1–39 (2012)

8. Rammstedt, B., John, O.: Measuring personality in one minute or less: A 10-item short version of the Big Five Inventory in English and German. J. Res. Pers. 41(1), 203–212 (2007)
9. Rentfrow, P.J., Gosling, S.D.: The do re mi's of everyday life: the structure and personality correlates of music preference. J. Pers. Soc. Psychol. 84, 1236–1253 (2003)
10. Rentfrow, P.J., McDonald, J.: Preference, personality, and emotion. In: Juslin, P., Slobada, J. (eds.) Handbook of Music and Emotion: Theory, Research, Applications, pp. 669–695 (2010)
11. Schein, A.I., Popescul, A., Ungar, L.H., Pennock, D.M.: Methods and metrics for cold-start recommendations. In: Proc. 25th Annual International ACMSIGIR Conf. Research and Development in Information Retrieval (2002)
12. Srivastava, R., Jiashi, F., Roy, S., Sim, T., Yan, S.: Don't Ask Me What I'm Like, Just Watch and Listen. In: ACM International Conference on Multimedia, ACMMM (to appear, 2012)
13. Tzanetakis, G., Cook, P.: Music genre classification of audio signals. IEEE T. Speech Audi. P. 10(5), 293–302 (2002)

Interactive Virtual Try-On Based on Real-Time Motion Capture

Xiaoyang Zhu, Shuxin Qin, Haitao Yu, Shuiying Ge,
Yiping Yang, and Yongshi Jiang

Integrated Information System Research Center,
Institute of Automation, Chinese Academy of Sciences,
Beijing, China

Abstract. In this paper, we present an augmented reality system for interactive virtual try-on of garments based on real-time motion capture. The system uses a commodity depth sensor to obtain depth images and joint motion data of a user. We first apply a novel evaluation method over two specific depth images to determine the user's body measurements, according to which garment models are deformed to fit his/her actual size. Torso joint of the selected garment model is translated to follow the user's position, while other joints are rotated to mimic the user's postures. Then the system superimposes the transformed model onto the same user in a live image sequence and move with him/her accurately. We also propose a method for handling model dangling artifacts due to the limitations of current tracking techniques in producing smooth, noise free motion data in real-time. The system can be used at user's home as well as retailer's shop to present an interactive try-on experience.

1   Introduction

Virtual try-on of garments is highly appealing and becoming more widespread due to its convenience and time saving for both consumers and retailers. For consumers, it helps narrow down the selection to only a few clothes without putting on them physically. For retailers, it can reduce the number of fitting rooms while let more customers try on more garments.

Due to the above-mentioned advantages, virtual try-on has reasonably good commercial potential in the garment market where several systems already been proposed. Cordier [1] provide a framework for online clothing stores that can adjust a standard 3D mannequin according to body measurements the user inputs, resize garments to fit the mannequin, and simulate garment movements using motion data. Then Responsive Mirror [2] enhances virtual fitting rooms with online social fashion comparisons. With the advent of commodity depth cameras, e.g., the Kinect sensor, new opportunities for virtual try-on emerge. It is reported in [3], users can interactively control personalized avatars with augmented clothes at home using the Kinect. Although fitting results of this system are good, users are required to enter or pass through a multi-camera setup to reconstruct 3D models of them. However reconstruction of good quality body

W. Lin et al. (Eds.): PCM 2012, LNCS 7674, pp. 616–627, 2012.

model is still an open problem, so that customers will hardly be able to recognize themselves and generally it requires manual editing to have realistic models [4].

In this paper, we propose an augmented reality system for interactive virtual try-on of garments using real-time motion capture. We first apply a novel full-body tracking method over data extracted from the Kinect's depth sensor to determine a user's body measurements and joint motion data in real time. Instead of augmenting reconstructed 3D model with virtual garments, we deform virtual clothes according to the evaluated body measurements and then superimpose them onto the same user in the live image sequence obtained from the Kinect's RGB camera. Using the tracked joint positions and orientations, the skeletally deformable garments can be interactively controlled by the user in front of this device. Compared to conventional virtual try-on systems, our system does not require any manual intervention and users can get more interactive try-on experience. The main contributions of our work are:

- Estimate a user's body measurements from only two depth images captured from the Kinect in real time.
- Employ linear regression forecasting method to replace uncertain tracking data of joints so as to reduce model dangling artifacts.
- Deform template garment models to fit the user's shape without additional skinning information.

2   Related Works

The main task of virtual try-on is to let garment models match with the user's figure in the live image sequence and at the same time be controlled by the user interactively. Because of the relatively huge database of clothing models and the real-time performance constraint, we need efficient deformation and animation methods to adapt the standard garment models to the same size as the user and allow skeletal motion to animate them with less artifacts. Below, we attempt to discuss algorithms that are most closely related to our goals and techniques.

2.1   Model Deformation

In order to augment garment models on anthropometrically different users, size-accurate representation of models is necessary. Nowadays most virtual models are either created by artists or obtained using 3D body scanning devices. But these approaches are time consuming and require expert knowledge. Cordier et al. [1] used a template model and interpolators to evaluate joint and shape parameters to get expected models. Kasap and Magnenat-Thalmann [5] use anthropometric measurement parameters to deform the template model, and eliminate the manual vertex labeling stage by using the existing per-vertex skinning weights attached to the model [6]. Our method is based on the same idea, but we simplify the problem by applying a novel method to evaluate user's body measurements from two depth images without user inputs.

2.2   Skeleton Animation

Common skeleton-driven skin deformation was first introduced by [7]. Since then, several different approaches to skeleton animation have emerged, such as physically based methods, capturing real subjects, example-based techniques and geometric methods [8]. Computationally the fastest technique, geometric method, is the most preferable one in real-time applications because it doesn't require high computational power, expensive hardware and production of a large number of examples. Considering that these constraints are also important for our virtual try-on system, in this section we will mostly focus on the skinning method that are subject to geometric skinning techniques.

The standard algorithm for low-cost skinning, in the category of geometric method, is linear blend skinning (LBS). Thanks to its well-known elbow-collapse and candy-wrapper artifacts, Log-Matrix Blending [9], Spherical Blending [10] and Dual Quaternions [8] have been proposed to improve its quality shortcomings. However, neither LBS nor its improvements properly handle stretching, where bones change length, nor twisting, where the skin twist along the length of a bone [11]. While these problems are common in the fitting process, we designed a two phases deforming method to manage the proper size of garment models.

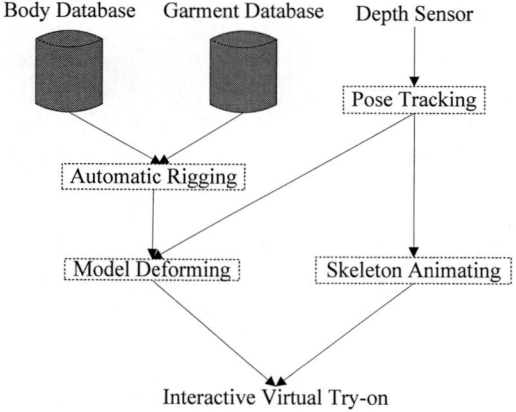

Fig. 1. Architecture of interactive virtual try-on system

3   System Overview

As shown in Fig. 1, four modules, the pose tracking, the automatic rigging, the model deforming and skeleton animating modules are included in our interactive virtual try-on system. Each of the four modules can either generate some necessary data (about body measurements or joint motion data) or deform the garment models to fit the user's body frame. As a prerequisite, garments models should be rigged automatically before deforming in the automatic rigging module. In the pose tracking module, joint positions and orientations are obtained by using data extracted from a depth sensor. Then body measurements, like arm length, can be estimated (See Section 4). Despite the apparent difficulty in building new garment geometries from the approximate body measurements within the real-time constraint, we show how this process is feasible through the garment model deforming module for practical applications in Section 5. To animate garments at an interactive rate, we apply skeleton-driven skin deformation to the selected garment model in the skeleton animating module.

3.1   Body and Garment Database

The body database contains two 3D mannequins for male and female gender, which refer to as template body models. They are manually generated only once in the model design stage and doesn't require any modifications afterwards. Template garment models in the other database can be created either by manipulate clothing patterns to desired positions of our body models [12] or reconstructed from data captured by laser scanners [13] or a set of surrounding cameras [3]. Fig. 2 shows our template body as well as several garment models.

Fig. 2. The template body and garment models

The template model is usually animated by transforming its underlying skeleton, which is a graph that consists of nodes (joints) and edges (bones). As a preprocessing step, we need to properly adjust a standard human skeleton to the template body and garment models, and specify the desired weight properties either by the user with sufficient 3D weight painting tools (e.g. Maya) or apply a rigging algorithm [14] on the mesh which calculates the skinning weights for all vertices automatically.

4 Pose Tracking

The pose tracking module provides information needed in the process of adapting the garment model in a way so it fits the user in the image sequence. As recent developments in sensor technologies allow for cheap and robust acquisition of depth images, Ganapathi et al. [15] have shown how to track full body motions using a single time-of-flight camera. We also use a consumer priced depth camera, i.e. the Microsoft Kinect, to acquire depth images of users, from which users' body measurements and postures can be determined by using the OpenNI library [16].

The OpenNI framework provides, among others, a high-level pose tracking module, which can be used for detecting the captured user and tracking his/her body joints [17]. The result is a complete 3D skeleton that accurately mimics the movements of the user in front of the sensor. Although the OpenNI tracking module produces positions and orientations of 24 joints, along with corresponding tracking confidences, we use only 15 joints (*Head, Neck, Torso, Left and Right Shoulder, L/R Elbow, L/R Wrist, L/R Hip, L/R Knee and L/R Ankle*) for garment deformation and 2 joints (*L/R Hand*) for interaction. Fig. 3 shows corresponding joints between the template model and captured user in the depth image.

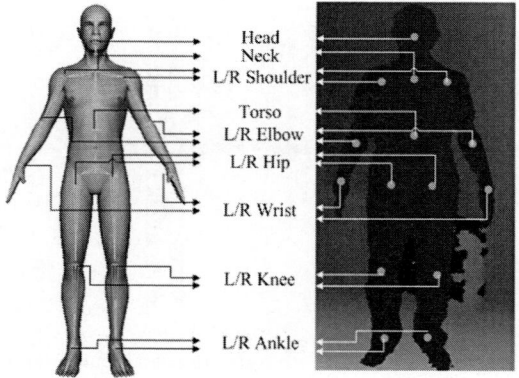

Fig. 3. Joints mapping between the template model and the depth map

In Section 4.1, we present a method for evaluating a user's body measurements from two depth images automatically. Due to the limitations of current tracking algorithms in producing smooth, noise free tracking data, linear regression forecasting method was used to replace missing tracking data of joints as described in Section 4.2.

4.1   Evaluate Body Measurements

Despite recent efforts devoted to using 3D human body scanners to generate accurate body measurements from a specific subject, limiting factors such as the inability to automatically integrate body scan data to application software exist [1]. One important feature of our virtual try-on system is its ability to get a user's body measurements from only two depth images (front and side) of the user in real time.

In addition to the *Surrender* pose (Fig. 4(a)) required by the OpenNI tracking module , we need the user to show the *Push* pose (Fig. 4(b)) in order to get the front and side depth images, from which we can obtain information about the user's body characteristics. More specifically, our pose tracking module requires the captured user to stay still in two specific calibration poses for a few seconds. In Fig. 4, the blue figure shows the captured user while the green balls indicate positions of the joints used for estimating body measurements.

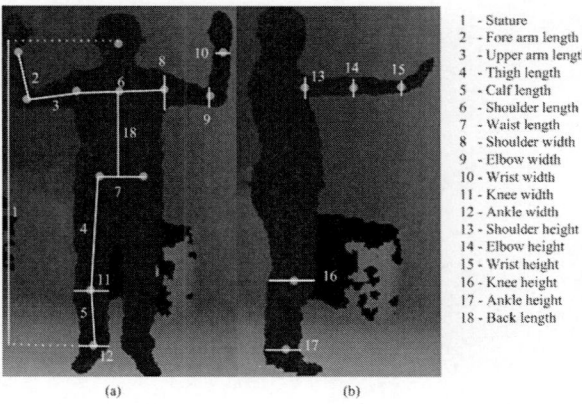

Fig. 4. (a)The *Surrender* pose, (b) the *Push* pose, and the major body measurement landmarks

The ISO7250 provides a description of anthropometric measurements and body landmarks that intended to serve as a guide primarily for tailors, designers etc [6]. Based on this standard and the two depth maps, several main body measurements (see Fig. 4) are extracted and calculated. While some body measurements are directly related to the distance between joints, others need to query the horizontal or vertical blue boundaries at the joint position in the depth images. This process is quite efficient, typically under a second to get all the 18 measurements on a modern midrange PC. This is essentially the information needed to deform the template garment models in the deforming module (See Section 5). For the sake of simplicity, we denote the 18 measurements of the captured user as $\hat{m}_i \, (i = 1, \cdots, 18)$, while the template models' measurements given as known qualities and denoted as $m_i \, (i = 1, \cdots, 18)$.

4.2   Replace Missing Tracking

During virtual trying on, the user interacts with various garment models that animated using real time motion capture data extracted from the depth sensor. Sometimes, the depth image obtained by the depth sensor is prone to missing values due to shadowing of the infrared data or when the user is outside the range of the sensor. In such cases, the user's immersive experience might be tarnished if the missing limbs are left dangling. Take the right hand for example, the OpenNI tracking module produces its positions and corresponding tracking confidences, from 0.0 to 1.0 (indicating uncertain to certain). In the upper part of Fig. 5, the blue line shows the right hand's y positions whose confidences equal to 1.0 while the red line for confidences less than 1.0, resulting in right hand dangling artifacts. Bleiweiss et al. [18] present a solution that fill in the uncertain tracking data with predefined idle animations. For interactive applications like virtual try-on systems, however, the user still can't have the feeling of full control and immediate feedback.

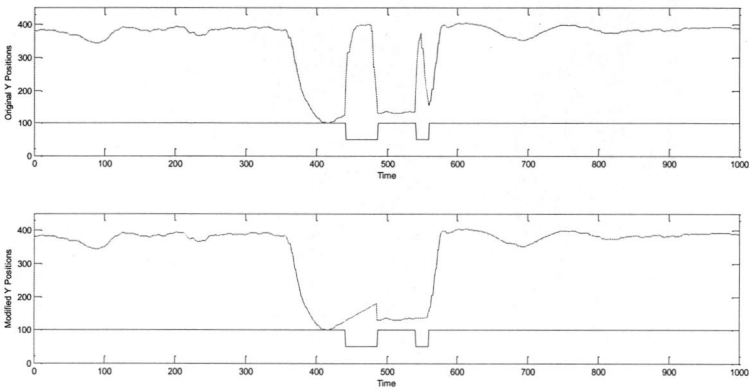

Fig. 5. The upper part shows the origin hand movement with certain (blue) and uncertain (red) values obtained from the tracking module. To get smoother hand movement, linear regression forecasting method is employed to replace uncertain values, as the lower part shows.

To resolve this, the joint that missing values is identified by its corresponding tracking confidence and linear regression forecasting method [19] is used to estimate its actual values. For time series: y_t $(t = 1, \cdots, n)$, we can build its corresponding linear regression forecasting model: $\hat{y}_t = \hat{\alpha} y_{t-1} + \hat{\beta}$, where $\hat{\alpha}$ and $\hat{\beta}$ can be calculated by using least squares method:

$$\hat{\alpha} = \frac{(n-1)\sum_{t=2}^{n} y_{t-1} y_t - \sum_{t=2}^{n} y_{t-1} \sum_{t=2}^{n} y_t}{(n-1)\sum_{t=2}^{n} y_{t-1}^2 - \left(\sum_{t=2}^{n} y_{t-1}\right)^2}, \tag{1}$$

$$\hat{\beta} = \frac{\sum_{t=2}^{n} y_t - \hat{\alpha} \sum_{t=2}^{n} y_{t-1}}{n-1}.$$ (2)

Using this method, we can get estimated position values when their corresponding confidences are less than 1.0. Lower part of Fig. 5 shows we can get smoother hand movement with uncertain values being replaced by using the presented method.

5 Garment Models Deforming

One of key challenges in virtual try-on is to manage the proper size of skeletally deformable garment models and follow the user's movement. Kavan et al. [8] vary a model's proportions without having to modify the model itself by separating the joint transformation into nonrigid and rigid parts and perform skinning in two phases. In the first phase, they resize the mesh in the rest-pose. In the second phase, rigid joint transformations are applied using dual quaternion skinning. However, this method suffer from stretching and twisting problems [11] which are common in the fitting process. In order to handle these artifacts, we use the regional deformation method [6] to rescale the rest-pose mesh according to evaluated body measurements only once, and then use motion capture data to transform the mesh to the shape of the user in the image sequence. Our method doesn't require additional design efforts and uses the same skinning information for animation that is already attached to the template model. Below, we will describe our method in detail.

5.1 Model Resizing

We apply the regional deformation method [6] to generate new models from rest-pose template mesh by using the below equation:

$$\mathbf{v}_i' = \mathbf{v}_i + \sum_{j=1}^{k} \mathbf{s}_j \mathbf{n}_i f_j \left(L(\mathbf{v}_i) \right).$$ (3)

Here, $\mathbf{v}_i'$ is the new position of $\mathbf{v}_i$ after deformation and $\mathbf{n}_i$ is the normal vector of $\mathbf{v}_i$ which is not changed after deformation because the deformation is in the same direction as the normal. k is the number of deformation functions which can be horizontal, vertical, or both. f_j is representing the jth deformation function and L is normalized local coordinate function of a vertex within a region. $\mathbf{s}_j = (s_{jx}, s_{jy}, s_{jz})$ is the scale factor of jth deformation function and each component separately defines the scale factor on the corresponding dimension. Our main task here is to define the scale factor $\mathbf{s}_j$ according to the body measurements.

Take the *Calf* for example, we can define the deformation region using three body measurements *Knee Width* , *Knee Height* and *Calf Length*, as shown in Fig. 6(a). Then $\mathbf{s}_j$ can be calculated in all three dimensions using the below equation:

$$s_{jx} = \alpha \frac{\hat{m}_{11}}{m_{11}}, s_{jy} = \beta \frac{\hat{m}_5}{m_5}, s_{jz} = \gamma \frac{\hat{m}_{16}}{m_{16}}, \qquad (4)$$

where parameter α, β and γ is used to adjust the proper ratio between $\hat{m}_i$ and m_i, indicating measurement of user and template model respectively. Based on our experiments, the value between 0.31-0.42 for α, β and γ would give a satisfactory result. Then using equation (3) and (4), we can deform the *Calf* region and get resized model, as shown in Fig. 6(b). Other joints can be deformed in the same manner and we can obtain garment models with the same size as the user in the image sequence. Then we apply the automatic rigging method [14] on the deformed models once again to adjust the skeleton positions and skin weights.

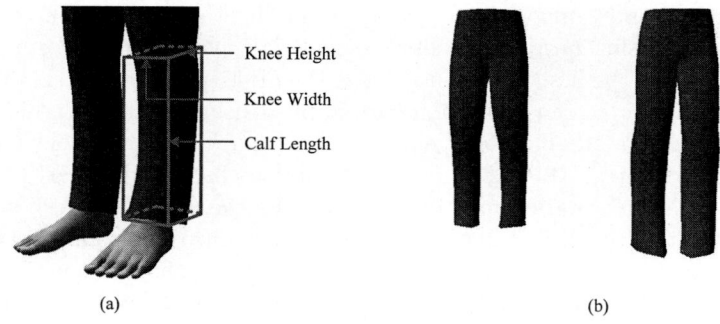

(a)   (b)

Fig. 6. (a) Deformation region of the *Calf*, and (b) its deformation result

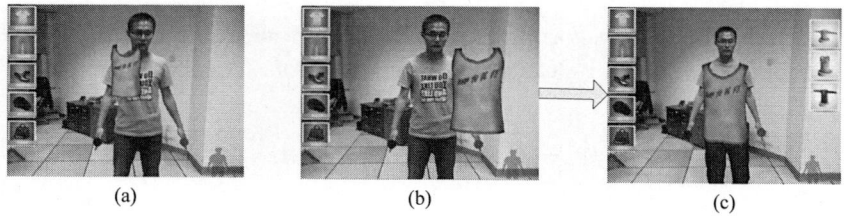

(a)   (b)   (c)

Fig. 7. *Left to right*: (a) wrong position and wrong size, (b) wrong position but right size, and (c) right position and right size

5.2   Model Transforming

When our virtual try-on system starts working, the initial state is shown in Fig. 7(a). In this situation, the garment model cannot fit the user's figure both in position and size. Fig. 7(b) shows the results after models been resized, with right size but wrong position. Then the left problem is to translate the model to the proper position and mimic the user's movement. Using the pose tracking module provided by the OpenNI framework, we can determine a user's *Torso* joint position $\mathbf{p}_T$ in the Kinect coordinate system at runtime. Then $\mathbf{p}_T$ can be transformed to $\mathbf{p}'_T$ in the camera coordinate system using the following equation:

$$\mathbf{p}'_T = T_{CK}\mathbf{p}_T, \tag{5}$$

where T_{CK} is the transformation from the Kinect coordinate system to the camera coordinate system. After that the garment model is translated to the same point, as shown in Fig. 7(c).

Finally, we apply the dual quaternion skinning method [8] to the resized model to mimic the movement of user in front of the Kinect sensor. Fig. 8 shows some fitting results of three users with different body size.

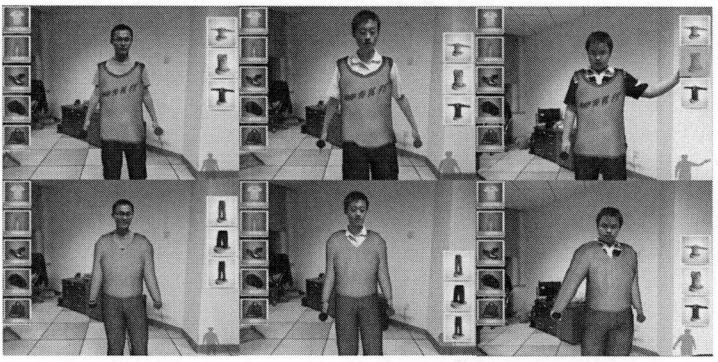

Fig. 8. Try-on results of three anthropometrically different users

6   Conclusions and Future Work

In this work we describe a tentative and affordable framework for virtual try-on at home. Color image sequence of the Microsoft Kinect is rendered as background and depth images as basis for further analysis. We apply a novel estimation method over two specific depth images to obtain a user's approximate body measurements, according to which template garment models are deformed to fit the user's actual figure without any manual intervention. Motion capture data is also extracted from depth images and used to animate garment models to follow user's movement in real time. The virtual garments are transformed so as to appear attached to the human frame in the color image sequence. In addition, we've developed a method for handling the dangling artifacts caused by uncertain tracking data. Finally, we set up an interactive virtual try-on system, where users can choose among many different types of garments and visualize them on their figure.

Nevertheless, there's still much room for improvement. Contrary to previous works, our approach uses skeleton animation method to animate garment models. In this process, we cannot use cloth simulation algorithms or collision detection methods, thus the system cannot get accurate animation results than physics based methods. In addition, we will handle the occlusion problem and display those parts of garments that are not occluded by the body. We expect that users can have immersive try-on experience in the future.

References

1. Cordier, F., Seo, H., Magnenat-Thalmann, N.: Made-to-measure technologies for an online clothing store. IEEE Computer Graphics and Applications 23(1), 38–48 (2003)
2. Zhang, W., Matsumoto, T., Liu, J., Chu, M., Begole, B.: An intelligent fitting room using multi-camera perception. In: Proceedings of the 13th International Conference on Intelligent User Interfaces, IUI 2008, pp. 60–69. ACM, New York (2008)
3. Hauswiesner, S., Straka, M., Reitmayr, G.: Free viewpoint virtual try-on with commodity depth cameras. In: Proceedings of the 10th International Conference on Virtual Reality Continuum and Its Applications in Industry, VRCAI 2011, pp. 23–30. ACM, New York (2011)
4. Yuan, M., Khan, I.R., Farbiz, F., Niswar, A., Huang, Z.: A mixed reality system for virtual glasses try-on. In: Proceedings of the 10th International Conference on Virtual Reality Continuum and Its Applications in Industry, VRCAI 2011, pp. 363–366. ACM, New York (2011)
5. Kasap, M., Magnenat-Thalmann, N.: Parameterized human body model for real-time applications. In: Proceedings of the 2007 International Conference on Cyberworlds, CW 2007, pp. 160–167. IEEE Computer Society, Washington, DC (2007)
6. Kasap, M., Magnenat-Thalmann, N.: Sizing avatars from skin weights. In: Proceedings of the 16th ACM Symposium on Virtual Reality Software and Technology, VRST 2009, pp. 123–126. ACM, New York (2009)
7. Magnenat-Thalmann, N., Laperrière, R., Thalmann, D.: Joint-dependent local deformations for hand animation and object grasping. In: Proceedings on Graphics Interface 1988, pp. 26–33. Canadian Information Processing Society, Toronto (1988)
8. Kavan, L., Collins, S., Žára, J., O'Sullivan, C.: Geometric skinning with approximate dual quaternion blending. ACM Trans. Graph. 27(4), 105:1–105:23 (2008)
9. Cordier, F., Magnenat-Thalmann, N.: A data-driven approach for real-time clothes simulation. In: Proceedings of the 12th Pacific Conference on Computer Graphics and Applications, PG 2004, pp. 257–266 (October 2004)
10. Kavan, L., Žára, J.: Spherical blend skinning: a real-time deformation of articulated models. In: Proceedings of the 2005 Symposium on Interactive 3D Graphics and Games, I3D 2005, pp. 9–16. ACM, New York (2005)
11. Jacobson, A., Sorkine, O.: Stretchable and twistable bones for skeletal shape deformation. In: Proceedings of the 2011 SIGGRAPH Asia Conference, SA 2011, pp. 165:1–165:8. ACM, New York (2011)
12. Meng, Y., Mok, P.Y., Jin, X.: Interactive virtual try-on clothing design systems. Comput. Aided Des. 42(4), 310–321 (2010)
13. Stoll, C., Gall, J., de Aguiar, E., Thrun, S., Theobalt, C.: Video-based reconstruction of animatable human characters. ACM Trans. Graph. 29(6), 139:1–139:10 (2010)

14. Baran, I., Popović, J.: Automatic rigging and animation of 3d characters. In: ACM SIGGRAPH 2007 Papers, SIGGRAPH 2007. ACM, New York (2007)
15. Ganapathi, V., Plagemann, C., Koller, D., Thrun, S.: Real time motion capture using a single time-of-flight camera. In: 2010 IEEE Conference on Computer Vision and Pattern Recognition, CVPR, pp. 755–762 (June 2010)
16. OpenNI: Open Natural Interface SDK (2012), http://www.openni.org
17. Alexiadis, D.S., Kelly, P., Daras, P., O'Connor, N.E., Boubekeur, T., Moussa, M.B.: Evaluating a dancer's performance using kinect-based skeleton tracking. In: Proceedings of the 19th ACM International Conference on Multimedia, MM 2011, pp. 659–662. ACM, New York (2011)
18. Bleiweiss, A., Eshar, D., Kutliroff, G., Lerner, A., Oshrat, Y., Yanai, Y.: Enhanced interactive gaming by blending full-body tracking and gesture animation. In: ACM SIGGRAPH ASIA 2010 Sketches, SA 2010, pp. 34:1–34:2. ACM, New York (2010)
19. Montgomery, D.C., Peck, E.A., Vining, G.G.: Introduction to Linear Regression Analysis, Solutions Manual. Wiley Series in Probability and Statistics. Wiley-Interscience (2007)

Distant Speaker Verification Using a Combined Family of MVDR Estimates

Bhargava Manevarte, Waquar Ahmad, and Rajesh M. Hegde

Department of Electrical Engineering,
Indian Institute of Technology Kanpur
rhegde@iitk.ac.in
http://202.3.77.107/mips/

Abstract. Distant speaker verification involves explicit spectral estimation of speech acquired over microphone arrays. The choice of the appropriate set of microphones is important here. In this paper we describe an implicit approach to minimum variance distortionless response (MVDR) spectral estimation of distant talking speech and its application in distant speaker verification. A mathematical formulation for computing an implicit spectral estimate for speech acquired over a uniform linear array (ULA) is first presented. This formulation is based on a simple mathematical relation between a fixed order MVDR spectral estimate, the harmonics in speech, and the noise power. This relationship is used for spectral modeling of distant talking speech by jointly combining a family of MVDR estimates and the number of elements in the ULA. The performance of the proposed implicit MVDR spectral estimation method is evaluated in terms of cepstral distance measure indicating improvements over the Fourier spectral estimates obtained from the individual elements of the ULA. Experiments on distant speaker verification using speech data from the NIST 2004 corpus indicate reasonable improvements when compared to conventional MFCC from the individual elements from the ULA.

1 Introduction

Microphone array processing [1], is gaining importance owing to its non intrusive nature in acquiring speech. Spatial filtering is usually employed in this context by exploiting the time delay of arrival (TDOA) between different microphones. Techniques like fixed and adaptive beam forming requires the selection of the right pair of microphones prior to spectral estimation of distant speech, making these approaches explicit in nature [1]. Methods such as the dual excitation model [1], have also combined explicit speech modeling with spatial filtering. In this work, the problem of distant speaker verification is viewed as a clean speech acquisition problem based upon a parameter model [2], followed by speaker verification. The proposed multi channel spectral estimation technique is based on the MVDR method [3–5]. It is implicit in nature since it directly computes the spectral estimate of speech from the output of a uniform linear array. It does

W. Lin et al. (Eds.): PCM 2012, LNCS 7674, pp. 628–638, 2012.

not involve the selection of the right pair of microphones as is done in explicit approaches. A mathematical formulation for computing an implicit spectral estimate for speech acquired from a uniform linear array (ULA) is presented in this paper. This formulation is based on a simple mathematical relation between a fixed order MVDR spectral estimate, the harmonics in speech, and the noise power. This relationship is used for spectral modeling of distant talking speech by jointly combining a family of MVDR estimates and the number of elements in the ULA. Once the spectral estimate is obtained the corresponding MFCC are computed and used in a distant speaker verification task. The rest of the paper is organized as follows. The effect of distance on the spectral estimation in typical reverberant room conditions is discussed first. A brief review of spectrum estimation for close talking speech using a family of MVDR estimates (CF-MVDR) [6], is presented next followed by a description of the proposed implicit approach to spectral estimation of distant talking speech. The implicit spectral estimation method is evaluated for its performance using average cepstral distance measures [7]. Experimental results on distant speaker verification on speech data from the NIST 2004 corpus [8], using features derived from the proposed method are listed. The paper concludes with a discussion on their significance.

2   Implicit Approach to Spectral Estimation of Distant Talking Speech

Spectral estimation of speech based on a parametric model usually uses a single microphone for acquiring speech data. However when an array of microphones is used selection of the appropriate microphone assumes importance [1]. More often it is the microphone that is closest to the speaker that gives the best performance for various speech processing tasks. However when spatial filtering techniques are used along with speech modeling as in [1], the selection of the right pair of microphones becomes important.

2.1   Explicit Spectral Estimation of Distant Talking Speech

In order to illustrate the explicit approach, we acquire speech sampled at 16 KHz using a uniform linear array (ULA) under reverberant conditions. The spectral estimates using the DFT and the MVDR method are computed for two elements of the ULA. The first element is at a distance of one meter while the second element is at a distance of two meters from the speech source. Figure 1 illustrates the DFT magnitude spectra (top) and the tenth order MVDR spectrum (bottom) of a close talking microphone (CTM) and the two elements of the ULA. Note that the microphone at a distance of one meter yields a spectra that is closest to the CTM. Hence it is intuitive to assume that any speech spectrum estimation method based on parametric modeling will have to explicitly select the microphone closest to the source. Similarly when speech modeling is combined with spatial filtering approaches one will have to explicitly select the pair of microphones that are closest to the speech source. In the succeeding sections

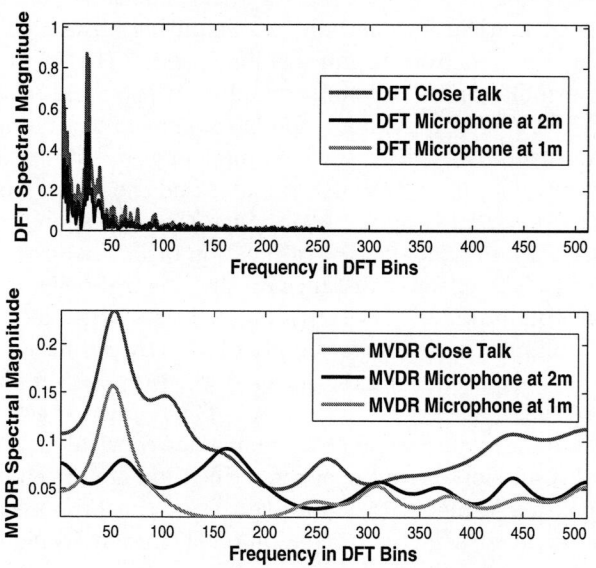

Fig. 1. Comparison of DFT (top) and MVDR (bottom) spectra of distant talking speech using a close talking microphone, microphone at a distance of one meter, and microphone at a distance of 2 meters

we focus only on the spectral estimation part and develop an Implicit approach to speech modeling without having to resort to explicit selection of microphones.

2.2 Implicit Approach to Mvdr Spectrum Estimation of Distant Talking Speech

Spectrum estimation of close talking speech using a family of MVDR estimates has been described in [6]. In this work, a simple relation between the MVDR spectrum of a particular MVDR order, signal variance, and noise variance has been presented for an exponential signal in white noise. In [6], the minimum variance spectral estimate of an exponential with amplitude Ψ_k in noise at the frequency ω_k is shown to be

$$R_M^{mvdr}(e^{j\omega}) = \frac{\sigma_w^2}{M} + |\Psi_k|^2 \tag{1}$$

Where M is the order of spectral estimate and σ_w^2 is the noise variance. The MVDR spectral estimate of noise has been shown to be

$$R_M^{mvdr}(e^{j\omega_l}) = \frac{\sigma_w^2}{M} \tag{2}$$

For more than one undamped complex exponential, and a large model order M, Equation 1, approximately holds at the frequencies corresponding to the exponentials. Extending this to speech signals modeled as a sum N complex exponentials with the frequencies ω_k being a integer multiple of the fundamental (pitch) frequency ω_0, we have

$$x(n) = \sum_{k=0}^{N-1} \Psi_k e^{j(\omega_k n + \psi_k)} \tag{3}$$

where $k=0,1,2,...,(N-1)$, are the frequency components of the signal. Assuming that the frequency components are known, the MVDR estimate can be computed at each of these frequencies using varying model orders for each microphone in the array. In explicit approaches, selection of the right microphone is an issue. Certain approaches like the closeness to the speech source and combining the spectral estimation with spatial filtering have been used before. In order to alleviate this problem we formulate an implicit approach as follows. Let us consider P microphones in an ULA. A single step MVDR spectral estimation is done by jointly combining the multiple microphones and the family of MVDR estimates (MVDR estimates of different order). Hence the approach is implicit in nature. Using Equation 1, the MVDR estimates at each ω_k, using varying model orders (M_1 to M_L), and at P different microphones, is given by

$$
\begin{aligned}
R_{M_{11}}^{mvdr}(e^{j\omega_k}) &= \frac{\sigma_{w1}^2}{M_1} + |\Psi_k|^2 + \epsilon_{11} \\
\cdots &= \cdots + \cdots + \cdots \\
R_{M_{1L}}^{mvdr}(e^{j\omega_k}) &= \frac{\sigma_{w1}^2}{M_L} + |\Psi_k|^2 + \epsilon_{1L} \\
\vdots &= \vdots + \vdots + \vdots \\
R_{M_{P1}}^{mvdr}(e^{j\omega_k}) &= \frac{\sigma_{wP}^2}{M_1} + |\Psi_k|^2 + \epsilon_{P1} \\
\cdots &= \cdots + \cdots + \cdots \\
R_{M_{PL}}^{mvdr}(e^{j\omega_k}) &= \frac{\sigma_{wP}^2}{M_L} + |\Psi_k|^2 + \epsilon_{PL}
\end{aligned}
$$

The above array of equations, can be written in a matrix form as

$$\mathbf{Y} = \mathbf{AX} + \epsilon \tag{4}$$

where

$$
Y = \begin{pmatrix}
R_{M_{11}}^{mvdr}(e^{j\omega_k}) & R_{M_{21}}^{mvdr}(e^{j\omega_k}) & \cdots & R_{M_{P1}}^{mvdr}(e^{j\omega_k}) \\
R_{M_{12}}^{mvdr}(e^{j\omega_k}) & R_{M_{22}}^{mvdr}(e^{j\omega_k}) & \cdots & R_{M_{P2}}^{mvdr}(e^{j\omega_k}) \\
\cdots & \cdots & & \cdots \\
R_{M_{1L}}^{mvdr}(e^{j\omega_k}) & R_{M_{2L}}^{mvdr}(e^{j\omega_k}) & \cdots & R_{M_{PL}}^{mvdr}(e^{j\omega_k})
\end{pmatrix}
$$

$$
X = \begin{pmatrix}
\sigma_{w1}^2 & \sigma_{w2}^2 & \cdots & \sigma_{wP}^2 \\
|\Psi_k|^2] & |\Psi_k|^2] & \cdots & |\Psi_k|^2]
\end{pmatrix}
$$

$$A = \begin{pmatrix} 1 & M_1 \\ 1 & M_2 \\ . & . \\ . & . \\ . & . \\ 1 & M_L \end{pmatrix}$$

In Equation 4, the matrix $\mathbf{X}$, can be estimated by minimizing the weighted norm of the error,

$$||\epsilon||^2_{\mathbf{W}} = ||\mathbf{Y} - \mathbf{AX}||^2_{\mathbf{W}} \tag{5}$$

The weighted least square solution to $\mathbf{X}$ is given by

$$\mathbf{X} = (\mathbf{A}^H \mathbf{WA})^{-1} \mathbf{A}^H \mathbf{WY}. \tag{6}$$

The matrix $\mathbf{W}$ is a diagonal matrix of weight vectors which can be computed

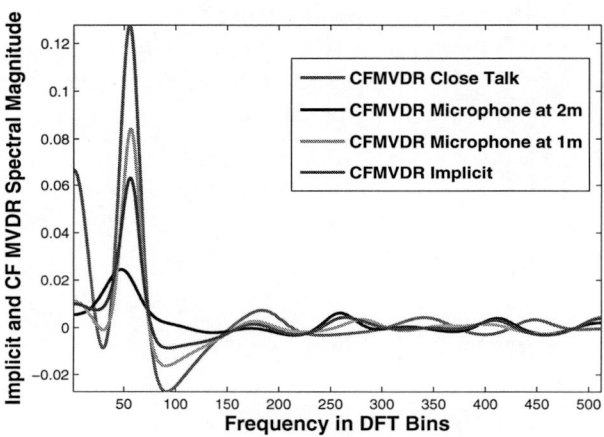

Fig. 2. Comparison of CF-MVDR spectra (Explicit) [6], and Implicit spectrum of distant talking speech using a close talking microphone, microphone at a distance of one meter, and microphone at a distance of 2 meters

using the knowledge of the MVDR spectral estimation error. For example, lower model orders can be assumed to have more error than higher model orders and this can be reflected in the choice of $\mathbf{W}$. Explicit approaches which use the CF-MVDR spectrum are indicated by CF-MVDR explicit, and the Implicit approach is indicated by the CF-MVDR Implicit in the ensuing discussions and plots.

2.3 Improving the Implicit Mvdr Spectral Estimate Using the Robust Error Norm

Although the least square error norm can be shown to be optimal for samples drawn from a Gaussian distribution, it is sensitive to outliers in a non-Gaussian

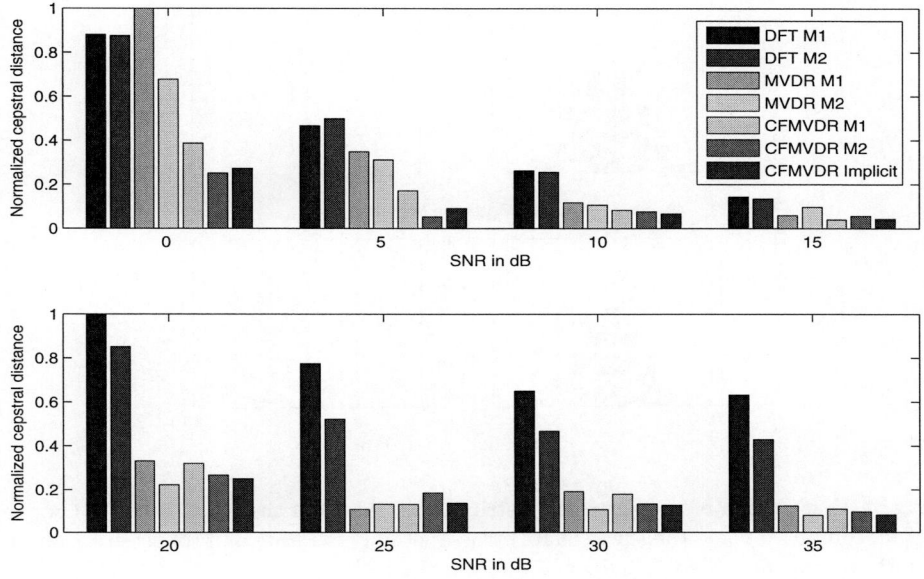

Fig. 3. Cepstral distance plots for SNR in the range of 0dB - 35 dB, for various spectral estimation methods at microphone 1 and 2 (Explicit) and the proposed Implicit approach

distribution. In this work we therefore use the robust error norm instead of least square error norm to reduce errors due to a few outliers with large measurement errors. The influence of an outlier is much larger than the other points because the least square estimator (LSE) weights the errors quadratically. Consequently, the robustness of LSE is poor. Hence the robust error norm method is used to improve the estimate by bounding the outliers as

$$||\epsilon_{robust}|| = \sum_{n=0}^{N-1} \rho(\epsilon_n) = \sum_{n=0}^{N-1} \rho(z_n - h_n(\hat{x})) \qquad (7)$$

where $\rho(.)$ measures the size of each individual residual $z_n - h_n(\hat{x})$. This measure should be selected such that above a given level of ϵ_n its influence is ruled out. In addition, a smooth $\rho(.)$ is considered so that numerical optimization of ϵ_{robust} is not too difficult. In order to illustrate the effectiveness of the robust error norm, average spectral error between the close talking microphone spectrum and the implicit MVDR spectrum is computed. The average error distributions (AED) at a SNR of 0 dB and 5 dB are illustrated in Figure 4. It can be noted that the AED of the implicit approach exhibits lesser variance when compared to the method of least squares.

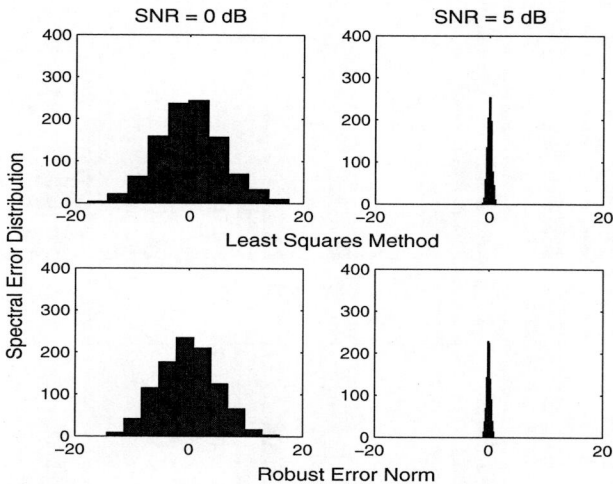

Fig. 4. Comparison of average error distributions (AED) of the Implicit MVDR spectrum, computed using the least square errors method (top row) and robust error norm (bottom row), at a SNR of 0 dB and 5 dB respectively

3   Performance Evaluation

In this Section, we evaluate the Implicit spectral estimation technique for its robustness to additive noise at various SNR using average cepstral distance plots [7]. Experimental results for distant speaker verification on a subset (8C-1C) condition of the NIST 2004 database [8], are also listed.

3.1   Robustness of the Implicit Mvdr Spectral Estimation

We compare the robustness of the MVDR, CF-MVDR and the conventional DFT based spectrum estimation techniques in the presence of white noise at different values of SNR using average cepstral distance. Thirty utterances from NIST 2004 corpus [8], recorded over a microphone array are picked randomly for analysis. White noise scaled by a factor is added to these sentences and the corresponding SNR computed. The normalized average cepstral distance between the clean and the noisy speech across all frames corresponding to the these sentences is then calculated for various values of SNR from 0 dB to 35 dB. Figure 3, illustrates the cepstral distance plot computed herein. A unit variance Gaussian normalization scheme is used in this context. It is clear from Figure 3, that average cepstral distance of the noisy speech cepstra from the clean speech cepstra is the least for the CF-MVDR technique when compared to the MVDR and DFT based spectral estimation techniques for explicit speech modeling of each microphone. It is also significant to note that the implicit approach to multi microphone speech modeling (Implicit CF-MVDR) yields the least cepstral error when compared to all other methods.

3.2 Experiments on Speaker Verification

The experimental setup for recording two channel data using a subset (8C-1C condition) of the NIST 2004 corpus [8], is first described. The recordings were

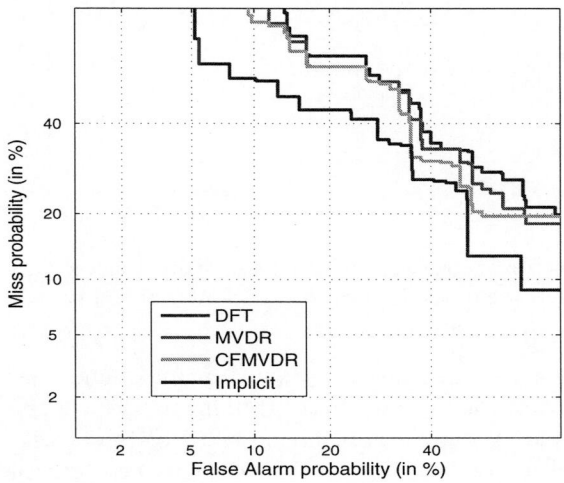

Fig. 5. The DET curves for speaker verification for different methods using microphone 1 with the the DET curve of the Implicit approach overlaid on it

made in a moderately reverberant 8.2m×3.6m×2.4m rectangular room containing a centrally located 4.8m×1.2m semi-elliptical table. The microphones were positioned at the center of the semi-elliptical table. The PC power supply fan was the predominant source of background noise. A four-element linear microphone array was placed in the center of the table.

In the 8C-1C condition of the NIST 2004 corpus, the test segments contained a whole speaker conversation side, and the model training material consisted of either one conversation side (of approximately 5 minutes) or 8 conversation sides, respectively. The data is part of the MIXER data corpus. The evaluation contains different languages and includes many trials for which the training and testing material consists of different languages. Also, there is a great variation in handset and channel type within the database.

The baseline system used in the experiments is a conventional GMM-UBM speaker verification system. A Gaussian mixture model (GMM) is trained by pooling data from many different speakers to create a universal background model(UBM) [9]. NIST 2002 SRE data was used for training the background

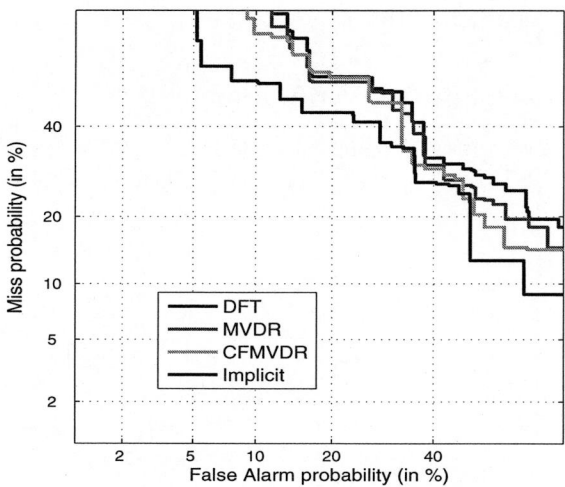

Fig. 6. The DET curves for speaker verification for different methods using microphone 2 with the the DET curve of the Implicit approach overlaid on it

models. The target speaker models are trained by maximum a posteriori(MAP) adaptation of the background model to the training data. For a given test sample, the accumulated and averaged log likelihood ratio for the target model and the background model is used as a score. The features used for the experiments in this system are the thirteen dimensional Mel frequency cepstral coefficients (MFCCs), without the zeroth order coefficient, and appended with velocity and acceleration coefficient's, resulting in thirty nine dimensional feature vectors. The features are modeled by 128 mixture component GMMs. Only the GMM means are adapted to the observed data.

The detection error trade-off (DET) plots for a subset of the NIST 2004 SRE data using features extracted from the three methods spectral estimation methods namely, DFT , MVDR, CF-MVDR (explicit) and the Implicit method are shown in Figures 5 and 6. Figure 5, illustrates the DET curves obtained using DFT (MFCC), MVDR (MVDR-MFCC), CF-MVDR (CFMVDR-MFCC) for microphone 1, and also using the Implicit (Implicit-MFCC) method for the distant speaker verification task. Similar DET curves for microphone 2, are illustrated in Figure 6, along with Implicit (Implicit-MFCC) method. Note that the implicit method performs better in terms of speaker verification performance when compared to the explicit approaches like MVDR-MFCC and CF-MVDR-MFCC computed on each microphone separately.

Figure 7, shows the DET curves for comparing CF-MVDR method for Microphone 1,2 and the Implicit approach for speaker verification system. From Figure 7, it is evident that features extracted from the implicit method perform reasonably better than those extracted from the CF-MVDR method on individual microphones in terms of the EER.

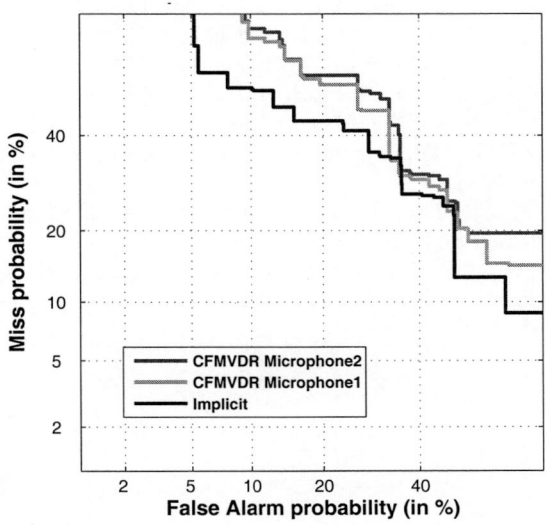

Fig. 7. DET Plot for comparing CFMVDR method for Microphone 1,2 and the Implicit approach for speaker verification

4   Conclusions

A mathematical approach to jointly combine a family of MVDR estimates and the number of elements in a ULA has been proposed in this work. Its application to distant speaker verification has also been discussed. The proposed approach to implicit spectrum estimation for distant talking speech has a twofold advantage. Using the proposed approach, a spectral estimate can be obtained from the output of an array of microphones without resorting to explicit approaches where the selection of the right microphone is an issue. When combined with spatial filtering, this technique can eliminate the need to select the right pair of microphones. Experiments on distant speaker verification indicate a reasonable performance improvement over the explicit approaches.

Acknowledgements. This work was supported by the BITCOE IIT Kanpur.

References

1. Brandstein, M., Ward, D.: Microphone Arrays: Signal processing Techniques and applications. Springer, Berlin (2001)
2. Stoica, P., Moses, R.: Spectral analysis of signals. Prentice Hall, NJ (2001)
3. Sherman, P.J., Lou, K.N.: On the family of ML spectral estimates for mixed spectrum identification. IEEE Transactions on Signal Processing 39(3), 644–655 (1991)
4. Murthi, M.N., Rao, B.D.: All-pole modeling of speech based on the minimum variance distortionless response spectrum. In: Asilomar Conference on Signals, Systems Computers, vol. 2, pp. 1061–1065 (1997)

5. Wolfel, M., McDonough, J.: Minimum variance distortionless response spectral estimation. IEEE Signal Processing Magazine 22(5), 117–126 (2005)
6. Hegde, R.M., Jin, Y., Rao, B.D.: Spectral Estimation of Voiced Speech using a Family of MVDR Estimates. In: IEEE International Conference on Acoustics, Speech and Signal Processing, ICASSP 2007, vol. 4, pp. 1069–1072 (2007)
7. Rabiner, L., Juang, B.H.: Fundamentals of speech recognition. Prentice-Hall Inc., NJ (1993)
8. NIST Speech Group, The 2004 NIST Speaker Recognition Evaluation Plan (2006), www.itl.nist.gov/iad/mig/tests/sre/2004/
9. Reynolds, D.A., Rose, R.C.: Robust Text-Independent Speaker Identification Using Gaussian Mixture Speaker Models. IEEE Transactions on Speech and Audio Processing 3, 72–83 (1995)

Spatio-temporal Visual Distortion and Rate Optimization for Video Coding

Fangzhen Hu, Li Su, Honggang Qi, and Qingming Huang

Graduate University of Chinese Academy of Sciences, Beijing, China
{fzhu,lsu,hgqi,qmhuang}@jdl.ac.cn

Abstract. Rate-distortion optimization (RDO) plays a significant role in video coding. However, in most RDO methods, the distortion measurement metrics consider only the spatial distortion of statistical pixel errors. People have concerns about not only the information of independent pixels, but also the spatial and temporal correlations between them. In order to make the distortion assessment more consistent with human perception, temporal information of the successive images and the characteristics of human visual perception should be considered as well. In this paper, we propose a rate-distortion model based on spatio-temporal video structural similarity (stVSSIM) index, which takes both spatial and temporal visual quality into account. Meanwhile, to obtain a reasonable trade-off between bit-rate and visual quality dynamically, a perceptual adaptive Lagrange multiplier selection method is presented. Simulation results show that the proposed method averagely reduces 20% bit-rate under the equal visual quality and the adaptive Lagrange multiplier can further improve the results.

Keywords: Video coding, Rate-distortion optimization, Spatio-temporal visual distortion assessment, Visual perception.

1 Introduction

In popular hybrid video coding standards, more and more coding modes are designed to improve the coding efficiency. For example, in the latest video coding standard H.264/AVC, there are more than 10 kinds of intra and inter modes. Which mode should be selected as the best mode is very important for the final coding performance. To obtain the best mode, the mode selection in the current video codec is usually determined by the rate-distortion optimization (RDO).

The RDO problem can be mathematically defined as following [1]:

$$min\{J\}, where\ J = D + \lambda \cdot R \tag{1}$$

where J is the rate-distortion (R-D) cost and R is bit-rate for a coding unit such as one macroblock. λ is the Lagrange multiplier (LM) which controls the trade-off between R and the distortion D.

In the past decades, many methods have been proposed to model the R-D characteristic for high efficient coding [1] [2]. The most popular R-D model which

W. Lin et al. (Eds.): PCM 2012, LNCS 7674, pp. 639–650, 2012.

is used in general hybrid video coding standards such as H.263 and H.264/AVC is proposed in [1] [2]. However, in this model the Lagrange multiplier is fixed and properties of input signal don't earn enough consideration. In order to achieve adaptivity, Chen proposed an adaptive Lagrange multiplier estimation method based on ρ-domain method [3] [4]. But R and D are directly included into λ calculation, which may be effected by error propagation. In [5], an adaptive RDO model using Laplace distribution of transformed residuals is described. However, the objective distortion metrics used for measuring video quality in the above methods such as sum of square error (SSE) or mean squared error (MSE) are poorly correlated with perceptual quality. Researches show that distorted images with nearly identical MSE may present totally different perceptual distortion [6].

Recently, to resolve this problem, many perceptual quality assessment metrics have been proposed. These metrics can replace the SSE in RDO process to improve the performance of the encoder. Among the various quality assessment metrics, the structural similarity (SSIM) index, which is proposed by Wang [7], has been shown to be effective and computationally efficient to quantify the compression artifacts. It has been introduced into motion estimation and mode selection of video coding. In [8], a statistical relationship between the SSIM and the bit-rate is developed based on experiments. In [9], a rate-SSIM curve is employed to describe the R-D relationship and a dynamic Lagrange multiplier is obtained by approximating the gradient descent of R-D points of encoded frames. Whereas two-pass encoding of the key frames brings more additional complexity to the encoder. The method in [10] derives the Lagrange multiplier adaptively by incorporating a statistical reduced-referenced SSIM model and a source-side information combined rate model into the RDO process. In [11], spatial visual attention of images is considered. However, the SSIM distortion metric in the methods mentioned above is merely used to measure distortion of each static frame and considers only the spatial information. Actually, the temporal information in the video also has a profound impact on human visual perception. So it is rational to introduce the video quality metrics with temporal information of successive images into the RDO problem.

In this paper, to achieve high visual performance, a spatio-temporal RDO model is proposed. In the new model, a spatio-temporal video quality assessment metric called stVSSIM is employed [12]. Different from other distortion metrics, stVSSIM utilizes motion information and structural similarity to assess the temporal and spatial video quality jointly. In particular, we incorporate the R-D model and distortion-QP (D-QP) model which are obtained from the macroblock statistical data of several sequences to derive the Lagrange multiplier. Meanwhile, we set up an adaptive adjusting model of Lagrange multiplier based on the spatio-temporal distortion model and human attention weighting to make a dynamic trade-off between visual distortion and bit-rate.

The rest of this paper is organized as follows. Firstly, we briefly describe the spatio-temporal visual distortion metric stVSSIM in Section 2. Secondly, we introduce the proposed new rate-distortion model based on stVSSIM and the adaptive Lagrange multiplier adjusting method in Section 3. Subsequently, the performance of the proposed model is shown in Section 4. Finally, conclusions are presented in the last section.

2   Spatio-temporal Video SSIM Index

In this section we will review the basic concept of stVSSIM [12] that is used in our proposed rate-distortion model. In stVSSIM, spatial and temporal quality assessments, SSIM [7] and SSIM3D [12], are calculated separately.

Suppose x and y are two image blocks from the nth frame of two videos, H and W are the height and width of x and y, respectively. Firstly, the spatial quality is calculated as follows:

$$SSIM(x, y) = \frac{(2\mu_x\mu_y + C_1)(2\sigma_{xy} + C_2)}{(\mu_x^2 + \mu_y^2 + C_1)(\sigma_x^2 + \sigma_y^2 + C_2)} \tag{2}$$

where μ_x, μ_y, σ_x^2 and σ_y^2 are the means, the variances of x and y, respectively, σ_{xy} is the covariance between x and y. The constants C_1, C_2 and C_3 are used to avoid instability [7].

To obtain the temporal quality, let X and Y denote two video blocks corresponding to x and y, $N-1$ is the number of frames in front of the nth frame, temporally. Then the following statistics of video blocks X and Y are calculated:

$$\mu_X = \sum_{k=1}^{N}\sum_{i=1}^{H}\sum_{j=1}^{W} w(i, j, k)X(i, j, k) \tag{3}$$

$$\sigma_X^2 = \sum_{k=1}^{N}\sum_{i=1}^{H}\sum_{j=1}^{W} w(i, j, k)(X(i, j, k) - \mu_X)^2 \tag{4}$$

$$\sigma_{XY} = \sum_{k=1}^{N}\sum_{i=1}^{H}\sum_{j=1}^{W} w(i, j, k)(X(i, j, k) - \mu_X)(Y(i, j, k) - \mu_Y) \tag{5}$$

where (i, j, k) is coordinate of pixels in the video blocks and w is a filter. Then the temporal quality between block x and y can be calculated as follows:

$$SSIM3D(x, y) = \frac{(2\mu_X\mu_Y + C_1)(2\sigma_{XY} + C_2)}{(\mu_X^2 + \mu_Y^2 + C_1)(\sigma_X^2 + \sigma_Y^2 + C_2)} \tag{6}$$

where the constants C_1 and C_2 are the same with (2).

Generally, we get several SSIM3D values depending on the number of filters used. In this paper, four filters are used. Then motion vectors of the video block are used to decide the best SSIM3D value.

At last, the spatio-temporal quality between x and y can be calculated as follows:

$$stVSSIM(x, y) = SSIM(x, y) \times SSIM3D(x, y) \tag{7}$$

The block size is typically 8×8 [7], and the final stVSSIM of the nth frame is the average of stVSSIM values of all blocks.

3   Proposed Rate-Distortion Optimization Model

In [7], we know that SSIM reflects the perceptual feature of human visual system (HVS). From Section 2, we realize that stVSSIM considers spatial assessment SSIM and temporal assessment SSIM3D, which indicates that stVSSIM tends to be a more complete perceptual metric compared with SSIM. Therefore, the stVSSIM-based distortion is introduced into our RDO model for more accurate estimation on visual quality of video.

3.1   stVSSIM-Based RDO Model (stRDO)

So as to incorporate the stVSSIM into the RDO model appropriately, the distortion metric $D_{stVSSIM}$ is defined as

$$D_{stVSSIM} = 1 - stVSSIM \tag{8}$$

Then the R-D cost in (1) is rewritten as

$$J = D_{stVSSIM} + \lambda \cdot R \tag{9}$$

Suppose R and $D_{stVSSIM}$ can be differentiable everywhere, the minimum of the R-D cost, J, is obtained by setting its derivative to zero:

$$\lambda = -\frac{dD_{stVSSIM}}{dR} \tag{10}$$

Equation (10) indicates that λ corresponds to the negative slope of the rate-distortion curve, which means that λ can be perfectly determined by the model of R and $D_{stVSSIM}$.

In previous literature, many methods use quantization parameter (QP) or other variables as a bridge variable between rate and distortion [3] [4] [5] [8] [11]. Namely, rate-QP (R-QP) and D-QP models are built in these methods. However, we find that this way may bring some fluctuations during our modeling process.

From the information theory, we know that there is a classic relationship between rate and distortion, which is presented in the Fig. 1. In Fig. 1, there are 9 sequences of QCIF format presented, and the rate-distortion curves keep simimlar shapes. However, if we merely model the relationship of rate and QP or that of distortion and QP, the constraint relationship between rate and distortion can't be guaranteed.

In this paper, we set up the model of rate and distortion to satisfy the rate-distortion curve. Besides, in order to obtain the Lagrange multiplier, QP is still used as the control variable in our model. In this case, we can model the relationship of rate and QP or relationship of distortion and QP.

Privious researches show that at sufficiently high rates, the source probability distribution can be approximated as uniform within each quantization interval and the distortion and QP relationship is given [13]. Therefore, we model relationship between distortion and QP in this paper. Through the R-D model and the D-QP model, we derive the formula of Lagrange multiplier.

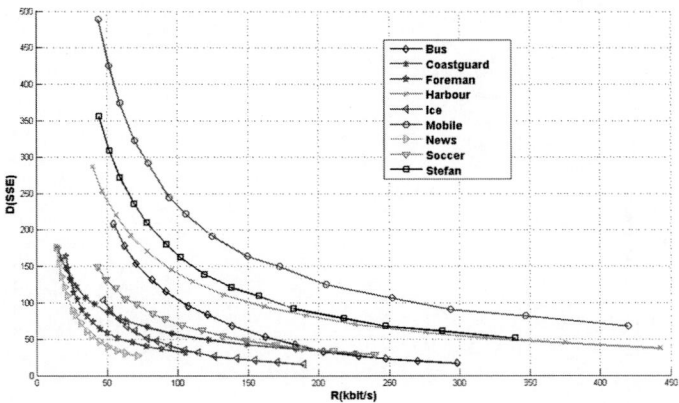

Fig. 1. Rate and distortion curves of 9 different sequences

Rate-Distortion Model Usually, in the RDO models which are based on given statistical data, the R-D data of frames is used. However, the RDO process is usually operated on macroblocks. Therefore, we use the statistical data of macroblocks to make the models much more precise.

Fig. 2 is the macroblock scatter diagram of $D_{stVSSIM}$ and R from 12 sequences. We get the R-D curve through data fitting:

$$R = \frac{1}{b} \log \left(\frac{D_{stVSSIM}}{a} \right) \qquad (11)$$

where a and b are fitted parameters.

Table 1. Performance with various QPs

	base-e	base-2
SSE	1.261	5.464
R-square	0.9508	0.7867
Adjusted R-square	0.9507	0.7864
RMSE	0.03898	0.08114

In our experiments, we discover that base-e can model the relationship of distortion and QP better than base-2. The comparison between base-e and base-2 is presented in Table 1. The SSE or RMSE value closer to 0 indicates a better fit, while R-square or Adjusted R-square with a value closer to 1 corresponds a better fit. Thus our R-D model in (11) can be rewritten as

$$R = \frac{1}{b} \ln \left(\frac{D_{stVSSIM}}{a} \right) \qquad (12)$$

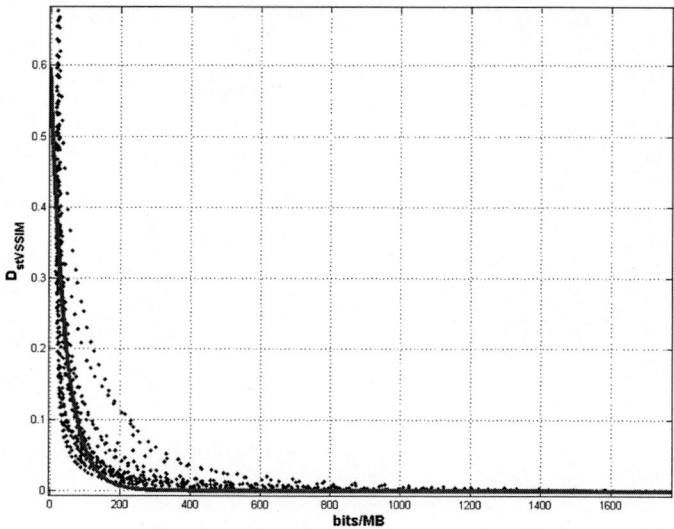

Fig. 2. Relationship between Rate and $D_{stVSSIM}$ of macroblocks

Distortion-QP Model. In [8], an exponential relationship of distortion and QP is presented:

$$D = k \cdot E[D] = \frac{k \cdot 2^{(QP-12)/3}}{3} \tag{13}$$

where k is the number of pixels in a macroblock, $E[D]$ is the expectation of distortion of one pixel.

Fig. 3 shows the macroblock scatter data of $D_{stVSSIM}$ and QP from 12 sequences of QCIF format.The fitted equation (14) depicts the relationship which is similar with (13).

$$D_{stVSSIM} = c \cdot e^{d \cdot QP} \tag{14}$$

where c and d are fitted parameters.

From (12) and (14), we derive

$$\frac{dD_{stVSSIM}}{dR} = a \cdot b \cdot e^{b \cdot R} = c \cdot b \cdot e^{d \cdot QP} \tag{15}$$

Derived from (10) and (15), the final λ can be determined as

$$\lambda = -c \cdot b \cdot e^{d \cdot QP} \tag{16}$$

From the fitted curves in Fig. 2 and Fig. 3, we get the approximate values of b, c, and d. In our experiments, the best approximate λ is

$$\lambda = 5.883 \times 10^{-3} \times 2.229 \times 10^{-2} \times e^{9.28 \times 10^{-2} \times (QP-15)} \tag{17}$$

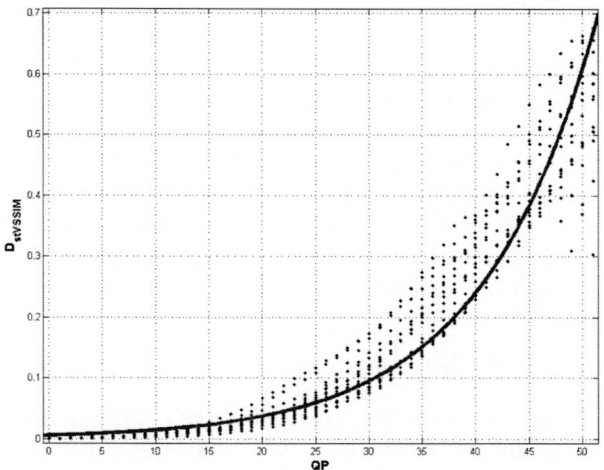

Fig. 3. Relationship between $D_{stVSSIM}$ QP of macroblocks

3.2 Adaptive Lagrange Multiplier Method

Lagrange multiplier λ in (17) is a fixed value for all sequences, which is not appropriate for different sequences with different content. It is necessary to do some adjustment to λ according to the content of sequences.

To make λ do a better adaption with the content of the video, some perceptual information of the video image is introduced in our RDO scheme. As people have different attention to different parts of one image [14], we employ the attention information to adjust λ to make it much more adaptive to the content of the image.

Suppose a_j is the attention value of an image pixel calculated by [14]. In fact, a_j contains the spatial and temporal attention. Thus, the attention weight of one macroblock is calculated as following:

$$w_i = \sum_{j \in M_i} a_j \tag{18}$$

where w_i is the attention weight of macroblock M_i.

When an image is encoded, for the parts of high attention, much more bits should be allocated and vice versa. Equation (9) indicates that higher rates correspond lower λ, which means for a macroblock, if it is highly noticed, the λ should be decreased. Thus we use the following method to adjust λ [15]:

$$\phi_i = \left(\frac{w_{avg}}{w_i} \right)^{\varphi} \tag{19}$$

$$\lambda_i' = \lambda \cdot \phi_i \tag{20}$$

where w_{avg} represents the average weight of all the macroblocks in the current frame, ϕ_i is the adjustment factor for macroblock M_i and λ_i' is the adaptive Lagrange multiplier for M_i.

4   Experiments

In this section, the proposed RDO scheme is verified in H.264/AVC reference software JM14.1 [16]. All the test QCIF video sequences are in YCbCr 4:2:0 format and encoded under baseline profile. For each sequence, 50 frames with one frame skipped are encoded with IPPP structure.

To make a thorough evaluation, the proposed stVSSIM rate-distortion (stRDO) model is compared with two H.264 compliant encoders. One is the MSE-based RDO adopted in the JM14.1 and the other is the SSIM-based RDO [8]. Then, we compare the results of stRDO using adaptive Lagrange multiplier or not.

4.1   Performance of Proposed Method without Adaptive LM

The R-D performance curves of the proposed stRDO method are shown in Fig. 4. These curves show that for all test sequences, the coding performance has been improved. Under higher bit-rate, the encoded visual quality is good for all methods. And our stRDO method improves the visual quality much more at high bit-rate. However, under lower bit-rate, the visual quality of these algorithms is rather different. The R-D curve of sequence *Foreman* indicates that our method require more bits, but the visual quality improves much more compared with the JM14.1. From the comparison between the proposed stRDO method and SSIM-based RDO method, we can see that the temporal information performs well in helping improve coding efficiency.

Table 2 shows the performance of our method in various QPs. It indicates that the rate reduction and the stVSSIM/SSIM gain for high bit-rate is much higher than that for low bit-rate. When compared with SSIM-based method, we observe that the rate reduction stabilize at around 18%. This may be explained by the temporal and motion information which is integrated into the stVSSIM. For the same sequence, no matter what QP it is, these two aspects information remain stable. Thus the rate reduction of different QPs stays the same.

Simulation results are shown in Table 3. On average, compared with JM14.1, the proposed RDO model achieves 2.93% stVSSIM or 8.36% SSIM visual quality gain and reduces 20.96% bit-rate. Meanwhile, compared with SSIM-based RDO model, it gains 1.97% stVSSIM or 6.51% SSIM visual quality and reduces 18.38% bit-rate. This improvement is due to the fact that stRDO select the best mode from perceptual point of view, resulting in more bits allocated to areas which are more sensitive to our visual systems. From Fig. 4 and Table 3, we find that in some sequences, such as *Foreman* and *Highway*, SSIM-based method performs not too well, whereas our method still keeps better performance, which means the temporal and motion information is fairly important.

In general, we think the improved performance of our stRDO method benefits from three main reasons. First, in our RDO scheme, besides spatial information of one sequence, temporal information is also considered at the same time. Second, we use the statistical macroblock data of several sequences to build our RDO model. Third, the motion between the frames is utilized to further improve the rate distribution among the MBs in consideration of HVS.

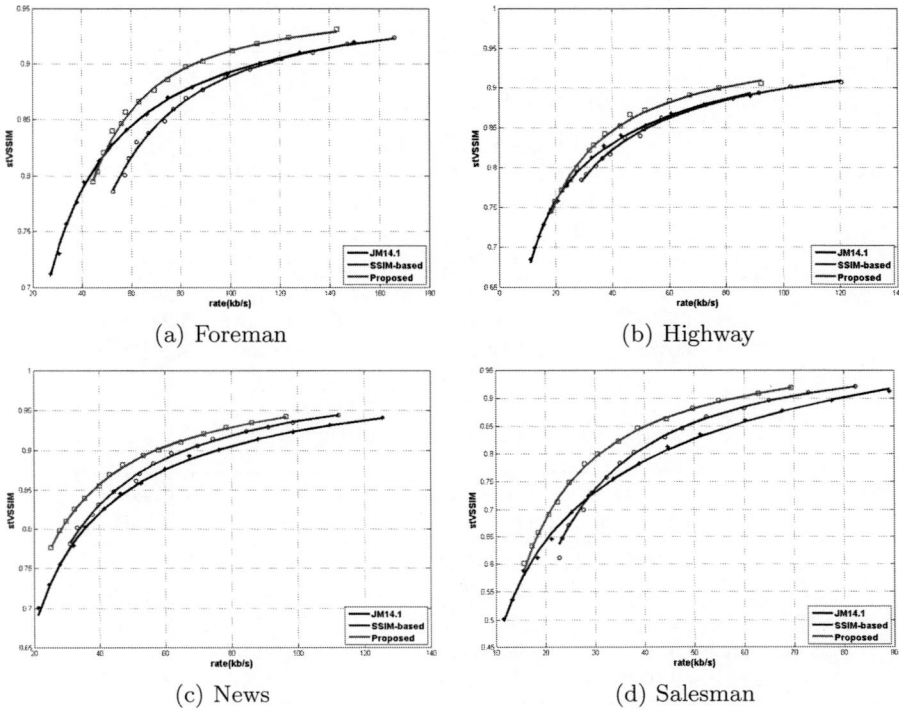

Fig. 4. Performance comparison: The proposed method presents better performance than JM14.1 and SSIM-based RDO

4.2   Performance of Adaptive LM Method

To show the advantage of our adaptive Lagrange multiplier method, the performance comparison between the stRDO without adaptive LM and stRDO using adaptive LM (stRDOLM) is presented in Table 4.

Table 4 shows that under the same bit-rate, the stVSSIM visual quality of the sequence *Foreman, News* and *Salesman* all have been improved in different extents. In case of the same visual quality, the bit-rate of *News* and *Salesman* have reduced and *Salesman* drops much more. When the SSIM visual quality is considered, it can be perceived all sequences have made an improvement.

However, our stRDOLM performs not too well on *Highway*. Since there is not too much motion information and attractive information in *Highway*, the attention information extracted from it is less accurate. This may result in the bit-rate increase.

On average, we can see that the bit-rate reduction is unconspicuous. There are two reasons. First, our adaptive Lagrange multiplier is used on the macroblocks within one frame, thus the adjustment is limited. Second, the attention information inside one frame is used while the attention information between frames is not considered. In a word, if the Lagrange multiplier is first adjusted through

Table 2. Performance with various QPs

QP	stRDO vs. JM14.1			stRDO vs. SSIM-based		
	ΔstVSSIM	ΔRate	ΔSSIM	ΔstVSSIM	ΔRate	ΔSSIM
28	+1.95%	-25.10%	+5.16%	+1.17%	-18.57%	+4.24%
29	+2.22%	-24.09%	+5.91%	+1.28%	-17.73%	+4.74%
30	+2.58%	-23.64%	+6.78%	+1.57%	-18.90%	+5.38%
31	+2.95%	-23.31%	+7.71%	+1.82%	-19.04%	+5.95%
32	+3.19%	-20.95%	+8.75%	+1.97%	-18.05%	+6.63%
33	+3.15%	-17.80%	+9.51%	+2.38%	-18.87%	+7.47%
34	+3.69%	-17.75%	+10.95%	+2.59%	-17.66%	+8.24%
35	+3.66%	-15.08%	+12.12%	+3.01%	-18.24%	+9.39%

Table 3. Simulation results of the stRDO

Sequence	stRDO vs. JM14.1			stRDO vs. SSIM-based		
	ΔstVSSIM	ΔRate	ΔSSIM	ΔstVSSIM	ΔRate	ΔSSIM
Foreman	+1.89%	-17.82%	+5.99%	+2.18%	-24.40%	+5.47%
Highway	+1.65%	-14.86%	+9.23%	+1.89%	-21.70%	+7.15%
News	+2.53%	-23.86%	+6.20%	+1.10%	-11.78%	+4.76%
Salesman	+5.63%	-27.32%	+12.03%	+2.72%	-15.66%	+8.64%
Average	+2.93%	-20.96%	+8.36%	+1.97%	-18.38%	+6.51%

Table 4. Simulation results of stRDO using adaptive LM

Sequence	stRDOLM vs. stRDO			stRDOLM vs. JM14.1		
	ΔstVSSIM	ΔRate	ΔSSIM	ΔstVSSIM	ΔRate	ΔSSIM
Foreman	+0.09%	-0.00%	+3.76%	+1.93%	-18.30%	+5.99%
Highway	-0.30%	+3.84%	+6.39%	+1.52%	-14.27%	+9.30%
News	+0.08%	-0.63%	+4.27%	+2.56%	-24.64%	+6.17%
Salesman	+0.74%	-4.19%	+7.48%	+6.21%	-30.81%	+12.15%
Average	+0.15%	-0.24%	+5.48%	+3.06%	-22.01%	+8.40%

the frame structure information and then regulated in the macroblock level, the results will be much better.

4.3 Subjective Quality Evaluation

Fig. 5 shows the original frame, H.264/AVC coded frame with the conventional RDO, H.264/AVC coded frame with the proposed stRDO method and H.264/AVC coded frame with the proposed stRDOLM method. It should be noted that the visual quality of the four circumstances are almost the same, while the stRDO and stRDOLM save much more bit-rates.

(a) Original   (b) MSE-based

(c) stRDO   (d) stRDOLM

Fig. 5. The 56th reconstructed frame from *News*. (b) Bits=3000, PSNR=36.799, SSIM=0.9689, stVSSIM=0.9419. (c) Bits=2800, PSNR=35.696, SSIM=0.9691, stVS-SIM=0.9420. (d) Bits=2712, PSNR=35.189, SSIM=0.9673, stVSSIM=0.9398.

5   Conclusions

In this paper, a spatio-temporal visual distortion and rate optimization method for video coding is presented. Firstly, the stVSSIM index is used as the distortion metric which is more consistent with the human perceptual distortion. Then, we derive new rate distortion model based on the spatio-temporal perceptual distortion. In the proposed RDO model, an exponential Lagrange multiplier is dynamically fitted for higher coding performance. Meanwhile, human attention of the image is used during encoding one macroblock to adjust the Lagrange multiplier to adapt the content of the sequences. Experimental results show that proposed RDO method improves the performance of video coding efficiently.

Acknowledgments. This work was supported in part by National Basic Research Program of China (973 Program): 2009CB320906, in part by National Natural Science Foundation of China: 61025011, 60833006, 61001177 and 61001108.

References

1. Sullivan, G.J., Wiegand, T.: Rate-distortion Optimization for Video Compression. IEEE Signal Process. Mag. 15(6), 74–90 (1998)
2. Wiegand, T., Girod, B.: Lagrangian Multiplier Selection in Hybrid Video Coder Control. In: IEEE Int. Conf. of Image Process., vol. 3, pp. 542–545 (2001)
3. He, Z., Kim, Y.K., Mitra, S.K.: Low-delay Rate Control for DCT Video Coding via ρ-domain Source Modeling. IEEE Trans. on Circuits Syst. for Video Tech. 11, 928–940 (2001)
4. Chen, L., Garbacea, I.: Adaptive Lambda Estimation in Lagrangian Rate-distortion Optimization for Video Coding. In: Visual Commun. Image Process., VCIP, vol. 6077, pp. 1–8 (2006)
5. Li, X., Oertel, N., Hutter, A., Kaup, A.: Laplace Distribution Based Lagrangian Rate Distortion Optimization for Hybrid Video Coding. IEEE Trans. on Circuits Syst. for Video Tech. 19(2), 193–205 (2009)
6. Wang, Z., Bovik, A.C.: Mean Squared Error: Love It or Leave It? A New Look at Signal Fidelity Measures. IEEE Signal Process. Mag. 26(1), 98–117 (2009)
7. Wang, Z., Bovik, A.C., Sheikh, H.R., Simoncelli, E.P.: Image Quality Assessment: From Error Visibility to Structural Similarity. IEEE Trans. on Image Process. 13(4), 600–612 (2004)
8. Yang, C., Leung, R., Po, L., Mai, Z.: An SSIM-optimal H.264/AVC Inter Frame Encoder. In: IEEE Proc. Intelligent Computing and Intelligent Systems, vol. 4, pp. 291–295 (2009)
9. Huang, Y., Ou, T., Su, P., Chen, H.: Perceptual Rate-distortion Optimization Using Structural Similarity Index as Quality Metric. IEEE Trans. on Circuits Syst. for Video Tech. 20 (2010) 1051-8215
10. Wang, S., Rehman, A., Wang, Z., Ma, S., Gao, W.: Rate-SSIM Optimization for Video Coding. In: IEEE Proc. Acoustics, Speech and Signal Processing, pp. 833–836 (2011)
11. Wang, X., Su, L., Huang, Q., Liu, C.: Visual Perception Based Lagrangian Rate Distortion Optimization for Video Coding. In: IEEE Int. Conf. of Image Process., pp. 1653–1656 (2011)
12. Moorthy, A.K., Bovik, A.C.: Efficient Motion Weighted Spatio-temporal Video SSIM Index. In: SPIE Proc. Human Vision and Electronic Imaging, vol. 7527, p. 72571 (2010)
13. Gish, H., Pierce, J.N.: Asymptotically Efficient Quantizing. IEEE Trans. on Information Theory 14, 676–683 (1968)
14. Liu, H., Jiang, S., Huang, Q., Xu, C.: A Generic Virtual Content Insertion System Based on Visual Attention Analysis. In: ACM Multimedia, pp. 379–388 (2008)
15. Wang, M., Ling, N.: Lagrangian Multiplier Based Joint Three-layer Rate Control for H.264/AVC. IEEE Signal Process. Letters 16(8), 679–682 (2009)
16. H.264 reference software JM14.1, http://iphome.hhi.de/suehring/tml/

View Synthesis Based on Background Update with Gaussian Mixture Model

Chao Yao, Yao Zhao, and Huihui Bai

Institute of Information Science, Beijing Jiaotong University, Beijing 100044, China
Beijing Key Laboratory of Advanced Information Science and Network Technology,
Beijing 100044, China
yaochao1986@gmail.com, {yzhao,hhbai}@bjtu.edu.cn

Abstract. View Synthesis is a key technique for 3-D video and free view video generation. In the traditional 3-D video and free view video, there have to be many real cameras to capture the scene at the large cost. With the help of the view synthesis technique, a limited number of cameras can achieve the goal of multi-view generation. However, some holes will appear in the synthesized views due to the 3-D warping process in the view synthesis system. These holes seriously affect the quality of the synthesized images, especially for the disocclusions which is caused from the occluded regions in the original view may become visible in the virtual view. In this paper, we focus on the disocclustion filling after 3-D warping in view synthesis system. An approach is proposed to fill the discocclusion by using the real background information covered in the original view, which is based on the observation that the covered information in the current frame may be visible in the next frames of the same view. In this approach, the stable texture and depth background reference frames are generated for the left and right view, respectively, which are based on the Gaussian Mixture Model (GMM). Then, in the view synthesis system, a stable background reference frame is merged by the left and right warped images with the corresponding texture and depth background reference frames. Finally, the merged frame is used to fill the disocclusion regions of each merged frame as the background reference frame. The experimental results show that the proposed scheme can achieve better objective quality, especially for the scene with moving objects.

Keywords: View Synthesis, Gaussian Mixture Model, Background Update, Depth-Image-Based-Render.

1 Introduction

In the past two decades, many techniques about 3-D video [1] have emerged with 3-D movies arising. In this context, a new 3-D data format is proposed to support the 3-D video [2], which is consist of the color texture image and the per-pixel-associated depth map. Based on this format, the technique of the view synthesis [3] with Depth-Image-Based-Render (DIBR) [4], which can generate

W. Lin et al. (Eds.): PCM 2012, LNCS 7674, pp. 651–660, 2012.

arbitrary virtual views between two views, has been applied in the 3-D system. Thus, in case of a limited number of camera sources, the multi-view video and free view video can be achieved. Compared with the traditional 3-D video, which is generated by multi-view videos, this new 3-D data can efficiently support the transmission in case of limited bandwidth. Owing to these benefits, 3-D video with the representation of depth has become an important topic in academic and industry.

However, a critical problem in the DIBR technique is how to deal with the hole regions after 3-D projection. For a higher quality of virtual view, view synthesis requires high-quality depth data. Whereas, it is difficult to get perfect depth maps in reality. Thus, the imperfect depth map (e.g., the depth discontinuity, which represents as the depth value is discontinuous among the adjacent pixels, while these pixels are on the same depth level in the scene.)will lead to some artifacts in the rendered image and decrease the quality of the image. To handle with the holes in render image, L. Zhang proposed to smooth the whole of the original depth map with a symmetric Gaussian filter in [5]. Then, in [6], an asymmetric filter was suggested to reduce the vertical edge artifacts compared with the symmetric filter. By using the lowpass filter, the depth pixels will be smoothed by the around pixels, but the changes of the depth value will also lead to the geometry distortion of the objects in the rendering image. With the intention to get rid of the geometry distortion, Chen et al. proposed an edge-dependent Gaussian filter to smooth the depth map while the depth on the boundary between the foreground and the background can be perserved [7], and Lee et al. utilized a lowpass adaptive Gaussian filter on the boundary of the objects [8] and corrected the depth value on the horizontal and vertical direction to avoid the distortion for objects. However, for these approaches, the typical artifacts can still be observed, especially for the case of large baseline.

Another problem is that, the regions covered by the foreground objects in the original image become visible in the virtual view, which represent as the disocclusion regions in the virtual view. For this problem which is caused by the change of the view, the approaches based on the depth pre-processing are not valid enough. Y. Zhao [9] proposed a SMART solution based on depth enhancement to reduce the background noise and foreground erosion, and it is efficient for the artifacts on the boundary of foreground objects in the rendering image while it is still limited on handling with the disocclusion. In [10], a background sprite is generated to fill the disocclusions, which is based on the regions covered in one frame will become visible in the other frames. Thus, the occluded regions can be filled with the real background information. But the performance of this method will be seriously affected in case of depth temporal inconsistency.

In this paper, we proposed an approach based on background updating to deal with the disocclusion in the rendering image. Given the depth temporal inconsistency, we introduce the Gaussian Mixture Model (GMM) into view synthesis system and apply it on the texture sequences and the depth sequences, respectively. Based on the GMM, a stable texture background reference frame and a stable depth background reference frame of each original view(e.g., the left view and the right view) can be generated. Using these reference frames, a stable virtual background reference frame, which is for the left warped view and the right warped view, respectively, will be generated to fill the disocclusion of each frame in the view synthesis system. Experiment results show that the performance of the proposed approach is better than the View Synthesis Reference Software (VSRS) in the objective test.

The rest of this paper is organized as follows. Section 2 reviews the conventional view synthesis framework. Section 3 introduces our proposed method. Experiment results are showed in Section 4. Finally, Section 5 concludes this paper.

2 View Synthesis Framework

View synthesis is an expanded application of Depth-Image-Based-Render technique, which employs the spatial geometry relationship to generate virtual views near to the original views. There are basically three steps in the view synthesis system, as shown in Fig.1: First, forward warp to the intermediary virtual view from the left and right original views, respectively; Second, merge both warped views to one view; Finally fill the holes in the merged view.

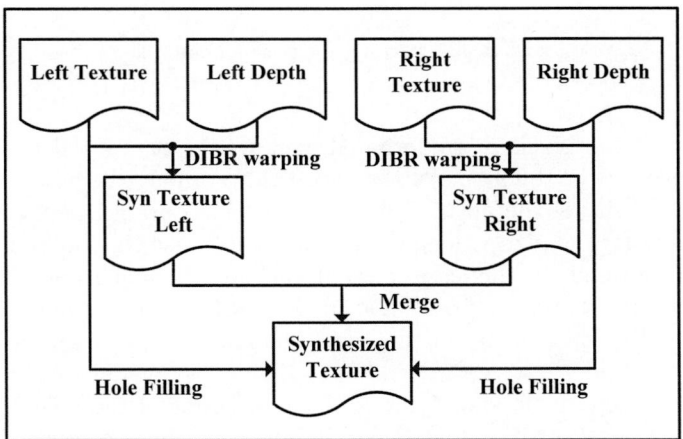

Fig. 1. View synthesis framework

For simplicity, we just take 1-D mode camera configuration for generating intermediary virtual view to illustrate the warping process, as shown in Fig.2. Under this camera configuration, the point O with the depth Z is projected onto the image plane, and its corresponding pixels in the left, the virtual center and the right view can be represented as $(x_l, y_l), (x_c, y_c)$ and (x_r, y_r), respectively. According to the space geometric relationship, we have the equation,

$$x_c = x_l - b \cdot \frac{f}{Z}, x_c = x_r + b \cdot \frac{f}{Z}, y_l = y_r = y_c \qquad (1)$$

where f specifies the focal length of the camera, Z is given the depth value in the left and right view, b is the value of the baseline distance between the reference camera and virtual camera.

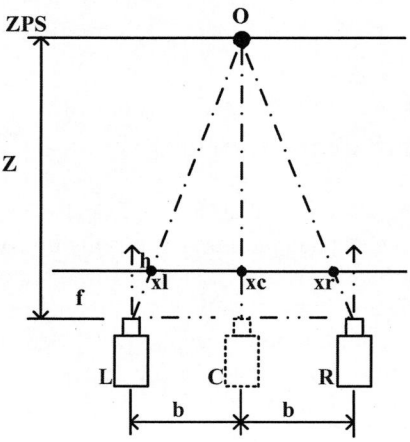

Fig. 2. 3D warping for parallel camera

Then, all of the pixels in the original view would be warped to the virtual view. However, if the difference of the depth value among the adjacent pixels is large, the disparity of the position where these pixels are warped will be large, too, especially for the pixels along the boundary between the foreground objects and the background. In this case, part of background which are not visible in the original view would be visible, shown as HOLE in the virtual view. Hence, for obtaining the high quality virtual view, the holes in the virtual view need to be filled.

The merge step in the view synthesis system is one of the hole-filling methods, which is based on the spatial correlation between two original views. In theory, the depth value in the left and right view are similar with each other, so the warped pixels are aligned in the virtual view. The disocclusion regions in the left warped view, should be not holes in the right warped view. Thus, the merge of two views can fill the disocclusion regions in the virtual view. In the merge step, first of all, a weight function is applied to calculate which of the two views is the major view. Then, the major view is taken as the domain view and the other view is used to fill the holes of the domain view as a reference view. At last, a relative well merged view will be got after the hole-filling with the linear pixel interpolation. But to fill the holes with the merge method, it requires that the alignment between the left view and the right view must be good enough, the depth map of the left view and the right view must be also in keep with each other. However, for the depth maps which are generated based on depth estimation without any post-processing, it is difficult to fill all of the holes perfectly.

3   Proposed Method

On the basis that the disocclusion is resulted from that the regions occluded by the foreground objects in the original view become visible in the virtual view, so it is available for that the occluded background information is used to fill the disocclusions in the virtual view.

(a) The original frame   (b) The background model

Fig. 3. The background model from the original sequences

3.1   Gaussian Mixture Model

The conventional approaches for getting the occluded background information include two types methods: One is based on the spatial relationship among different views, and another is based on the temporal relationship among the frames in one view. The methods based on the spatial relationship, in general, need an amount of cameras to capture the same scene, and the calibration of cameras is an essential step in all of methods. The accuracy of the calibration parameters will affect the correlation between the cameras, and limit the performance of the background updating. The methods based on the temporal relationship, is resulting from the observation that the regions occluded by the foreground objects in one frame while part of these regions become visible in the other frames. Thus, the methods based on the temporal relationship, by comparison, appear to be more applicable in case of view synthesis with limited cameras.

In the computer vision field, the Gaussian Mixture Model is a commonly used method to detect the moving objects [11][12][13], which has been widely applied to model the stable background. The Gaussian Mixture Model method performed at pixel level, for dividing the moving objects and stable background, each pixel of the scene is modeled independently by a mixture K (common as 3) Gaussian models, which are represented as the Gaussian distributions

$$p(x_t) = \sum_{i=1}^{K} \omega_{i,t} \cdot \eta(x_t, \mu_{i,t}, \Sigma_{i,t}) \tag{2}$$

where x_t represents the pixel value at the time t, $\omega_{i,t}$ is the ith Gaussian distribution's weight, which $\sum_{i}^{K} \omega_{i,t} = 1$, the $\mu_{i,t}$ and $\Sigma_{i,t}$ is the mean and the variance of the pixel x_t, respectively. These parameters form the basis for generating the most stable background.

Fig. 4. The virtual background reference frame

In the process of GMM, firstly, an empty set of models is initialized and at the time t_0, using the current pixel of the frame at time t_0. For the other frames, the corresponding pixels are used to match with the initialized K Gaussian model, and the matching condition is $|x_t - \mu_{i,t-1}| \leq 2.5\Sigma_{i,t-1}$(the ith model). If the condition is satisfied, the associated parameters of the matched model, e.g., the mean value μ_{it}, the variance value $\Sigma_{i,t}$ and the weight parameter $\omega_{i,t}$, will be updated and the pixel x_t is identified as the background pixel. The parameter updating regulation is

$$\mu_{i,t} = (1 - \rho)\mu_{i,t-1} + \rho x_t \tag{3}$$

$$\Sigma_{i,t} = (1 - \rho)\Sigma_{i,t-1} + \rho(x_t - \mu_{i,t})^2 \tag{4}$$

$$\begin{aligned} \omega_{i,t} &= (1 - \rho)\omega_{i,t-1} + \rho, \; for \, the \, matched \, model \\ \omega_{i,t} &= (1 - \rho)\omega_{i,t-1}, \; for \, the \, no \, mathced \, model \end{aligned} \tag{5}$$

$$\rho = \alpha \cdot \eta(x_t, \mu_{i,t}, \Sigma_{i,t}) \tag{6}$$

where α is the learning rate that pre-defined. Else, the Gaussian model with the minimum vale of $\omega_{i,t_0}/\Sigma_{i,t_0}$ is set as the matched Gaussian model, the associated parameters will remain unchanged, expect for the weight parameter $\omega_{i,t}$, which will be updated as the above regulation. In case of static background scene, which the background pixels keep according on time domain, so the final matched model generated as the regulation will be the most stable background reference frame, as shown in Fig.3.

3.2   View Synthesis with GMM

After the background updating by using some original frames, a stable background will be obtained as the reference frame for filling the disocclusion. In our approach, we apply the GMM on the original texture sequence and the depth sequence, respectively, and generate the stable texture background and the stable depth background.

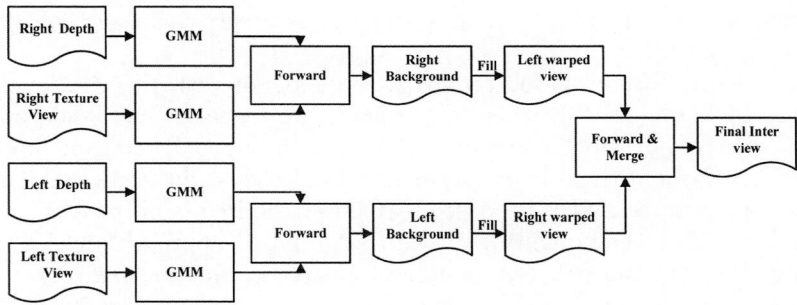

Fig. 5. Proposed scheme

As above mentioned, in view synthesis framework, the disocclusion is mostly filled in the merge step. But in case of bad alignment between the left view and the right view or bad depth maps, only part of disocclusion can be filled with the corresponding generated virtual view (e.g., the right warped image is used fill the left warped image.), imperfectly. Thus, if we can obtain an incomplete background reference frame, it is available for filling disocclusion in any case. So target on filling the disocclusion with the stable background reference frame after 3D warping, the texture background and the depth background for the left view and the right view will be generated, respectively. Using a pair of texture and depth backgrounds (e.g, the texture background and the depth background of the left·view), a virtual background reference frame can be generated as the reference frame of the virtual view, as shown in Fig.4. Although there are some holes in the virtual reference frame, which are due to the inaccurate depth map, most of background in the scene can be modeled in our approach. For each frame of the sequence, after 3D warping, the reference frame is used to fill the disocclusion as the followed description(we set the left view as an example)

1. First, generate the texture background and the depth background, respectively.

2. Second, warp the background to generate the virtual background reference frame.
3. Third, for each pixel in the virtual frame, if the pixel is a hole and it is not a hole in the reference frame, use the pixel of the reference frame to fill it.
4. Final, with the merge step in view synthesis, the other holes will be filled.

The complete framework about our proposed approach is shown in Fig.5.

4   Experiment Results

In this section, we compare our results with the MPEG view synthesis reference software (3.5) [14]. For evaluating the proposed scheme, three 3D video sequences, which provided by the HHI[15]:"Book arrival", "door flowers", and "outdoor". They have a resolution of 1024×768. The depth map of the sequences are generated with the MPEG depth estimation reference software(DERS) (5.1) based on graph cuts.

In this paper, the proposed approach is compared with the view synthesis reference software (VSRS). In our experiment, we generate the reference background texture and depth frames for each view in one GOP frames, the GOP size is set as 30 and there is no scene change. In the static scene, the gains of the results generated by the proposed method are limited, and there is no great difference on the visual quality between the proposed approach and VSRS, as shown in Fig.6(a) and (b). But in case of the scene with moving objects, the gains on the PSNR and SSIM become acheieved, as shown in Fig.6(c) and (d). In Table.1, the means value of PSNR and SSIM in the GOP are calculated and listed for the three test sequences. The "Original view"means the the real texture sequences captured by the real camera, and the "Virtual view"represents the generated virtual view, which is associated with the real camera position. As shown in Table.1, the proposed approach is better than VSRS on the objective measurement. Especially for the sequence "Book arrival"and the "outdoor", which are with translation motion in most of frames, the gains on PSNR and SSIM are more obvious, but the PSNR and SSIM values are limited by the imperfect depth maps. While for the "door flowers"sequence, the gains are limited. This is because there is the scene change in this sequence, the generated reference background frames failed to handle with the scene change.

Table 1. Result comparison on LN data

Sequence	Original view	Virtual view	PSNR(dB)		SSIM	
			VSRS	proposed	VSRS	proposed
BookArrival	08,10	09	20.9370	22.5039	0.7563	0.8295
Doorflowers	08,12	10	35.1954	35.2229	0.9836	0.9836
outdoor	06,08	07	27.4499	28.4314	0.8366	0.8466

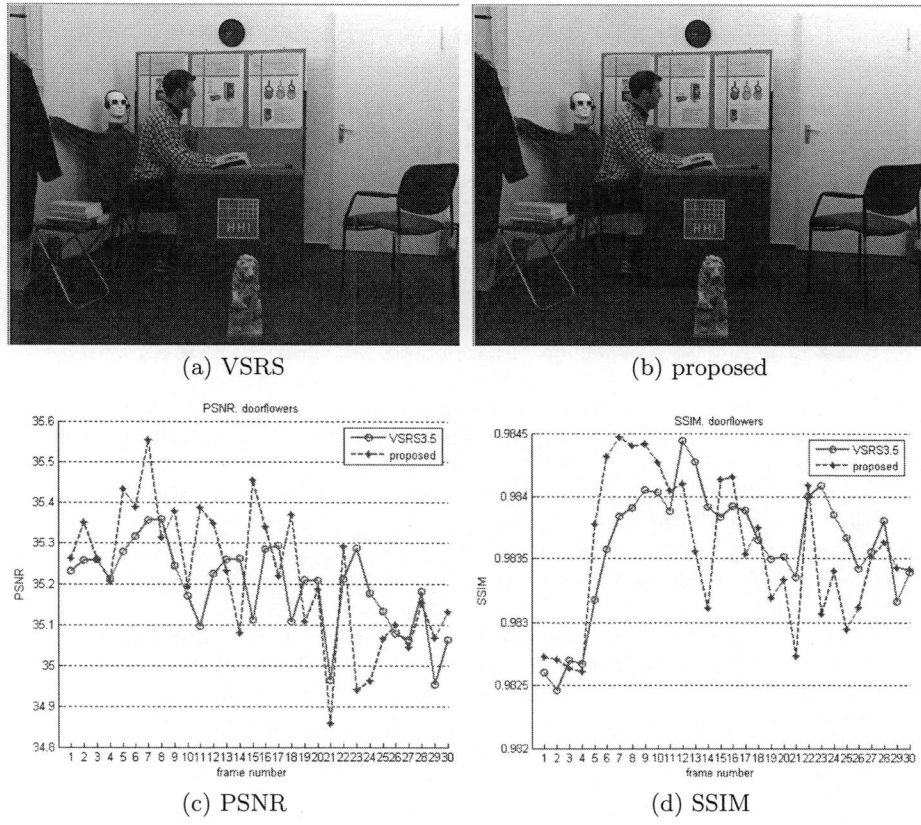

Fig. 6. The synthesized view

5   Conclusion

In this paper, we proposed an approach based on background updating with Gaussian Mixture Model for disocclusion filling. At pixel level, each pixel of the scene is modeled independently as the background or the foreground pixel. With the background model from the texture and the depth sequence, the best and the most stable background information can be obtained, and part of covered background information in one frame of the sequence will be recovered. With these texture and depth background, a warped background reference frame can be generated to fill the holes in the virtual view. Experimental results show that the objective quality of the generation virtual view can be improved, especially for the scene with moving objects. However, in case of the scene with no moving foreground objects, the gains of the results are limited. Otherwise, the method based on GMM, which is used to generate the stable background, is only available for the scene with rigid translational motion, it will fail to handle with the case of the scene changing. These problems will be addressed in our future work.

Acknowledgments. This work is supported by in part by National Natural Science Foundation of China (No.61025013, No.60903066, No.61210006), Beijing Natural Science Foundation (No.4112043, No.4102049), 973 Program (No.2012CB316401), Fundamental scientific research project(No.K12JB00200), Fundamental Research Funds for the Central Universities(No.2011JBM029).

References

1. Benzie, P., Watson, J., Surman, P., Rakkolainen, I., Hopf, K., Urey, H., Sainov, V., von Kopylow, C.: A survey of 3DTV displays: techniques and technologies. IEEE Trans. Circuits Syst. Video Technol. 17(11), 1647–1658 (2007)
2. Kubota, A., Smolic, A., Magnor, M., Tanimoto, M., Chen, T., Zhang, C.: Multiview imaging and 3DTV. IEEE Signal Process. Mag. 24(6), 10–21 (2007)
3. Müller, K., Smolic, A., Dix, K., Merkle, P., Kauff, P., Wiegand, T.: View synthesis for advanced 3D video systems. EURASIP Journal on Image and Video Processing 2008, 1–12 (2008)
4. Fehn, C.: A 3D-TV approach using depth-image-based rendering (DIBR). In: Proc. Visu., Imaging Image Process., VIIP, pp. 482–487 (2003)
5. Zhang, L., Tam, W.J., Wang, D.: Stereoscopic image generation based on depth images. In: International Conference on Image Processing, ICIP, vol. 5, pp. 2993–2996 (2004)
6. Zhang, L., Tam, W.J.: Stereoscopic image generation based on depth images for 3D TV. IEEE Transactions on Broadcasting 5, 2993–2996 (2004)
7. Chen, W.-Y., Chang, Y.-L., Lin, S.-F., Ding, L.-F., Chen, L.-G.: Efficient depth image based rendering with edge dependent depth filter and interpolation. In: Proc. IEEE Int. Conf. Multimedia Expo, Amsterdam, The Netherlans, pp. 1314–1317 (2005)
8. Lee, P.-J., Effendi: Nongeometric Distortion Smoothing Approach for Depth Map Preprocessing. IEEE Transactions on Multimedia 13(2), 246–254 (2011)
9. Zhao, Y., Zhu, C., Chen, Z., Tian, D., Yu, L.: Boundary Artifact Reduction in View Synthesis of 3D Video: From Perspective of Texture-Depth Alignment. IEEE Transactions on Broadcasting 57(2), 510–522 (2011)
10. Köppel, M., Ndjiki-Nya, P., Doshkov, D., Lakshman, H., Merkle, P., Müller, K., Wiegand, T.: Temporally consistent handling of disocclusions with texture synthesis for depth-image-based rendering. In: IEEE International Conference on Image Processing, ICIP, pp. 1809–1812 (2010)
11. Stauffer, C., Grimson, W.E.L.: Adaptive background mixture models for real-time tracking. In: IEEE Conference on Computer Vision and Pattern Recognition, vol. 2, pp. 246–252 (1999)
12. Lee, D.-S.: Effective Gaussian mixture learning for video background subtraction. IEEE Transactions on Pattern Analysis and Machine Intelligence 27(5), 827–832 (2005)
13. Haque, M., Murshed, M., Paul, M.: Improved Gaussian mixtures for robust object detection by adaptive multi-background generation. In: IEEE International Conference on Pattern Recognition, pp. 1–4 (2008)
14. Tanimoto, M., Fujii, T., Suzuki, K.: View synthesis algorithm in view synthesis reference software 3.5 (VSRS3.5) Document M16090, ISO/IEC JTC1/SC29/WG11 (MPEG) (May 2009)
15. Mobile3DTV, http://sp.cs.tut.fi/mobile3dtv/stereo-video/

Cloud-Based Image Compression via Subband-Based Reconstruction*

Zhongbo Shi[1], Xiaoyan Sun[2], and Feng Wu[2]

[1] University of Sience and Technology of China
Hefei, Anhui, China
stoneshi@mail.ustc.edu.cn
[2] Microsoft Research Asia,
Beijing, China
{xysun,fengwu}@microsoft.com

Abstract. In this paper, we propose a novel cloud-based image compression scheme. In contrast to traditional compression schemes, our scheme targets a new scenario that ensures large scale images in the cloud are always available. Thus, our proposed scheme makes use of not only the internal correlation, but also the external correlation between the target image and images in the cloud to achieve advanced coding performance. One the encoder side, two kinds of information, global and in-band local information, are extracted from the wavelet pyramids of the input image and compressed accordingly. On the decoder side, a subband-based reconstruction approach is proposed for hierarchically generating the reconstructed image from the compressed information and a large dataset in the cloud. Experimental results demonstrate that our proposed scheme achieves high objective and subjective qualities at high compression ratios given a large scale image dataset.

Keywords: image compression, cloud, wavelet, image reconstruction.

1 Introduction

Today's Internet contains billions of digital images. When combined with ubiquitous network access, today's users are becoming accustomed to being able to capture, store, share, and access digital images on demand. Instant, web-based image applications create new challenges as well as new opportunities for image compression that is an essential component in today's web services.

Image compression provides an efficient method for reducing the irrelevance and redundancy within images so as to store or transmit images in a much more efficient manner. Traditional image compression schemes, e.g. JPEG [1], JPEG2000 [2], and intra coding of H.264 [3], as well as HEVC [4], reduce the redundancy of an image using prediction-transform. The local correlation inside one image is explored using different sets of intra-prediction modes based on neighboring pixels or image blocks, followed by

---

* This work was done during Zhongbo Shi's internship with Microsoft Research Asia.

W. Lin et al. (Eds.): PCM 2012, LNCS 7674, pp. 661–673, 2012.

different kinds of transforms to further reduce irrelevance. The internal correlation of a single image has been investigated extensively for single image compression.

Image compression supported by external information has also been studied in depth. The well-known vector quantization (VQ) based image compression schemes achieve a high compression ratio by mapping the high dimensional vectors of images into a predefined external finite set of low dimensional vectors. However, as the supporting information, e.g. low dimensional vectors, is predefined, it is hard to tell whether the information is suitable and adequate enough for coding an input image or not.

With the rapid development of the Internet, researchers recently have noticed that the exploration of internet images provides a new way to solve some well-known research problems. For example, Hays et al. present promising research in which unknown regions of images are completed by searching similar images based on a scene descriptor [5]. Eitz et al. [6] and Chen et al [7] propose composing an image from a sketch-based search and synthesis. Subsequently, Weinzaepfel et al. [8] revealed that the SIFT (Scale-invariant feature transform) descriptors [9] that are widely used in image retrieval may lead to certain security issues as they can be used to interpret visual content and generate visually meaningful images. All these projects present promising results by taking advantage of large scale images over the Internet.

Inspired by web-based solutions, we propose a new cloud-based image compression scheme that aims to enable image compression by making use of the correlations not only inside one image but also between the image and an external image database hosted by a cloud. We further propose exploring the visual correlation between images using SIFT-based matching rather than MSE-based search. Two kinds of information, global and local information, are exacted from wavelet decomposed subbands and transmitted for each input image, respectively. The global information is the lowest subband signal that serves as the guidance of reconstruction. The local information is provided by the SIFT descriptors extracted from higher subbands that present the local characteristics of image regions. We then propose a corresponding subband-based reconstruction approach on the decoder side. According by the visual correlation exploit by in-band SIFT matching, our decoder generates a group of visually similar image patches. Assisted with the global information, we embed the high-frequency components of these patches into the corresponding subbands from bottom to top. In this way, a refined reconstruction image can be achieved.

The rest of this paper is organized as follows. Section 2 presents the overview of our scheme. Section 3 and Section 4 describe the details of the encoder and decoder, respectively. Experimental results are demonstrated in Section 5. Section 6 concludes this paper.

2   Overview of Our Scheme

Our proposed compression scheme exploits the external correlation between the input image and an image dataset based on the local features. The basic idea of our scheme is to descript an image on the encoder side but reconstruct it on the decoder side given a huge image dataset. In our compression scheme, we propose to descript an input image I using two kinds of information - global information G_I and local detailed information D_I. G_I provides a basic description of an image and serves as guidance for reconstruction. D_I helps to exploit the external visual correlation between images for recovering the local details.

The framework of our cloud-based image compression is shown in Fig. 1. There are two modules employed in the encoder. The subband-based information extraction module generates G_I and D_I, and the compound encoder compresses the information G_I and D_I into bitstream.

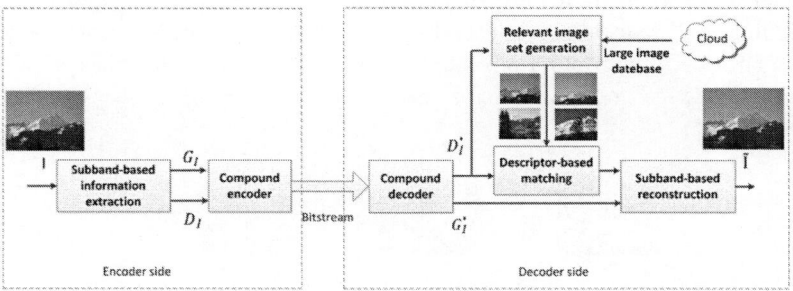

Fig. 1. Framework of our scheme

There are many ways to generate the global description of an input image. We employ wavelet-pyramid decomposition, which is widely used in signal decomposition and reconstruction, to extract G_I as shown in Fig. 1. For an input image I, we choose the lowest-frequency subband as G_I. Although lacking high-frequency details, it provides a rough global description of the input image.

We also extract the in-band local information D_I during the decomposition. Due to the robustness of SIFT descriptors in terms of identifying similar visual objects, we propose using the SIFT descriptors as D_I in our scheme. According to [10], the wavelet representation can be considered a special case of multi-scale space, where different subbands correspond to different scale planes. Thus, the multi-scale SIFT descriptors can be extracted from these subbands.

On the decoder side, we employ the corresponding subband-based approach to reconstruct an image from G_I and D_I. As shown in Fig. 1, after compound decoding, we get the decoded information G_I' and D_I'. Then the high relevant image set is generated using SIFT-based image retrieval, from which the highly correlated high frequency details are achieved thought SIFT-based matching. Finally, the retrieved high frequency subband information is integrated into G_I' gradually to generate the final reconstructed image.

3   Encoder

The encoding modules, subband-based information extraction, and the compound encoder shown in Fig.1 are introduced in this section.

3.1 Subband-Based Information Extraction

During the extraction, an input image is decomposed to reveal two kinds of information: the global information G_I and in-band local information D_I. For simplicity, we demonstrate a two-layer representation to explain our decomposition approach.

We adopt a wavelet representation to build a multi-scale space. As shown in Fig. 2, in the vertical dimension, wavelet decomposition (W module) is performed to generate different wavelet subbands where n denotes the index of the wavelet layer. After multiple iterations, a LL subband of limited spatial redundancy is generated as the global information G_I. In the horizontal dimension, we perform Gaussian filtering (F module in Fig. 2) sequentially to each LL subband. This produces a group of subscale planes. The SIFT descriptors are then extracted from the differences between the planes to get the in-band local description.

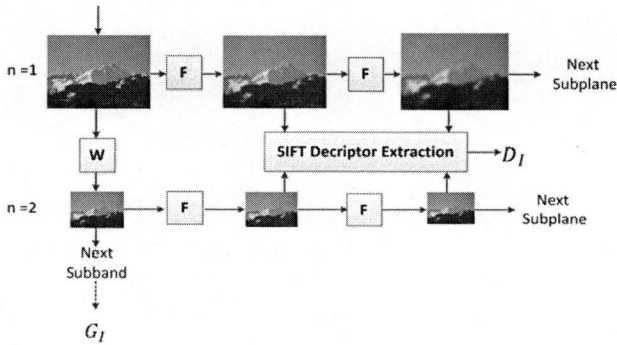

Fig. 2. Information extraction

A SIFT descriptor d_i is defined as:

$$d_i = (x_i, y_i, O_i, S_i, \boldsymbol{v}_i) \tag{1}$$

Here x_i and y_i are the spatial coordinates of the ith key point, which is one of the maxima or minima values of the difference signals. Additionally, O_i denotes the main orientation of gradient of the point, S_i is the scale information denoting the local region size covered by d_i, and $\boldsymbol{v}_i$ is a 128-dimension vector that characterizes the local region with gradient histogram in different directions. For more detailed information on SIFT generation, please refer to [9].

In our scheme, the total number of decomposition layers is 5 (n=0…4), where the original image can be regarded as layer 0. We select the LL subband from layer index $n = 4$ as G_I. D_I is the set of SIFT descriptors extracted from layer 1 to layer 4.

3.2 Subband Information Compression

As shown in Fig. 3, the compound encoder involves three different compression approaches for different inputs.

First, global information G_I, which can be regarded as a thumbnail of the input image, is coded as an image. We adopt a traditional image coding method (e.g. JPEG 2000) to compress it. The decoded version G_I' is used in the coding of D_I.

Second, we divide all extract descriptors into two groups, large-scale group (LG) and median-scale group (MG), to compress the in-band local information D_I. LG consists of the larger scale descriptors that can be extracted from G_I', so that no bit is needed for coding the descriptors in LG. The MG group consists of the rest of the descriptors.

For MG descriptors, the scalar parameters including coordinates, orientation and scale factor are first quantized using the scalar quantization module (Q module in Fig. 3) as:

$$\bar{x}_i = round(x_i),$$
$$\bar{y}_i = round(y_i),$$
$$\bar{O}_i = round(\log_2(\frac{O_i}{2\pi} \times 128)),$$
$$\bar{S}_i = \operatorname{argmin}_m(3 \times \log_2\left(\frac{S_i}{\sigma_0}\right) - T(m)),$$

where $\sigma_0 = 1.6 \times 2^{\left(\frac{1}{3}\right)}$ and $T(m) = \frac{3 \times m - 13}{16}, m = 0 \dots 15.$ (2)

Here, σ_0 is the initial derivation parameter of the Gaussian filter used in SIFT extraction, and $T(m)$ generates the quantization table for scale quantization. In this way, the orientation space is divided into 128 subparts and the scale space in an octave is divided into 16 subparts. Thus, the quantized orientations and scale factors can be represented and encoded by fixed-length arithmetic coding into 7 and 4 bits, respectively.

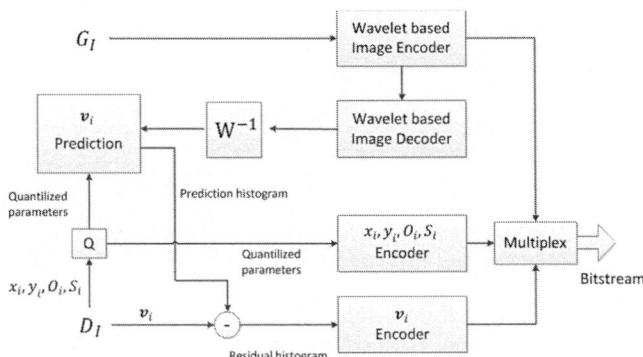

Fig. 3. Compound encoder

Let $\{d_i\}_n$ denote the descriptors extracted from layer n, we propose representing coordinates $\{(\bar{x}_i, \bar{y}_i)\}_n$ of $\{d_i\}_n$ in each layer n (n=1, 2, 3) in the form of a binary map and compressing the map using binary arithmetic coding. The resolution of the map is the same as that of this layer. The values of the map are defined as

$$b_n(\bar{x}_i, \bar{y}_i) = \begin{cases} 1, & if \ (\bar{x}_i, \bar{y}_i) \in \{d_i\}_n \\ 0, & otherwise \end{cases}.$$ (3)

Moreover, for each non-zero value in the map, an additional integer is used and coded by arithmetic coding to indicate the number of SIFT descriptors at this position, considering that a key point may have 4 main gradient orientations.

Third, we propose compressing the 128-dimension vectors $\{v_i\}$ using prediction-residual coding approach. The reference information for prediction comes from the up-sampled G'_l, as it provides a rough estimation to the original image. Fig. 4 measures the correlation between the original vector $\{v_i\}$ and the prediction vectors $\{v'_i\}$ that are extracted from the up-sampled G'_l according to the compressed coordinates, orientation and scale factor. In Fig. 4, the vertical axis denotes the prediction error e between v_i and v'_i, and the horizontal axis denotes the wavelet layer index.

$$e = \frac{\|v_i - v'_i\|}{\|v_i\|} \tag{4}$$

The parameter Q in Fig. 4 indicates the quality level of G'_l when coded by JPEG2000. The higher Q is, the better G'_l is achieved. The blue curve indexed as non-coded indicates the vectors extracted from G_l. Based on the results, we can see that v'_i and v_i are quite similar when the layer is larger than 4. We also observe that e increases when n decreases, but the correlation is still high for layer 2 and layer 3 since the average error is about 20% when Q is larger than 96. When n is smaller than 2, the correlation becomes low due to the lack of high frequency details in G'_l.

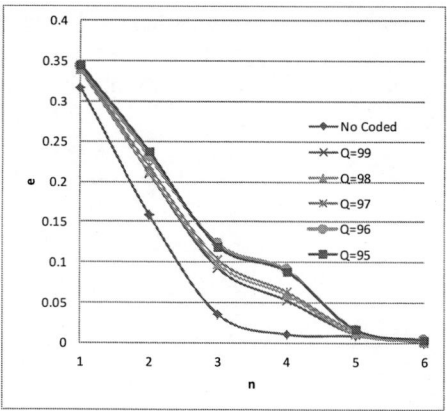

Fig. 4. The predicted error

Based on these observations, we propose predicting the original v_i by v'_i first, and then the residual histogram is quantized and encoded using context-based adaptive binary arithmetic coding (CABAC) [11]. Additionally, the parameter Q for compressing G_I is usually set high ($Q \geq 96$) to make the prediction effective.

We would like to point out that the descriptors from the highest subbands (n=1) are discarded in our compression scheme for two main reasons. First, the histogram in this layer is difficult to predict accurately, thus the residual vector costs a considerable number of bits; second, the scale factor in layer 1 is usually small, which means the image patches are too small to be utilized well in image reconstruction.

4   Decoder

As shown in Fig. 1, this section introduces the decoding modules including compound decoder, relevant image set generation, SIFT-based matching, and subband-based image reconstruct sequentially.

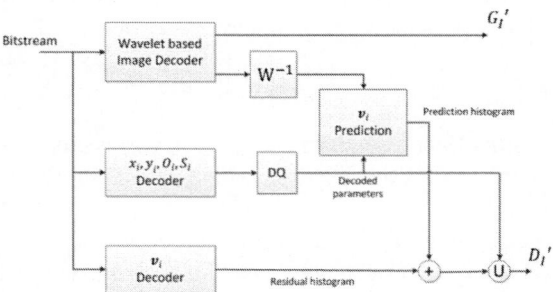

Fig. 5. Compound decoder

4.1   Compound Decoder

Corresponding to our encoder, the block diagram of our decoder is depicted in Fig. 5.

The wavelet-based image decoder outputs the decompressed G_i'. After arithmetic decoding, we get the quantized parameters and residual vectors. Then, the de-quantized orientation and scale factor can be achieved using scalar de-quantization module (DQ module in Fig. 5.) as

$$O_i' = \frac{2^{\overline{O_i}}}{128} \times 2\pi, \qquad S_i' = \frac{3 \times \bar{s}_i - 13}{16}. \tag{5}$$

Once all parameters are decoded, the prediction vectors $\{v_i'\}$ are extracted from G_i' in the same way as the encoder. Finally, we get the decoded vectors $\{\hat{v}_i\}$ by adding prediction vectors to the residual ones.

4.2   Relevant Image Set Generation

In this step, we retrieve the highly relevant images for reconstruction. The external correlation between images is exploited by visual word based matching [12]. We assume that the SIFT descriptors of all the images in the cloud have been extracted. We then randomly select 50 million descriptors with $S \geq 2$ and train them into 1M visual words thought the K-mean clustering. According to the Euclidian distance, each of the SIFT descriptors in the cloud are quantized into a visual word. In this way, an image is represented as a set of visual words.

The decoded SIFT descriptors are also quantized as visual words. Each visual word votes on its matched images. The images with higher voting scores are selected as highly relevant images for reconstruction. For detailed implementation on a similar image retrieve, please refer to [12] and [13].

4.3   SIFT-Based Matching

To further exploit the external correlation between the target image and the retrieved image set, we employ SIFT-based matching to improve the precision of visual word matching. According to the correlation between two matched descriptors, visually similar image patches can be generated.

Let Ω denote the set of all descriptors extracted from the relative image set. A decoded descriptor d_i' in D_I' achieves its counterpart d_a in Ω if

$$\frac{Dis(v_i', v_a)}{Dis(v_i', v_b)} > \alpha, \tag{6}$$

where $Dis(.)$ denotes the Euclidean distance between two vectors, v_i' is the vector of d_i', v_a and v_b are the nearest and second nearest vectors in Ω, respectively, and α is a constant factor of 1.5.

Once a decoded descriptor d_i' has a matched descriptor d_a in Ω, an image patch p_a can be extracted from the corresponding candidate image according to the coordinates and scale factor of d_a. In our scheme, p_a is a square image block centered at $(x_a, y_a) \in d_a$. The size of each patch is the same as the size of the region covered by d_a. According to [11], it can be calculated as:

$$BlockSize = S_a \times 12 \tag{7}$$

4.3.1   Subband-Based Reconstruction

In this module, the retrieved patches during SIFT-based matching are utilized to approximate the high frequency information of image reconstruction. Corresponding to the encoder, we employ a wavelet-pyramid structure to reconstruct the target image from the lower subband to higher ones. The reconstruction process of the two layers is illustrated in Fig. 6.

As shown in Fig. 6, the lowest LL subband in layer 4 (denoted as $I_{LL,4}'$) is initialized by G_I'. The other three high frequency subbands (LH, HL and HH subbands) are set to zero, that is $I_{LH,4}', I_{HL,4}'$ and $I_{HH,4}'$ are filled with zeros. Later, the values in these subbands will be updated using searching-based mapping according to $I_{LL,4}'$, which is similar to that in the image hallucination in the spatial domain [14].

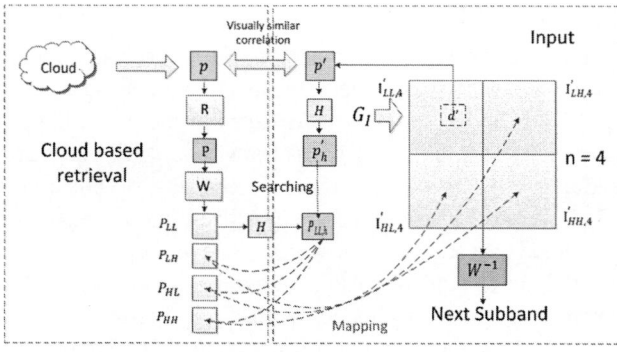

Fig. 6. Subband-based reconstruction

Before search-based matching, we employ a regulation module (R module in Fig. 6) to reduce the local geometric distortion between the matched patches as they may come from different viewpoints. Let $D'_{l,k}$ denote the set of descriptors extracted from layers of index $n \geq k$. Suppose we have a matched pair of descriptors $(d' \leftrightarrow d)$ where $d' \in D'_{l,4}$ and $d \in \Omega$, and accordingly we have a matched pair of patches $(p' \leftrightarrow p)$ where $p' \in I'_{LL,4}$ and p is the patched retrieved by d from the relevant image dataset. Then the geometric transformation between p' and p is approximated using a planar projection H with eight parameters. In our scheme, the parameters in H are estimated using the RANSAC method [15]. The estimate is performed by utilizing the matched locations of SIFT descriptors inside the two patches iteratively. At first, several pairs of SIFT locations are randomly selected to calculate H while others are used to verify H. For a location pair, if the Euclidean distance between them after H transformation is smaller than a given threshold, this pair is treated as an inlier to H; otherwise, it is outlier. H and the number of inlier are updated iteratively until no new location pairs become an inlier or they achieve the maximum number of iterations. Note that this estimation requires at least four pairs of SIFT locations; otherwise the H is equal to unitary matrix.

After the transformation, we get patch $P = H(p)$. P is then decomposed into four subbands, P_{LL}, P_{LH}, P_{HL} and P_{HH}, as shown in Fig. 6. The high frequency information in $I'_{LH,4}, I'_{HL,4}$ and $I'_{HH,4}$ is updated based on the correlation between p' and P_{LL} in the following three steps.

1. High pass filtering. The two patches, p' and P_{LL}, are high pass filtered (H module in Fig.6.) and generate the high frequency signals p'_h and $P_{LL,h}$ as
$$p_h = p - f(p),\qquad(10)$$
    where $f(\cdot)$ is the Gaussian filtering;

2. Block matching. For each $m \times m$ block B in p'_h, a similar block B_{LL} in $P_{LL,h}$ is retrieved by measuring the distance between the two blocks as

$$B_{LL} = argmin_{\forall B' \in P_{LL,h}}(|B, B'|),\qquad(11)$$

    where |.| denotes the sum of the absolute difference between the two blocks;

3. High frequency updating.   The blocks relevant to B in high frequency subbands $I'_{LH,4}, I'_{HL,4}$ and $I'_{HH,4}$ are updated by the collocated blocks to B_{LL} in P_{LH}, P_{HL} and P_{HH}, respectively.

Repeating these steps, the high-frequency information in $I'_{LH,4}, I'_{HL,4}$ and $I'_{HH,4}$ are generated gradually. Notice that the average values are utilized for overlapped positions.

After all the SIFT descriptors in $D'_{l,4}$ are processed, an inverse wavelet transform with $I'_{LL,4}, I'_{LH,4}, I'_{HL,4}$ and $I'_{HH,4}$ is performed to achieve higher LL subband $I'_{LL,3}$. Then the search-based mapping process repeats until the target image is fully reconstructed at the original resolution.

5   Experimental Results

We tested our cloud-based image compression scheme using two image dataset - the INRIA Holidays [16] dataset and the Zurich Building Database (ZubBud) [17]. We selected these two datasets for two reasons: First, these datasets are widely used in image index systems and are also utilized in [8] for image reconstruction; second, there are multiple images at the same place from different viewpoints.

Fig. 7. Test images (T op: Image 1-3; Bottom: Image 4-6)

In our test, we used 6 high-resolution input images for compression (as shown in Fig. 7) that were excluded from the search database. We used grey images for performance evaluation as the SIFT-based matching is performed only on the grey information in our current solution. We compared our scheme with the convention subband-based image compression scheme JPEG2000 [2]. In our scheme, an input image is encoded into a bitstream containing two parts - a compressed down-sampled image and a set of compressed in-band local SIFT descriptors. Table 1 illustrates the size of each part, the overall bpp (bit per pixel), and the reconstructed PSNR of our scheme. Additionally, the PSNR results of JPEG2000 and our scheme at the same bpp levels are also shown in Table 1. Our scheme achieved 2.15dB gain on average compared with JPEG2000.

Table 1. Objective comparison in bits and PSNR values

Image	Size	G_I (kB)	No. SIFT	D_I (kB)	bpp (bit/pix)	Ours PSNR (dB)	J2K PSNR (dB)	PSNR Gain (dB)
1	2816×2112	4.98	816	3.13	0.012	33.57	31.96	1.61
2	2560×1920	7.95	1104	3.99	0.029	22.00	20.76	1.24
3	1536×2048	3.99	855	3.10	0.018	26.49	23.09	3.4
4	1536×1152	1.93	376	1.42	0.015	29.27	26.61	2.66
5	1600×1200	3.00	634	2.33	0.022	22.32	21.67	0.65
6	2560×1920	4.87	913	3.44	0.014	29.11	25.75	3.36
Avg.		4.45	783	2.90	0.018	27.13	24.97	2.15

Fig. 8. Visual comparison (From left to right, images of original, JPEG2000, our scheme and relevant images)

Fig. 9. Samples when no similar images (From left to right, original P1, reconstructed P1, original P2, reconstructed P2)

We also evaluated the visual improvement of our proposed scheme. Some detailed samples extracted from the reconstructed images are shown in Fig. 8. One can observe that the reconstructed quality of JPEG2000 is visually poor and the artifacts left by compression are annoying. However, our reconstructed images have much better visual quality. The details in the mountain, clock, and windows are well preserved.

Our scheme has some limitations. Our scheme works well when similar images can be retrieved, but on the other hand generates smoothed images if no relevant image can be found. It is inefficient in recovering certain regions, such as face or small textures. Fig. 9 shows some examples when no similar images are accessible.

6   Conclusion

In this paper, we propose a cloud-based image compression scheme. This scheme aims to exploit the external correlation between the target image and the dataset in the cloud. We utilize wavelet-pyramid decomposition to extract two kinds of information for each input image. The compressed information helps the decoder to exploit the external correlation between the target image and the image dataset using SIFT-based matching. The reconstructed results demonstrate the effectiveness of our compression scheme in terms of generating visually pleasing images at a high compression ratio.

For future research, a better approach for decomposition, information compression and reconstruction should be investigated. Besides, a method for preserving people or certain object in scenes is another critical issue to be addressed.

References

1. Wallace, G.K.: The JPEG still picture compression standard. Communications of the ACM 34, 30–44 (1991)
2. Taubman, D.S., Marcellin, M.W.: JPEG2000: Image Compression Fundamentals, Standards, and Practice. Kluwer Academic Publishers (2001)
3. Wiegand, T., Sullivan, G.J., Bjontegaard, G., Luthra, A.: Overview of the H.264/AVC video coding standard. IEEE Trans. on Circuits and Systems for Video Technology 13, 560–576 (2003)
4. JCT-VC, WD6: Working Draft 6 of High-Efficiency Video Coding. JCTVC-H1003, JCT-VC Meeting, San Jose (February 2012)
5. Hays, J., Efros, A.A.: Scene completion using millions of photographs. ACM Trans. on Graphics 126 (2007)
6. Eitz, M., Richter, R., Hildebrand, K., Boubekeur, T., Alexa, M.: Photosketcher: interactive sketch-based image synthesis. IEEE Journal of Computer Graphics and Applications 31, 56–66 (2011)
7. Chen, T., Cheng, M.M., Tan, P., Shamir, A., Hu, S.M.: PhotoSketch: Internet image montage. In: ACM Proc. of SIGGRAPH ASIA (2009)
8. Weinzaepfel, P., Jegou, H., Perez, P.: Reconstructing an image from its local descriptors. In: IEEE Proc. of Computer Vision and Pattern Recognition, pp. 337–344 (2011)
9. Lowe, D.G.: Distinctive image features from scale-invariant keypoints. International Journal of Computer Vision 60, 91–110 (2004)

10. Lindegerg, T.: Scale-space theory: A basic tool for analyzing structures at different scales. Journal of Applied Statistics 21(2), 224–270 (1994)
11. Marpe, D., Schwartz, H., Wiegand, T.: Context-Based Adaptive Binary Arithmetic Coding in the H.264/AVC video compression standard. IEEE Trans. on CSVT 13(7), 620–636 (2003)
12. Zhou, W., Lu, Y., Li, H., Song, Y., Tian, Q.: Spatial coding for large scale partial-duplicate web image search. In: ACM Proc. of MM (2010)
13. Wu, Z., Ke, Q.F., Isard, M., Sun, J.: Bundling features for large scale partial-duplicate web image search. In: Proc. of IEEE Conference on Computer Vision and Pattern Recognition, pp. 25–32 (2009)
14. Xiong, Z., Sun, X., Wu, F.: Image hallucination with feature enhancement. In: Proc. IEEE Conf. Computer Vision and Pattern Recognition, pp. 2074–2081 (2009)
15. Fischler, M.A., Bolles, R.C.: Random sample consensus: a paradigm for model fitting with applications to image analysis and automated cartography. Communications of the ACM 24, 381–395 (1981)
16. Jégou, H., Douze, M.: INRIA Holiday dataset (2008),
    http://lear.inrialpes.fr/people/jegou/data.php
17. Eth-Zurich, Zurich building image database,
    http://www.vision.ee.ethz.ch/showroom/zubud/index.en.html

Image Primitive Coding and Visual Quality Assessment

Jian Zhang[1,*], Siwei Ma[2], Ruiqin Xiong[2], Debin Zhao[1], and Wen Gao[2]

[1] School of Computer Science and Technology, Harbin Institute of Technology,
Harbin 150001, P.R. China
{jzhangcs,dbzhao}@hit.edu.cn
[2] National Engineering Laboratory for Video Technology, Peking University,
Beijing 100871, P.R. China
{swma,rqxiong,wgao}@pku.edu.cn

Abstract. In this work, we introduce a new content-adaptive compression scheme, called image primitive coding, which exploits the input image for training a dictionary. The atoms composed of the learned dictionary are named as image primitives. The coding performance between the learned image primitives and the traditional DCT basis is compared, and demonstrates the potential of image primitive coding. Furthermore, a novel concept, entropy of primitives (EoP), is proposed for measuring image visual information. Some very interesting results about EoP are achieved and analyzed, which can be further studied for visual quality assessment.

Keywords: image coding, image primitive, visual information, visual quality assessment (VQA).

1 Introduction

With the accelerative growth of high-performance computers and electronic equipments, a great progress of image coding standards have been achieved. One of the important compression techniques is known as transform coding, which decomposes the image over a dictionary and provides compact image representation to obtain compression.

As we know, transform-based coding techniques generally make an assumption that the dictionary is fixed and is built in both the encoder and decoder. For example, in the JPEG [1] and JPEG2000 [2] compression standards, the dictionary considered is the DCT or wavelet, respectively.

The Sparseland model is an emerging and powerful method to describe signals based on the sparsity and redundancy of their representations [3] [4]. Obtaining an overcomplete dictionary from a set of signals allows us to represent them as a sparse linear combination of dictionary atoms. Pursuit algorithms are then used for signal decomposition.

---

* This work was supported in part by Major State Basic Research Development Program of China (973 Program, 2009CB320903), National Science Foundation (60833013, 61121002) and National High-tech R&D Program of China (863 Program, SS2012AA010805).

W. Lin et al. (Eds.): PCM 2012, LNCS 7674, pp. 674–685, 2012.
© Springer-Verlag Berlin Heidelberg 2012

As a matter of fact, the predetermined fixed dictionaries are targeted at general-purpose image compression. For a specific application, by utilizing content-specific dictionaries optimized for a specific class of images, compression schemes have been demonstrated to acquire substantial gains over fixed dictionaries. For instance, in [5], the authors propose an algorithm for facial image compression by exploiting a sparse approximation of the image patches over a set of pre-trained dictionaries. The task-aware compression method is shown to achieve a dramatic improvement over JPEG2000 for facial imagery. Recently, an algorithm based on iteration-tuned dictionaries (ITDs) for a specific class of images has also been proposed to encode the input image patches in [6], which is able to outperform JPEG and JPEG2000 convincingly for facial images.

It is obvious to see that the main drawback of the task-specific approaches is their loss of generality, only restricting them to encoding a specific class of images for which a suitable dictionary has been pre-learned. In this work, we introduce a new content-adaptive compression scheme, called image primitive coding, which exploits the input image for training a dictionary. The atoms composed of the learned dictionary are named as image primitives. We compare the coding performance between the learned image primitives and the traditional DCT basis, which demonstrate the potential of image primitive coding. Furthermore, a novel concept, entropy of primitives (EoP), is proposed for measuring image visual information. Some very interesting results about EoP are achieved and analyzed.

This paper is organized as follows: In section 2 we introduce the scheme of image primitive coding and sparse coding, and provide the performance between the learned image primitives and the traditional DCT basis in section 3. Based on image primitives, a novel concept, entropy of primitives (EoP), is proposed in section 4. Section 5 shows some very interesting results about EoP. We conclude and discuss some future directions in section 6.

2   Image Primitive Coding

In this section, we will introduce image primitive coding, showing how to achieve image primitives and how to utilize image primitives for coding. Then, a performance comparison of image representation between image primitive and DCT basis is conducted. Some conclusions are also drawn.

2.1   Image Primitive

The scheme of image primitive coding is established on the Sparseland model, which assumes that natural signals, such as images, admit a sparse decomposition over a redundant dictionary. More specifically, given a signal $\mathbf{x} \in \mathbb{R}^n$, this model suggests the existence of a specific dictionary (i.e., a matrix) $_\mathbf{S}$ which contains k prototype signals, also referred to as atoms. The model assumes that for $\mathbf{x}$, there exists a sparse linear combination of atoms from $\mathbf{D}$ that approximates it well. Put more formally, for $\forall \mathbf{x} \in \mathbb{R}^n$, $\exists a \in \mathbb{R}^k$ such that $\mathbf{x} \approx \mathbf{D} a$ and $\|a\|_0 \ll n$. The notion $\|\bullet\|_0$ is ℓ_0

norm, which counts the number of nonzero elements in a vector. We typically assume $k>n$, implying that the dictionary $\mathbf{D}$ is redundant to $\mathbf{x}$.

An overcomplete dictionary that leads to sparse representations can either be chosen as a pre-specified set of functions or designed by adapting its content to fit a given set of signal examples. In this work, we design an adaptive overcomplete dictionary for input image.

For an input image $\mathbf{X}$, the dictionary learning process starts by partitioning the image into many overlapped patches, which are denoted by $\mathbf{x}_1, \mathbf{x}_2, ..., \mathbf{x}_i$, $i = 1, 2, ..., N$. These patches are then collected as training samples. Assuming a local Sparse-Land model on image patches, the K-SVD dictionary training algorithm [7] is applied to the set of patches $\{\mathbf{x}_i\}$, generating a content adaptive dictionary $\mathbf{D}$:

$$\mathbf{D}, \{a_i\} = \underset{\mathbf{D}, \{a_i\}}{\operatorname{argmin}} \sum_k \left\| \mathbf{x}_i - \mathbf{D} \, a_i \right\|_2^2 \quad \text{s.t.} \quad \left\| a_i \right\|_0 < L \quad \forall i. \tag{1}$$

where $\{a_i\}$ are the sparse representation vectors for $\{\mathbf{x}_i\}$. In this paper, the atoms of dictionary $\mathbf{D}$ are named as image primitives. Fig. 1 gives an example of overcomplete DCT basis and a learned dictionary which is trained by 8×8 patches from Image *Lena*.

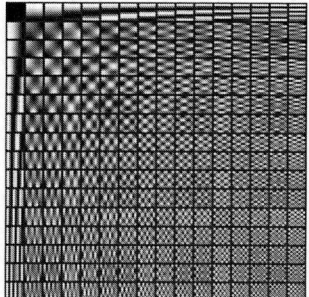 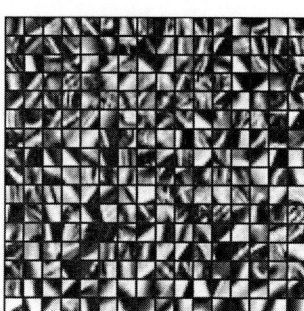

Fig. 1. Left: Overcomplete DCT base dictionary; Right: Dictionary trained over image patches

2.2   Sparse Coding

For a patch $\mathbf{x}_i$, the process of finding its sparse representation vector a_i with respect to a known overcomplete dictionary $\mathbf{D}$ is called sparse coding. As can be seen, owing to the overcompleteness, the null space of $\mathbf{D}$ introduces additional degrees of freedom in the choice of a_i, which can be exploited to improve its compressibility. To obtain the sparse representation, sparse coding can be formulated as

$$a_i = \underset{a_i}{\operatorname{argmin}} \left\| \mathbf{x}_i - \mathbf{D} \, a_i \right\|_2^2 \quad \text{s.t.} \quad \left\| a_i \right\|_0 < L \quad . \tag{2}$$

Though Problem (2) is NP-hard in general, it can be approximated by a wide range of techniques [4]. In this paper, we adopt orthogonal matching pursuit (OMP) [8] algorithm to solve (2) for its simplicity and efficiency.

3   Comparison between Image Primitive and DCT Basis

In order to prove the validity of image primitive coding scheme, this section gives the coding performance comparison between the image primitive and traditional DCT basis. The comparative setting is as follows. First, the trained dictionary composed of image primitives is produced by the previously mentioned algorithm to the coding image. The size of the trained overcomplete dictionary is set to 256, while the number of traditional DCT basis for 8×8 patches is 64. Then, split the coding image into some non-overlapped patches, and the size of image patch is set to 8×8. Next, for each patch, carry out the process of sparse coding with the trained overcomplete dictionary and traditional DCT basis by OMP. The number of image primitives to represent each patch (denoted by l) is fixed each time with the range from 1 to 10. Finally, the PSNR and SSIM [9] comparison curves with regarding to three test images (shown in Fig. 2) are presented by Figs. 3–5, and the visual reconstruction results of Image *Lena* by the trained overcomplete dictionary and traditional DCT are given in Figs. 6–7.

Fig. 2. Test Images. Left to right: *Lena* (512×512), *Airplane* (512×768), *Peppers* (512×512)

It is clear to see that the reconstructed image quality becomes better and better for the two types of dictionaries, as the number of image primitives to represent each patch l increases. Seen from Figs. 3–5, the values of PSNR and SSIM achieved by image primitives are both higher than those by the traditional DCT basis, especially in the case of low bit rate, i. e., when l is small. From Figs. 6–7, it is obvious that the visual quality of the reconstructed image by image primitives is much better than that by DCT basis with the same value of l. For instance, when $l = 3$, Fig. 6(c) has evident block artifacts, while the block artifacts in Fig. 7(c) are almost invisible.

One important observation from Fig. 7 is when $l > 4$, the reconstructed image is very close to the original image in visual perception. For example, one cannot distinguish between the original Image *Lena* and Fig. 7(f) visually. That means, as $l > 6$, it will add little visual information for human visual system.

Although the results of image primitive coding are encouraging, one key problem is that it requires transmitting the image primitive dictionary along with the compressed data. Thus, mining the trained dictionary structure and compressing the trained dictionary efficiently are very significant, which are also the directions of our future work. Fortunately, recent studies have shown that training sparse dictionary with Sparse K-SVD is possible, where each atom of dictionary is a sparse combination of atoms from pre-specified base, such as DCT or wavelet [10]. This technique allows relatively low-cost transmission of image primitives, thus greatly reducing the number of coding bits.

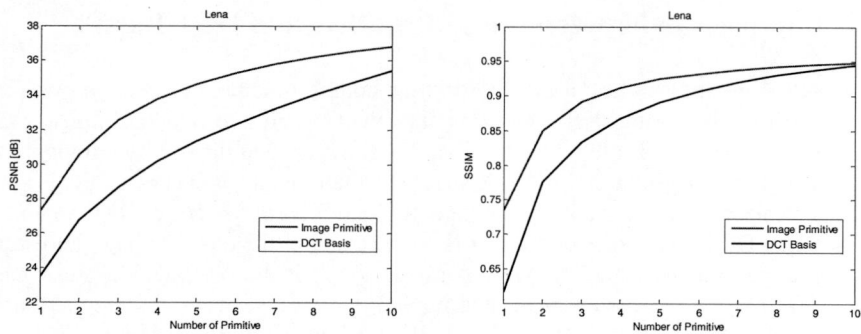

Fig. 3. PSNR and SSIM comparison curves for Image *Lena* with regarding to image primives and DCT basis

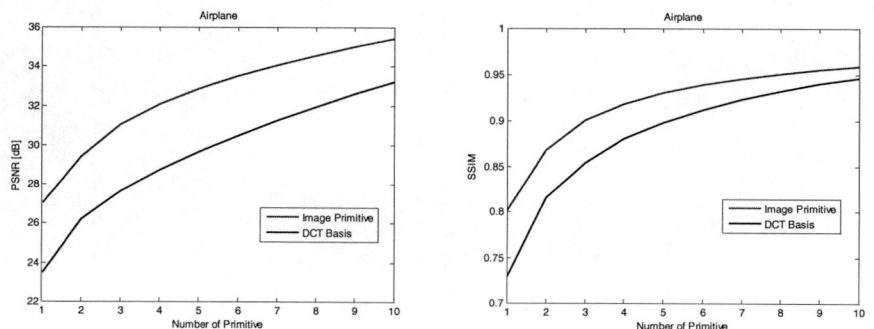

Fig. 4. PSNR and SSIM comparison curves for Image *Airplane* with regarding to image primives and DCT basis

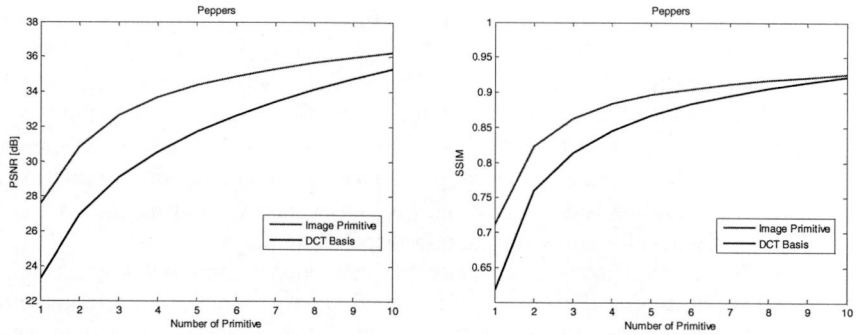

Fig. 5. PSNR and SSIM comparison curves for Image *Peppers* with regarding to image primives and DCT basis

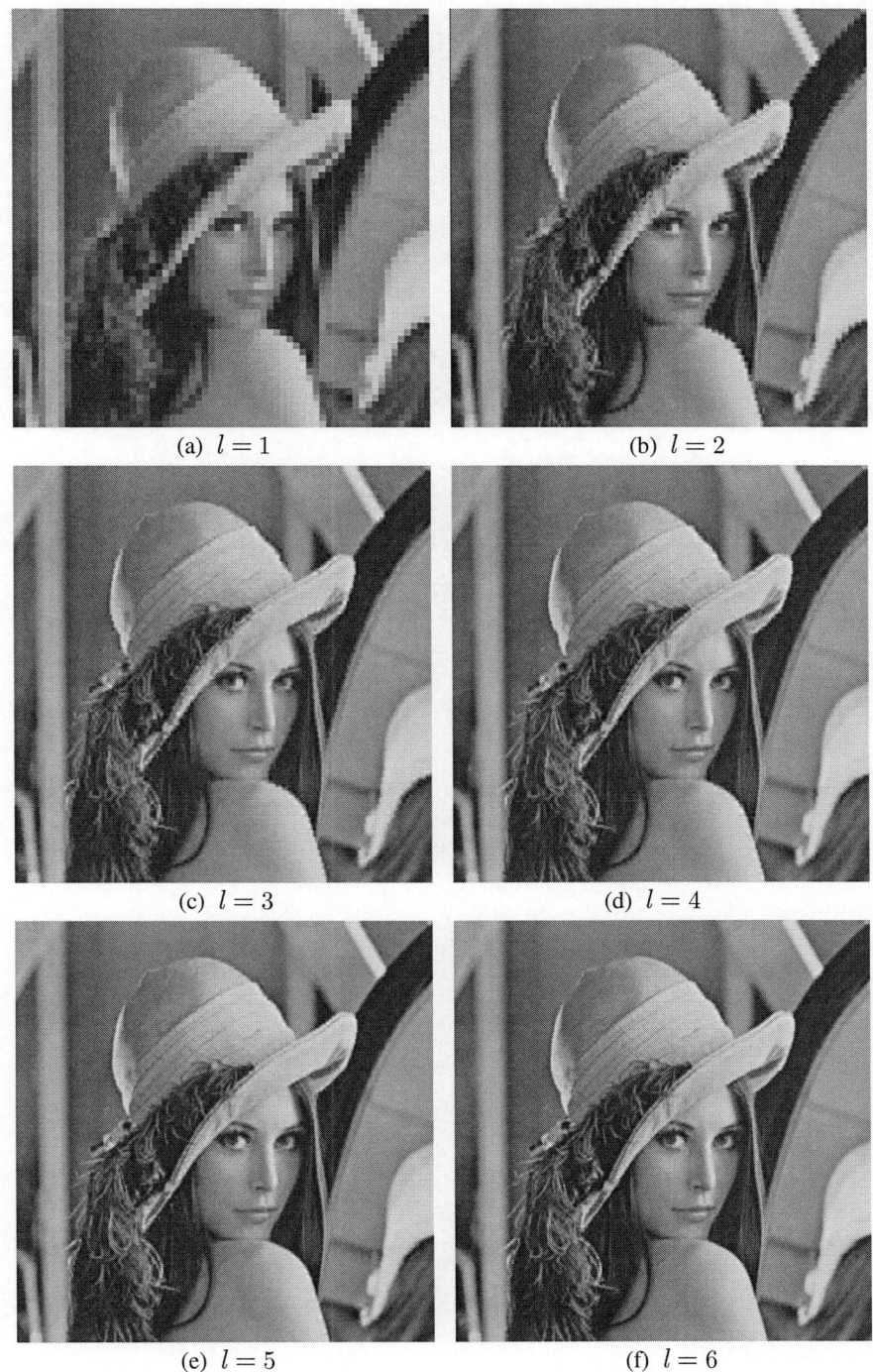

(a) $l = 1$ (b) $l = 2$

(c) $l = 3$ (d) $l = 4$

(e) $l = 5$ (f) $l = 6$

Fig. 6. Visual reconstruction results of Image *Lena* by traditional DCT basis when l equals from 1 to 6. Here, l denotes the number of image primitives to represent each patch.

(a) $l = 1$ (b) $l = 2$

(c) $l = 3$ (d) $l = 4$

(e) $l = 5$ (f) $l = 6$

Fig. 7. Visual reconstruction results of Image *Lena* by its trained image primitives when l equals from 1 to 6. Here, l denotes the number of image primitives to represent each patch.

4   Entropy of Primitive and Visual Quality Assessment

According to the above scheme of image primitive coding, in this section, a novel concept, namely, Entropy of Primitives (EoP) is put forward to measure the amount of image visual information, and some very interesting results about EoP are also provided. Our motivation is as follows. On one hand, a set of image primitives can be learned from an image. On the other hand, the image primitives can also be utilized to approximate the original image. It can be observed that an image with its image primitives have a good corresponding relationship. Therefore, we can measure the amount of visual information of images by the amount of information taken by image primitives. Here, we use the concept of entropy in Shannon theory to describe the amount of information. The details are provided below.

Take Image *Lena* (512×512), for example. There are four steps to calculate its EoP.

Step 1, image primitives are generated by the previously mentioned method. Here, the size of image patch is set to 8×8, and the number of image primitives is set to 256.

Step 2, divide Image *Lena* into non-overlapped image patches, with the patch number equaling $512 \times 512 / 64 = 4096$.

Step 3, for each patch, conduct the process of sparse coding using the trained image primitives, while the number of image primitives (denoted by l) to represent each patch is fixed, e. g., $l = 4$. Thus, the total number of image primitives used for describing the whole image is $tatal = 4096 \times 4 = 16384$. Further, the number of every image primitive used for sparse coding can be calculated, denoted by $num_i, i = 1, 2, ..., 256$. Therefore, the probability of each primitive can be expressed as $p_i = num_i / tatal$.

Step 4, according to Shannon Theory, the entropy of primitives (EoP) for Image *Lena* is written as $EoP = -\sum_i p_i \log(p_i)$. For instance, when $l = 4$, $EoP = 4.3183$.

5   Comparison of PSNR, SSIM and EoP

With the concept of EoP, what can we achieve? With the changes of image quality, what are the statistical laws of EoP? Can EoP be exploited to characterize the amount of visual information of an image? The followings will answer the above questions.

When l increases, the quality of reconstruction image becomes better. We can compute PSNR and SSIM for the reconstruction images. Given l, according to the procedures above, we can also compute EoP. Figs. 8–10 present the PSNR, SSIM and EoP results for three test images with respect to the number of image primitives to represent each patch, i. e., l.

We can achieve some very interesting observations from these experimental results.

a. The EoP curves are monotonically increasing with the number of image primitive l and gradually become flat.

b. When l reaches a certain point, 6 in the curve, the EoP value nearly gets to its peak and becomes stable thereafter. This shows that no more visual information could be supplied from the additional image primitive when l is larger than 6, which is in

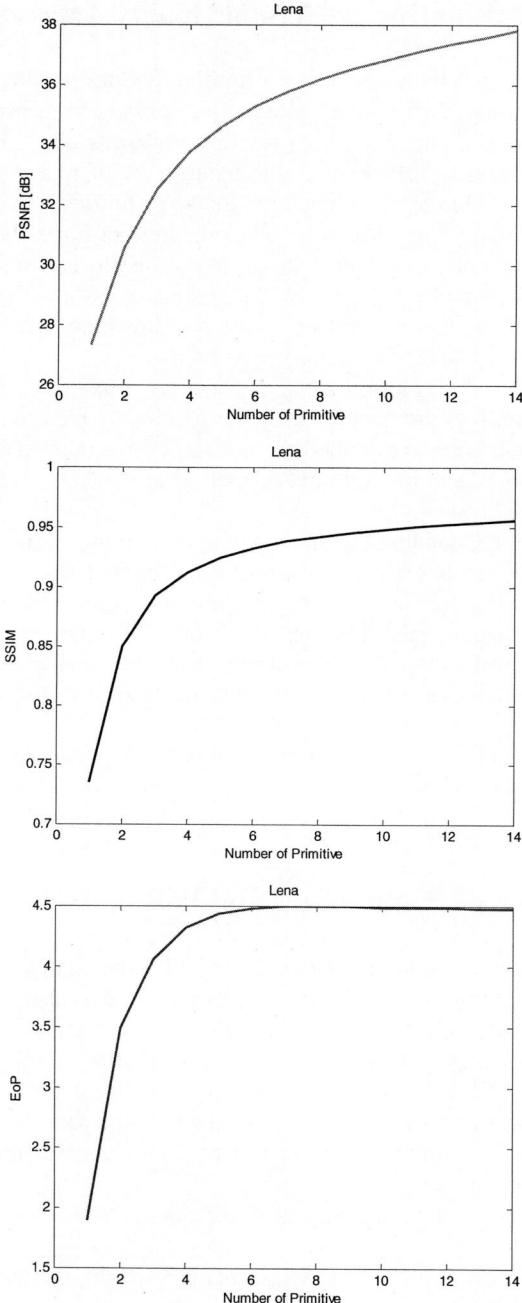

Fig. 8. PSNR, SSIM and EoP results for Image *Lena* with respect to the number of image primitives to represent each patch

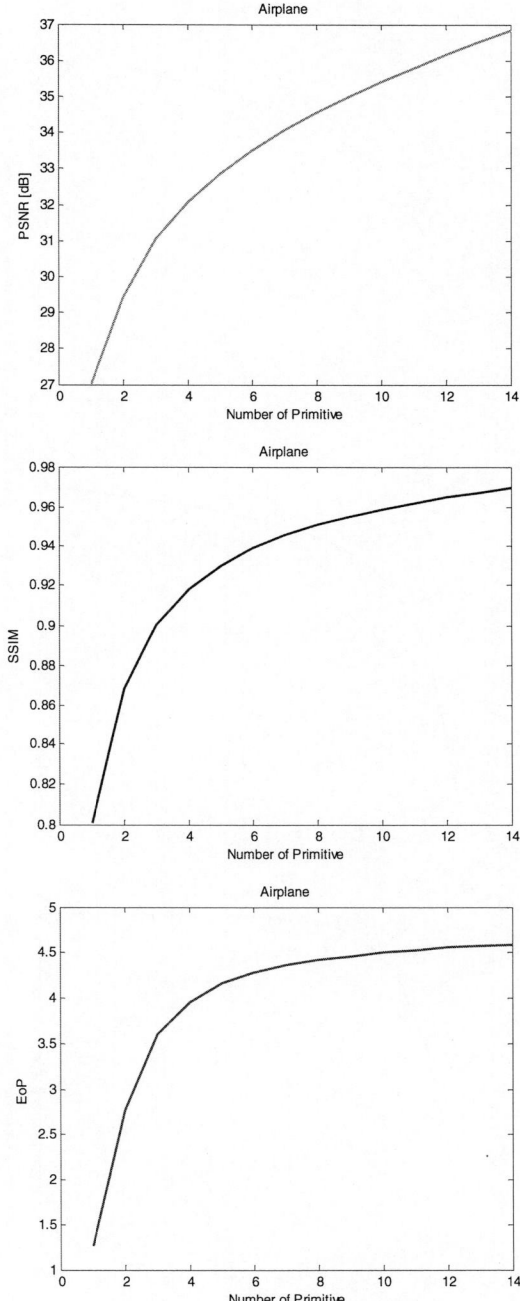

Fig. 9. PSNR, SSIM and EoP results for Image *Airplane* with respect to the number of image primitives to represent each patch

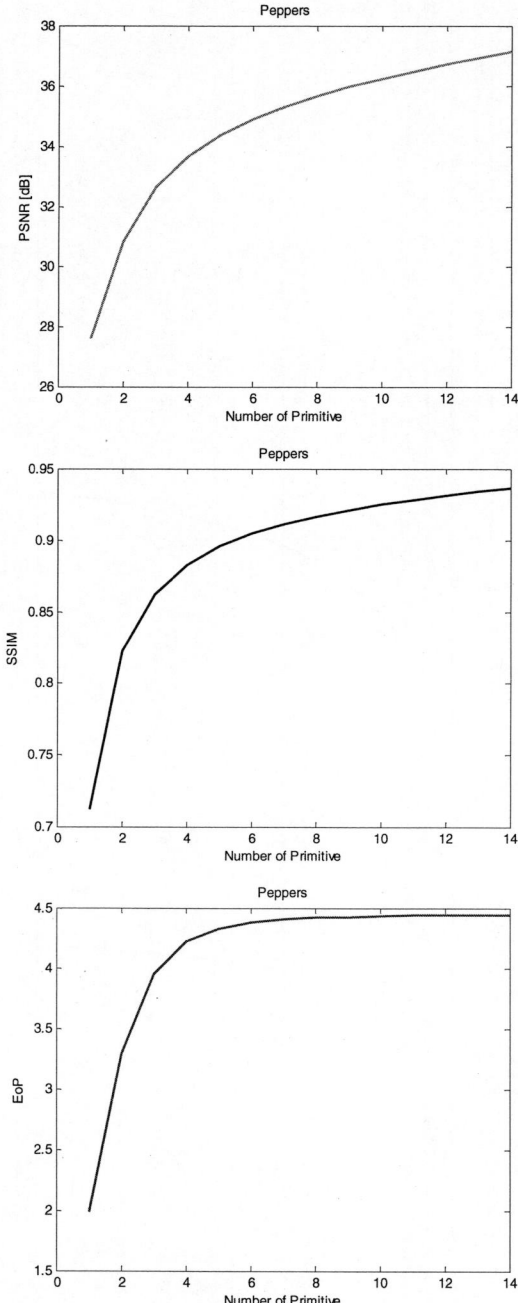

Fig. 10. PSNR, SSIM and EoP results for Image *Peppers* with respect to the number of image primitives to represent each patch

conformity with the foregoing conclusions. We illustrate this observation in Figs. 8–10. By contrast, the PSNR and SSIM curves are still increasing when $l \geq 6$.

Based on these two points, we can say that the proposed concept EoP can evaluate the visual information of images to some extent, which can be further exploited as a criterion for visual quality assessment.

6 Conclusions

In this work, a new content-adaptive compression scheme, called image primitive coding, is introduced and demonstrates the good potentials over the traditional DCT coding. Moreover, a novel concept based on image primitives, namely, entropy of primitives (EoP), is proposed for measuring image visual information. Some very interesting results about EoP are achieved and analyzed, which has a close relationship with visual quality assessment. Future work includes two aspects. For one thing, try to effectively compress image primitives by taking advantage of dictionary structure; for another, it is also very interesting to design a new algorithm for visual quality assessment with the study on EoP.

References

1. Pennebaker, W.B., Mitchell, J.L.: JPEG still image data compression standard. Springer, New York (1993)
2. Taubman, D.S., Marcellin, M.W.: JPEG2000: Image compression fundamentals, standards and practice. Kluwer Academic Publishers, Norwell (2001)
3. Elad, M., Aharon, M.: Image denoising via sparse and redundant representations over learned dictionaries. IEEE Trans. on Image Processing 15(12), 3736–3745 (2006)
4. Elad, M.: Sparse and redundant representations–From theory to applications in signal and image processing. Springer (2010)
5. Elad, M., Bryt, O.: Compression of facial images using the K-SVD algorithm. Journal of Visual Communication and Image Representation 19(4), 270–283 (2008)
6. Zepeda, J., Guillemot, C., Kijak, E.: Image Compression using the Iteration-Tuned and Aligned Dictionary. In: 36th IEEE International Conference on Acoustics, Speech, and Signal Processing, pp. 793–796. IEEE Press (2011)
7. Aharon, M., Elad, M., Bruckstein, A.M.: The K-SVD: An Algorithm for Designing of Overcomplete Dictionaries for Sparse Representation. IEEE Trans. on Signal Processing 54(11), 4311–4322 (2006)
8. Tropp, J.A., Gilber, A.A.: Signal Recovery from Random Measurements via Orthogonal Matching Pursuit. IEEE Trans. on Information Theory 53(12), 4655–4666 (2007)
9. Wang, Z., Bovik, A.C., Sheikh, H.R., Simoncelli, E.P.: Image quality assessment: From error visibility to structural similarity. IEEE Trans. on Image Processing 13(4), 600–612 (2004)
10. Rubinstein, R., Zibulevsky, M., Elad, M.: Double sparsity: learning sparse dictionaries for sparse signal approximation. IEEE Trans. on Signal Processing 58(3), 1553–1564 (2010)

A Flexible Directional Image Representation Using Pseudo Polar Fourier Transform Based DFBs

Siqi Shi, Xuemei Xie, Huihui Lu, Guangming Shi, Yazhong Zhang, and Yongbo Li

Key Laboratory of Intelligent Perception and Image Understanding of Ministry of Education, School of Electronic Engineering, Xidian University, Shaanxi, 710071, P.R. China
sqshi@mail.xdian.edu.cn

Abstract. This paper presents a kind of basis functions used for image directional representation, which are obtained from the pseudo polar Fourier transform-based directional filter banks (PPFT-DFBs). The basis functions so obtained have the attractive properties of i) flexible direction and ii) arbitrary number of subbands. More specifically, we give the derivation of the basis function from the equivalent directional filter of PPFT-DFBs. Further, we analyze the properties of basis functions and their corresponding basis images. Experiments are given to testify the flexibility of basis functions and their efficiency in directional representation.

Keywords: Directional representation, directional filter bank, pseudo polar Fourier transform, basis function.

1 Introduction

Directional information of images plays a key role in many image processing applications. The efficient directional representation, in some way, closely depends on the flexible and accurate frequency partitioning of images, which can capture the significant information with fewer basis functions. Lots of methods of directional representation have been proposed [1-8]. Wavelet transform [2] can effectively capture the point-singularity of images, whereas it fails to the curve-singularity. To obtain better directionality and anisotropy, many effective methods beyond wavelets are proposed, such as the ridgelet [3], the wedgelet [4], the curvelet [5] and the contourlet [1, 6], etc. Among them, some are constructed in the discrete domain by utilizing the multirate filter banks [6-8], considering the geometry and directionality in images are hided in the discrete data. The contourlet consists of Laplacian pyramid (LP) and directional filter bank (DFB). The DFB is implemented by two-channel filter banks cascaded in the manner of a tree-structure [8]. The basis of contourlet can achieve the directional description in 2^n subbands excluding the specific directions, namely the horizontal, vertical and diagonal directions. Although the horizontal and vertical directional subbands can be obtained in Ref. [7], the convenient implementation is desired in practice. Unfortunately, the fixed number of directional subbands is mainly caused by such DFBs with the cascaded tree-structure, which impose restrictions on the frequency partitioning. So, the flexible directionality of basis functions is expected for directional image representation.

W. Lin et al. (Eds.): PCM 2012, LNCS 7674, pp. 686–696, 2012.

This paper presents a kind of basis functions, which is derived based on PPFT-DFBs [9]. Due to the flexible frequency partitioning scheme of PPFT-DFBs, the derived basis functions can achieve the arbitrary number of directional subbands and the flexible directions. In this paper, we derive the basis functions via the equivalent directional filters of the PPFT-DFBs. Such kinds of directional filters can be interpreted as the overall result of 2-dimensional (2-D) filters combined with the PPFT [10]. Further, we discuss the directionality of basis functions and their corresponding basis images. The flexible direction of basis functions is illustrated by the comparison of basis images of PPFT-DFBs with those of the nonsubsampled contourlet (NSCT) [11]. Finally, two experiments of the nonlinear approximation (NLA) are given to testify the efficiency of the basis functions for directional representation. The first one reveals the influence of different numbers of subbands on the performance of NLA. The second one demonstrates the flexibility of the proposed basis functions for directional image representation.

2   The PPFT-DFBs

The PPFT-DFBs is obtained by applying 1-D filter banks to the modified PPFT [8]. The PPFT evaluates the 2-D Fourier transform on pseudo-polar grid (pp grid). The pp grid has a distribution in accordance with directional features of images, and consists of two basic subsets: the basically vertical (BV) and basically horizontal (BH) subsets. The subsets can be obtained by

$$BV = \begin{cases} \omega_y = \pi l / N & -N \le l < N, \\ \omega_x = \omega_y \cdot 2m / N & -N/2 \le m < N/2 \end{cases} \tag{1}$$

$$BH = \begin{cases} \omega_x = \pi l / N & -N \le l < N, \\ \omega_y = \omega_x \cdot 2m / N & -N/2 < m \le N/2 \end{cases} \tag{2}$$

The pp grid is illustrated in Fig. 1(a), where the filled disk refers to the BV subset and the circle refers to the BH subset. It is obviously that m represents the slope direction and l the radial direction. Figs. 1(b) and (c) show BV and BH subsets in the coordinates of (m,l).

Before employing the 1-D K-channel filter bank, we need to make some modification to the PPFT of the image. That is, a) combining the BV and BH subsets; b) adjusting the combined one into the region of $[-\pi,\pi]$ along the slope direction. Fig. 2(a) shows the modified PPFT and its frequency partitioning by the 1-D K-channel filter bank. In this figure, the horizontal axis is corresponding to the slope direction (refer to Fig. 1(a)). As the 1-D filter bank is employed along the horizontal axis, the Cartesian grid of PPFT is decomposed into K subbands with rectangle supports. Each rectangle region in Fig. 2(a) corresponds to a wedge-shaped support in Fig. 2(b). By doing so, the PPFT-DFBs can be obtained.

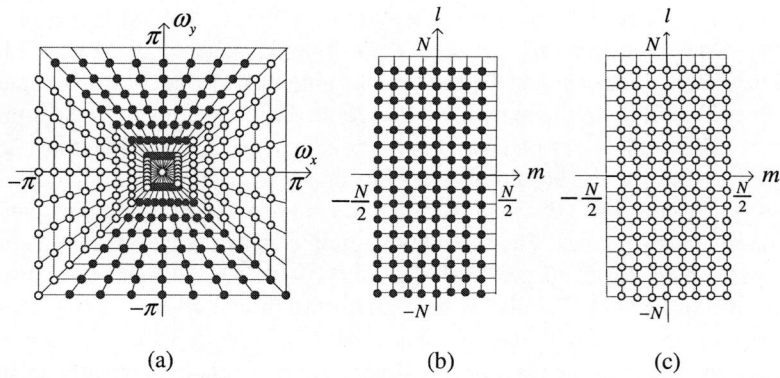

Fig. 1. The pp grid, (a) the filled disk refers to the BV subset and the circle is the BH subset, (b) BV subset and (c) BH subset in the coordinates of (m,l)

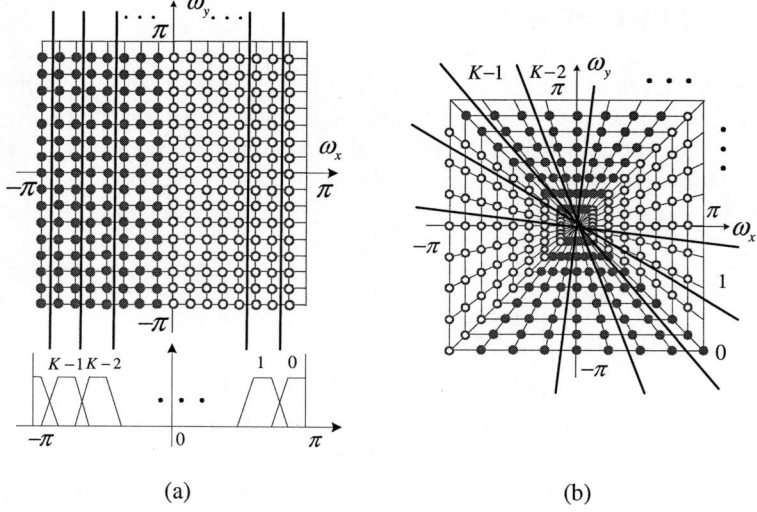

Fig. 2. Frequency partitioning by using 1-D K-channel filter banks, (a) applying an 1-D K-channel complex-valued filter bank to the modified PPFT, (b) the corresponding wedge-shaped subbands

3   Directional Representation of PPFT-DFBs

The DFB combined with the LP structure was proposed for a multiscale and multidirectional representation of images [1,6]. With the LP structure, the whole space in which an image lives can be divided into the approximation subspace for the coarse image and the detail subspace for the difference image. In the view of multi-resolution, it can be described as

$$V_{all} = V \oplus W \tag{3}$$

where V_{all} is the whole space, V the approximation subspace, and W the detail subspace. Fig. 3 shows the space partitioning, which is related with the frequency partitioning of the image. The dotted line is used for the partitioning of the directional subspaces which will be explained later on.

Since this paper focuses on the directional representation of the PPFT-DFBs, for easy discussion, we only consider the case where the PPFT-DFBs are applied to the finest detail subspace.

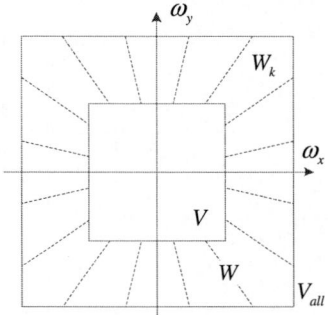

Fig. 3. Space partitioning, corresponding to frequency partitioning of the image

3.1 Multidirectional Decomposition

The multidirectional decomposition of an image can be achieved by applying a DFB. Thus, for the finest subspace (or the detail subspace), we have

$$W = \bigoplus_{k=0}^{K-1} W_k \tag{4}$$

where K is the number of the directional subspaces, k the index of the directional subspace, and W_k the k-th directional subspace of W. See Fig. 4 for the partitioning with the dotted line. Since, in this paper, we employ PPFT-DFBs in the LP structure, the partitioning of the subspaces can be more flexible in the direction, which is different with that in contourlet.

Further, the directional subspace W_k can be spanned by its basis functions as

$$W_k = \overline{\mathrm{Span}\left\{\varphi_{k,\mathbf{m}}\right\}_{\mathbf{m}\in\mathbb{Z}^2}}, \ 0 \le k \le K\text{-}1 \tag{5}$$

where $\mathbf{m}$ is the shifting position of the basis functions, $\left\{\varphi_{k,\mathbf{m}}\right\}_{\mathbf{m}\in\mathbb{Z}^2}$ is for the basis function $\varphi_{k,0}$ and its shifting versions.

In the PPFT-DFBs, the value of K depends on the number of channels of 1-D filter bank, and we can choose K as an arbitrary positive integer. Obviously, the larger the value of K is, the more accurate the directional representation of image. Moreover, one subband in any direction can be represented on one directional subspace, especially in the horizontal/vertical direction, due to the flexibility of the subspace partitioning.

3.2   Relationship of the Basis Function and the Directional Filter

Via the PPFT-DFBs, the detail subspace can be decomposed into directional subspaces. Thus, the basis functions $\{\varphi_{k,\mathbf{m}}\}_{\mathbf{m}\in\mathbb{Z}^2}$, which construct the directional subspaces W_k, must have closed relationship with directional filters of the PPFT-DFBs. To reveal this relationship, we present an equivalent structure, shown in Fig. 4.

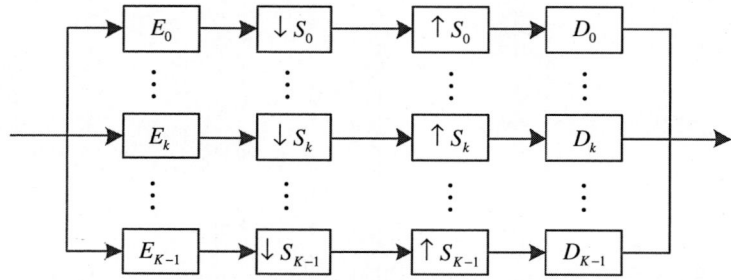

Fig. 4. Equivalent structure of the PPFT-DFBs with K subbands

In Fig. 4, the equivalent directional filters in the analysis and synthesis sections are respectively denoted by E_k and D_k, $0 \le k < K-1$. Different from that in the tree-structure, multi-stage structure (or indirect structure) [6-8], those directional filters of the PPFT-DFBs come from single-stage structure (or direct structure) with the manipulation of the 1-D filter bank in the PPFT domain. Such kind of filters can be regarded as the 2-D directional filters in the discrete Fourier transform, the translated domain of the PPFT.

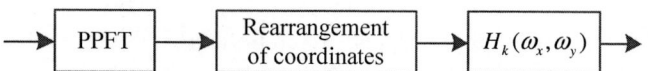

Fig. 5. Implementation structure of the directional filter E_k

Fig. 5 gives the implementation structure of one equivalent directional filter E_k from the k-th branch of the structure in Fig. 4. As more procedures, the input image is firstly translated in the PPFT domain and then rearranged in Cartesian coordinates, together with the adjustment of the period of 2π. A 2-D filter $H(\omega_x, \omega_y)$ with allpass in the direction of ω_y, referring to Fig. 2, is used to decompose the rearranged image,   and therefore obtain the corresponding wedge-shaped subband in the pp grid.

The basis functions and the equivalent directional filter have the following relationship

$$\left\{\varphi_{k,\mathbf{m}}\right\}_{\mathbf{m}\in\mathbb{Z}^2} \triangleq \left\{d_k\left[\mathbf{n}-\mathbf{S}_k\mathbf{m}\right]\right\}_{\mathbf{m}\in\mathbb{Z}^2} \qquad (6)$$

where d_k is the impulse response of the equivalent directional filter D_k, which is the dual filter of E_k. $\mathbf{S}_k$ indicates the sampling matrix in the k-channel. For the non-subsampled PPFT-DFBs, $\mathbf{S}_k$ is chosen as the unit matrix.

3.3   Basis Image

To describe the direction representation of the PPFT-DFBs more clearly, the basis images corresponding to the basis functions are presented for illustration. As an example, the basis images of the 8-band PPFT-DFBs, together with those of the 3-level NSCT, are given. For a better visual effect, all the basis images are displayed with the size of 64×64, in the following of this subsection.

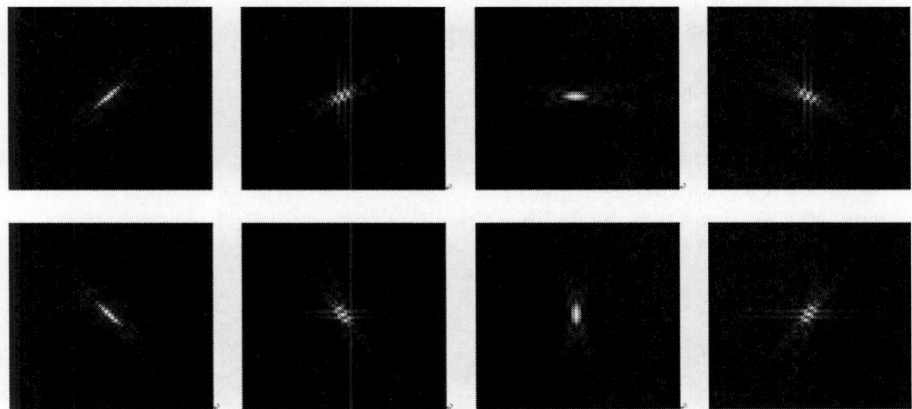

Fig. 6. Basis images of the 8-band PPFT- DFBs

Fig. 6 shows the basis images of the 8-subband PPFT-DFBs, where we can find the basis images in specific directions, such as horizontal, vertical, diagonal and anti-diagonal directions. In fact, any direction can be obtained if we properly choose the partitioning scheme of the PPFT-DFBs.

Here in this subsection, we also give the basis images of the 3-level NSCT for the comparison. It is equivalently 8 subbands. Fig. 7 shows the basis images. Due to the fixed frequency partitioning, the directions of the basis images are therefore fixed. There is no basis image falling in the specific directions as existed in the PPFT-DFBs. This degrades the flexibility of directional representation.

From the above we can see that, in the PPFT-DFBs, the flexibility on the direction of the basis functions can be obtained. To verify the flexible directional representation of the PPFT-DFBs, we will give two experiments of NLA to the difference image in the next section.

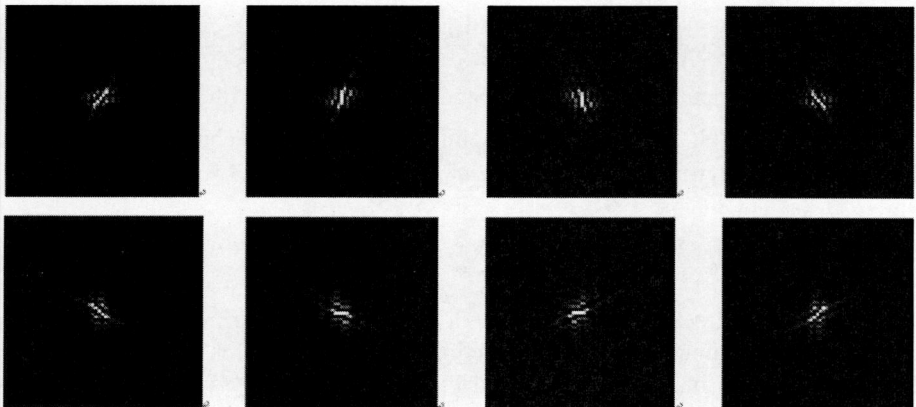

Fig. 7. Basis images of the 3-level NSCT

4   Simulations on Nonlinear Approximation

Two experiments of NLA are presented to evaluate the basis functions of the PPFT-DFBs in the directional representation. The first experiment tests the PPFT-DFBs with different numbers of subbands. And the influence of the number of subbands on the directional representation is analyzed. The second one compares the PPFT-DFBs with the NSCT, illustrating the flexible direction of the proposed basis functions.

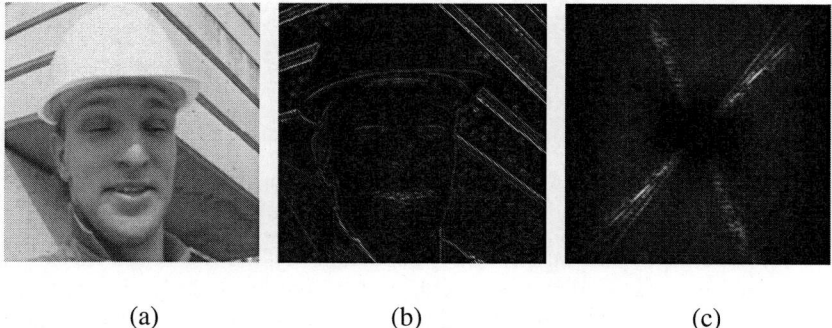

(a)   (b)   (c)

Fig. 8. (a) The original image; (b) and (c) the difference image and its frequency spectrum

The testing image used in both of two experiments is shown in Fig. 8(a). The difference image and its frequency spectrum are given in Figs. 8(b) and (c).

Some parameters used in the experiments are listed as follows. To obtain the difference image, the "9-7" biorthogonal filters are used in the LP stage. All the filters in PPFT-DFBs have the same length of 120. The filters in the contourlet are selected as the "pkva" filter with the size of "23-45" [12]. The number of most significant coefficients for the NLA is denoted by the ratio. In two experiments, the ratios are selected as 0.01%, 0.1% and 0.2%, respectively.

4.1   PPFT-DFBs with Different Numbers of Subbands

This experiment evaluates the NLA performance of PPFT-DFBs with different numbers of subbands. As an example, the cases of 6-band and 20-band are considered for the comparison. Figs. 9(a) and (b) respectively display the basis images of PPFT-DFBs in two cases, where all the six for 6-band and nine of twenty for 20-band. Figs. 9(c) and (d) show sequence of the approximation images reconstructed by two PPFT-DFBs, respectively.

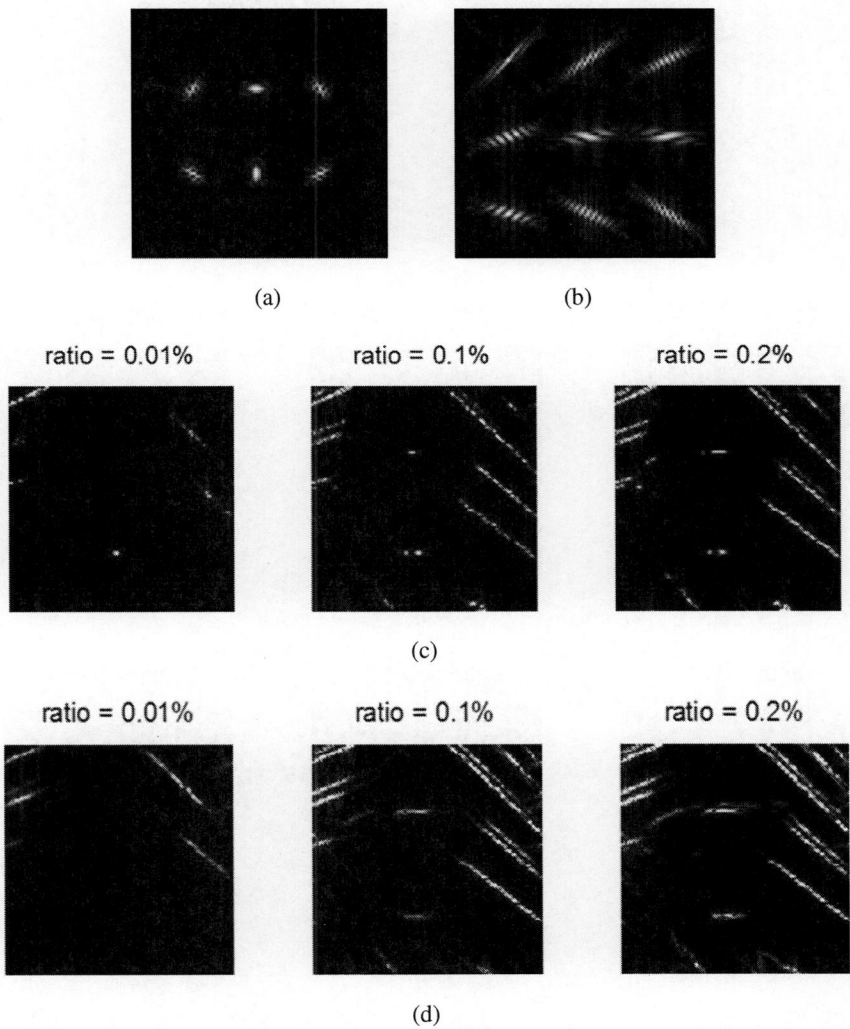

Fig. 9. (a) All six basis images of the 6-band PPFT-DFBs, (b) nine of twenty basis images of the 20-band case, sequence of the difference image "Foreman" approximated nonlinearly by (c) 6-band and (d) 20-band PPFT-DFBs

As Figs. 9(c) and (d) show, the visual quality of 20-band performs better than that of 6 subbands case. The reason is that the basis images of 20-band PPFT-DFBs are more flexible and precise on directional representation compared with that of 6-band case. The more the number of subbands is, the better the directional images representation.

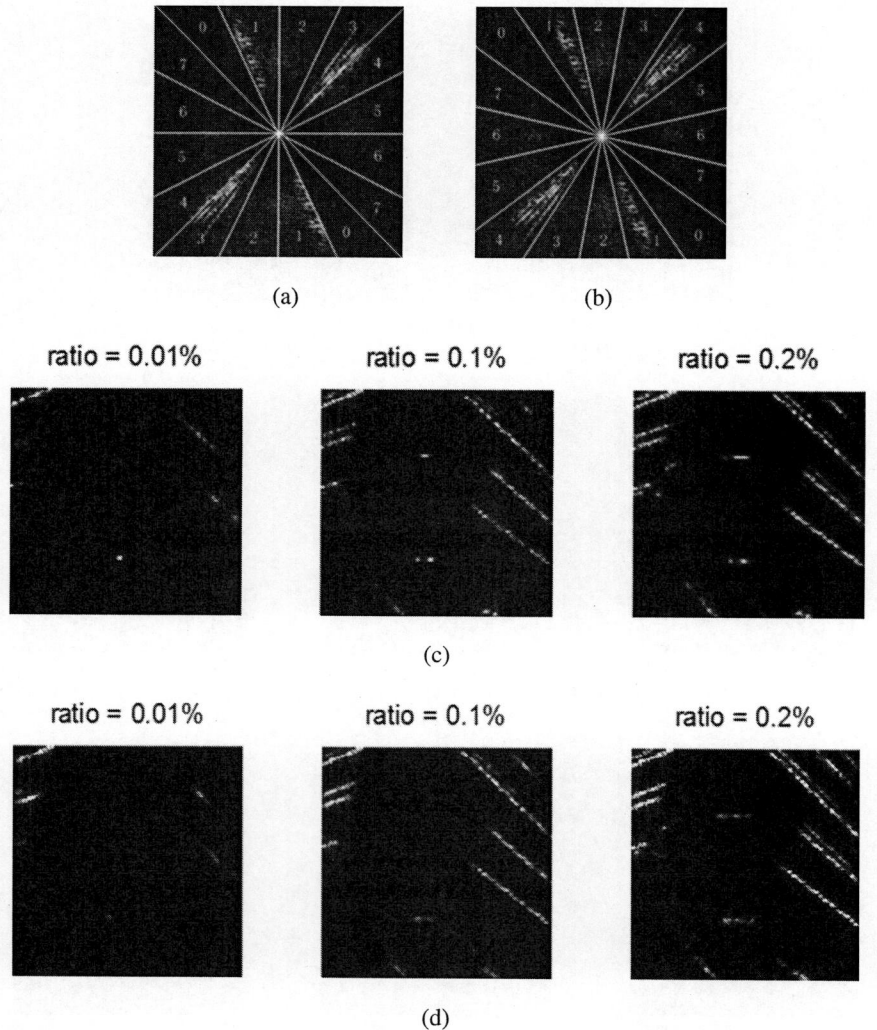

Fig. 10. The frequency partitioning scheme of (a) NSCT and (b) PPFT- DFBs, sequence of the difference image "Foreman" approximated nonlinearly by (c) the 3-level NSCT and (d) the 8-band PPFT- DFBs

4.2   Comparison between NSCT and PPFT-DFBs

This experiment evaluates the NLA performance of two kinds of basis functions: the proposed basis functions of the PPFT-DFBs and that of NSCT. As an example, we choose an 8-band PPFT-DFBs and a 3-level (equivalently, 8-band) NSCT for comparison, the basis images of which have been shown in Figs. 6 and 7 in Subsection 3.3. The frequency partitioning schemes of NSCT and PPFT-DFBs are respectively displayed in Figs. 10(a) and (b). Figs. 10(c) and (d) show sequence of the approximated images respectively by two kinds of basis functions.

It should be noted that most of the directional information can be captured by the individual subband of the PPFT-DFBs, respectively labeled as '1','2','4' and '6' in Fig. 10(b), which failed by the NSCT in Fig. 10(a). As seen in Figs. 10(c) and (d), the approximated images reconstructed by the PPFT-DFBs perform better in those directions, such as the horizontal, vertical and diagonal directions. So, the proposed basis functions have more flexible directions and are more efficient in the directional representation, compared with that of the NSCT.

5   Conclusion

In this paper, a kind of basis functions based on PPFT-DFBs is presented for the image representation. It has two attractive properties: flexible direction and arbitrary number of subbands, compared with the NSCT. In the future, study on the proposed basis functions and the related factors, such as the directional filter and the frequency partitioning, will be taken into account. Furthermore, the basis functions in the subsampled case are also to be considered.

Acknowledgements. This work was supported in part by the NSF of China under Grants 61072104, 61033004 and Doctoral Program Foundation of Institutions of Higher Education of China under Grants 20090203110003.

References

1. Do, M.N., Vetterli, M.: The Contourlet Transform: an Efficient Directional Multiresolution Image Representation. IEEE Transactions on Image Processing 14(12), 2091–2106 (2005)
2. Mallat, S.: A Wavelet Tour of Signal Processing, 2nd edn. Academic, New York (1998)
3. Donoho, D.L.: Orthonormal Ridgelets and Linear Singularities. SIAM Journal on Mathematical Analysis 31(5), 1062–1099 (1998)
4. Donoho, D.L.: Wedgelets: Nearly Minimax Estimation of Edges. The Annals of Statistics 27(3), 859–897 (1999)
5. Candes, E.J., Donoho, D.L.: Curvelets—A Surprisingly Effective Nonadaptive Representation for Objects with Edges. In: Cohen, A., Rabut, C., Schumaker, L.L. (eds.) Curves and Surfaces Fitting. Vanderbilt Univ. Press, Nashville (1999)
6. Do, M.N.: Directional Multiresolution Image Representations. Ph.D. dissertation, School Comput. Commun. Sci., Swiss Fed. Inst. Technol., Lausanne, Switzerland (2001)

7. Nguyen, T.T., Chauris, H.: Uniform Discrete Curvelet Transform. IEEE Transactions on Signal Processing 58(7), 3618–3634 (2010)
8. Bamberger, R.H., Smith, M.J.T.: A Filter Bank for the Directional Decomposition of Images: Theory and Design. IEEE Transactions on Signal Processing 40(4), 882–893 (1992)
9. Shi, G.M., Liang, L.L., Xie, X.M.: Design of Directional Filter Banks with Arbitrary Number of Subbands. IEEE Transactions on Signal Processing 57(12), 4936–4941 (2009)
10. Averbuch, A., Coifman, R.R., Donoho, D.L., Elad, M., Israeli, M.: Fast and Accurate Polar Fourier Transform. Applied and Computational Harmonic Analysis 21, 145–167 (2006)
11. Cunha, A.L., Zhou, J.P., Do, M.N.: The Nonsubsampled Contourlet Transform: Theory, Design, and Applications. IEEE Transactions on Image Processing 15(10), 3089–3101 (2006)
12. Phoong, S.M.C., Kim, W., Vaidyanathan, P.P., Ansari, R.: A New Class of Two-Channel Biorthogonal Filter Banks and Wavelet Bases. IEEE Transactions on Signal Processing 43(3), 649–665 (1995)

Location and Route Tracking in University from Photos without GPS Information

Lin Mingxia, Shichang Hu, Li Cuihua, Jin Taisong, and Zou Quan

School of Information Science and Technology, Xiamen University, Xiamen, P.R. China

Abstract. Location and route tracking is important for visitors and travelers, and it mainly depends on GPS information. However, GPS devices are not usually carried with by the travelers. Mobile phone with digital camera is the common standing item for people. We try to analyze the photos from mobile and compared to the known scenic, then predict the user location and accomplish the route tracking according the time and spatial information. In this paper, we choose our university as the scenic, and get good performance on daytime.

Keywords: Location, scene recognize, libD3C.

1   Introduction

Location-based services estimate your location in order to provide you with a more useful service, such as requesting the nearest business or service (an ATM or restaurant).Today, some web and mobile apps use GPS or publicly broadcast WiFi data from wireless access points to estimate location. A GPS receiver calculates its position by precisely timing the signals sent by GPS satellites high above the Earth. Although GPS is the most popular technology in location, it still has some drawbacks. In order to get your position, you need a GPS device, such as mobile smartphone with GPS navigation. GPS signal is another important factor and in some situation there is no signal such as indoor. In addition, mobile smartphone with GPS is constantly draining the battery when the GPS left on. It is trouble for travelers that they charge their mobile phone at any time. The obvious drawback of using GPS service is some people worry their personal information leakage and refuse it. To travelers they usually lose their direction when they travel to a new scenic especially to a large area and urgently need more detailed information about location. However GPS just tell them the scenic name, because large area to people maybe a small point to GPS.

In this paper we try to use a new way to resolve this problem. We analyze the photos from mobile and compared to the known scenic, then predict the user location and accomplish the route tracking according the time and spatial information. In our approach we use the scene recognition without GPS. Users who have mobile phone just with digital camera can accomplish it, and can get the next service. Otherwise, our approach can be used in automatically tag the scenic photos that web user upload and forget giving the tag. It is helpful to the photo retrieval application.

To predict the user location by the photos user supply accurately, in fact we do the scene recognition. Nowadays, there are many approaches in scene recognition especially outdoor scene recognition is proved to achieve high accuracy. Like mostly scene

W. Lin et al. (Eds.): PCM 2012, LNCS 7674, pp. 697–706, 2012.

recognition work, our work is divided into 2 steps: 1) we define the effective features then according to the selected features we abstract the features from the photos.2) based on the known scenic photos we use ensemble classifier to classify uploading photos and infer the detail location.

Our contribution is: 1) Our work is an important supplement approach on location of GPS when GPS can't work effectively. On the other hand, to travelers our work can tell the more detail position information than GPS. 2) Our work has practical value. We have built an application website and a dataset about our university scenic for our experiments (http://datamining.xmu.edu.cn/software/showhere/), the experiments show this method can get good performance on daytime. In the future, this app will offer further services such as tracking the travelers and giving some suggestion, allowing travelers sharing their travel .Maybe one day you can download it easily in apple store.

The paper is organized as follows. We will briefly introduce the prior related researches in Section 2, define features we selected in Section 3, ensemble classifier framework in Section 4, experimental evaluation in Section 5, and conclusions in Section 6.

2   Related Work

Early methods for scene recognition mainly used low-level image features such as color, texture, and shape. Vailaya[1] using the low-level feature like color histogram ,color coherence vector , edge direction-based features and so on to classify city images vs landscapes. In order to get satisfied accuracy, they think about the discriminative power of the following features.[2] also use low-level global features for image classification, different with [1] they think about a belief or confidence function among the available scene labels. [3] use color histograms as the image signature and a k-nearest neighbors scheme for classification. Color histogram computed by assigning all pixels in an image to a pre-computed universal color dictionary computed using k-means. Early approaches used low-level feature directly from the image in combination with supervised learning methods to classify images into several semantic classes. Therefore the main problem with these approaches is that they can't generalize from the training data to new scenes.

Oliva and Torralba[4] proposed a novel feature using coarsely localized spectral information they called spatial envelope. Although they bypasses the segmentation and the processing of individual objects or regions, they still used localized information so met the same problem above.

In order to reduce the gap between low-level and high-level image processing, other methods in term of the process humans do scene classification used semantic modeling to describe the image. Recent work has focused on the way generated from text mining, which termed bag-of-words. Fei-Fei and Perona [5] represent the image of a scene by a collection of local regions, denoted as codewords obtained by unsupervised learning. Although the traditional bag-of-words model works well for image classification, people empirically found that, this approach discard the information about the spatial layout of features and it is orderless.So it's drawback is capturing shapes or locating an object.

Researchers endeavored to extend bag-of-words method. Some researchers aimed to use PLSA[6-8]with local features. Some in term of the objective recognition approach to get some related information, such as [9,10,11], Spatial pyramid matching[12-13] is proved to get the most successful results.

3 Coding Descriptors

As we talked in section 2,SPM as an extension of the BOF model get remarkable success[22]in image classification. In these paper we will use an extension of the SPM approach called Locality-constrained Linear Coding(LLC)[21].

Typical SPM method partition the image into increasingly segment and computes the BOF histogram of each segment, finally using coding scheme convert all the histogram into vector representation of the image. Although typical SPM method have good performance in scene recognition, the obvious shortcoming is it has to use classifier with nonlinear Mercer kernels. So many researchers aim to obtaining nonlinear feature representations.LLC is the same.

LLC method think that locality is more essential than sparsity. Let X be a set of D-dimensional local descriptors extracted from an image, i.e. $x = [x_1, ..., x_N] \in R^{D \times N}$. $C = [C_1, ..., C_M] \in R^{D \times M}$,are the M cluster centers to be found, called codebook. $V = [V_1, ..., V_N]$ is the set of codes of X. LLC code can be introduced as follows.

$$\min_V \sum_{i=1}^{N} \|x_i - Cv_i\|^2 + \lambda \|u_i \odot v_i\|^2 \tag{1}$$

Subject to $card(v_i) = 1, \forall i$

Where $card(v_i) = 1$ is a cardinality constraint, meaning that only one elements of v_i is nonzero. $\odot$denotes element-wise multiplication, Note that $u_i \in R^M$is the locality adaptor that can present as follows:

$$u_i = \exp\left(\frac{dist(x_i, C)}{\sigma}\right) \tag{2}$$

$dist(x_i, C) = [dist(x_i, C_1), ..., dist(x_i, C_M)]^T$, $dist(x_i, C_j)$ is Euclidean distance between x_i and C_j, σ is a parameter used for adjusting u_i decay speed.

4 Dynamic Selection and Circulating Combination Based on Clustering

After feature selection and representation, we use classifier to distinguish the location of the photo. The traditional classifier such as SVM, decision tree, BP neural network can't get satisfied performance in scene recognition. At present, many researchers focus on classifier ensemble. Most of the experiments prove that the ensemble systems own the greater generalization capability than the individual classifier. We use a new classifier ensemble method that called dynamic selection and circulating combination based on clustering. Next we will introduce this method.

The method can be divided into two phase: In the first phase, in order to control the size of classifiers we employs k-means clustering to prune the whole set of the base classifiers. The second phase consists of ensemble backward sequential selection based on interrater agreement together with the framework of dynamic selection and circulating combination.

4.1   Reduction Strategy Based on k-Means Clustering

Zhou Zhihua [14] prove not all classifiers employed in the classifier ensemble can get the most effective performance. Therefore, we devote to utilizing some strategy to reduce the redundant classifiers before doing dynamic selection and circulating combination. In this paper, we utilize k-means clustering. Then we can obtain the subset of the classifiers which have the greater diversity each other.

The process is: First we train the classifier independently. We set vector $E_i = \{e_{i1}, ..., e_{i|O_{num}|}\}$ to represent the effect of a classifier I, e_{ij} is the effect of classifier I to the j example. The value of e_{ij} is only 1 or 0, it means correct or not. Then use vector space E clustering. At last, chooses the classifier which has the highest accuracy from every cluster. To complete the clustering, there are there important problems. One is how to represent the distance of two classifiers. Second is how many clusters we selected. Third is how to confirm the initial centroids. According to Giacinto and Roli[15] they define the distance of two classifiers which is defined as follow:

$$d(C_i, C_j) = 1 - P(C_{ifails}, C_{jfails}), \forall C_i, C_i \in T \tag{3}$$

where C_i and C_j are the classifiers, C_{ifails} and C_{jfails} are the fail set which C_i and C_j get, and $P(C_{ifails}, C_{jfails})$ is the possibility of misclassification intersection of the classifier C_i and the classifier C_j. It means the more misclassification intersection of the classifier the small distance of their two.

The number of clusters k we set $k = \frac{|T|}{2}$, where T is the classifiers set. We adopt random selection to initialize the centroids and the seed is fixed.

4.2   The Framework of Dynamic Selection and Circulating Combination

The disagreement measure between classifier is important to the dynamic selection and circulating combination. It is the key to classifier ensemble to get high accuracy. Acorrding to[16], we select interrater agreement κ to measure the disagreement. The interrater agreement κ can be defined as follows [16]:

Set classifiers ensemble $T = \{C_1 ..., C_t\}$, $\bar{p}$ is the average accuracy of the whole classifier, $Dis_{av} = \sum Dis_{ik}$, Dis_{ik} is the disagreement measure, $Dis_{ik} = \frac{N^{01}+N^{10}}{N}$, we represent the output of a classifier C_i as an N-dimensional binary vector, the detail see the Table 1.

Table 1. The Relationship between the pair of two classifier

	$C_k correct(1)$	$C_k wrong(0)$
$C_i correct(1)$	N^{11}	N^{10}
$C_i wrong(0)$	N^{01}	N^{00}

Total: $N = N^{11} + N^{10} + N^{01} + N^{00}$

$$\text{interrater agreement } K, k = 1 - \frac{1}{2\bar{p}(1-\bar{p})} Dis_{av} \qquad (4)$$

Note that K is depended on $\bar{p}$ and Dis_{av}, The smaller the value of K the greater disagreement.

Using the interrater agreement K mentioned above we present the framework of dynamic selection and circulating combination and ensemble backward sequential selection is embedded into the framework.

The algorithm of the framework of dynamic selection and circulating combination include 4 steps: (1) sets up the initial threshold of the accuracy $\theta = \theta_0$ and the interval $\Delta\theta$ that can control the procedure dynamically. Set the initial classifiers ensemble $S = T$, ensemble T is the process result of the first phase. (2)If $|S| > N_{threshold}$, set $S = S_{suboptimal}$ $N_{threshold}$ is the threshold in order to limit the number of the classifiers, $S_{suboptimal}$ is the optimal classifiers ensemble locality. (3)Ranks the classifiers according to the accuracy from high to low, if reduce the current classifier C_i can leads to smaller interrater agreement K and improve the accuracy then C_i will be cut from the ensemble T;(4) When the current ensemble accuracy exceeds the threshold θ,the algorithm end. Otherwise set $\theta = \theta - \Delta\theta$, repeat the above process.

5 Experiments

In this section, we report the experiments results on our dataset. Our dataset contains of 8 categories of our university scenes (see Fig.1). The average size of each image is approximately 480×640 pixels. The 8 categories are obtained by us from both personal photographs as well as the baidu image search engine. The 8 categories include the famous scenic spots or symbol building around our university. Our dataset has 115 samples and 21505 attributes. The experiments show the superiority of the model proposed in this paper.

As described in Fig.2, we build a website allow people to upload their photos and it will return the user where they are. Furthermore user can click 'Find in map' button to get the location in the map.

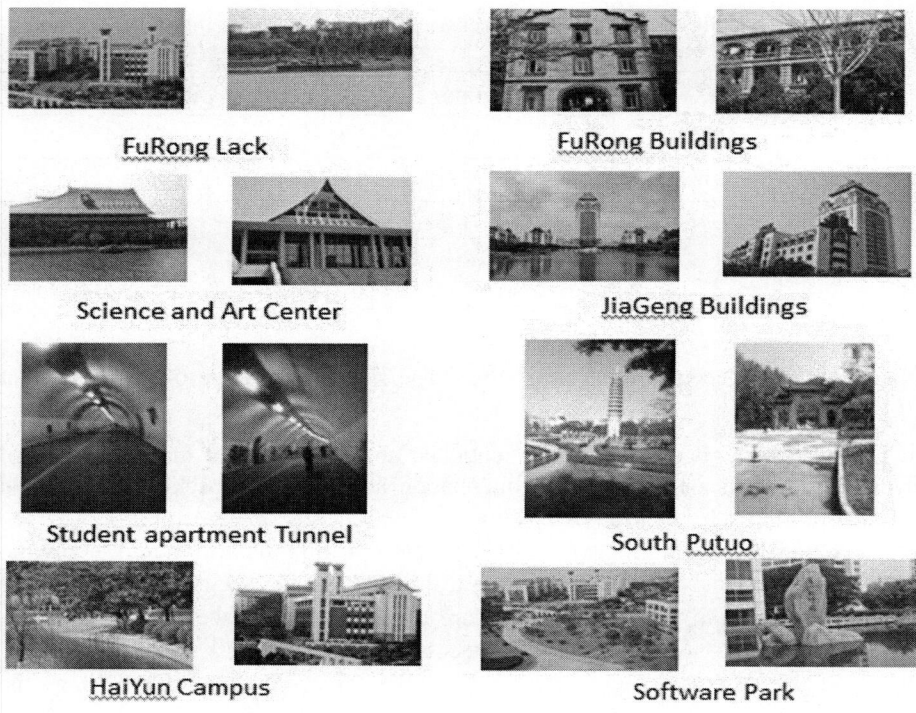

Fig. 1. Our dataset consists of 8 categories

Fig. 2. The Website of our application

LibD3C[23](see Fig.3) is a library for dynamic selection and circulating combination based on clustering. We test the proposed model we mention above in LibD3C.In order to compare the performance of it we also do the experiments in Liblinear[17], KNN and libSVM. The result is presented as Table 2.We can see our method perform better than other method. The results reported are the averages of ten times of 5-fold cross validation and the averages can evaluate the effect of the classification. The experiments cost 0.5 hours more than liblinear.

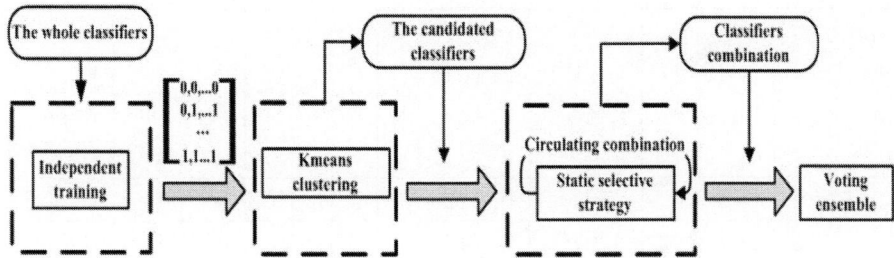

Fig. 3. The framework of LibD3C

Table 2. The Classification of our dataset

Method	Accuracy
liblinear	63.48%
libD3C	68.70%
KNN	48.09%
libSVM	50.74%

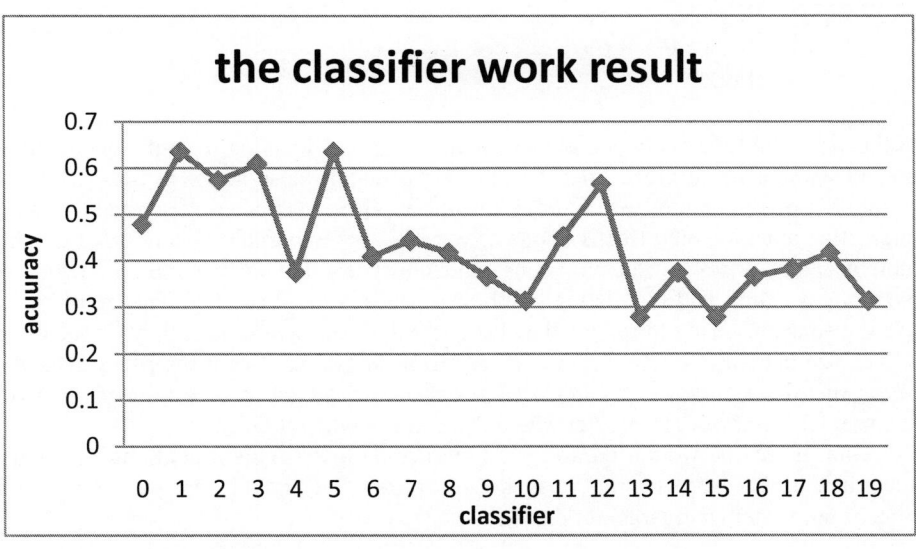

Fig. 4. The Accuracy of 19 classifiers work independ

In order to satisfy the necessary diversity, we set the initial classifiers ensemble 19 miscellaneous classifiers, including KNN[18],SVM[19], random forest, decision tree etc. The results show in Fig.4 reported the accuracy of 19 classifiers work independ.

In Table 3,it shows that our method perform in different major measurements including TP Rate, FP Rate[20], Precision, Recall[20], F-Measure, ROC Area.

Table 3. the Result of our method in each class

Class/ Measurement	TP Rate	FP Rate	Precision	Recall	F-Measure	ROC Area
1	0.8	0.07	0.632	0.8	0.706	0.865
2	0.417	0.019	0.714	0.417	0.526	0.699
3	0.273	0.019	0.6	0.273	0.375	0.627
4	0.4	0.01	0.8	0.4	0.533	0.695
5	0.571	0.009	0.8	0.571	0.667	0.781
6	0.923	0.01	0.923	0.923	0.923	0.957
7	0.884	0.292	0.644	0.884	0.745	0.796
8	0.25	0.009	0.5	0.25	0.333	0.62
averages weight	0.687	0.125	0.695	0.687	0.664	0.781

6   Conclusions

In this paper we address the problem of identifying user location from the photos they upload without using GPS. First we define the feature descriptors in SPM[21].It is simple but effective and very suitable for our application. Because user need in time interaction a simple but effective code scheme is very important. Secondly, to get the more accuracy of result we employ ensemble classifiers that work in the framework of dynamic selection and circulating combination based on clustering. This framework use k-means clustering to reduce the classifiers that can save time and avoid the classifiers size become too big. Experimental results show significant improves than liblinear, and the accuracy in 8 categories of our dataset all above 65%.It means that we can use our framework to predict where the user are without GPS.

In the future, we would like to dynamic trace the user route around our university according to the different time images user upload. We should improve the respond time of our system and large our dataset.

Acknowledgement. The work was supported by the Natural Science Foundation of China (No.61001013, No.61102136) and the Natural Science Foundation of Fujian Province of China (No.2011J05158, No.2011J01365).

References

1. Vailaya, A., Jain, A., Zhang, H.: On image classification: city vs. landscapes. landscapes. Pattern Recog. 31, 1921–1935 (1998)
2. Chang, E., Goh, K., Sychay, G., Wu, G.: Cbsa: Content-based soft annotation for multi-modal image retrieval using bayes point machines. IEEE Trans. on Circuits and Systems for Video Technology 13, 26–38 (2003)
3. Ulrich, I., Nourbakhsh, I.: Appearance-based place recog. For topological localization. In: IEEE Int. Conf. on Rob. and Automation, ICRA (2000)
4. Oliva, A., Torralba, A.: Modeling the shape of the scene: a holistic representation of the spatial envelope. Int. Journal of Comp. Vision 42, 145–175 (2001)
5. Fei-Fei, L., Perona, P.: A Bayesian Hierarchical Model for Learning Natural Scene Categories. In: IEEE Computer Society Conference on Computer Vision and Pattern Recognition, CVPR 2005 (2005)
6. Torralba, A.: LabelMe: Online Image Annotation and Applications. Proceedings of the IEEE 98(8), 1467–1484 (2010)
7. Torralba, A., Murphy, K.P., Freeman, W.T.: Using the forest to see the trees: exploiting context for visual object detection and localization. Communications of the ACM CACM Homepagearchive 53(3) (March 2010)
8. Grauman, K., Darrell, T.: Pyramid match kernels: Discriminative classification with sets of image features. In: Proc. ICCV (2005)
9. Espinace, P., Kollar, T., Soto, A., Roy, N.: Indoor Scene Recognition Through Object Detection. In: 2010 IEEE International Conference on Robotics and Automation, ICRA, May 3-7, pp. 1406–1413 (2010)
10. Baba, T., Chen, T.: Object-driven image group annotation. In: 2010 17th IEEE International Conference on Image Processing, ICIP, September 26-29, pp. 2641–2644 (2010)
11. Li, L.-J., Su, H., Xing, E.P., Fei-Fei, L.: Object bank: A high-level image representation for scene classification and semantic feature sparsification. In: Proceedings of the Neural Information Processing Systems, NIPS (2010)
12. Ergul, E., Arica, N.: Scene Classification Using Spatial Pyramid of Latent Topics. This Paper Appears in: 20th International Conference on Pattern Recognition, ICPR, August 23-26 (2010)
13. Elfiky, N.M., Khan, F.S., van de Weijer, J., Gonzalez, J.: Discriminative compact pyramids for object and scene recognition (September 24, 2011)
14. Zhou, Z., Wu, J., Tang, W.: Ensembling neural network: Many could be better than all. Artificial Intelligence 137(1-2), 239–263 (2002)
15. Giacinto, G., Roli, F.: An approach to the automatic design of multiple classifier system. Pattern Recognition Letters 22(1), 25–33 (2001)
16. Kuncheva, L.I., Whitaker, C.J.: Measures of diversity in classifier ensembles and their relationship with the ensemble accuracy. Machine Learning 51(2), 181–207 (2003)
17. Fan, R.-E., Chang, K.-W., Hsieh, C.-J., Wang, X.-R., Lin, C.-J.: LIBLINEAR: A Library for Large Linear Classification. The Journal of Machine Learning Research Archive 9, 1871–1874 (2008)

18. Boser, B.E., Guyon, I.M., Vapnik, V.N.: A training algorithm for optimal margin classifiers. In: Proceedings of the Fifth Annual Workshop on Computational Learning Theory, pp. 144–152. ACM, New York (1992)
19. Ghodselahi, A.: A Hybrid Support Vector Machine Ensemble Model for Credit Scoring. International Journal of Computer Applications 17(5), 1–5 (2011)
20. Lin, Z., Lai, Y., Lin, C., Xie, Y., Zou, Q.: Maintaining Internal Consistency of Report for Real-Time OLAP with Layer-Based View. In: Du, X., Fan, W., Wang, J., Peng, Z., Sharaf, M.A. (eds.) APWeb 2011. LNCS, vol. 6612, pp. 143–154. Springer, Heidelberg (2011)
21. Wang, J., Yang, J., Yu, K., Lv, F., Huang, T., Gong, Y.: Locality-constrained Linear Coding for Image Classification. In: 2010 IEEE Conference on Computer Vision and Pattern Recognition, CVPR, June 13-18 (2010)
22. Ji, R., Duan, L.Y., Chen, J., Yao, H., Yuan, J., Rui, Y., Gao, W.: Location Discriminative Vocabulary Coding for Mobile Landmark Search. International Journal of Computer Vision, 1–25 (2012)
23. Gao, Y., Wang, M., Tao, D., Dai, Q., Zhang, N.: Object Retrieval and Recognition with Hypergraph Analysis. In: IEEE TIP 2012 (2012)

Real-Time Viewfinder Composition Assessment and Recommendation to Mobile Photographing[*]

Chen Lujun[1], Yao Hongxun[1], Sun Xiaoshuai[1], and Zhang Hongming[2]

[1] Department of Computer Science and Engineering,
Harbin Institute of Technology, China
[2] NEC Laboratories China
h.yao@hit.edu.cn

Abstract. Mobile phone has been the major device for taking photos in our daily lives. In this paper, we create a novel iOS application called PhotoGuide to aid iPhone users for efficient photographing. The system automatically assesses the quality of the preview images from iPhone's camera using attention-based perceptual assessment method, based on which the users could find an optimized camera-view and distance for taking the photos. According to the feedback from the users, the system will adaptively change the parameters shifting to a personalized working mode, which is design to satisfy specialized photographing environments and personal preference. We also designed a friendly user interface to improve the user experience. Comprehensive user studies well indicate the significant improvement both in photographic effect and user's experience.

Keywords: Mobile phone camera, automatic view finding, perceptual photo assessment.

1 Introduction

With the advances in DSP technology, new breed of built-in features such as automatic focus(AF), face detection (FD) etc, have been embedded into digital cameras, which makes taking a sophisticated photos a piece of cake. However, recent studies have shown that the number of photos captured by mobile phone is growing rapidly with its convenience in recording life's fleeting moment. When first appearing in the mobile phone in 2002, camera now seems to have become an essential feature of mobile phone. A quarter of respondents said that if the phone's camera quality reaches to 600 million pixels they will only use the phone to take pictures according to a survey conducted by Schneider-kreuznach [5]. In some cases, 43% of people would be willing to appropriate replace their digital camera. Currently, only 32% of people will still prefer a digital camera. Users, especially in India and China, are willing to accept cell phone photography. In these countries, nearly 80% of the respondents are willing to

---

[*] This work was supported in part by the National Science Foundation of China (No. 61071180 & No. 61133003) and the program of NEC (CHINA) CO., LTD. (LC04-20111205-08).

W. Lin et al. (Eds.): PCM 2012, LNCS 7674, pp. 707–714, 2012.

use only cell phones to take pictures. India and China, more than half of respondents (60% and 52%) has been photographed several times a week using mobile phones and in the United States the proportion reaches to more than a quarter (26%), while in Germany, it is the lowest (12%). However, unlike taking photo with digital camera, user may find it difficult to take a good photo using the function offered by the mobile itself. All four countries above bear the idea that currently the photo quality of mobile phones on the market is unsatisfactory, which becomes the main reason why they don't want use camera phone to replace digital cameras. In this paper, we present PhotoGuide, an iPhone application to aid users for efficient photographing.

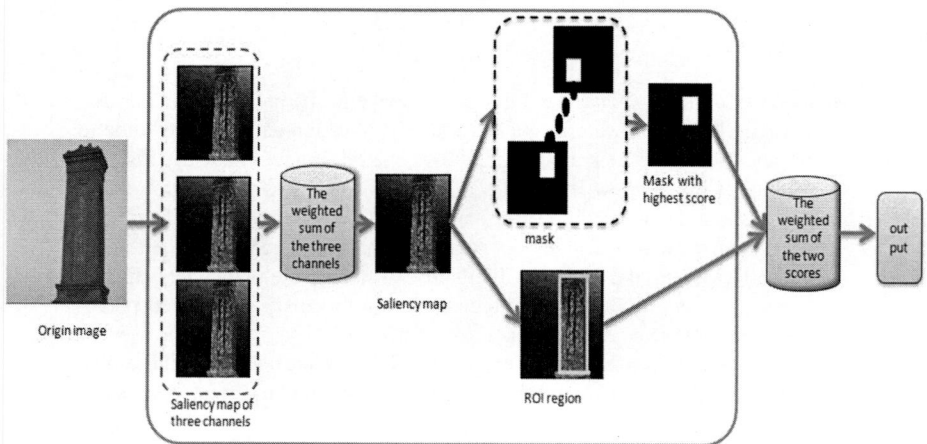

Fig. 1. The illustration of our system's work procedure

The main function of our system is to aid iPhone users to find an optimized camera-view and distance for taking the photos by using a computational algorithm based on real-time perceptual image assessment. Besides, considering various environments and personalized preference, the system will adaptively update the parameters to satisfy specialized user requirement.

2   Related Work

To aid users taking good photos with phone camera, firstly our system must solve the problem of real-time perceptual image quality assessment. This has always been the eyes of the beholder wise views about the issue of image assessment, and there always lacks an explicit or practical criterion which measures the goodness of a photo due to its complexity of photography and subjectivity in evaluation and difficulty in context modeling. Previews work like Chen *et al.* [1] proposed an intelligent photography system, which automatically and professionally generates user-favorite photos from a wide view or a continuous view sequence by mining the underlying knowledge and experience of the photographers from massively crawled professional photos.

Luo *et al.* [3] designed a photo quality assessment algorithm which first extracts the subject region from a photo, and then formulates a number of high level semantic features for photo quality classification. Ke *et al.* [4] proposed a high level semantic feature to match the people's perception of photo quality. Zhang *et al.* [5] develop a novel feature based IQA model called Riesz-transform based Feature Similarity metric (RFSIM) for image quality assessment. Chen *et al.* [7] develop an improved method which is called gradient-based structural similarity (GSSIM) based on the structural similarity (SSIM) which is more consistent to human visual system. Previous works of automatic image assessment adopt various image processing techniques such as image segmentation, Gaussian convolution, and DFT. These techniques are highly time-consuming, which makes them impossible to be directly applied in the mobile phone platform.

Our approach, instead of assessing a picture with a very complicated method, just pays attention to the saliency map of the image. We develop an extremely less time-consuming algorithm to get the saliency map of an image, and assess the picture with a method of compositional template matching. Therefore, our approach possesses several inherent advantages: 1) Our approach applies a less time-consuming algorithm, which meets the real-time requirement for mobile phones. 2) Because our approach is based on the method of template matching, users could generate their own templates to satisfy personalized preference.

3   System Framework

In this section, we will give a detailed introduction of our system's framework, which includes saliency map computation, compositional template matching, ROI segmentation, and personalized mask generation. A diagram illustration of our system is given in Figure 1.

3.1   Determinants of Assessment

Unlike professional photographer who wants to take rich artistic photos, the mobile users are more likely interested in recording fleeting life moments with their mobile phones. And this rules the two determinants of assessing photos taken with mobile phone: 1) whether the target object photographed is in a significant area. 2) Whether the target object is significant enough, namely whether ROI segment is in proper size.

Composition Assessment
Whether the target object photographed in a significant area is a problem of composition. Composition is the placement or arrangement of visual elements in a photograph [2]. Although there are no absolute rules that guarantee perfect composition for all photographs, there are nonetheless some heuristic principles which when applied properly suggest a composition that will be pleasing for most people.

We proposed a method of compositional template matching based on the saliency map to assess the placement or arrangement quality of the preview image. The templates are generated according to some heuristic principles which suggest a composition that will be pleasing for most people. First step of our approach is to compute saliency map with an efficient algorithm. We map the origin picture to the Lab color space, and the saliency map of each channel is given by:

$$S\_L(i,j) = \left[L(i,j) - \frac{1}{MN} \sum_{i=1}^{M} \sum_{j=1}^{N} L(i,j) \right]^2 \tag{1}$$

$$S\_a(i,j) = \left[a(i,j) - \frac{1}{MN} \sum_{i=1}^{M} \sum_{j=1}^{N} a(i,j) \right]^2 \tag{2}$$

$$S\_b(i,j) = \left[b(i,j) - \frac{1}{MN} \sum_{i=1}^{M} \sum_{j=1}^{N} b(i,j) \right]^2 \tag{3}$$

where M,N are the height and width of the image respectively, S_L, S_a, S_b are respectively saliency map of L, a, b channels. L (i,j) is the pixel value of L channel, and the same to the a and b channel. The finally saliency map is a weighted sum of S_L, S_a, S_b:

$$S(i,j) = \frac{1}{sum\_L} S\_L(i,j) + \frac{1}{sum\_a} S\_a(i,j) + \frac{1}{sum\_b} S\_b(i,j) \tag{4}$$

where sum_L, sum_a, sum_b are respectively the pixel sum of S_L, S_a, S_b. After obtaining the final saliency map, we compute the score of composition by:

$$f_a = max_{k=1\ to\ n} \sum_{i=1}^{M} \sum_{j=1}^{N} [S(i,j) * mask_k(i,j)] \tag{5}$$

ROI Assessment

Size of ROI segments represents an image's simplicity, which is a distinguishing factor in determining whether a photograph is professional or not [2]. In order to get the size of ROI segments, we reuse the saliency map. In the saliency map, we define for coordinate values, namely, Xmin, Xmax, Ymin, Ymax, which obtain a region A containing 80% intensity of the saliency map. We manually define the range of a good picture's ROI size as 80% to 20%. Then the ROI score can be computed as:

$$f_{ROI} = \begin{cases} 0.5 & 20\% < \frac{A}{MN} * 100\% < 80\% \\ \left(1 - \frac{A}{MN}\right) * 250\% & \frac{A}{MN} * 100\% > 80\% \\ \left(\frac{A}{MN}\right) * 250\% & \frac{A}{MN} * 100\% < 20\% \end{cases} \tag{6}$$

3.2　Personalized Template

Due to various environments and different personal taste, rules above may not fully capture personal taste. For example, some may prefer the target object in the center of the picture, but our system doesn't have this kind of template. These personalized features are described in this section:

We develop an approach of generating personalized template and adjusting parameters automatically according to the users' preference. The basic idea is simple reuse the four coordinate values, namely, Xmin, Xmax, Ymin, Ymax, to form a new template. A diagram illustration of the approach is shown in Figure 2.

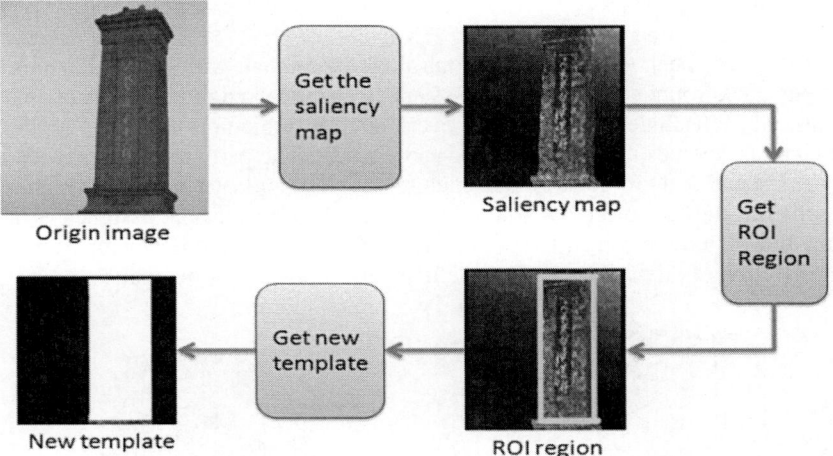

Fig. 2. The illustration of generating personalized template

4   User Interface

Figure 3 shows the user interface of the Photo Guide. There are five basic elements in the interface namely: a progress bar and a label in the top of the screen that shows the assessment result of the picture. The value of the progress bar and label will change automatically in real-time with the movement of the camera's view. In the process of taking picture, users just move the camera view and find the best view to press the OK button in the bottom of the interface. There is a ADJUST button beside the OK button, and if the   user find a view that he think is best but our system doesn't give a high assessment, then he may press it, in this way the system will generate a new mask giving the picture and other similar scene a high assessment.

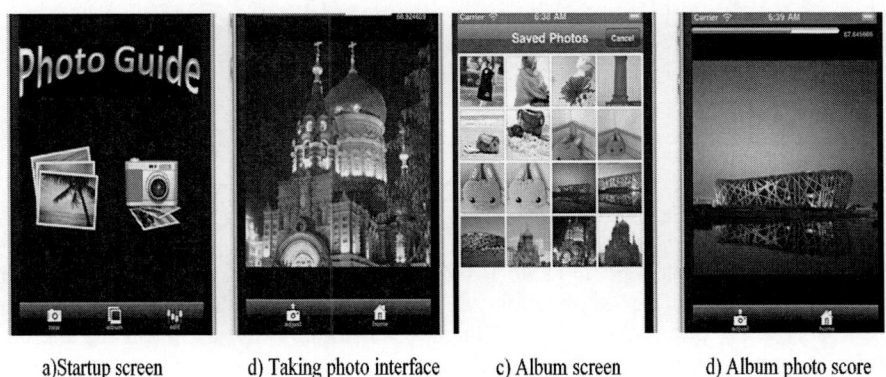

a)Startup screen   d) Taking photo interface   c) Album screen   d) Album photo score

Fig. 3. User Interface

5   User Experience

The system has been evaluated in a controlled experiment with 10 participants from different backgrounds (i.e. computer science, electrical engineering, mathematics). The task of each single-user is to take several groups of pictures using our application. The pictures' themes include landmark and portrait. The participants are divided into two groups and one group takes their picture with our application while the other with the camera interface offer by iPhone itself. Each participant is assigned a task of taking 100 pictures for each theme, namely 1000 pictures altogether for each group. The collection of all pictures is then evaluated by another 5 participants:

Fig. 4. A user is taking photos with our system

Table 1. Picture quality with our system

	Excellent	**Ordinary**	**Poor**
Landmark	71	417	12
Portrait	76	418	6

Table 2. Picture quality without our system

	Excellent	**Ordinary**	**Poor**
Landmark	53	350	97
Portrait	55	380	65

From the result showed in Table 1 and Table 2 we may draw the conclusion that participants who use our application can significantly avoid shooting poor pictures (with only 2.4% poor images on the theme of landmark and 1.2% on the theme of portrait) than those who use the origin camera interface (with 19.4% poor images on the theme of landmark and 13% on the theme of portrait). We may find that our system doesn't show an obvious performance in helping users shooting excellent photos (both close to 12% excellent pictures on the theme of landmark and 12% on the theme of portrait). The possible reason is that our templates are generated according to some heuristic principles that properly suggest a common composition and simplicity pleasing for most people, while to get an excellent picture we should be concerned about not only composition and simplicity but also some other rules of aesthetics such as color harmonization, intensity balance, and contrast and so on [2]. We also conduct an investigation of user experience and define three kind of experience as follows according to the feedback of our participants:

A: situation that user find a good view and the application give a high score.

B: situation that user find a good view but the system give a relatively low score, but after adjust the good view to generate new template, our system give a good score to the similar scene.

C: situation that user find a good view but the system give a relatively low score, but after adjust the good view to generate new template, our system still give a low score to the similar scene.

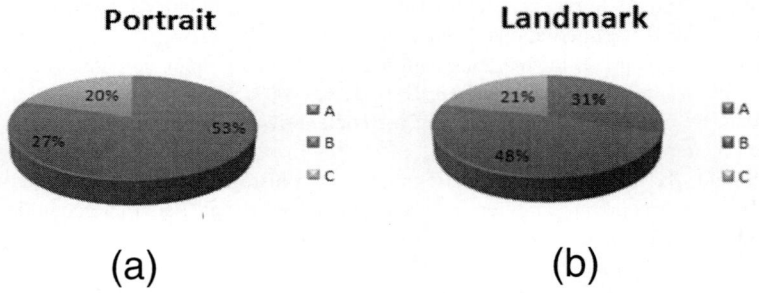

(a)   (b)

Fig. 5. The results of user experience on difference themes

Figure 5 (a) and (b) show the results of user experience on difference themes.

By comparing the diagrams in Figure 5, we can find that our system works better on the theme of portrait than that of landmark. The reason is that the target object is easy to be separated from background.

Situation C means that our system doesn't work, because the pictures are too complicated to foreground segment. Now we are developing new methods to solve those problems, and we will apply those methods to the new edition of our application.

6   Conclusion

In this paper, we presented a novel photographing mobile application based on real-time perceptual image assessment. Our system offers a great help to those who are not professional in taking a photo. We design a real-time perceptual image assessment algorithm, with which the system can guide users to find the best shooting distance and angles. Considering the personal preference and difference environment, the system allows user's feedback and will adaptively generate the new mask shifting to the personalized working mode.

The system can be competent to most situations, but in order to meet the requirements of real-time, we apply a low time-consuming algorithm and result in sometime the system may not work so well in more complicated background.

References

1. Cheng, B., Ni, B., Yan, S., Tian, Q.: Learning to Photograph. In: ACM MM (2010)
2. Yeh, C.-H., Ho, Y.-C., Barsky, B.A., Ouhyoung, M.: Personalized Photograph Ranking and Selection System. In: ACM MM (2010)
3. Luo, Y., Tang, X.: Photo and Video Quality Evaluation: Focusing on the Subject. In: Forsyth, D., Torr, P., Zisserman, A. (eds.) ECCV 2008, Part III. LNCS, vol. 5304, pp. 386–399. Springer, Heidelberg (2008)
4. Ke, Y., Tang, X., Jing, F.: The design of high-level features for photo quality assessment. In: IEEE International Conference on Computer Vision and Pattern Recognition (2006)
5. Zhang, L., Zhang, L., Mou, X.: A Feature Based Image Quality Assesment Metric Using Riesz Transforms. In: IEEE International Conference on Image Processing, pp. 321–324 (2010)
6. http://www.schneiderkreuznach.com/pdf/mobil_phone_study.pdf
7. Chen, G., Yang, C., Xie, S.: Gradient-Based Structural Similarity for Image Quality Assessment. In: IEEE International Conference on Image Processing, pp. 2929–2932 (2006)
8. Banerjee, S., Evans, B.L.: In-camera automation of photographic composition rules. IEEE Transactions on Image Processing 16, 1807–1820 (2007)
9. Avidan, S., Shamir, A.: Seam carving for content-aware image resizing. ACM Transactions on Graphics 26(3), 1–9 (2007)
10. Birchfield, S., Rangarajan, S.: Spatiograms versus histograms for region-based tracking. In: IEEE International Conference on Computer Vision and Pattern Recognition, vol. 2, pp. 1158–1163 (2005)

Instance-Level Landmark Labeling
via Multi-layer Superpixels

Yanyun Qu, Jiangjun Yang, Han Liu*, Yi Xie, and Cuihua Li

Computer Science Department, Xiamen University, 361005, P.R.China
{quyanyun,samual0920,ll.heal}@gmail.com, {csyxie,chli}@xmu.edu.cn

Abstract. Millions of place-specified photos are uploaded on the Internet. Landmark labeling is very important for place-specified image understanding, landmark retrieval and auto-annotation. In this paper, we aim at extracting and labeling a Landmark in an image. The novelty of our method is that we use multi-layer superpixels to effectively extract a Landmark. The multi-layer superpixels can be used to capture the context of scale space and the spatial coherency of neighboring superpixels. And the context constraints are enforced by Conditional Random Field. In our method, we firstly learn a SVM classifier which operates on the superpixels of the training data. Then we construct a $3D$ adjacent graph which links the superpixels not only in the same layer but also in the successive layers. Finally, we use Conditional Random Field to combine the supervision information with the context cues in order to label landmarks. We compare our method with the state-of-the-art methods on the landmark images which are collected from Flickr, and the experimental results show that our method has achieved the best detection precision and the best pixel-based precision-recall.

Keywords: landmark labeling, multi-layer superpixels, SVM, conditional random field, instance-level.

1 Introduction

The Internet provides unprecedented rich visual information, which makes it easy to search images by search engines such as Google images and Flickr. Moreover, the communities contribute millions of place-specified images which are taken of famous places from a multitude of viewpoints, at different time, and under variant weather conditions. Collecting and labeling these place-specified images are useful for many applications such as tourism, $3D$ reconstruction, landmark retrieval, automatically tagging, mapping the landmark image to the Google earth map, etc. In this paper, we focus on the landmark labeling. Fig.1 shows typical results of landmark labeling, the first row shows the original landmark images, and the second row shows the results of the landmark labeling.

In order to collect the landmark images, we use the landmark keywords such as "Statue of Liberty" to download the images from the Internet. But the obtained images are noisy and far away from our goal. And we face some challenges

---

* Corresponding author.

W. Lin et al. (Eds.): PCM 2012, LNCS 7674, pp. 715–725, 2012.

Fig. 1. Some results of the landmark labeling

to deal with the raw image collection: 1) Some downloaded images are not the desired landmark images, as shown in Fig.2 a); 2) The landmark is photographed in different viewpoints, which results in a variety of appearance, shown in Fig.2 c) d); 3) The landmark is shown in a variety of scale, shown in Fig. 2 b) c). These affect the performance of landmark labeling. Though the object detection has achieved considerable progress in recent years, these methods [1,2,3,4,5] cannot be directly applied to solve our problem, because the traditional object appearance models is operated on the complete object region and this model need combine with a sliding window searching scheme. Therefore, they are not effective to the images which are not similar to the training data, that is, it can't deal with the deformation, occlusion and viewpoint changes.

a)   b)   c)   d)

Fig. 2. Typical examples of the Statue of Liberty downloaded from the Flickr

In order to overcome these difficulties, we propose to utilize muti-layer superpixel to segment the landmark instead of searching the object in an image by a sliding window scheme. The core idea is to learn the superpixel classifier rather than the object classifier. A superpixel is a small region whose elements are similar, for example, the elements in a superpixel are similar in brightness, texture and color. Thus a superpixel is homogenous and stable. In our method, we first learn a SVM classifier which operates on the extracted superpixels. And then we construct a 3D adjacent graph which enforces the context constrains on these superpixels. Finally, we use Conditional Random Field (CRF) to extract object regions. The main contribution of this paper is to utilize the context of superpixel scale space to label the landmark in the instance level.

The rest of this paper is organized as follows. We introduce the related works in Section 2. We present the implementation of landmark labeling in Section 3. And we discuss the experimental results in Section 4. Finally we draw the conclusions in the last section.

2 Related Works

Our method is motivated by the rapid development of object detection and recognition. Face detection [1] and pedestrian detection [2] are the typical class-dependent object detection methods. These methods design the special features and classifiers for the special object classes. For example, the Adaboost classifier with Haar-like features is suitable to face detection, and the SVM classifier with HOG is very helpful to pedestrian detection. However, the class-dependent method may not be effective for other object class detection. Therefore, researchers pay attentions to designing the methods for the general object category detection in recent years. Fergus et al.[3,4] designed the constellation model for object categorization and used visual words to filter the Google image. Li et al. [5] built the OPTIMOL system based on an incremental learning framework to collect the images and update the category model. But there are three limits of these methods: 1) They localize an object by a bounding box which usually includes part of the background; 2) They are sensitive to the changes of object appearance which are caused by illumination, occlusion, scales and viewpoints; 3) The classifier learned from the complete pattern region is not robust to the change of object appearance. Fortunately, recent research success in superpixel-level categorization has shown a promise for object localization, in which one can label image pixels with the corresponding classes instead of roughly bounding an object with a rectangle. Shotton et al.[6] constructed semantic texton forests (STF) to learn the local representation. Fulkerson et al.[7] used superpixels to represent local features.

Moreover, our motivation of studying landmarks is influenced by the development of the landmark research which is a hot topic up to now. Lazebnike et al. [11] modeled and recognized the landmark, and they combined the $2D$ appearance and $3D$ geometric constraints to summarize the landmark images, and registered the landmark images to the $3D$ model of the landmark. Snavely et al.[8][9] did the research on $3D$ reconstruct of the landmark, and browed the landmark in $3D$ way. Quack et al.[13] mined the object and event from the community photo collection. Simon et al.[10] summarized the landmarks and obtained the canonical view images. Gammeter et al. [14] labeled the landmark by an unsupervised method. Li et al. [12] classified the landmark images in a large scale collection which combined the visual information with the text information. Ji et al. [22] designed a coding method for mobile landmark search. And the latest work [23][24] in image retrieval and annotation will inspire the landmark research. The integration of textual and visual information may improve performance of the landmark labeling, and the $3D$ landmark retrieval is also interesting.

In this paper, we aim at landmark labeling, which is critical to place-specified image understanding. Carolina et al.[16] used multiple segmentations and weakly supervised method to obtain the outline of the landmark. This method supposed that at least one segment should contain the object of interest. But the assumption was very difficult to achieve. Some experiments demonstrated that a good segmentation occurs after about 1000 segmentations for an image. In this paper, we learn a classifier on multi-layer superpixels rather than on the segments obtained by multiple segmentations, and enforce the spatial consistency on the multi-layer superpixels using CRF. Our method is robust to scales, illumination, occlusion and viewpoints.

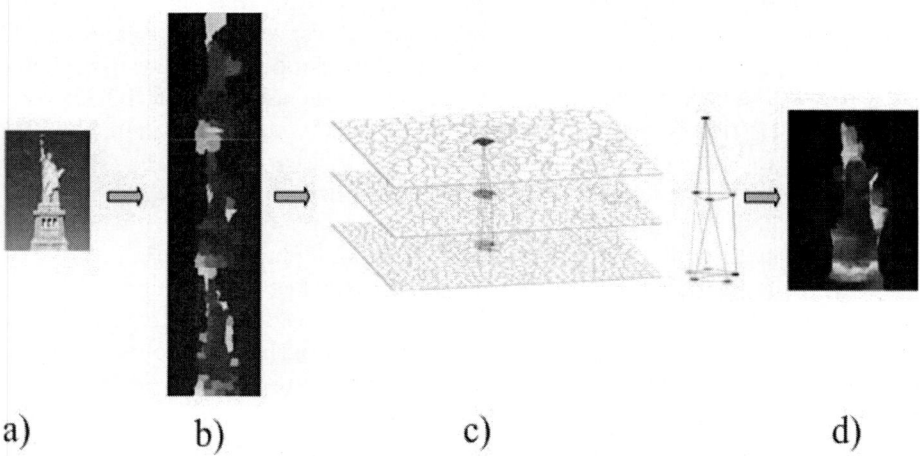

a)   b)   c)   d)

Fig. 3. The framework of the instance-level landmark labeling. a) The original image. b) The classification of the segments at three layers where the red color means a high probability of the corresponding superpixels belonging to the Statue of Liberty and the blue color means a high probability of the corresponding superpixels belonging to the background. c) 3D graph model on the multi-layer superpixels. d) The final obtained confidence map.

3   Implementation Details

The framework of our method is shown in Fig.3. We firstly obtain the superpixels at multiple layers by changing the number of segments at each layer, which is shown in Fig.3 b). Then a SVM classifier operating on the superpixels of the foreground object is learned on the labeled training data. After that, the confidence values of superpixels are computed according to the classifier. We employ the CRF [17] to enforce the spatial consistency on the adjacent superpixels both in the same layer and in the successive layers in the scale space, as shown in Fig.3 c). Finally, we obtain the class-specified label of an image, which is shown in Fig.3 d).

3.1   Landmark Collection

We search the landmark images by the Google image search engine and Flickr based on the keywords. Because the downloaded images are noisy, we follow the method proposed by Lazebnike et al.[11] to eliminate the irrelevant images and to summarize the landmark image. We finally obtain the landmark image cluster in which the landmark images are more similar in appearance. We label landmark objects manually, and the labeled landmark collections are used for the supervised learning and evaluation.

3.2   Superpixel Classification

In this subsection, we train a classifier on the superpixels rather than on the global object regions and compute the confidence value for each superpixel. We further consider the neighborhoods of superpixels in order to extract the landmark from the background. The problem is how many superpixels can form the landmark region. In order to solve this problem, we use multi-layer superpixels to capture the context of the superpixels of multiple layers in the scale space and extract a relative stable instance-level region for a landmark. In our method, we firstly use SLIC [19] to oversegment an image with different numbers of segments and obtain the multi-layer superpixels. We use the dense description to describe each pixel based on SIFT [20], and then employ the bag-of-words model (BOW) to describe these superpixels. These descriptors are then mapped to a vocabulary of "visual words" which are computed using vector quantization. The flowchart of the segment representation is shown in Fig. 4. Before representing a superpixel, we expand the superpixel region four more pixels in order to enforce the boundary information on the superpixel descriptor. Each superpixel is represented by a histogram of word frequencies, which is named a signature and denoted by v_i . Each superpixel is assigned the most frequent class label it contains.

In order to compute the confidence value of a superpixel, we train a SVM classifiers on these signatures $\{v_i\}_{i=1}^l$ in the training datasets. We learn a binary SVM classifier with the χ^2 kernel by using the labeled training data. The confidence value of a superpixel is computed as follows:

$$c(h) = \sum_{i=1}^{L} c_i exp(-gd_{\chi^2}^2(h, v_i)) \tag{1}$$

where h denotes the query superpixel signature, v_i denotes the support vector selected by SVM, c_i denotes the learned coefficients, g denotes a parameter selected by cross-validation, and the χ^2 distance $d_{\chi^2}^2(h, v_i)$ is defined as,

$$d_{\chi^2}^2(h, v_i) = \sum_{k=1}^{K} \frac{(h(k) - v_i(k))^2}{h(k) + v(k)} \tag{2}$$

In our experiments, we use 600 visual words, that is, $K = 600$. Because we perform the multiple segmentations, a pixel may belong to different segments. The confidence value of the pixel is the average confidence value of the several superpixels which contain it.

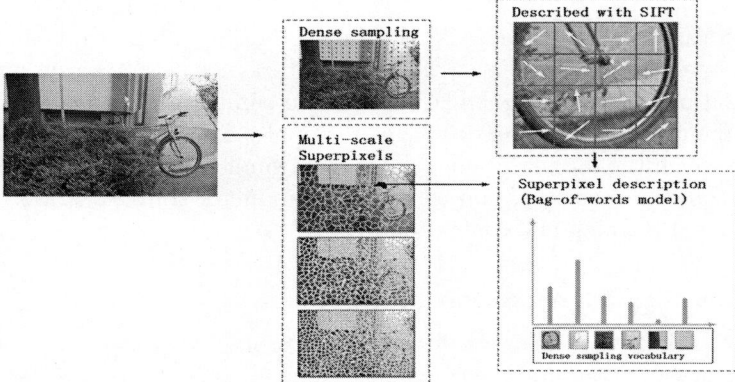

Fig. 4. The flowchart of superpixel's description with bag of words model

3.3   Graph Construction

In this subsection, we aim at utilizing the context of an image to solve how many superpixels the landmark is made up of. We observe that the boundary tends to be blurred with the increase of the superpixel size. Considering the spatial consistency between superpixels, we construct a 3D adjacent graph $G(V, E)$ to enforce the spatial constraints: V is the set of nodes which contain all the superpixels obtained by multiple segmentations; E is the set of edges which connects the pairs of neighboring superpixels (s_i, s_j) . The context cues are implied in the edges. There are two types of edges: horizontal edges and vertical edges. We connect any pair of superpixels in the same layer of an image with a horizontal edge if they share a boundary, and we connect any pair of superpixels between the successive layers in the scale space with a vertical edge if they share pixels. We add the vertical edges which enable our method to capture the context cues of multiple layers in the scale space and extract a stable instance-level region. Because our method utilizes the context of the superpixel scale space, it is not sensitive to the size of superpixels.

3.4   Inferring with CRF

We introduce CRF to combine the information obtained by the supervised learning and the context cues. Let $P(c|G, \omega, \nu)$ be the conditional probability of the set of the class label c assignments given the adjacent graph $G(S, E)$ and the weights ω and ν:

$$-log(P(c|G, \omega, \nu)) =$$

$$\sum_{s_i \in S} \psi(c_i|s_i) + \omega(\sum_{(s_i, s_j) \in E_h} \phi(c_i, c_j|s_i, s_j) + \nu \sum_{(s_i, s_j) \in E_v} \varphi(c_i, c_j|s_i, s_j)) \quad (3)$$

where E_h is the set of the horizontal edges, and E_v is the set of the vertical edges. There are two weights ω and ν used in our model: ω is the trade-off parameter between the unary potentials and the pairwise edge potentials, and ν is the trade-off parameter between the horizontal edge potentials and the vertical edge potentials. We use stochastic gradient descent to train the parameters ω and ν. We find in our experiments that the vertical edges have more contributions than horizontal edges, because the context of the multi-layer superpixels of the scale space is more important for object segmentation.

The unary potential $\psi(c_i|s_i)$ is defined by the confidence value obtained by using SVM which is operated on the superpixels. The horizontal pairwise edge potential ϕ is defined as:

$$\phi(c_i, c_j|s_i, s_j) = \frac{1}{1 + \|s_i - s_j\|} \qquad (c_i \neq c_j, (s_i, s_j) \in E_h), \qquad (4)$$

where $\|s_i - s_j\|$ is the norm of the color distance between superpixels in Lab color space. It is inversely proportional to the difference of the color between the two adjacent superpixels in the same superpixel layer. And the vertical pairwise edge potential φ is defined as:

$$\varphi(c_i, c_j|s_i, s_j) = \frac{|s_i \cap s_j|}{|s_i \cup s_j|} \qquad (c_i \neq c_j, (s_i, s_j) \in E_v) \qquad (5)$$

The vertical pairwise edge potential is the ratio of the intersection area and the union area of the pairwise superpixels.

Since the total number of the nodes in the graph is usually over a thousand, exact inference is intractable. Thus we employ the loopy belief propagation (LBP) [21] for approximate inference.

4   Experimental Results

In this section, we implement our method on the three landmark collections: the Statue of Liberty (738), Notre Dame (197) and the Triumphal arch (200). Each class set is split into two separate sets of images. One set is for training and the other set is for testing. We first evaluate our approach by the detection precision. The detection precision is defined as the ratio of the number of the regions correctly detected as landmark regions and the number of the ground truth landmarks. And the correct detection satisfies that the ratio of the intersection area and the union area between the detected region and the ground truth region is greater than 0.5. Our method achieves 100% detection precision on the three landmark collections.

Table 1. The comparison of the proposed method with different numbers of superpixel layers in terms of the recall=precision point [7]

the number of superpixel layer	Status of Liberty	Notre Dame	Triumphal arch
4	91.7%	94.0%	87.2%
5	92.4%	96.3%	**92.4%**
6	**95.8%**	**97.1%**	91.4%

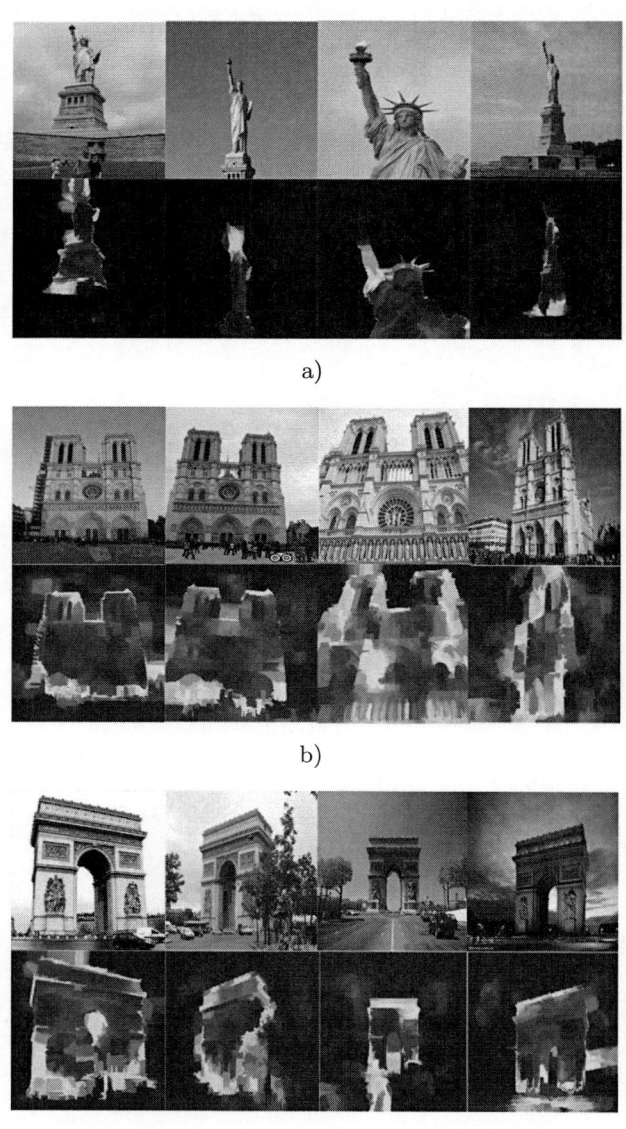

Fig. 5. The landmark label results. a) The Statue of Liberty labeling results. b) Notre Dame labeling results. c) The Triumphal arch labeling results.

Next, we evaluate our method in terms of pixel-based precision-recall, which is used by Fulkerson [7] to estimate the object localization accuracy. The point where the precision is equal to the recall is regarded as the criterion. Based on the ground-truth segmentation maps we count a pixel belonging to an object as a true positive when it is detected and as a false negative otherwise. The pixels incorrectly detected as object pixels are false positives.

We estimate the effect of the number of the superpixel layers. As shown in Table 1, with the increase of the number of the superpixel layers, the label performance is improved, and our method achieves the best performance when the number of the superpixel layers is equal to 6. Considering the trade-off between the performance and speed, we use five superpixel layers in our experiments. Fig. 5 shows some results of the instance-level segmentation of landmarks. The deeper red means a higher probability of the corresponding superpixels belonging to the Statue of Liberty and the deeper blue color means a higher probability of the corresponding superpixels belonging to the background. Table 1 and Fig.5 demonstrate that our method is effective. We also compare our method with two other methods based on multiple segmentations in terms of the detection precision: the class-specified unsupervised object discovery which is our previous work [15] and the weakly supervised method [16]. We implement three methods on the two landmark sets: the Statue of Liberty and Notre Dame. The results of Fig. 6 show that the supervised method is superior to the unsupervised method and the weakly supervised method, because the supervised method can learn more information from the training data.

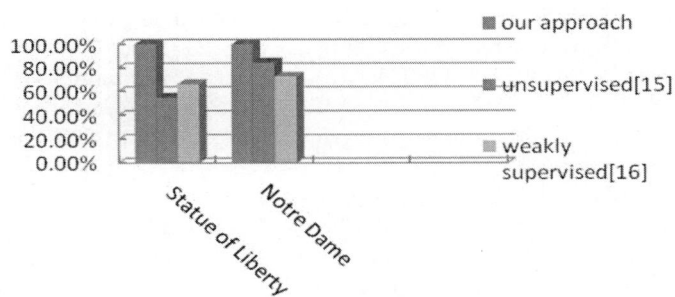

Fig. 6. Comparison of the detection precisions

5   Conclusions

In this paper, we have proposed to utilize the context of multiple superpixel layers to label the landmark in the instance level. We first perform multiple segmentations on each landmark images, and then learn the SVM classifier with the kernel on the superpixels of the training set. In order to utilize the context of multiple superpixel layers, we design a graph to enforce the context constraints. We define the edge link weights between pairwise adjacent superpixels belonging to the same superpixel layer as well as the edge link weights between pairwise adjacent superpixles belonging to the successive superpixel layers. After that, we implement CRF on the graph to fuse the obtained supervised information and the spatial information of superpixels. The experimental results have demonstrated that our method can label the landmark images along the outline of the landmark. And our method is also superior to the compared unsupervised method and the weakly supervised method.

Acknowledgments. This research work was supported by the Fundamental Research Funds for the Central Universities (2010121067, 2010121066), National Defence Basic Scientific Research program of China(B1420****55).

References

1. Viola, P., Jones, M.: Rapid object detection using a boosted cascade of simple features. In: Proceedings of the 2001 IEEE Computer Society Conference on Computer Vision and Pattern Recognition, CVPR 2001, vol. 1, pp. I-511–I-518 (2001)
2. Dalal, N., Triggs, B.: Histograms of oriented gradients for human detection. In: Proceeding of the IEEE Computer Society Conference on Computer Vision and Pattern Recognition, CVPR 2005, vol. 1, pp. 886–893 (2005)
3. Fergus, R., Perona, P., Zisserman, A.: A Visual Category Filter for Google Images. In: Pajdla, T., Matas, J. (eds.) ECCV 2004, Part I. LNCS, vol. 3021, pp. 242–256. Springer, Heidelberg (2004)
4. Fergus, R., Fei-Fei, L., Perona, P., Zisserman, A.: Learning object categories from google's image search. In: Tenth IEEE International Conference on Computer Vision, ICCV 2005, October 17-21, vol. 2, pp. 1816–1823 (2005)
5. Li, J., Wang, G., Fei-Fei, L.: OPTIMOL: automatic object picture collection via incremental model learning. Computer Vision and Pattern Recognition (2006)
6. Shotton, J., Johnson, M., Cipolla, R.: Semantic texton forests for image categorization and segmentation. In: CVPR, pp. 1–8 (2008)
7. Fulkerson, B., Vedaldi, A., Soatto, S.: Class segmentation and object localization with superpixel neighborhoods. In: ICCV, pp. 670–677 (2009)
8. Snavely, N., Seitz, S., Szeliski, R.: Photo tourism: Exploring photo collections in 3D. ACM Trans. on Graphics 25(3) (2006)
9. Snavely, N., Seitz, S.M., Szeliski, R.: Modeling the world from Internet photo collections. International Journal of Computer Vision 80(2), 189–210 (2008)
10. Simon, I., Snavely, N., Seitz, S.M.: Scene summarization for online image collections. In: ICCV (2007)
11. Li, X., Wu, C., Zach, C., Lazebnik, S., Frahm, J.-M.: Modeling and Recognition of Landmark Image Collections Using Iconic Scene Graphs. In: Forsyth, D., Torr, P., Zisserman, A. (eds.) ECCV 2008, Part I. LNCS, vol. 5302, pp. 427–440. Springer, Heidelberg (2008)
12. Li, Y., Crandall, D.J., Huttenlocher, D.P.: Landmark classification in large-scale image collections. In: ICCV (2009)
13. Quack, T., Leibe, B., Van Gool, L.: World-scale Mining of Objects and Events from Community Photo Collections. In: CIVR 2008, Niagara Falls, Canada, July 7-9 (2008)

14. Gammeter, S., Bossard, L., Quack, T., Van Gool, L.: I know what you did last summer: object-level auto-annotation of holiday snaps. In: ICCV 2009, Kyoto, Japan, September 27-October 4 (2009)
15. Liu, H., Qu, Y.: Exploiting context aware category discovery for image labeling. In: Proceedings of the Third International Conference on Internet Multimedia Computing and Service (2011)
16. Galleguillos, C., Babenko, B., Rabinovich, A., Belongie, S.: Weakly Supervised Object Localization with Stable Segmentations. In: Forsyth, D., Torr, P., Zisserman, A. (eds.) ECCV 2008, Part I. LNCS, vol. 5302, pp. 193–207. Springer, Heidelberg (2008)
17. Lafferty, J.D., McCallum, A., Pereira, F.C.N.: Conditional Random Fields: Probabilistic models for segmenting and labeling sequence data. In: ICML, pp. 282–289 (2001)
18. Oliva, A., Torralba, A.: Modeling the shape of the scene: a holistic representation of the spatial envelope. Int. J. Comput. Vision 42(3), 145–175 (2001)
19. Achanta, R., Shaji, A., Smith, K., Lucchi, A., Fua, P., Süsstrunk, S.: SLIC Superpixels (2010), http://ivrg.epfl.ch/supplementary_material/RK_SLICSuperpixels/index.html
20. Lowe, D.G.: Distinctive image features from scale-invariant keypoints. Int. J. Comput. Vision 60, 91–110 (2004)
21. Murphy, K.P., Weiss, Y., Jordan, M.I.: Loopy belief propagation for approximate inference: an empirical study. In: Uncertainty in Artificial Intelligence, Sweden, pp. 467–475 (1999)
22. Ji, R., Duan, L., Chen, J., Yao, H., Yuan, J., Rui, Y., Gao, W.: Location discriminative vocabulary coding for mobile landmark search. Int. J. Comput. Vision 96(3), 290–314 (2012)
23. Gao, Y., Wang, M., Zha, Z., Shen, J., Li, X., Wu, X.: Visual-textual joint relevance learning for tag-based social image search. IEEE Transactions on Image Processing (in press)
24. Gao, Y., Wang, M., Zha, Z., Shen, J., Tian, Q., Dai, Q., Zhang, N.: Less is more: Efficient 3D object retrieval with query view selection. IEEE Transactions on Multimedia 13(5), 1007–1018 (2011)

Location Based Robust Audio Watermarking Algorithm for Social TV System[*]

Di Chang[1], Xia Zhang[2,**], Qiong Liu[3], Ge Gao[1], and Yue Wu[1]

[1] Department of Computer Science, Wuhan University, Wuhan China
[2] School Physics & information Engineering of Jianghan University, Wuhan, China
[3] Department of Electronics & Information Engineering,
Huazhong University of Science & Technology, Wuhan, China

Abstract. There is a big gap between TV and social network in conventional Social Networking Services. The mobile terminals cannot get the interactive URL from TV broadcasting automatically and the social network cannot get the location information of TV customers at the same time. To bridge the two kind of media, the information of value-added services hiding in the real-time audio stream of TV programs is transmitted. In this paper, the robust audio watermarking algorithm for social TV system is proposed, which analyze the character of background noise in the air channel, modify the energy coefficients of adjacent frequency bands in DCT domain of original audio carrier, and realize the recycling embedding of synchronization signal and watermarking information into original audio carrier. The experimental results indicate that, the proposed algorithm has a good hidden effect, and it is robust to air-channel background noise attack in transmitting process, AD/DA conversion, common signal processing, etc. In a conclusion, the proposed algorithm could put together TV and social network, which are separated before, and provide new idea for social TV system in its true sense.

Keywords: Social TV，Audio，Watermarking，DCT.

1   Introduction

Recently the research work on web multimedia has been investigated widely [1][2][3][4]. Social network systems are popular for the emerging web media applications. The TV is separated from the social network systems in current Social TV System. The customers cannot automatically establish the connection to the interactive URL in the social network systems. They should get the interactive URL from the TV by hearing or vision, and input the URL to connect to the social network.

There is a big gap between TV and social network in conventional Social Network Services. To bridge the two media, the information of value-added services hiding in

---

[*] Supported by National Nature Science Foundation of China (61202470), Planning Project of Innovative Experiment of National Undergraduate (111048652, 1210486060), and Science and Technology Research of keystone Projects of Educational Commission of Hubei Province (D20123405).
[**] Corresponding author.

W. Lin et al. (Eds.): PCM 2012, LNCS 7674, pp. 726–738, 2012.

the real-time audio stream of TV programs is transmitted. As can be seen in Fig.1, the Interactive URL is embed as a watermark in streamed audio in step 1 to 3, then the streamed audio is distributed through TV broadcasting channel in step 4 and 5. The mobile terminals record the streamed audio and get the interactive URL from it. Finally, the mobile terminals and the social network system exchange the location information of the customers and the interactive information in step 7 and 8.

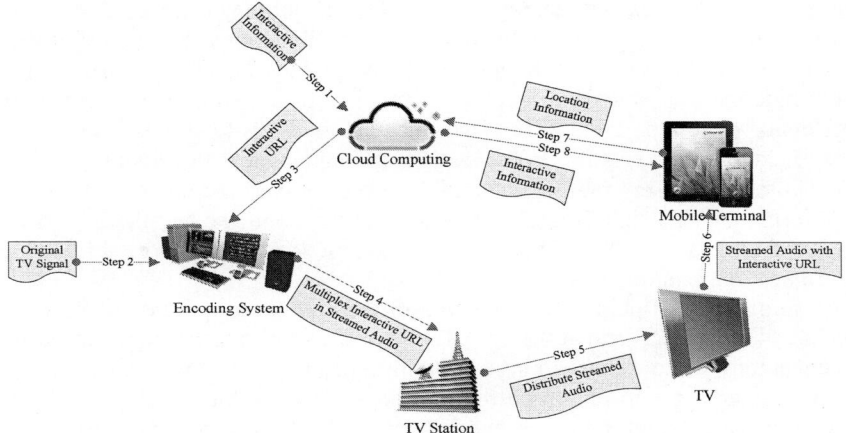

Fig. 1. New Social TV System

Audio digital watermarking, which is associated with location information, served as the main method to realize the social TV system, is widely researched and used nowadays.

Recently, pirated products of the field of air-channel audio transmission, mainly from the theater, concert hall and other public places were recorded by means of the hidden recorders, which makes airborne audio watermarking of great research value. However, in addition to a complex of A/D, D/A conversion, the audio watermarking transmitting via air channel, will be influenced by the facts of air noise, source volume and where the recording equipment placed. What's more, the audio work also may suffer from resample attacks, format conversion attacks (such as MP3 compression) and other attacks.

As for resampling attacks, the algorithm [5] can resist the resampling attack. However, it could not resist the additive noise attacks, such as MP3 compression and low pass filtering attacks. Of course, the algorithms in [6] have a very good robustness to adding noise attacks, but cannot resist resampling attacks. Algorithm in [7] uses the maxima of the audio low-frequency sub-band to locate the watermark embedding area, it takes sample of which the length is 4096 points before and after the anchor of the audio section to take the FFT transform, and exchange the low-frequency sub-band coefficients in the DFT domain to embed watermark. Thus, the watermark information is embedded in only a small portion of samples of the audio signal, that is, the samples before and after the anchor point, while the information is not evenly distributed among the entire audio signal. Also, the algorithm in [8] can resist strong geometric transformation attacks by repeatedly embedding the same watermark in different parts of the audio. The side information is used to solve the attacking problem which is based on "Resample" mode [9]. Due to the introduction of the side information, the computation of watermark detection is greatly reduced.

Audio digital watermarking disseminated in digital channel is relatively mature. However, the audio signals transmitted in the air will suffer from various aspects of attacks. Compared with digital channels, researches in air channel have much less.

At first, Steinbach and his colleagues[10] in German carried research, by setting a number of different spacing ranging from 5~400cm, and they used 4 different microphones to study the 5 types of audio watermarking technology, but the experiment is too small, and difficult to apply in practice. Subsequently, Japan's Tachibana et al [11] tried to hide the watermark into public environment in real time such as the music at music concerts, it is possible to hide 64b message in a 30s-long music clips, but the effect of extraction is general. In the straight-through cable transmission, Xiang Shijun [12] used the energy ratio method of three paragraphs, and embedded a string of 32b information. Though Xiang's extraction results were better, the experimental capacity is also too small, and hard to apply tin practice, what's more, it's of higher synchronization requirements.

To summarize, for public dissemination of the audio, the question of how to improve the hiding effects and at the same time increase the capacity, remains a difficult problem among audio watermarking algorithms [13][14]. In this paper, we propose an audio watermarking algorithm for airborne which can resist various attacks. As shown in Fig. 2, when transmitting in air, audio signal suffers many influences from outside [15][16], the main problems are pointed in [17].

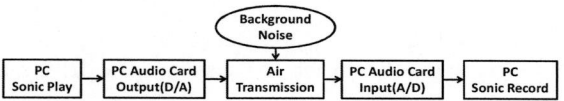

Fig. 2. Audio signal's transmitting model via air channel

2 Basic Theory of Digital Audio Watermarking Algorithm

A general outline of the system involved in the proposed scheme is shown in Fig.3. Its core algorithm consists of the following 3 parts: the watermark embedded algorithm, the synchronization embedded algorithms, and the watermark extracted algorithm.In the following section, each part of the algorithm is introduced and analyzed.

2.1 Watermark Embedding Algorithm

There are many kinds of classification of audio watermark algorithms. From the view of implementation, they can be divided into time-domain and transform-domain algorithms. Compared with the other, transform domain-based algorithm is more robust. The key of transform domain watermarking algorithm is to find a particular transform domain, making the original information changes little in the time domain before and after embedding watermark, but change greater in particular transform domain.

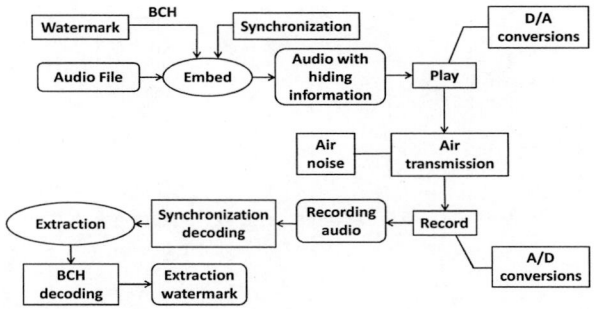

Fig. 3. Diagram of watermarking algorithm

Based on the double-DCT transform, the encoded watermark information by BCH is embedded into the original audio's the transform domain, then transforming inversely, getting the audio with the watermark. The overall process is shown in Fig. 4.

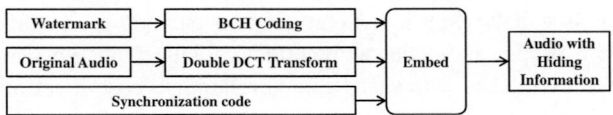

Fig. 4. Diagram of embedding algorithm

Encode the original watermark information $data(i)$, $0 \leq i \leq length(data)$ by BCH, to get the watermark information $code(i)$, $1 \leq i \leq length(code)$ after coding. Embedding it to the double DCT domain of audio signal and inverse double DCT transform, therefore, the audio signal with the watermark information can be got.

The specifics are as follows. Framing the original audio signal, there are 2048 sampling points each for a frame, it is denoted by N. Take DCT transformation for the first time on N, you can get the frequency domain coefficients of N, denoted by N'. Set watermark embedding factor S, T, according to the sampling rate FS, calculate $S' = \lfloor 2048 \cdot S / FS \rfloor$, $T' = \lfloor 2048 \cdot T / FS \rfloor$, where, $\lfloor x \rfloor$ is the rounding of x. Remove part of the coefficients of N': $P = N'(i)$, $S' \leq i \leq T'$, put P on the second DCT transform and get P'. The watermark embedding adjustment coefficient is λ, the embedding segmentation point is $mid = \lfloor (S' - T') / 2 \rfloor$. After encoding the watermark information is $data(i)$, specific embedding strategy are as follows:

1. If $code(i) = 0$, then modify the coefficient as (1) shows, the result is in Fig.5.

$$P'(i) = P'(i) / \lambda, \quad 1 \leq i \leq mid \tag{1}$$

2. If $code(i) = 1$, then modify the coefficient as (2) shows, the result is in Fig.6.

$$P'(i) = P'(i) / \lambda, \quad mid + 1 \leq i \leq S' - T' \tag{2}$$

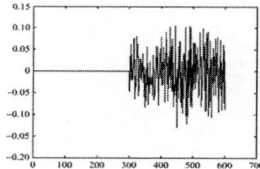

Fig. 5. Watermark '0' coefficients in Double DCT Domain

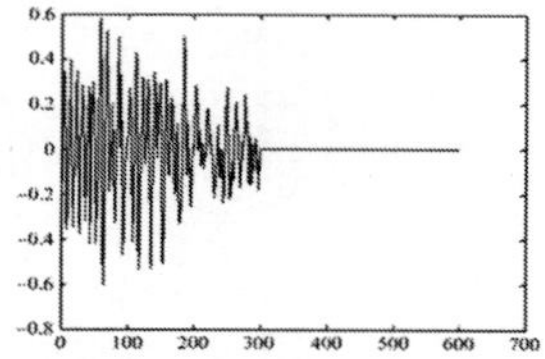

Fig. 6. Watermark '1' coefficients in Double DCT Domain

2.2   Synchronization Code Embedding Algorithm

Synchronization occupies an important position in communication systems occupies an important position. Whether Sync's performance is good or bad, will directly affect the quality of communication system, and at the same time affect the normal communication directly. Barker code sequence can effectively avoid the dislocating situation, thus it is widely used in synchronization technology. In this section, sync signal algorithm is proposed, which can be effectively used in the air-spread channel.

Barker code is a sequence with sharp autocorrelation, whose function is shown as:

$$r_{a,a}(\tau) = \frac{1}{n}\sum_{i=1}^{n} a_i a_{i+\tau} \tag{3}$$

Where, a_i represents the value of i-th bit of Barker code, combined with the form of 12 Barker code, (4) is available.

$$r_{a,a}(\tau) = \begin{cases} 12 & \tau = 0 \\ 0, \pm 1, \pm 2 & \tau = 1, 2, \cdots, 11 \\ 0 & \tau \geq 12 \end{cases} \tag{4}$$

It can be conducted   from (4) that, if there occurs dislocation between testing sequence and the Barker code sequence, or there are some differences, the value of $r_{a,a}(\tau)$ will be very small, typically less than 5; Only when the sequence to be tested are identical with the Barker code sequence, the maximum of $r_{a,a}(\tau)$ will reach 12.

Through our research and extensive testing, Barker code as synchronization sequences are as well suited for this part of the synchronization signal algorithm.

Embed the Sync signal at every started 3 frames of each loop, and following confidential steganographic information. Hence, forming a loop, embed it repeatedly.

Divide the 3 frames of synchronization signal segment into 12 parts, and embed in 12 Barker code in turn. There are 512 samples in each part, 512 samples were divided into embedded areas and buffer zones, there are 256 sampling points both in the embedded area and the buffer zone. Buffer technology can effectively avoid the intersymbol interference. If there is no buffer zone among the embedded areas, the adjacent embedded areas will interfere with each other, due to the factors such as the sensitivity of recording devices, it will result in an error message of Barker code, thus it   will cause greater interference in extraction of synchronization signal, that is the so-called Inter-symbol interference. The synchronization signal structure diagram is shown in Fig.7

| Embedded | Buffer | Embedded | Buffer | ...... | Embedded | Buffer |

Fig. 7. Synchronous signal embedded policies

A large number of experimental results show that background noise in the air has a lower frequency, and the weak nature of the energy, the MATLAB simulation spectrum is shown in Fig. 8. In order to avoid air noise attack, we choose to embed the synchronized signal in the intermediate frequency domain of the original audio signal. By modifying the coefficients of the energy in the intermediate frequency of the DCT domain, we can achieve in embedding synchronization signals, and ensure that the synchronization signal can resist the attack of background noise in air.

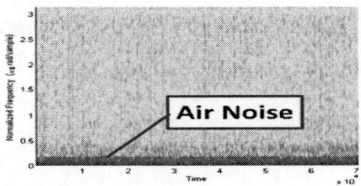

Fig. 8. Simulated spectrum in MATLAB

Specific embedded sync signal method is as follows. Set the low frequency range factors s, t, intermediate frequency range factors l, m, make DCT transform to the embedded areas, obtain a DCT-domain coefficient $x(i)$. Calculate the maximum energy of low-frequency coefficients which is Max', shown in (5).

$$Max' = \max(|x(i)|) \tag{5}$$

Where, $x(i)$, $s \leq i \leq t$, represent the low frequency coefficient in DCT domain, max(.) represents the function to calculate the maximum. Then calculate the average energy $Aver$ of the high-frequency coefficients, shown in (6).

$$Aver = \sum_{i=l}^{m} |x(i)| / (m-l+1) \tag{6}$$

Then, set the embedding strength factor θ, the higher θ is, the better the performance of synchronization is, but it has a worse effect of hiding. Test results showed that when $\theta = 0.5$, the combined effect was the best. Specific embedding method is shown in (7). If the j-bit Barker code meets the condition of $a_j = 1$, then suppress the intermediate frequency energy coefficient. If the j-bit Barker code meets the condition of $a_j = 0$, then enhance the intermediate frequency energy coefficient, according to the embedding strength factor θ.

$$x(i) = \begin{cases} 0 & a_j = 1 \\ Max'/\,Aver * x(i) * \theta & a_j = 0 \end{cases} \tag{7}$$

Where, $x(i)$, $l \le i \le m$ represent the intermediate frequency factor in DCT domain. 0 and 1, respectively, are embedded in a Barker code of the DCT-domain spectrum.

2.3   Key Performance Analysis of the Embedded Algorithms

Analysis of SNR
When embedding watermarks in audio signals, the value of SNR will inevitably be affected. Usually use decibels (dB) as a unit, and the higher SNR is the better the audio product is. The method of how to calculate the value of SNR is shown in (8). The Sound of the International Union requires that, the change of signal's SNR value must be greater than 20dB before and after watermark embedding. Experimental results show that the in this algorithm, the average SNR is greater than 20.00dB.

$$SNR = -10\log_{10}\left(\frac{\|F - F'\|^2}{\|F\|^2}\right) \tag{8}$$

Where, F is original signal, F' is the audio signal which contains hidden information. It can be easily seen that basically audio signal waveforms are of the same, there is almost no impact in hearing.

Analysis of Embedding Capacity
Embedding capacity is the number of bits which are embedded into the audio carrier signal in unit time; the unit is expressed by bps. The expression of algorithm's embedding capacity is shown as:

$$B = \frac{R}{k \cdot (S' - T') \cdot L} \qquad (bps) \tag{9}$$

Where, R represents signal sampling rate, L represents the length of coefficients in single DCT transform domain which is used for watermark embedding. S' and T' are the address parameters of double DCT coefficients. k is the ratio between the lengths of single DCT variation domain coefficients and the length of double DCT variation domain coefficients. Experimental results show that, take the signal of which the sampling rate is 44.1 KHz for example, the frame size is 2048 sampling points, in this algorithm the embedding capacity is approximately 22.0 bps.

2.4   Watermark Extracting Algorithm

The watermarking extracting algorithm flow is shown in Fig.9.

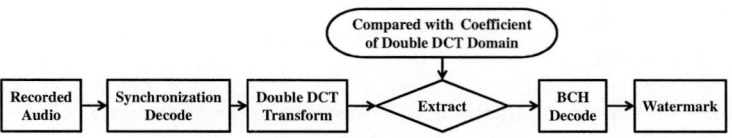

Fig. 9. Diagram of extraction algorithm

Firstly, extract the synchronization code of the audio, and then take double DCT transform (specific flow please see watermark embedding algorithm), by comparing double DCT domain coefficient, and extract the embedded information, then apply BCH decoding to the information, finally we can get the watermark information.

Synchronization Decoding
From the starting position of the audio signal, 32 sampling points are for the synchronization signal decoding step, select 12-512 sampling points and divide them into 12 segments as the signal to be decoded.

After dividing the sync signal region into segments which are to be decoded, make the DCT transform, calculate the max coefficient Max' of the low-frequency energy, and the average energy of high-frequency coefficients $Aver$. Set the extracting threshold mul, synchronized signal extracted was shown in (10).

$$b_j = \begin{cases} 0 & Max'/Aver \le mul \\ 1 & Max'/Aver \ge mul \end{cases} \tag{10}$$

As shown in (11), define function $r(a,b)$.

$$r(a,b) = \sum_{i=1}^{12} a_i \cdot b_i \tag{11}$$

Set the threshold $bark\_mul$, and calculate the value of the function, if $r(a,b) \ge bark\_mul$, then we find one of the synchronization signals, that is, find the appropriate starting position of the confidential information, and record it.

Detection of Watermark Algorithm
After determining the synchronization information of the audio signal to be detected, the audio signal can be segmented according to audio signal segmentation rules when embedding watermark, then separate the segments of the signal and take the double DCT transformation. Record the double-DCT domain coefficient as $P'(i), 1 \le i \le length(P')$. The breakpoint of the watermark is recorded as $mid = \lfloor length(P')/2 \rfloor$, such as (12), (13) shown in extracting hidden information.

$$E_0 = \sum_{i=1}^{mid} P'(i) \tag{12}$$

$$E_1 = \sum_{i=mid+1}^{length(P')} P'(i) \tag{13}$$

1) If $E_0 < E_1$, $code[i] = 0$;
2) If $E_0 \geq E_1$, $code[i] = 1$.

At this time, we can obtain the hidden information sequence $code[i]$, $0 \leq i < length$. After the BCH error correction in the decoding of the sequence, we get the watermark $data(i)$, $1 \leq i \leq length(data)$.

3   Experimental Result

3.1   Testing Environment and Test Cases

Test environment is shown in Table 1.

Table 1. Test Environment

Hardware	Playback Device	Record Device		Audio Card
	Edifier PT R201T08	ISK BM-800 Microphone		ALC655
Software	Player		Recorder	
	Windows Media Player 10		Cool Edit Pro 2.1	
Distance	0.2m, 0.9m, 1.9m, etc. (between microphone and player)			
Volume	30%, 50%, 100%, etc.			
Orientation	Standard angle is 0°(microphone directly facing at player); Shifting angle is 0°, ±30°, ±60°, ±90°			
Situation	Lab Situation (with background noise of 15dB-25dB)			

A vase samples shown in Table 2, whose sampling rate is 44.1 KHz, is used for test the validity and properties of the algorithm.

Table 2. Test Samples

Samples	Length of Time	Characteristic
Pop.wav	1:45	a wide spectrum
Folk.wav	1:39	First half signal mainly with low frequency, second half mainly with high frequency
Song1.wav	1:52	Male Singer with medium music accompaniment
Song2.wav	1:49	Female Singer with light music accompaniment
Mix.wav	1:26	Symphony with super bass and strong intensity of background music

3.2   The Impact of Distance and Volume

In order to test the impact of different distance and volume on error rate, we select different distance ranging from 0.2m to 1.8m, and different volume ranging from 30% to 100%, then under various environment, we test the proposed algorithm's error rate. The results are shown in Table 3 and Table 4.

Table 3. The Error Rate in Different Situation Without BCH

Situation Samples	Volume: 30%			Volume:50%			Volume:100%		
	0.2m	0.9m	1.8m	0.2m	0.9m	1.8m	0.2m	0.9m	1.8m
Pop.wav	3.12%	3.26%	4.21%	2.50%	5.46%	4.98%	4.10%	2.98%	3.90%
Folk.wav	4.30%	2.89%	2.31%	2.86%	3.16%	2.37%	5.08%	5.82%	4.78%
Song1.wav	2.10%	0.96%	1.98%	4.71%	4.09%	3.16%	0.94%	2.36%	4.02%
Song2.wav	2.27%	1.49%	1.08%	3.15%	3.24%	1.03%	4.15%	3.41%	1.88%
Mix.wav	1.09%	5.02%	2.92%	1.25%	1.98%	1.78%	2.99%	1.49%	3.19%

Table 4. The Error Rate in Different Situation With BCH

Situation Samples	Volume: 30%			Volume:50%			Volume:100%		
	0.2m	0.9m	1.8m	0.2m	0.9m	1.8m	0.2m	0.9m	1.8m
Pop.wav	2.09%	2.59%	2.46%	1.47%	4.21%	3.16%	2.02%	2.10%	3.02%
Folk.wav	3.10%	2.16%	1.78%	1.12%	2.46%	1.82%	4.60%	4.16%	3.90%
Song1.wav	0.97%	0.87%	1.67%	4.06%	3.36%	2.19%	0.80%	1.49%	3.26%
Song2.wav	2.12%	1.10%	0.96%	1.94%	2.12%	0.68%	3.25%	2.51%	0.93%
Mix.wav	1.04%	3.80%	2.12%	0.87%	0.88%	1.09%	1.34%	0.78%	2.28%

The test results indicate that under environment with different distance and volume, the algorithm proposed in this paper has a very low bit error rate, and the average accuracy can be 97.82%. And using BCH code will get lower bit error rate.

3.3   The Impact of Orientation

In order to test the impact of different orientation between play device and recorder, we select different orientation ranging from 0° to 90°, and test error rate under these environments. The results are shown in Table 5.

Table 5. The Error Rate under Situation with Different Orientation

Oriental Samples	0°		±45°		±90°	
	Without BCH	With BCH	Without BCH	With BCH	Without BCH	With BCH
Pop.wav	1.94%	0.56%	2.59%	0.79%	3.01%	2.01%
Folk.wav	2.28%	0.84%	3.87%	1.37%	3.95%	1.20%
Song1.wav	3.93%	2.81%	3.98%	2.10%	4.79%	2.92%
Song2.wav	3.89%	2.96%	3.38%	1.92%	4.04%	3.02%
Mix.wav	4.01%	2.35%	4.36%	2.92%	3.93%	1.87%

The test results show that the changing of orientation between devices has little influence to detect watermarking, and taking BCH code can promote the performance.

3.4   Test of Robustness against the Attacks

In order to test the robustness of the proposed algorithm, the attacks of regular signal processing, resample attack. And the bit error rate in the following attacks was shown in Table 6 and Fig.10.

Table 6. The Error Rate in the Attacks of Regular Signal Processing

Attack / Samples	Normalize	Re-quantization $16\rightarrow32\rightarrow16\,b$	Low Pass $11.025kHz$
Pop.wav	0.00%	0.01%	0.01%
Folk.wav	0.01%	0.00%	0.01%
Song1.wav	0.01%	0.02%	0.00%
Song2.wav	0.00%	0.01%	0.02%
Mix.wav	0.02%	0.00%	0.01%

The test results indicate that the proposed algorithm can resist from the attacks of regular signal processing which include Normalize, Re-quantization, Low Pass Filer($11.025kHz$), etc.

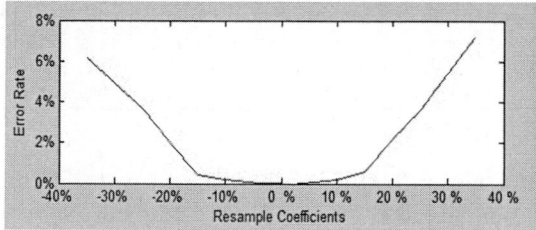

Fig. 10. The Error Rate in the Resample Attack

The test results show that the proposed algorithm has been able to resist against the resample attack whose coefficients is approximately 30% with good the robustness of the proposed algorithm.

3.5   Test of Contrastive Experiment

A real test environment of playing, recording is built as the same as Table 1, except that the orientation is set from the offset of $\pm\,30°$ to   0°. Under this experiment environment, our algorithm and the algorithm [18][19] are tested and compared, Table 7 shows comparing result.

Table 7. bit error rate in real evironment

Comparing Algorithm / Samples	Proposed Algorithm	Algorithm [18]	Algorithm [19]
Pop.wav	0.67%	1.82%	0.98%
Folk.wav	1.25%	2.29%	2.94%
Song1.wav	0.74%	1.21%	3.21%
Song2.wav	0.45%	0.99%	1.08%
Mix.wav	0.86%	1.76%	3.71%

As can be seen in Table 7, our algorithm can not only keep superior performance, but also be against attack of A/D, D/A, air noise without increasing bit error rate. Generally speaking, our algorithm has better robust performance [18][19].

3.6   Test Conclusion

Judging from the experimental data, the proposed algorithm can resist not only the attack of AD/DA conversion and background noise in air, but also the interference of various factors such as distance, orientation and volume. Moreover, the proposed algorithm has been able to resist from the resample attacks whose coefficients is about 30%, the attacks of regular signal processing. The algorithm can also increase correction rate and robust, so it is appropriate to apply into the practical situation.

4   Summary

In this paper, asynchronous code algorithm is proposed, it can automatically modify the intensity of embedded sync signal under situations with different delay between playing and recording, which help sync code to increase the quality of hidden information. The embedding algorithm can resist the attack of AD/DA conversion and the interference of background noise in air, so these features increase the algorithm's robustness. The proposed algorithm has been capable to resist against the resample attacks whose coefficients is about 30%, the attacks of regular signal processing, etc. Furthermore, the error rate ranges from 2% to 6%, so the algorithm can be applied in social TV situation.

References

1. Gao, Y., Wang, M., Zha, Z., Shen, J., Li, X., Wu, X.: Visual-Textual Joint Relevance Learning for Tag-Based Social Image Search. IEEE Transactions on Image Processing (in press)
2. Gao, Y., Tang, J., Hong, R., Dai, Q., Chua, T.-S., Jain, R.: W2Go: A Travel Guidance System by Automatic Landmark Ranking. In: ACM Conference on Multimedia, pp. 123–132 (2010)
3. Gao, Y., Wang, M., Luan, H., Shen, J., Yan, S., Tao, D.: Tag-Based Social Image Search with Visual-Text Joint Hypergraph Learning. In: ACM Conference on Multimedia, pp. 1517–1520 (2011)
4. Ji, R., Duan, L.Y., Chen, J., Yao, H., Yuan, J., Rui, Y., Gao, W.: Location Discriminative Vocabulary Coding for Mobile Landmark Search. International Journal of Computer Vision, 1–25 (2012)
5. Zhang, X.: Audio watermarking algorithm for public information transmission. Journal of Computer Applications 29(9), 2323–2326 (2009)
6. Guhl, D., Lu, A., Bender, W.: Echo Hiding. In: Anderson, R. (ed.) IH 1996. LNCS, vol. 1174, pp. 295–315. Springer, Heidelberg (1996)
7. Lei, Z., Yan, B.: Narrowband-Based Audio Watermarking with Self-Synchronization. Chinese Journal of Computers 31(7), 1283–1290 (2008)
8. You, S., Bai, S.: Audio information hiding algorithm resisting DA/AD conversions. Computer Engineering and Applications 44(7), 113–116 (2008)
9. Kim, W.G., Lee, J.C., Lee, W.D.: An audio Watermarking scheme with hidden signatures. In: International Conference on Signal Processing, Beijing (2000)

10. Steinebach, M., Lang, A., Dittmann, J., et al.: Audio watermarking quality evaluation: Robustness to DA/AD processes. In: Proceedings of the International Conference on Information Technology: Coding and Computing, Washington, pp. 100–103 (2002)
11. Tachibana, R.: Audio watermarking for live performance. In: Security and Watermarking of Multimedia Contents V, pp. 32–43 (2003)
12. Xiang, S., Huang, J., Yang, R.: Time-Scale Invariant Audio Watermarking Based on the Statistical Features in Time Domain. In: Camenisch, J.L., Collberg, C.S., Johnson, N.F., Sallee, P. (eds.) IH 2006. LNCS, vol. 4437, pp. 93–108. Springer, Heidelberg (2007)
13. Yeo, I.K., Kim, H.J.: Modified patchwork algorithm: A novel audio watermarking scheme. IEEE Trans. on Speech and Audio Processing 11(4), 381–386 (2003)
14. Ji, R., Yao, H., Sun, X., Liu, W., Tian, Q.: Task-Dependent Visual Codebook Compression. IEEE Transactions on Image Processing, 1
15. Li, W., Xue, X., Lu, P.: Robust audio watermarking based on rhythm region detection. IEEE Electronics Letters 4l(4), 218–219 (2005)
16. Learning to Distribute Vocabulary Indexing for Scalable Visual Search. IEEE Transactions on Multimedia
17. Li, W., Xue, X., Lu, P.: Localized audio watermarking technique robust against time-scale modification. IEEE Trans. on Muhimedia 8(2), 60–69 (2006)
18. Xia, Z., Di, C., Wei, G., et al.: An Audio Steganography Algorithm Based on Air-Channel Transmitting. Journal of Wuhan University (Natural Science Edition) 57(6), 499–505 (2011)
19. Zhang, X., Chang, D., Yang, W., et al.: An Audio Digital Watermarking Algorithm Transmitted via Air Channel in Double DCT Domain. In: The 2nd International Conference on Multimedia Technology, pp. 2926–2930 (July 2011)

Combining SIFT and Global Features
for Web Image Classification

Qimin Cheng[1,*], Yue Wen[2], Zheng-Jun Zha[3], Xihua Chen[1], and Zhenfeng Shao[4]

[1] The Department of Electronics and Information Engineering/Wuhan National Laboratory for
Optoelectronics, Huazhong university of Science and technology, Wuhan 430074, China
[2] Department of Automation, Tsinghua University, Beijing, 100086, China
[3] School of Computing National University of Singapore, 117417, Singpaore
[4] State Key Laboratory for Information Engineering in Surveying,
Mapping, and Remote Sensing, Wuhan University, Wuhan 430079, China
chengqm@hust.edu.cn

Abstract. Nowadays, web images are rapidly increasing with the development of
internet technology. This situation leads to the difficulties on effective and efficient image retrieval from mass data under web environment. In this paper, we
propose a web images classification method by integrating SIFT features of the
images with global features. First, Locality Sensitive Hashing (LSH) is adopted
for local feature extraction by embedding the SIFT feature vector. Then, other
global features, such as color, texture or shape feature, are extracted. Support
Vector Machine (SVM) is employed for image classification by using these two
types of features respectively. The two classification results are integrated by
decision-level fusion to get the final classification result. Experimental results on
a web image dataset show that the proposed method is able to improve the performance of web images classification.

Keywords: Web image classification, SVM, LSH, decision-level fusion.

1 Introduction

In recent decades, extensive research efforts have been dedicated to image retrieval and
classification [1-6]. With the fast development of Internet technology, web image
search and classification [7-8] has been a hot research area these days. For
image retrieval, image feature descriptors are vital to achieve satisfied content-based
image classification performance [9-11]. SIFT [12] (Scale Invariant Feature) operator
has been widely used in image classification, retrieval and target identification for its
scale, intensity and orientation invariant [13-16]. Moreover, SIFT is effective and
robust in affine transformation and noise suppression. However, there are two disadvantages in real practical application, i.e. it loses the global features and is
time-consuming to match a large number of key points.

To address the shortage of SIFT in image global feature description, many image
classification methods [17-18] with the combination of the SIFT feature and global
features have been proposed recently. By integrating color-based features and the SIFT

---

* Corresponding author.

W. Lin et al. (Eds.): PCM 2012, LNCS 7674, pp. 739–747, 2012.

feature, some methods such as SIFT-CCH [17] and Transformed color SIFT [18] can be superior to traditional approaches. It is noted that direct fusion of these two features may result in the curse of dimensionality, which may decrease the final classification performance [19].

Considering the expensive time consuming problem, the transformation from the SIFT key points distribution to its eigenvectors can be effective on reduction of computational cost. For example, the Bag-of-Words approach [20] quantifies the SIFT key points in a feature vector.

In this work, we propose an SVM-based feature fusion method for web image classification. We employ LSH to embed the SIFT features and color features in hashing codes, and then the SVM classifier is used to classify images using these two types of features respectively. A decision-level information fusion is applied to generate the final classification results to evaluate the performance of the proposed method. We have conducted experiments on the web images crawled from internet. Experimental results demonstrate that the proposed method not only improves the classification performance, but also provides better robustness and expansibility.

2   Related Work

2.1   SIFT Feature

SIFT is able to describe image local features by extracting texture information around the robust points in the specially constructed multi-scale space, which includes the following steps [12]:

(1) Local extreme point detection and orientation: every point was compared with its neighboring 26 points and decided whether it can be an extreme point after the DOG (Difference-of-Gaussian) space was constructed. The DOG construction method can be illustrated as formula (1):

$$D(x, y, \sigma) = (G(x, y, k\sigma) - G(x, y, \sigma)) * I(x, y) \tag{1}$$

where $G(x, y, \sigma) = \dfrac{1}{2\pi\sigma^2} e^{-(x^2+y^2)/2\sigma^2}$, once these extreme points were obtained, the scale and location of the key points can be determined by second-order Taylor expansion of the aforementioned scale space function. Then the extreme points with low contrast ratio and unstable edge response points were removed to enhance the resistance to noise immunity.

(2) Key point orientation determining: in order for rotation invariant, Gradient direction distribution of key point neighborhood pixels was used to obtain the necessary orientation parameter. Its norm and direction can be acquired by using the convolution of original image and Gaussian kernel.

(3) Generation of key point descriptor: to insure rotation invariant, the coordinate was revolved to the direction coordinated with the key point, then a 8×8 pixels window centered on the point and its 4 sub windows (4×4 pixels) was constructed. Gradient histograms of 8 directions were calculated. Finally a 128 dimension vector data can be obtained from a key point and the SIFT eigenvector was determined after normalization, which can eliminate the influence of illumination.

2.2   LSH

SIFT features can be regarded as a collection of key points and each key point is illustrated by a 128 dimension eigenvector. However, large scale key points may lead to huge amount of computation which limits the further computation. Local Sensitive Hashing (LSH) [21] has been widely used to deal with this problem. LSH is a classical proximity search algorithm, and its basic idea can be described as follows: a group of Hash function family $H = \{h_1, h_2, ..., h_g\}$ was used to build several Hash tables. Similar points will increase the probability of conflict. In this way the similar points is more likely to be picked up into the same slot. For any point $p \in R^d$, the p-stable distribution based LSH [22] atomic hash function can be defined in formula (2):

$$h(p) = \left\lfloor \frac{A*p + b}{W} \right\rfloor \mod 2 = \{0, 1\} \tag{2}$$

Where $A \in R^d$ is the random vector which meets the standard normal distribution, W is the window size controlling the distance, b is the random value of uniform distribution $U[0, W)$. After processing, the values would be binary (0 or 1) and can be used for constructing the normalized histogram of SIFT eigenvector.

2.3   Multi-feature Fusion Algorithm

Multi-feature fusion methods can be classified into two groups [23]: highly coupled methods and low coupled methods. Figure 1 shows the basic procedure of the multi-feature fusion methods. Highly coupled methods, also called direct fusion, usually integrate a variety of eigenvectors and rebuild a new one, i.e. apply fusion directly for eigenvectors f_1 and f_2 and then form a new eigenvector $f = (f_1, f_2)$. Though the method is common and easy to be implemented, the disadvantages including large differences between two eigenvectors, the curse of dimensionality and high dimension feature submerging the lower one [19] still exist. Low coupled methods, also called decision-level fusion, often extract the decision information contained in the different intermediate results in advance, and then integrate all these decision information to get the final classification result.

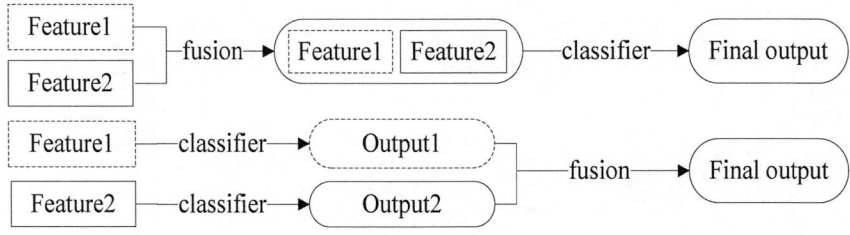

Fig. 1. A schematic illustration of the direct fusion and decision-level fusion methods

3   Image Classification by Integrating SIFT and Color Features

In this section, a SVM-based SIFT feature and color feature decision-level fusion method was introduced. The global color feature of images were extracted in the HSV color space, the SIFT eigenvectors were extracted and embedded into a histogram vector using LSH. Then the probability of the image belonging to a specific class was the gathered by SVM classifier. Finally, the multi-feature decision-level fusion was applied to generate the final classification results.

3.1   Color Feature Extraction

HSV color space is more appropriate for image application demand compared to traditional RGB color space due to its conformation with human visual perception. Quantization for HSV space is often needed to lower the computational complexity. In this paper the non-interval quantization was employed considering the color range and human visual perception. The three components, H, S and V, were divided into 8 intervals, 3 intervals, and 3 intervals respectively. According to the quantization levels and human visual sensitivity towards HSV color space, the three components were combined with different weights, and then the 72 dimension color eigenvector of HSV color space were extracted.

3.2   Feature Quantization Using LSH

In this step, LSH is employed to further quantify the features. The detailed steps of the histogram construction can be described as following procedures:

(1) Let B Hash atoms represent a SIFT feature point vector, generates B binary values as hash value in the range of $[0, 2^B)$. Then build a hash table with the length of 2^B and regard the final Hash table as the initial feature;

(2)   Iterate step (1) M times and obtain M histograms with 2^B dimension;

(3) Iterate step (1) and step (2) N times and get histograms with $N \times 2^B$ dimension. Then a higher dimension histogram vector with $N \times 2^B$ dimension is constructed.

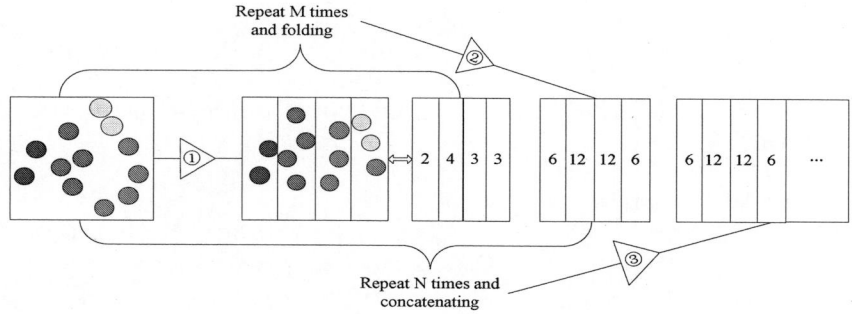

Fig. 2. Flowchart of using LSH to embed SIFT feature set into a histogram

3.3 SVM-Based Decision-Level Classification by Integrating SIFT and Color Features

Multiple SVMs are trained by using the training data, and all images can be classified by using SIFT feature and color feature respectively. Based on the class probability of each image, a decision-level fusion of multiple features is conducted. The algorithm procedure of decision-level fusion of SIFT and color features is shown in Figure 3.

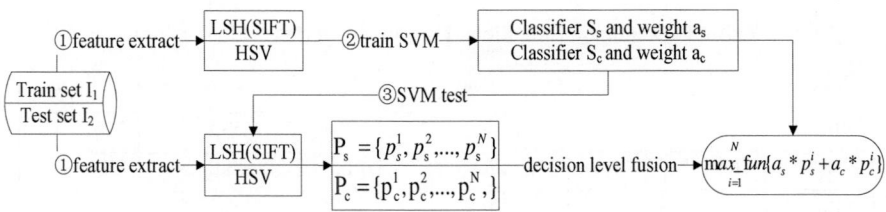

Fig. 3. Flowchart of fusing SIFT and HSV based on SVM

Let N denotes the class number of images in database I, I_1 represents training dataset and I_2 represents testing dataset respectively. Two classifier, S_s and S_c, can be trained by using SIFT feature and color feature respectively, where the associated weights are a_s and a_c. The calculation of a_s and a_c can be described as the following procedures:

(1) Divide dataset I_1 into $I_{10}, I_{11}, ..., I_{1k}$ evenly. For each $I_{1i}, i \in [0,k]$, Two classifier, S_s and S_c, are obtained by training its corresponding SIFT feature and HSV feature;

(2) Use $I_{1i}, i \in [0,k]$ to test the two classifier, S_s and S_c, obtained in the last step and record accurate classification numbers N_s 和 N_c;

(3) Repeat step (2). The final weights a_s and a_c are calculated by:
$a_s = N_s /(N_s + N_c)$, $a_c = N_c /(N_s + N_c)$;

By using the two classifiers, S_s and S_c, each image can be classified into a certain class with the possibilities of $P_s = \{p_s^1, p_s^2, ..., p_s^N\}$ and $P_c = \{p_c^1, p_c^2, ..., p_c^N\}$, and the final classification results t can be calculated by formula (3):

$$t = \max_i \{\alpha_s \times p_s^i + \alpha_c \times p_c^i\} \qquad (3)$$

It is safely to draw a conclusion that the decision-level fusion algorithm mentioned above has good extensibility. For example, it can merge other global feature such as shape and special relationship more conveniently and describe the global feature of images more comprehensively. Thus the performance of classification can be improved effectively.

4   Experimental Results

4.1   Testing Dataset

In this work, a web image dataset composed of 13719 images from 11 categories are crawled from internet.The detailed information of all the 11 categories is given in Table 1. Figure 4 illustrates a group of examples from the testing dataset.

Table 1. Detailed information of the 11 categories testing dataset

class	building	car-body	car-interior	dog	Dolphin	elephant
number	878	916	354	4170	395	722
class	chart	laptop	character	phone	indoor	all
number	384	2127	1564	1285	924	13719

Fig. 4. A group of examples of the testing image database

4.2   Experimental Results

In our experiments, 30% samples from each class are selected as training set, and all other images are acted as testing data. The LIBSVM [24] is employed to implement SVM-based classification. Experimental results are shown in Figure 5.

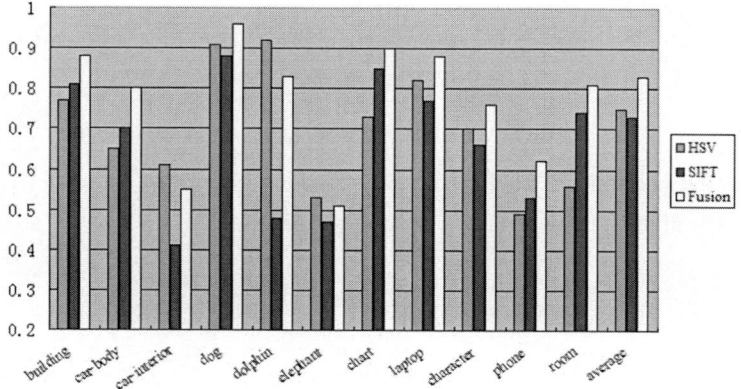

Fig. 5. Classification accuracy comparison of different features

In our experiments, classification accuracy based on color feature, SIFT feature and fusion of both features are compared. As illustrated in Figure 5, compared with single feature, we get better classification performance by using decision-level fusion. The superiority of decision-level fusion can be attributed to two aspects: the adoption of LSH in high-dimension histogram vector derived from SIFT eigenvectors for the sake of decreasing the influence on accuracy and the utilization of low-coupled decision -level fusion which extract the decision information contained in the different inter- mediate results beforehand to guarantee better image classification. An example of image classification result is shown in Figure 6.

Fig. 6. Example of image classification using our method

5   Conclusions

In this paper, we proposed a web image classification method by combining two types of features by using decision-level fusion strategy. In our experiments, a dataset composed of 13719 web images which were crawled from internet was used to test classification performance of the proposed method. To further verify its validation, classification accuracy of our fusion strategy was compared with that of single global or local feature. Experimental results proved that the decision-level fusion strategy of the proposed algorithm can not only provide higher classification accuracy but also better robustness and expansibility.

Future work involves extending the proposed algorithm to more applications with more flexible feature selection and fusion strategy and decreasing information loss in the procedure of features vector data reduction to improve efficiency.

Acknowledgements. Our research was supported by National Basic Research Program of China (973 Program(No.2010CB731800) and National Natural Science Foundation program (No.61172174).

References

1. Zha, Z.-J., Wang, M., et al.: Interactive Video Indexing with Statistical Active Learning. IEEE Trans. on Multimedia 14(1), 17–27 (2012)
2. Zha, Z.-J., Yang, L., et al.: Visual Query Suggestion. In: Proc. of the ACM International Conference on Multimedia, pp. 15–24 (2009)
3. Ji, R., Yao, H., Xie, X., Tian, Q.: Vocabulary Hierarchy Optimization and Transfer for Scalable Image Search. IEEE Multimedia Magazine 18(3), 66–77 (2011)
4. Ji, R., Yao, H., Liu, W., Sun, X., Tian, Q.: Task Dependent Visual Codebook Compression. IEEE Transactions on Image Processing 21(4), 2282–2293 (2011)
5. Wang, M., Yang, K., Hua, X.-S., Zhang, H.-J.: Towards Relevant and Diverse Search of Social Images. IEEE Transactions on Multimedia 12(8), 829–842 (2010)
6. Wang, M., Hua, X.-S., Hong, R., Tang, J., Qi, G.-J., Song, Y.: Unified Video Annotation Via Multi-Graph Learning. IEEE Transactions on Circuits and Systems for Video Technology 19(5), 733–746 (2009)
7. Wang, M., Hong, R., Li, G., Zha, Z.-J., Yan, S., Chua, T.-S.: Event Driven Web Video Summarization by Tag Localization and Key-Shot Identification. IEEE Transactions on Multimedia 14(4), 975–985 (2012)
8. Gao, Y., Wang, M., Zha, Z., Shen, J., Li, X., Wu, X.: Visual-Textual Joint Relevance Learning for Tag-Based Social Image Search. IEEE Transactions on Image Processing (in press)
9. Gao, Y., Wang, M., Zha, Z., Tian, Q., Dai, Q., Zhang, N.: Less is More: Efficient 3D Object Retrieval with Query View Selection. IEEE Transactions on Multimedia 11(5), 1007–1018 (2011)
10. Gao, Y., Wang, M., Tao, D., Ji, R., Dai, Q.: 3D Object Retrieval and Recognition with Hypergraph Analysis. IEEE Transactions on Image Processing 21(4), 4290–4303 (2012)
11. Gao, Y., Tang, J., Hong, R., Yan, S., Dai, Q., Zhang, N., Chua, T.-S.: Camera Constraint-Free View-Based 3D Object Retrieval. IEEE Transactions on Image Processing 21(4), 2269–2281 (2012)
12. Lowe, D.G.: Distinctive Image Features from Scale-Invariant KeyPoints. International Journal of Computer Vision 60(2), 91–110 (2004)
13. Banerjee, B., Bhattacharjee, T., Chowdhury, N.: Image Object Classification Using Scale Invariant Feature Transform Descriptor with Support Vector Machine Classifier with Histogram Intersection Kernel. In: Das, V.V., Vijaykumar, R. (eds.) ICT 2010. CCIS, vol. 101, pp. 443–448. Springer, Heidelberg (2010)
14. Jia, S., Xiao, N., Jie, Z.: Trademark Image Retrieval Algorithm Based on SIFT Feature. In: Yang, Y., Ma, M. (eds.) Green Communications and Networks. LNEE, vol. 113, pp. 201–207. Springer, Heidelberg (2012)

15. Cho, M., Park, H.: A Robust Keypoints Matching Strategy for SIFT: An Application to Face Recognition. In: Leung, C.S., Lee, M., Chan, J.H. (eds.) ICONIP 2009, Part I. LNCS, vol. 5863, pp. 716–723. Springer, Heidelberg (2009)
16. Liu, X., Li, P.: An Iris Recognition Approach with SIFT Descriptors. In: Huang, D.-S., Gan, Y., Gupta, P., Gromiha, M.M. (eds.) ICIC 2011. LNCS, vol. 6839, pp. 427–434. Springer, Heidelberg (2012)
17. Ancuti, C., Bekaert, P.: SIFT-CCH: Increasing the SIFT distinctness by Color Co-occurrence Histograms. Image and Signal Processing and Analysis 23, 130–135 (2007)
18. Abdel-Hakim, A.E., Farag, A.A.: CSIFT: A SIFT Descriptor with Color Invariant Characteristics. In: IEEE Computer Society Conference Computer Vision and Pattern Recognition, vol. 2, pp. 1978–1983 (2006)
19. Tommasi, T., Orabona, F., Caputo, B.: Discriminative cue integration for medical image annotation. Pattern Recognition Letters 29, 4283–4286 (2010)
20. Wu, L., Luo, S., Sun, W., Zheng, X.: Integrating ILSR to Bag-of-Visual Words Model Based on Sparse Codes of SIFT Features Representations. Pattern Recognition 23, 4283–4286 (2008)
21. Indyk, P., Motwani, R.: Approximate nearest neighbours: Towards removing the curse of dimensionality. In: Proc. of the 30th ACM Symposium on Theory of Computing, pp. 604–613 (1998)
22. Datar, M., Immorlica, N., Indyk, P.: Locality-Sensitive Hashing Scheme Based on p-Stable Distributions. In: Proc. of the 20th Symposium on Computational Geometry, pp. 53–265 (2004)
23. Clark, J., Yuille, A.: Data fusion for sensory information processing systems. Kluwer Academic Publisher (1999)
24. Chang, C.-C., Lin, C.-J.: LIBSVM: a library for support vector machines, http://www.csie.ntu.edu.tw/~cjlin/libsvm

An Interactive Semi-supervised Approach for Automatic Image Annotation

Yanhui Xiao, Zhenfeng Zhu, Nan Liu, and Yao Zhao

Institute of Information Science,
Beijing Jiaotong University,
Beijing, China
xiaoyanhui@gmail.com, {zhfzhu,yzhao,05112073}@bjtu.edu.cn

Abstract. Automatic image annotation (AIA) is an effective technique to bridge the semantic gap between low level image features and high level semantics. However, most of the existing AIA approaches failed to consider the use of unlabeled data. In this paper, we present an interactive semi-supervised approach for AIA by integrating graph propagation model and kernel canonical correlation analysis (KCCA) together. We aim to jointly utilize the keywords associated with labeled and selected unlabeled images to annotate the residual unlabeled images. Toward this goal, we firstly estimate the annotations of unlabeled images by the consistency-driven graph propagation model. Then, the KCCA is applied to seek the semantic consistency between the two concurrent visual and textual features. In addition, the unlabeled image with highest semantic consistency is selected into the training set. Thus, with the enlarged training set, the potential of the semantic consistency between visual and textual representations could be boosted. Some experiments carried out on two standard databases validate the effectiveness of the proposed method.

Keywords: Automatic image annotation, kernel canonical correlation analysis, graph propagation.

1 Introduction

Nowadays, the number of digital images has been growing rapidly on world wide web due to the popularity of digital cameras and online community such as Flickr and Picasa. Therefore, there is an increasing demand to efficiently manage and retrieve these large number of images. As a promising solution to facilitate the image retrieval and management system, automatic image annotation (AIA), which aims at automatically assigning the images with a set of textual words, has become an active research area in recent years and extensive efforts have been made.

Some popular works posed AIA as a generative model problem, which can be further divided into topic model and mixture model. Specifically, the main

W. Lin et al. (Eds.): PCM 2012, LNCS 7674, pp. 748–758, 2012.

idea of topic model is to annotate images as samples from a specific mixture of topics such as latent Dirichlet allocation [1], probabilistic latent semantic analysis [2] and hierarchical Dirichlet processes [3]. In addition, mixture models [4,5] estimate a joint distribution for local image features and annotations. To annotate an image, these models computed the conditional probability over keywords given the visual features by normalizing the joint likelihood. Furthermore, several approaches called discriminative models [6,7] learn a separate classifier for each label, and use it to predict whether the new image belongs to the class of images that are annotated with the label. Moreover, several approaches [8,9] have employed nearest neighbor matching techniques to find a set of visually similar images for a given image, and thereby used keywords of neighbor images to annotate the given image.

Recently, the graph-based methods have attracted much attention in image annotation due to their effectiveness and efficiency. [10] utilized graph propagation model(GPM) to propagate the keywords from the labeled images to the unlabeled images by visual similarities. The drawback with this approach is that it does not take into account the inherent correlations among multiple keywords. To alleviate the problem, [11] proposed an adaptive GPM method which utilized keyword correlations to improve the annotations. As the crux of the matter of an effective GPM method, the similarity estimation is capable of mining the data structure and describing the intrinsic semantic consistency between visual and textual representations. However, most of these previous studies only concerned the utilizations of visual similarity and textual similarity, respectively. Since the similar caption often reflects similar images which are annotated with similar labels, the annotation ability could be boosted by maximizing the consistency between visual and textual modalities.

To address the above issue, in this paper, we propose an interactive semi-supervised algorithm by incorporating GPM and Kernel canonical correlation analysis (KCCA) into a unified scheme, named ISSA, to propagate the keywords from labeled data to unlabeled data in the sematic space. In particular, the proposed ISSA method consists of two steps, i.e. label estimation and semantic consistency measure. In the label estimation step, the GPM based on KCCA, in which the similarity between images is estimated in the latent space, is employed to annotate the unlabeled images. In addition, the candidate annotations are refined by word co-occurrence frequency. Furthermore, in the semantic consistency measure step, KCCA is utilized to measure the consistency between visual semantic and textual semantic in the latent semantic space. Subsequently, the unlabeled image with the highest semantic consistency are selected into the training set and the estimation step is rerun until all the unlabeled images are annotated. Iteratively enlarging the training set can be seen as a bootstrapping way. Hence, the ISSA not only may connect the visual and textual modalities with maximal consistency in the semantic space but also could automatically annotate images in an iterative reinforcement way.

2   The Similarity Estimation

It is very important for GPM to estimate the similarity between images, which reflects the understanding of the data structure and boosts to mine the potential knowledge. In this section, we first introduce some notation which will be used in the rest of the paper, and then outline the main idea of KCCA. Finally, the details of the KCCA based similarity estimation method will be given.

2.1   Preliminaries

To begin with some definitions, suppose there are n classes. Let $\mathcal{N} = \{1, \ldots, n\}$ denote the set of class labels. Let $\mathcal{X} = \{x_i\}_{i=1,\ldots l,\ldots,l+u} \in \mathbb{R}^d$ denotes a given dataset where the first l samples are labeled data and the remaining u ones are unlabeled, usually $l \ll u$. We use $y_i \in \mathcal{Y}(\mathbb{R}^{l+u})$ to denote the label of x_i. We assume $y_1, \ldots, y_l$ are known, and the task is to compute $y_{l+1}, \ldots, y_{l+u}$. In the following discussions, we use $\mathcal{L} = \{1, \ldots, l\}$ and $\mathcal{U} = \{l+1, \ldots, l+u\}$ to denote labeled and unlabeled data indexing set respectively. We define $Y \in \mathbb{R}^{(l+u) \times c}$ is the initial label matrix, i.e., for $i \in \mathcal{L}$, $Y_{ij} = \begin{cases} 1 \ if \ j \in y_i \\ 0 \ if \ j \notin y_i \end{cases} (j \in \mathcal{N})$, and $Y_{ij} = 0$ for $i \in \mathcal{U}$.

Based on the collected dataset $\mathcal{X}$, an undirected graph $\mathcal{G}(\mathcal{E}, \mathcal{V})$ can be constructed, where the vertex set $\mathcal{V} = \{v_i\}_{i=1,\ldots,(l+u)}$ represents the visual feature vectors for all x_i and $\mathcal{E} = \{(v_i, v_j)\}_{i,j=1,\ldots,(l+u)}$ denotes the edge set. Particularly, a well-defined weight $s_{ij} \in S$ is assigned to the edge $(v_i, v_j) \in \mathcal{E}$ connecting input pairs (x_i, x_j) to reflect the magnitude of strength of linkage.

Given the above dataset, let $\mathcal{V}$ and $\mathcal{Y}$ be visual and textual views, i.e. two attribute sets, for the identical data. In order to identify nonlinearly correlated projections between the two views, let ϕ be the feature space mapping of visual view and φ be the feature space mapping of textual view into a higher dimensional feature space, respectively. Denote $\phi(\mathcal{V}) = (\phi(v_1), \cdots, \phi(v_{(l+u)}))$ the feature space mapping applied to visual view and $\varphi(\mathcal{Y}) = (\varphi(y_1), \cdots, \varphi(y_{(l+u)}))$ as the feature space mapping of textual view.

2.2   KCCA

As one of the most popular statistical tools, canonical correlation analysis(CCA) [12] finds a pair of linear transformations one for each of the sets of variables such that when the set of variables are transformed the corresponding co-ordinates are maximally correlated. To overcome the drawback of linear CCA in extracting nonlinear correlation spaces, the KCCA [13], offers an alternate solution by first projecting the input space into a higher dimensional feature space by some nonlinear mapping function. Fig.1 illustrates that image visual and textual features are projected into a latent semantic space with maximal correlation by KCCA.

We define a kernel function on v: $K_v(v_i, v_j) = < \phi(v_i), \phi(v_j) >$ where $< \cdot, \cdot >$ is the dot product (similarly for y). The essence of KCCA is to search

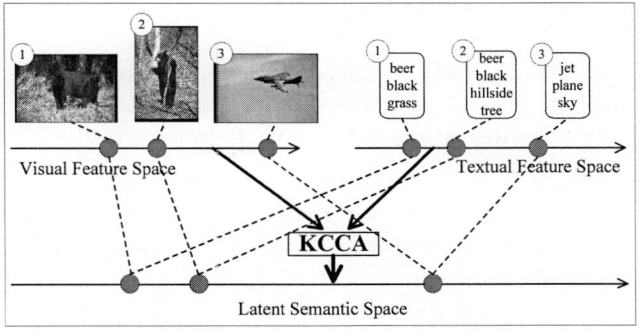

Fig. 1. Illustration of projections in KCCA

for projection vectors w_v and w_y that lie in the span of $\phi(v)$ and $\varphi(y)$: $w_v = \sum_{i=1}^{(l+u)} \alpha_i \phi(v_i) = \phi(\mathcal{V})\alpha^T$ and $w_y = \sum_{i=1}^{(l+u)} \beta_i \varphi(y_i) = \varphi(Y)\beta^T$. Denote the kernel matrices K_v and K_y, we wish to optimize

$$\max_{\alpha,\beta} \frac{\alpha^T K_v K_y \beta}{\sqrt{(\alpha^T K_v{}^2 \alpha) \cdot (\beta^T K_y{}^2 \beta)}}.$$

By some mathematical manipulation like in [13], the solutions yield the corresponding generalized eigenvalue problem, i.e. Eq.1 and Eq.2.

$$(K_v + \kappa I)^{-1} K_y (K_y + \kappa I)^{-1} K_v \alpha = \lambda^2 \alpha \tag{1}$$

$$\beta = \frac{1}{\lambda}(K_y + \kappa I)^{-1} K_v \alpha \tag{2}$$

The eigenvectors α and β associated with the top k eigenvalues then form the basis A and B, where $A = [\alpha^1 \dots \alpha^k]$ and $B = [\beta^1 \dots \beta^k]$ are the solutions to KCCA. I and κ are identity matrix and regularization factor, respectively.

2.3   The Similarity Estimation Based on KCCA

The similarity estimation in ISSA is to build a weighted graph whose nodes correspond to labeled and unlabeled images and edges reflect the similarities between images like in [10]. Furthermore, [13] proved that the similarity between instances can be better estimated by projecting data into the latent semantic space with KCCA. That is, it can maximize the consistency by seeking a latent space between visual semantic and textual semantic, while minimizing the diversity in the words to describe the same object. Therefore, the similarity estimation based on KCCA is defined as

$$s_{ij} = exp\left\{-\frac{d(K_v(v_i, \mathcal{V})A, K_v(v_j, \mathcal{V})A)}{2\sigma_1^2}\right\} \cdot exp\left\{-\frac{d(K_y(y_i, Y)B, K_y(y_j, Y)B)}{2\sigma_2^2}\right\}, \tag{3}$$

where $d(\cdot, \cdot)$ is the distance measure which will be further described in detail in Section 4.2, σ_1 and σ_2 are two parameters that control the decrease rate of the function.

3   The Interactive AIA Algorithm

The main idea of ISSA algorithm is that the labels of the unlabeled images are iteratively estimated by an interactive way which is mainly composed of two steps, i.e., label estimation and semantic consistency measure.

Label Estimation: Estimate the annotations for all unlabeled images ($x_i \in \mathcal{U}$) based on the updated training set in the previous semantic consistency measure step. Note that the first iteration uses the original training set to compute the label estimation step.

Semantic Consistency Measure: Select the unlabeled image with the highest semantic consistency from the unlabeled set $\mathcal{U}$ to further enlarge the training set $\mathcal{L}$ by the semantic consistency of unlabeled images.

3.1   Label Estimation

Given the labeled training set, the label estimation step like in [14] aims to propagate keywords from the annotated images to the unlabeled images based on their visual similarities. Specifically, it is an iterative graph propagation process defined as

$$R(t+1) = \gamma S \times R(t) + (1-\gamma)Y, \tag{4}$$

where R is a $(1+u) \times n$ dimensional matrix whose element R_{ij} represents the confidence of image i belonging to j_{th} class, and t denotes the number of iterations. Note that the first iteration for $R(t)$ (i.e. $t = 0$) is equal to Y. In addition, Y mentioned in Section 2.1 is the initial label matrix obtained from prior knowledge, S is the similarity matrix between images. In order to ensure the GPM algorithm's convergence, the similarity matrix $S = [s_{ij}]_{(1+u)\times(1+u)}$ similar to [10] should be normalized by $S = D^{-1/2}SD^{-1/2}$, where D is a diagonal matrix and $D_{ii} = \sum_{j=1}^{(1+u)} s_{ij}$. The parameter Y provides prior label information for the propagation process, and the latter S describes the data distribution over all the labeled and unlabeled data. γ is a tradeoff between the visual correlation and prior confidence. It shows in [14] that Eq.4 converges to a steady state, i.e., $R^* = (1-\gamma)(I - \gamma S)^{-1}Y$. Labels with highest confidence in convergent matrix R^* are selected as the final annotations for unlabeled data.

In order to combine the prior confidence of candidate annotations and word relations jointly, we use the cooccurrence frequency of labels in the training dataset similar to [15] which used word cooccurrence to refine the original annotations. Let $\mathcal{W}(w_i, w_j)$ be the correlation of words w_i and w_j. That is,

$$W(w_i, w_j) = \begin{cases} 0 & num(w_i, w_j) = 0 \\ \frac{num(w_i,w_j)}{min(num(w_i),num(w_j))} & num(w_i, w_j) \neq 0 \end{cases} \tag{5}$$

where $num(w_i, w_j)$ is the number of the images annotated by both words w_i and w_j, $num(w_i)$ and $num(w_j)$ are the number of images only labeled with words w_i and w_j, respectively. The word correlation matrix is used to refine the label prior by $Y = Y \times \mathcal{W}$.

3.2   Semantic Consistency Measure

The goal of this step is to select the unlabeled image with highest semantic consistency from the unlabeled images set $\mathcal{U}$. We map the vectors of unlabeled image i in $\mathcal{V}$ and $\mathcal{Y}$ to the latent space based on KCCA and utilize the Euclidean distance between the projected vectors as a similarity score. Thus, the semantic consistency score could be obtained as:

$$c_i = exp(-||K_v(v_i, \mathcal{V})A - K_y(y_i, Y)B||_2^2), \tag{6}$$

where $|| \cdot ||_2$ is the Euclidean norm. Since the visual semantic is expected to be as close as the textual semantic, the unlabeled image with highest semantic consistency score will be utilized to enlarge the training image set. By rerunning the estimation step, the training set can be gradually increased in a bootstrapping way, and the unlabeled images will be fully annotated by the most relevant keywords based on the maximal visual-textual consistency of unlabeled images versus labeled samples.

Table 1. The ISSA algorithm

Input: The initial label matrix Y, the word correlation matrix W, the visual kernel K_v and initial textual kernel K_y.
Initialize:
$\mathcal{L} \leftarrow \{labeled\ images\}$, $\mathcal{U} \leftarrow \{unlabeled\ images\}$.
while $\mathcal{U} \neq \emptyset$ **do**
　　% Label Estimation
　　Obtain A and B by solving Eq.1 and Eq.2 based on $\mathcal{L}$.
　　for all $i \in \mathcal{L} \cup \mathcal{U}$ **do**
　　　　Compute the similarity matrix S according to Eq.3.
　　end
　　$Y_r = Y \times W$. %Refine the annotation priors.
　　$R(0) = Y_r$.
　　Iterate $R(t + 1) = \gamma S \times R(t) + (1 - \gamma)Y_r$ until convergence to the steady state R^*.
　　for all $i \in \mathcal{U}$ **do**
　　　　Decide the label of y_i with highest confidence according to R^*.
　　end
　　% *Semantic Consistency Measure*
　　Update the textual kernel K_y.
　　for all $i \in \mathcal{U}$ **do**
　　　　$c_i = ||K_v(v_i, \mathcal{V})A - K_y(y_i, Y)B||_2$.
　　end
　　$I = \{$ The image with highest semantic consistency$\}$.
　　$\mathcal{L} = \mathcal{L} \cup I$.
　　$\mathcal{U} = \mathcal{U} - I$.
　　Update the label matrix Y.
end
Output: $\{y_i\}_{i=l+1,...,l+u}$.

The ISSA utilizes an interactive process to iteratively annotate the unlabeled images from visual features to a set of keywords. The proposed ISSA algorithm is summarized in Table 1. To acquire the coefficient vectors A and B, we employ the linear kernel and Gaussian kernel for textual and visual modality, respectively. Furthermore, the labels with highest confidences are selected as the annotations for each unlabeled image according to the convergent matrix R^*. Thus, based on the GPM, we are able to use the similarity consistency matrix C to select the most possible unlabeled image according to consistency score of the image to enlarge the training set. Finally, all the unlabeled images will be annotated with highest sematic consistency.

4   Experimental Results and Analysis

4.1   Data Sets and Feature Extraction

Two publicly available data sets (Corel5K and IAPR TC12) are used to evaluate the performance of the ISSA and compare with other state-of-the-art models.

Corel5K. It was firstly unitized by Barnard et al. [16] and has become an important benchmark data set in the image retrieval area. To evaluate the performance on ISSA, a series of experiments are conducted on 5000 images. In particular, we select 4500 images with 1 to 5 keywords as training set and the remainder as testing data. Totally, 374 words are manually labeled for the training set, which results in an average of 3.5 words for each image.

IAPR TC12. This set is a collection of 20,000 images and its size is suitable to evaluate the scalability of annotation algorithms. However, since the annotations are free-flowing captions, keywords need to be extracted by using natural language techniques. Thus, we use the same annotation for each image as in [8]. That is, there are 291 keywords (an average 4.7 words for each image) exploited as keyword dictionary.

A variety of global features, including RGB, LAB, and HSV color histograms with 16 bins for each color channel and 512-dimensional Gist features [17], are utilized in our scheme to characterize the color distribution and spatial arrangement of image, respectively. [9] showed that combining global and saliency color features could improve the performance of AIA. Hence, we extract the similar saliency features for each color space as a complement of global representation. In addition, with respect to the local visual representation, SIFT features are densely extracted on a multi-scale grid and further form a 3000-dimensional bag of visual words for each image by k-means quantization, which is built by the training set. To compute the distances between the features, we utilize χ^2 as the base metric for SIFT and $L1$ for the others.

The evaluation measures based on precision, recall, and F1 are utilized to evaluate the performance of the proposed AIA Algorithm. The precision and recall are denoted by $precision = B/A$ and $recall = B/C$, where A is the number of the images automatically annotated with a given keyword; B is the total of images correctly annotated with this keyword; and C is the number of

Table 2. Annotation performance on Corel5K and IAPR TC12

Method	Corel5K				IAPR TC12			
	P	R	$F1$	$N+$	P	R	$F1$	$N+$
SML[5]	0.23	0.29	0.26	137	–	–	–	–
GLM[18]	0.22	0.25	0.23	121	–	–	–	–
TGLM[11]	0.25	0.29	0.27	131	–	–	–	–
En-CRF[7]	0.32	0.33	0.32	148	–	–	–	–
MBRM[4]	0.24	0.25	0.24	122	0.24	0.23	0.23	233
LASSO[8]	0.24	0.29	0.26	127	0.28	0.29	0.28	246
JEC[8]	0.27	0.32	0.29	139	0.28	0.29	0.28	250
GS[9]	0.30	0.33	0.31	146	0.32	0.29	0.30	252
ISSA	0.28	0.37	0.32	150	0.37	0.28	0.32	253

– denotes that the author did not provide the data for this measure. $N+$ is utilized to denote the number of keywords with non-zero recall value.

the images with ground truth annotation of this keyword. The F1 is given by $F1 = 2 \times Precision \times Recall/(Precision + Recall)$.

4.2 Experimental Results

Following the same experiment setting of GS[9], we annotate each unlabeled image with the 5 most relevant keywords. The performance comparisons of the proposed ISSA algorithm with other annotation approaches, including SML[5], original graph learning model (GLM)[18], TGLM[11], MBRM[4], LASSO[8], JEC[8], En-CRF [7] and GS, are given in Table 2.

We can explicitly obverse that the proposed method convincingly outperforms other previous works since the potentials of obtaining the semantic consistency between visual and textual representations are fully explored. Particularly, compared with GLM and TGLM on Corel5K, ISSA achieves an evident improvement on precision, recall and specially for the words with positive recall. It indicates that the proposed interactive semi-supervised algorithm can fully exploit intrinsic semantic consistency between the two concurrent visual and textual modalities in the latent semantic space and improve the performance. Although the state-of-the-art method, GS, achieves the most promising results, group structure and the sparsity number utilized in this scheme seem to be unavailable for the practical applications.

The distance measure for the similarity matrix S is a crux of the GPM methods. Therefore, the proposed distance measure is compared with $L1$ and χ^2 metric for all of the features, respectively, which are illustrated in Fig. 2. It is clear that the proposed metric outperforms the other metric in both Corel5K and IAPR TC12 owing to better modeling the similarity among each image. Thus, we employ χ^2 for the SIFT feature and $L1$ for others to compute the similarity matrix S in our scheme unless special specification.

To evaluate the effect of size of the training set on the performance of the proposed ISSA, a series of experiments are conducted by the number of training images $n = 500, 1000, 1500, 2000, 2500, 3000, 3500, 4000, 4500$ for Corel5K and

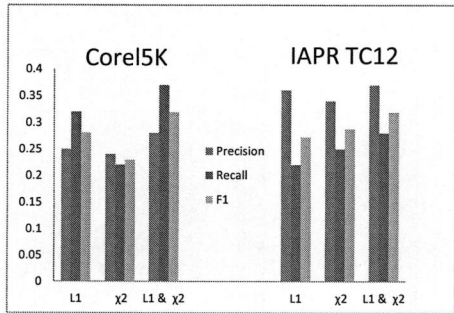

Fig. 2. Comparison of the three metric schemes

$n = 2000, 4000, 6000, 8000, 10000, 12000, 14000, 16000, 18000$ for IAPR TC12, respectively. Since the images in one folder are generally collected by semantic similarity, the images in one folder can be supposed to belong to one category. Thus, there are 50 categories in Corel5K set and 41 categories in IAPR TC12. Actually these images are not well grouped, but images in the same folder are relatively similar. The training images are randomly selected from each folder and the proposed method is employed on these data. In the experiment, such procedure is repeated 10 times and the result is the average. Fig. 3 shows the results of precision, recall and F1. It is obvious that with increasing number of training image, the performance is also increasing. But the results are more stabled in Corel5K than in IAPR TC12. It may be that the images in Corel5K are more perfectly grouped in each folder than these in IAPR TC12. Thus, not enough training data is provided for the ISSA algorithm to approximate the keywords for the unlabeled images. However, with a small quantity of annotated training images, the proposed ISSA algorithm is even better than some other annotation models with the whole of training set.

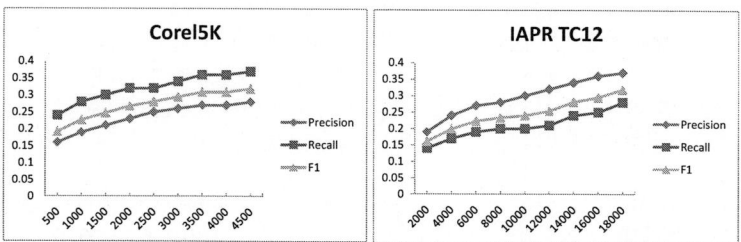

Fig. 3. Influence of the number of training images on the proposed ISSA algorithm

In Fig.4 we show some examples of the annotations and corresponding ground truth for several images in Corel5K and IAPR TC12, demonstrating the promising performance of the proposed ISSA algorithm. It is notable that some images (e. g. the first image in second row) are annotated much more keywords (i.e. tree and tourist)than those by manually labeled by human beings. Actually, some of

Predicted keywords	polar bear tundra snow cubs	cars tracks turn prototype formula	water sand sky desert beach	f-16 jet plane runway sky	tree beach palm water people	iguana marine lizard water rocks
Ground Truth	bear polar snow tundra	cars tracks turn prototype	sky water	sky jet plane	tree beach people palm	water iguana marine
Predicted keywords	table people restaurant tree tourist	people man shelter forest roof	man balcony stage woman spectator	mountain sky range desert landscape	woman jean tee-shirt shop bag	sky mountain landscape bush llama
Ground Truth	people restaurant table	forest man people roof shelter	man spectator stage woman	desert landscape mountain sky	bag jean shop tee-shirt woman	bush llama landscape mountain sky

Fig. 4. The keywords annotated by the proposed ISSA versus ground truth for images from Corel5K (first row) and IAPR TC12 (second row). Although redundancies may misinterpret the images, some keywords explain them well.

these annotated keywords frequently appear in the similar images, which may result in some misinterpretation of image contents. However, on the other hands, they may enhance the representation ability of these images compared with the simple ground truth that may be ignored by humans.

5 Conclusions

In this paper, we propose an ISSA algorithm for AIA by incorporating GPM and KCCA into a unified scheme. In ISSA, the intrinsic semantic consistency between the two concurrent visual and textual modalities is fully exploited in the latent semantic space by KCCA. Furthermore, since the unlabeled image with highest semantic consistency is selected into the training set, the unlabeled images can be iteratively annotated by a bootstrapping way. The experiments conducted on standardized datasets have demonstrated the effectiveness of the proposed algorithm.

Acknowledgments. This work was supported in part by 973 Program (No. 2012CB316400), the National Science Foundation of China (No. 61025013, 61172129), Beijing Municipal Natural Science Foundation (No. 4112043), and Fundamental Research Funds for the Central Universities (No.2012JBZ012).

References

1. Barnard, K., Duygulu, P., Forsyth, D., de Freitas, N., Blei, D.M., Jordan, M.I.: Matching words and pictures. J. Mach. Learn. Res., 1107–1135 (2003)
2. Monay, F., Gatica-Perez, D.: Plsa-based image auto-annotation: constraining the latent space. In: Proceedings of the 12th Annual ACM International Conference on Multimedia, pp. 348–351. ACM (2004)

3. Yakhnenko, O., Honavar, V.: Annotating images and image objects using a hierarchical dirichlet process model. In: Proceedings of the 9th International Workshop on Multimedia Data Mining: Held in Conjunction with the ACM SIGKDD 2008, pp. 1–7. ACM (2008)

4. Feng, S., Manmatha, R., Lavrenko, V.: Multiple bernoulli relevance models for image and video annotation. In: CVPR, vol. 2, pp. 1002–1009 (2004)

5. Carneiro, G., Chan, A.B., Moreno, P.J., Vasconcelos, N.: Supervised learning of semantic classes for image annotation and retrieval. IEEE Trans. Pattern Anal. Mach. Intell. 29, 394–410 (2007)

6. Grangier, D., Bengio, S.: A discriminative kernel-based approach to rank images from text queries. TPAMI 30, 1371–1384 (2008)

7. Xu, X., Jiang, Y., Peng, L., Xue, X., Zhou, Z.: Ensemble approach based on conditional random field for multi-label image and video annotation. In: MM, pp. 1377–1380. ACM (2011)

8. Makadia, A., Pavlovic, V., Kumar, S.: A New Baseline for Image Annotation. In: Forsyth, D., Torr, P., Zisserman, A. (eds.) ECCV 2008, Part III. LNCS, vol. 5304, pp. 316–329. Springer, Heidelberg (2008)

9. Zhang, S., Huang, J., Huang, Y., Yu, Y., Li, H., Metaxas, D.: Automatic image annotation using group sparsity. In: CVPR, pp. 3312–3319 (2010)

10. He, J., Li, M., Zhang, H., Tong, H., Zhang, C.: Manifold-ranking based image retrieval. In: Proceedings of the 12th Annual ACM International Conference on Multimedia, pp. 9–16. ACM (2004)

11. Liu, J., Li, M., Liu, Q., Lu, H., Ma, S.: Image annotation via graph learning. Pattern Recognition 42, 218–228 (2009)

12. Hotelling, H.: Relations Between Two Sets of Variates. Biometrika 28, 321–377 (1936)

13. Hardoon, D.R., Saunders, C., Szedmak, S., Shawe-Taylor, J.: A Correlation Approach for Automatic Image Annotation. In: Li, X., Zaïane, O.R., Li, Z.-H. (eds.) ADMA 2006. LNCS (LNAI), vol. 4093, pp. 681–692. Springer, Heidelberg (2006)

14. Zhou, D., Bousquet, O., Lal, T.N., Weston, J., Schölkopf, B.: Learning with local and global consistency. In: Advances in Neural Information Processing Systems 16, pp. 321–328. MIT Press (2004)

15. Wang, C., Jing, F., Zhang, L., Zhang, H.J.: Image annotation refinement using random walk with restarts. In: MM, MULTIMEDIA 2006, New York, NY, USA, pp. 647–650 (2006)

16. Duygulu, P., Barnard, K., de Freitas, J.F.G., Forsyth, D.: Object Recognition as Machine Translation: Learning a Lexicon for a Fixed Image Vocabulary. In: Heyden, A., Sparr, G., Nielsen, M., Johansen, P. (eds.) ECCV 2002, Part IV. LNCS, vol. 2353, pp. 97–112. Springer, Heidelberg (2002)

17. Oliva, A., Torralba, A.: Modeling the shape of the scene: A holistic representation of the spatial envelope. In: ICCV, vol. 42, pp. 145–175 (2001)

18. Tong, H., He, J., Li, M., Ma, W.Y., Zhang, H.J., Zhang, C.: Manifold-ranking-based keyword propagation for image retrieval. EURASIP J. Appl. Signal Process., 190 (2006)

Cross-Media Semantics Mining Based on Sparse Canonical Correlation Analysis and Relevance Feedback[*]

Hong Zhang and Xiaoming Liu

College of Computer Science & Technology
Wuhan University of Science & Technology, 430065, China
zhanghong_zju@yahoo.com.cn

Abstract. Cross-media learning is a new hot topic in multimedia content analysis and retrieval. Because multimedia data of different modalities are heterogeneous in feature space and there exists the well-know semantic gap, one of the most challenging issues for cross-media learning is to mine underlying semantics and estimate cross-media correlation. In this paper we propose a cross-media semantics mining approach based on Sparse Canonical Correlation Analysis and relevance feedback. First, we analyze sparse canonical correlation between low-level feature matrices of different modalities in training stage, and construct a Multimodal Sparse Subspace where both canonical correlation and most meaningful features are preserved; then based on geometric distance in the subspace we estimate cross-media correlation and enable cross-media retrieval; also we provide long-term relevance feedback strategy for performance optimization. Our approach is tested with general multimedia data, including image, audio and text. Experiment and comparison results are encouraging and show that the performance of our approach is effective.

Keywords: Sparse CCA, Cross-media retrieval, Relevance Feedback.

1   Introduction

In recent years, cross-media retrieval has become a new hot topic in the area of multimedia content analysis and retrieval [1][2][3]. In cross-media retrieval system, users can query similar multimedia objects whose modalities may not be the same as that of the query example. This happens in real world retrievals. For example, a user has a picture of zither, and he wants to know what it sounds like when it is played. In this case most existing content-based multimedia retrieval systems can't meet the user's need [4][5][11], while he/she can get the answer with cross-media retrieval system.

The main challenging issue for cross-media retrieval is how to measure cross-media semantic correlation based on heterogeneous multimedia features [12]. We can estimate the similarity between two images by calculating how close they are in color,

---

[*] This work is supported by National Natural Science Foundation of China (No.61003127).

W. Lin et al. (Eds.): PCM 2012, LNCS 7674, pp. 759–768, 2012.
© Springer-Verlag Berlin Heidelberg 2012

shape or texture. But it is difficult to calculate the distance between visual feature vector of an image and auditory feature vector of an audio clip. A few research has proposed effective methods to solve the correlation measure problem for cross-media retrieval in the past five years, including: nonlinear semantic subspace mapping [1][6], graph-based correlation fusion [3], text-based methods, and so on. For example, Yang et al. proposed a distance measure between heterogeneous Multimedia Documents which consisted of text, image or audio samples, and constructed a MMD semantic subspace for cross-media retrieval [1]. In our previous work [6], we employed Canonical Correlation Analysis (CCA) to compute canonical correlation between visual feature matrix and auditory feature matrix, and calculated an isomorphic subspace where the correlation learned was preserved.

Different from above researches, this paper proposes a cross-media semantics mining algorithm based on Sparse Canonical Correlation Analysis (SCCA), and provides performance optimization strategy with long-term relevance feedback. First, SCCA is used to explore sparse canonical correlation among training data, including text, image and audio, and then an isomorphic subspace is built for multimodal data representation; secondly, to further narrow the semantic gap, we make use of long-term relevance feedback, and fuse prior knowledge learned from user interactions into the subspace. In this way, cross-media retrieval performance is periodically improved. The main difference between this paper and most previous research is that: we focus on the sparisity property when calculating how multimedia data of different modalities are statistically correlated, which filtrates minor correlations.

The rest of this paper is organized as follows. In section 2, we describe how to build multimodal sparse subspace based on the method of SCCA. Section 3 describes cross-media retrieval algorithm with long-term relevance feedback, and how to enable cross-media retrieval with new data. Experiments and comparisons are presented in section 4, and section 5 gives conclusion and future work.

2   Construction of Multimodal Sparse Subspace

In our previous work, Canonical Correlation Analysis (CCA) was used to find a map to the optimal isomorphic subspace where canonical correlation is maximally preserved. However, when the dimension of low-level feature is very high it is important to preserve meaningful correlations instead of all of them. Therefore, in this section, we focus on how to find sparse mapping vectors during feature correlation analysis.

2.1   Sparse Canonical Correlation Analysis

CCA is a classical method to explore statistical correlation between two sets of variables [7], and it has been used for the analysis of multimedia data [6]. The underlying ideas of CCA are as follows: it looks for two basis vectors for two sets of variables such that the correlation between the projections onto the basis vectors is mutually maximized.

Given two data sets X and Y of dimensions $n \times p_1$ and $n \times p_2$ on the same set of n observations, we assume that the columns of X and Y have been standardized to have mean zero and standard deviation one. CCA calculates linear combinations of the variables in X and Y that are maximally correlated with each other. Let $u \in \mathbb{R}^{p_1}$ and $v \in \mathbb{R}^{p_2}$ denote canonical vectors which maximize the correlation between Xu and Yv, CCA is to solve the following extremum problem:

$$\max \; u^T X^T Yv$$
$$s.t. \; u^T X^T Xu = 1, \; v^T Y^T Yv = 1 \tag{1}$$

The main challenging issue of CCA is that it is not appropriate when $p_1, p_2 \approx n$ or $p_1, p_2 \gg n$. Then Sparse Canonical Correlation Analysis (SCCA) was proposed to address the problem [8], and its objective function takes the following form:

$$\max \; u^T X^T Yv$$
$$s.t. \; \|u\|_2 \le 1, \; \|v\|_2 \le 1, \; P_1(u) \le c_1, \; P_2(v) \le c_2 \tag{2}$$

where P_1, P_2 are convex and non-smooth sparsity-inducing penalty functions that yield sparse u, v. And the constraints $\|u\|_2 \le 1$, $\|v\|_2 \le 1$ are convex relaxations of the quality constraints.

Paper [8] studied two specific forms of the penalty P (either P_1 or P_2) with structure of l_1-norm penalty and the chain-structured fused lasso penalty, which resulted in unique canonical vectors, even when $p_1, p_2 \gg n$. With u fixed, the criterion is convex in v, and with v fixed, it is convex in u.

It has been shown that SCCA can be applied to content-based multimedia data analysis and retrieval. For example, paper [9] used SCCA to find a set of "acoustically meaningful" tags that were correlated with a chosen feature-based representation of audio content, and as a result, their supervised auto-tagging system better modeled the selected tags. paper [10] found words that had a high correlation with the audio feature representation, and annotated songs with semantically meaningful words so as to retrieve relevant songs based on a text query.

2.2   Construction of Multimodal Sparse Subspace

SCCA has been seldom used for multimodal content analysis. In this section, we focus on correlation mining among heterogeneous multimodal data, including text, image and audio. Based on SCCA method, we build a multimodal sparse subspace where all training data reside and underlying correlations are maximally preserved.

Formally, let $X \in \mathbb{R}^{n \times p_1}$ denote image feature matrix, and $Y \in \mathbb{R}^{n \times p_2}$ denote textural feature matrix. Then the objective function to solve image canonical vector u and text canonical vector v is the same as function (2) in subsection 2.1. Here canonical vectors u and v define a linear combination of visual features in X that is correlated with a linear combination of textural features in Y. Elements of u and that equal zero indicate features in X and Y that are not involved in the linear combinations.

In this application the solution vector v can be interpreted as a mapping of words to weights where a high weight implies that a given word is highly correlated with the image feature representation. Thus we impose sparsity on v. For the ease of illustration, we assume:

$$P_1(u) = \|u\|_1 \tag{3}$$

$$P_2(v) = \sum_j |v_j| + \sum_j |v_j - v_{j-1}| \tag{4}$$

where $P_1(u)$ is an L_1 penalty and $P_2(v)$ is a fused lasso penalty [8].

To substitute Eq.(3) and Eq.(4) for $P_1(u)$ and $P_2(v)$ in the objective function (2), the optimized sparse canonical vectors u and v can be calculated with the algorithm proposed in paper [8]. And accordingly, image feature matrix and text feature matrix can be mapped to the sparse subspace.

We use similar process to analyze underlying correlation between audio and text and between image and audio training data. Simultaneously, we choose the same dimensionality when calculating sparse vectors for text and audio. In this way, all training data are mapped into the Multimodal Sparse Subspace (MSS).

3   Cross-Media Retrieval with Long-Term Relevance Feedback

Since text, image and audio data are represented with vectors in the MSS, we can estimate cross-media correlation according to the Euclidean distance. However, because of the well-known semantic gap, Euclidean distance measure results in the MSS are not always consistent with high-level semantics. Thus we utilize user interaction to optimize cross-media retrieval results. In this section, we propose a geometrically motivated long-term RF strategy, which could be used to periodically refine previous learning results and improve overall retrieval performance.

3.1   The Algorithm

Let $\Omega = \{s_1, s_2, ..., s_m\}$ be the whole training set, including text, image and audio, and $m = |\Omega|$ is the number of all samples. We construct a weighted adjacency graph $G(V, E)$ according to distance measure in the MSS: for any sample s_i, there is a corresponding vertex $V_i \in G(V, E)$ and for any two vertices $V_i, V_j \in G(V, E)$, we put an edge between them with distance τ_{ij} which is defined as follows:

$$\tau_{ij} = \begin{cases} \|s_i - s_j\|, & if \ \|s_i - s_j\| < \varepsilon \\ \infty, & otherwise \end{cases} \tag{5}$$

where ε is a suitable constant reflecting the definition of locality, and $\|s_i - s_j\|$ is their distance in the MSS. In this way, nearby data points are connected with an edge if they are "close" enough. To model the global geometrical structure, we define the length of a path as the sum of all pair wise distances along the path, and replace distance τ_{ij} with the shortest path between s_i and s_j using Dijkstra's algorithm.

Then for a query example user submits, we find its nearest neighbors (which could be text, image and audio) by distance τ_{ij} and return them as query results. Let P and N denote the positive and negative results user labeled respectively, and then the distance matrix $[\tau_{ij}]$ is refined with:

$$\tau_{ij} = \begin{cases} \tau_{ij}/f_1, & if \ (s_i, s_j \in P) \\ \tau_{ij} \times f_2, & if \ (s_i \in P, s_j \in N) \end{cases} \tag{6}$$

where f_1, f_2 are suitable constants greater than 1. As the user interacts with the retrieval system, the distance matrix $[\tau_{ij}]$ will gradually be improved, and better reflect the distances in semantic space.

Based on distance matrix $[\tau_{ij}]$, we define the weights of edges are as follows:

$$w_{ij} = \begin{cases} \exp(-\tau_{ij}/t), & if \ \tau_{ij} < \rho \\ 0, & otherwise \end{cases} \tag{7}$$

where t, ρ are suitable constants.

Let $S^* = \{s_1^*, s_2^*, ..., s_m^*\}$ denote updated coordinate vectors of $\Omega = \{s_1, s_2, ..., s_m\}$ in the MSS after user interactions are integrated. Considering the locality preserving property and the nonlinear manifold structure on the graph, we use Laplacian Eigenmaps to calculate S^*. It's reasonable that a "good" map to S^* should minimize the objective function $\sum (s_i^* - s_j^*)^2 W_{ij}$, which incurs a heavy penalty if neighboring points s_i and s_j are mapped far apart. And we have $\sum (s_i^* - s_j^*)^2 W_{ij} = 2(S^*)^T L S^*$ where $L = D - W$ is a Laplacian matrix and D is a diagonal matrix defined as $D_{ii} = \sum_j w_{ji}$. Thus the minimization problems is:

$$\arg \min_{S^T S = I} (S^*)^T L S^* \tag{8}$$

Therefore, S^* can be obtained by eigen-decomposition of L. In summary, the cross-media retrieval algorithm with long-term RF is stated below:

Step 1. Compute MSS with SCCA method for training set $S = \{s_i\}, i \in [1, ..., m]$ including text, image and audio;
Step 2. Construct the weighted adjacency graph $G(V, E)$ based on distance τ_{ij} in the MSS, then for each query example, return its nearest neighbors by the value of τ_{ij};
Step 3. After each round of query refine matrix $[\tau_{ij}]$ with (6) according to positive and negative results, then after certain times of retrieval, calculate the weight matrix $[w_{ij}]$ with equation (7), and get the Laplacian matrix L in (8);
Step 4. Compute $V = [v^1, v^2, ... v^c]$ in which $v^1, v^2, ... v^c$ are eigenvectors obtained from c minimum non-zero eigenvalues of (8), then for sample s_i its updated MSS coordinates s_i^* is calculated by $s_i^* = (v_i^1, v_i^2, ..., v_i^c)$ where v_i^j is the ith entry of eigenvector v^j.

Algorithm 1. Cross-media Retrieval Algorithm with Long-term RF

As users interact with the system all positive and negative results are recorded in system log and used to refine distance matrix $[\tau_{ij}]$. Accordingly, the MSS can be periodically optimized.

3.2 Cross-Media Retrieval with New Data

When the query example r is inside training set, the system finds its k-nearest neighbors in the MSS, ranks them by distance in ascending order, and returns to the user as query results. On the other hand, when the query example r is out of training set it needs to be mapped into the MSS, then the retrieval process is the same as before.

Our mapping algorithm is based on correlation analysis of whole training data, so it is difficult to map a single new query example r into the MSS in the same way training data does. Therefore, we make use of short-term RF to calculate the coordinates of r in the MSS. Our approach is as follows:

- Find r's k-nearest neighbors $\Omega_k = \{s_1, s_2, ..., s_k\}$ of the same modality according to low-level feature distance, and return Ω to the user as query results;

- Let P denote positive examples user marked from Ω, and y_i denote the coordinates of positive example $s_i \in P$ in the MSS, $f(i,r)$ denote the similarity between sample s_i and the query example r which is in inverse proportion to the low-level distance, the coordinates of r in the MSS are given by:

$$y_r = \sum_{y_i \in P} y_i \frac{f(i,r)}{\sum_P f(i,r)} \qquad (9)$$

4 Experiment and Comparisons

The collected dataset consists of 15 Image-Audio-Text categories, such as piano, zither, dog, bird, explosion, car, tiger, goal, etc. And for each Image-Audio-Text category there are 60 images, 30 audio records and 40 text records. These datasets are collected from Multimedia Cyclopaedia, educational and E-business Webpages (e.g. http://encarta.msn.com and http://www.animalbehaviorarchive.org/), and so on.

The extracted visual features include Color Histogram (in HSV space), CCV, and Tamura Texture. Auditory features are made up of Centroid, Rolloff, Spectral Flux and Root Mean Square. Audio is a kind of time series data, so the dimensionalities of combined auditory feature vectors are inconsistent. We employ Fuzzy Clustering algorithm [6] on auditory features for dimension reduction to get isomorphic feature vectors, and require collected audio clips not exceed 7 seconds. For text records, we use TF/IDF feature. If the returned result and the query example are in the same semantic category, it is regarded as a correct result.

To accumulate prior knowledge and refine the MSS with long-term relevance feedback, we perform 10 times of retrieval with different query examples for each category, and provide two positive and two negative examples in each query.

All experimental results listed below are obtained after the MSS is refined with one round of long-term relevance feedback.

4.1   Multimodal Retrieval in the MSS

First, we run multimodal retrieval in the MSS to test overall retrieval performance. When users submit a query example we find its k-nearest neighbors in the MSS according to distance τ_{ij} in Eq.(5). Thus, returned results could be text, image and audio, and we name it as multimodal retrieval. In our experiments we generate 8 random text queries, 8 random image queries and 8 random audio queries for each category. Figure 1 shows average multimodal retrieval results, including query by text example, query by audio example and query by image example.

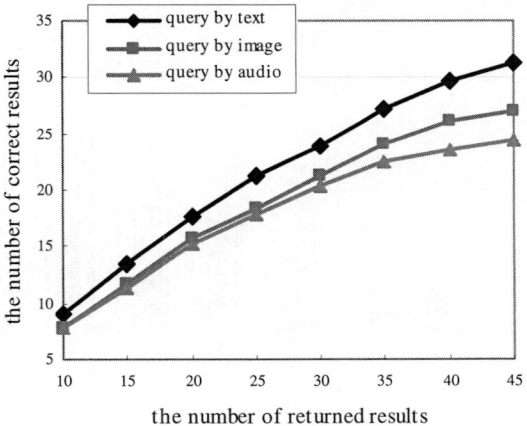

Fig. 1. Multimodal retrieval results with different query examples

In Figure 1 "the number of correct results" means total number of correct returned text, image and audio samples. It can be seen from Figure 1 that three kinds of multimodal retrieval achieve good results on the whole. And zooming into details, we notice that (1) query by text obtains better results than query by image and query by audio; (2) query by image is close to query by audio, and the former slightly outperforms the latter when the number of returned results is bigger than 30. This is mainly because: text itself expresses certain semantics, and it is easier to estimate text-image and text-audio correlation than image-audio correlation; besides, in training dataset audio clips are not more 7 seconds, and accordingly auditory features are comparatively more consistent than visual features.

4.2   Performance Comparison of Image-Audio Cross-Media Retrieval

To further evaluate the effectiveness of our approach, we perform cross-media retrieval between image and audio in the MSS, and compare our approach with CCA based method in [6] and KCCA based method in [2]. Figure 2(a) shows precision performance comparison results of querying image by audio example, and Figure 2(b) shows those of querying audio by image example.

(a) query image by audio example

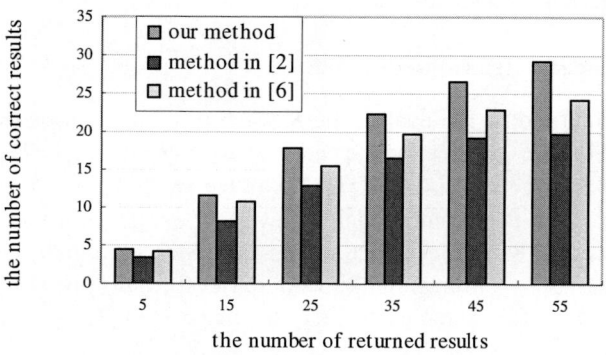

the number of returned results

(b) query audio by image example

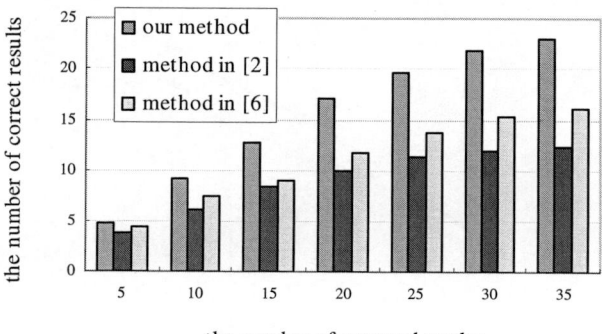

the number of returned results

Fig. 2. (a)(b) A comparison of our algorithm with CCA based method in [6] and KCCA based method in [2] for image-audio cross media retrieval

We observe that our algorithm consistently outperforms the methods in [2][6]. In our method the number of correct results is 17.8 in Figure 2.(a) when the number of returned results is 25 and is 19.6 in Figure 2.(b). This is mainly because: KCCA method maps two datasets into higher dimensional space via implicit nonlinear mapping, and then a traditional CCA is performed; as we described in section 2.1 when the dimensionality of features is much bigger than the number of samples CCA is less effective in correlation mining. The method of SCCA successfully finds sparse canonical vectors that identify most correlated features from high-dimensional feature vectors during subspace mapping.

4.3   Query Example Out of Training Set

We also test the retrieval performance when query examples are out of training set. We use the method in section 3.2 to calculate the coordinates in the MSS for new data. Table 1 shows average results of image-audio cross-media retrieval by example of new image or new audio without long-term relevance feedback.

Table 1. Image-audio cross-media retrieval results with new query examples

scope query	5	10	15	20	25	30	35	40
query image by new audio	4.13	7.85	10.17	13.11	15.37	17.67	19.60	20.32
query audio by new image	3.85	7.23	10.10	12.56	14.93	16.43	17.23	18.36

The first row in Table 1 means the number of returned results, and the other two rows are the number of correct results when the query examples of image or audio are out of database. Although querying results by new data are slightly weaker than those by training data, the results in Table 1. are good on the whole. As can be seen, the proposed approach is fairly robust when dealing with new query examples, and the retrieval performance is encouraging. Moreover, when new data are mapped into the MSS long-term relevance feedback can also be used for performance optimization with new data.

5   Conclusions and Future Work

In this paper, we propose an effective approach to mine cross-media semantics for retrieval. Different from most single modality retrieval methods, we explore sparse canonical correlation from multimodal data which are heterogeneous in feature spaces. And based on correlation measure we further propose long-term relevance feedback strategy to periodically improve cross-media retrieval performance. Sparse correlation works well on finding meaningful features when the dimensions of multimodal features are relatively high. Experiment results are encouraging and show that our approach is effective both on database samples and new query examples out of database. Structural information has been proved effective to optimize the objective function of SCCA in some applications, such as biological data. And future work mainly includes further study on structural information exploration from low-level features and the fusion of the structural information into the SCCA description.

References

1. Yang, Y., Zhuang, Y., Wu, F., Pan, Y.: Harmonizing Hierarchical Manifolds for Multimedia Document Semantics Understanding and Cross-media Retrieval. IEEE Transactions on Multimedia 10(3), 437–446 (2008)
2. Zhang, H., Liu, X.: Boosting Multimodal Semantic Understanding by Local Similarity Adaptation and Global Correlation Propagation. In: Qiu, G., Lam, K.M., Kiya, H., Xue, X.-Y., Kuo, C.-C.J., Lew, M.S. (eds.) PCM 2010, Part I. LNCS, vol. 6297, pp. 148–158. Springer, Heidelberg (2010)
3. Zhuang, Y., Yang, Y., Wu, F.: Mining Semantic Correlation of Heterogeneous Multimedia Data for Cross-media Retrieval. IEEE Transactions on Multimedia 10(2), 221–229 (2008)
4. Lew, M.: Content Based Multimedia Information Retrieval: State of the Art and Challenges. ACM Transactions on Multimedia Computing, Communications and Applications 2(1), 1–19 (2006)

5. He, X., Ma, W.Y., Zhang, H.J.: Learning an Image Manifold for Retrieval. In: Proceedings of ACM Multimedia Conference (2004)

6. Zhang, H., Weng, J.: Measuring Multi-modality Similarities Via Subspace Learning for Cross-Media Retrieval. In: Zhuang, Y.-T., Yang, S.-Q., Rui, Y., He, Q. (eds.) PCM 2006. LNCS, vol. 4261, pp. 979–988. Springer, Heidelberg (2006)

7. Hotelling, H.: Relations Between Two Sets of Variates. Biometrika, 321–377 (1936)

8. Witten, D.M., Tibshirani, R.: Extensions of sparse canonical correlation analysis, with applications to genomic data. Statistical Applications in Genetics and Molecular Biology 8(1) (2009)

9. Torres, D.A.: Using sparse CCA for vocabulary selection. M.S. University of California, San Diego (2009)

10. Torres, D.A., Turnbull, D., Barrington, L., Sriperumbudur, B.K., Lanckriet, G.: Finding Musically Meaningful Words by Sparse CCA. In: NIPS Workshop on Music, Brain & Cognition (2007)

11. Zhang, R., Zhang, Z.: Effective Image Retrieval based on Hidden Concept Discovery in Image Database. IEEE Transactions on Image Processing 16(2), 562–572 (2007)

12. Yang, Y., Nie, F., Xu, D., Luo, J., Zhuang, Y., Pan, Y.: A multimedia retrieval framework based on semi-supervised ranking and relevance feedback. IEEE Transactions on Pattern Analysis and Machine Intelligence 34(4), 723–742 (2012)

What Happened Near Big Ben: Event-Driven Landmark Mining from Flickr

Weiqing Min[1,2], Bing-Kun Bao[1,2], and Changsheng Xu[1,2]

[1] National Lab of Pattern Recognition, Institute of Automation, CAS,
Beijing 100190, China
[2] China-Singapore Institute of Digital Media, Singapore, 119613, Singapore
{wqmin,csxu}@nlpr.ia.ac.cn, bingkunbao@gmail.com

Abstract. The fast development of Internet and personal electronic devices has led to a dramatic growth of landmark images available on social media sites such as Flickr. With their informative and attractive content, landmark images have received considerable attention in multimedia research community. Most of existing methods focus on exploring landmark images by their spatial distribution, while largely ignoring the temporal aspect. Through digging the temporal information in the shared images, we can reveal the series of historical moments of landmarks, which could be useful for social studies and attractive to tourists. In this paper, we propose a scheme named Landmark Timeline Construction(LTC), which automatically mines and selects diverse images on historical events of a landmark simply from Flickr. In our scheme, Time Interval Selection Algorithm is proposed to handle the limitation of the existing methods on the fixed time interval by assigning the optimal ones to different tags. The experimental results demonstrate the effectiveness of our methods.

Keywords: landmark timeline construction, event, aging theory.

1 Introduction

With the rapid development of photo-sharing web sites, we have witnessed the explosive growth of images available on the Internet. Among these images, landmark images are part of the most informative and attractive ones that have been widely studied in recent years. Many landmark images have been taken at special moments with their unique physical, cultural and historical features. Therefore, exploring and organizing them is useful and interesting, since they can not only help users to deeply understand the cultural value and social function of these landmarks from temporal aspect, but also be applied for tour recommendation and visualization.

Most of existing works have focused on the summary of landmark images in a local area(e.g. [7] [8] [10] [12]) or at global scale(e.g. [4] [15]). They employed content and context information from Flickr to select representative landmark images. These methods can show users some representative views of each landmark within a special geographic area, but fail to provide users more about

W. Lin et al. (Eds.): PCM 2012, LNCS 7674, pp. 769–778, 2012.

historical moments of a landmark, as they largely disregard the temporal information from landmark images.

In this paper, we propose a novel scheme named Landmark Timeline Construction(LTC) for mining diverse images on historical moments simply from Flickr. Fig. 1 shows the constructed Big Ben timeline by LTC on Flickr. Through those images, we can easily learn what happened near Big Ben in the past. For example, in 2008-04-12, an Marathon race happened near Big Ben. It is obvious that the most challenging step of this scheme is the historical event detection. There are some existing methods [9] [3] for extracting event tags from tag set. In particular, [3] detected event tags of Flickr data by discretizing the continuous time into time sequence with a fixed time interval. Although it can roughly obtain the distribution of each tag's occurrences, the performance heavily relies on the selection of the time interval, that is, if the time interval is too small or too large, the occurrence of certain tags in the peak (bursty) interval may not suddenly increase compared with those of adjacent intervals. Therefore, it is crucial to automatically assign each tag an optimal time interval. More specifically, for event tags, the time interval should be equal to the length of peak (bursty) period, while for non-event tags, it can be set as any value[1]. To this concern, we present a Time Interval Selection Algorithm by seeking the length of peak (bursty) period for each tag.

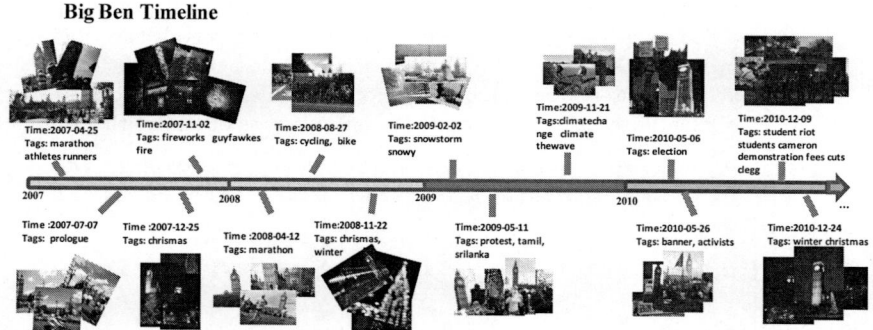

Fig. 1. The example of Big Ben timeline from 2007 to 2010 using our LTC

Our main contributions of this paper can be summarized as follows:
- To the best of our knowledge, this is the first attempt to mine the historical moments of landmarks from Flickr. The obtained images not only can help users to deeply understand the histories of landmarks, but also can be applied into tour recommendation and visualization.

- We propose a new scheme named Landmark Timeline Construction(LTC), which can automatically mine and select the diverse images on historical events of a landmark.

---

[1] Please note that we analyze the tags in the length of one year every time and assume that the event tag only has one peak (bursty) period during a year.

- A new Time Interval Selection Algorithm is presented to handle the limitation of the existing methods which depend on a fixed time interval by seeking the optimal ones.

The rest of this paper is organized as follows. Section 2 details the LTC framework and the proposed Optimal Time Interval Selection Algorithm. The experiment results are reported in Section 3. We conclude the paper with future work in Section 4.

2   Landmark Timeline Construction

There are three steps in the proposed Landmark Timeline Construction: event tag detection, event tag clustering, and image retrieval & reranking, shown in Fig. 2. Given a certain landmark, a set of related images together with their attached tags and upload time are collected by searching the name of the landmark on Flickr. In event tag detection, the Time Interval Selection Algorithm is proposed to assign different intervals to tags, and aging theory is utilized to calculate the bursty weight of each tag. In event tag clustering, the top 50 tags with the highest bursty weights are then grouped together by considering tag occurrences, the word similarity and the temporal similarity. In image retrieval & reranking, the relevant images are retrieved using manifold ranking by querying the tags from the same cluster, and re-ranked using diverse relevance ranking.

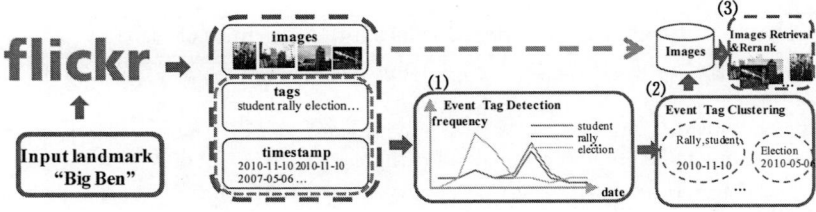

Fig. 2. The framework of LTC

There are some notations in this paper. For a certain landmark, a set of related images crawled from Flickr is denoted as $X = \{x_1, \cdots, x_n, \cdots, x_{|x|}\}$. Each image x_n is combined with an upload time t_n and a set of attached tags $C_n \subset C$, where $C = \{c_1, \cdots, c_k, \cdots, c_{|c|}\}$ is the tag set including all the attached tags.

2.1   Event Tag Detection

As aforementioned, when an event happened, hundreds of relevant images would be uploaded to Flickr with tags related to that event. Thus, the variation of tag occurrence on images along the time sequence can help us to detect those events. To calculate the tag occurrence, the time interval is introduced to discretize the continuous time. Considering that the peak (bursty) period of each tag is an optimal selection for the time interval, we present Time Interval Selection Algorithm to seek the peak (bursty) period for each tag, especially the event ones.

Let $I = < T_s, T_e >$ be a time range of one year, where T_s and T_e denote the start and the end time of I respectively. $S = \{s_j | j = 1, \cdots, |s|\}$ denotes a set of time interval values in an ascending order. In our work, S is set as $\{1, \cdots, 30\}$, and the unit is one day. When the time interval is defined as s_j, the m-th time segmentation is $I_m = < i_m, i_m + s_j >, m = 1, 2, \cdots, |m|$, where $i_0 = T_s$, and $T_e - i_{|m|} \leq s_j$. Let $F(c_k, j, m)$ be the occurrence of tag c_k on different users in m-th time segmentation I_m when the time interval is defined as s_j. Our target is to seek the optimal time interval s_{j^*} for c_k.

Obviously, if the time interval varies to be smaller than the length of peak period, the tag occurrence will decrease significantly; while if the time interval moves in the opposite direction, the tag occurrence will increase slowly. Thus, the optimal time interval should be close to the length of peak period. In particular, $F(c_k, j^*, m)$ is close to $F(c_k, j^* + j, m), j = 1, 2, \cdots$ and much higher than $F(c_k, j^* - 1, m)$. Let the threshold be σ, and we have,

$$\begin{cases} \frac{\max_m F(c_k, j^*, m) - \max_m F(c_k, j^* - 1, m)}{\max_m F(c_k, j^* - 1, m)} > \alpha, \\ \frac{\max_m F(c_k, j^* + j + 1, m) - \max_m F(c_k, j^* + j, m)}{\max_m F(c_k, j^* + j, m)} \leq \sigma, \quad j = 1, 2, \cdots, |j| - j^* - 1. \end{cases} \quad (1)$$

Algorithm 1. Optimal time interval selection algorithm (OTIS)

Input: tag set $C = \{c_k | k = 1, \cdots, |c|\}$, time interval set $S = \{s_j | j = 1, \cdots, |s|\}$, threshold σ

Output: the optimal time intervals for all the tags $\overline{S}^* = \{\overline{s}_k^*, k = 1, \cdots, |c|\}$, where $\overline{s}_k^*$ indicates the optimal time interval value for tag c_k.

1: **for** $k = 1$ to $|c|$
2: **Initialization**
   $j = |s|, F = \max_m F(c_k, j, m), k^* = |s| - 1, F^* = \max_m F(c_k, j^*, m), ratio = \frac{F - F^*}{F^*}$
3: **while** $ratio \leq \sigma$ and $j^* > 1$
4:   $j^* = j^* - 1;$
5:   $F = F^*, F^* = \max_m F(c_k, j^*, m), ratio = \frac{F - F^*}{F^*}$
6: **end while**
7:   $\overline{s}_k^* = s_{j^*}$
8: **end for**
9: **return** $\overline{S}^*$.

Based on Eqn. (1), Optimal Time Interval Selection Algorithm (OTIS) is proposed in Alg. 1 with the output of the optimal time interval $\overline{S}^*$ for tag set C. Then, aging theory is applied to assign the bursty weight w_k to tag c_k by following [1] [2].

2.2 Event Tag Clustering

Clustering is a widely accepted method of event detection on a set of keywords [14]. There exist many cluster methods, such as k-means, mean-shift, etc. The most critical step is to calculate the similarities between those elements (e.g. tags in our case). In our scheme, we take three kinds of similarities into consideration, that is,

- Similarities on tags by occurrences on the same period, referred to as S_1.
- Semantic similarity on tags according to Wordnet::similarity [13], referred to as S_2.
- Temporal similarity on tags according to upload time, referred to as S_3.
  Tag occurrence similarity between c_k and c_q can be computed as [3]:

$$S_1 = \frac{N(c_k, c_q)}{\min(N(c_k), N(c_q))} \tag{2}$$

where $N(c_k)$ and $N(c_q)$ are the numbers of images associated with tag c_k and c_q respectively, $N(c_k, c_q)$ is the number of images associated with both tag c_k and c_q.

S_2 is calculated by Wordnet::similarity, a widely used software package to measure the semantic similarity between words from Wordnet [5].

The temporal similarity S_3 indicates the correlation between bursty periods of two tags. With known of the optimal time intervals $\bar{s}_k^\star$ and $\bar{s}_q^\star$ for tags c_k and c_q, the bursty periods of them are the time segmentations with highest tags' occurrences. Thus, the indexes for those time segmentations are

$$\begin{cases} m_k = \max_m F(c_k, \bar{s}_k^\star, m), \\ m_q = \max_m F(c_q, \bar{s}_q^\star, m). \end{cases}$$

Then, the bursty periods of c_k and c_q are

$$\begin{cases} I_{m_k} = <i_{m_k}, i_{m_k} + \bar{s}_k^\star>, \\ I_{m_q} = <i_{m_q}, i_{m_q} + \bar{s}_q^\star> . \end{cases}$$

The temporal similarity S_3 can be defined as

$$S_3 = H(I_{m_k}, I_{m_q}) = \begin{cases} 1 & if \quad (I_{m_k} \cap I_{m_q}) \neq \phi \\ 0 & otherwise. \end{cases}$$

Eqn. (3) combines these three kinds of similarities into $S(c_k, c_q)$,

$$S(c_k, c_q) = (\alpha S_1(c_k, c_q) + \beta S_2(c_k, c_q)) S_3(c_k, c_q) \tag{3}$$

where α and β are the weights assigned to S_1 and S_2 respectively, and $\alpha + \beta = 1$

At last, we use k-means to cluster top 50 tags in each year for every landmark into $|E|$ clusters, that is, $E = \{E_1, \cdots, E_m, \cdots, E_{|E|}\}$, where $E_m = \{c_1^m, \cdots, c_q^m, \cdots, c_{|m|}^m\}$ indicates the m-th tag cluster, c_q^m denotes the q-th tag in this cluster, and $|m|$ denotes the number of tags in the m-th cluster.

2.3   Image Retrieval and Re-ranking

In order to obtain the relevant and diverse images for each event of landmarks, the relevant images are retrieved using manifold ranking [6] by querying tags from the same cluster, and the diverse images are assigned with high re-ranking scores by using diverse relevance ranking [11]. For sake of simplification, we take the m-th tag cluster E_m as an illustration.

For image set $X = \{x_1, \cdots, x_n, \cdots, x_{|x|}\}$, denote $y = [y_1, \cdots, y_n, \cdots, y_{|x|}]^T \in \Re^{|x|}$, where $y_n = \frac{\hat{n}}{|x|}$, if n-th image's tags include $\hat{n}$ tags from E_m. Let $f = [f_1, \cdots, f_n, \cdots, f_{|x|}]^T \in \Re^{|x|}$ be the ranking value of X. By following manifold ranking, f can be optimized by

$$f^\star = \min_f (f^T L f + \lambda \|f - r\|^2) \tag{4}$$

where $L = I - D^{-1/2} W D^{-1/2}$, D is a diagonal matrix with its element $D_{ii} = \sum_j W_{ij}$. W_{ij} denotes the visual similarity between two images.

To output diverse images in the retrieval results, we re-rank the retrieved images using Diverse Relevance Ranking (DRR) method [11]. DRR generates a ranking list by a greedy ordering algorithm to optimize average diverse precision, extended from the conventional average precision. At last, the top images with highest ranking scores are selected as the output of LTC.

3   Experiment

In this section, we systematically elaborate our LTC scheme on 5 landmarks, including Big Ben, Statue of Liberty, Golden Gate Bridge, Lincoln Memorial and Eiffel Tower. The images together with their attached tags and upload time are crawled from Flickr by searching the names of the landmarks and constraining the upload time as "from Jan 01, 2007 to Dec 31, 2010". Table 1 shows the statistics of the collected dataset.

Table 1. The statistics of our collected Flickr data

Landmark	♯image	♯tag	♯unique tag	♯user
Big Ben	64785	589924	26695	17571
Statue of Liberty	77202	453656	29526	14556
Golden Gate Bridge	113712	724864	31452	16907
Lincoln Memorial	31687	221431	11466	30543
Eiffel Tower	91818	500323	29838	15490

To demonstrate the performances of our proposed OTIS algorithm and LTC scheme, we conduct objective evaluation for OTIS algorithm and user study for LTC respectively.

3.1 Experiment on OTIS Algorithm

OTIS algorithm optimizes a time interval for each tag, and then aging theory detects the event ones from the tag set with their own time intervals. Obviously, the bad time interval could result in increasing the bursty weights of the non-event tags. Thus, we demonstrate the top tags with high bursty weights from aging theory to show the effectiveness of OTIS algorithm.

We compare our proposed OTIS algorithms, tag occurrence on different users with optimal scale (referred to "OTIS"), with three methods: tag occurrence on different images with fixed scale (referred to "IT-F"), tag occurrence on different users with fixed scale (referred to "UT-F") and tag occurrence on different images with optimal scale (referred to "IT-O"). We select three scales of time interval for I-tag with Fixed-scale and U-tag with Fixed-scale respectively, that is, 5 days, 10 days and 15 days. So, there are totally 7 baselines: IT-F-5, IT-F-10, IT-F-15, UT-F-5, UT-F-10, UT-F-15, IT-O.

Also, we asked for 10 participants to annotate the top 10 tags with "event tag" and "non-event tag" for our method as well as the baselines. For one tag, if more than 6 participants thought it is relevant to an event, the ground truth of it is set as event tag. We compare all the results with the precision metric.

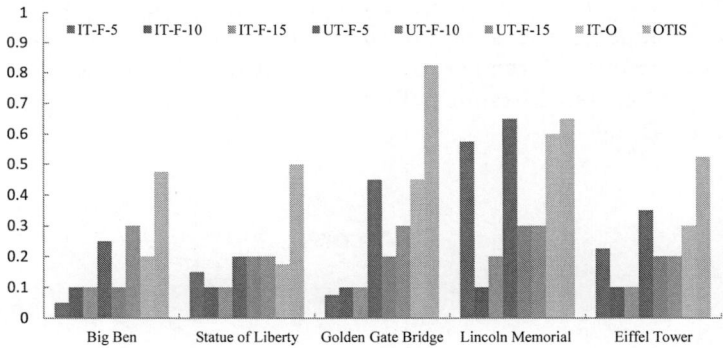

Fig. 3. P@10 for 5 landmarks

Fig. 3 shows P@10 results of each landmark. From them, we can see that for the same fixed-scale, the methods using UT is better than using IT since UT is more discriminative than IT. We can also see that IT-O performs better than IT-F-5,IT-F-10,IT-F-15 and OTIS performs better than UT-F-5, UT-F-10, UT-F-15, due to the optimal time interval selection of each tag. Compared with other methods, our OTIS algorithm achieves much better performance because we select the optimal time interval of each tag considering the tag occurrence on users.

Table 2 shows the extracted top 10 tags in 2010 from Big Ben. Again, our method performs better than others.

Table 2. Top 10 tags for each method

Methods	Tags[1]
IT-F-5	*protest*, gold, france, french, louvrepyramid, paris, londra, bigbus, ducktour, jaan
IT-F-10	*protest*, *riot*, *student*, dayx, cameron, *violence*, graffiti, kettle, clegg, *journalism*
IT-F-15	cheapside, bus, fleetstreet, jamess, mallst, marylestrand, pall, church, sugarquary, themall
UT-F-5	london, *protest*, londoneye, thames, *police*, *winter*, night, *riot*, *christmas*, eye
UT-F-10	*protest*, night, sky, towerbridge, houses, *riot*, *police*, clock, square, wheel
UT-F-15	*winter*, light, *police*, *chrismas*, towerbridge, autumn, buidlings, skyline, ligth, lights
IT-O	*protest*, accd, art, artcenter, artstudio, center, design, fieldtrip, graphic, graphicdesign
OTIS	*winter*, *student*, *riot*, *christmas*, *election*, *students*, soho, autumn, cameron, tube

[1] higher weight tags appear further to the left and tags in black font are event tags.

3.2 Experiment on LTC Scheme

LTC provides users top three images for each event on every landmark. We also utilize the aforementioned three methods to compare with ours. Considering that the results of time interval with 5 days achieve better than that with 10 and 15 days in three landmarks, we only experiment on IT-F-5, UT-F-5, IT-O, and our LTC.

The comparative user studies are conducted as follows. 20 participants are asked to score each obtained image with: 1) 0: if it is not relevant to the landmark; 2) 0.33: if it is not relevant to a landmark-based event; 3) 0.66: if it is not diverse with the previous ones from the same event; 4) 1: if participant is satisfied with it. The average scores of all the events from 5 landmarks in baselines and our scheme are show in Fig. 4. As shown in the results from Fig. 4, our LTC 's score is the highest compared with other methods, that is, most participants agreed that LTC has the better performance, which clearly demonstrates the effectiveness of our LTC scheme. As an example, Table 3 shows results of our LTC on mining Golden Gate Bridge.

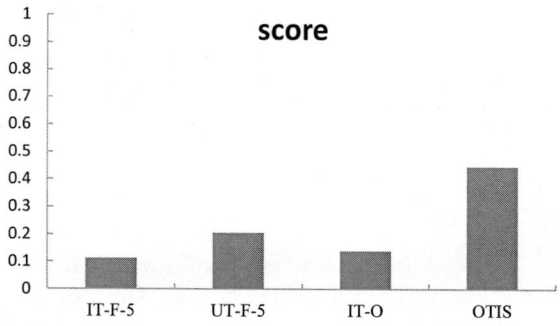

Fig. 4. Evaluation on the effectiveness of LTC

As shown in the experimental evaluation and comparison with other methods, the proposed LTC is effective. It is worthy of noting that there are some limitations. Take Big Ben as an example, by checking their associated images, we find that there are 6 irrelevant events. These non-event clusters mainly contain too

Table 3. Golden Gate Bridge result of LTC

Event Tags	Time	Photos
airshow blueangels fleetweek fleet angels week jet navy therock planes usnavy jets	10/4/2007~ 10/8/2007	
biking	9/14/2007 ~ 9/16/2007	
birthday	9/22/2007	
airshow angels fleetweek jet week blueangels fleet jets plane formation angel blueangles	10/09/2008 ~ 10/13/2008	
tibet protest torch freetibet olympics free olympic	4/7/2008 ~ 4/9/2008	
marathon running	8/3/2008, 8/4/2008	
blueangels fleetweek airshow angels jet navy	10/7/2009 ~ 10/15/2009	
week fleet airplane jet angels jets show air plane unitedairlines sfbayarea crowd boeing airshow	10/7/2010~ 10/11/2010	

many images which are uploaded by only few persons at a special time interval. Although our approach considers the user information, yet under this extreme occasion, the UT value is also very large, which leads to wrongly detection of them as events.

4   Conclusions

In this paper, we have proposed a new scheme named Landmark Timeline Construction (LTC) to automatically mine and select the diverse images on historical event of a landmark. In this scheme, a new time interval selection algorithm was presented to handle the limitation of the existing methods which depend on a fixed time interval by seeking the optimal ones. Also, the experimental results have demonstrated the effectiveness of our method. In our future work, we will apply the proposed scheme into tour recommendation and visualization.

Acknowledgement. This work was supported by National Program on Key Basic Research Project (973 Program, Project No. 2012CB316304), the National Natural Science Foundation of China (Grant No. 61201374, 90920303, 61003161), China Postdoctoral Science Foundation (Grant No. 2011M500430).

References

1. Chen, C.C., Chen, Y.-T., Sun, Y., Chen, M.C.: Life Cycle Modeling of News Events Using Aging Theory. In: Lavrač, N., Gamberger, D., Todorovski, L., Blockeel, H. (eds.) ECML 2003. LNCS (LNAI), vol. 2837, pp. 47–59. Springer, Heidelberg (2003)
2. Chen, K., Luesukprasert, L., Chou, S., et al.: Hot topic extraction based on timeline analysis and multidimensional sentence modeling. IEEE Transactions on Knowledge and Data Engineering 19(8), 1016–1025 (2007)
3. Chen, L., Roy, A.: Event detection from flickr data through wavelet-based spatial analysis. In: Proceedings of the 18th ACM Conference on Information and Knowledge Management, pp. 523–532. ACM (2009)
4. Crandall, D., Backstrom, L., Huttenlocher, D., Kleinberg, J.: Mapping the world's photos. In: Proceedings of the 18th International Conference on World Wide Web, pp. 761–770. ACM (2009)
5. Fellbaum, C.: Wordnet. In: Theory and Applications of Ontology: Computer Applications, pp. 231–243 (2010)
6. He, J., Li, M., Zhang, H., Tong, H., Zhang, C.: Manifold-ranking based image retrieval. In: Proceedings of the 12th Annual ACM International Conference on Multimedia, pp. 9–16. ACM (2004)
7. Kennedy, L., Naaman, M.: Generating diverse and representative image search results for landmarks. In: Proceeding of the 17th International Conference on World Wide Web, pp. 297–306. ACM (2008)
8. Kennedy, L., Naaman, M., Ahern, S., Nair, R., Rattenbury, T.: How flickr helps us make sense of the world: context and content in community-contributed media collections. In: Proceedings of the 15th International Conference on Multimedia, pp. 631–640. ACM (2007)
9. Rattenbury, T., Good, N., Naaman, M.: Towards automatic extraction of event and place semantics from flickr tags. In: Proceedings of the 30th Annual International ACM SIGIR Conference on Research and Development in Information Retrieval, pp. 103–110. ACM (2007)
10. Rudinac, S., Hanjalic, A., Larson, M.: Finding representative and diverse community contributed images to create visual summaries of geographic areas. In: Proceedings of the 19th ACM International Conference on Multimedia, pp. 1109–1112. ACM (2011)
11. Wang, M., Yang, K., Hua, X., Zhang, H.: Towards a relevant and diverse search of social images. IEEE Transactions on Multimedia 12(8), 829–842 (2010)
12. Weyand, T., Leibe, B.: Discovering favorite views of popular places with iconoid shift. In: 2011 IEEE International Conference on Computer Vision, ICCV, pp. 1132–1139. IEEE (2011)
13. Yang, D., Powers, D.: Measuring semantic similarity in the taxonomy of wordnet. In: Proceedings of the Twenty-Eighth Australasian Conference on Computer Science, vol. 38, pp. 315–322. Australian Computer Society, Inc. (2005)
14. Yang, Y., Pierce, T., Carbonell, J.: A study of retrospective and on-line event detection. In: Proceedings of the 21st Annual International ACM SIGIR Conference on Research and Development in Information Retrieval, pp. 28–36. ACM (1998)
15. Zheng, Y., Zhao, M., Song, Y., Adam, H., Buddemeier, U., Bissacco, A., Brucher, F., Chua, T., Neven, H.: Tour the world: building a web-scale landmark recognition engine. In: IEEE Conference on Computer Vision and Pattern Recognition, CVPR 2009, pp. 1085–1092. IEEE (2009)

Image Ranking via Attribute Boosted Hypergraph

Zhou Yu, Siliang Tang, Yin Zhang, and Jian Shao

College of Computer Science, Zhejiang University
Hangzhou, 310027, P.R. China
{yuz,jshao,zhangyin98}@zju.edu.cn, siliang.tang@gmail.com

Abstract. Recently, the visual attribute of images is becoming a research focus in computer vision and multimedia retrieval areas due to
its describable or human-nameable nature for image understanding. In
this paper, the visual attribute is utilized to boost the result of image
ranking. To well modeling the images along with their visual attributes,
hypergraph is used to integrate the visual attributes with low-level features of images. After that, we perform a ranking algorithm on the hypergraph. The experiment conducted on Animal with Attribute(AwA)
dataset demonstrate the effectiveness of our proposed approach.

Keywords: Visual Attribute, Hypergraph, Image Ranking.

1   Introduction

With the rapid growth of Internet, increasing amount of image data are available
every moment. How to retrieve similar images among these data is becoming a
significant challenge. Traditional retrieval method is based on the manually annotated labels or tags around the images. Under this setting, image retrieval
problem is converted to traditional text retrieval problem. However, this strategy is becoming more and more difficult as the number of unlabeled images
grows exponentially and even most annotated tags are somehow incorrect or
meaningless.

Content-based image retrieval (CBIR) or query-by-example (QBE) is implemented for a long time for image retrieval in past years. For content-based image
retrieval, the extracted visual features are compared to find most similar images
from the database. Hence, the accuracy of the retrieval heavily depends on the
representation of features. However, it has been observed that there exists a semantic gap between high-level label features and low-level visual features [18].
To improve the accuracy of query results in human understanding, it is better
to introduce some other additional cues for image retrieval.

In recent years, *visual attributes* have become a major focus in computer vision
and multimedia retrieval areas. Differ from high-level manually annotated tags
and low-level extracted visual features, visual attributes are commonly regarded
as a middle-level cue that are able to bridge low-level image features and high-
level object classes. It has been demonstrated that visual attributes are beneficial
for improving the performance of image understanding [9, 15].

W. Lin et al. (Eds.): PCM 2012, LNCS 7674, pp. 779–789, 2012.

As demonstrated in [11], the CBIR problem can be formulated as a hypergraph ranking problem, in which images are taken as vertices in a weighted hypergraph. Taking each image as a 'centroid' vertex, each hyperedge is formed by a centroid and its k-nearest neighbours in the low-level feature space. The retrieval procedure starts with an user feedback or an active learning step. After the feedback images are provided, a transductive inference approach is executed and return the final ranked results.

In this paper, we focus on the problem of how to improve the hypergraph ranking performance. We propose an attribute boosted hypergraph. Specifically, when constructing hypergraph, besides the correlations of images, the visual attributes of images are also considered in order to boost the understanding of images and improve ranking result. Given an image dataset, a visual attribute can be taken as a high-order relation shared by a group of images, therefore it is natural to construct a hyperedge in the hypergraph to encode the high-order relation by a shared visual attribute among images. That is to say, all the images with a same visual attribute are associated with a hyperedge.

Unlike the high-level conceptual tags and low-level visual features, visual attributes are describable, for example, "*bear*" and "*gorilla*" may share the same visual attribute "*black*" even they do not belong to a same category. Nevertheless, two images sharing the same attribute may have distinct semantics. To make the visual attribute relationship more quantitatively precise, when assigning a visual attribute to a image, a relative score could be also used to describe the degree of a image belonging to a given visual attribute. During the construction of hypergraph by visual attributes, the values of visual attributes are not binary (has an attribute or has not an attribute). On the contrary, each visual attribute is divided into several levels. For example, the attribute "*black*" can be divided into several levels, such as "*very black*", "*black*", "*a little black*" and "*not black*" according to the relative score of each image sharing this visual attribute. A hyperedge is generated to associate all of images with the same level of a given visual attribute. We argue that the introduction of visual attributes could boost image retrieval since visual attributes actually encode a high-order correlation between images.

The rest of the paper is organized as follows. In section 2, we review the related work on attribute learning and hypergraph ranking . In section 3, we present our attribute boosted hypergraph and ranking algorithm . In section 4, we demonstrate the performance of our algorithm on benchmark dataset. The conclusion and future work are given in the last section.

2   Related Work

2.1   Attribute Learning

Due to the characteristic of human-nameable of visual attribute, attribute-based algorithm has shown excellent effect in object recognition and image understanding. Attribute is used to strengthen face verification [14], object recognition [8], generating natural language descriptions from unfamiliar images [13], facilitation of "zero-shot" transfer learning [15], and prediction of the relative strength of an attribute with respect to other novel images [17]. For examples, [15] proposed direct attribute prediction (DAP) and indirect attribute prediction (IAP) for attribute-based classification by transferring information between disjoint training and test classes.

In this paper, we are interested in the utilization of visual attributes to encode the high-order correlations among images for image ranking and retrieval.

2.2   Graph and Hypergraph Construction

Graph is a foundational structure to describe the correlations between objects. A hypergraph is a graph in which one edge (hyperedge) can connect more than two vertices. This characteristic enables the hypergraph to represent complex and higher-order relations which are difficult to be represented in traditional undirected or directed graphs.

In many real-world problems, hypergraph is commonly used. social media computing, machine learning, IC design [12] and parallel computing [7, 10].

2.3   Graph and Hypergraph Ranking Algorithm

Our work is related to graph and hypergraph ranking algorithms [1, 2, 6, 20, 21].

In [21], a manifold ranking algorithm is proposed with respect to the geometrical structure of data. Random walking on a weighted graph is performed and stops at a stable state. In [2], utilizing the weighted graph like [21], a ranking function is regularized.

In recent years, hypergraph is becoming a research focus due to its outstanding expression on high order information. In [6], a hypergraph clustering algorithm based on high order similarity is proposed. In [20], a integrated methodology of hypergraph is generalized, including normalized cut, random walk, spectral partitioning, transductive inference on hypergraph. Inspired by [20], ranking algorithm on hypergraph are proposed in [5, 11].

3   Attribute Boosted Hypergraph

3.1   Notation and Problem Definitions

Assume that we have a image dataset X containing n images, on each image, visual features are extracted for each image in X and generate a feature matrix $F \in \mathbb{R}^{n \times d}$ where d is the dimension of extracted feature. Additional, a visual attribute set $\mathcal{A}$ containing m human-named visual attributes are generated. For each image(category) in X, if it's labeled by a visual attribute $a \in \mathcal{A}$, a relative score indicating the degree on this visual attribute is set. Thus, a image(category)-attribute matrix C is obtained. As described in section 1, each visual attribute can be divided into several levels. The number of levels of visual attributes is l and the C is quantized to C_l. According to the visual attributes and low-level visual features, we can utilize hyperedge to encode the high-order correlation between images by visual attributes and low-level features, and construct a hypergraph.

Let $G(V, E, w)$ denote a hypergraph where V is the set of vertices, E is the set of hyperedges, w is the weights for each hyperedge. Each hyperedge $e \in E$ connects a subset of V to encode a certain high-order correlation among images, its degree is defined as $\delta(e) = |e|$, that is, the cardinally of e. For a vertex $v \in V$, its degree is defined as $d(v) = \sum_{e \in E | v \in e} w(e)$. We then define an incidence matrix $H \in \mathbb{R}^{|V| \times |E|}$ whose element $h(v, e)$ is set to a certain value if $v \in e$ and 0 otherwise. Then the degree of each vertex and each hyperedge are re-defined as follows:

$$d(v) = \sum_{e \in E} w(e) h(v, e) \tag{1}$$

$$\delta(e) = \sum_{v \in V} h(v, e) \tag{2}$$

$D_e \in \mathbb{R}^{|E| \times |E|}$, $D_v \in \mathbb{R}^{|V| \times |V|}$ and $W \in \mathbb{R}^{|E| \times |E|}$ denote the three diagonal matrices consisting of degrees of hyperedges, degrees of vertices and hyperedge weights.

Our attribute boosted hypergraph has *one* kind of vertices and *two* kinds of hyperedges. That is to say, each vertex is denoted as a image, and two kinds of hyperedge connects a set of vertices (images) when those vertices (images) are visually similar or have a same visual attribute with a same level.

The schema of our attribute boosted hypergraph ranking is as follows: given a query vertex q from V, other vertices are initially ranked according to their correlations to the query q. Assume that query vector $q = [q_1, q_2, ..., q_{i-1}, q_i, q_{i+1}, ...q_{|V|}]^T$, and q_i denotes the query image's index in V and is set to 1. Unlike the settings in [5, 11], the query vector q has only 1 nonzero element in our application since the input query is a single image. $f = [f_1, f_2, ..., f_{|V|}]^T$ are the corresponding ranked score learned from transductive inference on the hypergraph [20]. The motivation of hypergraph ranking is to find most of favorite images to query q.

3.2   The Construction of Attribute Boosted Hypergraph

As discussed before, the visually similar images can be associated by a hyperedge. In this paper, visual attributes are also utilized to form hyperedges connecting the images with a same visual attribute level for the construction of hypergraph. In our hypergraph, two kinds of hyperedges E^1 and E^2 are defined in hypergraph, e.g., $E = E^1 \bigcup E^2$. The detail of two kinds of hyperedges are explained as follows:

- *Visual attribute hyperedge E^1*: edges in set E^1 connect the vertices (images) that has a same attribute with a same level. Since each attribute $a \in \mathcal{A}$ is divided into m levels, given each level of an attribute, a hyperedge is constructed to denote the correlations between a certain attribute. By this way, we obtain attribute hyperedge set E^1, $|E^1| = m * l$. All hyperedges in E^1 has equivalent importance. Hence, We set weights to all of them to be 1.

- *low-level feature similarity hyperedge E^2*: edges in set E^2 connect the images that are visually similar. We take each images as a *centroid* vertex and construct a hyperedge by itself and its k-nearest neighbours, $|E^2| = |V|$. To maintain the relative similarity within every two vertices, the *probabilistic hypergraph* method [11] is conducted in this paper.

Same as E^1 and E^2, two kinds of overall incidence matrix H can be also defined: the incidence matrix of visual attribute H^1 and the incidence matrix of low-level visual similarity H^2.

H^1 is defined as:

$$H^1(v_i, e_j) = \begin{cases} 1 & \text{if } v_i \in e_j \\ 0 & \text{otherwise} \end{cases} \tag{3}$$

For incidence matrix of visual attribute H^1, each vertex v_i is assigned to a hyperedge e_j with a binary value since every vertex is connected by a hyperedge is of equivalent importance. However, for the incidence matrix of low-level visual similarity H^2, since the k-nearest neighbours of each vertex v_i is at different degree of importance, the *probabilistic* incidence matrix is conducted to obtain

$$H^2(v_i, e_j) = \begin{cases} A(j, i) & \text{if } v_i \in e_j \\ 0 & \text{otherwise} \end{cases} \tag{4}$$

Here, A is the affinity matrix that $A(i, j) = exp(-\frac{Dis(i,j)}{\overline{D}})$. $Dis(i, j)$ denotes the metric distance of two vertices at visual feature space and $\overline{D}$ the average distance.

The final incidence matrix H is integrated with the two incidence matrices H^1 and H^2, i.e., $H = [H^1 \quad H^2] \in \mathbb{R}^{|V| \times (|E^1| + |E^2|)}$.

The corresponding D_v, D_e and W are respectively defined as:

$$W = \begin{bmatrix} W^1 & 0 \\ 0 & \lambda W^2 \end{bmatrix} \qquad D_v = \begin{bmatrix} D_v^1 & 0 \\ 0 & D_v^2 \end{bmatrix} \qquad D_e = \begin{bmatrix} D_e^1 & 0 \\ 0 & D_e^2 \end{bmatrix} \tag{5}$$

where $\lambda > 0$ is the regularization parameter which controls the influence of attribute hyperedges.

3.3 Attribute Boosted Hypergraph Ranking

Some researches have shown how to perform ranking on hypergraph [5, 11, 20]. The cost function can be defined as:

$$\begin{aligned} \Omega(f) &= \frac{1}{2} \sum_{e \in E} \sum_{u, v \in e} \frac{w(e)h(u,e)h(v,2)}{\delta(e)} \left|\left| \frac{f(u)}{\sqrt{d(u)}} - \frac{f(v)}{\sqrt{d(v)}} \right|\right|^2 + \mu \|f - q\|^2 \\ &= \sum_{u \in V} f^2(u) \sum_{e \in E} \frac{w(e)h(u,e)}{d(u)} \sum_{v \in E} \frac{h(v,e)}{\delta(e)} + \mu \|f - q\|^2 \\ &= - \sum_{e \in E} \sum_{u, v \in e} \frac{f(u)h(u,e)w(e)h(v,e)f(v)}{\sqrt{d(u)d(v)}\delta(e)} + \mu \|f - q\|^2 \end{aligned} \tag{6}$$

where $\mu > 0$ is a regularization parameter and ranked score vector f is obtained when $\Omega(f)$ is minimized. Substitute Equation 1,2 into 6 and defining a matrix $\Lambda = D_v^{-\frac{1}{2}} HWDe^{-1}H^T D_v^{-\frac{1}{2}}$, Equation 6 can be rewrite as follows:

$$\Omega(f) = f^T(I - \Lambda)f + \mu\|f - q\|^2 \tag{7}$$

Differentiating $\Omega(f)$, we have

$$f = \frac{\mu}{1+\mu}(I - \frac{\mu}{1+\mu}\Lambda)^{-1}q \tag{8}$$

Thus, when the query vector q is taken as a input, after transductive inference on the hypergraph, we can obtain the expected ranked score vector f. In the end, we sort f in descending order, the favorite images to the query q can be found.

To summarize, the overall procedure of our attribute boosted hypergraph ranking algorithm is shown in Algorithm 1

Algorithm 1. Attribute boosted Hypergraph Ranking

Input: feature matrix F; quantitative image-attribute correlation matrix C_l; k is the number of in the k-nearest neighbours affnity matrix construction; query vector q

Output: ranked score vector f to query q

1. Construct affinity matrix A for F by calculating k-nearest neighbours.
2. Construct E^1 with the matrix C_l, construct E^2 with the affinity matrix we obtain in Step 1.
3. Construct H^1 and H^2 using Equation 3 and 4, $H = [H^1 \ H^2]$.
4. Calculate D_v, D_e, W using Equation 5 and then compute Λ.

return ranked score vector f by Equation 8.

---

4   Experimental Results

In this section, we evaluate the performance of our attribute boosted hypergraph ranking and compare it with other state-of-the-art hypergraph based ranking algorithms.

4.1   DataSet and Evaluation Criterion

To evaluate the performance of our proposed algorithm, we conduct experiments on a real-world image dataset Animals with Attributes(AwA) [15].

AwA contains 30475 images of 50 animal categories and 85 visual attributes. Each image is labeled by a category and corresponding relate visual attributes, each visual attribute with a relative score is assigned to each category. For each images, 6 kinds of visual features are extracted: 2,688-D Color Histogram, 252-D HOG [4], 2,000-D LSS [18], 2,000-D SIFT [16], 2,000-D RGSIFT [19], 2000-D SURF [3] descriptors.

To evaluate the performance of ranking result. We use the *precision vs scope* and *precision vs recall* curves similar with [11].

The ground truth is defined as : for each query image, we calculate its Euclidean distance with all images in the database by their visual features and return the k-nearest neighbours.

4.2 Experimental Setup

For the AwA dataset with 30,475 images, we build a hypergraph. To compare with our proposed attribute boosted probabilistic hypergraph ranking algorithm(APHR), another 2 types of hypergraph ranking algorithms are implemented: one is traditional hypergraph ranking with hyperedges on low-level visual features (HR), that is to say, incidence matrix is binary; the other one is probabilistic hypergraph with hyperedges on low-level visual features (PHR) and the elementss in incidence matrix are probabilistic. Additionally, we implement a attribute boosted HR algorithm (the incidence matrix H^2 is binary) and name it AHR.

For the traditional HR and PHR, the visual feature hyperedges are defined as: for each *centroid* image, its 49 nearest neighbours along with it form a hyperedges. That is, the cardinally of each hyperedge is 50.

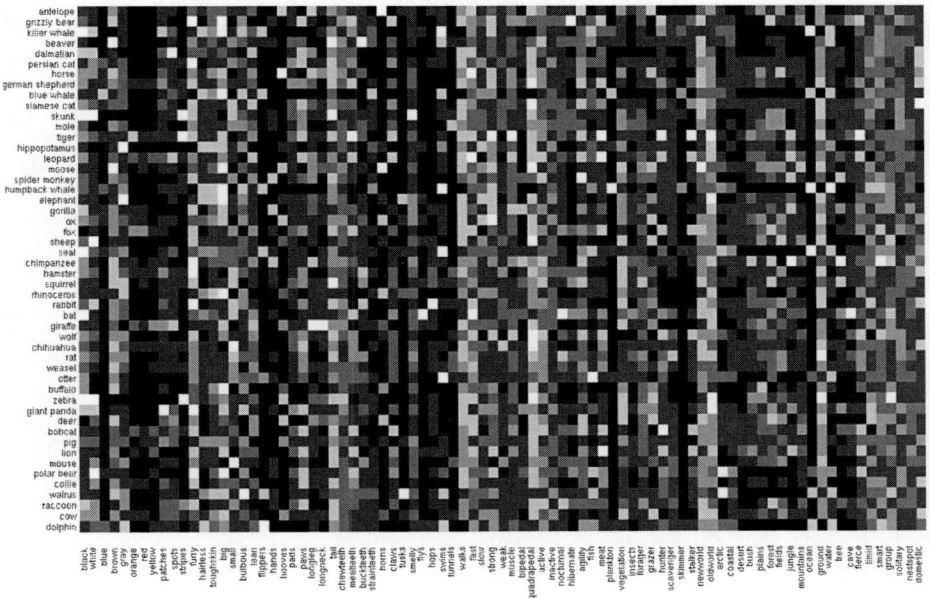

Fig. 1. Category-attribute matrix of AwA dataset. The colors show the degree of the visual attribute on the corresponding category. If it's dark, the category has a weak association with this visual attribute and otherwise, the association is strong.

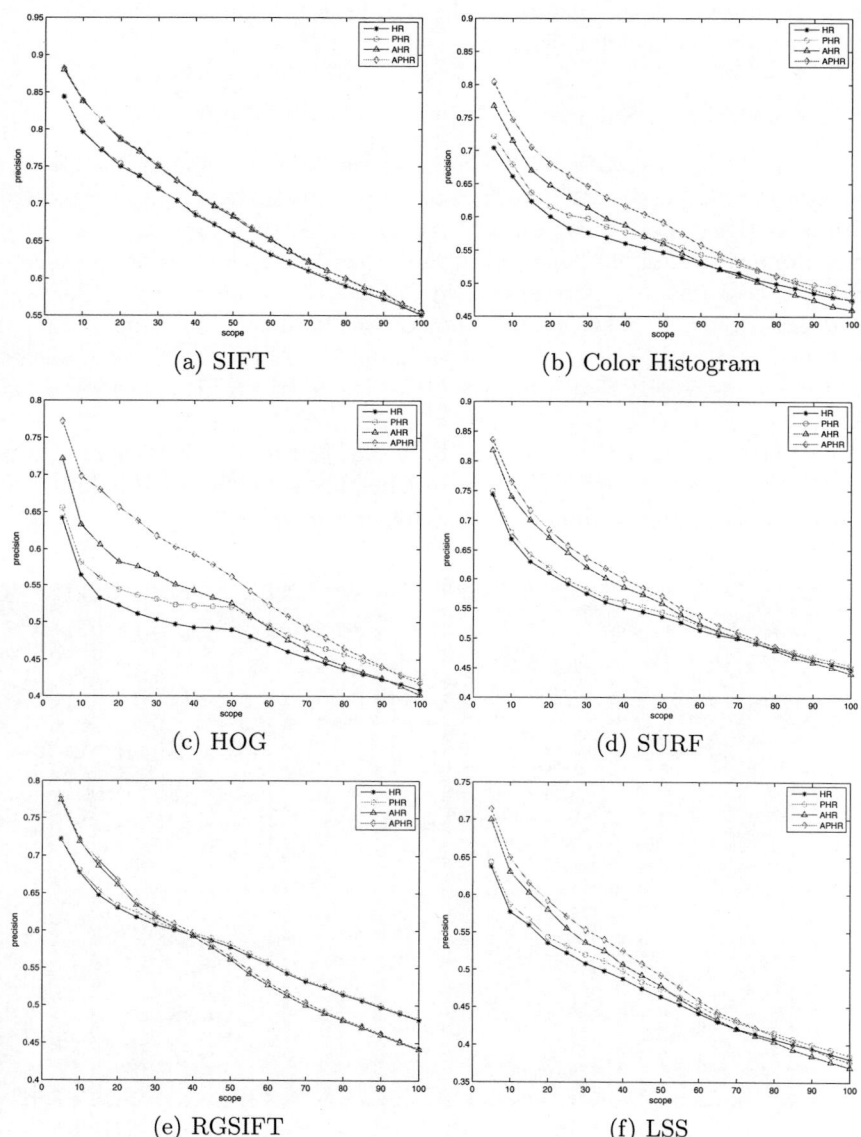

Fig. 2. *Precision vs scope* curve for different type of visual features on the ground truth of k-nearest neighbours

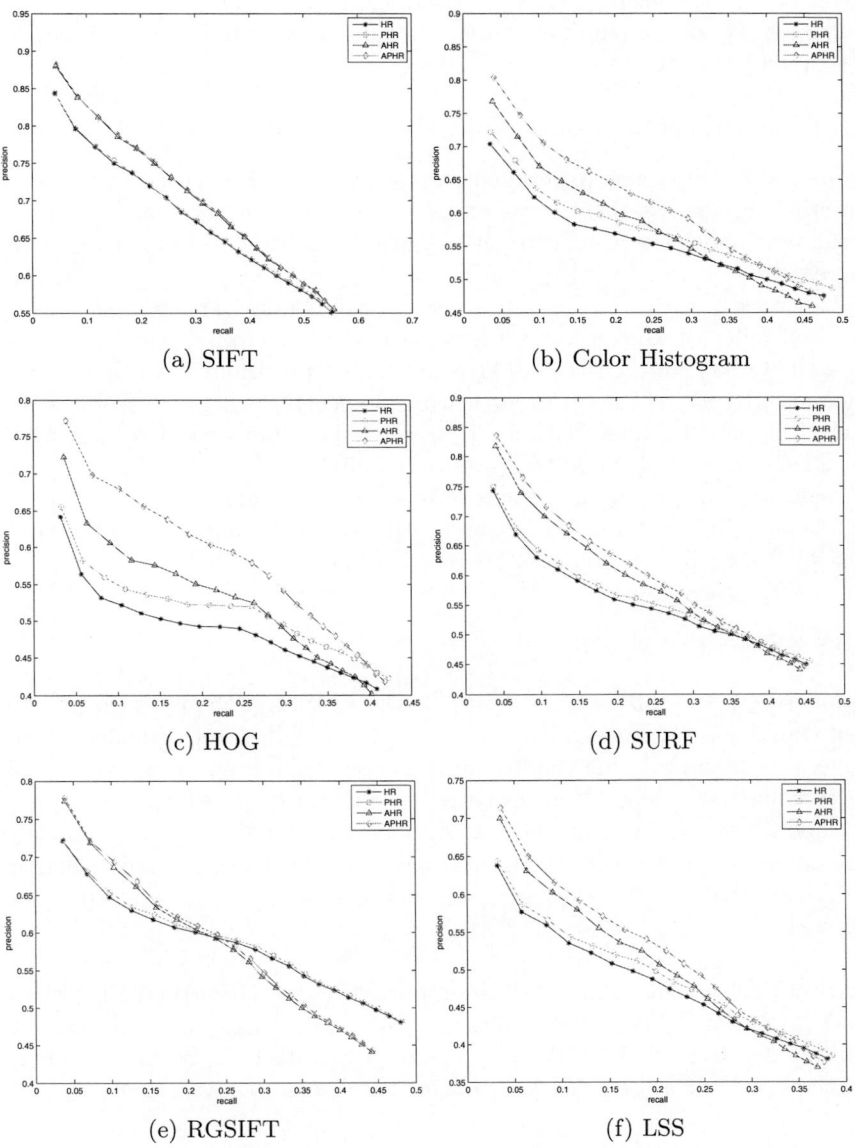

Fig. 3. *Precision vs recall* curve for different type of visual features on the ground truth of k-nearest neighbours

For our attribute boosted AHR and APHR, the visual attribute hyperedges are defined as: for each visual attribute, it's divided into 6 levels and the category-attribute matrix is shown in Fig 1. Since the AwA dataset has 85 visual attribute, we get totally 510 visual attribute hyperedges.

The regularization parameter μ is set to 0.5 as used in [5] and λ is set to 0.4 as a tuned parameter.

4.3   Experimental Results Analysis

We perform comparison experiments on different type of visual features under two criterions: *precision vs scope* and *precision vs recall*. For each criterion, we calculate it under the ground truth of k-nearest neighbours. Finally, we analyze the result.

The scope ranges from 5 $\sim$ 100 nearest neighbours. The *precision vs scope* curves of different kinds of visual features under the ground truth is as follows: Fig 2 show that our APHR and AHR get higher precisions than the traditional HR and PHR algorithm on every feature. Especially when the scope is within a relatively small radius (within 20), our attribute boosted algorithms: APHR and AHR are 3% $\sim$ 10% better than the traditional HR and PHR.

Then, we demonstrate the result of *precision vs recall* curves:

As shown in Fig 3, out APHR and AHR algorithm outperform the HR and PHR by 2% $\sim$ 10% on precision for recall < 0.2.

5   Conclusion

In this paper, we propose an attribute boosted hypergraph approach to improve image ranking performance. By introducing the middle-level visual attributes on images, the high-order information in the hypergraph is enriched which leads to a better understanding of images correlation and a more precise ranking result. We conduct experiments on the real *Animal with Attribute* (AwA) dataset and compare our approach with the traditional hypergraph ranking algorithms without visual attributes. The result demonstrates the effectiveness of our proposed approach.

Acknowledgement. This work is supported by the HEGAOJI Project under grant No.2010ZX01042-002-003-001, the National Natural Science Foundation of China No. 61105074, 61103099, the China Postdoctoral Science Foundation, and the Fundamental Research Funds for the Central Universities.

References

1. Agarwal, S.: Ranking on graph data. In: Machine Learning International Workshop Then Conference, vol. 23, p. 25 (2006)
2. Agarwal, S., Branson, K., Belongie, S.: Higher order learning with graphs. In: Proceedings of the 23rd International Conference on Machine Learning, ICML, pp. 17–24. ACM (2006)

3. Bay, H., Tuytelaars, T., Van Gool, L.: SURF: Speeded Up Robust Features. In: Leonardis, A., Bischof, H., Pinz, A. (eds.) ECCV 2006, Part I. LNCS, vol. 3951, pp. 404–417. Springer, Heidelberg (2006)
4. Bosch, A., Zisserman, A., Munoz, X.: Representing shape with a spatial pyramid kernel. In: Proceedings of the 6th ACM International Conference on Image and Video Retrieval, pp. 401–408. ACM (2007)
5. Bu, J., Tan, S., Chen, C., Wang, C., Wu, H., Zhang, L., He, X.: Music recommendation by unified hypergraph: combining social media information and music content. In: Proceedings of the International Conference on Multimedia, pp. 391–400. ACM (2010)
6. Bulò, S.R., Pelillo, M.: A game-theoretic approach to hypergraph clustering. In: Advances in Neural Information Processing Systems, NIPS, vol. 22, pp. 1571–1579 (2009)
7. Catalyürek, Ü.V., Aykanat, C.: Hypergraph model for mapping repeated sparse matrix-vector product computations onto multicomputers (1995)
8. Farhadi, A., Endres, I., Hoiem, D.: Attribute-centric recognition for cross-category generalization. In: IEEE Conference on Computer Vision and Pattern Recognition, CVPR, pp. 2352–2359. IEEE (2010)
9. Ferrari, V., Zisserman, A.: Learning visual attributes. In: Advances in Neural Information Processing Systems, NIPS (2008)
10. Hendrickson, B., Kolda, T.G.: Graph partitioning models for parallel computing. Parallel Computing 26(12), 1519–1534 (2000)
11. Huang, Y., Liu, Q., Zhang, S., Metaxas, D.N.: Image retrieval via probabilistic hypergraph ranking. In: IEEE Conference on Computer Vision and Pattern Recognition, CVPR, pp. 3376–3383. IEEE (2010)
12. Karypis, G., Aggarwal, R., Kumar, V., Shekhar, S.: Multilevel hypergraph partitioning: applications in vlsi domain. IEEE Transactions on Very Large Scale Integration Systems, VLSI 7(1), 69–79 (1999)
13. Kulkarni, G., Premraj, V., Dhar, S., Li, S., Choi, Y., Berg, A.C., Berg, T.L.: Baby talk: Understanding and generating simple image descriptions. In: IEEE Conference on Computer Vision and Pattern Recognition, CVPR, pp. 1601–1608. IEEE (2011)
14. Kumar, N., Berg, A., Belhumeur, P., Nayar, S.: Describable visual attributes for face verification and image search. IEEE Transactions on Pattern Analysis and Machine Intelligence, PAMI (99), 1 (2011)
15. Lampert, C.H., Nickisch, H., Harmeling, S.: Learning to detect unseen object classes by between-class attribute transfer. In: IEEE Conference on Computer Vision and Pattern Recognition, CVPR, pp. 951–958. IEEE (2009)
16. Lowe, D.G.: Distinctive image features from scale-invariant keypoints. International Journal of Computer Vision, IJCV 60(2), 91–110 (2004)
17. Osherson, D.N., Stern, J., Wilkie, O., Stob, M., Smith, E.E.: Default probability. Cognitive Science 15(2), 251–269 (1991)
18. Shechtman, E., Irani, M.: Matching local self-similarities across images and videos. In: IEEE Conference on Computer Vision and Pattern Recognition, CVPR, pp. 1–8. IEEE (2007)
19. Van de Sande, K., Gevers, T., Snoek, C.: Evaluation of color descriptors for object and scene recognition. In: IEEE Conference on Computer Vision and Pattern Recognition, CVPR, pp. 1–8. IEEE (2008)
20. Zhou, D., Huang, J., Scholkopf, B.: Learning with hypergraphs: Clustering, classification, and embedding. In: Advances in Neural Information Processing Systems, NIPS, vol. 19, p. 1601 (2007)
21. Zhou, D., Weston, J., Gretton, A., Bousquet, O., Schölkopf, B.: Ranking on data manifolds. In: Advances in Neural Information Processing Systems, NIPS, vol. 16, pp. 169–176 (2004)

Structural Context-Aware Cross Media Recommendation

Zhenming Yuan, Kai Yu, Jia Zhang, and Hong Pan

School of Information Science and Engineering,
Hangzhou Normal University,
310036 Hangzhou, China
{zmyuan,yk,zhangjia,chin}@hznu.edu.cn

Abstract. Traditional tensor factorization based context-aware collaborative filtering considers the context as homogeneous ones, which uses vectorization to implement the factorization as the single context version while ignoring many structural interactions between the heterogeneous contexts. However, cross media data in digital libraries have common and distinctive context, which can be used to discover the latent structural grouping semantics to improve the diversity of recommendation. In this paper, we propose a structural context-aware feature selection framework for cross media recommendation. Firstly, the TUCKER based tensor factorization is conducted on the N-dimensional user-item-content tensor. Then the hidden structural representation are defined as the solution of the structural sparse coding with the loss function by regularizing the terms according to some principle context components, which are optimally selected by the structural grouping sparsity (MtBGS) method. Finally, the top n items with the highest n prediction probabilities are recommended for specific user. Experiments conducted on a cross media dataset based on Douban.com show the effectiveness of diversity for cross media recommendation.

Keywords: Structural Grouping Sparsity, Cross Media Recommendation, Tensor Factorization, Feature Selection.

1   Introduction

There are huge collections of heterogeneous media data from social Web sites, digital libraries, and mobile internet Apps. Many social behaviors can be reflected by integrating these heterogeneous media data, which also can be used to provide cross media recommendations. For examples, Amazon would like to recommend not only the books, but also the relevant videos and electronics, etc. In the social Web site, like Douban.com, the users in the social networks share and comment the books, the movies, and the music, as well as are willing to read the recommendations across these three types of data. Different from the traditional collaborative filtering-based or content-based single media recommendation systems, in such cross-media recommendation system, the recommended items may come from different data sources. The recommendation results do not need to be of the same media type the user ever visited or tagged. For example, the user once read the book "Facebook: The Missing Manual", then the system may recommend the movie "The social network".

W. Lin et al. (Eds.): PCM 2012, LNCS 7674, pp. 790–800, 2012.
© Springer-Verlag Berlin Heidelberg 2012

From the view of recommendation data, current commercial recommendations can be classified into three types [1]: collaborative filtering based recommendation [2], content based recommendation[3], and hybrid based recommendation, in which collaborative filtering based method is the most popular one. From the view of algorithms, there are neighbor-based, graph-based, and matrix factorization-based recommendation algorithms [4]. In order to improve the accuracy of recommendation, lots of features representing context prior have been included [5], which usually have high dimensionality, high order, and large scale. Those high-dimensional features are often composed of different types of media data interrelated everywhere, and may describe various aspects of characteristics. However, most of the recommendation systems only consider the features as the homogenous ones, as well as lack of the ability of recommendation across different media sources. The recommendation of different types of item in the commercial systems, such as Amazon, is only based on the habits of users' actions, while ignoring the implicit content of the items.

In recent years, cross-domain recommendation began to be concerned [6]. In this area, the definition of cross-domain recommendation is to recommend the items or users in a target domain system referenced by the recommend model discovered in a source domain system. There are two categories of cross-domain recommendation methods. One is to combine the two domain systems into one system, and make recommendation using the traditional one-domain method [7]. The other is to use transfer learning to construct the bridge from source domain to target domain [8]. Usually, both of them face the problems of partly overlap of the items and the users.

Actually there is one category of recommendation systems, in which there is one user group with different groups of items. We call such system as the cross media recommendation. In those systems, different users may favor in different types of media data. Here, each group of media data can have its own features, while different groups can also share some common characteristics. For example, in the digital library, there are rich types of digitalized media data, such as the books, the movies, and the pictures. At the same time, different user in the digital library may focus on one or more types of media data, which usually have different characteristics or metadata, as well as many common attributes, such as the title, the authors, the tags, the ratings, and the publish or product year, etc. One of the essential challenges to be solved in cross media recommendation is to make recommendation of different types of media data for specific persons to maximize the diversity of media types as well as keeping good recommendation accuracy. To get such goal, we should discover the relations and interactions among the different features of the cross media data, and settle the sparsity and the high-dimensional heterogeneous features problems simultaneously.

In this paper, a structural context-aware feature selection framework for cross media recommendation is proposed. Firstly, the TUCKER based tensor factorization is conducted on the user-item-content tensor. Then the hidden structural representation is defined as the solution of the structural sparse coding with the loss function by regularizing the terms according to some principle context components. We recommend the top n items with the highest n prediction probability estimated by kNN clustering.

The remainder of the paper is organized as follows. In section 2, we first introduce the problem setting for cross media recommendation and the tensor factorization model for latent cross media feature modeling. In section 3, we describe how to find the probability prediction for users by learning the structural sparse-based feature selection using the selection of heterogeneous features with multi-label boosting by structural grouping sparsity (MtBGS) method [10]. We experimentally validate the effectiveness and the diversity of the algorithm for cross media recommendation in Section 4 and conclude the paper in Section 5.

2 Representation and Factorization of Cross Media Data

2.1 Tensor Representation of Cross Media Data

Without loss of generality, we consider there are two types of media data set in the recommendation system, $\mathbf{X}_A$ and $\mathbf{X}_B$, which are two feature matrixes for two homogeneous media data. There are n items in $\mathbf{X}_A=\{x_i, i=1,\ldots,n\}$, where $x_i=\{x_{i1},\ldots,x_{it_A}\}$ represents the t_A features (tags) of each item x_i. And there are also m items with t_B features in $\mathbf{X}_B$. It is reasonably that there are many common features (tags) among two features sets. So we fuse the two matrixes into one big feature matrix by preserving the heterogeneous features while extracting the homogeneous features, that is:

$$F = (F_A - F_A \cap F_B) \cup (F_B - F_A \cap F_B) \cup (F_A \cap F_B) \tag{1}$$

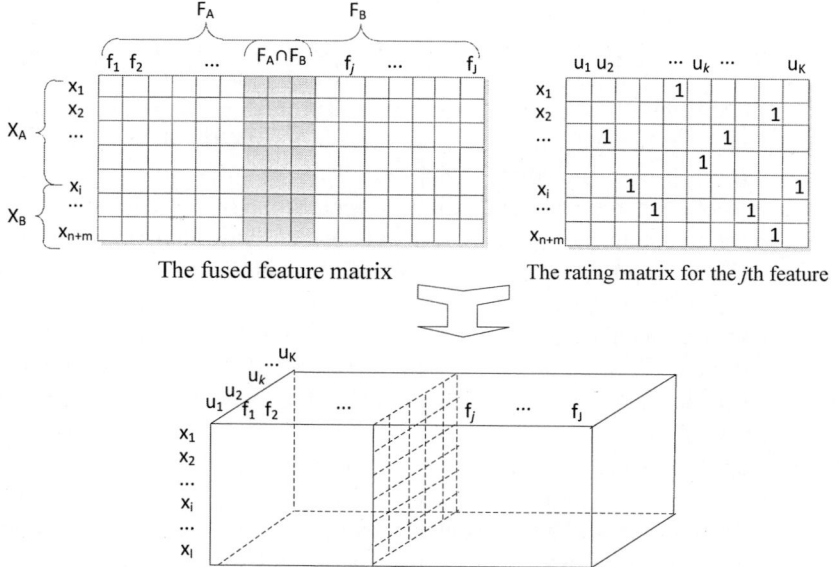

Fig. 1. The configuration of the 3-order cross-media tensor

where F is the feature set of the fused features, F_A and F_B are the feature sets of $\mathbf{X}_A$ and $\mathbf{X}_B$ separately. For example, in Douban.com social network Website, the features of the books are composed of title, authors, publisher, price, and thousands of tags, etc. While the features of the movies are composed of title, authors, director, actors, and thousands of tags, etc. We can find there are many common features, like title and authors, and there are also more different features, like actors and tags. The fused feature matrix concatenate two feature sets into one big feature set, and filled with the whole items. It is obviously there exists feature overlap between two item sets, which can be used to construct the bridge for cross media data.

In addition to the feature matrix, the jth feature of the ith item is associated with K-dimensional rating vector, $y_i = \{y_{ij1}, \ldots, y_{ijK}\}^T \in \{0,1\}^K$, where $y_{ijk} = 1$ if the jth feature in the ith item has been rated by the kth user and $y_{ijk} = 0$ otherwise. Then we can build a tensor representation, $\mathcal{A}$, of the cross media data. Unlike the rating matrix in traditional collaborative filtering, a tensor is a multidimensional array. In our problem, 3-way or 3-order tensor is an element of the tensor product of three vector spaces, which are the user, the item, and the content feature coordinates.

2.2   Tensor Factorization Based on TUCKER Decomposition

In traditional model based collaborative filtering recommendation systems, the rating matrix can be decomposed into a sum of rank-1 matrices by SVD or Funk-SVD [23] methods, which is called Latent Factor Model (LFM). However, in this paper the cross media data is a high-order tensor or multidimensional array, which has the characteristics of sparsity and high-dimension. The tensor is very sparse because users' rating actions only cover little items with little tags. When we consider all of the tags and metadata as the features, the number of features, J, is much larger than the number of training items, I, and the number of users, K. Same with Latent Factor Model, sparse representation can play an important role in such problem. All of the heterogeneous features from different views or domains can be unified as a consensus representation for the cross-media semantics. And they also can be factorized into some latent spaces with structured sparsity that can be exploited to simultaneously learn a low-dimensional latent space [11].   There are two types of tensor decompositions used most in application. The first model is currently known as the CANDECOMP-PARAFAC (CP) model [12]. The second one is called TUCKER model [13]. Both of them can be considered as higher-order generalizations of the matrix SVD or PCA. Here, we use TUCKER model to factorize the cross media tensor.

Given the $I \times J \times K$ cross media tensor defined in Section 2.1, $\mathcal{A}$, the TUCKER model [13] is a decomposition of the form:

$$\mathcal{A} = \sum_{i=1}^{R_1} \sum_{j=1}^{R_2} \sum_{k=1}^{R_3} \delta_{ijk}(u_i \circ v_j \circ w_k) \tag{2}$$

where $R_1 \leq I, R_2 \leq J, R_3 \leq K, u_i \in \mathbb{R}^{R_1}, v_j \in \mathbb{R}^{R_2}, w_k \in \mathbb{R}^{R_3}$ for all i,j,k. The tensor, $\mathcal{S} = (\delta_{ijk})$, is called the *core tensor*. When the u_i, v_j, and w_k are columns from orthogonal matrices $\mathbf{U}, \mathbf{V}, \mathbf{W}$, the TUCKER model is referred to as the High-Order Singular Value Decomposition (HOSVD). By taking the SVD of each of the flattening matrices, the HOSVD always exists, and the approximate of the original tensor can be expressed as the n-mode multiplication of the *core tensor* with three orthogonal matrices:

$$\mathcal{A} = \mathcal{S} \times_1 \mathbf{U} \times_2 \mathbf{V} \times_3 \mathbf{W} \tag{3}$$

where $\mathcal{A}, \mathcal{S} \in \mathbb{R}^{I \times J \times K}$, $\mathbf{U} \in \mathbb{R}^{I \times I}$, $\mathbf{V} \in \mathbb{R}^{J \times J}$, $\mathbf{W} \in \mathbb{R}^{K \times K}$, and $\times_n$ operation is n-mode product. Such tensor algebra defines multi-linear operators over the set of vector spaces, which is composed of the item space, $\mathbf{U}$, the feature space, $\mathbf{V}$, and the user space $\mathbf{W}$. Further, the high-order interaction information in heterogeneous features can be captured based on the decomposition results.

3   Probability Prediction and Recommendation Based on Structural Sparse-Based Feature Selection

3.1   Structural Sparse-Based Feature Selection

The dimension of the features in recommendation system is very high, which lead to the pairwise correlation between the group of features is also very high. According to the former researches of natural image and video analysis, the user and item preferences of the recommendation system can be well approximated by a small subset of features from the large sparse cross media matrix. The process of finding a good latent interaction along with the subset of corresponding latent preference modeling features is known as sparse-based feature selection.

Many efficient approaches to find a sparse representation for the data have been developed in computer vision and multimedia retrieval. The basic idea of sparse-based feature selection is to impose a structural sparse penalty to select discriminative features [10,14,15]. One popular penalty is the $l1$-norm, also called *lasso*, least absolution shrinkage and selection operator [16], which makes the learning mode both sparse and interpretable. However, under the circumstances discussed above, *lasso* tends to individually select only one of the pairwise correlated features and does not induce the group effect. In our problem, the grouped feature is an important concern to facilitate a model's interpretability. For example, in heterogeneous cross-media features, a grouped feature represent on domain feature with homogeneous data. More recently, *elastic net* [17] and *group lasso* [18] are proposed to get the grouped features by imposing $l1$-norm and $l2$-norm penalties. However, the *group lasso* does not yield sparsity within a group. That is, if the selection coefficients of a group are nonzero, the selection coefficient of each feature within that group will all be nonzero. Motivated by Wu, *et al.* [19], we use a framework of multi-label boosting by the selection of heterogeneous features with structural grouping sparsity (MtBGS), which utilize the structure priors between heterogeneous and homogeneous features for latent cross media modeling.

3.2   Structural Sparse-Based Feature Selection Learning

As mentioned in section 2, three rank-1 tensors are factorized by TUCKER-based tensor decomposition, in which $\mathbf{U}$ represents the user preferences space, $\mathbf{V}$ represents the item preferences space, and W represents the context features space. In order to find the latent relationships among these spaces, we reconstruct the item-context feature matrix, $\mathbf{X}$, and the user-item rating indicator matrix, $\mathbf{Y}$, from the factorized spaces. The latent context correlation between the items and the features can be reconstructed in terms of the sum of the core tensor $\mathcal{S}$ multiplied by $\mathbf{U}$ and $\mathbf{V}$, as well as the latent rating correlation between the items and the users can be reconstructed in terms of the sum of the core tensor $\mathcal{S}$ multiplied by $\mathbf{V}$ and $\mathbf{W}$.

$$\mathbf{X} = \sum_{i=1}^{R_1} \sum_{j=1}^{R_2} \delta_{ijk}(\mathbf{u}_i °\mathbf{v}_j) \tag{4}$$

$$\mathbf{Y} = \sum_{i=1}^{R_1} \sum_{k=1}^{R_3} \delta_{ijk}(\mathbf{u}_i °\mathbf{w}_k) \tag{5}$$

where $\mathbf{X} \in \mathbb{R}^{I \times J}$, $\mathbf{Y} \in \mathbb{R}^{I \times K}$. Intuitively, $\mathbf{X} = \{\mathbf{x}_i, i = 1, ..., I\}$ represents the context features of total I items. Each item, such as the book, the movie, or the music, is associated with J-dimensional heterogeneous context feature,

$$\mathbf{x}_i = \{\mathbf{x}_{i1}, ..., \mathbf{x}_{iJ}\}^T \in \mathbb{R}^J \tag{6}$$

where J represents the dimensionality of features and is the dimension of F in equation (1). We consider $\mathbf{X}$ of I labeled items as the $I \times J$ training set to learn the sparse-based feature selection. At the same time, $\mathbf{Y} = \{y_j, j=1, ..., K\}$ and

$$y_j = \{y_{j1}, ..., y_{jK}\}^T \in \{0,1\}^K \tag{7}$$

represents the K-dimensional rating vector for jth items given by total K users. By taking the user's ratings as the labels, we consider matrix $\mathbf{Y}$ as the $I \times K$ rating label indicator matrix.

Suppose that the extracted J-dimensional heterogeneous features are divided into L disjoint groups of homogeneous features, with J_l the number of features in the lth group, $\sum_{l=1}^{L} J_l = J$. We use a matrix $\mathbf{X}_l \in R^{I \times J_l}$ to represent the features of the training data corresponding to the lth group, with corresponding coefficient vector $\beta_{kl} \in R^{J_l}$ ($l = 1, ..., L$) for the kth user.

Let $\beta_k = (\beta_{k1}^T, ..., \beta_{kL}^T)^T$ be the entire coefficient vector for the kth user, we have

$$\mathbf{X}\beta_k = \sum_{l=1}^{L} \mathbf{X}_l \beta_{kl} \tag{8}$$

The task we should do is to training a fitting procedure δ to estimate the coefficients $\hat{\beta}(\delta)$. For the kth user, we tend to train a regression method $\hat{\beta}_k(\delta)$ to select its corresponding discriminative features. Traditionally, the *ridge regression* use $l2$-norm to avoid overfitting and *lasso* uses $l1$-norm to produce sparsity on $\hat{\beta}_k(\delta)$. To fully utilize the correlations between users, MtBGS learning method [19] is used to utilize the latent information hidden in the similar users to boost the performance of recommendation.

Given the kth user and his corresponding rating vector $\mathbf{Y}(:,k)$, the regression model of MtBGS is defined as follows:

$$\min_{\hat{\beta}_k} \left\| \mathbf{Y}(:,k) - \sum_{l=1}^{L} \mathbf{x}_l \hat{\beta}_{kl} \right\|_2^2 + \lambda_1 \sum_{l=1}^{L} \left\| \hat{\beta}_{kl} \right\|_2 + \lambda_2 \left\| \hat{\beta}_k \right\|_1 \tag{9}$$

where $\lambda_1 \sum_{l=1}^{L} \|\hat{\beta}_{kl}\|_2 + \lambda_2 \|\hat{\beta}_k\|_1$ is the regularizer term, and is called the structural grouping penalty. There are two steps of the regularized regression with structural grouping penalty. The first is to select the groups of homogeneous features for the kth user. The second is to identify the subgroup within each selected group. We suppose the lth group is selected and the coefficients $\beta_{kl} = \theta_{kl} = (\theta_1, \theta_2, \dots, \theta_{p_l})$. Through the subgradient of (9), this can be determined by minimizing

$$J(t) = \sum_{m=1}^{p_l} \left(\frac{\theta_m}{\|\theta_{kl}\|}\right)^2 \tag{10}$$

where to $t_m = sign(\theta_m) \in [-1,1]$, and if $J(\hat{t}) > 1$, the lth group is selected. Then the following criterion is used to identify the subgroup of homogeneous features in the lth group:

$$\min_{\theta_m} \left\|r_{kl} - \sum_{m=1}^{p_l} X_m^l \theta_m\right\|_2^2 + \lambda_1 \|\theta_{jl}\|_2 + \lambda_2 \sum_{m=1}^{p_l} \|\theta_m\|_1 \tag{11}$$

where X_m^l is the corresponding p_l-dimensional homogeneous features of kth user, $r_{kl} = Y(:,k) - \sum_{i \neq l} X_i \beta_{ki}$ is the partial residual when the lth group is removed. This regression model with the structural grouping sparsity can be optimized by the Gauss-Seidel Coordinate Descent method [20].

3.3   Probability Prediction for Recommendation

Let $\hat{\beta}_k$ be the solution of equation (9), we predict $\hat{y}_u$ as the probability of the rating prediction of unlabeled item X^u by the kth user:

$$\hat{y}_u = X^u \hat{\beta}_k \tag{12}$$

where $\hat{y}_u \in \mathbb{R}^J$ is the probability predictions for J features of the unlabeled item X^u.

In order to take advantage of the correlations among the users, like the paper of Wu, et al. [19], the curds and whey (C&W) method is used to boost the prediction process. A linear combination $\widetilde{y_u} = B\hat{y}_u$ replaces the correlated probabilities, and the estimated indicators $\widetilde{y_u}$ are given by:

$$\widetilde{y_u} = B\hat{y}_u = C^{-1}WCX\hat{\beta}_k \tag{13}$$

where X is the selected features, C is the $K \times K$ matrix whose rows are the indicator canonical coordinates output by canonical correlation analysis (CCA), and W is a diagonal matrix whose diagonal elements $\varpi_k (k=1,2,\dots,K)$ are computed by the correlation coefficient in CCA [22].

Neighborhood models are further adapted to recommend Top-n items by means of a kNN (k-nearest-neighborhood) approach. For the kth user, we consider the top n items predicted by k that have the maximum prediction probability. Unlike the traditional item-based or user-based methods, we use the probability instead of the rating. And the kNN approach discards the items with very poor probability, thus decreasing noise for improving the quality of recommendations. We recommend the top n items with the highest n prediction probability as:

$$\max_n \sum_{j=1}^{J} \{\widetilde{y_{n_J}} | \widetilde{y_{n_J}} > \sigma\}. \tag{14}$$

where $\widetilde{y_{n_J}}$ is the probability of the jth feature of the nth item for the kth user, and σ is a threshold which control the diversity of the homogeneous feature groups.

4   Experiments and Results

4.1   Dataset

Traditional standard recommendation datasets are used to verify the rating prediction accuracy or Top-n recommendation in homogeneous data. So we built a cross media dataset, which is a subset of Douban (http://www.douban.com). Douban is a social website in China, which focuses on share the information on books, movies and music. All the ratings and comments are committed by users.

The whole dataset has 5000 users, 226109 books, 67708 movies and 165470 pieces of music. There are totally 1105 unique tags with high ratings and 3976317 rates in the dataset. The 1105 heterogeneous features were extracted and concatenated as the content feature vector for each item. We manually divide the features into 20 categories. Each of them represents homogeneous features and sequentially arrayed in the feature vector. Details of features, dimensionality are listed in Table.1.

Table 1. The examples of the first four feature groups

Group Names	# of features	Content feature (tag) examples
Country/ regions	40	Japan, America, China, UK, Hong Kong, French, Taiwan, Germany
Types	65	Novel, Drama, Literature, Cartoon, Foreign Literature, Culture, Comedy, Movie, Documentary, Animation, Biography, Essays
Genres	30	Pop, JPop, Electronic, Rock, OST, Ballad, Jazz, Popular
Emotions	80	Classic, Philosophy, Thriller, Art, Science fiction, Terror, Reasoning, Religion, Love

We randomly sampled 500 users, 500 books, 200 movies, and 300 pieces of music for each dataset. About 15% of the data in the dataset are randomly selected out as training data. Some of them are included in the training data while some are not. This process was repeated ten times to generate 10 random training and test groups. The average performances in terms of recall and diversity score are evaluated.

4.2   Parameter Tuning

The vector coefficient $\hat{\beta}$ in Equation (10) needs to be tuned. It is used to select the user's corresponding discriminative features. Note that, to develop a personalized recommendation method, different features are used for different people. Therefore, the parameter tuning process is performing separately for each user. As described in Section 3, a fitting procedure δ is trained in order to estimate the vector coefficient $\hat{\beta}$.

4.3   Comparison of Diversity

Diversity is an important metric to consider the performance of our recommendation system. It represents how widely the system can recommend across the different types of media data.

For Top-n recommendation, we choose n items which have the highest ratings in the test set as the chosen items. Then the results produced by the proposed method are compared with the chosen items. For each type of media, the recall ratio can be calculated as follows:

$$recall_i = \frac{num\_rec_i}{num\_chosen_i} \tag{15}$$

where num_rec_i is the number of items recommended in the ith type of media, and num_chosen_i is the number of items chosen by the volunteers which are rated with the highest n ratings.

The diversity is defined as the weighted average recall ratio.

$$diversity = \frac{\sum_{i=1}^{m} recall_i * num\_chosen_i}{\sum_{i=1}^{m} num\_chosen_i} \tag{16}$$

where m is the number of types of cross media data. We test the precision ratio and diversity with respect to two parameters: number of neighbor kNN and number of features used in tensor factorization. We test the proposed technique with a different number of neighbors (10, 20, 30, and 50 neighbors). The results of a Top-20 recommendation are shown in Fig. 2. From the results, the diversity is inversely proportional to the precision, which is consistent with the common sense. And our method has relatively uniform properties under different number of neighbors.

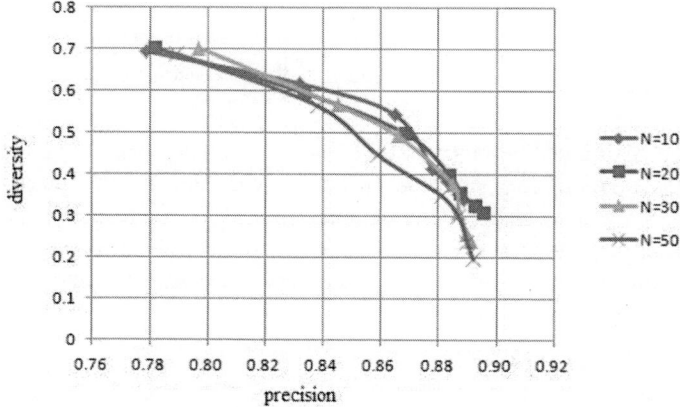

Fig. 2. Diversity and precision for different number of neighbors of Top-20 recommendation

The second experiment is to compare the diversity with a heuristic-based technique [21]. The number of neighbors in kNN is 20, and a top-20 recommendation is evaluated. The result is shown in Fig. 3. Our proposed method can get a larger diversity than the heuristic-based technique with the same precision.

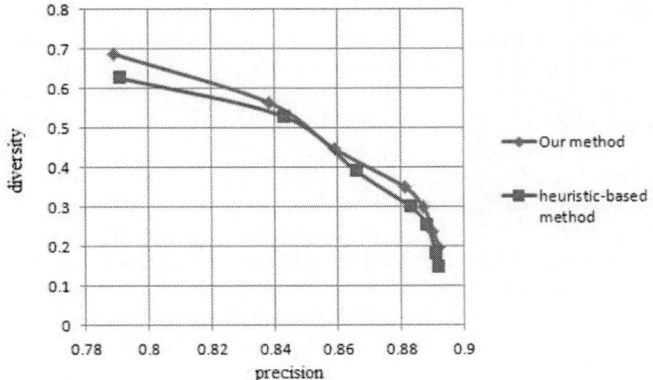

Fig. 3. Comparison of the proposed method and heuristic-based method

5   Conclusion

This paper proposes a structural context-aware collaborative filtering framework for cross media recommendation. The item-context matrix and item-user rating matrix are factorized by TUCKER based tensor decomposition. And the multi-label boosting by structural grouping sparsity is used to select the feature groups and the subset of homogeneous features in one group. Finally, the Top-n items are recommended according to the prediction probability estimated by the regression. Experiments on our own cross media dataset show that the framework has good diversity ability as well as good recommendation accuracy.

Acknowledgement. This research is supported by the 211 Key Project of Ministry of Education of Chi-na (Project of China Academic Digital Associative Library, No. 201003017, No. 201003018), Zhejiang Provincial Natural Science Foundation of China (Grant No. Z12F020027, Y1101129).

References

1. Ricci, F., Rokach, L., Shapira, B., Kantor, P.: Recommender Systems Handbook. Springer (2010)
2. Koren, Y., Bell, R.: Advances in collaborative filtering. In: Recommender Systems Handbook. Springer (2010)
3. Pazzani, M.J., Billsus, D.: Content-Based Recommendation Systems. In: Brusilovsky, P., Kobsa, A., Nejdl, W. (eds.) The Adaptive Web. LNCS, vol. 4321, pp. 325–341. Springer, Heidelberg (2007)
4. Koren, Y., Bell, R., Volinsky, C.: Matrix factorization techniques for recommender systems. Computer 42(8), 30–37 (2009)

5. Ma, H., Zhou, T.C., Michael, R.L., King, I.: Improving recommender systems by incorporating social contextual information. ACM Transactions on Information Systems 29(2), 9 (2011)
6. Ignacio, F.T., Iván, C., Marius, K., Francesco, R.: Cross-domain Recommender Systems: A Survey of the State of the Art. In: Proceedings of the 2nd Spanish Conference on Information Retrieval, CERI 2012, Valencia, Spain (2012)
7. Li, B., Yang, Q., Xue, X.: Can movies and books collaborative? Cross-domain collaborative filtering for sparsity reduction. In: Proceedings of the 21st International Joint Conference on Artificial Intelligence, IJCAI 2009, San Francisco, CA, USA, pp. 2052–2057 (2009)
8. Li, B., Yang, Q.: Transfer learning for collaborative filtering via a rating-matrix generative model. In: Proceedings of the 26th Annual International Conference on Machine Learning, ICML 2009, New York, NY, USA, pp. 617–624 (2009)
9. Su, Y.M., Hsu, P.Y., Pai, N.Y.: An approach to discover and recommend cross-domain bridge-keywords in document banks. The Electronic Library 28(5), 669–687 (2010)
10. Wu, F., Han, Y.H., Liu, X., Shao, J., Zhuang, Y.T., Zhang, Z.F.: The Heterogeneous feature selection with structural sparsity for multimedia annotation and hashing: A survey. International Journal of Multimedia Information Retrieval 1(1), 3–15 (2012)
11. Jia, Y., Salzmann, M., Darrell, T.: Factorized latent spaces with structured sparsity. In: Proceedings of the Conference on Neural Information Processing Systems, NIPS, vol. 23. MIT Press (2010)
12. Harshman, R.A.: Foundations of the PARAFAC procedure: models and conditions for an "explanatory" multimodal factor analysis. University of California at Los Angeles (1970)
13. Tucker, L.R.: Some mathematical notes on three-mode factor analysis. Psychometrika 31(3), 279–311 (1996)
14. Wright, J., Yang, A., Ganesh, A., Sastry, S., Ma, Y.: Robust face recognition via sparse representation. IEEE Trans. Pattern Anal. Mach. Intell. 31(2), 210–227 (2009)
15. Cao, L., Luo, J., Liang, F., Huang, T.: Heterogeneous feature machines for visual recognition. In: Proceedings of the IEEE International Conference on Computer Vision, ICCV, Kyoto, Japan, pp. 1095–1102 (2009)
16. Tibshirani, R.: Regression shrinkage and selection via the lasso. J. R. Stat. Soc. Ser. B (Statistical Methodology) 58(1), 267–288 (1996)
17. Zou, H., Hastie, T.: Regularization and variable selection via the elastic net. J. R. Stat. Soc. Ser. B (Statistical Methodology) 67(2), 301–320 (2005)
18. Yuan, M., Lin, Y.: Model selection and estimation in regression with grouped variables. J. R. Stat. Soc. Ser. B (Methodological) 68(1), 49–67 (2006)
19. Wu, F., Han, Y., Tian, Q., Zhuang, Y.: Multi-label boosting for image annotation by structural grouping sparsity. In: Proceedings of the 2010 ACM International Conference on Multimedia, ACMMM, New York, NY, USA, pp. 15–24 (2010)
20. Shevade, S., Keerthi, S.: A simple and efficient algorithm for gene selection using sparse logistic regression. Bioinformatics 19(17), 2246–2253 (2003)
21. Adomavicius, G., Kwon, Y.O.: Improving Aggregate Recommendation Diversity Using Ranking-Based Techniques. IEEE Transactions on Knowledge and Data Engineering 24(5), 896–911 (2012)
22. Hotelling, H.: Relations between two sets of variates. Biometrika 28(3), 321–377 (1936)
23. Funk, S.: Netflix update: Try this at home (2006),
http://sifter.org/?simon/journal/20061211.html
24. Karatzoglou, A., Amatriain, X., Baltrunas, L., Oliver, N.: Multiverse recommendation: n-dimensional tensor factorization for context-aware collaborative filtering. In: Proc. of the 4th ACM Conference on Recommender Systems, pp. 79–86 (2010)
25. Lew, M., Sebe, N., Djeraba, C., Jain, R.: Content-based multimedia information retrieval: state-of-the-art and challenges. ACM Transactions on Multimedia Computing, Communication, and Applications 2(1), 1–19 (2006)

Spherical Soft Assignment: Improving Image Representation in Content-Based Image Retrieval

Liefu Ai, Junqing Yu[*], and Tao Guan

School of Computer Science & Technology,
Huazhong University of Science and Technology, 430074, Wuhan, China
ailiefuhu@gmail.com, yjqing@hust.edu.cn, qd_gt@126.com

Abstract. Image representation is essential to performance of content-based image retrieval. VLAD has been proved to be superior to BOF. However, hard assignment is utilized in VLAD, which does not consider codeword uncertainty and codeword plausibility. In this paper, each cluster associated to visual word is defined as a hyper-sphere. The radius is denoted as the distance from visual word to the farthest feature point. Spherical soft assignment is proposed to adaptively assign a local feature to close visual words according to corresponding radius. Spherical soft assignment and a descriptor-space soft assignment of state of the art are applied to VLAD. Experiments on multiple datasets demonstrate that the proposed spherical soft assignment can noticeably improve VLAD image representation in image retrieval and be superior to the descriptor-space soft assignment.

Keywords: Image Retrieval, Image Representation, Soft Assignment.

1   Introduction

With the rapid development of Internet and multimedia technology, multimedia information especially picture and image is growing explosively. These large database and the demands of people retrieve similar and favorite images pose enormous challenge to image retrieval systems. To gain accurate query results, image representation is the key point.

Bag-of-Feature image representation (BOF) [1] is popular for image retrieval and categorization applications. However, to achieve good accuracy and efficiency, the dimension of BOF need to be high [2] [3] [4], usually up to a million dimensions. The memory requirement of BOF limits the number of image can be handled in practice. Based on BOF and Fisher kernel [5], Jegou et al. [6] develops vectors of locally aggregated descriptors (VLAD), VLAD create a compact global image representation by aggregating vector residuals of local SIFT [7] descriptors quantized to a small set of codebook. VLAD obtains significant superior performance than BOF with lower dimensionality. To remove outlier features lie close to the boundary between 2 visual words, Chen et al. [8] discards all the features whose distances are above 90% on the

---

[*] Corresponding author.

W. Lin et al. (Eds.): PCM 2012, LNCS 7674, pp. 801–810, 2012.
© Springer-Verlag Berlin Heidelberg 2012

distribution of distances. VLAD commonly consists of SIFT feature extraction, visual codebook creation, feature assignment and vector residuals aggregating. Hard assignment is utilized in VLAD, which assigns local feature to the nearest visual word.

Hard assignment does not consider codeword uncertainty and codeword plausibility, often introduce large quantization error. To alleviate these drawbacks, a kernel based soft assignment [9] [10] is proposed, which assigns every local feature to all visual words and computes corresponding weight of the local feature to different visual words. In [11], to reduce quantization error, a soft assignment is proposed by assigning every local feature to k nearest neighbor visual words. The corresponding weight is computed based on Gaussian Mixture Models (GMM) [12]. Similarity, in [13], a localized soft assignment is proposed by only considering the k nearest neighbor visual words of a local feature and set its distances to the remain visual words as infinite. Given a local feature, the method of computing weight is similar to the work in [11], but sum of the weights to all visual words equals to 1.

In this paper, built on the work of VLAD, we propose spherical soft assignment which adaptively assigns a local feature to visual words in the neighborhood. In the procedure of learning visual codebook, a distance radius is calculated for every visual word based on the distribution of Euclidian distance. Then, a local feature is adaptively assigned to close visual words according to the radius. Consequently, the corresponding weight for each close visual word is calculated. To show the improvement of image representation by spherical soft assignment in content-based image retrieval, it is applied to VLAD and evaluated on different datasets. The detail process is presented in following sections.

The rest of this paper is organized as follows: relate work is introduced in section 2; section 3 presents our approach of spherical soft assignment, which adaptively assigns a local feature to similar visual words in feature space; section 4 reports the results of experiments, followed by conclusions section 5.

2   Related Work

This section reviews VLAD that produce vector representation of image from a set of local feature and descriptor-space soft assignment of allocating a local feature to different visual words.

2.1   VLAD

In [6], VLAD is proposed to represent image by aggregating local features in feature space. Let c_i ($c_i \in R^d$) denote a visual word, where d is the dimensionality of a local feature, and x_i ($x_i \in R^d$) denote the ith local feature in an image. Similar to BOF, a codebook $C = \{c_1, ... c_k\}$ of k visual words is learned by K-Means on a local feature set. Each local feature x_i is allocated to the nearest visual word $c_j = NN(x_i)$ and vector residual x_i-$c_j$is calculated. For a visual word c_j, the sum of all the vector residuals constitutes the jth sub vector v_j of VLAD. The sub vector v_j is computed as the following formula:

$$v_j = \sum_{x \text{ such that } v_j = NN(x)} x - c_j \tag{1}$$

where x denotes the local features in an image that allocated to visual word c_j. All aggregated vector residuals of k visual words are concentrated together forming the VLAD image representation. The dimension of VLAD is $D = k \times d$. Comparing to BOF, VLAD can attain better retrieval performance by using a much smaller set of codebook. Typically, the value of k ranges from $k = 16$ to $k = 256$. For a compact representation, principal component analysis (PCA) and product quantization (PQ) [14] are applied to VLAD for content-based image retrieval.

2.2   Descriptor-Space Soft Assignment

In [11], a descriptor dependent soft assignment on the distribution of Euclidean distance between the feature point and the visual words is investigated to reduce quantization error during hard assignment. It considers that the weight vector can localize the feature point more precisely in SIFT feature space. Each feature point x_i is allocated to r nearest visual words, denoted with $Rnn(x_i)$. The weight of x_i to visual word c_j is compute as the following formula:

$$w_{ij} = \frac{\exp(-\frac{d_{ij}^2}{2\sigma^2})}{\sum_{c_j \in Rnn(x_i)} \exp(-\frac{d_{ij}^2}{2\sigma^2})} \tag{2}$$

where d_{ij} denotes the Euclidian distance from x_i to visual word c_j; σ is a parameter needed to be evaluated with experiment. Typically, the value of r is 3 and σ^2 is 6250. Then, a local feature is represented by an r-vector, which is L_1 normalized.

This soft assignment has been implemented and applied to VLAD. We will compare with our approach in experiment.

3   Spherical Soft Assignment

In this section, we propose our method to allocating a local feature to close visual words adaptively and weights computing of a local feature to corresponding visual words. Then, spherical soft assignment is applied to VLAD.

3.1   Spherical Soft Assignment

We propose spherical soft assignment based on the distance distribution of every visual word. A codebook $C = \{c_1, \dots c_i, \dots c_k\}$ ($c_i \in R^d$) of k visual words is first learned with K-Means. For each cluster, the local feature farthest from the visual word is found and the Euclidian distance is denoted as r_i ($i = 1, \dots k$). Consequently, r_i as the radius, a hyper-sphere for each cluster is constructed in local feature space.

A local feature is assigned to close visual words according to the spatial positional relationship between the local feature and hyper-spheres.

For a local feature x_i ($x_i \in R^d$), let b_{ij} ($b_{ij} = 0$ or 1, $j = 1, \ldots k$) denotes whether it is assigned to the jth visual word. 1 denotes x_i is allocated to c_j, otherwise, b_{ij} is 0. The mechanism of spherical soft assignment is defined as follows:

$$b_{ij} = \begin{cases} 0 & \text{when } d(x_i, c_j) > r_j \\ 1 & \text{when } d(x_i, c_j) \leq r_j \end{cases} \tag{3}$$

where $d(x_i, c_j)$ denotes the Euclidean distance between local feature x_i and visual word c_j.

Due to the difference between learning feature set and retrieval dataset, there may be a situation that a local feature in new coming image is not allocated to any visual word according to Formula (3). To ensure a local feature x_i can be allocated to at least a visual word, x_i is assigned to the nearest visual word among the distance to all the visual words when b_{ij} is 0 for all visual words. The formula is as follows:

$$b_{ij} = 1 \quad j = \arg \min_{j=1,\ldots,k} d(x_i, c_j) \tag{4}$$

with spherical soft assignment, a local feature can be adaptively assigned to at least one visual word.

Comparing to descriptor-space soft assignment which empirically allocating a local feature to fixed knn nearest visual words, spherical soft assignment doesn't need to consider any empirical parameter and assigns local feature to close visual words according to distance distribution of every cluster. Spherical soft assignment is more flexible. We will experimentally demonstrate that spherical soft assignment outperforms descriptor-space soft assignment in image retrieval.

3.2   Weight Computing

For a local feature x_i, let w_{ij} denotes the weight with respect to visual word c_j. For each cluster, assuming that the distances between local feature and the visual word is Gaussian distribution. The weight w_{ij} can be computed as the following formula:

$$w_{ij} = b_{ij} \times \exp\left(-\frac{d_{ij}}{2\sigma^2}\right) \tag{5}$$

where d_{ij} denotes the Euclidian distance between local feature x_i and visual word c_j; σ denotes the uniform parameter for all clusters. The value of σ will be given with experiment to attain the best performance in image retrieval.

The weight of local feature x_i associated to k visual words can be represented by a k vector $w_i = (w_{i1}, w_{i2}, \ldots, w_{ik})$. To make sure the sum of w_{ij} for x_i equal to 1, the weight vector w_i need to be L1 normalized. Then, Formula (5) is optimized as the follows:

$$w_{ij} = \begin{cases} \dfrac{b_{ij} \times \exp\left(-\dfrac{d_{ij}}{2\,\sigma^2}\right)}{\sum_{j=1}^{k} b_{ij} \times \exp\left(-\dfrac{d_{ij}}{2\,\sigma^2}\right)} & \text{when } b_{ij} \neq 0 \\[4mm] 0 & \text{when } b_{ij} = 0 \end{cases} \tag{6}$$

3.3   Appling to VLAD

When spherical soft assignment is applied to VLAD, as for VLAD, a codebook $C = \{c_1, \dots c_k\}$ is firstly learned. Every local feature x_i ($x_i \in R^d$) then is assigned to close visual words with spherical soft assignment. Vector residual between x_i and c_j is proportional to $x_i - c_j$ with corresponding weight w_{ij}. For visual word c_j, the sum of all the vector residuals constitutes the jth sub vector v_j of VLAD. The formula (1) of computing sub vector v_j of VLAD is updated as the following formula:

$$v_j = \sum_{x_i \text{such that } b_{ij}=1} w_{ij} \times (x_i - c_j) \tag{7}$$

where x_i denotes the local features assigned to visual word c_j with spherical soft assignment, w_{ij} denotes the weight of local feature x_i associated to visual word c_j. Then, similarity to VLAD, all aggregated vector residuals v_j of k visual words are concentrated together forming the new VLAD image representation. The dimension of new VLAD is also k × d. We will experimentally demonstrate the improvement on image representation with spherical soft assignment in image retrieval.

4   Experiments

In this section, we firstly evaluate the parameter σ for constructing new VLAD image representation in image retrieval. Then, we provide a comparison with VLAD and descriptor-space soft assignment on different image dataset.

Our work is built on the VLAD, so the procedure after generating VLAD image representation follows that in VLAD, including PCA to reduce the dimension of VLAD and PQ to increase the speed of retrieval.

Typically, the number of visual word k ranges from $k = 16$ to $k = 256$, the larger number of visual words, the higher dimension of VLAD. VLAD of higher dimensionality can increase the discrimination of image representation in image retrieval, but suffer from more error when dimensional reduction, while VLAD of lower dimension can reduce error of dimensional reduction, but the discrimination turn into drawback. In [6], the authors experimentally demonstrate that the best value of k is 64 in terms of the trade-off between retrieval accuracy and error of dimension reduction on the datasets of INRIA Holidays and University of Kentucky Benchmark. So we set the number of visual words k=64 in all our experiments. We use SIFT descriptor of 128 dimensionality to describe visual words and local features of all images in both datasets of INRIA Holidays and University of Kentucky Benchmark.

4.1   Dataset

The INRIA Holidays Dataset [15]

This is a collection of 1491 holiday images, which is divided into 500 groups. The first image of each group is the query image and the correct retrieval results are the other images of the group. Total vectors in dataset are used as training set and database set. The accuracy is measured by mean Average Precision (mAP).

The University of Kentucky Benchmark (UKbench) [16]

This is a collection of 10200 object images, which is divided into 2550 groups. Each object is represented by 4 images. Each images of this dataset is the query image. The commonly used evaluation metric counts the average number of relevant images in corresponding group (including the query itself). Total vectors in dataset are used as training set and database set. The accuracy is measured by Recall@4.

4.2   Parameter Evaluating

Appling our approach of spherical soft assignment to VLAD, Table 1 and Table 2 show the retrieval performance of VLAD with different parameter σ^2 for number of visual words k=64 on Holidays dataset and UKbench.

Table 1. Comparing of different parameter for mAP of VLAD representation with spherical soft assignment, before and after dimension reduction by PCA on Holidays dataset

k	D	σ^2	Holidays dataset (mAP)			
			D	D'=128	D'=64	D'=32
64	8192	2250	0.551	0.561	0.533	0.491
64	**8192**	**2500**	**0.553**	**0.558**	**0.533**	**0.493**
64	8192	2750	0.546	0.559	0.533	0.491
64	8192	3000	0.542	0.556	0.534	0.490
64	8192	3500	0.537	0.556	0.534	0.488

Table 2. Comparing of different parameter for recall of VLAD representation with spherical soft assignment, before and after dimension reduction by PCA on UKbench

k	D	σ^2	UKbench (recall@4)			
			D	D'=128	D'=64	D'=32
64	8192	2250	3.036	3.098	3.000	2.835
64	8192	2500	3.042	3.102	3.004	2.839
64	8192	2750	3.048	3.107	3.007	2.842
64	**8192**	**3000**	**3.052**	**3.110**	**3.011**	**2.846**
64	8192	3500	3.058	3.109	3.010	2.843

The evaluation is performed without PQ scheme at this step. Here, we put an emphasis on evaluating the best value of σ^2 for k=64 and the performance obtained after dimensionality reduction. It can be seen from Table 1 and Table 2 that the performance of VLAD changed very little as the varied parameter σ. For Holidays dataset, the best accuracy is attained when $\sigma^2 = 2500$, while VLAD attains the best performance on UKbench dataset when $\sigma^2 = 3000$. We use $\sigma^2 = 2500$ for Holidays dataset and $\sigma^2 = 3000$ for UKbench dataset in next experiments.

4.3   Comparison with the State of the Art

The descriptor-space soft assignment in [11] is implemented and applied to VLAD, which is compared with our approach and existing VLAD in this section.

Table 3 and Table 4 compare different image representation on 2 datasets: VLAD, VLAD with descriptor-space soft assignment and VLAD with our approach of spherical soft assignment.

There are 2 parameters in VLAD with descriptor-space soft assignment: r and σ^2, where r denotes the number of visual word that a local feature is assigned to, σ^2 is the parameter to be used in computing weight. The value of these 2 parameters is the optimal value given by Ref [11]. The $D' = 128, ADC\ 16 \times 8$ indicates that image representation is divided into 16 sub vectors and each sub vector is encoded with 8 bit binary code. Asymmetric Distance Computing (ADC) in PQ [14] is used to image search.

Table 3. Performance comparison of different image representation, before, after dimension and using ADC on Holidays dataset

Descriptor	k	D	Holidays dataset (mAP)				
			D	D'=128	D'=64	D'=32	D'=128 ADC 16 × 8
VLAD	64	8192	0.526	0.510	0.478	0.420	0.456
Ref[11], r=3 $\sigma^2 = 6250$	64	8192	0.497	0.510	0.491	0.463	0.451
Our Approach $\sigma^2 = 2500$	64	8192	0.553	0.558	0.553	0.493	0.499

Table 4. Performance comparison of different image representation, before, after dimension and using ADC on UKbench

Descriptor	k	D	UKbench (recall@4)				
			D	D'=128	D'=64	D'=32	D'=128 ADC 16 × 8
VLAD	64	8192	2.964	3.063	2.951	2.785	2.592
Ref[11], r=3 $\sigma^2 = 6250$	64	8192	2.871	2.983	2.928	2.780	2.609
Our Approach $\sigma^2 = 3000$	64	8192	3.052	3.110	3.011	2.846	2.809

It can be seen from Table 3 and Table 4 that VLAD with our approach noticeably outperforms existing VLAD on both Holidays and UKbench. Furthermore, comparing to existing VLAD, the influence of dimension reduction is less weak to accuracy with spherical soft assignment. Table 3 and Table 4 also show that our approach is significantly superior to descriptor-space soft assignment in Ref [11]. The recall of existing VLAD is slightly different from that reported in [6], because the method to feature extraction is different.

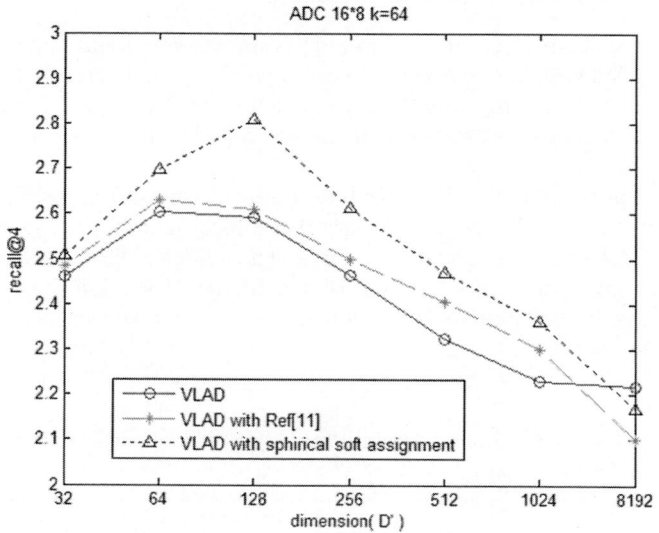

Fig. 1. Performance of different image representation by ADC searching on UKbench, before and after dimension reduction by PCA

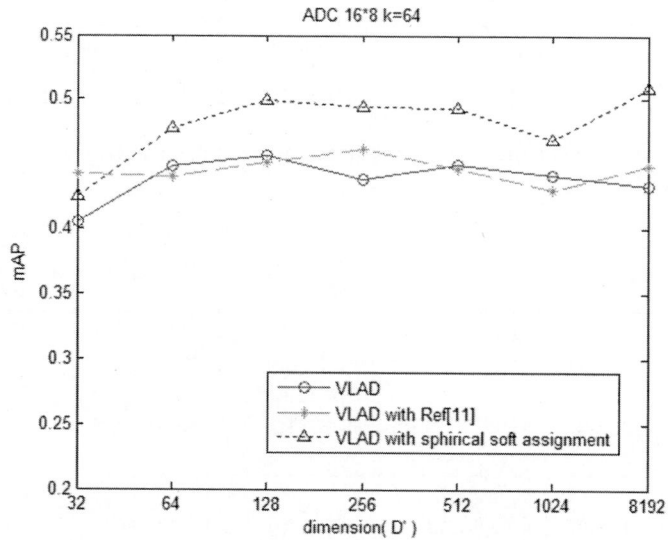

Fig. 2. Performance of different image representation by ADC searching on Holidays, before and after dimension reduction by PCA

Image representation is reduced to different dimension. Then PQ with fixed 16 Bytes is used to encode the image representation of various dimensions. The retrieval performance of ADC searching on different image representation with various dimensionalities is compared on UKbench (Figure 1) and Holiday dataset (Figure 2). ADC searching uses distance between feature point and cluster center to approximate distance between 2 feature points, so that the speed of image retrieval is increased.

From Figure 1 and Figure 2, we can observe that VLAD with spherical soft assignment is significantly superior to both existing VLAD and VLAD with Ref [11] on UKbench and Holidays dataset. Consequently, it indicates that spherical soft assignment outperforms descriptor-space soft assignment.

5   Conclusion

In view of the importance of image representation to content-based image retrieval, optimized VLAD image representation with spherical soft assignment is developed. By spherical soft assignment, a local feature is assigned to the visual words that contain the local feature in the boundary of hyper-sphere. Comparing to descriptor-space soft assignment, spherical soft assignment can adaptively assign local feature to close visual words. It is more practical for different real data. Experimental results show that spherical soft assignment can noticeably improve accuracy of image retrieval and outperform descriptor-space soft assignment. Soft assignment does not change the dimension of VLAD, so the memory usage is the same as VLAD. This paper mainly emphasizes on the improvement on image representation and search accuracy, due to weight computing procedure, efficiency of generating VLAD is slightly inferior to existing VLAD with hard assignment. In future work, we will jointly optimize on the tradeoff between accuracy and efficiency. Also, we will evaluate performance of VLAD with proposed spherical soft assignment on more large scale image dataset.

Acknowledgment. This paper is financially supported by the National Natural Science Foundation of China (NSFC) under Grant No. 60903095, 61202300 and 61272202.

References

1. Josef, S., Andrew, Z.: Video Google: A Text Retrieval Approach to Object Matching in Videos. In: IEEE International Conference on Computer Vision, ICCV, pp. 1470–1477 (2003)
2. Herve, J., Matthijs, D., Cordelia, S.: Improving Bag-of-Features for Large Scale Image Search. International Journal of Computer Vision, IJCV 87(3), 316–326 (2010)
3. David, N., Henrik, S.: Scalable Recognition with a Vocabulary Tree. In: IEEE Conference on Computer Vision and Pattern Recognition, CVPR, pp. 2161–2168 (2006)
4. James, P., Ondrej, C., Michael, I., et al.: Object retrieval with large vocabularies and fast spatial matching. In: IEEE Conference on Computer Vision and Pattern Recognition, CVPR, pp. 1–8 (2007), doi:10.1109/CVPR.2007.383172

5. Florent, P., Christopher, D.: Fisher Kernels on Visual Vocabularies for Image Categorization. In: IEEE Conference on Computer Vision and Pattern Recognition, CVPR, pp. 1–8 (2007), doi:10.1109/CVPR.2007.383266

6. Herve, J., Matthijs, D., Cordelia, S., et al.: Aggregating local descriptors into a compact image representation. In: IEEE Conference on Computer Vision and Pattern Recognition, CVPR, pp. 3304–3311 (2010)

7. David, G.L.: Distinctive Image Feature from Scale-Invariant Keypoints. International Journal of Computer Vision, IJCV 60(2), 91–100 (2004)

8. David, C., Sam, T., Vijay, C., et al.: Residual Enhanced Visual Vectors for On-Device Image Matching. In: 45th Asilomar Conference on Signals, Systems and Computers, ASILOMAR, pp. 850–854 (2011)

9. van Gemert, J.C., Geusebroek, J.-M., Veenman, C.J., Smeulders, A.W.M.: Kernel Codebooks for Scene Categorization. In: Forsyth, D., Torr, P., Zisserman, A. (eds.) ECCV 2008, Part III. LNCS, vol. 5304, pp. 696–709. Springer, Heidelberg (2008)

10. van Gemert, J.C., Veenman, C.J., Smeulders, A.W.M.: Visual Word Ambiguity. IEEE Transactions on Pattern Analysis and Machine Intelligence 32(7), 1271–1283 (2010)

11. James, P., Ondrej, C., Michael, I., et al.: Lost in Quantization: Improving Particular Object Retrieval in Large Scale Image Databases. In: IEEE Conference on Computer Vision and Pattern Recognition, CVPR, pp. 1–8 (2008)

12. Christopher, M.B.: Pattern Recognition and Machine Learning. Springer, Heidelberg (2006)

13. Linqiao, L., Lei, W., Xinwang, L.: In Defense of Soft-assignment Coding. In: IEEE International Conference on Computer Vision, ICCV, pp. 2486–2493 (2011)

14. Herve, J., Matthijs, D., Cordelia, S.: Product quantization for nearest neighbor search. IEEE Transactions on Pattern Analysis and Machine Intelligence 33(1), 117–128 (2010)

15. Jegou, H., Douze, M., Schmid, C.: Hamming Embedding and Weak Geometric Consistency for Large Scale Image Search. In: Forsyth, D., Torr, P., Zisserman, A. (eds.) ECCV 2008, Part I. LNCS, vol. 5302, pp. 304–317. Springer, Heidelberg (2008)

16. UKbench descriptor, http://bigimbaz.inrialpes.fr/herve/ukbench_descriptors/

Fast Pedestrian Detection
Based on Sliding Window Filtering

Feidie Liang[1], Dong Wang[2], Yang Liu[2], Youcheng Jiang[1], and Sheng Tang[1]

[1] Adavanced Computing Research Laboratory, Beijing Key Laboratory of Mobile Computing
and Pervasive Device, Institute of Computing Technology,
Chinese Academy of Sciences, Beijing, China
{liangfeidie,jiangyoucheng,ts}@ict.ac.cn
[2] Huawei Technologies Co., Ltd, Beijing, China
{dave.wangdong,ethan.liuyang}@huawei.com

Abstract. Pedestrian detection is a fundamental problem in video surveillance. An overwhelming majority of existing detection methods are based on sliding windows with exhaustive multi-scale scanning over the whole frame images which can achieve good accuracy but suffer from expensive computational cost. To reduce the complexity significantly while keeping high accuracy, in this paper, we propose an effective and efficient pedestrian detection method based on sliding windows with well-designed multi-scale scanning over candidate regions instead of whole frames. The candidate regions can be obtained through three main steps: (1) foreground extraction by using a fast background subtraction model to remove large number of static regions since pedestrians are usually keeping moving; (2) region merging and filtering through clustering foreground pixels to avoid over-partitioned or too large regions of non-pedestrian; (3) well-designed multi-scale scanning by exploiting the size information of current region to avoid useless scales. Therefore, through utilization of motion and size information, we can not only speed up the detection through reducing large number of windows, but also improve the accuracy of detection through eliminating many false positive regions. Our experiments on two public datasets have verified that our method outperforms the state-of-the-art methods in both speed and accuracy of detection.

Keywords: Pedestrian detection, Video surveillance, Background subtraction, Sliding window.

1 Introduction

Pedestrian detection is a fundamental problem in video surveillance since it is a key procedure for successive tracking, action recognition, personal identification and abnormal events detection. In the last decade, most researches focused on improving the detection accuracy and made significant progresses. However, an assignable byproduct of the increased detection accuracy is the quicker increased computation cost, which makes the pedestrian detection further far from real-time processing. Especially in video surveillance, embedded computers are usually adopted to perform pedestrian detection thus the computation capability is very limited. Meanwhile, many

W. Lin et al. (Eds.): PCM 2012, LNCS 7674, pp. 811–822, 2012.

applications require real-time accurate pedestrian detection in video surveillance, so a big challenge is how to improve the speed of state-of-the-art methods without sacrificing the detection accuracy.

One of the most successful approaches for pedestrian detection is the sliding window paradigm, which uses a sliding window to scan over an image exhaustively in scale-space, and classify each window individually [1, 2]. The results of the Pascal Visual Object Classes Challenge from 2005 to 2010 [3] and recent researches [4-7] show that this approach can achieve better detection accuracy than other approaches. However, due to the large number of possible target locations and pedestrian sizes in an image, enormous windows are extracted for further classification to detect all possible pedestrians. For example, the number of dense multi-scale (scale step is 1.05, sliding window size is 64×128 pixels, scanning stride is 8 pixels) sliding windows is about 25,900 on an image with resolution of 640×480 pixels. In general, the number of sliding windows grows as O(n4) for images of size n×n, which makes it computationally too expensive to exhaustively classify all of them, especially for those with high dimension features.

In recent years, many acceleration methods have been proposed to increase the detection speed by shortening the time of classification stage. For example, cascade strategy is adopted in [8, 9] so that most negative sliding windows can be rejected in the early stages of the cascade classification. Branch and bound search introduced in [10] can speed up the classification speed by trying to only focus on the image regions which have the highest possibility of containing pedestrian. However, this type of optimization can't reduce the time of other stages in sliding window paradigm (e.g. collecting features), which may become performance bottlenecks after applying these optimizing methods. Another optimizing direction is to reduce the number of sliding windows. For example, the authors of [11] combined the image pyramid and classifier pyramid to reduce the number of sliding windows with only a little reduction of detection accuracy. Coarse-to-fine detection scheme [12] can also be used to reduce the number of sliding windows, but the detection of small pedestrians is sacrificed.

In order to reduce the complexity significantly while keeping high accuracy, in this paper, we propose a novel multi-strategy filtering method to reduce the number of sliding windows. First, we apply sliding window technique merely on regions containing moving objects in the video. For video surveillance, the cameras are usually stationary most of time, so moving objects can be extracted by normal background subtraction methods. Then, besides the foreground information, we adopt clustering techniques incorporated with spatial information to form the image regions to be detected, so that the negative effects of noises on the number of windows and the fragmentation problem can be reduced to some extent. Finally, during the multi-scale scanning process, we exploit the size information of regions to avoid useless scales, hence further reduce the number of windows. Combining all these three windows filtering strategies, our method can greatly reduce the number of windows, thus achieve much faster detection speed. Meanwhile, our method can get better detection accuracy since most negative windows are filtered out before classification, hence reduces the false positive rate. Our experiments on two public datasets show that our method improves both speed and detection accuracy in comparison with the state-of-the-art methods. Most importantly, our method can achieves near real-time detection rate on both datasets, which is about 12 FPS (frames per second) on 768×576 images and 26 FPS on 384×288 images on average.

2   Related Work

As an early work, Papageorgiou et al. [13] and Viola et al. [9] have showed great success of sliding window paradigm for object detection. Based on sliding window paradigm, Dalal and Triggs [2] use HOG descriptors and SVM to build a pedestrian detector. By tuning the parameters of their HOG features, they find the best configuration for pedestrian detection through a variety of feature configurations on a challenging dataset of human figures. By combining HOG and Local Binary Pattern (LBP) as the feature set, Wang et al. [7] propose to use a global detector for whole sliding windows and part detectors for local regions in sliding windows which can well handling partial occlusion. Felzenszwalb et al. [6] build an object detection system based on mixtures of multi-scale deformable part models, which also combines the HOG and sliding window. This system achieves the best results in the PASCAL object detection challenges [3]. In summary, as a dense version of the dominating SIFT [14] feature, HOG and sliding window have shown great success in object detection and recognition [4, 5] despite its low detection speed.

In order to decrease the run-time, Qiang et al. [8] use a computationally efficient rejection chain classifier like [9] to fast filter out false alarms, with HOG based on variable size of blocks as its input feature. This method combined AdaBoost feature selection and integral image can effectively accelerate the computation speed. Lampert et al. [10] propose an efficient sub-window search (ESS) method for object localization, the method relies on a branch-and-bound scheme to find the global optimum of a quality function over all possible sub-images in the possible candidate images and can return the same object locations as the traditional sliding window approach can. Dollár et al. [11] proposed a method called FPDW which uses a step size of an entire octave to build a sparsely multi-scale image pyramid, and at each octave, multiple features introduced in [15] are approximated and a classifier pyramid is used. This approach can achieve nearly the same accuracy as using densely multi-scale image pyramids, with nearly the same speed as using a classifier pyramid applied to an image at a single scale. Wei et al. [12] propose a multi-resolution framework which uses a coarse-to-fine feature hierarchy to represent different resolutions. Then the lower resolution features are used to reject the majority of negative windows, leaving a relatively small number of windows to be processed in higher resolutions. The performance of this approach is good but small size of pedestrians will be lost. All these methods can somehow decrease the run-time of multi-scale detection, but still far from real-time processing. The reported fastest detection speed is about 6 fps for detecting pedestrians at least 100 pixels high and 3 fps for detecting pedestrians over 50 pixels on 640×480 image [11], much lower than the speed of our method as aforementioned.

Different with the existing acceleration methods, our approach mainly takes advantage of the motion information to increase the pedestrian detection speed of sliding windows based on the observation that pedestrians are usually keeping moving in video surveillance. Moreover, because most of our acceleration methods are applied in the early stages of generating sliding windows, our method can be combined with other existing approaches which accelerate classification stage to further improve the detection speed.

3   Our Method

The fast pedestrian detection based on sliding window method is illustrated in Fig. 1. In detection stage, we choose HOG as feature descriptors and Linear SVM as our classifier for their great success in object detection area. In the following, we describe the multi-strategy filtering method in details.

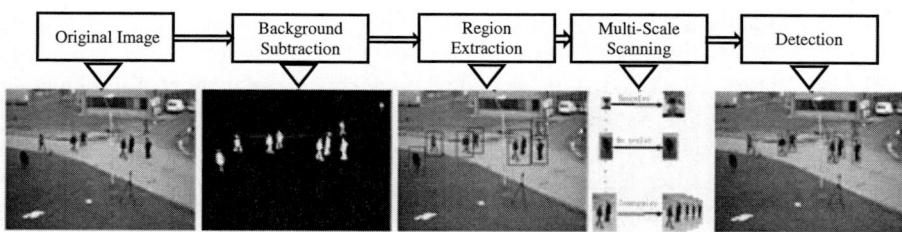

Fig. 1. Framework of our method

3.1   Background Subtraction

Pedestrians are usually walking in video surveillance. Although they may stop walking for a while, they won't keep static for a long time. Based on this observation, we first use a fast and simple background model to filter out most non-motion pixels. We choose the ViBe [16] model to perform background subtraction. Compared to other background models, this model is appropriate for our method for four reasons: (1) It can fast separate foreground pixels from the background by combining random process to the background subtraction process. (2) It only needs a single frame to initialize the model which is necessary to start pedestrian detection without latency. (3) It uses information of neighborhood pixels to update the model which will achieve good accuracy to get foreground pixels. (4) The objects will be treated as foreground if they stop moving for a short period of time. (It is hard and not common for pedestrians to keep absolutely static for a long time especially in video surveillance, so no additional steps are needed to handle this case.)

After background subtraction, morphology operations are used to eliminate small noises like salt and pepper noises caused by sensors, compression artifacts.

3.2   Region Extraction

The foreground pixels obtained by background subtraction can't be directly used because rectangular regions are required to apply sliding window method. An intuitive solution to the generation of candidate rectangular regions is to cluster all adjacent foreground pixels and then generate different rectangular regions with the pixels in each cluster. However, this solution is not perfect because of the following issues.

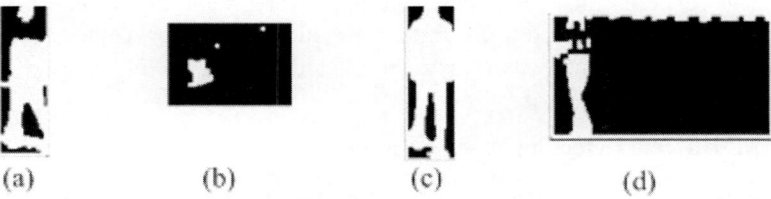

(a)   (b)   (c)   (d)

Fig. 2. Example of (a) fragments (b) noises (c) extracted region too close to the edge of pedestrian to get right HOG features (d) superfluous region caused by noises

At first, pedestrian may be fragmented into several separated elements such as the pedestrian in Fig.2 (a). For example, parts of pedestrian may temporally obstructed by the trees or fences; portions of a pedestrian may be accidentally very similar to objects in the background. In these cases, a pedestrian may not be detected or may be detected as multiple pedestrians because it is fragmented and each part is classified separately. Therefore, we introduce a clustering method which measures the similarity of two pixels in different regions. If the similarity is less than a given threshold $C_{threshold}$, these pixels need to be put into the same cluster. The similarity can be defined by distance or colors. In experiments, we find the Manhattan Distance is appropriated for our method with low computational complexity and good accuracy.

Secondly, there are some noises with relatively large areas as shown in Fig.2 (b), which cannot be removed by morphology operations. If we treat such noises as moving objects, both the size and the number of candidate regions may increase. But these regions affirmatively contain only noises other than pedestrians. Therefore, we use the size information of a pedestrian to further remove this kind of noise as follows. We set a size threshold $R_{threshold}$ for the candidate regions. All the small candidate regions are filtered out if their widths are less than $R_{threshold}$ or their heights are less than $R_{threshold} \times 2$. The height threshold is chosen to double the value of the width threshold which is consistent with most of real aspect ratio of pedestrians. By choosing the suitable value for $R_{threshold}$, most candidate regions that only contain noises can be filtered out.

Thirdly, because the neighboring pixels to the pedestrians are usually necessary to extract the HOG features of the pedestrians, sliding window method can't be directly applied to the generated candidate regions since the peripheral pixels of a candidate region have not sufficient neighboring information. Fig.2 (c) shows an example of this case. Thus in our approach, each candidate regions is extended by $(\varepsilon_x, \varepsilon_y)$ before sliding window step, where $(\varepsilon_x, \varepsilon_y)$ stands for the extended width and height at both directions respectively. The extension enlarges the size of candidate regions thus increases the number of sliding windows, but the improved detection accuracy is worthy of this cost.

In some cases, the noises can't be filtered out by our noise filtering methods, for example a long waving stripe around pedestrians like Fig.2 (d). This type of noises enlarges candidate regions thus more sliding windows than necessary need to be classified. To filter out these additional sliding windows, the proportion of foreground pixels in the sliding windows is taken as a factor to filter out some sliding windows. In other words, only those windows with higher foreground pixels ratio than a threshold $F_{threshold}$ will be passed to for further detection. This filter method is reasonable and many negative sliding windows can be filtered out.

3.3   Multi-scale Detection Based on Region

After subtracting the candidate rectangular regions from each frame image, the sub-images in the corresponding regions will be treated as separate images and applied traditional multi-scale sliding window methods. We also only adopt downscaling when producing the image pyramid for each sub-image to avoid the high cost of upscaling. However, there is an exception that the sub-images need to be firstly upscaled if they are too small to contain one sliding window. The scale factor ς_l can be calculated by the following equation:

$$\varsigma_l = max\left\{\frac{SW.w}{RR.w}, \frac{SW.h}{RR.h}, 1\right\} \tag{1}$$

where SW.w and SW.h are the width and height of the sliding window; RR.w and RR.h denote the width and height of the sub-images respectively. This upscaling step helps to detect out some small size pedestrians. Meanwhile, the cost of this step is not much since only small sub-images are limitedly upscaled.

Because the size and aspect ratio are different for different sub-image, we can't use fixed downscale range in downscaling process. In our approach, the downscale range ς_s is calculated for each sub-image during runtime by using the following equation:

$$\varsigma_s = max\{min\left\{\frac{RR.w}{SW.w}, \frac{RR.h}{SW.h}\right\}, 1\} \tag{2}$$

4   Experiments

Our experiments focus on PETS2009 (dataset S2, L1, view_001)[1] consisting of 794 frames and total 4893 pedestrians and CAVIAR (dataset "ShopAssistant2cor")[2] consisting of 3700 frames and total 8740 pedestrians. The video resolution of PETS2009 is 768×576 and pedestrians' height varies from 35 to 160 pixels. The video resolution of CAVIAR is 384×288 and pedestrians' height varies from 34 to 148 pixels.

---

[1] http://www.cvg.rdg.ac.uk/PETS2009/a.html
[2] http://groups.inf.ed.ac.uk/vision/CAVIAR/CAVIARDATA1/

Recall, precision and F-measure are used as accuracy metrics to quantitatively compare our approach with other existing ones. Taking TP as the number of true positives, FP as the number of false positives, and P is the number of positives in the test dataset, recall is defined by R=TP/P and precision is defined by Pr=TP/(TP+FP). F-measure is the harmonic mean between recall and precision and defined by F-measure=(2×R×Pr)/(R+Pr). For F-measure, larger value means better detection accuracy. We choose to use recall-precision curve (RPC, recall against 1-precision) to do the comparison in a more informative picture. After getting the detected windows reported as containing a pedestrian, PASCAL criterion is adopted to distinguish true positive windows from false positive ones. The detected window is accepted as a true positive only if the areas overlap of this window and a ground truth exceeds 50%.

Our experiments are done on a computer with a 2.3GHz Core i5 processor and 4GB main memory. All our code is implemented in C language. The related parameters of both HOG and SVM are the same as [2]. The model is trained off-line on INRIA static image pedestrian dataset which includes 2416 positive and 1218 negative images.

4.1   Determination of the Parameters

Several parameters are introduced in our approach. Just as discussed in Section 3.2, both the detection speed and accuracy are related to these parameters. Therefore we need carefully choose values for them. We use F-measure (stands for accuracy) and the number of generated sliding windows (stands for speed) to choose the value on PET2009 dataset. To separately study the impact of the value of a parameter on the speed and accuracy, the other parameters are chosen to be a fixed value based on our experiences as following:

- Distance threshold to cluster foreground pixels: $C_{threshold}=15$;
- Size threshold to filter out small regions: $R_{threshold}=10$;
- Extension width and height for regions: $\varepsilon_x=\varepsilon_y=15$;
- Foreground ratio threshold: $F_{threshold}=0.14$.

Fig.3 (a) shows the impact of $C_{threshold}$ on F-measure and number of generated sliding windows. From the figure, we can see that the number of sliding windows fast increases as the value of $C_{threshold}$ is increased. It is reasonable because more foreground pixels are clustered together thus larger candidate regions are generated. For F-measure, the relation is more complicate. When increasing the value of $C_{threshold}$, on one hand, part of the fragmented pedestrians has more chances to be clustered together thus get better detection accuracy; however on the other hand, some noises or other moving objects may also be clustered into the same clusters of pedestrians, which cause larger candidate regions along with more potential false positive results. As a result of the two factors, F-measure firstly sharply goes up when increasing the value of $C_{threshold}$ from 1, and then slowly goes down after getting the highest value when $C_{threshold}$ is 15.

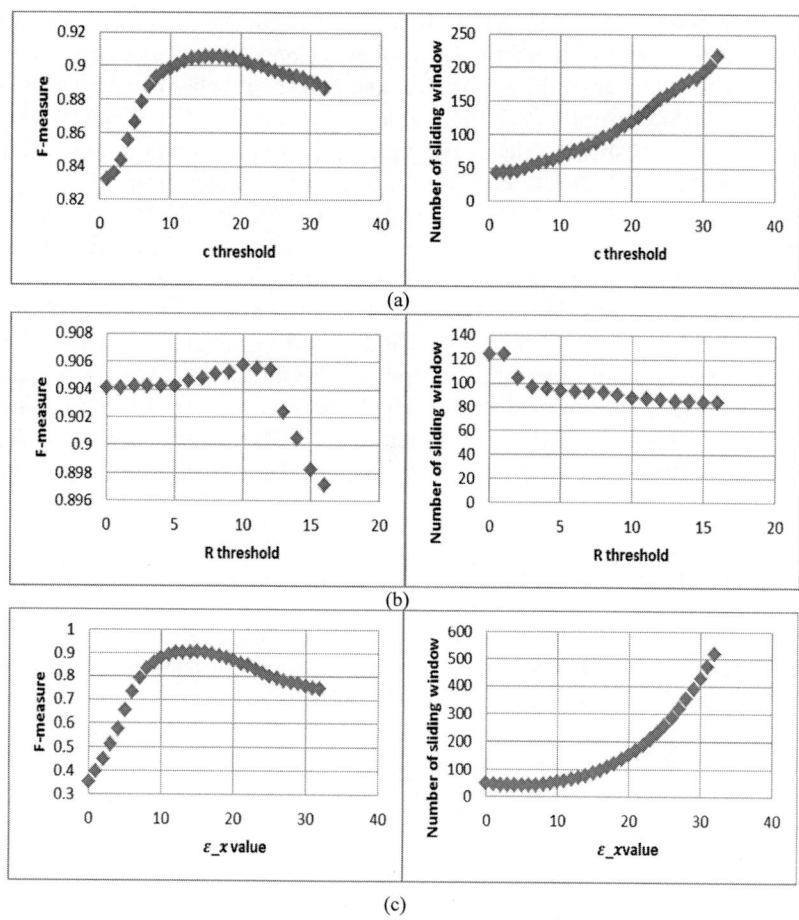

Fig. 3. F-measure and number of sliding windows for different value of (a) $C_{threshold}$ (b) $R_{threshold}$ (c) ε_x (We only show the results on PETS2009, for the reason that the impact of these parameters on F-measure and number of generated sliding windows is almost the same for those 2 datasets except that the concrete values are different.)

Since using larger value for $R_{threshold}$ can filter out more small candidate regions, the number of sliding windows decreases as the increasing of $R_{threshold}$'s value, just as showed in Fig.3 (b). Although selecting larger value for $R_{threshold}$ can filter out more negative regions, true positive regions may also be filtered out. From Fig.3 (b), we can see that the highest F-measure is obtained when the value of $R_{threshold}$ is 10.

For simplification, we use the same value for ε_x and ε_y. It is not surprising that the number of sliding windows sharply increases with the increasing value of ε_x. However, it is not intuitive for the left curve in Fig.3 (c). The gradient information of the neighborhood pixels outside the pedestrian's contour is necessary to collect concrete HOG features, thus we can get higher F-measure when increasing the value of ε_x from 0. However, just as the same reason of $C_{threshold}$, larger candidate regions caused by larger ε_x also cause more potential false positive results. Therefore, F-measure slowly decreases when the value of ε_x is greater than 15. This value is reasonable because in our training dataset, the average height of pedestrians is around 34×98 and the size of sliding window is 64×128.

The value of $F_{threshold}$ is set to be 0.14 according to our experiments on the background subtraction model: the proportion of foreground pixels of a pedestrian in a window is no less than 0.14.

4.2 Comparison with Other Methods

We compare our approach with Dalal and Triggs' (D&T) [2] approach and Dollár's FPDW [11] approach. We choose these two approaches to do comparison because D&T is the most classical approach for pedestrian detection and FPDW is the fastest approach based on sliding window paradigm according to the best of our knowledge.

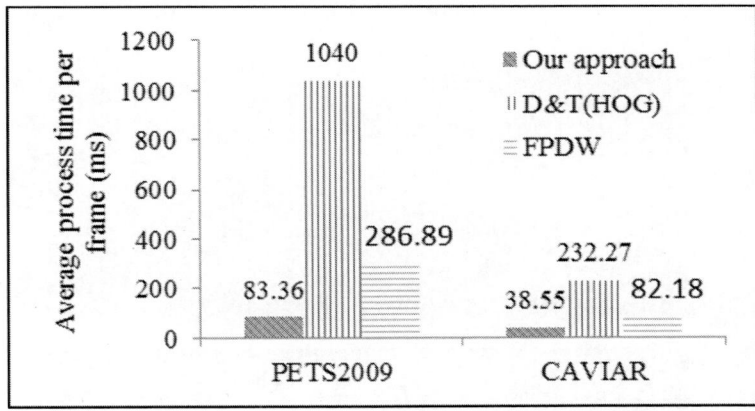

Fig. 4. Average process time per frame of our approach, D&T and FPDW on PETS2009 and CAVIAR

Fig.4 compares the average process time per frame of our approach, D&T and FPDW on PETS2009 and CAVIAR datasets. We can see that our approach is the fastest one. Our approach can achieve about 12 FPS on PETS2009, while D&T and FPDW can only achieve about 1 FPS and 3 FPS respectively. Because the video resolution of CAVIAR is lower than PETS2009, the processing time is much shorter. On CAVIAR, the detection speed of our approach is about 26 FPS, much faster than that of D&T and FPDW which are about 4 FPS and 12 FPS respectively. The speed advantage of our method mainly comes from the reduced number of windows needed to be detected through our sliding window filtering strategies. For example, the average number of sliding windows per frame on PETS2009 can be reduced from about 42,000 to 88 by our filtering strategies. Thus the cost of both features collecting and classifying of the removed windows is saved. Although background subtraction and region extraction introduce a bit of overhead, this overhead is much less than the saved time. For example, the average overhead of background subtraction and region extraction on CAVIAR is about 8.84ms and 5.52ms per frame respectively, whereas the HOG detection time is reduced from 232.27ms to 23.89ms, about 9.72 times of improvement.

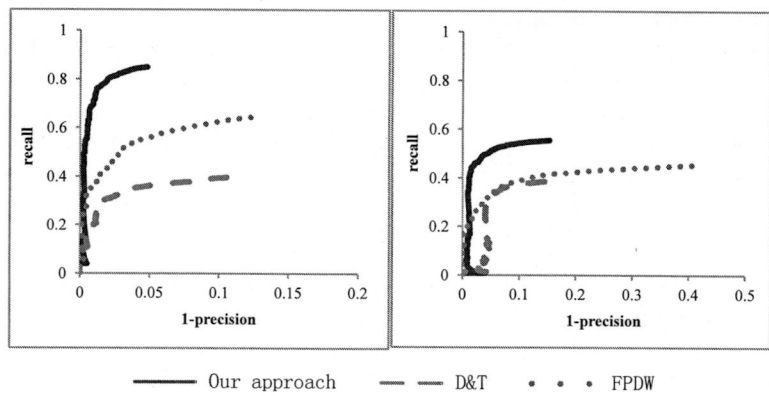

Fig. 5. RPC for (a) PETS2009 (b) CAVIAR

Fig. 6. Detection results of our approach on (a) PETS2009 (b) CAVIAR

From the RPC showed in Fig.5, we can see that our approach can get better detection accuracy than D&T and FPDW on both datasets. For example, the highest F-measure got by our approach is 0.906 on PETS2009, which is improved by 22% and 62% against FPDW (0.742) and D&T (0.559) respectively. The improvement of accuracy comes from two sides: (1) there are less false positive windows since most negative windows have been filtered out by our filtering strategies; (2) we can detected out some small size pedestrians as we have upscaling step during the multi-scale detection process. If we don't use the upscaling step, the F-measure will decrease from 0.906 to 0.43 on PETS09 and from 0.669 to 0.34 on CAVIAR. We also notice that all the three approaches are not good on CAVIAR dataset because the training dataset (mostly outdoors and seldom occlusions) is very different from CAVIAR dataset (all indoors and many occlusions). Fig.6 shows some detection results of our approach on the two datasets.

5   Conclusion

In this paper, we propose a fast pedestrian detection method by applying sliding window only on the regions containing moving objects. By reducing the number of sliding windows to be classified by combining filtering strategies based on motion and size information of the video, our method overcomes the speed drawback of sliding window paradigm without sacrificing the accuracy of detection. Our experimental results on two public datasets show that our proposed method can achieve near real-time detection rate, which is much faster than the state-of-the-art methods. Meanwhile, the accuracy of detection is also improved.

In the future, we plan to integrate other acceleration orthogonal methods (e.g. cascade method) to our system to further speed up the whole process to satisfy the real-time requirements for applications with higher video quality. Besides, how to achieve high accuracy of detection on diverse datasets of different domains through domain adaption technique is also our future work.

Acknowledgement. This work was supported in part by the   National Nature Science Foundation of China (61173054, 61271428); and Co-building Program of Beijing Municipal Education Commission.

References

1. Dalal, N.: Finding people in images and videos. Institute National Polytechnique de Grenoble (2006)
2. Dalal, N., Triggs, B.: Histograms of oriented gradients for human detection. In: IEEE Conference on Computer Vision and Pattern Recognition, CVPR, pp. 886–893 (2005)
3. Everingham, M., et al.: The PASCAL Visual Object Classes Challenge 2010 (VOC 2010) Results, http://www.pascal-network.org/challenges/VOC/voc2010/workshop/index.html
4. Dollar, P., et al.: Pedestrian detection: A benchmark. In: IEEE Conference on Computer Vision and Pattern Recognition, CVPR, pp. 304–311 (2009)
5. Enzweiler, M., Gavrila, D.M.: Monocular Pedestrian Detection: Survey and Experiments. IEEE Transactions on Pattern Analysis and Machine Intelligence, PAMI 31(12), 2179–2195 (2009)
6. Felzenszwalb, P.F., et al.: Object Detection with Discriminatively Trained Part-Based Models. IEEE Transactions on Pattern Analysis and Machine Intelligence, PAMI 32(9), 1627–1645 (2010)
7. Wang, X., Han, T.X., Yan, S.: An HOG-LBP human detector with partial occlusion handling. In: IEEE International Conference on Computer Vision, ICCV, pp. 32–39 (2009)

8. Qiang, Z., et al.: Fast Human Detection Using a Cascade of Histograms of Oriented Gradients. In: IEEE Conference on Computer Vision and Pattern Recognition, CVPR, pp. 1491–1498 (2006)
9. Viola, P., Jones, M.: Rapid object detection using a boosted cascade of simple features. In: IEEE Conference on Computer Vision and Pattern Recognition, CVPR (2001)
10. Lampert, C.H., Blaschko, M.B., Hofmann, T.: Beyond sliding windows: Object localization by efficient subwindow search. In: IEEE Conference on Computer Vision and Pattern Recognition, CVPR, pp. 1–8 (2008)
11. Dollár, P., Belongie, S., Perona, P.: The Fastest Pedestrian Detector in the West. In: British Machine Vision Conference, BMVC (2010)
12. Wei, Z., Zelinsky, G., Samaras, D.: Real-time Accurate Object Detection using Multiple Resolutions. In: IEEE International Conference on Computer Vision, ICCV, pp. 1–8. IEEE (2007)
13. Papageorgiou, C., Poggio, T.: A Trainable System for Object Detection. International Journal of Computer Vision, IJCV 38 (2000)
14. Lowe, D.G.: Distinctive image features from scale-invariant keypoints. International Journal of Computer Vision, IJCV 60(2), 91–110 (2004)
15. Dollár, P., et al.: Integral Channel Features. In: British Machine Vision Conference, BMVC (2009)
16. Barnich, O., Van Droogenbroeck, M.: ViBe: a universal background subtraction algorithm for video sequences. IEEE Transactions on Image Process., ITIP 20(6), 1709–1724 (2011)

The Research of the Face's Depth Information Generation Technology Based on the Candide Model

Jiang Taiping, Zhang Lei, and Zhang Xuefeng

School of Computer Science, Anhui University of Technology, Ma'anshan, China
{Jtp2008,zxf_06}@ahut.edu.cn, imagesuper@163.com

Abstract. Now in the 2D to 3D conversion of the many movie scenes, the obtained depth information is not satisfied because of its inaccuracy and poor stereoscopic result. The paper has provided a simple and effective approach to convert a specific two-dimensional face image to the three-dimensional face image. Firstly the Candide model is adopted as the common 3D face model. Then the global transformation and partial transformation are implemented by adjusting the control points of the Candide model in order to obtain the specific face 3D mesh model by the maximal match between the face picture and the model. Finally the specific face mesh model can match better with the 2d face by the mesh's vertex regularization and the NURBS surface fitting method, and then the accurate face depth information can be generated from the face mesh model.

Keywords: Candide model,2D to 3D,NURBS surface,depth information.

1 Introduction

In daily communication, the face plays the most impressive role in the whole body and it is also the most discriminative index of individual identity identification. In the virtual world of computer, face can play a role as a carrier of people's expressions and language and it is also the important channel of people's mutual communication. Actually, different faces have the similar parts. For example, outline of the face can be viewed as an ellipse, the position of the eyebrows, eyes, nose, mouth and other organs in the distribution of the whole face is relatively stable, and these organs also share the same properties. As a result, General face model is a collection of these same characteristics, reflecting the structure of the human face. However, there exist objectively individual differences among facial features, some of which are extremely obvious, though it appears that the two are just like the twins, they still have their own unique properties in some respects. Therefore, in the 2D to 3D conversion, it is critical to generate accurate depth information.

At present, in terms of the 2D to 3D[1] conversion, at first, the body need to be separated from the scene by the object segmentation, then give a depth value of the whole person. However, the experiments prove that three-dimensional sense is not strong.Even in some ways three-dimensional specific face models can be generated with high accuracy, the cost of the equipment is expensive and the price is high while the range of applications is limited. It should achieve such a goal finally to generate face depth information in the 2D to 3D conversion technology:1) a realistic image can

W. Lin et al. (Eds.): PCM 2012, LNCS 7674, pp. 823–831, 2012.

be produced. 2) different types of face can be applied. 3) the matches should be to the greatest extent. In order to achieve these goals above, the paper puts forward a interactive method for face depth information on the basis of Candide model after extracting the 2D face via Smart Cutout, so as to ensure the realism and accuracy of the generated 3D face.

2   Generic Model Introduction

Candide model [2] [3] is a kind of widely used parametric face the standard models in the face study, which is designed originally in order to achieve the model code of the face and has already developed to the 3rd edition (ie, Candide-3) . Candide-3 is compatible with the facial animation parameters and face definition parameters in MPEG, widely used in face modeling. Figure 1 is a triangular grid graph of Candide-3 model composed of 113 vertices and 168 surfaces which can be controlled through a series of global and partial action unit.

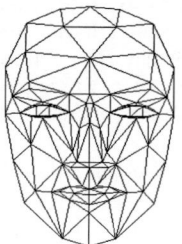 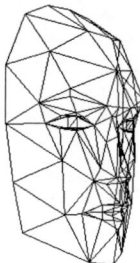

Fig. 1. Candide-3 model

Candide-3 model is a standardized 3D face model. As a result, different people faces need to be adjusted accordingly. At present, mostly manual adjustment measures are taken to work on the study based on Candide modeling methods, besides rarely there exists any precise positioning analysis according to the points in the Candide model. By analyzing the characteristics of the multi-level face images, combining with Candide-3 model feature points and interrelationship, the paper analysis and locates Facial organs. According to the feature points in the model images are analyzed to ensure the key feature points. The model and the face can be matched to the maximum extent by adjusting feature points of Candide-3 model to the appropriate location.

3   Feature Point Extraction and Model Matching

3.1   The Key Feature Points Extraction

In terms of face, the process of determining facial feature points automatically is just the process of identifying the organs and the outlines of the face. While it is easy to identify the exact locations of facial feature points from an image, it is quite difficult for the computer. The face has a complex three-dimensional surface structure. The two-dimensional images by taking photo of the face are quite different in different poses, facial expressions and lighting conditions. Now there is no more effective way to extract facial feature points automatically, leaving automatic extraction so difficult. The extraction of feature points in this paper includes the generic face mesh model and feature points extraction from specific facial photo. The definition of the feature points on the generic face mesh model can be calibrated in the Candide model. The feature points in the facial photo are extracted with the method of feature point template manual interaction.

(1) extraction of feature points from face image

At present there is not yet a uniform standard about the facial feature points. Face definition parameters FDP provides the relevant of the facial feature points. Moreover, MPEG-4 standard[4] defines the 84 individual facial feature points of the FDP and also divides them into 11 groups by region. Face can be divided into forehead, eyes, nose, cheeks, mouth, chin and face outline seven regions based on the structural features of the face, with reference to the regional distribution of facial feature points in the FDP. By comparing with the used Candide-3 model it can be known that some parts of the face need to be emphasized precisely, but the locations of the feature points defined by FDP are nor precise enough or enough in quantity. As a result, the quantity and the positions of the feature points of the eyebrows, eyes, mouth and other parts need to be revised on the basis of FDP. 64 feature points of the front face are extracted via experimental analysis finally. The classification of feature points according to facial area is shown in Table 1.

Table 1. Distribution of the number of facial feature points

face	The number of points
Eyebrow	4×2
Eyes	6×2
Nose	11
Forehead Cheeks	3
The outer ontour	16
Mouth	9
Chin	5
In total	64

(2) Universal calibration of feature points though the 3D face mesh model

This paper chooses improved Candide-3 model as a generic 3D face model, which clearly describes the contours of the face, cheeks, eyes, nose, mouth and other features. According to the number of facial feature points listed in table 1, referring to the definition of the FDP feature points the feature points of the Candide model are calibrated. 64 vertex that can best express the characteristics of frontal face are selected from the 113 vertices as feature points. Side of the model forms from rotating the positive model around the y axis. As is shown in Figure 2,where white dots are the calibration feature points, the rest vertices made up of intersected facets are non-feature points.

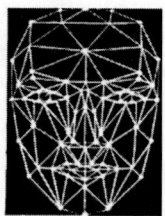
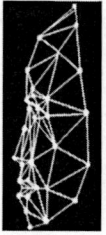

(a) the feature points of frontal face model   (b) the feature points of face's side

Fig. 2. The definition of the feature points in generic face model

3.2   Adjustment of the Face Mesh Model

After extracting feature points, we can adapt shape of the generic face mesh model to a specific face. This process is decomposed into two steps in the paper: global transformation and partial transformation.

(1) global transformation

Set P (X, Y, Z) as some point in Candide-3 model, the point P '(X', Y ', Z') as the point P corresponding to the target point. Point P does the rigid motion [4] from infinitesimal Euler angles to its target point, which can be described as follow:

$$
\begin{bmatrix} X' \\ Y' \\ Z' \end{bmatrix} = \begin{bmatrix} 1 & -\Delta\theta_z & \Delta\theta_y \\ \Delta\theta_z & 1 & -\Delta\theta_x \\ -\Delta\theta_y & \Delta\theta_x & 1 \end{bmatrix} \begin{bmatrix} S_x & 0 & 0 \\ 0 & S_y & 0 \\ 0 & 0 & S_z \end{bmatrix} \begin{bmatrix} X \\ Y \\ Z \end{bmatrix} + \begin{bmatrix} T_x \\ T_y \\ T_z \end{bmatrix}
\tag{1}
$$

$\theta x, \theta y, \theta z$ stand for rotation angles around the X, Y and Z axis respectively; Sx, Sy, Sz are the corresponding scale factors; $(Tx\ Ty\ Tz)^T$ is the translation vector. Global transformation can be equivalent as the parameter estimates of these nine sports. Translation vector can be work out by calculating the distance between the 3D face model and the center of 2D face after vertical insinuate. Pm stands for the center of the mouth, Pl stands for the central point of left eye, Pr stands for the central point of the right eye and Pc stands for the of the two eyes. Pl', Pr', Pc', Pm' are just corresponding feature points of the 2D projection in the 3D face model. Therefore, the scaling factor Sx and Sy can have the following definition:

$$
\begin{cases} S_x = \|P_l - P_r\| / \|P_l' - P_r'\| \\ S_y = \|P_c - P_m\| / \|P_c' - P_m'\| \end{cases}
\tag{2}
$$

In planar images, the depth of the face is not visible. No matter which direction is chosen for observation the result is the same. Approximation is used in the paper. It is considered that the expansion and depth extensions of the grid model in the vertical and horizontal directions are basically consistent with the actual face, so the scaling factor

Sz of the third dimension of the actual face sets the application of linear expansion as the average of Sx and Sy, which is:

$$S_z = \frac{S_x + S_y}{2} \tag{3}$$

(2) partial transformation
The most important facial features in this paper are the eyebrows, chin, eyes and mouth. In order to make the 3D face model and the 2D face a perfect match. Partial adjustments to the 3D mesh model are required according to different situations. 8 eyebrows nodes in Figure 3 replace 8 eyebrows nodes extracted from 2D face. The locations of the eyebrows node in the 3D face mesh model are adjusted to coincide with those of the eyebrows node in the 2D face. In the replacement of the chin, 5 chin nodes of the 3D face mesh model should be consistent with chin contour extracted from the 2D face through the telescopic movement.

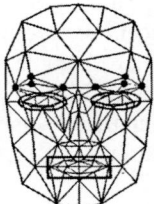

Fig. 3. Partial adjustment of the region

3.3   Adjustment of Non-feature Point

Model adjustments include mainly the adjustment of the feature points and the adjustment of non-feature points. It is necessary to adjust and determine the location of the non-feature points after adjusting three-dimensional coordinates of the model feature points. With free-form deformation, interpolation of scattered data columns, and elastic matching non-feature points can be adjusted. However, these methods have their shortcoming. For example, free-form deformation algorithm is relatively complex, radial basis function interpolates smoothly but it can not guarantee smooth interpolation. In this paper, it is improved on the basis of the aforementioned methods that based on sub-regional difference method. Based on sub-regional difference method [4], specific face model forms through the amendment of the generic face model. The correction algorithm is described as follows: First, determine the location of the reference point; then get the spatial location of feature points on the face model after adjusted; finally, set these feature points as the boundary, use the linear mapping in the regions to get corresponding position in the adjusted face model of non-feature points in the original face model.

Set points in the generic 3D face mesh model as $\{P_g(i)\}$, where $i = 1,2, ..., n$ represents the serial number of the points ;set points in the adjusted face model as $\{P_p(i)\}$. Set displacement of points from face model to those of the adjusted generic 3D face model as follows:

$$\Delta P(i) = P_p(i) - P_g(i) \tag{4}$$

According to the space geometry theorem, the space displacement of the point is equal to the sum of displacements in each direction:

$$\Delta P(i) = \overrightarrow{\Delta x(i)} + \overrightarrow{\Delta y(i)} + \overrightarrow{\Delta z(i)} \tag{5}$$

As is known from Equation 4 and Equation 5:

$$P_p(i) = P_g(i) + \Delta P(i) = P_g(i) + \overrightarrow{\Delta x(i)} + \overrightarrow{\Delta y(i)} + \overrightarrow{\Delta z(i)} \tag{6}$$

It can be drawn from the formula 6, the adjustment of the generic 3D face mesh model should be decomposed as the adjustments in x, y, and z directions respectively. Location information provided by the 2D face image can be adjusted in the x, y direction; adjustment in the z-axis direction can work on the location information of the face side view, or with artificial visual method.

After the location information of feature points in the adjusted generic model is got, it can be considered as a benchmark to fix the position of non-feature points in the model. In terms of a feature point P in the grid model, it is gotten from the position of the direction of the two most adjacent feature points in the x, y, and z-direction correction value interpolation basis. For example, P is some point in the mesh model, assuming that the two feature points in the x-axis direction adjacent the location coordinates in the model are xa and xb, in the new model is adjusted to xa' and xb' ,and the correction value on the x-axis direction by a linear mapping is:

$$x_p' = \frac{(x_p - x_a)(x_b' - x_a')}{(x_b - x_a)} + x_a' \tag{7}$$

4   The Generation of the Depth Information

4.1   NURBS Fitting Face Mesh Model

The test on 2D movie scenes or photos human face in accordance with the self-correction method of the feature point extraction and calculation of non-feature points achieve good results. Figure 4(a) is a generic 3D face mesh model .With 2D face images that matches the frontal face image (Figure 4 (b) below) and the side face inclined at an angle, its adjustment images (Figure 4 (c) below).

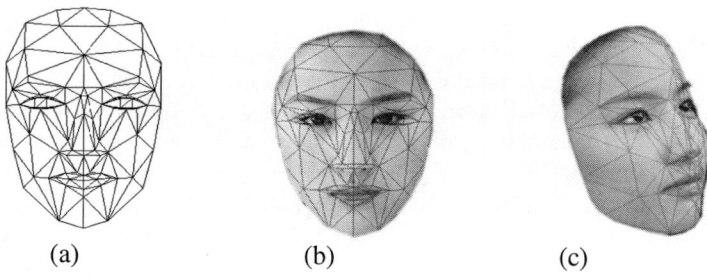

(a)   (b)   (c)

Fig. 4. The matching results of generic 3D face model and 2D image

Although 3D face mesh model obtained by matching can describe the broad contours of the face, it can not reflect specifically the smooth arc of the face. At the moment we use NURBS surfaces[5] fitting face mesh model to enable it approach the face more perfectly, to lay the foundation to generate accurate depth information of the face. Since the distribution of triangle mesh vertex in Candide model is irregular, to use non-uniform rational B-spline fitting face surface, there's necessary to transfer mesh model into a two-dimensional array grid model. According to the facial features some new vertices are needed to be identified. The new vertices and original vertices control point array together. In terms of any two given points of the mesh model $V_1(x, y, z)$ and $V_2(x, y, z)$, set the new interpolation point as $V(x, y, z)$.Therefore according to the linear interpolation method:

$$V(x, y) = (1 - a)V_1(x, y) + aV_2(x, y), (0 \leq a \leq 1)$$

$$V(z) = (1 - b)V_1(z) + bV_2(z) \tag{8}$$

$V(x, y)$ stands for coordinates of vertex $V(x, y)$; $V(z)$ stands for the z coordinate of the vertex V.

As is shown in Figure 5, t, location of interpolation points $V(x, y, z)$ change as he parameters a and b values change. To control over changes of the curve more precisely, new different control points between the two points can be gotten by using different parameters.

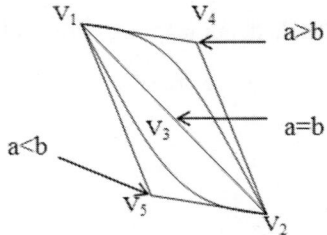

Fig. 5. B-spline curves fitting

Control lattice specific face mesh by interpolation, given the control lattice P_{ij} (i = 0,1 ..., n; j = 0,1, ..., m), the corresponding weights ω_{ij}, u and v direction vector : u_0, u_1 ...u_{n+k+1} and $v_0, v_1 ... v_{n+k+1}$, the grid model of rational B-spline surfaces for:

$$P(u, v) = \frac{\sum_{i=0}^{n} \sum_{j=0}^{m} \omega_{ij} P_{ij} B_{i,k}(u) B_{j,l}(v)}{\sum_{i=0}^{n} \sum_{j=0}^{m} \omega_{ij} B_{i,k}(u) B_{j,l}(v)} \quad (u_k \leq u \leq u_{n+1}, v_l \leq v \leq v_{m+1}) \tag{9}$$

4.2   The Creation of Face's Depth Generation Information

It can be seen from the calculation above that the depth value associated with each point is relevant to its value in the X-axis. Let us suppose feature points in adjusted facial mesh model would obtain the maximum and minimum, respectively Pmax and Pmin in the Z-axis, P(z) represents the value of curved surface's point. Then the scene should be analyzed to give the face a appropriate depth value [a,b], assuming the depth value d associated with the point P. Based on relative proportional relationship:

$$\frac{P(z) - P_{min}(z)}{P_{max}(z) - P_{min}(z)} = \frac{d - a}{b - a} \qquad (10)$$

It can be concluded from the derivation:

$$d = \frac{(P(z) - P_{min}(z))(b - a)}{P_{max}(z) - P_{min}(z)} + a \qquad (11)$$

The depth value of established NURBS curved surface will be given on the basis of the calculation above, for example, the depth value of front face is endowed with 235~145 (i.e. a=235,b=145) and the depth map is shown as 6(a); the value of side face is 240~150 (i.e. a=240. b=150) and the depth map is shown as 6(b).

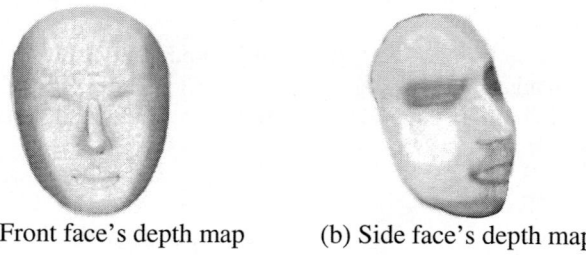

(a) Front face's depth map   (b) Side face's depth map

Fig. 6. The face's depth map

5   Conclusion

This paper, in regardless of illumination or other image noise jamming, supposes one simple and paper method of facial information creation in the conversion from 2D to 3D, based on Candide generic mesh model. Firstly, interactive approach will be used to acquire future points in generic facial model and 2D face. Secondly, generic facial model will be processed in the form of global transformation and local transformation. Thirdly, non-future points will be adjusted according to sub-region difference method and linear interpolation method will be adopted to obtain coordinate in Z-axis. Finally, specific depth values will be given to two points which are maximum and minimum in Z-axis according to the scene. Also, depth values of other points will be created automatically. Compared with other approaches, the innovation of this paper is that candied generic model can be matched with different 2D faces through global transformation and local transformation. In terms of its influences, people as a whole are normally be given a depth value in the transition from 2D to 3D, which may exert a paper effect to some extent. The facial depth data with using approaches proposed by this paper is satisfied because it will achieve evident stereo effect and strong sense of reality. However, there still have some issues for this paper to undertake. For examples, future points taken from pictures can be created into models automatically, thereby reducing manual work. Issues such as improving automaticity and reality need be concerned as well.

References

1. Dai, Q., Li, T.: Method based on human-computer interaction plane video transfer three-dimensional video. Chinese patent number: ZL200810102033.1 (September 2008)
2. Act, Y., Wei, X., Sheng, W.: Face adaptive 3D modeling. Computer Engineering and Applications 46(19) (2010)
3. Zhang, X., Zhi-Yong, L., Hua, B., Chen, Y.-Y.: The photo synthetic 3D face from the positive side. Computer Applications 20(7), 42–45 (2000)
4. Gang, W.: Modeling, method study on automatically leaflets frontal face photo-based 3D Face. Nanjing University of Technology and Engineering, 6–11, 50–55 (2008)
5. Yin, Y.: 3D face wireframe model of NURBS surface fitting. Digital Technology and Mechanical Processes, 15–17 (October 2009)
6. Jiang, T., Wang, S., Zhan, T.: Generation of Depth Information Based on Motion Estimation. Computer Technology and Development (10) (2010)
7. Sheng, Y., Sadka, A.H., Kondoz, A.M.: Automatic 3D face synthesis using single video frame. IEEE Electronics Letters 40(19) (September 2004)
8. Ahlberg: CANDIDE-3 an updated parameterized face. Report No. LiTH-ISY-R-2326, Dept. of Electrical Engineering, Linkoping University, Sweden (2001)

Action Segmentation in Dance Videos

Han Tingting[1], Yao Hongxun[1,*], Sun Xiaoshuai[1], and Liu Guoyi[2]

[1] School of Computer Science and Technology, Harbin Institute of Technology, China
[2] NEC Laboratories China
h.yao@hit.edu.cn

Abstract. In this paper, we consider the problem of segmentation of dance videos with unconstrained background. A dynamic saliency detection algorithm is adopted to achieve a fast extraction of the videos' action characteristics, which is robust to the background movements and unexpected distractions. We calculate the saliency of the frame differences and select the maximum within every frame to plot a maximum saliency curve, which reflects the movement along the whole video. After filtered with the frequency filter, the influence of macro body movements is eliminated significantly. We detect the local minimums of the smoothed saliency curve as the boundaries of the segmentations. We test our method on various well annotated dance videos. The experimental results demonstrate the superior performance and robustness of the proposed approach.

Keywords: Action segmentation, action extraction, action boundary detection, visual saliency, dance video.

1 Introduction

In recent years, problems on video analysis concentrate on human actions more and more [1, 2, 3]. As a typical kind of video all composed of human movement, dance video will cause topics worth studying. By the time, the segmentation of dance videos will also become a quite meaningful studying point. It may help to implement intelligent video browsing based on action units. Besides, most studies on action recognition are based on action clips generated manually, so the automatic segmentation process will become a very practical method to reduce the manual work.

To deal with traditional video segmentation problem, there are usually two steps. The first step is to detect the shot boundaries. Many classical algorithms have been proposed to address this problem including algorithms based on color histogram differences [4], edge change ratio [5], algorithms specialized on fades [6] and so on. Until recent years, there are still many researchers exploring new methods [7, 8, 9]. The second step is to extract key frames from the shots. Some of existing algorithms simply take the middle or the marginal frame of the shot as the key frames [10].

---
[*] The work was supported by the National Natural Science Foundation of China (61071180, 61133003), the Defence Advance Research Project of China (40401040204) and NEC (China) Co. Ltd. Project (LC04_20121205-08).

W. Lin et al. (Eds.): PCM 2012, LNCS 7674, pp. 832–840, 2012.

Ngo [11] creates a new frame using mosaic as the key frame. Wolf [12] takes an approach of motion analysis to decide the key frames. Among recent work for action recognition, much effort focuses on the event detection approach. The algorithms predict the event by evaluating a classifier function at segments to be detected [13, 14, 15]. Besides, other techniques such as change-points detection technique, work by performing a sequence of change-point analysis [16]. Action segmentation has also been studied from analyzing periodicity of cyclic events [17, 18]. Algorithms on action recognition were designed based on supervised learning [19, 20]. However, these methods typically have high time complexities.

Different from common video segmentation, the segmentation of dance videos throws out a new challenging problem to us, that is, how to segment the video into meaningful action units accurately.

In this paper, we propose a fast and robust method to segment dance videos with unconstraint background according to the action clues. In order to precisely localize the boundary frame of dance actions, the first essential step is to separate the foreground dancing actions from the unrestricted background scenes. As the background is unrestricted, it might either be purely static or contain large dynamic changes caused by camera motions. Traditional motion compensation methods take little effect on such scenarios, in which foreground actions occupy a large percentage of video motions and there exist other distractions such as caption texts or company logos. The other challenge lies in the complexity of dance actions. Take *Latin* for example, a single beat dance contains large movements of the whole body and several macro movements from each body parts such as head shaking and arm swing.

To deal with the challenge of foreground/background separation, we propose a method to represent the foreground dancing action using dynamic visual saliency, which is proved to be fast and robust to various camera motions and the interference from caption and subtitle texts. As for the action complexity issue, we adopt a straightforward frequency domain filtering approach to illuminate the noises caused by macro body movements in order to provide a smooth feature flow for action segmentation and further rhythm analysis.

The remainder of the paper is organized as follows. In Section 2, we first overview the proposed method, and then we describe the details. Section 3 shows the experimental results of rhythm analysis and action driven segmentation on various kinds of dance videos. Finally, we conclude the paper and discuss the direction of our future work.

2   Method

The overview of the proposed approach is shown in Fig. 1. Firstly, we describe dance actions using dynamic saliency in order to implement the fast and robust action extraction from the unconstraint background. After that, we can get a curve of saliency as the description of the dance actions. Then, we detect the local minimums of the saliency curve as the boundaries of actions, which indicate the local minimums of the movements. In order to improve the accuracy of the detection result, we execute noise reduction based on the saliency curve in advance. At the end of the process, we can get the smaller video clips with meaningful dancing actions embedded.

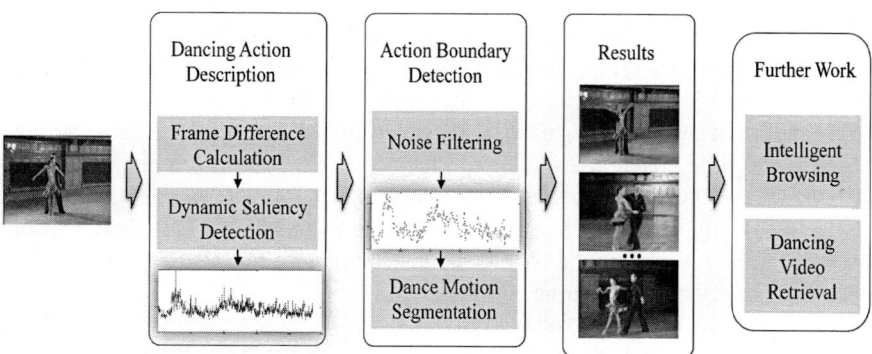

Fig. 1. The framework of action segmentation in dance videos

2.1   Describing Dancing Action Using Dynamic Saliency

In our study, most subjects agree that the action of the dancers is much more salient compared with background movements in all kinds of dance videos, which inspired us to use a well-known quantitative visual attention measure, namely visual saliency, to represent the foreground dancing actions. There are many off-the-shelf approaches to compute signal saliency [18][19][20]. Hou *et al.* [19] proposed Spectral Residual (**SR**) approach based on Fourier Transform, which is purely unsupervised and able to detect salient objects rapidly. After that, Guo *et al.* [20] further simplified the original SR approach by using Phase preserving inverse Fourier Transform (**PFT**). Considering the factors on both computational efficiency and biological plausibility, we design our dynamic saliency detection algorithm using a **PFT**-like strategy:

$$f(x, y) = F\left(I_i(x, y) - I_{i-n}(x, y)\right) \tag{1}$$

$$S(x, y) = \left\| F^{-1}\left(e^{i \cdot P(f(x, y))}\right) \right\| \tag{2}$$

where I_i is the ith video frame, F is the Fourier Transform and F^{-1} the inverse Fourier Transform, $P(f)$ represents the phase spectrum of f. In order to minimize the influence of static visual appearance and only extract the salient dancing actions, we take frame differences as the input data instead of the original RGB images. Some examples of saliency detection results are shown in Fig. 2. Both of the two video sequences contain large background motions caused by rapid camera movements. The visualized results clearly show that only the background is restrained effectively in the dynamic saliency map, which demonstrate the effectiveness of our proposed action extraction strategy and also its robustness against the background motions.

Note that, we have also tried to use traditional motion compensation methods, such as **SIFT-RANSAC**, to illuminate the influences of the background movements. Firstly, mosaic the neighboring frames by aligning the background. Then, carry out the frame difference to get the foreground extraction. However, these methods performed very poor due to two main factors: 1. The actions of the dancers occupy a large percentage of video motions which makes it harder for global motion estimation; 2. The appearance of the background scenes has very large variations which might offer either too many or too few feature points for homography computation. Other issues such as subtitles can also affect the compensation performance. Fortunately, all above issues could be well handled by our proposed strategy.

In Fig. 3, we can observe that the maximum saliency values of the video frames show very obvious rhythmicity which we think is related with the rhythm of the dance actions themselves. This interesting appearance gives us an important clue for action driven dance video segmentation.

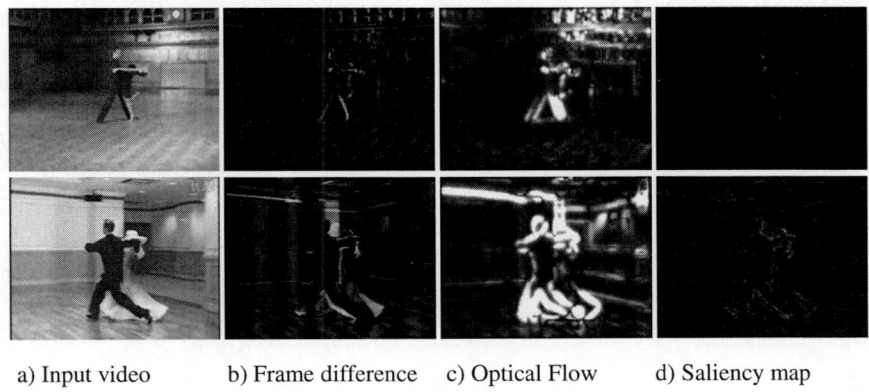

   a) Input video   b) Frame difference   c) Optical Flow   d) Saliency map

Fig. 2. Examples of dynamic saliency detection

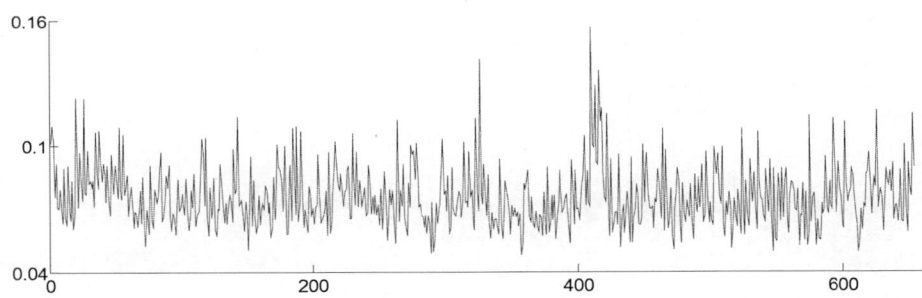

Fig. 3. The maximum saliency value of each frame in a typical dance video sequence

2.2 Noise Filtering and Action Boundary Detection

To our knowledge, typical dances usually have their unique rhythms. Within one rhythm, it is consist of large movements of the dancers which might lead to larger saliency values. Between two beats, it is usually a pause lasting for a short time or macro body movements like waving arms and macro writhes of body which has smaller saliency relatively. Inspired by these factors, we propose a method to segment the video into subsections by detecting the local minimal values of saliency. However, it is still difficult to precisely localize the boundary frame. Considering the curve, it is not that surprising to associate the problem with signal noise reduction. When processing signal noise, frequency filtering is the most common and effective method.

Therefore, based on the maximum saliency value, we utilize a filter to get a smooth saliency curve before the boundary detection.

The procedure of our method can be summarized as follows:

— Transform the maximum saliency values to frequency domain with Fourier Transform.
— Set a threshold for the frequency curve in order to eliminate the component whose frequency is higher than the threshold.
— Detect the local minimum using a sliding window over the recovered signal of inverse Fourier Transform.
— Check the points to make sure that they are minimal points we need instead of the boundary of the sliding window.

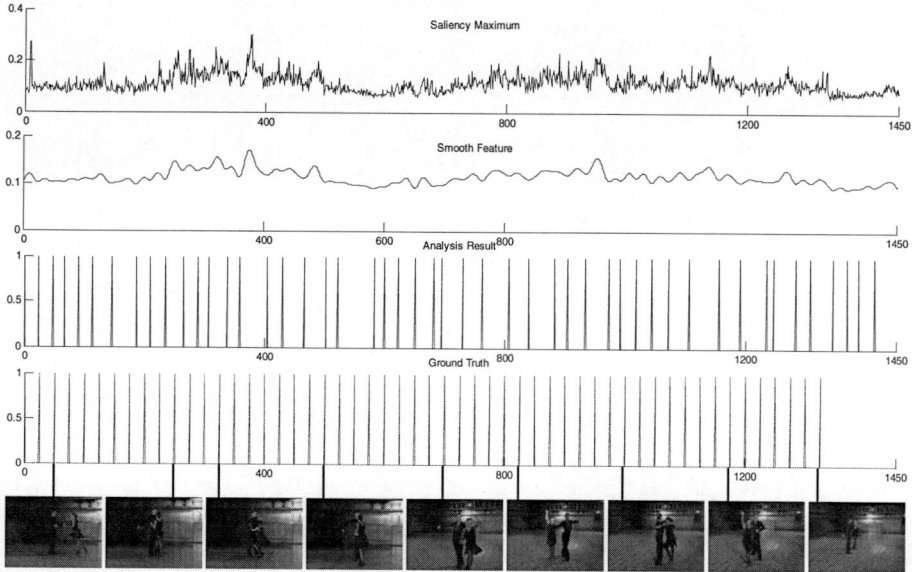

Fig. 4. Action driven dance video segmentation (Line 1, raw maximum saliency data; line 2, smoothed saliency after filtering; line 3, segmentation results produced by the proposed method; line 4, the referential results labeled by hands; line 5, some examples of the boundary frames)

Some examples of segmentation results are shown in Fig. 4. The smoothed saliency curve shows the rhythm more clearly after eliminating the influence of macro body movements, which makes it much easier to localize the boundary of each segment. The result of our proposed method and the ground truth are both visualized in Fig. 4. It shows that the proposed method performs very well in segmenting the dance videos with dynamically changing background caused by camera motions and other distractions appeared in the video unexpectedly. Quantitative analysis of the video segmentation results will be presented in Sec 3.

In addition, when changing the threshold for filtering, we can get various smoothed results in varying degrees. The larger the threshold is set, the more influence of the macro body movements will be retained and the more boundaries will be detected. Note that, we have also taken the sum of saliency as the raw data to be filtered and further applied to video segmentations. The result is not as good as that produced by the maximum saliency values.

3 Experiment and Result

In order to examine the feasibility of our approach and to evaluate its performance, videos of multiple dances are collected and annotated. Then, we implement the method recommended above and some other comparison experiment. We test these methods on the video set and get the ROC curve. At last, the results and some phenomena are analyzed in detail at the end of this chapter.

3.1 Data Collection

We have collected and annotated 27 videos with 10 kinds of dances used for teaching to form a regular dataset for implementing and evaluating the proposed action driven video segmentation method. The detailed information of the dance video dataset is listed in Table 1.

Table 1. Testing videos used in the experiment

Name	Quantity	Frames	mm:ss	Cuts
Cha Cha	3	2657	02:51	143
Foxtrot	3	2654	02:55	93
Jive	2	1629	01:47	81
Paso Doble	2	3966	02:54	108
Quick Step	3	2332	02:34	121
Rumba	2	3753	02:46	108
Samba	2	3094	02:23	110
Tango	3	2454	02:42	116
Viennese Waltz	2	1643	01:49	103
Waltz	5	6251	06:55	218

3.2 Comparison Experiment

For comparisons, we set several extra experiments including methods based on the frame differences directly and the method proposed by Wolf [12] based on motion analysis. Here, we haven't compared our method to traditional approaches of shot cut problems, because the data we collect used for teaching has only one shot in each video, there's no need to detect the shot boundary additionally.

We set a threshold to the frame differences and reset the values below the threshold to zero. Then, we make two different decisions to find the cut points, one is to find the mid-points(**MP**) of the zero regions as the cut points, and the other is to find catastrophe points(**CP**) as the detection results.

Wolf's method calculates the optical flow filed first and then measures the movement using the sum of modules in the current frame. Similar to our method, he detects the local minimums of the movement values as the key frame.

3.3   Evaluation Metric

In order to quantify the performance of the methods, we use *Precision* and *Recall* scores similar with traditional video segmentation problem. Considering the differences between shot detection and human action composed video's cut detection, our evaluation tolerates the error of seven frames around the points detected by the algorithms when identifying the match between the detected cut and the labeled cut.

$$Recall = |GT \cap Seg| / GT \tag{3}$$

$$Precision = |GT \cap Seg| / Seg \tag{4}$$

where **GT** is the set of labeled cuts, and **Seg** is the set of cuts detected by the programs. The term | **GT** ∩ **Seg** | represents the number of the labeled samples which are correctly detected. By varying the threshold of the frame differences or the filters, we can get the ROC curves for all approaches mentioned above, as shown in Fig.5.

3.4   Result Analysis

It is clear to see from Fig.5 that our method and Wolf's method [12] both have much better performance on the testing videos than **MP** and **CP** on both recall and precision. We can also observe a very strange phenomenon that there are no curves in interval (0.6, 1]. After analyzing carefully, we think the possible reasons are as follows. With the increase of the threshold, the cut points increase gradually, which causes the recall value becomes larger and larger and then achieves the maximum. After that, the cut points will decrease when the threshold value becomes too large and this will result in the decrease of the recall value. However, although the recall value is maximal, the simplicity and coarseness of the algorithms make it difficult to achieve higher recall value.

What's more, our approach performs better than Wolf's, although there are few points matched between the two curves, which may result from the manual annotating error. The area under the curve of our approach is 6.5 percent larger than his. Besides, what's worth specially mentioning is that our method takes 0.007717 seconds to deal with one frame, the time cost is so little that our method can achieve real-time performance. However, Wolf's method involves large time complexities. According to our observation, if we set the iterations to 16 when calculating the optical flow field, it will get acceptable result in both time cost and optical flow density. But even so, it takes 0.332733 seconds to process one frame and the time cost is more than 40 times than our method. It follows that our method has much better efficiency than Wolf's method.

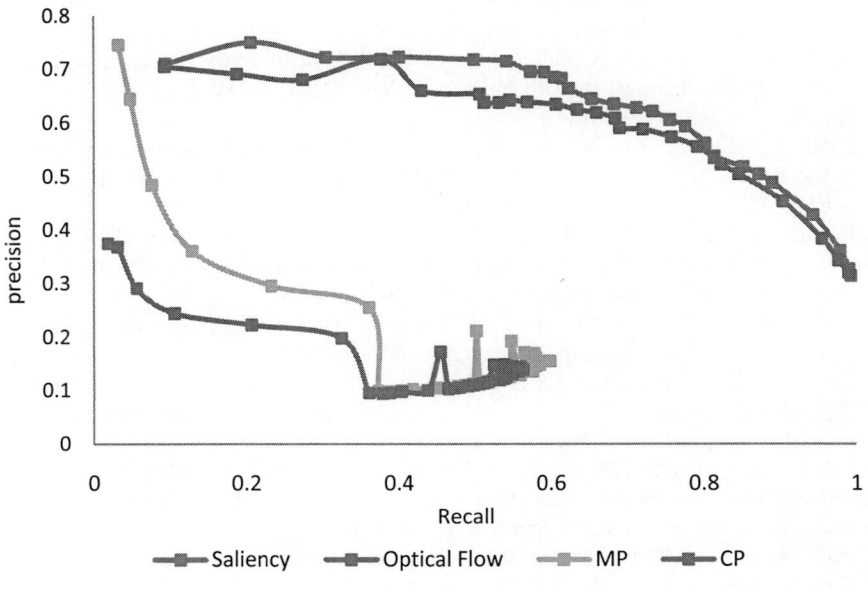

Fig. 5. ROC Curves

4 Conclusion and Future Work

In this paper, we have proposed a dance video segmentation method based on dynamic visual saliency. We calculate the maximal dynamic saliency of every frame to represent the movement within the current shot. It works fast and has been proved robust enough to background motions and other distractions such as captions and subtitles. Utilizing frequency filtering, we eliminate the negative effects generated by macro body movements. The experimental results tested on the dataset demonstrate the effectiveness and robustness of our method.

In our future work, we will build an intelligent dance video browsing system based on the video segmentation algorithm due to its rapidness. The browser will automatically segment the videos into short action segments in real time, and allow the viewers to drag videos forward or backward based on action units instead of time units. Another feasible work is to build a dance video retrieval system based on the action units, combining with existing retrieval methods.

References

1. Jiang, X., Khosla, A., Lin, A., Guibas, L., Li, F.: Human action recognition by learning bases of action attributes and parts. In: ICCV, pp. 1331–1338 (2011)
2. Dexter, E., Laptev, I., Perez, P.: View-Independent Action Recognition from Temporal Self-Similarities. IEEE TPAMI 33(1), 172–185 (2011)

3. Ji, R., Yao, H., Sun, X.: Actor-independent action search using spatiotemporal vocabulary with appearance hashing. Pattern Recognition 44(3), 624–638 (2011)
4. Voreczky, J.S., Rowe, L.A.: Comparison of Video Shot Boundary Detection Techniques. In: Storage and Retrieval for Still Image and Video Databases IV. Proc. SPIE, vol. 2664, pp. 170–179 (January 1996)
5. Zabih, R., Miller, J., Mai, K.: A Featured-based Algorithm for Detecting and Classifying Scene Breaks. In: Proc. ACM Multimedia 1995, San Francisco, CA, pp. 189–200 (November 1995)
6. Lienhart, R., Kuhmunch, C., Effelsberg, W.: On the Detection and Recognition of Television Commercials. In: Proceedings of the International Conference on Multimedia Computing and Systems, Ontario, Canada, pp. 509–516 (June 1997)
7. Bai, L., Lao, S.Y., Liu, H.T., Bu, J.: Video shot boundary detection using petri-net. In: Proc. Int. Conf. Mach. Learning Cybern., pp. 3047–3051 (2008)
8. Chang, Y., Lee, D.J., Hong, Y., Archibald, J.: Unsupervised video shot detection using clustering ensemble with a color global scale invariant feature transform descriptor. EURASIP J. Image Video Process., 1–10 (2008)
9. Baber, J., Afzulpurkar, N., Dailey, M.N., Bakhtyar, M.: Shot Boundary Detection from Videos Using Entropy and Local Descriptor. In: Proceedings of 17th International Conference Digital Signal Processing, pp. 6–8 (July 2011)
10. Pentland, et al.: Video and Image Semantics, Advanced Tools for Telecommunications. IEEE Multimedia (Summer 1994)
11. Ngo, C.W.: Analysis of Spatio-temporal Slice for Video Content Representation. PH.D. thesis (2000)
12. Wolf, W.: Key Frame Selection by Motion Analysis. In: Proc. IEEE Int. Conf. Acoust., Speech and Signal Proc. (1996)
13. Ke, Y., Sukthankar, R., Hebert, M.: Event detection in crowded videos. In: ICCV (2007)
14. Duchenne, O., Laptev, I., Sivic, J., Bach, F.R., Ponce, J.: Automatic annotation of human actions in video. In: ICCV (2009)
15. Nguyen, M.H., Simon, T., De la Torre, F., Cohn, J.: Action unit detection with segment-based SVMs. In: CVPR (2010)
16. Harchaoui, Z., Bach, F., Moulines, E.: Kernel change-point analysis. In: NIPS (2009)
17. Cutler, R., Davis, L.: Robust real-time periodic motion detection, analysis, and applications. IEEE TPAMI 22(8), 781–796 (2000)
18. Pogalin, E., Smeulders, A., Thean, A.: Visual quasi-periodicity. In: CVPR (2008)
19. Le, Q.V., Zou, W.Y., Yeung, S.Y., Ng, A.Y.: Learning hierarchical invariant spatio-temporal features for action recognition with independent subspace analysis. In: CVPR (2011)
20. Liu, J., Kuipers, B., Savarese, S.: Recognizing Human Action by Attributes. In: CVPR (2011)
21. Itti, L., Koch, C., Niebur, E., et al.: A Model of Saliency-based Visual Attention for Rapid Scene Analysis. IEEE TPAMI 20(11), 1254–1259 (1998)
22. Hou, X., Zhang, L.: Saliency Detection: A Spectral Residual Approach. In: CVPR (2007)
23. Guo, C., Ma, Q., Zhang, L.: Spatio-temporal Saliency Detection using Phase Spectrum of Quaternion Fourier Transform. In: CVPR (2008)

Topology Adaptation Based on Mobile Agent in Unstructured P2P Networks

XiangJun Shen[1], PeiYing Gu[1], Zheng-Jun Zha[2], and JiMing Chen[1]

[1] School of Computer Science and Telecommunication Engineering,
Jiangsu University, Zhenjiang, 212013, China
xjshen@ujs.edu.cn
[2] School of Computing, National University of Singapore, Singapore

Abstract. Peer-to-Peer (P2P) network has shown encouraging capacity in facilitating multimedia communication over Internet. This paper focuses on the topology adaptation in P2P networks. A new topology adaptation approach based on mobile agent is proposed to resolve the congestion caused by resource location in unstructured P2P networks. In our approach, peers direct mobile agent to migrate to the potential congestion peers based on their neighbors' characteristics including processing capacity and connectedness. Thus congestion can be found effectively and the topology optimization mechanism is then used to resolve the congestions. Simulation results show that the proposed method can improve networks topology, avoid congestions effectively and increase the efficiency of resource location.

Keywords: P2P, congestion, mobile agent, topology optimization.

1 Introduction

With the rapid development of large-scal storage, high performance computation, and broadband network technology, the information transferred on Internet goes beyond pure text, and consists of increasing multimedia communication, which makes video, image, audio, text as one kind and provides richer user experience. Recently, Peer-to-Peer (P2P) technology has been developed to facilitate multimedia communication over Internet. Contrast to traditional Client-Server networks, P2P networks, including structured and unstructured P2P networks, can share their resources, bandwidth, processing capacity and storage space with other peers [1]. P2P networks facilitate many applications, such as file sharing, distributed computing and video streaming, etc [2]. The distributed characteristics of P2P networks, especially the unstructured networks, pose difficulty in resource location. To address this problem, several protocols have been proposed, such as random walk [3], APS [4]. However, the heterogeneity of peer capacities and uneven distribution of data objects among peers may lead to congestion in weaker peers, which have serious influence on the performance of search protocols [5]. Load balancing is thus proposed to balance the loads and avoid congestion in P2P network [6–12].

W. Lin et al. (Eds.): PCM 2012, LNCS 7674, pp. 841–849, 2012.

Existing load balancing methods can be classified into two categories, i.e., topology adaptation and topology maintaining approaches, according to whether the topology structure changes. The topology adaptation methods change the topology structure to make capable peers possess high node degree, so that they can process more search queries. For example, in Gia [6], the topology is adapted based on the peers' level of satisfaction, therefore more capable peers could link to more peers. In DANTE [7] the topology is changed depending on peers' attractiveness which makes the average degree of the peers with the highest capacity very close to the maximum number of possible connections. In these protocols, if the rate of query generation accelerates, the central peers will become congested quickly. On the other hand, the topology maintaining methods, this subclass of methods balances the network loads by reassigning excessive incoming loads of overloaded peers to capable peers. In [8, 9] peers exchange messages of load information periodically in order to make decisions on load balancing, but the message exchanges result in high communication latency and thus deteriorate the performance of the system. Mobile agent technology provides a new solution in the topology maintaining methods to support load balancing for its merits of high flexibility, low network traffic as well as less communication latency [10]. In [11, 12], agent moves in the network randomly to look for overloaded peers.

In this paper we propose a topology adaptation approach based on mobile agent in unstructured P2P networks. Every Peer in the network collects its neighbors' local information such as processing capacity and connectedness. The mobile agent is directed by such local information to migrate among the possible congested neighbor peers. Once the mobile agent migrates to a peer and detects the possible congestion in it, the mobile agent will launch a topology optimization mechanism. Thus our method can discover congestions in time and avoid congestions by reconnecting excessive links to other capable peers. Simulation results show that the proposed method can improve networks topology, avoid congestions effectively and increase the efficiency of resource location.

This paper is organized as follows: Section 2 describes the topology adaptation protocol. Section 3 presents the simulation results. The paper is concluded in section 4.

2   Topology Adaptive Protocol

To make full use of peers' capacity, the reconnection mechanism is used in our work to grant capable peers possess more neighbors. At the same time, the mobile agent is used to avoid those capable peers possess too many neighbors which lead to congestion. In this section, we firstly introduce the topology optimization mechanism based on the mobile agent. Then we introduce the reconnection mechanism which is launched by the peers themselves.

2.1   Mobile Agent Based Topology Optimization Mechanism

According to the reconnection mechanism which will be introduced in the next section, the higher a peer's capacity is, the more neighbors a peer would possess. So the higher capacity peers with large number of neighbors will become congested peers more easily than lower capacity peers. Based on the analysis above, the mobile agent is designed in this paper to migrate among these peers with high connectedness and high capacity to optimize the topology structure. As the network is unstructured and the mobile agent does not know where those peers are, a parameter called attractiveness is introduced in our method to direct the mobile agent to migrate to the possible congested peers. The procedure of topology optimization is introduced as follows.

Table 1. An Example neighbor-table of a peer with five neighbors

Neighbor	Capacity	Connectedness	Attractiveness
P_1	1	6	6
P_2	0.1	3	0.3
P_3	10	7.5	75
P_4	100	14	1400
P_5	100	12.5	1250

Each peer maintains a neighbor-table which records the connectedness [13] and capacity of its neighbors. Table 1 gives an example neighbor-table of a peer. And the attractiveness of every neighbor peer is computed by the formula 1.

$$A_i = \chi(i, k_c) \times C_i \tag{1}$$

where $\chi(i, k_c)$ denotes the connectedness of peer P_i, and C_i is the capacity of P_i. The larger A_i is, the more likely the mobile agent migrates to P_i.
And the connectedness of P_i in P2P network is computed as follows.

$$\chi(i, k_c) = \sum_{h=1}^{h=k_c} \frac{N(i, h)}{h^\delta} \tag{2}$$

$N(i, h)$ denotes the set of peers that are h hops away from P_i, k_c is the lookahead parameter for the connectedness of P_i, δ is a control parameter.

The mobile agent chooses its next visiting-peer from the current peer's Neighbor-Table. Assuming the current peer is P_i, then the next visiting-peer is P_m.

$$P_m = \underset{j \in N_i - (N_i \cap R)}{argmax} A_j \tag{3}$$

where N_i is the set of neighbors of P_i, R is the set of recently visited peers by the mobile agent. And P_m is the peer with maximum attractiveness and not in the set of R.

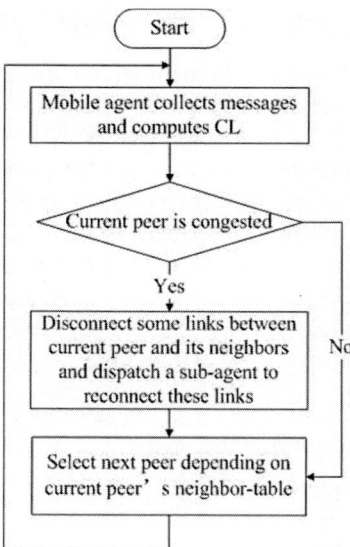

Fig. 1. Mobile agent based topology optimization procedure

Applying this migration strategy, the mobile agent is directed to migrate among the most likely congested peers. Thus we can detect the congestion situation in the network more quickly. We use the congestion level (CL) [14] to predict whether a peer is congested or not. And the value of CL of peer P_i at time t is computed as:

$$CL_i(t) = \frac{1 + Q_i(t)}{C_i} \tag{4}$$

where $Q_i(t)$ denotes the number of queries that are waiting for being processed in P_i's input buffer at time t. C_i represents the processing capacity of P_i. Equation 4 reflects the waiting time a walker would spend if it is forwarded to the peer P_i.

The mobile agent judges whether a peer is congested or not by comparing the value of CL with two thresholds B_t and U_t, and then changes the load state of the peer at the same time. In our algorithm, each peer has three load states: under-loaded, normal-loaded and over-loaded and the variable *flag* is used to represent these three states.

$$flag_i = \begin{cases} -1, & CL_i <= B_t \\ 0, & B_t < CL_i < U_t \\ 1, & CL_i >= U_t \end{cases} \tag{5}$$

For each peer, if *flag* $= +1$, it means the peer is over-loaded and congested. In this case, the peer will refuse any connection request. If *flag* $= -1$, it indicates the peer is under-loaded and the peer accepts connection requests. If *flag* $= 0$, it indicates the peer is normal-loaded. In this case, the peer determines whether to accept connection requests or not based on its previous load state. If the peer's previous load state is over-loaded, it will refuse the connection requests. Otherwise it will accept the connection requests.

When the mobile agent arrives at a peer, it detects if the peer is congested by collecting the number of queries that are waiting for being processed in the input buffer and then computing the congestion level of current peer. When the mobile agent finds a congested peer, some connections would be reconnected to the peers with spare capacity. To fulfill the task of reconnection, a sub-agent which is dispatched by the mobile agent is used. After dispatching a sub-agent, the mobile agent migrates to the next peer. The sub-agent then searches the peers with spare capacity through breadth-first traversal method, and then links the redundant connections to those peers. The sub-agent's life will be terminated when the reconnection process finishes.

The whole topology optimization procedure on mobile agent is shown in Fig.1.

2.2   Reconnection Mechanism

To make full use of the capacity of capable peers, every peer triggers the reconnection mechanism periodically. Peers reconnect themselves to the most capable peers who are chosen from a set of candidate peers. Similar with DANTE [7], to build the candidate peer set, the initiator peer, assumed as peer P_i, launches a Look-For-Peer message to start a new reconnection process. And the message is sent in the network through random walk method with a bounded TTL (time to live). When the TTL expires, the list of peers with spare capacity in the propagation path of Look-For-Peer message are sent to P_i and become the elements of candidate set. The candidate set is marked as S_i. P_i then chooses the peer with the highest spare capacity, named M_i, from set S_i, and then takes it out from the set S_i. If M_i can accept the reconnection request, then P_i disconnects its weakest neighbor and connects itself to M_i. This process repeats till the predefined number of reconnection peers has reached or the peer that has the highest capacity in the set M_i is weaker than the others neighbor of P_i.

Obviously, the above reconnection mechanism would change the overlay topology structure from random to a centralized one. Peers in the centralized topology structure could find resource effectively since they may just need one or two more hops to obtain the resource. But the center peers would become congested more easily, which will decrease the efficiency of resource location. To avoid congestions in such center peers, we proposed a mobile agent based on topology optimization approach which is introduced in the previous section. The combination of two methods can fulfill load balancing and effective resource location.

3   Simulation Results

In our simulation, a P2P simulator, which was implemented in python, was designed based on Gnutella protocol. It had $10,000$ peers. Every peer handled about 10 connections at the beginning. And each peer held 50 different resources.

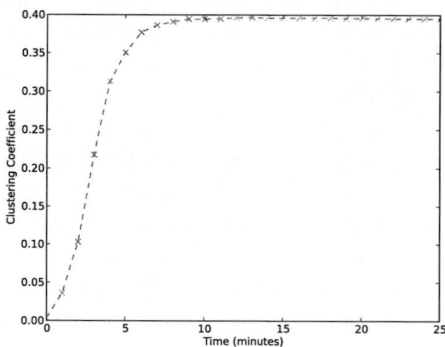

Fig. 2. The change of topology structure represented by the clustering coefficient

All resources in the system were equally popular, and the replication of resources was uniform. In such a system, we assumed the replication factor of all resources was 0.01. Then a query would be answered by 10000×0.01 peers. The heterogeneity characteristic of P2P networks in processing capacity is presented in Table 2. This distribution was obtained from the measure of the Gnutella peer reported in [15]. The capacity of peer P_i was marked as c_i which is expressed in resources processed per micro-second. Assuming there are n resources in P_i, the time spent in processing a query in P_i is $t_{proc} = n/c_i$.

Table 2. Peer processing capacity distribution in the simulator

Percentage of peers (%)	Processing capacity c_i
20	0.1
45	1
30	10
4.9	100
0.1	1000

The load of the system was caused by the resource lookups initiated by the network peers. Each peer was assigned a query generation rate q, thus peer P_i could generate q_i queries per second. In our simulation, we assumed that all peers in our system had the same query generation rate, which was set as 0.1. We used random walkers to search resources. To initiate a query request, the requestor randomly sent out 3 query walkers to its neighbors. The TTL of each walker was set as 8. The TTL of the Look-For-Peer message was set as 30, and the predefined number of reconnection peers was 5. The two thresholds U_t and B_t were set as 0.1 and 0.05 respectively.

To observe the effect of topology adaptation, Clustering Coefficient (CC) [16], a metric that shows the degree of centralization of the P2P network was used.

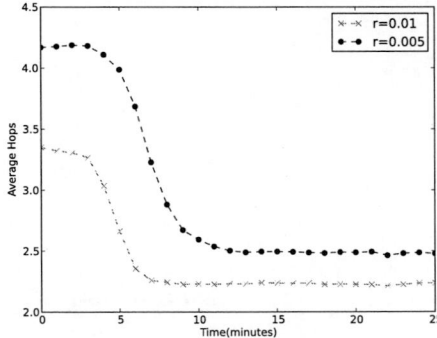

Fig. 3. Average search lengths change under two different replication factors

We modelled the p2p network as $G = (V, E)$, where G is an undirected graph, V is the set of peers and E is the set of links between peers. The clustering coefficient CC_i of P_i, is computed as follows:

$$CC_i = \frac{|(N_i \times N_i) \cap E|}{k_i(k_i - 1)} \quad (6)$$

Where N_i is the set of neighbors of P_i, $k_i = |N_i|$. The following equation computes the clustering coefficient of the entire network, which is denoted as CC:

$$CC = \frac{1}{|V|} \sum_{i \in V} CC_i \quad (7)$$

It is obvious that $0 \leq CC \leq 1$. The closer CC is to 1, the more centralized the topology is.

Fig. 2 shows how the overlay topology structure improves in our proposed method. We used the change of clustering coefficient to illustrate the improvement. At the beginning, the value of CC was quite small for the network maintained a randomly topology structure. With time going, the clustering coefficient became bigger, and finally reached a stable value. That means the topology adaptation protocol made the topology structure more centralized. The value of CC was smaller than 1 for the mobile agent based load balancing mechanism prevented too much peers connecting with the central nodes.

Fig. 3 shows another example of improvement in the resource location efficiency in our proposed method. We demonstrate the improvement in two different replication factor, $r = 0.01$ and $r = 0.005$. We can see from the figure that after a few reconnections the average hops in both replication factors decreased sharply, and reached to a small value between 2 and 3. It shows that the efficiency of resource location increases as the average search length decreases by applying our proposed method.

Fig.4 illustrates how the mobile agent migrates through the network, which is the most important part in our algorithm. The average visiting times is used

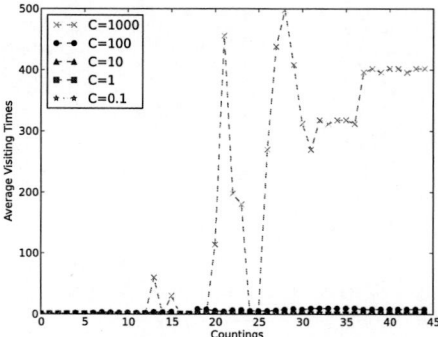

Fig. 4. The average visiting times that the mobile agent visits to different capacity peers in every 10000 visiting times

to evaluate the visiting frequencies of the mobile agent in different groups of processing capacity peers. The average visiting times in each type of processing capacity peers is defined as follows.

$$AVT_j = \frac{CP_j}{n_j} \tag{8}$$

Where n_j is the number of peers that have the same capacity processing j, CP_j is the total number of visiting times in the peers of processing capacity j when 10,000 peers are visited by the mobile agent. AVT_j is the average visiting times in the peers of capacity j counted in 10,000 peers visited by the agent. From the figure, we can see that the average visiting times that the mobile agent visited the group of different processing capacity peers changed over time. Initially, the average visiting times that the mobile agent visited all peers were almost the same. With the agent keeping moving on the network, the average visiting times that the mobile agent accessed to the most capable peers gradually increased. And finally the mobile agent moved almost only in those capable peers. It demonstrated that the mobile agent migrated through the most capable peers and could find the congestions in those peers more quickly.

4   Conclusion

In this paper, we have proposed a mobile agent based topology adaptation method in unstructured P2P networks. The mobile agent is directed by peers on their neighbors' characteristics, including processing capacity and connectedness, to migrate to the potential congestion peers. Thus congestion can be found effectively and the topology optimization mechanism is then used to resolve the congestions. Simulation results show that the proposed method can improve networks topology, avoid congestions effectively and increase the efficiency of resource location.

Acknowledgments. This work was funded in part by the National Natural Science Foundation of China(No.61005017); Natural Science Foundation of the Jiangsu Higher Education Institutions of China(10KJB520005); Senior Talent of Jiangsu University(No. 1283000347).

References

1. Thampi, S.M., Sekaran, K.C.: Survey of search and replication schemes in unstructured P2P networks. Network Protocols and Algorithms 2(1), 93–131 (2010)
2. Cai, K.: Survey of search and optimization of P2P networks. Peer-to-Peer Network and Applications 4(3), 211–218 (2011)
3. Lv, Q., Cao, P., Cohen, E., Li, K., Shenker, S.: Search and replication in unstructured peer-to-peer networks. In: Proc. 16th International Conference on Supercomputing, pp. 84–95 (2002)
4. Tsoumakos, D., Roussopoulos, N.: Adaptive Probabilistic Search for Peer-to-Peer Networks. In: 3rd IEEE Intl. Conf. on P2P Computing, pp. 102–109 (2003)
5. Lv, Q., Ratnasamy, S., Shenker, S.: Can Heterogeneity Make Gnutella Scalable? In: Druschel, P., Kaashoek, M.F., Rowstron, A. (eds.) IPTPS 2002. LNCS, vol. 2429, pp. 94–103. Springer, Heidelberg (2002)
6. Chawathe, Y., Ratnasamy, S., Lanham, N., Shenker, S.: Making Gnutella-like P2P systems scalable. In: Proc. ACM SIGCOMM, pp. 407–418 (2003)
7. Merino, L.R., Anta, A.F., Lópze, L., Cholvi, V.: Self-managed topologies in P2P networks. Computer Networks 53(10), 1722–1736 (2009)
8. Cardellini, V., Colajanni, M., Yu, P.S.: Dynamic Load Balancing on Web-server Systems. IEEE Internet Computing 3(3), 28–39 (1999)
9. Schlossnagle, T.: The Backhand Project: Load balancing and Monitoring Apache Web Clusters. In: Proc. Apache Con Europe (2000)
10. Nehra, N., Patel, R.B., Bhat, V.K.: Load Balancing in Heterogeneous P2P Systems using Mobile Agents. International Journal of Applied Science, Engineering and Technology 2(3), 108–113 (2006)
11. Bhardwaj, R., Dixit, V.S., Upadhyay, A.K.: A Propound Method for Agent Based Dynamic Load Balancing Algorithm for Heterogeneous P2P Systems. In: Intl. Conf. on Intelligent Agent and Multi-Agent Systems, pp. 1–4 (2009)
12. Hui, L., Fei, S.: An Improved Load Balancing Algorithm for P2P System Based on Mobile Agent. In: Proc. AIMSEC, pp. 2791–2794 (2011)
13. Dasgupta, P.: A Multi-agent Mechanism for Topology Balancing in Unstructured P2P Networks. In: Proc. IEEE/WIC/ACM Intl. Conf. on Intelligent Agent Technology, pp. 389–392 (2006)
14. Kwong, K.W., Tsang, D.H.K.: A Congestion-Aware Search Protocol for Unstructured Peer-to-Peer Networks. In: Cao, J., Yang, L.T., Guo, M., Lau, F. (eds.) ISPA 2004. LNCS, vol. 3358, pp. 319–329. Springer, Heidelberg (2004)
15. Saroiu, S., Gummadi, P.K., Gribble, S.D.: A measurement study of peer-to-peer file sharing systems. In: MMCN 2002, pp. 156–170 (2002)
16. Strogatz, S.H., Watts, D.J.: Collective dynamics of small-world networks. Nature 393, 440–442 (1998)

Accurate Pedestrian Counting System Based on Local Features

Yu Peng[1], Min Xu[2], Zefeng Ni[2], Jesse S. Jin[3,4], and Suhuai Luo[1]

[1] School of DICT, University of Newcastle, NSW, Australia
{Yu.Peng,Suhuai.Luo}@uon.edu.au
[2] Faculty of Engineering & I.T. University of Technology, Sydney, Australia
{Min.Xu,Zefeng.Ni}@uts.edu.au
[3] Centre for Quantum Computation & Intelligent Systems,
University of Technology, Sydney
[4] School of Software, Tianjin University, China
jesse@cse.unsw.edu.au

Abstract. Accurate pedestrian counting are challenging in real-world due to occlusions, pedestrians' overlays or camera view sensitive. In this paper, we propose an accurate and robust pedestrian detection and counting system to address these problems. Our proposed method is group-based, where the count of people in a dense moving group is estimated as a whole. Moving groups containing single or several pedestrians are discriminated from other moving objects. Our method utilizes 9 features of each moving group within a video frame to estimate the pedestrian number in each group. Pedestrian counts are optimized by a novel tracking method, which is based on an analysis of moving groups match, split or merge. Comparison experiments with other two current methods on three benchmark surveillance videos show the effectiveness of our proposed method.

Keywords: Pedestrian detection and counting, feature extraction, classification.

1 Introduction

Various approaches to pedestrian detection and counting have been proposed in last twenty years. These methods usually fall in one of three categories: based on global features of video frame, based on individual detection and counting and based on moving pedestrian group detection and counting.

Researchers utilized global features of the whole frame, such as texture information [4], fractal dimension [4] and invariant orthonormal Chebyshev moments [6] to estimate pedestrian numbers on each frame. However, global features are highly sensitive to illumination changes. Therefore, these methods can hardly work well in outdoor environment, where lighting changes much at different times. Moreover, these methods can only estimate the approximate numbers of pedestrians in the video frame.

W. Lin et al. (Eds.): PCM 2012, LNCS 7674, pp. 850–860, 2012.

Afterwards, human appearance models were usually used in individual detection and counting. These methods usually slide the whole video frame with scalable window and classify the window image, after train classifiers based on extracted features with machine learning methods. Based on pedestrian body shape, [7] proposed a pedestrian detector based on Histogram of Oriented Gradient (HOG) descriptor [1]. Though the authors demonstrated the impressive pedestrian detection performance, this method is of expensive computation and sensitive to camera angles and very limited in the occlusion cases. In [8], a method based on face detection and tracking was proposed. Free camera viewpoint is achieved. Moreover, using the face as reference rather than the entire body can be more reliable because faces are generally not obscured from surveillance cameras. However, the method is invalid when pedestrians do not face to camera. In [9], authors trained classifiers based on HOG features of heads and shoulders with Adaboost framework to detect people in each frame. Method based on head detection is more robust than face detection based methods, as it does not require pedestrians to face to camera. However, both the two methods cannot obtain promising result when video definition is low or environment is complex, as both face and head are very small.

Besides mentioned limitations, another major drawback of most methods based on individual detection and counting is that they assume there is a distinct visual separation between individuals. Strictly depending on this assumption, aforementioned methods of individual detection work well. However, this assumption is not the normal case in surveillance videos. On the other hand, pedestrians are severely occluded and visually inseparable.

On the other hand, group-based methods count the pedestrian number for each moving groups, after segment moving objects from background. [10][11] provided a method using geometric projections to estimate pedestrian numbers in moving groups. The method required prior knowledge of camera setting and accurate camera calibration to learn estimation for pedestrian number. The method showed promising results in both urban and indoor environment. However, the prior knowledge is usually unavailable in reality. The method in [12] assumed that each pedestrian, on average, has a particular number of corners and determined pedestrian number in a moving group through analyzing detected corners. However, due to many factors such as camera angle, distance from people to camera and video definition, number of corners detected on each pedestrian varies much. [13] proposed a method that extracts features based on foreground segmentation and edge detection. Though the authors demonstrated their method took into account feature normalization to deal with perspective projection and different camera orientation, the method was violated much by the edges detected from background. Moreover, homograph calculation required in this method is annoying. The methods [14], [15] extracted several features from each detected moving groups. Based on these features, classifier was trained using neural network or a linear model. However, like most of aforementioned methods, these methods determine the pedestrian number of moving group with the assumption that segmented foregrounds are pedestrians. In surveillance video, no foreground segmentation method can segment pedestrians only. Discriminating pedestrians from other segmented objects such as moving vehicles, shaking tree branches and running cats, should have not been ignored.

Our proposed method is group-based, where the count of people in a dense moving group is estimated as a whole. Detected moving groups containing single or several pedestrians are discriminated from other detected moving objects. Our method utilized 9 features of each moving group within a video frame to estimate the pedestrian number in each group. Tracking of moving groups with a novel analysis of group merge or split is performed to improve the pedestrian counting. Our proposed method is evaluated on three benchmark videos: two videos are from PETS2009 [2] and the other one is from Town Centre Database [3]. The comparison experiments with Histogram of Gradient (HOG) based method and local features based method demonstrate the effectiveness of our method.

The remainder of the paper is structured as follows. We provide an overview of our method in section 2. Section 3 describes moving objects detection and features extraction. We introduce the procedure of moving group tracking in section 4. Comparison experiments with other popular methods are demonstrated in section 5. The paper is concluded in section 6.

2   Method Overview

As shown in Fig.1, our method consists of two stages: training and testing. In training stage, extended Gaussian mixture model is implemented on frames for foreground segmentation. The method then removes noise from segmented foreground as well as keeps informative pixels by median filter. Contours are detected on frame, followed by up-right bounding rectangle detection for these contours. Therefore, all detected rectangles indicate moving objects, which include single pedestrian, several pedestrians or other objects. Relevant features are extracted from each moving rectangle.

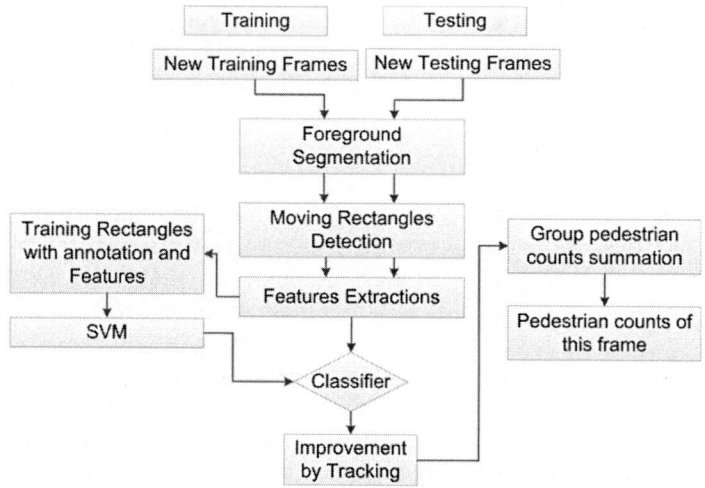

Fig. 1. Method Overview

Moreover, moving rectangles are annotated manually as follow: rectangle including single pedestrian is annotated with 1, rectangle including several pedestrian are annotated with pedestrian number in this rectangle, which we found usually from 2 to 10, and rectangles of other objects are annotated with 0. Annotated rectangles with extracted features are learned by Support Vector Machine (SVM) for training classifier. In testing stage, rectangles are detected and features extracted from testing frames using the same methods in training stage. The rectangles with extracted features are classified by trained classifier. Classified pedestrian number of each moving rectangle is optimized by rectangles tracking, which is based on a novel analysis of rectangles split and merge. The total pedestrian number of the image is the summation of pedestrian numbers of all rectangles, as shown in Fig. 2.

Fig. 2. Pedestrian counts is the summation of estimated counts of all moving groups

3   Rectangle Detection and Features Extraction

Our method detects rectangles of contours, after segments foreground using extended Gaussian mixture model. 9 high relevant features are then extracted from each rectangle.

3.1   Extended Gaussian Mixture Model

A foreign object appearing in the scene will be represented by some additional components with low weights and high variances. After implement EGMM on frames, moving objects are segmented from background. After utilizing median filter to remove noises from segmented results, we detect contours and find up-right rectangles to separate these rectangles. Those detected rectangles contain pedestrians as well as other objects such as pigeons and moving waste paper. In order to discriminate those rectangles as well as tell pedestrian numbers within them, we train classifier based on extracted rectangle features.

3.2   Features Extraction

9 highly relevant features are extracted from each rectangle in order to estimate the number of pedestrians in this rectangle. Please note here we define rectangle containing no pedestrian with pedestrian count 0. All features are investigated on binary image obtained from foreground segmentation and noise removal, which are described in last section. These features are:

·Grid Index: According to our observation, rectangles contain same numbers of pedestrians on different locations of frame have different appearances. Both the two rectangles contain two pedestrians while they might be with different sizes because the distances from them to camera are different. Instead of using the locations of rectangles, we divide every frame into 10*10 grids and indicate the grids, to which rectangles belong:

$$argminDD=Rx,-Gix,y, i\in\{1,\ldots,100\} \tag{1}$$

rectangles belong D is the distance between rectangle center $R(x,y)$ and grid ter $G_i(x,y)$. Taking the advantage of grid indication, our method is robust to videos of different definitions.

Width and Height: Rather than using areas of rectangles in previous methods[14-15], we adopt both relative width and height as features. Since pedestrians usually walk up-right, even rectangles of other objects are with the similar areas of pedestrian rectangles. Moreover, we take into account various video definitions. The relative width W and height H are defined as:

$$W=WidthFrameWidth, \qquad H=HeightFrameHeight \tag{2}$$

where $Width$ and $Height$ are the width and height of moving rectangle, respectively, while $FrameWidth$ and $FrameHeight$ are the width and height of video frame, respectively.

·Density: Density is used to describe the Foreground Pixels (FPs) density of each rectangle using:

$$DS=F/N \tag{3}$$

where F is the number of FPs in the rectangle and N is the number of all pixels in the rectangle.

·Density Variance: Besides the FPs density information, we should note that FPs in rectangles with same pedestrian numbers usually distribute with some common characteristics. Therefore, we utilize FP density variance as a clue to discriminate rectangles with different pedestrian numbers. To obtain this feature, each rectangle is divided into $n*n$ equal-size sub-blocks. Let g_i denote the foreground pixel number in sub-block i, and DS is the FP density described in (3). Then, the density variance V_g is defined as:

$$Vg=i=1n|gi-DS|n2*DS \tag{4}$$

where n^2 is the number of sub-blocks, e.g., $n = 4$ in our experiment.

Horizontal Mean, Horizontal Variance, Vertical Mean, and Vertical Variance: Due to the pedestrian shape and walking posture, some characteristics of rectangles can be described by Horizontal FP Mean(HM), Horizontal FP Variance(HV), Vertical FP Mean(VM), and Vertical FP Variance(VV):

$$HM = F/Width \qquad HV = \frac{\sum_{i=1}^{Width}|I_i - HM|}{Width*HM}$$

$$VM = F/Heigh \qquad VV = \frac{\sum_{j=1}^{Height}|I_j - VM|}{Height*VM} \tag{5}$$

In training stage, all rectangles are annotated manually with 0, 1, 2,..., 10. With above extracted features, classifier is trained using SVM. We use libsvm with radial basis function kernel [17].

4   Improved Counting with Pedestrians Tracking

Our method treats each frame of video as independent of one another, estimating the pedestrian number based on features extracted from each moving rectangles. Although some tracking techniques such as Kalman filter could smooth the rectangle trajectory, the splits and merges of rectangles are ignored. In our method, we track rectangles based on the analysis of match, split and merge.

We first detect matches between rectangles in two consecutive frames. Given two rectangles A, B, two rectangles match is defined as:

$$D(A,B) < \frac{\sqrt{(A_W^2 + A_H^2)} + \sqrt{(B_W^2 + B_H^2)}}{2}$$

$$0.8 < \frac{B_W*B_H}{A_W*A_H} < 1.2 \tag{6}$$

where $D(A,B)$ is the distances between centers of A and B, A_W, A_H, B_W and B_H are width and height of rectangle A, width and height of rectangle B, respectively.

After matched rectangles are found, left rectangles are split or merged. To match A_n, A_m in previous frame and B in current frame, we combine A_n and A_m to a joined region $M_A = A_n \cup A_m$. If M_A and B satisfy (10), we determine A_n, A_m in pervious frame merge into B in current frame. To match B in previous frame and A_n, A_m in current frame, we we combine A_n and A_m to a joined region $S_A = A_n \cap A_m$. If B and S_A satisfy (10), we determine A_n, A_m in current frame are split from into B in previous frame.

By taking advantage of rectangles tracking, the pedestrian counting is improved. The pedestrian counting of current rectangles is optimized by the historical records of this rectangle according to the following four cases:

·No match: If no matched rectangle is found in previous frame, we only consider the current pedestrian counts of this rectangle.

·Direct match: If directly matched rectangle in previous is found, we take the current pedestrian counts as the median value of the counting record, which include current counting and maximum -9 historical counts.

·Merge: If two rectangles A_n ,A_m are found in previous frame for one rectangle B in current frame. A new counts record is formed by summing corresponding counts in the two lists of A_n and A_m. We take current pedestrian counts as the median value of this new record, which include current counts and maximum -9 historical counts.

·Split: If one rectangles B are found in previous frame for one rectangle A_n,A_m in current frame. The current pedestrian counts are considered as:

$$C_{A_n}^o = (C_B * \frac{R_{A_n}}{R_{A_n}+R_{A_m}} + C_{A_n}) \qquad C_{A_m}^o = (C_B * \frac{R_{A_m}}{R_{A_n}+R_{A_m}} + C_{A_m})/2 \qquad (7)$$

Where $C_{A_n}^o$ and $C_{A_m}^o$ are optimized pedestrian counting, C_B is pedestrian counts of B, R_{A_n} and R_{A_m} are areas of A_n and A_m, C_{A_n} and C_{A_m} are current pedestrian counts.

5   Experiment and Discussion

In this section, we analyze the performance of our method. Experiments were performed on three benchmark surveillance videos: two videos are from PETS 2009 [2] and the other one comes from Town Centre Database [3], and compared with two current methods: fastHOG[9] and Crowd Counting using Multiple Local Features (CCMLF) [14]. Thanks to the opened source code of fastHOG, we save much time. The three scenes analysed contain groups of pedestrians ranging from 0 to 10. Note that 10 is the maximum size of one group, not the total number of pedestrians in the frame. The total pedestrian count on a frame is the summation of the numbers of pedestrians within all the groups. All experiments were implemented on a Intel(R) Core(TM)2 Duo CPU 3.00GHz 2.00 GB memory PC. Please refer to the supplementary material or via this link   http://www.youtube.com/watch?v=wENabEdKDZo to watch demonstration video.

5.1   Classifier Training

As aforementioned, we used three videos in the experiment. Two videos come from PETS2009, the other one is from Town Centre Database. PETS2009 is a set of 768*576 pixels JPEG image sequences in outdoor condition. It has 4 subsets, each subset contains several sequences and each sequence contains from 4 up to 8 views. We choose view 1 from subject 1, sequence 1 scenario and view 1 from subject 2, sequence 1 scenario to create two 768*576 at 20 fps videos. We name these two videos as PETS2009_1 and PETS2009_2. Town Centre Database contains a video of a busy town canter street. The video is high definition (1920*1080 at 25fps). This video was used to test pedestrian detection and tracking performance in [18, 19].

The lengths of the three videos (PETS2009_1, PETS2009_2 and TownCentre Video) are 1584 frames, 478 frames, and 7500 frames. In order to collect training data, we implemented rectangle detection algorithm on the first halves of these videos, respectively, as described in method overview. After classifier trained, we tested our method on the second halves of these three videos. As described in Table 1, we collected 3919 rectangles, 997 rectangles, and 45614 rectangles from 793 frames of PETS2009_1, 239 frames of PETS2009_2, and 3750 frames of Town Centre Video. After extracting 9 features from each binary rectangle, we manually annotated these rectangles with pedestrian numbers (0 to 10). Most detected rectangles from PETS2009_1 contain 0 to 4 pedestrians, as pedestrians in PETS2009_1 are usually sparse. Most rectangles detected from PETS2009_2 contain more pedestrians, which numbers of which ranged from 0 to 10, as pedestrian groups are usually dense in PETS2009_2. The pedestrian numbers of detected rectangles from TownCentre distribute evenly as TownCentre contains much more frames than previous two videos.

Table 1. Detected rectangles with counts annotations for training classifier

Video	TF	DR	PN0	PN1	PN2	PN3	PN4	PN5	PN6	PN7	PN8	PN9	PN10
PETS2009_1	792	3919	409	2446	801	230	26	5	1	0	1	0	0
PETS2009_2	239	997	268	134	112	37	109	229	72	58	9	21	48
TownCentre	3750	45614	4500	24560	10549	1243	2690	1267	569	108	48	50	30

*TF denotes Training Frames, DR denotes Detected Rectangles, PNx denotes pedestrian number in rectangle is x

After finishing annotation, we input all extracted features and pedestrian numbers into libsvm [17] for training classifier.

In this section, we assess the performance of the proposed method against fastHOG[9] and CCMLF [14], via testing on the second halves of the three videos. Moreover, in order to demonstrate the benefits brought about by rectangles tracking, we also investigate the proposed method without rectangles tracking. Please note that CCMLF [14] assume all detected blob are pedestrian rather than filter out detected moving objects from pedestrian blobs. Actually, this problem exists in many current pedestrian detection and counting methods. In order to make comparison experiments valid, we add background objects discrimination into CCMLF using the features and training method in CCMLF.

5.2   Comparison Evaluation

Manually counted ground truth of each frame is compared with the total estimated counts of our proposed method, of fastHOG, and of adaptive CCMLF, tested on the second halves of the three videos. Fig. 3, Fig. 4 and Fig. 5 depict the comparisons. Referring to the three figures, the red line describes ground truth pedestrian numbers per frame throughout the entire video. The blue, green, and black lines represent differences between estimated pedestrian counts and ground truth per frame throughout the entire video using our proposed method, fastHOG and CCMLF, respectively.

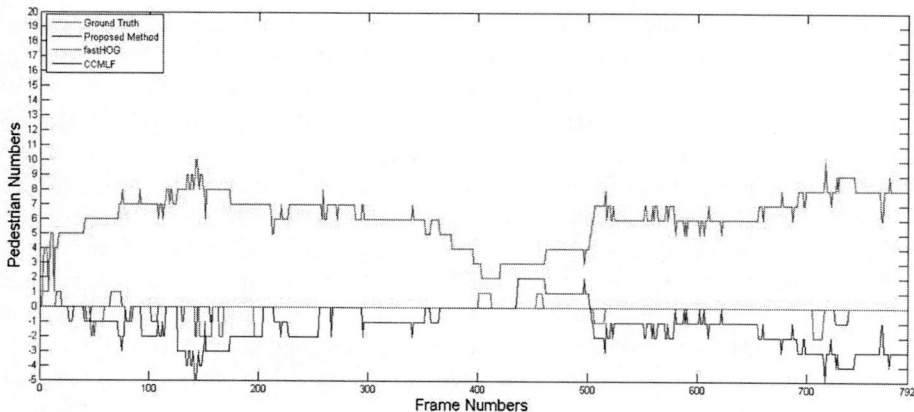

Fig. 3. Comparison evaluation of three methods by testing on PETS2009_1

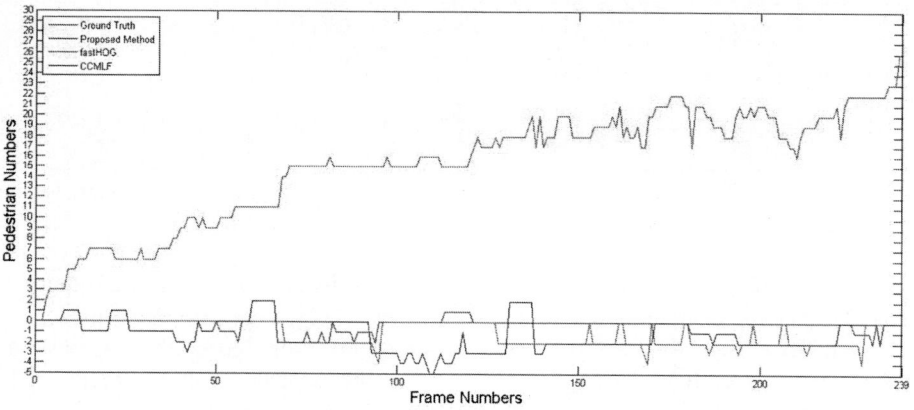

Fig. 4. Comparison evaluation of three methods by testing on PETS2009_2

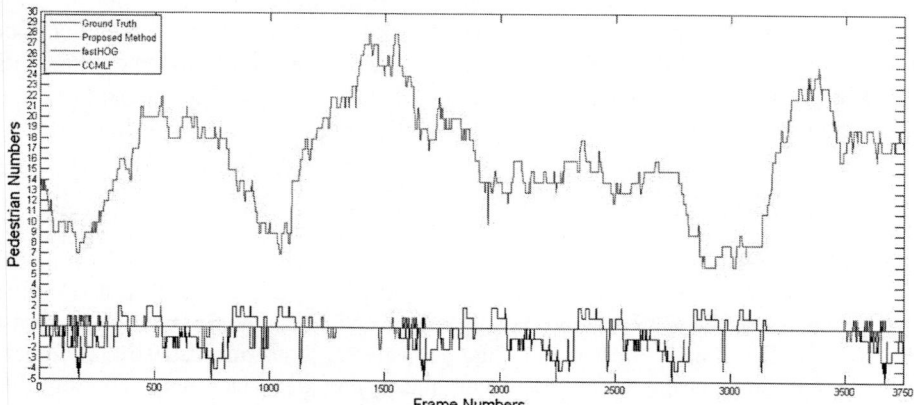

Fig. 5. Comparison evaluation of three methods by testing on TownCenter

Fig. 3 illustrates the case of PET12008_1 video. The video is usually sparse that contains 1 to 10 pedestrians per frame. The proposed method (blue line) and fastHOG (green line) work much better than CCMLF (back line). Moreover, our method is more stable than fastHOG. For example, around frame 150 and frame 700, fastHOG is prone to make miss-detections, which are usually caused by pedestrians overlay. Fig.4 describes the case of PET12008_2 video, which usually contains pedestrian crowds of high density. The CCMCL (back line) is still unstable in this case. fastHOG (green line) usually miss much pedestrians as occlusion while the proposed method (blue line) works well. However, for example, around frame 90, mistakes are made by proposed method when the pedestrian densities of rectangles are too high. Fig.5 depicts the case of TownCenter video, which contains a complicated scenario than that of previous videos. CCMCL (back line) works badly in this case. fastHOG (green line) works well as the pedestrians usually work sparsely but still miss pedestrians when occlusions happen. The proposed method works well. However, a drawback of proposed method should be noted that it cannot deal well with stationary pedestrian. For example, around frame 1200, our method detects and counts the pedestrian correctly when he walks into the view of camera. But our method misses it after the pedestrian stops on the centre of street without any action.

6   Conclusion and Future Work

We have presented a novel method that estimates the numbers of pedestrians in surveillance videos. We first extract moving objects from background per frame. Based on extracted 9 features from each moving object, each object is classified into with 0 to 10 pedestrians. A novel tracking method is proposed to improve the estimated pedestrian counts. The total pedestrian number per frame is the summation of pedestrian counts of detected rectangles. The effectiveness of the proposed method is demonstrated by comparing with two other methods on three benchmark surveillance videos.

Acknowledgement. This work is supported by Chinese Scholarship Council (CSC)-Newcastle Joint Scholarship.

References

1. Dalal, N.: Histogram of oriented gradients for human detection. In: CVPR IEEE, France, vol. 1, pp. 886–893 (2005)
2. PETS 2009 Benchmark Data (2009), http://www.cvg.rdg.ac.uk/PETS2009/ (accessed April 26, 2012)
3. Town Center Database (2010), http://www.robots.ox.ac.uk/ActiveVision/Research/Projects/2009bbenfold_headpose/project.html#datasets (accessed April 26, 2012)
4. Marana, A.N., Velastin, S.A., Costa, L.F., Lotufo, R.A.: Automatic estimation of crowd density using texture. Safety Science 28(3), 165–175 (1998), doi:10.1016/s0925-7535(97)00081-7

5. Marana, A.N., Da Fontoura Costa, L., Lotufo, R.A., Velastin, S.A.: Estimating crowd density with Minkowski fractal dimension. In: Proceedings of the 1999 IEEE International Conference on Acoustics, Speech, and Signal Processing, March 15-19, vol. 3526, pp. 3521–3524 (1999), doi:10.1109/icassp.1999.757602

6. Rahmalan, H., Nixon, M.S., Carter, J.N.: On crowd density estimation for surveillance. IET Seminar Digests 2006(11434), 540–545 (2006)

7. Dalal, N., Triggs, B.: Histograms of oriented gradients for human detection. In: IEEE Computer Society Conference on Computer Vision and Pattern Recognition, CVPR 2005, June 25, vol. 881, pp. 886–893 (2005), doi:10.1109/cvpr.2005.177

8. Zhao, X., Delleandrea, E., Chen, L.: A People Counting System Based on Face Detection and Tracking in a Video. Paper Presented at the Proceedings of the 2009 Sixth IEEE International Conference on Advanced Video and Signal Based Surveillance (2009)

9. Min, L., Zhaoxiang, Z., Kaiqi, H., Tieniu, T.: Estimating the number of people in crowded scenes by MID based foreground segmentation and head-shoulder detection. In: 19th International Conference on Pattern Recognition, ICPR 2008, December 8-11, pp. 1–4 (2008), doi:10.1109/icpr.2008.4761705

10. Rodriguez, M.D., Shah, M.: Detecting and segmenting humans in crowded scenes. Paper Presented at the Proceedings of the 15th International Conference on Multimedia, Augsburg, German (2007)

11. Kilambi, P., Ribnick, E., Joshi, A.J., Masoud, O., Papanikolopoulos, N.: Estimating pedestrian counts in groups. Computer Vision and Image Understanding 110(1), 43–59 (2008), doi:10.1016/j.cviu.2007.02.003

12. Albiol, A., Silla, M.J., Albiol, A., Mossi, J.M.: Video analysis using corner motion statistics. In: IEEE International Workshop on Performance Evaluation of Tracking and Surveillance, pp. 31–28 (2009)

13. Kong, D., Gray, D., Tao, H.: Counting Pedestrians in Crowds Using Viewpoint Invariant Training. British Machine Vision Association (2005)

14. Ryan, D., Denman, S., Fookes, C., Sridharan, S.: Crowd Counting Using Multiple Local Features. Paper Presented at the Proceedings of the 2009 Digital Image Computing: Techniques and Applications (2009)

15. Ryan, D., Denman, S., Fookes, C., Sridharan, S.: Crowd Counting Using Group Tracking and Local Features. Paper Presented at the Proceedings of the 2010 7th IEEE International Conference on Advanced Video and Signal Based Surveillance (2010)

16. Zivkovic, Z., van der Heijden, F.: Efficient adaptive density estimation per image pixel for the task of background subtraction. Pattern Recognition Letters 27(7), 773–780 (2006), doi:10.1016/j.patrec.2005.11.005

17. Chang, C.-C., Lin, C.-J.: LIBSVM: A library for support vector machines. ACM Trans. Intell. Syst. Technol. 2(3), 1–27 (2011), doi:10.1145/1961189.1961199

18. Prisacariu, V., Reid, I.: fastHOG - a real-time GPU implementation of HOG. Department of Engineering Science, Oxford University (2009)

19. Benfold, B., Reid, I.: Stable multi-target tracking in real-time surveillance video. In: 2011 IEEE Conference on Computer Vision and Pattern Recognition, CVPR, June 20-25, pp. 3457–3464 (2011), doi:10.1109/cvpr.2011.5995667

Two Dimensional K-SVD
for the Analysis Sparse Dictionary

Yunhui Shi, Na Qi, Baocai Yin, and Wenpeng Ding

Beijing Key Laboratory of Multimedia and Intelligent Software Technology
College of Computer Science and Technology
Beijing University of Technology, 100124, Beijing, China
q1987n@emails.bjut.edu.cn,
{syhzm,ybc,wpding}@bjut.edu.cn

Abstract. Analysis sparse model has been successfully used for a variety of tasks such as image denoising, deblurring, and most recently compressed sensing, so it arouses much attention. K-SVD is a mature dictionary learning approach for the analysis sparse model. However, it represents images as one dimension signals, which results in mistakes of spatial correlations. In this paper, we propose a novel analysis sparse model, where analysis dictionary derived from two analysis operators which act on an image, leading to a sparse outcome. And a two dimensional K-SVD (2D-KSVD) is proposed to train the analysis sparse dictionaries. Experiments on image denoising validate that the proposed analysis dictionary can express more image spatial and frequency characteristics and by using the dictionary, the two dimension analysis sparse model outperforms the traditional analysis model in terms of PSNR.

Keywords: Sparse Representation, 2D K-SVD, Analysis-Based Sparse Model, Dictionary Learning.

1   Introduction

Signal models are fundamental for handling various tasks, such as compression, sampling, recovering, and more. A very popular approach to signal modeling is the synthesis-based sparse representation model $D\alpha = x$, where a signal $x \in R^d$ is assumed to be composed as a linear combination of a few atoms from a given dictionary $D \in R^{d \times n}$ [1]. In the past decade, this model has a wide range of application, such as image compressing [2], and super-resolution reconstruction [3]. The concentrates on this model are obtaining the dictionary from signal examples and getting the state-of-the-art sparse results when given dictionary. Some dictionary learning approaches including K-SVD [4], sparse coding, etc. are relatively mature. The sparse representation approaches can get a sparse solution about the inverse problem $\min_{x} \|x\|_0$ *subject to* $y = Dx$, where $\|x\|_0$ is the count of the non-zeros in x, which is used to show the sparsity and the dimension of the subspace the signal belongs to.

W. Lin et al. (Eds.): PCM 2012, LNCS 7674, pp. 861–871, 2012.
© Springer-Verlag Berlin Heidelberg 2012

The synthesis-based sparse model has been extensively studied and has been a well established field, while the alternative analysis-based sparse model has been aside untouched[5]. The analysis model is defined as $\|\Omega x\|_0 = p - l$, where $\Omega \in R^{p \times d}$ is a linear operation, and l is the co-sparsity of the analysis signal x. There will be some zeros in Ωx. Compared to the numbers of non-zeros in the synthesis model, the numbers of zeros show sparsity and define the subspace the signal x belongs to. Similar to the sparse dictionary D in the synthesis sparse model, Ω is an analysis dictionary in the analysis model, and the corresponding inverse problem is $\min_x \|x - y\|_2$ *subject to* $\|\Omega x\|_0 = p - l$.

Recently, analysis models have been successfully used for a variety of signal processing tasks such as image denoising, deblurring, and most recently compressed sensing [6], so the analysis sparse model has also aroused attention. The researches of analysis model are focused on two aspects. One aspect is the application [7][8].In [7], the analysis prior models the coefficients obtained by applying the forward transform to the signal. And they compare analysis and synthesis l1-norm regularization with overcomplete transforms for denoising and deconvolutions. The work in [8] is also used in image deconvolution and image restoration. They model the analysis coefficients as a strictly sparse vector plus a Gaussian correction term. At the end, they use iterated marginal minimization to solve the inverse problem. The other aspect is the analysis dictionary learning approach [9][10][11][12]. The authors of [10] suggest that learning Ω one row at a time, identifying directions that are orthogonal to a set of the training data. However, the approach is used in randomized initialization, so it will lose its efficiency rapidly when the dictionary grows. The work proposed in [11] includes two greedy pursuit algorithms for the dictionary learning based on the co-sparsity and the error control, and a penalty function for the dictionary update stage. However, the work in [12] adopts co-rank of the desired co-support rather than co-sparsity to control the iteration condition and thus the actual number of vanishing coefficients in the output representation may be larger than co-rank.

In this paper, we focus on analysis dictionary learning. We propose an anchored dictionary learning approach named 2D-KSVD for image. Why do we introduce the two dimension model? As we know, the signal or images have certain relevance in adjacent area, and we should make full use of the relevance. For example in order to compress, the relevance needs to be removed, while in the sparse dictionary constructing, redundant information needs to be introduced according to it. The relevance is directional in image differing from signal. Learning dictionary from a set of vectors reshaped from patches may introduce unnecessary relevance. For instance, the first row has little or no relevance with the last row of the patch. However, once the patch is reshaped to a vector in column direction, it may be regarded that the first row and the last row have relevance in the process of learning dictionary. The apparent drawback exists in the traditional dictionary learning. So we introduce the two dimensional dictionary learning. Experiments demonstrate that 2D-KSVD can better reflect image spatial and frequency characteristics and reduce the unnecessary redundant, and two dimension analysis sparse-coding algorithm outperforms traditional method in denoising.

The rest of this paper is organized as follow. The two dimension analysis model, the two dimension analysis sparse-coding and 2D K-SVD algorithm are described in Section 2. To verify the validity of our model, experiment results are shown in Section 3. Finally, we make a conclusion and describe the future work in Section 4.

2   The Two Dimensional K-SVD Dictionary Learning

2.1   Notations

For the formula and symbols easily comprehended, we give some notations here. $\|x\|_*$ is defined as the count of non-zeros of matrix x. $\bar{x}, \bar{y}, \bar{z}$ respectively represent the reshaped vectors of the matrix x, y, z. $\forall x, x(i, j)$ is its (i, j)-th entry. $\|x\|_F$ is noted as Frobenius norm. $\|x\|_0$ is l_0 norm. † means pseudo-inverse.

2.2   The Two Dimension Analysis Model

With respect to a given patch $x \in R^{d_1 \times d_1}$, we build the two dimension analysis model as $\left\| \Omega_1 x \Omega_2^T \right\|_* = p - l$, where $\Omega_1 \in R^{p_1 \times d_1}$ and $\Omega_2 \in R^{p_2 \times d_1}$ are two dimensional analysis redundant dictionaries defined as horizontal dictionary and vertical dictionary, and $p = p_1 \times p_2$. Similar to the co-sparsity in [5][6][9][11], we define l as the co-sparsity of matrix. Generally, for a given patch x, firstly we expect the sparsity in the horizontal direction, which means $\left\| \Omega_1 x_j \right\|_0 = p_1 - l_1$. x_j is the j th column of the patch x, and the co-support Λ of x_j is the set of $l_1 = |\Lambda|$ rows that are orthogonal to it [11]. And we also expect the sparsity in vertical direction, so we transpose $\Omega_1 x$ to get $z = (\Omega_1 x)^T$, in the same way $\left\| \Omega_2 z_j \right\|_0 = p_2 - l_2$, where z_j is the j th column of the patch $(\Omega_1 x)^T$, in other words z_j is the j th row of $\Omega_1 x$. So the sparsity of the original patch in another direction can be promised, and the co-support Λ of z_j is the set of $l_2 = |\Lambda|$ rows that are orthogonal to it. Summarize the above operation, we expect $\Omega_2 (\Omega_1 x)^T$ to sparse, which can be rewritten as $\Omega_1 x \Omega_2^T$.

The following equation (1) means that $\bar{y} = \Omega_0 \bar{x}$ can be rewritten as $y = \Omega_1 x \Omega_2^T$, where $\bar{x}$ is the reshaped vector of x in the column or row direction, and Ω_0 can be computed by Ω_1, Ω_2^T.

$$y(i,j) = \sum_l \Omega_1(i,l)(x\Omega_2^T)(l,j) = \sum_l \Omega_1(i,l)\sum_k x(l,k)\Omega_2^T(k,j)$$

$$= \sum_l \sum_k \Omega_1(i,l)\Omega_2^T(k,j)x(l,k) = \sum_l \sum_k (\Omega_1(i,l)\Omega_2^T(k,j))x(l,k) \tag{1}$$

So $\left\|\Omega_1 x \Omega_2^T\right\|_* = p - l$ can lead to $\left\|\Omega_0 \bar{x}\right\|_0 = p - l$. However, in some condition, $\exists\ \Omega_1' \neq \Omega_1, \Omega_2' \neq \Omega_2$, $y = \Omega_1' x (\Omega_2')^T$ .It proves that $\bar{y} = \Omega_0 \bar{x}$ and $y = \Omega_1 x \Omega_2^T$ are not completely equivalent.

2.3 The Analysis Sparse-Coding

The analysis sparse-coding is the fundamental of the dictionary learning, so we give the two dimension analysis sparse-coding. When given Ω_1, Ω_2 , and x, its analysis coefficient $\Omega_1 x I$ has equivalent co-sparsity to $\Omega_{10} \bar{x}$, where I is identity matrix, and Ω_{10} is computed by Ω_1 and I using the equation (1).The co-sparsity of global patch can be obtained by $\Omega_1 x \Omega_2^T$. In traditional analysis sparse model, the co-rank of a signal $\bar{x}$ with co-support Λ is defined as the rank of Ω_Λ in [12]. The dimension of the subspace the signal belongs to denoted as r , is small, namely $r << d_1$. The co-rank of $\bar{x}$ is $d_1 - r$. The co-sparsity l is used to control the iteration in [11], while the co-rank is used in [12] and the latter outperforms the former. So we use the co-rank model like [12]. For x and Ω_1 , there is $\Omega_{1\Lambda}$ such that $\Omega_{1\Lambda} x_j = \vec{0}$ .The rank of $\Omega_{1\Lambda}$ is obtained. However, a given patch y is always contaminated by noises. In this paper, we refer such a model $y = x + v$, where v is a zero-mean white-Gaussian additive noise patch. So we can find x by solving the following optimization problem:

$$\hat{x} = \arg\min_{x,\Lambda_1,\Lambda_2} \left\|x - y\right\|_F^2, subject\ \ to\ \ \Omega_{1\Lambda_1} x_{j_1} = 0, rank(\Omega_{1\Lambda_1}) = d_1 - r_1$$

$$\Omega_{2\Lambda_2} z_{j_2} = 0, rank(\Omega_{2\Lambda_2}) = d_1 - r_2 \tag{2}$$

$$z = (\Omega_1 x)^T, 1 \leq j_1 \leq d_1, 1 \leq j_2 \leq p_1$$

Where r_1, r_2 represent the dimension of the subspaces that the signal x_{j_1} and z_{j_2} belong to respectively. $d_1 - r_1$ and $d_1 - r_2$ respectively illustrate the rank of $\Omega_{1\Lambda_1}$ and $\Omega_{2\Lambda_2}$,in a sense they represent the co-sparsity of the patch. We define the above problem as the two dimension analysis sparse-coding or analysis-pursuit problem.

Although the above problem is difficult to solve, it can be converted to the problem that can be solve by Backward Greedy(BG) Algorithm and the Optimized-BG(OBG) Algorithm mentioned in [11][12]. The problem is defined as follows:

$$\hat{X} = \arg\min_{X,\Lambda} rank(\Omega_\Lambda), subject \quad to \quad \Omega_\Lambda X = 0, \|X - Y\|_F^2 < \varepsilon \qquad (3)$$

Where ε is error tolerance, related to noise power, and $X = \begin{bmatrix} \bar{x} \\ \bar{z} \end{bmatrix}, Y = \begin{bmatrix} \bar{y} \\ \bar{u} \end{bmatrix}$, $\bar{u}$ is the

reshaped vector of $u = \Omega_1 y^T$. Ω is combined by Ω_1 and Ω_2 as follows:

$$\Omega = \begin{bmatrix} \Omega_A & 0 \\ 0 & \Omega_B \end{bmatrix} \qquad (4)$$

where $\Omega_A = diag\underbrace{(\Omega_1, \Omega_1 \cdots, \Omega_1)}_{d_1}, \Omega_B = diag\underbrace{(\Omega_2, \Omega_2 \cdots, \Omega_2)}_{p_1}$. The dimension of Ω

is $R_1 \times R_2$, $R_1 = p_1 \times d_1 + p_2 \times p_1$, $R_2 = d_1 \times d_1 + d_1 \times p_1$. By solving the problem (3), we can get $\hat{X}$. The first K th ($K = d_1 \times d_1$) rows of $\hat{X}$ is the recovered $\bar{x}$, and then the recovered x can be reshaped by $\bar{x}$. A detail of the resulting algorithm is given in Table 1.

Table 1. Two Dimension Analysis Sparse-coding

Algorithm: Two Dimension Analysis Sparse-coding
1. Input: Analysis Dictionary Ω_1, Ω_2, a patch y, η, and σ. σ depends on the noise energy, and error tolerance $\varepsilon = \eta * \sigma$
2. Construct Ω and Y
3. Solve $\hat{X} = \arg\min_{X,\Lambda} rank(\Omega_\Lambda), subject \quad to \quad \Omega_\Lambda X = 0, \|X - Y\|_F^2 < \varepsilon$
4. Reshape the K -th rows of $\hat{X}$ to get the recovered patch $\hat{x}$.
5. Output: The patch $\hat{x}$

To obtain the two dictionaries, we should consider the following two optimized problems:

$$\hat{x}_j^1 = \arg\min_{x_j^1, \Lambda_1} \|x_j^1 - y_j\|_2$$

$$subject \quad to \quad \Omega_{1\Lambda_1} x_j^1 = 0, rank(\Omega_{1\Lambda_1}) = d_1 - r_1 \qquad (5)$$

$$\hat{x}_j^2 = \arg\min_{x_j^2, \Lambda_2} \left\| x_j^2 - z_j \right\|_2$$

$$subject \ to \Omega_{2\Lambda_2} x_j^2 = 0, rank(\Omega_{2\Lambda_2}) = d_1 - r_2, z_j = (\Omega_1 x)_j^T \tag{6}$$

Where y_j and z_j respectively represent the j th column of patch y and z , and x_j^1 and x_j^2 respectively represent the recovered column. We can use pursuit approaches to solve the above two problems, such as BG and OBG mentioned in [11][12]. The above two problems are fundamentals of the two dimensional K-SVD problem presented in the following section.

2.4   2D-KSVD

Now, we turn to describe the two dimensional K-SVD algorithm used for analysis learning. We consider the following setting: Given a training set $II = [y^{(1)}, y^{(2)}, ... y^{(M)}] \in R^{d_1 \times M_0}$, where $y^{(i)}$ is a $d_1 \times d_1$ patch, and $M_0 = d_1 \times M$, we assume that every example $y^{(i)}$ is a noisy version of a patch residing in an r -dimensional subspace related to the dictionary Ω_0 . Thus $y^{(i)} = x^{(i)} + v^{(i)}$, where $v^{(i)}$ is a zero-mean white-Gaussian additive noise patch, and $x^{(i)}$ satisfies a co-rank of $d - r$ with respect to the dictionary Ω_1, Ω_2 .We aim at learning two dimensional dictionaries from the training set. Then we formulate the following optimization task:

$$\{\hat{\Omega}_1, \hat{\Omega}_2, \hat{I}\} = \arg\min_{I, \Omega_1, \Omega_2} \left\| I - II \right\|_F^2 ,$$

$$subject \ to \ \ \Omega_{1\Lambda_1} x_{j_1}^{(i)} = 0, rank(\Omega_{1\Lambda_1}) = d_1 - r_1, 1 \le i \le M_0, 1 \le j_1 \le d_1$$

$$\Omega_{2\Lambda_2} z_{j_2}^{(l)} = 0, rank(\Omega_{2\Lambda_2}) = d_1 - r_2, 1 \le j_2 \le p_1 \tag{7}$$

$$z^{(l)} = (\Omega_1 x^{(l)})^T, 1 \le l \le M_1, M_1 = p_1 \times M$$

$$\left\| w_{k_1}^{(1)} \right\|_2 = 1, \left\| w_{k_2}^{(2)} \right\|_2 = 1, 1 \le k_1 \le p_1, 1 \le k_2 \le p_2$$

where $x_{j_1}^{(i)}$ is the j_1 th column of the patch $x^{(i)}$, and $z_{j_2}^{(l)}$ is the j_2 th column of the patch $z^{(l)}$. $w_{k_1}^{(1)}$ is the k_1 th row of Ω_1 and $w_{k_2}^{(2)}$ is the k_2 th row of Ω_2 .To solve this problem(7), we separate it to two sub-learning problems which refer to the problem (5) and (6). Then we need to get the new training set from the original training set. Each column from the original patch is a member of the first new training set. Then we solve the following optimized problem (8) by the two-phase block-coordinate relaxation approach [11][12]. After we get $\hat{\Omega}_1$, we form second training set. $\hat{\Omega}_1$ multiplying the every patch in the original set II to get a new patch $\hat{\Omega}_1 y^{(i)}$, the second set consists of the columns of $(\hat{\Omega}_1 y^{(i)})^T$. We use traditional dictionary training method to get dictionary $\hat{\Omega}_2$ once again. Every learning process is to solve the following problem:

$$\{\hat{\Omega}, \hat{X}, \{\Lambda_i\}_{i=1}^{M_0}\} = Arg \min \|X - Y\|_F^2$$

$$Subject \quad to \qquad \Omega_{\Lambda_i} x_i = 0, Rank(\Omega_{\Lambda_i}) = d_1 - r_1, \forall 1 \le i \le M_0 \qquad (8)$$

$$\|w_j\|_2 = 1, \forall 1 \le j \le p$$

where Y is every new set whose member is a vector. The initialization of Ω_1 and Ω_2 are similar to the approach mentioned in [11][12]. In the first learning, we can use the co-rank to control the stopping condition. For the convenience solving, we can use error threshold related to the noise power in the second learning. In short, this paper emphasizes on the two dimension analysis sparse model and the two dimension analysis sparse-coding. To validate the above model and algorithm, we give the following experiment results.

3   Experiment Results

In this section, we present a set of experiment results with the proposed two dimension analysis model. In the first section we show results on the synthetic patch in the model, and in the second section we show results for piecewise-constant images with two dimension analysis sparse-coding and 2D-KSVD. Experiment results confirm the validity of two dimension sparse analysis model.

3.1   Experiment I

First, we assume two dimension dictionaries Ω_1 and Ω_2 are known. And we set $rank(\Omega_{1\Lambda_1}) = d_1 - r_1$, $rank(\Omega_{2\Lambda_2}) = d_1 - r_2$. The patch can be synthesized by the following equation:

$$x = (u - \Omega_{1\Lambda_1}{}^+ \Omega_{1\Lambda_1} u \Omega_{2\Lambda_2}{}^T (\Omega_{2\Lambda_2}{}^T)^+) \qquad (9)$$

where u is a random patch. By using the equation (1), Ω_0 and $\Omega_{0\Lambda}$ can be obtained by Ω_1, Ω_2 and $\Omega_{1\Lambda_1}, \Omega_{2\Lambda_2}$ separately. And the result of x by using the equation (9) is equivalent to $\bar{x} = (I - \Omega_{0\Lambda}{}^+ \Omega_{0\Lambda})\bar{u}$.

As shown in part (a) of Figure 1, Ω_1, Ω_2 are initialized by $\Omega_{DIF} \in R^{10 \times 5}$ and Ω_0 is shown in next. Then we set $r_1 = 1$, $r_2 = 1$, and get $\Omega_{1\Lambda_1}$ and $\Omega_{2\Lambda_2}$ by choosing $l_1 = 5 - r_1 = 4$ and $l_2 = 5 - r_2 = 4$ rows from Ω_1, Ω_2 at random. So we generate 1000 unit-norm analysis patches satisfying the equation (9). A set of such randomly created image patches, satisfying $\left\| \Omega_{0\Lambda} \bar{x} \right\|_0 = 16$, is shown in last part of figure 1(a). However, the part (b) presents the histogram of the effective co-sparsity, which is larger than 16, because Ω_1, Ω_2 are initialized by Ω_{DIF}, which is not in-general position.

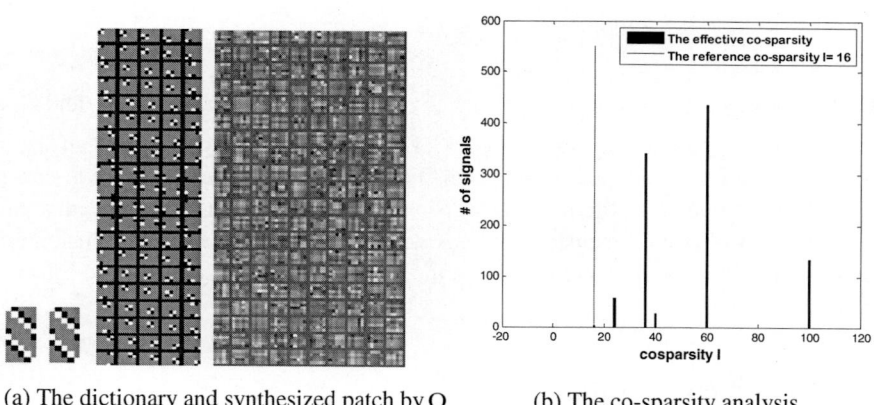

(a) The dictionary and synthesized patch by Ω_{DIF} (b) The co-sparsity analysis

Fig. 1. Synthetic experiment on the DIF dictionary and co-sparsity analysis

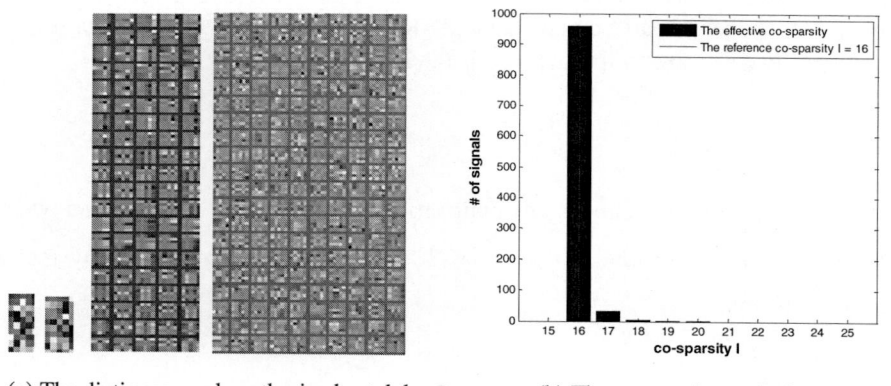

(a) The dictionary and synthesized patch by Ω_{Random} (b) The co-sparsity analysis

Fig. 2. Synthetic experiment on the random dictionary and co-sparsity analysis

Next, we choose Ω_1, Ω_2 known as random Gaussian entries and the experiment setting is the same to the above experiment. The results are shown in figure 2(a): Ω_1 , Ω_2 , Ω_0 by using the equation(1),and the analysis patches satisfying $\|\Omega_{0\wedge}\bar{x}\|_0 = 16$. In figure2(b), the histogram of the effective co-sparsity is presented to show that more than 95% of co-sparsity are equal to 16. It demonstrates although Ω_1 , Ω_2 are initialized by Ω_{random} , which is in-general position, the actual co-sparsity is not strictly to the rank of $\Omega_{0\wedge}$, which differs from the traditional situation. The relationship between the rank of Ω_1, Ω_2 and the rank of Ω_0 is required to explore.

3.2   Experiment II

Now, we present experimental results for a piecewise-constant (PWC) image, aiming at evaluating the effect of the proposed 2D-KSVD approach, and comparing the denoising result of [12] and the proposed two dimension analysis sparse coding.

First, we get a piecewise-image shown in the upper of the left column of figure 3. Then we extract all possible 5×5 image patches from a 256×256 PWC image contaminated by noise $\sigma = 5$ ($PSNR = 34.1397dB$). The contaminated image is shown in the lower of the left column of figure 3.We randomly choose 20,000 "active"

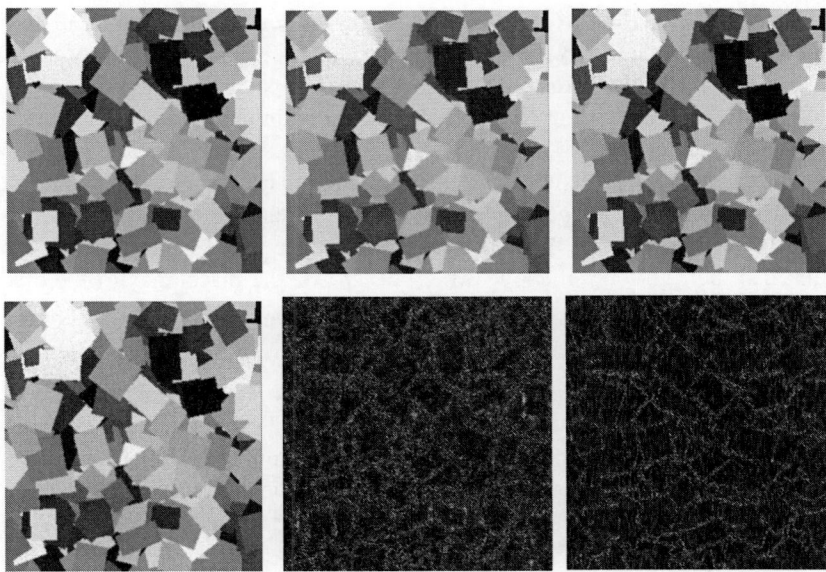

Fig. 3. The denoise experiment on the piecewise-constant image: the noisy image with PSNR=34.1397dB(Left), PSNR=36.5320dB(Center[12]), PSNR=38.4969dB (Right(proposed))

patches for the dictionary training, and apply 100 iterations of the Analysis K-SVD on this training set to learn an analysis dictionary Ω of size 100×25, and assuming recovered patches residing in 4-dimensional subspaces. And we apply 100 iterations of 2D-KSVD on this training set to get Ω_1 and Ω_2 of size 10×5, and assuming recovered columns of the patches residing in 1-dimensional subspace. By using the equation (1), Ω_0 can be obtained. Ω and Ω_0 are shown in figure 4.

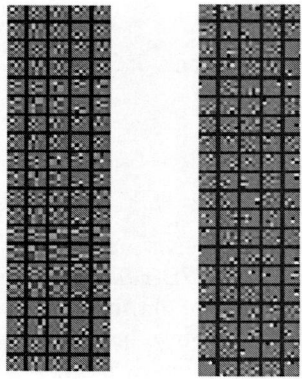

Fig. 4. The dictionary result Ω_0 by using 2D-KSVD and the dictionary result Ω by [12]

Next, we use the learned analysis dictionary to denoise each patch of the entire image. We use the analysis sparse-coding in [12] and our proposed analysis sparse-coding respectively to compare the results. The patch denosing stage is followed by averaging the overlapping patch recoveries to obtain the final denoised image. The results in the center column are results by using [12] and the absolute errors are displayed in range [0, 20].The results in the right column are our results. The resulting of PSNRs of the denoised images are 36.5320dB for [12] and 38.4969dB for our proposed approach. We observe that the absolute errors of edge in the center one are more apparent than the right one. It shows when Ω grows, the inaccuracy of the dictionary increases. So the denoising effect is not well. And we can see Ω_0 can better reflect image spatial and frequency characteristics. By the way, we reproduce the approach in [12] and implant it to our model, our target is to evaluate whether our proposed model is effective. Our proposed model can more easily capture the spatial and frequency characteristic of image and can reduce unnecessary dictionary learning mistakes, which caused by reshaping the patch to a vector to increase the unnecessary correlation.

4   Conclusion

In this paper, we propose a novel analysis sparse model which has stronger ability to represent image. And the two dimensional dictionary learned by using 2D-KSVD can better reflect image spatial and frequency characteristics. Two dimension analysis sparse-coding outperforms the traditional analysis sparse-coding in denoising. At present, the two dimension analysis dictionary learning proposed is converted to two traditional dictionary learning problem to solve. More effective dictionary learning approaches for the two dimension analysis sparse model and the two dimension analysis sparse-coding are left for future research. And which application could benefit from the analysis model remains to be seen.

Acknowledgments. This paper is supported by 973 Program (2011CB302703), the National Natural Science Foundation of China (No. 60825203, 61033004, 60973056, 61170103, 61003182, U0935004), Beijing Natural Science Foundation (4102009, 4112007).

References

1. Bruckstein, A.M., Donoho, D.L., Elad, M.: From sparse solutions of systems of equations to sparse modeling of signals and images. SIAM Review 51(1), 34–81 (2009)
2. Horev, I., Bryt, O., Rubinstein, R.: Adaptive image compression using sparse dictionaries. In: 2012 19th International Conference on Systems Signals and Image Processing, IWSSIP, pp. 592–595 (2012)
3. Yang, J.C., John, W., Ma, Y., Huang, T.: Image super-resolution as a sparse representation of raw image patches. In: Proceedings of IEEE Conference on Computer Vision and Pattern Recognition, CVPR 2008, Anchorage, Alaska, pp. 333–340 (2008)
4. Aharon, M., Elad, M., Bruckstein, A.: K-SVD: an algorithm for designing overcomplete dictionaries for sparse representation. IEEE Transactions on Signal Processing 54(11), 4311–4322 (2006)
5. Elad, M., Milanfar, P., Rubinstein, R.: Analysis versus synthesis in signal priors. Inverse Problems 23(3), 947–968 (2007)
6. Nam, S., Davies, M.E., Elad, M., Gribonval, R.: Cosparse analysis modeling-uniqueness and algorithms. In: 2011 IEEE International Conference on Acoustics, Speech and Signal Processing, ICASSP, pp. 5804–5807 (2011)
7. Selesnick, I.W., Figueiredo, M.A.T.: Signal restoration with overcomplete wavelet transforms: comparison of analysis and synthesis priors. In: Proc. SPIE, Wavelets XIII, vol. 7446, p. 74460D (September 04, 2009), doi:10.1117/12.826663
8. Portilla, J.: Image restoration through L0 analysis-based sparse optimization in tight frames. In: Proceedings of the 2009 16th IEEE International Conference on Image Processing, ICIP 2009, pp. 3909–3912 (2009)
9. Nam, S., Davies, M.E., Elad, M., Gribonval, R.: The Cosparse Analysis Model and Algorithms. To Appear in Applied and Computational Harmonic Analysis (2012), http://www.cs.technion.ac.il/~elad/publications/journals/
10. Ophir, B., Elad, M., Bertin, N., Plumbley, M.D.: Sequential minimal eigenvalues – an approach to analysis dictionary learning. In: Proceedings of EUSIPCO (2011)
11. Rubinstein, R., Peleg, T., Elad, M.: K-SVD Dictionary Learning for the Analysis Co-Sparse Model. In: ICASSP, Kyoto, Japan, March 25-30 (2012)
12. Rubinstein, R., Peleg, T., Elad, M.: Analysis K-SVD: A Dictionary-Learning Algorithm for the Analysis Sparse Model. Submitted to IEEE Trans. on Signal Processing (2012), http://www.cs.technion.ac.il/~elad/publications/journals/

The Method for Constructing Block Sparse Measurement Matrix Based on Orthogonal Vectors[*]

Ruizhen Zhao[1,2], Zhou Qin[1,2], and Jinhui Tang[3]

[1] Institute of Information Science, Beijing Jiaotong University,
Beijing 100044, China
[2] Key Laboratory of Advanced Information Science and Network
Technology of Beijing, Beijing 100044, China
[3] School of Computer Science, Nanjing University of Science and Technology,
Nanjing 210094, China

Abstract. Compressive sensing is a new way of information processing which recover the original signal through acquiring much fewer measurements with a measurement matrix. The measurement matrix has an important effect in signal sampling and reconstruction algorithm. However, there are two main problems in currently existing matrices: the difficulty of hardware implementation and high computation complexity. In this paper, we proposed a class of highly sparse and deterministic scrambled block measurement matrices based on orthogonal vectors (SBOV). It could improve sensing efficiency and reduce computation complexity. Those matrices constructed by the proposed method only need very little memory space and they could be easily implemented in hardware due to their simple entries. Some experiments show the better imaging performance comparable to scrambled block Hadamard matrix (SBH) and dense partial Hadamard matrix. SBOV matrices are simpler and sparser than SBH matrix.

Keywords: compressive sensing, measurement matrix, orthogonal vectors, block and sparse matrix.

1   Introduction

In recent years, a great of attention has been paid to the new method of data acquisition compressive sensing (CS) [1], [2]. The idea of CS is that signal sampling and data compression are implemented at the same time. Sparse signal or compressive signal can be recovered by few measurements. Due to the large amount of data in image and video signal, CS is usually used in imaging applications when the measurement is very costly. Some image processing algorithms

---

[*] This work is supported by National Natural Science Foundation of China (61073079, 61103059) and the Fundamental Research Funds for the Central Universities (2011 JBM216).

W. Lin et al. (Eds.): PCM 2012, LNCS 7674, pp. 872–879, 2012.

based on CS are applied in many areas. For example, Fourier transform matrix is applied in MRI [3] and binary random matrix in single pixel camera [4]. In order to solve the algorithm problem of high dimension, Gan proposed the method based on block technology [5]. It can improve computation speed when using block measurement matrix. Despite the above mentioned works, there still exists a huge gap between the CS theory and applications. Therefore, how to construct simple and efficient measurement matrices is an important problem.

The measurement matrix plays an important role in measurement acquiring and signal reconstruction and it is one of the most important parts in CS. In order to meet practical requirements, the measurement matrix are generally expected to have the following properties: (1) The strong incoherence between measurement and sparse basis; (2) the number of measurements for perfect reconstruction is close to the theo-retical bound; (3) fast sampling and reconstruction; (4) low memory space and simple entries, easily hardware implement.

At present, there are many measurement matrices in theory, but few of them can satisfy the above four conditions. The first family is dense random matrices, e.g. Gaussian i.i.d matrix [1]. They can offer strong incoherence and optimal number of measurement. But they are impractical for image applications due to huge memory space and high computational complexity. The second family is deterministic structured matrices such as Toeplitz matrix [6]. They have fixed structure and simple elements, which are easily implemented for hardware. But in order to obtain good performance, they need more measurements and smaller sparsity, which leads to high computational complexity. The third family is matrices generated from orthogonal matrices such as partial Hadamard matrix [7] and partial Fourier matrix. Their reconstruction effect and computational complexity are better. However they are still hard with hardware im-plementation due to the huge memory space. The fourth family is random sparse matrices, e.g. binary random sparse matrix [8] and the very sparse matrix [9]. Due to random elements, they still need much memory space. The fifth family is structured sparse matrices, e.g. block polynomial deterministic matrix and scrambled block Hadamard (SBH) matrix [10], [11]. They are sparse and structured but the size of its block is not too small. There are tens of nonzero in each column. Its computational efficiency and memory space are still a little high.

In order to overcome the disadvantages of above measurement matrices, we pro-posed a way of constructing simple and efficient measurement matrix: scrambled block sparse structure based on orthogonal vectors (SBOV). The rows of a matrix which are orthogonal could improve reconstruction effect [12].We firstly constructed some low dimension orthogonal vectors with entries 1 or -1. Each vector is regarded as a block and a sub-matrix is constructed with the diagonal block. Then we merged some sub-matrices. Finally the measurement matrix was constructed through randomly permuting the columns. Those matrices are highly sparse and easily implemented for hardware due to the advantages of low memory space, simple entries and fast computation. The most important advantage is that those matrices could get better reconstruction results than SBH matrix.

The remainder of this paper is organized as follows. Section 2 introduces the back-ground of CS. Section 3 describes our method of constructing SBOV matrices. In section 4, simulations are shown to verify the validity of the proposed method. Section 5 is the conclusion.

2   Background and CS Theory

Suppose that a signal $x \in R^N$ is sparse in some transform domain $\Psi \in R^{N \times N}$. This means $x = \Psi\alpha$, and α only has K nonzero entries. K is called as the sparsity of signal α. For images, we usually choose the DCT as transform domain. Then we use a measurement matrix $\Phi \in R^{M \times N}(M \leq N)$, which is incoherent with Φ, to sample a signal and obtain a measurement vector. That is $y = \Phi x = \Phi\Psi\alpha$ and $y \in R^M$. The CS theory states that a signal can be reconstructed by taking only $M = O(k \log N)$ measurements.

The sampling process is a linear projection, but reconstruction algorithm is non-linear. The reconstruction process is expressed as

$$\min \left\| \alpha \right\|_0 \quad s.t. \quad y = \Phi\Psi\alpha = \Theta\alpha . \tag{1}$$

Due to the signal is sparse under the transform domain Psi, the sparsest solution for (1) is possible if Φ and Ψ are incoherent. The problem of ℓ_0 norm is generally an NP-hard problem. An alternative solution procedure is to minimize the ℓ_1 norm:

$$\min \left\| \alpha \right\|_1 \quad s.t. \quad y = \Phi\Psi\alpha = \Theta\alpha . \tag{2}$$

This is equally to a convex programming problem [13]. The matching pursuit algorithm [14] can be used to solve the problem.

Measurement matrix not only affects the performance of acquiring measurements, it also plays important role in the reconstruction algorithm. In this paper, we focused on the construction of sampling matrix for imaging applications. So measurement matrix is required to have the following properties. (1) near optimal number of measurements; (2) strong mutual incoherence; (3) low computation complexity and memory space; (4) simple entries for easy hardware implementation.

None of the existing measurement matrix can satisfy all of the above mentioned properties. The Gaussian matrix offers optimal performance, but it is impractical for applications for $O(MN)$ memory space which is too high. Toeplitz matrix is structured and contains simple entries, but it needs $ck \log^3(N/\delta)$ measurements for reconstruction. Partial orthogonal matrix needs $O(MN)$ memory space and the random selection of partial rows will reduce incoherence. SBH matrix, the size of its block is at least 32. The memory space is BN.

3   Scrambled Block Sparse Matrix Based on Orthogonal Vectors

Now we suppose orthogonal vectors are $r_1, r_2, \ldots r_s$. Their dimension is $1 \times b$ and entries are 1 and -1. Every vector r_i can produce a block diagonal sub-matrix

B_i and the number of blocks is N/b. Then we merge sub-matrices in parallel to form a big matrix. Finally permute the columns and randomly select partial rows. The measurement matrix is written as $\boldsymbol{\Phi} = \boldsymbol{Q_M B P_N}, \boldsymbol{B} = [\boldsymbol{B_1; B_2; \cdots ; B_N}]$, where $\boldsymbol{P_N}$ represents the randomly permuting and $\boldsymbol{Q_M}$ represents picking up M rows of $\boldsymbol{B P_N}$ uniform at random. Without loss of generality, we suppose $s = 2, b = 4$ and select two orthogonal vectors of four vectors: $r_1 = (1, 1, -1, -1)$, $r_2 = (-1, 1, 1, -1)$. So the form of $\boldsymbol{B} = [\boldsymbol{B_1; B_2}]$ is shown as Fig. 1. The number of blocks in every $N/b \times N$ sub-matrix is N/b. The size of $\boldsymbol{B}$ is $sN/b \times N$.

$$B = \begin{bmatrix} \begin{pmatrix} 1\ 1\ -1\ -1 & & & \\ & 1\ 1\ -1\ -1 & & \\ & & \ddots & \\ & & & 1\ 1\ -1\ -1 \end{pmatrix} \\ \begin{pmatrix} -1\ 1\ 1\ -1 & & & \\ & -1\ 1\ 1\ -1 & & \\ & & \ddots & \\ & & & -1\ 1\ 1\ -1 \end{pmatrix} \end{bmatrix}$$

Fig. 1. An example of SBOV matrix

3.1 The Comparison of Property between SBOV Matrix and SBH Matrix

In this paper, we construct block sparse matrix based on orthogonal vectors. Due to these orthogonal vectors, the mutual incoherence and the incoherence between mea-surements are both enhanced. Thus the reconstruction effect will be improved. The proposed matrix is highly sparse. It has only Mb nonzero entries and the proportion of sparsity is b/N. In contrast, in order to get good reconstruction effect, the size of B in SBH matrix is at least 32. Their sensing time are s and B, computation complexity are Ms and $M \log B$, memory space are Mb and NB respectively. Therefore the SBOV matrices can improve sensing efficiency and reduce computation complexity and is easier for hardware implementation.

3.2 The Influence of Parameters S and b

We mainly construct measurement matrices based on parameters b and s. Different b and s influence the size and performance of measurement matrix. So when how big the parameters are, measurement matrix is the best?

From the aspect of sparsity and computation efficiency, b could not be too large. Measuring a signal with blocked matrix is equal to measuring a segmented signal with small matrix. In each sub-matrix, every diagonal vector measures a length b of the signal and gets a measurement. When b is too large,the number of the signals is relative too small, which will affect reconstruction precision. But when b is too small,the number of the blocks of sub-matrix is too large, which will also decrease the re-construction efficiency.

When b is fixed, number of blocks is fixed. There are b orthogonal vectors for $1 \times b$ vector.The smaller the number of vectors is, the less memory space is consumed. But the larger the number of vectors is, the more mutual incoherence will be obtained.

When the size of measurement matrix is fixed, that is, M,N are fixed and b is also fixed, the size of parameter s influences rows of $(BP)_N$. The rows of each sub-matrix are N/b and the rows of the large matrix are sN/b. We must promise the premise of$sN/b \geq M$, so $s \geq bM/N$.

When we randomly select M rows from sN/b, the mutual incoherence will be reduced. When sN/b is larger, the reconstruction effect is worse. On condition that promising a fixed number of rows, we pick up the number of orthogonal vectors so as to sN/b is slightly larger than M. This will lead to reducing the least mutual incoherence. Now we verify the validity through simulation results.

4   Simulation Result

In this section, we constructed some measurement matrices using the proposed method. In order to compare our results, we also implement SBH matrix and PH matrix which provide good reconstruction effect. SBH matrix is generated by $b \times b$ small Hadamard block matrix and then randomly permuting the columns and finally pick up M rows. The size of b is 32. PH matrix is generated from dense Hadamard matrix by randomly choosing M rows. In this simulation, we select 256×256 Lena image signal and DCT sparse transformation and OMP reconstruction algorithm. So $N = 256$, for convenience, we suppose $M = 128$. In promise of high sparsity, we constructed one matrix using $b = 1$, $s = 1$; two matrices using $b = 2, s = 1, 2$; three matrices using $b = 4, s = 2, 3, 4$; four matrices using $b = 8, s = 4, 5, 8$. Finally when $b = 4, s = 2$ and $b = 8, s = 4$ we use nonorthogonal vectors to construct two matrices NOV1 and NOV2. The rows and diagonal blocks of matrix $\boldsymbol{BP}_N$ are shown in Table. 1. We call measurement matrices which are generated from matrix $\boldsymbol{BP}_N$ after randomly choosing M rows as $b_i s_i$, e.g. $b = 2, s = 2$ is denoted as $b_2 s_2$.

Now we reconstruct image using measurement matrix of $b_i s_i$ and SBH and PH. We compare the PSNR of of reconstruction image.

From Table 2, the reconstruction effect of SBH matrix is comparable to that of PH matrix at much lower implementation cost. Most of the matrices used the proposed method show better performance than SBH matrix. When b and s are are different values respectively, reconstruction effect are different from each other.

Table 1. When $M = 128$, the size of matrix $\boldsymbol{BP}_N$ using our method

b,s	Number of diagonal blocks	Number of rows
$b = 1, s = 1$	256	256
$b = 2, s = 1$	128	128
$b = 2, s = 2$	128	256
$b = 4, s = 2$	64	128
$NOV1$	64	128
$b = 4, s = 3$	64	192
$b = 4, s = 4$	64	256
$b = 8, s = 4$	32	128
$NOV2$	32	128
$b = 8, s = 5$	32	160
$b = 8, s = 8$	32	256

Table 2. The PSNR of Lena image using each measurement matrix when $M/N = 0.5$

measurement matrix	PH	SBH	b_1s_1	b_2s_1	b_2s_2	b_4s_2
PSNR(dB)	23.71	23.15	18.03	25.64	21.85	27.85
NOV1	b_4s_3	b_4s_4	b_8s_4	NOV2	b_8s_5	b_8s_8
25.16	26.56	22.42	26.29	24.14	24.57	24.12

(1) The size of b will influence reconstruction effect. E.g. matrix b_8s_4 and b_4s_2 differ in the length of orthogonal vectors and we can see the bad reconstruction effect from Table 2. So we hope the parameter b is not too large.

(2) The size of b indirectly determine the number of diagonal blocks of each sub-matrix. When $b = 1$, the reconstruction effect is bad. Matrix b_2s_2 and b_4s_4 differ in number of diagonal blocks and we can see the bad reconstruction effect from Table 2. So we hope the parameter is not too small.

(3)The vectors in every sub-matrix are orthogonal for each other can improve re-construction effect. E.g. the performance of b_4s_2 is superior to NOV1 and b_8s_4 is superior to NOV2.

(4) We suppose the size of matrix we want to get is $M \times N$. When the rows of matrix $\boldsymbol{BP}_N$ the rows of matrix differ greatly with M, the reconstruction effect is weak. E.g. the reconstruction effect of b_4s_2, b_4s_3, b_4s_4 are weaker in turn.

The main reason the method in this paper is superior to SBH matrix is we can choose suitable orthogonal vectors and suitable number of vectors according to the number of measurements. We try to construct $\boldsymbol{BP}_N$ when the number of rows is slightly larger than the number of measurements or equal to the number of measurements. So we can reduce or avoid degradation of performance when randomly choosing partial rows. When the length of a signal is fixed, the number of measurements is diversified.

From the above analysis, we should synthesize the parameters when we want acquire the optimal measurement matrix. As shown inTable 2, the PSNR of b_4s_2 is the best. The reconstruction images of all matrices are shown in Fig. reffig:2.

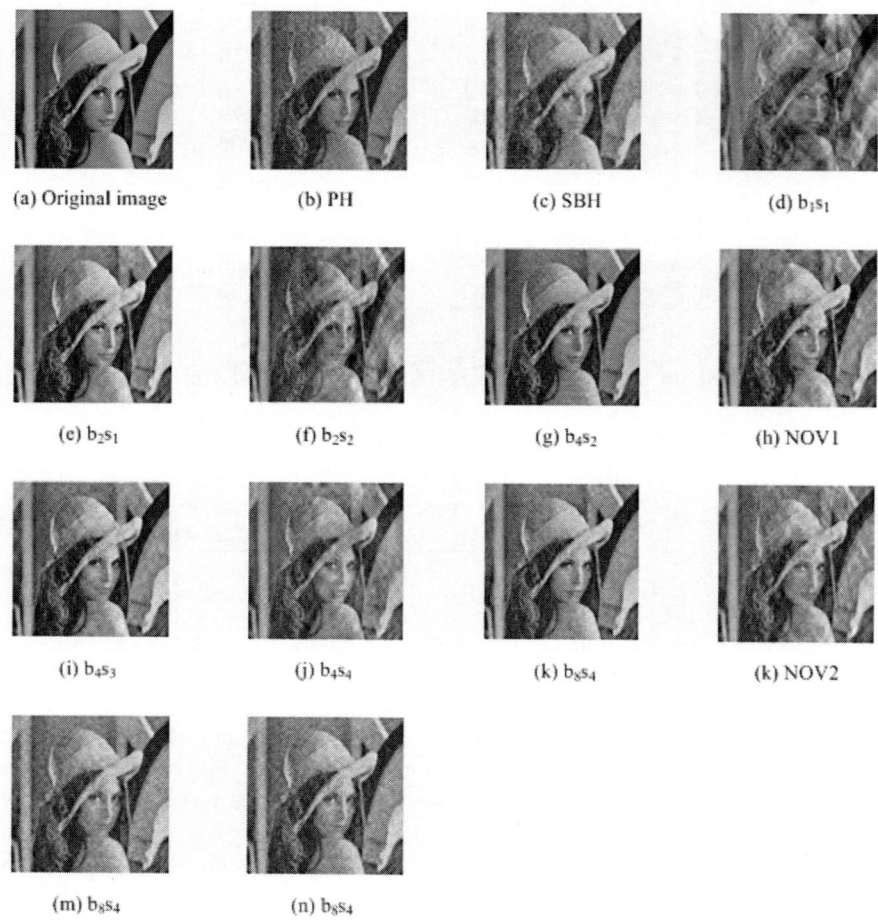

(a) Original image   (b) PH   (c) SBH   (d) b_1s_1

(e) b_2s_1 (f) b_2s_2 (g) b_4s_2 (h) NOV1

(i) b_4s_3 (j) b_4s_4 (k) b_8s_4 (k) NOV2

(m) b_8s_4 (n) b_8s_4

Fig. 2. The reconstruction images using all matrices with its size of 128×256

5   Conclusion

We proposed a method for constructing block sparse measurement matrix based on orthogonal vectors (SBOV). Those matrices are simple and highly sparse and are useful for compressive imaging applications. They are sparser than SBH matrix, so they can improve sensing efficiency and reduce computation complexity. When we commendably choose the length and number of orthogonal vectors, the reconstruction result of the proposed matrix is superior to SBH and PH matrix. The entries of matrices are 1,-1 and 0. Therefore they are easily implemented in hardware.

References

1. Donoho, D.L.: Compressive sensing. IEEE Trans. Inform. Theory 52, 1229–1306 (2006)
2. Candès, E., Romberg, J., Tao, T.: Robust uncertainty principles: Exact signal reconstruction from highly imcomplete frequency information. IEEE Trans. Inform. Theory 52, 489–509 (2006)
3. Lustig, M., Santos, D.D.J., Pauly, J.: Compressed sensing MRI. IEEE Signal Processing Magazine 25, 72–82 (2008)
4. Duarte, F., Davenport, M.A.: Single pixel imaging via compressive sampling. IEEE Signal Processing Magazine 25, 83–91 (2008)
5. Gan, L.: Block compressed sensing of natural images. In: 15th International Conference on Digtial Signal Processing, pp. 403–406 (2007)
6. Bajwa, W., Haupt, J.: Toeplitz-structured compressed sensing matrices. In: Proceedings of IEEE Workshop on Statistical Signal Processing, pp. 294–298 (2007)
7. Tsaig, Y., Donoho, D.: Extensions of compressed sensing. Signal Processing 86, 549–571 (2006)
8. Yu, K., Guo, X.: Compressive sensing with sparse measurement matrices. In: IEEE 73rd Conference on Vehicular Technology (2011)
9. Fang, H., Zhang, Q.B., Wei, S.: Method of image reconstruction based on very sparse random projection. Computer Engineering and Applications 43, 25–27 (2007)
10. Li, X., Zhao, R., Hu, S.: Blocked polynomial deterministic matrix for compressed sensing. In: 2010 International Conference on Wireless Communications, Networking and Mobile Computing (2010)
11. Gan, L., Do, T., Tran, T.D.: Fast compressive imaging using scrambled block hadamard ensemble. In: Proc. EUSIPCO (2008)
12. Lin, X., Lu, G., Yan, J., Lin, W.: Measurement matrix of compressive sensing based on Gram-Schmidt Orthogonalization. In: 2011 Sixth International Conference on Image and Graphics, pp. 205–210 (2011)
13. Candès, E., Romberg, J.: Robust signal recovery from incomplete observations. In: Proc. of International Conference of Image Processing, pp. 1281–1284 (2006)
14. Tropp, J.A.: Greed is good: Algorithm results for sparse approximation. IEEE Trans. Inform. Theory 50, 2231–2242 (2004)

Author Index